PRESBYTERIANS IN THE GREAT WAR.

MONUMENTAL HONOUR ROLL.

WORK COMPLETED AFTER SIX YEARS.

A monumental volume, which has just been completed in the Press, is: "The Presbyterian Church in Ireland Roll of Honour, 1914-1919," published under the auspices of the Presbyterian Historical Society of Ireland, Church House, Belfast. It is a work that has obviously entailed great care in research and compilation, and is a book of the highest historic value and interest to the Presbyterian Church, whose members played so prominent and gallant a part in the World War. It is a large sized volume, of 340 pages, in strong, blue-coloured cloth binding, having in the centre of the front cover the symbolic arms of the Church (the Burning Bush), and the motto "Ardens Sed Virens," wrought in gold. The frontispiece is a singularly artistic photograph showing in uniform the Right Rev. Major-General Simms, C.B., C.M.G., D.D., LL.D., K.H.C., Principal Chaplain to the Forces, 1914-1919; Moderator of the General Assembly, 1919-20. The printers, Messrs. W. & G. Baird, Ltd., Royal Avenue, are to be congratulated upon the handsome manner in which the book has been printed and turned out, the workmanship being in every way worthy of the object.

The scheme for the preparation of this monumental Roll, originated shortly after the outbreak of the war, when the Rev. W. J. Baird, B.A. (minister of Agnes Street Presbyterian Church), as Convener of the State of Religion Committee, suggested that arrangements should be made for the preparation of rolls of honour in connection with the various congregations, and a return of same made to the General Assembly. It was most interesting to observe the growth of the movement, which was taken up with universal enthusiasm, and had not a little influence in furthering recruiting among the young people of the Church who had the encouragement of realising how great an interest would be taken in their welfare when absent from home and friends. The preparation of the full roll, which has just been completed, has been in progress since the year 1915, under the direction of Rev. Mr. Baird, convener; and Messrs. J. W. Kernohan and A. G. Crawford, the energetic hon. secretaries of the Presbyterian Historical Society. Reference is made in the preface to the debt of gratitude which the Church owes to Miss Jean Craig, of the Historical Society, "for her persistent labour in collecting, revising, and classifying the various congregational lists, and for correcting the proofs."

DR. MACMILLAN'S FOREWORD.

Recognition is also paid to the valued services of Rev. John Macmillan, D.D., for "the suitable Foreword." We give the opening portion of the Foreword (to which the initials "J. M." are appended), which will convey an idea of the masterly style in which it is written, and its suitability to the noble purpose to which it is dedicated—
"War of the World: a ruthless horde forswear
Agreements that themselves had signed and sealed;
Reverted to the plane of primal Hun,
They hurl the brand, deal the assassin's stroke.
They terrorise the weak, profane the Home,
Degrade it to the kennel and the stye.
They mock the wounded, mutilate the child;
They shell the Hospital by land and sea,
And, at distress of stragglers on the wave,
Raise the insensate laughter of the fiend,
Defiant of the laws of earth and Heaven;
Eclipsing Attila, "the scourge of God,"
Their paragon in deeds nefarious
Which demons only were supposed to do.
They turn to dust the spoils of Time, they quench
The lamp that centuries had trimmed;
Liege, Bruxelles, Mons, Rheims, Louvain recall
The fate of Alexandria, what time
Her priceless parchments fed the fires that served
Her public baths for half a year. For this
The centuries since then have mourned; and what
This Christian century has seen the race
Of men, who have not forfeited the right
To be accounted human, shall deplore.

Herein are those who shared the great defence
Raised as a rampart 'gainst the fatal tide
That jeopardised the Freedom of the World,
And drew its dreaded course towards the Home
And all for which it stood in Days of Peace."

Then there follows graceful and merited tribute to those who "left the harvest and their fathers' fields; kissed their mothers, sisters, lovers, wives; yielded their love of liberty and life;" who "left the Academic Halls . . . left Brief and Bar; exchanged the Forum for the Camp; they left the School of Esculap, the microscope, the rostrum, and the desk, and grasped the sword;" who "left the cure of souls in fitting hands, exchanged the Gown and Bands for uniform . . . and cheered the men with prayer and Psalm and with familiar word, that served their Brother in command of all who bore the Maltese Cross." Nor are forgotten, in this heart-stirring poetic eulogium, "The Lady of the Lamp," and "the Women who remained at home, and found means to serve in divers ways." And last, though far from least:—
"In the Holy Place, the Church at home
Made earnest pleading, wrestling in the fight;
And souls elect ne'er failed to meet at hour
Of week-night prayer, to sing their Hymn, and leave
Their loved ones 'neath the care of boundless Heaven . . .
So, those who worked at home and prayed, and kept
The hearth alight, and those who longed to go,
And were debarred by Providence, but nursed
The soldier-spirit in their hearts, have share
Alike with those who marched with bannered host
And fought, whom now we hail as our defence
In danger's hour. To God be praise for all!"

THE LOYALTY OF THE CHURCH.

From its earliest days—from the times of Milton and Cromwell—the Presbyterian Church in Ireland has always been conspicuous for its steadfast and devoted loyalty to the Crown and Constitution. It has a notable and untarnished history in this respect; and it did not fail to maintain its great traditions in the war that so many of its gallant sons—and daughters too—helped to bring to a victorious conclusion. From the manse to the humblest country cottage, thousands instantly responded all over the country to the great call; and a large proportion paid the supreme sacrifice or suffered grievous wounds, that the Peace we now enjoy might be achieved. Their names are now immortalised for all time in this permanent "Roll of Honour," which will take an honoured and permanent place in the archives of the Church whose sons and daughters so nobly distinguished themselves, "counting not the cost."

The roll contains upwards of 24,000 names, but it is pointed out that for various reasons it is incomplete. Some congregations did not make returns, while others were late in commencing to keep a register, with the result that many names were not recorded. Further, in the large industrial populations, especially in Belfast, large numbers of Presbyterian young men joined the colours who were not actively identified with church life, and whose names did not, in consequence, find their way to the congregational lists. It is estimated that probably about 2,000 names are wanting, which would bring the Irish Presbyterian representation in the great line of defence up to 26,000.

The roll sets out the name of each member, his (or her) home address, the rank in which he (or she) served the regiment, battalion, or unit, and under the head of "Remarks" states if wounded or killed, and also gives the decorations where such are awarded, and these are certainly very numerous. The "Manse Roll of Honour," which is included in the volume, contains the names of the ministers and sons of ministers who served either as chaplains or in the fighting ranks; and also the names of daughters of ministers, with the position they occupied, and where they served, together with the honours bestowed. There are two cases where no less than five sons from the one manse did service, these being sons of the late Rev. Dr. Wright, Newtownards, and the Rev. S. Matthews. Wicklow. There are numerous instances of four, three, and two sons from the one family having played their part in the great fight for freedom. The names of the members of the United Free Church in Ireland who took part also find a place in the historic record. The "Manse" section of the work was arranged by the present Moderator, the Right Rev. Dr. W. J. Lowe, M.A., who is now in America with the Irish deputation from the Church to the Pan-Presbyterian Conference, and two of whose sons served—Lieut. Alfred Lowe, with the 5th Battalion Royal Irish Regiment, and Lieut. John A. Lowe, with the American Army.

There is an admirable system of arrangement which enables the names to be easily referred to. They are placed alphabetically under their respective congregations, and the congregations are similarly placed under the Presbyteries to which they belong. It is only necessary to look up the Presbytery to which the congregation belongs, and the rest is simple.

Copies of the volume, of which only a limited number of copies have been issued, will find a place in the libraries and academic headquarters of the principal towns of the United Kingdom. The authorities of the War Museum, London, have invited and will be presented with a copy; while others are being sent to the Free Library, the Assembly's College, the M'Crea-Magee College, the Presbyterian Historical Society, Trinity College, Dublin, and similar institutions.—"Belfast Telegraph."

Copies to be had at two guineas each, apply to Presbyterian Historical Society, Church House, Belfast.

The Right Rev. Major-General John M. Simms, C.B. C.M.G. D.D. LL.D. K.H.C.
Principal Chaplain. 1914-1919.
Moderator of the General Assembly. 1919-1920.

The Presbyterian Church in Ireland.

ROLL OF HONOUR.

1914—1919.

The Presbyterian Historical Society of Ireland,

CHURCH HOUSE, BELFAST.

Cover illustration:
The 2nd Battalion The Royal Munster Fusiliers at Loos-September 25th 1915.

The Naval & Military Press Ltd

Published by
The Naval & Military Press Ltd
5 Riverside, Brambleside, Bellbrook
Industrial Estate, Uckfield, East Sussex,
TN22 1QQ England
Tel: +44 (0) 1825 749494
Fax: +44 (0) 1825 765701
www.naval-military-press.com
www.military-genealogy.com
www.militarymaproom.com

In reprinting in facsimile from the original, any imperfections are inevitably reproduced and the quality may fall short of modern type and cartographic standards.

THE FOREWORD.

WAR OF THE WORLD: a ruthless horde forswear
  Agreements that themselves had signed and sealed;
Reverted to the plane of primal Hun,
They hurl the brand, deal the assassin's stroke,
They terrorise the weak, profane the Home,
Degrade it to the kennel and the stye.
They mock the wounded, mutilate the child:
They shell the Hospital by land and sea,
And, at distress of strugglers on the wave,
Raise the insensate laughter of the fiend,
Defiant of the laws of earth and HEAVEN;
Eclipsing Attila, "the scourge of GOD,"
Their paragon in deeds nefarious
Which demons only were supposed to do.
They turn to dust the spoils of Time, they quench
The lamp that centuries had trimmed:
Liége, Bruxelles, Mons, Rheims, Louvain recall
The fate of Alexandria, what time
Her priceless parchments fed the fires that served
Her public baths for half-a-year. For this
The centuries since then have mourned: and what
This Christian century has seen the race
Of men, who have not forfeited the right
To be accounted human, shall deplore.

HEREIN are those who shared the great defence
Raised as a rampart 'gainst the fatal tide
That jeopardised the Freedom of the World,
And drew its dreaded course towards the Home
And all for which it stood in Days of Peace.

THEY left the harvest and their fathers' fields,
They kissed their mothers, sisters, lovers, wives;
Yielded their love of liberty and life
To rule of Camp—then hurtling bolts of death.
The men of skill in every craft stood forth,
And sons of humbler toil, as brave in heart,
Awaited not the second call to arms.
From loom and mart, from mine and forge they flocked
As to their windows doves: as drops of dew
Obey the signal of th' awakening Morn
And countless stand resplendent in array:
As Highland clan that saw the Fiery Cross
And heard the blood-call, and an army rose
Out of the ground and sped to trysting-place.
So from Dominion of the West, from 'neath
The Southern Cross, from whence the British Flag
In silken folds floats o'er the Commonwealth,
As volunteers of GOD's great Host to help
Of Motherland they come to save mankind:—
In Flanders and in France, in Pharaoh's land,
And in the cradle of the race, and where
The Aegean plied its fatal lure, and where
Olympus viewed a fallen race and King
Perfidious on classic seat, and where
The CHRIST pursued His high campaign to set
The captive free, the Spoiler's pow'r o'erthrow
And bring assurance to the heart that LOVE
Shall triumph in the end and reign for aye.
  They never failed their leader, never quailed
In face of hopeless task; nay, oft surpassed
Command, achieving "the impossible."
And now a lowly bed, a Cross perchance
With poppies and with roses red, token
Of richer harvests from their sacrifice,
Are all that's seen by outer eye; but yet
Their deeds shall live in storied page and song
Whilst love of Freedom lives and Time endures.

THEY left the Academic Halls and laid
The scholar's promise by, left Brief and Bar,
Exchanged the Forum for the Camp: they left
The School of Aesculap, the microscope,
The rostrum and the desk, and grasped the sword.
They drew their comrades to the ranks and called them
Brothers, whom they led and whom they loved,
With whom they shared their comforts and their gifts;
Transformed the erstwhile name of "Officers,"
Who boasted that they were not "Soldiers," and
Whose boast was true!
  They leaped the parapet
And faced the rain of death and gained the end
Assigned by high command, without a trace
Of fear save for their men: they hid the wounds
Themselves received and soothed the pain of hurt
In others, and rejoiced as one by one
Returned and answered call.
  The hero of the strife,
The youth with shoulder-strap and single Star:
The second Star was won and then the Cross
By valour matchless—so despatch declared—
And onward still he strove from Star to Star.
We pictured him receiving from the King
The badge of merit, in his early Home
Congratulations of his friends, and then
The Day of Peace and honours it would bring.
He passed instead into his FATHER's House
Above—a smile upon his face, a word
Of fond farewell upon his lips that moved
As if to tell discharge had come, had heard
The CAPTAIN's call. Short was the step to rest
Of hand and heart and brain and eye and ear.
Him now we see white-robed, the palm-decked Cross
Exchanged for Crown, rejoicing in the life
Immortal and the strength that never fails.

THEY left the cure of souls in fitting hands,
Exchanged the Gown and Bands for uniform,
And with the benison of Mother-Church
They served their Brother in command of all
Who bore the Maltese Cross. They cheered the men
With Prayer and Psalm and with familiar word,
That stirred the echoes of a hallowed past
And girded for the final test: they mourned
The dead, and message sent to hearts bereaved
That made them thankful for a hero's death
And service rendered to a sacred cause.
They proved as valiant as the combatant,
And shared with him the honours of the field.

THE FOREWORD.

APOLLO'S shafts the Dragon slew, they said,
In Greece when Greece was wise : the sons
Of Aesculap the Dragon slew with beams of light,
Evoked from crucible of darksome toil,
And won by eager searchers for the Truth ;
And health preserved amid the countless host
Of foes unseen, and healed the septic wound,
Assuaging pain with tenderness and skill,
Soldiers as brave as served in Britain's day,

To EVERY MAN his work, the Scripture saith :
According to their bent or whither told—
Some served on wing and eyes supplied on sea
And shore : and other some, as playthings of the deep,
Submerged at will and won a vantage ground
From whence to deal the unexpected stroke :
And some as silent watchers on the wave
Forestalled the impending raid and swept the main
Of boasted Fleet and brigand ship : of some
The burden was of troops, of staff of life
To man and beast—a burden nobly borne
By Service Corps : and never multitudes
In field or camp fared half so well as they.

THE LADY OF THE LAMP outlives the storm
That swept o'er Euxine's troubled marge : her light
Glows brighter with the years and leads a train
Of sisters dedicate to high emprise—
To heal the wounds that man inflicts on man,
Cast soothing shadows on the couch of pain,
To quicken hearts by touch of human love
That gives assurances of LOVE DIVINE ;
And bid the hopeless be of hope and live.
Of all the forms that moved upon that stage
So tragic from the first to last, so fraught
With fateful blundering, she wears the palm
For vision clear, for voice creative, and
For skill to snatch a triumph from defeat,

And wrest his trophies from the god of war,
The Lady of the Lamp stands first of all.
She led a train who followed in her steps
And multiplied her presence and her smile,
That brought both life and hope to broken men
Full five-and-sixty years ago.

AND WOMEN who remained at home found means
To serve in divers ways, they turned the thread
To uses manifold their love inspired ;
They organised their sisters into bands
And companies that week by week despatched
Their gifts to Trench and Camp and Hospital
And those who suffered in captivity:
As sweet as manna they, fragrant as herbs
In garden of their childhood far away.

AND IN THE HOLY PLACE the CHURCH at home
Made earnest pleading, wrestling in the fight ;
And souls elect ne'er failed to meet at hour
Of week-night prayer to sing their Hymn and leave
Their loved ones 'neath the care of boundless HEAVEN.

The ANCIENT ORDINANCE gave equal share
To those who went to battle and to those
Who stayed where duty kept them,
As they guarded what was there to guard
And to prepare to welcome back again
The weary warriors to hearths still lit
And warmed with glow of love and gratitude ;
So those who worked at home and prayed and kept
The hearth a-light, and those who longed to go
And were debarred by Providence but nursed
The soldier-spirit in their hearts, have share
Alike with those who marched with bannered host
And fought, whom now we hail as our defence
In danger's hour. To GOD be praise for all !

J. M.

THE Roll of Honour contains over 24,000 names. For various reasons it is far from complete. Several congregations made no returns, while others were late in commencing to keep a register, with the result that names were not recorded. In large industrial populations, especially in Belfast, large numbers of Presbyterian young men joined the colours who were not identified with Church life, and whose names therefore did not find their way to our congregational lists. It is calculated that probably 2,000 names are wanting, so that our representation in the great line of defence numbered above 26,000 men.

In the preparation of the Roll the Church owes a debt of gratitude to Miss Jean Craig, of the Historical Society, for her patient, persistent labour in collecting, revising, and classifying the various congregational lists and for correcting the proofs ; and to the Rev. John Macmillan, D.D., for the above suitable Foreword.

W. J. BAIRD, CONVENER.

A. G. CRAWFORD, } HON. SECS.,
J. W. KERNOHAN, } PRESBYTERIAN HISTORICAL SOCIETY.

Congregational Roll of Honour.

The names are arranged alphabetically under Congregations, and the Congregations similarly under Presbyteries. First ascertain the Presbytery to which the Congregation belongs.

AHOGHILL PRESBYTERY.

Name.	Home Address.	Rank.	Regiment, Battalion or Unit.	Remarks.
AHOGHILL, BROOKSIDE.				
Calderwood, Adam	Cullybackey	Private	8th R.I.R.	Wounded.
Coulter, Thos.	Ballymulroy	Rifleman	12th R.I.R.	
Dewart, A.		Private	12th R.I.R.	Wounded.
Ervine, Saml.	Ahoghill	Lance-Corporal	3rd Wiltshire Regt.	Killed.
Henry, Thos.	Ahoghill	Private	16th R.I.R.	W'ded and Pris.
McKeown, Robt.	Finkilta	Private	Seaforth Highlanders	Twice Wounded.
Willshow, Wm. Jas.	Drumrankin	Private	16th Batt. R.I.R.	
COLONIALS.				
Crawford, Jack		Private	N.Z. Forces	
Holmes, S. E.	Ballyconnelly	Major	A.V.C.	
Megaughin, Robt.	Ballybeg, Ahoghill	Signaller	116 Batt. Can.	
Orr, J. M.	Ahoghill	Private	Can. F.A.	
AHOGHILL, TRINITY CHURCH.				
Barr, Hugh	Galgorm	Private	A. & S. Highldrs.	
Dickey, Nathaniel	Ballybollan	Gunner	R.I.R.	
Dickey, Wm.	Ballybollan	Driver	R.G.A.	
Donnan, Samuel	Ahoghill	Private	A.S.C.	
Donnan, William A.	Ahoghill	Corporal	R.I.R.	
Glass, Robt.	Ballyconnolly	Private	R.I.R.	Died Pris. of War.
Graham, Thos. Duff	Ahoghill	Captain	R.A.M.C.	Wounded.
Hill, Frank	Gloonan Lodge	Lieutenant	A.S.C.	
Johnston, Saml.	Ahoghill	Private	R. Scots	Mons Star, W'ded.
Kennedy, Alexr.	Buick Row	Private	R.I.R.	Killed in Action.
Love, James	Ahoghill	Sergeant	R.A.F.	
Luke, Archie	Ahoghill	Private	R.I.R.	Wounded.
Luke, Wm.	Ahoghill	Private	R.I.R.	Wounded.
Luke, Alexr.	Ahoghill	Private	R.I.R.	Killed in Action.
McCord, Robt. Neill Ballagh		Surgeon	R.N.	
McFadden, Robt.	Clohogue	Private	R.I. Fus.	
McFadden, Wm.	Clohogue	Private	R.F.A.	
McMaster, Harry.	Killyless	Sapper	R.E.	Wounded.
McMaster, Saml.	Killyless	Private	R.I.R.	Killed in Action.
McMaster, Wm. Jas.	Tullygarley	Private	R.I.R.	
McMaster, Wm. R.	Tullygarley	Private	R.I.R.	Wounded.
McNeill, J.	Ahoghill	Private	R. Scots	Killed in Action.
Magill, Robt.	Galgorm	Private	R.E.	
Moody, Alexr.	Ahoghill	Rifleman	R.I.R.	
Moore, Hugh	Galgorm	Rifleman	R.I.R.	
Perry, Saml. H.	Ahoghill	Private	R.I.R.	
Ramsay, Wm.	Ahoghill	Lance-Corporal	R.I.R.	
Rock, George	Ahoghill	Private	R.I.R.	
Sands, Adam	Finkiltagh	Corporal	M.G.C.	
Scullion, Saml.	Lisnafillan	Bugler	R.I.R.	
Wilson, Wm.	Clohogue	Private	A. & S. Highldrs.	
COLONIALS & U.S.A. FORCES.				
Coulter, Stafford John	Ballymacilroy	Lance-Corporal	Am. E.F.	
Dickey, John	Ballybolan	Corporal	N.Z.	
Houston, David	Carmacmoin	Private	N.Z.	Killed in Action.
McMaster, James	Killyless	Corporal	Canadians	
Marshall, J.	Longstone	Private	N.Z.	
Ramsay, Saml. M.	Ahoghill	Private	Canadians	
Small, Robt.	Ahoghill	Private	Candians	Accidentally Killed
Wallace, Saml.	Ahoghill	Private	Canadians	Twice Wounded.

AHOGHILL PRESBYTERY. CHURCHTOWN.

Name.	Home Address.	Rank.	Regiment, Battalion or Unit.	Remarks.
CHURCHTOWN.				
Agnew, Robert	Drumard	Private	10th R.I.F.	Wounded.
Bloomfield, John	Drumark	Private	R. Inn. Fus.	Wounded.
Caldwell, Alex.	Lislea	Private	R. Inn. Fus.	Wounded.
Davidson, R. J.	Drumoolish	Private	R.A.M.C.	
Dempsey, John	Tamlaght O'Crilly	Private	R.F.A.	
Douthirt, John	Tamlaght O'Crilly	Corporal	Despatch Rider	M.C.
Forgrave, Jas.	Upperlands	Private	R.G.A.	
Gamble, Alex.	Dungleady	Sergeant	36th Ulster Div.	Wounded.
Halliday, Jas.	Moyagney	Private	R.I. Fus.	Wounded.
Kelso, Jas.	Upperlands	Private	R.I. Fus.	Wounded, Prisoner
Kelso, John	Drumlane	Private		
Montgomery, Thos.	Portglenone	Private	R.I. Fus.	Prisoner.
Mulholland, H. C., M.B., D.P.H.	Churchtown Manse	Captain	R.A.M.C.	Wounded and Mentioned in D'patches
Nelson, Jack	Killymuck	Private	R.G.A.	
Nelson, James	Lislea	Private	R.I. Fus.	Wounded.
Rowe, John	Drumoolish	Private	R.I. Fus.	Killed in Action.
Rowe, Saml.	Drumoolish	Private	R.I. Fus.	Wounded 3 times. Killed in Action.
Stewart, Jack	Killygullib	Private	R.I. Fus.	Killed in Action.
Turner, Alex.	Drumard	Private	R.I. Fus.	Wounded.
COLONIAL FORCES.				
Agnew, Stewart	Drumnacannon	Private	Australian E.F.	Killed in Action.
Bolton, Sloan	Moneysallin House	Private	Austn. Light Horse	Wounded, D.M.C.
Kelso, Joseph	Drumlane	Private	N.Z. Force	Wounded.
Wallace, James	Lisnagrot	Private	Australians	
Wilson, Wm.	Dungleady			
GRANGE.				
Bankhead, Robt.	Taylorstown	Private	11th R.I.R.	
Campbell, James	Kilnock	Private	11th R.I.R.	Prisoner.
Clarke, Robt. John	Taylorstown	Private	11th R.I.R.	Killed in Action.
Cunningham, Robert	Kilnock	Private	M.G.C., 16th Batt.	
Graham, Thomas	Kilnock	Private	R.A.F.	
Green, Samuel	Taylorstown	Private	11th R.I.R.	
Hamill, Alex.	Taylorstown	Private	20th R.I.R.	Died.
Hamill, Shepherd	Taylorstown	Private	11th R.I.R.	Died.
McBride, Thos.	Muckrim	Private	11th R.I.R.	Died of Wounds.
McKee, John	Taylorstown	Private	11th R.I.R.	W'ded & Gassed.
McKee, William	Taylorstown	Private	North Irish Horse	
Pollock, Sam	Taylorstown	Private	11th R.I.R.	Wounded.
Robinson, Edward	Taylorstown	Private	1st R.I.R.	Killed in Action.
Shaw, John	Kilnock	Lance-Corporal	1st R.I.R.	Wounded.
Surgenor, James	Taylorstown	Coy. Sergt.-Major	1st R.I.R.	Died of Wounds.
KILLYMURRIS.				
Bradly, James	Glarryford	Gunner	R.G.A.	
Calderwood, Hugh	Glenbuck	Driver	R.A.S.C.	
Calderwood, Matthew	Carclinty	Corporal	I.G.	
Calderwood, Robt. J.	Carclinty	Driver	R.A.S.C.	
Calderwood, Wm.				
Calderwood, Wilson	Dunalney			
Compton, Thos. R.	Tullyreagh	Private		
Devlin, Samuel	Dromore			
Devlin, Wm.	Killycowan			
Dickey, Robt.	Kilcreen	Private	R.A.F.	
Erwin, James	Dromona			
Gaston, Andrew	Killagan	Captain	R.A.M.C.	
Gaston, David	Killagan	Captain	R.A.M.C.	
Gaston, James	Killagan	Captain	4th Suffolks	
Houston, Thos.	Killagan	Captain	R.A.M.C.	
Kenny, Wm.	Dunminning	Driver	R.F.A.	
Kinnear, Robt.	Glarryford	Private	N.I.H.	
Lewis, Matthew	Dunminning			
Linton, Andrew	Killycowan	Private		
McAlonan, Thos.	Killycowan	Private	R.I. Hussars	
McClelland, R. L.	Killagan			
McHendry, Saml.	Killagan	Seaman	R.N.	
McMurry, Andrew	Killagan	Private		
McWhirter, John	Killycowan	Private		
McWilliam, Samuel	Glarryford	Private	R.I.R.	
Madill, Saml. H.	Crankill			
Mairs, Wm.	Killagan	Private	R.I.R.	
Parke, David	Glarryford	Private	Scots Guards	
Park, John Jas.	Crankill	Lieut.-Corporal	R.I.V's	

AHOGHILL PRESBYTERY. KILLYMURRIS.

Name.	Home Address.	Rank.	Regiment, Battalion or Unit.	Remarks.
Park, Wm.	Ballywatermy	Private		
Pollock, Robt.	Killycowan	Private	Scots Guards	
Smyth, James	Dunalney	Rifleman	R.I.R.	
Smyth, Thos.	Dunalney	Rifleman	R.I.R.	
Strange, Robt.	Carnlea	Private	R.I.R.	
Strange, Wm. J.	Glarryford	Private	R.I.R.	
Wilson, Thos.	Glarryford	Private	R.I.R.	
Wylie, David	Tullygrawley	Private		
Wylie, James	Tullygrawley	Private		
Wylie, Wm.	Tullygrawley	Private		
COLONIAL FORCES.				
Bradshaw, William	Glarryford	Private	Australians	
Calderwood, Thos.	Glarryford	Gunner	Canadian F.A.	
Hunter, Jas. S.	Dunminning	Private	Australian E.F.	
Hyndman, John	Dromore	Private	Australian E.F.	
Linton, Wm.	Killagan	Private	Canadians	
Lynn, James	Killagan	Private	Canadians	
Lynn, R. J.	Killagan	Lance-Corporal	Can. M.R.	
Russell, John M.	Tullygrawley	Sergeant	A.E.F.	
THIRD PORTGLENONE.				
Black, Henry	Portglenone	Private	R. Inn. Fus.	
Bonter, Robt.	Portglenone	Private	R.A.F.	
Carleton, Robt.	Portglenone	Private	R. Inn. Fus.	
Holmes, Robt.	Portglenone	Private	R.D. Fus.	
Law, William	Portglenone	Private	R. Inn. Fus.	Killed in Action.
McLean, Alex.	Portglenone	Private	R. Inn. Fus.	Killed in Action.
McNeill, James	Portglenone	Private	R. Inn. Fus.	Wounded.
Moffett, Alex.	Portglenone	Private	R. Irish Rifles	
Montgomery, Robt.	Portglenone	Private	R.A.F.	
Nickle, James	Portglenone	Private	I. Guards	
Ross, Robt.	Portglenone	Gunner	R.F.A.	
Stewart, James	Portglenone	Lieutenant	N. Surgeon	
Stronge, Archibald	Portglenone	Private	Gordon Highldrs.	Wounded.
Williamson, Henry	Portglenone	Private	Seaforth Highldrs.	Wounded.
RASHARKIN.				
Anderson, Robt.	Rasharkin	Private	R.I.R.	
Anderson, Saml.	Rasharkin	Private	A.S.C.	
Brown, Matthew	Rasharkin	Private	R.I.R.	
Campbell, Robt.	Rasharkin	Private	R.I.R.	Killed in Action.
Glasgow, Joseph	Rasharkin	Private	R.F.A.	
Gordon, James	Rasharkin	Private	N.I.H.	
Harkness, Joseph	Rasharkin	Private	R.A.F.	
Harkness, Tom	Rasharkin	Private	R.A.F.	
Johnston, Jas.	Rasharkin	Private	N.I.H.	
Kennedy, James	Rasharkin	Private	R.I.F.	
Killough, George	Rasharkin	Private	N.I.H.	Died.
Kirkwood, Thos.	Rasharkin	Private	H.L.I.	
Kyle, Robt. Y.	Rasharkin	Private	R.I.R.	
Kyle, Thos.	Rasharkin	Private	R.I.R.	
McAllion, Jack	Rasharkin	Private	Seaforth Highldrs.	
McCahon, Hugh	Rasharkin	Private	N.I.H.	
McCaughey, Jas.	Rasharkin	Private	R.I.R.	
McCaughey, John	Rasharkin	Private	R.I.R.	
McHenry, Joseph	Rasharkin	Lieut.	R.I.R.	
McIntyre, Robt.	Rasharkin	Sergeant	R.I.F.	
McMillan, Jas.	Rasharkin	Rifleman	R.I.R.	
McNeill, Saml.	Rasharkin	Private	R.I.F.	Killed in Action.
Montgomery, Wm. J.	Rasharkin	Corporal	R.I.F.	
Reid, Chas.	Rasharkin	Private	N.I.H.	
Simpson, Alex.	Rasharkin	Private	Siege Battery	Killed in Action.
Smyth, Thos.	Rasharkin	Private	R.I.F.	
Wilson, George	Rasharkin	Private	R.F.A.	
Wilson, Saml.	Rasharkin	Gunner	R.F.A.	
Wilson, Wm.	Rasharkin	Sergeant	R.I.F.	Killed in Action.
Wilson, Wm. J.	Rasharkin	Sergeant	H.L.I.	
Wylie, Edward	Rasharkin	Rifleman	R.I.R.	
COLONIAL FORCES.				
Kirkpatrick, Leslie	Rasharkin	Private	Canadian F.A.	Killed in Action.
McCaughren, Wm.	Rasharkin	Private	Australians	Killed in Action.
Peacock, Alex.	Rasharkin	Private	Australians	
Taylor, John	Rasharkin	Private	N.Z. Force	

ARDS PRESBYTERY.

Name.	Home Address.	Rank.	Regiment, Battalion, or Unit.	Remarks.
BALLYBLACK.				
Allen, Robt.	Ballyblack	Rifleman	3rd R.I.R.	
Calderwood, Thomas	5 John St., N'ards	Rifleman	13th R.I.R.	Prisoner, Died.
Graham, Rev. Robert	Ballyblack Manse	Chaplain		
McCutcheon, Wm.			R.A.F.	
McKeague, Jas.	Ballywittacock	Rifleman	8th R.I.R.	Wounded.
McMillan, Hugh	Drumawhey	Rifleman	18th R.I.R.	Gassed.
McMurray, Jas.	Ballyblack	Rifleman	8th R.I.R.	Wounded.
Murray, Samuel	Ballyblack	Rifleman	20th R.I.R.	Killed in Action.
Murray, Sidney	Ballyblack	Rifleman	18th R.I.R.	Wounded.
Rankin, John A.	Loughries	Trooper	N.I.H.	Prisoner.
Ritchie, Jas.	Ballyblack	Sergeant	R.I. Fus.	
Shanks, Hugh	Loughries	Rifleman	13th R.I.R.	Killed in Action.
Torney, Jas.	Ballywittacock	Rifleman	2nd R.I.R.	
Waugh, David	Ballyblack	Fitter Q.M.S.	R.G.A.	
COLONIAL FORCES.				
Patton, Saml.	Crossnamuckley	Trooper	N.Z. Mounted Rifles	Died.
Stoupe, Davidson		Sergeant	1st Well. Batt. N.Z.	Wounded, D.C.M.
BALLYGILBERT.				
Alexander, Saml.	Ballymoney	A.B.S.	R.N.	
Alexander, W. J.	Ballymoney	A.B.S.	Naval Reserve	
Boyd, James	Ballydavey	Private	R.I.R.	
Campbell, David	Crawfordsburn	Private		
Clarke, Joseph	Ballyrobert	Private	R.F.A.	
Coey, Wm.	Craigavad	Private	R.I.R.	
Davidson, John A.	Ballygilbert	P.O.	R.N.	
Davidson, Robert	Ballygilbert	Driver	A.S.C.	
Davidson, Wm.	Ballygilbert	Driver	R.E.	
Eley, Wm.	Ballygilbert	Private	R.I.R.	Wounded 4 times.
Ellison, Robert	Ballyrobert	Private	R.I.R.	
Hamilton, Walton	Crawfordsburn	Private	20th R.I.R.	
Hoey, Robert	Crawfordsburn	Private	15th R.I.R.	
Howden, James	Ballyrobert	Private	18th R.I.R.	
Hughes, J.	Ballymullan	Corporal	208 Brass Band	
Irwin, Chas.	Ballyrobert			
Irwin, David	Ballyrobert			Killed in Action.
Johnston, John	Ballymullan	Private	R.I.R.	
Kennedy, John	Crawfordsburn	Private	13th R.I.R.	Wounded.
Lindsay, Jas.	Crawfordsburn			
McClements, Alex.	Crawfordsburn	Private	R.I.R.	Killed in Action.
McDowell, Wm.	Crawfordsburn	Private	R.I. Fus.	Died in France.
Macfarlane, John	Ballydavey	Private	R.I.R.	
McKee, W. J.	Ballysallagh	Sergeant	Signalling Corps	
Macormac, Saml.	Ballysallagh	Lieutenant	R.A.M.C.	
McWha, Albert				
McWha, George				
McWha, Hugh				
McWha, James				
Malcolm, R. H.				Wounded.
Malcolm, W. H.	Craigavad	A.B.S.	R.N.	
Milligen, Hugh	Ballymoney			Killed in Action.
Moffett, Samuel	Clandeboye	Private	11th R.I.R.	Killed in Action.
Nelson, Albert	Crawfordsburn	Private		
Page, Albert	Crawfordsburn	Private		
Pyper, Thos. W.	Crawfordsburn	Sergt.-Major	N.I.H.	
Rollins, H. E.	Ballyrobert	Private	R.I.R.	
Rowney, Andrew	Crawfordsburn	Sergeant	R.I.R.	Wounded twice.
Rowney, Samuel	Crawfordsburn	Lance-Corporal	R.I.R.	
Taylor, W. E.	Ballyrobert	Private	R.E.	Killed in Action.
Torrens, Jas.	Ballymullan			Killed in Action.
Ward, John S.	Crawfordsburn			
Ward, Thos.	Crawfordsburn	Sapper	R.E.	
Warnock, Hugh	Crawfordsburn			
COLONIAL FORCES.				
Finlay, Andrew C.	Ballymullan	Private	N.Z. Force	
McDowell, Robt.	Crawfordsburn	Private	Can. Force	Killed in Action.
Macormac, Fred S.	Ballysallagh	Lieutenant	R.A.M.C.	
Rowney, Wm.	Crawfordsburn	Sergt.-Major	Can. M. Rifles	D.C.M.
BALLYGRAINEY.				
Alexander, Robt.	Cottown	Lance-Corporal	R.I.R.	Killed in Action.
Alexander, Wm.	Cottown	Private	R.I.R.	Killed in Action.
Beattie, John	Cottown	Private	R.I.R.	Wounded.
Bennett, James	Granshaw	Private	R.I.R.	Wounded.
Campbell, David	Cottown	Private	R.I.R.	Wounded.
Campbell, Wash.	Cottown	Private	R.I.R.	Killed in Action.

ARDS PRESBYTERY. BALLYGRAINEY.

Name.	Home Address.	Rank.	Regiment, Battalion, or Unit.	Remarks.
Frew, Joseph	Cottown	Private	A.S.C.	
Gaw, John	Ballycrochan	Sergeant	R.I.R.	Wounded.
Hanna, Thos.	Cottown	Lieutenant	A.S.C.	
Keating, John	Cottown	Private	R.I.R.	Killed in Action.
McCauley, Adam	Cottown	Private	R.I.R.	
McCauley, Wm. Robt.	Cottown	Private	R.I.R.	Prisoner of War.
McClelland, Jas.	Cottown	Private	R.I.R.	Killed in Action.
McClelland, Jas. A.	Cottown	Private	R.I.R.	Killed in Action.
McClelland, Saml. D.	Ballygrainey	Private	R.I.R.	
McClelland, Wm. John	Cottown	Private	R.I.R.	Prisoner of War.
McGimpsey, Jas.	Cottown	Private	R.I.R.	Wounded.
McWhinney, Robt. J.	Granshaw	Lieutenant	R.F.A.	
Melville, Gordon	Ballygrainey	Private	R.A.F.	
Montgomery, Andrew	Cottown	Private	R.I.R.	Killed in Action.
Moore, Thos	Ballygrainey	Lance-Corporal	A.S.C.	
Simpson, Thomas	Cottown	Private	R.A.F.	
Torrens, Jas. Claude	Granshaw	Lieutenant	M.G.C.	Killed in Action.
Wilson, Jas.	Cottown	Private	R.I.R.	

COLONIAL AND U.S.A. FORCES.

Name.	Home Address.	Rank.	Regiment, Battalion, or Unit.	Remarks.
Alexander, David	Cottown	Private	American Forces	
Alexander, James	Cottown	Private	American Forces	
Alexander, Wm.	Cottown	Private	American Forces	
McMillan, Thos.	Cottown	Private	N.Z.R.	
Taylor, John	Granshaw	Private	N.Z.R.	
Taylor, Thomas	Granshaw	Private	N.Z.R.	
Torrens, W. B.	Granshaw	Officer	American Forces	

FIRST BALLYWALTER.

Name.	Home Address.	Rank.	Regiment, Battalion, or Unit.	Remarks.
McCormick, William	Springvale	Private	2nd Hants.	
McCullough, Wallace	Ballywalter	Private	7th Tank. Batt.	Wounded.
Murland, Geo.	Ballywalter	Sapper	R.E.	
Scott, Chas. B.	Ballyobrian	Private.	Can. F.A.	

SECOND BALLYWALTER.

Name.	Home Address.	Rank.	Regiment, Battalion, or Unit.	Remarks.
Cromie, Alex.	Whitechurch	Private	8/9 R.I.R.	
Cromie, David	Ballywalter	Private	13th R.I.R.	Killed in Action.
Cromie, Robt. Jas.	Ballywalter	Private	E. Yorkshire Regt.	
Cromie, Thos.	Ballywalter	Private	11/13 R.I.R.	Wounded.
Dickson, Wm. Henry	Ganaway	Private	H.Q. 37th Div.	
Gunning, James	Ballywalter	Private	11th R.I.R.	
Gunning, Walter	Ballywalter	Lance-Corporal	13th R.I.R.	Killed in Action.
Hamilton, Saml.	Ballywalter	Private	R.I.R.	Wounded.
Harper, Hugh	Ballywalter	Seaman	R.N.	
Hunter, Wm.	Carrowdore	Private	11/13 R.I.R.	
Johnston, David	Dunover	Private	R.I.R.	
Lemon, Hugh	Ballywalter	Private	16th R.I.R.	
Lemon, Wm.	Ballywalter	Private	R.I. Fus.	
McCappin, Thos.	Ballywalter	C.P.O.	R.N.	
McDowell, Wm.	Ballywalter	Private	11th R.I.R.	Wounded.
O'Neill, John	Ballywalter	Private	13th R.I.R.	Killed in Action.
O'Neill, Samuel	Ballywalter	Private	H.Q. R.I.R.	
O'Neill, Wm.	Ballywalter	Private	20th R.I.R.	
Orr, Frank	Ballyhaskin	Private	3rd R.I.R.	
Orr, Hugh	Ballyhaskin	A.B.	R.N.	
Orr, John	Ballyhaskin	Private	12th R.I.R.	Killed in Action.
Reid, Wm.	Springvale	Private	A.S.C.	
Thompson, Robt.	Ballyferris	C.M.S.	K's.O.R. Lancasters	Killed in Action.
Thompson, R. J.	Ballywalter	Seaman	R.N.	
White, Gordon	Ballywalter	Lance-Corporal	8/9 R.I.R.	Killed in Action.
Young, Andrew	Dunover	Ship's Corporal	R.N.	

COLONIAL FORCES.

Name.	Home Address.	Rank.	Regiment, Battalion, or Unit.	Remarks.
Boyle, Alexander	Kilbright	Private	Australians	
Dorrian, James	Ballywalter	Private	Canadians	Killed in Action.
Dorrian, John	Ballywalter	Private	Canadians	
Harper, John	Ballywalter	Private	Canadians	Twice Wounded.
Orr, Andrew	Ballyhaskin	Private	Canadians	Killed in Action.
Orr, Nicholas	Ballyhaskin	Private	Canadians	

FIRST BANGOR.

Name.	Home Address.	Rank.	Regiment, Battalion, or Unit.	Remarks.
Agnew, Alex.	Castle Lodge	Rifleman	13th R.I. Rifles	Wounded.
Agnew, Edward	Demesne,	Lance-Corporal	R. Irish Rifles	Wounded.
Agnew, Harry	Demesne,	A.C.M.	R.A.F.	
Agnew, John	26 Victoria Road	C.Q.M.S.	R. Irish Rifles.	
Anderson, Robert	Albert Street	Private	R.I. Rifles	Killed in Action.
Angus, Samuel	28 Gray's Hill	C. Sgt.-Major	13th R.I. Rifles.	
Austin, Harry	92 University St., Belfast	A.B.	Royal Navy	
Austin, William	College Avenue	A.B.	Royal Navy	

ARDS PRESBYTERY.   FIRST BANGOR.

Name.	Home Address.	Rank.	Regiment, Battalion, or Unit.	Remarks.
Barbour, Wm.	54 Ballymagee Street	Driver	2nd Co. R.A.M.C.	
Beattie, W. H.	120 Seacliff Road	2nd Lieutenant	3rd R.I. Rifles	
Bell, P. S.	Farnham Road	Captain	A.S.C.	
Bell, Wm. R.	College Avenue	Captain	12th R.I. Rifles	M.C.
Black, A. M.	Bryansburn Road	Corporal	R.E. Signals	
Black, Hugh	Bryansburn Road	Private	M.T., A.S.C.	
Black, James	Bryansburn Road	C.Q.M.S.	The Black Watch	
Blair, A. E.	Seacliff Road	2/Lieut.	3rd Leinster Regt.	
Brand, Norman	The Bungalow, Ballyholme Road	A/Capt.	4th Hussars (Res.)	
Brown, A. V. L.	8 Belfast Terrace	Lieutenant	6th R.I. Rifles	Wounded.
Brown, Francis	8 Belfast Terrace	2/Lieutenant		Killed in Action.
Brown, Fred. A. J.	8 Belfast Terrace	L. Seaman	Royal Navy	
Brown, Leo	Demesne	Private	10th Corps Cyclists' Bn.	
Burns, Bertie	Waverley Drive	Driver	R.A.S.C., M.T.	
Burns, David McC.	Waverley Drive	Lance/Corporal	R.I. Rifles	
Campbell, Alex.	Abbey Street	Rifleman	R. Irish Rifles	Killed in Action.
Campbell, Archibald	Dufferin Avenue	Corporal	M.T., R.A.S.C.	
Campbell, J. D.	Hamilton Road	Lt.-Commander	R.N.V.R.	Ment. in Despatches
Campbell, John	14 Sunbury Avenue, Bloomfield, Belfast	Sergeant	14th R.I. Rifles	Twice Wounded.
Cooke, Wm.	25 Albert Street	Sapper	R.E., 89th Field Co.	Wounded.
Corbett, Wm.	45 Prospect Road	Sapper	R.E.	Twice wounded.
Cosgrove, H. H.	Daisy Hill, Banbridge	Captain	4th R. Irish Fus.	
Dobbs, Walter	Downshire Road	Cadet	A.S.C.	
Dudgeon, John E.	16 Ward Avenue	Sub-Lieutenant	R.N.V.R.	
Fairbairn, Alex.	19 Victoria Road	1st Class Petty Officer	Royal Navy	
Freeman, Wm.	Brunswick Road	C.S.M.	R.G.A.	
Gilmore, Robt.	14 Lr. Cargill St., Belfast	Lance-Corporal	2nd R.I. Rifles	
Girvan, C.	Ward Avenue	M. Mariner	Mercantile Marine	Meritorious Service Medal.
Graham, Chas.	The Lodge, Northland House, Dungannon	S.S. Major	5th R.I. Lancers	Twice Wounded. D.C.M. & M.M.
Graham, Robt.	72 Church Street	Lance-Corporal	R.I. Rifles	Wounded.
Gray, Alex.	9 Railwayview Street	Corporal	18th R.I. Rifles	Wounded.
Gray, Arthur	9 Railwayview Street	Gunner	E. Bn. 7th Res. Bgde. R.F.A.	
Gray, James	9 Railwayview Street	Rifleman	13th R.I. Rifles	
Gray, John, Sen.	16a Church Street	Driver	R.A.S.C.	
Gray, John, Jun.	16a Church Street	Private	R.A.S.C.	
Gray, Robt.	16a Church Street	Private	R. Irish Rifles	Killed in Action.
Greenwood, A. V.	59 Main Street	Private	R.A.M.C.	
Greenwood, J. E.	59 Main Street	Corporal	R.A.M.C.	M.M. Killed in Action.
Hannay, Herbert	37 Prospect Road	Driver	A.S.C.	
Hanna, Robert	23 Victoria Road	Private	18th R.I. Rifles	
Hardy, Frank	98 Castle Street	Private	R.A.F.	
Henderson, Walter	Downshire Road	Corporal	R.E.	
Henry, Thomas	Southwell Road	Gunner	13th Tanks	Twice Wounded.
Hollywood, Arthur	"Bayswater"	Lieutenant	9th R. Irish Fus.	Killed in Action.
Hollywood, Gerald	Princetown Road	Lieutenant	8th R. Irish Regt.	
Hollywood, James	"Bayswater"	2nd Lieutenant	12th R.I. Rifles	Killed in Action.
Holmes, John M.	Hamilton Road	Lieutenant	R.N.R.	
Holmes, Wm.	Downshire Road, H'wood	Chief E.R.A.	Royal Navy	Died.
Houston, Henry	26 Holborn Avenue	Rifleman	13th R.I. Rifles	Wounded.
Houston, Thos.	Castlemount	Rifleman	R.I. Rifles	
Houston, Wm	26 Holborn Avenue	Private	M.T., R.A.S.C.	
Hutchinson, J.	29 Brunswick Road	A.B.	Royal Navy	
Irvine, Duncan	Brisbane	2/Lieutenant	M.M.G.	Wounded.
Johnston, Albert	Ballymagee Street	Rifleman	17th R.I. Rifles	
Keenan, Wm. H.	10 Bingham Street	Captain	Machine Gun Corps	Ment. in Des.
Lawson, W. J.	41 Belfast Road, Bangor	Corporal	10th R.I. Rifles	Twice wounded.
Legge, Robert	14 Beatrice Road	Sapper	R.E.	
Lightbody, John	Ballymaconnell	Private	Royal Marines	
Lindsay, Hugh	47 & 49 Ballymagee St.	Driver	8th Aux. Horse Trans. R.A.S.C.	
Lindsay, Wm.	Beatrice Road	Private	13th R.I. Rifles	Wounded.
Lowry, Alex.	Bingham Street	Rifleman	18th R.I. Rifles	
Lowry, Herbert	Orlock	Private	13th R.I. Rifles	Wounded.
Lowry, Samuel	Bingham Street	Rifleman	10th R.I. Rifles	Wounded.
McAlpine, Geo. T.	Beatrice Avenue	Rifleman	R. Irish Rifles	Killed in Action.
McCauley, Wm. R.	94 Castle Street	Private	13th R.I. Rifles	
McClure, Samuel	46 Abbey Street	Rifleman	2nd R.I. Rifles	Twice Wounded.
McCready, Andrew	Castle Square	Rifleman	13th R.I. Rifles	Killed in Action.
McCready, Nathaniel	The Windmill, B'home	Rifleman	13th R.I. Rifles	Killed in Action.
McCready, Robert N.	Donaghadee Road	2nd Lieutenant	R. Irish Rifles	
McFeeters, Jack	College Avenue	L/Bombdr.	65 Siege Battery R.G.A.	
McGilton, David John	71 Railwayview Street	Lieutenant	R.I. Rifles	
McGilton, James	71 Railwayview Street	2/Lieutenant	8/9 R.I. Rifles	Killed in Action.
McCletchie, Wm. B.	Clifton Road	Sergeant	13th R.I. Rifles	
McMurray, Alex.	28 Dufferin Avenue	1st Class Stoker	Royal Navy	Killed in Action.
McMurray, Robert	28 Dufferin Avenue	1st Class Stoker	Royal Navy	
McMurray, Robert G.	Clifton Road	2/Lieutenant	R.F.C.	
McMurray, Thomas	Clifton Road	Private	13th R.I. Rifles	Three times Wd.
McNair, Robert	Primacy	Corporal	13th R.I. Rifles	Killed in Action.
McQuoid, Jim	102 Seacliff Road	Lieutenant	R. Irish Rifles	
McQuoid, Louis	102 Seacliff Road	A. L.-Sergeant	21st Glamorgan Yeomanry	Wounded.

ARDS PRESBYTERY. FIRST BANGOR.

Name.	Home Address.	Rank.	Regiment, Battalion, or Unit.	Remarks.
McQuoid, Urell	102 Seacliff Road			Killed in Action.
Maginnis, Andrew F.	3 Victoria Road	Lieutenant	Royal Navy	
Maginnis, Alex.	3 Victoria Road	Sergeant	7th M.G.C.	
Major, A.	80 Castle Street	A.C. 2	R.A.F.	
Major, James	13 Beatrice Avenue	Driver	2nd Co. R.A.S.C.	
Major, Wm.	80 Castle Street	Driver	M.T., R.A.S.C.	
Major, Wm. J.	60 Abbey Street	Rifleman	6th R.I. Rifles	Twice Wounded.
Malcolm, Wm.	The Hill, Groomsport	Driver	A.S.C.	Killed in Action.
Mann, Frazer	Railwayview Street	Sergeant	13th R.I. Rifles	Killed in Action.
Manning, F. E. B.	Ballyholme Road	Lieutenant	M.G.C., Army of Occupation, Egypt.	Wounded.
Martin, Wm.	Clandeboye, Co. Down	Private	R.I. Rifles	Wounded.
Martin, Wm. Herbert	Princetown Road	Sergeant	N. Irish Horse	
Mathers, Samuel	84 Castle Street	3rd Air Mechanic	R.A.F.	
Meek, Jack	71 Clifton Road	Midshipman	R.N.V.R.	
Meek, Wm. J.	71 Clifton Road	Lieutenant	R.N.V.R.	
Milliken, Jas., Jun.	8 Farnham Road	Lieutenant	R.I. Rifles	M.C.
Mitchell, Marcus	Queen's Parade	Lieutenant	11th R.I. Rifles	M.C. Wounded.
Miskelly, Thos.	King Street	Rifleman	13th R.I. Rifles	Killed in Action.
Miskelly, W. J.	Castle Square	Private	R. Scottish Fus.	
Moag, Charles	Rathgael	Trooper	N. Irish Horse	
Moorehead, J. F.	Princetown Road	Captain	R.A.S.C.	
Morrison, Fred. W.	Windsor Avenue	Lieutenant	M.G.C.	Wounded.
Morrison, Saml. M'G.	Windsor Avenue	Lieutenant	8th Cheshire	Wounded.
Mulholland, John	Ballymagee Street	Corporal	R.A.S.C.	
Orr, John	Castle Street	Rifleman	11th R.I. Rifles	Killed in Action.
Orr, Norman	39 Castlemount	Gunner	119 Siege Batt. R.G.A.	Wounded.
Orr, Samuel	16 Hopefield Ave, Belfast	Private	Army Ord. Corps	
Patterson, John W.	5 Prospect Road	Major	R.E.	D.S.O.
Patterson, Thos.	Castle Street	Private	13th R.I.R., attd. M.G.C.	Killed in Action.
Patton, Graham	Downshire Road	Major	R.A.M.C. T.F.	
Polson, John D.	68 Southwell Road	Telegraphist	Royal Navy	
Pollock, Clifford	Donaghadee Road	Lieutenant	R. Irish Fus.	
Rea, S. P.	Esplanade, Bangor	Captain	R.A.M.C.	Ment. in Des.
Reid, Thomas J.	43 Queen's Parade	Private	R. Irish Rifles	
Ritchie, Hugh	48 William St., N'ards	Private	R.F.A.	Twice Wounded.
Ritchie, John	19 Railwayview Street	Private	R.A.M.C.	
Ritchie, Thomas	10 Central Avenue	Private	Royal Marines	
Rogan, Patrick	55 Victoria Road	Seaman	Royal Navy	
Rowley, Thomas	Clandeboye	Rifleman	R.I. Rifles	
Savage, Alex., Sen.	17 Crosbie Street	Private	R. Marine Labour Corps	
Scott, Geo. B.	9 Bingham Street	Corporal	R.A.F.	
Scott, Harden	Station Ho., B'hinch	Lieutenant	R.F.C.	M.C. Killed in Action.
Scott, John	Bryansburn Road	Captain	R.A.M.C.	
Scott, Wm.	Croft Street		R.N.	Killed in Action
Seeton, A.	Ballyholme		Mercantile Marine	
Shanks, John	Ballymagee Street	Lieutenant	R.I. Rifles	Wounded.
Small, Thomas	Ballyholme Road	R.Q.M.S.	13th R.I. Rifles	Ment. in Des.
Smiley, Harry	8 Albert Street	Private	R.A.F.	
Smiley, Wm.	29 May Avenue	Corporal	R.A.S.C.	
Smith, Herbert	Farnham Park	Captain	R.A.M.C.	
Smith, S. A.	21 Beatrice Road	Sergeant	R.E.	M.M.
Stevenson, James	Gray's Hill	Private	R. Irish Rifles	
Stitt, Robert P.	5 Beatrice Road	A.B.	Royal Navy	
Stockman, Saml.	88 Chamberlayne Road, London	Major	R.A.M.C.	
Thompson, Stafford	Downshire Road	Private	M.T., A.S.C.	
Thompson, Stewart	Abbey Street	Private	R.A.M.C.	
Trotter, Chas.	Castle Street	Driver	R.A.S.C.	
Tyrrell, John Marcus	The Cairn, Ballyholme	Captain	R.A.F.	M.C. Killed in Action.
Tyrrell, Walter Alex.	The Cairn, Ballyholme	Captain	R.A.F.	M.C. Killed in Action.
Tyrrell, Wm. Ross	The Cairn, Ballyholme	Lt.-Colonel	R.A.M.C.	D.S.O. and Bar, Croix-de-Guerre, M.C.
Walkington, Tony	3 Belgravia	2nd Lieutenant	R.F.C.	
Wilson, Jack A.	Strathmona	Lance-Corporal	12th R.I. Rifles	
Wilson, Jas. M.	Strathmona	Corporal	R.E. (Signals)	
Wilson, Nial	Groomsport Road	L.A.C Wireless Op.	R.A.F.	
COLONIAL AND U.S.A. FORCES.				
Agnew, George	Demesne, Bangor	Private	1st Can. Motor Transport	
Alexander, Louis	Edmonton	Sergeant	49th Bn. C.E.F.	
Anderson, David	Albert Street, Bangor	Private	C.E.F.	Killed in Action.
Brown, J. Birch	Prospect Road, Bangor	2nd Lieutenant	Indian Army	
Dobbs, Jack	Downshire Road	Lieutenant	S.A. Remounts	
Francis, A. W.	3 Victoria Road	Private	N.Z.E.F.	
Graham, A.	Kansas, U.S.A.	1st Sergeant	N.Y. Scottish Highldrs.	
Graham, Samuel	Pittsburg, U.S.A.	Gunnery Sergeant	U.S. Marines	
Hanna, Robert B.	Queen's Parade	Private	Austr. E. Force	Killed in Action.
Harden, James	Ballynahinch	Sergeant	U.S.A. Army	Croix-de-Guerre.

ARDS PRESBYTERY.　　　　　　　　　　　　　　　　　　　　　　　　　　　　　　　　　　　FIRST BANGOR.

Name.	Home Address.	Rank.	Regiment, Battalion, or Unit.	Remarks.
Hennessy, James	Donaghadee Road	R.S.M.	24th Bn. Canadians	M.M. Killed in Action.
Holmes, A. M.	Auckland, N.Z.	Private	N.Z. R.A.M.C.	
Holmes, D. G.	Victoria, B.C.	Sergeant	7th Canadians	
Houston, James	Canterbury, N.Z.	Private	N.Z. Rifles	
Jackson, George	Toronto, Can.	Sergeant	13th R.I.R.	
Kennedy, Robert Foster	New York	Major	R.A.M.C.	
McBride, Wm. A.	Brunswick Rd., Bangor	Signaller	39th Battery C.F.A.	Wounded.
McCoy, Rev. William	80 Princetown Road		U.S. Navy	
McMillan, Hugh	59 Gray's Hill	Corporal	N.Z. Engineers	M.M. Wounded.
McMillan, Robt. J.	N.S. Wales	Private	18th Bn. Aust. Infantry	Killed in Action.
Matthews, Charles	Ballygrainey	Corporal	N.Z. Force	M.M. Twice Wd.
Ritchie, John	48 William St., N'ards	Private	N.Z. Force	Wounded.
Robinson, J. Scott	64 Dufferin Avenue	Private	S.A. L. Inft.	
Scott, Daniel	Bingham Street	Private	P.P Can. L. Inft.	Killed in Action.
Scott, Wm.	Bryansburn Road	Lieutenant	52nd Sikhs F.F.	
Stevenson, Harry	Groomsport Road	Sapper	2nd Can. Engineers	Wounded.
Stewart, Jas.	2 Central Avenue	Private	31st Can. Inft.	Killed in Action.
Wright, David S.	Ballyholme	Sergt.-Major	8th Can. M.G.C.	
Wright, Robert	Ballyholme	Private	N.Z.E.F.	
BANGOR, HAMILTON ROAD.				
Baxter, Harry	15 Ward Avenue	Private	R.M.L.I.	
Bell, Austin	45 Holborn Avenue	Sergt-Major	16th Batt. R.I.R.	Killed in Action.
Bell, Alex.	55 Railwayview Street	Steward	H.M.H.S. Magic II	
Berkeley, Lowry E.	Ardmore	Lieutenant	Connaught Rangers	Wounded.
Brown, Hugh	4 Bryansburn Road	Driver	R.A.S.C.	
Burroughs, Thos. J.	3 Mount Royal	Captain	13th R.I.R.	
Claney, John	80 Ballymagee Street	Trooper	Fortgary Horse	
Claney, Robert M.	80 Ballymagee Street	Private	Princess Patricia's L.I.	Killed in Action.
Claney, S. M.	80 Ballymagee Street	Lieutenant		
Combe, George	Gray's Hill	Sergeant	13th R.I.R.	
Godson, Harry	Gray's Hill	Sergeant	R.A.M.C.	
Gorman, W. J. R.	Bridge Street	Private	4th Canadians, 11th R.B.	Killed in Action.
Halliday, John	Church Street	Private	R.A.M.C.	
Hayes, John	Castle Street	Private	R.A.M.C.	
Hughes, Bert.	Ballyholme	Private	14th R.I.R. (Y.C.V. 1)	Killed in Action.
Hughes, Willie	Ballyholme	Private	14th R.I.R. (Y.C.V. 1)	Killed in Action.
McCartney, James	Ballymagee Street	A.S.	Submarine E56	
McChesney, John	King Street	Private	13th R.I.R.	
McClune, John	Castle Street	Sergeant	R.A.M.C.	
McCready, Robert, Jr.	Springfield Road	P.O.	R.N.A.S.	
McGimpsey, Thos., Jr	Sheridan Drive	Private	M.T., A.S.C.	
McGimpsey, Wm.	Sheridan Drive	P.O.	R.N.A.S	
Oliver, John	Church Street	Seaman	H.M. Monitor	
Paton, Frank	Ardmore	Q.M. Sergeant	18th R.I.R.	
Rea, David	Broadway	Private	18th R.I.R.	
Templeton, George	Southwell Road	Major	2nd R.I.R.	
Thompson, Wm. J.	King Street	Rifleman	12th R.I.R.	
BANGOR, TRINITY CHURCH.				
Beattie, Hugh	27 Beatrice Road	Private	R.I.Rifles	Wounded.
Beattie, John	41 Crosbie Street	Private	R.I.Rifles	
Breeze, John	35 Hamilton Road	Sergeant	16th R.I. Rifles	
Brown, David	22 Dufferin Avenue	Stoker	R.N.	
Brown, James	46 Albert Street	Private	R.I. Rifles	
Carruthers, Andrew	41 Crosbie Street	Private	R.I. Rifles	
Caughey, W. F.	Ranfurly Avenue	2nd Lieutenant	R.I.R.	Wounded.
Caulfield, J. N.	28 Albert Street	Sapper	R.I. Regiment	
Caulfield, R. H.	28 Albert Street	Private	R.I. Regiment	
Chambers, Joseph A.	45 Gray's Hill	Private	16th R.I. Rifles	
Cheyne, J. D. E.	Downshire Road	Lieutenant	Royal Garrison Artillery	
Clarke, Robert	39 Ballyholme Road	Private	R.A.M.C.	Wounded.
Conway, James	28 Castle Square	Private	R.I.R.	
Conway, Robert	28 Castle Square	Private	R.I.R.	
Conway, Wm. C.	28 Castle Square	Private	12th R.I.R.	Wounded.
Crawford, James	20 Alfred Street	Private	12th R.I.R.	
Crawford, Samuel	20 Alfred Street	Private	R.A.F.	
Davidson, A. F.	39 Victoria Road	Driver	Motor Transport	
Davidson, W. F.	39 Victoria Road	Driver	Motor Transport	
Dickson, Hugh	34 Church Street	Private	16th R.I.R.	
Dickson, Reuben	15 Victoria Road	Private	R.I.R.	
Foster, James M.	10 Beatrice Road	Corporal	Royal Air F.	
Fowler, Andrew	3 King Street	Gunner	Royal Navy	
Gordon, Robert	41 Church Street	Lance-Corporal	1st R.I.R.	
Gordon, Sandford	41 Church Street	Private	R.I.R.	Wounded.
Gorman, Albert	3 King Street	Private	13th R.I.R.	
Gorman, James	3 King Street	Private	13th R.I.R.	
Gorman, Samuel	3 King Street	Cook	A.D.M. Stores	Wounded.
Hanna, J. B.	47 Queen's Parade	Major	R.A.M.C.	
Hassan, Alex.	1 Brunswick Road	Stoker	R N.	Drowned.
Hassan, James	1 Brunswick Road	Driver	Armoured Car	

ARDS PRESBYTERY.   TRINITY CHURCH, BANGOR.

Name.	Home Address.	Rank.	Regiment, Battalion, or Unit.	Remarks.
Hassan, Wm.	1 Brunswick Road	...	R.N.	
Hoppes, James	3 Beatrice Avenue	Private	Garr. Art.	
Irwin, Norman	6 Ward Avenue	2nd Lieutenant	R.I.R.	
Legge, Norman	7 Southwell Road	Private	B.M.T.D.	Wounded.
Lindsay, Alex.	15 Victoria Road	Mechanic	R.A.F.	
Lowry, Alex.	35 Hamilton Road	Corporal	13th R.I.R.	Wounded.
Lowry, George	35 Hamilton Road	Private	17th R.I.R.	
Lyttle, Bertie	56 Seacliff Road	Private	13th R.I.R.	Died.
McAlpine, R. A.	36 Church Street	Sergt.-Major	A.S.C.	
McCaw, Andrew	10 Castle Street	Private	13th R.I.R.	
McCaw, James	37 Belfast Road	Corporal	Labour Batt.	
McCaw, John	37 Church Street	Corporal	R.I. Regt.	Wounded 3 times.
McClements, Samuel	20 Abbey Street	Gunner	Siege Battery	Wounded.
McClurg, James	4 Beatrice Avenue	Private	R.A.M.C.	
McKee, Wm.	Castle Cottages	Private	R.I.R.	
McMahon, Hugh	51 Victoria Road	Private	A.S.C.	
McMahon, Thos.	4 Primrose Street	Lance-Corporal	13th R.I.R.	
McNeill, H. H.	Springfield Road	2nd Lieutenant	R.I.R.	
McNeilly, Samuel	51 Castle Street	Private	R.I.R.	Wounded.
Magowan, Wm.	19 Alfred Street	Sergeant	R.I.R.	Wounded.
Mansfield, Jas. A.	Dufferin Villas	2nd Lieutenant	R.I.R.	
Mansfield, W. A.	Dufferin Villas	Trooper	N.I.H.	
Marshall, Stanley	Princetown Villas	P. Officer	Armoured Car	
Maxwell, S. W.	Seacliff Road	Private	Siege Battery	
Milne, George	25 Beatrice Road	Private	R.I.R.	Died.
Montgomery, John	47 Prospect Road	Private	R.I.R.	
Morrow, Edward	Seaview	2nd Lieutenant	24th R.I.R.	
Newell, Hugh	6 Castle Square	Private	R.I.R.	Killed in Action.
Newell, Leslie	6 Castle Square	Private	R.I.R.	Killed in Action.
Newell, Thos.	6 Castle Square	Sapper	R.E.	
Nicholson, J. C.	Mornington Park	Captain	R.A.M.C.	
Palmer, James	17 Holborn Avenue	Seaman	Mer. Marine	Drowned.
Patterson, Thos.	40 Botanic Road	Private	13th R.I.R.	Killed in Action.
Pollock, Clifford	34 Donaghadee Road	Lieutenant	R.I. Fus.	
Ritchie, Wm.	11 Crosby Street	Sergeant	A.S.C.	
Rowley, John	17 May Avenue	...		
Russell, David	Ballymagee	Driver	A.S.C.	
Savage, Andrew	16 Castle Square	Private	R.I.R.	
Savage, David	16 Castle Square	Private	King's Liverpool Regt.	
Savage, Robert	41 Prospect Road	2nd Lieutenant	10th R.I.R.	
Scott, David	21 Crosby Street	Private	16th R.I.R.	Prisoner.
Sheldon, R. H.	51 Castle Street	Attendant	R.A.M.C.	
Skimin, Captain	40 Holborn Avenue	Captain	Transport Service	Drowned.
Skimin, George	29 Crosby Street	Private	R.I.R.	Wounded.
Stewart, A. Knowles	Baymount	Lieutenant	Royal Engineers	
Storey, J. C.	51 Castle Street	Private	R.I.R.	
Todd, Thomas	48 Castle Street	Private	R.I.R.	Wounded.
Watterson, John	46 Castle Square	Corporal	13th R.I.R.	Wounded.
Wightman, Jas.	4 Castle Street	Corporal	A.S.C.	
Wright, Victor	82 Abbey Street	Private	36 T.R. Batt.	
	COLONIAL FORCES.			
Gordon, James	3 Broadway, Bangor	Private	Australian Force	
Gordon, Mark	3 Broadway, Bangor	Private	Australian Force	
Gorman, Alex.	3 King Street	...	Canadian Force	Wounded.
Harvey, Robert	18 Belfast Road	Driver	4th Canadian Force	
Jordan, Robert	39 Beatrice Road	Private	Australian Force	Killed in Action.
Legge, William	7 Southwell Road	Private	Canadian Force	Wounded.
Lindsay, Albert	15 Victoria Road	Private	Canadian Infty.	
Lindsay, Robert	15 Victoria Road	...	Canadian F.A.	
Neill, J. Wilson	1 Windsor Avenue	Captain	1st Can. Mounted Rifles	
Newell, Walter	6 Castle Square	Private	Canadian Infty.	
Oliver, Samuel	70 Church Street	Private	Canadian Infty.	
	CARROWDORE.			
Bailie, Samuel	Ballyboley	Private	R.I.R.	
Barclay, James	Cairney Hill	Sergeant	R.I.R.	Wounded.
Beck, Hugh	Sloanstown	...		
Burrows, James C.	Carrowdore	Private	R.I.R.	Wounded.
Ewart, Frank	Ganaway	Surgeon	R.N.	O.B.E.
McClure, Rev. William	Carrowdore	C.F.	R.A.C.D.	
McClure, W. S.	Ballyhaskin	Private	R.A.M.C.	
Morrow, James	Carrowdore	Private	R.I.R.	Killed in Action.
Morrow, Thomas	Carrowdore	Private	R.I.R.	
Morrow, Samuel	Carrowdore	Private	R.I.R.	Wounded.
Reid, Samuel	Ballyboley	Private	R.I.R.	Wounded.
Robson, James	Carrowdore	Private	R.I.R.	
Taylor, James	Carrowdore	Private	Bute Artillery	
White, Samuel	Carrowdore	Private	R.I.R.	Wounded
Woods, Robert	Carrowdore	...	R.N.	
Workman, W. E. H.	Carrowdore Castle	Major		

ARDS PRESBYTERY. CARROWDORE.

Name.	Home Address.	Rank.	Regiment, Battalion, or Unit.	Remarks.
	COLONIAL AND U.S.A. FORCES.			
Hamilton, Thomas	Ballyboley	Private	Can. Force	
McConnell, E.	Drumfad	Private	Aust. Force	
McConnell, James	Drumfad	Private	Can. Force	
McDermott,	Carrowdore	Private	Can. Force	
Reid, John	Ballyboley	Driver	Can. Force	
Reid, James	Carrowdore	Private	U.S.A. Force	
Shanks, Robert T.	Ballyboley	Private	Can. Force	Wounded.
	CLOUGHEY.			
Barbour, R. Stanley	Red House	Lieutenant	R.A. Force	
Donnan, James	Cloughey	Private	11th R.I.R.	
Donnan, James	Cloughey	Seaman	H.M.S. Donegal	
Finnegan, Wm.	Drummerdon	Seaman	H.M.S. Tiger	
Monan, James	Ardminan	Private	R.I.R.	
Palmer, James	Cloughey	Lance-Corporal	16th R.I.R.	D.C.M. Wounded.
Thompson, James	Kirkeston	Private	13th R.I.R.	Killed in Action.
	COLONIAL AND U.S.A. FORCES.			
Donnan, Thomas	Cloughey	Private	N.Z. Infantry	Killed in Action.
McQuitty, George	Kirkeston, Cloughey	Private	8th Canadian Infantry	Prisoner of War.
McQuitty, James	Kirkeston, Cloughey	Corporal	Tasmanian Forces	Wounded.
Thompson, Wm.	Kirkeston, Cloughey	Private	U.S.A. Army	
	CONLIG.			
Aiken, Edward	Conlig	Private	1st Bn. R.I. Rifles	Killed in Action.
Ballard, James T.	Conlig	Private	Labour Corps	
Brown, James	Church St., N'ards	Private	12th Bn. R.I.R.	Prisoner, released.
Burns, George	Conlig	Private	1st R.I.R.	Killed in Action.
Burns, James	Conlig	Private	1st Bn. R.I.R.	Died.
Burns, John	Conlig	Private	R. Innis Fus.	Wounded.
Burns, Wm. T.	Conlig	Seaman	R.N. (T.B.D.)	
Cairns, Wm.	Conlig	Private		
Carlisle, Alex.	Conlig	Private	9th R.I. Rifles	Killed in Action.
Carlisle, James	Conlig	Private	4th R.I.R.	Twice Wounded.
Conway, Fredk.	Conlig	Private	13th R.I.R.	Prisoner, released.
Dickson, Joseph	Conlig	Private	A.S.C.	
Dickson, Reuben	Conlig	2nd Lieutenant	N.I. Horse	
Gamble, David	Conlig	Private	1st R.I. Rifles	Prisoner, Killed in attempting escape.
Gore, John	Conlig	Private	Labour Corps	
Gore, Bertie	Conlig	Private	R.I. Rifles	
Hamilton, Samuel	Conlig	Sergeant	M.G.C.	Wounded.
Lightbody, James	Conlig	Private	11th R.I. Rifles	Wounded.
Lightbody, James	Conlig	Lance-Corporal	2nd King's Liverpool Regt.	
McCamley, Wm.	Conlig	Private	20th R.I.R.	
McClements, Alex.	Conlig	Private	14th R.I.R.	Missing, believed killed.
McGimpsey, John	Conlig	Sergeant	4th R.I.R.	Wounded.
Montgomery, Hugh	Conlig	Sapper	Royal Engineers	
Montgomery, John	Conlig	Sergeant	1st & 12th R.Innis.Fus. M.G.C.	Died of Wounds.
Montgomery, Joseph	Conlig	Private	11th R.I. Rifles	Wounded.
Montgomery, Thos.	Conlig	Private	11th R.I.R.	Killed in Action.
Montgomery, William	Conlig	Private	4th R.I. Rifles	
Nelson, James	Conlig	Corporal	R.E.	Wounded.
Rea, Hugh	Conlig	Gunner	R.F.A. (106th Brigade)	
Sloan, William	Conlig	Private	11th R.I. Rifles	Killed in Action.
Stone, Robert	Conlig	Private	13th R.I. Rifles	Killed in Action.
Stone, Wm., Senr.	Conlig	Private	R.F.A.	
Stone, Wm., Junr.	Conlig	Private	20th R.I.R.	
Welsh, Hugh	Conlig	Private	11th R.I.R.	Killed in Action.
	COLONIAL AND U.S.A. FORCES.			
Gamble, Alex.	Auckland, N.Z.	Gunner	N.Z. Field Art. (2nd Brig.)	
Gibson, Wm.		Private	N.Z. Forces	
Ladley, Wm.		Private	U.S.A. Forces	
	DONAGHADEE.			
Boyd, Samuel	Portavo	Stoker P.O.	R.N.	
Boyd, Thomas F.	Portavo	Torpedo Gunner	R.N.	
Boyd, William J.	Portavo	Sergeant	13th Batt. R.I.R.	Wounded.
Fullerton, John	Donaghadee	Private	2nd Artists' Rifles	
Fullerton, Marcus	Donaghadee	Lieutenant	K.A.R.	
Fullerton, Peter	Donaghadee	3rd Officer	H.M.T. Sutton Hall	
Gilliland, John	Donaghadee	Midshipman	R.N.V.R.	
Hamilton, William	Donaghadee	Private	A.S.C.	
Haseldine, Frederick				
Herron, William	Donaghadee	Sergeant	R.E.	M.M.

ARDS PRESBYTERY. DONAGHADEE.

Name.	Home Address.	Rank.	Regiment, Battalion, or Unit.	Remarks.
Herron, John	Donaghadee	Corporal	A.S.C.	
Heybourne, William	Donaghadee	Staff Sergt.	3rd R.I.R.	
Keith, Andrew	Ballyvester	Sergeant	11/13 R.I.R.	M.M. Wounded.
Keith, Thomas	Ballyvester	Private	R.I.R.	Killed in Action.
McPeake, Herbert	Donaghadee	Corporal	12th R.I.R.	D.C.M. Wounded.
McCullough, James	Donaghadee	Private	4th R.I.R.	Killed in Action.
McCullough, John	Donaghadee	Private	4th R.I.R.	Wounded.
Magill, Albert	Ballyvester	Rifleman	2nd R.I.R.	
Moore, David D.	Donaghadee	Captain	R.I.R.	
Muckle, James Smith	Donaghadee	Gunner	R.G.A.	
Mulholland, I. A.	Donaghadee	Major	R.I.R.	M.C., Frch Croix-de-Guerre with Palm. Twice ment. in Despatches.
Mulholland, H.H.	Donaghadee	Major	R.A.M.C	
Mulholland, D. O.	Donaghadee	Major	Connaught Rangers, R.A.F.	Ment. in Des.
Mulholland, G. P.	Donaghadee	Lieutenant	R.A.F.	Fatiche-de-Guerra.
Patton, Thos. McBride	Ballywilliam	Private	R.I.R.	Died of Wounds.
Robinson, James	Cannyreagh	Private	12th R.I.R.	Died of Wounds.
Walker, William M.	Donaghadee	Major	R.A.M.C.	M.C., Mons Star.
Walker, S. Howard	Donaghadee	Lieutenant	R.I. Regt., T.M.B.	Ment. in Des.
COLONIAL AND U.S.A. FORCES.				
Brown, John H.	S. Africa	Private	S.A.R.E.	
Hamilton, John C.	Donaghadee	Private	Canadian A.M.C.	
Hamilton, P. K.	Donaghadee	Private	Canadian M.R.	Wounded.
Keath, W. James	Ballyvester	Sergeant	Canadian 1st Div.	M.M. and Bar.
Sloan, Jas. Finlay	Donaghadee	Private	Atago M.R.	Wounded.
Sloan, Wm.	Donaghadee	Private	U.S. V.C.	
Taylor, Samuel	Cannyreagh	Private	Canadian M.R.	Died of Wounds.
DONAGHADEE, SHORE STREET.				
Agnew, John	Donaghadee			
Angus, Akel	Donaghadee			
Angus, Alex.	Donaghadee			
Angus, Francis	Donaghadee	Private		
Angus, George	Donaghadee	Rifleman	R.I.R.	Wounded.
Angus, Haisley	Donaghadee	Rifleman		Wounded.
Angus, James	Bangor			Killed in Action.
Angus, John B.	Bangor	Rifleman		Killed in Action.
Angus, Robert	Bangor			Killed in Action.
Angus, Samuel	Bangor	Sergt.-Major	R.I.R.	
Angus, Thomas	Donaghadee		R.I.F.	Prisoner of War.
Angus, Wm.	Donaghadee			Killed in Action.
Angus, Wm.	Donaghadee			
Bunting, James	Donaghadee	Sergeant	A.S.C.	
Bunting, John	Donaghadee	A.B.	R.N.	
Bunting, Robert	Donaghadee	Corporal	R.I.R.	Wounded.
Campbell, Alex.	Donaghadee	Lance-Corporal	R.I.R.	Killed in Action.
Campbell, Wm.	Portavo, Donaghadee			
Clegg, Matthew	Donaghadee	Rifleman	R.I.R.	
Clegg, Richard	Donaghadee	Private	A.S.C.	
Clegg, Robert	Copeland Island	Lieutenant		
Clegg, Robert	Shore Street	Rifleman	R.I.R.	
Donnen, John	Donaghadee			
Foster, Robert	Donaghadee	Rifleman	R.I.R.	Wounded.
Fullerton, David	Donaghadee			
Fullerton, Robert				
Fulton, Edward	Donaghadee			
Galway, James	Donaghadee	Corporal	K.O.S.B.	3 times Wounded.
Gaw, John	Donaghadee	Lance-Corporal	R.I.R.	
Girvan, Alex.	Donaghadee	Driver	R.E.	Wounded.
Gray, Alex.	Donaghadee	Corporal	R.I.R.	Wounded.
Haisley, Samuel	Donaghadee	Private	R.E.	
Hamil, Peter	Donaghadee	Rifleman	R.I.R.	Wounded.
Hamilton, Andrew	Donaghadee	A.B.	R.N.	Wounded.
Harper, Wm.	Donaghadee	Sergeant		
Harper, Wm.	Donaghadee	Captain	I.W.T.	
Herron, Samuel	Donaghadee			
Kennedy, Morris	Donaghadee	A.B.		
Kennedy, Thos.	Donaghadee	C. Officer		
Lennon, James	Donaghadee	Private	R.E.	Wounded.
Lennon, Thos.	Donaghadee	Private	A.O.C.	
Lindsay, Andrew	Donaghadee			
Lindsay, Francis W.		Rifleman	R.I.R.	
London, Benjamin	Donaghadee	Sergeant	Black Watch	
London, Henry				
McCullough, John	Donaghadee	Rifleman	R.I.R.	Killed in Action.
McCutcheon, Jas.	Donaghadee	Rifleman	R.I.R.	Wounded.
McDowell, Fergus	Donaghadee	Rifleman	R.I.R.	Wounded.
McDowell, John		A.B.		
McGaffin, Jas.	Ballyhoy, Donaghadee	Private		Killed in Action.

ARDS PRESBYTERY.   SHORE STREET, DONAGHADEE.

Name.	Home Address.	Rank.	Regiment, Battalion, or Unit.	Remarks
McGaffin, Robert	Ballyhoy, Donaghadee	...	...	Killed in Action.
Magowan, Alex.	...	Driver	A.S.C.	Wounded.
Magowan, Robert	...	...	...	...
Magowan, Thos.	...	...	...	Killed in Action.
Mateer, Robert	Ballywilliam	Private	...	Killed in Action.
Melville, Wm.	Donaghadee	Private	R. Inn. Fus.	Wounded.
Menown, And.	...	...	...	Wounded.
Moderate, Henry	Donaghadee	Private	Tanks	Wounded.
Moore, Wm.	Donaghadee	Driver	R.E.	
Morrow, John	Herdstown, Donaghadee	Rifleman	R.I.R.	Wounded.
Patton, John	...	...	...	Prisoner.
Patton, Robert	...	Rifleman	R.I.R.	Killed in Action.
Patton, Wm.	...	...	...	Killed in Action.
Robinson, Robert	Donaghadee	...	...	
Semple, Hugh	Donaghadee	...	...	Prisoner
Semple, James	Herdstown	Private	...	Killed in Action.
Semple, Robert	East Street	Rifleman	R.I.R.	Killed in Action.
Semple, Wm.	East Street	...	...	Killed in Action.
Semple, Wm.	Manor Street	...	...	
Strain, John	Herdstown	Driver	M.G.C.	
Tanner, Wm.	Donaghadee	...	...	Killed in Action.
Thompson, Chas.	Donaghadee	...	...	Killed in Action.
COLONIAL FORCE.				
Campbell, David	Donaghadee	Private	Canadians	
McMillan, Alex.	Donaghadee	Corporal	Canadians	Wounded.
GLASTRY.				
Bailie, D.	Ballyhalbert	Lance-Corporal	R.I.R.	
Bailie, H. S.	Portavogie	Private	R.S.F.	Killed in Action.
Bailie, J.	Ballyhalbert	Rifleman	R.I.R.	
Bailie, T.	Ballyhalbert	Private	M.G.C.	Wounded.
Bell, R. S. S.	Ballyhalbert	Private	B.E.F.	
Bell, T.	Ballyhalbert	Lance-Corporal	R.I.R.	
Boyd, D. H.	Ballyhalbert	Leading Stoker	R.N.	
Boyd, W.	Ballyhalbert	Private	M.G.C.	
Browne, H.	Ballyfrench	Rifleman	R.I.R.	
Caughey, J.	Rureagh	Rifleman	R.I.R.	Wounded.
Caughey, W.	Rureagh	Rifleman	R.I.R.	Wounded.
Donnan, H.	Ballyfrench	Rifleman	R.I.R.	Gassed.
Ennis, R.	Ballyhalbert	Leading Stoker	R.N.	Killed in Action.
Gowan, G.	Portavogie	Private	R. Innis. F.	
Hagan, J.	Ballyeasboro	Lance-Corporal	R.I.R.	Wounded.
Hanna, W.	Ballyeasboro	Sergeant	R.I.R.	Killed in Action.
Harpur, W. J.	Ballyhalbert	Rifleman	R.I.R.	
Henry, J.	Glastry	Rifleman	R.I.R.	
Hughes, R.	Portavogie	Lieutenant	R.N.R.	
Mahood, J. P.	Portavogie	Corporal	R.I.R.	
McCormack, R.	Portavogie	Leading Stoker	R.N.	
Moreland, J.	Glastry	Stoker	R.N.R.	Killed in Action.
Orr, J.	Ballyhalbert	Leading Stoker	R.N.R.	
Smith, J. B.	Portavogie	Lieutenant	R.N.R.	
Thompson, J.	Ballyhalbert	Leading Seaman	R.N.R.	
Thompson, R. J.	Ballyhalbert	Leading Seaman	R.N.R.	
Thompson, T. H.	Ballyhalbert	Rifleman	R.I.R.	
Warnock, W. W.	Ballygraffin	Lieutenant	R.I.R.	
Warnock, J.	Ballygraffin	Driver	R.A.S.C.	Awarded M.M.
Young, A.	Ballyhalbert	P.O.	R.N.	
Young, S.	Ballyhalbert	Leading Stoker	R.N.R.	
Young, W. J.	Ballyhalbert	Leading Seaman	R.N.R.	Wounded.
COLONIAL AND U.S.A. FORCES.				
Bailie, R.	Ballyhalbert	Private	C.E.F.	
Bell, J.	Ballyhalbert	Private	U.S. Army	
Bell, P.	Ballyhalbert	Private	C.E.F.	
Caughey, S. W.	Ballyhalbert	Sergeant	C.E.F.	
Donnan, T.	Ballyfrench	Private	U.S. Army	
Hill, R.	Glastry	Private	A.E.F.	
Hughes, J.	Portavogie	Rifleman	C.E.F.	Awarded M.M.
Johnston, H. T.	Ballyfrench	Private	U.S. Army	
Johnston, J. G.	Ballyfrench	Private	U.S. Army	
Johnston, W.	Ballyfrench	Private	U.S. Army	
Keag, R.	Echlinville	Sergeant	U.S. Army	
Palmer, J.	Ballyhalbert	Seaman	U.S.A. N.R.	
Palmer, R.	Ballyeasboro	Sergeant	C.E.F.	
Palmer, W.	Portavogie	Private	C.E.F.	Wounded.
Ritchie, A. F.	Ballyhalbert	Private	C.M.C.	
Ritchie, H. G.	Ballyhalbert	Private	C.E.F.	
Smiley, J.	Glastry	Sergt.-Major	C.M.T.	
Tibbs, H.	Ballyeasboro	Corporal	U.S. Army	

ARDS PRESBYTERY.   TRINITY CHURCH, GREYABBEY.

Name.	Home Address.	Rank.	Regiment, Battalion, or Unit.	Remarks.
	GREYABBEY, TRINITY CHURCH.			
Armour, James	Greyabbey	Private	R.I.R.	
Bowden, Samuel	Tullycaney, Greyabbey	Private	N.I.H.	
Davidson, Walter	Greyabbey	Sergeant	Gordon Highlanders	
Finlay, John	Islands, Greyabbey	Corporal	King's Life Guards	
Hunter, Wm.	Greyabbey	Private	R.I.R.	
McCallum, Hugh	Greyabbey	Sergt.-Major	R.I.R.	Killed in Action.
McCready, Samuel	Greyabbey	Private	R.I.R.	
McCready, Wm. John	Greyabbey	Private	R.I.R.	
McGimpsey, James	Greyabbey	Private	9th Royal Scots	Killed in Action.
McKay, John	Greyabbey	Private	R.I.R.	
Pritchard, John	Tullycaney, Greyabbey	Private	R.I.R.	
	COLONIAL AND U.S.A. FORCES.			
Atchison, John		Private	Canadian Army	
Hamilton, Jas.		Sergeant	Canadian Army	Killed in Action.
Stewart, Wm. S.		Private	Australian Contgt.	
	GROOMSPORT.			
Apperson, Geo. J.	Seabreeze, Ballyholme, Bangor	Captain	13th R.I. Rifles	Twice Wounded. Awarded M.C.
Apperson, Wm.	Seabreeze, Ballyholme	Private	13th R.I. Rifles	
Barrons, Patrick	Groomsport	Private	13th R.I. Rifles	
Barrons, Alexr.	Groomsport	Lance-Corporal	R.I. Rifles	Wounded.
Blakeley, Hugh	Groomsport	Private	13th R.I. Rifles	Wounded.
Brewer, Harry H.	Sheridan Villas, B'holme	Lieutenant	Durham Light Infantry	Twice Wounded. Croix-de-Guerre.
Gardner, Campbell	Groomsport	Lieutenant	Gen. Ser. Recruiting Officer	
Graham, Wm.	Ballymaconnell Road, Bangor	Private	A.S.C.	
Graham, Thos.	Ballymaconnell Road, Bangor	Private	12th R.I. Rifles	
Hamilton, John N.	Groomsport	Private	13th R.I. Rifles	
Hamilton, Samuel	Groomsport	Private	12th R.I. Rifles	Wounded.
Kennedy, John R.	Groomsport	Apprentice	H.M. Transport	T'pedoed in Action.
Kingan, Thos. D.	Glenganagh, Bangor	Lieutenant	13th R.I. Rifles	Wounded.
Legate, Rev. John N. M.	Groomsport Manse, B'ngor	Captain	C.F.	
Lightbody, John	Portavoe, Donaghadee	Private	R.M.L.I.	
Lightbody, Wm.	Portavoe, Donaghadee	Private	R.I. Rifles	Twice wounded.
McCullough, W. J.	Ballymacormick, Bangor	A.B.	H.M.S. Erin	
McDowell, John	Windmill Ho., B'holme	Private	14th R.I.R. and Tanks Corps	
Mailey, James	B'maconnell Rd., Bangor	Private	13th R.I. Rifles	Wounded.
Montgomery, A. C.	Ballyholme Ho., Bangor	Private	Black Watch	
Mooney, Alexr.	Balloo, Groomsport	Private	12th R.I. Rifles	
Orr, James	Groomsport	Private	Cheshire Regt.	Killed in Action.
Orr, Wm.	Groomsport	A.B.	H.M.S. Sydney	
Parke, Jos. B.	Sheridan Drive, B'holme	Lieutenant	18th R.I. Rifles	
Parker, Francis	B'maconnell Ho., Bangor	Private	13th R.I. Rifles	
Patton, Robt.	Glenganagh Cot., Bangor	Private	13th R.I. Rifles	Wounded.
Savage, Alexr.	Donaghadee Rd., Bangor	Sapper	R.E.	
Somers, John	Groomsport	Private	Seaforth Highlanders	Wounded 4 times.
	COLONIAL FORCE.			
Mooney, Hugh	Ballymaconnell Road	Corporal	Canadian Infantry	Wounded.
	HELEN'S BAY.			
Buchan, R.	Coastguard Station	Stoker R.N.	R.N.	
Eley, Wm.		Private	R.I.R.	Wounded.
Hamilton, J. E.	The Manse	Captain	R.A. Ch.D.	Awarded M.C.
Harper, G.	Etna Lodge	Private	R.I.R.	
Hopkins, —	Helen's Bay	Sergeant	R. Innis. Fus.	Awarded M.M.
Liddell, G.	Helen's Bay	Lance-Corporal	13th R.I.R.	
Livingstone-Learmonth, B. L.	Helen's Bay	Captain	R.A.M.C.	
Roaney, Wm.	Helen's Bay	Sergeant	P.P.L.I.	Awarded D.C.M.
Ross, D.	Dunrobin	Lieutenant	R.G.A.	
Workman, R.	Craigdarragh	Major	R.I.R.	Wounded.
Workman, E.	Craigdarragh	Captain	R.I.F.	
Russell, D.	Helen's Bay	Sergeant	U.S.A. Q.U. Corps	
	FIRST HOLYWOOD.			
Allan, Jack	The Kinnegar, Holywood	2nd Lieutenant	R.F.C.	Awarded D.C.M.
Anderson, Albert	High Street, Holywood	2nd Lieutenant	R.I. Rifles	Killed in Action.
Anderson, Cecil	The Kinnegar, Holywood	Private	R.I. Rifles	
Anderson, Samuel	Newtownards	2nd Lieutenant	R.I. Rifles	
Black, Samuel	Redburn Lodge	Q.M. Sergeant	10th R.I. Rifles	Ment. in Des.
Blakley, John	Trevor Street	Private	35th M.G.C.	
Boyd, Hugh	Downshire Road	Sergeant	18th R.I. Rifles	

ARDS PRESBYTERY. FIRST HOLYWOOD.

Name.	Home Address.	Rank.	Regiment, Battalion, or Unit.	Remarks.
Brown, Robert L. G.	Bellvue	Private	A.S.C.	
Brown, Nathaniel	Bellvue	Trooper	N.I.H.	
Burrows, W. F.	Belfast Road	Private	A.S.C.	
Calwell, Theo. L.	Spafield	Lieutenant	R.F.	Awarded M.C. Killed in Action.
Calwell, Walter H.	Spafield	2nd Lieutenant	5th R.I. Rifles	Killed in Action.
Calwell, William	Spafield	Captain	Doctor R.A.M.C.	
Caughey, James	Downshire Road	Pioneer Sergeant	20th R.I. Rifles	
Caughey, Samuel	Downshire Road	Private	R.I. Rifles	
Chambers, James	Belfast Road	Private	R.I. Regt.	
Cowan, Alex.	Marino, Co. Down	Trooper	N.I.H.	
Cowan, James	Marino, Co. Down	Driver	Motor Transport	
Dickson, Roland	High Street	2nd Airman	R.F.C.	
Dougan, John	Victoria Road	Gunner	R.E. M.G.C.	
Dougan, W. J. H.	Victoria Road	Sapper	121 Field Co. R.E.	
Emerson, Samuel	The Kinnegar	Corporal	R.I. Rifles	
Ferguson, R. H.	High Street	Lieutenant	9th K.O.V.L.I.	
Fitzsimmons, Henry	Hill Street	A 13	R.N.	
Fitzsimmons, William	Hill Street	Private	R.I. Rifles	
Forsythe, Jack	Plasmerdyn	Cadet	R.I. Rifles	
Forsythe, William	Plasmerdyn	2nd Lieutenant	R.I. Rifles	
Francis, Dick	Shore Street	Private	R.F.C.	
Galbraith, George	Ballykeel, Holywood	Private	A.S.C.	
Graham, Henry	Spencer Street	Sapper	R.E.	
Graham, Hugh	Spencer Street	Private	R.I. Rifles	Killed in Action.
Graham, Sam	Spencer Street	Leading Seaman	H.M.S. Leander	
Graham, John	Spencer Street	Rifleman	R.I. Rifles	
Greenlees, John	Ballycultra	Private	R.E.	
Hunter, John D.	Botanic Av., Belfast	Q.M. Sergt.-Major	R.I. Rifles	
Hunter, Robert	Marine Parade	Private	King's Liverpool Regt.	
Johnston, James	Church View	2nd Lieutenant	R.I. Rifles	
Kenney, Robert	Ballymiscaw	Private	R.I. Rifles	
Lynch, Thos. A.	Church Avenue	Private	11th Royal Scottish Fusiliers	
McBride, William	Seacliffe Road, Bangor	Driver	A.S.C.	
McCall, William	Downshire Road	2nd Lieutenant	R.I. Rifles	
McDowell, William	Whinny Hill		R.F.C.	
McFadden, David	Knocknagoney	Sapper	121 R.E.	
McKeag, Harry	Trevor Street	Private	13th Middlesex Regt.	
McKibbin, Henry	Spencer Street	Private	R.I. Rifles	
McKibbin, Joseph	Spencer Street	Private	14th R.I. Rifles	Missing, believed killed.
McKibbin, William	Spencer Street	Gunner	H.M.S. Emperor of India	
McLarty, Duncan	Spencer Street	Sapper	11th R.E.	
McLintie, F. J.	Spencer Street	Sergt.-Major	Battery	
McMurray, David	Bath Terrace	Private	M.T. A.S.C.	
Macartney, William	Plasmerdyn	Private	Irish Guards	
Mackey, John J.	The Kinnegar	Co. Sergt.-Major	14th R.I. Rifles	
Magill, Edgar	Marino, Co. Down	Gunner	Tank Corps	
Magill, Joseph	Marino, Co. Down	Petty Officer	H.M.S. Colossus	
Magill, Thomas S.	Marino, Co. Down	Gunner	H.M.S.Q. 26	
Magill, William	Marino, Co. Down	Stoker	H.M.S. Sutlej	
Malcolm, Samuel	High Street	Rifleman	13th R.I. Rifles	
Malcolm, Walter	High Street	Rifleman	8th R.I. Rifles	Prisoner of War
Megaw, David	The Strand	Sergeant	K.O.S.B.	Awarded M.M.
Mulholland, John	Trevor Street	Rifleman	R.I. Rifles	
Murdock, Alex.	Spencer Street	Rifleman	R.I. Rifles	
Murdock, Henry	Spencer Street	Rifleman	R.I. Rifles	Killed in Action.
Murdock, Samuel	Spencer Street	Rifleman	R.I Rifles	Died of Wounds.
Murray, James	Glenside	Private	Armoured Cars	
Nelson, Tom	Stewart's Place	Driver	R.I. Rifles	
Nelson, James	Stewart's Place	Private	K.O. Roy. Lancashire Regt.	
Pettigrew, George	Ballymenoch	Private	R.I. Rifles	
Pettigrew, Robert	Ballymenoch	Private	R.I Rifles	
Purdy, David	36 Camden St., Belfast	Private	R.E.	
Purdy, Hugh	36 Camden St., Belfast	Private	R.I. Rifles	
Purdy, W. M.	36 Camden St., Belfast	Private	A.F.C.	
Rea, Thomas	Ballykeel	Private	Royal Navy	Prisoner of War.
Richardson, Sam	Church Road	Gunner		
Richardson, Thomas	Church Road	Private	M.G.C.	Killed in Action.
Rollins, Harold E.	Brook Street	Private	R.I. Rifles	
Simpson, John	Shore Road	Rifleman	R.I. Rifles	
Smyth, Harry P.	The Kinnegar	Sergeant	R.I. Rifles	
Tait, Douglas	Bellevue	Sergeant	R.I. Rifles	
Tait, Joseph S.	Bellevue	Sergeant	School of Instruction	
Templeton, James	Trevor Street	Lance-Corporal	R.I. Rifles	
Templeton, Robert	Trevor Street	Private	M.G.C.	
Thompson, Alfred	Churchfield	Trooper	N.I.H., M.M.P.	
Waterfield, James	Spencer Street	Acting Bombardier	H.M.S. Dreadnought	
White, Alex.	Bath Terrace	Stoker	Royal Navy	
White, James	The Strand	Rifleman	R.I. Rifles	Prisoner of War.
White, Robert G.	The Strand	Private	R.I. Rifles	
Wilson, Hugh	Downshire Road	Rifleman	R.I. Rifles	
Wilson, William C.	Downshire Road	Rifleman	R.I. Rifles	Killed in Action.
Woods, Jack	Churchfield	Lieutenant	R.N.R.	

ARDS PRESBYTERY. FIRST HOLYWOOD.

Name.	Home Address.	Rank.	Regiment, Battalion, or Unit.	Remarks.
Woods, Norman H.	Churchfield	Lieutenant	Innis. Fus.	Awarded M.C. Killed in Action.
Woods, W. E. G.	Churchfield	Signaller	Black Watch	
COLONIAL FORCES.				
Erskine, Clifford	High Street, Holywood	Corporal	1st N.Z. Rifles	
Gray, Thompson	Moorpark, Holywood	Private	Canadians	Died of Wounds.
Keating, David	Mertoun Hall	Private	Canadians	
Legate, Charles M.	Spafield, Holywood	Private	Australians	Killed in Action.
Legate, Harry H.	Spafield, Holywood	Private	Canadian Scottish	
Magill, Isaac	Marino, Co. Down	Private	Canadians	
Orr, Robert	The Hill	Private	6th Canadian M.G.C.	
Russell, Wm.	Ballymenoch	Private	Canadian Batt.	
KIRCUBBIN.				
Adams, Alfred		Private	R. Irish Rifles	
Brown, Harris	Innishargie	Rifleman	18th Batt. R.I.R.	
Campbell, Thomas	Kirkcubbin	Surgeon Prob.	R.N.	
Campbell, Wm.	Kirkcubbin	Lieut. Com.	R.N.R.	D.S. Cross.
Dodds, James	Kirkcubbin	2nd Mate	Mercantile M.	
Filson, Andrew	Kirkcubbin	Farrier Sergt.	A.S.C.	
Fitzsimmons, Ralston	Kirkcubbin	Private	R.I.R.	Killed in Action.
Fitzsimmons, Robert	Kirkcubbin	Private	R.I.R.	
Lawther, Robert	Kirkcubbin	Leading Stoker	R.N.	
McClements, John	Nunsquarter	Staff Sergt.	R. Irish Regiment	
McClements, Thos.	Nunsquarter	Private	A.S.C., Seaforth Highldrs.	
McClements, Thomas		Captain	Mercantile Marine	
McClements, Samuel		2nd Engineer	Mercantile Marine	
McMaster, David	Blackstaff	Private	13th R.I.R.	Killed in Action.
McMillan, David	Kirkcubbin	Corporal	2nd R. Dublin Fus.	M.M Killed in Action.
Maxwell, Jack	Evansban		Red Cross, France	
Maxwell, Wm.	Ballygraffin	Private	A.S.C.	
Patterson, Wm.		Seaman	Mercantile Marine	
Savage, James	Kirkcubbin	Private	R.E.	
Shaw, Brown, M.B.	Kirkcubbin	Fleet Surgeon	R.N.	
Shaw, Fred.	Kirkcubbin	Captain	Mercantile Marine	
Sinclair, Alex.	Kirkcubbin	Sergeant	13th Batt. R.I.R.	
Sinclair, John	Kirkcubbin	Private	13th R.I.R.	Killed in Action.
Weir, David	Mountstewart	Private	A.S.C.	
Wilson, Thos.	Kirkcubbin	Sergeant	13th Batt. R.I.R.	
Woods, Wm.	Blackabbey	Private	R. North Lanc.	Died in Hospital.
COLONIAL AND U.S.A. FORCES.				
Connor, John		Private	U.S. Army	
Donnan, Wm.		Private	Canadian Infantry	Killed in Action.
McMaster, Alex.		Private	Canadian Cavalry	
MILLISLE AND BALLYCOPELAND.				
Baird, Robert	Craigboy, Donaghadee	Private		
Bennett, W. James	Ballycopeland	Private		
Boyd, Wm.	Ballyhaskin	2nd Lieutenant	7th Hussars, Mesopotamia	
Boyle, Samuel	Millisle	Gunner	S.A.R.B.	
Boyle, Thomas	Gannaway	Private	R.I.R.	
Brown, David	Millisle	Private	R. Engineers	
Drennan, David J.	Ballyrolly	Lance-Corporal	Cameron Highlanders	
Drennan, Jas. A.	Ballyrolly	Private	R.I. Fusiliers	Died from Wounds.
Finlay, Hugh	Millisle	Leading Stoker	R.N.	
Finlay, Robert	Millisle	Private	5th Batt. R.I.R.	
Francis, John	Drumawhey, N'ards	Private	Transport Service A.I.F.	
Jamison, George	Millisle	Corporal	16th Batt. R.I.R.	
Jamison, James	Millisle		H.M. Transport	Died.
Jamison, Robt. M.	Millisle	2nd Lieutenant	R.A.F.	Awd. Flying Cross
Jamison, Samuel	Millisle	2nd Lieutenant	1st Batt. R.I.R.	
Keith, Thomas	Ballyhaskin	Corporal	A.I.F.	Awarded D.C.M.
McGimpsey, Hugh	Ballyvester	Private	A.S.C.	
McGimpsey, James	Ballyvester	Private	R.I.R.	
McGimpsey, Robt.	Ballycopeland	Private	R.I.R.	Killed in France.
McGowan, David	Gannaway	Private	R.A.S.C.	
McKee, Robert	Grange	Gunner	R.G.A.	
Nesbitt, David	Millisle	Private	Inns of Court O.T.C.	
Nesbitt, Thos.	Millisle	2nd Lieutenant	23rd Cheshire Regt.	
O'Neill, John	Ballyvester	Private	R.I.R.	
Sandford, John	Millisle	Private	R.I.R.	
Shanks, David	Millisle	Private	R.I.R.	
Walker, Samuel	Ballymacruise	Private	1st Batt. R.I. Fus.	
COLONIAL FORCES.				
Bitcon, Wm.	Ballycopeland	Sergeant	47th Batt. A Co. Canadians	

ARDS PRESBYTERY.   MILLISLE AND BALLYCOPELAND.

Name.	Home Address.	Rank.	Regiment, Battalion, or Unit.	Remarks.
BITCON, HARRY	Ballycopeland	Private	47th Batt. Canadians	
BOYD, DAVID	Ballycopeland	Private	Canadian Forces	
BROWN, ANDREW	Millisle	Private	Aus. Military Force	
BROWN, THOS.	Millisle		10th Batt. Canadians	
JAMISON, DAVID J.	Millisle	Private	4th Batt. C.M.R.	
McKEE, DAVID J.	Grange, Millisle	Lance-Corporal	4th Can. Artillery	
McKEE, JAMES	Grange, Millisle	Sergeant	Canadian Forces	Killed in Action.
MARTIN, ROBERT	Drumfad	Private	Canadian Forces	
TREAN, FREDK.	Craigboy	Private	Australian Forces	
WALKER, JOHN	Ballymacruise, Millisle	Sapper	No. 2 Batt Can. Ry. Troops	
FIRST NEWTOWNARDS.				
ACHESON, JOSEPH	Newtownards	Sergt.-Major	14th R.I.R.	
ADAIR, EDWARD	Newtownards	Private	11th R. Innis. Fus.	Killed in Action.
ADAIR, JAMES	Newtownards	Gunner	R.F. Artillery	Wounded.
ANDERSON, JAMES	Newtownards	Private	8th R.I.R.	
ANDERSON, WILLIAM	Newtownards	Private	1st R.I.R.	
BROWN, WILLIAM	Newtownards	Private	18th R.I.R.	
BRETT, EDWARD	Newtownards	Trooper	N.I. Horse	
CARSER, JAMES	Newtownards	Private	6th Highland L.I.	Killed in Action.
COLVILLE, JAMES	Victoria Avenue	Private	Royal Air Force	
COPELAND, T. SYDNEY	Westmount	2nd Lieutenant	N.I. Horse	
CRAWFORD, EDWARD	Newtownards	Corporal	13th R.I.R.	
CRAWFORD, T. J.	Newtownards	Corporal	13th R.I.R.	
DICKSON, ALEXANDER	Newtownards	2nd Lieutenant	18th R.I.R.	
DOGGART, THOMAS	Newtownards	Lance-Corporal	5th R. Irish Regt.	
DONALDSON, HUGH	Newtownards	Private	A.S. Corps	
DOOLEN, THOMAS	Newtownards	Private	A.S. Corps	
DORMAN, WILLIAM	Newtownards	Private	9th R. Innis. Fus.	
DORRIAN, THOMAS	Newtownards	Private	10th R.I.R.	
DOUGLAS, JOHN	Newtownards	Private	13th R.I.R.	
EDGAR, S.	Newtownards	Private	18th R.I.R.	
FERGUSON, HUGH	Newtownards	Coastguard Signaller	Royal Navy	
FERGUSON, JAMES C.	Newtownards	Lieutenant	Army Service Corps	
FERGUSON, WILLIAM J.	Newtownards	Private	Army Service Corps	
FOSTER, JAMES	Newtownards	Private	R.I.R.	
GIBSON, JAMES	Newtownards	Corporal	Royal Engineers	Awarded M.M.
GIBSON, WILLIAM	Newtownards	Lance-Corporal	Royal Engineers	Wound. Awd. M.M.
GILMORE, JOHN	Newtownards	Private	18th R.I.R.	
GORDON, JAMES K.	Newtownards	Lance-Corporal	17th R.I.R.	
GRAHAM, JAMES	Newtownards	Private	20th R.I.R.	
HARRIS, ANDREW	Newtownards	Private	2nd R.I.R.	
HARRIS, THOMAS		Private		Killed in Action.
HERON, JAMES	Newtownards	Com. Sergt.-Major	17th R.I.R.	
JARDINE, JAMES F.	Newtownards	A.M.	R.N.A.S.	
KEENAN, SAMUEL	Newtownards	Sergeant	13th R.I.R.	
KELLY, JAMES	Newtownards	Private	18th R.I.R.	
McBRIDE, NATHANIEL	Newtownards	Private	3rd R.I.R.	
McGIMPSEY, BERTIE	Newtownards	Private	Royal Air Force	
McGIMPSEY, JOHN G.	Newtownards	Private	18th R.I.R.	Twice Wounded.
McGIMPSEY, JULIUS	Newtownards	Private	18th R.I.R.	
McGIMPSEY, WILLIAM	Newtownards	Private	13th R.I.R.	Prisoner of War.
McGIMPSEY, WILLIAM	Newtownards	Private	9th R.I.R.	
McGREECHAN, DANIEL	Newtownards	Private	20th R.I.R.	
McGREECHAN, JOHN	Newtownards	Lance-Corporal	4th R.I.R.	
McGREECHAN, R. J.	Newtownards	Lance-Corporal	4th R.I.R.	
McMASTER, WILLIAM	Newtownards	Private	18th R.I.R.	
MAJOR, DAVID	Newtownards	Private	16th R.I.R.	
MENAGH, ANDREW	Newtownards	Private	18th R.I.R.	
MILLAR, WILLIAM	Newtownards	Private	8th R.I.R.	Died of Wounds.
MONTGOMERY, JOHN	Newtownards	Private	9th R. Inniskillings	
MONTGOMERY, SAMUEL	Newtownards	Private	15th R.I.R.	
MOORE, JAMES	Newtownards	Private	10th R.I.R.	
MURPHY, HERBERT	Newtownards	Pioneer	Royal Engineers	
O'LONE, JOHN	Loughries	Regt. Q.M. Sergt.	R.I.R.	Re-enlisted at outbreak of War at age of 73 years. Ment. in Des.
O'LONE, ROBERT JAMES	Loughries	Captain	2nd R.I.R.	Killed in Action.
O'LONE, WILLIAM PERCY	Loughries	Captain	2nd R.I.R.	D.C.M. Killed in Action.
ORR, HAMILTON	Loughries	Lieutenant	18th R.I.R.	
ORR, THOMAS	Loughries	Sergeant	N.I. Horse	
O'PREY, HENRY	Loughries	Private	R. Marine Artillery	
PARKES, FRED	Loughries	Private	14th R.I.R.	Killed in Action.
PATTERSON, ALEX.	Drumkirk	1st Class Mechanic	R.A.F.	
PURDY, HUGH	Drumkirk	Corporal	R.F.A.	
PURDY, JAMES	Drumkirk	Private	R.A.M.C.	
QUINN, THOMAS	Killearn	Private	13th R.I.R.	Killed in Action.
QUINN, WILLIAM	Newtownards	Private	13th R.I.R.	
ROBINSON, SAMUEL	Newtownards	Private	19th R.I.R.	
SCOTT, J. A.	Newtownards	Trooper	N.I. Horse	
SIMPSON, WILLIAM	Newtownards	Lance-Corporal	13th R.I.R.	Killed in Action.

ARDS PRESBYTERY.   FIRST NEWTOWNARDS.

Name.	Home Address.	Rank.	Regiment, Battalion, or Unit.	Remarks.
Skimmon, Alex.	Newtownards	Private	Royal Engineers	Wounded. Awd. Croix-de-Guerre.
Sloane, Zena	Newtownards	Lieutenant	Royal Engineers.	
Smith, James	Newtownards	Private	13th R.I.R.	Killed in Action.
Spiers, H.	Newtownards	Private	2nd Scots Guards	
Stevenson, James	Newtownards	Private	4th R.I.R.	Killed in Action.
Stevenson, William	Newtownards	Private	18th R.I.R.	
Stewart, James	Newtownards	Driver	A.S. Corps	
Thompson, David John	Newtownards	Lance-Corporal	13th R.I.R.	Killed in Action.
Thompson, W. J.	Newtownards	Corporal	13th R.I.R.	Killed in Action.
Wilson, William	Newtownards	Bombardier	R.F. Artillery	
Wright, Alfred James	The Manse, N'ards	Lieutenant	9th R. Innis Fus.	
Wright, Matthew John	The Manse, N'ards	2nd Lieutenant	14th R.I.R.	Killed in Action.
Wright, R. P. Maxwell	The Manse, N'ards	Lieutenant	Royal Engineers	
Wright, William M.	The Manse, N'ards	Captain	13th R.I.R.	Wounded.
COLONIAL FORCES.				
Apperson, James	81 South Street	Lieutenant	8th Canadians	Wounded. M.C.
Brown, C. S.	Newtownards	Gunner	2nd African F.A.	
Colville, R. J.	Newtownards	Private	2nd Can. Inf. Brig.	
Ferguson, Francis	Newtownards	Private	24th Canadians	Wounded.
Francis, James	Newtownards	Private	7th Canadians	
Jamison, Samuel	Newtownards	Private	2nd New Zealanders	Wounded 3 times.
Major, Robert	Newtownards	Lance-Corporal	32nd Canadians	
McGimpsey, David	East Street	Private	15th Batt. A.E.F.	Prisoner of War.
McGimpsey, James C.	East Street	Private	8th Canadians	Killed in Action.
Patterson, William	Drumkirk	Private	1st S. A. Inf.	
Scott, Robert	Newtownards	Private	4th Canadians	
Scott, Samuel	Newtownards	Saddler	1st Canadians	
Scott, William F.	69 South Street	Private	1st S. Af. Inf.	Wounded.
NEWTOWNARDS, REGENT STREET.				
Chambers, George	Mill Street	Private	20th R.I. Rifles	Killed in Action.
Ferris, David	Church Street	Sergt.-Major	5th R.I. Rifles	Killed in Action.
Gilliland, Thos.	Wallace Street	Private	13th R.I. Rifles	Killed in Action.
Haddick, Thos.	Victoria Avenue	Lieutenant	Leinster Regt.	
McCord, Robert	Bangor Road	Private	13th R.I. Rifles	
Millar, Wm.	William Street	Private	13th R.I. Rifles	
Nevin, George	Court Street	Private	20th R.I. Rifles	
Patterson, W. J.	Balfour Street	Corporal	13th R.I. Rifles	Killed in Action.
Perry, George	William Street	Private	Artillery	
Rodgers,	Britannia Place	Q.M. Sergeant	5th R.I. Rifles	
Smyth, N. R.	Court Street	Private	13th R.I. Rifles	
Stratton, D. J.	Balfour Street	Com. Sergt.-Major	Royal Engineers	Died.
Williamson, Joshua	Britannia Place	Private	Cyclists' Corps	
SECOND NEWTOWNARDS.				
Aicken, Alexander	Newtownards	Sergeant	A.S.C.	
Algie, James	Newtownards	Sergt.-Major	R.F. Artillery	
Beattie, Samuel	Newtownards	Sergeant	R. Innisl Fusiliers	
Beattie, Thomas	Newtownards	Driver	Motor Trans. Corps	
Beattie, William	Newtownards		Machine Gun Corps	
Beattie, William	Newtownards	Private	13th R.I. Rifles	
Cahoon, David	Newtownards	Private	13th R.I. Rifles	Wounded.
Cahoon, James	Newtownards	Private	18th R.I. Rifles	
Campbell, William	Newtownards	Sergeant	13th R.I. Rifles	
Carnduff, Robert	Newtownards	Private	13th R.I. Rifles	Wounded.
Clarke, James	Newtownards	Private	R. Scots Fusiliers	Wounded.
Clarke, John	Newtownards	Gunner	R.F. Artillery	Wounded.
Crooks, Samuel	Newtownards	Able Seaman	R. Navy	Died in Hospital.
Doggart, John	Newtownards	Driver	A.S.C.	
Doggart, Maurice	Newtownards	Private	18th R.I. Rifles	Wounded.
Doggart, Robert	Newtownards	Private	R.A.M.C.	
Doggart, William L.	Newtownards	Sapper	R. Engineers	
Ferguson, Shaw	Newtownards	Private	R.A.M.C.	
Filson, Charles	Newtownards		Mechanical Transport	
Finlay, Hugh	Newtownards	Corporal	R. Innis. Fusiliers	M.C. Wounded.
Foster, Alexander	Newtownards	Private	13th R.I. Rifles	
Foster, John	Newtownards	Private	13th R.I. Rifles	
Foster, Thomas	Newtownards	Private	18th R.I. Rifles	
Galway, Robert Jas.	Newtownards	Private	20th R.I. Rifles	
Gamble, John L.	Newtownards	Sergeant	18th R.I. Rifles	Wounded.
Gamble, Robert	Newtownards	Driver	A.S.C.	
Garrett, William	Newtownards	Sergeant	A.S.C.	
Gilliland, John	Newtownards	Private	13th R.I. Rifles	Wd. Pris. of War.
Gilliland, Robert	Newtownards	Private	13th R.I. Rifles	
Gordon, Sl. H.	Newtownards	Private	13th R.I. Rifles	Killed in Action.
Gray, Robert	Newtownards	Corporal	R.F. Artillery	
Harvey, John	Newtownards	Private	13th R.I. Rifles	Died.
Hay, Andrew McL.	Newtownards	Private	3rd Manchester Regt.	
Heron, John	Newtownards	Sapper	R. Engineers	

ARDS PRESBYTERY.   SECOND NEWTOWNARDS.

Name.	Home Address.	Rank.	Regiment, Battalion, or Unit.	Remarks.
Iago, Francis	Newtownards	Lieutenant	R. Navy	
Irvine, James	Newtownards	Private	4th R.I. Rifles	Wounded.
Irvine, Thomas	Newtownards	Private	K.O.S.B.	Wounded.
Johnston, Hugh	Newtownards		R.I. Fus.	
Kerr, Thomas H.	Newtownards	Sergeant	13th R.I. Rifles	Wounded.
Lightbody, Robert	Newtownards	Private	R. Innis. Fusiliers	Killed in Action.
Long, David	Newtownards	Private	R. Irish Fusiliers	Wounded.
Long, William	Newtownards	Gunner	R.F. Artillery	Wounded.
McCann, Robert	Newtownards	Lance-Corporal	12th R.I Rifles	
McClure, Joseph	Newtownards	Gunner	Royal Navy	
McConnell, Hugh	Newtownards	Private	R. Irish Fusiliers	Wounded. Died.
McConnell, Isaac	Newtownards	Private	Royal Scots Fusiliers	
McDowell, Alexander	Belfast	Private	King's Liverpool Regt.	
McIlroy, William	Newtownards	Corporal	R. Innis. Fusiliers	Wounded.
McKibben, David	Newtownards	Private	9th R.I. Rifles	
McKibben, Hamilton	Newtownards	Private	7th R.I. Rifles	
McKibben, Hamilton, Jun.	Newtownards	Private	5th R.I Rifles	
McKnight, Harry	Newtownards		Mechanical Transport	
McMeekin, Hugh	Newtownards	Private	18th R.I. Rifles	
McMeekin, James	Newtownards	Private	13th R.I. Rifles	
Majury, David	Newtownards	Lance-Corporal	5th R.I. Rifles	
Mawhinney, James	Newtownards	Private	4th R.I. Rifles	Wounded.
Montgomery, Andrew	Newtownards	Driver	R.E.	
Montgomery, William	Newtownards	Private	Highland Light Infantry	Killed in Action.
Moore, Hamilton	Newtownards	Corporal	3rd R.I. Rifles	Died.
Moorehead, Saml. James	Newtownards	Sergeant	4th R.I. Rifles	Prisoner.
Morrison, William	Newtownards	Pioneer	R. Engineers	
Murphy, John	Newtownards	Sergeant	R.I. Rifles	Wounded.
Newell, Charles	Newtownards	Private	13th R.I. Rifles	Killed in Action.
Newell, Thomas	Newtownards	Private	12th R.I. Rifles	Killed in Action.
Paden, Wm. H. R.	Newtownards	Corporal	18th R.I. Rifles	Killed in Action.
Pagen, John	Newtownards	Private	18th R.I. Rifles	Wounded.
Patterson, John	Newtownards	Private	R. Innis. Fusiliers	Wounded.
Rowley, James	Newtownards	Bomber	11th R.I. Rifles	Wounded.
Rowley, John Bell	Newtownards	Private	12th R.I. Rifles	Wounded.
Rutherford, John	Newtownards	Corporal	13th R.I. Rifles	
Savage, Edwin	Newtownards	Private	18th R.I. Rifles	Wounded.
Savage, Robert	Newtownards	Corporal	M.G.C.	
Snodden, James	Newtownards	Sergt.-Major	R. Innis. Fusiliers	M.C. Wounded.
Strain, Wm. R.	Newtownards	Corporal	3rd R.I. Rifles	Wounded.
Stratton, George	Newtownards	Private	4th R.I. Rifles	
Telford, Nelson	Newtownards	Private	R. Innis. Fusiliers	
Wallace, James	Newtownards	Private	2nd R.I. Rifles	
Woods, Alex.	Newtownards	Private	4th R.I. Rifles	Wounded.
Woods, David	Newtownards	Private	4th R.I. Rifles	Twice Wounded.
Woods, Hugh	Newtownards	Sergeant	18th R.I. Rifles	
Woods, Thomas	Newtownards	Lance-Corporal	13th R.I. Rifles	Wounded.
COLONIAL FORCE.				
Ferguson, David Mc.	Toronto	Private	Can. Inft.	
NEWTOWNARDS, GREENWELL STREET.				
Aicken, Thomas	12 Corry's Quarter	Gunner	R.N.	
Algie, Robert	124 Greenwell Street	Seaman	R.N.	Killed in Action.
Allen, Robert	28 John Street Lane	Private	13th R.I.R.	Killed in Action.
Allen, Robert Hugh	18 Frederick Street	Rifleman	13th R.I.R.	Wounded.
Allen, William	69 East Street	Private	19th R.I.R.	
Allen, Wm. John	18 Frederick Street	Private	R. Scots Fusiliers	
Anderson, Samuel	47 Frederick Street	Rifleman	4th R.I.R.	
Anderson, Thos. J.	47 Frederick Street	Private	9th R.I.F.	
Anderson, Wm.	39 Townhead Street Stevenston. G'gow	Private	R.F. Corps	
Armour, James	116 Greenwell Street	Private	7th R.I.R.	
Armour, James	28 South Street	Private	15th R.I.R.	
Armour, Wm. Hugh	Ballyrea, Newtownards	Sapper	R. Engineers	
Barr, Wm.	3 Greenwell Lane	Private	A.S. Corps	
Beattie, Thos.	39 West Street	Driver	A.S.C.	
Beckett, Wm.	East Street	Corporal	2nd R.I.R.	D.C.M.
Beggs, Wm.	4 Lte. Francis Street	Private	5th R.I.F.	
Bell, David	22 Wallace's St., No. 1	Private	13th R.I.R.	Killed in Action.
Bell, Hugh	4 Market Street	Private	A.S. Corps	
Bell, John	4 Market Street	Corporal	4th R.I.R.	
Bell, Robert	4 Market Street	Artificer	A.S. Corps	
Bell, Wm.	102 East Street	Private	13th R.I.R.	
Bennett, David J.	203 Mill Street	Private	12th R.I.R.	
Bennett, Edward	11 Pound Street	Corporal	13th R.I.R.	Killed in Action.
Bennett, Hamilton	11 Pound Street	Private	M.G. Corps	Killed in Action.
Bennett, John	11 Pound Street	Sergeant	6th R.I.R.	
Bennett, Wm.	13 L. Francis Street	Gunner	R.F.A.	
Boal, Wm.	11 Balfour Street	Private	2nd Scots Guards	Died a P.O.W.
Bowden, David	100 Templemore Street Belfast	Private	R.I. Fus.	

ARDS PRESBYTERY.   GREENWELL STREET, NEWTOWNARDS.

Name.	Home Address.	Rank.	Regiment, Battalion, or Unit.	Remarks.
Brown, George	19 East Street	Driver	A.S. Corps	
Buckley, Wm. A.	37 South Street	Gunner	R.F. Artillery	
Boyd, William	81 William Street	Private	4th R.I.R.	Killed in Action.
Boyd, Joshua	17 Frederick Street	Rifleman	12th R.I.R.	
Boyd, John	19 Frederick Street	Private	Labour Corps	Wounded.
Boyd Saml. Jas.	8 Mark Street	Private	14th Royal Scots, attached 98th Light Railway Crew Co., R. Engineers	
Caddell, Wm.	7 Queen Street	Private	4th Devons	
Calderwood, Thos.	5 John Street	Private	13th R.I.R.	Died a P.O.W.
Cargo, John	29 Frederick Street	Gunner	R.F. Artillery	
Carlett, Wm.	41 Church Street	Seaman	H.M.S. Resolution	
Carr, Richard	23 Ford Street	Private	3rd R.I.R.	
Caughey, Wm.	38 Frederick Street	Corporal	3rd R.S.F.	
Chambers, Edward	17 Mill Street	Deck Boy	H.M.T. "Joseph Connell"	
Chambers, Geo.	17 Mill Street	Private	2nd R.I.R.	Died a P.O.W.
Chambers, Henry	17 Mill Street	Private	A.S. Corps	
Clarke, David	27 Shuttlefield	Private	8th R.I.R.	
Clarke, Hugh	36 South Street	Corporal	L.E. Engs.	
Clarke, Wm.	17 Mill Street	Private	12th R.I.R.	
Close, Thos.	11 Victoria Avenue	2nd Private	R. Air Force	
Coates, George	High Street	Private	1st R.I.R.	
Coffey, John	Bootown Road	Lance-Corporal	10th R.I.R.	
Copeland, David	64 Greenwell Street	Private	Royal Welsh Fus.	
Conkey, Robt.	Dundonald	Gunner	R.G.A.	
Cowan, Joseph	9 Church Terrace	Corporal	18th R.I.R.	
Crothers, Henry	42 Up. Movilla Street	Private	13th R.I.R.	
Crothers, Joseph	42 Up. Movilla Street	Private	13th R.I.R.	
Crothers, Joseph	42 Up. Movilla Street	Private	5th R.I.R.	
Cummings, Alex.	48 Wallace's St. (2)	Private	5th R.I.R.	
Dempster, Saml.	5 Russell Place	Private	8th R.I.R.	
Doggart, Thos. Watters	Greenwell Street	Private	Connaught Rangers	1914-1915 Medal.
Donaldson, Adam	25 Victoria Avenue	Private	M. Gun Corps	Killed in Action.
Donaldson, John	25 Victoria Avenue	Private	36th Division Hut Co.	
Donaldson, Thos.	20 Thomas Street	Private	13th R.I.R.	
Donnelly, Alex.	62 Francis Street	Drummer	D.O.W. Regt.	
Donnelly, John	62 Francis Street	Private	2nd R.I. Fus.	
Dorrian, Isaac	33a John Street	Corporal	13th R.I.R.	
Dorrian, Wm.	16 Pound Street	Sergeant	4th R.I.R.	
Dorrian, Thos.	69 Movilla Street	Lance-Corporal	5th R.I.F.	
Dickson, Wm.	32 Thomas Street	Private	Scottish Rifles	Wounded & Gassed
Dunn, Robert	Newtownards	Stoker	H.M.S. Leopard	
Eadie, Wm.	8 Zion Place	Private	A.S.C. M.T.	
Eagleson, David	Ballywatticock, N'ards	Gunner	R.N.	
Edmunds, D.	124 Mill Street	Private	R. Innis. Fus.	
Ennis, Andrew	34 Wallace's Street (2)	Private	Tank Corps	
Ennis, Thos.	34 Wallace's Street (2)	Private	16th R.I.R.	1915 Medal.
Ennis, Wm.	6 Court Street	Private	4th R.I.R.	
Farley, Robert	108 Mill Street	Sapper	R. Engineers	
Fenton, Alfred	116 Mill Street	Private	A.S. Corps	
Ferguson, David	43 Pound Street	Private	9th R. Innis. Fus.	
Ferguson, James	33 West Street	Private	12th A. & S. Highlanders	
Ferguson, John	30 Thomas Street	Corporal	8/9th R.I.R.	M.M.
Finlay, Wm. Jas.	69 Mark Street	Sapper	R. Engineers	
Fryars, Wm.	27 Queen Street	Private	2nd R.I.R.	Killed in Action.
Fullerton, John	26 Court Street	Private	4th R.I.R.	Killed in Action.
Fullerton, Robert	26 Court Street	Private	R.F. Corps	
Gamble, David	Cronstown, N'ards	Private	1st R.I. Fus.	Killed. P.O.W.
Gaw, John	97 Greenwell Street	Private	17th R.I.R.	
Gebbie, Hugh	5 Zion Place	Lance-Corporal	2nd R.I.R.	Wounded.
George, Robert	123 Mark Street	Rifleman	4th R.I.R.	Wd. Mons Star.
Gibson, Alex.	32 Movilla Street	Private	3rd R.I.R.	Killed in Action.
Gibson, Hugh	21 Ford Street	Private	5th R.I.R.	
Gibson, Samuel	23 Movilla Street	Private	12th R.I.R.	
Gibson, Wm. Jas.	166 Greenwell Street	Private	13th R.I.R.	Killed in Action.
Gilmore, Samuel	27 George's Street	Private	1st R.I.R.	Killed in Action.
Gordon, Arthur	47 West Street	Private	4th R.I.R.	
Gordon, James	47 West Street	Private	1st I. Guards	
Gordon, Samuel	5 Russell Place	Sapper	110th R. Engineers	
Gorman, Charles	11 Windmill Row	Private	1st R.I.R.	Killed in Action.
Gorman, David	11 Windmill Row	Private	3rd R.I.R.	
Gorman, James	11 Windmill Row	Private	1/8th Scots Rifles	Killed in Action.
Gourley, Henry	71 Church Street	Private	3rd R.I.R.	
Gourley, Thos.	71 Church Street	Private	1st R.I.F.	
Gracie, James	81 Church Street	Private	13th R.I.R.	
Graham, David	3 Thomas Street	Sergeant	A.S. Corps	
Graham, Hugh	128 Greenwell Street	Leading Stoker	H.M.S. Tiger	
Graham, James	3 Mary Street	Private	13th R.I.R.	
Graham, James	58 Up. Movilla Street	Private	4th R.I.R.	
Graham, John	2 Wallace's Street (2)	Sergeant	6th R. Innis. Fus.	D.C.M. Wd. twice.
Graham, William	8 Windmill Row	Private	4th R.I.R.	
Gray, Wm. John	28 Frederick Street	Private	1st H.L.I.	
Gray, Saml. Jas.	28 Frederick Street	Driver	R.F. Artillery	
Green, Richard	95 Movilla Street	Private	16th R.I.R.	

ARDS PRESBYTERY.   GREENWELL STREET, NEWTOWNARDS.

Name.	Home Address.	Rank.	Regiment, Battalion, or Unit.	Remarks.
Green, Thomas	111 Mill Street	Sapper	R. Engineers	
Hanna, Alex.	71 Greenwell Street	Private	13th R.I.R.	
Hanna, John	25 Robert Street	Private	1st R. Dublin Fus.	Killed in Action.
Hanna, John	8 Zion Place	Private	10th R.I.F.	
Hanna, Thomas	98 Greenwell Street	Private	13th R.I.R.	
Hanna, Wm.	98 Greenwell Street	Private	R. Engineers	
Harris, Isaac	Movilla	Private	M.T. Coy.	
Harvey, David	9 Up. Movilla Street	Private	5th Seaforth Highlanders	Killed in Action.
Henderson, Wm. Jas.	Ballyrogan, N'ards	Private	A.S.C. (Remounts)	
Hollinger, J. W.	18 Court Street	Private	A.O. Corps	
Hutchinson, James	126 Mill Street	Private	L. Corps	
Hutchinson, John	126 Mill Street	Private	A.S.C.	
Irvine, Alex.	2 Court Street	Private	A.S.C.	
Irvine, James	93 Church Street	Driver	R.A.M.C.	
Irvine, Samuel	22 Mary Street	Sergeant	13th R.I.R.	
Jamison, Samuel	50 Church Street	Private	4th R.I.R.	
Jamison, Thomas	118 Greenwell Street	Private	13th R.I.R.	
Job, Joseph	29 Marquis Street	Private	A.S.C., M.T.	
Johnston, Edward	Sunnyside, Victoria Av.	Private	5th R.I.R.	
Johnston, James		Private	R.I.R.	
Johnston, John	33 Mill Street	Private	A.S.C., M.T.	
Johnston, John	19 Church Street	Sergeant	13th R.I.R.	
Johnston, Robert	33 Mill Street	Private	1st R.I.R.	Killed in Action.
Johnston, Thomas	19 Church Street	Drummer	3rd Innis. Fus.	
Johnstone, Thomas	34 Francis Street	Private	1st R.I.R.	
Johnston, W. J.	33 Mill Street	Private	12th R.I.R.	
Johnston, W. J.	19 Church Street	Private	33rd R.B. Section, 3rd Army	
Johnston, George	Sunnyside, Victoria Av.	Private	4th R.I.R.	Wounded.
Jeffrey, Jacob	85 Movilla Street	Private	1st R.I.R.	
Keenan, Robert	83 Church Street	Drummer	4th Hants.	
Kielty, David Jas.	49 East Street	Private	2nd R.I.R.	Died of Wounds.
Kelly, Edward	34 Movilla Street	Private	1st R.I.R.	Killed in Action.
Kelly, Wm. George	55 Wallace's St. (No. 2)	Private	13th R.I.R.	Killed in Action.
Kerr, Hugh	14 Kimberley Buildings	Lance-Corporal	Royal Engineers	Died of Wounds.
Killen, Samuel	6 Court Street	Private	Labour Corps	
Kinghan, Robert	25 Hillview Terrace	Private	2nd Seaforth Highlanders	Mons Star. Wd.
Kirk, Frank	97 Greenwell Street	Private	13th R.I.R.	
Kisby, John	69 Mill Street	Rifleman	11th R.I.R.	
Kisby, W. H.	Newtownards	Lance-Corporal	A.S.C. 661 Coy.	
Larmour, Samuel	56 Movilla Street	Private	11th Innis. Fus.	
Logan, Wm. James	54 East Street	Private	4th R.I.R.	
Long, John	29 Wallace's St. (No. 2)	Private	6th Black Watch	
Long, Robert	29 Wallace's St. (No. 2)	Lance-Corporal	Military Foot Police	
Lowry, John	Ballywatticock	Private	18th R.I.R.	
Lowry, Robert	Ballywatticock	Lance-Corporal	13th R.I.R.	Killed in Action.
Lowry, William	24 Wallace's St. (No. 1)	Private	9th A. & S. Highlanders	
Lockhart, Robt., Sen.	9 Thomas Street	Private	R. Army Ordnance Corps	Twice Wounded.
Lockhart, Robt., Jun.	9 Thomas Street	Signaller	15th Devons	
McAvoy, Edward	4 Talbot Street	Private	13th R.I. Rifles	Died of Wounds.
McAvoy, John	140 Mill Street	Private	13th R.I. Rifles	Killed in Action.
McAvoy, Patrick	51 William Street	Rifleman	3rd R.I.R.	
McBlain, James	48 Movilla Street	Signaller	16th R.I. Rifles	
McBlain, Stewart	66 Movilla Street	Private	3rd Innis. Fus.	
McBride, Edward	Ballywittacock	Driver	36th Machine Gun Corps	
McCalpine, Frank	180 Mill Street	Corporal	R. Garrison Artillery	Killed in Action.
McCalpine, James	Canada	A.B. Seaman		
McCalpine, Wm.	24 Wallace's St. (2)	Private	Rifle Brigade	
McCandless, James	9 Queen Street	Private	2nd R.I. Rifles	Killed in Action.
McCann, Thos.	37 Church Street	Private	9th R.I. Fus.	Killed in Action.
McCartney, Robert	4 Talbot Street	Private	13th R.I. Rifles	Killed in Action.
McChesney, John	54 East Street	Private	13th R.I. Rifles	Died.
McClelland, James	14 Pound Street	Private	3rd R.I.R.	Killed in Action.
McClements, Joseph	59 Little Francis Street	Private	1st Rifle Brigade	
McClements, Robert	59 Little Francis Street	Private	15th R.I.R.	
McClinton, George	59 Frederick Street	Private	2nd R. Innis. Fus.	
McClure, Thos.	163 Greenwell Street	Private	2nd R. Innis. Fus.	
McCoy, Wm. James	Ballybarnes Cottages	Lance-Corporal	13th R.I. Rifles	Died.
McCready, Thos.	21 Ford Street	Corporal	38th R. Field Artillery	
McCullough, Alfred	34 Church Street	Private	9th Scot. Rifles	
McCullough, Geo.	8 West Street	Drummer	4th Hants.	
McDade, William	40 Thomas Street	Private	4th R.I. Rifles	
McDowell, Joseph	81 Balfour Street	Private	13th R.I. Rifles	
McDowell, Samuel	10 Balfour Street	Private	3rd R.I. Rifles	
McDowell, Thos.	84 Greenwell Street	Private	R.I. Fusiliers	
McGilton, James	76 Movilla Street	Lance-Corporal	12th H.L. Infty.	
McGrath, Joseph	19 Balfour Street	Private	13th R.I. Rifles	
McKee, Andrew	27 North Street	Sergeant	7th R.I. Rifles	
McKee, Fred.	77 Greenwell Street	Private	14th R.I. Rifles	Killed in Action.
McKee, James	27 North Street	Private	9th Innis. Fus.	
McKee, James	88 Little Francis Street	Private	Labour Corps	
McKee, Robert	101 Mill Street	Lance-Corporal	2nd R.I. Rifles	Killed in Action.
McKee, Wm.	15 John Street Lane	Sergeant	B/159 Brigade R.F.A.	
McKeown, Charles	105 Mill Street	Private	3rd R.I. Rifles	Killed in Action.
McKeown, James	105 Mill Street	Private	13th R.I. Rifles	

(20)

ARDS PRESBYTERY. GREENWELL STREET, NEWTOWNARDS.

Name.	Home Address.	Rank.	Regiment, Battalion, or Unit.	Remarks.
MACKEY, JAMES	64 South Street	Private	4th R.I. Rifles	Died of Wounds.
McKIBBEN, JOHN HILL	47 Robert Street	Corporal	1st R.I. Rifles	Killed in Action.
McKIBBEN, WM. JAS.	47 Robert Street	Private	2nd R.I. Rifles	
McKIMM, ROBERT	Windmill Row	Private	164th P.O.W. Co.	
McKITTRICK, R. J.	10 Wallace's Street	Private	2nd R.I. Rifles	
McKITTRICK, WM.	8 Short Street	Private	13th R.I. Rifles	Killed in Action.
McKNIGHT, JAS.	18 Wallace's St. (1)	Private	8th R.I. Regt.	
McKNIGHT, JOHN	23 South Street	Sergeant	13th R.I. Rifles	
McKEE, WILLIAM	141 Mill Street	Private	11th R. Innis. Fus.	
McMORREN, JAMES	27 Balfour Street	Lieutenant	9th R.I. Fus.	
McMORREN, JOHN	27 Balfour Street	Chief Engineer	Transport S.S. Risaldar	
McNEILLY, ALEX.	19 Greenwell Street	Private	R. Artillery	
McNEILLY, ROBERT	Scotland	Private	3rd R.I. Rifles	
McQUISTON, WM.	76 Up. Movilla Street	Private	13th R.I. Rifles	Killed in Action.
McCREADY, SAMUEL	31 Wallace's St. (2)	Private	R.I.R.	Wounded.
McCREADY, JOHN	9 Wallace's St. (2)	Private	R. Irish Fus.	Wounded 5 times.
McCREADY, ALEX.	9 Wallace's St. (2)	Private	R.I.R.	
McCULLY, WM.	22 James Street	Rifleman	11th R.I.R.	Prisoner
McKEE, JAMES	88 Little Francis St.	Sapper	I.W.T., R.E.	
McKEE, GEORGE	116 Mill Street	Gunner	H.M.S. "Repulse"	
McGILTON, JAMES	5 Canal Row	Corporal	R. Engineers	
McGILTON, EDWARD	124 Mill Street	Rifleman	18th R.I.R.	Wounded.
McROBERTS, THOS.		Corporal	R.I.R.	Wounded twice.
McROBERTS, WM.		Driver	R.E.	
MALONE, JAMES	16 Robert Street	Lance-Corporal	H. Light Inft.	Wd. Mons Ribbon.
MATIER, H. W.	Court Street	Lance-Corporal	16th R.I.R.	
MAJOR, D. J.	47 William Street	Private	19th R.I.R.	
MARSHALL, JAMES	33 Greenwell Street	Private	5th R.I.R.	
MARSHALL, ROBERT	33 Greenwell Street	Private	R. Innis. Fus.	Killed in Action.
MARTIN, JAMES	Little Francis Street	Private	6th R.I.F.	Killed in Action.
MARTIN, JOHN	East Street	Private	1st R.I.R.	Killed in Action.
MATHERS, THOMPSON	163 Greenwell Street	Private	2nd R.I.R.	Killed in Action.
MATIER, DANIEL	59 Little Francis Street	Corporal	2nd R.I.R.	Killed in Action.
MAWHINNEY, JAS. H.	52 Little Francis Street	2nd Engineer	Transport S.	
MAXWELL, WM.	15 Frederick Street	Private	A.S.C.	
MAYNE, JAMES	12 Mary Street Lane	Gunner	H.M.S. "Revenge"	
MAYNE, JOHN	12 Mary Street Lane	Private	4th R.I.R.	
MAYNE, ROBERT	12 Mary Street Lane	Private	13th R.I.R.	
MAYNE, THOMAS	12 Mary Street Lane	Private	13th R.I.R.	
MENAGH, ADAM	10 Church Street	Private	10th R. Innis. Fus.	
MENAGH, ALEX.	10 Church Street	Private	18th R. Innis. Fus.	
MEREDITH, GEORGE	34 Francis Street	Corporal	1st R.I.R.	
MEREDITH, JAMES	34 Francis Street	Sergeant	1st R.I.R.	
MEREDITH, J.	34 Francis Street	Private	2nd Innis Fus.	
MILLAR, ROBT.	54 Mill Street	Private	13th R.I.R.	
MILLAR, JAS. ALEX.	70 Elgin Crescent, London		R. Air Force	
MILLS, DAVID	29 Robert Street	Sergeant	2nd R.I.R.	
MISKELLY, SAMUEL	4 Ivy Grove, Chapman St., Hulme, Manchester	Private	19th Manchesters	
MODERATE, HARRY	13 Up. Court Street	Rifleman	13th R.I.R.	
MONTGOMERY, JOHN	24 Mary Street	Private	12th R.I.R.	
MOORE, WILLIAM	154 Greenwell Street	Lance-Corporal	6th R.I.R.	Killed in Action.
MORRISON, HENRY	1 East Street	Sergeant	R.A.F.	
MORRISON, JOHN	54 Mill Street	Gunner	R.F. Art.	
MULLAN, DAVID	19 Movilla Street	Private	13th R.I.R.	Killed in Action.
MULLAN, HUGH	19 Movilla Street	Private	R. Scots Fus.	Died of Wounds.
MULLAN, JAMES	6 Darragh's Lane	Rifleman	4th R.I.R.	Killed in Action.
MULLEN, WM.	47 Movilla Street	Private	1st R.I.R.	
MURRAY, WALTER	68 Mill Street	Bugler	Duke of Cornwall L.I.	
NEWELL, THOS.	140 Greenwell Street	Sapper	R. Engineers	
OLIVER, GEORGE	20 Wallace's St. (2)	Lance-Corporal	3rd R.I. Rifles	
O'NEILL, JAMES A.	34 William Street	Private	13th R.I. Rifles	
O'NEILL, JOHN	34 William Street	Corporal	13th R.I. Rifles	Killed in Action.
O'NEILL, WILLIAM	34 William Street	Private	K.O.S.B.	Killed in Action.
O'NEILL, JOSEPH	24 Frederick Street	Gunner	R. Garr. Artillery	
ORME, JAMES	173 Neill Street	Private	14th R.I. Rifles	
ORME, ROBERT	45 North Street	Private	4th R.I. Rifles	
ORR, WM. JAS.	40 Wallace's St. (2)	Private	2nd R. Irish Fus.	
ORR, WM. J.	40 Wallace's St. (2)	Lance-Corporal	3rd R.I. Rifles	
OWENS, HUGH HENRY	Thomas Street	Private	12th R.I. Rifles	
PAGEN, ALEX.	89 Mill Street	Private	11th R.I. Rifles	Killed in Action.
PALMER, ALEX.	18 Kimberley Bldgs.	Private	15th R.I. Rifles	Died of Wounds.
POOLE, ROBT. JAS.	5 Greenwell Street	Private	4th R.I. Rifles	
POOLE, WM.	5 Greenwell Street	Private	13th R.I. Rifles	
PINNONS, JOHN	55 Balfour Street	Private	Royal Air Force	
RANKIN, JAMES	34 Movilla Street	Private	12th R.I. Rifles	
RANKIN, JOHN	34 Movilla Street	Lance-Corporal	13th K. Royal Rifles	
RANKIN, ROBERT	34 Movilla Street	2nd Lieutenant	3rd South Staffords	M.M., M.C.
REID, JAMES	130 East Street	Sapper	R. Engineers	
RITCHIE, ROBERT	East Street	Private	4th R.I. Rifles	
ROBB, ANDREW	36 John Street	Private	9th R.I. Rifles	
ROBB, DAVID	28 Wallace's St. (1)	Private	2nd R.I. Rifles	
ROBB, JOHN	26 Mill Street	Private	1st H.L. Infantry	
ROBINSON, ALEX.	3 Lower Mary Street	Private	13th R.I. Rifles	Killed in Action.

ARDS PRESBYTERY. GREENWELL STREET, NEWTOWNARDS.

Name.	Home Address.	Rank.	Regiment, Battalion, or Unit.	Remarks.
Robson, Robert	52 Frederick Street	Private	A.S. Corps	Killed in Action.
Robson, Wm.	Castle Place	Driver	16th R.F. Artillery	
Russell, James	3 Circular Row	Private	2nd R. Innis. Fus.	Military Medal.
Russell, John	36 Frederick Street	Sergeant	4th R.I. Rifles	
Russell, John	13 Circular Row	Private	13th R.I. Rifles	Killed in Action.
Russell, Joseph	47 King St., Bangor	Private	4th R.I. Rifles	
Russell, Robert	13 Circular Row	Private	2nd R. Irish Fus.	
Russell, Samuel	13 Circular Row	Corporal	1st R.I. Rifles	
Russell, Wm.	55 Church Street	Gunner	R.G. Artillery	
Russell, Wm.	56 South Street	Rifleman	13th R.I. Rifles	
Seeds, Thos.	29 West Street	Lance-Corporal	5th R.I. Rifles	
Shaw, Henry	8 Queen Street	Private	5th R.F. Artillery	Killed in Action.
Sheppherd, John	52 Wallace's St. (2)	Private	13th R.I. Rifles	Killed in Action.
Sheppherd, Robert	52 Wallace's St. (2)	Sapper	R. Engineers	
Sheppherd, Wm.	52 Wallace's St. (2)	Gunner	R.G. Artillery	
Smyth, David	87 Mill Street	Co. S.-Major	2nd R.I. Rifles	Died.
Smyth, George	87 Mill Street	Private	A.S. Corps	
Smyth, Wm. John	105 Mark Street	Sapper	R. Engineers	
Smyth, Wm.	48 Regent Street	Private	12th R.I. Rifles	Killed in Action.
Stevenson, William	50 Movilla Street	Private	5th R.I. Rifles	
Stratton, Samuel	Wallace's Street (2)	Gunner	H.M.S. Peking	
Shields, James	6 Church Terrace	Private	4th R.I. Rifles	
Scott, David	92 Mill Street	Rifleman	3rd R.I. Rifles	
Tate, Adam	167 Mill Street	Private	3rd R.I. Rifles	
Thompson, Alex.	1 Zion Place	Private	R.A. Force	
Thompson, David	63 Church Street	Private	12th R.I. Rifles	
Thompson, David	54 William Street	Corporal	4th R.I. Rifles	
Thompson, John	1 Zion Place	Private	13th L. Corps	
Thompson, Samuel	151 Greenwell Street	Stoker	H.M.S. Tiger	
Trueman, Thomas	32 Frederick Street	Private	4th R.I. Rifles	D.C.M.
Tweed, David	154 Greenwell Street	Private	8th R.I. Regt.	
Thompson, James	8 Church Street	Private	15th R.I. Fus.	Twice Wounded.
Thompson, Alexr.	13 Windmill Row	Rifleman	4th R.I.R.	
Todd, Hugh		Sergt.-Major	2nd R.I.R.	Gassed, Victory Medal & 2 stars.
Vance, Alex.	19 Greenwell Street	Private	2nd R. Innis. Fus.	
Vance, James	19 Greenwell Street	Private	13th R.I. Rifles	Missing.
Vance, Wm.	West Street	Private	2nd R.I. Rifles	Killed in Action.
Vance, Wm.	8 Windmill Row	Private	2nd R.I. Rifles	
Walker, Saml.	77 Church Street	Driver	R.F. Artillery	Killed in Action.
Weir, Joseph	112 Mill Street	Private	1st R.I. Rifles	
Weir, Nathaniel	13 Lower Mary Street	Sapper	R. Engineers	
Weir, Watson	81 William Street	Private	9th R.I. Fus.	
Weir, Wm.	4 Russell Place	Private	11th R.I.R.	Wounded.
White, David	19 Wallace's St. (2)	Sergeant	13th R.I. Rifles	
White, James	18 William Street	Gunner	C.M.B's. (Base)	
Whitla, James	3 Wallace's St. (2)	Private	16th R.I. Rifles	Military Medal.
Wilson, James	61 Church Street	Private	R.A.M.C.	
Wilson, James F.	29 Victoria Avenue	Driver	A.S. Corps	
Wilson, Samuel	70 William Street	Driver	A.S. Corps	
Wright, Alfred	41 West Street	Private	15th R.I. Rifles	
Wright, Jas.	74 Up. Movilla Street	Private	13th R.I. Rifles	Killed in Action.
Wright, James		Private	M.T., A.S.C.	
Wright, John	138 Mill Street	Private	R. Air Force	
Weir, John	formerly 81 William St. now 70 Paris St., Belfast	Rifleman	1st R.I.R.	Wounded twice.
Wright, Samuel	2 Robert Street	Sergeant	2nd R.I.R.	Wounded.
Young, James	44 William Street	Lance-Corporal	12th R.I. Rifles	Killed in Action.

COLONIAL AND U.S.A. FORCES.

Name.	Home Address.	Rank.	Regiment, Battalion, or Unit.	Remarks.
Beattie, David H.	22 James Street	Private	R.A.F., United States	
Beck, James	Ballyblack	Private	Otago, New Zealand	Missing, believed killed.
Boyce, Thomas	15 John Street	Sapper	2nd Canadian Engineers	
Dorman, John	33 East Street	Corporal	28th Canadian Infantry	Escaped when P.O.W.
Hare, Joseph	15 Kimberley Bldgs.	Corporal	8th Canadian Infantry	
Kirk, John	67 Mark Street	Private	75th Canadian Infantry	
Major, R.	47 William Street	Sergeant	28th Canadians	
Moore, Hugh	12 Greenwell Street	Private	46th Canadian Infantry	Killed in Action.
McAlpine, George	24 Wallace's St. (2)	Private	4th South African Infantry	Killed in Action.
McDowell, James	82 Greenwell Street	Private	208th Canadian Rifles	
McMillan, Robert	93 Greenwell Street	Private	16th Canadian Scottish Inf.	Died.
Orme, William	37 North Street	Private	14th Canadian Infantry	
Robinson, Hugh	41 Church Street	Corporal	Canadian Infantry	
Smyth, Hugh	87 Mill Street	Private	13th R. Highland Infantry	
Tomlinson, James	Ontario, Canada	Private	Canadian Army Medical Co., Training Depot 2	
White, Alex.	18 Mary Street	Private	1st Canadian Infantry	Died of Wounds.
Willis, Wm. McCowatt	75 Victoria Avenue	Sergeant	Canadian Infantry	Military Medal.

ARDS PRESBYTERY.   PORTAFERRY.

Name.	Home Address.	Rank.	Regiment, Battalion, or Unit.	Remarks.
PORTAFERRY.				
Bailie, James	Priestown	Corporal	13th R.I.R.	Killed in Action.
Caughey, Wm.	Church Street	Corporal	13th R.I.R.	
Cavan, Thomas	Kearney	Gunner	H.M.S. Leviathan	
Dodds, Alex.	Ballybrannigan	Private	10th R.I.R.	Killed in Action.
Dodds, Wm. J.	The Square		R.A.F.	
Donaldson, Andrew	Thomastown	Private	13th R.I.R.	Killed in Action.
Gowan, George	Kearney	Private	A.S.C.	
Hanna, Wm.	The Shore	Sergeant	1st R.I.R.	Killed in Action.
Moreland, Andrew	Corrock	Private	8th R.I.R.	
Moreland, David	Corrock		H.M.S. Pembroke	
McCluskey, Hugh	Ballyblack	Private	18th R.I.R.	Wounded.
McCluskey, Wm. J.	Ballyblack	Private	13th R.I.R.	Died in Training.
McDonnell, Alex.	The Shore	Signaller	294th R.G.A.	Killed in Action.
McDonnell, David John	Ballygalget	Private	18th R.I.R.	Killed in Action.
McDonnell, James	The Shore	Captain	17th R.I.R.	Wounded.
McMullan, Wm.	Ballyward	Corporal	13th R.I.R.	Wounded.
McNeice, John	Quinton	Signaller	7th R.I.R.	
Savage, Edward	Barr Hall	Corporal	8th R.I.R.	Wounded twice.
Savage, John	Bar Hall	Engineer	H.M.S. Minneapolis	
Savage, Langtry	Bar Hall		8th R.I.R.	Wounded twice.
Savage, H. Leslie	Bar Hall	Cadet	R. Air F.	
Torney, Wm.	High Street	Private	13th R.I.R.	
Witherspoon, Geo.	Church Street	Private	Italian E.F. Transport Ser.	
COLONIAL FORCES.				
Bailie, Harry R.	Priestown		N.Z., Canterbury Regt.	
Kelly, David	Ferry Street		Canadian A.S.C.	
Moreland, Robert	Corrock		47th Canadians	Wounded.
Savage, Wm.	Bar Hall		N.Z.E.F., Dardanelles	Wounded.
Wilson, Albert, M.D.	The Square	Captain	R.A.M.C., B.E.F., Africa	
Wilson, Parke	The Square		Canadian A.S.C.	Wounded.

ARMAGH PRESBYTERY.

Name.	Home Address.	Rank.	Regiment, Battalion or Unit.	Remarks.
AHOREY.				
Clements, James	Ahorey	Private	R.I.R.	
Clements, Thomas	Ahorey	Sergeant	R.I.F.	M.M. Star. Killed in Action.
Cullen, Wm.	Ahorey	Private	R. Scots. F.	Wounded.
Grundle, Albert	Cornascriebe	Sergeant	R.I.F.	Wounded.
Jeffers, James	Scotland	Sergeant		Wounded.
Marshall, John	Ballyloughan	Private	R.I.F.	M.M. and Star. Killed in Action.
COLONIAL AND U.S.A. FORCES.				
Jeffers, Isaac	U.S.A.	Private	U.S.E.F.	
Thompson, James	New Zealand	Private	N.Z.E.F.	
FIRST ARMAGH.				
Anderson, S. M.	Victoria Street	Lieutenant	9th R.I.F.	Died.
Blair, Harold	Barrack Hill	Private	R.E.	
Bratten, James	Tyra	Sergeant	9th R.I.F.	
Briggs, John J.	Milford	Sergeant	3rd R.I.F.	Prisoner of War.
Brittain, Ernest	Barrack Hill	Sergeant	9th R.I.F.	Wounded.
Brown, Robert	Sunnymede	Lieut.-Col.	R.A.M.C.	
Clarke, Wm.	Ballmagalliah	Driver	R.I.F.	
Clarke, W. J.	Tyra	Private		Prisoner of War.
Ferris, Skelton		2nd Lieutenant	R.A.F.	
Ferris, Wm.	The Mall	Lieutenant	Black Watch	Wounded.
Foster, Charles	Dobbin Street	Lieutenant	R. Innis. Fus.	Wounded.
Gallagher, George H.	Newry Road	Private	R.I.F.	
Gallagher, Wm.	Newry Road	Private	R.I.F.	
Hopkins, John	Gaol Square	Sergeant	R.I.F.	D.C.M.
Hutton, Charles	Market Street	Air Mechanic	R.A.F.	
Hutton, William	Market Street	Air Mechanic	R.A.F.	
Irwin, Robert J.	Boyd's Row	Driver	9th R.I.F.	Wounded.
Kerr, William		Private	9th R.I.F.	
Leeman, P. G.	Victoria Street	Captain	R.A.M.C.	M.C.
Leeman, R.	Victoria Street	Captain	R.A.S.C.	
M'Alister, Jack	Railway House	Private	9th R.I.F.	

ARMAGH PRESBYTERY. — FIRST ARMAGH.

Name.	Home Address.	Rank.	Regiment, Battalion or Unit.	Remarks.
MACARTNEY, G.	Killuncy	Private	Post Office Rifles	Wounded.
McATEER, WM.	Gaol Square	Private	9th R.I.F.	Killed in Action.
McATEER, ALEX.	Gaol Square	Private	R.I. Rifles	Wounded.
McDOUGALL, JOHN	Scotch Street	Private	Irish Guards	
McKENNALL, JOHN	Killylinn	Trooper	North Irish Horse	
McLAUCHLAN, J. S.	Milford	Corporal	R.I.F.	Wounded.
McLAUCHLAN, WM.	Milford	Private	R.I.R.	Killed in Action.
MAHAFFEY, T. H.	Tower Hill	Captain	R.A.M.C.	Men. in Despatches
MAHAFFEY, WILLIAM	Tower Hill	Bombardier	R.G.A.	
MILLER, R. C.	Drumsill	Lieutenant	R.F.A.	
MOFFETT, ROBERT	Albert Place	Private	M.D.P.	
REYNOR, SAMUEL	Gaol Square	Private	R.I.F.	Wounded.
SLEATOR, CLYDE	Railway Street	Air Mechanic	R.A.F.	
THOMSON, BERTRAM	Abbey Street	Lieutenant	R.G.A.	
THOMSON, LEX	Abbey Street	Private	A.O.C.	
TODD, FREDERICK	Milford	Private	R.I.F.	
TODD, HAROLD	Milford	Corporal	R.A.M.C.	
TRIMBLE, ALAN	English Street	Corporal	R.E.	
TRIMBLE, CHARLES	English Street	Lieutenant	R.F.A.	Wounded.
COLONIAL FORCES.				
BOYD, HERBERT	English Street	Corporal	Can. Engineers	
FARLEY, A. F. M.	Thomas Street	Private	Can. A.V.C.	
McKENNAL, THOMAS	Killylinn	Private	P.P. Can. L.I.	Killed in Action.
MAGILL, SAM.	Newry Road	Private	Can. Engineers	
MAXWELL, FRED.	English Street	Private	Austral. E.F.	
MAXWELL, ROBERT	English Street	Private	Can. E.F.	
SLOAN, JAMES	Tullygarron	Private	Can. Engineers	
STUART, HERBERT	Tower Hill	Corporal	Can. R.A.M.C.	Killed in Action.
THIRD ARMAGH.				
BALLANTINE, THOS.	Drumad	Private	R.I.F.	Killed in Action.
BELL, WM.	Lonsdale Street	Private	R.A.F.	
BRIENS, JOHN	Lonsdale Street	Private	R.I.F.	
CARSON, JAMES	Milford	Private	R.I.F.	Wounded.
CARSON, ROBERT	Milford	Sergeant	R.I.F.	
DAWSON, J. E.	Armagh	Private	I.G.	
DOBBIN SAMUEL	Milford		R.N.	
ELLIOTT, HENRY	Armagh	Private	R.I.F.	Killed in Action.
ELLIOTT, JAMES	Armagh	Private	R.I.F.	
ELIOTT, ROBERT B.	Armagh	Captain	R.A.M.C.	
FRAZER, WM.	Milford	Private	R.I.F.	
GRANT, WM.	Milford	Private	A.S.C.	
GRAY, JOSEPH	Milford	Corporal	R.I.F.	
GRAY, PERCY W.	Armagh	Private	R.A.M.C.	Killed in Action.
GRAY, ROBERT	Armagh	Private	R.A.M.C.	
HADDEN, RALPH	Cavanaraw	Private	N.F.	
HALL, JAS.	Armagh	Private	R.I.F.	Killed in Action.
HANSON, WM.	Cloughfin	Private	R.I.F.	
HAWTHORNE, ALEX.	Kildarton	Private	R.I.F.	Killed in Action.
HAWTHORNE, GEO.	Kildarton	Sergeant	R.I.F.	
JONES, JAS.	Armagh	Private	R.I.F.	
KIRKWOOD, GEO.	Milford	Sergeant	R.I.F.	
LESTER, JAS.	Lonsdale Street	Private	R.I.F.	
McCARTNEY, ALEX.	Scotch Street	Private	R.I.F.	
McCARTNEY, GEO.	Drumad	Private	R.I.F.	
McCLELLAND, THOS.	Irish Street	Private	R.I.F.	
McLOUGHLIN, HERBERT	Armagh	Private	R.I.F.	
MAGILL, WM.	Mullinure	Private	R.I.F.	
MOORE, WM.	Castle Street	Private	R.I.F.	
PORTER, SAMUEL CLAUDE	Abbey Street	Private	R.A.F.	
PROCTOR, JOHN	Edward Street	Private	R.I.F.	Died.
RITCHIE, JAMES	Newry Road	Private	R.I.F.	
ROLSTON, WILLIAM	Armagh	Private	R. Irish Fus.	
SIMPSON, JAS. ROSS	Ballinahone	Private	R. Irish Fus.	
SLEATOR, ROBERT	Armagh	Lieutenant	R. Irish Fus.	Died.
SMITH, HUGH M.	Armagh	Private	R. Irish Fus.	Killed in Action.
WALKER, CECIL	Barrack Street	Private	R.A.F.	
WALLACE, W. G.	Milford	Private	R. Irish Fus.	
WILSON, JOHN	Lonsdale Street	Private	R. Irish Fus.	
WILSON, JOCK	Lonsdale Street	Private	R.I.R.	
WILSON, ROBERT	Lonsdale Street	Private	R.F.A.	
COLONIAL FORCES.				
BARTHOLOMEW, WM.		Private	Canadians	
ELLIOTT, B. G.	Armagh	Captain	4th Batt. East Lancs.	
ELLIOTT, CHAS. J.	Armagh	Lieutenant	17th Australian A.S.C.	
GRAY, JAMES	Armagh	Private	Canadians	
HALLIDAY, RICHARD	Milford, Armagh	Private	Canadians	Killed in Action.
HUTCHINSON, JAMES	Milford, Armagh	Private	Canadians	
McKEE, ROBERT		Private	C.C.S.	Killed in Action.

ARMAGH PRESBYTERY.   THIRD ARMAGH.

Name.	Home Address.	Rank.	Regiment, Battalion or Unit.	Remarks.
Rea, William	Armagh	Private	Canadians	
Shields, Allen	Armagh	Private	Canadians	
Vogan, Robert	Armagh	Private	C.R.F.A.	
ARMAGHBRAGUE.				
Armstrong, W. J.	Darkley	Sergeant	16th R.I.F.	Wounded.
Chambers, Samuel	Darkley	Private	R.I.F.	Killed in Action.
Duffy, James	Darkley	Lance-Corporal	R.I.F.	
Frame, James	Darkley	Private	R.I.F.	
Graham, Joseph H.	Armaghbrague	Private	R.I.F.	
Kennedy, Robt. J.	Armaghbrague	Sergeant	R.E.	
Morton, David	Darkley	Private	R.I.F.	
Reaney, Robert	Darkley	Private	9th R.I.F.	Killed in Action.
Reaney, Wm.	Darkley	Lance-Corporal	9th R.I.F.	
Semple, R. J.	Darkley	Sergeant	R.I.F.	
Shilliday, Joseph	Darkley	Lance-Corporal	R.I.F.	
COLONIAL FORCES.				
Duffy, Joseph	Darkley	Private	Can. E.F.	
Duffy, Wm.	Darkley	Private	Can. E.F.	Wounded.
Moorcroft, Wm.	Aughnagurgan	Private	Can. E.F.	
BENBURB.				
Irwin, Bob	Benburb	Private	9th R. Inn. Fus.	Killed in Action.
Smith, Sam.	Derrycreevy	Lance-Corporal	9th R. Inn. Fus.	Killed in Action.
CALEDON.				
Clow, Jas. Moncrieff	Mill Cottage, Tynan	Private	76th M.G.C.	Killed in Action.
Dillen, Hugh	Huddersfield, England	Private	E. Lanc.	
Dillen, James	Huddersfield, England	Gunner	R.F.A.	
Duncan, Norman	Caledon	Private	R. Marines	
Forde, Ernest	Main Street, Caledon	Private	9th R. Inn. F.	
Forde, Fred.	Main Street, Caledon	Private	9th R. Inn. F.	
Graham, Wm.	Ballymena	Private	9th R. Inn. F.	
Hamilton, John	Caledon	Private	9th R. Inn. F.	Killed in Action.
McCoy, Robert	Main Street, Caledon	Private	R.I.F.	
Robinson, Henry	Caledon	Sergeant	Scottish Regt.	Died of Wounds.
Sanderson, Thos. J.	Main Street, Caledon	Private	A.S.C.	
Shannon, Robt.	Ramaket	Private	9th R. Inn. F.	
Sloan, Anthony	Ballygawley	Private	9th R. Inn. F.	
Sparks, David	Armagh Road	Private	9th R. Inn. F.	
Steenson, Samuel	Caledon	Private	9th R. Inn. F.	Died of Wounds.
Symington, Robert	Caledon		R.N.	
Whitelock, Alfred	Caledon	Private	9th R. Inn. F.	
Whitelock, Robert	Caledon	1st Stoker	R.N.	
Wilkin, Thos. A.	Tannaghlane	Sergeant	B.W.	M.M.
Wilkin, Wm.	Tannaghlane	2nd Lieutenant	R.M.F.	
COLONIAL FORCES.				
Brodie, Hugh	Mill Cottage, Tynan	Corporal	49th Can.	
Garmany, Hans	S. Africa	2nd Lieutenant	S.A. A.S.C.	
Gordon, Ben	Canada	Private	Can. Force	
Graham, Henry	Canada	Lieutenant	Winnipeg Rifles	
Graham, Thos.	Caledon	Cadet	Can. R.A.F.	
CLADYMORE.				
Dougan, Andrew	Lisnagat	Private	R.E.	
Gilmore, McClelland	Ballylane	Private	R.I.F.	Died of Wounds.
McClenaghan, W. S.	Cladybeg	Corporal		Wounded.
COLONIAL AND U.S.A. FORCES.				
Gilmore, Robert	Ballylane	Private	C.E.F.	
Graham, Saml. J.	Enagh	Private	C.E.F.	
Menary, Jas. Gray	Enagh	Mechanic	U.S.E.F.	Wounded.
Taylor, John	Cladymore	Private	Can. Railway	
CLARE.				
Armstrong, Wm. Jas.	Ballyshiel	Gunner	R.G.A.	
Caughey, Wm.	Ballyshiel	Private	R.I.R.	Wounded.
Copeland, D. H.	Ballyshiel	Private	R.I.F.	Wounded.
Hamilton, James	Ballyshiel	Gunner	R.G.A.	
Hamilton, Richard	Ballyshiel	Private	H.L.I.	
Hamilton, Wm.	Ballyshiel	Gunner	R.F.A.	
Henry, Robt. J.	Clare	Private	10th R.I.R.	Wounded.
Mitchell, John	Ballyshiel	Private	R.A.M.C.	
Purdy, Robt. John	Mullinary	Private	4th C.M.R.	Killed in Action.

ARMAGH PRESBYTERY. **CLARE.**

Name.	Home Address.	Rank.	Regiment, Battalion or Unit.	Remarks.
Thompson, Fred.	Clare	Private	R.A.M.C.	
Tweedie, John	Drummamather	Corporal	Transport	Killed.
Watson, Jas.	Ballyshiel	Lieutenant	3rd R.I.F.	Killed in Action.
COLONIAL FORCES.				
Dickson, Thos. H.	38 Shaftesbury Avenue	Private	3rd Can. Division	
Dickson, Wm. M.	38 Shaftesbury Avenue	Private	3rd Can. Division	
Greenlee, John W.	Marlacoo	Private	16th Can. Division	
Greenlee, Samuel	Marlacoo	Private	16th Can. Division	
DRUMMINIS.				
Browne, Saml. J.	The Rocks	Private	9th R.I.F.	Killed in Action.
Cochrane, Thos.	Derryraine	Rifleman	R.I.R.	Killed in Action.
Graham, Abraham	Ternascobe	Private	9th R.I.F.	Killed in Action.
MacLaughlin, Rev. D.	The Manse, Drumminis	Captain	C.F.	M.M.
MacLaughlin, Alex. Wilson	The Manse, Drumminis	2nd Lieutenant	R.A.F.	Wounded 5 times, Killed in Action, Mons Ribbon & Star.
COLONIAL FORCES.				
McCartney, Samuel	Vancouver	Private	Canadian Army	
McKew, Robert	Vancouver	Private	Canadian Army	
FIRST KEADY.				
Acheson, John	Mowillian	2nd Lieutenant	R.G.A.	
Adams, George	Tulinamallogue	Private	R.G.A.	Killed in Action.
Adams, Robt. Henry	Tullinamallogue	Private	R. Irish Fus.	
Breadnor, Thos.	Kelereavy, Keady	Sergt.-Major	R.G.A.	
Broomfield, Saml.	Moneyquin	Private	R. Irish Fus.	
Dunlop, A. Crawford	Annemount	2nd Lieutenant	R.A.F.	Wounded.
Dunlop, John L.	Annemount	Captain	R.A.M.C.	
Dunlop, Robt. B.	Annemount	Major	R.E.	Wounded twice.
Dunlop, Wm. L.	Annemount	Captain	R.A.M.C.	
Foster, James	Kelcreevy, Armagh	Private	R. Irish Fus.	
Ireland, David	Moneyquin	Private	R. Irish Fus.	
McBride, Wm.	Roan	Private	R. Inn. Fus.	Killed in Action.
McIlrath, Robert A.	Kelereavy	Gunner	108th Inft.	Killed in Action.
Mann, Joseph	Bachelors' Walk	Private	I. Guards	Killed in Action.
Watson, Max.	Crossmore	Lance-Corporal	Young Citizens	
COLONIAL FORCES.				
Gibson, Geo. A.	Bachelors' Walk	Private	1st Can. Div.	
Keys, Albert E.	Aughavilly	Private	1st S.A. Inft.	Killed in Action.
Keys, Fred. D. J.	Aughavilly	Private	1st S.A. Inft.	Wounded twice.
McCarten, R. J.	Mowillian	Private	75th Overseas Batt.	Died in Trenches.
McCarten, Saml. John	Mowillian	Private	208th Can. Batt.	
McCarten, Wm. Jas.	Mowillian	Private	208th Can. Batt.	
McCullough, Wm.	Fernalay	Private	Can. Mt. Inft.	Killed in Action.
Mann, Wm. J.	Tullinamallogue	Private	Can. Mt. Rifles	
Watson, Chas. G.	Crossmore	Private	S.A. F. Amb.	
SECOND KEADY.				
Bates, James	Main Street	Private	3rd Batt. R.I.R.	
Cummins, William	Meeting Street	A.B.	H.M.S. Inconstant	
Dalzell, Andrew	Cannagh, Castleblayney	Private		
Doran, Robert	Caramoyle	Private	1st Batt. R.I.F.	
Graham, Joseph	Darkley	Private	9th Batt. R.I.F.	
Huston, Samuel	Dunlargue	Private	9th Batt. R.I.F.	
Maxwell, Samuel	Main Street	Private	Scots Guards	Killed in Action.
McWilliams, J.	Victoria Square	Lance-Corporal	9th Batt. R.I.F.	
Reilly, Fred. A.	Main Street	Private	R.A.M.C.	
Roddy, James	Dunlargue	Private	3rd Batt. Cameron Hldrs.	
Roddy, William	Caramoyle	Private	14th (S) Batt. R.I.R.	Killed in Action.
Small, Hugh A	Main Street	2nd Lieutenant	20th (S) King's Liv. Regt.	M.C. Killed in Action.
Walker, William J.	Main Street	Private	R.A.M.C.	
COLONIAL FORCES.				
Maxwell, James	Main Street	Private	7th Batt. Canadian Engineers	
Nesbitt, Andrew	Cannagh, Castleblayney	Private	Canadian Royal Artillery	
Robinson, Thomas J.	Darkley	Private	56th Batt. C.E.F.	
Robinson, Walker A.	Darkley	Private	75th Batt. C.E.F.	Killed in Action.
Roddy, Hugh	Caramoyle	Private	38th Canadian Batt.	Killed in Action.
Walker, Alfred	Main Street	Private	South Rhodesian Volunteers	
Walker, John A.	Main Street	Private	4th South African Infantry	Killed in Action.
Walker, Samuel F.	Main Street	Private	3rd South African Infantry	Killed in Action.
Walker, Thomas F.	Main Street	Private	2nd South African Rifles	Died.

ARMAGH PRESBYTERY. KNAPPAGH.

Name.	Home Address.	Rank.	Regiment, Battalion or Unit.	Remarks.
KNAPPAGH.				
Anderson, John	Killylea	Private	R.A.F.	
Draften, Andrew	Drumgar	Private	R.I.F.	Killed in Action.
Nelson, Thomas	Killylea	Private	Ulster Volunteers	M.C.
LOUGHGALL.				
Elliott, John	Ardress, Loughgall	Sapper	R.E.	
Elliott, Thomas	Ardress, Loughgall	Private	9th Batt. R.I.F.	Twice Wounded.
Elliott, William	Ardress, Loughgall	Gunner	R.G.A.	Wounded.
English, William	Kinnego, Loughgall	Private	9th Batt. R.I.F.	Wounded.
Irwin, Archibald	Kinnego, Loughgall	Bombardier	R.F.A.	
Irwin, Christopher	Kinnego, Loughgall	Bombardier	R.F.A.	
Marshall, David L.	Bond Hill, Loughgall	Sergeant	9th Batt. R.I.F.	Prisoner.
FIRST MARKETHILL.				
Adair, James	Markethill	Seaman	H.M.S. Hindustan	
Armstrong, Thomas	Seboughan	Private	9th Batt. R.I. Fusiliers	Wounded.
Beattie, Thomas	Markethill	Private	2nd Batt. R.I. Fusiliers	Killed in Action.
Frame Alfred	Ballymacaulay	Private	2nd Batt. R. Innis. Fusiliers	Killed in Action.
Fullerton, William	Tanaghmore	Private	Royal Field Artillery	
Hooks, John	Markethill	Private	9th Batt. R.I. Fusiliers	Wounded.
Mackenzie, Angus	Markethill	Private	Mechanical Motor Transport	Wounded.
Mackenzie, Duncan	Markethill	Private	Royal Army Medical Corps	
McStay, Joseph	Mullabrack	Private	9th Batt. R.I. Fusiliers	W'ded and Killed.
McStay, Ludovic	Mullabrack	Private	Royal Engineers	
Magill, Matthew	Markethill	Lance-Corporal	1st Batt. Loyal North Lancs.	Wounded 4 times.
Miscampbell, John	Edenkennedy	Lance-Corporal	Army Service Corps	
Moore, Henry, R. D.	Manse	Lance-Corporal	Officers' Training Corps	
Moore, Rutherford, W.	Manse	Assistant Paymaster	H.M.S. Dominion	
Small, Alexander	Lattery	2nd Lieutenant	10th Batt. R.I. Fusiliers	
Small, Walter	Lattery	2nd Lieutenant	Royal Scots Fusiliers	Killed.
Spence, David	Markethill	Lance-Corporal	19th Batt. R.I. Rifles	
Taylor, David	Markethill	Private	Canadian Artillery	
Taylor, George	Markethill	Lieutenant	R. Innis. Fusiliers	
Willis, George	Mullabrack	Private	Royal Engineers	
MOY.				
Aird, Archibald	Charlemont	2nd Lieutenant	London I.R.	Killed in Action.
Allen, Wm. John	Charlemont	Private	R.A.S.C. (M.T.)	
Gray, John	Donedade	Private	Irish Guards	Killed in Action.
Gray, James	Donedade	Private	R. Inn. F.	
Gillon, Samuel	Tullygoney	Private	Wiltshire Regt.	Wounded.
Johnston, Godfrey	Mullaghbuoy	Private	Signalling Corps	
McCrea, John	Trewmount	Private	5th Lancers	
Meenagh, John	Moy	Private	H.L.I.	
Morrison, Hugh R.	Moy	Private	R.A.S.C.	Wounded.
Morrison, Joseph D.	Moy	Lance-Corporal	R. Inn. F.	Killed in Action.
COLONIAL AND U.S.A. FORCES.				
Patterson, Robert	Grange, Moy	Private	Canadians	Wounded.
Reid, James	Charlemont	Lieutenant	U.S. Air F.	Missing.
Reid, Thomas	Charlemont	Private	U.S. Army	
Reid, Henry	Charlemont	Private	U.S. Army	
FIRST PORTADOWN.				
Acheson, John E.	Dunavon	Lieutenant	Liverpool Regt.	Prisoner.
Adamson, George	Park Road			Killed in Action.
Aitcheson, Joseph R.	Park Road		R.N.	
Barr, Arthur	Henry Street	Sergeant	3rd R.I.R	
Barr, Edward	Henry Street	Sapper	R.E.	
Barr, Joseph	Henry Street	Private	1st R.I.R.	
Baxter, Reginald	Parkmount	Artificer	R.N.	
Bell, Chas. D.	Millicent Terrace	Surgeon	R.N.	
Best, David	Bocombra	Sergeant	R Inn. F.	
Brew, John G.	Rathlin	Major	9th R.I.F.	Died of Wounds.
Bright, Norman	Edenderry	Captain	R.A.M.C.	
Brown, Wm. J.	Montague Street	Sergt.-Major		Killed in Action.
Bryars, J. G.	Jervis Street	Private	R.A.S.C. (M.T.)	
Bryars, James	Jervis Street	Private	R.A.S.C.	
Bryson, Harold S.	Dirleton	Sapper	R.E.	
Bryson, Hugh P.	Dirleton	2nd Lieutenant	Tank Corps	M.C and Croix- de Guerre.
Clow, Malcom P.	Feddal House	Ambulance Driver	Red Cross	Died.
Cochrane, Jack	Atkinson's Avenue	Sergeant	R.D.C.	
Copeland, Wm.	Hanover Street	Sergeant	R.F.A.	Died of Wounds.
Crosbie, Thomas	Mahon House	Captain	9th R.I.F.	Killed in Action. M.C.
Crozier, John	Portmore Street	Staff Sergeant	Army Shop	

ARMAGH PRESBYTERY. FIRST PORTADOWN.

Name.	Home Address.	Rank.	Regiment, Battalion or Unit.	Remarks.
Crozier, Wm.	Charles Street	Sergeant	R.F.A.	
Dale, James	Carleton Street	Sergt.-Major	R.E.	
Davis, James	Lurgan Road	Sapper	R.E.	
Davison, Wm.	Bridge Street	Corporal	R.A.P.C.	
Gardiner, James T.	Annagh	2nd Lieutenant	R.I.R.	Died of Wounds.
Gibson, Jack	Windsor Lodge	Captain	9th R. Inn. F.	
Gibson, John Edgar	Gilford Road	Captain	9th R. Inn. F.	
Gibson, Thomas	Windsor Lodge	2nd Lieutenant	R.G.A.	
Graham, Albert	Carrickblacker Road	Private	9th R.I.F.	Killed in Action.
Graham, Thomas	Carrickblacker Road	Gunner	R.F.A.	
Hamilton, John	Seagoe	Private	9th R.I.F.	
Hanna, Henry	Edward Street	Lieutenant	K.O.S.B.	
Hughes, John	Jarvis Street	Private	9th R.I.F.	
Hutcheson, Ernest	Market Street	2nd Lieutenant		
Jennings, John	West Street			
Jennings, Rowan	West Street	Private	11th Tank Corps	
Jennings, Samuel	West Street			
Keith, John	Jervis Street	Sergeant	9th R.I.F.	M.S.M.
Kidd, Alex.	Francis Street	Private	3rd R.I.F.	
King, R. F. M. A.		Private	4th R.I.F.	
Livingstone, M.		Sergeant		
Lynas, James	Moyallon	Private	26th B.W.	
McClelland, Robert	Park Road	Private	R.A.S.C.	
McCullagh, James	Irwin Street	Sergeant	9th R.I.F.	M.M.
Magowan, Andrew	Park Road	Corporal	9th R.I.F.	Killed in Action. M.M.
Millar, Edward	Seagoe			
Millar, George	Seagoe	Private	5th R.I.F.	
Millar, Henry	Seagoe			
Orr, David	Bridge Street	Corporal	9th R.I.F.	M.M. Killed in Action.
Palmer, James	Victoria Terrace	Private	9th R.I.F.	
Patterson, David	High Street	Private	9th R.I.F.	
Rutherford, Herbert	Bannview House		N.I.H.	Prisoner.
Sergeant, Wm. Henry	Edenderry		R.N.	
Sloan, A. Gerrard	Ballyworkan House	Cadet	D.U. O.T.C.	
Smith, Alex.				
Smith, R. F., M.A.	Jervis Street	Private	3rd R.I.F.	
Stevenson, Wm.	High Street	Sergeant	9th R.I.F.	M.M.
Stewart, Wm.	Alma Terrace	Sapper	R.E.	M.M.
Tate, George				
Tate, James	Railway Street	Lance-Corporal	4th R.I.R.	
Tate, Samuel				
Todd, Francis	Sandy Row	Private		Killed in Action.
Todd, Robert	Sandy Row	Private	2nd R.I.F (Egypt)	
Turner, Edward		Private	5th R.I.F.	
Turner, Wm.		Lance-Corporal	R.E.	
Vaughan, Thos.	Seagoe	Sergeant	N.I.H.	Prisoner at Mons.
Vaughan, Walter	Seagoe	Trooper	N.I.H.	
Walker, Fred.	Parkmount	Private		Wounded.
Walker, John	Parkmount	Private	1st R.I.F.	Wounded.
Walker, John	King Street	Private	1st R.I.F. (Egypt)	
Walker, Wm. J.	Prospect House	Private	R.I.F.	
Wilson, Thos. H.	Drumcree	Private	1/1 Bucks.	
COLONIAL FORCES.				
Banks, Orston			Canadian Army	
Baxter, David			Canadian Army	
Bright, David		Captain	Canadian Army	
Bright, James		Engineer	S. African Army	
Crozier, James	Charles Street	Private	1st Canadian Army	
Gibson, Joseph			Canadian Army	
Gibson, Thomas			Canadian Army	
Gordon, Thos. A.		Sergeant	Canadian Army	
Knipe, John			Canadian Army	
Stevenson, Thos.			Canadian Army	
Sprott, Robert			N.Z.	
Whitehead, Robert			Canadian Army	
Whitehead, Victor			Canadian Army	
Wilson, Robert			Canadian Army	
PORTADOWN, ARMAGH ROAD.				
Battersby, S. J.	West Street		R.A.M.C.	
Bowles, H.	Montague Street		A.S.C.	
Bowles, W.	Montague Street	Private	9th Batt. R.I.F.	Killed in Action.
Clarke, H.	Charles Street	Private	5th Batt. R.I.F.	
Clarke, S	Parkmount	Private	5th Batt. R.I.F.	
Clarke, T. H.	Parkmount	Private	5th Batt. R.I.F.	
Clarke, W.	Parkmount	Private	H.M.S. Colossus	
Cochrane, J.	Jervis Street	Private	9th Batt. R.I.F.	
Cooke, E.	Victoria Terrace	Private	Cyclists' Corps	

ARMAGH PRESBYTERY.   ARMAGH ROAD, PORTADOWN.

Name.	Home Address.	Rank.	Regiment, Battalion or Unit.	Remarks.
Cooke, J.	8 Cecil Street	Private	9th Batt. R.I.F.	
Cooke, J.	Garvaghy Road	Private	9th Batt. R.I.F.	
Corkin, J.	Jervis Street	Private	9th Batt. R.I.F.	
Espie, H.	Tavanagh Terrace	Private	9th Batt. R.I.F.	
Espie, T.	Tavanagh Terrace	2nd Lieutenant	9th Batt. R.I.F.	
Ferguson, J. A.	South Street	Private	9th Batt. R.I.F.	
Forbes, D.	Thomas Street	Private		
Fulton, J. W. V.	Church Place		O.T.C. (R.H.A.)	
Gibson, D.	Thomas Street	Private	2nd Batt. R.I.F.	
Gordon, R.	Cecil Street	Private	5th Batt. R.I.F.	Wounded.
Gordon, W.	Castle Avenue	Sergeant	9th Batt. R.I.F.	Killed in Action.
Gregg, J.	John Street	Private	9th Batt. R.I.F.	
Hunter, R. W.	William Street	Private	A.O.C.	
Hutchinson, J.	Carleton Street	Private	9th Batt. R.I.F.	Killed in Action.
Jackson, W.	Union Street	Private	4th Batt. R.I.F.	
Jones, H.	Annaghhill	Private	9th Batt. R.I.F.	Wounded.
Jones, J.	Parkmount	Private	9th Batt. R.I.F.	Wounded.
Joyce, J.	Atkinson Avenue	Private	9th Batt. R.I.F.	Killed in Action.
Joyce, T.	Atkinson Avenue	Private	9th Batt. R.I.F.	
Joyce, W. J.	Atkinson Avenue	Private	9th Batt. R.I.F.	
Lappin, G.	West Street	Private	Inniskilling Dragoons	
Leeman, E.	Mandeville Street	Private	9th Batt. R.I.F.	Wounded.
Leeman, E.	Meadow Lane	Private	4th Batt. R.I.F.	Prisoner.
Logan, V.	Hanover Street	Private	10th Batt. R.I.F.	Prisoner.
Lyttle, J.	King Street	Private	B. Co. R.I.F.	Killed in Action.
McCullough, S.	David Street	Private	3rd Batt. Sherwood Foresters	
Monahan, H.	South Street	Private	16th Batt. R.I.F.	
McNeece	Burnbrae Avenue	Sergeant	Canadian Engineers	
Morton, D.	Thomas Street		R.E.	Killed in Action.
Perry, R. J.	Manse	Corporal		
Pickering, J.	Armagh Road	Private	10th Res. Batt. R.I.F.	
Radcliffe, D.	West Street	Private	10th Batt. R.I.F.	
Ritchie, F.	Park Road	Private		
Ritchie, Sergeant	Bridge Street			
Rowan, A.	Coronation Street	Private	9th Batt. R.I.F.	Killed in Action.
Shanks, W.	South Street	Private	3rd Batt. R.I.F.	
Shanks, W. J.	Hanover Street	Private	3rd Batt. R.I.F.	
Shannon, A. C.	Erin Crescent		P.P.C.L.J.	
Stoops, J.	Lisliskey	Private		
Stratton, J.	Park Road		H.M.S. Natal	Killed in Action.
Walker, J.	Annagh Terrace			
Watson, F	James Street	Private	R.E.	
Willis, J.	Union Street	Private	9th Batt. R.I.F.	
REDROCK.				
Bell, Wm. George	Derryraine	Lance-Corporal	9th R.I.F.	Wounded.
Frazer, James	Cavanagrove	Private	10th Bedfords	
Gray, Herbert	Outlack	Private	9th R.I.F.	Wounded 3 times.
McConnell, Clarke	Cavanagrove	Private	R.F.A.	
McConnell, James	Cavanagrove	Private	4th Canadians	Wounded.
Megarrity, Jackson	Collone	Private	9th R.I.F.	
RICHHILL.				
Beck, John	Hamiltonstown	Private	R.I.F.	
Craig, Wm.	Hockley	Private	R.I.F.	
Deans, Theodore John	The Manse	2nd Lieutenant	Indian Army	
Graham, Andrew	Richhill	Private	R.I.F.	Killed in Action.
Hutchinson, Jas. Alex.	Drumman	Private	R.I.F.	Died of Wounds.
Hutchinson, John	Drumman	Corporal	R.I.F.	Killed in Action.
McAlister, James	Cavan, Richhill	Private	R.I.F.	
McAlister, Simon	Cavan, Richhill	Private	Can. E.F.	Killed in Action.
McMahon, Harry	Ballinahinch	2nd Lieutenant	Indian Army	
McMahon, John A.	Ballinahinch	2nd Lieutenant	M.G.C.	
Parks, Wm. Jas.	Ballygrubney	Sergeant	Canadian E.F.	
Smith, Albert Ed.	Drumman	Driver	R.E.	
Welshman, J.	Hockley	Private	R.I.F.	
TARTARAGHAN.				
Graham, Samuel John	Tartaraghan	Private	9th R. Inn. Fus.	Wounded.
Rogers, Wm. John	Tartaraghan	A.B.	R.N.	Killed.
Trueman, Francis	Tartaraghan	Corporal	49th M.G. Corps	Wounded.
Trueman, William	Tartaraghan	Private	9th R. Inn. Fus.	
TASSAGH.				
Cunningham, Joseph	Killyfaddy	Sergeant	R. Irish Fus.	Twice Wounded.
Ferguson, Wm.	Balleer	Private	R. Irish Fus.	Killed in Action.

ARMAGH PRESBYTERY. TASSAGH.

Name.	Home Address.	Rank.	Regiment, Battalion or Unit.	Remarks.
Johnston, Wm. J.	Tullybrone	Lance-Corporal	R. Irish Fus.	
McMorran, Hugh	Tassagh	Lance-Corporal	N.I.H.	
McMorran, David	Tassagh	Gunner	R.F.A.	
Sleator, Harry	Iskymeadow	Sapper	R.E.	
Sleator, James	Iskymeadow	Private	R. Irish Fus.	Killed in Action.
VINECASH.				
Robinson, Samuel	Scotch St., Portadown	Private		

ATHLONE PRESBYTERY.

Name.	Home Address.	Rank.	Regiment, Battalion or Unit.	Remarks.
ATHLONE.				
Goodfellow, Tom Y.	4 Auburn Terrace	Sapper	R.E.	
Hutchinson, J.	Burgess & Co., Athlone	Bombardier	R.F.A.	Killed in Action.
Smith, A. R.	1 Garden Vale	Engineer	U.S. Air Service	
Smith, George	1 Garden Vale	Corporal	R.F.A.	
Snowden, James	Galashiels, Scotland		R.N.	
BALLINASLOE.				
Aitkin, Adam McL.	Hernesbrooke	Private	R.A.F.	
Aitkin, James	Woodlawn	2nd Lieutenant	R.A.F.	Killed.
Davidson, John W.	Ivy Lodge	Private	R.D. Fus.	Killed.
Elliott, George M.	The Manse	Captain	R.A.M.C	
Elliott, Oliver G.	The Manse	Private	12th R. Scots	
Elliott, Robert	The Manse	Lieutenant	Cameron Highlanders	
Giffin, Samuel	Ballinasloe	Private	Field Telegraph	
Hay, James	Clonbruk	2nd Lieutenant	Northumberland Fusiliers	Killed in Action.
Hutchins, W. J.	Ballinasloe	Sergeant	Connaught Rangers	Wounded.
Martin, H.	Ballinasloe	Colonel	R.A.M.C.	
Morrison, James	Ballinasloe	Private	Field Telegraph	
Petrie, W.	Ballinasoe	Private	R.A.F.	
Rutherford, Cecil	Ballinasloe	Captain	R.A.M.C.	
Rutherford, Gascoyne	Ballinasloe	Lieutenant	R.A.	
Thompson, Robert	Ballinasloe	Sergeant	R.I.R.	Wounded.
Tracy, Cantrell	Ballinasloe	Captain	R.A.V C.	Wounded.
Wood, H. W.		Corporal	R.I.R.	M. Medal. W'ded.
COLONIAL FORCES.				
Bagnal, George	Calgary	Private	Canadians	
Boden, Chesney	Adelaide	Private	Australian	Wounded.
Bookless, John	Bloomfontein	2nd Lieutenant	S. African	
Garrett, Charles	Vancouver	Private	Canadians	
CORBOY.				
Allen, W.	Lisardowling	Sergeant	S. Ir. Horse	Wounded.
Burke, B. W.	Treel	Surgeon Probationer	R.N.	
Caldwell, S. A.	Corboy Manse	Bombardier	R.F.A.	Wounded.
Little, W. F.	Crieve	Gunner	R.F.A.	Wounded.
Morrison, H. N.	Edgeworthstown	N. Instructor	R.N.	
Morrison, J. A.	Edgeworthstown	Lieutenant	R. Inn. Fus.	
Wilson-Slator, H. B.	White Hill	Major	R.D. Fus.	Wounded.
COLONIAL FORCES.				
Allen, A. W.	Richardstown	Corporal	Canadians	Killed in Action.
Allen, J. J.	Carne	Private	Canadians	
ENNIS.				
Carroll, Wm.	Eden Vale	Private	Cavalry Regt.	Killed in Action.
Johnston, W. J.	Ballymena	Lieutenant	R. Engineers	
Nightingale, Wm.	Ennis	Private	Munster Fus.	Wounded.
Scott, Norman	The Manse, Ennis	Sergeant	R.A.F.	
GALWAY.				
Anderson, Alex. B.Sc.	University Cottage	Lieutenant	4th Connaught Rangers	Prisoner of War.
Anderson, Walter Thomas	Millbrook House	Sub-Lieutenant	R.N.V.R.	L.D.S.
Bruce, Wm. H.	Galway	Petty Officer	R.N.	

ATHLONE PRESBYTERY. GALWAY.

Name.	Home Address.	Rank.	Regiment, Battalion or Unit.	Remarks.
GIRVIN, JAMES	The Docks	Lance-Corporal	2nd S. Lancers	Prisoner.
HAIRE, W. F.	Newcastle, Galway	Captain	R.A.M.C.	
PERRY, S.	Galway	Major	R.G.A.	
COLONIAL FORCE.				
MILNE, ARTHUR	Scrahallia Lodge	Gunner	1st Can. Heavy Battery	
MILNE, ED. R.	Scrahallia Lodge	Captain	10th Can. Infantry	Thrice Wounded. D.C.M. and Bar.
MILNE, ROBT. M.	Scrahallia Lodge	Sergeant	R. Can. Dragoons	
LONGFORD.				
CRERAR, JOHN	Longford	Sapper	R.E.	
FERGUSON, HERBERT A.	25 Alma St., Derry	Private	10th R. Inn. Fus.	Prisoner
LEYBURN, JAS. H.		Trooper	N.I.H.	
RENTOUL, ALFRED H.	Longford	Captain	R.A.M.C.	
WILSON, GILBERT R.	Longford	Lieutenant	R.A.M.C.	
MULLINGAR AND MOYVORE.				
BAMFORD, JAMES	Rochfort Bridge	Sergeant	R.M.F.	
McDOWELL, WM.	Tubberdaly	Guardsman	G.G.	Twice Wounded.
MILLS, JOHN	Clonbrin	Private	Inn. Fus.	1915 Ribbon.
MILLS, ROBT. JAS.	Clonbrin	Gunner	R.F.A.	Killed in Action.
MILLS, THOS.	Clonbrin	Lance-Corporal	Inn. Fus.	
ROSCOMMON AND CREGGS.				
HAGGART, ROBERT	Mote Park	Private	Northumberland Fus.	Died of Wounds.
SATCHWELL, RALPH	Mount Mary	2nd Lieutenant	R.G.A.	Killed in Action.

BAILIEBOROUGH PRESBYTERY.

Name.	Home Address.	Rank.	Regiment, Battalion or Unit.	Remarks.
BAILIEBOROUGH, TRINITY CHURCH.				
FELL, THOMAS	Carnalynch	Rifleman	11/13th Batt. R.I.R.	Gassed.
BLANIGAN, WILLIAM R.	Lisnalskey	Private	7th Batt. Royal Irish Regt.	
FLEMING, GREER	Carnalynch	Private	7th Batt. Royal Irish Regt.	
HANNA, HENRY	Corlurgan		Royal Innis. Fus.	Wounded.
LEINSTER, GEORGE	Pottledufl	Rifleman	Royal Irish Rifles	
WILSON, CHARLES	Carangarve	Corporal	88th Co. R.G.A.	
WILSON, FREDERICK	Dromecarrow		7rh Batt. Royal Irish Regt.	Gassed.
BALLYJAMESDUFF.				
ANDERSON, WM.	Ahalohan	Private	N.I.H.	
BUCHANAN, JOSEPH	Clarinda	Private	3rd Reserve Batt. I.G.	
BYERS, JOSEPH	Ahagashel	Private	9th R.I. Fus.	Prisoner.
GAMBLE, GILBERT	Ballyjamesduff	Sapper	R.E.	
MORROW, ROBERT EVANS	Rockville	Private	R.A.M.C.	Died.
BELLASIS AND SEAFIN.				
BYERS, ROBERT	Stramaquirty	Private	Irish Rifles	
BYERS, SAMUEL	Stramaquirty	Sergeant	Irish Rifles	Wounded.
McILWAINE, HOWARD	Killinkere	Corporal	S. Irish Horse	
WILSON, DAVID	Seafin	Private	S. Irish Horse	
WILSON, JOHN JAS.	Drumagoland	Private	Irish Rifles	Wounded.
WILSON, WM.	Drumagoland	Private	Signalman	
COLONIAL FORCE.				
CHAMBERS, ROBERT	Billis	Private	Canadians	
CHAMBERS, SAMUEL	Billis	Private	Canadians	Killed in Action.
CORLEA.				
ANDERSON, JOHN	Lisclougher	Gunner	R.F.A.	
ANDERSON, THOS. HENRY	Lisclougher	Lance-Corporal	Wireless	
FORDE, GEORGE	Derrygooney	Private	Can. Force	
HEGAN, JAMES	Mountain Lodge	Sergeant	N. Hants.	
IRWIN, THOS. W	Lacken	Private	Aust. Force	
WELLWOOD, SAMUEL	Lacken	Private	2nd I. Guards	Wounded. Died Pris. in Germany.
WYLIE, JAS. BROWN	Castleblayney	Surgeon Prob.	R.N.	

BAILIEBOROUGH PRESBYTERY.   CORLEA.

Name.	Home Address.	Rank.	Regiment, Battalion or Unit.	Remarks.
CORVALLEY.				
Nelson, David	Longfield, Carrickmacross	Gunner	Royal Field Artillery	Died of Wounds.
ERVEY.				
McMurray, Herbert Joseph	Kingscourt	Driver	R.F.A.	
Ramsay, Charles	Cabra, Kingscourt	Trooper	Scots Greys	
Shannon, William	Ravagh, Kingscourt	Trooper	S. Irish Horse	
KELLS, CO. MEATH.				
Downie, Wm.	Kells	Sergeant		
Hamilton, Thos.	Kells	Sergeant		Wounded.
McElwaine, James	Balrath	Lance-Corporal	A.S.C.	
Millar, John	Navan	Private	Cam. High.	Killed in Action.
Millar, Wm.	Navan	Private	Black Watch	Wounded.
Tease, John	Balrath	Sergeant	Irish Guards	Wounded.
SHERCOCK.				
Clisdell, John Edw.		Private	12th R. Inn. Fus. and Chinese Labour Corps	
White, James		Private	R.I.R.	
Middleton, Saml.		Private	American Army	

BALLYBAY PRESBYTERY.

Name.	Home Address.	Rank.	Regiment, Battalion or Unit.	Remarks.
FIRST BALLYBAY.				
Carson, Ralph	Ballybay	Private	R. Fus.	
Hagan, Samuel	Crievagh	Wheeler	A.S.C.	
Latimer, David		Private	2nd R.I.F.	
Latimer, John	Lisgorran	Lance-Corporal	1st R.I.F.	Wounded.
Latimer, Thomas	Lisgorran	Private	Trench M.B.	Wounded.
Maguire, S.	Laragh	Sergeant	R.I.F.	Wounded.
Miller, Albert	Ballybay	Corporal	1st Innis. F.	Wounded.
Miller, Thomas	Ballybay	Private	Gordon Highlanders	Killed in Action.
Shiels, Robt. J.	Crosskea	Private	9th R.I.F.	Killed in Action.
Shiels, Samuel			9th R.I.F.	Drowned in R.M.S. Leinster.
Templeton, James	Ednafirkin	Coy. Sergt.-Major	2nd R.I.F.	Killed in Action.
Templeton, Robert	Ednafirkin		9th R.I.F.	Killed in Action.
COLONIAL FORCES.				
Cuming, D. R.	Ballybay	Private	31st Canadians	Wounded.
Cuming, J. H.	Ballybay	Private	31st Canadians	Wounded.
Harper, J. L.	Moninton	Private	N.Z. Force	
Miller, John	Moninton		Canadian T.S.	
SECOND BALLLYBAY.				
Boyd, Thomas M.	The Crescent, Ballybay	Lieutenant	R.A.M.C.	
Brown, Samuel	Drumfaldra		12th Lancers	
Carlisle, J. Craig	Sunnybank	2nd Lieutenant	Machine Gun Corps	
Garling, George	Main Street	Trooper	Machine Gun Corps	
Harkness, Fred. C.	Glenmount	2nd Lieutenant	9th Batt. R.I.R.	
Livingstone, George	Main Street	Gunner	Royal G.A.	
McWilliams, Richard	Creevelands	Trooper	North Irish Horse	
McWilliams, Samuel	Creevelands	Lance-Corporal	9th Batt. R.I.F.	Wounded.
McWilliams, Thomas	Creévelands	Corporal	9th Batt. R.I.F.	Wounded.
Nesbitt, George	Tyrardon	Sergeant	North Irish Horse	
Nesbitt, William	Tappa	Private	North Irish Horse	
Potts, Louis	Drumgrole	Private	North Irish Horse	
Ross, Samuel	Belfast	Private	10th Batt. R.I.R.	
Steen, George	Corkeeran	Private	Scottish Rifles	Wounded.
Wilson, John	Corbrack	Lance-Corporal	R.I.F.	
Wilson, Sydney	Corbrack	Private	9th R.I.F.	Killed in Action.
Wylie, David	Knockamuddy	Private	K.L.R.	Wounded.
FIRST CASTLEBLAYNEY.				
Adair, Samuel	Carrickaslane			Wounded.
Bailie, Joseph Smythe	Tullyvin	Corporal		
Duffy, Samuel	Castleblayney			

BALLYBAY PRESBYTERY.   FIRST CASTLEBLAYNEY.

Name	Home Address.	Rank.	Regiment, Battalion or Unit.	Remarks.
George, John	Tullyharnett	Corporal	R.E.	
Gillespie, John, LL.B.	Castleblayney	Captain	R.F.A.	Wounded.
Graham, Edward	Derrycreevy		R. Inn. Fus.	Gassed.
Groves, Joseph	Castleblayney	Corporal	R.I.F.	Killed.
Harrison, Robert	Tullyrahan		R. Inn. Fus	
Harrison, Thomas	Tullyrahan		R Inn. Fus.	
Harvey, John	Anyart		R.F.A.	Wounded.
King, George	Tullyvin	Corporal	S.C. R.E.	
King, Jas. H.	Tullyvin	Sergt.-Major	N.I.H.	
King, Thomas	Tullyvin	Sergeant	R.I.F.	
Livingston, William	Castleblayney		N.I.H.	Gassed.
McCullough, George	Castleblayney		R.I. Fus.	
Martin, Samuel	Anyart			
Martin, William	Cairntra		N.I.H.	
Morrison, Howard S.	Castleblayney	Lieutenant	R.G.A.	Wounded.
Smythe, R. Hastings	The Manse, Castleblayney	Captain	R.A.M.C.	Gassed.
Sommerville, James	Castleblayney		R.I.F.	
Sommerville, Samuel	Castleblayney		R.I.F.	Killed.
Watson, Harry	Castleblayney	Corporal	N.I.H.	
White, Thomas	Castleblayney		R.I.F.	
White, Edwin	Castleblayney		R.N.	
COLONIAL FORCES.				
Bartholemew, W. G.	Castleblayney		Canadian Force	Wounded.
Blackwood, James	Ballinarea		Canadian Force	Killed.
Campbell, William	Castleblayney		Canadian Force	Gassed.
Crozier, Edwin	Castleblayney	Lieutenant	Canadian Force	Killed.
King, Samuel H.	Winnipeg		Canadian Force	
McClelland, John	Castleblayney		Canadian Force	
McClelland, Wm.			Canadian Force	Wounded.
Watson, John	Castleblayney		South Africa	
White, Samuel	Tullinearly		Canadian Force	Killed.
CREGGAN AND BROOMFIELD.				
Brown, William	Clohog, Co. Armagh	Sergeant	American E.F.	
Clements, Thomas	Freeduff, Co. Armagh	Private	2nd Scots Guards	Killed in Action.
Donaldson, Randal	Clohog, Co. Armagh	Private	U.S. Inft.	
McCullagh, George	Clohog, Co. Armagh	Private	R.E.	
McCully, A. L., M.B.	England	Captain	R.A.M.C.	
McCully, M. C.		Private	S. African Reg.	
Preston, Josias	Camlough, Co. Armagh	Private	Scots Guards	Killed in Action.
Speers, Samuel	Cullyhanna, Co. Armagh	Private	R.I.F.	Killed in Action.
Stitt, U. J.	Ashfield, Co. Armagh	Lieut.-Commander	R.N.	
DERRYVALLEY.				
Douglass, Herbert	Shantonagh	Lance-Corporal	3rd R.I.F.	Wounded, Died.
Evans, John	Caddagh	Gunner	R.G.A.	Wounded.
Gilliland, Ernest	Corfad	Sergt.-Major	N.I.H.	
Irwin, Samuel	Cumry House, Ballybay	Sapper	R.E.	
Roland, James	Lisgorran			
COLONIAL FORCES.				
Douglas, A.	Cordevlis, Ballybay	Private	16th Can. Scottish	
Greer, J. N.	Tullycarbet, Ballybay	Q. Master Sergt.	43rd Canadians	
FRANKFORD, GARMANY'S GROVE.				
Allen, Victor Ballagh	Killycracken	Corporal	Army Pay Corps	
Birch, Robert	Tattinclave	Private	R.F. Artillery	
Brook, Frank	Castleblayney	Lieut.-Colonel	K.O.Y.L.I.	M.C., D.S.O. & Bar.
Crozier, Samuel	Longfield	Trooper	North Irish Horse	
George, John Thomas	Castleblayney	Driver	R.F. Artillery	Wounded.
Knox, Robert A.	Dromore	Lance-Corporal	R.I. Rifles	Prisoner of War.
Maguire, John	Castleblayney	Private	H.L. Infantry	Wounded & D'char.
McBride, Samuel	Tullycollive	Private	R.G. Artillery	
Rankin, Macauley	Drumagelvin	Private	R.I. Rifles	Prisoner of War & reported dead.
Stephenson, Wm. H.	Church-hill	Private	R.I. Fusiliers	
Wilson, Wm. F.	Castleblayney	Captain	R.A.M.C.	M.C.
DRUMKEEN.				
Armstrong, Wm.	Drumkeen, Newbliss	Private	I. Guards	M.M. Killed in Act.
Armstrong, Wm.	Drumate Lodge, Newbliss	Private	London Irish Home Force	
Lester, Ralph	Swan's Cross P.O.	Private	M.T.	
Thompson, John Robert	Drumkeen, Newbliss	Private	Can. Force	Killed in Action.
Thompson, Wm. Coote	Drumkeen, Newbliss	Private	Can. Force	

BALLYBAY PRESBYTERY.   LOUGHMOURNE AND CRIEVE.

Name.	Home Address.	Rank.	Regiment, Battalion or Unit.	Remarks.
LOUGHMOURNE AND CRIEVE.				
Burgess, Josiah	Loughmourne	Private	N.I.H.	Mons Medal.
McBride, Joseph	Crieve, Ballybay	Sergeant	2nd D.C.L.I.	Twice Wounded. Escaped Prisoner. Men. in D'patches.
McBride, Robert	Crieve, Ballybay	Sergt.-Major	9th R.Ir. Fus.	D.C.M., M.M. Wounded.
McBride, Wm.	Crieve, Ballybay	Corporal	9th R. Ir. Fus.	M.M., Wounded & Prisoner.
Mills, Wm.		Private	N.I.H.	Died.
Monaghan, S. R.		Sergeant	Can. F.A.	M.M. Killed in Act.
Somerville, Thomas	Crieve	Private	R. Irish Regt.	M.M. Wounded.
McKELVEY'S GROVE.				
Shiveral, Samuel			English Regt.	Killed in Action.
McMahon, John			Canadian Force	
Seymour, Robert			Canadian Force	
Seymour, Samuel			Canadian Force	
Seymour, Wm. John			Australian Force	
Thompson, James			Canadian Force	
Thompson, Wm.			Canadian Force	
Thompson, Wm., Jun.				
Thompson, Wm. J.				
ROCKCORRY.				
Hawthorne, Cecil	Tallybrook	Private	R.I.R.	
Ross, Walter John	Fairfield	Private	R.I.R.	

BALLYMENA PRESBYTERY.

Name.	Home Address.	Rank.	Regiment, Battalion or Unit.	Remarks.
FIRST AHOGHILL.				
Aiken, Fred.	Ahoghill	Petty Officer	R. Navy	
Bell, Matthew	Lisnafillan	Private	R. I Fus.	
Bell, Samuel James	Lisnafillan	Private	R.I. Rifles	
Blair, James	Drumrammer	Private	R.I. Rifles	
Cameron David	Corbally	Private	R.I. Rifles	Killed in Action.
Chesney, Wm. M'Meekin	Kilcurry	Captain	R.A.M.C.	Military Cross.
Christie, Mark	Killybegs	Private	R. Navy	
Forbes, George	Moneydollog	Private	North Irish Horse	
Forbes, John	Moneydollog	Private	North Irish Horse	Killed in Action.
Fullerton, Fred	Ballymena	Private	R.I. Rifles	
Fullerton, George	Ballymena	Private	R.I. Rifles	
Fullerton, Jonathan	Ballymena	Private	R.I Rifles	
Fullerton, Herbert	Ballymena	Private	R.I. Rifles	
Gillespie, James	Carmegrim	Private	H.L.I.	Killed in Action.
Greer, William	Ahoghill	Private	R.I. Rifles	Killed in Action.
Hamilton, John C.	Cloughogue	Private	R.I. Rifles	
Hamilton, Samuel	Ballymacilroy	Private	R.I. Rifles	
Houston, Leslie	Ballymena	Private	R.I. Fusiliers	Killed in Action.
Johnston, Samuel	Ahoghill	Private	R.I. Rifles	
Kennedy, John	Castletown	Private	R.M. Fusiliers	Wounded.
Kernohan, Bob	Ahoghill	Private	20th Hussars	
Kernohan, Hugh	Tullygarley	Private	R.I. Rifles	
Leith, George	Ballyconnelly	Private	R.I. Rifles	
McConachie, Alex.	Ballyboland	Private	R.I. Rifles	
M'Loughlin, Fred. Jas.	Ahoghill	Private	R.I. Rifles	
M'Master, Charles	Ballylummin	Private	Gordon Highlanders	
McMaster, John	Moneydollog	Private	R.I. Rifles	
MacMillan, Robert	Cloughogue	Private	R.I. Rifles	
McNeilly, Kennedy	Castletown	Private	R. Navy	
Maginnis, William	Ballymena	Private	R.I. Rifles	
Moody, Thomas	Ballyconnelly	Private	R.I. Rifles	
Orr, John	Killybegs	1st Stoker	R. Navy	
Perry, Harry	Galgorm	Private	North Irish Horse	
Perry, William	Galgorm	Sergeant	Royal Engineers	
Picken, Thomas	Slatt	Private	R.I. Rifles	
Scullion, Alex.	Ballymena	Private	Highland Light Infantry	
Scullion, Matthew	Ballymena	Private	R.I. Rifles	
Scullion, Samuel	Ballymena	Private	R.I. Rifles	
Scullion, Samuel John	Ballymena	Private	R.I. Rifles	

BALLYMENA PRESBYTERY.   FIRST AHOGHILL.

Name.	Home Address.	Rank.	Regiment, Battalion or Unit.	Remarks.
Shaw, Andrew	Slatt	Private	R.I. Rifles	
Sloan, John	Gloonan	Private	R.I. Rifles	
Sloan, Robert	Gloonan	Private	R.I. Rifles	
Small, William	Gloonan	Private	R.I. Rifles	
Smyth, John	Cloughwater	2nd Lieutenant	R.I. Rifles	Killed in Action.
Stevely, Samuel	Gloonan	Private	R.I. Rifles	Killed in Action.
Stevenson, Robert	Tullygarley	Private	H.L.I.	
Wilson, John	Galgorm	Captain	R.A.M.C.	
Wilson, Owen	Galgorm	Captain	R.A.M.C.	
COLONIAL FORCES.				
Blair, James	Glenhue	Private	Canadian	
Burnett, James	Ballylummin	Private	New Zealand	
Cameron, John	Gloonan	Private	New Zealand	
Clarke, James	Ballylummin	Private	Canadian	Killed in Action.
Clarke, William	Ballylummin	Private	Canadian	
Craig, Alex.	Drumrammer	Private	New Zealand	
Craig, David	Drumrammer	Private	New Zealand	
Craig, John	Killybeg	Private	Canadian	Killed in Action.
Craig, Samuel	Killybeg	Private	Canadian	
Kernohan, Andrew	Moyasset	Private	Canadian	
Kilpatrick, William	Ballylummin	Captain	Royal Engineers	
McDowell William John	Straid	Private	Canadian	
Mark, Johnston	Gloonan	Private	New Zealand	
Mitchell, David	Gracehill	Lieutenant	Canadian	
Newell, Robert	Craignageerah	Private	Northumberland F.	Killed in Action.
Nicholl, John	Craignageerah	Private	Canadian	
Nicholl, Robert	Craignageerah	Private	Canadian	
Robinson, Archie	Gloonan	Private	Canadian	
Thompson, William	Cloughogue	Private	New Zealand	
SECOND ANTRIM.				
Beattie, Robert J.	Hurtletoot	Private	11th R.I.R.	Killed in Action.
Beresford, Samuel	Antrim	Private	N.I.H.	
Boal, John Kirk	Antrim House	Captain	1st R.I. Fus.	Killed in Action.
Clark, Chas. W.	New Lodge, Muckamore	2nd Lieutenant	N.I.H.	
Clark, Henry	Dungonnell, Antrim	Private	N.I.H.	
Dalton, David	The Cottage, Greenmount	Private	R.E.	
Dalton, David, Jun.	The Cottage, Greenmount	Private	R.N.	
Erwin, Francis	Muckamore	Private	11th R.I.R	
Esler, Robert	Antrim	Private	11th R.I.R.	
Graham, Norman	Clonlee, Muckamore	Captain	R.A.M.C.	M.C.
Holmes, J. M.	Inglerea Tce., Antrim		R.N.	
Holmes, William	Inglerea Tce., Antrim		R.N.	
Hunter, Robt. T.	Mt. Oriel, Antrim	Private	29 R. Fus.	
Huston, Alfred	Antrim	Private	N.I.H.	
Kelly, Henry	Parkhall, Antrim	Private	A.S.C.	
Kelly, J. Alex.	Ardnaveigh, Antrim	Sergt.-Major	11th R.I.R.	D.C.M.
Kirkpatrick, Jas.	Hurtletoot	Private	11th R.I.R.	
Kirkwood, Francis R.	Muckamore	Private	Signalling Coy. R.E.	
McAloney, Wm. M.	Dunsilly	Private	12th R.I.R.	
McCormick, Robert	Antrim	Private	9th R. Inn. Fus.	
Malseed, John	Belfast Bank House, Antrim	Private	Cadet Corps	
Montgomery George	New Lodge, Muckamore	Sergeant	14th R.I.R.	M.M.
Montgomery, Hugh	The Lodge, Spring Farm	Boy	R.N.	
Montgomery, Wm.	The Lodge, Spring Farm	Private	16th R.I.R.	
Roberts, John R.	Antrim		R.N.	
Steele, Samuel	Steeple, Antrim	Private	9th R.I.R.	
Taggart, Andrew	Irishtown, Antrim	Private	11th R.I.R.	
Thompson, John	Castle Street, Antrim	Private	11th R.I.R.	Killed in Action.
Thompson, Samuel	Castle Street, Antrim	Private	11th R.I.R.	
Williamson, Edward	Fountain Street, Antrim		R.A.F.	
Williamson, Fred.	Fountain Street, Antrim		11th R.I.R.	Killed in Action.
Williamson, Samuel	Fountain Street, Antrim	Private	N.I.H.	
Williamson, Thomas	Fountain Street, Antrim		R.E.	M.M.
COLONIAL FORCES.				
Gray, Nathaniel		Lieutenant	190th Canadian Force	
Holmes, A. M.	Inglerea Tce., Antrim	Private	N.Z. Hosp. France	
Holmes, D. G.	Inglerea Tce., Antrim	Private	1st Canadian Force	
Huston, Robert	Pietersburg, S.A.	Private	S.A. (Pietersburg Command)	
Kirk, J. Coleman	Antrim	Corporal	49th Can. E.F.	Killed in Action.
Kirkwood, Wm. H.	Muckamore	Private	27th Can. E.F.	Killed in Action.
McDowell, Joseph	Ladyhill, Antrim	Private	Aust. E.F.	
McKeown, Wm. M.	Muckamore	Private	12th Brigade Can. F.A.	
Murdock, Wm.	Donegore	Private	S.A. E. Force	
Wilson, John	Irishtown		N.Z. E.F.	

BALLYMENA PRESBYTERY. FIRST BALLYMENA.

FIRST BALLYMENA.

Name.	Home Address.	Rank.	Regiment, Battalion or Unit.	Remarks.
ADRAIN, WM. KEARNS	Ballymena	Lieutenant	R.I.R.	Killed in Action.
ABERNETHY, TITUS	Ballymena	Private	R.I.R.	
AIKEN, WM.	Ballymena	Private	A.S.C.	
AIKEN, JOHN	Ballymena	Private	N.I.H.	
ALLEN, WM.	Dunyradden	Private	R.I.R.	Killed in Action.
ANDERSON, R. B.	Ballymena	Officer	R.N.R.	
BAMBER, ROBERT	Ballyloughan	Private	R.A.F.	
BARCLAY, OLIVER	Ballymena	Private	R. Inn. F.	
BARR, JAMES	Ballymena	Lance-Corporal	R.I.R.	
BARR, WM.	Ballymena	Private	R.A.F.	
BELL, JOSEPH	Ballymena	Private	R.I.R.	Killed in Action.
BELL, HERBERT	Dunderg	Private	R.A.F.	
BODEN, JOHN	Slatt	Private	R.I.R.	Died on Ac. Ser.
BOYD, SAMUEL	Ballymena	Private	R.A.M.C.	
CAIRNS, WM.	Ballymena	Private	R.I.R.	
CAIRNS, DAVID	Ballymena	Private	R.I.R.	
CARSON, MATTHEW	Ballymarlow	Private	R.A.F.	
CARUTH, ALEX. C.	Ballymena	Lieutenant	Gurkha Rifles	
CATHCART, WM.	Tullygarley	Lance-Corporal	R.E.	
CATHCART, ALEX.	Tullygarley	Lance-Corporal	R.G.A.	
CATHCART, WILLIAM	Tullygarley	Lance-Corporal	West Riding	
CATHCART, ROBERT	Tullygarley		R.N.	Killed.
CATHCART, JOHN	Tullygarley	Private	Royal Scots	Killed in Action.
CATHCART, DAVID	Slatt	Lieutenant	West Kents	Killed in Action.
CATHCART, JOHN	Ballymena	Private	A.S.C.	
CHESNEY, GEORGE	Ballymena	Captain	R.A.M.C.	
CLARKE, NATHANIEL	Tullygarley	Private	R.F.A.	
COOKE, JAMES	Ballyloughan	Lance-Corporal	R.E.	
COOKE, ALEX.	Ballymena	Private	R.I.R.	
COOKE, THOMAS H.	Ballymena	Private	R.I.R.	Killed in Action.
COWAN, ADAM	Ballymena	Lieutenant		Killed in Action.
CRAWFORD, JOHN	Ballymena	Private	R.E.	
CRAWFORD, CHAS. D.	Ballymena		R.N.	
CRAWFORD, JOHN	Ballymena	Lieutenant	R.I.R.	
CRAWFORD, ROBERT	Ballymena	Lieutenant	R.I.R.	
CROTHERS, WM.	Ballymena	Private	A.S.C.	
CUMMING, SAMUEL	Ballymena	Sergeant	R.I.R.	
DAVISON, EDWARD	Ballymena	Private	R.I.R.	
DAVISON, J. H.	Ballymena	Captain	R.A.M.C.	
DARRAGH, JAMES	Ballycraigy	Lieutenant	Duke of Wellington	Killed in Action.
DARRAGH, MATTHEW	Ballycraigy	Lieutenant	Duke of Wellington	Killed in Action.
DARRAGH, JOHN	Ballycraigy	Private	R.IK.D.	Killed in Action.
EAGLESON, ROBERT	Ballymena	Private	R.A.M.C.	
FERGUSON, WM.	Ballymena	Lieutenant	R.I.R.	
FISHER, JACK	Ballymena	Private	N.I.H.	
FRANCEY, JOSEPH	Ballymena		R.N.	
FRANCEY, JAS.	Slatt	Lieutenant	R.I.R.	
FRANCEY, JAS.	Ballymena	Private	R.G.A.	
FRANCEY, JAS.	Ballymena	Private	R.IK.F.	Killed in Action.
FRANCEY, WM.	Ballymena		R.IK.F.	Killed in Action.
GIBSON, MATTHEW	Slatt	Private	R.I.R.	
GIBSON, JOHN	Slatt	Corporal	R.I.R.	
GIBSON, DAVID	Slatt	Private	R.I.R.	Killed in Action.
GORDON, WM.	Ballymarlow	Corporal	R.I.R.	
HAMILL, ROBERT	Ballymena	Private	R.E.	
HAMILL, ANDREW	Ballymena	Private	R.A.F.	
HANNA, GEORGE	Ballymena	Private	R.I.R.	
HASLETT, M.C., T. S.	Ballymena	Lieutenant	R.I.R.	Killed in Action.
HATTON, JOHN	Ballymena	Lieutenant	West Y. Regt.	
HOGG, WM.	Tullygarley	Private	R.E.	
HOGG, DAVID	Tullygarley	Private	A. & S.H.	
HOGG, SAMUEL	Tullygarley	Private	R.A.F.	
HOUSTON, JOSEPH	Ballymena	Private	M.M.P.	Died on Act. Ser.
KINNEAR, ROBERT	Ballymena		N.I.H.	
KYLE, JAS. T.	Ballymena	Captain	R.A.M.C.	
LEETCH, SAMUEL	Ballymena	Private	R.A.M.C.	
LEETCH, WILLIAM	Ballymena	Lance-Corporal	R.I.R.	
LENNOX, JAMES	Ballymena	Private	R.I.R.	Killed in Action.
LOGAN, SAMUEL	Ballymena	Private	R.I.R.	Killed in Action.
LORMER, JOHN	Galgorm Parks	Private	R.IK.F.	
LORMER, GEO.	Ballymena	Private	R.A.F.	
LORMER, JOHN	Ballymena	Private	A.S.C.	
MACAULAY, ROBERT	Ballymarlow	Private	R.I.R.	
MARCUS, THOMAS	Ballymena	Private	N. Lanc. R.	
MARCUS, ALEX.	Ballymena	Private	R.I.R.	
MEHAFFY, N. C.	Ballymena	Lance-Corporal	R.E.	
MEHAFFY, HARRY	Ballymena	Private	N.I.H.	
MONTGOMERY, THOS.	Ballymena	Private	N.I.H.	
MONTGOMERY, ALEX.	Kirkinriola	Private	R.I.R.	Killed in Action.
MOORE, SAMUEL	Ballymena		R.N.	
MORROW, JOSEPH	Ballee	Private	R.I.R.	
MORROW, HUGH	Ballee	Private	R.A.F.	

(36)

BALLYMENA PRESBYTERY.

FIRST BALLYMENA.

Name.	Home Address.	Rank.	Regiment, Battalion or Unit.	Remarks.
Millar, Henry	Tullygarley	Private	R.I.R.	
Millar, Wm. J.	Tullygarley	Private	Lanc. F.	
Millar, Alex.	Tullygarley	Private	R.I.R.	
Millar, Wm. J.	Tullygarley	Private	R.I.R.	
Millar, Thos.	Ballymena	Private	R.I.F.	
Millar, John	Ballymena	Lieutenant	R.I.R.	
Millar, Samuel	Ballymena	Private		
Millar, Hugh	Liminary	Private	R.S.F.	
Millar, Wm.	Brodamount	Private	R.A.F.	
McAteer, Thomas	Ballymena	Private	N.I.H.	
McAteer, Wilson	Ballymena	Private	R.I.R.	
McAteer, Archy	Ballymena	Private	R.G.A.	
McAteer, James	Ballymena		R.I.R.	
McAteer, Adam	Ballymena	Private	R.I.K.F.	Killed in Action.
McAteer, Natl.	Ballymena	Private	Mahow Cavalry	Killed in Action.
McCallion, Jas.	Ballymena	Sergeant	H.L.I.	
McCallion, Robt. K.	Ballymena	Private	R.I.R.	
McCallion, David	Ballymena	Private	R.I.F.	
McCarroll, James	Ballylesson	Private	R.E.	
McCarroll, John	Ballylesson	Lance-Corporal	R.I.R.	
McCartney, Wm.	Ballymena	Sergeant	R.I.K.F.	
McCartney, John	Ballymena	Private	N.I.H.	
McCaughey, James	Carninny	Private	R.I.R	
McCaw, Robt. R.	Ballymena	Private	R.I.R.	
McClurkin, Fred.	Ballymena		R.N.	
McConnell, Geo. S.	Ballymena	Private	A.S.C.	
M'Connell, A. J.	Ballymena	Captain	R.A.M.C.	
McConnell, Daniel W.	Ballymena	Private	R.F.C.	Died on Act. Ser.
McCready, Jas.	Ballymena	Private	R.A.F.	
McFetridge, Jas.	Ballymena	Private	R.I.F.	
McFetridge, Samuel	Ballymena	Lance-Corporal	R.I.R.	
McGall, John	Ballymena	Private	R.I.R.	
McIlwaine, Jas.	Dunfane	Corporal	R.I.R.	
McIlwaine, Wm.	Dunfane	Private	R.A.F.	
McIlwaine, Alex.	Dunfane	Private	R.N.	
McIlwaine, Anderson	Dunfane	Private	R.I.R.	Died of Wounds
McKee, James	Ballymena	Private	H.L.I.	
McNeice, Wm. J.	Ballymena	Private	R.I.R.	Killed in Action.
McQuitty, James	Ballylesson	Sergeant	R.I.R.	
McShane, Frank	Ballymena		R.I.R.	
Parke, Robert	Ballymena	Private	A.S.C.	
Parke, Jun., Robert	Ballymena	Private	R.I.K.F.	
Patterson, John	Ballymena	Private	Black Watch	
Rainey, William	Ballymena	Private	R.I.R.	
Reid, Hugh	Ballymena	Private	R.I.R.	
Robinson, Robert	Ballymena	Private	A. & S.H.	
Russell, Saml. E.	Ballymena	Private	R.I.R.	
Russell, Jas. L.	Ballymena	Lance-Corporal	R. In. F.	
Smyth, Arthur	Ballymena	Private	N.I.H.	
Smyth, Robert	Ballymena	Sergeant	W. Guards	
Spence, John	Ballymena	Private	R.I.R	
Spence, Wm. J.	Ballymena	Private	R.I.R.	Died on Act. Ser.
Stewart, Natl.	Tullygarley	Private	E. Surrey R.	
Stewart, Jas.	Tullygarley	Private	R.A.F.	
Suiter, Jas.	Ballymena	Private	R.I.R.	
Telford, Wm.	Tullygarley	Sergeant	R.I.K.F.	
Telford, John	Ballyloughan	Private	R.I.R.	
Watson, Goodlet H.	Ballymena		R.N.R.	
Weir, Jas. A.	Ballymena	Private	Cardiff City B.	
Weir, Harry W.	Ballymena	Captain	R.A.M.C.	
Wilson, Andrew	Ballymena	Private	R.I.R.	Killed in Action.
Wilson, John H.	Ballymena	Private	7 Coy. 75th T.R.B.	Died on Act. Ser.
Wilson, Geo. H.	Tullygarley	Captain	R.G.A.	
Wilson, Ben.	Tullygarley		R.N.	
Wilson, Malcolm O.	Ballymena	Captain	R.A.M.C.	
Wilson, Samuel	Ballymena	Sergeant	R.I.F.	
Wilson, Charles	Ballymena	Private	R.I.R.	
Wilson, Thomas	Ballymena	Private	A.S.C.	
Wilson, Geo. W.	Ballymena	Lieutenant	A.S.C.	
Woodburn, Jas.	Crebilly	Private	R.G.A.	
Wylie, John	Ballymena	Lieutenant	King's Liverpool	
Young, Henry	Galgorm Castle	Colonel	Indian Army	
COLONIAL FORCES.				
Allen, Robert	Dunyraden	Private	C.F.A.	
Allen, Samuel	Dunyraden	Sergeant	C.E.F.	
Beatty, Samuel	Ballygarvey	Private	C.E.F.	
Blair, Harry	Ballymena	Private	C.E.F.	
Cathcart, David	Tullygarley	Private	A.I.F.	
Wilson, Esler	Ballymena	Private	N.Z. Ex. F.	
Gillespie, Robert	Ballymena	Private	C.F.A.	
Gillespie, Thos. B.	Ballymena		West Af. F.	
Gordon, James	Ballymarlow	Private	C.E.F.	Killed in Action.

BALLYMENA PRESBYTERY. FIRST BALLYMENA.

Name.	Home Address.	Rank.	Regiment, Battalion or Unit.	Remarks.
Gordon, Charles	Ballymarlow	Private	C.E.F.	Killed in Action.
Kennedy, John	Ballylesson	Sergeant	C.E.F.	
Mehaffy, Wm. H.	Ballymena	Lance-Corporal	C.E.F.	
McNeilly, Arthur	Ballymena	Sergeant	C.E.F.	
Penny, Samuel	Ballymena	Private	C.E.F.	
Rea, William	Tullygarley	Private	Anzacs	Died of Wounds.
Simpson, Wm. B.	Dunfane	Private	C.E.F.	
Suiter, John	Ballymena	Private	C.E.F.	
Sutter, Samuel	Ballymena	Private	C.E.F.	
Wilson, W. O.	Ballymena	Captain	R.A.M.C., West Af. F.	

SECOND BALLYMENA.

Name.	Home Address.	Rank.	Regiment, Battalion or Unit.	Remarks.
Bailie, Joseph	Princess Street	Trooper	N.I.H.	
Black, George	Robert Street	Driver	R.F.A.	
Black, John	Robert Street	Gunner	R.F.A.	
Black, Robert	Robert Street	Driver	R.F.A.	
Blair, Wm.	Galgorm Street	Lance-Corporal	R.I.R.	Died of Wounds.
Bonnar, Alex.	Henry Street	Private	R.F.A.	
Bonnar, Joseph	Kintullagh Terrace	Private	Wiltshire Regt.	
Campbell, Matthew	Garfield Place,	Private	R.A.M.C.	
Currie, Wm.	William Street	Private	R.I.R.	
Eagleson Robert	Bridge Street		R.A.M.C.	
Eagleson, Wilson	Bridge Street		R.A.F.	
Galloway, James	Bridge Street Place	Private	12th R.I.R.	
Galloway, Joseph	Bridge Street Place		R.A.F.	
Galloway, Thomas	Bridge Street Place		2nd R.I.R.	
Gaston, Andrew	Clarence Street	Private	5th Inft. Brigade	
Gaston, Robert	Clarence Street		Labour Batt.	
Giffin. Wm.	Mount Street		L.N. Lancers	Died of Wounds.
Graham, John	Galgorm Street	Private	16th R.I.R.	
Graham, Samuel	Galgorm Street	Private	12th R.I.R.	
Grant, John, Jun.	Galgorm	Private	12th R.I.R.	Killed in Action.
Grant, Wm.	Railway Cottages	Sergeant	12th R.I.R.	Killed in Action.
Herbison, James	Hill Street		A.S.C.	
Herbison, John	Ballymoney Street	Private	16th R.I.R.	
Herbison, Samuel	Ballymoney Street	Private	12th R.I.R.	
Herbison, Wm.	Ballymoney Street		R.N.	
Houston, Clarke	Galgorm Street	Private	2nd R.I. Fus.	
Hughes, Alex.	Warden Street	Private	M.G. Corps	
Kennedy, Bertie	Waveney Avenue		R.A.F.	
Kernohan, James	Queen Street		R.A.F.	
King, James	Springwell Street	Private	12th R.I.R.	Killed in Action.
Lamont, John	Galgorm	Private	12th R.I.R.	
Larkin, Thomas	Hill Street	Private	M.G. Corps	
Larkin, Wm.	Hill Street	Private	Cyclists' Corps	
Little, Robert	Prospect Place	Private	R.I. Fus.	Killed in Action.
McAteer, Francis	Greenvale Street		M.G. Corps	
McAteer, James	Greenvale Street	Trooper	N.I.H.	
McCauley, James	Edward Street		M.G. Corps	
McCauley, John	Bridge Street	Private	R.E.	
McCauley, Joseph	Edward Street		Garrison G. Coy.	
McCauley, Joseph, Jun.	Edward Street	Private	12th R.I.R.	
McCauley, Wm. J.	Bridge Street	Private	R.I.R.	
McClean, Samuel	Springwell Street	Private	12th R.I.R.	
McClean, Wm.	Springwell Street	Private	14th R.I.R.	
McCollum, Thos.	Park Head	Lance-Corporal	R.I.R.	Killed in Action.
McCullough, Robt.	Bridge Street	Private	12th R.I.R.	
McDonald, Albert	Broughshane Street	Private	1st R.I.R.	Killed in Action.
McIlroy, Samuel	Fenagh		4th Scottish Rifles	Killed in Action.
McKane, Wm. A.	Park Street		Labour Corps	
McMullan, Wm.	Queen Street	Private	12th R.I.R.	
Magee, Robert	Queen Street	Private	12th R.I.R.	Killed in Action.
Magee, Wm. J.	Queen Street	Private	12th R.I.R.	
Marshall, Herbert	Springwell Street	Lance-Corporal	2nd R.I.R.	
Millar, Hugh	Albert Place	Private	R.I. Fus.	
Montgomery, Henry	Killyflugh	Private	2nd B. Watch	Killed in Action.
Moody, James	Park Street			
Murphy, Robert	Leighinmohr		R.N.	
Neely, Samuel	Park Head	Private	R.I.R.	Killed in Action.
Nicholl, Hugh	Bridge St. Place	Private	2nd R.I.R.	Killed in Action.
Orr, Matthew	Patrick Place	Private	1st I. Guards	
Patton, Wm.	Galgorm Street	Private	12th R.I.R.	
Peacock, Wm. J.	Kirkinriola	Gunner	R.G.A.	
Rea, James	Hope Street		R.A.M.C.	
Reilly, Robert, Jun.	Princess Street		R.E.	
Richmond, Wm. J.	Garfield Place	Trooper	N.I.H.	
Robinson, Geo.	Prospect Place	Private	12th R.I.R.	
Rock, James	Ballygarvey	Private	12th R.I.R.	
Ross, Bertie	Bridge Street		R.A.F.	
Ross, Robert	High Street		R.A.F.	
Steele, Robert	Clonavon Terrace		R.E.	
Steele, Samuel	Clonavon Terrace	Trooper	N.I.H.	
Stewart, John	Waveney Avenue	Private	12th R.I.R.	

BALLYMENA PRESBYTERY. SECOND BALLYMENA.

Name.	Home Address.	Rank.	Regiment, Battalion or Unit.	Remarks.
Stewart, Joseph	Waveney Avenue		Labour Corps	
Thompson, Alex.	Galgorm Street	Private	R.I. Fus.	
Thompson, John	Galgorm Street	Private	R.I.R.	
Torbitt, Jack	Moat Road	Corporal	12th R.I.R.	
Torbitt, Robert	Moat Road	Private	15th R.I.R.	
Wilson, James	Killyflugh	Private	12th R.I.R	
Wilson, John	Killyflugh	Private	3rd R.I.R.	
Wilson, Thomas	Killyflugh	Private	12th R.I.R.	Died in Germany.
Wilson, Wm.	Killyflugh	Private	20th R.I.R.	
Wright, Alex.	Moat Road		R.A.F.	
Wright, John	Carninny	Private	3rd R.I.R.	

WEST CHURCH, BALLYMENA.

Name.	Home Address.	Rank.	Regiment, Battalion or Unit.	Remarks.
Allison, W. J.	Ballymena	Private	R. Inn. Fus.	
Andrews, Arthur	Ballymena	Lieutenant	R. Irish Fus.	Wounded.
Andrews, Fred. S.	Ballymena	Lieutenant	R Inn. Fus	
Andrews, W. J. M.	Ballymena	2nd Lieutenant	R.A.F.	Killed in Action.
Ballintine, Wm.	Ballymena	Private	R.A.M.C.	
Bartholomew, Alex.	Ballymena	Private	R. Inn. Fus.	M.M. and Russian Cross of St.George
Bartholomew, John	Ballymena	Private	Field Ambulance	
Bartholomew, Wm.	Ballymena	Private	M.G.C.	
Beatty, George	Ballymena	Trooper	N.I.H.	
Bell, Alex.	Ballymena	Captain	15th London Regt.	
Bellis, A.	Ballymena	Petty Officer	R.N	
Boal, J. G.	Ballymena	Surgeon	R.N.	
Brown, David	Ballymena	Quartermaster		
Brown, John	Ballymena		R.N.	
Caruth, Gordon	Ballymena	Lieutenant	R.I.R.	Killed in Action.
Clarke, Henry	Ballymena	Private	R.I. Regt.	
Clarke, Jerry	Ballymena	Private	10th Cav. Corps	
Courtney, Robt.	Ballymena	Private	R.I.R.	Died.
Craig, James	Ballymena	Drummer	R. Inn Fus	
Craig, William	Ballymena	Private	R. Inn. Fus.	Wounded.
Currie, Samuel	Ballymena	Sergeant	12th R.I.R.	Killed in Action.
Dempsey, John	Ballymena	Private	Seaforth Highldrs.	Wounded.
Dempsey, Robert	Ballymena	Private	Scottish Rifles	
Dempsey, Thomas	Ballymena	Sergeant	Gordon Highldrs.	
Dunn, John	Ballymena	Private	R.I.F.	
Elliott, James	Ballymena	Private	R.I.R.	
Elliott, James	Ballymena	Gunner	R.F.A.	D.C.M.
Ferguson, James	Ballymena	2nd Lieutenant	R.G.A.	Wounded.
Getty, Ernest	Ballymena	Gunner	R.F.A.	
Gillespie, James	Ballymena	Private	M.G. Corps	
Gillespie, Wm.	Ballymena	Private	M.G. Corps	
Gordon, Robert	Ballymena	Rifleman	12th R.I.R.	
Graham, W. J.	Ballymena	Sergeant	R. Inn. Fus.	
Grant, Alex.	Ballymena	Private	R.A.F.	
Harkness, Thos.	Ballymena	Lance-Corporal	R.I.R.	
Henry, Walter	Ballymena	Sapper	R.E	
Herbison, J. B.	Ballyloughin	Private	Imperial Camel Corps	
Herbison, J. S.	Ballyloughin	Private		Died.
Johnston, W. F.	Ballymena	Lieutenant	R.E.	
Leitch, Wm.	Ballymena	Sergeant	R.I.R.	
Lynn, Wm.	Ballymena	Private	R.I.R.	
McAdorey, Matthew	Ballymena	Rifleman	R.I.R.	Wounded.
McClelland, John	Ballymena	Lance-Corporal	R. Marines	
McCook, John	Ballymena	Private	R.E.	
McDonnell, Campbell	Ballymena	Gunner	R.G.A.	
McGowan, J.	Ballymena	Private	R.I.R.	
McIlroy, James	Ballymena	Sergeant	N.I H.	
McKeegan, T.	Ballymena	Trooper	N.I.H.	
McVeigh, Wm.	Ballymena	Lance-Corporal	R.I.R.	Wounded.
Magregor, Wm.	Ballymena	Trooper	N.I.H.	
Martin, G. B.	Ballymena	Major	Oxford & Bucks Light Inft.	M.C.
Millar, R. W.	Ballymena	Sergeant	Can. Mt. Rifles	
Millar, S. R.	Ballymena	2nd Lieutenant	R. Inn. Fus.	Wounded.
Millar, Wm.	Ballymena	Private	R. I. Fus.	
Montgomery, John	Ballymena	Lieutenant	R.A.F.	
Moore, Robert	Ballymena	Gunner	R.G.A.	
Nevin, Wm.	Ballymena	Lance-Sergeant	R.I.R.	
O'Neill, George	Ballymena	Private	R.I.R.	
O'Neill, John	Ballymena	Gunner	R.F.A.	
O'Neill, Wm.	Ballymena	Private	R.I.R.	
Rainey, Alex.	Ballymena	Private	R.I.R.	
Rainey, Wm.	Ballymena	Lance-Corporal	R.I.R.	
Rankin, John	Ballymena	Sapper	R.I.R.	
Rowan, James	Ballymena	Private	R.I.R.	
Rowan, T.		Gunner	R.F.A.	
Simpson, Hugh		Lieutenant	172 Labour Coy.	
Skillen, Fred.	Ballymena	Lieutenant	King's Liv. Regt.	
Smith, Thos.	Slatt	Private	R. Inn. Fus.	
Stewart, John	Ballymena	Captain	R.A.M.C.	Wounded.

BALLYMENA PRESBYTERY. **WEST CHURCH, BALLYMENA.**

Name.	Home Address.	Rank.	Regiment, Battalion or Unit.	Remarks.
Stewart, Thomas	Ballymena	Rifleman	R.I.R.	
Stewart, W. H., Rev.	Ballymena	Captain	Chaplain	
Stewart, Wm. J.	Ballymena	Corporal	R.I.R.	
Tennent, Frank	Ballymena	Private	R.I.R.	Wounded.
Warden, James	Ballymena		R.N.	
Warnick, John	Ballymena	Rifleman	R.I.R.	
Warnick, Thos.	Ballymena	Private	R.A.F.	
Wilson, Jack	Ballymena		R.N.	
Wilson, Jas. W.	Ballymena	Lance-Corporal	R.E.	
Wilson, John	Ballymena	Private	R.I.R.	
Wilson, John C.	Ballymena	Captain	R.A.M.C.	
Wilson, R. B.	Ballymena	Private	Welsh Regt.	
Wilson, Samuel	Ballymena	Private	N.I.H.	
Wilson, Wm.		Sergeant	P.B.T.	
Woodside, Cecil		Captain	R.A.M.C.	
Wray, John		Gunner	R.F.A.	
Wylie, John		Corporal	R. Inn. Fus.	Wounded.
Wylie, Robert		Pioneer	R.E.	
WELLINGTON STREET, BALLYMENA.				
Agnew John	Cromkill, Ballymena	Lance-Corporal	R.I.R.	Wounded.
Allen, Robert	Ballymena	Private	R.I.R.	
Allen, Samuel	Teeshan, Ballymena	Private	R.I.R.	Wounded.
Anderson, Jack	Ballymena	Private	R.I.R.	Wounded.
Anderson, James	Ballymena	Cadet	N.I.H.	
Anderson, John	Ballymena	Private	R.E.	Gassed.
Anderson, John	Ballymena	Private	R.I.R.	Wounded.
Anderson, Joseph	Ballymena	Trooper	N.I.H.	
Armstrong, Robert	Ballymena	Private	R.I. Fus.	Wounded
Armstrong, Wm.	Ballymena	Private	Black Watch	Killed.
Barr, Archie	Ballymena	Mechanic	R.A. Force	
Barr, John	Ballymena	Private	R.I.R.	Killed
Barr, Matthew	Cromkill	Private	R.I.R.	Killed.
Barr, Robert	Ballymena	Private	Tank Corps	Prisoner of War.
Black, Alex.	Ballymena	Private	R.I.R.	Wounded.
Blair, James	Ballymena	Private	R.E.	
Boal, James S.	Tullygarley, Ballymena	Lieutenant	R.G. Artillery	Died of Wounds.
Boyd, Robert	Ballymena	Private	R.I.R.	
Boyd, Waller	Ballymena	Gunner	R.G.A.	
Brown, William	Ballymena	Sergeant	R.I.R.	
Cairns, Norman	Ballymena	Private	R.I. Fus.	
Cairns, Wm.	Ballymena	Sergeant	R.I. Fus.	
Carlton, James	Ballymena	Driver	R. Transport	
Carlton, James	Ballymena	Mechanic	R.A. Force	
Chambers, Robt. J.	Ballymena	Lance-Corporal	R.I.R.	Wounded.
Chambers, Vincent	Ballymena	Lance-Corporal	R.I.R.	Wounded.
Clarke, James	Ballymena	Private	R.I.R.	
Clarke, John	Ballymena	Captain	R.A.M.C.	Killed
Clarke, Robert	Ballymena	Private	R.I.R.	
Coulter, Thos.	Ballymena	Private	R.F.A.	Killed.
Davison, John	Ballymena	Sergeant	R.I.R.	
Dempster, Wm.	Ballymena	Sergeant	Cameron Highlanders	Wounded.
Dickey, Wm.	Ballymena	Private	R.I.R.	
Ellis, Samuel	Ballymena	Air Mechanic	R.A.F.	
Finlay, Hugh	Ballymena	Private	R.A.F.	
Finlay, Wm.	Ballymena	Private	R. Inn. Fus	Wounded.
Foster, Samuel	Ballymena	Private	R.I. Fus.	Wounded.
Foster, Samuel	Ballymena	Private	Labour Corps	
Francey, James	Ballee, Ballymena	Private	N.I.H.	Prisoner of War.
Garret, Stafford	Ballymena	Private	Northumberland Fus.	
Gillen, John	Ballymena	Private	R.A.M.C.	
Gillespie, Wm.	Ballycraigy, Ballymena	Trooper	N.I.H.	
Gilliland, Robert	Ballymena	Corporal	R.I.R.	
Gray, David	Ballymena	Private	R.I.R.	Killed.
Gray, Hugh	Teeshan, Ballymena	Private	Black Watch	
Gray, Robert	Ballymena	Private	R.I.R.	
Greer, Alex.	Ballymena	Private	R.I.R.	Prisoner of War.
Hamill, Samuel C.	Ballymena	Driver	R.E.	
Hamilton, David	Ballymena	Sapper	R.E.	
Hamilton, John	Ballymena	Private	R.I.F.	Prisoner of War.
Harrison, James	Cromkill, Ballymena	Driver	Tank Corps	Gassed.
Henry, William	Slatt, Ballymena	Private	R.I.R.	Wounded.
Herbison, James	Ballymena	Corporal	R.I. Regt.	Prisoner of War
Herbison, John	Ballymena	Private	R.I.R.	Wounded.
Herbison, Robert	Ballymena	Sergeant	R.I.R.	Killed.
Kelso, George	Ballymena	Sergeant	R.I.R.	Wounded.
Kernohan, Robert	Ballymena	Private		Killed.
Knox, James	Ballymena	Private	R.I.R.	Wounded.
Knox, John	Ballymena	Private	R.I.R.	Killed.
Knox, Joseph		Air Mechanic	R.A.F.	
Lamont, Arthur	Ballymena			
Lamont, James	Ballymena	Private	R.I.R.	
Leith, James	Cloughouge, Ballymena	Driver	A.S.C.	Wounded.

BALLYMENA PRESBYTERY.   WELLINGTON STREET, BALLYMENA.

Name.	Home Address.	Rank.	Regiment, Battalion or Unit.	Remarks.
McCartney, David	Ballymena	Air Mechanic	R.A.F.	
McCartney, Stafford	Ballymena	Stoker	R.N.	
McCutcheon, John	Ballymena	Lieutenant	R.A.M.C.	
McDowell, Hugh	Ballymena	Private	R.I.R.	Died of Wounds.
McFadden, Robt.	Ballymena	Private	R. Inn. Fus.	Wounded.
McFadden, Wm.	Ballymena	Driver	D.A.C.	
McFall, Daniel	Ballymena	Private	R.I.R.	Killed.
McFall, Robert	Ballymena	Private	R.I.R.	Prisoner of War.
McFall, Thomas	Ballymena	Private	R.A.F.	
McNeice, Alex.	Ballymena	Petty Officer	R.N.	
McNeice, Alex.	Ballymena	Private	R.I.R.	Wounded.
McNeice, Archie	Ballymena	Air Mechanic	R.A.F.	
McNeice, Daniel	Ballymena	Private	R.I.R.	Killed.
McNeice, Wm. Jas.	Ballymena	Lance-Corporal	R.E.	
McQuiston, Andrew	Ballymena	Private	R.I.R.	Wounded.
McQuiston, Norman	Ballymena	Air Mechanic	R.A.F.	
McWhirter, James	Ballymena	Private	R.A.M.C.	
McWhirter, James	Ballymena	Private	Irish Guards	Prisoner of War.
McWhirter, J.	Ballymena	Private	Mounted Transport	
Magill, Hugh	Ballymena	Private	R.I.R.	Wounded.
Mark, George	Ballymena	Private	R.I. Fus.	Killed.
Mark, John	Kirkinriola, Ballymena	Private	Labour Corps	
Martin, Joseph	Ballymena	Private	R.I.R.	Killed.
Millar, John	Ballymena	Private	R.I.R.	
Millar, Samuel	Ballymena	Private	R.I.R.	Wounded.
Moody, Alex.	Ballymena	Private	R. Innis. Fus.	
Moore, Wm.	Ballymena	Joiner	R.N.	
Morrison, James	Ballymena	Staff-Sergeant	R.E.	Wounded.
Mullen, James	Ballymena	Air Mechanic	R.A.F.	
Murray, Albert	Ballee, Ballymena			Gassed.
Murray, Wm.	Ballee, Ballymena			Wounded.
O'Loan, James	Ballymena	Private	R.I.R.	Prisoner of War.
Ramsey, Samuel	Ballee, Ballymena	Lance-Corporal	R.I.R.	Wounded.
Scullion, Matthew	Ballymena	Air Mechanic	R.A.F.	
Scullion, Samuel	Ballymena	Private	R.A.F.	
Shaw, John	Ballymena	Trooper	N.I.H.	
Smyth, Hugh	Cromkill, Ballymena	Private	R. Inn. Fus.	
Smyth, Robert	Cromkill, Ballymena	Private	M. Gun Corps	D.C.M.
Smyth, Samuel	Ballymena	Private	R.I. Fus.	Killed.
Smyth, William	Cromkill, Ballymena	Sapper	R.E.	
Steele, George	Ballymena	Private	R.I.R.	Wounded.
Steele, Thomas	Ballymena	Private	R.I.R.	Wounded.
Stewart, Hugh	Teeshan, Ballymena	Private	R.I.R.	
Strahan, John D.	Killybegs, Ballymena			
Taylor, David	Galgorm Parks	Private	R.I.R.	Died in Germany.
Taylor, John	Galgorm Parks	Lieutenant	R.I. Fus.	M.C.
Thomson, James	Ballymena	Private	R.I.R.	Wounded.
Thomson, James	Ballee, Ballymena	Corporal	R.I.R.	Killed.
Thomson, John B.	Ballee, Ballymena	Lance-Corporal	R.I.R.	
Thomson, Samuel	Ballymena	Private	R.I.R.	
Todd, Hugh	Ballymena	Lieut.-commander	R.N.R.	Died.
Todd, Leonard	Ballymena	Private	R.I.R.	
Tweed, Charles	Ballymena	Private	Argyle & S. Highldrs.	Wounded.
Tweed, Robert	Ballymena	Private	R. Innis. Fus.	Wounded.
Wallace, David	Cromkill, Ballymena	Private	Irish Guards	Wounded.
Wallace, James	Ballymena	Sergeant	Irish Guards	Killed.
Wallace, John	Ballymena	Private	Argyle & S. Highldrs.	Wounded.
Welsh, Harry	Ballee, Ballymena	Trooper	N.I. Horse	
Wilson, John	Kirkinriola	Private	Labour Corps	Wounded.
Young, Jack	Ballymena	Lieutenant	R.I. Fus.	Wounded.
Young, Wm.	Ballymena	Driver	A.S.C.	
COLONIAL AND U.S.A. FORCES.				
Boyd, John M.	Australia	Major	Light Horse Regt.	M.C.
Boyd, Norman	Australia	Private	A.M.C.	
Craig, Samuel	Canada	Private	8th Canadians	
Finlay, Samuel	Canada	Private	8th Canadians	Killed.
Francey, Thos.	Canada	Driver	Can. A.S.C.	Wounded.
Galloway, Hugh	S. Africa	Private	S.A. Rifles	
Hamilton, Alex.	Canada	Private	52nd Canadians	
Kennedy, Samuel	U.S.A.	Private	Texas Contgt.	
Linton, James	Canada	Gunner	Can. F.A.	Wounded.
Mann, Samuel	Canada	Private	23rd Res. Can.	Gassed.
Montgomery, Allan	Canada	Private	Winnipeg Rifles	Killed.
Montgomery, Robert	Canada	Private	Winnipeg Rifles	Wounded.
McCartney, Samuel	Canada	Private	P.P.C. L.I.	
McCartney, Stafford	Canada	Private	52nd Can.	Wounded.
McDowell, John C.	Canada	Lieutenant	P.P.C. L.I.	M.M.
McNeice, Archie	Canada	Sergeant	Can. R.A.M.C.	Killed.
McNeice, Jas. H.	Canada	Private	8th Canadians	
McNeice, Robt. J.	Canada	Private	8th Canadians	Killed.
McNeice, Samuel	Canada	Private	8th Canadians	Wounded.
McNeilly, Duncan	Australia	Lance-Corporal	Aus. Ex. Force	Died of Wounds.

BALLYMENA PRESBYTERY.　　　　　　　　　　　　　　　　　WELLINGTON STREET, BALLYMENA.

Name.	Home Address.	Rank.	Regiment, Battalion or Unit.	Remarks.
McNeilly, Samuel	Australia	Sergeant	Aus. Ex. Force	Wounded.
Rainey, Robert	Canada	Sapper	Can. Rail Troops	
Rainey, Wm.	Canada	Private	1st Canadians	
Ross, Wm.	Australia	Private	Aus. Ex. Force	Wounded.
Skillen, Arthur	New Zealand	Private	Otago Inft. Batt.	Gassed.
Taylor, Alex.	Canada	Sapper	1st Can.	
Tuff, Thomas	Canada	Gunner	Can. F.A.	Wounded.
Wallace, Samuel	Australia	Private	Aus. Ex. Force	Killed.
Welsh, Walker	N. Zealand	Private	Otago Inft. Batt.	
HARRYVILLE, BALLYMENA.				
Allen, David	Alfred Street, Ballymena	Private	R.I.R.	
Bell, John	Queen Street, Ballymena	Private	R.I.R.	Wounded.
Blair, John	Queen Street, Ballymena	Private	Irish Guards	Wounded.
Cathcart, Henry	Queen Street, Ballymena	Driver	R.E.	
Clarke, Wm.	Railway St., Ballymena	Corporal	R.A.M.C.	Prisoner.
Connor, Alex.	Waring St., Ballymena	Corporal	R.I.R.	Wounded.
Duncan, Alex.	Ballymarlow Ho., B'mena	Captain	R.A.M.C.	
Ferguson, Samuel	Ladysmith Tce., B'mena	Private	R.I.R.	
Foster, David	Ballylesson, Ballymena	Able Seaman	R.N.	Lost at Sea.
Fulton, Wm.	Casement St., Ballymena	Private	Canadian Force	Killed in Action.
Gardener, Robert	Waring St., Ballymena	Private	Gordon Highldrs.	Wounded.
Gillen, John	Douglas Tce., Ballymena	Private	R. Inn. Fus.	Wounded.
Gillen, Robert	Crebilly, Ballymena	Private	R.I.R.	Wounded.
Hanna, Samuel J.	Waveney Rd., B'mena	Private	N.I. Horse	
Harrison, —		Private	Tank Corps	Wounded.
Henry, John	Patrick Place, B'mena	Private	R.I.R.	Wounded.
Houston, Leslie	Queen St., Ballymena	Private	R.I.R.	Killed in Action.
Jamison, David	Greenvale St., Ballymena	Private	R.I.R.	Killed in Action.
Jamison, James H.	Greenvale St., Ballymena	Private	R.I.R.	Wounded.
Kennedy, Frank	Larne St., Balymena	Private	R.I.R.	
Kennedy, James	Galgorm St., Ballymena	Private	A.S.C.	Wounded.
Kennedy, Peter	Larne St., Ballymena	Able Seaman	R.N.	Lost on 'Q. Mary.''
Kernohan, Geo.	Casement St., Ballymena	Private	R.I.R.	
Millar, Lockhart	Larne St., Ballymena	Private	R.I.R.	
Millar, Samuel	Larne St., Ballymena	Corporal	R.I.R.	Killed in Action.
Mullan, Hugh	Queen St., Ballymena	Private	R.I.R.	Wounded.
Murphy, Andrew	Park St., Ballymena	Private	Canadian Corps	
Murphy, Wm.	Park St., Ballymena	Private	R. Irish Fus.	Wounded.
Montgomery, Alex.	Casement St., Ballymena	Private	R.I.R.	Killed in Action.
Montgomery, Joseph	Casement St., Ballymena	Private	R.I.R.	Wounded.
McCarley, Wm.	Casement St., Ballymena	Private	R. Irish Fus.	M. Medal.
McClean, Alfred	Casement St., Ballymena	Trooper	N.I. Horse	
McClelland, Wm.	Crumkill, Ballymena	Private	R.I.R.	
McElroy, Wm.	Waring St., Ballymena	Private	R.I.R.	
McIlroy, Charles	Casement St., Ballymena	Private	R.I.R.	Gassed.
McIvor, Hugh		Private	R.A. Force	
McNabney, John	Larne St,. Ballymena	Sergeant	R. Engineers	M. Medal with Bar
McNabney, Samuel	Larne Street, Ballymena	Private	R. Engneers	
Rainey, Anthony	Cullybackey Rd., B'mena	Private	A.S.C.	
Rainey, John		Private	R.I.R.	
Richardson, Alex.	Alfred St., Ballymena	Private	R.I.R.	Wounded.
Richardson, Joseph	Alfred St., Ballymena	Private	R.I.R.	Killed in Action.
Smyth, Alex.	Waring St., Ballymena	Private	R.I.R.	Prisoner.
Smyth, David	Waring St., Ballymena	Private	R.I.R.	Prisoner.
Sutters, Matthew	Queen St., Ballymena	Private	R.A.M.C.	
Telford, W. F.	Thomas St., Ballymena	Captain	London Fus.	M. Cross.
Vint, F. W.	Waveney Rd·, B'mena	Lieutenant	R. Irish Fus.	Wounded.
Vint, James	Waveney Rd., B'mena	Lieutenant	R. Garrison Artillery	Wounded. M.C.
Wasson, Thos.	Ballycraigy, Ballymena	Private	R.I.R.	
FIRST BROUGHSHANE.				
Acheson, David R.	Knockboy	Lieutenant	R.A.M.C.	
Acheson, Jas. A.	Knockboy	Lieutenant	R.F.A.	
Acheson, Samuel	Dunaird	Captain	R.A.M.C.	
Alexander, John	Coreen,	Private		
Armstrong, John	Bushyfield	2nd Lieutenant	R.I.R.	
Armstrong, Robert	Rokeel	Aircraftsman	R.N.A.F.	
Currie, Wm. Jas.	Loughloughan	Gunner	R.H.A.	
Dickey, Robert	Broughshane	Private	R.E.F.	
Fleck, Wm.	Broughshane	Private	Siege Battery	
Gibson, James	Rathsherry	Private	R.A.F.	
Gilchrist, David	Dunaird		R.N.	
Gilchrist, John	Dunaird	Private	N.I.H.	
Gilchrist, Wm.	Broughshane	Private	R.I.R.	
Johnston, John J.	Elgany	Private	Brigade.	Wounded.
McBride, A. Stewart	Tullymore Cottage	Private	A.S.C. M.T.	
McBurney, Frank	Ballylig	Gunner	R.H.A.	
McCaughey, F. H.	Broughshane	Captain	R.A.M.C.	
McClure, Robert	Broughshane	Sergeant	A.S.C.	
McClure, Wm.	Broughshane	Sergeant	R.I.R.	
McCosh, Robert	Kenbally	Corporal	R.E.	

BALLYMENA PRESBYTERY.   FIRST BROUGHSHANE.

Name.	Home Address.	Rank.	Regiment, Battalion or Unit.	Remarks.
McCully, James	Caugherty	Private	R.I.R.	
McCully, John	Caugherty	Rifleman	18th R.I.R.	
McTurk, Wm. John	Pollee		R.N. Mine Sweeping	
Mawhinnie, John	Little Ballymena	Private	Argyle & S. Highldrs.	
Mitchell, Rev. D. R.	The Manse	Captain	C.F. 10th R.I.R.	
Montford, John	Lisnamurricane	Cadet	N.I.H.	
Peden, Robert G.	Ballymena	Private	A.S.C. M.T.	
Ritchie, David	Ballylig	Private	R.I.R.	Killed in Action.
Ritchie, James	Ballylig	Private	N.I.H.	
Robinson, James	Rokeel	Lieutenant	12th R.I.R.	
Robinson, Wm. J.	Rokeel	Corporal	N.I.H.	Killed in Action.
Taggart, Ben.	Knockboy	Trooper	N.I.H.	
Welsh, David	Elgany	Private	N.I.H.	
Wilson, J. B.	Knowehead	Major-General	R.A.M.C.	
COLONIAL AND U.S.A. FORCES.				
Armstrong, Andrew	Pollee	Private	N.Z.	Killed in Action.
Cameron, Robert Hugh	Ballycloughan	Rifleman	N.Z. R.B.	Missing.
Hutchinson, James	Coreen	Private	N.Z.	Wounded.
Hutchinson, Thomas	Coreen	Private	N.Z.	
McBride, Wm. J.	Coreen	Private	N.Z.	Wounded.
McBride, Moses	Coreen	Private	N.Z 2nd Otago	Killed in Action.
McBride, Samuel	Coreen	P.O.	American Navy	
McCully, A.	Caugherty	Private	N.Z.E.F.	
McCosh, Samuel		Private	Canadians	
Maybin, Richmond	Dunaird	Private	Canadians	Killed in Action.
Smith, Thomas	Rokeel	Private	Can. Artillery	
SECOND BROUGHSHANE.				
Adair, J.	Rathkeel	Private	North Irish Horse	
Alexander, John	Ballygarvey	Private	R.I.R.	
Auld, Robert	Broughshane	Private	A.S.C. M.T.	
Barr, J.	Broughshane	Private	N.I.H.	
Barr, W.	Broughshane	Private	R.I.R.	Wounded.
Brennan, J.	Broughshane	Private	R.E.	
Craig, J.	Kenbally	Private	R.I.R.	Wounded.
Crawford, S.	Tullymore	Private	N.I.H.	
Crawford, —	Broughshane	Seaman	H.M.S. Calliope	
Currie, W. J.	Ballylig	Private	R.F.A.	
Davidson, Robert	Broughshane	Private	R.I.R.	
Dempster, W.	Broughshane		M.G.C.	D.C.M. Killed.
Dunbar, D.	Broughshane	Bugler	R.I.R.	Killed.
Gibson, J. M.	Broughshane	Captain	R.A.M.C.	
Grahamslaw, A.	Broughshane	Private	K.O.S.B.	Killed.
Grahamslaw, W.	Broughshane	Private	A.S.C. M.T.	
Gribben, James	Broughshane	Private	R.A.F.	
Gribben, S.	Broughshane	Private	Black Watch	Killed.
Heggarty, R.	Lower Broughshane	Seaman		
Hill, M.	Broughshane	Private	R.I.R.	Killed.
Ireland, Geo.	Ballygarvey	Lance-Corporal	R.I.R.	Killed.
Lamont, F.	Broughshane	Private	R.A.F.	
Lynn, Alex.	Broughshane	Private	N.I.H.	
McClean, A.	Pollee	Private	R.I.R.	
McClintock, A	Broughshane	Private	A.S.C. M.T.	
McClintock, D.	Broughshane	Private	A.S.C. M.T.	Killed.
McClintock, J.	Broughshane	Private	A.S.C. M.T.	
McKay, W.	Ballylig	Private	Hussars	
McIlveen, J.	Broughshane	Seaman	H.M.S. Calliope	
Martin, J.	Rathkeel	Captain	R.A.M.C.	
Maybin, J.	Lower Broughshane	Private	R.I.R.	Killed.
Moffett, Thos.				
O'Neill, J.	Broughshane	Lance-Corporal	Cycle Corps	Wounded.
Peters, Joe	Tullymore	Private	R.I.R.	Killed.
Peters, R.	Tullymore	Private	R. Innis. Fus.	
Power, J.	Broughshane	Leading Stoker	H.M.S. Hawke	Killed.
Power, W.	Broughshane	Private	R.I.R.	Wounded.
Redmond, M.	Broughshane	Private	R.I.R.	
Reid, Thomas	Ballycloughan	Sergeant	R.I.R.	Killed.
Shearer, S.	Broughshane			
Smyth, S. L.	Broughshane			Killed.
Townsley, J.	Broughshane	Private	A.S.C.	
Watson, Rev. A.		Chaplain		
COLONIAL FORCES.				
Crawford, S.	Broughshane	Private	Canad. Forestry	
Crawford, Thos.	Tullymore	Private	Canad. M.G.C.	Killed.
Gribben, A.	Broughshane	Private	N.Z.F.	
Gribben, Alex.	Broughshane	Private	N.Z.F.	
Gribben, F.	Broughshane	Private	N·Z.F	
Gribben, R.	Broughshane	Private	N.Z.F.	Killed.
Ireland, J.	Ballygarvey	Private	Canadians	

BALLYMENA PRESBYTERY.   SECOND BROUGHSHANE.

Name.	Home Address.	Rank.	Regiment, Battalion or Unit.	Remarks.
Lamont, George	Broughshane	Private	Canad. A.S.C.	
McCullagh, T.	Ballylig	Private	Austral. R.E.	
McMaster, J.	Ballygelly	Lance-Corporal	Canadians	Killed.
Patterson, J. J.	Drummack	Private	Canad. R.A.M.C.	
BUCKNA.				
Adams, Joseph	Carnstroan	Lieutenant	R.A.M.C.	M.C.
Adams, Samuel K.	Ballyligpatrick	Captain	R.A.M.C.	
Bonnar, John	Tullough	Private	R.I.R.	Killed in Action.
Bonnar, Wm. M.	Tullough	Driver	R.I.R.	
Boyle, Wm.	Upper Buckna	Trooper	North Irish Horse	
Campbell, Robert	Longmore	Private	H.M.S. Sentinel	
Campbell, William	Longmore	Corporal	H.M.S. Concord	
Clarke, Harry	Ballinacaird	Private	Inniskilling Fusiliers	Killed in Action.
Clarke, William	Ballinacaird	Trooper	North Irish Horse	
Currie, Samuel	Rocavan	Private	Royal Scots	
Currie, Wm. James	Magheramully	Private	R.F. Artillery	
Davidson, David	Rocavan	Engineer	Royal Engineers	
Davidson, John	Ballinacaird	Private	A. & S. Highlanders	
Davidson, Wm. John	Rocavan	Corporal	R.I.R.	
Garret, David	Tamneybrack	Lance-Corporal	R. Irish Rifles	
Garret, James	Tamneybrack	Private	R. Irish Rifles	Killed in Action.
Gordon, John	Aughacully	Private	Munster Fusiliers	
Greer, Joseph	Drumack	Lance-Corporal	Gordon Highlanders	
Jamieson, David	Buckna	Private	Irish Guards	Wounded.
Kennedy, David	Blackstown	Trooper	N.I. Horse	
Logan, John	Greenhill	Corporal	R.I. Rifles	
Martin, John	Glenside	Private	R.I. Rifles	
McCauley, William	Ballinacaird	Rifleman	R.I.R.	
McColm, John	Blackstown	Private	Inniskilling Fus.	
McColm, William	Blackstown	Private	Inniskilling Fus.	Killed in Action.
McCullagh, Alex.	Aughafatten	Gunner	R.F.A.	
McCurdy, John	Rocavan	Lieutenant	R.A.M.C.	
McMaster, Frank	Upper Buckna	Private	R.I. Rifles	Wounded.
Moorehead, Wm. J.	Ballinacaird	Private	A. & S. Hussars	
Ramsay, James	Drumlickney	Private	R.I. Fusiliers	
Ramsay, Robert	Drumlickney	Private	Royal Scots	
Ramsay, John	Drumlickney	Private	N.I.H.	
Rea, James	Ballyligpatrick	Private	C.A.S.C.	
Rea, Wm. Hugh	Rocavan	Rifleman	R.I.R.	
Robinson, David	Ballinacaird	Private	5th Lancers	Killed in Action.
Robinson, Robert	Ballinacaird	Trooper	N.I.H.	
Robinson, William	Tamneybrack	Lance-Corporal	5th Lancers	
Shaw, Joseph	Loughconnolly	Trooper	N.I.H.	
Sterling, Robert	Drumack	Private	Scottish Rifles	
Stewart, John	Crevamoy	Private	R.G.A.	Killed in Action.
Stewart, Matthew	Crevamoy	Gunner	R.G.A.	
Wallace, Samuel	Kilnacolpagh	Private	N.I.H.	
COLONIAL FORCES.				
Cruickshank, Robert	Kilnacolpagh	Private	Can. F.A.	Wounded.
Currie, James	Lisnamurrican	Lance-Corporal	Auckland Inft. Batt.	
Graham, Nathaniel	Blackstown	Lance-Corporal	Can. Ex. Force	
Hamilton, Wm.	Loughcomly	Private	Can. Ex. Force	
Hood, Archie	Rocavan	Private	3rd Can Ex Force	
Hood, George	Rocavan	Private	42nd Batt. R.H. Can.	
Martin, R.	Ballyligpatrick	Private	3rd Can. Div.	
Miller, Geo.	Glenside	Private	N. Zealand Rifles	
McAleese, Thomas	Rocavan	Private	Can. Mt. Rifles	
McCullagh, Wm.	Tamneybrake	Private	Canadian Force	
Rea, Wm. J.	Rocavan	Rifleman	Can. Div. Supply Co.	
Redmond, C.	Aughafatten	Private	13th Coy. N.Z.E. Force	
Robinson, Jack S.	Tamneybrack	Private	N. Zealanders	Killed in Action.
Robinson, Wm.	Ballinacaird	Lance-Corporal	N.Z. R.B.	
Smythe, Jack	Tamneybrack	Private	N.Z. R.B.	Killed in Action.
Turtle, Joseph	Ballyligpatrick	Private	Can. Ex. Force	
Wray, Robert	Tamneybrack	Private	Can. Ex. Force	
CARNALBANA.				
Baird, Alex.	Carnalbana, Ballymena	Private		
Carson, David	Carnalbana, Ballymena	Private		Wounded.
Conly, Andrew	Drumcrew, Carnalbana	Private		
Conly, Wm.	Drumcrew, Carnalbana			
Finlay, Tom	Carnalbana	Private	Argyle & Suth. Highldrs.	Killed in Action.
McAuley, Wm.	Carnalbana, Ballymena	Private	R.I.R.	Wounded.
McClure, David	Deerpark, Glenarm	Private	Winnipeg Regt.	
Morrow, David	Drumcrew, Carnalbana	Lieutenant	Winnipeg Regt.	
Morrow, James	Drumcrew, Carnalbana	Private	Winnipeg Regt.	
Morrow, Robert	Drumcrew, Carnalbana	Private	Winipeg Regt.	
Purdy, Hugh	Carnalbana, Ballymena	Private	R.I.R.	
Purdy, Wm.	Carnalbana, Ballymena	Private	R.I.R.	Wounded.

BALLYMENA PRESBYTERY. CARNALBANA.

Name.	Home Address.	Rank.	Regiment, Battalion or Unit.	Remarks.
Rea, James	Carnalbana, Ballymena	Private	R.I.R.	Killed in Action.
Rea, James, Jun.	Drumcrew	Lance-Corporal	R.I.R.	Killed in Action.
Steele, George	Cariff, Carnalbana	Private	Innis. Fus.	Killed in Action.
Steele, William	Cariff, Carnalbana	Private	Innis. Fus.	
Wilson, Alex.	Deerpark, Glenarm	Private	R.I.R.	
Wilson, Edmond	Deerpark, Glenarm	Private	R.I.R.	
Wilson, Wm.	Deerpark, Glenarm	Private	R.I.R.	Killed in Action.

CLOUGH, CO. ANTRIM.

Name.	Home Address.	Rank.	Regiment, Battalion or Unit.	Remarks.
Adams, Wm.	Carnmore	Private	R.F.A.	
Blair, John	Drumadoan	Corporal	R.I.R.	
Boyd, Wm.	Carnlea	Lance-Corporal	R. Inn. Fus.	
Crawford, Jas. E.	Clough	Lieutenant		Russian Medal. Wounded in Russia
Cubitt, Thomas	Glenleslie	Private	R.A. Force	
Dunseath, Geo.	Fernacussog	Private	R.F.A.	
Erwin, Wm. Jas.	Forcess	Private	A.S.C.	
Ferguson, Harry	Carnlea	Private	N.I.H.	
Finlay, Wm. H.	Forcess	Lieutenant	R.I.R.	
Galbraith, James	Carnlea	Private	Royal Scots	Prisoner of War.
Graham, Andrew	Ballyreagh	Private	N.I.G.	Died of Wounds.
Graham, James	Ballyreagh	Private	N.I.H.	
Hall, Richard	Clough Manse	Captain	Chaplain	
Johnston, Hugh Hall	Ballyreagh	Private	N.I.H.	
Johnston, Thomas	Ballyreagh	Private	R.I.R.	Killed in Action.
Kyle, Henry D.		Private	R.A.F.	
Linton, Alex.	Dougery	Private	R.I.R.	Prisoner of War.
Linton, David	Artnacrea	Private	R.I.R.	Killed in Action.
Linton, Robt. Jas.	Artnacrea	Private	R.G.A.	
Linton, Samuel	Artnacrea	Corporal	T.M. Battery	Wounded, M.M., & D.C.M.
McCart, Robert	Forcess	Private	R. Inn. Fus.	
McCleery, Andrew	Tullykittagh	Private	R.A.F.	
McClelland, Thos.	Kinflea	Private	R.A.F.	
Mitchell, John	Springmount	Private	R. Inn. Fus.	Wounded.
Murphy, Jas.	Drumadoon	Private	R. Scots	Wounded.
Nichol, David	Drumagrove	Private	R.E.	
Orr, Frederick	Drumbare	Lance-Corporal	Cam. Highdrs.	Killed in Action.
Robinson, Wm. H.	Springmount	Private	R.I.R.	
Swan, Wm.	Drumbare	Private	R.I. Fus.	Wounded.
Walker, Robt.	Dunboght	Private	N.I.H.	
Watt, Robert	Forcess	Private	N.I.H.	Prisoner of War.
White, Robt. Jas.	Carnbeg?	Private	R. Irish Fus.	

COLONIAL AND U.S.A. FORCES.

Name.	Home Address.	Rank.	Regiment, Battalion or Unit.	Remarks.
Crawford, John M.	Tullykittagh	Private	Can. Ex. Force	
Crawford, Robert	Glenleslie	Private	N.Z. R.B.	
Galbraith, George	Carnlea	Private	Canadian D.A.C.	
Galbraith, Robert	Carnlea	Private	N.Z. Rifles	Died of Wounds.
Linton, Wm. G.	Cloughmills	Sergeant	Canadian Ex. Force	Wounded.
McFetridge, John	Eglish	Private	N.Z. Mounted Rifles	
Nicholl, Robert	Drumagrove	Private	U.S. Army	
Orr, Jack	Forcess	Private	Canadian Ex. F.	
Orr, Thomas	Forcess	Corporal	Canadian Ry. Troops	
Rea, Andrew	Cloughgaldonagh	Private	Canadian Ex. F.	
Walker, John	Dunbought	Private	U.S. Army	
Watt, Wm.	Forcess	Private	Canadian Ex. F.	Wounded. Died Pris. in Germany.

CLOUGHWATER.

Name.	Home Address.	Rank.	Regiment, Battalion or Unit.	Remarks.
Adams, Robert	Lisnacrogher	Private	R.I.R.	
Baird, Alex.	Lisnacrogher	Private	R.I.R.	
Bell, Rev. John	Bally	Lieutenant	Seaforth Highldrs.	
Bell, Samuel	Bally	Captain	R.I.R.	
Black, James	Clinty	Private	R.I.R.	
Boyd, Samuel	Ballyreagh	Private	R.E.	Wounded.
Cherry, Alex.	Craigywarren	Corporal	Argyle & Suth. Highldrs.	
Dickson, James	Craigywarren	Private	R.I.R.	
Dickson, John	Craigywarren	Private	R.I.R.	Killed in Action.
Dickson, Wm.	Craigywarren	Private	R.I.R.	Wounded.
Donly, Speers Jack	Clinty	Signaller	R.I.R.	
Hamilton, Robert	Kirkinriola	Private	Argyle & Suth. Highldrs.	Killed in Action.
Hamilton, Tom	Kirkinriola	Private	R.I.R.	Killed in Action.
Hamilton, Wm.	Kirkinriola	Private	R.I.R.	
Herbison, Alex.	Derneveagh	Private	R. Irish Fus.	Wounded.
Herbison, Robert C.	Drumfin	Private	N.I.H.	
Kelly, David	Craigywarren	Corporal	N.I.H.	
McBurney, John	Drumfin	Private	R.I.R.	
McCay, Samuel	Inchamph	2nd Lieutenant	R.I.R.	Wounded.
McClintock, Joseph	Killygore	Private	N.I.H.	
McCullough, Thomas	Craigywarren	Private	R.I.R.	
McFall, Daniel	Dunfane	Private	R.I.R.	Killed in Action.
McFall, Denny	Craigywarren	Private	R.I.R.	Killed in Action.

BALLYMENA PRESBYTERY. — CLOUGHWATER.

Name.	Home Address.	Rank.	Regiment, Battalion or Unit.	Remarks.
McFall, James	Dunfane	Private	R.I.R.	Killed in Action.
McFall, John	Dunfane	Private	R.A.F.	
McFall, Robert	Craigywarren	Private	R.I.R.	
McKelvey, John	Rathkenny	Private	R.I.R.	Wounded.
Marcus, Wm. Jas.	Carncoagh	Sapper	R.E.	Wounded.
Patterson, James	Carncoagh	Private	R.I.R.	Killed in Action.
Patterson, Robert	Carncoagh	Private	R.I.R.	
Patton, Ernest	Cloughwater Manse	Lieutenant	London Regiment	
Patton, Noel W.	Cloughwater Manse	Lieutenant	19th R.I.R.	
Patton, T. W., B.A.	Cloughwater Manse	2nd Lieutenant	5th R. Ir. F.	Invalided.
Richmond W. John	Rathkenny	Private	N.I.H.	
Shaw, James	Killygore	Private	R.I.R.	Killed in Action.
Smith, Josias	Dungall	Private	R. Inn. Fus.	
Smith, Robert	Carncoagh	Private	R.I.R.	Wounded.
Smith, Tom	Dungall	Private	Seaforth Highldrs.	Killed in Action.
Smith, William	Carncoagh	Private	R.I.R.	Invalided.
Smyth, John	Dungall	2nd Lieutenant	R.I.R.	Killed in Action.
Smyth, Wm. T.	Dungall	Lieutenant	R. Inn. Fus.	Wounded.
Taggart, W. Jas.	Craigywarren	Rifleman	King's R. Rifles	Killed in Action.
Wallace, James	Bally	Sergeant	London Regt.	Wounded.
Whiteside, James	Craigywarren	Corporal	Dragoon Guards	Twice Wounded.
Whiteside, Thomas	Craigywarren	Corporal	R.F.A.	Wounded.
Whiteside, Wm.	Eglish	Private	R.I.R.	Killed in Action.
Wisner, John	Lisnacrogher	Private	R.I.R.	

COLONIAL AND U.S.A. FORCES.

Name.	Home Address.	Rank.	Regiment, Battalion or Unit.	Remarks.
Adams, David	Lisnacrogher	Private	Canadians	
Black, Josias	Clinty	Driver	Aust. Mtd. Div.	
Donly, Robt. J.	Clinty	Corporal	U.S. Inft.	
Donly Wm.	Clinty	Corporal	U.S. Inft.	
McCay, John	Inchamph		Canadians	
McCay, Robert	Inchamph		N.Z. Force	
McKay, James	Rathkenny		Aust. Transport Coy.	
McNeill, John	Carncoagh		N.Z. Force	
Ritchie, John	Carncoagh		N.Z. Force	Killed in Action.
Ritchie, Wm. John	Carncoagh		Can. Engineers	
Strahan Robt.	Dunbought		N.Z. Force	
Strahan, Thos.	Dunbought		N.Z. Force	
Wallace, Richard	Bally	Bombardier	Can. Am. Column	
Wallace, Robert	Bally	Driver	Can. Am. Column	

CONNOR.

Name.	Home Address.	Rank.	Regiment, Battalion or Unit.	Remarks.
Allen, Reuben	Connor	Lieutenant	R.F.A.	Killed in Action.
Barclay, James	Barnish, Kells	Private	1st Gordon Highldrs.	Wounded.
Barnett, James	Ballymaceven, Kells	Private	I.G.	
Brownlees, John	Ballymaceven, Kells	Trooper	N.I.H.	
Caldwell, Robert M.	Ross, Kells	Private	12th R.I.R.	Wounded.
Caldwell, Thos. Fry	Ross, Kells	Private	Mechanical Transport	Wounded.
Carmichael, John	Tannybrake, Kells	Private	A. & S. Highldrs.	
Carmichael, Robert	Tannybrake, Kells	Private	2nd Black Watch	
Cathcart, John	Kells	Lieutenant	R.A.M.C.	
Cupples, Hugh G.	Kells	Private	N.I.H.	
Cupples, Jeremiah	Lisnevenagh, Kells	Farrier	N.I.H.	
Faulkner, Edward	Kells	Lance-Corporal	3rd R.I. Fus.	
Foster, David	Ballymarlow, Ballymena	Seaman	R.N.	Killed.
Foster, Robert	Liminary, Kells	Private	7th R.I.R.	
Francey, David	Lisnevenagh, Kells	Trooper	8th Hussars	
Francey, Robert J.	Lisnevenagh, Kells	Private	11th R.I.R.	
Francey, W. J.	Lisnevenagh, Kells	Private	11th R.I.R.	
Gamble, Francis	Kells	Private	12th R.I.R.	Killed in Action.
Gamble, Samuel	Kells	Private	20th R.I.R.	
Glenholmes, James	Ballycowan, Kells	Lance-Corporal	18th R.I.R.	
Glenholmes, John	Ballycowan, Kells	Private	8th R.I.R.	Killed in Action.
Graham, Charles	Connor	Rifleman	15th R.I.R.	
Graham, Wm.	Connor	Driver	R.E.	
Greer, Robt. H.	Ross, Kells	Pioneer	R.E.	
Hanna, George B.	Kildrum, Kells	Lieutenant	R.A.M.C.	
Hanna, Kennedy	Lisnevenagh, Kells	Private	18th R.I.R.	
Hanna, Robert	Lisnevenagh, Kells	Private	11th R.I.R.	
Herron, Robert J.	Tully, Kells	Corporal	M.M. Police	
Kirkwood, Robert	Kells	Lance-Corporal	12th R.I.R.	Died.
Kirkwood, Wm.	Kells	Private	R. Vet. Corps	Wounded.
McAteer, David	Ballymaceven, Kells	Private	17th R.I.R.	
McAteer, Wm.	Ballymaceven, Kells	Private	8th R.I. Fus.	
McAteer, Wm.	Ballymaceven, Kells	Private	Scots Guards	
McCartney, Matthew	Crumbkill, Ballymena	Trooper	N.I.H.	
McCluney, Wasson	Artnagullion, Kells	Private	8th Seaforth Highldrs.	
McCreedy, Hugh	Ross, Kells	Private	16th R.I.R.	Wounded.
McKee, James	Connor	Private	36th High. L. Inft.	
McKillen, David	Ross, Kells	Private	14th R.I.R.	Wounded.
McLean, William	Ballymaceven, Kells	Bombardier	27th R.F.A.	
McMurray, Geo.	Tannybrook, Kells	Lance-Corporal	12th R.I.R.	Killed in Action.

BALLYMENA PRESBYTERY. CONNOR.

Name.	Home Address.	Rank.	Regiment, Battalion or Unit.	Remarks.
McMurray, James	Tannybrook, Kells	Private	12th R.I.R.	
McMurray, Thomas	Tannybrook, Kells	Trooper	R. Inn. Dragoons	
Maybin, John A.	Gilgad, Kells	Lance-Corporal	R.A.M.C.	
Robinson, John	Ross, Kells	Stoker	R.N.	
Shaw, Robert	Ferniskey, Kells	Sergeant	R. Inn. Fus.	Wounded.
Shaw, Wm. John	Ferniskey, Kells	Sapper	R.E.	Wounded.
Smith, Herbert	Cross, Kells	Shoeing-smith	24th E. Lanc.	
Thompson, Alex.	Kildrum, Kells	Private	R.E.	
Thompson, David	Kildrum, Kells	Rifleman	12th R.I.R.	Wounded.
Thompson, James	Connor	Rifleman	6th R.I.R.	
Thompson, Robt. C.	Kildrum	Driver	R.E.	
Wilson, James	Connor	Private	11th R.I.R.	
Wilson, Matthew	Tardree, Kells	Rifleman	15th R.I.R.	
Wilson, Samuel	Lisnevenagh	Private	11th R.I.R.	Wounded.
Wilson, Samuel	Tardree, Kells	Rifleman	19th R.I.R.	
Wilson, Thomas S.	Connor	Private	11th R.I.R.	
COLONIAL FORCES.				
Allen, Samuel	Antrim	Private	Lord Strathcona's Horse	
Allen, Thomas	Kildrum, Kells	Private	Canadians	
Barr, Adam	Tanneybrake, Kells		54th Canadians	
Blain, John	Kells	Private	92nd Canadians	
Craig, John	Ferniskey, Kells	Private	Canadians	
Cupples, Thomas	Kells	Private	Canadians	
Currie, David	Castlegore, Kells			
Dalrymple, Wm. Frew	Kells	Sergeant	Aust. Light Horse	Wounded.
Duncan, Andrew	Carnearney, Kells	Lieutenant	Canadians	Killed in Action.
Duncan, James	Carnearney, Kells	Private	Canadians	
Duncan, Stewart	Carnearney, Kells	Driver	6th Field Co. Can.	
Francey, Geo.	Kells	Private	14th Canadians	Killed in Action.
Hanna, Richard	Kildrum, Kells	Private	Canadians	
Johnston, John	Connor	Private	5th Canadians	
McGimpsey, Robert	Kells	Private	Canadians	
McKillen, Robert	Tanneybrook, Kells	Private	Canadians	
McMeekin, Geo.	Ballymaceven, Kells	Sapper	Can. Engineers	
Magill, Samuel	Kells	Private	1st Canadians	
Mehaffey, John J.	Ross, Kells	Private	Can. A.S.C.	
Meneely, Robert	Kells	Private	Canadians	
Mewhan, Wm.	Kells	Private	Can. A.S.C.	Wounded.
Mitchell, David	Gracehill, Ballymena	Private	Canadians	
Nimmon, Wm.	Kells	Private	Lord Strathcona's Horse	
Stevenson, Thomas	Kells	Private	Canadians	
Thompson, Jas.	Connor	Gunner	Australian Imp. Force	
Wilson, Wm.	Connor	Private	Canadians	
CUNINGHAM MEMORIAL				
Allen, Samuel	Fenagh	Rifleman	R.I.R.	
Burby, W. J.	Carclinty	Sapper	R.E.	
Calderwood, Adam	Cullybackey	Rifleman	R.I.R. and R.A.S.C.	Wounded.
Calderwood, John	Cullybackey		Canadians	
Carson, Andrew	Craigs	Rifleman	2nd Batt. R.I.R.	M.M.
Carson, John	Craigs		U.S.A.	Killed in Action.
Craig, James	Craigs	Trooper	N.I.H.	
Craig, Thomas	Craigs	Trooper	N.I.H.	
Craig, William	Artibrannon	Rifleman	R.I.R.	
Duff, James	Craigs	Rifleman	R.I.R.	
Forgrove, William	Cullybackey	Rifleman	12th R.I.R.	Killed in Action.
Frater, John	Cullybackey	Rifleman	R.I.R.	Killed Accid. Ex.
Gordon, John	Hillmount	Rifleman	R.I.R.	
Grant, James	Hillmount	Rifleman	R.I.R.	
Hall, George	Cullybackey	Private	Tank Corps	Wounded.
Herbison, James	Cullybackey	Private	R. Inn. Fus.	Killed in Action.
Herbison, Tom	Craigs	Rifleman	R.I.R.	
Herbison, Wm.	Craigs	Sapper	R.E.	
Hutchison, Rev. W. H.	Cullybackey	Captain	Attd. 1st R.I.R.	M.C.
Irwin, Henry H.	Ballyclose		Australians	
Irwin, John	Ballyclose	Rifleman	R.I.R.	
Irwin, Robert	Ballyclose	Private	Irish Guards	
Jackson, Andrew	Cullybackey		Canadians	
Jackson, George	Cullybackey		Canadians	
Johnston, Hugh	Hillmount	Rifleman	R.I.R.	
Johnston, John	Hillmount	Rifleman	R.I.R.	
Kennedy, Robert John	Galgorm Parks	Trooper	N.I.H.	
Kennedy, William				
Kernohan, Alex.	Cullybackey	Rifleman	16th R.I.R.	
Kernohan, David	Cullybackey	Rifleman	2nd R.I.R.	
Kerr, Henry	Grouba		Canadians	Killed in Action.
Kirkpatrick, Wilson	Craigs	Rifleman	R.I.R.	Pris. of War, Wnded
Laverty, Alex.	Hillmount	Rifleman	R.I.R.	
Laverty, Alec	Hillmount	Rifleman	R.I.R.	Killed in Action.
Laverty, Arthur	Hillmount	Rifleman	R.I.R.	
Laverty, Artie	Hillmount	Lance-Corporal	12th R.I.R.	Killed in Action.

BALLYMENA PRESBYTERY. CUNINGHAM MEMORIAL.

Name.	Home Address.	Rank.	Regiment, Battalion or Unit.	Remarks.
Leith, Hugh	Cullybackey	Rifleman	R.I.R.	
Letters, Robert	Cullybackey	Corporal	R.G.A. & R.A.S.C.	
Letters, Robert, Jun.	Cullybackey	Sergeant	R.I.R.	Killed in Action.
Logan, Joe	Cullybackey	Rifleman	R.I.R.	
Loughridge, David	Cullybackey	Rifleman	R.I.R.	
McAleese, Alex.	Cullybackey	Private	R.G.A.	
McCartney, Robert R.	Craigs	Rifleman	R.I.R.	Killed in Action.
McCord, Samuel			U.S.A.	Killed in Action.
McCracken, Robert	Cullybackey	Rifleman	R.I.R.	Killed in Action.
McCrory, Samuel	Dunnygarron		U.S.A.	
McGowan, James, Jun.	Ballymena	Private	Black Watch	Killed in Action.
McIlrath, Albert	Fenagh	Rifleman	R.I.R.	Wounded.
McIlrath, Andrew	Fenagh	Rifleman	12th R.I.R.	Wounded.
McIlroy, John	Fenagh	Rifleman	Scottish Rifles	Killed in Action.
McIvor, Robert	Dunnygarron	Lieutenant	R.I. Regt.	Wounded.
McKelvey, Edward	Cullybackey		Canadians	
McKelvey, Samuel	Cullybackey		Canadians	
McWhirter, Samuel	Galgorm Parks		Canadians	
Mairs, John			Australians	
Marwood, James	Cullybackey	Rifleman	R.I.R.	
Marwood, Robert	Cullybackey	Rifleman	R.I.R.	
Miller, Andrew	Cullybackey	Rifleman	R.I.R.	Wounded.
Millar, Ben.	Hillmount	Rifleman	R.I.R.	Killed in Action.
Millar, James F.	Cullybackey	Rifleman	R.I.R	Wounded.
Millar, William	Cullybackey	Rifleman	R.I.R.	
Montgomery, Simpson	Cullybackey	Rifleman	R.I.R.	Killed in Action.
Murdock, Alec.	Hillmount	Private	R.A.M.C.	
Orr, William	Dreen	Rifleman	2nd R.I.R.	
Ramsay, William	Cullybackey	Rifleman	R.I.R.	Wounded.
Robinson, H.				
Rock, David	Hillmount	Rifleman	R.I.R.	
Rock, R. J.	Hillmount	Rifleman	R.I.R.	
Saunderson, Edward	Cullybackey	Rifleman	R.I.R.	
Simpson, Bertie	Cullybackey	Private	H.L.I.	
Simpson, Tom	Cullybackey	Private	H.L.I.	M.M.
Stevenson, William	Crankill	Corporal	N.I.H.	
Stirling, William				
Thompson, Gerald	Cullybackey	A.B.S.	R.N.	
Thompson, John	Corbally	Private	R.I.R.	
Turtle, Edward	Cullybackey		Canadians	
Turtle, John	Cullybackey	Private	Black Watch	
Turtle, Maybin	Cullybackey		R. Marines	
Watt, Harry	Hillmount	Rifleman	R.I.R.	Wounded twice.
Watt, John	Hillmount	Rifleman	R.I.R.	
Watt, Samuel	Hillmount	Rifleman	R.I.R.	Gassed.
Welsh, Harry	Cullybackey	Trooper	N.I.H.	
Wilson, James			Canadians	
Wilson, Robert			Canadians	Killed in Action.
Wright, Thomas	Galgorm Parks		Canadians	Wounded.

CUSHENDALL.

Name.	Home Address.	Rank.	Regiment, Battalion or Unit.	Remarks.
Barbour, John	Cushendun	Private		Killed in Action.
Griffin, Daniel G.	Coast Guard Stn., C'dall	Boatman	R.N.	
Orr, Arthur	Waterfoot, Glenariff	Petty Officer	R.N.	
Robinson, Charles	Cushendun	Private	Inniskilling Fus-	Killed in Action
Stewart, Jas. Maxwell	Cushendall	Private	North Irish Horse	

GLENARM.

Name.	Home Address.	Rank.	Regiment, Battalion or Unit.	Remarks.
Black, Charles	Glenarm	Private	R.I.R.	Wounded.
Brown, John	Glenarm	Stoker	R.N. Reserve	
Campbell, Andrew	Doonan	Private	2nd R.I.R.	Killed in Action.
Campbell, Robert	Doonan	Private	A. & S. Highldrs.	
Clarke, James	Glenarm Park	Bombardier	Ayrshire R.H.A.	
Craig, James	Carnlough	Petty Officer	R.N.	
Crawford, Wm. G.	Dickeystown	Private	N.I.H.	Wounded.
Crawford, Samuel	Dickeystown	Sergeant	5th Lancers	W'ded. Missing.
Currell, James	Carnlough	Captain	R.A.M.C.	
Dunlop, David	Carnlough	Engineer	R.N.R.	Drowned.
Dunlop, Robert	Carnlough	Private	R.A.F.	
Duncan, Richard	Glenarm	Petty Officer	R.N.R.	
English, Jack	Carnlough	Q.M. Sergt.	20th R.I.R.	
Hunter, Allan	Glenarm	Private	M.G. Corps	
Hunter, James	Glenarm	Lieutenant	R.N.	
McCalmont, James	Glenarm	Petty Officer	R.N.R.	
McKay, Wm.	Glenarm	Private	R.I.R.	
McRoberts, Thomas	Glenarm	Petty Officer	R.N.R.	
Morrow, John	Glenarm	Private	9th R.I.R.	
Orr, Alex.	Glenarm	Private	12th R.I.R.	Wounded.
Shaw, Daniel	Duntogue	Private	R.I.R.	
Stewart, John	Mullaghconnoly	Private	12th R.I.R.	Wounded.
Taggart, Andrew	Feystown	Private	10th R.I.R.	Killed in Action.
Wright, James	Doonan	Private	M.G. Corps	

BALLYMENA PRESBYTERY.   GLENARM.

Name.	Home Address.	Rank.	Regiment, Battalion or Unit.	Remarks.
COLONIAL FORCES.				
Black, James	Glenarm	Private	N.Z. Force	
Hunter, James	Little Deerpark	Private	N.Z. Force	
Lindsay, Wm. G.	Glenarm	Private	N.Z. Force	Killed in Action.
Montgomery, James	Old Church	Private	Can. Force	Wounded.
Wilson, Andrew	Munie	Private	N.Z. Force	Killed in Action.
Wilson, David	Deerpark	Private	Can. Force	
Wilson, William	Deerpark	Private	Can. Force	
GLENWHERRY.				
Crowe, Agnew	Glen Head	Private	R.I.R.	Killed in Action.
Esler, John	Cross	Private	R.N.	
Esler, Patrick Maybin	Cross	Private	N.I.H.	
Esler, Wm. John	Cross	Private	Vet. Corps, Egypt	
Fleck, David	Greenhill	Lieutenant	R.I.R.	Wounded.
Hoey, Andrew	Mistyburn		R.N.	
McCrea, Robert	Liminary		R.I.R.	
McKibbin, Kirk	Glenwherry	Lieutenant	R.I.R.	
McKibbin, Thomas	Glenwherry	Lieutenant	R.I. Regiment	
Norwood, David	Bogtown		R.I.R.	
Robinson, James	Kinneygallough		N.I.H.	
Robinson, Thomas	Kinneygallough		N.I.H.	
COLONIAL FORCES.				
Esler, Andrew	Whaupstown	Private	16th Batt. Can. Engineers	Wounded.
Esler, Samuel	Whaupstown	Private	1st Can. Pioneers	
McCullough, John	Whaupstown	Private	Can. Engineers	
Service, Samuel		Drummer	7th Batt. B.C.	
Service, W. J.		Sergt.-Major	4th Can. Division	
Stewart, Samuel	Kerney Hill	Private	Lord Strathcona's Horse	
Strange, Samuel	Crosshill	Private	Can. Engineers	
KELLS AND ESKYLANE.				
Agnew, John	Tannaghmore	Private	12th R.I.R.	Killed in Action.
Agnew, Samuel	Tannaghmore	Private	Seaforth Highldrs.	Wounded.
Armstrong, Robert	Gilgad	Private	11th R.I.R.	Wounded.
Armstrong, Wm.	Gilgad	Private	11th R.I.R.	
Beattie, Richard M.	Cross Moorfields	Private	R. Scottish Fus.	
Buick, Robert	Kildrum	Private	11th R.I.R.	Wounded.
Caldwell, John	Ross Lodge	2nd Lieutenant	18th R.I.R.	
Caldwell, Samuel	Ross Lodge	Sergeant	11th R.I.R.	Killed in Action.
Caldwell, Robert	Edenvale	Private	11th R.I.R.	
Cameron, John	Ballymacvea	Private	18th R.I.R.	
Cameron, Wm.	Ballymacvea	Private	R. Irish Fus.	
Carson, John	Carnaught	Sergt.-Major	Black Watch	Wounded.
Cooper, Robert	Tullynamullen	Private	11th R.I.R.	Killed in Action.
Creelman, Wm.	Crumkill		R.N.	
Dinsmore, Gardner	Greenfield	Lieutenant	R. Innis. Fus.	
Dinsmore, J. F.	Greenfield	Lieutenant	R. Innis. Fus.	
Fisher, Hugh	Kells	Private	R. Scottish Fus.	Killed in Action.
Fisher, John	Kells	Sergt.-Major	4th Dragoons Guards	
Fisher, Samuel J.	Kells	Private	4th Dragoon Guards	Wounded.
Hamilton, James	Tully	Private	R.A.F.	
Hamilton, Wm.	Ballycowan	Lieutenant	R.A.F.	
Hanna, David	Old Green	Private	12th R.I.R.	
Hanna, James	Crumkill	Private	N.I.H.	Wounded.
Hanna, Robert	Creavillyvally	Private	Cycling Corps	
Hanna, Wm.	Old Green	Corporal	12th R.I.R.	
Laird, Samuel	Kells	Private	18th R.I.R.	
McCartney, John	Crumkill	Private	12th R.I.R.	
McCartney, Wm.	Crumkill	Lance-Corporal	12th R.I.R.	
McKee, Robert	Tullynamullen	Private	11th R.I.R.	
McKee, Samuel	Tullynamullen	Private	12th R.I.R.	Wounded.
McKee, William	Ross, Kells	Private	K.O.S.B.	Killed in Action.
McLean, Wm.	Kells	Private	11th R.I.R.	Killed in Action.
Mairs, Alexander	Kellswater	Stoker	R.N.	Drowned.
Mawhinney, Samuel	Old Green	Lance-Corporal	11th R.I.R.	Died of Wounds.
Moore, Matthew	Tullynamullen	Private	R. Scottish Fus.	
Ramsay, John	Kells	Sergeant	12th R.I.R.	
Shaw, Gibson	Tullynamullen	Private	12th R.I.R.	
Swann, Samuel	Tannaghmore, Rans'town	Private	11th R.I.R.	Killed in Action.
Thompson, John	Crumkill	Private	11th R.I.R.	Killed in Action.
Wilson, James	Ballymarlowe	Private	5th R.I.R.	
Wray, Samuel	Kells	Private	N.I.H.	Wounded.

BALLYMENA PRESBYTERY.   KELLS AND ESKYLANE.

Name.	Home Address.	Rank.	Regiment, Battalion or Unit.	Remarks.
COLONIAL FORCES.				
Carlisle, Alex.	Tullynamullen	Private	Can. E.F.	
Cupples, David	Kells	Private	Can. E.F.	Killed in Action.
Currie, Nathaniel	Ballymacvea	Private	Can. E.F.	
Francey, Robert	Ross	Private	Austln. Horse	
Gillen, A.	Moorfields	Sergt.-Major	Indian Army	M.C.
McIlroy, Tom	Tullynamullen	Private	Can. E.F.	
Maybin, James	Liminary	Private	Can. E.F.	
Topping, Nathaniel	Connor	Private	Can. E.F.	Wounded.
Torrens, John	Connor	Private	Aust. E.F.	
Wilson, Geo.	Ballymarlowe	Private	Can. EF.	
Wray, Robert	Kells	Private	Can. E.F.	
NEWTOWNCROMMELIN.				
Gilmore, J. J. A., B.A.	Warbeck Road, London	Lieutenant	R.A.F.	
Gilmore, Wm., M.B.	Woodvale	Captain	R.A.M.C.	
Gordon, Malcolm	Glenleslie	Private	R.A.F.	
Kerr, Isaac	Skerry East	Corporal	R. Scots	Killed in Action.
Kerr Wm.	Skerry East	Private	R. Scots	Killed in Action.
McCartney, James	Cargan	Trooper	Household Batt.	Killed in Action.
McCartney, John	Cargan	Private	Gordon Highlanders	
McCartney, Wm.	Cargan	Private	H.L.I.	Killed in Action.
McQuitty, Robert J.	Cargan	Private	R.E.	
McQuitty, Wm.	Cargan	Private	Scotch Guards	Twice Wounded.
Quate, Robert	Parkmore	Private	R.I.R.	Died.
Scott, John	Parkmore	Trooper	N.I.H.	Killed in Action.
Steede, James	Skerry East	Signaller	R. Inn. Fus.	
Walker, William	Skerry East	Private	R.I.R.	Wounded.
FIRST PORTGLENONE.				
Baird, William	Killycoogan	Private	R. Inn .Fus.	
Calwell, Joseph	Tamlaght	Private	11th Hussars	
Clarke, G.	Garvaghy	Corporal	H.L.A.	
Clarke, R. D.	Garvaghy	Corporal	A.A.S.	
Clarke, Wm.	Garvaghy	Private	Royal Scots	Killed in Action.
Connaughty, Hugh	Garvaghy	Private	R.I.R.	
Connaughty, Robert	Garvaghy	Private	11th R.I.R.	
Coulter, Alex.	Tullnahinin	Private	I.G.	Killed in Action.
Dunlop, Alex.	Mullinsallagh	Private	12th R.I.R.	
Dysart, Archie	Aughnacleagh	Private		
Fleming, Barkley	Garvaghy	Private	36th R.I.R.	Wounded.
Haire, R.		Private	11th Hants	
Kilpatrick, Wm.	Finkitagh	Driver	R.F.A.	Died Pris. of War.
Lamont, James	Lisrodden	Driver	A. Transport	Wounded.
Lamont, Robert	Killycoogan	Driver	16th R. Inn. Fus.	Wounded.
McIlrath, Andrew	Island Cottage	Engineer	R.N.	
Marshall, Samuel	Garvaghy	Private	N.I.H.	
Montgomery, Thomas	Mount Horan	Private	9th R. Inn. Fus.	Prisoner.
Reynolds, Wm.	Tyanee	Private	N.I.H.	
Steele, David	Gortfadd	Private	16th R.I.R.	
Taylor, Robert		Private	3rd A & S. Highldrs.	
COLONIAL & U.S.A. FORCES.				
Andrews John	Portglenone	Private	Can. F.A.	Wounded.
Clarke, James	Garvaghy	Private	U.S. Army	
Clements, John	Innisrush	Corporal	T.A., U.S. Army	
Kyle, S. W.	Tyanee House	Corporal	Wellington, N.Z., Force	
Kyle, Thos.	Tyanee House	Corporal	Otago Regt., N.Z. Force	
McCaughey, Charles	Ballymacpeake	Driver	U.S. Army	
McCaughey, Wm.	Ballymacpeake	Corporal	Canadians	W'ded. D.C.M.
Montgomery, Harry	Slavanagh	Private	20th Can. B.E.F.	
Patton, Archie	Tyanee	Rifleman	N.Z. R.B.	Killed in Action.
Patton, James	Tyanee	Private	Aust. I.F.	Wounded.
Scott, James	Portglenone	Private	U.S. Army	
RANDALSTOWN OLD.				
Allen, James	Lenagh	Private	11th R.I.R.	
Anderson, S. A.	Shane St., Randalstown	Private	11th R.I.R.	
Anderson, W. H.	Shane St., Randalstown	Private	11th R.I.R.	Killed in Action.
Beattie, Robert	Mountshalgus		R.N.	
Bell, Andrew	Ballygrooby	Private	14th R.I.R.	Killed in Action.
Bell, James	Ballygrooby	Private	14th R.I.R.	Killed in Action.

BALLYMENA PRESBYTERY.   RANDALSTOWN OLD.

Name.	Home Address.	Rank.	Regiment, Battalion or Unit.	Remarks.
Bell, Robert	Ballylurgan	Private	11th R.I.R.	
Brown, John	Main Street	Private	11th R.I.R.	Wounded.
Carson, Francis	Terrygowan	Captain	R.A.M.C.	
Clarke, Robert J.	Groggan	Private	11th R.I.R.	
Clotworthy, Andrew	Aughaloughan	Private		
Clotworthy, James	Aughaloughan	Private		
Coulter, Thomas	Feehogue	Private	11th R.I.R.	
Cullen, Wm.	Feehogue	Private	11th R.I.R.	Wounded.
Deans, Joseph	Feehogue	Private	11th R.I.R.	Died.
Edgar, James	Magheralane	Private	A.S.C.	
Edgar, John	Magheralane	Private	A.S.C.	
Ewart, Henry	Feehogue	Private	11th R.I.R.	Wounded.
Foster, John	Caddy	Private	11th R.I.R.	Killed in Action.
Gourley, David	Ballygrooby	Private	11th R.I.R.	
Gourley, David J.	Main Street	2nd Lieutenant	11th R.I.R.	
Hamilton, John	Ballygrooby	Private	11th R.I.R.	
Harpur, Samuel	Magheralane	Private	10th R.I. Fus.	
Harpur, Thomas	Magheralane	Private	N.I.H.	
Hogg, James	Caddy	Private	11th R.I.R.	
Holmes, Henry	Feehogue	Private	B. Watch	Wounded.
Houston, John	Feehogue	Private	11th R.I.R.	
Houston, Robert	Feehogue	Private	R.F.A.	Wounded.
Houston, Robert, Jun.	Feehogue	Private	11th R.I.R.	
Houston, Wm.	Feehogue	Private	11th R.I.R.	Died in Germany.
Hume, James	Main Street	Private	11th R.I.R.	Wounded.
Letson, J. W.	Croggan	Private	A.S.C.	
Letson, T. A.	Croggan	Private	A.S.C.	
Letson, W. H.	Croggan	Private	12th R.I.R.	
Logan, David	Caddy	Private	11th R.I.R.	Wounded.
McAndrew, Hector	Ballygrooby	Private	11th R.I.R.	Killed in Action.
McBurney, Thomas	Feehogue	Private	11th R.I.R.	Wounded.
McCombes, Henry	Croggan	Private	1st R.I.R.	Wounded.
McFadden, John	Feehogue	Private	11th R.I.R.	
McKinstry, Chalmers	Randalstown	Private	6th B. Watch	
McKinstry, Herbert	Randalstown	Lieutenant	18th R.I.R.	
McKinstry, Joseph	Randalstown	Lieutenant	Wilt. Regt.	
McMullan, James	Ballylurgan	Private	11th R.I.R.	
McMullan, Samuel	Ballylurgan	Private	11th R.I.R.	
McMurray, James	Ballygrooby	Private	11th R.I.R.	Wounded.
Magill, Robert	Ballytresna	Private	11th R.I.R.	Killed in Action.
Magill, Thomas	Ballytresna	Private	11th R.I.R.	
Millar, Hugh	Feehogue	Private	11th R.I.R.	Wounded.
Millar, Thomas	Caddy	Private	11th R.I.R.	Killed in Action.
Nimmons, Alex.	Leitrim	Private	12th R. Inn. Fus.	Wounded.
Osborne, Wm.	Craigmore	Private	11th R.I.R.	Killed in Action.
Pollock, James	Craigmore	Private	11th R.I.R.	
Richardson, George	Ballygrooby		R.F.A.	
Scott, Herbert J.	Main Street		A.S.C., M.T.	
Stewart, Francis	Main Street		11th R.I.R.	
Stewart, James	Main Street	Private	11th R.I.R.	Killed in Action.
Stewart, William	Main Street	Private	11th R.I.R.	Prisoner.
Stewart, Wm.	Main Street	Private	11th R.I.R.	
Storey, David	Feehogue	Private	11th R.I.R.	Wounded.
Storey, Joseph	Feehogue	Private	11th R.I.R.	Wounded.
Storey, Robert	Feehogue		R.A.F.	
Thompson, Thomas	Andraid	Private	A.S.C.	
Thompson, Wilfred	Andraid		N.I.H.	
Whiteside, Samuel	Ballytresna		11th R.I.R.	Missing.
COLONIAL FORCES.				
Anderson, Albert	Shane Street		Can. E.F.	Wounded.
Anderson, R. J.	Shane Street		Can. E.F.	
Edgar, Samuel	Magheralane		Can. E.F.	
Hill, George	Ballylurgan		Can. E.F.	
Houston, Alex.			N.Z. Med. Corps	
Hughes, Arthur	Maghereagh		Aust. E.F.	
Jamison, Robert	Ballely		Can. E.F.	
Jamison, Wm.	Ballely		Aust. E.F.	Killed in Action.
Little, Arthur	Ballylurgan		Can. E.F.	
McCaughey, David	Caddy		Can. E.F.	
Neeson, James	Magherabeg		Can. E.F.	
O'Neill, James	Caddy		Can. E.F.	
Rainey, James	Leitrim		Can. E.F.	Killed in Action.
Rainey, John	Leitrim		Can. E.F.	
Robinson, Wm.	Moneynick		Can. E.F.	
Stewart, Samuel	Main Street		Can. E.F.	Wounded.
Storey, Wm.	Feehogue		Can. E.F.	
Thompson, Robert	Andraid		N.Z. E.F.	

BANBRIDGE PRESBYTERY.

Name.	Home Address.	Rank.	Regiment, Battalion or Unit.	Remarks.
FIRST AND SECOND ANAGHLONE.				
Andrews, Robert	Ballynafern	Sub-Lieutenant	R.I.R.	Killed.
Gordon, John	Banbridge	Sapper	R.E.	
Hamilton, W. George	Shanaghan	Captain	Foraging Dept.	
McMurray, Thomas	Cappy	Machine Gunner	R.I.R.	Wounded.
Ritchie, Cecil	Lisnasliggan	Driver	M.T.	
Wills, Joseph J.	Tanvally	Rifleman	R.I.R.	Wounded.
BALLYDOWN.				
Barnet, Robert	Prospect Tce., Banbridge	Private	R.I. Rifles	Killed in Action.
Barr, Robt. Jas.	Dromore Rd., Banbridge	Private	13th Batt. R.I.R.	Killed in Action.
Boyd, Henry	Law's Row, Banbridge	Sergeant	R.I.R.	
Finney, John	Corbet, Banbridge	Lieutenant	11th Batt. R. Inn. Fus.	M.C. Died in Hosp.
Gardine, James	Banbridge	Private	R Irish Fus.	
Gardine, Joseph	Banbridge	Private	R.I. Rifles	
Gilchrist, Sandy	Law's Row, Banbridge	Private	R.I.R.	
McKee, John	Dromore Rd., Banbridge	Private	N.I. Horse	
Maxwell, Ernest	Rilley St., Banbridge	Private	R.I.R.	
Maxwell Herbert	Rilley St., Banbridge	Private	Liverpool Rifles	Wounded.
Murland, Tom	Ballydown	Private	5th Batt. R.I.R.	
Radcliffe, Fred	Cleagh, Banbridge	Private	Despatch Rider	
Radcliffe, James	Cleagh, Banbridge	A.B.	R.N.	
Rogers James	Banbridge	Private	R.I.R.	
Stewart, Samuel	Railway St., Banbridge	Private	Anti-Aircraft Section, Egypt	
Waterson, David	Tullyconnought	Private	R.E.	Wounded twice.
BANBRIDGE, BANNSIDE,				
Adair, Ben	Drumnavaddy	Private	14th Batt. R.I.R.	W'ded and Dis.
Adamson, Joseph	Ferguson's Row	Private	13th Batt. R.I.R.	Killed in Action.
Allen, J.		Private	R.I.R.	
Anderson, J. C.	Roselawn	Captain	R.A.M.C	
Anderson, J. Geo.	Roselawn	Captain	R.A.M.C.	Missing. M.C.
Anthony, Wm.	Seapatrick	Private	R. Irish Fus. and R.I.R.	
Burns, H.	Fort Street	Sergeant	R.I.R.	
Chambers, Thos.	Dromore Street	Trooper	N.I.H.	
Chambers, Wm.	Dromore Street	Sergeant	N.I.H.	
Dale, Alex.	Seapatrick	Private	13th Batt. R.I.R.	Killed in Action.
Dale, David	Railway Street	Private	13th Batt. R.I.R.	Killed in Action.
Dale, John	Seapatrick	Private	13th Batt. R.I.R.	Killed in Action.
Harvey, J. B.	Church Street	Trooper	N.I. Horse	
Harvey, J. H.	Newry Street	Cadet	R.A. Force	
Lyle, Harry	Church Street	Private	18th Batt. R.I.R.	
McCready, S. J.	Kenlis Court	Driver	A.S.C., 84th Brigade	
McCullagh, H.		Rifleman	R.G.A.	
McGrath, John	Weir's Row, Seapatrick	Private	R. Irish Fus.	Killed in Action.
Morton, Bertie	Enville	Private	King's Liverpool Regt.	Killed in Action.
Morton, Jack	Enville	Lieutenant		
Morton, Reginald	Enville	Lieutenant	9th Batt. R.I.R.	Prisoner of War.
Mulligan, Thos.	The Straits	Rifleman	R.I.R.	
Paxton, Albert	Hill Street	Private	R.I.F.	
Pheonix George	Lurgan Road	Engineer	R.A.F.	
Radcliffe, J. A. Douglas	Mountain View Terrace	Captain	R.A.M.C.	
Scott, Edward	Seapatrick	Private	14th Batt. R.I.R.	Wounded.
Scott, H. Hope	The Manse	Captain	R.A.M.C.	Wounded.
Scott, John	Seapatrick	Private	14th Batt. R.I.R.	Wounded.
Scott, Robert	Ballydown	Corporal	150 Field Co. R.E.	
Shannon, John	Ashley Street	Private	1st Batt. R.I.R.	W'ded and Dis.
Shannon, Wm.	Ashley Street	Private	1st Batt. R.I.R.	Wounded.
Stewart, Raymond	Windsor Terrace		R.A.F.	
Thompson, Leslie	Ferguson's Row	Signalman	18th Batt. R.I.R.	
COLONIAL FORCES.				
Gillespie, Morris	Newry St., Banbridge	Private	Canadian Troops	
Henry, Wm. N.	Edenderry Tce., B'bridge	Private	Canadian Troops	
Kennedy, Robert	Mount Royal	Private	57th Batt. Canadian Inft.	
Kilpatrick, Joseph	Banbridge	Private	Canadian Troops	
BANBRIDGE, SCARVA STREET.				
Anderson, Alf. J.	Edenmore	Lieutenant	13th Batt. R.I.R.	
Ardery, Frank B.	Ballyvally	Lance-Corporal	11th Batt. R.I.R.	
Banks, W. P.	Newry Street	Private	Res. 1st R.R. Cavalry	
Banks, Orson	Newry Street	Private	2nd Batt. Scots Guards	
Bell, Edmund	Ferguson's Row	Private	16th Batt. R.I.R.	
Bell, James	Bridge Street	Private	13th Batt. R.I.R.	
Bell, Joseph	Newry Street	Sergeant	6th Service Batt. R.I.R.	Killed in Action.
Bell, Hugh	Dromore Street	Private	4th Batt. R.I.F.	Killed in Action.
Bell, William	Newry Street	Private	13th Batt. R.I.R.	Killed in Action.
Bell, William	Dromore Street	Private	4th Batt. R.I.F.	

BANBRIDGE PRESBYTERY. SCARVA STREET, BANBRIDGE.

Name.	Home Address.	Rank.	Regiment, Battalion or Unit.	Remarks.
Cargin, Wilfred	Railway Street	Private	R. Inn. Fus.	
Cargin, W. J.	Railway Street	Bombardier	R.F.A.	Wounded.
Carson, Charles	Newry Street	Private	B Coy. 10th R.I.F.	
Carson, John	Newry Street	Private	R. Irish Horse	
Carson, William	Newry Street	Private	8th Royal Engineers	
Chambers, Edward	Anderson Street	Private	R. Inn. Fus.	
Chambers, Thomas	Seapatrick	Private	18th Batt. R.I.R.	Wounded.
Clegg, Ernest	Dromore Street	Private	A. 10th Batt. R.I.R.	Pris. in Germany.
Coburn, J. G.	Fountainville	Sub-Lieutenant	R.N.D. Public Schools Batt.	Wounded.
Coburn, D. Norman	Newry Road	Cadet	R.I.R.	
Craig, George	Rathfriland Street	Sergeant	91st Batt. R.F.A.	Killed in Action.
Craig, John	Newry Street	Private	16th Batt. R.I.R.	
Craig, William	Huntley	Private	13th Batt. R.I.R.	
Crawford, James	Bridge Street	Private	A. 10th Batt. R.I.F.	
Crawford, John	Bridge Street	Private	13th Batt. R.I.R.	Killed in Action.
Crothers, Robert, M.B.	Donard View	Captain	R.A.M.C.	
Currie, Thomas	Railway Street	Private	16th Batt. R.I.R.	
Derby, George	Lurgan Road	Private	13th Batt. R.I.R.	Killed in Action.
Dickson, I. A.	Bridge Street		Sec. A.M., Royal Flying Corps	
Emerson, David	Church Street	Private	18th Batt. R.I.R.	Wounded.
Emerson, William S.	Church Street	Lance-Corporal	Royal Engineers	
Emerson, Joseph	Reilly Street	Private	13th Batt. R.I.R.	Killed in Action.
Ewart, Jonathan	Scarva Road	Private	13th Batt. R.I.R.	
Ewart, Thomas	Railway Street	Private	13th Batt. R.I.R.	
Ferguson, John	Newry Street	Private	I.C.L.C.	
Finlay, Ernest, M.B.	Newry Street	Captain	R.A.M.C.	
Fleming, Wm.	Bridge Street	Corporal	Despatch Rider	
Giffen, James	Reilly Street	Private	35th Batt. R.F.A.	
Hampson, Alexander	Scarva Road	Private	13th Batt. R.I.R.	
Harvey, I. H.	Newry Street	Corporal	71st Field Ambulance	
Hawthorne, John	Reilly Street	Private	5th Batt. R.I.R.	Killed in Action.
Hawthorne, Thomas	Reilly Street	Sergeant	5th Batt. R.I.R.	
Hyslop, William	Reilly Street	Private	5th Batt. R.I.R.	
Lyons, Thomas	Seapatrick	Private	13th Batt. R.I.R.	
Lyttle, David	Scarva Street	Private	6th Service Batt. R.I.R.	
Lyttle, Fred	Scarva Street	Private	13th Batt. R.I.R.	
Morgan, Robert	Scarva Street	Private	R.A.F.	
McCabrey, Robert	Lenaderg	Private	13th Batt. R.I.R.	Killed in Action.
McCabrey, T. Nelson	Lenaderg	Private	17th Batt. R.I.R.	
McCallister, Joseph	Kenlis Street	Private	13th Batt. R.I.R.	Killed in Action.
McClimond, John	Newry Street	Rifleman	7th Batt. R.I.R.	Killed in Action.
McClimond, Wm.	Newry Street	Private	1st R.I.F.	Wounded.
McComb, George	Kenlis Street	Private	16th Batt. R.I.R.	
McComb, James	Kenlis Street	Private	5th Batt. R.I.R.	
McCracken, Albert	Victoria Street	Rifleman	13th Batt. R.I.R.	
McCracken, Francis	Victoria Street	Rifleman	13th Batt. R.I.R.	
McCracken, James	Victoria Street	Sergeant	18th Batt. R.I.R.	
McKee, Fred	Scarva Street	Sergeant	Att. A.G.S.	
McKee, Robert	Scarva Street	Private	161 Batt. Signal Corps	
McNeight, Alex.	Reilly Street	Sergeant	13th Batt. R.I.R.	Killed in Action.
McWilliam, Wm. N.	Newry Street	2nd Lieutenant	Royal G. Artillery	
Patterson, Andrew	Victoria Street	Private	A.S.C., M.T.	
Pepper, John	Brookfield	Private	18th Batt. R.I.R.	
Porter, William	Rathfriland Street	Private	3rd Batt R.G.A.	
Potts, W. A., M.R.C.V.S.	Newry Street	Captain	Veterinary Dept.	
Preston, John	Scarva Street	Sergeant	R.M.F.	Killed in Action.
Robinson, James	Rathfriland Street	Private	R.I. Guards	
Robinson, Thomas	Rathfriland Street	Private	Cameron Highldrs.	W'ded and Dis.
Rowney, Alfred	Bridge Street	Private	2nd Batt. R.I.F.	
Simms, J. J.	Bridge Street	2nd Lieutenant	R.I.R.	
Simms, H. C.	Bridge Street	Private	R.G.A.	Killed in Action.
Simms, R. B.	Bridge Street	Cadet		
Simms, F. C.	Bridge Street	Cadet		
Shooter, W. A.	Rathfriland Street	2nd Lieutenant	R.I.R.	
Shooter, R.	Rathfriland Street	Rifleman	15th Batt. R.I.R.	
Smyth, R. S., M.D.	Brookfield	Major	R.A.M.C.	Died.
Smyth, E. F.	Brookfield	Major	11th Batt. R.I.R.	M.C. Killed in Act.
Smyth, Ernest	Lenaderg	Sergeant	6th Batt. R.I.R.	
Smyth, Harold	Lenaderg	Rifleman	13th Batt. R.I.R.	Pris. in Germany.
Templeton, Wm.	Kilpike	Sergeant	13th Batt. R.I.R.	
White, Ernest	Rathfriland Street	Private	5th Dragoon Guards	Gassed and Dis.
White, Joseph	Rathfriland Street	Sergeant	5th Batt. R.I.R.	Wounded.
Wilson, W. A.	Lurgan Road	Rifleman	13th Batt. R.I.R.	Missing.
Wilson, Samuel	Seapatrick	Rifleman	13th Batt. R.I.R.	Killed in Action.
COLONIAL FORCES.				
Derby, Hugh	Windsor Tce., Banbridge	Sergeant	Canadians	
Derby, Joseph	Windsor Tce., Banbridge	Private	Canadians	
Kinley, James		Private	Can. Dragoons	
McMullan, Hubert	Newry Street	Sergt.-Major	Aust. I. Force	
McMullan, T. H.	Newry Street	Captain	Aust. I. Force	
Power, A. C.	Bridge Street	Private	Can. Inft.	
Power, George	Bridge Street	Private	Can. Ex. Force	
Power, Wm. F.	Bridge Street	2nd Lieutenant	Can. Ex. Force	Promoted on Field.

BANBRIDGE PRESBYTERY. **DONACLONEY.**

Name.	Home Address.	Rank.	Regiment, Battalion or Unit.	Remarks.
DONACLONEY.				
ALEXANDER, JAMES	Moygannon	Private	R.I.R.	
ALEXANDER, WILLIAM	Donacloney	Private	16th R.I.R.	Killed in Action.
ALEXANDER, WM. J.	Ballynabraggett	Private	16th R.I.R.	Wounded.
ANDREWS, FRANK	Annaghanoon	Private	10th R.I.F.	Killed in Action.
ARLOW, DAVID	Blackscull, Dromore	Private	R.I.F.	
ARLOW, JAMES	Blackscull, Dromore	Private	1st Batt. Irish Guards	
ARLOW, SAMUEL J.	Blackscull, Dromore	Private	10th R.I.F.	Killed in Action.
ARMSTRONG, THOS. J.	Donacloney	Private	R.A.M.C.	
BEATTIE, EDWARD	Donacloney	Private	16th Batt. R.I.R.	
CAIRNS, HARRY	Donacloney	Private	10th R.I.F.	
CAIRNS, ROBERT	Donacloney	Lance-Corporal	13th R.I.R.	Killed in Action.
CHAMBERS, SAMUEL	Ballylough, Laurencet'n	Lieutenant	R.G.A.	
CLARKE, JAMES	Donacloney	Sergeant	R.I.R.	Wounded.
CLARKE, JOSEPH	Donacloney	Private	16th R.I.R.	
CLARKE, SAMUEL	Donacloney	Private	R.I.R.	
CLARKE, SAMUEL J.	Donacloney	Private	R.A.M.C.	
CLARKE, THOMAS	Donacloney	Private	R.A.M.C.	
CLARKE, WM.	Donacloney	Private	R.A.M.C.	
CLARKE, WM. J.	Donacloney	Private	3rd North. Fus.	
DIAMOND, SAMUEL J.	Ballynabraggett	Lieutenant	R.I.F.	
DOWDS, JOSEPH	Donacloney	Private	20th R.I.R.	Killed in Action.
HAMILTON, EWART	Ballynabraggett	Private	North Irish Horse	
HAMILTON, JACOB	Donacloney	Private	10th R.I.R.	Wounded.
HAMILTON, ROBERT	Donacloney	Sergeant	13th R.I.R.	Killed in Action.
HOUSTON, ROBERT	Donacloney	Private	N.I.H.	
HUMPHRIES, GEORGE	Donacloney	Private	16th R.I.R.	
KENNEDY, SAMUEL	Blackscull, Dromore	Private	16th R.I.R.	Wounded.
LYTTLE, WM.	Lisnasure	Private	R.F.A.	Killed in Action.
MACARTNEY, JAMES	Donacloney	Private	10th R.I.F.	Killed in Action.
McDOWELL, WM. JOHN	Ballykelly, Banbridge	Private	10th R.I.F.	Twice Wounded.
McKANE, SAMUEL J.	Moygannon	Driver	N.I.H.	Wounded.
MOUNT, JAMES	Blackscull, Dromore	Private	R.I.R.	Wounded.
SHANKS, MICHAEL	Blackscull, Dromore	Private	R.I.R.	
TOPPING, JAMES	Donacloney	Private	13th R.I.R.	Certificate
TOWELL, HARVEY	Moygannon, Donacloney	Lieutenant	R.I.R.	Wounded.
TOWELL, WILLIE	Moygannon, Donacloney		R.A.M.C.	M.C.
COLONIAL & U.S.A. FORCES.				
ANDERSON, GEORGE	Lenaderg, Banbridge	Private	American E.F.	
HYLANDS, ROBERT	Moygannon, Donacloney	Private	American E.F.	Killed in Action.
McDOWELL, ANDREW	Ballykelly, Banbridge	Lieutenant	Canadian E.F.	
McKANE, WESLEY	Moygannon, Donacloney	Private	Australian E.F.	
MORGAN, GEORGE	Moygannon	Private	Australian E.F.	Killed in Action.
SHEPHERD, DAVID	Blackscull, Dromore	Private	Canadians	
WESTMORE, MAJOR	Ballynabraggett, Lurgan		Canadians	
GARVAGHY.				
BAILIE, ARCHIBALD	Fedney	2nd Lieutenant	12th Inn. Fus.	
BAILIE, WM.	Fedney	2nd Lieutenant	M.G. Corps	
BAIRD, WM. F.	Garvaghy Manse	Driver	R.H.A.	
McCULLOUGH, SAMUEL	Fedney	Private	5th Canadians	
McCULLOUGH, W. T.	Fedney	Private	A.S.C.	
McGREGOR, J. A.	Carnew	Rifleman	17th R.I.R.	
McMURRAY, JOSEPH	Garvaghy	Driver	R.G.A.	
MAGOWAN, WM. M.	Garvaghy	Sapper	R.E.	
MEEK, M.	Carnew	Gunner	R.F.A.	
SPENCE, ERNEST	Fedney			
GILFORD.				
BARTLEY, CECIL	Gilford	Lance-Corporal	19th Hussars	Wounded.
BEATTIE, JOHN	Kernon, Gilford	Private	Inn. Fus.	
BOYCE, JOHN	Dunbarton, Gilford	Sergeant	16th R.I.R.	
BOYCE, WM.	Dunbarton, Gilford	Corporal	16th R.I.R.	Wounded.
BROWN, W. H.	Kernon, Gilford	Private	20th R.I.R.	
BROWNLEE, JOSEPH	Drumairn	Private	R.I.R.	Prisoner of War.
BROWNLEE, N.	Drumairn	Corporal	Inn Fusiliers	Wounded.
BURNS, GEORGE	Dunbarton, Gilford	Lance-Corporal	13th R.I.R.	Wounded.
COCHRANE, J. S.	Gilford (Manse)	Lieutenant	18th R.I.R.	Wounded.
COCHRANE, WM. E.	Gilford (Manse)	Corporal	10th R. Ir. Fusiliers	
DAVIDSON, THOMAS	Dunbarton, Gilford	Private	Inn. Fus.	W'ded and Dis.
DAVIDSON, WM.	Loughans, Gilford	Lance-Corporal	4th R.I. Fus.	Wounded.
DONALDSON, JOSEPH	Gilford	Private	Inn. Fus.	Wounded.
FOWLER R. McG.	Madden, Gilford	Private	N.I. Horse	
GRACEY, SAMUEL	Dunbarton, Gilford	Sergeant	2nd R.I.R.	Twice Wounded.
GRAHAM, JOSEPH	Gilford	Corporal	2nd R.I.R.	Prisoner of War.
HILLEN, JOSEPH	Gilford	Private	Inn. Fus.	W'ded. Lost eye.
JOYCE, J. G.	Gilford	Corporal	S.A. Scottish	
JOYCE, JAMES	Gilford		Army Postal Service	
KINLEY, SAMUEL	Gilford	Corporal	A.S.C.	

BANBRIDGE PRESBYTERY.

GILFORD.

Name.	Home Address.	Rank.	Regiment, Battalion or Unit.	Remarks.
Kinley, Joseph	Gilford	Private	A.S.C.	
Kinley, David	Gilford	Lieutenant	Welsh Fusiliers	Wounded.
Kinley, Thomas	Gilford	Sergeant	A.S.C.	
McCart, Joseph	Dunbarton, Gilford	Private	2nd Inn. Fus.	Killed in Action.
McCart, John	Drumairn, Gilford	Private	Inn. Fus.	Wounded.
McCart, William	Drumairn, Gilford	Corporal	R. Ir. Fus.	
Nelson, Stephen	Drumairn, Gilford	Private	13th R. Ir. Rifles	
Pillor, Samuel	Dunbarton, Gilford	Private	16th R.I.R.	
Ruddock, John	Gilford	Private	13th R.I.R.	
Steele, Thomas	Dunbarton, Gilford	Lieutenant	R.N.S.	Lost in Laurentic.
Stewart, G. S.	Manse, Gilford	Private	S.A. Scottish	Wounded. Lost leg and eye.
Whiteside, Wm.	Gilford	Private	16th R.I.R.	
Wilson, David	Dunbarton, Gilford	Private	10th R. Ir. Fus.	Wounded.
COLONIAL FORCES.				
Harvey, James				
Pink, Charles	Gilford	Private	Canadians	
Ross, R. S.	Gilford	Sergeant	Can. Engineers	
	Manse	Lieutenant	Canadians	Wounded.
GLASCAR				
Fitzsimmons, Joseph				
Lusk, Sam. Finlay	Emdale	Private	A.S.C.	
McAnuff, John	Loughbrickland	Captain	R.A.M.C.	
McAnuff, Robert	Ringolish	Private	R.I.R.	
McFadden, Wm. John	Ringolish		R.N.	
McGowan, David	Glascar	Private	R.I.R.	Killed in Action.
McKinstry, Robert	Glascar		R.N.	Killed in Action.
Sands, John	Granshaw	Private	A.S.C.	
Simpson, James	Ballinaskeagh	Private	A·S·C.	
Sterritt, Andrew	Glascar	Private	R.I.R.	Killed in Action.
Sterritt, John	Ballinaskeagh	Private	R.F.C.	
Todd, Ralph	Gilford	Sergeant	R.I.R.	
Watt, Isaac	Glascar	Cadet	R.F.C.	
Watt, John	Brookvale	Private	R.I.R.	Killed in Action.
Watt, Wm.	Glascar	Private	R.I.R.	Killed in Action.
	Brookvale	Private	N.I.H.	Military Medal.
COLONIAL AND U.S.A. FORCES.				
Mitchell, George		Private	American Force	
Shepherd, Samuel		Private	Canadian Inftry.	
Trimble, John		Private	Canadian Inftry.	
Watt, Hugh		Private	American Force	
KATESBRIDGE.				
Copes, Joseph	Katesbridge	Private	R.I. Rifles	
Massey, William	Katesbridge	Private	R.I. Rifles	
McElroy, David	Katesbridge	Private	R.I. Fusiliers	Twice Wounded.
McElroy, William S.	Katesbridge	Lieutenant	R.A.M.C.	
Speir, George	Katesbridge	Private	Canadian Exp. Force	Missing. Bel. Kld.
Wilson, David	Katesbridge	Private	R.I. Rifles	
Wilson, Joseph S.	Katesbridge	Private	R.I. Rifles	
LOUGHBRICKLAND.				
Anderson, John Alex.	Clay, Banbridge	Private	R.I.R.	Wounded.
Beck, James	Caskum, L'brickland	Sergeant	R.M. Light Inft.	
Buller, Hugh F.	Brickland, L'brickland	Sergt.-Major	R. Welsh Fus.	
Buller, Wm.	Brickland, L'brickland	Cadet	O.Y.C.	
Campbell, David	Loughbrickland	Sergeant	R.I.R.	Wounded.
Fitsimmons, Wm.	Loughbrickland	Private	R.I.R.	
Gibney, Alex.	Derrydrummuck	Private	Grenadier Guards	Wounded.
Hawthorne, David	Ballygowan, Banbridge	Private	R.I.R.	Killed in Action.
Hawthorne, Joseph	Ballygowan, Banbridge	Corporal	R.I.R.	
Hawthorne, Wm. Jas.	Loughbrickland	Sergeant	R.I.R.	Killed in Action.
Heslip, Isaac	Caskum, L'brickland	Major	R.I.R.	
Holmes, Wm.	Brickland, L'brickland	Private	R.I.R.	Killed in Action.
Houston, John	Loughbrickland	Private	R.I.R.	Killed in Action.
Hoy, Richard	Loughadian, L'brickland	Private	R.I.R.	
Ledlie, Wm.	Loughbrickland	Captain	R.A. Force	
Lister, Henry	Loughbrickland	Private	R.I.R.	
Lister, Samuel	Loughbrickland	Private	R.I.R.	
McAllister, David	Clay, Banbridge	Private	R.I.R.	Wounded.
Marshall, Joseph	Shankill, L'brickland	Corporal	R.I.R.	Wounded.
Nicholl, David	Bovennett, L'brickland	Private	R.I.R.	
Porter, Joseph	Caskum, L'brickland	Private	Grenadier Guards	
Reid, Thos. S. (Rev.)	The Manse, L'brickland	Captain	Army Chaplain	

BANBRIDGE PRESBYTERY. **LOUGHBRICKLAND.**

Name.	Home Address.	Rank.	Regiment, Battalion or Unit.	Remarks.
	COLONIAL FORCES.			
BEATTY, ALEX.	Newry Street, Banbridge	Private	Canadian Cont.	
BELL, HUGH	Dooghery, Banbridge	Rifleman	Canadian Cont.	Killed in Action.
BELL, JOHN	Brague, L'brickland	Private	Canadian Cont.	
BELL, ROBERT	Brague, L'brickland	Gunner	Can. F.A.	
	MAGHERALLY.			
AGNEW, JOHN	Mullafernaghan	Lieutenant	8th S.A. L.R.O. Corps	
ARLOW, SAMUEL	Mullafernaghan		5th R.I.R.	Killed in Action.
CRAWFORD, GEORGE	Ballievey	Lance-Corporal	E.A.M.R.	
CRAWFORD, THOMAS	Ballievey	Trooper	E.A.M.R.	
COPELAND, JOHN H.	Tullyrain		R.G. Artillery	
COULTER, JAMES	Magherally	Private	20th Batt. R.I.R.	Wounded.
CULLY, WM. J.	Scolvan	Driver	Motor Transport	
CULLY, ALBERT	Scolvan		R.F. Corps	
CUMMINS, ELEAZER	Mullafernaghan	Rifleman	6th Batt. R.I.R.	
CUMMINS, WM.	Mullafernaghan	Sapper	Royal Engineers	
DAVISON, SAMUEL	Tullyhenan	Sergeant	16th Batt. R.I.R.	
DERBY, ROBERT	Kilmacrew	Rifleman	13th Batt. R.I.R.	Wounded.
DICKSON, WM.	Mullafernaghan	Driver	R.F. Artillery	
EWART, JOSEPH	Tullyhenan	Gunner	R.G.A.	
GIBSON, JOHN	Edenordinary	Coy. Sergt.-Major	16th R.I.R.	
GIBSON, ROBERT	Edenordinary	Sergeant	2nd R.I.R.	
GIBSON, JOSEPH	Edenordinary	Rifleman	20th Batt. R.I.R.	
HAMILTON, S. G.	Ballycross	Corporal	R.G.A.	
JARDINE, CHARLES	Banbridge	Lance-Corporal	9th Batt. R.I.R.	
JARDINE, SAMUEL	Banbridge	Private	1st Batt. A & S. Highldrs.	
JOHNSTON, W. S.	Edenordinary	Private	44th Batt. Canadian	Died of Wounds.
KING, GEORGE	Castlevennon	Gunner	71st. Siege Bat.S.A.H.A.	
KNOX, GEORGE	Tullyhenan	Gunner	R.G. Artillery	Killed in Action.
MILLIGAN, ALEXANDER	Tullyear		5th Batt. R.I.R.	Killed in Action.
MULLIGAN, SAMUEL	Magherally	Sergeant	5th Batt. R.I.R.	
MULLIGAN, THOMAS	Ballydown	Private	Police Hut, 35 Aux.	
MULLIGAN, WM.	Tullyear	Private	10th Army Corps	
McCLENAGHAN, ROBERT	Edenordinary	Private	16th Batt. R.I.R.	
MULLIGAN, JAMES	Magherally	Lance-Corporal	3rd Res. Batt. R.I.R.	
McCALDIN, DAVID	Lisnaward	Private	R.I. Rifles	
NELSON, JOHN	Knockgorm	Private	Cycle Corps	Died in Training.
PEPPER, JOHN	Drumnagalley	Private	M.G. Corps	
RUSSELL GERALD	Drumneath	Private	64th Batt. Canad. Force	
RUSSELL, HUGH	Magerally	Private	5th Batt. R.I.R.	
SLOAN, SAMUEL	Mullafernaghan	Operator	Wireless, R.F.C.	
SMYTH, S. D.	Killaney	Corporal	16th R.I.R.	Wounded.
TAYLOR, NATHANIEL	Shanrod	Eng. Artificer	H.M.S. "Natal"	Killed in explosion.
	NEWMILLS (CO. DOWN).			
ADAMSON, ALEXANDER	Ballydougan	Sergeant	1st Batt. Irish Guards	
BOYCE, DAVID	Ballydougan	Private	16th R.I.R.	
BOYCE, WM. HENRY	Ballydougan	Sergeant	16th R.I.R.	
BOYCE, WM. JAMES	Ballydougan	Private	R.I.R.	
BOYCE, ISAAC	Ballydougan	Private	R.I.F.	
BOYCE, JOSEPH HENRY	Ballydougan	Private	R.I.R.	
BROWN, THOS. ANDERSON	Ballynagarrick	Signaller	Royal Innis. Fusiliers	
CALVERT, JOSEPH	Bleary	Private	16th R.I.R.	Wounded.
CALVERT, JOHN	Bleary	Private		
CHAMBERS, JAS. ORR	Ballynagarrick	Sergeant	11th R.I.R.	Wounded.
CUNNINGHAM, SAML. MATTHEW	Ballynagarrick	Sergeant	16th R.I.R.	
CUNNINGHAM, SAMUEL	Clare	Corporal	16th R.I.R.	Wounded.
DAWSON, RICHARD	Ballydougan	Gunner	R.G.A.	
DOAK, JOSEPH	Ballynagarrick	Private	R.I.F.	Wounded.
ENGLAND, JAS. RITCHIE	Ballydougan	Rifleman	16th R.I.R.	
HAMILTON, ALEXANDER	Ballydougan	Rifleman	16th R.I.R.	
HOLMES, WALTER	Ballynagarrick	Private	R.A.S.C.	Wounded.
LUNDY, HUGH	Moyallon	Private	R.I.R.	
McCLEARY, SAMUEL BOYD	Bleary	Rifleman	1st Batt. R.I.R.	Wounded.
McCORMICK, WILLIAM	Ballynagarrick	Lance-Corporal	London. Ir. Rifles	
McGRATTAN, WM. JAS.	Knocknamuckley	Private	16th R.I.R.	Killed in Action.
MORROW, ALEXANDER	Clare, Co. Down	Staff Captain	16th Bn. Co. of London Regt.	
	COLONIAL FORCES.			
MAXWELL, JOHN	Bleary, Co. Down	Sergeant	1st Canadian Cavalry Regt.	
MORROW, GEORGE	Clare, Co. Down	Private	26th Canterbury Reinforce.	Wounded.
TOAL, GEORGE	Brackagh, Co. Armagh	Private	South Africa	
TOPPING, JAMES	Ballynagarrick, Co. Down	Private	Lord Strathcona's Horse	Wounded.
	POYNTZPASS AND SCARVA.			
BICKER, ANDREW	Poyntzpass	Private	2nd R.I. Fusiliers	
BICKER, DAVID	Poyntzpass	Private	2nd Batt. R.I.F.	Wounded.
BICKER, GEORGE	Poyntzpass	Private	5th R.I. Fusiliers	

BANBRIDGE PRESBYTERY.

POYNTZPASS AND SCARVA.

Name.	Home Address.	Rank.	Regiment, Battalion or Unit.	Remarks.
BICKER, JAMES	Killysavan, Poyntzpass	Private	1st Royal Fusiliers	
CHAMBERS, JAMES	Scarva	Private	3rd Batt. North Hants.	
CHAMBERS, JOSEPH	Scarva	Private	1st Royal Fusiliers	
COLE, HENRY S.	Aughlish	Private	12th Machine Gun Corps	
DENNY, JOHN T.	Mintlone, Scarva	A. Seaman	H.M.N. R.M. Barracks	
FLECK, JAMES	Scarva	L. Seaman	H.M.S. "Oak"	
FLECK, JOHN	Scarva	Private	R. Marine Artillery	
GRAHAM, WILLIAM	Poyntzpass	Private	2nd Royal Inniskillings	Wounded.
HAMMOND, D. J.	Legananny	Private	1st Royal Munster Fusiliers	Prisoner of War.
JOHNSTON, ROBERT	Mintlone, Scarva	Private	295th Brigade R.F.A.	
LOUGHLIN, FRED	Lochadian	Drummer	204th Batt. C.E.F.	
McCLEMENTS, GEORGE	Poyntzpass	Private	36th Div. Royal Engineers	
MINNIS, W. F.	Loughadian	Private	10th Batt. R.I. Rifles	
MOODY, EDWARD	Mintlone, Scarva	Private	16th R.I.R.	Wounded.
MORROW, WILLIAM	Poyntzpass	Corporal	9th R.I. Fusiliers	Killed in Action.
PURDY, JAS. A.	Poyntzpass	Private	R.I. Fusiliers	Wounded.
SLOAN, WILLIAM	Terryhoogan	Private	9th Batt. R.I. Fusiliers	

TANDRAGEE.

Name.	Home Address.	Rank.	Regiment, Battalion or Unit.	Remarks.
ADAIR, ALLEN	Mullintur	Private	R.I. Fus.	
ASTON, LOUIS	Tandragee	Private	R.I.R.	Wounded.
BAIRD, WM.	Tandragee	A.B.	R.N.	
DICKSON, GEORGE	Tandragee	2nd Lieutenant	R.I Fus.	Wounded.
DICKSON, HENRY	Tandragee	2nd Lieutenant	R.I. Fus.	Prisoner of War.
FERGUSON, JAMES	Tandragee	Private	R.I. Fus.	
FERGUSON, JOHN	Tandragee	Private	R.I. Fus.	Wounded.
FERRIS, HENRY	Tandragee	Private	R.A.M.C.	Wounded.
FERRIS, JOHN	Tandragee	Private	R.I. Fus.	
FINLAY, THOMAS	Tandragee	Private	R. Dragoon Gds.	
HADDEN, JAMES	Tandragee	Private	R.I. Fus.	
HANNA, EDWIN	Tandragee	Private	R.I. Fus.	Wounded.
HUNTER, WM.	Tandragee	Private	R.I. Fus.	Killed in Action.
McCULLOUGH, D.	Tandragee	Sergeant	R.I. Fus.	
McCULLOUGH, ROBERT	Tandragee	Private	A.S.C.	
McCULLOUGH, WM. ALEX.	Tandragee	Trooper	R.I.D. Guards	Wounded.
McKEE, HERBERT	Tandragee	Sergeant	R.I. Fus.	
NEWMAN, W. J.	Tandragee	Private	R I. Fus.	
NEWMAN, W. J., JUN.	Tandragee	Private	R.I. Fus.	Twice Wounded.
PALMER, DAVID A.	Tandragee	Captain	R.D. Fus.	M.C.
PALMER, KENNEDY A.	Tandragee	2nd A.M.	R. Air Force	
PALMER, SAMUEL W.	Tandragee	Lieutenant	R.D. Fus.	
ROBINSON, ARCHIE	Tandragee	Private	R.A.M.C.	
ROBINSON, R. J.	Tandragee	Private	R.F.A.	
STEWART, THOS. D.	Tandragee	Corporal	A.S.C.	
WALKER, JOHN	Ballymore	Corporal	R.I.R.	
WHITE, WM. J.	Tandragee	Private	A.S.C.	Died in Hospital.
WILLIAMSON, DAVID	Tandragee	Private	R.I.R.	Killed in Action.
WILSON, JAMES	Tandragee	Private	R.I. Fus.	Wounded.

COLONIAL FORCES.

Name.	Home Address.	Rank.	Regiment, Battalion or Unit.	Remarks.
ASTON, THOS.	Tandragee	Private	Canadians	
ASTON, WM.	Tandragee	Private	Canadians	
FINLAY, ISAAC	Tandragee	Private	Canadians	

TULLYLISH

Name.	Home Address.	Rank.	Regiment, Battalion or Unit.	Remarks.
BAKER, WILLIAM	Banbridge	Private	Royal I. Rifles	
BOYCE, DAVID	Ballynagarrick, Gilford	Private	Royal I. Rifles	
BROWNE, HUGH (REV.)	Strathmiglo, Scotland	Major	Chaplain	
BROWNE, JOHN	Whitelands, Gilford	Trooper	N.I. Horse	
CAMERON, FRED.	Tullyraine, L'town	Private	R.I. Rifles	
CAMERON, JAMES	Tullyraine, L'town	Private	R.I. Rifles	
COPELAND, NORMAN	Drumnascamph, L'town	Private	R.I. Rifles	Killed in Action.
CRAIG GEORGE	Coose, Laurencetown	Private	R.I. Rifles	
CRAIG, WILLIAM	Coose, Laurencetown	Trooper	N.I. Horse	
CRAIG, WILLIAM	Lenaderg, Banbridge	Private	R.I. Rifles	Wounded.
DICKSON, J. M.	Lenaderg, Banbridge	Major	R.F.A.	
DICKSON, MOSES	Tullyraine, L'town	Private	R.I. Rifles	
ENGLISH, JIM	Lenaderg, Banbridge	Private	R.I. Rifles	Killed in Action.
FORSYTHE, HUGH	Lenaderg, Banbridge	Private	R.A.	Killed in Action.
GORDON, NORMAN	Drumnascamph, L'town	Private	R.I. Rifles	
GORDON, WILLIAM	Drumnascamph, L'town	Private	Cameron Highlanders	Missing.
HARVEY, JACK	Banbridge	Private	R.A.M.C.	
HEWITT, NORMAN	Laurencetown	Private	Royal I. Rifles	Missing.
HODGEN, JAMES	Drumnascamph, L'town	Private	Royal I. Rifles	
HODGEN, THOMAS	Drumnascamph, L'town	Private	Inniskilling Fus.	
JARDINE, ROBERT	Drumnascamph, L'town	Private	R.I. Rifles	
JOHNSTON, HOWARD	Lenaderg, Banbridge	Private	Canadian R.A.M.C.	
JOHNSTON, SAMUEL	Lenaderg, Banbridge	Private	R.I. Rifles	
KELSO, FRED	Lenaderg, Banbridge	Lieutenant	R.I. Rifles	M.M. Wounded
KERR, EDMUND	Laurencetown	Private	R.I. Rifles	Wounded.
KERR, JOHN	Drumnascamph, L'town	Private	R.I. Rifles	Wounded.

BANBRIDGE PRESBYTERY.   TULLYLISH.

Name.	Home Address.	Rank.	Regiment, Battalion or Unit.	Remarks.
Kerr, Joseph	Drumnascamph, L'town	Private	R.I. Rifles	Wounded.
Lindsay, Fred.	Lenaderg, Banbridge	Sergeant	Inniskilling Fus.	Died of Wounds.
Lindsay, James	Lenaderg, Banbridge	Private	Inniskilling Fus.	Wounded.
Lindsay, John	Lenaderg, Banbridge	Private	R.I. Rifles	Wounded.
Mack, Willie	Seapatrick, Banbridge	Private	R.I. Rifles	
Martin, Hugh	Lenaderg, Banbridge	Private	R.I. Rifles	Wounded.
Moore, Harry	Banford, Gilford	Private	R.I. Rifles	
Moore, Willie	Banford, Gilford	Sergeant	R.I. Rifles	
Morgan, George	Donacloney, Lurgan	Private	Aust. Contgt.	M.M. Killed in Act.
Morton, John	Lenaderg, Banbridge	Private	Naval Flying Corps	
Murray, John	Drumnascamph, L'town	Sergeant	R.I. Rifles	Wounded.
McEnarney, John	Drumnascamph, L'town	A.B.	Royal Navy	
McEnarney, Willie	Drumnascamph, L'town	Private	R.I. Rifles	Killed in Action.
Orr, James	Kilpike, Banbridge	Private	R.I. Rifles	
Orr, James	Ballykelly, Banbridge	Private	R.I. Rifles	Wounded.
Orr, Samuel	Ballykelly, Banbridge	Private	R.I. Rifles	Wounded.
Orr, Samuel	Seapatrick, Banbridge	Private	R.I. Rifles	
Orr, William	Ballykelly, Banbridge	Private	R.I. Rifles	
Orr, William	Banbridge	Private	R.I. Rifles	Killed in Action.
Orr, William J.	Seapatrick, Banbridge	Private	R.I. Rifles	Killed in Action.
Parke, Joseph	Keonan Lurgan	Lieutenant	R.I. Rifles	
Phoenix, William	Stranmillis, Belfast	Sergeant	R.E.	M.M. Killed in Act.
Preston, Andrew	Lenaderg, Banbridge	Private	R.I. Rifles	
Preston, John	Seapatrick, Banbridge	Sergeant	Inniskilling Fus.	Missing.
Rogers, G. M.	Hazelbank, Banbridge	Lieutenant	R.I. Rifles	Killed in Action.
Walker, Laurence	Lenaderg, Banbridge	Private	R.I. Rifles	Killed in Action.
Wills, John	Kernon, Gilford	Private	R.I. Rifles	Wounded.
Wilson, Stewart	Lenaderg, Banbridge	Private	R.I Rifles	Wounded.

BELFAST PRESBYTERY.

Name.	Home Address.	Rank.	Regiment, Battalion or Unit.	Remarks.
	AGNES STREET.			
Adair, Francis	14 Wimbledon Street	Private	R.I. Rifles	Killed in Action.
Adair, Robert	Agnes Street	Private		
Adgey, Thomas	223 Hillman Street	Lance-Corporal	6th Coy. R.E.	
Agnew, Daniel	22 Brownlow Street			
Aicken, William	34 Hazelfield Street	Private	4th Hussars	
Alexander, J.	72 Matchett Street			
Allen, John	17 Acton Street	Private	15th R.I.R.	
Allen, William	6 Wellwynne Street	Private	R.S. Cycle Battn.	Wounded.
Anderson, L.	Springmount Street	Private	R.I. Fusiliers	Wounded.
Anderson, Robert	12 Wellwynne Street	Private	R. Innis. Fus.	
Andrews, Gilbert	5 Woodvale Road	Lance-Corporal	Machine Gun Battn.	
Andrews, William	5 Woodvale Road	Rifleman	8th Innis. Fus.	
Ardis, Samuel	23 Daisyfield Street	Driver	65th Brigade A.F.A.	
Arlow, John	Crumlin Road	Trooper	1st N.I.H.	
Armstrong, William	23 Yarrow Street			Killed.
Armstrong, William J.	20 Sancroft Street	Private	R.I.R.	
Ashe, William	22 Acton Street	Corporal	16th R.I.R.	
Atkinson, Thomas	15 Blaney Street	Private	2nd R.I. Rifles	Killed.
Bailey, James	82 Fortingale Street	Private	R.I. Fus.	
Bailey, William	82 Fortingale Street	Lance-Corporal	5th R. Innis. Fus·	
Baird, Alfred	12 Wellwynne Street	Rifleman	10th R.I.R.	Twice Wounded.
Baird, William	28 Brookvale Avenue	Engineer	R.N.T. Service	Twice Torpedoed.
Ballentine, Daniel	20 Agnes Street	Trooper	7th Cavalry Corps	Wounded.
Ballentine, Charles	20 Agnes Street		M.T.A.S.C.	
Bambridge, Robert	11 Upper Meenan Street	Sapper	Royal Engineers	
Barnes, Joseph	14 Alloa Street		N. Irish Horse	
Barnett, Bertie	1a Lyle Street	Driver	12th R.I.R.	Prisoner of War.
Barnett, Ernest	1a Lyle Street	Private	8th Black Watch	Killed in Action.
Barnett, Robert	1a Lyle Street	Private	Black Watch	
Barnett, William T.	1a Lyle Street	Private	3rd Light Horse	
Barr, Samuel	13 Twickenham Street	Private	2nd Batt. R.D. Fus.	
Beattie, Benjamin	10 Manor Drive	Sapper	Royal Engineers	
Beattie, Samuel	10 Manor Drive	Sapper	Royal Engineers	
Beattie, William	57 Bristol Street	A.B.	H.M.S. "Hope"	
Beckett, Thomas	18 Eton Street	Rifleman	2nd Batt. R.I.R.	
Beckett, William	8 Eton Street	Driver	R.F.A.	
Beggs, Samuel	4 Woodburn Street			
Beggs, William	4 Woodburn Street	Lance-Corporal	R.I.R.	
Bennett, R. S.	22 Wellwynne Street	Corporal	Field Bakery, A.S.C.	
Bennett, John	11 Conlig Street			
Bell, Andrew	115 Fortingale Street	Private	Seaforth Highlanders	
Bell, Clements	41 Lonsdale Street	Seaman	Australian Supplies	
Bell, William S.	41 Lonsdale Street	Private	M.T. A.S.C.	

BELFAST PRESBYTERY.   AGNES STREET.

Name.	Home Address.	Rank.	Regiment, Battalion or Unit.	Remarks.
Bell, Samuel	115 Fortingale Street	Private	1st R.I.R.	Died of Wounds
Bell, Thomas	115 Fortingale, Street	Private	R.A.M.C.	
Bell, Wm. J.	4 Bristol Street	Private	10th R.I.R.	Killed.
Bell, Wm. J.	80 M'Tier Street	Rifleman	1st R.I.R.	
Blackwood, George	43 Beechpark Street	Private	17th R.I.R.	Killed.
Boyd, William, R.I.C.	Craven Street	Sergeant	Irish Guards	Killed in Action.
Boyd, William	67 Downing Street			
Boyles, Andrew	62 Glenfarne Street	Private		
Boyles, Thomas	62 Glenfarne Street	Stoker	H.M.S. "Geranium"	
Boyles, William J.	62 Glenfarne Street	Private		
Bowman, A.	35 Mountview Street	Gunner	9th R.F.A.	
Brabazon, H. G.	11 Bootle Street	Private	R.A.M.C.	
Brown, Alexander	5 Perth Street	Cyclist	10th Divisional Corps	
Brown, Andrew	9 Alaska Street	Private	150 R.E.	
Brown, George	26 Klondyke Street	Coy. Sergt-Major	R. Munster Fus.	
Brown, Samuel	7 Alloa Street	Private	29th Canadian Battn.	Wounded.
Brown, Wm.	63 Fortingale Street	Private	8th R. Ir. Fus.	Wounded.
Brownlie, George	7 Kendal Street	Private	M.T. A.S.C.	
Bryans, George	14 Rosewood Street	Private	Canadian Infantry	
Buller, Thos.	90 Fortingale Street	Private	R M.L.C.	
Buchanan, George	72 Upper Charleville St.	Private	R. Ir. Fus.	
Buchanan, James	72 Upper Charleville St.	Private	1st R.I.R.	
Burgess, Richard	122 Sugarfield Street	Rifleman	9th R.I. Rifles	Wounded.
Burns, Isaac	63 Brownlow Street			Killed.
Cairney, Andrew	6 Crystal Terrace	Private	R.F.C.	
Cairns, Joseph	24 Ohio Street	Driver	A.S.C.	
Cairns, William	24 Ohio Street	Private	R. Ir. Fus.	
Calderwood, W.	6 Israel Street	Driver	A S.C.	
Caldwell, James	2 Jersey Street		H.M.S. "Olympic"	
Cameron, C.	148 Argyle Street	Lance-Corporal	1st R.I. Rifles	
Campbell, Edwin	163 Crimea Street	Private	9th R.I. Rifles	
Campbell, James Alexander	11 Bisley Street	Private	2 Corps Troops M.T.	
Campbell, William	76 Fortingale Street	Sapper	A.S.C.	
Campbell, William	96 M'Tier Street	Lance-Corporal	Machine Gun C.	
Campbell, Thomas	48 Bowness Street	Driver	A.S.C.	
Campbell, John	96 M'Tier Street	Private	Tank Corps	
Campbell, William J.	38 Moscow Street	Private	R.I.R.	
Carlisle, F. E.	13 Tilly Street	Trooper	N.I.H.	
Catherwood, Joseph	1 Herron's Row,	Rifleman	9th R.I.R.	Prisoner of War.
Cartmill, Thomas	13 Brennan Street	Private	R.A.F	
Chambers, Robert	7 Raleigh Street	Private	R.I.R.	
Clarke, David	41 Paris Street	Corporal	18th R.I. Rifles	
Clarke, John	41 Paris Street	Private	Salonika Forces	Died.
Clarke, John	23 Hemsworth Street	Sapper	2nd R.I. Rifles	
Clarke, Samuel	Hopeton Street			
Clarke, S. J.	84 Bristol Street	Driver	A.S.C.	
Close, Wm. J.	82 Snugville Street			
Coates, J. M.	72 Fortingale Street	Private	Machine Gun Corps	
Coates, James F.	67 Fortingale Street	L.Br.	R.F.A.	
Coe, John H.	66 Malvern Street	Private	V.C.R.	Wounded.
Colgan, Isaac	85 Fortingale Street	Private	2nd R. Ir. Fus.	
Collins, Thomas	13 Enfield Street	Corporal	Div. Headquarters	
Connor, William	44 Ninth Street	Lance-Corporal	R.E.	
Connery, Samuel	117 Brookmount Street			
Cox, James	85 Fortingale Street	Stoker	H.M.S. "Aubrietia"	
Crawford, J. K.	83 Brookmount Street	Private	8th Otago Co. N.Z.	
Crawford, Robert	3 Upper Meenan Street	Corporal	16th R.I. Rifles	
Cree, A.	42 Bristol Street	Lance-Corporal	A.V.C.	
Crothers, T.	Agnes Street	Private	14th R.I. Rifles	
Culbert, James	21 Dunn Street	Sergeant	6th R.I.R.	Killed.
Curry, Edward	6 Aberdeen Street	Cyclist	10th Cyclist Battalion	
Curry, Nathaniel	6 Aberdeen Street	Gunner	19th R.F.A.	Died.
Cush, Nathaniel	57 Downing Street	Lance-Corporal	17th R.I. Rifles	
Crocket, J.	95 Crimea Street	Private		
Dalton, William	92 Oregon Street		H.M.S. "Boadicea"	
Davey, Henry	20 Vistula Street	Private	16th Ulster Division	
Dewar, Alexander	2 Haldane Street	Rifleman	8th R.I. Rifles	
Dewar, Alexander	1 Glentilt Street	Private	8th R.I. Rifles	
Dewar, Mark	1 Glentilt Street	Private	9th R.I. Rifles	
Dickey, J.	48 Ottawa Street	Driver	A.S.C.	
Dickey, Samuel	48 Ottawa Street	Sapper	I.W.T. R.E.	
Dickson, Robert	12 Chief Street	Sergeant	Cyclist Corps	
Ditty, S.	66 Belgrave Street	Private	3rd R.I. Fus.	
Duffin, Lawrence	60 Fortingale Street	Driver	A.S.C.	
Dixon, Richard	49 Kendal Street	Rifleman	10th R.I.R.	Killed in Action.
Dobson, Alexander	16 Roe Street	Driver	R.E.	
Dobson, John	16 Roe Street	2nd Lieutenant		Killed in Action.
Dobson, Robert	20 Haldane Street	Driver	R.E.	
Donaldson, George	27 Ballyclare Street	Private	R A.M.C.	
Doyle, Frank	13 Shannon Street	Private	R.C.D.	
Doyle, Robert M.	13 Shannon Street	Sapper	R.E.	
Dorman, Andrew	27 Ambleside Street	Private		
Dorman, James	27 Ambleside Street	Private	R.D. Fus.	
Duff, Allen	13 Hillview Street	Private	M.T. A.S.C.	

BELFAST PRESBYTERY. **AGNES STREET.**

Name.	Home Address.	Rank.	Regiment, Battalion or Unit.	Remarks.
Duff, Hugh	13 Hillview Street	Sergeant	R.F.A.	
Dunbar, R.	20 Haldane Street	Rifleman	15th R.I. Rifles	
Edmundson, Robt. Hy.	79 Snugville Street	Private	371 Forestry Coy.	
Elwood, William	15 Huss Street		H.M.S. "John Dunn"	
Evans, S. A.	119 Manor Street		H.M.S. "Satellite"	
Ewing, John A.	53 Stratheden Street	Lieutenant		
Fairfield, Samuel	3 Nore Street	Private	51st Welsh Regt	
Ferguson, Herbert	12 Upper Charleville St.	Private	14th R.I. Rifles	
Ferguson, Thomas	20 Sylvan Street	Private	R.A.M.C.	
Ferguson, George	20 Sylvan Street	Private	R.G.A.	
Finlay, William	110 Bellevue Street	Sergeant	15th R.I. Rifles	
Fluke, M.	80 Paris Street	Private	2nd R.I. Rifles	
Forsythe, James	34 Hopeton Street	Private	R. Munster Fus.	
Forsythe, William	9 Everton Street	Private	10th R.I. Rifles	
Fullerton, James	30 Bann Street	Private	12th R.I. Rifles	
Gault, William	37 Battenberg Street	Wheeler	A.S.C.	
Gettinby, James	31 Bridge End	Private	R.A.F.	
Gibson, David	43 Snugville Street	Private	Irish Guards	
Gibson, John	43 Snugville Street	Private	17th R.I. Rifles	
Gibson, Joseph	44 Brownlow Street	Sapper	Works Coy. R.E.	
Gibson, James	13 Alaska Street	Private		Killed in Action.
Gibson, Thomas John	9 Alaska Street	Private		Killed in Action.
Gibson, R. J.	63 Brussels Street	Private	A.S.C.	
Gibson, Samuel	37 Beresford Street	Private	5th R.I.R.	Killed in Action.
Gibson, Thomas	9 Alaska Street	Driver	Aust. I. Force	
Gibson, William	15 Huss Street	Sapper	R.E.	Wounded.
Gilchrist, Richard	22 Glentilt Street	Private		
Gill, William	179 Cupar Street	Sapper	36 R.E.	
Gilliland, David	46 Ottawa Street	Private	1st R.I. Fus.	Killed in Action.
Gordon, Samuel	38 Wimbledon Street	Private	5th R.I.R.	
Gordon, Thomas	3 Woburn Street	Driver	A Coy. M.G.C.	
Gordon, William	21 Ottawa Street	Corporal	7th R. Inn. Fus.	Killed in Action.
Gourley, Robt Alex.	17 Richmond Street	Private	R.A.M.C.	
Gowdy, William	7 Raleigh Street	Corporal	121 Coy. R.E.	
Graham, William John	11 Springmount Street	Rifleman	15th R.I. Rifles	Killed in Action.
Graham, Thomas	47 Carnan Street	Private	2nd Canadians	
Grainger, Alfred	9 Charleville Street	Private	Black Watch	Killed in Action.
Grainger, J.	44 Bristol Street	Gunner	R.F.A.	
Grainger, Robert	181 Cambrai Street	Private	9th R.I. Rifles	
Grainger, William James	9 Charleville Street	Corporal	9th R.I.R.	
Gray, John	280 Springfield Road	Rifleman	2nd R.I. Rifles	
Gray, Samuel	80 Fortingale Street	Sergeant	A.S.C.	
Greer, Alexander	189 Agnes Street			
Greer, James	15 Avoca Street	Sergeant	S.A.M.C.	
Greer, James	18 Ballycarry Street	Lance-Corporal	R.I.R.	Prisoner of War.
Hamill, James				
Hamill, Samuel	10 Richmond Street			
Hamill, William J.	5 Beresford Street	Private	182 Labour Coy.	
Hamilton, Ernest	6 Glenfarne Street	Sergeant	R.D. Fus.	
Hamilton, John	11 Glentilt Place	Gunner	R.H. R.F.A.	
Harbinson, R. Parker	26 Orient Gardens	Corporal	A.S.C.	
Harbinson, William Alex.	26 Orient Gardens	Private	A.S.C.	
Harris, William	81 Silvio Street	Rifleman	13th R.I. Rifles	
Harrison, William	80 Fortingale Street	Rifleman	R.I.R.	
Harrison, William	18 Ulverston Street		R.A.M.C.	Prisoner of War.
Hayes, William John	3 Brownlow Street			
Henderson, F. G.	18 Bray Street	Driver	A.S.C.	
Henderson, Robt. J.	30 Louisa Street	Lance-Corporal	1st R.I. Rifles	Wounded.
Herron, Albert	187 Snugville Street			Killed in Action.
Herron, Henry	9 Springmount Street	Private	R.I. Fus.	
Herron, Walter	23 Roseleigh Street	Private	R.I.R.	
Higginson, J.	43 Arkwright Street	Sergeant	16th R.I.Rifles	
Hillian, Alexander	14 Upper Malvern St.	Driver	36th Ulster Division	Died of Wounds.
Hogg, James	30 Lawnbrook Avenue		A.S.C.	
Hogg, Nathaniel	195 Crimea Street	Rifleman	16th T.R. Battn.	
Hollywood, David	260 Crumlin Road	Private	R.A.M.C.	
Hollywood, M.,	260 Crumlin Road	Driver	A.S.C.	
Hood, John	88 Fortingale Street	Gunner	R.F.A.	
Hood, Samuel	88 Fortingale Street	Corporal Wheeler	A.S.C.	
Hoy, George	137 Fortingale Street	Sapper	R.E.	Killed in Action.
Hoy, Hugh M.	8 Summer Street	Rifleman	16th R.I.R.	
Hoy, Samuel E.	11 Brookmount Street	Driver	A.S.C.	Wounded.
Howarth, Alfred	67 Emerson Street	Corporal	5th Coy. R.E.	
Howells, William H.	10 Ohio Street			Killed.
Hume, James	27 Tudor Place	Sergeant	36 Btn Machine G.C.	D.C.M., M.M.
Hume, William	27 Tudor Place		H.M.S. "Olympic"	
Hume, Thomas	27 Tudor Place	Private	R.I. Rifles	
Humphries, George	14 Glenfarne Street	Corporal	17th R.I. Rifles	
Hunter, John	54 Leadbetter Street	Sergeant	R.I. Rifles	Wounded. M.M.
Hunter, John	23 Malvern Street			
Hunter, William	36 Silvio Street	Corporal	R.I.R.	
Hunter, William	8 Summer Street	Sergeant	16th R.I.R.	Died of Wounds.
Hyndman, H.	Fortingale Street	Gunner	R.I. Rifles	
Ireland, James	274 Old Lodge Road	Lance-Corporal	R.I. Rifles	Killed.

BELFAST PRESBYTERY. AGNES STREET.

Name.	Home Address.	Rank.	Regiment, Battalion or Unit.	Remarks.
IRELAND, JOHN	18 Eton Street	Private	15th R.I. Rifles	Accid. Drowned.
IRELAND, WILLIAM	18 Eton Street	Private	Seaforth Highlanders	Killed in Action.
IRVINE, R.	45 Downing Street		R.A.M.C.	
IRVINE, R. J.	25 Ballymoney Street		R.A.M.C.	
IRVINE, SAMUEL	45 Downing Street	Lance-Corporal	15th R.I. Rifles	
IRWIN, WM. DAVID	42 Battenberg Street	Sergeant	R.I.R.	Killed in Action.
JACKSON, J.	93 Crimea Street	Private		
JOHNSTON, ALEXANDER C.	12 Queensland Street	Private	Machine Gun Corps	
JOHNSTON, ALLEN	117 Fortingale Street	Private	R.Ir. Fus.	
JOHNSTON, ARTHUR	44 Crosby Street	Private	R.I.R.	
JOHNSTON, JOHN	42 Arkwright Street	Cyclist	10th Corps	
JOHNSTON, ROBERT	108 Westmoreland Street	Rifleman	R.I.R.	
JOHNSTON, SAMUEL	144 Silvio Street	Private	R.I. Fus.	
JOHNSTON, SAMUEL	11 Springmount Street	Private	R.I. Fus.	
JOHNSTON, THOMAS	15 Huss Street	Private	10th R. Innis. Fus.	
JORDAN, SAMUEL	25 Perth Street	Sergeant	R.I.R.	Prisoner of War.
JORDAN, WILLIAM	25 Perth Street	Corporal	107 Trench Mortar	Prisoner of War.
KEERS, JOSEPH G.	65 Willowbank Street	Private	R.I.R.	
KELLY, JOHN	11 Perth Street	Private	M.G.C.	Killed in Action.
KENNEDY, ROBERT	8 Eton Street	Private	18th R.I.R.	Killed.
KENNEDY, ROBERT	17 Winchester Street	Private	R.A.F.	
KILPATRICK, R.	1 Eccles Street	Sergeant	108 Brigade Co.	Wounded.
KING, JOSEPH	24 Chatsworth Street	Private	6th Dragoons	
KIRK, ALEXANDER	114 Agnes Street	Sergeant	R.A.M.C.	Prisoner of War.
KIRKPATRICK, JOHN	2 Coniston Street	Private	K.L.M.C.H.	
KYLE, EDWARD	108 Westmoreland Street	Seaman	H.M.S. "Valhalla"	
LARMOUR, WILLIAM	38 Glenfarne Street	Bugler	9th R.I.R.	Killed in Action.
LAUGHLIN, FRANCIS	24 Blaney Street	Private	6th R.I. Fus.	
LAW, ALEXANDER	40 Esmond Street	Driver	A.S.C.	
LAW, JAMES	40 Esmond Street	Private	R. Innis. Fus.	
LAW, STEWART	40 Esmond Street	Bombardier	R.F.A.	
LENNON, ROBERT	35 Court Street	Private	19th R.I. Rifles	
LENNON T. G.	35 Court Street	A.B.	H.M.S. "Erin"	
LIGGETT, WILLIAM	9 Battenberg Street	Private	M.T. A.S.C.	
LITTLE, DANIEL	45 Glenfarne Street	Bandsman	R. Ir. Fus.	
LONSDALE, RICHARD	4 Woodburn Street			
LOUGHINS, DAVID	26 Wellwynne Street	Private	1st R.I.R.	Killed in Action.
LYLE, D.	8 Hillview Street	Private	R. Innis. Fus.	
LYLE, JAMES	40 Avoca Street	Col.-Sergeant	3rd R.I. Rifles	
LYLE, SAMUEL	40 Avoca Street	Private	109th Brigade Observers.	
LYNN, WILLIAM	57 Bristol Street		2nd R. Innis Fus.	Killed in Action.
LYNN, JOHN	57 Bristol Street	3rd Air Mechanic	R.A.F.	
McALLISTER, JAMES	41 Arkwright Street	Private	18th R.I. Rifles	
McARTHUR, WILLIAM	19 Bowness Street	Private	R.A.M.C.	
McBRIDE, ARTHUR	74 Eglinton Street	Private		
McCANDLESS, ROBERT	23 Bradford Street	Private	8th North. Fus.	
McCARROLL, R. H.	Everton Villa	Captain	9th Lincolns	
McCLELLAND, R. J.	35 Upper Townsend St.	Stoker	H.M.S. "Vigilant"	
McCLENAGHAN, THOMAS	36 Springmount Street	Private	Labour Co.	
McCLURE, J.	4 Shaftesbury Street	Private	R.A.F.	
McCLURE, T.	4 Shaftesbury Street	Private	Labour Co.	
McCLURG, GEORGE	120 Fortingale Street	Private		
McCLURG, THOMAS	120 Fortingale Street	Private	2nd R. Inn. F.	Killed in Action.
McCOMB, ANDREW	"Roseville"	Private	R.I. Rifles	
McCOMB, DR. SAMUEL	"Albertville"	Captain	R.A.M.C.	
McCOMB, THOMAS	"Roseville"	Captain	R.G.A.	
McCONNELL, JOSEPH	102 Short Strand	Sergeant	R.I.R.	
McCORMICK, ARCHIBALD	29 Sancroft Street			Killed.
McCORMICK, WILLIAM	85 Fortingale Street	Private	62nd Coy. S.G.	
McCOURT, RICHARD	25 Upper Charleville St.			Killed in Action.
McCOURT, T. J. C.	26 Upper Charleville St.	Private	M.T.A.S.C.	
McCREA, SAMUEL	48 Queensland Street	Sergeant	A.P.O.	
McCREEDY, DAVID	43 Alloa Street	A.B.	H.M.S. "Lion"	
McCREEDY, DAVID	44 Upper Charleville St.	Co. Q.M.S.	14th Lab. Co.	
McCREEDY, GEORGE	44 Upper Charleville St.			
McCREEDY, RICHARD	44 Upper Charleville St.			
McCUULLOGH, ALEXANDER	56 Cliftonpark Avenue	Captain	Mercantile Marine	Torpedoed, Died.
McCULLOUGH, FRANCIS	42 Downing Street			Killed.
McCULLOUGH, SAMUEL	21 Everton Street	Private	R.I. Rifles	
McCULLOUGH, WILLIAM	21 Everton Street			
McCUTCHEON, R.	27 Meenan Street	Private	R.A.F.	
McCUTCHEON, WILLIAM	153 Spamount Street	Corporal	Artizan Co.	
McDONALD, ROBERT	60 Rosapenna Street	Gunner	R.F.A.	Died of Wounds.
McDONALD, WILLIAM	60 Rosapenna Street		Lanc. Fus.	Killed.
McDOWELL, DAVID	24 Moscow Street	Private	Area Employment Co.	
McDOWELL, THOMAS	26 Upper Charleville St.	Private	A.S.C.	
McDOWELL, CHARLES		Driver	A.S.C.	
McFARLANE, ANDREW	18 Sancroft Street	Private	R.I.R.	
McFARLAND, JAMES	46 Crimea Street	Rifleman	136th Div. Reinforcement	
McFARLAND, WILLIAM	46 Crimea Street	Private	R. Ir. Fus.	
McGEAGH, ROBERT	6 Bristol Street	Private	Infantry Brigade	
McGRATH, MATTHEW	42 Keswick Street			
McGREGOR, DAVID	17 Blaney Street	Driver	A.S.C.	
McILVEEN, R. J.	14 Meenan Street	Stoker	H.M.S. "Inflexible"	

BELFAST PRESBYTERY.   AGNES STREET.

Name.	Home Address.	Rank.	Regiment, Battalion or Unit.	Remarks.
McIlwaine, Henry	14 Acton Street	Private	Artizan Co.	
McIlwaine, James	14 Acton Street			Killed in Action.
McIlwaine, Robert	14 Acton Street	Sergeant	Irish Guards	
McIlwaine, William	4 Tenth Street	Private	H.S. Labour Co.	
McIlwaine, James	110 Bristol Street	Lance-Corporal	M.F.P.	
McKaye, R.	54 Brownlow Street	Private	A.S.C.	
McKee, Henry	59 Agnes Street	Lance-Corporal	2rd S. Lanc.	1914-15 Medal.
McKee, James	59 Agnes Street		Mercantile Marine	
McKee, Samuel	59 Agnes Street	Private	R.M.L.S.	Mons Star.
McKee, James	92 Fortingale Street	Rifleman	R.I.R.	
McKee, John	92 Fortingale Street	Private	R. Innis. Fus.	
McKee, Reggie	4 Glanworth Street	Corporal	14th R.I. Rifles	
McKee, Victor	4 Glanworth Street	Private	1st R.I.R.	Prisoner of War.
McKenna, James	14 Killarney Street	Private		
McKnight, William	18 McCandless Street	Private	19th R.I. Rifles	
McLarnon, Robert	7 Sydney Street West	Private		Killed in Action.
McLaughlin, James	80 North Queen Street			
McLaughlin, Robert	80 North Queen Street			
McLaughlin, Henry	80 North Queen Street			
McLean, Jack	Alexandra Villa	Private	5th Corps R.E.	
McMaster, Matthew	107 Conlig Street	Private	16th Artizan Co.	
McMaster, Thomas	94 Percy Street		Royal Navy	
McMillan, Andrew	Penrith Street	3rd A.M.	R.A.F.	
McMillan, J.	35 Ashmore Street	Private	A.S.C.	
McMillan, Robert	Crimea Street	Sapper	R.E.	
McMillan, Samuel	Crimea Street	Private	R.I.R.	
McMillan, Thomas	Crimea Street	Rifleman	R.I.R.	
McMullan, Andrew	68 Fortingale Street	Driver	A.S.C.	
McMullan, Robert	47 Tenth Street	Private	R.I.R.	
McNeice, Thomas	21 Blaney Street	Private	R.M.L.C.	
McPherson, S.	5 Bristol Street	Rifleman	Trench Mortar Batt.	
McTaggart, William	25 Richmond Street	Private	3rd R.I.R.	Killed in Action.
McVeigh, Henry	143 Crumlin Road	Private		
McWilliams, William		Rifleman	5th R.I.R.	
Macartney, George	77 Bristol Street			
Mack, John	224 Old Lodge Road	Driver	R.F.A.	
Mack, Samuel	224 Old Lodge Road	Private	Attd. Cyclist Battalion	
Macklin, Victor	11 Glentilt Street	Rifleman	R.I. Rifles	
Magill, W. E.	11 Eighth Street			
Magowan, John	32 Bristol Street	Sergeant	18th R.I. Rifles	
Magowan, William M.	22 Baden-Powell Street	Corporal	R.E.	
Malcolmson, William	4 Glenfarne Street	Corporal	5th Field Bakery	
Martin, David	8 Beresford Street	Driver	A.S.C.	
Martin, Edward	44 Bristol Street	Private	22nd Queen's	
Martin, David	44 Bristol Street	Driver	A.S.C.	
Martin, John	44 Bristol Street	Private		
Martin, Robinson	23 Forster Street	Regl. D.	R.E.	
Martin, Robert	23 Agnes Street	Driver	A.S.C.	
Martin, Edward Victor	23 Agnes Street	Private	R.A.F.	
Maze, William J.	92 Crimea Street			Killed.
Mechan, William	47 Bowness Street	Rifleman	47th Division	
Megarry, Hugh	9 Forster Street	Corporal	R.I. Rifles	Wounded.
Mehaffey, John	Oldpark Road			
Midgley, H.	223 Hillman Street	Sapper	R.E.	
Miller, Samuel J.	Choir, Agnes Street	Lance-Corporal	49th Canadians	
Miller, Thos.	19 Crimea Street	Private	R. Ir. Fus.	
Millen, Herbert	23 Charleville Street	Rifleman	15th R.I.R.	Killed.
Milligan, John	169 Agnes Street	Leading Stoker	H.M.S. "Dartmouth"	
Milligan, William	74 Percy Street	Chief P.O.	H.M.S. "Bellerophon"	
Milne, James	114 Agnes Street	Gunner	R.G.A.	
Milne, William	114 Agnes Street	Gunner	148th R.F.A.	
Minnis, James	161 Ainsworth Avenue	Private	R.A.F.	
Minnis, Robert	161 Ainsworth Avenue	Private	R.A.M.C.	
Minnis, Herbert	161 Ainsworth Avenue	Driver	R.F.A., 36th Div.	
Mitchell, Alexander	18 Agnes Street	Lieutenant	11th N. Staffs.	
Montgomery, James	160 Snugville Street	Private	R.I.R.	Died.
Montgomery, William	160 Snugville Street	Private	R. Inn. Fus.	Killed in Action.
Montgomery, Henry	35 Raleigh Street	Private	A.O.C.	
Montgomery, William	89 Sydney Street W.	Rifleman	R.I.R.	Prisoner of War.
Moody, Robert	87 Palmer Street	Rifleman	2nd R.I. Rifles	Prisoner of War.
Moore, Robert	44 Hillview Street	Private	R. West Kents	Wounded.
Moore, Joseph	44 Hillview Street	Private	Black Watch	Wounded.
Moore, Richard	44 Hillview Street	Trooper	N.I.H.	Died.
Moore, John	22 Jaffa Street			
Moore, William J.	8 Eton Street	Sergeant	R.I. Rifles	W'ded and Gassed.
Moore, William John	67 Upper Charleville St.	Private	N.Z.E.F.	
Moore, Thomas	67 Upper Charleville St.	Private	C.T.B. N.Z.E.F.	
Moore, Samuel	44 Hillview Street	Corporal	R.I. Rifles	Wounded.
Morrow, Samuel	32 Fourth Street	Gunner	R.F.A.	
Morton, William	40 Bristol Street	Rifleman	R.I. Rifles	
Morton W.	40 Bristol Street	Rifleman	R.I. Rifles	
Morton, H.	40 Bristol Street	Rifleman	A.S.C.	
Morton, John	40 Bristol Street	A.B.	H.M.S. "Collingwood"	
Mulholland, William	18 Dover Street	Private	M.T. A.S.C.	

BELFAST PRESBYTERY.   AGNES STREET.

Name.	Home Address.	Rank.	Regiment, Battalion or Unit.	Remarks.
Mulholland, William	22 Danube Street	Private	A.S.C.	
Neill, William	86 Fortingale Street	Private		
Nesbitt, William	15 Dunn Street	Driver	C.F.A.	
Nixon, Matthew	126 Tennent Street	Rifleman	R.I. Rifles	
Norwood, David	5 Queensland Street	Private	49th Canadians	
Norwood, David	65 Berlin Street	Rifleman	Labour Corps	
Officer, Arthur	46 Aberdeen Street		R.M.E.	
Officer, Arthur	135 Manor Street	Private	1st Canadians	Killed in Action.
Officer, R.	4 Pernau Street			
Officer, Samuel	135 Manor Street	Rifleman	15th R.I. Rifles	
Officer, William	135 Manor Street	Private	14th R. Montreal Regt.	Killed in Action.
Orr, Charles	110 Crimea Street	Rifleman	R. Ir. Fus.	
Orr, William	110 Crimea Street	Private	Area Employment Co.	
Orr, Robert	110 Crimea Street	Private	R.G.A.	
Orr, James	111 Bristol Street	Private	R.I. Rifles	
Orr, Samuel	12 Beresford Street			Killed in Action.
Orr, William J.	12 Beresford Street	Private	2nd R. Lancs. Regt.	
Orr, Robert James	12 Beresford Street		H.M.S. "Calypoo"	
Orr, D.	7 Gracehill Street	Private	31st M.G.C.	
Patterson, Alexander	Percy Street	Private	1st R. Ir. Fus.	
Patterson, Thomas	1 Shaftesbury Street	Private	R.I. Rifles	
Peacock, James H.	56 Glenwood Street	Driver	R.E.	
Peoples, John	2 Pernau Street		6th R.I. Rifles	
Porter, Ernest	6 Shannon Street	Private	1st R.I. Rifles	Killed in Action.
Pritchard, George	74 Fortingale Street	Private	A.S.C., Ulster Div.	
Priestly, John A.	28 Ravenhill Street		R.M. H.M.S. "Temeraire"	Died.
Purdy, William J.	Corporation Square	Private	14th R.I. Rifles	
Quigg, William John	16 Bisley Street	Private	7th Border Regt.	
Rankin, William	10 Glentilt Street	Private	R.D.C.	
Reid, Robert	12 Shaftesbury Street	Private	R.I. Rifles	
Reilly, Louis	107 Fortingale Street	Private	R.I. Rifles	
Reilly, William	122 Fortingale Street	Private	M.T. A.S.C.	
Richmond, John	22 Hemsworth Street	Private		Killed.
Richmond, James	22 Hemsworth Street	Private		
Robinson, Charles	17 Blaney Street	Driver	A.S.C.	
Robinson, Mark D.	8 Dunn Street	Sergeant	Recruiting	
Robinson, Martin	23 Foster Street	Driver	R.E.	
Robinson, Richard	8 Beresford Street			
Robinson, William	8 Beresford Street	Sergeant	R. Innis. Fus.	
Rodgers, James	10 Bristol Street	Sergeant	4th Batt. M.G.C.	Killed in Action.
Rodgers, Wm.	10 Bristol Street	Sergeant	R. Engineers	
Rodgers, John R.	10 Bristol Street	Captain	R. Irish Guards	
Rodgers, R.	10 Bristol Street		Mercantile Marine	
Rodgers, Samuel R.	10 Bristol Street		Mercantile Marine	
Rogerson, Hy. J.	112 Bristol Street		A.S.C.	
Rourke, William J.	10 Glentilt Place	Co. Sergt. Major	R.I. Rifles	
Rourke, A. D.	10 Glentilt Place	Private	Black Watch	
Russell, David	20 Yarrow Street	Q.M.S.	R.A.M.C.	
Russell, Thomas	21 Ambleside Street	Driver	A.S.C.	Killed.
Robertson, Robert	40 Annadale Street	Private	R.A.M.C.	
Rosco, Alfred	4 Glenfarne Street	Private	R.I.R.	
Roulestone, Robert J., R.I.C.	Craven Street	Sergt.-Major	Irish Guards	
Ross, James	2 Dunn Street	Rifleman	19th R.I. Rifles	
Savage, Henry	112 Bristol Street	Private	R.I. Rifles	Died.
Savage, Robert	9 Lyle Street	Lance-Corporal	49th Field Ambulance	
Scott, Robert James	66 Queensland Street	Lance-Corporal	1st R.I. Rifles	
Scott, William	30 Coniston Street	Sapper	R.E.	Killed in Action.
Scott, William	4 Annadale Street	Sergeant	R.I.R.	Killed in Action.
Sefton, D	58 Westland Street	Private	R.F.A.	
Shannon, Edward	42 Hillview Street	Private		Gassed, Died.
Shaw, John	17 Baden-Powell Street	Sapper	Signalling Corps	
Shaw, Joseph	Ballyutoag	Private	4th Batt. Tank Corps	
Shaw, William J.	112 Tennent Street	Private	Scottish Rifles	
Simpson, F. J.	75 Cavehill Road	Sergeant	N.I. Horse	
Simpson, James	23 Atlantic Avenue	Lieutenant	R.I. Rifles	
Smart, James	37 Brownlow Street	Gunner	Machine Gun Corps	
Smith, Albert	13 Acton Street	Private	R.I. Fus.	Killed in Action.
Smith, Edmund	45 Weir Street	Driver	R.F.A.	
Smith, John	111 Bray Street	Private	36th Reserve Corps	Died.
Smith, Samuel	185 Crimea Street		R.M.E.	
Smyth, Andrew	223 Crumlin Road	A.B.	H.M.S. "Irvine"	
Smyth, Andrew	20 Baden-Powell Street	Sergeant	15th R.I. Rifles	
Smyth, James	68 Fortingale Street	Gunner	I. Exp. Force	
Smyth, James	63 Malvern Street	Rifleman	R.I. Rifles	
Smyth, James	24 Rosewood Street			
Smyth, John Kennedy	223 Crumlin Road	Sergeant	R.A.F.	
Smyth, Robert	42 Perth Street	Corporal	R.I.R.	Killed.
Smyth, Thomas J.	347 Crumlin Road	Private	R.I. Rifles	
Smyth, William	64 Groomsport Street	Private	15th R.I. Rifles	
Smyth, Wilson	2 Anglesea Street	Corporal	1st R. Inn. Fus.	Killed in Action.
Spence, William	224 Shankill Road	Private	R.I. Rifles	
Stewart, William	Choir, Agnes Street		Y.M.C.A.	
Stitt, Thomas	16 Snugville Street			
Stockman, Robert	14 Paris Street	Private	2nd R. Inn. Fus.	

(63)

BELFAST PRESBYTERY. **AGNES STREET.**

Name.	Home Address.	Rank.	Regiment, Battalion or Unit.	Remarks.
Stockman, William	14 Paris Street	Seaman	H.M.S. " Humber "	
Teeny, William Hy.	57 Harrybrook Street	Sapper	Ulster Division	
Telford, James	20 Liffey Street	Private	R. Inn. Fus.	
Taggart, Robert	28 Shannon Street	Rifleman	London Irish Rifles	
Taggart, William	54 Jaffa Street	Private	15th R.I.R.	Killed.
Taggart, William	25 Richmond Street	Private	5th R.I. Rifles	
Tate, Robert	203 Tennent Street	1st A.M.	R.A.F.	
Taylor, Adam	43 Upper Charleville St.	Private	M.T. A.S.C.	
Taylor, John	43 Upper Charleville St.	Private	15th R.I. Rifles	
Tinsley, George	29 Winchester Street	Sapper	R.E.	
Tinsley, Hugh	29 Winchester Street	Private	M.T.	
Tinsley, John	29 Winchester Street		S.S. " Mahia "	M.M. and G.S.M.
Thompson, Albert Edward	31 Pernau Street	Private	4th R.I. Rifles	
Thompson, David Samuel	31 Pernau Street	Private	2nd R.I. Fus.	
Thompson, George	124 Agnes Street	Rifleman	Signalling Corps	
Thompson, John	31 Pernau Street	Private	R. Marine L. Infantry	
Thompson, Joseph	1 Herron's Row	Private	R. Warwick Rifles	
Thompson, Joseph	19 Nore Street	Sapper	C.R.T.	
Thompson, Joshua M.	31 Pernau Street	Private	18th R.I. Rifles	
Thompson, Richard H.	21 Dunn Street	Sergeant	10th R.I. Rifles	
Thompson, Robert	13 Rusholme Street	Private	R.A.F.	
Thompson, Robert	31 Pernau Street	Private	18th R.I. Rifles	
Thompson, William	15 Huss Street	Rifleman	R.I. Rifles	
Thompson, William Thomas	31 Pernau Street			R.I. Rifles
Todd, George	15 Foster Street	Private	R.F.A.	
Todd, James	79 Crumlin Road	Private	R.F.C.	
Todd, Nathaniel	63 Fortingale Street	Private	8th R.I. Fus.	
Todd, Robert	79 Crumlin Road	Rifleman	R.I. Rifles	
Toland, Robert	2 Bristol Street	Private	2nd Garrison R.I. Regt.	
Trainor, Edward H.	110 Fortingale Street	Gunner	R.F.A.	
Trainor, Jeremiah	110 Fortingale Street	Private	Labour Co.	
Trainor, James	103 Fortingale Street	Private		Died in France.
Trainor, James	108 Fortingale Street	A.B.	H.M.S. " Dublin."	
Trainor, William	108 Fortingale Street	Sergeant	16th R.I. Rifles	
Trimble, James	180 Agnes Street	Sergeant	Armoured Car Brigade	
Tully, David	95 Bristol Street	Seaman	R. Navy	Drowned.
Tully, George	95 Bristol Street	Rifleman	R.I. Rifles	
Tully, William	95 Bristol Street	Private	1st R. Inn. Fus.	Killed.
Tully, Joseph	95 Bristol Street	Private	R.A.F.	
Turtle, Thomas	34 Esmond Street	Private	9th R.I. Rifles	
Twynam, James	6 Beresford Street	Sapper	R.E.	
Ussher, James	18 Jersey Street	Lance-Corporal	19th R.I.R.	Killed.
Vincent, Harry	50 Old Lodge Road	Private	R. Innis. Fus.	
Wade, Robert	Agnes Street	Private	R. Inn. Fus.	
Waddell, H.	102 Agnes Street	Sergeant	R.A.F.	Mons Star, W'ded twice.
Walker, Alexander	96 North Howard Street		R. Navy	
Walker, George	126 Bristol Street	Private	8th R.I.R.	Killed.
Walker, Robert	77 Fortingale Street	Rifleman	R.I. Rifles	
Walker, Thomas	77 Fortingale Street	Rifleman	R.I. Rifles	
Walker, William	126 Bristol Street	Signaller	R.I. Rifles	
Wallace, Alexander	24 Brennan Street	Private	A.S.C.	
Wallace, James	37 Brownlow Street	Driver	R.F.A.	
Ward, Alfred Thomas	31 Ballymena Street	Sergeant	R.I. Fus.	M.M., Q.S.A., K.S.A. and G.S.M.
Warden, Samuel	103 Fortingale Street	Gunner	R.G.A.	
Warnock, Charles	70 Beresford Street			Killed.
Warnock, William	1 Richmond Street		2nd R. Inn. Fus.	Killed.
Watt, David A.	78 Agnes Street	Sapper	2nd Can. R. Troops	
Watt, William	197 Crimea Street	Driver	M.T. A.S.C.	
Watters, John	40 Langford Street	Private	4th Royal Fus.	
Watters, James W.	80 Joseph Street		2nd R. Inn. Fus.	
Watters, John	80 Joseph Street		2nd R.I. Rifles	
Watters, Robert W.	80 Joseph Street		10th R.I. Rifles	
Watters, William	80 Joseph Street		2nd R.I. Rifles	
Watson, William	31 Sancroft Street	Private	R. Marine L. Inft.	
Weldon, James	34 Disraeli Street	Rifleman	R.I. Rifles	Prisoner of War.
Weldon, John	34 Disraeli Street	Mjr. Bugler	R.I. Rifles	
Welsh, S. J.	92 Crimea Street	Rifleman	R.I. Rifles	
West, David	65 Fortingale Street	Rifleman	R.I. Rifles	
West, Isaac	65 Fortingale Street	Rifleman	8th R.I. Rifles	Killed in Action.
White, William	20 Sylvan Street	Private	A.S.C.	Died.
Whiteside, John	108 Agnes Street	Private	R. Ir. Fus.	
Wilkinson, Kennedy	1 Bristol Street	Private	2nd R.I. Rifles	
Williamson, James	65 Manor Street	Private	R. Engineers	
Williamson, John	65 Manor Street		H.M.S. " New Zealand "	
Williamson, Thomas	14 Wellwynne Street	Private	224 Employment Company	
Wilson, Edward	90 Fortingale Street	Driver	D.A.C.	
Wilson, Henry	90 Fortingale Street	Private	7th R. Ir. Fus.	
Wilson, Matthew	81 Hopeton Street	Rifleman	15th R.I.R.	Killed in Action.
Wilson, Samuel	81 Hopeton Street	Rifleman	14th R.I. Rifles	
Wilson, Hugh	127 Fortingale Street	Rifleman	17th R.I. Rifles	
Wilson, Samuel	90 Fortingale Street	Gunner	Tank Corps	
Woodside, Hugh	83 Conlig Street	Private	A.S.C.	

BELFAST PRESBYTERY. AGNES STREET.

Name.	Home Address.	Rank.	Regiment, Battalion or Unit.	Remarks.
Wright, James	71 Denmark Street	Signaller	16th Northumberland Fus.	
Wylie, William	Ivydene, Kingsmere Av.	Lance-Corporal	Cyclist Corps	
Young, Robert	Salisbury Drive	Rifleman	15th R.I.R.	Wounded.
Young, Adam	16 Upper Canning Street	Private	M.T. A.S.C.	
	ALBERT STREET.			
Adair, J. S.	Century Street	Lieutenant	11/13 R.I.R.	Prisoner of War.
Adair, Thomas	Century Street	Lieutenant	10th Bedfordshire Regt.	Died of Wounds.
Adair, Samuel	Charleville Street	Private	4th Dragoon Guards	Wounded.
Alexander, James	Harrybrook Street	Sergeant	17th R.I.R.	Mer. S.M.
Adams, John	Agnes Street	Private	15th R.I.R.	
Andrews, Martin	Shankill Road	Private	14th R.I.R.	
Andrews, David	Shankill Road	Private	M.T.	
Boyd, Alexander	Craigmore Street	Private	A.S.C.	Wounded.
Brownlee, Lawson McK.	Percy Street	Petty Officer	Dunster Force	Russ. C. of St.G.
Boyce, Joseph	Argyle Street	Private	9th R.I.R.	
Browne, Thomas	Roden Street	Private	R.I.R.	
Bell, W. J.	Burnaby Street	Private	10th R.I.R.	
Boyd, Hugh	Hopeton Street	Private	1st R.I.R.	Wounded.
Burns, Robert	Mountcollyer Street	Private	14th R.I.R.	Wounded.
Butler, John	Ashmore Street	Private	9th R.I.R.	
Butler, Alexander	Ashmore Street	Private	R. Inn. Fus.	
Boyd, Samuel	Craigmore Street	Private	10th R.I.R.	Wounded.
Black, David	Sugarfield Street	Private	A.S.C.	
Beck, W. A.	Knutsford Drive	Surgeon Prob.	R.N.V.R.	
Campbell, Samuel	Grosvenor Road	Major	R.A.M.C.	
Currie, Albert	Battenberg Street		Navy	
Campbell, Joseph	Roden Street		15th R.I.R.	
Campbell, William	Whiteville Terrace		M.T.	
Currie, David	Battenberg Street	Private	A.S.C.	
Chambers, W. J.	Fifth Street	Gunner	Navy	
Chambers, James	Fifth Street	Private	3rd R.I.R.	Wounded.
Crowe, John	Craven Street	Sergeant	R.I. Regt.	Wounded.
Chambers, Thomas	Mountcashel Street	Private	R.E.	
Chambers, George	Fifth Street	Private	6th R.I.R.	
Cummings, W. H.	Wigton Street	Private	4th R.I.R.	
Creighton, John	North Howard Street	Private	9th R.I.R.	
Campbell, John	Rosebank Street	Lance-Corporal	9th R. Inn. Fus.	Killed.
Campbell, William	Roden Street		Navy	
Campbell, Hamilton	Roden Street		Navy (Marines)	
Campbell, Thomas	Roden Street	Private	10th R.I.R.	
Campbell, James	Roden Street	Private	10th R.I.R.	
Campbell, Samuel	Roden Street	Private	9th R.I.R.	
Craig, W. J.	Cupar Street		Navy	
Caston, D. M.	Ashmore Street	Private	8th R.I.R.	
Davis, William	Jaffa Street	Engineer	R. Navy	
Duke, John, Junr.	Fifth Street	Private	R.I.R.	
Esler, William R.	Harcourt Street	Private	9th Fusiliers	
Edwards, Robert	Urney Street	Private	9th R.I.R.	
Elwood, Alexander	Balmoral Street	Staff Sergt.-Major	A.S.C.	M.M.
Forsythe, John	Meenan Street	Private	R.I.R.	
Fulton, William	Bristol Street	Private	R.I.R.	
Fraser, William	Beverley Street		R. Navy	
Galbraith, Samuel	Shankill Road	Private	A.S.C.	
Greenwood, Albert	Newington Avenue	Private	R.A.M.C.	
Graham, Robert	Rathlin Street	Private	R.I.R.	
Gilmour, David	Carmel Street	Private	M.T.	
Gracey, William	Chadwick Street	Private	M.T.	
Glass, William	Tennyson Street	2nd Lieutenant	R.N.V.R.	
Gourley, Ernest	Tennent Street	Private	R.A.F.	
Gihon, William	Adela Place	Lance-Corporal	14th R.I.R.	Killed.
Gibson, Harry	Northumberland St.	Sapper	R.E.	
Gibson, Herbert E.	Northumberland Street	Chief P.O.	Navy	
Giffen, Watson	Dunluce Avenue	Private	R. Inn. Fus.	
Glasgow, Robert	Fourth Street	Gunner	R.F.A.	Killed.
Glasgow, Thomas	Fourth Street	Private	R.A.M.C.	Wounded.
Graham, James	Circus Villas	2nd Lieutenant	R.A.F.	
Graham, Willie	Bray Street	Driver	A.S.C.	
Greenwood, John E.	Newington Avenue	Corporal	R.A.M.C.	M.M. Killed.
Hanna, Albert	Albertville Drive	Private	15th R.I.R.	
Hanna, William	Albertvile Drive	Private	R.A.M.C.	
Hall, David	Drew Street	Private	R.F.A.	Killed.
Hanna, William	Northumberland Street		Navy	
Halliday, Thomas	Ormeau Road	2nd Lieutenant	9th R.I.R.	Killed.
Hargrove, Samuel	Grosvenor Road	Private	R.E.	
Harkness, Hugh	Argyle Place	Private	R.I.R.	Died in France.
Hoey, William R.	Grosvenor Road	Private	10th R.I.R.	Killed.
Huston, Thomas	Brookmount Street	Private	9th R.I.R.	
Hunter, David	Percy Street	Private	R.A.M.C.	
Hunter, John E.	Northumberland Street	Sergeant	14th R.I.R.	Killed.
Hall, Robert	Tyne Street	Sergeant	R.A.M.C.	M.M.
Hogg, David	Sugarfield Street		16th R.I.R.	
Henry, Thomas	Meenan Street	Private	R.I.R.	Invalided.

BELFAST PRESBYTERY.   **ALBERT STREET.**

Name.	Home Address.	Rank.	Regiment, Battalion or Unit.	Remarks.
Isdell, John	Groomsport Street	Private	A.O.C.	
Johnson, Joe	Shankill Road		14th R.I.R.	
Johnson, Samuel	Glenwood Street	Sergeant	A.S.C.	
Johnson, Thomas	Shankill Road	Private	14th R.I.R.	
Johnson, Harry	Burnaby Street	Private	3rd R. Inn. Fus.	
Johnson, Willie	College Place North	Cadet	R.G.A.	
Jamison, Robert	Dover Street		N.I.H.	
Kelly, John	Buckingham Street	Corporal	10th R.I.R.	Wounded.
Kelso, Robert	Cupar Street	Private	R.E.	
Kennedy, Albert V.	Roosevelt Street		R.N.V.R.	
Kilpatrick, Robert	Old Lodge Road		R. Inn. Fus.	
Laughlin, Albert	Battenberg Street	Private	14th R.I.R.	Killed.
Laughlin, Robert	Battenberg Street	Private	A.S.C.	
Lavery, Victor	Merkland Street	Private	R.I.R.	
Lilley, Andrew	Brookmount Street	Private	R.E.	
Magee, John	Roosevelt Street		14th R.I.R.	
Martin, Robert	Springfield Road		Navy	
Meek, Robert	Donegall Road	Private	R. Inn. Fus.	
Mooney, Edward	Cupar Street	Private	9th R.I.R.	Killed.
Morrison, John	Ashmore Street		9th R.I.R.	
Morrison, W. J.	Glenwood Street	Corporal	1st R. Inn. Fus.	Killed.
Mullan, Joseph	Argyle Street	Private	9th R.I.R.	Wounded.
Murray, Robert	Cupar Street	Private	R.I.R.	
Mattison, David	Emerson Street		R.E.	
Mitchell, J. Howard	Strangemore Terrace		Dunster Force	Killed.
Macauley, Thomas	Springfield Road	Private	14th R.I.R.	
McAllister, Joseph	Argyle Street		9th R.I.R.	Killed.
McClure, W. J.	Ashmore Street		R.G.A.	
McClune, John	Buckingham Street	Private	6th R. Inn. Fus.	Wounded.
McCracken, Joseph	Hopeton Street	Private	14th R.I.R.	Killed.
McCabe, Bertie	Donegall Avenue	Private	14th R.I.R.	
McClure, Samuel	Rockville Street	Gunner	R.F.A.	Prisoner of War.
McClurg, James	Tyne Street	Private	10th R.I.R.	
McConnell, William	Fourth Street	Private	R.A.M.C.	
McConnell, John	Fourth Street	Private	9th R.I.R.	
McCarron, Samuel	Mayo Street	Corporal	R.A.M.C.	
McClune, James	Buckingham Street		12th R. Inn. Fus.	
McDowell, W. J.	Dover Street	Private	9th R.I.R.	
McDowell, James	Ashmore Street	Private	9th R.I.R.	
McDowell, Robert	Ashmore Street	Private	R.F.A.	
McGrath, Henry	Ashmore Street	Private	9th R.I.R.	
McGrath, James	Connaught Street	Private	16th R.I.R.	Killed.
McIlroy, William	Damascus Street	Private	R.A.M.C.	
McIlroy, James	Damascus Street	Gunner	R.G.A.	
McIlroy, John	Damascus Street	Private	4th R.I.R.	
McIlveen, Ernest	Lawnview Street	Private	R.A.F.	
McKee, Thomas	Ashmore Street	Private	9th R.I.R.	Killed.
McKinstry, William	Bootle Street		14th R.I.R.	
McMullan, John	Northumberland Street	Private	R.A.M.C.	
McMullan, Thomas	Northumberland Street	Warrant Officer	Navy	
McMaster, John	Enfield Street	Sergeant	N.I.H.	
McMaster, David	Roden Street	Private	8th R.I.R.	
McNeice, Wesley	Merkland Street	Corporal	12th R.I.R.	
McNeice, John	Hudson Street	Private	M.T.	
McTighe, R. J.	Carmel Street	Private	6th R.I.R.	Prisoner of War.
Nugent, Arthur	Percy Street	Private	10th R.I.R.	
Nicholl, Robert	Lawnbrook Avenue		2nd R. Inn. Fus.	Killed.
Nicholl, Edward	Lawnbrook Avenue	Signaller	9th R.I.R.	Wounded.
Nelson, James	Belair Street	Private	R.E.	
Nugent, James	Percy Street		2nd R. Inn. Fus.	Killed.
Olliver, John	North Howard Street	Sergeant	19th R.I.R.	
Olliver, Thomas	North Howard Street	Private	13th R.I.R.	
Patterson, D. Knox	Toronto Terrace	Captain	R.I. Fusiliers	
Peacock, William	Percy Street	Private	R.E.	
Robinson, Thomas	Seventh Street	Private	6th R.I.R.	
Reid, Percy	Wilmont Terrace	Driver	Tank Corps	Wounded.
Robinson, Richard	Nassau Street	Private	14th R.I.R.	
Robinson, Thomas, Junr.	Seventh Street	Private	1st R.I.R.	
Robinson, John	Conway Street	Private	9th R.I.R.	
Robinson, Robert	Wilton Street	Private	R.A.M.C.	
Robinson, William	Lawnbrook Avenue		4th R. Inn. Fus.	
Russell, Archibald	Mountview Street	Sergeant	1st R.I.R.	Killed.
Russell, Joseph	Mountview Street	Private	6th Black Watch	
Rogers, Charles	Urney Street	Private	9th R.I.R.	
Reid, Robert	Agnes Street		16th R.I.R.	
Ruddock, Samuel	Enston Street	Private	8th R.I.R.	
Smith, R.	Lawnbrook Avenue		1st Wiltshire Regt.	Wounded.
Strong, James	Glenwood Street		R. Inn. Fus.	
Smith, Andrew I.	Bedeque Street		R. London Fus.	
Smith, David	Bellevue Street	Private	R.E.	
Spence, David	Meenan Street	Private	10th R.I. Fus.	Wounded.
Sloan, Henry	Sixth Street	Engineer	Navy	
Sloan, Alex.	Sixth Street	Private	R.A.M.C.	
Smith, Hubert R.	Dunluce Avenue	Private	14th R.I.R.	Prisoner of War.

BELFAST PRESBYTERY. ALBERT STREET.

Name.	Home Address.	Rank.	Regiment, Battalion or Unit.	Remarks.
STEAD, JAMES	Cambrai Street	Private	Grenadier Guards	Invalided.
SPENCE, JAMES	Meenan Street	Private	1st R.I.R.	Wounded, M.M. & Mons Medal.
SHANNON, HERBERT	Bellevue Street	Private	8th R.I.R.	
SMITH, THOMAS	Burnaby Street	Private	10th R.I.R.	Killed.
SPENCE, ROBERT	Meenan Street	Private	18th R.I.R.	
STEPHENSON, THOMAS	Eccles Street	Private	R.I.R.	
THOMPSON, ROBERT	Shankill Road	C.Q.M.S.	A.S.C.	
THOMPSON, MATTHEW	Lawnbrook Avenue	Private	9th R.I.R.	Wounded.
TEMPLETON, JAMES	Cupar Street		R. Inn. Fus.	Killed.
TODD, WILLIAM	Hawthorne Street	Private	8th R. Inn. Fus.	Killed.
THOMPSON, WILLIAM	Glenwood Street		Navy	
TODD, WILLIAM A.	Grosvenor Road	Private	9th R.I. Fus.	Prisoner of War.
TWEED, WILLIAM	Magdala Street	Corporal	R.E.	
TWEED, DAVID	Magdala Street	Driver	R.F.A.	
TATE, DAVID	Dundee Street	Private	A. & S. Highlanders	
WILLIAMSON, HARRY	Northumberland Street	Private	9th R.I.R.	Invalided.
WATSON, JAMES	Botanic Avenue	2nd Lieutenant	14th R.I.R.	Killed.
WILSON, ROBERT	Azamor Street	Private	9th R.I.R.	
WILSON, JOHN	Woodvale Road	P.O.	Navy	
WAUGH, THOMAS	Conway Street	Private	5th R.I.R.	Wounded.
WHITESIDE, WILLIE	Canmore Street		Navy	
WHITESIDE, DAVID	Canmore Street	Private	5th R.I.R.	Killed.
WHITESIDE, GEORGE	Canmore Street	Private	2nd R. Inn. Fus.	Wounded.
WRIGHT, ALEXANDER	Grosvenor Road	Private	3rd Cheshires	
WILSON, WILLIAM	Azamor Street	Gunner	R.G.A.	
WILSON, ROBERT	Clifford Street	Private	M.T.	
WALLACE, JAMES G.	Cupar Street	Private	8th R.I.R.	Prisoner of War.
WALKER, HERBERT	Agnes Street	Private	R.N.A.S.	
WILKINSON, DAVID	Lanark Street	Private	A.S.C.	
WHITESIDE, DAVID, SENR.	Canmore Street	Private	9th R.I.R.	
WILLIAMSON, JOHN	Northumberland Street	Private	R.A.F.	
YOUNG, FRED	Madras Street	Private	King's R. Rifles	Killed.
COLONIAL FORCES.				
ADAIR, WILLIAM	Up. Charleville St.		Canadian R.A.M.C.	
CAMPBELL, GEORGE	Ballygomartin Road		Canadian Ex. Force	
CROSIER, DAVID	James Street		Canadian Sig. Corps	
ERSKINE, ADAM	Northumberland Street		S.A. Scottish Inft.	
GREER, JOHN, B.A.,B.E.	Springfield Road		Canadian Eng. Corps	
HOEY, STEWART	Grosvenor Road		Princess Patricia's L.I.	Wounded.
KELSO, JOHN	Cupar Street	Private	Princess Patricia's L.I.	Killed.
KING, MATTHEW	Sydney Street W.		Australian Inft.	
MORRISON, J. A.	Grosvenor Road		S.A. Field Telegraph Corps	
McCLUSKEY, JAMES	Pollard Street		Australian Inft.	Wounded.
McILROY, JAMES	Enfield Street		58th Batt. Canadian Force	
McNAB, JOHN, B.A.	Agnes Street	Captain	Chaplain Canadians	
NIXON, EDWARD	Eccles Street		Australian Exp. Force	Killed.
WILSON, HARRY	Chambers Street		Canadian Exp. Force	
WILSON, JAMES	Woodvale Road		Canadian Exp. Force	Killed.
ARGYLE PLACE.				
ADAIR, WILLIAM	98 Bray Street	1st Class Mechanic	R.N.A.S.	
ADAMS, JAMES	48 Perth Street	Sapper	Royal Engineers	
ADAMS, SAMUEL	209 Cupar Street	Private	R.I. Fus.	Wounded.
ALLEN, JOHN	17 Acton Street	Private	9th R.I. Rifles	Wounded.
ANNSLEY, JOHN	33 Columbia Street	Sergeant	14th Batt. (Y.C.V.) R.I.R.	Wounded.
AUSTIN, GEORGE	24 Fleetwood Street	Corporal	A.S.C.	
BARBOUR, JAMES	16 Court Street	Sapper	R.E.	Wounded.
BEATTIE, WILLIAM	12 Ninth Street	Private	R.I. Rifles	Killed in Action.
BEGGS, JOHN	398 Oldpark Road	Private	R.I.R. & Labour Corps	Died.
BEGGS, JOSEPH	40 Tobergill Street	Corporal	R.I. Fus.	
BLAIR, ALFRED	115 Bellevue Street	Private	R.I. Rifles	
BRADY, JOHN	165 Cambrai Street	Driver	A.S.C.	
BRADY, ROBERT	165 Cambrai Street	Private	R.I. Rifles	Killed in Action.
BROWN, THOMAS FLETCHER	204 Shankill Road	2nd Lieutenant	7th Manchester Regt.	Killed in Action.
BROWN, WILLIAM H.	21 Woodvale Road	Lance-Corporal	R.E.	
CARMICHAEL, HERBERT K.	19 Glenvale Street	Private	R.A.F.	
CARMICHAEL, ROBERT	19 Glenvale Street	Sergeant	15th Batt. R.I.R.	Killed in Action.
CARMICHAEL, VICTOR	19 Glenvale Street	Sergeant	Seaforth Highlanders	Military Medal.
CLARKE, WILLIAM	27 Ainsworth Avenue	Driver	A.S.C.	
CRAWFORD, MATTHEW	24 Mossvale Street	Trooper	North Irish Horse	Wounded.
CURRY, WILLIAM	5 Kirk Street	Sapper	R.E.	Wounded.
DORNAN, SAMUEL	46 Westland Street	Sapper	R.E.	
DUFF, ANDREW	60 Wilton Street	Private	9th Batt. R.I.R.	
DUNCAN, THOMAS	40 Rathlin Street	Private	7th S. Lanc. Regt.	Wounded.
DUNCAN, WILLIAM	37 Thorndyke Avenue	Private	R. Inn. Fus.	Killed in Action.
EASTON, SAMUEL	65 Matchett Street	Private	11th Batt. R.I.R.	Killed in Action.
FERRIS, ALEXANDER	176 Sugarfield Street	Private	9th Batt. R.I.R.	Wounded.
FINLAY, SAMUEL	18 Eighth Street	Private	A.S.C. M.T.	Wounded.
FOX, GEORGE	80 Weir Street	Private	R.I. Fus.	Wounded.
GEDDIS, ERNEST	249 Mayo Street	Signaller	9th Batt. R.I.R.	

BELFAST PRESBYTERY. ARGYLE PLACE.

Name.	Home Address.	Rank.	Regiment, Battalion or Unit.	Remarks.
Geddis, James	249 Mayo Street	Corporal	9th Batt. R.I.R.	Wd. & Pris. of War.
Gibson, Isaac	42 Tennent Street	Chief Engine-room A.	Royal Navy	Lost in Sub. K17.
Gibson, Thomas	42 Tennent Street	Engine-room A.	Royal Navy	
Gray, Hugh	280 Springfield Road	1st Class Stoker	R.N.	
Gray, John	280 Springfield Road	Signaller	9th Batt. R.I.R.	M.M.
Gray, Robert J.	147 Cambrai Street	Private	Seaforth Highlanders	Killed in Action.
Graham, George	140 Ainsworth Avenue	Private	15th Batt. R.I.R.	
Gresham, John M.	47 Ambleside Street	Stoker	H.M.S. Ebro	
Gorman, William	25 Mountjoy Street	Sapper	R.E.	
Hanna, Samuel	40 Danube Street	Private	M.T. A.S.C.	
Hastings, Adam John	59 Hopeton Street	Sergeant	16th Batt. R.I.R.	
Herald, Charles	13 Penrith Street	Private	R. Dub. Fus.	Wounded.
Hill, Samuel	80 Up. Charleville St.	Private	11th Batt. R.I.R.	Wounded.
Hillis, Thomas K.	84 Wilton Street	Private	M.T. A.S.C.	
Hoey, Charles M.	84 Wilton Street	Driver	M.T. A.S.C.	
Hoy, Samuel	43 Kendal Street	Sergeant	9th Batt. R.I.R.	
Howard, Charles	5 Eia Street	Engineer Lieutenant	R.N.R.	
Jackson, James	34 Rosewood Street	Q.M. Sergeant	13th Batt. R.I.R.	
Johnston, John	485 Oldpark Road	Private	R.A.M.C.	
Johnston, Joseph	348 Shankill Road	Corporal	14th Batt. R.I.R.	
Johnston, William J.	22 Columbia Street	Driver	136 Batty. R.F.A.	
Kelly, John Henry	5 Jersey Street	Sergt.-Major	15th Batt. R.I.R.	M.C., Pris. of War.
King, Thomas	43 Bowness Street	Sergeant	6th Batt. R.I.R.	
Kirk, Albert	16 Springfield Village	Driver	A.S.C.	
Kirk, James	16 Springfield Village	Private	9th Batt. R.I.R.	Killed in Action.
Laverty, Andrew	86 Riga Street	Gun-Layer	H.M.S. "Thunderer," R.N.	
Lee, Richard	15 Shannon Street	Private	16th R.I.R.	
Legg, Albert J.	64 Dover Street	Battery Fitter	R.F.A.	
Legg, John	64 Dover Street	A.B.	H.M.S. "City of Oxford"	
Legge, Robert J.	16 Tennyson Street	Corporal	1st Batt. R.I.R.	Wounded.
Lewis, Samuel J., Junr.	28 Wimbledon Street	Private	14th Batt. R.I.R.	Killed in Action.
Lewis, Samuel J.	28 Wimbledon Street	Sapper	R.E.	
Lindsay, John	44 Carnan Street	Corporal	9th Batt. R.I.R.	
Lynas, John	46 Woodvale Street	Private	2nd Batt. R. Inn. Fus.	Died.
Macauley, William	6 Eccles Street	Private	15th Batt. R.I.R.	
Machesney, George	6 Berlin Street	Sub-Lieutenant	R.N.R.	
Machesney, James	6 Berlin Street	Sergeant	16th Batt. R.I.R.	Gassed.
Madine, Peter	90 Ainsworth Avenue	Private	2nd Batt. R.I.R.	
Madine, William J.	90 Ainsworth Avenue	Private	2nd Batt. R.I.R.	
Magill, James	21 Jersey Street	Private	M.T. A.S.C.	
Moore, Robert McConnell	227 Springfield Road	2nd Lieutenant	R. I. Rifles	M.M., Killed in Act.
Morrison, David	13 Southland Street	Corporal	9th Batt. R.I.R.	Killed in Action.
McCallum, Alexander	90 Ainsworth Avenue	Trooper	2nd Life Guards	Killed in Action.
McCleery, James	1 Heather Street	Private	M.T. A.S.C.	
McConnell, William	6 Mountcashel Street	Private	9th Batt. R.I.R.	Wd. & Pris. of W.
McCracken, Archibald	38 Bann Street	Sapper	R.E.	
McCracken, James	38 Bann Street	Bombardier	R.F.A.	
McCracken, Samuel	38 Bann Street	Private	West Yorks	
McIlveen, John	66 Westland Street	Sergeant	14th Batt. R.I.R.	M.M. 2 Bars, French M.M.
McIlveen, William	66 Westland Street	Sergt.-Major	14th Batt. R.I.R.	D.C.M. 2 Bars, Killed in Action.
McIlwaine, Nevin	69 Palmer Street	Sergeant	South Lancs. Regt.	Wounded, Gassed.
McIlwaine, Samuel	69 Palmer Street	Sapper	R.E.	
McIlwaine, Thomas	69 Palmer Street	Private	Irish Guards	
McKee, Thomas	5 Lawnview Street	Driver	A.S.C.	
McKegherty, Atchinson	Ardoyne Village	Signaller	14th Batt. R.I.R.	
McKinney, Andrew	129 Cupar Street	Private	Army Medical Corps	
McKnight, James	236 Cupar Street	Private	9th Batt. R.I.R.	Killed in Action.
McManus, William C.	49 Lawnbrook Avenue	Private	9th Batt. R.I.R.	
McMullan, William	44 Woodvale Avenue	Private	9th Batt. R.I.R.	
McQueen, James Alex.	15 Bellevue Street	Private	9th Batt. R.I.R.	
McQueen, William R.	15 Bellevue Street	Private	R.A.M.C.	
Miskimmon, John	241 Springfield Road	Private	R.A.F.	
Neill, Alexander	101 Sugarfield Street	Lance-Corporal	9th Batt. R.I.R.	M.M., Pris. of W.
Nelson, Harry	228 Springfield Road	Sapper	R.E.	Wounded.
Nesbitt, William	21 Brookmount Street	Sergeant	Armoured Car Section.	
Nevin, John	46 Charleville Street	Private	15th Batt. R.I.R.	
Peoples, John	52 Riga Street	Private	R.I. Fus.	Wounded.
Pilson, Samuel	125 Canmore Street	Sapper	R.E.	Killed in Action.
Porter, James	20 Bowness Street	Private	15th Batt. R.I.R.	
Porter, John	20 Bowness Street	Private	15th Batt. R.I.R.	Wounded.
Porter, Robert	78 Glenwood Street	Private	9th Batt. R.I.R.	Wounded.
Porter, William J.	78 Glenwood Street	Private	R.M.L.I.	
Porter, William J.	20 Bowness Street	Private	15th Batt. R.I.R.	
Reford, Lewis	16 Court Street	A.B.	Royal Navy	
Reilly, Frederick	36 Queensland Street	Lance-Corporal	R.I. Rifles	
Reilly, William	36 Queensland Street	Sapper	R.E.	
Scott, Samuel	36 Perth Street	Corporal	M.T. A.S.C.	
Scroggie, David	18 Eighth Street	Private	R.M.L.I.	
Scroggie, Ephraim	18 Eighth Street	Driver	122nd Batty. R.F.A.	Gassed.
Scoggie, Frederick	18 Eighth Street	A.B.	R.N., Trawler Section	
Scroggie, John	18 Eighth Street	Private	11th Batt. R.I.R.	
Scroggie, William	18 Eighth Street	Stoker	Royal Navy	Wounded.

BELFAST PRESBYTERY. ARGYLE PLACE.

Name.	Home Address.	Rank.	Regiment, Battalion or Unit.	Remarks.
Smyth, Joseph	49 Gt. Patrick Street	Lance-Corporal	9th Batt. Black Watch	Killed in Action.
Spence, Joseph	5 Huss Street	Private	R.I. Rifles	
Sweeney, Richard E.	Cliftonville Road	S.Q.M. Sergt.-Major	A.S.C.	Died.
Tedford, Robert H.	22 Blaney Street	Private	9th Batt. R.I.R.	Wounded.
Telford, Hugh	37 Seventh Street	Private	R.I. Rifles	
Telford, James	181 Bellevue Street	Private	R.I. Rifles	
Wallace, William J.	398 Shankill Road	Private	R.I. Rifles	
White, James	45 Seventh Street	Private	R. Inn. Fus.	Killed in Action.
White, John	45 Seventh Street	Driver	M.T. A.S.C.	Wounded.
Whiteside, David	58 Canmore Street	Sapper	R.E.	
Whiteside, David, Junr.	58 Canmore Street	Private	2nd Batt. R.I.R.	Killed in Action.
Whiteside, George	58 Canmore Street	Private	2nd Batt. R. Inn. Fus.	Wounded.
Whiteside, Robert S.	58 Canmore Street	Private	M.T. A.S.C.	
Whiteside, William	58 Canmore Street	Private	R.M.L.I.	Wounded.
Wigston, Francis	37 Urney Street	Private	R.I. Rifles	
Wigston, Francis, Junr.	37 Urney Street	Private	R.I. Rifles	
Wigston, William	37 Urney Street	Private	2nd Batt. R.I.R.	Died of Wounds.
Winnington, William	92 Bray Street	Trooper	North Irish Horse	
Woods, John	Holywood	Lieutenant	R.V.N.R.	
Woods, Norman H.	Holywood	Lieutenant	R. Inn. Fus.	M.C., Killed in Act.
Woods, William E. G.	Holywood	Signaller	6th Batt. Black Watch	Wounded.
COLONIAL FORCES.				
Campbell, Daniel	Cliftonville Circus	Private	Canadian Forestry Corps	Wounded 5 times.
Geddis, Frank	249 Mayo Street	Private	N.Z. Force	
Gibson, Alex.	42 Tennent Street	Private	Can. Scottish	Gassed.
Moore, Thomas	227 Springfield Road	Sergeant	Can. R.A.M.C.	M. Medal.
McCreanor, Thos.	32 Rosebank Street	Private	8th Can. Inft.	Killed in Action.
McCreanor, Wm. J.	32 Rosebank Street	Private	27th Can. Inft.	Wounded.
Smyth, David	206 Ravenhill Road	Corporal	Can. Seaforth Highldrs.	Wounded.
Taylor, David	Woodvale Park	Private	Can. A.S.C.	
BALLYMACARRETT.				
Alcorn, Robert J.	15 Maymount Street			
Anderson, Wm. J.	264 Newtownards Road		Royal Navy	
Arnold, Thomas	92 Madrid Street			
Auld, Andrew	88 Up. Newtownards Rd.			
Auld, Thomas	88 Up. Newtownards Rd.			
Barker, Edward				
Barker, George				
Baxter, Albert	56 The Mount	Lance-Corporal	R.I. Fusiliers	
Baxter, Edgar A.	56 The Mount	Lieutenant	S. Lancs. Regt.	
Baxter, Samuel J.	56 The Mount	Air Mechanic	R.A.F.	
Brown, John	3 Ailsa Terrace	Captain	R.I.R.	M.C., Killed in Act.
Brown, John	72 Ogilvie Street	Private	R.I.R.	
Brown, John N.				
Cathcart, Dr.	Ruperta Ho., N'ards Rd.		R.A.M.C.	
Cleland, Ernest				
Craig, James	64 Mount Street	Private	R.I.R.	
Crommie, John W.	58 Castlereagh Road			
Devlin, Robinson	Fire Station, A'bridge Rd.			
Devlin, Robinson, Jun.	Fire Station, A'bridge Rd.	Private	R.I.R.	
Dornan, James	74 Templemore Avenue	Corporal	A.S.C.	
Dornan, Robert	74 Templemore Avenue	Sergt.-Major	A.S.C.	
Dornan, William	74 Templemore Avenue	Sapper	R.E.	
Ferguson, John				
Gillespie, H. V.	12 Castlereagh Street			
Gilmer, James	51 Richardson Street	Corporal	R.I.R.	
Gordon, William				
Halliday, Fred	85 Ogilvie Street			
Henderson, A.				
Jackson, John	10 The Mount	Corporal	9th R.I.R.	Wounded.
Jackson, William	10 The Mount	Private	14th R.I.R. (Y.C.V.)	Killed.
Johnstone, Samuel				
Jordan, William J.				
Jameson, S. D.	Hillmount, K'breda Rd.			
Kingsberry, Wm.				
Kirk, Alister	The Pines, N'breda			
Kirk, Stanley	The Pines, N'breda			
Kirkpatrick, James	The Farm, Orangefield	Lieutenant	R.N.	
Laird, W. A.	2 Temple Street	Private	R.I.R.	
Lewis, Hugh D.	The Lodge, Orangefield	Private	R.I.R.	
Lewis, Samuel	The Lodge, Orangefield	Driver	Army Transport	
Livingstone, John	159 Avoniel Road			
Livingstone, William	159 Avoniel Road			Killed in Action.
Logan, David	80 Dee Street			
Logan, Henry	80 Dee Street			
Logan, James	80 Dee Street			
Long, J. K.	2 Castlereagh Road			
McCabe, Denis				
McCabe, Denis, Jun.				
McCabe, John				

BELFAST PRESBYTERY.　　　　　　　　　　　　　　　　　　　　　　　　　　　　　　　　　　　**BALLYMACARRETT.**

Name.	Home Address.	Rank.	Regiment, Battalion or Unit.	Remarks.
McCann, Thomas	255 Mountpottinger Rd.	Farrier Sergt.-Major	R.F.A.	M.S.M.
McCann, William	255 Mountpottonger Rd.	Private	Worcester Regt.	
McCracken, Henry Joy	Austinville, Bloomfield	Lieutenant	R.A.F.	Died on Service.
McCrea, John	49 Omeath Street	Lieutenant		
McDowell, Isaac	15 Chatsworth Street			
McFall, James	22 Mayflower Street	Private		Wounded.
McFarlane, Donald	7 Frank Street			
McFarlane, Neill	7 Frank Street			Wounded.
McKillen, David	264a Newtownards Rd.			
McRoberts, Joseph	3 Daisyfield Terrace			
McRoberts, Robert M.	3 Daisyfield Terrace	Private	R.A.M.C.	
McTear, Samuel	18 Clara Street			
McIlveen, William				
Maginnis, Hugh				
Miller, J.				
Mitchell, James	121 The Mount	Lieutenant		
Moore, Archie	Ashley House	Captain		Wounded.
Moore, Willie	Ashley House			Killed in Action.
Moore, Hugh	80 Woodstock Road			
Mullan, John	91 Grove Street East	Private		
Mullan, John, Jun.	91 Grove Street East	Private		
Neely, R.	Edenderry U' N'ards Rd.			
Nicholl, Joseph D.	Ailsa Ter., Holywood Rd.	Captain		
Pettigrew, Andrew	68 Jocelyn Avenue	Sergeant	R.E.	
Pettigrew, John				
Pinkerton, George	7 Temple Street			
Ritchie, Arthur				
Shanks, Hiram	67 Madrid Street	Gunner	H.M.S. Corea	
Spence, William	203 Albertbridge Road	Private	14th R.I.R.	Killed in Action.
Steele, Thomas	9 The Mount			
Torrington, James	53 Nevis Avenue			
White, James				
Wilson, John	32 Irwin Avenue			
Yeates, James	84 The Mount	Eng. Lieutenant	R.N.R.	
Yeates, Robert	84 The Mount	Sergt.-Major		
Yeates, Thomas	84 The Mount	Sergeant		
BALLYSILLAN.				
Adair, David		Private	9th R.I.F.	
Adair, Francis		Private	9th R.I.F.	
Adams, Alexander		Private	2nd R. In. Fus.	Wounded.
Adams, Robert		Private	4th Seaforth Highlanders	
Agnew, Robert		Private	15th R.I.R.	
Agnew, Samuel		Private	55th Coy. R.E.	Wounded.
Allen, Robert		Private	15th R.I.R.	
Allen, Thomas		Private	15th R.I.R.	
Armstrong, Robert		Private	R. In. Fus.	
Armstrong, William J.		Trooper	6th R. In. Dragoons	
Baird, William			9th R.I.F.	Killed.
Ballagh, Samuel				Killed.
Beattie, David		Private	2nd Irish Guards	
Bell, George		Drummer	2nd R.I.F.	
Bell, Henry Cooke		Sergeant	110th F.A., R.A.M.C.	
Bell, Matt. Arlow		Private	14th R.I.R. (Y.C.V.)	
Bell, Samuel		Private	5th R.I.R.	Wounded.
Bell, William		Private	3rd R. In. Fus.	Killed.
Boal, Edwin S.		Private	14th R.I.R (Y.C.V.)	
Boal, Harry		Private	Canadian Grenadier Guards	Wounded.
Boal, John			15th R.I.R.	
Boal, Robert		Private	6th R.I.F.	
Boville, Robert				Killed.
Boville, James				Killed.
Boyd, James		Private	15th R.I.R.	
Boyd, Samuel		Private	6th R.I.R.	
Brown, Joseph		Private	14th R.I.R. (Y.C.V.)	
Brownlee, Joseph		Private	15th R.I.R.	
Burgess, James		Private	15th R.I.R.	
Burns, William		Private	15th R.I.R.	
Cairns, Hugh		Private	15th R.I.R.	
Caldwell, Andrew		Private	Scottish Rifles	
Caldwell, Samuel Andrew		Private	110th F.A., R.A.M.C.	
Campbell, William		Lieut.-Commander	R.N.R.	D.S.C.
Campbell, Henry		Private	110th F.A., R.A.M.C.	
Campbell, Hugh		Corporal	17th F.A., R.A.M.C.	Wounded.
Campbell, James		Sergeant	7th King's Own Regt.	
Campbell, Samuel		Private	15th R.I.R.	
Campbell, Samuel		Private	17th F.A., R.A.M.C.	
Campbell, William		Private	36th Div. Cyclist Corps	
Clarke, Thomas		Lance-Corporal	King's Own Yorkshire L.I.	
Collins, Samuel		Private	R.M.L.I.	
Coulter, John R.		Private	15th R.I.R.	
Crawford, George		Private	5th R.I.F.	
Crawford, James Armour		Sergeant	1st Irish Guards	Wounded.

BELFAST PRESBYTERY. BALLYSILLAN.

Name.	Home Address.	Rank.	Regiment, Battalion or Unit.	Remarks.
Crawford, John	...	Private	3rd R.I.F.	Wounded.
Creavy, William	...	...	...	Killed.
Downey, James	...	Private	15th R.I.R.	
Falloon, Albert V.	...	Private	R.M., H.M.S. "Exmouth"	
Falloon, James	...	Private	122nd Coy. R.E.	
Ferris, Samuel	...	Private	2nd R.I.R.	Killed in Action.
Ferris, William Robert	...	Private	R.A.M.C.	
Flanagan, Alexander	...	Sergeant	15th R.I.R.	
Flanagan, George	...	Private	2nd/6th Black Watch	
Flanagan, Samuel	...	Private	14th R.I.R. (Y.C.V.)	
Fletcher, J.	...	Lance-Corporal	8th R. In. Fus.	
Fletcher, William J.	...	Private	17th R.I.R.	
French, Robert James	...	Private	15th R.I.R.	
Gailey, James Leitch	...	Sergeant	R.A.M.C.	
Gailey, Andrew James	...	...	...	
Gailey, John T.	...	...	...	
Gault, Joseph B.	...	Private	15th R.I.R.	
Gibson, James	...	Private	15th R.I.R.	
Giffen, John	...	Private	15th R.I.R.	
Giffen, Samuel	...	Private	15th R.I.R.	
Giffen, Samuel	...	Private	14th R.I.R. (Y.C.V.)	
Giffen, Thomas	...	...	...	Killed.
Goudy, James	...	Private	4th R.I.R.	
Grattan, Joseph	...	Private	15th R.I.R.	
Haire, Hans	...	Private	15th R.I.R.	
Haire, R.	...	Gunner	2nd Battery R.G.A.	
Haire, Samuel	...	Private	R. In. Fus.	
Hanvey, John	...	Private	15th R.I.R.	
Harbinson, James	...	Private	A.S.C.	
Harper, Robert	...	Gunner	69th Co., R.G.A.	
Hawkins, William	...	Sergeant	15th R.I.R.	
Herdman, Thomas	...	Sergeant	A.S.C.	
Hill, James	...	Stoker	H.M.S. "Roxburgh"	
Hutchinson, William	...	...	...	Killed.
Johnston, Fred. L.	...	C.Q.-M.S.	R.I.R.	
Kennedy, William Henry	...	Private	4th Seaforth Highlanders	
Kell, Robert	...	...	1st Canadian Pioneers	
Kerr, Thomas	...	Private	15th R.I.R.	
Kinkead, Alfred H.	...	Private	15th R.I.R.	
Kinnon, Robert	...	Corporal	15th R.I.R.	
Kirkwood, Albert	...	Bombardier	25th Battery R.F.A.	
Kirkwood, James	...	Engineer-Artificer	R.N.R., H.M.S. "Leven"	
Kyle, Alexander	...	Private	11th R.I.R.	
Lawlor, Alexander	...	Gunner	Canadian R.F.A.	
Lawlor, James	...	Private	2nd R.I.F.	Wounded.
Lawlor, Samuel	...	...	8th Canadian Rangers	
Leslie, David	...	Private	16th R.I.R.	
Lewis, James	...	Private	17th R.I.R.	
Lewis, Alexander	...	...	...	Killed.
Lynass, George	...	Private	17th R.I.R.	
Lynass, William John	...	Private	15th R.I.R.	
Magee, John	...	Gunner	Canadian R.F.A.	
Magee, William J.	...	Stoker	H.M.S. "Kent"	
Magilton, Valentine	...	...	R.N.	
Mann, Alexander	...	Private	9th R.I.R.	
Martin, John	...	...	...	Killed.
Matthewson, James, Sen.	...	Private	9th R.I.R.	
Matthewson, James, Jun.	...	Private	15th R.I.R.	
Matthewson, Samuel	...	Private	6th Cameron Highlanders	
Matthewson, William	...	Private	36th U. Div. Train A.S.C.	
Millar, Sinclair	...	Lieutenant	R.A.M.C.	
Moore, William John	...	Private	3rd R.I.R.	
Murdie, S.	...	Gunner	54th Brigade R.F.A.	
Murdock, Hamilton	...	Private	R. In. Fus.	
Murray, Matthew	...	Private	15th R.I.R.	
McAdam, Ernest	...	Lance-Corporal	9th R. In. Fus.	
McAdam, Samuel	...	Private	5th R. In. Fus.	
McClay, Joseph J.	...	Private	R.A.S.C.	
McClinton, Samuel	...	Private	1st Irish Guards	Killed in Action.
McCord, Alexander	...	Private	17th R.I.R.	
McCormick, Andrew	...	Corporal	1st R.I.R.	
McCormick, Robert J.	...	Private	4th R.I.R.	
McCormick, Samuel	...	Gunner	25th Battery R.F.A.	
McCracken, David	...	Private	15th R.I.R.	
McCracken, John F.	...	Private	15th R.I.R.	
McCracken, William	...	Private	15th R.I.R.	
McCracken, William Hoy	...	Private	44th Canadians	
McCreight, Thomas	...	Private	7th Batt. 1st B. Col. Regt.	
McCullough, David	...	Private	15th R.I.R.	
McCullough, Isaac	...	Private	4th R.I.R.	
McCurley, David	...	Private	15th R.I.R.	
McCurley, Samuel	...	Private	15th R.I.R.	
McCurley, William	...	Sergeant	15th R.I.R.	
McDowell, Albert	...	2nd Lieutenant	5th R.I.R.	

BELFAST PRESBYTERY.   BALLYSILLAN.

Name.	Home Address.	Rank.	Regiment, Battalion or Unit.	Remarks.
McDowell, Frank	... ...	Trooper	N.I.H.	
McDowell, Samuel	... ...	Lance-Corporal	15th R.I.R.	
McDowell, William	... ...	Trooper	N.I.H.	
McIlhare, Alexander	... ...	Gunner	1st Battery R.G.A.	
McIlhare, David	... ...	Private	2nd R.I.R.	Wounded.
McIlhare, Samuel	... ...	Private	3rd R.I.R.	
McIlrath, Edward	... ...	Private	9th R.I.R.	
McIlrath, James	... ...	Petty Officer	H.M.S. "Nottingham"	
McIlrath, James	... ...	Private	15th R.I.R.	
McIlwaine, John	... ...	Private	36th U. Div. Train A.S.C.	
McKee, David	... ...	Private	18th R.I.R.	
McLarnon, Samuel	... ...	Private	17th R.I.R.	
McLarnon, Matthew	... ...	...	...	Killed.
McMillen, John	... ...	Private	H.M.S. "Highflyer"	
McMurray, James Edward	... ...	Private	15th R.I.R.	
McVeigh, Richard	... ...	Lance-Corporal	15th R.I.R.	
Neill, William	... ...	Private	14th R.I.R. (Y.C.V.)	
Nesbitt, Agnew	... ...	Gunner	1st R.G.A.	
Nesbitt, John	... ...	Trooper	6th R. In. Dragoons	
Nesbitt, William	... ...	Gunner	1st Battery R.G.A.	
O'Hara, Thomas	... ...	Lance-Corporal	1st R.I.R.	
Parfitt, William J.	... ...	Private	3rd Rifle Brigade	Killed.
Pedlow, William J.	... ...	Bugler	15th R.I.R.	
Peoples, Alexander	... ...	Private	15th R.I.R.	
Phillips, Robert	... ...	...	...	Killed.
Pollock, John	... ...	Private	2nd R.I.R.	
Porter, Samuel	... ...	Private	15th R.I.R.	
Quigley, George	... ...	Private	15th R.I.R.	
Ramsey, James	... ...	Private	15th R.I.R.	
Ramsey, Matthew	... ...	...	2nd Duke of Wellington Regt.	
Ramsey, William	... ...	Private	5th R. In. Fus.	
Rea, William H.	... ...	Stoker	R.N., H.M.S. "Invincible"	
Reid, Arthur	... ...	...	...	Killed.
Ritchie, Alexander	... ...	Private	Canadian Ex. Force	
Ritchie, Benjamin	... ...	Lance-Corporal	15th R.I.R.	
Ritchie, John	... ...	Private	Can. E. Force	
Ritchie, William	... ...	Sergeant	125th Battery R.F.A.	
Rodgerson, Henry	... ...	Private	15th R.I.R.	
Salters, Robert	... ...	Sergeant	36th U. Div. Train A.S.C.	
Savage, Edgar	... ...	Private	14th R.I.R. (Y.C.V.)	
Savage, J. H.	... ...	Private	32nd F.A., R.A.M.C.	
Seeds, John	... ...	Private	9th R.I.R.	
Seeds, Samuel	... ...	Private	15th R.I.R.	
Shaw, James	... ...	Private	9th R.I.R.	
Smyth, William David	... ...	Private	5th R.I.R.	
Spratt, David	... ...	Private	15th R.I.R.	
Spratt, James	... ...	Private	15th R.I.R.	
Stevenson, Alexander	... ...	Stoker	H.M.S. "Chatham"	
Stevenson, W.	... ...	Private	32nd F.A., R.A.M.C.	
Stewart, James	... ...	Private	15th R.I.R.	
Stewart, John	... ...	Private	15th R.I.R.	
Stewart, Joseph W.	... ...	Private	15th R.I.R.	
Stewart, Matthew	... ...	Private	15th R.I.R.	
Stewart, Samuel	... ...	Private	15th R.I.R.	
Stewart, William	... ...	Private	15th R.I.R.	
Taylor, Andrew	... ...	Sergeant	13th R. In. Fus.	
Templeton, James	... ...	Stoker	H.M.S. "Hibernia"	
Thompson, Arthur	... ...	...	...	Killed.
Thompson, James	... ...	Private	15th R.I.R.	
Thompson, Robert	... ...	Private	4th R.I.R.	
Thompson, William L.	... ...	Private	9th R.I.R.	
Toland, John	... ...	Private	2nd R. In. Fus.	
Todd, Robert	... ...	Private	122nd Field Coy., R.E.	
Todd, Thomas	... ...	Private	122nd Field Coy., R.E.	
Walker, Robert	... ...	Private	10th Western Can. Regt.	Missing.
Walker, Roland	... ...	Private	15th R.I.R.	
Wallace, Edward	... ...	Private	2nd R.I.R.	Wounded.
White, George	... ...	Private	15th R.I.R.	
White, Hugh Henry	... ...	Private	2nd Irish Guards	
White, Shannon	... ...	Corporal	2nd Irish Guards	
Wilkinson, Hugh	... ...	Private	4th R. In. Fus.	
Wilkinson, Robert	... ...	Private	2nd R. In. Fus.	
Wilkinson, William	... ...	Lance-Corporal	1st Cheshire Regt.	
Wilson, W. M.	... ...	Trooper	N.I.H., F.M.	
Wright, David	... ...	Private	15th R.I.R.	
Wright, John	... ...	Sergeant	N.I.H.	
Wright, Samuel	... ...	Private	2nd R.I.R.	
Young, David	... ...	Private	2nd R. In. Fus.	Wounded.
Younger, J.	... ...	Driver	25th Battery R.F.A.	
BELMONT.				
Auld, A.	... ...	Private	...	
Barr, W. M.	... ...	Lance-Corporal	...	
Beck, A.	... ...	Private	...	

BELFAST PRESBYTERY. BELMONT.

Name.	Home Address.	Rank.	Regiment, Battalion or Unit.	Remarks.
Bell, S. R.		Cadet		
Benson, S.		Corporal		
Bickerstaffe, F.		Driver		
Bickerstaffe, W. J.		Lance-Corporal		
Blackwood, A. T.		Captain		
Blackwood, T. A.		Captain		
Boyd, C. J.		Lieutenant		
Boucher, F. J.		Captain		
Boucher, E. R.		2nd Lieutenant		
Buick, H. F.		Sergeant		
Buick, J. G. Fred.		Gunner		
Bingham, Samuel			R.I.F.	Killed.
Brown, William			R.I.F.	
Campbell, J.		Corporal		
Campbell, Kenneth M.			Canadian Force	Killed in Action.
Cathcart, J.		Private		
Chase, C. D.		Captain		M.C.
Clarke, J.		Gunner		
Clarke, E.		Gunner		
Colville, William				
Colville, T. J.		Private		
Colville, R. F.		C.S.M.		
Cooper, W.		Sergeant		
Crabbe, J. M.		Engineer		
Crabbe, J.		Engineer		
Craig, Sir James, Bart.		Lieut.-Colonel		
Crawford, H. C.		Captain		
Cochrane, Robert			R.F.A.	Accid. Drowned.
Dickson, W. W.		Captain		
Dickson, H. L.		Captain		
Dickson, C.		Lieutenant		M.C.
Doherty, R.		Lance-Corporal		
Dickson, John		Lieutenant	R.A.F.	Killed in Action.
Dunwoody, E.		2nd Lieutenant		
Dunwoody, H. H.		2nd Lieutenant	R.I.F.	Killed in Action.
Edwards, W. V.		Captain	R.D.F.	Killed in Action.
Ewing, A. McA.		Cadet		
Erskine, George		Corporal	R.I.R.	Killed in Action.
Ferguson, T.		Rifleman		
Gill, David		Rifleman	R.I.R.	
Gill, J.		Lance-Corporal		
Gill, George			N.I.H.	
Gilmore, C.		Corporal		
Gordon, R.		Driver		
Haire, J. C.		Lance-Corporal		
Harris, J. F.		Cadet		
Henderson, Samuel			R.I.R.	
Harrison, J.		A.B.		
Irvine, Adam		Private		
Irvine, A.		Private		
Irvine, I.		1st Class P.O.		
Irvine, Hugh R.		Lieutenant		
Johnston, Elliott		Captain	R.I.R.	M.C., K'd. in Action
Jackson, J. F.		Lance-Corporal		
Jamison, D.		A.B.		
Jebb, William		Private		
Jebb, Thomas		Private		
Kelly, G.		Private		
Kelly, W. B.		Lieutenant		
Kelly, J.		Private		
Kelly, J. L.		Private		
Kerr, A.		Lance-Corporal		
Killen, S.		Private		
Knox, B.		Rifleman		
Knox, F. K.		2nd Lieutenant		
Lawther, F.		Driver		
Lecky, J.		Private		
Lewis, W. R.		Stoker	R.N.	
Lemon, D. Archibald		Lieutenant	R.I.R.	Killed in Action.
Lindsay, D. C.		Captain		
Long, M.		Private		
Long, J.		Private		
Long, E.		Private		
MacBride, T. G.		Lieutenant		
MacBride, Norman			R.G.A.	
MacColl, George E.		Major	R.I.R.	Killed in Action.
MacColl, H. F.		Midshipman		
McCormick, F.		Trooper		
McConnell, William C.		Lieutenant	R.I.R.	Killed in Action.
MacDermott, W.		Captain		
MacDermott, R. W.		2nd Lieutenant	R.I.R.	Killed in Action.
MacDermott, J. C.		Lieutenant		M.C.
McDonald, W. W.		Private		
McDowell, G.		Private		
McDowell, W.		Private		

BELFAST PRESBYTERY.   BELMONT.

Name.	Home Address.	Rank.	Regiment, Battalion or Unit.	Remarks.
McDowell, J.	...	Corporal	...	...
McDowell, S. S.	...	Captain	...	...
McDowell, James	...	Corporal	...	...
McFarland, R.	...	Captain	...	...
McGonigal, R.	...	Captain	...	M.C. and Bar.
McGregor, R.	...	Sergeant	...	...
McIlree, W.	...	Private	...	...
McIlree, Henry	...	...	R.I.R.	...
McIvor, R. J.	...	Lieutenant	...	...
McKee, William D.	...	Lieutenant	R.I.R.	Killed in Action.
McKee, James	...	Captain	...	D.S.O.
McKibben, A. J.	...	Sergeant	...	...
McKitterick, A.	...	Private	...	...
McLeod, J.	...	Cadet	...	...
McMaster, H.	...	Surgeon-Lieutenant	...	...
McNab, S.	...	Sergeant	...	...
Macpherson, I. D.	...	Trooper	...	...
Macpherson, W. A. S.	...	Captain	...	M.C.
Magowan, W.	...	Private	...	...
Maxton, L. G.	...	Captain	...	...
Moore, J. M.	...	Lance-Corporal	...	...
Moore, James S.	...	Seaman	...	...
Murdock, J.	...	Private	...	...
Murdock, R.	...	Private	...	...
Ogle, J.	...	Private	...	...
Ogle, D.	...	Private	...	...
Ogle, T.	...	Private	...	...
O'Neill, C.	...	A.B.	...	...
Orchard, R. C.	...	Lieutenant	...	...
Orchard, W. S.	...	Private	...	...
Pottinger, J.	...	Chief Stoker	...	C.P.O.
Ramsay, Charles	...	Captain	...	...
Ramage, George N.	...	Comm. R.R.	...	R.D. Kd. in Action.
Reid, W.	...	Private	...	...
Reid, C.	...	Private	...	...
Reid, S.	...	Private	...	...
Reid, William	...	...	R.A.F.	...
Ritchie, J.	...	Private	...	...
Robinson, J.	...	Private	...	...
Robson, D.	...	Corporal	...	...
Scott, William	...	Captain	...	D.S.O., M.C.
Scott, J. P.	...	Midshipman	...	...
Shaw, R. M.	...	Sergeant	...	...
Sherlock, J.	...	Rifleman	...	...
Sherlock, David	...	...	R.E.	...
Smith, G.	...	Private	...	M.M.
Swinson, L. F.	...	Bombardier	...	...
Swinson, S.	...	...	...	...
Tait, H. J.	...	Lance-Corporal	...	...
Tattersall, G. S.	...	Sergeant	...	...
Tedford, J.	...	Private	...	...
Tedford, A.	...	Driver	...	...
Thompson, J.	...	Captain	...	...
Thompson, E. W.	...	Sergeant	...	...
Walker, J.	...	Private	...	...
Warrick, J.	...	Private	...	...
Warrick, T. P.	...	Lance-Corporal	...	...
Watson, J.	...	Sergeant	...	...
Watson, S. K.	...	Private	...	...
Watson, F. W.	...	Lieutenant	...	M.C.
Workman, Edward	...	Lieutenant	R.I.R.	P. of War, M.C.
Watts, Robert	...	Captain	R.I.R.	M.C. and Bar.
Webb, W.	...	Private	...	...
Wright, T.	...	Driver	...	...
BERRY STREET.				
Adair, Brian	Central Fire Station	Sergt.-Major	R.I.R.	...
Brown, David	29 Bute Street	Lance-Corporal	R.I. Fus.	...
Brown, Samuel	50 Delhi Street	Captain	R.A.M.C.	M.C.
Campbell, Robert	286 L. Broadway	Private	A.S.C.	...
Cooke, John	42 Cooke Street	2nd Lieutenant	R.I.R.	...
Currie, Allan	Central Hall	Private	R. Dub. Fus.	...
Fergie, Charles	10 Hopeton Street	Private	R.I.R.	Wounded.
Fergie, John	10 Hopeton Street	Private	R.I.R.	...
Fleming, Matthew	20 Dock Street	Private	R.I. Fus.	...
Hanley, Henry	114 Wilton Street	Private	R.I.R.	...
Hanna, John	18 Sherbrook Street	Private	R.I.R.	...
Jamison, David	65 Hopeton Street	Private	Mch. Transport	...
Jamison, George	65 Hopeton Street	Private	R.E.	...
Jamison, John	65 Hopeton Street	Sergt.-Major	R.I.R.	...
Jamison, John	76 Hopeton Street	Lance-Corporal	R.I.R.	...
Long, Robert	50 Bankmore Street	...	Royal Navy	...
Louden, John	140 Peter's Hill	Private	R.I.R.	...
Lyons, John	44 Peveril Street	...	Royal Navy	Killed in Action.

BELFAST PRESBYTERY. BERRY STREET.

Name.	Home Address.	Rank.	Regiment, Battalion or Unit.	Remarks.
Lynas, John	46 Woodvale Street	Private	R. Inn. Fus.	Died of Gas Poison
Monteith, Robert	98 York Street	2nd Lieutenant	R.I.R.	Prisoner of War.
McCammon, John	42 Carlisle Street	Lance-Corporal	R.I.R.	Wounded.
McConnell, Hugh	191 Snugville Street	Private	A.S.C.	Wounded.
McCoubrey, David	9 Abercorn Street	Lance-Corporal	R.I.R.	
McCoubrey, John	9 Abercorn Street	Sergeant	R.I.R.	Killed in Action.
McLean, Robert George	34 Fortuna Street	Private	R.I.R.	Killed in Action.
McQuoid, James	5 Clondara Terrace	Private	A.S.C.	
McQuoid, William	5 Clondara Terrace	Private	R.I.R.	
McQuoid, William	105 Westmoreland Street	Private	N.I. Horse	
McVeigh, Samuel	117 Nelson Street	Sergeant	R.I.R.	Killed in Action.
Patrick, David	4 Alloa Street		Royal Navy	
Rankin, Hugh	5 St. Jude's Avenue	Lance-Corporal	R.I.R.	
Rankin, Matthew	5 St. Jude's Avenue	2nd Lieutenant	R.I.R.	
Rea, Charles	32 Hardcastle Street	Private		
Rea, David	32 Hardcastle Street	Private	R.E.	
Russell, Wm. G.	12 Beech Street	Private	Irish Guards	Wounded.
Sheriff, John	14 Victoria Avenue	Corporal	R.I.R.	
Shields, Arthur	38 Dunvegan Street	Private	R.I.R.	Killed in Action.
Shields, James	38 Dunvegan Street		Royal Navy	
Smith, John	10 Adam Street	Corporal	N.I. Horse	Missing.
Spence, James	83 Devonshire Street	Private	R.E.	
Spence, Robert	83 Devonshire Street	Private	R.I.R.	Killed in Action.
Spence, Thomas	83 Devonshire Street	Private	A.S.C.	
Spence, William	83 Devonshire Street	Private	Inn. Fus.	Wounded.
Stewart, Joseph	Ulster Bank (Waring St.)	Private	R. Air Force	
Thomson, James	86 Cliftonpark Avenue		Royal Navy	
Thomson, John	86 Cliftonpark Avenue	Private	A.S.C.	
Wiseman, Herbert	15 Oldpark Road		Royal Navy	
Wiseman, Robert	2 Buller Street	Private	R.I.R.	Wounded.
COLONIAL FORCES.				
Caldwell, David	30 Arundel Street		Can. A.S.C.	
Caldwell, Robert	30 Arundel Street		52nd Canadians	
McKittrick, David	20 Cullingtree Street			Wounded.
McKittrick, Irwin	20 Cullingtree Street			Gassed.
Smith, Reuben	7 Thorndale Avenue			
BETHANY (AGNES STREET).				
Adgey, Thomas	13 Columbia Street	Private	R.E.	
Allen, John	57 Dundee Street	Private	9th R.I.R.	
Andrews, James	17 Rosewood Street	Private		
Armstrong, Wm.	37 Daisyfield Street	Private	R.A.M.C.	Wounded.
Banks, William	15 Albany Street	Private	R.I.R.	Wounded.
Beattie, Alex.	5 Oregon Street	Private	7th R. Inn. Fus.	Wounded.
Boyd, Thomas	34 Howe Street	Private	R.A.O.C.	
Campbell, Michael	139 Snugville Street	Stoker	Naval Reserve	
Carson, John	46 Orkney Street	Sergeant	9th R.I.R.	
Chestnutt, Joseph	100 Ainsworth Avenue	Private	R.E.	
Cunningham, Robert	82 Emerson Street	Private	R.I.R.	
Ellis, Samuel	274 Crimea Street	Private	1st R.I.R.	
Finlay, John	29 Landscape	Private	14th R.I.R.	
Gordon, Gawn	33 Courtrai Street	Lance-Corporal	Cameronian Highldrs.	Killed in Action.
Gordon, James	33 Courtrai Street	Sergeant	R. Inn. Fus.	W'ded and Pris.
Grattan, George	57 Dundee Street	Private	R.I.R.	
Gray, John	302 Conway Street	Private	R.A.M.C.	Prisoner.
Hayes, Wilson	9 Dunmoyle Street	Private	14th R.I.R.	
Holden, Henry	59 Dundee Street	Private	9th R.I.R.	Killed in Action.
Hughes, James	70 Lawnbrook Avenue	Private	7th Inn. Fus.	
Hylands, John	173 Leopold Street	Private	R.E.	Killed in Action.
Johnston, Edward	29 Fortingale Street	Private	R.A.F.	
Johnston, Robert	29 Fortingale Street	Private	Black Watch	Killed in Action.
Johnston, Samuel	50 Langford Street	Private	1st R.I.R.	Wounded.
Johnston, Samuel	50 Langford Street	Private	9th R.I.R.	
Johnston, William	164 Snugville Street	Private	14th R.I.R.	Killed in Action.
Jordan, Robert	42 Glenfarne Street	Private	9th R.I.R.	Wounded.
Kerr, Wm. P.	Crumlin Road	Private	R.A.M.C.	
Kirk, Edward	8 Craig's Terrace	Private	9th R.I.R.	
Kirk, Wm.	8 Craig's Terrace	Private	15th R.I.R.	
Knox, John	30 Thorndale Avenue	Lieutenant	R. Inn. Fus.	Killed in Action.
Lewis, Albert	90 Agnes Street	Sergeant	R.A.M.C.	
Lewis, Ernest	90 Agnes Street	Private	15th R.I.R.	
Lindsay, William	41 M'Candless Street	Private	15th R.I.R.	Killed in Action.
McAlpine, Wm.	329 Springfield Road	Engineer		Prisoner.
McClarnon, Robert John	31 Raleigh Street	Private	16th R.I.R.	Wounded.
McIlwaine, Hugh	274 Crimea Street	Private	3rd Inn. Fus.	Wounded.
McIlwaine, John	22 Haldane Street	Private	R.I.R.	Wounded.
McIlwaine, Robert	274 Crimea Street	Private	2nd Inn. Fus.	Wounded.
McIlwrath, Robert	5 Up. Meenan Street	Private	A.S.C.	
McIntyre, David	8 Bootle Street	Private	9th R.I.R.	
McRoberts, Frank	5 Northumberland St.	Private	1st R.I.R.	Wounded.
Mann, John	58 Esmond Street	Private	15th R.I.R.	Wounded.
Mann, Robert	58 Esmond Street	Private	9th Inn. Fus.	Killed in Action.

(75)

BELFAST PRESBYTERY. BETHANY.

NAME.	HOME ADDRESS.	RANK.	REGIMENT, BATTALION OR UNIT.	REMARKS.
MATTHEWS, JAMES	6 Wimbledon Street	Q.-Master	9th R.I.R.	Gassed.
MILLAR, GEO. G.	22 Raleigh Street	Private	13th R.I.R.	
MURRAY, GEORGE	Eglish, Cliftonville Circus	Private	N.I.H. and R.I. Regt.	Killed in Action.
NUGENT, ARTHUR	31 Percy Street	Private	R.E.	
NUGENT, JAMES	31 Percy Street	Private	2nd R. Inn. Fus.	Killed in Action.
NUGENT, JOHN	31 Percy Street	Private	R.F.A.	
NUGENT, JOSEPH	31 Percy Street	Private	Merch. Transport	
NUGENT, ROBERT	31 Percy Street	Private	1st Inn. Fus.	Killed in Action.
PALMER, WM.	27 Glenfarne Street	Sergeant	R.A.M.C.	
REAVY, JOHN	43 Glenfarne Street	Private	15th R.I.R.	
REID, ANDREW	22 Raleigh Street	Private	15th R.I.R.	
ROBINSON, JAMES	282 Crimea Street	Private	Merch. Transport	
ROGERS, WM.	280 Crimea Street	Private	1st Black Watch	Prisoner.
RUSSELL, THOMAS	34 Ottawa Street	Sergeant	R.E.	Wounded.
SMYTH, A.	21 Rusholme Street	Private	15th R.I.R.	Killed in Action.
SMYTH, SAMUEL	21 Rusholme Street	Private	Merch. Transport	
SMYTH, THOMAS	21 Rusholme Street	Sergeant	R.I.R.	Wounded.
STEVENSON, WM.	12 Southport Street	Private	15th R.I.R.	
STEWART, JOSEPH	17 Raleigh Street	Private	11th Inn. Fus.	Wounded.
THOMPSON, ROBERT	45 Westmoreland Street	Private	Merch. Transport	
THOMPSON, THOMAS	45 Westmoreland Street	Private	R.A.M.C.	
TOWNSLEY, JOHN	20 Century Street	Private	15th R.I.R.	Wounded.
TOWNSLEY, WILLIAM	20 Century Street	Private	14th R.I.R.	
TOWNSLEY, WILSON	20 Century Street	Private	14th R.I.R.	Wounded.
WILLIAMSON, ARCHIBALD	108 Crumlin Road	Private	R. Inn. Fus.	Killed in Action.
WILSON, A.		Private	9th R.I.R.	
WILSON, WM.		Private	R.E.	
YORKE, FRED	10 Roe Street	Private	R.A.M.C.	
YORKE, JAMES	10 Roe Street	Private	R.A.F.	
BLOOMFIELD.				
ADAIR, SAMUEL	34 Grampian Avenue	Private	10th Inn. Fus.	
AGNEW, WILLIAM	21 Ulsterdale Street	Private	14th R.I.R.	Killed in Action.
ALLEN, ROBERT H.	47 Woodcot Avenue	Private	A.S.C.	Died in Hospital.
ASHE, ROBERT J.	14 Kensington Avenue	Driver	A.S.C.	
ATKINSON, ROBERT	44 Woodcot Avenue	Private	8th R.I.R.	Killed in Action.
ATKINSON, THOMAS	44 Woodcot Avenue	Private	9th F.A. R.A.M.C.	1914 Star.
BALNAVE, DAVID	86 Bread Street East	Private	A. & S. Highlanders	W'ded, Mons. M.
BAMFORD, JAMES	17 Cyprus Gardens	Wireless Operator		
BELL, WM. J.	33 Bloomfield Street	Private	8th R.I.R.	Wounded.
BELSHAW, JOHN	49 Cheviot Avenue	Private	14th R.I.R.	
BLACK, JOHN	32 Belmont Avenue		L.M., R.N.A.S.	
BOYD, BRIAN	10 Cyprus Gardens	Lieutenant	14th R.I.R.	Killed in Action.
BOYD, WILLIAM	39 Bread Street East	Private	10th R.I.R.	Wounded.
BOYD, ROBERT J.	39 Bread Street East	Stoker	R.N.	
BOWDEN, WILLIAM	9 Grace Avenue	Private	14th R.I.R.	
BROWN, HENRY	48 Bloomfield Street	Private	8th R.I.R.	
BROWN, GEORGE	48 Bloomfield Street	Private	4th R.I.R.	
CAMPBELL, GEORGE	85 Cheviot Avenue	Signaller	R.E.	
CHAPMAN, WM. O.	Edenderry Cot., Omagh	Private	R.A.M.C.	
CLARKE, JOHN	52 Tamar Street	R.M.L.I.	R.N.	
COULTER, THOMAS	6 Glenvarlock Street	Driver	A.S.C.	
CONNOLLY, CHARLES	77 Belmont Church Rd.	Lance-Corporal	14th R.I.R.	W'ded and Pris.
COCHRANE, MATT.	31 Finvoy Street	3rd A.M.	R.A.F.	
DALTON, JOHN	120 Bloomfield Avenue	Sergeant	R.G.A.	
DICKSON, JAMES	34 Avondale Street	Sergeant	Chinese Labour Corps	
DUNCAN, LOWRY S.	Vive Villas Up. N'ards R.	Temp. Captain	12th R.I.R.	M.C. and bar, W'd, Order de Leopold and Croix-de-G.
EDWARDS, ANDREW	9 Roseberry Street	Corporal	Grenadier Guards	
ELDER, ROBERT C.	31 Bread Street East	Stoker	R.N.	Lost in Jutland B.
ELLISON, ROBERT G.	7 Elmdale Street	C.Q.M.S.	R. Irish Fus.	Wounded.
ELLISON, WM. S.	7 Elmdale Street	Driver	R.F.A.	
GLENDINNING, ROBERT A.	116 My Lady's Road	Private	10th R.I.R.	
GORDON, WILLIAM	17 Moorgate Street	Engineer	R.N.	Medal and Bar.
GRAHAM, ANDREW	57 Montrose Street	Private	19th R.I.R.	
GRAY, FREDK.	17 Carew Street	Private	8th R.I.R.	
GRAY, HENRY	17 Carew Street	Private	1 R. Inn. Fus.	
GRAY, SAMUEL	17 Carew Street	Private	1 R. Inn. Fus.	Killed in Action.
GRAY, WM.	11 Clara Crescent		R.N.	
GRAY, HENRY	12 Carew Street		School of Marine Observers	
GREEN, FREDK.	88 Dunraven Avenue	Private	2nd R.I.R.	
GREGG, JOSEPH	90 Bread Street East	Private		
HENDRY, JAMES	49 Cheviot Avenue	Lance-Corporal	R.E.	
HENDRY, WILLIAM	49 Cheviot Avenue	Private	5th R. Inn. Fus.	
HOUSTON, THOS.	23 Cyprus Gardens	Lieutenant	1st R. Irish Fus.	M.C., Prisoner.
JACKSON, HENRY	436 Newtownards Rd.	Private	8th R.I.R.	
JACKSON, JAMES	436 Newtownards Road	Gunner	Mechanical Transport	
JOHNSTON, ALBERT	22 Ulsterdale Street	A.B.	R.N.	
KELLS, ROBERT	25 Kerrsland Crescent	Corporal R.M.L.I.	R.N.	Wounded.
KERR, HUGH SLOAN	40 Martinez Avenue	E.R.A., R.N.R.	R.N.	Killed in Action.
LAIRD, ALEX.	151 Belmont Road	Private	R.E.	Killed in Action.
LECKY, DAVID	29 Welland Street	Private	R. Inn. Fus.	Wounded.
LEMON, THOS. J.	33 Moorgate Street	Driver	A.S.C.	

BELFAST PRESBYTERY. BLOOMFIELD.

Name.	Home Address.	Rank.	Regiment, Battalion or Unit.	Remarks.
Miness, Harold	45 Lichfield Avenue	P.O.	R.N.	
Moore, Alex.	1 Erskine Street	A.B.	R.N.	
Moore, Henry	1 Erskine Street	C.Q.M.S.	16th R.I.R.	Gassed.
Morrison, Fredk.	1 Cyprus Park	Lieutenant	R.I.R.	Wounded.
Morrison, Samuel	1 Cyprus Park	Lieutenant	1/25 London Regt.	
Morrison, Wm. A.	52 Dunraven Avenue	Private	8/9 R.I.R.	
Morrison, Ernest W.	52 Dunraven Avenue	Private	8/9 R.I.R.	
Morrison, Sydney	52 Dunraven Avenue	Private	3rd Hussars	
Munn, John	Roslyn, North Road		R.A.M.C.	
McAllen, George	75 Grove Street East	Private	10th R.I.R.	Killed in Action.
McBurney, Henry C.	10 Oakland Avenue	Sapper	R.E.	
McCurdy, James W.	8 Grace Avenue	Private	17 Cyclist Batt.	
McCullough, Stanley	22 Bloomfield Street	Wireless Operator	R.A.F.	
McDowell, Wm. J.	26 Cyprus Park	Lieutenant	15th R.I.R.	M.C., Wounded.
McGimpsey, Malcolm	20 Woodcot Avenue	Stoker	R.N.	
McGimpsey, John	20 Woodcot Avenue	Private	18th R.I.R.	
McIntyre, Albert	Finnary, North Road	Private	R.A.F.	
McKelvey, Robert	124 Hyndford Street	Lieutenant	1/6 R. Highlanders	M.M., Wounded.
McMaster, Chas.	Rose Lodge, U. N'ards Rd.	Captain	7th R.I.R.	Killed in Action.
McMaster, Lendrick	Rose Lodge, U. N'ards Rd.	Lieutenant	16th R.I.R.	Wounded.
Patton, James	23 Bloomfield Street	Private	10th R.I.R.	Wounded.
Peck, George	13 Ravenscroft Avenue	E.R.A.	R.N.	
Primrose, David	110 Bryson Street	Cyclist	36 Signalling Corps	
Quinleven, John	85 Bread Street East	Private	R.E.	
Reid, John	137 Hyndford Street	Private	R.F.A.	
Ritchie, David	Ogstonville Earlswood R.	Dispenser	R.A.M.C.	
Robinson, Joseph	7 Cheviot Street	Joiner	R.N.	
Rowan, Robert	311 Albertbridge Road	Private	3 Seaforth Highldrs.	
Ruddock, Samuel	44 Mayflower Street	Private	8th R.I.R.	
Saunders, Wm.	6 Chater Street	Private		Died.
Shields, David W.	96 Dunraven Avenue	Private	8th R.I.R.	Killed in Action.
Smith, Arthur P.	Wellington, Wingrove Gds.	Lieutenant	14th R.I.R.	Wded, Men. in Des.
Steele, Alex. K.	58 Lichfield Avenue	Lance-Corporal	14th R.I.R.	
Steele, Joseph	58 Lichfield Avenue	E.R.A.	R.N.	
Stewart, James	9 Manderson Street	Private	8th R.I.R.	
Stewart, Wm.	59 Isoline Street	Private	2 R.I. Fus.	
Stirling, Albert	5 Greenville Avenue	Private	R.A.F.	
Stuart, James D.	2 Woodcot Avenue	Private	16th R.I.R.	
Tate, Allen	65 Island Street	Sapper	R.E.	
Tate, George	65 Island Street	Corporal	R.I.R.	
Taylor, Richard		Signaller	18th R.I.R.	
Thompson, George	12 Kensington Avenue	Lance-Corporal		Killed in Action.
Todd, Robert J.	1 Greenville Avenue	Private	20th R.I.R.	Died on Service.
Walker, John	Hawarden	Despatch Rider	A.S.C.	
Wright, Fredk. J.	19 Bloomfield Street	Sergeant	Huzzars	Killed in Action.
Wylie, Fredk.	8 Factory Street	Private	R.E.	
COLONIAL FORCES.				
Jackson, Hugh	83 Cheviot Avenue	Private	49th Canadians	Killed in Action.
Stuart, Wm.	2 Woodcot Avenue	Sergeant	26th Can. E.F.	
BROADWAY.				
Adamson, George	555 Donegall Road	Private	Seaforth Highldrs.	Wounded.
Adamson, Wm.	555 Donegall Road	Lance-Corporal	14th R.I.R.	
Anderson, James	Lecale Street	Private	Machine Gun Corps	Wounded.
Anderson, T.	15 Rockmore Road	Driver	R.E.	
Anderson, W.	38 Broadway	Driver	A.S.C.	
Baxter, N.	251 Mayo Street	Driver	R.E.	
Black, James	93 Donegall Avenue	Private	9th R.I.R.	Killed in Action.
Black, James		Private	A.S.C.	
Brady, Robert	563 Donegall Road	Private	R.E.	
Burns, W. J.	549 Donegall Road	Rifleman	10th R.I.R.	
Carnegie, T.	Willowbank, Falls Rd.	Sergeant	13th Hussars	Conduct Medal.
Clarke, A.	22 Irwell Street	Corporal	15th R.I.R.	W'ded and Pris.
Clarke, H.	22 Irwell Street	Private	10th R.I.R.	Killed in Action.
Clarke, W.	22 Irwell Street	Driver	A.S.C.	
Collins, D.	Maryburn, Andersonstown	Private	Black Watch	Killed in Action.
Coulter, John	Norfolk Drive	Sapper	R.E.	Wounded.
Coulter, Joseph	Norfolk Drive	Driver	R.E.	Wounded.
Davidson, George	Lake Glen	Private	10th R.I.R., A.S.C.	
Davidson, Jas.	Lake Glen	Private	R.E.	Died of Wounds.
Davidson, T.	Lake Glen	Air Mechanic	R.A. Force	
Davidson, W. M.	St. James's Park	Private	A.S.C.	
Dawson, C.	356 Donegall Road	Private	5th R.I.R.	Wounded.
Dawson, George	356 Donegall Road	Driver	10th R.I.R.	
Dawson, H. B.	356 Donegall Road	Rifleman	10th R.I.R.	
Dawson, R. J.	356 Donegall Road	Signaller	10th R.I.R.	
Dodds, —	23 Rockview Street	Private	10th R.I.R.	Wounded.
Doherty, Isaac	Braemar Street	Rifleman	9th R.I.R.	
Donaghy, A.	Rockview Street	Rifleman	10th R.I.R.	Wounded.
Donning, Harold	25 Roden Street	Private	14th R.I.R.	
Duffield, Harry	Ballyhackamore	Private	A.S.C.	

BELFAST PRESBYTERY. BROADWAY.

Name.	Home Address.	Rank.	Regiment, Battalion, or Unit.	Remarks.
Duffield, Hugh	Ballyhackamore	Staff-Sergeant	A.S.C.	
Dynes, George	8 Lecale Street	Private	10th R.I.R.	
Dynes, John	8 Lecale Street	Private	9th R.I.R.	Killed in Action.
Foster, John	38 Thames Street	Private	17th R.I.R.	
Getty, James	Clondara Terrace	Private	R.F.C.	
Gordon, C. D.	14 Milner Street	Sergeant	R.E.	
Graham, A.	3 Broadway	Bugler	17th R.I.R.	
Graham, E.	3 Broadway	Signaller	10th R.I.R.	
Graham, John	8 Brighton Street	Shipwright	R.N.	
Gray, D.	224 Grosvenor Road	Shipwright	R.N.	
Gray, R.	224 Grosvenor Road	Sergeant	10th R.I.R.	
Gray, Constable	Springfield Rd. Barracks	Private	10th R.I.R.	Killed in Action.
Hall, A.	39 Thames Street	Lance-Corporal	R.A.M.C.	Prisoner.
Hall, A. W.	2 Irwell Street	Driver	10th R.I.R.	
Hall, Isaac	39 Thames Street	Private	8th Machine Gun Corps	
Hoy, Samuel	Ballydownfine	Private	R.I.R.	Killed in Action.
Heenan, Thomas	34 Lecale Street	Stoker	R.N.	
Hill, D.	2 Thames Street	Rifleman	17th R.I.R.	
Hill, H.	2 Thames Street	Private	7th R. Sussex Regt.	
Holland, Geo.	Lawnbrook Avenue	Private	1st Cheshire Regt.	Prisoner.
Horner, George	Donegall Road	Private	Seaforth Highldrs.	Killed in Action.
Jackson, S.	Whiterock Road	Private	10th R.I.R.	
Johnston, Albert	Lake Glen	Private	Black Watch	
Johnston, Geo.	Euterpe Street	Co. Sergt.-Major	10th R.I.R.	
Johnston, William	Donegall Road	Private	N.I.H.	
Johnston, W. H.		Rifleman	R.I. Fus.	Wounded.
Kennedy, Wm.	64 Excise Street	Private	8th R.I.R.	W'ded & Pris.
Kerr, R.	11 Rockdale Street	Gunner	R.F.A.	
Laughlin, R.	24 Lecale Street	Private	10th Batt. Border Regt.	
Lucas, James	Braemar Street		R.I. Fus.	
Lucas, Joseph	Braemar Street		Tank Corps	
Lucas, Thomas	Braemar Street		10th R.I.R.	
McAllister, R.	7 Fallswater Street	Rifleman	10th R.I.R.	Wounded.
McAllister, S.	7 Fallswater Street	Private	R.A.M.C.	Killed.
McCracken, John	369 Donegall Road	Private	A.S.C.	
McCune, W. S.	Donegall Road	Private	2nd R.I. Fus.	
McDowell, John	15 Tennyson Street	Rifleman	12th R.I.R.	Killed in Action.
McFadden, John	Upton Cottages	Private	R.I. Fus.	Prisoner.
McGeagh, C.	229 Springfield Road	Rifleman	R.I.R.	
McGowan, —	20 Braemar Street	Sergeant	Machine Gun Corps	
McKee, G.	5 Broadway	Sergeant	9th Inn. Fus.	Wounded.
McKee, Samuel	5 Broadway	Private	14th R.I.R.	
McKee, W.	5 Broadway	Private	Dragoon Guards	
McKeen, W.	3 Brighton Street	Rifleman	10th R.I.R.	
McMillan N.	Nansen Street	Driver	A.S.C.	
McQuoid, James	Clondara Terrace	Corporal	A.S.C.	
McQuoid, Wm.	Clondara Terrace	Private	N.I.H.	
Magee, W.	Upton Cottages	Corporal	Black Watch	
Magill, A.	19 Rockdale Street	Private	10th R.I.R.	
Maguire, James	17 Drew Street	Private	R.E.	
Marshall, W.	60 Braemar Street	Rifleman	10th R.I.R.	Killed in Action.
Martin, H.	36 Broadway	Driver	M.G. Corps	
Mercer, G.	Irwell Street	Sergeant	17th R.I.R.	
Millen, Ashley	107 Roden Street	Private	15th R.I.R.	Died Pris. in G.
Millen, Ernest	107 Roden Street	Sergeant	15th R.I.R.	
Millen, Nelson	40 Nansen Street	Sergeant	A.S.C.	
Millen, Thos.	107 Roden Street	Private	R. Marines	
Millar, Thos.	28 Broadway	Gunner	H.M.S. Majestic	Drowned.
Minford, George	19 Rockdale Street	Private		
Minford, John	19 Rockdale Street	Private	16th R.I.R.	
Moles, H.	11 Fallswater Street	Rifleman	10th R.I.R.	
Moody, S.	54 Coolfin Street	Gunner	M.G. Corps	
Moore, R.	56 Lecale Street	Private	10th R.I.R.	
Morrison, John	Andersonstown	Gunner	R.H.A.	
Montgomery, Joseph	64 Braemar Street	Rifleman	10th R.I.R.	Killed in Action.
Musgrave, F.	1 Rockmore Road	Driver	A.S.C.	
Morris, T.	20 Tavanagh Street	Private	10th R.I.R.	
Nutt, Alex.	70 Maryville Street	Private	10th R.I.R.	
Nutt, James	23 Islandbawn Street	Sergeant	E. Lancashire Regt.	
Nutt, Mark	70 Maryville Street	Private	10th R.I.R.	Killed in Action.
Nutt, Robert	70 Maryville Street	Private	10th R.I.R.	
Ogilvie, J.	25 Fallswater Street	Driver	A.S.C.	
Purdy, Harry	15 Thames Street	Private	10th R.I.R.	Killed in Action.
Purdy, W.	15 Thames Street	Rifleman	10th R.I.R.	
Rainey, T.	Andersonstown	Rifleman	10th R.I.R.	
Rainey, W.	Andersonstown	Private	M.T. A.S.C.	
Rankin, R.	58 Thames Street	Lance-Corporal	10th R.I.R.	
Reid, A.	571 Donegall Road	Driver	R.F.A.	
Reid, Joseph	571 Donegall Road	Private	10th R.I.R.	
Shannon, Jas.	Shankill Road	Private	N.I.H.	Wounded.
Shields, D.	215 Ainsworth Avenue	Private	M.T. A.S.C.	
Sinclair, Edward	36 Broadway	Private	10th R.I.R.	Killed in Action.
Sinclair, James	8 Thames Street	Private	7th R. Inn. Fus.	
Sinclair, James	35 Braemar Street	Private	4th R. Inn. Fus.	

BELFAST PRESBYTERY.   BROADWAY.

NAME.	HOME ADDRESS.	RANK.	REGIMENT, BATTALION OR UNIT.	REMARKS.
SMYTH, R.	15 Rockdale Street	Sapper	R.E.	
SPRATT, S. J.	Thames Street	Lance-Corporal	2nd R.I.R.	Killed in Action.
STEAD, H.	1 Irwell Street	Sergeant	A.S.C.	
STEWART, W.	29 Thames Street	Lance-Corporal	3rd R.I.R.	
TEDFORD, W.	23 Brassey Street	Private	M.T. A.S.C.	
THOMPSON, HERBERT	Andersonstown	Private	A.S.C.	Killed.
TODD, HAROLD	Lake Glen	Private	2nd Yorkshire Regt.	M.M., K'd in Act.
WATSON, THOMAS	Locan Street	Sergeant	M.G.C.	M.M., Wounded.
WALLWIN, H.	61 Braemar Street	Fitter	R.F.A.	
WILLIS, J. J.	1 Monarch Street	Corporal	10th R.I.R.	
WILSON, GEORGE	20 Irwell Street	Sapper	R.E.	
WILSON, JAMES	61 Braemar Street	Sapper	Depot Co.	
WILSON, T.	Donegall Road	Private	10th R.I.R.	
WRIGHT, ALEX.	Upton Cottages	Farrier	11th R.I.R.	
WHARRY, JAMES	30 Thames Street	Private	11th R.I.R.	Died in France.
COLONIAL FORCES.				
ANDERSON, JAMES	38 Broadway		46th Canadians	Killed in Action.
CARNEGIE, J.	Willowbank, Falls Road	Sapper	Can. Engineers	
McCRACKEN, S.	359 Donegall Road	Private	27th Canadians	Killed in Action.
MAGILL, J.	Lower Broadway	Private	Can. M.G. Corps	
MARTIN, J.	36 Broadway	Private	11th Can. M.G. Corps	
MARTIN, W.	36 Broadway	Private	3rd Can. M.G. Corps	
CARNMONEY.				
ABERNETHY, ISRAEL	Carnmoney	Rifleman	12th Batt. R.I.R.	Wounded.
ANDREWS, WILLIAM	Carnmoney	Rifleman	12th Batt. R.I.R.	Died of Wounds.
BARNETT, DANIEL	Carnmoney	Rifleman	12th Batt. R.I.R.	
BARR, ANDREW	Carnmoney	Private	R.A.M.C.	
BARR, WM. JOHN	Carnmoney	Rifleman	14th Batt. R.I.R.	Wounded.
BEATTY, DAVID	Ballyearl	2nd Lieutenant	R.N.V.R.	Killed.
BEGGS, JAMES	Glengormley	Corporal	12th Batt. R.I.R.	
BEGGS, ROBERT	Whitewell	Rifleman	12th Batt. R.I.R.	
BLAIN, JOHN	Carnmoney	Rifleman	12th Batt. R.I.R.	Wounded.
BLAIR, SAMUEL	Mossley	Corporal	12th Batt. R.I.R.	Wounded.
BLAIR, WILLIAM	Mossley	Rifleman	12th Batt. R.I.R.	
BOYD, ALEX.	Mossley	Rifleman	12th Batt. R.I.R.	
BOYD, DAVID	Mossley	Lance-Corporal	R.E.	
BRADLEY, ROBERT	Carntall	Sergeant	2nd Inn. Fus.	
BRENNAN, JAMES	Carnmoney	Rifleman	12th Batt. R.I.R.	Missing.
BRYSON, JOSIAS	Ballyduff	Sergt.-Major	12th Batt. R.I.R.	Wounded.
BURNEY, WILLIAM	Carnmoney	Lance-Corporal	A.S.C.	
CALDWELL, JAMES	Ballyduff	Sergeant	12th Batt. R.I.R.	Killed.
CALDWELL, ROBERT	Ballyduff	Private	R.E.	
CURRIE, SAMUEL	Ballyhenry	Driver	R.E.	
DARRAGH, GEORGE	Mossley	Engineer	R.N. Transport Ser.	
DARRAGH, WILLIAM	Mossley	Lance-Corporal	12th Batt. R.I.R.	Wounded.
DAVIDSON, JAMES	Glengormley	Rifleman	16th Batt. R.I.R.	
DAVIDSON, JAS. JOHNSTON	Carnmoney	Rifleman	9th Batt. R.I.R.	
DAVIDSON, JOHN	Glengormley	Rifleman	2nd Batt. R.I. Fus.	
DAVIDSON, LAURENCE	Glengormley	Rifleman	12th Batt. R.I.R.	Wounded.
DAVIDSON, WM.	Glengormley	Lance-Corporal	16th Batt. R.I.R.	
DUNLOP, ALEC.	Carnmoney	Rifleman	12th Batt. R.I.R.	Wounded.
DUNN, JEREMIAH	Mossley	Lance-Corporal	R.E.	Wounded.
DUNN, WM. B.		Driver	A.S.C.	
FARQUAHAR, JOHN	Monkstown	Corporal	R. Inn. Fus.	Wounded.
FORSYTHE, JAMES	Carnmoney	Rifleman	12th Batt. R.I.R.	Killed.
FORSYTHE, THOMAS	Carnmoney	Rifleman	12th Batt. R.I.R.	Wounded.
FORSYTHE, WM.	Carnmoney	Lance-Corporal	20th Batt. R.I.R.	
GIHON, ANDREW	Whitewell	Private	A.S.C.	
GILLESPIE, JOHN	Ballyvesey	Seaman	R.N.	
GILLESPIE, WM.	Ballyvesey	Rifleman	12th Batt. R.I.R.	Wounded.
GORDON, JOHN	Whitewell	Lance-Corporal	1st Batt. Inn. Fus.	Killed.
HAMILL, THOMAS	Ballyhenry	Rifleman	12th Batt. R.I.R.	
HAMILL, THOS., JUN.	Ballyvesey	Rifleman	12th Batt. R.I.R.	
HAMILTON, JAMES	Carnmoney	Rifleman	12th Batt. R.I.R.	Invalided home.
HERON, ROBERT		Private	R. Flying Corps	
HOUSTON, DR. JOHN CARSON	Jordanstown	Captain	R.A.M.C.	
HOUSTON, WM. WYLIE	Jordanstown	2nd Lieutenant	R.E.	Killed.
HUNTER, ANDREW	Carnmoney	Lance-Corporal	12th Batt. R.I.R.	
HUNTER, JOSEPH	Carnmoney	Private	Seaforth Highldrs.	
JOHNSTON, WM. S.	Ballyduff	Gunner	R.N.	
KERR, ROBERT	Carnmoney	Private	A.S.C.	
KERR, THOS. JOSEPH	Mossley	Sergeant	R.F.A.	
LOUGHRIDGE, JOHN	Whitewell	Captain	R.A.M.C.	
LYLE, SAMUEL	Monkstown	Rifleman	12th Batt. R.I.R.	
LYLE, WILLIAM	Ballyvesey	Lieutenant	18th Batt. R.I.R.	
McCLEERY, JAMES	Mossley	Lance-Corporal	9th Batt. R.I.R.	Wounded.
McCOMBE, HUGH	Carnmoney	Gunner	R.F.A.	
McCREA, SAMUEL	Ballycraigy	Sergt.-Major	2nd R.I.R.	Wounded, D.C.M.
McCREA, WILLIAM	Ballycraigy	2nd Lieutenant	1st Rifle Brigade	Wounded, M.M.
McCULLOUGH, SAMUEL	Glengormley	Trooper	N.I. Horse	

BELFAST PRESBYTERY. **CARNMONEY.**

Name.	Home Address.	Rank.	Regiment, Battalion or Unit.	Remarks.
McGarrell, David J.	Monkstown	Seaman	R.N.	
McIlwaine, James	Carnmoney	Private	18th Batt. R.I.R.	
McKinlay, James	Whitewell	Trooper	N.I.H.	
McKinney, Thos. Geo.	Ballyvesey	Private	R. Fus.	Died of Wounds.
McMaster, Thos.	Whitewell	Rifleman	18th Batt. R.I.R.	
Manice, John	Ballyhenry	Rifleman	12th Batt. R.I.R.	Wounded.
Manice, Thos.	Ballyhenry	Corporal	Inn. Fus.	Wounded.
Manice, Wm.	Ballyhenry	Rifleman	12th Batt. R.I.R.	Wounded.
Menary, Charles	Ballyhenry	Lance-Corporal	14th Batt. R.I.R.	
Montgomery, John	Mossley	Rifleman	14th Batt. R.I.R.	
Montgomery, John	Mossley	Sergeant	North'land Fus.	
Montgomery, Robert	Mossley	Sergeant	12th Batt. R.I.R.	
Montgomery, Thos.	Mossley	Sergeant	A.V.C.	
Paisley, Joseph	Carnmoney	Private	10th Innis Fus	
Ramsey, Wm. John	Cloughfern	Rifleman	12th Batt. R.I.R.	Wounded, M.M.
Rea, Wm.	Mossley	Rifleman	12th Batt. R.I.R.	
Robb, David	Carnmoney	Rifleman	19th Batt. R.I.R.	
Robb, Hugh	Carnmoney	Private	Seaforth Highldrs.	Wounded.
Robb, Wm.	Carnmoney	Rifleman	2nd Batt. R.I.R.	Killed.
Robinson, John	Ballyduff	Rifleman	12th Batt. R.I.R.	Wounded.
Robinson, Joseph	Carntall	Rifleman	12th Batt. R.I.R.	
Robinson, Robert	Ballyduff	Private	Machine Gun	
Robinson, Samuel	Ballyduff	Rifleman	12th Batt. R.I.R.	Killed.
Smith, Henry	Carnmoney	Private	Seaforth Highldrs.	Killed.
Smith, Dr. James M.	Ballyhone	Captain	R.A.M.C.	
Stevenson, Joseph	Glengormley	Rifleman	12th Batt. R.I.R.	Wounded, M.M.
Stewart, John	Carnmoney	Stoker	R.N.	
Stewart, Joseph	Carnmoney	Rifleman	12th Batt. R.I.R.	Wounded.
Stewart, Wm.	Carnmoney	Rifleman	2nd Batt. R.I.R.	
Strange, Hugh	Ballyhenry	Rifleman	3rd Batt. R.I.R.	
Strange, Samuel	Ballyhenry	Trooper	N.I.H.	
Tate, James	Glengormley	Sergeant	11th Batt. R.I.R.	
Tate, Wm.	Glengormley	Sergeant	18th Batt. R.I.R.	
Watson, James	Ballycraigy	Sapper	R.E.	
Whittley, Gavin	King's Moss	Corporal	1st Inn. Fus.	Killed.
Wilson, Arthur	Carnmoney	Private	4th Inn. Fus.	
Wilson, Sydney	Mossley	Rifleman	12th Batt. R.I.R.	
Wiseman, Hubert	Carnmoney	O.D. Seaman	R.N.	
COLONIAL FORCES.				
Blair, Alex.	Mossley	Private	Canadians	Wounded.
Burney, Hugh Waterworth	Carnmoney	Private	Canadians	Killed.
Burney, Josias	Carnmoney	Sergeant	S. African M.R.	
Cunningham, Robert	Carntall	Private	Canadians	
Louden, James		Private	N.Z. Rifle Brigade	
Smith, George T.	Ballyhone	Trooper	N.Z. M. Inftry.	Wounded.
Smith, James	Hightown	Lance-Corporal	Can. Cameron Highldrs.	Wounded.
CASTLEREAGH.				
Aicken, William	Lower Castlereagh	Private	R.I.R.	Wounded.
Bennett, Samuel	Lower Castlereagh	Corporal	R.I.R.	Wounded.
Bennett, William	Lower Castlereagh	Private	R.I.R.	
Boyd, Claud	Knock Village	Private	R.I.R.	
Campbell, John Forsyth	City View, Cregagh	Sergeant	R.S.	Prisoner of War, Died of Wounds.
Campbell, Thomas	Castlereagh	Stoker	R.N.	
Campbell, George	Castlereagh	Private	R.I.R.	Wounded.
Carlile, George	3 Twickenham Street	Private	S.H.	M.M., K'd in Act.
Crawford, Herbert	Glenview, Carnamuck	2nd Lieutenant	5th Lancers	
Glover, James	Lower Castlereagh	Driver	R.F.A.	
Harvey, John Forsyth	Downshire Road	Captain	R.I.F.	Killed in Action.
Hedley, William	Ballykeel	Corporal	R.I.R.	Wounded.
Hewitt, David John	Castlereagh P.O.	Corporal	R.I.R.	Killed in Action.
Hewitt, James O'Neill	Ards View	Captain	R.I.F.	Croix-de-Guerre.
Jamison, James	Castlereagh	Rifleman	R.I.R.	Killed in Action.
Lamont, John	Lisleen	Trooper	N.I.H.	
McClune, William	Lower Castlereagh	Rifleman	R.I.R.	Wounded.
McClune, Hugh	Lower Castlereagh	Rifleman	R.I.R.	Wounded.
McClune, John	Lower Castlereagh	Rifleman	R.I.R.	Prisoner of War.
McKelvey, Robert	124 Hyndford Street	Private	R.B.W.	
McMinn, Samuel	Newtownbreda	Trooper	N.I.H.	Wounded.
McMinn, William	Newtownbreda	Private	Y.C.V.	Killed in Action.
Magill, John	Ballykeel	Rifleman	R.I.R.	Killed in Action.
McQuoid, James	23 Eversleigh Street	Petty Officer	R.N.	
Martin, John	Beechhill	Corporal	R.I.R.	Wounded.
Millar, John Forsythe	Castlereagh House	Sapper	R.D.R.	
Morrow, James A.	Newtownbreda	Rifleman	R.I.R.	Wounded.
Morrow, Jim	Newtownbreda	Rifleman	R.I.R.	Wounded.
Patterson, J. Clawson	5 South Parade	2nd Lieutenant	R.I.R.	
Patterson, Jack W.	5 South Parade	Private	R.I.R.	Wounded
Patterson, Harold J.	5 South Parade	Private	Y.C.V.	Killed in Action.
Rainey, James	Castlereagh	Trooper	N.I.H.	Wounded.

BELFAST PRESBYTERY. CASTLEREAGH.

Name.	Home Address.	Rank.	Regiment, Battalion or Unit.	Remarks.
Rainey, Robert	Crossnacreevy	Private	R.I.R.	Wounded.
Scott, William	Crossnacreevy	Driver	R.F.A.	
Smith, Thomas	35 Moneyrea Street	Private	R.I.R.	Wounded.
Smith, Walter	35 Moneyrea Street	Private	R.I.R.	W'ded & Pris. of W.
CASTLETON.				
Adair, Bryan	Loughview Villas	Sergt.-Major	Royal Rifles	
Anderson, James	5 Harrisburgh Street			
Anderson, Robert		Private	9th Inn. Fus.	Killed in Action.
Anderson, Wm.	127 Alexandra Park Av.	Engineer	R.N.	
Anderson, Wm.	20 Belmont Avenue	Private	Royal Rifles	
Anderson, Wm.	5 Harrisburg Street			
Baxter, Robert	Dee Street			
Beggs, Robert				
Bell, Wm.				
Best, John	2 Hogarth Street		R.N.	
Best, Samuel L.	2 Hogarth Street	Stoker	R.N.	
Black, Alex.	195 York Road			
Black, James	195 York Road			
Black, Robert	195 York Road	Driver	9th Batt R.I.R.	
Black, Thos.	195 York Road	Private	Infantry Brigade	
Bourke, Thos.	147 York Road			
Brecke, Edward	140 Cosgrave Street			
Brolly, William	4 Pittsburg Street	Corporal	2nd Inn. Fus.	Killed in Action.
Brooks, John	Skegoniel Street			
Brown, Alfred	1 Mountcollyer Avenue			
Brown, Fred.	1 Mountcollyer Avenue	Sapper	R.E.	
Brown, Wilfred	166 North Queen Street	Sapper	R.E.	
Brown, Wm. Ernest	166 North Queen Street		R.N.	
Bruce, George	46 Seaview Street			
Brymner, Robert	York Road	Sergeant	A.S.C.	
Carrick, Wm. Jas.	2 Victoria Gardens			
Coskery, Joseph	Hughenden Avenue			
Craig, Barton	108 Alexandra Park Av.	Driver	A.S.C.	
Craig, David	108 Alexandra Park Av.			
Craig, Robert		Gunner	R.F.A.	
Creighton, Wm. J.	Mt. Vernon Cottage	Private	Labour Corps	
Cullen, James	27 Glencollyer Street	Private	No. 1 Base Supply Depot	
Cullen, Thos.	27 Glencollyer Street	Driver	R.E.	
Cumming, Alex.	84 Mountcollyer Avenue			
Davidson, Wm.	183 Alexandra Park Av.			
Doak, Gerald	41 Glandore Avenue			
Douglas, John A.	6 Brougham Street			
Duff, John	15 Deacon Street	Lieutenant	1st Inn. Fus.	Killed in Action.
Dunlop, Alex.	Ritchie Street			
Dunlop, Samuel	Ritchie Street			
Dunlop, William John				
Elder, Charles	25 New North Queen St.	Trooper	N.I.H.	Killed in Action.
Elder, Wm.	25 New North Queen St.			
Fee, James	34 Harrisburg Street			
Fee, Samuel	34 Harrisburg Street	Stoker	R.N.	Killed in Action.
Ferguson, Henry		Rifleman	R.I.R.	
Ferguson, Wm.		Corporal		
Fraser, Wm.	Deerpark Avenue	2nd Lieutenant	B. Watch	Killed in Action.
Freebairn, Thos.		Engineer	Canadians	Killed in Action.
Fulton, John	108 Mountcollyer Street			
Glen, James	10 Queen Victoria Gdns.	Driver	R.I. Rifles	
Gray, Wm. C.	Cora-Linn, Cliftonville			
Guy, George	3 Ivan Street			
Guy, Wm.	3 Ivan Street			
Hamilton, Harry	1 Mineral Street	Stoker	R.N.	
Hamilton, James	1 Mineral Street			
Hamilton, R. J.	1 Mineral Street			
Heathwood, Joseph	Parkmount Street			
Hill, John		Private	R.I. Fus.	
Hillis, Joseph	143 Garmoyle Terrace			
Horner, George	7 New North Queen St.	Rifleman	R.I.R.	
Horner, Wm.	7 New North Queen St.	Stoker	R.N.	
Houston, John	42 Brougham Street	Private	R.I.R.	
Hunter, John				
Hunter, Nelson	31 Bute Street			
Hunter, Robert	41 New North Queen St.		Canadians	Killed in Action.
Hutchinson, Ronald	147 York Road		H.L.I.	Killed in Action.
Ingram, Samuel M.	Hanna Street			
Jamieson, John	52 Harrisburg Street	Sapper	R.E.	
Johnston, Henry	9 St. Vincent Street	Sapper	R.E.	
Johnston, John	9 St. Vincent Street			
Keenan, John				
Kennedy, John G.	Loughview Villas			
Kennedy, Joseph	4 Rokeby Villas			
Kennedy, Peter	30 Ritchie Street	Stoker	R.N.	Killed in Action.
Kennedy, Robt. Jas.				
Kennedy, Wm.				

BELFAST PRESBYTERY. CASTLETON.

Name.	Home Address.	Rank.	Regiment, Battalion or Unit.	Remarks.
Kirkwood, George	2 Alexandra Park Ave.	Private	14th R.I.R.	Killed in Action.
Lunn, George	57 Seaview Street	...	...	...
McPhelimey, Robert	Hollywood View Terrace	...	...	...
McAuley, Robert	12 Deacon Street	...	...	...
McBride, Robert	35 Glasgow Street	...	...	...
McBride, Thos. H.	35 Glasgow Street	...	...	...
McBride, Victor	35 Glasgow Street	Private	R.I.R.	Killed in Action.
McBride, W. J.	35 Glasgow Street	...	...	...
McCall, Samuel	Gainsboro' Drive	Private	14th R.I.R.	Killed in Action.
McCallum, A.	Alexandra Avenue	...	...	...
McCann, Frank	23 Glasgow Street	...	...	...
McCann, James	25 Ritchie Street	Lance-Corporal	1st Inn. Fus.	Killed in Action.
McCartney, James	103 Alexandra Park Av.	...	...	...
McClure, Samuel J.	Whiteabbey	Gunner	R.F.A.	Killed in Action.
McClure, Thos. J.	Rosalee, Whiteabbey	...	...	...
McCrea, Hedley V.	7 Fortview Terrace	...	...	...
McCullough, John	Gara Terrace	...	...	...
McGarvey, Thomas	46 Seaview Street	...	...	...
McGirr, W. J.	107 Glencollyer Street	...	...	...
McKee, James	26 Fife Street	...	...	...
McKelvey, Jack	Loughview Villas	...	...	...
McKeown, Hugh	19 Gainsboro Drive	...	...	...
McKnight, Henry	38 Rowan Street	...	...	...
McKnight, James	38 Rowan Street	...	...	...
McKnight, John	38 Rowan Street	...	...	...
McKnight, Samuel	38 Rowan Street	...	...	...
McKnight, Thomas	38 Rowan Street	...	...	...
McKnight, Wm.	37 Ship Street	...	...	...
McMeekin, Thomas	Mountcollyer Street	Rifleman	15th R.I.R.	Killed in Action.
McNabb, Hugh	Mountcollyer Street	...	...	...
McVeigh, S.	17 Crosscollyer Street	...	...	...
Magill, James	35 Up. Canning Street	...	...	...
Mawhinney, Samuel	Cosgrave Street	...	...	...
Melvin, George	15 Ivan Street	...	...	...
Millar, Harry	78 Fortwilliam Parade	...	...	...
Millar, Herbert	78 Fortwilliam Parade	...	...	...
Millar, William	30 Atlantic Avenue	...	...	...
Moody, Arnold	16 Moyola Street	Private	R.M.L.I.	...
Moody, David	16 Moyola Street	Signaller	15th Batt. R.I.R.	...
Moody, Wm.	16 Moyola Street	Private	R.I.R.	...
Moore, Hugh	Weaver Street	Private	...	...
Moore, Robert	33 Gainsboro' Drive	Private	R.I.R.	...
Moore, Samuel	33 Gainsboro' Drive	Private	R.I.R.	...
Murdock, John	...	...	15th R.I.R.	Killed in Action.
Murdough, James	Fife Street	...	...	...
Murdough, Richard	Fife Street	...	...	...
Myers, Alex.	Fife Street	...	...	...
Myers, Wm.	Fife Street	...	...	...
Myers, Walter S.	48 Fife Street	Sapper	R.E.	Killed in Action.
Neill, James	59 Victoria Terrace	...	...	...
Neill, William	59 Victoria Terrace	...	...	...
Nelson, William	Seaview Street	Sapper	R.E.	Killed in Action.
Nesbitt, John	40 Parkmount Street	...	...	...
Palmer, John	York Road	Sergeant	2nd R.I.R.	Killed in Action.
Park, James	77 Mountcollyer Rd.	...	...	...
Partington, John	131 Alexandra Park Av.	...	...	...
Patterson, William	York Road	...	...	...
Pollock, David	...	Rifleman	15th R.I.R.	Killed in Action.
Pollock, James	Deacon Street	...	...	...
Pollock, Smyth	Deacon Street	...	...	...
Pratt, Wm.	Harrisburgh Street	...	...	...
Reid, James	28 Rowan Street	...	1st Inn. Fus.	Killed in Action.
Robinson, James	Mineral Street	...	...	...
Robinson, Thomas	Mineral Street	...	R.E.	Killed in Action.
Rosbottom, Thomas	Ayr Street	...	...	...
Scott, Wm.	...	...	R.N.	Killed in Action.
Semple, Robert	Alexandra Park Ave.	...	...	...
Seymour, Hugh	197 York Road	...	...	...
Smith, Alex.	Lansdowne Road	Private	14th R.I.R.	Killed in Action.
Smith, Wm.	Lansdowne Road	...	...	...
Spence, James	Shore Road	Rifleman	12th R.I.R.	Killed in Action.
Steel, Alex.	...	...	...	Killed in Action.
Stewart, Robert	...	...	...	...
Stone, William	Seaview Street	...	...	...
Thompson, S. B.	5 Seaview Street	...	...	...
Trimble, A.	1 York Road	...	...	...
Trimble, H.	1 York Road	...	...	...
Trimble, John	1 York Road	...	...	...
Vance, James	22 St. Vincent Street	...	...	...
Walker, Andrew	Glasgow Street	...	R.E.	Killed in Action.
Walker, John	Glasgow Street	...	...	...
Waring, James	5 Loughview Villas	...	...	...
Waring, John	5 Loughview Villas	...	...	...
Watson, John Alex.	10 Deacon Street	...	...	...

BELFAST PRESBYTERY.   CASTLETON.

Name.	Home Address.	Rank.	Regiment, Battalion or Unit.	Remarks.
Watson, W. H.	10 Deacon Street	...	...	...
Williamson, John	Dee Street	...	...	...
Williamson, Samuel	Dee Street	...	9th R.I.R.	Killed in Action.
Williamson, Wm.	Dee Street	...	...	...
Worlin, W. J.	...	...	N.F.	...
Wright, John	38 Seaview Street	...	...	Killed in Action.
Young, John	19 St. Aubyn Street	...	...	...
CLIFTON STREET.				
Adair, Ernest	1 Gt. Patrick Street	Trooper	N.I.H.	Wounded.
Adair, Ernest J.	35 Bedeque Street	Private	R.I. Rifles	Wounded.
Adair, Graham	1 Gt. Patrick Street	Private	R. Inn. Fus.	Wounded.
Adair, Robert	1 Gt. Patrick Street	Sergeant	R. Inn. Fus.	Killed in Action.
Aicken, David	3 Thistle Street, Dundee	Armr. Staff-Sergeant	A.O. Corps	
Anderson, Cecil W.	3 Thorndale Avenue	Private	R.I. Rifles	
Archibald, James	8 Thorndale Avenue	Sapper	R.E.	
Armstrong, Andrew	5 Dundee Street	Private	R.I. Rifles	
Armstrong, Robert	59 Mayo Street	Private	R.I. Rifles	Wounded.
Auld, Archie	25 Dagmar Street	Private	R.I. Rifles	
Ball, David	59 Humber Street	Private	R.I. Rifles	Wounded.
Ball, Hugh	60 Wigton Street	Bugler	R.I. Rifles	
Ball, John	5 Hanover Street	Private	R.I. Rifles	
Beattie, Robert	49 Silvio Street	Private	R.I. Fus.	Wounded.
Bothwell, James	64 Israel Street	Private	R.E.	
Bothwell, John	64 Israel Street	A.B.	R.N.	
Boyle, Alex.	4 London Street	Private	R.I. Rifles	
Brizzell, Samuel	12 Trafalgar Street	Private	R.E.	Killed in Action.
Brizzell, William	12 Trafalgar Street	Private	R.I. Rifles	Killed in Action.
Brown, James	47 Jersey Street	Private	R.I. Rifles	
Cairns, Samuel	19 North Ann Street	Private	Irish Guards	Wounded.
Campbell, James	17 Derry Street	Gunner	R.F.A.	
Carton, James	7 Singleton Street	Private	R.I. Rifles	D.C.M.
Childs, Edward	43 Paxton Street	Driver	R.F.A.	
Childs, James	43 Paxton Street	Gunner	R.F.A.	
Cinnamon, James	27 Mayo Street	Private	R.I. Rifles	
Colquhoun, David	6 Broadbent Street	Corporal	R.I. Rifles	
Colquhoun, James	6 Broadbent Street	Sapper	R.E.	
Colquhoun, William	6 Broadbent Street	Private	R.I. Rifles	
Cox, James	15 Broadbent Street	Stoker	R.N.	
Craig, David	4 Denmark Street	Private	M.T. A.S.C.	
Cree, William	21 Denmark Street	Corporal	R.I. Rifles	
Cunningham, Thomas	33 Drew Street	Coy. Sergt.-Major	R. Inn. Fus.	Wounded.
Curry, Saml. J.	8 Walton Street	Private	R.I. Rifles	
Doake, Samuel J.	7 Cosgrave Street	Private	R.I. Rifles	
Douglas, John	24 Bradford Street	Sergeant	R.I. Rifles	
English, Alex.	60 Foreman Street	Private	R. Inn. Fus.	Killed in Action.
Ellison, William	38 Warkworth Street	Corporal	R.I. Rifles	
Gibson, John	12 Trafalgar Street	Private	R.I. Rifles	
Gillespie, Robt. F.	64 Clanchattan Street	Trooper	N.I.H.	
Gourley, William	3 Sunwich Street	Private	R.I. Rifles	Wounded.
Harper, Gibson	40 Up. Townsend Street	Driver	M.T. A.S.C.	
Harper, Thomas	99 Northumberland St.	Private	R.I. Rifles	
Harper, William	40 Up. Townsend Street	Private	R.I. Rifles	
Hart, James	71 Hopeton Street	Private	R.I. Rifles	
Hart, William	71 Hopeton Street	Driver	A.S.C.	
Henderson, John	36 Linfield Road	Private	R.I. Rifles	
Hill, Thos. John	37 Eastland Street	Private	R.I. Rifles	
Hill, Thos. Joseph	37 Eastland Street	Private	King's Liverpool Regt.	
Houston, Wright	53 Dagmar Street	Sergeant	A.V. Corps	
Hunter, Thomas	80 Old Lodge Road	Private	R. Inn. Fus.	Killed in Action.
Hunter, William J.	80 Old Lodge Road	Private	R.I. Rifles	
Jordan, Thos. L.	34 Hogarth Street	Private	R. Inn. Fus.	
Kelso, George	24 Court Street	2nd Engineer	R.N.A.S.	
Kelso, Joseph	65 Penrith Street	Private	R.I. Rifles	Wounded.
Kirk, James	10 Coyle Street	Stoker	R.N.	
Kirk, Matthew	10 Coyle Street	Private	R.I. Rifles	Died of Wounds, Prisoner of War.
Kirkwood, James	32 Up. Canning St.	Private	R.I. Rifles	Wounded.
Laird, Joseph	20 Bandon Street	Private	Seaforth Highlanders	
Lea, Claude M.	6 Edenderry Gardens	Lieutenant	Machine Gun Corps	Wounded.
Lochart, James	46 Vistula Street	Private	R. Inn. Fus.	
Lochart, William	46 Vistula Street	Driver	R.E.	
Lowden, Norman	3 Easton Avenue	2nd Lieutenant	T.M. Battery	Killed in Action.
Lowden, Sydney	3 Easton Avenue	Lieutenant	West Yorks Regt.	Wounded.
Lyle, John	83 Wall Street	Private	R.I. Rifles	
Maguire, Robert	9 Harrybrook Street	Private	R.I. Rifles	
Majury, Andrew	19 Castle Lane	Private	Black Watch	
Majury, Thomas	19 Castle Lane	Sergeant	N.I.H.	
Matthews, William	26 Regent Street	Driver	R.F.A.	
Mitchell, John	262 Crimea Street	Corporal	M.F. Police	Wounded.
Morrow, Edwin E.	44 Clifton Street	2nd Lieutenant	R.F. Corps	
McClean, Alex.	72 Hopeton Street	Private	R.F. Corps	
McConnell, David J.	10 Glentilt Place	Private	A.S.C.	

BELFAST PRESBYTERY. **CLIFTON STREET.**

Name.	Home Address.	Rank.	Regiment, Battalion or Unit.	Remarks.
McCormick, James	23 Leadbetter Street	Driver	A.S.C.	
McCormick, Samuel	23 Leadbetter Street	Driver	A.S.C.	
McCormick, William J.	23 Leadbetter Street	Private	R.I. Rifles	Killed in Action.
McIlwaine, Alex.	44 McClure Street	Sapper	R.E.	Wounded.
McIvor, Lawrence	8 Walton Street	Private	R.I. Rifles	
McKenzie, Albert	Ashley View,	Trooper	N.I.H.	Wounded.
McKenzie, David	Ashley View	Driver	R.A.M.C.	
McKenzie, Wm. J.	Cliftonville Circus	Trooper	N.I.H.	Wounded.
McRoberts, Hugh	36 Victoria Gardens	Sergeant	R.E.	Awarded Croix-de-Guerre.
Nesbitt, Robert W.	6 Athol Street	Sapper	R.E.	
Nesbitt, Joseph, T.C.	6 Athol Street	Private	Grenadier Guards	
Orr, James B.	25 Dock Street	Trooper	5th Hussars	
Orr, William D.	25 Dock Street	Gunner	R.F.A.	
Patterson, Robert	5 Alaska Street	Private	R.I. Rifles	Died.
Perry, James	40 Regent Street	Sergeant	M.F. Police	Wounded.
Priestley, James R.	46 Old Lodge Road	Sergt.-Major	R. Munster Fus.	Wounded.
Priestley, William A.	46 Old Lodge Road	Private	A.S.C.	
Rainey, Alex.	72 Limestone Road	Private	7th Northants Regt.	Killed in Action.
Rainey, Hugh	72 Limestone Road	Driver	M.T. A.S.C.	
Rainey, William	72 Limestone Road	Trooper	S.I. Horse	
Rainey, Willaim	63 Bristol Street	2nd Lieutenant	R.I. Rifles	
Rea, Hugh	40 Sunnyside Street	Private	A.S.C.	
Reid, Francis C.	120 Old Lodge Road	Private	R.I. Rifles	
Richmond, Alex.	66 Foreman Street	Private	R. Irish Fus.	
Richmond, Henry	66 Foreman Street	Private	R.E.	
Savage, Wm. J.	39 Havana Street	2nd Lieutenant	R.I. Rifles	
Sayles, James P.	42 Cardigan Drive	2nd Lieutenant	R.I. Rifles	Wounded.
Service, David	98 Snugville Street	Corporal	R.A.M.C.	M.M.
Stevenson, Henry	24 Shaftesbury Avenue	Private	8th Welsh Regt.	Wounded.
Stevenson, John	24 Shaftesbury Avenue	Lance-Corporal	R.A.M.C.	
Stevenson, Thomas	24 Shaftesbury Avenue	Private	R.I. Rifles	
Stevenson, Joseph	31 Tennent Street	Private	R.I. Rifles	Killed in Action.
Storey, Thomas H.	28 Fairview Street	Corporal	R.I. Rifles	M.M.
Taylor, James	35 Ruth Street	A.B.	R.N.	
Telford, James	11 Summerhill Street	Stoker	R.N.	
Templeton, Robert M.	7 Alaska Street	Private	R.I. Rifles	Killed in Action.
Thompson, John	99 Crimea Street	Private	R.I. Rifles	
Thompson, Samuel	7 Boyne Street	Private	East Lanc. Regt.	
Warnock, Thomas	228 Conway Street	Driver	A.S.C.	
Wright, John	105 St. Leonards Street	Private	R.I. Rifles	Killed in Action.
Young, James	76 Hanover Street	Driver	A.S.C.	
COLONIAL & U.S.A. FORCES.				
Adair, Hugh	1 Gt. Patrick Street	Private	Canadian Inft.	
Armstrong, James	Cliftonville Circus	Private	South Africa Regt.	
Armstrong, Robert	6 Hanover Street	Private	Canadian Inft.	Wounded.
Houston, Fred	28 Albertville Drive	Private	Canadian Inft.	Wounded.
Jamison, Caulfield	5 Agnes Street	Private	Canadian Inft.	Wounded.
McMaster, David	83 Cromac Street	Sergeant	R.A.M.C., Canadian Forces	
Skelton, Wm. J.	139 Riga Street	Private	Canadian Inft.	Wounded.
Stevenson, Hugh	24 Shaftesbury Avenue	Sergeant	2nd Engineers, U.S.A. Forces	
CLIFTONVILLE.				
Adair, Henry	40 Shannon Street	Private	R.I.R.	
Adair, John	43 Shannon Street	Cook	R.N.	
Adams, John	5 Liffey Street	Private	R.I.R.	
Armstrong, Wm.	187 Up. Meadow Street	Private	N.I.H.	Wounded.
Baird, Alex.	80 Up. Meadow Street	Gunner	R.N.	Killed in Action.
Baird, David	80 Up. Meadow Street	Private	R.I.R.	Killed in Action.
Beatty, John	142 Manor Street	2nd Lieutenant	N.I.H.	
Bell, Geo.	28 Nore Street	Cadet	R.N.	
Bell, James	28 Nore Street	Private	R.I.R.	Died in Hospital.
Bell, Wm. Jas.	28 Nore Street	Private	R.I.R.	Killed in Action.
Black, Fred	6 Southport Street	Private	R.I.R.	Killed in Action.
Boyd, James S.	42 Indiana Avenue	Lance-Corporal	Black Watch	Killed in Action. Mons Star.
Boyle, David	13 Up. Charleville St.	Private	R.I.R.	
Brown, Wm.	41 Brookhill Avenue	Lance-Corporal	R.I.R.	
Calvert, Louis N.	Knutsford Drive	Private	R.I.R.	Killed in Action.
Calvert, Norman	Knutsford Drive	Private	R.I.R.	
Calvert, Wm.	Knutsford Drive	2nd Lieutenant	R.I.R.	Killed in Action.
Campbell, William	21 Summerhill Street	Lance-Corporal	R.I.R.	
Carson, John	294 Crumlin Road	2nd Lieutenant	N.I.H.	
Chapman, W. O.	6 Clifton Crescent	Private	R.A.M.C.	
Chase, Nubie	47 Mountview Street	A.B.S.	R.N.	
Clements, W. H.	Knutsford Drive	2nd Lieutenant	Dublin Fus.	Killed in Action.
Coleman, W. J.	5 Southport Street	Private	R.I.R.	
Crawford, J. R.	9 Cliftonville Avenue	Captain	Black Watch	
Crothers, Edwin	21 Albertville Drive	Private	R.A.M.C.	
Crozier, F. Howard	Brookhill Avenue	Sur. Sub-Lieuten'nt	R.N.V.R.	
Darragh, George	13 Up. Charleville St.	Corporal	R.I.R.	

BELFAST PRESBYTERY. CLIFTONVILLE.

Name.	Home Address.	Rank.	Regiment, Battalion or Unit.	Remarks.
Darragh, Hugh	13 Up. Charleville St.	Sergeant	R.I.R.	
Darragh, Kendal	11 Hopefield Avenue	2nd Lieutenant	R.I.R.	Wounded.
Darragh, Samuel	13 Up. Charleville St.	Private	R.I.R.	
Darragh, William	13 Up. Charleville St.	Private	R.I.R.	
Donald, Samuel	33 Beechpark Street	Private	R.I.R.	
Dunlop, Stewart	Dunart, Kelvin Parade	Private	R.I.R.	
Eakin, John	15 Tavanagh Street	Transport Driver	A.S.C.	
Elliott, Samuel	31 Clifton Crescent	Private	R.I.R.	
Gailey, Norman	35 Atlantic Avenue	Private	R.I.R.	
Gaylor, Stanley	23 Groomsport Street	Lance-Corporal	R.I.R.	
Gray, H.	Vilette, Downshire Road	Trooper	N.I.H.	
Harrison, J.	6 Ashville, Skegoniel Av.	Private	N.A. Service	Cross of St. Michael Cross of St. Geo., D.C.M.
Horton, A.	Fitzroy Avenue	A.B.S.	R.N.	
Howard, F.	2 Elmgrove Villas	Private	R.I.R.	
Hull, R. B.	16 Cliftonville Road	Lieutenant	Welsh Fus.	
Hutchinson, Isaac	190 Cliftonville Road	Private	R.I.R.	
Johnston, E.	1 Hazelnut Street	Trooper	Lancers	
Johnston, John	7 Nore Street	Trooper	N.I.H.	
Johnston, John	7 Nore Street	Gunner	R.A.	
Kennedy, William	90 Cliftonpark Avenue	Sergeant	R.I.R.	
Kernohan, Wm.	225 Crumlin Road	A.B.S.	R.N.	
King, Norman	31 Cliftonville Road	Private	R.I.R.	Prisoner of War.
Kirkpatrick, Joseph	14 Liffey Street	Private	R.I.R.	Killed in Action.
Lindsay, Joseph	21 Shannon Street	Private	R.I.R.	Wounded.
Lyle, John	21 Nore Street	Sergeant	R.I.R.	Died.
Lyle, Samuel	21 Nore Street	Private	R.I.R.	
Mairs, D.	1 Strangemore Terrace	Major	A.S.C.	
Marshall, M. H.	12 Courtrai Street	Private	R.I.R.	
Millar, Harding	16 Easton Crescent	2nd Lieutenant	R.I.R.	Killed in Action.
Millar, Laurence	16 Easton Crescent	Private	R.I.R.	
Moffett, George	10 Derg Street	Sergeant	R.I.R.	
Moody, James	134 Hillman Street	Private	R.I.R.	
Morton, Bertie	7 Indiana Avenue	2nd Lieutenant	Black Watch	
McCullough, Archie	26 Newington Avenue	Private	R.I.R.	
McDowell, William	34 Derg Street	Engineer	R.N.	Killed in Action.
McGookin, W. D.	28 Newport Street	2nd Lieutenant	R.I.R.	K'd. in Act., D.S.M.
McGuiness, Henry	12 Courtrai Street	Private	R.I.R.	
Orr, F. E.	Old Cavehill Road	Private	R.I.R.	
Palmer, George			R.I.R.	
Palmer, Robert			R.I.R.	
Price, Henry	4 Up. Charleville Street	Trooper	N.I. Horse	
Purdy, Jas. H.	62 Cliftonpark Avenue	Private	R.I.R.	Killed in Action.
Purdy, J. C. M.	62 Cliftonpark Avenue	Engineer	R.N.	
Ross, James	17 Nore Street	Private	R.I.R.	
Ross, John	17 Nore Street	Private	R.I.R.	
Ross, T. G.	17 Nore Street	Private	R.I.R.	
Saunders, Harry	127 Oldpark Road	Private	R.I.R.	
Saunders, J. A.	127 Oldpark Road	C.S.M.	R.I.R.	Killed in Action.
Shannon, A.	194 Cliftonville Road	Private	R.I.R.	
Shannon, Robert	194 Cliftonville Raad	Private	R.I.R.	Killed in Action.
Sherman, Wm.	58 Foyle Street	Private	R.I.R.	
Simms, H.	11 Beechnut Street	Private	R.I.R.	
Smyth, T. E.	125 Oldpark Road	P.O. Sorter	Pioneers	
Spence, Thos.	37 Eia Street	Private	R.I.R.	
Ward, Gerald	113 Limestone Road	2nd Lieutenant	R.E.	
Watson, John J.	88 Oldpark Road	Private	14th R.I.R.	Killed in Action.
Watterson, J. A.	36 Vicinage Park		R.A.M.C.	
Wilkin, Thos.	13 Easton Crescent	2nd Lieutenant	Black Watch	M.M.
Wilkin, Wm.	13 Easton Crescent	2nd Lieutenant	N.I.H.	
COLONIAL FORCES.				
Calvert, Murray	Knutsford Drive	Trooper	Australian E.F.	
Gray, D.	Vilette, Downshire Road	Private	Canadian E.F.	
Quigley, Andrew	53 Cavehill Road	Sergeant	S. African Force	Prisoner of War.
Quigley, Arthur	53 Cavehill Road	2nd Lieutenant	Canadian E.F.	
Walker, Hugh	Cliftonville Road	Private	Canadians	
Wilson, James L.	2 Summer Street	Private	Canadians	
Wilson, John	8 Cliftonville Street	Trooper	S.A. L.H.	
COLLEGE SQUARE.				
Baird, J. Archie	71 Oldpark Road,	Captain	9th Batt. Cheshires	Prisoner of War.
Bell, Wm. James	87 University Avenue	2nd Lieutenant	5th Batt. R.I. Regt.	
Burnside, William	88 Durham Street	Driver	R.E.	Wounded.
Clarke, James	Donegall Road	Private	10th R.I.R.	Wounded.
Creelman, Wm. J.	217 Roden Street	Sapper	S10 Signal Section	
Cupples, Wm.	93 Cliftonpark Avenue	Captain	2nd Batt. R. Inn. Fus.	Missing.
Dickson, David				
Dickson, James				
Donaldson, James M.	8 Cairo Street	Lance-Corporal	17th Batt. R.I.R.	
Edmonds, Hugh	207 Grosvenor Street	Private	A.S.C.	

BELFAST PRESBYTERY. COLLEGE SQUARE.

Name.	Home Address.	Rank.	Regiment, Battalion or Unit.	Remarks.
Ferguson, Thomas	56 Little Distillery St.	Private	10th Batt. R.I.R.	
Finlay, Henry	20 M'Adam Street	Private	10th Batt. R.I.R.	
Finlay, Thomas	20 M'Adam Street	Mechanic	R.N.A.S.	
Fryer, Samuel	12 Roosevelt Street	Corporal	R.E.	
Fryer, Thomas	12 Roosevelt Street	Private	Y.C.V.	
Hamill, George	11 Halliday's Road	2nd Lieutenant	3rd Suffolk Regt.	Wounded.
Hamill, John	11 Halliday's Road	Private	R.E.	Wounded.
Johnston, Albert	Lake Glen, A'sonstown	Private	6th Black Watch	Wounded.
Keenan, Wm.	Hutchinson Street	Lance-Corporal	19th Batt. R.I.R.	Killed.
Killen, James McG.	33 Hutchinson Street	Private	R.I.R.	
Kindness, Wm.	83 Roden Street	Private	4th R.I. Fus.	Wounded.
Liggett, John	76 Cromwell Road			
Lindsay, Herbert	248 Donegall Road	Private	19th Batt. R.I.R.	Wounded.
Lindsay, Wm. McQuitty	248 Donegall Road	Private	R.A.M.C.	
Moffett, John Lewers	15 Wilmont Terrace	Chief Engineer	R.N.	
Mehaffey, John	96 Roden Street	Private	16th Pioneers R.I.R.	
Mehaffey, David	96 Roden Street	Private	19th Batt. R.I.R.	
Mehaffey, Bertie	96 Roden Street	A. Seaman	R.N.	
Macauley, Maurice	21 Camden Street	2nd Lieutenant	17th Batt. R.I.R.	
Macauley, Cyril K.	21 Camden Street	Lieutenant	9th Batt. R.I.R.	Wounded.
Moore, Wm. J. B.	26 Rutland Street	Corporal	14th Batt. R.I.R.	
Moore, Robt. Charles	26 Rutland Street	Lance-Corporal	14th Batt. R.I.R.	Wounded.
Montgomery, Albert H.	11 Rugby Parade	Private	14th R.I.R.	
Montgomery, Jas. T.	11 Rugby Parade	Private	A. & S. Highldrs.	Lost eye, W'ded.
Montgomery, John	11 Rugby Parade	Sec. Comdr.	South African	
Megaw, Geo. L.	55 Botanic Avenue	Private	C.A.S.C., Supplies	
Macarthur, Peter, M.B.	47 University Street	Surgeon	R.N.	
Macauley, Thos. H.	21 Camden Street	Cadet	R.I.R.	
Magee, Joseph	26 Dickson Street	Private	R.I.R.	
Macarthur, Jas., M.B., B.A., B.A.O.	47 University Street	Captain	R.A.M.C., R.F.A.	
Macarthur, John	47 University Street	4th Officer	H.M.S. Carrigan Head	
McConnell, Arthur E.	Stranmillis House	Captain	20th Batt. R.I.R.	Wounded.
McGuigan, Arthur	28 Titania Street	Gunner	Field Artilery	
McGuigan, Samuel	28 Titania Street	Private	R.I.R.	Prisoner of War.
McGuigan, William	28 Titania Street	Private	R.I.R.	
McKee, Wm. Jas.	83 Frenchpark Street	Sergt.-Major	10th Batt. R.I.R.	
McKee, Thomas John	Roden Street	Private	R.I. Rifles	
McCann, William	8 Symons Street	Private	2nd Batt. R.I. Fus.	Wounded.
McBride, Robert	Ravenhill Park	Sapper	36th Div. R.E.	
McGregor, Duncan	31 Devonshire Street	Leading Seaman	R.N.	
Neill, John	College Street West	Private	R.I.R.	Wounded.
Philips, Wm. A.	35 Buckingham Street	Coy. Sergt.-Major	R.E.	D.C.M.
Ross, Rex.	20 Linview Street	Corporal	1st Batt. R.I.R.	Killed.
Robinson, Frank	150 Roden Street	Private	16th Batt. R.I.R.	Wounded.
Stewart, John	39 Distillery Street	2nd Lieutenant	10th Batt. R.I.R.	
Stewart, James	39 Distillery Street	Lance-Corporal	S.B.A.C., Caterpillar Section	
Stewart, George	39 Distillery Street	Rifleman	8th and 9th Batt. R.I.R.	Wounded.
Sterling, James	70 Cedar Avenue	2nd Lieutenant	Cameron Highlanders	Wounded.
Sterling, Samuel	70 Cedar Avenue	Private	Irish Guards	Accidentally killed.
Scott, John, M.B., B.A., B.A.O.	39 Bryansburn Rd., Bgor	Surgeon Captain	R.A.M.C.	
Sterritt, Samuel	Devonshire Street	Private	R.E.	
Sterritt, Robert	Devonshire Street	Private	14th R.I.R.	
Sterritt, William	Devonshire Street	Private	R.I.R.	
Templeton, Samuel	48 Roden Street	Private	Mechanical Transport	Wounded.
Williams, Henry	79 Excise Street	Lance-Corporal	Royal Fusiliers	Wounded.
Walker, Samuel T.	Crescent Buildings	Sergeant	Ulster Division	Wounded.
Wylie, Wm. Smyth	51 Roden Street	Private	2nd R. Inn. Fus.	Killed.
Wilson, W. J.	47 Dover Street	Private	Northumberland Fus.	Wounded.
COLONIAL FORCES.				
Gass, William D.	1 Stranmillis Park	Private	Australians	
Megaw, Geo. L.	55 Botanic Avenue	Private	Can. A.S.C.	
Skelly, Robert		Sergeant	Canadian Artillery	
Stewart, Robert H.	39 Distillery Street	2nd Lieutenant	Canadians	
Stewart, Wm.	39 Distillery Street	Private	Canadians	
COOKE CENTENARY.				
Adair, John	23 Spring Street	Sapper	R.E. 36, R.I.R.	
Allen, Thomas Campbell	31 Kimberley Street	Private	18th H.L.I.	Killed.
Ashe, Samuel	21 Gypsy Street	Private	R.I.R.	
Austin, Hubert Morrell	6 Cranmore Gardens	2nd Lieutenant	H.L.I.	Killed.
Austin, James M.A.	6 Cranmore Gardens	2nd Lieutenant	13th Manchester Regt.	Killed.
Banford, James	28 Primrose Street	Sergeant	M.G. Corps	
Bennison, Douglas	127 M'Clure Street	Sapper	R.E.	
Bennison, James	127 M'Clure Street	Sapper	R.E.	
Bestwick, Jonathan W.	6 Fernwood Street		R.M.L.I.	
Biggerstaff, John	40 Somerset Street	Private	T.Q.Y. Cheshire Regt.	
Black, William	99 Delhi Street	Gunner	R.F.A.	
Bleakley, Robert	151 Stranmillis Road	Corporal	3rd R.I.R.	
Boston, Alexander	28 Primrose Street	Rifleman	15th R.I.R.	
Boyd, Cecil V.	Claremount, Ardenlee Av.	2nd Lieutenant	R.I.R.	Killed.
Boyd, Clifford R.	Claremount, Ardenlee Av.	Lieutenant	R.A.F.	R.I.

BELFAST PRESBYTERY. COOKE CENTENARY.

Name.	Home Address.	Rank.	Regiment, Battalion or Unit.	Remarks.
Brown, Samuel	115 Agincourt Avenue	Rifleman	14th R.I.R. (Y.C.V.)	Killed.
Bryson, James	22 Raby Street	Sergeant	R.A.S.C.	
Bryson, William	22 Raby Street	Sub.-Lieutenant	H.M.S. Doris	
Burns, Samuel	13 Balfour Avenue	Sergeant	14th R.I.R. (Y.C.V.)	
Busby, Charles	208 Ormeau Road	Rifleman	10th R.I.R.	
Campbell, John	21 Somerset Street	Rifleman	8th R.I.R.	Killed.
Clair, William	7 Ardmore Avenue	Seaman	H.M.S. Hogue	Killed.
Clawson, Hugh	55 Ballarat Street	Farrier	9th R.I.R.	
Cooke, George	Ardmine, Ravenhill Rd.	Gunner	R.G.A.	
Courtney, Archibald	Ravenhill Road	Rifleman	R.I. Fusiliers	
Courtney, John	Ravenhill Road	Gunner	R.N.R.	
Craig, John J.	27 Somerset Street	Private	7th R.I.R.	
Craig, Robert	27 Somerset Street	Private	R.I.F.	
Craig, Thomas	27 Somerset Street	Seaman	H.M.S. Gloucester	
Crothers, James A.	Belvoir Tce., Ormeau Rd.	Sergeant	R.I.R.	
Cunningham, David	9 Parkmore Street	Private	R.E.	
Cunningham, Hugh	11 Bryansford Street	Private	R.E.	
Dailey, John	1 Fernwood Street	Rifleman	8th R.I.R.	
Davies, Alexander M.	Botanic Gardens	Rifleman	9th R.I.R.	
Davies, John J.	Botanic Gardens	Rifleman	Machine Gun Corps	
Davison, Robert	Ormeau Road	Lieutenant	12th King's Liverpool Regt.	M.C. Killed
Dickey, Robert	48 College Park Avenue	Lt. Engineer	R.N.R.	
Dickson, Frank	35 Farnham Street	Rifleman	10th R.I.R.	Killed.
Dickson, Joseph	58 Somerset Street	Rifleman	R.F.A.	
Dornan, John	Malcolm's Lane		R.N.	
Dornan, Wm. James	Malcolm's Lane	Bugler	1st Batt. R.I.R.	
Downey, Victor	100 Deramore Avenue	Lance-Corporal	R.I.F.	
Downing, James	South Parade	2nd Lieutenant	6th R.I. Regt.	Killed.
English, David	Buncrana, Ormeau Road	Sergeant	14th R.I.R. (Y.C.V.)	Killed.
Finlay, John	14 Kimberley Street	Private	36th Div. Res. Co.	
Fulton, T. Stevenson, M.D. D.P.H.	Valere, Rosetta Park	Captain	R.A.M.C.	
Gibson, Albert Henry	7 Devonshire Villas	2nd Lieutenant	9th R.I. Fus.	Killed.
Gibson, George, C.A.	7 Devonshire Villas	Warrant Officer		
Gibson, Robert	7 Devonshire Villas	Lance-Corporal	R.I.R.	
Gilbert, John B.	Heathcot, North Parade	Captain	Nigerian W.A. Force	
Gilchrist, John	Dunedin, Ravenhill Gdns.	Private	Intelligence Sec. Brigade	
Gilchrist, Thomas	Dunedin, Ravenhill Gdns.	Sergeant	R.I. Rifles	
Graham, Robert	Arden, Ardenlee Avenue	Gunner	R.F.A.	
Gray, Robert John	Landores, Ormeau Road	Corporal	20th Royal Fusiliers	Killed.
Hamilton, Robert	58 North Parade	Sergeant	R.I. Fus.	
Hanna, James	39 Haypark Avenue	Company Sergt. M.	1st R. Inn. Fus.	Killed.
Harbinson, Parker	Ashbank, Ardenlee Av.	Corporal	36th R.I.R.	
Harrison, David	20 Rushfield Avenue	Seaman	H.M.S. Bonaventure	
Harrison, Edmund	20 Rushfield Avenue	Rifleman	15th R.I.R.	
Harrison, James B.	20 Rushfield Avenue	Seaman	H.M.S. Monitor	
Harvey, F. L. James	1 Skegoniel Avenue	Sergeant	R. Inn. Fus.	
Harvey, James B.	1 Skegoniel Avenue	Sergeant	N.I. Horse	
Henry, C. Earnest	21 South Parade	Corporal	14th R.I.R.	
Henry, Maurice	21 South Parade	Lieutenant	114 Mahrattas	
Henry, Samuel	Seventh St., Shankill Rd.	Rifleman	R.I.R.	
Hill, James A.	23 Ardmore Avenue	Private	R.A.F.	
Hill, William J.	23 Ardmore Avenue	Private	R.A.F.	
Hinton, Thomas	33 Somerset Street	Stoker	H.M.S. Resolution	
Hiscocks, John C.	37 Haypark Avenue	Pioneer Signal	H.M.S.	
Jackson, Harold M.	Ravenhill Road	Lance-Corporal	Motor Transport	
Jeffers, Arthur H.	Ahorey, Ardenlee Avenue	Private	R. Inn. Fus.	
Jeffers, George	Ahorey, Ardenlee Avenue	Staff Sergeant	Motor Transport	M.S.M.
Jeffers, Walter	Ahorey, Ardenlee Avenue	Corporal	Motor Transport	M.S.M.
Jordan, George	115 Walmer Street	Shoer	South Notts Hussars	
Jordan, John	115 Walmer Street	1st Stoker	R.N.	
Jordan, Thomas	115 Walmer Street	Rifleman	16th R.I.R.	
Kerr, William		Rifleman	Irish Guards	
Ligget, Andrew	125 Walmer Street	Private	Motor Transport	
Ligget, Andrew	125 Walmer Street	Driver	R.A.S.C.	
Lyons, James S.	Valere, Rosetta Park	Captain	R. Lanc. Fus.	M.C.
Lyons, Robert Victor	Valere, Rosetta Park	2nd Lieutenant	14th R.I. Rifles	Killed.
Lyons, William Thos.	Valere, Rosetta Park	Captain	8th R. Lanc. Fus.	Killed, M..C
Macdonald, George	27 Deramore Avenue	Petty Officer	R.N.A.S.	Rus. Order of St. George, 3 Medals, Medal.
MacFarlane, Joseph		Lance-Corporal		
Magill, John	8 Penrose Street	Corporal	R.A.S.C.	
Magill, John	8 Penrose Street	Rifleman	15th R.I.R.	
Magowan, Alex.	56 Somerset Street	Staff Sergeant	R.F.A.	D.C.M.
Magowan, James	56 Somerset Street	Leading Stoker	H.M.S. Cerebus	
Mann, James Ure	34 South Parade	Lieutenant	9th R. Sussex Regt.	M.C.
Marshall, Alex.	Ardenlee House	Major	Machine Gun Corps	
Marshall, David	Ardenlee House	Sergeant	14th R.I.R.	Killed.
Marshall, James	Ardenlee House	Lieutenant	Machine Gun Corps	
Martin, Barry	Ashburn, Ravenhill Rd.	Corporal	14th R.I.R.	
Mason, William	60 Delhi Street	Rifleman	14th R.I.R.	Killed.
Milliken, John	27 Gipsy Street	Driver	16th M.G.C.	
Moore, Thomas	Ormeau Park	Lance-Sergeant	M.G.C.	
Morrow, Robert	63 Ormeau Road	Rifleman	14th R.I.R.	Killed.
McClure, John	Ashbank Ardenlee Av.	Sergeant	14th R.I.R.	

BELFAST PRESBYTERY.   COOKE CENTENARY.

Name.	Home Address.	Rank.	Regiment, Battalion or Unit.	Remarks.
McConchie, James F.	Stranraer	2nd Lieutenant	2/5th K.O.S.B.	
McCullough, William	66 Haypark Avenue	Corporal	1st R.I.R.	
McLoughlin, Annesley		Sergeant	9th Batt. R. Inn. Fus.	
McMinn, Martin	6 Walmer Street	Bombardier	R.F.A.	
McMordie, Frank	30 South Parade	Sergeant	R.E.	
McMordie, James Wilson	30 South Parade	2nd Lieutenant	9th K.O.Y.L.I.	Killed.
Nicholl, Alfred S.	3 St. Jude's Avenue	Brig. Bomb. Officer	13th R.I.R.	Killed.
Osborne, William	101 Walmer Street	Private	R.A.F.	
Paton, William M.	71 South Parade	Corporal	19th Worcester Regt.	Killed.
Pollock, John	39 Raby Street	Private	3rd R.I.R. (Reserve)	
Reid, Robert	100 University Street	Private	R.A.S.C.	
Robie, James	Drummond, R'hill Rd.	Private	3rd R.I.F.	
Rowney, John	14 Delaware Street	Sergeant	R.E.	
Roy, Alex.	St. Helens, F'ville Av.	Trooper	N.I.H.	
Roy, David	St. Helens, F'ville Av.	2nd Lieutenant	16th R.I.R.	
Roy, Hugh St. Clair	St. Helens, F'ville Av.	Captain	R.A.F.	
Russell, Angus	8 Agra Street	Lance-Corporal	8th R.I.R.	
Russell, Charles	8 Agra Street	Private	R.A.S.C.	
Schneider, Alex.	Ormeau Road	Lieutenant	Indian Army	
Scott, George B.	82 Kimberley Street	Corporal	93rd A. & S. Highldrs.	
Scott, Joseph	138 Ormeau Road	Engineer	H.M.S. Blake	
Scott, Robert	31 Somerset Street	Rifleman	8th R.I.R.	
Scougall, John A.	7 Gipsy Street	Private	4th Corps School of Instruc.	
Shearer, Thomas	3 St. Jude's Avenue	Lieutenant	12th R.I.R.	
Shields, John	112 Ormeau Road	Private	R.A.S.C.	
Smyth, William John	28 Penrose Street	Rifleman	R.I.R.	
Steele, Alex.	22 Somerset Street	Private	R.A.S.C.	
Sterritt, James	7 Gypsy Street	Seaman	H.M. Submarines	
Sterritt, William J.	7 Gypsy Street	Lance-Corporal	10th R.I.R.	
Stevenson, Cecil Y.	2 Ravenhill Terrace	Captain	R.E.	
Stevenson, Walter, M.B.	2 Ravenhill Terrace	Major	R.A.M.C.	
Stoopes, Norman	45 Farnham Street	Sapper	14th R.I.R.	
Strain, Charles	Beechmount, Rosetta Pk.		Transport	
Strain, George Herbert	Beechmount, Rosetta Pk.	Corporal	37th King's Liverpool Regt.	M.M., Killed.
Welsh, William	12 Dromara Street	Private	Army Cyclist Corps	M.M.
Welton, Samuel	14 Agra Street	Private	R. Inn. Fus.	
Wilkin, James Cecil	65 Rugby Avenue	Lieutenant	18th R.I.R.	
Wilkinson, Robert J.	94 North Parade	2nd Lieutenant	R.A.F.	
Wilson, Charles H.		2nd Lieutenant	R.A.M.C.	
Wilson, H. Pringle	39 Rugby Road	2nd Lieutenant	Warwickshire Regt.	Killed.
Wilson, William M.B.	Hampton Park	Captain	R.A.M.C.	
Windrim, Arthur	4 South Parade			
Winnington, Albert	Alexandra Park Avenue	Private	R.A.S.C.	
Winnington, James A.	Alexandra Park Avenue	Trooper	N.I. Horse	
Witherspoon, Valentine	35 Walmer Street	Private	M.T. R.A.S.C.	
COLONIAL AND U.S.A. FORCES.				
Adair, Hugh			New Zealand E.F.	Killed.
Clendinning, W. George	Delaware Street		3rd Div. Can. Engineers	Killed.
Doran, Fred. Will.	Ardenlee Avenue		Canadian E.F.	
Downing, Alexander	45 South Parade	Private	231st Can. Highldrs.	
Graham, David		Private	Canadians	
Guiler, John H.	89 Ormeau Road	Signaller	54th Canadian Infty.	
Henry, William	Seventh St. Shankill Rd.	Bugler	Canadian Mtd. Rifles	
Jeffers, James	Ardenlee Avenue	Lieutenant	American Red Cross	
Marshall, Andrew J.	83 Haypark Avenue		American E.F.	
Moore, Alick	Rushfield Avenue	S.Q.M.S.	2nd Batt. Canadians	
McDowell, Robert H. M.	Ravenhill Park	Private	72 Seaforth Highldrs. (Can.)	
McClean, Hugh	7 Devonshire Villas	Private	19th Canadians	
McClean, Robert H.	7 Devonshire Villas	Cadet	Canadians	
McSpadden, Thomas	Westminster Street		Canadian E.F.	
Stewart, William H.	10 North Parade	Gunner	Australian F.A.	
CREGAGH.				
Cochrane, Brownlow		Private	R.I.R.	
Copeland, Thomas			R.N.	
Courtney, Samuel		Private	R.A.M.C.	
Ellison, Willie		Private	R. Marines	
Foster, John			R.N.	Drowned.
Gibson, Robert J.		Private	A.S.C.	
Gibson, Samuel Orr		Private	Seaforth Highlanders	
Greer, Fred. W.		Private	14th R.I.R.	Killed in Action.
Grimson, F.		Lieutenant	R.A.M.C.	
Harper, Charles		Private	9th N. Staffords	
Harper, Joseph		Sergeant	8th R.I.F.	Killed in Action.
Hill, W. J. McC.		Private	M.T. A.S.C.	
McAnally, William		Private	1st R.I.R.	
McCartney, James			R.N.	
McCartney, John			R.N.	
McCaw, Joseph		Sergeant	Stafford Regt.	Killed in Action.
McCullough, James		Private	R.E.	
McDougal, Thomas		Private	King's Liverpool Regt.	

BELFAST PRESBYTERY. CREGAGH.

Name.	Home Address.	Rank.	Regiment, Battalion or Unit.	Remarks.
McKinley, Hugh	...	Private	1st R.I.R.	Killed in Action.
McLean, James	...	Private	R. Marines	
Maxwell, James	...	...	R.N.	
Mills, Leonard	...	Private	17th R.I.R.	
Morrow, R. C.	...	Private	Innisk. Dragoons	
Parker, D. J.	...	...	R.N.	
Parker, J. E.	...	...	R.N.	
Patterson, Samuel	...	...	R.A.F.	
Patterson, Samuel	...	Private	A.S.C.	
Pearce, Andrew	...	Private	N.I.H	
Perry, Robert	...	Private	R.E.	
Phillips, Thomas	...	Private	M.T. A.S.C.	
Pierce, Thomas	...	...	R.N.	
Pierce, William John	...	Private	R.I.R.	
Poag, James	...	Lance-Corporal	R.I.R.	Killed in Action.
Poag, Robert	...	Private	R.G.A.	Killed in Action.
Poag, William	...	Private	R. Marines	
Reid, David	...	Private	16th R.I.R.	
Reid, William	...	Private	R.F.A.	
Reynolds, Jim	...	Private	King's Shropshire Lt. Inf.	
Simms, John McKeen	...	Private	R. In. Fus.	Killed.
Simms, Robert J.	...	...	R.N.	
Simms, Thomas	...	Sergeant	R.I.R.	
Sterling, Robert	...	Private	A.S.C.	
Walsh, Charles	...	Lance-Corporal	R.I.R.	
Wilson, James Bryson	...	...	R.N.	
Wilson, John	...	Private	N.I.H.	
Woodside, Charles	...	...	N.I.H.	Died.
Woodside, Wallace	...	Corporal	16th R.I.R. (Y.C.V.)	Died of Wounds.
	COLONIAL FORCES.			
Dalzell, A.	...	Lance-Corporal	7th Can. Mounted Rifles	
Stewart, H. J.	...	Private	14th Can. E.F.	Killed in Action.
	CRESCENT.			
Adair, H. Drummond	40 Botanic Avenue	Cadet	O.T. Corps	
Aitkenhead, George	20 Spruce Street	Private	King's Royal Rifles	
Allan, Samuel D.	20 Maryville Street	Private	R.I.R.	
Allen, Ernest	20 Maryville Street	Private	A.S.C. M.F.	Killed.
Allen, Samuel D.	20 Maryville Street	Private	R. Flying Corps	
Auld, William	194 Blythe Street	Private	2/9th A. & S. Highldrs.	
Barbour, James	13 Salisbury Street	Trooper	N.I.H.	
Barbour, Robert	13 Salisbury Street	Trooper	N.I.H.	
Barrett, Benjamin	49 Vernon Street	Sergt.-Major	107th Grenade Brigade	Wounded.
Baxter, William	51 Lake Street	Private	R.I.R.	
Blair, Hugh	77 M'Clure Street	Lance-Corporal	14th Batt. R.I.R.	
Bleakley, Edward	13 Jerusalem Street	Private	R.I. Fus.	Killed.
Boland, Charles	21 Gosford Street	Private	R.A.M.C.	Wounded.
Boland, Alexander	21 Gosford Street	Private	10th Batt. R.I. Rifles	Killled.
Bratton, George	28 Pine Street	Private	10th Batt. R.I. Rifles	Killed.
Bratton, John	28 Pine Street	Private	Motor Transport	
Broad, Alwyn	5 Ireton Street	Lance-Corporal	3rd Batt. R.I.R.	
Brown, Thomas	23 Beech Street	Driver	A.S.C.	
Brown, W. D.	23 Beech Street	Gunner	R.G.A.	
Burns, George	54 Beech Street	Private	109th Field Ambulance	
Burns, William	54 Beech Street	Private	10th Batt. R.I.R.	
Byers, R. J.	15 Walnut Street	Rifleman	8th Batt. R.I.R.	Wounded.
Calwell, David	26 M'Adam Street	Private	47th Batt. R. Inn.	Killed.
Calvert, de la Varty	93 University Avenue	Sergt.-Major	3rd R.I. Fus.	
Campbell, R. J.	17 Virginia Street	Private	R.E.	
Carmichael, R. D.	10 Blackwood Street	Sergeant	8/9 Batt. R.I. Rifles	
Chancellor, John	10 Norwood Street	Private	17th Batt. R.I. Rifles	
Collins, Ernest	Silvergrove Street	Private	Tank Corps	
Colville, James	27 Wolseley Street	Private	Royal Marines	Wounded.
Craig, Samuel	22 Penrose Street	Lance-Corporal	R.E.	
Craig, John	...	Sapper	R.E.	
Cullen, James	Canada	Doctor	60th Battery C.F.A.	
Cumberland, Joseph	52 Silvergrove Street	Private	R.E.	
Curragh, Ernest	6 Kinallon Street	Private	59 Div. M.T. A.S.C.	
Dodds, James	25 Spruce Street	Private	17th Batt. R.I.R.	Killed.
Donald, David A.	8 Wellington Street	Private	3rd Batt. R.I.R.	Wounded.
Donald, Henry W.	8 Wellington Street	Boy	533 Durham Q.	
Dowling, James	Rea Anna, M'boro Park	2nd Lieutenant	10th Batt. R.I.R.	Wounded.
Dumigan, John	10 Lavinia Street	Corporal	2nd Dragoons, R. Scots Greys.	
English, W. G.	28 Rugby Road	2nd Lieutenant	17th Batt. R.I.R.	Wounded.
Ervine, George G.	2 Magdala Street	Petty Officer	R.N.A.S.	
Ervine, W. J.	2 Magdala Street	Sergeant	8th Batt. R.I.R.	Killed.
Forbes, William	5 Strandview Street	2nd Lieutenant	R.A.F.	
Ferris, J. S.	29 Colenso Parade	Cadet	R.A.F.	
Finlay, J.	12 Copeland Street	Private	16th Batt. R.I.R.	
Frew, Philip W.	Trough Road	2nd Lieutenant	12th Batt. R.I.R.	Wounded.
Gibson, Samuel	95 Maryville Street	Private	Motor Transport	Wounded.

BELFAST PRESBYTERY. CRESCENT.

NAME.	HOME ADDRESS.	RANK.	REGIMENT, BATTALION OR UNIT.	REMARKS.
GORDON, FREDERICK	...	Private	R.F.A.	
GORDON, DAVID	...	Private	2nd Batt. R. Inn. Fus.	Died of Wounds.
GRACEY, STANLEY	8 Rossmore Avenue	2nd Private	Royal Flying Corps	
GREER, JAMES	95 Roden Street	Rifleman	8th Batt. R.I.R.	
GREER, JOHN	95 Roden Street	Corporal	4th R. Inn. Fus.	
GREER, THOMAS	95 Roden Street	Private	4th Batt. R.I. Fus.	Wounded.
HANNA, JAMES	1 Maryville Street	Private	R.I.R.	Prisoner of War.
HANNA, ROBERT	1 Maryville Street	Lance-Corporal	9th Batt. R.I.R.	Wounded.
HANNA, WM. J.	1 Maryville Street	Private	Labour Coy.	
HANNA, SAMUEL	14 Spruce Street	Private	19th Batt. R.I.R.	
HAWTHORNE, JOHN	331 Ravenhill Road	Cadet	R.A.F.	
HAYES, ROBERT	68 Balfour Avenue	Private	14th Batt. R.I.R.	
HERDMAN, HENRY	11 Elm Street	Private	10th Batt. R.I.R.	
HERDMAN, JOHN	11 Elm Street	Private	10th Batt. R.I.R.	
HERDMAN, THOMAS	11 Elm Street	Private	10th Batt. Welsh Pioneers	
HERDMAN, WILLIAM	11 Elm Street	Private	A.S.C.	
HILDITCH, HENRY	1 Oak Street	Private	Indian Motor Transport	Died from illness.
HILL, JAMES	9 Lancefield Road	Lieutenant	1st Torquay Div. R.A.M.C.	
HOGG, HENRY	The Croft, Park Road	Sapper	R.E.	Wounded.
HOLMES, GEORGE	15 Essex Street	Private	14th Batt. R.I.R.	
HOY, RICHARD	6 Gosford Street	Private	14th Batt. R.I.R.	Wounded.
HUNTER, J. D.	44 Botanic Avenue	Q.M.-Sergeant	13th Batt. R.I.R.	Wounded.
HUNTER, WALTER	24 Ava Street	Sergeant	10th Batt. R.I.R.	Wounded.
JACKSON, JOHN	80 Edinburgh Street	Driver	A.S.C.	
JACKSON, SAMUEL	80 Edinburgh Street	Driver	M.T. A.S.C.	
JAMISON, WILLIAM	43 Fitzroy Avenue	Sergeant	2/18th Batt. London I.R.	
JOHNSTON, W. J.	20 Powerscourt Street	Sergeant	6th Batt. R.I.R.	Wounded.
KERR, WM. J.	15 Essex Street	Private	Labour Coy.	
KILDEA, JAMES W.	15 Elgin Street	Driver	Motor Transport	
KINNEN, HENRY	85 Craigmore Street	Private	R.A.F.	
KINNEN, JAMES	85 Craigmore Street	Private	R.I.R.	
LAW, W. E. R.	90 Cromwell Road	Private	6th Inn. Dragoons	
LEEBURN, ROBERT	5 Copeland Street	Driver	R.F.A.	
LIVINGSTONE, S. H.	15 Collingwood Avenue	1st Petty Officer	Mess 6, H.M.S. Hope	
LOCKHART, ALFRED	6 Crescent Gardens	Private	6th Batt. R.I.R.	
LONG, JOHN	16 Kinallon Street	Rifleman	20th Batt. R.I.R.	Died of Wounds.
LORD, JAMES	53 Beech Street	Private	N.I.H.	
LOWRY, WILLIAM	13 Donnybrook Street	Driver	A.S.C.	
LYNN, SAMUEL	8 Silvergrove Street	Private	10th Batt. R.I.R.	Wounded.
MACKEY, J. J.	Holywood	Sergt.-Major	14th Batt. R.I.R.	D.C.M.
MARSHALL, ALEX. W.	81 Craigmore Street	Private	2nd Batt. R.I.R.	Wounded.
MARSHALL, ANDREW	81 Craigmore Street	Private	R.A.F.	
MARSHALL, R. S.	81 Craigmore Street	Private	R.I.R.	
MARTIN, JAMES	5 Spruce Street	Sapper	R.E.	
MARTIN, JOHN	5 Spruce Street	Private	8/9th Batt. R.I.R.	
MARTIN, HUGH	5 Spruce Street	Private	18th Batt. R.I.R.	
MATTISON, CHARLES	33 Combermere Street	Driver	R.F.A.	Died.
MAULTSAID, JAMES	44 Melrose Street	Lance-Sergeant	14th Batt. R.I.R.	
McCANDLESS, CHARLES	56 Coolderry Street	Private	14th Field Ambulance	
McCARROL, WILLIAM	50 Spruce Street	Private	6th Batt. R.I.F.	
McCLEAN, WILLIAM	...	Rifleman	R.F.A.	
McCLUNE, JAMES	5 Craigmore Street	Private	10th Batt. R.I.R.	Wounded.
McCLUNE, JOHN	5 Craigmore Street	Driver	23 F.A. R.A.M.C.	
McCLUNE, WM.	29 Rutland Street	Private	R.A.S.C.	
McCONE, JOHN	11 Landseer Street	...	H.M.S. Carpathia	
McCONE, S. H.	11 Landseer Street	Private	R.I.R.	
McCONE, THOMAS	11 Landseer Street	Private	R. Inn. Fus.	
McCORD, JOHN R.	20 Craigmore Street	Private	19th Batt. R.I.R.	Wounded.
McCORD, WILLIAM	20 Craigmore Street	Private	R.A.F.	
McCOUBRIE, W. J.	5 St. Andrew's Square	Private	2nd Batt. R.I. Fus.	Died.
McCOUBRIE, MOSES	5 St. Andrew's Square	Sergeant	Irish Guards	Wounded.
McCULLOUGH, JAMES	19 Agincourt Avenue	Private	10th Batt. R.I.R.	Killed.
McCORMICK, R.	5 Arundel Street	Gunner	H.M.S. Carmelia	
McEWAN, NORMAN	60 Burmah Street	Private	9th Seaforths	
McILVEEN, JOHN	...	Private	10th Batt. R.I.R.	
McGRATH, ROBERT	59 Craigmore Street	Sergeant	R. Inn. Fus.	Wounded.
McKAY, CHARLES	11 Apsley Street	Private	R.A.M.C.	
McKAY, JAMES	11 Apsley Street	Private	10th Batt. R.I.R.	
McKNIGHT, JOHN	37 Scott Street	Private	4th Batt. R.I.R.	
McKNIGHT, THOMAS	37 Kensington Street	Private	Motor Transport	
McMANUS, DAVID	24 Penrose Street	Shoeing Smith	N.I.H.	
McMANUS, JOHN F.	24 Penrose Street	Private	2nd Batt. R.I. Fus.	M.M.
McMANUS, THOMAS	24 Penrose Street	Private	11th Batt. R. Dub. Fus.	Killed.
McPHERSON, W. J.	69 Pine Street	Corporal	1st Garrison Regt.	
McQUISTON, THOMAS	42 Coolderry Street	Private	16th Batt. R.I.R.	
McVEIGH, ALBERT	97 University Avenue	Private	36th Div. Signal Section	
McVEIGH, HERBERT	97 University Avenue	Private	R.A.F.	
McVEIGH, RICHARD	97 University Avenue	Private	10th Batt. R.I.R.	Wounded.
McVEIGH, STEWART	97 University Avenue	Lance-Corporal	16th Batt. R.I.R.	Wounded.
McVEIGH, WALTER	97 University Avenue	Gunner	R.F.A.	Wounded.
McVEIGH, WILLIAM	97 University Avenue	Private	10th Batt. R.I.R.	
McVEY, JAMES	67 Burmah Street	Gunner	H.M.S. Hope	Killed.
McGAW, JOHN	45 Hartington Street	Gunner	R.G.A.	
MERCER, W. CONN	34 Candahar Street	Driver	Motor Transport	

BELFAST PRESBYTERY. **CRESCENT.**

Name.	Home Address.	Rank.	Regiment, Battalion or Unit.	Remarks.
Milling, S. Craig	22 Penrose Street	Private	R.E.	
Millveigh, Robert	24 Naples Street	Driver	Motor Transport	
Molyneaux, George	10 Ulsterville Gardens	Lieutenant	R.F.C.	Killed.
Morgan, Cecil B.	70 Stranmillis Road	2nd Private	R.F.C.	
Nelson, Wm. R.	50 Silvergrove Street	Private	R.I.R.	
Nickels, Walter	29 Jerusalem Street	Petty Officer	15th Squad. R.N.A.S.	
Nickels, Henry	8 Burmah Street	Trooper	N.I.H.	
Parker, Isaac	71 Howard Street South	Gunner	Machine Gun Corps, R.I.R.	Killed.
Patterson, Samuel	9 Thalia Street	Lance-Corporal	10th Batt. R.I.R.	Wounded.
Pinion, F. M.	4 Toronto Terrace	Private	A.S.C.	
Pinion, W. R.	4 Toronto Terrace	Private	A.S.C.	
Pollins, Wm.	72 Stranmillis Gardens	Gunner	R.F.A.	Killed.
Porter, Hugh	3 Essex Street	Private	R.A.M.C.	M.M.
Porter, James	3 Essex Street	Private	Seaforth Highldrs.	Killed.
Porter, John	3 Essex Street	Private	R.I.R.	Wounded.
Porter, William	3 Essex Street	Private	3/5th Batt. Seaforth Higldrs.	Wounded.
Proctor, John	Rea-Anna, M'boro Park	Gunner	R.G.A.	
Rainey, Adam	12 Lawrence Street	Sergeant	H.L.I.	
Reaney, Robert	62 McClure Street	Sailor	H.M.S. Diligence	
Reaney, James	62 M'Clure Street	Sailor	H.M.S. Benbow	
Redmond, Samuel	49 Chadolly Street	Sergeant	6th Batt. R.I. Fus.	
Ritchie, Walter	20 Schomberg Street	Private	15th Batt. R.I.R.	Prisoner of War.
Robertson, Thomas	6 M'Adam Street	Private	2nd Batt. R.I.R.	
Rowan, Samuel	19 Cameron Street	Private	Seaforth Highldrs.	Wounded.
Russell, Andrew	8 Gordon Terrace	Private	10th Batt. R.I.R.	
Russell, George	8 Gordon Terrace	Private	10th Batt. R.I.R.	Wounded.
Russell, George	7 Auburn Street	Driver	A.S.C.	
Russell, William	7 Auburn Street	Trooper	Irish Guards	
Rutherford, Isaac	79 Chadwick Street	Gunner	H.M.S. Lion	
Scott, Wm. J.	12 Pine Street	Sergeant	14th Batt. R.I.R.	Killed.
Short, Hugh	4 Curzon Street	Private	110th Field Am., R.I.R.	Wounded.
Speers, George	7 Auburn Street	Private	Warwickshire Territorials	
Speers, William	7 Auburn Street	Trooper	Irish Guards	Killed.
Smith, W. J.	43 Rutland Street	Trooper	8th King's R.I. Hussars	
Spence, Wm. A.	21 Elm Street	Private	109th Field Ambulance	
Stuart, John	56 Carmel Street	Private	1st Batt. Irish Guards	Killed.
Sullivan, John	7 Copeland Street	Private	18th Batt. R.I.R.	Wounded.
Taylor, J. B.	36 Peveril Street	Rifleman	10th Batt. R.I.R.	
Templeton, Ernest	22 Silvergrove Street	Gunner	Tank Corps	
Thompson, Charles	56 Beech Street	Private	3rd Batt. R.I. Fus.	Wounded.
Thompson, David	59 Craigmore Street	Private	4th Batt. R.I.R.	Killed.
Thompson, James	59 Craigmore Street	Private	10th Batt. R.I.R.	Wounded.
Thompson, Joseph	59 Craigmore Street	Major	R. Inn. Fus.	
Thompson, Richard	36 Peveril Street	Rifleman	R.I.R.	Died of Wounds.
Thompson, Robert	59 Craigmore Street	Sergeant	R.E.	M.M.
Thompson, Robert	56 Beech Street	Private	A.S.C.	
Thompson, William	59 Craigmore Street	Gunner	42nd Battery R.F.A.	
White, Wm. J.	56 Beech Street	Sergeant	R.I.R.	Wounded.
Wilson, Francis	18 Craigmore Street	Private	2nd Batt. R.A.F.	Wounded.
Wilson, Joseph	18 Craigmore Street	Private	10th Batt. R.I.R.	
Wilson, Thomas	12 Apsley Street	Corporal	R.I.R.	
Wilson, William	12 Apsley Street	Private	10th Batt. R.I.R.	Killed.
Wilson, Thomas	18 Craigmore Street	Private	2nd Batt. R.A.F.	
Wylie, Robert	12 Pine Street	Sergeant	6th Batt. Armd. Car Unit	M.M., G.C.
Yool, W. Munro	19 Gt. Victoria Street	Lieutenant	R.F.C.	
COLONIAL FORCES.				
Alexander, Louis	25 Magdala Street	Private	R. Can. O. Corps	Wounded.
Barrett, A.	49 Vernon Street	Trooper	1st Can. M.M.P.	
Gordon, Harry A.	Canada	Private	Can. M'Clean Kilties	
Gordon, Thos. E.	Canada	Private	Can. McClean Kilties	Killed in Action.
Hilditch, John H.	1 Oak Street	Private	Can. E.F.	
Hilditch, Thos.	1 Oak Street	Private	3rd Canadians	
Johnston, George	28 University Street	Lance-Corporal	19th Can. Inft.	Wounded.
Larmour, Robert	Camden Street	Private	P. Pat. Can. L.I.	Killed in Action.
Morgan, Wm.	70 Stranmillis Road	Trooper	Can. Horse	
Phillips, Wm. J.	15 Albertbridge Road	Sapper	S.A. Regt.	
Thompson, Adrian	71 University Avenue	Gunner	S.A. F.A.	
CRUMLIN ROAD.				
Bailie, Joseph	15 Disraeli Street	Private	R.I.R.	
Beresford, John	Ardoyne Lodge	Sergeant	R.I.R.	
Birney, George	49 Rosebank Street	Private	R. Inn. Fus.	Wounded twice.
Birney, William	49 Rosebank Street	Private	R.I. Fus.	Wounded.
Blevings, Robert	53 Rosebank Street	Private	R.I.R.	
Booth, George	11 Wimbledon Street	Private	15th R.I.R.	Prisoner.
Booth, Hudson	11 Wimbledon Street	Private	14th Y.C.V.	Killed in Action.
Cathcart, John	272 Cambrai Street	Private	R.A.F.	
Chambers, Herbert J. K.	3 Beechpark Street	Private	9th R.I.R.	
Cooper, Andrew				
Cooper, Bertie				
Coulter, Samuel	49 Matchett Street			Killed in Action.

BELFAST PRESBYTERY.   CRUMLIN ROAD.

Name.	Home Address.	Rank.	Regiment, Battalion or Unit.	Remarks.
COWDEN, THOMAS	5 Tudor Place	R.Q.M.S.	R.I.R.	
COWDEN, THOMAS, JUN.	5 Tudor Place	Lance-Corporal	R.I.R.	
COWDEN, SAMUEL	5 Tudor Place	Sergeant	R.I.R.	Prisoner.
CREGHAN, HENRY	54 Sydney Street W.	Private	Canadians	Wounded and Pris.
CROTHERS, ALEX.	86 Louisa Street		6th R.I.R.	
CROTHERS, THOMAS	86 Louisa Street		R.I.R.	
DONALDSON, JONATHAN				
DORNAN, HENRY	66 Cambrai Street	Private	R.I.R.	Killed in Action.
DORNAN, JAMES	66 Cambrai Street	Private	R.I.R.	
DOWDS, H. H.				
GILCHRIST, J.				
GRAINGER, WILLIAM	175 Leopold Street	Private	R.A.M.C.	Killed in Action.
HAMILL, DAVID				
HAMILL, SAMUEL				
HAMILTON, JAMES				
HANLEY DAVID	10 Rosapenna Street	Lance-Corporal	14th R.I.R.	Killed in Action.
HARRIS, JAMES	63 Bryson Street	Private	Rocky Mt. Rangers	Wounded.
HARRIS, LEONARD	63 Bryson Street	Private	R.E.	Wounded.
HILL, ARTHUR				
HOGG, SAMUEL				
HOUSTON, J. R.				
HOUSTON, THOS.	175 Snugville Street	Private	R.I.R.	Died in France.
HUMPHREY, DAVID	172 Cambrai Street	Rifleman	15th R.I.R.	Wounded & Gassed
HUMPHREY, JOHN McC.	172 Cambrai Street	A.B.	R.N.	
HUMPHREY, SAMUEL	172 Cambrai Street	Rifleman	10th R.I.R.	Prisoner.
HUMPHREY, WILLIAM	172 Cambrai Street	Corporal	15th R.I.R.	M.M.
IRVINE, ROBERT	152 Leopold Street	Lance-Corporal	R.I.R.	Killed in Action.
JONNSTON, JAMES	104 Cambrai Street	Sergeant	Irish Guards	Killed in Action.
JOHNSTON, THOMAS	44 Rosebank Street	Private	M.T. A.S.C.	
JORDAN, THOMAS	6 Avonbeg Street	Corporal	R.I. Regt.	
KENNEDY, ROBERT				
KERR, SAMUEL				
KILLOW, THOMAS	41 Sydney Street W.	Lance-Corporal	R.A.F.	
LAWSON, WILLIAM				
LLOYD, EDWARD	39 Avonbeg Street	Sergeant	Armoured Car Brigade	
LOWRY, THOMAS				
McAVOY, FRED.	153 Mayo Street	Private	R.I.R.	
McAVOY, JAMES	153 Mayo Street	Sergeant	R.I.R.	Wounded 4 times.
McAVOY, JOHN	153 Mayo Street	A.B.	R.N.	
McCABE, T.				
McCARTNEY, ISAAC				
McCARTNEY, ROBERT	44 Broom Street	Private	R.F.A.	
McCHESNEY, ANDREW	59 Everton Street	Private	R. Marines	1914 Medal.
McCHESNEY, WM. A.	59 Everton Street	Private	8th R.I.R.	Killed in Action.
McCLEAN, DAVID	3 Everton Street	Private	R.I.R.	
McCRACKEN, DAVID				
McEVOY, THOMAS P.	14 Sydney Street W.	Sapper	R.E.	
McEVOY, WM. J.	14 Sydney Street W.	Private	8th Inn. Fus.	Killed in Action.
McGRAND, SAMUEL	107 Cambrai Street	Private	R.F.A.	
McLARNON, GEORGE				
McMASTER, DAVID	Oldpark Road	Sergeant	14th C. Battery	M. Medal.
McMASTER, FRED.	Oldpark Road	Private	D.C.L.I., 1st Batt.	
McMASTER, WILLIAM	Oldpark Road	Private	1st R. Inn. Fus.	
McQUISTON, DAVID				
McQUISTON, THOMAS	259 Crumlin Road	Private	R.I.R.	Prisoner.
MAGOWAN, CHARLES	48 Vistula Street	Driver	R.F.A.	G.S.M. & V. Medal.
MAGOWAN, JOHN	48 Vistula Street	Stoker	H.M.S. Chatham	1914-15 Star, G.S.M. & Vic. M.
MAGOWAN, ROBERT	48 Vistula Street	Stoker	H.M. Submarine 8	1914-15 Star, G.S.M. & Vic. M.
MAGOWAN, WILLIAM	48 Vistula Street	A.B.	H.M.S. Endymion	
MAGUIRE, JOHN	37 Geoffrey Street	Corporal	2nd R.I.R.	Wounded twice.
MAGUIRE, SAMUEL E.	37 Geoffrey Street	Private	8th R.I.R.	Wounded.
MAGUIRE, WM.	37 Geoffrey Street	Private	R.A.M.C.	Wounded.
MARTIN, DAVID	55 Byron Street			
MARTIN, WM.				
MAYBEN, JACK	Mayo Street			
MILLAR, GEORGE	179 Crumlin Road	Rifleman	15th R.I.R.	Wounded twice.
MILLAR, THOMAS S.	179 Crumlin Road	Sergeant	R.A.S.C.	
MOFFETT, FRED.				
MULHOLLAND, DAVID	41 Havana Street	Private	R.I.R.	Killed in Action
MULHOLLAND, JAMES	41 Havana Street	Private	R.A.F.	
MURRAY, HENRY	38 Groomsport Street	Sergeant	R.I.R.	Wounded, Ment in Despatches.
PARK, SAMUEL	18 Baden Powell Street	Private	1st G. Highldrs.	Prisoner 4 years.
PATTON, JOSEPH				
PORTER, GEORGE	3 Beechpark Street	Private	Artificer R.N.	
PORTER, HUGH	3 Beechpark Street	Private	R.F.A.	Wounded.
PORTER, JAMES	3 Beechpark Street	Private	Hussars	
PORTER, JOHN	3 Beechpark Street	Private	R.E.	Gassed 3 times.
RANKIN, JOHN				
RANKIN, THOMAS				
REA, THOMAS				
REAVEY, JACK				

BELFAST PRESBYTERY. CRUMLIN ROAD.

NAME.	HOME ADDRESS.	RANK.	REGIMENT, BATTALION OR UNIT.	REMARKS.
RONEY, HERBERT	15 Buller Street	Corporal	8th R.I.R.	Wounded 3 times.
ROY, DAVID				
ROY, GEORGE				
ROY, HUGH				
ROY, JOSEPH				
SAVAGE, ANDREW P.	5 Columbia Street	Private	109th F.A., R.A.M.C.	
SEMPLE, HUGH	32 Santiago Street	Private	R.F.A.	
SEYMOUR, FRANK H.	25 Sydney Street W.	Sergeant	R.E.	
SEYMOUR, PERCY	25 Sydney Street W.	Private	R. Fus.	Gassed.
SEYMOUR, ROBERT	25 Sydney Street W.	Sergeant	R.F.A.	
SEYMOUR, ROBERT E.	25 Sydney Street W.	Lance-Corporal	R.D. Fus.	Wounded.
SHAW, GEORGE				
SHAW, WILLIAM				
SILCOCK, JOHN	44 Rathlin Street	Private	M.T. A.S.C.	Wounded.
SKINNER, JOHN				
SMYTH, FRED.	32 Ponsonby Avenue	Private	E. African R.A.M.C.	
SMYTH, JOHN				
SMYTH, SAMUEL	32 Ponsonby Avenue	Private	5th F. Am., A.S.C.	M.M., Ment. Des.
STIRLING, RALPH	3 Rosapenna Street	Private	R.I.R.	Wounded.
THOMPSON, JOHN				
TOUGHER, JOHN				
TOUGHER, ROBERT				
TRAINER, JOHN	3 Louisa Street	Lance-Corporal	19th R.I.R.	Wounded.
TUMULTY, ROBERT				
WALSH, JOHN				
WILLIAMSON, THOMAS				
WILSON, JOHN				
YOUNG, HENRY	105 Bray Street	Lance-Corporal		Drowned.
COLONIAL FORCE.				
ADAIR, WILLIAM H.		Private	10th Canadians	Prisoner.
ALLAN, WILLIAM K.		Sergeant	Canadians	
CURRY, ROBERT J.	248 Crumlin Road	Private	44th Canadians	Killed in Action.
CURRY, WILLIAM	248 Crumlin Road	Private	Canadian R.A.M.C.	
IRWIN, ROBERT	62 Woodvale Road	Private	R.E., Canadians	
MIDDLETON, JOHN	102 Cambrai Street	Private	Canadian F.A.	Wounded.
ORR, WILLIAM	263 Tennent Street	Private	8th Canadian Reserve	
ROWNEY, ALEX.	Toronto	Private	Canadian S.S., R.A.M.C.	
McAVOY, ALBERT	Toronto	Private	84th Canadians	Wounded.
McCHESNEY, FRED.	Toronto	Private	Canadians	
DONEGALL PASS.				
BARR, DAVID	10 Bagot Street	Private	R.I.R.	Wounded & Dischd.
BASSETT, ROBERT	Elm Street	Private	R. Sussex Regt.	Killed in Action.
COLLINS, JOSEPH	24 Ormeau Street		R.N.	
COLLINS, WILLIAM	24 Ormeau Street	Private	R.I.R.	Wounded & Dischd.
DICKSON, JAMES	6 Stroud Street	Private	R.I.R.	
DUNLOP, CHARLES	Ballyholme Ho., Bangor	Lieutenant	R. Inn. Fus.	Died of Wounds.
DUNSEATH, SAMUEL	2 Coyle Place	Private	R.I.R.	Wounded.
FOREMAN, THOMAS	Knockbracken	Trooper	N.I.H	
GALBRAITH, W. J.		Private	R. Inn. Fus.	Wounded.
GOURLEY, RICHARD	27 Elm Street	Private	R. Inn. Fus.	
HALL, HARRY	13 Lonsdale Street	Lieutenant	R.I.R.	Killed in Action.
HALLIDAY, THOMAS	Beech Street	Lieutenant	R.I.R.	Killed in Action.
HAMILTON, JOHN	38 Rainey Street	Sergeant	R.I.R.	Killed in Action.
HAWTHORNE, JAMES	24 M'Clure Street	Private	R.E.	
HAYES, SAMUEL	23 Hatfield Street	Private	R.I.R.	Killed in Action.
HAZLETT, FRANCIS	Kimberley Street	Private	R.I.R.	Killed in Action.
HOGG, BRYSON, M.D.	135 Ormeau Road		R.N.	
HOGG, GERALD, M.D.	135 Ormeau Road		R.I.R.	
IRVINE, JS. MAGEE	15 Fitzroy Avenue	Private	R.I. Fus.	
IRWIN, ROBERT	79 Balfour Avenue	Private	R.I.R.	Wounded.
IRWIN, WM.	79 Balfour Avenue	Private	R.I.R.	Killed in Action.
JESS, DANIEL	44 Selby Street	Private	R.I.R.	Died of Wounds.
JONES, ELIAS	56 River Terrace		R.I.R.	Killed in Action.
KITSON, J.		Corporal	R.I.R.	Killed in Action.
KYDD, GEO. E.	21 Abbott Street	Private	8th London Regt.	Wounded.
KYDD, SAMUEL	21 Abbott Street	Lieutenant	R. Berks	Wounded.
LONGRIDGE, DAVID	1 Essex Street	Private	R. Inn. Fus.	
MACKEY, HUGH	9 Damascus Street	Private	R.A.M.C.	
MACKEY, THOMAS	9 Damascus Street	Private	R.A.M.C.	
MARTIN, ERNEST	7 Haywood Avenue	P.O.G.M.	R.N.	
MILLER, WM.	29 Elm Street	Private	R.A.M.C.	
MOTHERWELL, JAS. G.	34 Shaftesbury Avenue	Private	Dorset Regt.	Died of Cholera, in Baghdad.
McALISTER, HERBERT	19 Abbott Street	Private	R.I.R.	
McALISTER, WM.	19 Abbott Street	Private	R.I.R.	Wounded.
McAULEY, ANDREW	96 River Terrace	Private	R.A.M.C.	
McCOLLAM, JAMES	28 Peveril Street	Private	R.I.R.	Killed in Action.
McCOLLAM, JOHN	28 Peveril Street	Sergeant	R.I.R.	Killed in Action.
McILREAVY, FRED.	61 Lavinia Street	Private	R.A.M.C.	
McCONNELL, JAS.	10 Penrose Street	Private	R.I.R.	

BELFAST PRESBYTERY.   DONEGALL PASS.

Name.	Home Address.	Rank.	Regiment, Battalion or Unit.	Remarks.
McConnell, Wm. L.	10 Penrose Street	Corporal	R.I.R.	Wounded.
McCollough, Wm.	53 Gt. Northern Street	Private	R.I.R.	Wounded.
McKernan, Fred	38 Auburn Street	Private	R.F.A.	
McReynolds, W. F.	4 Ivanhoe Street	Private	R.I.R.	Wounded.
McWilliams, Stewart	2 Coyle Place	Sergeant	R. Inn. Fus.	Died of Wounds.
McWilliams, Wm.	2 Coyle Place	Lieutenant	R. Inn. Fus.	
Nixon, Charles	13 Curzon Street	Private	R.I. Fus.	Killed in Action.
Nixon, James	13 Curzon Street	Trooper	N.I.H.	
Patterson, James	25 Peveril Street	Private	R.E.	
Patterson, Robert	73 Pine Street	Private	Labour Corps	
Patterson, Wm.	73 Pine Street	Corporal	R.I.R.	Killed in Action.
Scott, Robert	3 Charlotte Street	Private	R.I.R.	Killed in Action.
Scott, Norman	36 Damascus Street	Private	R. Inn. Fus.	Wounded.
Scott, Albert	36 Damascus Street	Private		
Scott, Fred.	3 Charlotte Street	Private	R.I.R.	Wounded.
Scott, Harry	3 Charlotte Street	Private	R.I.R.	Wounded.
Scott, Walter	3 Charlotte Street	Private	R.I.R.	
Sloan, James	11 Fernwood Street	Private	R.I.R.	Prisoner of War.
Shaw, Martin	80 Cromwell Road	Lieutenant	R.G.A., Cameroons	M.C.
Shaw, Thomas	80 Cromwell Road	Private	R.I.R.	
Shaw, William	80 Cromwell Road	Lieutenant	R.I.R.	
Stewart, Walter	155 Roden Street	Sergeant	R. Inn. Fus.	Wounded.
Topping, Andrew	29 Elm Street	Private	A. & S. Highldrs.	
Taylor, Harry	10 Cooke Street	Private	Cameron Highldrs.	Wounded.
Taylor, James	10 Cooke Street	Private	R.E.	Wounded.
Thompson, Richard	6 Kimberley Street	Sergeant	R.I.R.	Wounded.
Wilson, Wm. A.	Peveril Street	Private	R.I.R.	
Woods, Wm.	43 Abbott Street	Private	R.I.R.	
Wright, John B.	107 Agincourt Avenue	Private	Machine Gun Corps	Died of Wounds.
Yeates, Andrew	52 Agincourt Avenue	Sergeant	R.I.R.	Killed in Action.
Yeates, Hugh	52 Agincourt Avenue	Sergeant	R.I.R.	Wounded.
Young, Leslie	6 Bagot Street	Private	R. Inn. Fus.	Wd., Pris. of War.
Young, Marshall	6 Bagot Street	Private	R. Inn. Fus.	
McBride, George	35 Essex Street		R.A.M.C.	Wounded.
COLONIAL & U.S.A. FORCES.				
Anderson, Isaac		Private	R.A.M.C., Canadians	
Dewar, James	109 University Street	Private	48th Highldrs., Canadians	Gassed, Died.
Fitzsimons, Samuel	Donegall Road	Private	A.S.C., Canadians	
Gourley, William	27 Elm Street	Private	Canadians	Killed in Action.
McAlister, Robert	62 Howard St. South	Corporal	Canadians	Killed in Action.
McAlister, Samuel			Canadians	Killed in Action.
McKernan, Thos.	38 Auburn Street		American Army	
Wright, Samuel	42 Sunnyside Street		Canadians	Killed in Action.
DONEGALL ROAD.				
Adamson, Wm.	4 Coolmore Street	Corporal	R.I.R.	
Bailie, J. H.	366 Donegall Road	Lance-Corporal	R.I.R.	Wounded.
Bateson, Hugh	34 Thalia Street	Driver	A.S.C.	Killed in Action.
Beattie, Wm.	30 Gaffikin Street	Private	R.I.R.	Killed in Action.
Black, Robert	41 Teutonic Street	Private	R.I. Fus.	
Boyd, James	97 Ormeau Road	Corporal	R.I.R.	
Boyd, Thomas	97 Ormeau Road	Private	R.I.R.	Wounded.
Brennan, Willie	254 Donegall Road	Private	N.I.H.	
Brown, Fred.	31 City Street	Private	R.E.	
Brown, Samuel	31 City Street		R.N.	
Brush, James	61 Eureka Street	Private	R.I.R.	
Burns, Robert	25 Coolbeg Street	Rifleman	R.I.R.	Prisoner.
Campbell, Wm.	31 Lisburn Avenue	Private	R.I. Regt.	
Campbell, Willie	203 Springfield Road		R.N.	
Carlisle, Herbert	24 Dorchester Street	Private	I.G.	Killed in Action.
Carlisle, Thos.	10 Utility Street	Private	R.I.R.	
Caswell, John	99 Abingdon Street	Private	R.I.R.	
Caswell, Joseph	99 Abingdon Street	Bugler	R.I.R.	Prisoner.
Caswell, William	99 Abingdon Street	Sergeant	R.I.R.	Missing.
Cassells, Sam.	117 Donegall Avenue	Rifleman	R.I.R.	Killed in Action.
Chambers, Joseph	11 Renfrew Street	Sergeant	R.F.A.	Died.
Clarke, John	13 Egeria Street	Rifleman	R.I.R.	Prisoner.
Clarke, Sam	13 Egeria Street	Private	R.I. Fus.	
Clarke, Wm.	29 Blythe Street	Sergeant	R.E.	M.M. and Cert.
Connor, James	131 Blythe Street	Private	Lanc. Fus.	
Coote, James	245 Roden Street	Private	R. Inn. Fus.	
Corry, Thos.	28 Barrington Street	Corporal	A.S.C.	
Creelman, Willie	217 Roden Street	Sapper	R.E.	
Crooks, David	30 Utility Street	Rifleman	R.I.R.	
Culbert, Robert	Buckingham Street	Private	R.I.R.	Killed in Action.
Davis, William	103 Charles Street South	Private	R.I.R.	Died.
Donaghy, Adam	22 Lower Rockview St.	Private	R.I.R.	Wounded & Dischd.
Dalzell, Robert	99 Donegall Road	Private	R.I. Fus.	Killed in Action.
Donald, William	168 Utility Street	Lance-Corporal	R.I. Fus.	
Donald, Sam	168 Utility Street	Private	R.I. Fus.	Wounded.
Dawson, John	356 Donegall Road	Seaman	R.N.	Lost at Sea.

BELFAST PRESBYTERY. DONEGALL ROAD.

Name.	Home Address.	Rank.	Regiment, Battalion or Unit.	Remarks.
Dawson, Henry	356 Donegall Road	Private	R.I.R.	Wounded.
Dawson, Charles	356 Donegall Road	Rifleman	R.I.R.	Wounded.
Dawson, Robert J.	356 Donegall Road	Signaller	R.I.R.	Wounded.
Dawson, George	356 Donegall Road	Driver	Machine G. Corps	Wounded.
Dron, William	8 Donegall Avenue	Gunner	R.G.A.	
Eakins, Richard	42 Lindsay Street	Private	R.A.M.C.	
Eakins, Fred.	42 Lindsay Street	Private		Prisoner of War.
Fuller, Harry	65 Devonshire Street	Sergeant	R.S. Regt.	
Ferris, Fred.	7 Symons Street	Private	R.F.A.	Wounded.
Ferguson, George A.	25 Wolseley Street		Flying Corps	
Gray, John	94 Donegall Road	Private	Royal Marines	Killed in Action.
Grahame, James	17 Magnetic Street	Rifleman	R.I.R.	
Greer, Hugh	19 Madrid Street	Private	A.S.C.	Wounded.
Gamble, James	50 Burnaby Street	Rifleman	R.I.R.	
Greer, Willie	59 Donegall Avenue	Private	R.I.R.	
Howard, David	21 Sandymount Street	Sergeant	R.I.R.	Twice Wd.' Cert.
Hannah, Robert	47 Abingdon Street	Lance-Corporal	R.I.R.	Wounded.
Houston, Robert	44 Auburn Street	Private	R.I.R.	Wounded.
Howie, Richard	68 Lindsay Street	Sergeant	Machine G. Corps	
Howie, Walter	68 Lindsay Street	Private	Irish Guards	Killed in Action.
Hill, Sam.	26 Symons Street	Driver	Salonica, R.F.A.	
Hoy, George	84 Utility Street	Private	R.I. Fus.	Prisoner.
Howard, J. A.	Norfolk Drive	2nd Engineer	H.M.S. Transport	
Henry, Samuel	147 Blythe Street	Sergeant	R.I.R.	
Johnston, Willie	34 Coolbeg Street	Private	Rifles	
Johnston, Joseph	34 Coolbeg Street	Private	R.I.R.	Wounded.
Johnston, Hugh	34 Coolbeg Street	Rifleman	R.I.R.	
Johnston, George	7 Euterpe Street	Sergeant	R.I.R.	
Johnston, John	20 Thalia Street	Driver	A.S.C.	
Jameson, Sam	123 Sandy Row	Corporal	R. Inn. Fus.	
Keep, Francis	42 Coolfin Street	Private	R.A.M.C.	
Kilpatrick, James	247 Donegall Road	Private	R.A.M.C.	
Kenning, John	39 Sandhurst Drive	Q.M. Sergeant	R.I.R.	
Kirkpatrick, John	207 Matilda Street	Sergeant	R.I. Fus.	
Kennedy, John	43 Virginia Street	Trooper	N.I.H.	
Lambert, William	143 Blythe Street	Corporal	R.I.R.	
Lovell, Joe	20 Barrington Street	Bombardier	R.I.R.	
Lowry, Willie	81 Donegall Road	A.B.	R.N.	
Leathem, Jas. Edward	1 Westminster Street		A.S.C.	
Leitch, William	5 Matilda Street	Private	R.I.R.	Killed in Action.
Lamont, J.	39 Coolfin Street	Rifleman	R.I.R.	
Leslie, Alex.	48 Boyne Square		R.N.	
Maxwell, R. J.	178 Blythe Street	Rifleman	R.I.R.	
McCurdy, John	15 Charleville Avenue	A.B.	R.N.	
McGregor, Duncan	32 Boyd Street	A.B.	R.N.	
McCarthy, Wm. J.	13 Coolfin Street	Private	R.I. Fus.	Wounded.
McCarthy, Andrew	13 Coolfin Street	Sapper	R.E.	Wounded.
McKeown, James	34 Coolfin Street	Sapper	R.E.	Killed in Action.
Macquiston, Samuel	91 Clementine Street	Rifleman	R.I.R.	Killed in Action.
McCrory, Joseph	63 Utility Street	Corporal	R.I.R.	
Martin, John A.	133 Blythe Street	Sapper	R.E.	
Magee, Alexander	123 Sandy Row	Private	A. Ord. Corps	Killed in Action.
McClean, William	42 Turin Street	Seaman	R.N.	Drowned.
McClean, Thomas	42 Turin Street	Private	R.I.R.	
Molyneux, John	32 Tavanagh Street	Stoker	R.N.	
Mateer, Robert	9 Aughrim Street	Rifleman	R.I.R.	Prisoner.
McBride, David	91 Clementine Street	Sapper	R.I. Fus.	Killed in Action.
Murray, Willie	8 Drew Street	Private	Innis. Dragoons	
McAllum, Sam	71 Excise Street	Private	Motor Transport	
Nutt, John	34 Rockview Street	Lance-Corporal	R.I.R.	Military Medal.
Potts, James	61 Lindsay Street	Private	R.I.R.	
Pollock, Isaac	10 Lawyer Street	Stoker	R.N.	
Pollock, Henry	30 Albion Street	A.B.	R.N.	
Pollock, Frederick	30 Albion Street		Air Service	
Pollock, Thomas	40 Auburn Street	Rifleman	R.I.R.	
Parker, Isaac	201 Donegall Road	Gunner	R.I.R.	Killed in Action.
Patterson, Sam	29 Beit Street	Boy Cook	R.N.	
Redpath, John	89 Roden Street	Private	R.I. Fus.	
Redpath, William	89 Roden Street	Rifleman	R.I.R.	
Reid, Robert	18 Electric Street	Sergeant	A. & S. Highldrs.	
Reid, William	31 Britannic Street	Private	R.I.R.	
Reid, Charles	13 Matilda Street	Rifleman	R.I.R.	
Reid, Robert	13 Matilda Street	Rifleman	R.I.R.	Died of Wounds.
Reid, Andrew	13 Matilda Street	Lance-Corporal	R.I.R.	Certificate.
Ross, Jack	4 Donegall Road	Gunner	R.F.A.	
Smyth, Samuel J.	79 Lindsay Street	Private	A. & S. Highldrs.	Killed.
Stewart, Sam	133 Dunluce Avenue	Sergeant	R.I.R.	
Stewart, Matthew	133 Dunluce Avenue	Staff-Sergeant	A.P.O.	
Shaw, John	34 Donegall Avenue	Private	R.I.R.	Wounded.
Smyth, Willie	101 Donegall Pass	Private	R.I.R.	
Stewart, George	16 Egeria Street	Corporal	R.I.R.	
Stirling, James	38 Fourth Street	Driver	R.F.A.	
Shirlow, Alex.	47 Majestic Street	Private	R.I.R.	
Service, Robert	54 Rockview Street	Sergeant	R.I.R.	Wounded.

BELFAST PRESBYTERY. **DONEGALL ROAD.**

Name.	Home Address.	Rank.	Regiment, Battalion or Unit.	Remarks.
Scott, Reginald	33 Donegall Avenue	Gunner	R.F.A.	Wounded.
Scott, John C.	33 Donegall Avenue	Driver	A.S.C.	Wounded.
Stoddart, William	76 Roden Street	Gunner	R.N.	
Stevens, R. J.	178 Blythe Street	Private	A.S.C.	
Scott, Thomas	14 Pandora Street	Stoker	R.N.	
Smyth, David	10 Balmoral Street	Private	Seaforth Highldrs.	
Thompson, John	14 Divis Drive	Private	R.I. Rifles	
Turner, William	40 Electric Street	Sapper	R.E.	
Watt, Robert	70 Coolfin Street	Private	R.I. Fus.	Killed in Action.
Watt, David	143 Kitchener Street	Private	A. & S. Highldrs.	Killed in Action.
Watt, Joseph	81 Hunter Street	Sergeant	R.I.R.	Wounded.
Wilson, Thomas	Ashley Avenue	Private	R. Inn. Fus.	
Wilson, Willie	Utility Street	Rifleman	R.I.R.	Prisoner.
Wilkinson, Abie	58 Selby Street	Rifleman	R.I.R.	Prisoner.
Wilkinson, John	58 Selby Street	Private	A.S.C.	
Wilkinson, Robert	10 Symons Street	Lance-Corporal	R.I. Fus.	Prisoner of War.
Woods, John	135 M'Clure Street	Lance-Corporal	R.I. Fus.	
Woods, Willie	135 M'Clure Street	Private	R.I. Fus.	
Wilkinson, Francis G.	190 Donegall Avenue	Private	Irish Guards	
Withers, John	69 Blythe Street	A.M.	R.F.C.	
Wilkinson, Robert J.	60 Egmont Street	Private	A.M. Corps	
Wilson, Charles	31 Ulsterville Avenue	Captain	K.S.L.I.	
COLONIAL FORCES.				
Bailie, Thomas	155 Donegall Road		Canadian F. Amb.	
Boyd, Alex.		Private	Canadian Div.	
Boyd, John		Sapper	Australians	
Eakins, James		Gunner	Canadian Div.	
Eakins, John		Sapper	Canadian Eng.	
Lamont, Wm.	39 Coolfin Street	Lance-Corporal	Australian I.F.	
Sloan, Wm.	170 Donegall Road	Private	Canadian Cont.	Killed in Action.
Smylie, Hugh	31 Maryville Street	Private	Australian I.F.	
DUNCAIRN.				
Adeley, Gerald Graham	Ben Eaden	Major	Royal Air Force	Wounded.
Adeley, Wm. Lawrence	Ben Eaden	Captain	A.S.C.	Wounded.
Aiken, Thomas	129 Up. Canning Street	Gunner	R.F.A.	
Allen, Isaac		Rifleman	R.I. Rifles	
Andison, Jas. Stewart	230 Cliftonville Road	Private	K.O.S.B.	Killed in Action.
Angus, John	126 Hillman Street	Lance-Corporal	R.E.	M.M. and Bar.
Arthur, Ian	Orient Gardens	Rifleman	R.I. Rifles	
Blackburn, John	Castleton Street	Gunner	R.G.A.	Died.
Blair, James S.	Oldpark Road	Lance-Corporal	R.I. Rifles	Wounded.
Boylan, John	Annadale Street	Rifleman	R.I. Rifles	Killed in Action.
Brown, C. B.	Brookvale Street	Gunner	Tank Corps	Wounded, M.M.
Brown, John	Brookvale Street	2nd Lieutenant	3rd S. Lancs. R.	Wounded.
Brown, H. W.	Brookvale Street	Lieutenant	4th W. Yorks R. (S.R.)	Wounded.
Brownlie, James		Private	M.T. A.S.C.	
Campbell, R. B.	Up. Meadow Street	Signaller	R.I. Rifles	Killed.
Carton, James	Singleton Street	Sergeant	R.I. Rifles	D.C.M., French and Belgian Medals.
Clarke, John K.	Manse Strabane	Lieutenant	R. Air Force	Killed in Action.
Corbett, James	57 Cedar Avenue	Lieutenant	K.O. Liverpool R.	Wounded.
Craig, Hugh M.	Chichester Park	Gunner	R.G.A.	Wounded.
Crockett, John	Templemore Pk. L'derry	Captain	R.I. Fus.	
Crothers, William	Hillman Street	Gunner	R.H.A.	
Darroch, Duncan	Hillman Street	Rifleman	R.I. Rifles	Wd., Pris. of War.
Davidson, Wm.	Alexandra Park Avenue	Rifleman	R.I. Rifles	Wounded.
Dick, Robert	Henryville Street	A.B. Seaman	R.N.	
Doak, John J.	Cosgrove Street	Trooper	N.I.H.	Wounded.
Donaghey, D.	Spamount Street	Signaller	R.I. Rifles	
Dorward, James	Stranmillis Gardens	Lieutenant	Munster Fus.	Wounded.
Drennan, Wm. J.	Lepper Street	Rifleman	R.I. Rifles	Wounded.
Duncan, Wm.	Walbeck Street	Sergeant	A.S.C.	
Dunn, J. Herbert	Wellesley Avenue	2nd Lieutenant	R. Ir. Fus.	Wounded.
Dunn, Walter		Private	London Irish	
Dunseith, Albert V.	Ashley Park	Corporal	R.I. Fus.	Wounded.
Edgar, James	Crimea Street	P.O.	R.N.A.S.	
Edgar, John Maxwell	Crimea Street	Private	R.A.M.C.	
Erskine, Wm. A.	Up. Canning Street	Rifleman	R.I. Rifles	Killed in Action.
Ewing, John	Stratheden Street	2nd Lieutenant	R.I. Rifles	M.M.
Fry, Robert	Hartwell Street	Sapper	R.E.	
Fryers, Albert	Oldpark	A.B. Seaman	R.N.	
Fryers, Wm. G. T.	Oldpark	Private	R. Marines	
Gamble, John	Shercock, Co. Cavan	C.S.M.	R.E.	
Gibb, John	Chestnutt Gardens	Rifleman	R.I. Rifles	Wounded.
Gibson, John	Chestnutt Gardens	Rifleman	R.I. Rifles	Wounded.
Gibson, Matt. H.	Chestnutt Gardens	Lieutenant	R.I. Rifles	M.C., Kd. in Act.
Gillespie, David	Donegall Square S.	Sergeant	A.S.C.	
Girvan, Walter	Woodland Avenue	2nd Lieutenant	Black Watch	French M.M.
Girvan, Wm. D.	Arlington Street	Rifleman	R.I. Rifles	Killed in Action.
Gordon, John	Shandon Street	Corporal	M.G.C.	Killed in Action.

BELFAST PRESBYTERY. DUNCAIRN.

NAME.	HOME ADDRESS.	RANK.	REGIMENT, BATTALION OR UNIT.	REMARKS.
GOURLEY, DANIEL	Arlington Street	Rifleman	R.I. Rifles	
GRAHAM, FRED.	Oldpark Road	Private	Cameron Highldrs.	Killed in Action.
GRAHAM, WILLIAM	Oldpark Road	Rifleman	R.I. Rifles	
GRAY, THOMAS	...	Rifleman	R.I. Rifles	
HAMILTON, JOSEPH	...	Rifleman	R.I. Rifles	
HAYES, JOHN	Shandon Street	Rifleman	R.I. Rifles	
HAYES, WM	Shandon Street	Private	R.I. Fus.	
HENDRON, J.	Dublin Road	Sergeant	R.I. Rifles	Wounded.
HILL, SAMUEL	12 Marsden Gardens	Sergeant	R.A.M.C.	Wounded.
IRWIN, NORMAN	Richmond	Gunner	R.G.A.	
IRWIN, W. W.	Victoria Gardens	Trooper	N.I.H.	Wounded.
JACKSON, CULBERTSON	Lower Crescent	Lieutenant	R.I. Rifles	M.C., Wounded.
JACKSON, J. SINCLAIR	Lower Crescent	Lieutenant	R.E.	M.C., Wounded.
JACKSON, MAURICE	Lower Crescent	Captain	R. Inn. Fus.	Wounded.
KELLY, WILLIAM	Hillman Street	2nd Lieutenant	R.I. Rifles	
KENNEDY, ERNEST	Moyola Street	Gunner	R.F.A.	
KENNEDY, SAMUEL J.	Moyola Street	Private	R.I. Rifles	Wounded.
KENNEDY, J. V.	Hartwell Street	Rifleman	R.I. Rifles	
KERR, CECIL H.	Orient Gardens	Lieutenant	R. Ir. Fus.	M.C., Croix.de-G., Men. twice Des.
KERR, ROBERT A.	Orient Gardens	Captain	R.A.M.C.	M.C.
LEES, LOWRY	Hughenden Avenue	Sergeant	Lond. Scott.	Killed in Action.
LEMON, WM. J.	Crumlin Road	Lance-Corporal	Tank Corps	
LIGGETT, ROBERT	Manor Street	C.Q.M.S.	R.I. Rifles	
LOGAN, HARRY L.	Castleton Gardens	2nd Lieutenant	18th Lond. Ir. Rifles	
LOGAN, JACK W.	Castleton Gardens	Trooper	N.I.H.	
LOGAN, JAMES F.	Castleton Gardens	Sergeant	R.I. Rifles	Wounded.
LOWE, ALFRED	Crescent Gardens	Lieutenant	R. Ir. Regt.	
McARTHUR, JAMES	Duncairn Gardens	Sergeant	R.I. Rifles	Wounded.
McCALLISTER, ROBERT	Hillman Street	Corporal	R.I. Rifles	Wd. and Prisoner.
McCAMMOND, CECIL	Donegall Park	2nd Lieutenant	R.I. Rifles	Wounded.
McCAMMOND, W. E. C.	Donegall Park	Lieut.-Colonel	R.I. Rifles	
McCAULEY, S.	Springfield Road	Private	R.F.A.	Wounded.
McCLEERY, J. M.	Old Cavehill Road	Flight-Commander	R.N.A.S.	
McCLELLAND, HAROLD	Linden Gardens	Driver	M.T. A.S.C.	
McCONNELL, R. J.	...	Lieutenant	R.A.M.C.	
McCRACKEN, SAMUEL	Mervue Street	Rifleman	R.I. Rifles	Wounded.
McCUTCHEON, WILLIAM	Spamount Street	Corporal	R.E.	
McDOWELL, JAMES	Spamount Street	Rifleman	R.I. Rifles	Wounded.
McDOWELL, JOHN BECK	Stranmillis Road	Lance-Corporal	R.F. (U.D.S)	Killed in Action.
McEWAN, HENRY C.	Clifton Crescent	Captain	R.G.A.	
McILVEEN, J. HERBERT	Parkmount Road	Private	M.T. A.S.C.	
McKEE, ALEXR.	Antrim Road	C.S.M.	Tank Corps	
McKENDRICK, ANDREW	Chichester Avenue	Corporal	Black Watch	Killed in Action.
McNAB, WILLIAM	Evolina Street	Private	Tank Corps	Wounded.
McNAMEE, JOHN	Cavour Street	Rifleman	R.I. Rifles	
MAGILL, ROBERT M.	Cavehill Road	Trooper	N.I.H.	
MAHAFFY, LEO	Antrim Road	Gunner	R.G.A.	
MAXWELL, STANLEY W.	Limestone Road	2nd Lieutenant	R.I. Rifles	Died Pris.in Ger.
MAYNES, GEORGE	Hillman Street	Driver	M.T. A.S.C.	
MAXWELL, WILFRID	Limestone Road	2nd Lieutenant	A.S.C.	
MILLAR, MATT HENRY	Glandore Avenue	Private	Tank Corps	
MONTGOMERY, LANCELOT	Antrim Road	Rifleman	R.I. Rifles	Wounded.
MONTGOMERY, SYDNEY W.	Somerton Road	Lance-Corporal	N.I.H.	Gassed.
MOORE, A. R.	Arlington Street	Rifleman	R.I. Rifles	
MOORE, F. W.	London	Private	R.F.	
MOORE, ROBERT M.	Glandore Gardens	2nd Lieutenant	R. Ir. F.	Prisoner of War.
MOORE, ROBERT T.	Up. Meadow Street	Rifleman	R.I. Rifles	Wounded.
MOORHEAD, JOSHUA	St. Paul's Street	Private	Machine Gun Corps	
MOORHEAD, MATTHEW	St. Paul's Street	Private	R.A.M.C.	
MOORHEAD, WM. JOHN	St. Paul's Street	Rifleman	R.I. Rifles	Wounded.
MOORHEAD, THOMAS	St. Paul's Street	Stoker	R.N.R.	Torpedoed.
MORRISON, A.	Spamount Street	Rifleman	R.I. Rifles	Wounded.
MORROW, JOHN S.	Eia House	Major	R.A.M.C.	
MORTON, W. SIDNEY	Atlantic Avenue	Private	A.S.C.	
MOUTRAY, ALEXANDER	Annadale Street	Rifleman	R.I. Rifles	
NICOLL, HARRY	Hopefield Avenue	Rifleman	R.I. Rifles	Killed in Action.
NIXON, CECIL	Hopefield Avenue	Corporal	R.I.R.	
NIXON, HAROLD P.	Hopefield Avenue	2nd Lieutenant	Wiltshire Regt.	Killed in Action.
NORRIS, W.	Grosvenor Road	Sergeant	R.I. Rifles	
ORR, FRANK	Crimea Street	Rifleman	R.I. Rifles	Killed in Action.
ORR, ROBERT	...	Sergeant	Royal Scots	
OSBORNE, H. CORRY	Hopefield Terrace	2nd Lieutenant	West Yorks R.	Killed in Action.
PATTERSON, ARTHUR	Singleton Street	A.B. Seaman	R.N.	
PATTERSON, HAROLD	Singleton Street	Private	R. Air Force	
PATTERSON, JAMES	Singleton Street	A.B. Seaman	R.N.	
PATTERSON, JOHN	Sheridan Street	Corporal	A.S.C.	
PICKEN, ANDREW	Richmond	Driver	M.T. A.S.C.	
PICKEN, SAMUEL E.	Richmond	Captain	R.A.M.C.	M.C.
PURDY, W. J.	Church Street	Rifleman	R.I. Rifles	Wounded.
RAE, JAMES	Hogarth Street	Rifleman	R.I. Rifles	Wounded.
RAINEY, WM.	Up. Meadow Street	Rifleman	R.I. Rifles	
RAMSEY, THOS.	...	A.B. Seaman	R.N.	
RANKIN, HUGH	Limestone Road	Lance-Corporal	R.I. Rifles	

BELFAST PRESBYTERY. — DUNCAIRN.

Name.	Home Address.	Rank.	Regiment, Battalion or Unit.	Remarks.
Rankin, Matthew	Limestone Road	Lieutenant	R.I. Rifles	
Rea, Wm. Q.	Richmond	2nd Lieutenant	R.I. Rifles	Prisoner of War.
Ritchie, Ernest A.		Private	R.A.M.C.	
Ritchie, W.		Sergeant	R.F.A.	
Rodgers, Wm.	Duncairn Gardens	Driver	A.S.C.	
Ronaldson, George R.	Cliftonville Circus	Rifleman	R.I. Rifles	Wounded.
Ronaldson, Harry	"	Lieutenant	I.W.T., R.E.	
Ronaldson, Jas. G.	Cliftonville Circus	2nd Lieutenant	R.W. Surrey Regt.	Killed in Action.
Ronaldson, Richard G.	Cliftonville Circus	Q.M.S.	Scot. Nat. Res.	
Sayers, Arthur C.	Vicinage Park	Lance-Corporal	R.I. Rifles	Wounded.
Shields, Fred.	Carlisle Circus	Captain	R.A.M.C.	
Shields, W. J.	Carlisle Circus	Lieutenant	A.D.S.	
Sinclair, D. J. O.	Hopefield House	Captain	R. Ir. F.	Wounded.
Sinclair, T. C.	Hopefield House	Colonel	R.A.	Wounded.
Skelly, Hugh	Stratheden Street	Gunner	R.F.A.	
Slade, Chas. Gordon	Hopefield Avenue	2nd Lieutenant	Beds. R.	
Smith, Archie	Marsden Gardens	Private	R. Ir. F.	
Smith, Jas. H.	Marsden Gardens	Corporal	R.I. Rifles	Wounded.
Spence, John			R.N.R.	
Spence, Robert L.	Halliday's Road	Rifleman	R.I. Rifles	Prisoner of War.
Spence, Wm.	Joy Street	Rifleman	R.I. Rifles	
Stewart, Thomas	Osborne Street	Rifleman	R.I. Rifles	Prisoner of War.
Stewart, Wm. Jas.	Shandon Street	Rifleman	R.I. Rifles and R. Air. F.	
Stewart, Wm. John	New Lodge Road	Rifleman	R.I. Rifles	Wd., Pris. of War.
Strange, James	Alexandra Avenue	Staff Sergeant	R.I. Rifles	
Strange, Samuel, Junr.	Carnmoney	Trooper	N.I. Horse and Scots Greys	
Strange, Samuel	Coventry Street	A.B. Seaman	R.N.	Killed in Action.
Stuart, George G.	Cliftonville Avenue	Bombardier	R.G.A.	Wounded.
Tweedie, Fred.	Antrim Road	Rifleman	R.I. Rifles	
Tyrell, John Marcus	Bangor, Co. Down	Captain	R.I.F., att. R.A.F.	Killed in Action.
Tyrell, Walter Alex.	Bangor, Co. Down	Flight-Commander	R.A.F.	Killed in Action.
Tyrell, Wm.	Bangor, Co. Down	Lieut.-Colonel	R.A.M.C.	M.C. and D.S.O.
Vint, Lionel H.	Brookvale Avenue	2nd Lieutenant	R.A.F.	
Walsh, John E.	Brookvale Avenue	Rifleman	R.I. Rifles	
Wilson, Tom	Thorndale Avenue	Gunner	R.G.A.	Killed in Action.
Wilson, Wyndham	Allworthy Avenue	Gunner	R.F.A.	
Winters, S.	Walbeck Street	Private	R.I.R.	Wd., Pris. of War.
Wylie, John	Up. Meadow Street	Private	Div. Cyclist Corps, R.A.F.	
Wylie, Stuart	Up. Meadow Street	Sergeant	R.I. Rifles	Wd., Pris. of War.
Wylie, James	Up. Meadow Street	Private	R.A.M.C.	
Young, James R.	Chichester Park	Captain	A.S.C.	
COLONIAL FORCES.				
Barron, Fred.	Fortwilliam Park	Sergeant	Canadian Con.	
Bickerstaff, William	Halliday's Road	Corporal	P.P. C.L.I.	Wounded, Died.
Dorman, A.	Stratheden Street	Private	Can. Ex. F.	Killed in Action.
Dunseith, A. V.		Private	S.Af. Md. Inft.	
Kerr, F. J.	Orient Gardens	Corporal	N.Z. Division	
McNab, John	Evolina Street	Corporal	Can. Ex. F.	Killed in Action.
Millar, Samuel J.	Glandore Avenue	Corporal	Can. Ex. F.	Wounded.
Montgomery, Jas. A.	Somerton Road	R.Q.M.S.	Can. Con.	Wounded.
Spence, John A.	Crumlin Road	Private	Can. A.M.C.	
DUNMURRY.				
Agnew, David	Dunmurry	Staff-Sergeant	A.S.C.	
Agnew, James	Dunmurry	Private	2nd R.I.R.	Killed in Action.
Agnew, John	Dunmurry	Sergeant	2nd R.I. Fus.	
Agnew, Thomas	Dunmurry	A.B.	R.N.	
Agnew, William	Dunmurry	Farrier	A.S.C.	M.M.
Agnew, William	Dunmurry	Sapper	R.E.	D.C.M., M.M.
Anderson, David M.	The Park, Dunmurry	Captain	5th R.I.R.	Wounded.
Anderson, Robert N.	The Park, Dunmurry	Lieutenant	2nd Cav. Reserve	
Anderson, Wm. A.	The Park, Dunmurry	Captain	R.A.M.C.	French Decoration
Arnold, John C.	The Manse, Dunmurry	Captain	1st Tyneside I. Brigade	Wounded.
Beggs, James	Dunmurry	Private	18th R.I.R.	
Bell, Wm. John	Suffolk, Dunmurry	Private	A.S.C.	
Bickerstaff, Thomas	Red Hill, Dunmurry	Private	11th R.I.R.	
Bothwell, T. H.	Mill Row, Dunmurry	Private	9th R.I.R.	Killed in Action.
Chambers, Joseph	Stewartstown Road	Private	11th R.I.R.	W'ded and Died.
Clarke, Adam	Milfort Av., Dunmurry	Private	9th R. Inn. Fus.	W'ded and Died.
Crooks, Joseph	Milfort Av., Dunmurry	Private	2nd R. Scots	
Crowe, Thomas	Mill Row, Dunmurry	Private	11th R.I.R.	
Duff, Joseph	Mill Row, Dunmurry	Private	11th R.I.R.	
Finlay, David H.	Duniris	Sergeant	9th R.I.R.	Wounded.
Fullerton, James	Strower Row, Dunmurry	Private	11th R.I.R.	Wounded.
Gillian, Samuel	Suffolk, Dunmurry	Private	R.A.F.	
Gillian, William	Suffolk, Dunmurry	Private	11th R.I.R.	
Gillian, William	Dunmurry	Private	11th R.I.R.	
Gillian, Wm. J.	Dunmurry	Private	11th R.I.R.	
Gregg, Robert	Suffolk, Dunmurry	Private	R.A.F.	
Hamilton, John D.	Dunmurry	Private	11th R.I.R.	
Hanna, Frank Leslie	Finaghy, Dunmurry	Lieutenant	Argyle & S. Highdrs.	Died in Hospital.

BELFAST PRESBYTERY. DUNMURRY.

Name.	Home Address.	Rank.	Regiment, Battalion or Unit.	Remarks.
Hanna, Wm. Tyrrell (Dr.)	Finaghy, Dunmurry	Lance-Corporal	R.A.S.C.	Wounded.
Harris, James	Milfort Av., Dunmurry	Private	5th R.I.R.	Wounded.
Hill, Samuel	Maryville Terrace	Private	11th R.I.R.	Wounded.
Hunter, S. R.	Rosemount, Dunmurry	Captain	R.A.M.C.	
Hyndman, James	Suffolk, Dunmurry	Private	11th R.I.R.	Died in France.
Hyndman, Robert J.	Suffolk, Dunmurry	Private	11th R.I.R.	
Irvine, Robert	Mt. Pleasant, Dunmurry	Private	11th R.I.R.	Wounded.
Irvine, Wm.	Mt. Pleasant, Dunmurry	Private	Scottish Fus.	Wounded.
Jack, Wm.	Conway, Dunmurry	Private	A.S.C.	
Kean, James	Railway St., Dunmurry	Private	2nd R. Inn. Fus.	Wounded.
Kennedy, Alex.	Mill Row, Dunmurry	Private	11th R.I.R.	
Kinnaird, J. L.	Lismoyne, Dunmurry	Captain	R.I.R.	
Logan, John	Larkfield, Dunmurry	Private	R. Inn. Fus.	
McClelland, John	Dispensary Hill	Sergt.-Major	Prince of Wales' Own	Wounded.
McComb, David	Milfort Av., Dunmurry	Private	A.S.C.	Wounded.
McCosh, Robert J.	Ladybrook, Dunmurry	Private	2nd R.I.R.	
McCosh, Samuel	Ladybrook, Dunmurry	Private	11th R.I.R.	
McCracken, Robert	Mill View, Dunmurry	Private	18th R.I.R.	
McDonald, Samuel	Fortfield, Dunmurry	Lance-Corporal	11th R.I.R.	
McFarlane, Wm. B.	Waterloo, Dunmurry	Sergeant	M. Foot Police	
McIlwaine, Samuel	Conway, Dunmurry	Private	R.I.R.	
McKechnie, Robert	Dunmurry	Lance-Corporal	11th R.I.R.	Killed in Action.
McKeown, Wm.	Dunmurry	Sergeant	11th R.I.R.	Killed in Action.
Magee, Wm.	Poleglass	Stoker	H.M.T.	
Marshall, James	Fairview, Dunmurry	Sergeant	10th R.I.R.	
Millar, Wm.	Dunmurry	Private		W'ded and Died.
Mitchell, Alex.	Innisfallen, Dunmurry	Trooper	N.I.H.	Wounded.
Murdoch, Samuel	Seymour Hill, Dunmurry	Private	11th R.I.R.	Prisoner.
Palmer, Francis	Fortfield, Dunmurry	A.C.	R.A.F.	
Patterson, John	Dunmurry	Private	11th R.I.R.	Wounded.
Pullins, William	Lambeg, Dunmurry		1st R.I.R.	Wounded.
Rennix, Edward	Maryville Tce., Dunmurry	Lance-Corporal	11th R.I.R.	Killed in Action.
Tannahill, Harry A.	Trinity Gds., Dunmurry	Corporal	11th R.I.R.	M.M., Wounded.
Tannahill, Robert	Trinity Gds., Dunmurry	Private	11th R.I.R.	Wounded.
Taylor, Wm.	Station View, Dunmurry	Private	R. Inn. Fus.	Wounded.
Thompson, Edward	Poleglass, Dunmurry	Private	18th R.I.R.	
Thompson, Edward, Junr.	Dunmurry	Private	4th Inn. Fus.	Killed in Action.
Thompson, Edward	Poleglass, Dunmurry	A.C.	R.A.F.	
Thompson, Thos.	Milfort Av., Dunmurry	Private		
Thompson, Thos., Junr.	Milfort Av., Dunmurry	Private	A.S.C.	
Todd, John	Suffolk, Dunmurry	Private	11th R.I.R.	
Todd, Robert	Suffolk, Dunmurry	A.C.	R.A.F.	
Wallace, James	Dunmurry	Lance-Corporal	R.I.R.	Missing.
Young, Geo. C.	Dunmurry	A.C.	R.A.F.	
COLONIAL & U.S.A. FORCES.				
Bell, John A.	Suffolk	Private	U.S.A.	
Finlay, Thos. D.	Dunmurry	Private	S. African Inft.	
Holden, A. R.	Salisbury Place	Private	Aust. I.F.	
MacVicker, Leon	Thorndale	Lieutenant	S.S.A., French Army	
Rainey, James	Dunmurry	Private	2nd Canadians	Killed in Action.
Reid, Wm.	Suffolk	Private	2nd Canadians	Wounded.
Tannahill, John S.	Dunmurry	Private	2nd Canadians	
EGLINTON STREET.				
Allen, Robert	190 Agnes Street	Corporal	N.I.H.	
Bill, David	5 Conlon Street	Private	6th R.I.R.	
Blackstock, David D.	91 Duncairn Gardens	A.S. Major	14th R.I.R.	
Blair, John		Private	N.I.H.	
Blundell, Edward	1 Trinity Street	Private	Cycling Corps	
Brown, Samuel	25 Howe Street	1st Stoker	R.N. Reserves	
Christie, David	47 Up. Charleville St.	A.B.	H.M.S. Dublin	
Clarke, Samuel	55 Hopeton Street	Lance-Corporal	6th R. Highldrs.	
Clokey, Edmund Hy.	1 Crumlin Terrace	Major	Machine Gun Corps	M.C.
Cobain, James	3 Evelyn Gardens	Private	14th R.I.R.	Died.
Crothers, Edwin J.	Albertville Drive	Corporal	R.A.M.C.	
Cunningham, James	18 Castleton Gardens	Private	14th R.I.R.	
Cunningham, Francis	18 Castleton Gardens	Cadet	N.I.H.	
Eno, John	22 Avonbeg Street	Private	R.I.R.	
Gray, John	22 Moyola Street	Lieutenant	Canadian Infantry	Killed in Action.
Harvey, David	55 Christopher Street	Private	8/9 R.I.R.	
Karr, Alfred E.	18 Carlisle Street	Private	7th R.I. Regt.	
Karr, Robert J.	18 Carlisle Street	2nd Engineer Officer	H.M.S. Monitor	
Karr, William H.	18 Carlisle Street	Lieutenant	R.F.A.	
Kirker, David	62 Christopher Street	A.B.	H.M.S. Implacable	
Knight, Robert Gregg	55 Rosemount Gardens	Private	R.A.F.	
Love, Thos. Edmund	32 Thorndale Avenue	Private	13/15 London Regt.	
McAllister, Alex.	62 Berlin Street	Corporal	N.I.H.	
McAllister, George A.	62 Berlin Street	Private	14th R.I.R.	
McAllister, Wm. A.	62 Berlin Street	Private	14th R.I.R.	
McCleery, James	131 Snugville Street	Sapper	R.E.	
McClements, Wm. Jas.	15 Leadbetter Street	Private	15th R.I.R.	Killed in Action.

BELFAST PRESBYTERY.   EGLINTON STREET.

Name.	Home Address.	Rank.	Regiment, Battalion or Unit.	Remarks.
McClure, Charles	7 Lonsdale Street	Private	Irish Guards	
McClurg, James	236 Old Lodge Road	Corporal	N.I.H.	
McConnell, Wm. J.	167 Crimea Street	A.B.	H.M.S. Ardent	Accid. Drowned.
McConnell, Andrew	167 Crimea Street	Private	22nd Manchesters	
McCullough, Wm. G.	32 Thorndale Avenue	Sapper	Army Sig. Co., R.E.	
McFall, Daniel	5 Conlon Street	Private	R.A.F.	
McFall, Thomas	5 Conlon Street	Private	6th R.I.R.	
McQuitty, Wm. J. C.	Kennet Place	Lance-Corporal	Machine Gun Corps	M.M.
Miskelly, Wm. James		A.B.	H.M.S. Benbow	
Mitchell, John		Private	R.I.R.	
Orr, Alexander	50 Jocelyn Avenue	Private	1/6 Black Watch	Killed in Action.
Osborough, Alan Henry	13 Eglinton Street	Lieutenant	12th R.I.R.	
Osborough, Edwin James	13 Eglinton Street	Corporal	12th R.I.R.	
Osborough, Wm. Andrew	13 Eglinton Street	Private	R.A.S.C.	
Prentice, Alexander	13 Glenfarne Street	Lance-Corporal	121st Field Co., R.E.	
Quinn, Wm. James	43 Hatfield Street	Corporal	Res. Sig. Co., R.E.	
Rea, William	9 Ratcliffe Street	Sergeant	R.F.A.	
Rea, Johnston	9 Ratcliffe Street	Private	R.A.F.	
Rea, Thomas	9 Ratcliffe Street	Sergeant	10th R.I.R.	
Rogerson, Henry	112 Bristol Street	Corporal	3rd Co. A.S.C.	
Simpson, John D. H.	208 Old Lodge Road	Private	19th R.I.R.	
Simpson, Thomas	208 Old Lodge Road	Private	Royal Air Force	
Smyth, James	4 Elmgrove Terrace	Petty Officer	R.N.A.F.	
Smyth, John	4 Elmgrove Terrace	Private	2nd R.I.R.	
Spratt, John	45 Brussels Street	Private	R.A.F.	
Stewart, John	3 Klondyke Street	Private	15th R.I.R.	Killed in Action.
Symms, Walter Geo.	208 Old Lodge Road	Corporal	3rd Co. A.S.C.	1st Cl. Order St.G.
Todd, Thomas	30 Up. Glenfarne Street	Private	N.I.H.	
Williamson, David	176 Snugville Street	Sapper	R.E.	
Wilson, Charles H.	14 Cliftonville Road	Captain	Lanc. Fus.	
EKENHEAD.				
Adair, Robert	90 Hillman Street	Private	R. Inn. Fus.	Wounded.
Adair, Samuel	90 Hillman Street	Sergeant	African Mtd. Rifles	
Adair, William	90 Hillman Street	Private	A.S.C.	
Adams, William	143 Spamount Street	Private	R.A.S.	
Baillie, Frank	4 Carlisle Street		R.N.	
Bagshaw, James	49 Hillman Street	Sergeant	15th R.I.R.	
Bole, George	10 Meadow Street	Private	R. Warwicks	Wounded.
Boal, Robert	13 Derg Street	Trooper	N.I.H.	
Bond, Isaac	16 Donore Street	Private	A.S.C.	
Boyd, David	205 Old Lodge Road	Corporal	5th R.I.R.	
Browne, Wm. R.	34 Springmount Street		R.N.	
Caddell, James	25 Spencer Street	Corporal	17th R.I.R.	
Campbell, Joseph			African Rifles	
Campbell, Robert B.	222 Up. Meadow Street	Private	14th R.I.R.	Missing.
Clarke, Wilfred	70 Rosevale Street	Private	R.I.R.	Killed in Action.
Corry, Alexander	90 Mountcollyer Avenue	Trooper	N.I.H.	
Craig, John	63 Mountcollyer Street	Private	14th R.I.R.	
Craig, Joseph	63 Mountcollyer Street	Private	9th R.I.R.	Wounded.
Creighton, Robert	Henderson Avenue	Lance-Corporal	14th R.I.R.	
Dickey, James	81 Mountcollyer Avenue		R.N.	
Fee, John	4 Carlisle Street	Driver	A.S.C.	
Ferguson, Thomas	3 Ballycarry Street	Sapper	R.E.	
Ferguson, William	193 Cambrai Street	Private	A.S.C.	
Forsythe, Joseph	68 Enfield Street	Rifleman	5th R.I.R.	
Foster, Robert J.	Spencer Street	Rifleman	15th R.I.R.	
Galloway, John	86 Mervue Street	Driver	R.A.F.	Wounded.
Galloway, Wm.	86 Mervue Street		R.N.	
Galway, Fred.	6 Duncairn Gardens		R.N.	
Gray, W. J.		Private	10th R.I.R.	Wounded.
Henderson, Robert	Cranmore Avenue			
Henderson, Wm.			R.N.	
Herron, John	39 Mountcollyer Avenue		H.M. Transport	
Herron, William	39 Mountcollyer Avenue	Private	A.O.C.	
Hume, Wm. J.	15 Up. Mervue Street			
Hutchinson, Robert	318 Shankill Road	Private	14th R.I.R.	
Irvine, Edward	36 Spencer Street	Private	R.F.A.	
Keenan, Wm. J.	25 Shankill Road	Private	14th Canadian Inft.	Killed in Action.
Kennedy, Robert J.	2 Singleton Street	Private	52nd F. Ambulance	
McCalmont, Joseph	48 Hillman Street	Rifleman	15th R.I.R.	
McCleery, Samuel	44 Perth Street	Lance-Corporal	15th R.I.R.	Killed in Action.
McCrea, James	73 Wall Street			
McIntosh, Thomas	32 Hanover Street	Corporal	Scottish Rifles	Wounded.
McKee, Alex.	20 Madison Avenue	Lieutenant	10th R.I.R.	Killed in Action.
Melville, Wm.	29 Bentinck Street		R.N.	
Montgomery, Fred.	92 Gainsboro' Drive		Naval A.S.	
Ogilby, Wm.	239 York Street	Private	Labour Corps	
Patterson, J.	5 Osborne Street	Private	R.F.A.	
Roberts, Edward		Private	R.A.S.	
Sewell, William	68 Henry Street	Private	R.E.	
Smith, James	60 Hooker Street	Private	R.A.M.C.	
Smythe, Chas. F.	Ashton Street	Sergeant	6th R.I.R.	

BELFAST PRESBYTERY.

EKENHEAD.

Name.	Home Address.	Rank.	Regiment, Battalion or Unit.	Remarks.
STEWART, WM.	...	...	R.N.	
THOMPSON, DAVID	...	...	R.N.	
THOMPSON, HUGH	15 Valentine Street	Private	7th R.I.R.	
TYRIE, ANDREW	198 Up. Meadow Street	Lance-Corporal	14th R.I.R.	Wounded.
WILSON, FRANCIS	20 Queensland Street	Rifleman	12th R.I.R.	Wounded.
WILSON, JAMES	20 Queensland Street	Bombardier	R.G.A.	Prisoner of War.
WILSON, JAMES, SEN.	20 Queensland Street	Rifleman	17th R.I.R.	Wounded.
WILSON, THOMAS J.	22 McCandless Street			

COLONIAL & U.S.A. FORCES.

Name.	Home Address.	Rank.	Regiment, Battalion or Unit.	Remarks.
AHARA, SAMUEL	...	Private	Canadian Engineers	
AHARA, MATTHEW	...	Lance-Corporal	Canadian Engineers	
DAVIDSON, SAMUEL	...	Sergeant	Canadian Engineers	
DOUGLAS, WM. H.	...	Sapper	Canadian Engineers	
FERGUSON, MURRAY	...	Private	American Infr.	
McAULEY, WM.	...	Private	Canadian Engineers	
WILSON, ADAM	...	Sapper	Aust. Engineers	M.M.

ELMWOOD.

Name.	Home Address.	Rank.	Regiment, Battalion or Unit.	Remarks.
AGNEW, KENNETH	Adelaide Park	Private	1st R.I.R.	Killed in Action.
ANDERSON, H. McDONNELL	Fitzwilliam Street	2nd Lieutenant	5th R. Northld. Fus.	Died of Wounds.
ANDERSON, WILLIAM	Fitzwilliam Street	2nd Lieutenant	4th R. Northld. Fus.	
BEATTIE, H. H.	Upper Crescent	Captain	Northampton Regt.	
BECK, STANLEY	Windsor Gardens	Lance-Corporal	18th R. Fus.	
BLACKWOOD, A. T.	Dunelin	Lieutenant	8th R.I.R.	
BLACKWOOD, T. A.	Dunelin	Lieutenant	8th R.I.R.	
BOUCHER, MAXWELL S.	Botanic Avenue	Lieutenant	A.S.C.	
BROWN, FRANCIS DALE	...	Private	5th R.I.R.	
BROWN, WM. CAMPBELL	...	Private	3rd R.I. Fus.	
CLARK, FRANK JEFFREY	Fitzwilliam Street	L· Sergeant	6th Black Watch	
CORRY, ROBERT P.	Longhurst	Lieutenant	A.S.C.	
CRYMBLE, JOHN G.	College Green	2nd Lieutenant	9th R.I. Fus.	Died of Wounds.
CUMMINGS, DAVID	Claremont Street	Private	14th R.I.R.	Killed in Action.
CURRAN, HERBERT	Myrtlefield Park	Private	23rd R.I. Fus.	Killed in Action
CURRAN, LANCELOT E.	Myrtlefield Park		R.A.F.	
CURRAN, WM.	Myrtlefield Park	Private	23rd R.I. Fus.	
DORWARD, JAMES	Stranmillis	2nd Lieutenant	13th R.I.R.	
DOUGLAS, HUGH A.	Elmwood Avenue	Lieutenant	R.N.	
FORBES, JOHN DONALD	Cadogan Park	2nd Lieutenant	10th Lanc. Fus.	Killed in Action.
FORBES, MURRAY	Cadogan Park	Captain	10th R.I.R., S.B.	
FORBES, ROBERT H.	Cadogan Park	Captain	5th R.I.R., M.G.C.	
FRASER, ALISTER S.	Thirlestane	Capt. and Adj.	O.T.C., Q.U.B.	
GILBERT, ROBERT STEVEN	Deramore Drive	2nd Lieutenant	R.A.F.	
GILMOUR, WALLACE	Ulsterville Avenue	Lieutenant	A.S.C.	
HANNA, FRANK LESLIE	Finaghy Park	Lieutenant	A. & S. Highldrs.	Killed in Action.
HANNA, TYRRELL	Finaghy Park	Lance-Corporal	A.S.C. M.T.	
HAY, BARKLEY	27 Dunluce Avenue	Aeroplane Inspector	A.I.D.	
HAY, SYDNEY	27 Dunluce Avenue	Engineer	H.M.T. Saxon Monarch	
HERON, S. M.	College Park	Sapper	R.E.	
HOLMES, JAMES McA.	Marlborough Park	Staff Surgeon	R.N.	D.S.O.
HOLMES, JOHN V.	Rugby Road	Captain	R.A.M.C.	
HOLMES, T. S. S.	University Road	Lieutenant	R.A.M.C.	
HOLMES, WM. P.	Stranmillis Road	2nd Lieutenant	M.G.C.	
IMRIE, W.	Belgravia Avenue	Private	A.O.C.	
INGLIS, HARRY W.	Adelaide Park	Captain	4th S. Staffordshire Regt.	
INGLIS, J. NORMAN	Adelaide Park	Lieutenant	6th R.I.R.	
IRELAND, DENIS L.	Malone Park	Captain	3rd R. Irish Fus.	Killed in Action.
IRELAND, RALPH	Malone Park	Lieut. Commander	R.N.	Killed in Action.
KERTLAND, EDWIN B.	Mount Pleasant	2nd Lieutenant	3rd R. Irish Fus.	Killed in Action.
McCULLOUGH, JOHN	Dunluce Avenue	Major	21st Middlesex Regt.	
McKENZIE, W. R.	University Road	Captain	R.A.M.C.	
McKINSTRY, JAMES M.	Rugby Road	2nd Lieutenant	12th R. Inn. Fus.	Died of Wounds.
McKINSTRY, JOHN	Rugby Road	2nd Lieutenant	11th R.I.R.	
McKINSTRY, ROBERT NOEL	Rugby Road	Surgeon	R.N.	
McLEAN, ROBERT	...	Corporal	A.S.C.	Killed in Action.
McMULLEN, ERIC H.	Eglantine Avenue	Corporal	R.E.	Killed in Action.
McMULLAN, GEORGE	Lennoxvale	Captain	R.A.M.C.	
McMULLAN, JOHN B.	Eglantine Avenue	2nd Lieutenant	Cheshire Regt.	
McMULLAN, ROBERT W.	Lennoxvale	2nd Lieutenant	7th Northld. Fus.	
MOFFATT, DOUGLAS M.	...	Captain	R.A.M.C.	M.C.
MONTGOMERY, ALEX.	Gt. Victoria Street	Captain	R.A.M.C.	
MOORE, CHAS. C.	University Street	Captain	1st Essex Regt.	
MOORE, DAVID B.	University Street	Captain	18th R.I.R.	
MOORE, J. HAMILTON	University Street	Chief Engineer	R.N.T.S.	
MORTON, W. B.	Notting Hill	2nd Lieutenant	O.T.C., Q.U.B.	
PRINGLE, JAMES A.	64 Eglantine Avenue	Vol. Driver	B. Red Cross	
PRINGLE, KENNETH	64 Eglantine Avenue		O.T.C., T.C.D.	
REYNOLDS, JAS. A.	Marlborough Park	2nd Lieutenant	7th R. Irish Fus.	Died.
ROBB, CAMPBELL	38 Eglantine Avenue	Captain	R.A.M.C.	
ROBB, JAS. J.	38 Eglantine Avenue	Major	I.M.S.	

BELFAST PRESBYTERY. ELMWOOD.

Name.	Home Address.	Rank.	Regiment, Battalion or Unit.	Remarks.
Sinclair, Geo. S.	Adelaide Park	2nd Lieutenant	5th R.I.R.	Killed in Action.
Sinclair, Herbert D.	Adelaide Park	2nd Lieutenant	5th R.I.R.	
Stephens, John K.	Sans Souci	Lieutenant	R.E.	
Taylor, D. Robertson	University Road	Lieutenant	R.A.M.C.	
Taylor, Alfred S.	Windsor Park	Captain	R.A.M.C.	Killed in Action.
Walker, R. H.	College Park	Cadet	R.A.F.	
Wight, John	Stranmillis Road	Cadet	O.T.C.	
Wilson, Gregg	Deramore Drive	Major	Com. O.T.C.	O.B.E.
Wilson, Jas. Oswald	Windsor Park	2nd Lieutenant	R.F.A.	
Wilson, R. Dempster	Windsor Park	Lieutenant	A.S.C.	
Workman, James	Notting Hill	Lieut.-Colonel	R.F.A.	
Yeates, Stanley	Derryvolgie Avenue	2nd Lieutenant	12th R.I.R.	
COLONIAL FORCES.				
Beck, Fred. Chas.		Lance-Sergt.	Can. Contingent	
McCullough, Hugh F.		Piper	2nd Transvaal Scots Regt.	
McMullen, John		Major	Natal Light Horse	
Milroy, R. P.		Bombardier	S.A. Artillery	
Moffatt, Geo. Baird		Captain	2nd S.A. Labour Regt.	

FISHERWICK.

The following have made the supreme sacrifice in the Great War—August, 1914, to November, 1918:—

Name.	Name.	Name.	Name.
Andrews, David	Geddis, George	Mitchell, Arthur G.	Russell, William J.
Beatty, William	Gould, William	Morrow, Hugh Gelston	Stevenson, William
Cooke, Charles Ernest	Gordon, James	McReynolds, J. Archibald	Turnbull, Alex. M.
Davey, William E.	Hemphill, Andrew	McKee, Henry	Wallace, James
Donaldson, Robert	Hamilton, David	McFarlane, Samuel	Walsh, J. Herbert
Donnelly, Fred.	Kerr, Robert Ernest	Owens, Alfred	Wilkinson, D. Stanley
Fisher, Hugh Bell	Morgan, William	Ramsey, John	

These are held in honour who have served their country in her time of need:—

Name.	Name.	Name.	Name.
Alexander, George	Dunn, William	Matthews, Charles	Scott, Walter
Allen, John	Farrow, Kenneth	Maxwell, Edward	Scott, Alexander
Allen, David	Ferguson, R.	Mayrs, Thomas Y. K.	Shanks, William J.
Allen, Thomas	Finlay, A. R. Gayer	Mayrs, E. Brice	Sherrard, John C.
Allsopp, George	Flanagan, John	Meneilly, Hugh	Sloan, Frank
Allsopp, Henry	Forbes, William	Miller, Albert E.	Smith, Robert H.
Allsopp, Francis	Frew, Philip	Millar, William McM.	Spence, John
Allsopp, Reginald	Gardiner, John	Mitchell, A. B.	Spratt, Moody
Armour, Alexander	Geddis, John	Mooney, J. S.	Stewart, William
Armour, William	Gerard, Ernest James	Moore, George S.	Stevenson, Andrew M.
Backler, Charles	Gillespie, W. McL.	Moore, Herbert S. L.	Strathdee, Ernest A.
Baillie, Thomas	Graham, W. F.	Morrow, James	Tate, Robert
Baillie, William	Graham, N. B.	Mortimer, David T.	Titterington, Henry G.
Baillie, John	Graham, D. F.	Murphy, William S.	Titterington, James
Barker, Frederick	Green, Robert	McAuley, Thomas	Titterington, A. E.
Baxter, Norman	Green, William Davey	McConnell, Arthur E.	Titterington, H. John
Beath, R. Maitland	Greenlee, Robert M.	McCorkell, William	Thompson, S. H. Hall
Bell, F.	Greer, William A.	McCorkell, Herbert	Thompson, Terence
Black, Edward	Hamilton, Cecil W.	McKee, Samuel K.	Thompson, Robert L.
Bodel, George W.	Hamilton, James	McKee, Thomas B.	Thompson, John R.
Bryson, G. Herbert	Hamilton, Scott	McKee, Herbert N.	Thompson, Robert
Bulloch, Ronald A. N.	Hardy, Thomas J.	McKinstry, Joseph	Thompson, William L.
Burrows, Thomas A.	Haslett, Ernest	McKinstry, Herbert	Thompson, James Stanley
Cathcart, Henry	Haslett, Victor	McKinstry, Chalmers	Thompson, Thomas Charles
Clarke, William	Haslett, W. B.	McMullan, Robert J.	Thompson, Joseph
Collins, Ingram D.	Houston, Samuel	McMullan, Samuel	Turnbull, M. Harper
Corry, David	Ingram, James	McMurray, Thomas	Verner, Henry Wilson
Corry, Richard	Irwin, S. T.	McNeill, William M.	Vaughan, Thomas
Cosgrove, Henry H.	Jeffrey, John	McReynolds, James C.	Wade, James
Crawford, Frederick H.	Jeffrey, George	Neill, James	Wallace, Alexander
Crawford, Stewart W. K.	Johnstone, Edgar	Neill, William	Wallace, John
Crothers, Walter	Kerr, Robert	Neill, John	Warnock, J. Edmund
Crothers, Harold	Kinghan, Samuel M.	Nevin, Hubert	Warren, Thomas J.
Currie, John	Knox, Ernest M.	Nevin, Francis	Wheeler, Donald R.
Currie, Harold	Kyle, D.	Nevin, Ernest	Wheeler, Arthur R.
Daley, William J.	Legate, Charles M.	Palmer, H. H.	Wheller, James R.
Daley, Samuel	Leitch, James F. L.	Patterson, Robert E.	Wilkinson, Robin
Davey, Fredk. C.	Macaulay, Thomas H.	Poots, James	Wilkinson, Richard W.
Davey, Thomas H.	Malcomson, Arthur J.	Rainey, Sydney	Wilson, William
Dickie, Charles	Martin, David	Rainey, W. M.	Wilson, C. L.
Doig, Fredk. G.	Martin, Leslie	Riddell, Robert	Wilson, Herbert
Donaldson, James N.	Martin, Victor	Robinson, James R. D.	Yarr, John L.
Donnelly, Leslie	Martin, Fredk.	Ross, Cyril H.	
Dugan, Cyril	Martin, A. Johnston	Ross, D. Hampton	
Duncan, George	Martin, A. Henry	Scott, William J.	

BELFAST PRESBYTERY. FITZROY AVENUE.

Name.	Home Address.	Rank.	Regiment, Battalion or Unit.	Remarks.
	FITZROY AVENUE.			
Baillie, Hugh M.				Killed in Action.
Baillie, Robert, Jun.				Wounded.
Baxter, William				
Bell, Wm.				
Bill, John A.				Killed in Action.
Buchanan, James				
Buchanan, Thomas				
Burnside, Edw. Edmond				Killed in Action.
Campbell, Dr. Boyd				
Campbell, James A.				Wounded.
Chesney, Wm., M.D.				Wounded.
Colquhoun, J. W. C.				
Colquhoun, Wm.				
Cowper, Wm. H.				Wounded.
Cronne, Fred. W.				
Crossey, Mark				Wounded.
Crossey, Wm. Ed.				Wounded.
Culbert, Joseph				Wounded.
Davidson, Duncan M.				Killed in Action.
Davidson, Norman				Wounded.
English, Wm.				
Frew, Philip W.				
Gailey, Robert				Wounded.
Gillespie, Alex. P.				
Glass, Geo. Shaw, M.B.				
Gorman, Thomas Sidney				
Graham, Wm. Rennie				Killed in Action.
Harris, Chas. E.				
Harris, Eccles				
Hogg, Dr. Bryson				
Hogg, Gerald, M.B.				
Hunter, Jack				Wounded.
Jackson, Culbertson				Wounded.
Jackson, J. Sinclair				Wounded.
Jackson, Maurice				Wounded.
Johnston, Eric				Wounded and Pris.
Johnston, R. Stanley				
Johnston, Thos. A.				
Kilpatrick N. Barbour				
King, Norman				Wounded.
King, Jack M.				
Legge, W. Norman				Died of Wounds.
Lindsay, Maurice				Killed in Action.
Loney, Alex.				
Loney, Charles Albert				
Loney, James				
McBride, Wilson, W.				Killed in Action.
McCleery, Hector				
McCleery, James				
McCleery, Wm.				
McClinton, Fred. W.				
McClinton, J. Stuart				Killed in Action.
McClinton, Norman				
McCord, R. Neill B.		Surgeon		
McCullough, Fredk. J.				Killed in Action.
McCullough, Ira A. C.				
McFadden, G. D. F.				
McLaughlin, Hugh M.				
McLaughlin, John				Killed in Action.
Martin, Sidney Todd				Killed in Action.
Martin, Norman				
O'Neill, James B.				
Orchin, Charles				Wounded.
Patton, Alex. Dunn				
Patton, John H. A.				
Patton, Wm. Frances				Wounded and Pris.
Press, Wm.				
Rea, Cecil A.				Wounded.
Sinclair, Samuel				Wounded.
Sinton, Dr. John Alex.				**VICTORIA CROSS.**
Smith, Howard				Wounded.
Smyth, Gordon Dill Long				Killed in Action.
Smyth, J. A.				
Taylor, Samuel				Wounded.
Thomson, Dr. W. W. D.				
Wightman, Brice M.				
Wightman, David A.				
Wightman, Geo. F.				
Wightman, Herbert				Killed in Action.
Wightman, Wm. V.				Wounded.
Wilson, Jack F.				Wounded.
Wilson, Wm. Bell				Killed in Action.
Wright, Robert				Killed in Action.

BELFAST PRESBYTERY. FORTWILLIAM PARK.

Name.	Home Address.	Rank.	Regiment, Battalion or Unit.	Remarks.
	FORTWILLIAM PARK.			
ALEXANDER, DREW	Lansdowne, L'downe Rd.	Sub-Lieutenant	R.N.V.R.	
ALEXANDER, JIM	Lansdowne, L'downe Rd.	Sub-Lieutenant	R.N.V.R.	
ANDREWS, D. ERNEST	Rathgola, Glenburn Pk.	2nd Lieutenant	2/94 Indian Army	Previously 1st R.I.R. Wounded.
ARCHIBALD, WALTER	Glen Alva, Cliftonville	Lieutenant	M.G.C., R. Dub. Fus.	
BELL, CHARLES	Marine Villas, G'dore Av.	Trooper	N.I.H.	
BLAIR, ANDREW	Daddystown	Leading Shipwright	H.M.S. Almanzora	
BLAKLEY, ROBERT J.	5 Manilla Tce, S'neil Av.	Sergt.-Major	Irish Cavalry Depot	
BREAKEY, WILLIAM	Elmwood, Chichester Pk.	Major	Army Ordnance Dept.	
BREAKEY, S. FRANK, M.B.	Elmwood, Chichester Pk.	Lieutenant	R.A.M.C.	
BROWN, ARCHIBALD	Warwick, Cavehill Rd.	2nd Lieutenant	7th R.I. Rifles	
BROWN, HUGH C.	Warwick, Cavehill Rd.	Signaller	R.A.M.C.	
BYERS, ROBERT J.	62 Newington Av.	Writer	H.M.S. Canopus	
BYERS, SAMUEL A.	62 Newington Av.	Armourer	H.M.S. Conqueror	
CALDWELL, SAMUEL A. G.	29 Cliftonville Av.	Bombardier	R.F.A.	
CAMPBELL, JACK	36 Hopefield Avenue	2nd Lieutenant	1st R. Inn. Fus.	Wounded.
CAMPBELL, JOHN C.	Cairn-Lynn, D'gall Pk.	Trooper	N.I.H.	
CAMPBELL, SAMUEL, M.B.	Caverna, C'chester Rd.	Major	R.A.M.C.	
CARSE, JAMES	9 Richmond Crescent	Eng. Sub-Lieutenant	R.N.R.	
CARSE, WILLIAM F.	9 Richmond Crescent	Trooper	N.I.H.	
CARSON, WILLIAM J. W.	Old Cavehill Road	2nd Lieutenant	14th R.I. Rifles	Missing sup. Killed.
CLARK, H. DOUGLAS	Fortwilliam Park	Lieutenant	8th A. & S. Highldrs.	
COOKE, NORMAN	4 Fortwilliam Terrace	Private	M.T.	
COOPER, JACK	St. Helens, L'downe Rd.	2nd Lieutenant	9th R. Inn. Fus.	Wounded.
COSKERY, JOSEPH	19 Hughenden Avenue	Private	2/6th R. Highldrs.Bk. Watch	
CRAIG, WILLIAM	Sunnyside, Antrim Rd.	Captain	H.M.T. Harbury	Drowned at Sea.
DALZELL, JOHN S.	Brymar, Castle Avenue	Lieutenant	R.E.	
DAVISON, ALEC	Kenbella, Antrim Rd.	2nd Lieutenant	1st R.I. Rifles	Prisoner of War.
DAVISON, CECIL	Kenbella, Antrim Rd.	Sub-Lieutenant	R.N.V.R.	
DAVISON, GEORGE	Lisbawn, Parkmount Rd.	Driver	M.T., R.E.	
DAVISON, THOS. H.	Lisbawn, Parkmount Rd.	Corporal	T.S., 14th R.I. Rifles	
DAVISON, WM. JOHN	Lisbawn, Parkmount Rd.	Chief Officer		
DOUGALL, ROBERT	Staunton, Taunton Av.	Trooper	N.I.H.	
DUDGEON, EDWARD C.	5 Glantane Street	Sergeant	R.E.	M.M., D.C.M.
DUNSEITH, BERTIE	Brooklands, Ashley Gns.	Trooper	N.I.H.	
ELLIOTT, E. HUGO	The Towers, D'gall Pk.	2nd Lieutenant	R.G.A.	
ELLIOTT, JOHN S.	The Towers, D'gall Pk.	Lieutenant	13th R.I. Rifles	Wounded.
ERSKINE, JACK	Longwood, Whitehouse	Lieutenant	R.E.	D.C.M.
FERGUSON, JAMES	Kilkeran, Salisbury Gns.	Major	R.E.	
FERGUSON, MATTHEW	47 Cedar Avenue	Captain	Transport Service	
FERGUSON, MATTHEW, JUNR.	47 Cedar Avenue		Transport Service	
FERGUSON, ROBERT A.	47 Cedar Avenue	Chief Officer	Transport Service	
FERGUSON, WILLIE G.	Parkmount Road	Signaller	464th Battery R.F.A.	Killed in Action.
FERRIS, J. LINDSAY	23 Rosemount Gardens	Lieutenant	M.G.C., R.I. Rifles	Wounded.
FERRIS, JOHN	5 Madison Avenue	Chief Officer	Transport Service	
FREW, ARTHUR	15 Indiana Avenue	Sergeant	N.I.H.	
GETTY, ROBERT H.	5 Indiana Avenue	Corporal	51st Devonshire Regt.	
GIBSON, LAWSON A. B.	1 Bellevue Tce., Shore Rd.	Private	M.T. A.S.C.	Gassed.
GLASS, JOHN B.	14 Camberwell Terrace	Lieutenant	R.A.F.	
GLASS, WILLIAM	Barrule, Parkmount Rd.	2nd Lieutenant	6th R. Highldrs. B.Watch (T)	Killed in Action.
HANNA, ROBERT	2 Hopefield Terrace	Captain	Transport Service	
HARPER, ALEC.	Chichester House	2nd Lieutenant	3rd Seaforth Highlanders	
HARPER, LOUIS	Chichester House	Lieutenant	R.A.F.	Wounded.
HARPER, R. FOSTER D.	Chichester House	Engineer		
HARPER, WILLIAM	Chichester House	Driver	M.T.S.	
HARVEY, JAMES	Cloughfin, Skegoniel Av.	Sergeant	N.I.H.	
HARVEY, LESLIE	Cloughfin, Skegoniel Av.	Sergeant	R. Irish Fus.	
HARVEY, WILLIAM J., M.B.	Tilmanston, Waterloo Gs.	Captain	R.A.M.C.	
HENRY, MOSES, M.B.	Ben Vista, Antrim Rd.	Captain	R.A.M.C.	
HOUSTON, JOHN	2 Fortview Terrace	Rifleman	R.I. Rifles	
HUTTON, HENRY	21 Salisbury Avenue	Engineer		
HUTTON, JIM	21 Salisbury Avenue	Cadet	R.A.F.	Wounded.
HYNDMAN, J. VALENTINE	Lisanore, Antrim Rd.	Captain	14th R.I. Rifles	Died of Wounds.
HYNDMAN, NORMAN	Lisanore, Antrim Road	Rifleman	14th R.I. Rifles	
JACKSON, LESTER	St. Helier's, Cavehill Rd.	Rifleman	14th R.I. Rifles	Died of Wounds or Killed in Action.
JOHNSTON, SAMUEL J.	49 Cedar Avenue	Sergeant	2nd R.I. Rifles	M.M. & Bar, gassed
JOHNSTON, SAMUEL	Ramore, Castle Park	Trooper	N.I.H.	
JONES, EDWIN	Linden, Bristol Avenue	P.O.	H.M.T.B.D. Redpole	
KANE, HUGH S.	15 Hughenden Avenue	Captain	Transport Service	
KELSO, SHAW	The Cottage, T'town Av.		A.V.C.	
KERR, CECIL	38 Victoria Gardens	Ship's Boy		
LEES, JAMES	Cranareen, Castle Park	Corporal	R.E.	M.M. and M.S.M.
LEES, JAMES LOWRY	Drumadoon, Castle Park	Captain	6th Batt. Tank Corps	M.C., Kd. in Act.
LEES, WILLIAM	Drumadoon, Castle Park	1st Class Air Mech.	R.A.F.	
LUNDY, ROBERT W.	13 Jubilee Avenue	Midshipman	R.N.R.	
McCOMB, HARRY	Dunedin, Antrim Road	2nd Lieutenant	R. Inn. F.	Wounded.
McCOMB, S. WILSON, M.B.	Dunedin, Antrim Road	Captain	R.A.M.C.	
McCURDY, WILL	Tieve Tara, F'william Pk.	Captain	M.T.S.	
McFARLANE, JOSEPH Y.	34 Ophir Gardens	Driver	M.T.	
McKAY, DOUGLAS	Old Cavehill Road	Lieutenant	R.A.F.	Wounded.
McKEE, REGINALD	4 Glanworth Street	Lance-Corporal	14th R.I. Rifles	

BELFAST PRESBYTERY. FORTWILLIAM PARK.

Name.	Home Address.	Rank.	Regiment, Battalion or Unit.	Remarks.
McKee, Victor	4 Glanworth Street	Trooper	N.I.H.	
McLees, Ernest	41 Queen Victoria Gdns.	Driver	M.T.S., R.E.	
Malone, Bristow M.	Entroya, F'william Pk.	2nd Lieutenant	9th R. Inn. Fus.	Missing, bel. killed.
Malone, William A.	Entroya, F'william Pk.	2nd Lieutenant	13th Cheshires	Died of Wds., Pris.
Miskimmin, Herbert	Culmore, Glenburn Park	2nd Lieutenant	M.G.C.	Wounded.
Moir, David	Baltic Villas, G'dore Av.	Trooper	N.I.H.	Wounded.
Moir, George	Baltic Villas, G'dore Av.	Captain	R.A.F.	
Moir, Stewart	Baltic Villas, G'dore Av.	Trooper	N.I.H. and R.A.F.	
Montgomery, Charles	Lancetta, Antrim Rd.	Midshipman	R.N.V.R.	
Moore, Cecil G.	Lismara, Salisbury Av.	Lieutenant	R.G.A.	
Moore, James R.	Clonlee, Glenburn Park	Captain	Transport Service	Sank German Sub.
Morton, Charlie	Simla, Glastonbury Av.	Trooper	N.I.H.	
Munro, George K.	39 Kansas Avenue	Engineer Lieut.	R.N.R.	
Nesbitt, Jim	8 Salisbury Avenue	Trooper	N.I.H.	Wounded.
Orr, Samuel	16 Hopefield Avenue	Private	Army Ordnance Corps	
Paisley, D. Gordon	30 Madison Avenue	Private	L.G.S. 1/6th R. Highldrs. Black Watch	Killed in Action.
Paisley, Edgar	30 Madison Avenue	Private	2/6th R. Highldrs. B. Watch	Wounded.
Pinkerton, E. Dudley R.	Oak Lodge, Cedar Av.	Lieutenant	3rd London Ir. Rifles	Wounded.
Pinkerton, John	87 Henderson Avenue	Sapper	122nd Field Co. R.E.	Prisoner of War.
Robb, Bertie	Kirk-Brughean	Lieutenant	R.A.F.	
Robb, Victor Harold	Kirk-Brughean	Lieutenant	14th R.I. Rifles	Died of Wounds.
Rusk, Jack	Winterdene, Cavehill Rd.	Trooper	N.I. Horse	
Sloan, Samuel	71 Fortwilliam Parade	Mechanic	R.A. Force	
Smiley, Robert	18 Chichester Avenue	Engineer	R.N.R.	
Smiley, Samuel T.	18 Chichester Avenue	Navigating Lieut.	H.M.S. Arabis	Drowned at Sea.
Stewart, William H.	13 Willowbank Street	2nd Lieutenant	11th R. Inn. Fus.	Killed in Action.
Suffern, Robert	Aislaby, Donegall Park	Captain	Transport Service	Drowned.
Taggart, Alfred C.	Ben Vista, Antrim Rd.	Capt. and Adjutant	7th R. Inn. Fus.	Wounded and Ged.
Taggart, Robert S., M.B.	Ben Vista, Antrim Rd.	Captain	R.A.M.C.	
Taggart, Wm. J., M.B.	3 Glandore Park	Lieutenant	R.A.M.C.	Attached Mes. E.F.
Taylor, Charles H.	10 Camberwell Terrace	C.Q.M.S.	12th R. Inn. Fus.	
Todd, Albert Edward	Clarinda, F'william Pk.	2nd Lieutenant	R.I. Rifles	M.C.
Todd, Charles	Cavehill Road	Engineer	Transport Service	
Veitch, Robert A.	23 Madison Avenue	Lieutenant	R.I. Rifles	Wounded.
Vint, Robert W., M.B.	36 Kansas Avenue	Captain	R.A.M.C.	Attached Mes E.F.
COLONIAL & U.S.A. FORCES.				
Adams, Wm. A.	50 Glantane Street	Private	Canadians	
Coskery, Tom	19 Hughenden Avenue	Private	Canadians	
Kelso-Shaw, James	The Cottage, T'ton Av.	Private	Canadians	
McKee, Percy	4 Glanworth Street	Sergeant	Canadians	
Pinkerton, Robert	87 Henderson Avenue	Private	Australians	Wounded.
Robb, Edwin	Kirk-Brughean	Private	Canadians	Gassed.
Smiley, David Nelson	18 Chichester Avenue	Quartermaster	U.S.A. Army	
Smiley, Wm. G.	18 Chichester Avenue	Gunner	Australian F.A.	Wounded.
Smith, Alfred J.	2 Castleton Terrace	Private	Canadians	
Smith, Charles H.	2 Castleton Terrace	Sergeant	Canadians	
Tattersall, G. Stanley	132 Limestone Road	Gunner	Australian F.A.	Wounded.
Todd, Ernest Victor	Fortwilliam Park	Private	New Zealand E.F.	Killed in Action.
FOUNTAINVILLE.				
Allen, James G.	114 Matilda Street	Rifleman	R.I.R.	
Aiken, James	81 Hunter Street	Gunner	R.G.A.	
Aiken, John	81 Hunter Street	Private	R.I.F.	
Anderson, John	15 Napier Street	Driver	E.B.	
Beattie, David	10 Gaffikin Street	Driver	N.I.H.	
Beattie, John	17 Thorn Street	Private	R.E.	
Beattie, William	10 Gaffikin Street	Driver	A.S.C.	
Bee, Wallace	44 City Street	Q.-master Sergt.	R.A.M.C.	
Bell, William	15 Utility Street	Private	R.W.F.	
Blakeley, David	43 Edinburgh Street	A.B.	H.M.S.	
Boal, Joseph	189 Matilda Street	Private	A.S.C.	
Bradley, Ernest	108 Clementine Street	Rifleman	R.I.R.	
Bradley, Frederick	108 Clementine Street	Private	R.A.F.	
Bradley, James	108 Clementine Street	Private	T.R.C.	
Brennan, Allen	66 City Street	Private	S.A.I.	
Brown, James	118 Blythe Street	Sapper	R.E.	
Brown, John	55 Gaffikin Street	Private	R.A.M.C.	
Brown, Martin	50 Essex Street	Sergt.-Major	R.I.R.	Died.
Brown, Norman	50 Essex Street	Sergeant	R.I.R.	D.C.
Brown, Robert	118 Blythe Street	Private	R.I.R.	Killed in Action.
Brown, William	118 Blythe Street	Private	A.V.C.	
Burns, Robert	22 Walnut Street	Sergeant	R.I.R.	
Cameron, James	9 Cairo Street	Sergeant	Y.C.V.	
Campbell, Alex.	9 Eblana Street	Corporal	R.A.F.	
Campbell, Herbert	9 Eblana Street	Sergeant	R.I.F.	
Cardwell, Henry	25 University Road	Private	R.A.M.C.	
Carroll, James	33 Renfrew Street	Private	K.O.Y.R.I.	
Caul, James	32 Magdala Street	Lance-Corporal	R.I.R.	
Caul, John	32 Magdala Street	Sapper	R.E.	
Cheyne, Hugh	43 Combermere Street	Private	A.S.C.	

BELFAST PRESBYTERY. **FOUNTAINVILLE.**

Name.	Home Address.	Rank.	Regiment, Battalion or Unit.	Remarks.
Cochrane, Maxwell	139 Rugby Avenue	Private	R.I.R.	Killed in Action.
Coleman, Norman	3 Donnybrook Street	Private	R.A.F.	
Connor, Samuel	14 Taylor Street	Private	R.I.R.	Killed in Action.
Courtney, Samuel	3 Rowland Street	Private	R.I.R.	Killed in Action.
Craig, A. Victor	1 Napier Street	Major	R.A.M.C.	M.C.
Craig, William	13 Brookland Street	Corporal	A.S.C.	
Crothers, Samuel	6 Chambers Street	Sapper	R.E.	
Currie, Harry	41 M'Clure Street	Private	A.S.C.	
Curry, John	12 Fortuna Street	Rifleman	R.I.R.	
Curry, Samuel	12 Fortuna Street	A.B.	H.M.S.	
Dickson, William	92 Matilda Street	Private	R.I.F.	Died.
Doak, Thomas	8 Oban Street	Private	N.F.	
Donald, Charles	94 Clementine Street	Private	R.I.R.	
Donald, James	94 Clementine Street	Private	R.I.F.	
Donaldson, Robert	80 Clementine Street	Private	R.I.R.	
Dorman, Charles	5 Aughrim Street	A.B.	H.M.S.	Died.
Dougan, William	9 Blondin Street	Private	B.K.	
Duddy, Joseph	164 Dunluce Avenue	Driver	C.E.	
Duddy, Robert J.	164 Dunluce Avenue	Private	R.A.M.C.	
Duff, William	3 Chilworth Buildings	Private	R.I.F.	
Duffin, Herbert	34 Boyne Square	Private	A.S.C.	
Edmondson, William	114 Matilda Street	Private	R.I.F.	Killed in Action.
Fairbairn, Henry	156 Matilda Street	Private	R.I.F.	
Frame, George	53 Gaffikin Street	Corporal	R.I.R.	
Freeman, David	41 Gaffikin Street	Private	R.I.R.	
Fryars, Hugh	108 Matilda Street	Sapper	R.E.	
Fulton, James	38 Brookland Street	Sergeant	E.S.C.	Died.
Gallagher, John	112 Utility Street	Private	R.I.R.	Killed in Action.
Gardiner, Thomas	81 Britannic Street	Rifleman	R.I.R.	
Glasgow, William	4 Belgravia Avenue	Sergt.-Major		D.C.M.
Glendinning, Thomas	13 Powerscourt Street	Private	R.I.R.	
Graham, James	6 Chambers Street	Rifleman	R.I.R.	
Grant, James	94 Donegall Road	Private	R.I.R.	
Greer, James	22 Colchester Street	Private	L.C.	
Hadden, Ernest	11 Magdala Street	Private	R.I.R.	Died of Wounds.
Hamilton, Alex.	68 Surrey Street	Rifleman	R.I.R.	
Hamilton, Bertie	38 Glenalpin Street	Private	R.I.R.	
Hamilton, Robert	38 Glenalpin Street	Sergeant	A.S.C.	
Hanna, Robert	51 Abingdon Street	Private	R.I.R.	
Harbinson, David	10 Sturgeon Street	Driver	A.S.C.	
Harbinson, David	59 Gaffikin Street	Private	R.D.C.	
Harbinson, Samuel	25 Lincoln Place	Lance-Corporal	R.I.F.	
Heenan, Joshua	113 Donegall Road	Private	L.R.	
Higginson, William	41 Donegall Road	Stoker	H.M.S.	
Houston, William	27 Gaffikin Street	Private	L.C.	
Hoy, David	112 Matilda Street	Private	R.I.R.	Died.
Hoy, Thomas	90 Matilda Street	Private	R.A.F.	
Hutchinson, John	45 Majestic Street	A.B.	H.M.S.	
Hutchinson, William	50 Blythe Street	Private	R.I.R.	
Irvine, Joseph	17 Coolbeg Street	Rifleman	R.I.R.	
Irvine, Smith	113 Donegall Road	Private	R.A.F.	
Irvine, William	17 Coolbeg Street	Corporal	R.F.A.	
Jest, Thomas	19 Linfield Road	Signaller	R.M.F.	
Jordan, Johnston	44 Hardcastle Street	Lieutenant	R.I.R.	
Keir, Herbert	49 Magdala Street	Lance-Corporal	R.I.R.	
Keyes, William	8 Thorn Street	A.B.	H.M.S.	
Kyle, James	12 Coolderry Street	Stoker	H.M.S.	
Lewis, Wm. J.	169 Ormeau Road	Private	C.I.	Died of Wounds.
Lyttle, James	51 Abingdon Street	Private	R.I.F.	
Lyttle, Robert	51 Abingdon Street	Private	R.A.M.C.	
Lyttle, William J.	4 Coolfin Street	Sergeant	R.A.F.	
Magill, John	2 Lawyer Street	Private	H.L.I.	
Magill, Thomas	2 Lawyer Street	Rifleman	R.I.R.	
Martin, Samuel	10 Pandora Street	Corporal	R.I.R.	
Maxwell, Edward	18 Carmel Street	Private	P.M.D.	
Millar, Henry	91 Blythe Street	Private	Hussars	
Montgomery, William	10 Burnaby Street	Private	A.S.C.	
Moore, Edmond	12 St. Andrew's Square	Lance-Corporal	R.I.R.	
Moore, William	135 Donegall Avenue	Private	A.S.C.	
Morrison, Thomas	50 City Street	Corporal	R.I.R.	
Morton, Samuel	53 Rugby Road	Private	M.T.	
McClean, Abraham	22 Clementine Street	Private	R.I.R.	Killed in Action.
McClean, Robert	22 Clementine Street	Private	R.I.F.	
McCone, John	233 Donegall Road	Lance-Corporal	R.I.F.	
McCone, Samuel	233 Donegall Road	Corporal	R.I.R.	
McCone, Thomas	233 Donegall Road	Sergeant	R.I.F.	
McCoubrey, Samuel	27 Powerscourt Street	Lance-Corporal	R.E.	
McCune, James	27 Cairo Street	Lance-Corporal	Y.C.V.	Killed in Action.
McDougal, David	42 Hurst Street	Sergeant	R.E.	
McHenry, Joseph	Gt. Victoria Street	2nd Lieutenant	R.I.R.	
McKee, A. Grey	8 Belgravia	Surg.-Lieutenant	R.N.	
McLernon, John	36 McClure Street	Sapper	I.W.T.R.	
McVeagh, Thomas	18 Canterbury Street	Private	R.I.F.	
Nellins, Joseph	15 Thorn Street	Driver	R.F.A.	

BELFAST PRESBYTERY.   FOUNTAINVILLE.

NAME.	HOME ADDRESS.	RANK.	REGIMENT, BATTALION OR UNIT.	REMARKS.
NESBITT, JOHN	107 University Avenue	A.B.	H.M.S.	
NESBITT, ROBERT	21 Coolfin Street	Gunner	A.C.	
PATTERSON, ROBERT	79 University Avenue	Private	B.W.	Died.
PATTERSON, SAMUEL	79 University Avenue	Private	C.P.	
PEDEN, JOHN	23 Vernon Street	Driver	R.E.	
PEDLOW, WILLIAM	4 Gaffikin Street	Private	A.F.C.	
REDFERN, JOSEPH	20 Matilda Street	Private	M.G.C.	
RODGERS, ALBERT	21 Penrose Street	Sapper	S.A.C.	
RODGERS, GILBERT	21 Penrose Street	Sapper	R.E.	
SAUNDERS, ROBERT	38 Posnett Street	Corporal	C.F.A.	
SCOTT, DAVID	259 Matilda Street	Private	R.M.L.I.	
SCOTT, HAMILTON	259 Matilda Street	Sapper	C.E.	
SHANKS, JOSEPH	67 Carmel Street	Sergeant	R.I.R.	
SHIELDS, WILLIAM	8 Watson Street	Gunner	G.A.	
SIMMS, WILLIAM	23 Linfield Road	Driver	R.F.A.B.	
SMITH, DOUGLAS	45 Dunluce Avenue	Chief Mechanic	R.A.F.	
SMITH, FRANK	45 Dunluce Avenue	Corporal	R.E.	
STANFIELD, SAMUEL	30 Sandhurst Drive	Lance-Corporal	R.A.R.	
SUTCLIFFE, ARCHIBALD	207 Dunluce Avenue	Sapper	A.P.O.	
STEWART, JOHN	64 Hardcastle Street	Rifleman	R.I.R.	
THOMPSON, FRANCIS	193 Matilda Street	Private	R.A.F.	
TOPPING, ROBERT	12 Lindsay Street	Rifleman	R.I.R.	
WALKER, JAMES	10 Eblana Street	Corporal	F.S.C.	
WARREN, JAMES	44 Palestine Street	Private	C.R.B.	
WARWICK, RICHARD	75 University Street	Private	Wilts	
WARWICK, SAMUEL	75 University Street	2nd Lieutenant	R.I.R.	
WATT, JOSEPH	81 Hunter Street	Sergeant	M.G.C.	
WILSON, DAVID	93 Blythe Street	Corporal	A.S.C.	
YOUNG, SAMUEL	94 Rugby Avenue	Private	R.I.R.	
GREAT VICTORIA STREET.				
ABERNETHY, JAMES	43 Lavinia Street	Private	R.A.F.	
ABERNETHY, JOHN	43 Lavinia Street	Private	R.A.F.	
ADAMS, HUGH	Coyle's Place	Private	R.A.M.C.	
ADAMS, WILLIAM	Coyle's Place	Lieutenant	R.F.A.	
ADDLEY, WM.	176 Utility Street	Private	R.I.R.	
AGNEW, WM. H.	9 Hurst Street	Private	R.I.R.	
AIKIN, JAMES	81 Hunter Street	Private	R.I.R.	
ALEXANDER, THOMAS	16 Ormeau Street	Private	R.I.R.	
ALVAN, SAMUEL	38 Aughrim Street	Private	R.I.R.	
ANDERSON, FRANK	73 Britannic Street	Private	R. Inn. Fus.	
ANDERSON, GEORGE	48 Glenalpin Street	A.B.	R.N.	
ANDERSON, JOHN	48 Glenalpin Street	Private	R.F.C.	M.C., Croix-de-G.
ANDERSON, MATTHEW	53 Norwood Street	Private	R. Inn. Fus.	
ANDERSON, MARCUS	48 Glenalpin Street	Private	R.I.R.	
ANDERSON, RONALD	24 Abingdon Street	Private	R.I.R.	Killed in Action.
ANDERSON, WM.	38 City Street	Private	R.I.R.	Killed in Action.
ANDERSON, WM. JOHN	40 Howard St. S	Private	R. Inn. Fus.	
ASHFIELD, JOHN	49 Boyne Square	Private	R. Inn. Fus.	
ASHFIELD, JOSEPH	49 Boyne Square	Private	R. Inn. Fus.	Killed in Action.
ATKINSON, ROBERT	38 Hunter Street	Private	R.I.R.	Died of Wounds.
AXTELL, THOMAS	31 Elaine Street	Private	Lond. Scott.	Killed in Action.
AXTELL, WILLIAM	31 Elaine Street	Private	Lond. Scott.	
BAILIE, JAMES	366 Donegall Road	Private	R. Inn. Fus.	
BAILIE, JOHN H.	37 Boyne Square	Lance-Corporal	R.I.R.	
BAILIE, SAMUEL	459 Donegall Road	Private	R. Inn. Fus.	
BAIRD, ALEX.	8 Combermere Street	Private	R.I.R.	
BAIRD, FRED.	48 Carmel Street	Private	R.A.F.	
BAIRD, JAMES	48 Carmel Street	Private	R.A.F.	
BAIRD, SAMUEL	124 Fitzroy Avenue	Assist. Paymaster	R.N.	
BAKER, CHARLES	21 City Street	Private	R.I.R.	
BAKER, WILLIAM	1 Glenalpin Street	Private	R. Inn. Fus.	Died of Wounds.
BARRETT, GEORGE	159 Matilda Street	Private	R.I.R.	
BATEMAN, JAMES	1 Glenalpin Street	Private	R.I.R.	
BEATTIE, HENRY	65 Haypark Avenue	A.B.	R.N.	Order of St. Stanislaus and Silver Medal by Czar.
BEATTIE, JOHN	59 Donegall Road	Private	R.F.A.	
BEATTIE, WILLIAM	69 Donegall Road	Private	R.E.	
BEATTIE, WILLIAM	65 Haypark Avenue	A.B.	R.N.	Decorated by Czar, S.M., Order of St. Stanislaus.
BEATTIE, ROBERT	38 Teutonic Street	Private	R.G.A.	Died of Wounds.
BELL, GEORGE	194 Donegall Avenue	Private	R.I.R.	Killed in Action.
BELL, JAMES	28 Glenalpin Street	Private	R.A.M.C.	
BELL, JOHN	56 Glenalpin Street	Private	R. Inn. Fus.	
BELL, ROBERT	28 Glenalpin Street	Private	R. Inn. Fus.	
BELL, THOMAS	194 Donegall Avenue	Gunner	R.F.A.	Killed in Action.
BELL, WM. J.	51 Delhi Street	Private	R.A.M.C.	
BENNETT, WALLACE	50 Jerusalem Street	A.B.	R.N.	
BENNETT, WM. JAMES	2 Martin Street	Private	R. Inn. Fus.	
BELSHAW, WILLIAM	43 Clementine Street	Private	R.I.R.	
BINGHAM, THOMAS	4 Schomberg Street	Private	R.I.R.	
BINGHAM, WM. J.	4 Schomberg Street	Private	R.I.R.	

BELFAST PRESBYTERY. **GREAT VICTORIA STREET.**

Name.	Home Address.	Rank.	Regiment, Battalion or Unit.	Remarks.
BLACK, J. CLARENCE	34 Albion Street	Private	R.I.R.	Killed in Action.
BLACK, JOHN	34 Albion Street	Private	R.I.R.	
BLACK, JOSEPH	34 Britannic Street	Private	R.I.R.	
BLACK, JOSEPH	48 Matilda Street	Private	R. Inn. Fus.	
BLACK, WM. E.	34 Boyne Square	Private	R.I.R.	
BLOOMER, JOHN	59 Malcolm Street	Private	R.I.R.	
BLOOMER, WILLIAM	59 Malcolm Street	Private	R.I.R.	
BLOOMER, WILLIAM	228 Matilda Street	Private	R. Inn. Fus.	Killed in Action.
BOND, ROBERT	99 Donegall Road	A.B.	R.N.	
BENFIELD, EDDIE	63 Melrose Street	Private	R.I.R.	
BOWEN, HUGH	21 Cambrai Street	Private	R. Inn. Fus.	
BOWERS, HUGH	65 Eglantine Avenue	Private	R.I.R.	
BOYCE, JOSEPH	18 Wolseley Street	Private	Rifle Brig.	Lost both eyes.
BOYD, JOHN	9 Lavinia Street	Private	R.I.R.	
BOYD, ROBERT	34 Albion Street	Private	R.I.R.	
BRIDGETT, SAM. J.	18 Majestic Street	Corporal	A.S.C.	
BRADSHAW, HAMILTON	8 Sherbrook Street	Private	R.I.R.	Died of Wounds.
BRADSHAW, HENRY	70 Britannic Street	Private	R. Inn. Fus.	Killed in Action.
BRADSHAW, JOHN	30 Norwood Street	Private	A.S.C.	Killed in Action.
BRADSHAW, JOSEPH	1 Ratcliffe Street	Private	R. Inn. Fus.	Killed in Action.
BRADSHAW, THOMAS	8 Scott Street	Private	R.I.R.	Died of Wounds.
BRADSHAW, THOS. H.	58 Rowland Street	Private	R.I.R.	
BRIGGS, ANDREW	31 Balfour Avenue	Corporal	A.S.C.	
BROWN, GEORGE	27 Matilda Street	Private	R.I.R.	
BROWN, JOHN	19 City Street	Private	R.I.R.	Killed in Action.
BROWN, JOHN JAMES	72 M'Clure Street	Private	R.F.A.	
BROWN, ROBERT J.	4 Castlereagh Street	Private	R.I.R.	
BROWN, SAMUEL	19 City Street	Private	R.I.R.	
BRUCE, ROBERT	4 Albion Street	Private	R. Inn. Fus.	Prisoner.
BRUCE, SANDY	4 Albion Street	Private	R.I.R.	
BRYANS, ROBERT	3 Linfield Road	Private	R.I.R.	
BURNS, DAVID	172 Utility Street	Private	R. Inn. Fus.	
BURNS, JOHN	11 Gay Street	Private	R. Inn. Fus.	
BURNS, JOSEPH	11 Gay Street	Private	R. Inn. Fus.	Killed in Action
BUSBY, JOSEPH	19 Atlantic Avenue	Private	R.I. Fus.	
BUTLER, DAVID	133 Hunter Street	Private	R.I.R.	
BYERS, JOSEPH	9 Delhi Street	Private	R.I.R.	
CAHILL, JOHN R.	111 Dunluce Avenue	A.C.	R.A.F.	
CAIRNS, JOSEPH	62 Donegall Road	Private	R.I.R.	Died from Exposure
CAIRNS, ROY	1 Abingdon Street	A.B.	R.N.	Lost on 'Russell.'
CALDWELL, JOHN	195 Matilda Street	Private	R. Inn. Fus.	Died of Wounds.
CALDWELL, JOSEPH	195 Matilda Street	Private	R. Inn. Fus.	
CALDWELL, WM. JAMES	195 Matilda Street	Private	R.I.R.	
CAMPBELL, GEORGE	39 Kensington Street	Private	R.I.R.	
CAMPBELL, JAS. L.	201 Roden Street	J.C.C.	R.N.	
CAMPBELL, JOHN	38 Lawyer Street	Private	R.I.R.	Killed in Action.
CAMPBELL, REGGIE	13 Ratcliffe Street	Private	A.S.C.	
CAMPBELL, ROBERT	53 Farnham Street	Private	N.I.H.	
CAMPBELL, WM.	53 Farnham Street	Gunner	R.F.A.	Prisoner, Died.
CARDWELL, HARRY	16 Claremont Street	Private	R.I.R.	
CARDWELL, JAMES	12 Primitive Street	Private	R.I.R.	
CARLISLE, JOHN	76 Clementine Street	A.B.	R.N.	Killed in Action.
CARSWELL, JOHN	130 Durham Street	Sergeant	R.I.R.	Prisoner.
CARROLL, JOHN	42 Essex Street	Private	R.I.R.	Died of Wounds.
CARROLL, WM.	42 Essex Street	Corporal	R.I.R.	Died of Wounds.
CARSON, SAMUEL	5 Blythe Street	Private	R.F.A.	
CARSON, THOMAS	5 Blythe Street	Private	R.F.A.	
CASKEY, DAVID	38 Britannic Street	Private	R. Inn. Fus.	
CASSELLS, CHARLES	24 Coolbeg Street	Private	R.I.R.	
CASSELLS, EDDIE	170 Donegall Road	Private	R.I.R.	
CASSELLS, JOSEPH	170 Donegall Road	Gunner	R.F.A.	
CASSELLS, WM.	9 Adelaide Avenue	Private	A.S.C.	
CASH, JAMES	83 Egmont Street	Private	R.I.R.	
CASH, ROBERT	83 Egmont Street	Private	R.I.R.	
CASWELL JAMES	179 Sandy Row	Private	R.I.R.	
CASWELL, JOHN	18 Napier Street	Sergeant	R.I.R.	
CATHERS, JAMES	53 Rowland Street	Private	R.I.R.	
CATHERS, ROBERT	53 Rowland Street	Private	R. Ir. Fus.	
CATHERWOOD, HENRY	18 Pandora Street	Private	R.I.R.	
CAUGHEY, JAMES	61 Britannic Street	Private	R.I.R.	
CAULFIELD, WM.	23 Rutland Street	Private	R. Inn. Drag.	
CHALMERS, PETER	3 Northbrook Street	Sergeant	A.S.C.	
CHAMBERS, HUGH K.	59 Charles Street S.	Private	R.I.R.	
CHAMBERS, THOS.	59 Charles Street S.	Private	R.I.R.	
CLARKE, JACKSON	14 Hurst Street	Sergeant	R.I.R.	
CLARKE, JAMES	29 Hartington Street	A.B.	R.N.	
CLARKE, JAMES	29 Bentham Street	Private	R.I.R.	
CLARKE, JOHN A.	47 Fallswater Street	Private	R.I.R.	
CLARKE, SAMUEL J.	5 Lavinia Street	Sergeant	R.I.R.	
CLARKE, WM.	29 Blythe Street	Sergeant	R.E.	M.S.M.
CLARKSON, HUGH S.	10 Brassey Street	Gunner	R.F.A.	
CLEGG, GEORGE	25 Renfrew Street	Private	Queen's Huss.	
CLEGG, GEORGE A.	4 Renfrew Street	Private	R.I.R.	
CLEGG, ROBERT	4 Canterbury Street	Sapper	R.E.	

(108)

BELFAST PRESBYTERY.   GREAT VICTORIA STREET.

NAME.	HOME ADDRESS.	RANK.	REGIMENT, BATTALION OR UNIT.	REMARKS.
CLEGG, ROBERT	19 Apsley Street	Private	R.I.R.	
CLELAND, THOMAS	11 Albion Street	Private	S. Lancs.	
CLELLAND, THOMAS	62 Donegall Road	Private	R.I.R.	
CLEMENTS, ROBERT J.	33 Hunter Street	Private	R.I.R.	
CLOVERLEY, DAVID	13 Mayne Street	Private	R.I.R.	
CLOTWORTHY, JOHN	53 Rowland Street	Private	A. Res.	
CLULOW, JAMES	33 Cussick Street	Private	R.I.R.	
CLULOW, THOMAS	2 Lawyer Street	Private	S. Lancs.	Killed in Action.
COBBAN, JOHN	18 Cranmore Avenue	Private	K.O.S.B.	
COLLINS, CHAS. H.	62 Howard Street S.	Gunner	R.F.A.	
COLVILLE, JOHN	159 Ormeau Road	Private	R. Inn. Fus.	
CONDY, JAMES	14 Balfour Avenue	Private	R.I.R.	
CONNERY, JOHN	44 Matilda Street	Sapper	R.E.	
CONNERY, WM. JAS.	44 Matilda Street	Private	R. Lancs.	
CONNOR, FRANK	19 Matilda Street	Private	R.I.R.	
COOTE, JOHN	52 Boyne Square	Private	R.I.R.	
COOTE, JOSEPH	52 Boyne Square	Private	R. Inn. Fus.	Died of Wounds.
COOTE, SAMUEL	52 Boyne Square	Private	A.S.C.	
CORRY, THOMAS	68 Bentham Street	Private	R.A.F.	
COSTLEY, JOHN	39 Wesley Street	Private	R.I.R.	
COULTER, ROBERT	64 Tate's Avenue	Private	R.I.R.	
COURTNEY, SAMUEL	11 Curzon Street	Private	R.I.R.	
COWAN, ALEX.	4 Albion Street	A.B.	R.N.	
COWAN, SAMUEL	4 Albion Street	Private	R. Inn. Fus.	
COWAN, WILLIAM	16 Albion Street	Private	Cheshires	
COWDEN, SAMUEL	21 Taylor Street	Private	R.I.R.	
COWDEN, SAMUEL C.	21 Taylor Street	Private	R.I.R.	
COWDEN, THOS. E.	21 Taylor Street	Private	R.I.R.	
CRAWFORD, HUGH	130 Durham Street	Private	R.I.R.	
CRAWFORD, HUGH	10 Barton Street	A.B.	R.N.	Lost at Sea.
CRAWFORD, HUGH L.	3 Coyle's Place	A.B.	R.N.R.	Lost on "Hawke."
CRAWFORD, JONATHAN	3 Coyle's Place	Bugler	R.I.R.	
CRAWFORD, THOS.	130 Durham Street	Private	R. Inn. Fus.	Killed in Action.
CRAWFORD, THOS. J.	159 M'Clure Street	Lieutenant	R.I.R.	
CRAWFORD, WM.	8 Hurst Street	Private	R.I.R.	
CRAWFORD, WM.	130 Durham Street	Private	Sig. Corps	
CRAWFORD, WM. ROBT.	95 M'Clure Street	Private	R.I.R.	
CRAIG, DAVID	6 Mayne Street	Sapper	R.E.	
CRAIG, ROBERT	26 Glenalpin Street	Gunner	R.F.A.	
CREAN, CHARLES	12 Shaftesbury Av.	Corporal	R.I.R.	
CROOKS, DAVID	30 Utility Street	Private	R.I.R.	
CROOKS, THOMAS	42 Sandy Row	Gunner	R.F.A.	
CROSSIE, ALEX. T.	5 City Street	Private	R.I.R.	
CULLY, JOSEPH	69 Broom Street	Sapper	R.E.	
CUNNINGHAM, GEORGE	61 Excise Street	A.B.	R.N.	
CURRIE, ALBERT	212 Roden Street	Private	R.I.R.	
CURRIE, CHARLES	104 Matilda Street	Private	R.I.R.	Killed in Action.
CURRY, WILLIAM	6 Mabel Street	Private	R.I.R.	
DALEY, WM. L.	5 Lt. Brunswick St.	Corporal	R.I.R.	
DALZELL, ROBERT J.	99 Donegall Road	Private	R.I.R.	Died of Wounds.
DAVIDSON, ALBERT E.	12 Southview Street	Private	Dub. Fus.	Lost both legs and one arm.
DICK, JOHN	45 Lavinia Street	Sergeant	A.S.C.	
DICKSON, ROBERT	20 Gaffikin Street	Gunner	R.F.A.	Killed in Action.
DIXON, BEN.	51 Ormeau Road	Private	R.I.R.	
DIXON, JOHN H.	51 Ormeau Road	Corporal	R.I.R.	Killed in Action.
DIXON, JOSEPH	51 Ormeau Road	Private	R. Inn. Fus.	
DOAKE, SAMUEL	80 Farnham Street	Private	N.I.H.	
DOGGART, WM. L.	13 Ridgway Street	Sapper	R.E.	
DORAN, THOS.	6 Wolseley Street	Sergeant	R.I.R.	
DORNAN, GEORGE	6 Boyne Square	Private	Scots Guards	Killed in Action.
DORNAN, JAMES	6 Boyne Square	Private	R.I.R.	
DORRINGTON, JAMES	154 Utility Street	Private	R. Inn. Fus.	
DORRITY, WILLIAM	29 Elaine Street	Private	R.I.R.	Killed in Action.
DOWSE, ALEX.	81 Clementine Street	A.B.	R.N.	
DRENNAN, GEORGE	11 Norwood Street	Corporal	R. Inn. Fus.	
DUFF, GEORGE	60 Brookfield Street	Private	R.I.R.	
DUNBAR, HUGH G.	99 Charles Street S.	Private	R.I.R.	
DUNBAR, JAMES	99 Charles Street S.	Corporal	R. Inn. Fus.	
DUNBAR, WM.	99 Charles Street S.	Private	R.I.R.	
DUNSEATH, JAMES	23 Brassey Street	Private	R.I.R.	
DUNSEITH, JOHN	92 Sandy Row	Private	London Rifles	
EDMONDSON, WM.	32 Scott Street	Private	R.I.R.	
EDWARDS, SAMUEL	21 Kensington Street	Private	R. Inn. Fus.	
ELLIOTT, EDWARD	16 Boyne Square	Private	R.I.R.	
ELLIOTT, JAMES	16 Boyne Square	Private	R. Ir. Fus.	
ELLIOTT, WILLIAM	16 Boyne Square	Private	R. Inn. Fus.	
ELLIS, ALEX.	16 Ormeau Street	Private	R.I.R.	
ELLIS, JAMES	16 Ormeau Street	Private	A.S.C.	
ELLIS, JAMES	69 Jerusalem Street	Private	R.I.R.	
ELLIS, MAXWELL	69 Jerusalem Street	Private	A.S.C.	
EMERSON, HERBERT	52 Wellington Park	Major	R.A.M.C.	
EMERSON, SAMUEL	4 Moore's Place	Corporal	R. Inn. Fus.	Killed in Action.
ERSKINE, DAVID	13 Ratcliffe Street	Private	S.A.H.	

BELFAST PRESBYTERY.   **GREAT VICTORIA STREET.**

NAME.	HOME ADDRESS.	RANK.	REGIMENT, BATTALION OR UNIT.	REMARKS.
EVANS, ROBERT	1 Kensington Street	Private	R.I.R.	
FAULKNER, THOMAS	10 Somerset Street	Private	Irish Guards	Killed in Action.
FERGUSON, MATT. H.	24 Beech Street	Corporal	R.I.R.	Killed in Action.
FERRIS, JOSEPH	43 Kensington Street	Private	R.I.R.	
FERRIS, SAMUEL	43 Kensington Street	Private	Irish Guards	
FINLAY, JOSEPH	11 Virginia Street	Private	R.I.R.	
FINN, HERBERT	1 Taylor Street	Private	R.I.R.	
FISHER, JAMES	66 Grosvenor Road	Private	A.S.C.	
FISHER, JOHN	66 Grosvenor Road	Private	Welsh Fus.	
FISHER, JOHN	57 Carmel Street	Private	R.I.R.	
FISHER, JOHN	19 Clementine Street	Private	R.I.R.	
FISHER, WM. JAMES	19 Clementine Street	Private	A.S.C.	
FITZSIMON, JAMES	172 Roden Street	Sergeant	R.I.R.	M.M.
FITZSIMON, JOHN H.	172 Roden Street	Corporal	R.I.R.	Killed in Action.
FITZSIMON, S. E. ERNEST	172 Roden Street	Major	R.I.R.	M.B.E.
FORDE, ROBERT	13 Linfield Street		R.A. Vet Corps	Died.
FORDYCE, WM.	56 Posnett Street	Private	R.I.R.	Killed in Action.
FOWKE, ROBERT	47 Hartington Street	Corporal	C.P.B.	
FOWKE, ROBERT	9 Salisbury Street	Sub-Lieutenant	R.I.R.	
FULLERTON, ARTHUR	19 Craigmore Street	Sub-Lieutenant	R.N.	
FULLERTON, HUGH	19 Craigmore Street	Sergeant	R.I.R.	
FULLERTON, WM.	19 Craigmore Street	Sergt.-Major	R.I.R.	
FRYERS, DAVID	108 Matilda Street	Private	R.I.R.	
FRYERS, HUGH	108 Matilda Street	Private	R.I.R.	
GALLAGHER, JOHN	11 M'Adam Street	Private	R. Inn. Fus.	Killed in Action.
GAMBLE, DAVID	18 Barrack Street	Private	N.I.H.	
GAMBLE, SAMUEL	30 Cable Street	Private	R. Inn. Fus.	
GARDINER, ROBERT H.	102 Bentham Street	Private	R.I.R.	Killed in Action.
GAVIN, CHARLES H.	18 Fitzroy Avenue	Lieutenant	K.O.S.B.	
GEARY, GEORGE	4 Beggs Street	A.B.	R.N.	
GEDDES, GEORGE	31 Combermere Street	Private	R.I.R.	
GEDDES, JAMES	31 Combermere Street	Private	R.I.R.	
GEDDIS, JOHN	2 Lawyer Street	Private	R.I.R.	
GETTY, ALEXANDER	20 Hatfield Street	Private	R.I.R.	
GIBSON, GEORGE	36 Linfield Road	Private	R.I.R.	
GIBSON, WM.	28 Rowland Street	Private	A.S.C.	Killed in Action.
GILMORE, EDWARD	34 Albion Street	Private	R.I.R.	
GILMORE, JAMES	34 Albion Street	Private	R.I.R.	
GLOVER, SAMUEL	21 Prospect Street	Private	A.S.C.	
GOODWIN, GEORGE	20 Schomberg Street	Sergeant	R.G.A.	
GRAHAM, ALEX.	35 Lavinia Street	Private	R.I.R.	
GRAHAM, GEORGE L.	234 Woodstock Road	Lieutenant	R. Inn. Fus.	Killed in Action.
GRAHAM, JOHN	18 Hugh Street	Sapper	R.E.	Accid. Killed.
GRAHAM, JOHN	30 Hurst Street	Sergeant	R.I.R.	Killed in Action.
GRAHAM, WM.	29 Colchester Street	Corporal	R.I.R.	Killed in Action.
GRAHAM, WM. JAS.	29 Colchester Street	Private	R.I.R.	
GRANGE, JOHN	72 Agincourt Avenue	Private	R.I.R.	
GREEN, MATTHEW	4 City Street	Private	R.I.R.	
GREER, WM. A.	138 Stranmillis Road	Corporal	R.I.R.	M.M.
GREGG, ROBERT	108 Maryville Street	Sergeant	R.I.R.	
GRIFFITHS, LOUIS	2 Lawyer Street	Private	R.I.R.	
HALE, THOMAS	56 Boyne Square	Private	R.I.R.	
HALE, THOMAS	122 Matilda Street	Private	R.I.R.	
HALL, ROBERT	17 Apsley Street	Private	R. Inn. Fus.	
HALL, THOMAS	48 Glenalpin Street	Corporal	R. Inn. Fus.	
HAMILTON, HENRY	Ballyhackamore	Private	R. Inn. Fus.	
HAMILTON, ROBERT	115 Dunluce Avenue	Private	R.I.R.	
HAMMOND, JAMES	8 Matilda Street	Private	R.I.R.	
HAMMOND, ROBERT	8 Matilda Street	Corporal	R.I.R.	
HAMMOND, WM.	8 Matilda Street	Gunner	R.F.A.	
HANNA, GORDON	56 Norwood Street	Private	R.I.R.	
HANNA, SAMUEL	21 Bruce Street	Private	R.I.R.	
HARPER, ROBERT	17 Bagot Street	Private	K. Hussars	
HARRISON, HUGH D.	7 Artana Street	Corporal	R.I.R.	Killed in Action.
HARRISON, JAMES	10 Somerset Street	Private	Irish Guards	
HARROW, JOHN	45 Albion Street	Private	R.A.S.C.	
HARVEY, GEORGE	41 Dunvegan Street	Private	A.S.C.	
HAYES, JOSEPH	76 M'Clure Street	Sergeant	R. Inn. Fus.	
HEGARTY, THOMAS	26 Moore's Place	Private	R.I.R.	
HENRY, CHARLES	54 Essex Street	Corporal	R. Inn. Fus.	
HENRY, ROBERT	Drumard	Private	R.I.R.	
HENRY, WILLIAM	1 Lisburn Road	Lieutenant	R. Irish Fus.	
HETHERTON, DAVID	117 Vernon Street	Private	R.I.R.	
HILLAND, JOSEPH	43 Renfrew Street	A.B.	R.N.	Lost on "Cressy."
HINTON, EDWARD	47 Magnetic Street	Minesweeper		
HOLMES, ALBERT	25 Albion Street	Private	R.I.R.	
HOLMES, HUGH	48 Blythe Street	Private	R.I.R.	
HOLMES, ROBERT	25 Wesley Street	Private	R.I.R.	
HOPKINS, JOHN	7 Willowfield Drive	Private	Inf. Brigade	
HOUSTON, FRED.	13 Albion Street	Private	R.I.R.	Killed in Action.
HUGHES, JAMES	47 Combermere Street	Private	R.I.R.	
HUGHES, WM. JAMES	146 Sandy Row	Private	R.I.R.	
HULL, JAMES	257 Matilda Street	Private	R.I.R.	
HULL, ROBERT	151 Donegall Road	Sapper	R.E.	

BELFAST PRESBYTERY. GREAT VICTORIA STREET.

Name.	Home Address.	Rank.	Regiment, Battalion or Unit.	Remarks.
Hull, Robert	151 Donegall Road	Corporal	R.I.R.	
Hull, Samuel	46 Westbourne Street	A.B.	R.N.	
Hyles, David	10 Scott Street	Sergeant	R.I.R.	D.C.M., Died of W.
Hyndman, Robert	259 Matilda Street	Sergeant	R.I.R.	
Irvine, Francis	5 Taylor Street	Private	R.I.R.	
Irwin, Charles	4 Clementine Street	Private	R.I.R.	
Irwin, Charles	61 Ormeau Road	Private	R.I.R.	
Irwin, Robert	20 Hatfield Street	Private	Arg. & Suth. Highldrs.	
Irwin, Thomas H.	125 University Avenue	Corporal	R.I.R.	
Irwin, William J.	18 Hatfield Street	Lieutenant	R.A.M.C.	
Jack, Harry	54 Farnham Street	Sapper	R.E.	
Jackson, Thomas	36 Posnett Street	Private	R.I.R.	
Jamieson, James	47 Skipton Street	Gunner	R.G.A.	
Jamieson, Lindsay	441 Lisburn Road	Private	N I.H.	
Jenkins, Samuel	210 Roden Street	A.B.	R.N.	
Johnston, Albert	15 Britannic Street	Private	A.S.C.	
Johnstone, John	36 Hatfield Street	Sapper	R.E.	
Jones, Charles C.	31 Balfour Avenue	Private	Arg. & Suth. Highldrs.	
Jones, Robert C.	31 Balfour Avenue	Private	N.I.H.	
Kelly, Andrew	40 Hardcastle Street	Private	R.I.R.	
Kelly, William	40 Hardcastle Street	Private	A.S.C.	
Kennedy, Robert	3 Apsley Street	Private	R.I.R.	
Kennedy, Robert	24 Camden Street	Private	R. Ir. Gds.	
Kennedy, William	24 Camden Street	Gunner	R.G.A.	
Kernaghan, William	13 Walnut Street	Lieutenant	R.I.R.	Killed in Action.
Kernohan, William	149 Roden Street	Corporal	R.E.	
Kerr, Arthur	18 Botanic Avenue	Private	R.I.R.	
Keyes, Thomas	202 Donegall Avenue	Private	R. Inn. Fus.	
Kildea, Alex.	6 Tate's Avenue	Private	R.I.R.	
Kirkham, Henry	8 Balmoral Street	Private	R. Inn. Fus.	
Kirkwood, George	88 Howard Street S.	Private	R. Inn. Fus.	
Kirkwood, William	88 Howard Street S.	Sergeant	R.I.R.	
Kyle, John	8 Balmoral Street	Private	R. Ir. Fus.	
Lackey, William	1 Coolfin Street	Private	R.I.R.	
Law, James	4 Britannic Street	Private	R.I.R.	
Lawson, William J.	36 Ashbourne Street	Private	R.I.R.	
Lees, John	35 Albion Street	Private	R. Inn. Fus.	
Leith, William J.	16 Dorchester Street	Gunner	R.F.A.	
Lennon, Samuel	16 Napier Street	Private	R.I.R.	
Lennox, John	36 Scott Street	Private	R.I.R.	Prisoner.
Leslie, Joseph	79 Roden Street	Private	R.I.R.	
Liddle, Gordon	3 Pakenham Street	Sergeant	R. Inn. Fus.	
Lightbody, Edgar	38 University Avenue	Private	R.C.D.	
Lightbody, George	38 University Avenue	Private	A.S.C.	
Lord, David	35 Lavinia Street	Private	K. Huss.	
Louden, Marcus	146 University Street	Private	R.I.R.	
Lowry, Robert	4 Hurst Street		Lab. Batt.	
Lowry, William	4 Hurst Street	Private	R.I.R.	Died of Wounds.
Lucas, Thomas	85 Edinburgh Street	Private	R.I.R.	
Lucas, William James	1 Fox's Row	Private	R.I.R.	
Lyons, Archibald	19 Lt. Victoria Street	Private	R. Inn. Fus.	Killed in Action.
Macartney, John	18 Bentham Street	Private	R.I.R.	Killed in Action.
Macaulay, Wm. James	145 M'Clure Street	Private	Cycling Corps	
Mack, Chris.	14 Walnut Street	Bugler	R.I.R.	
Mack, James A.	19 Grosvenor Road	A.B.	R.N.	
Mack, Jonathan C.	14 Walnut Street	Private	R.N.A.S.	
Mackey, Edward	65 Joy Street	Private	R.I.R.	
Mackey, Samuel	19 Wellwood Street	Sapper	R.E.	
Magill, Samuel	16 Damascus Street	Private	R.I.R.	
Magill, Samuel	38 Bankmore Street	Private	A.S.C.	
Magowan, Alex.	41 Edinburgh Street		Military Police	
Magowan, Robert	41 Edinburgh Street	Private	King's R.R.	
Magowan, William	21 Fortuna Street	Private	R.I.R.	
Martin, David	56 Agra Street		R. Air F.	
Martin, David	31 Silvergrove Street	Corporal	R.I.R.	
Martin, Ernest	19 Hunter Street	Private	R. Air F.	
Martin, James	16 Cromwell Road	P. Officer	R.N.	
Martin, Joseph	112 Matilda Street	Private	North. Fus.	
Martin, Robert	16 Cromwell Road	Private	R.I.R.	
Martin, Robert	65 Glenalpin Street	Corporal	R.I.R.	
Martin, Thomas	56 Agra Street	Private	Can. H.	
Martin, William	19 Hunter Street	Private	R.I.R.	
Matthews, Harold W.	Cranmore Gardens	Driver	B.R.C.S.	
Maxwell, Forbes	36 Adelaide Avenue	Private	R. Inn. Fus.	
Maxwell, George	36 Adelaide Avenue	Sapper	R.E.	
Maxwell, William James	59 Utility Street	Private	R.I.R.	Killed in Action.
Megaw, James	2 Primitive Street	Private	R.I.R.	
Meharry, John	49 Donegall Pass	Private	R. Inn. Fus.	
Melville, William	194 Donegall Avenue	Sapper	R.E.	
Mercer, Robert	346 Woodstock Road	Private	R.I.R.	M.M.
Mercer, Walter	6 Swiss Street	Private	Gordon Highlanders	
Millar, Hugh	65 Howard Street S.	Sapper	R.E.	
Millar, Joshua	19 Beit Street	Private	R.I.R.	
Millar, Marcus	70 Maryville Street	Private	R. Inn. Fus.	

BELFAST PRESBYTERY. **GREAT VICTORIA STREET.**

Name.	Home Address.	Rank.	Regiment, Battalion or Unit.	Remarks.
Millar, Robert	70 Maryville Street	Private	R.I.R.	
Millar, Robert J.	19 Beit Street	Sergeant	R.I.R.	Killed in Action.
Milligan, Sydney	13 Albion Street	Private	R.I.R.	
Minnis, William	126 Blythe Street	Private	R.I.R.	
Mitchell, George	16 Abingdon Street	Private	R.I.R.	Died from Exposure
Mitchell, Hugh	16 Abingdon Street	Private	R. Air F.	
Mitchell, John	27 Scott Street	Private	R.I.R.	
Moffett, Samuel	76 Palestine Street	Sapper	R.E.	
Molloy, James	30 Hurst Street	A.B.	R.N.	Lost on "Hawke."
Mooney, Herbert	44 Hatfield Street	Private	R.I.R.	
Moore, Edward	76 Dunluce Avenue	Private	R.I.R.	
Moore, Fred.	17 Ratcliffe Street	Private	R.I.R.	
Moore, Fred. Wm.	32 Madrid Street	Private	London R. F.	Killed in Action.
Moore, Harold S. L.	2 Dublin Street	Private	B.W.I. Regt.	
Moore, Harry	4 Napier Street	Sapper	R.E.	
Moore, James	4 Napier Street	Private	R.I.R.	
Moore, John	19 City Street	Private	R.I.R.	Killed in Action.
Moore, Robert	51 Eureka Street	Private	R.I.R.	
Moore, William	41 Bentham Street	Private	R.I.R.	
Moreland, Henry	18 Pine Street	Sergeant	R.I.R.	
Moreland, John	18 Pine Street	Private	R. Inn. Fus.	
Morrison, Alex.	3 Renfrew Street	Private	R.I.R.	
Morrison, George	3 Renfrew Street	Private	P.P.R.	
Morrison, Joseph	3 Renfrew Street	Private	P.P.R.	
Morrison, Thomas	20 Harmony Street	Private	R.I.R.	
Morrow, James	45 Albion Street		Cadet Corps	
Morrow, James M.	59 Wellesley Avenue	Private	R.I.R.	
Morrow, John	162 Blythe Street	Private	R.I.R.	
Moss, Charles	10 Penrose Street	Private	R.I.R.	
Mulholland, Herbert	150 Rugby Avenue	Private	R.I.R.	
Mulholland, Robt. Jas.	6 Curzon Street	Sapper	R.E.	Killed in Action.
Mullan, Thomas	62 Rowland Street	Private	R.I.R.	Killed in Action.
Murdoch, Henry	4 Glenalpin Street	Private	R. Inn. Fus.	
Murdock, James	212 Roden Street	Sergeant	Cheshires	Prisoner.
Murphy, Henry	40 Eureka Street	A.B.	R.N.	
Murphy, Hugh	8 Lawyer Street	Private	R.I.R.	Died of Wounds.
Murphy, John	8 Lawyer Street	Private	R.I.R.	
McAlister, Edward	48 Rowland Street	Private	R.I.R.	
McAlister, George	8 Scott Street	Private	R.I.R.	
McAllister, John	7 Gaffikin Street	Private	R. Inn. Fus.	
McAllister, Wm. George	7 Gaffikin Street	Corporal	R.I.R.	Killed in Action.
McAlpine, George F.	179 Sandy Row	Private	R.I.R.	
McAnoy, John	75 Maryville Street	Corporal	R.I.R.	Died, Prisoner.
McAnoy, Joseph	75 Maryville Street	Sergeant	R.I.R.	
McAteer, Thomas	33 Ava Avenue	Private	N.I.H.	
McAuley, James	145 M'Clure Street	Private	R.I.R.	Killed in Action.
McAuley, William	145 M'Clure Street	Gunner	R.F.A.	
McBride, James	9 Adelaide Street	Private	A.S.C.	
McBride, Samuel	145 Matilda Street	Private	R.I.R.	
McCabe, Thomas	34 Hope Street	Private	R.I.R.	
McCaldon, John	15 Barton Street	Private	R. Inn. Fus.	
McCandless, Robert	60 Excise Street	Sergeant	R.I.R.	Killed in Action.
McCartney, Samuel	28 Lawnview Street	Private	R. Inn. Fus.	Killed in Action.
McCaugherty, David	30 Hurst Street	A.B.	R.N.	Lost on "Hawke."
McClay, Andrew	93 Britannic Street	Private	R.I.R.	
McClay, Andrew	12 Glenbank Place	Private	R. Inn. Fus.	
McClure, Walter	23 Coolfin Street		Labour Corps	
McColl, Malcolm	Rose Cottage, Finaghy	Corporal	R.I.R.	Killed in Action.
McConkey, John	22 Matilda Street	Private	R. Inn. Fus.	
McConkey, Joseph	68 Bentham Street	Private	R.I.R.	
McComb, William J.	92 Tate's Avenue	Private	R.I.R.	
McConnell, William J.	108 Sandy Row	Private	R.I.R.	Killed in Action.
McCormack, William	Marlborough Park	Private	R.I.R.	
McCormack, William	2 Athol Street	Private	A.S.C.	
McCormick, William	39 Beit Street	Sapper	R.E.	
McCormick, Nat.	11 Matilda Street	Private	R.I.R.	
McCourt, David	51 Teutonic Street	Sergeant	R.I.R.	
McCracken, Wm. George	4 Renfrew Street	Private	R.I.R.	
McCracken, Wm. Jas.	20 Albion Street	Private	R.A.M.C.	
McCrea, Robert	17 Selina Street	Private	R.A.M.C.	Killed in Action.
McCrossan, Robert J.	138 Utility Street	Corporal	R.I.R.	
McCullough, Jas. F.	63 Up. Charleville St.	Private	R.I.R.	M.M.
McCullough, James	124 University Avenue	Private	R.I.R.	
McCully, William	67 Cromac Street	Private	R.I.R.	
McCutcheon, George	40 Rathcool Street	Private	A.S.C.	
McCutcheon, James	40 Rathcool Street	Private	A.S.C.	
McCutcheon, Joseph	40 Rathcool Street	Private	R. Inn. Fus.	
McDermid, George	10 Chadwick Street	Private	A.S.C.	
McDonald, John	13 Lismain Street		Cycle Corps	Died in Asylum.
McDowell, A. Balfour	16 Cromwell Road	Private	R.I.R.	
McDowell, Charles	27 Upton Street	Private	R. Inn. Fus.	
McDowell, David	10 Barton Street	A.B.	R.N.	
McDowell, Robert	10 Barton Street	Private	R. Inn. Fus.	
McDowell, William James	92 Selby Street	Private	R. Inn. Fus.	Killed in Action.

BELFAST PRESBYTERY.   GREAT VICTORIA STREET.

Name.	Home Address.	Rank.	Regiment, Battalion or Unit.	Remarks.
McDowell, William J.	Rose Cot., Coyle's Place	Lieutenant	R. Inn. Fus.	
McElroy, Samuel	20 Linfield Road	Private	R.I.R.	
McElroy, Samuel	154 Ormeau Road	Private	R. Ir. Fus.	
McElroy, William	71 Coolbeg Street	Private	R.I.R.	
McElroy, William	154 Ormeau Road	Private	R.I.R.	Killed in Action.
McEwan, Arthur	30 Ashbourne Street	Engineer	R.N.	Lost at Sea.
McEwan, David	30 Ashbourne Street	Sergeant	R.I.R.	Killed in Action.
McEwan, William	30 Ashbourne Street		Cycle Corps	
McGowan, Samuel	41 Edinburgh Street	Private	A.S.C.	
McGuigan, Edward	33 Elm Street	Sergeant	R.I.R.	
McHarry, James	49 Donegall Pass	Private	R. Inn. Fus.	
McIlroy, James	61 Damascus Street	Private	R.I.R.	
McIlroy, John	61 Damascus Street	Private	R.I.R.	
McIlroy, Walter	41 Vernon Street	Bugler	R.I.R.	Accidental Death.
McIlroy, William	61 Damascus Street	Sergeant	R.I.R.	
McIlroy, William	15 Ferndale Street	Sergeant	R.I.R.	
McIlveen, Robert	103 Matilda Street	Private	Dragoon Guards	
McIlveen, Samuel	27 Prospect Street	Private	R.I.R.	
McIlwaine, Samuel	45 Beit Street	Sapper	R.E.	
McIlwaine, William	103 Matilda Street	Private	Dragoon Guards	
McIntosh, Joseph	122 Sandy Row	Sergeant	R.I.R.	D.C.M.
McKee, Edward	16 Donegall Road	Private	R.I.R.	
McKee, James	35 Fife Street	Private	R.I.R.	
McKee, John	67 Palestine Street	Private	R.I.R.	
McKee, Joseph	16 Donegall Road	Private	R.I.R.	
McKee, Samuel C.	3 South Parade	Captain	A.S.C.	
McKee, Thomas	16 Donegall Road	Private	A.S.C.	
McKee, William	67 Palestine Street	Private	R.I.R.	
McKee, William Jas.	15 Wigton Street	Sergeant	R.E.	
McKee, William John	16 Donegall Road	Sergt.-Major	R.E.	
McKenzie, John	1 Lisburn Road	Asst. Paymaster	R.N.	
McKeown, James	48 Boyne Square	Private	R.I.R.	
McKinlay, Alex.	3 Rutland Street	Corporal	Machine Gun Corps	
McKinney, Thos. W.	6 Hunter Street	Private	R. Inn. Fus.	
McKissick, James	71 Clementine Street	Private	R.I.R.	Killed in Action.
McLenaghan, Robt. J.	12 Curzon Street	Sapper	R.E.	
McLenaghan, Wm. F.	12 Curzon Street	Private	N.I.H.	
McLeod, Samuel	88 Charles Street S.	Private	R. Inn. Fus.	
McNaughton, Ross	20 Dunluce Avenue	Private	A.S.C.	D.C.M.
McNeilly, Edward	3 Lisburn Avenue	Fireman	M.M.S.	
McMaster, James	12 Blythe Street	Private	R.I.R.	
McMorran, Thomas	66 Lagan Street	Private	R.I.R.	
McMillan, John	6 Albion Street	Private	R.I.R.	
McMillan, William	17 Madrid Street	Gunner	R.G.A.	
McMurray, Joseph	24 Essex Street	Sergeant	R.F.A.	Killed in Action.
McQuilkin, John	37 Hatfield Street	A.B.	R.N.	
McQuoid, James	27 Kenmare Street	Private	R.I.R.	
Neill, Hugh	45 Linfield Road	Private	R. Inn. Fus.	
Neill, James	6 Scott Street	Private	Cheshires	
Neill, Robert	4 Lt. Brunswick Street	Private	R.I.R.	
Neill, Thomas	99 Donegall Avenue	Private	R.I.R.	
Nelson, David G.	68 Donegall Pass	A.B.	R.N.	
Nelson, James	9 Salisbury Street	A.B.	R.N.R.	
Nesbitt, Ben.	48 River Terrace	Sergeant	R.I.R.	
Nesbitt, David	99 Charles Street S.	Private	R.I.R.	
Nesbitt, Thomas	99 Charles Street S.	Private	Cameron Highldrs.	
Newbold, George	19 Glenariffe Street	Private	R.I.R.	
Nixon, James	59 Israel Street	Private	R.A.M.C.	
Noble, Henry	89 Malone Avenue	Lieutenant	H.L. Inf.	
Oliver, David	82 Balfour Avenue	Sapper	R.E.	
Ormsby, Nicholson	6 College Sq. E.	Lieutenant	A.S.C.	
Orr, Andrew	33 Essex Street	Private	R.I.R.	
Orr, Stanley	140 University Street	Lieutenant	North Lancs.	
Owens, Samuel	170 Utility Street	A.B.	R.N.	Lost on Form'able.
O'Hara, Robert	90 Fitzroy Avenue	Private	R. Inn. Fus.	Killed in Action.
O'Neill, John H.	6 College Square E.	Captain	R.A.M.C.	
Palmer, Peter	9 M'Adam Street	Sergeant	S.A. Inft.	
Paskitt, James	48 M'Adam Street	Private	R.I.R.	
Patterson, Samuel	71 Tate's Avenue	A.B.	R.N.	
Patton, Andrew	52 Bentham Street	Private	R.I.R.	
Patton, James	52 Bentham Street	Corporal	R.I.R.	Killed in Action.
Patton, John	21 Windsor Street	Private	R. Inn. Fus.	Died of Wounds.
Patton, John	33 Excise Street	Private	A.S.C.	
Patton, Leslie	11 Northbrook Street	Private	R.I.R.	
Patton, Thomas	99 Vernon Street	Sergeant	R.I.R.	Killed in Action.
Paull, James G.	25 Botanic Avenue	Lieutenant	A.S.C.	
Peattie, William	111 Dunluce Avenue	Sapper	R.E.	
Peel, Wm. Jas.	34 Utility Street	Private	R.I.R.	
Pollock, Fred.	30 Albion Street	Gunner	R.A. Force	
Pollock, Henry	30 Albion Street	A.B.	R.N.	
Pollock, Isaac	30 Albion Street	A.B.	R.N.	
Pollock, James	68 Donegall Road	Private	R.I.R.	
Pollock, John	68 Donegall Road	Private	R.I.R.	
Pollock, William A.	68 Donegall Road	Corporal	R.I.R.	

BELFAST PRESBYTERY.   GREAT VICTORIA STREET.

Name.	Home Address.	Rank.	Regiment, Battalion or Unit.	Remarks.
Prenter, William M.	31 Outram Street	Private	R. Inn. Fus.	
Price, William J.	75 Rowland Street	Corporal	Welsh Borderers	
Purdy, David	66 Rutland Street	Lieutenant	R. Inn. Fus.	
Quigley, Henry	64 Posnett Street	Private	R. Inn. Fus.	
Rainey, William	54 Rainey Street	Sergeant	R.I.R.	
Rankin, Albert	26 Eblana Street	Private	R.I.R.	
Rankin, John	26 Eblana Street	Lance-Corporal	R.I.R.	Killed in Action.
Rea, Albert A.	5 City Street	Private	A.S.C.	
Rea, William	12 Windsor Street	Private	R.I.R.	Died of Wounds.
Reid, Andrew	26 Railway Street	Sapper	R.E.	
Reid, William	31 Howard Street S.	Gunner	R.G.A.	
Reilly, James H.	42 Pine Street	Private	N.I.H.	Killed in Action.
Reilly, John	42 Pine Street	Private	R. Inn. Fus.	
Reims, Henry	15 Combermere Street	Private	N.I.H.	
Reynolds, William	99 Mountpottinger Rd.	Sapper	R.E.	
Rice, James	66 Sandy Row	A.B.	R.N.	
Richardson, George	49 Abingdon Street	Private	R.I.R.	
Richardson, Isaac	49 Abingdon Street	Private	R.I.R.	Killed in Action.
Richardson, John	2 Carmel Street	Private	R. Inn. Fus.	
Ritchie, John	3 Bootle Street	Private	R.I.R.	
Ritchie, Samuel	73 Palestine Street	Sapper	R.E.	
Robinson, David	108 Matilda Street	Private	R. Inn. Fus.	Killed in Action.
Robinson, David W.	47 Abbott Street	Corporal	R.I.R.	Killed in Action.
Robinson, Robert	4 Boyne Street	Gunner	R.F.A.	Killed in Action.
Robinson, Samuel	108 Matilda Street	Gunner	R.F.A.	
Robinson, Thomas	24 Maryville Street	Private	R.I.R.	
Robinson, William	24 Maryville Street	Gunner	R.G.A.	
Ross, R. Campbell	6 Cameron Street	Private	R.I.R.	Killed in Action.
Ross, Walter	110 University Street	Q.M. Sergt.	R. Ir. Fus.	
Rowan, Andrew	30 Coolderry Street	Private	R.I.R.	
Ruddock, Thomas	9 Glenalpin Street	Private	R.M.L.I.	
Rush, Hugh	69 Eureka Street	Private	R.I.R.	
Rush, John	69 Eureka Street	Private	R.M.F.	
Russell, William	22 Palestine Street	Private	R.I.R.	
Saunderson, Samuel	3 Gay Street	Gunner	R.F.A.	
Savage, Henry	37 Auburn Street	Private	Royal Scots	
Scott, Albert	90 Fitzroy Avenue	Private	R. Inn. Fus.	
Scott, George	115 Matilda Street	Sapper	R.E.	
Scott, James H.	107 Britannic Street	Private	P.P.R.	
Scott, James H.	108 University Avenue	Lieutenant	Royal Worcs.	
Scott, Walter	18 Botanic Avenue	Lieutenant	R.I.R.	Killed in Action.
Shaw, Alex.	21 Renfrew Street	Engineer	R.N.	
Shaw, Andrew	91 Egmont Street	Private	R.I.R.	
Shaw, John	91 Egmont Street	Private	R.I.R.	
Shaw, John K.	11 Northbrook Street	Private	R.I.R.	
Shaw, Robert H.	91 Egmont Street	Private	R.I.R.	Killed in Action.
Shields, William	8 Watson Street	Private	H.A.	
Shirlow, Robert J.	12 Southview Street	Private	R.I.R.	
Simms, Henry	33 Abingdon Street	Private	R.I.R.	
Sinclair, Edward	16 Beggs Street	Sergeant	R. Inn. Fus.	Killed in Action, D.C.M.
Sloane, James	17 Peveril Street	Engineer	R.N.	
Sloane, Matthew	56 Britannic Street	Private	R.I.R.	
Sloane, Robert	17 Peveril Street	Private	R. Inn. Fus.	
Sloane, Robert G.	148 Rugby Avenue	Private	R. Air F.	
Sloane, Samuel	4 Renfrew Street	Private	R.I.R.	
Sloane, Samuel	42 Pretoria Street	Sergeant	A.S.C.	
Small, David	115 Vernon Street	Private	R.I.R.	
Smith, Samuel J.	58 Coolfin Street	Private	Arg. & Suth. Highldrs.	Died of Wounds.
Smylie, David	1 Ratcliffe Street	Sapper	R.E.	
Smylie, Robret	1 Ratcliffe Street	Private	R. Inn. Fus.	Killed in Action.
Smylie, William J.	108 Lindsay Street	Private	R. Inn. Fus.	Killed in Action.
Smyth, Charles	13 Lisburn Road	Private	R.I.R.	Killed in Action.
Smyth, Charles	Colin Villa	Private	R.I.R.	
Smyth, James F.	Colin Villa	Private	A.S.C.	Killed in Action.
Smyth, Samuel	Stockman's Lane	Private	Arg. & Suth. Highldrs.	
Smyth, William	1 Thorn Street	Private	R.I.R.	
Smyth, William J.	43 Rutland Street	Private	N.I.H.	
Sparrow, James A.	8 Kensington Street	Private	R.I.R.	Killed in Action.
Spence, George	21 Dromara Street	Private	R.I.R.	
Spence, Francis Jas.	18 Sunnyside Street	Private	R.I.R.	
Spence, John Alex.	95 Tate's Avenue	Engineer		M.M.
Spence, John	21 Dromara Street	Private	R. Inn. Fus.	
Spence, William	65 Tate's Avenue	Private	R.A.M.C.	
Spence, William John	95 Tate's Avenue	Gunner	R.G.A.	
Sprott, Robert	12 Charles Street S.	Private	R.I.R.	Died of Wounds.
Sprott, Thomas	12 Charles Street S.	Private	R.I.R.	
Spurr, George A.	73 Clementine Street	Private	K.R.R.	Killed in Action.
Stalker, John	38 Bankmore Street	Sergeant	R.I.R.	
Stanley, Harry	Knockbreda Road			Torpedoed.
Stanley, John C.	Knockbreda Road	Private	R.I.R.	
Stanley, Robert O.	Knockbreda Road	Lieutenant	Welsh Fus.	Killed in Action.
Stead, Hugh	214 Donegall Road	Sergeant	R.I.R.	
Stead, William	214 Donegall Road	A.B.	R.N.	

(114)

BELFAST PRESBYTERY. GREAT VICTORIA STREET.

Name.	Home Address.	Rank.	Regiment, Battalion or Unit.	Remarks.
Stephenson, Andrew M.	26 Fitzwilliam Street	Private	R.I.R.	M.M.
Stephenson, Thomas B.	26 Fitzwilliam Street	Lieutenant	R.I.R.	M.C. and Bar.
Stephenson, William	26 Fitzwilliam Street	Sergeant	R.I.R.	Killed in Action.
Stevens, Jas. A.	16 Mount Street	Private	H.L.I.	
Stevenson, James	42 Elm Street	Private	R.A.S.C.	
Storey, Samuel	49 Clementine Street	Private	R.I.R.	
Stranaghan, Robert	18 Lake Street	Private	R.I.R.	
Stratton, William J.	185 Sandy Row	Private	R.I.R.	
Surplus, Thomas	72 Devonshire Street	Private	R.I.R.	
Sutherland, Henry	4 Mayne Street	Private	Scots Fus.	
Switzer, Albert	11 Primrose Street	Gunner	R.F.A.	
Taggart, Joseph	13 Landseer Street	Private	R.I.R.	
Tate, James	21 Taylor Street	Private	R.I.R.	Died of Wounds.
Taylor, Edward A.	70 University Street	Lieutenant	H.L.I.	
Taylor, William J.	17 Apsley Street	Gunner	R.F.A.	
Teuton, James	1 Canterbury Street	Sergeant	R.I.R.	
Thompson, Edward T.	5 Malone Place	Private	R.I.R.	
Thompson, James	72 Howard Street S.	Sapper	R.E.	
Thompson, James	23 Magdala Street	Private	R.I.R.	
Thompson, John	3 Windsor Street	Private	R.I.R.	Killed in Action.
Thompson, John	20 Linfield Road	Private	R. Inn. Fus.	
Thompson, Moses	14 Balmoral Street	Private	A.S.C.	Died in Camp.
Thompson, Robert	27 Deramore Avenue	Sapper	R.E.	
Thompson, William	71 M'Clure Street	Private	R.Air F.	
Thompson, William Jas.	11 Walnut Street	Private	A.S.C.	
Thorsby, Robert	18 Ormeau Street	Private	R.I.R.	
Tipping, John	18 Hardcastle Street	Private	R.I.R.	
Todd, Robert	7 Blakely Street	Private	R.I.R.	
Todd, Thomas	7 Blakely Street	Private	R.I.R.	
Todd, Thomas	4 Kenmare Street	Corporal	R.I.R.	
Toman, William	23 Magdala Street	Private	R.I.R.	
Topping, A. Fred.	243 Roden Street	Private	R. Air F.	
Torrans, John	29 Sandy Row	Private	R.I.R.	
Torrans, Samuel	18 Pine Street	Private	R.I.R.	Killed in Action.
Walker, Thomas B.	81 City Street	Private	R.I.R.	
Wallace, Hugh	154 Lisburn Road	Gunner	R.F.A.	
Wallace, John	131 Vernon Street	Private	N.I.H.	Died of Wounds.
Warburton, Wm.	51 Maryville Street	Engineer	R.N.	
Warde, John	6 Curzon Street	Q.M. Sergt.	R.I.R.	
Watson, George	6 Linview Street	Private	R.A.M.C.	
Watson, James	3 Posnett Street	Private	R.I.R.	Killed in Action.
Watson, William	38 Albion Street	Private	Tank Corps	
Watters, John	157 Vernon Street	Private	R.I.R.	
Weatherup, James	3 Lisburn Avenue	Fireman	M.M.S.	
Weatherup, Thomas	3 Lisburn Avenue	Sapper	R.E.	
Webster, Joseph	10 Britannic Street	Private	R.I.R.	
White, Albert	123 Ormeau Road	Private	R.I.R.	
White, Ernest	123 Ormeau Road	Sapper	R.E.	
White, Robert	123 Ormeau Road	Private	R.I.R.	
Williamson, Andrew	18 Pandora Street	Private	A.S.C.	Died in Camp.
Williamson, George	40 Coolfin Street	Gunner	R.G.A.	Died in Hospital.
Williamson, George	40 Coolfin Street	Private	R.I.R.	
Williamson, Frank	4 Combermere Street	Private	R.I.R.	
Williamson, Thomas S.	4 Combermere Street	Private	Cycle Corps	
Williamson, Thomas W.	20 Britannic Street	Private	R. Inn. Fus.	Died in Hospital.
Williamson, William G.	30 Renfrew Street	Private	M.G.C.	
Willis, Samuel	30 Donegall Road	Private	R.I.R.	
Willis, Tom.	20 Hurst Street	A.B.	R.N.	
Wilson, Edward	3 Glentoran Street	Private	R.I.R.	
Wilson, George	251 Roden Street	Private	Cycle Corps	
Wilson, Henry	251 Roden Street	Sergeant	R.I.R.	
Wilson, James	3 Posnett Street	Private	R.I.R.	
Wilson, James	10 Thalia Street	Private	R.I.R.	
Wilson, James	4 Walnut Street	Private	C.P.B.	
Wilson, John	251 Roden Street	Sapper	R.E.	
Wilson, John K.	13 Brassey Street	Private	A.S.C.	
Wilson, Robert	13 Brassey Street	Sergeant	R. Inn. Fus.	
Wilson, Robert	1 St. Andrew's Square	Q.M. Sergt.	R. Inn. Fus.	M.S.M.
Wilson, Robert G.	47 Teutonic Street	Private	R. Ir. Fus.	
Wilson, Samuel	60 Donegall Road	Private	A.S.C.	
Wilson, William	60 Donegall Road	Private	R.I.R.	
Wilson, William G.	3 Palmerston Street	Private	R.I.R.	
Wilson, William J.	17 Sunnyside Street	Lance-Corporal	R.E.	M.M.
Witherow, George	130 Rugby Avenue	Private	A.S.C.	
Woods, Frank	64 Pine Street	A.B.	R.N.	
Woods, Hamilton	64 Pine Street	Private	R.A.M.C.	
Wright, Albert	8 Brassey Street	Private	R.I.R.	
Wright, James	35 Lisburn Avenue	Private	R.I.R.	
Wright, Samuel	35 Lisburn Avenue	Private	R. Air F.	
Wylie, Edward	Rose Cottage, Finaghy	Corporal	R.E.	Killed in Action.
Young, John	138 Lower Broadway	Private	R.I.R.	
Young, Robert	232 Roden Street	Sergeant	R. Inn. Fus.	Prisoner.
Young, William	138 Lower Broadway	A.B.	R.N.	

BELFAST PRESBYTERY. GREAT VICTORIA STREET.

Name.	Home Address.	Rank.	Regiment, Battalion or Unit.	Remarks.
	COLONIAL FORCES.			
Carse, David A.	11 Ireton Street	Private	Austral. Forces	
Carse, Norman Reg.	11 Ireton Street	Private	Austral. Forces	Killed in Action.
Carse, Sydney C. G.	11 Ireton Street	Private	Austral. Forces	Killed in Action.
Dick, John	7 Ventry Street	Private	2nd Canadians	
Doran, William	6 Wolseley Street	Sergt.-Major	U.S. Forces	
Green, Joseph	10 Hartington Street	Private	P.P. Regt.	Killed in Action.
Haslett, James	137 Dunluce Avenue	Private	P.P. Regt.	
Johnston, William	15 Britannic Street	Sapper	Canadian Engineers	
Keir, Alex. Ed.	Ivy Cottage, The Dub	Private	Canadian Forces	Killed in Action.
Martin, Albert L.	15 Tate's Avenue	Private	P.P. Regt.	
Miller, Albert E.	4 Stranmillis Park	Corporal	P.P. Regt.	
McClean, William J.	2 Belgravia Avenue	Private	Canadian F.A.	
Scott, James H.	107 Britannic Street	Private	Canadian R.R.	
	HOLYWOOD, HIGH STREET.			
Allan, Lowry B.	Holywood	Lieutenant	10th R. Dub. Fus.	
Anderson, Albert S.	Holywood	2nd Lieutenant	13th R. Inn. Fus.	Killed in Action.
Bell, Alex.	Holywood	Private	R.E.	
Bradshawe, J. M.	Holywood	Private	R.F.A.	
Brown, Robert	Holywood	Private	6th Black Watch	
Brown, Samuel	Holywood	Private	R.A.Y.	
Brown, William	Holywood	Surgeon	R.N.	
Burnside, Fred. W.	Holywood	2nd Lieutenant	19th R.I.R.	
Carpenter, C. H. V.	Holywood	Corporal	Rifle Brigade	
Curley, Robert	Holywood	2nd Lieutenant	6th R. Highldrs.	
Dunn, Hubert	Holywood	Surgeon	R.N.	
Elliott, W. Terence	Holywood	2nd Lieutenant	6th R. Highldrs.	
Ferguson, James	Holywood	Private	2nd R. Irish Fus.	
Ferguson, Samuel	Holywood	Private	13th R.I.R.	Killed in Action.
Galway, Wm.	Holywood	Private	13th R.I.R.	Killed in Action.
Galway, Wm.	Holywood	Private	13th R. Ir. R.	
Green, Wm.		Sergeant	20th R. Ir. R.	
Hanna, Robert	Holywood	Private	5th R. Ir. R.	
Hume, George	Cultra	Captain	5th R. Ir. R.	
Kemp, Jas. W. L.	Holywood	2nd Lieutenant	16th R. Irish R.	
Kemp, William F.		Lieutenant	R. Naval Air Force	
Long, John	Holywood	Captain	14th R. Ir. R.	
McIldowie, George	Craigavad	Captain	R.E.	
McIldowie, John D.	Craigavad	Lieutenant	11th R. Ir. Fus.	
Mackie, James	Holywood	Private	Black Watch	
Malcolm, Hugh	Holywood	Private	13th R. Ir. R.	Prisoner.
Martin, Donald, M.D.	Holywood	Private	M.T. A.S.C.	
Megaw, Wm.	Holywood	Sergeant	13th R. Ir. R.	
Osborough, W. T.	Holywood	Lance-Corporal	10th R. Ir. F.	
Parke, J. Beatty	Holywood	2nd Lieutenant	18th R. Ir. R.	
Parkhill, J. Stillwell	Holywood	Sapper	R.E.	
Patterson, Adam	Holywood	Sergeant	13th R. Ir. R.	
Patterson, J. W.	Holywood	2nd Lieutenant	R.E.	
Perry, Wm. R.	Holywood	Captain	King's Liverpool	
Pollock, John	Marino	Lieutenant	13th R. Ir. R.	Killed in Action.
Robb, John	Cultra	Private	R.N.R.	
Shannon, James	Holywood	Private	R.E.	
Shannon, Wm.	Holywood	Private	R. Ir. R.	
Steele, James	Holywood	Private	51st Queen's W. Surrey	Killed in Action.
Thompson, W. J.	Holywood	Lieutenant	A.S.C.	
Todd, Alex.	Holywood	Private	9th R. Ir. F.	Wounded.
White, W. Brownlow	Holywood		R.N.R.	
Workman, Arthur	Cultra	Lieutenant	5th R. Ir. R.	
	COLONIAL FORCE.			
Hanna, Samuel		Private	Canadian Highldrs.	
Kemp, Walter F.		Colonel	16th Canadians	
	HYDE PARK			
Campbell, William	Ballyvesey	Flight Lieutenant	R.A.F.	
Carruth, John	Hyde Park	2nd Lieutenant		Killed in Action.
Carruth, Matthew	Hyde Park	2nd Lieutenant		Killed in Action.
Fullerton, James	Hyde Park	Lance-Corporal	Northumberland Fus.	
Fullerton, Samuel	Hyde Park	Driver	R.F.A.	
Fullerton, Wm.	Hyde Park	Rifleman	R.I.R.	
Graham, Wm.	Hyde Park	Private	M.G.C.	
Hamill, Wm. F.	Hyde Park	Private	R.E.	
Kerr, Andrew	Hyde Park	Private	R. Marines	
McMillan, Samuel	Hightown	Private	12th R.I.R.	
Magee, Edward	Craigavogan	Lance-Corporal	12th R.I.R.	Killed in Action.
Mawhinney, Joseph		Corporal	7th Can. Inft. Brigade	
Mulholland, John	Hyde Park	Private	R.I.R.	
Templeton, John	Hydepark	Private	R. Irish Fus.	
Thompson, Robert	Hyde Park	Lance-Corporal	15th R.I.R.	

(116)

BELFAST PRESBYTERY. KNOCK.

Name.	Home Address.	Rank.	Regiment, Battalion or Unit.	Remarks.
KNOCK.				
Baillie, John S.	Marathon, Green Road	Paymaster Sub-Lt.	R.N.R.	
Bailie, Thomas	...	...	...	
Baillie, Wm. B.	Marathon, Green Road	A/Captain	R.I. Regt.	Wd., Ment in Des.
Boyd, James A.	Shieling, Green Road	Captain	Essex Regt.	
Boyd, Jim	...	...	...	
Boyd, John M.	Shieling, Green Road	Lieutenant	Canadian E.F.	Wounded.
Boyd, W. Ryder	Shieling, Green Road	Lieutenant	R. Inn. Fus.	
Brand, Andrew	...	...	...	
Burnet, Henry W.	...	...	...	Killed in Action.
Byers, David	...	...	...	
Byers, Nat. McC.	...	...	...	
Campbell, Alex.	...	...	...	
Campbell, James	...	...	...	Killed in Action.
Crawford, Henry	...	...	...	
Curry, Ernest	...	...	...	
Farrell, Stanley K.	...	...	...	Killed in Action.
Farrell, Wm. E.	...	...	...	
Ferris, Wm. S.	Sandown Park	Lieutenant	2nd R.I.R.	Killed in Action.
Foster, Rigby	Holywood Road	Lieutenant	R.I.R.	Wounded.
Foster, Roy	Holywood Road	Lieutenant	Hampshire Regt.	Twice Wounded.
Gamble, Albert	...	...	...	
Gordon, John	Kensington Park, Knock	Lieutenant	M.G.C.	
Graham, Alex.	Stormount	Sergt.-Major	M.T. A.S.C.	
Graham, Joseph	...	...	...	Killed in Action.
Graham, Nathaniel	...	Private	M.T. A.S.C.	
Graham, Samuel	...	...	...	
Graham, William	...	...	...	
Hanna, Musgrave	...	...	...	
Hanna, Robert	...	...	...	
Houston, George	Ballyhackamore	Private	A.I.F.	Killed in Action.
Hunter, Wm. J.	...	...	...	
Irwin, E. Stanley	...	...	...	
Irwin, Leslie T.	...	...	...	
King, Robert	...	...	...	
Lewis, Herbert J.	Glenallen, Dundela Av.	Lieutenant	Black Watch and R.A.S.C.	Wounded.
McCahon, Robert	Wyncroft, Knock	Lieutenant	R.E.	Died of Wounds.
McCaw, William	47 Atlantic Avenue	Sergeant	8th R.I. Rifles	Killed in Action.
MacDonald, S. F. C.	...	...	...	
MacFarland, Jos. Y.	...	...	...	
MacIntyre, John	Whittingham Villa	Sergeant	R.I. Rifles	Disabled.
MacIntyre, Robert	Whittingham Villa	Lieutenant	11th East Yorks	Died.
McMaster, Charles	Rose Lodge, Bloomfield	Captain	R.I.R.	Kd. in Act., M.C.
McMaster, Lendrick	Rose Lodge, Bloomfield	Lieutenant	R.I.R.	Wounded.
Marshall, Samuel H.	Ardcolm, Knock	Captain	Black Watch (R.H.)	
Morrow, Kenneth	...	...	...	
Neill, Albert	...	...	...	
Park, Andrew	Belmont Church Road	Driver	R.E.	
Park, Jacob	Belmont Church Road	Private	3/5 Seaforth Highldrs.	Died of Wounds.
Peddie, Robert	...	...	...	
Shaw, James Alex.	...	...	...	Killed in Action.
Shaw, Thomas	...	...	...	
Sinclair, Walter	...	...	...	
Sinclair, William	...	...	...	
Tate, Edward	...	...	...	
Tate, Hugh	...	...	...	
Taylor, Joseph S.	...	...	...	
Watson, Thomas M.	...	...	...	Killed in Action.
White, Thomas	...	...	...	
Wilson, Robert C.	...	Private	M.T. A.S.C.	
MACRORY MEMORIAL.				
Adair, Jack	Cavehill Road	Private	R.A.M.C.	
Agnew, David	Mountcollyer Street	A.B.	R.N.	
Agnew, W. R.	Gainsborough Drive	Corporal	R.A.M.C.	
Alexander, John	Dargle Street	Private	R.I.R.	
Allen, Andrew	Up. Meadow Street	Private	R.A.F.	
Bamford, John	Cosgrave Street	Private	A.S.C.	
Barker, F. J.	Cliftonpark Avenue	Corporal	R.E.	
Beattie, James S.	Hillman Street	Sergeant	R.G.A.	
Beggs, Harry	New Lodge Road	Sergeant	R.I.R.	
Beggs, John B.	New Lodge Road	Sergeant	R.I.R.	Wounded.
Beggs, Thos.	New Lodge Road	Sergeant	R.I.R.	
Boyd, Henry	Hillman Street	Sergeant	R.A.M.C.	Drowned.
Boyd, Wm.	Hillman Street	Air Craftsman	R.A.F.	
Bradley, John	Henderson Avenue	Private	R.A.F.	
Brown, Hugh	Ilchester Street	A.B.	R.N.	
Calvert, Richard	Spamount Street	Private	R.I.R.	Wounded.
Campbell, James	Duncairn Gardens	Private	R.I.R.	
Campbell, Nesbitt	Duncairn Gardens	Private	R.I.R.	Killed.
Campbell, Tom	Antrim Road	Private	H.M.T.	

BELFAST PRESBYTERY.   MACRORY MEMORIAL.

Name.	Home Address.	Rank.	Regiment, Battalion or Unit.	Remarks.
Cathcart, William	...	Lance-Corporal	R.E.	
Clarke, W. T.	Cosgrave Street	Lance-Corporal	London Regt.	
Cooke, Wm. M.	Deacon Street	Sergeant	18th K's R.R.	Wounded, D.C.M.
Crooks, Geo. F.	Meadow Street	Private	R.I.R.	
Davis, Wm. A.	Belfast	Private	R.I.R.	
Dean, W. J.	Brookhill Avenue	Captain	R.E.	
Dixon, G. S.	Belfast	Private	R.I.R.	
Dunlop, Stuart	York Street	S.P.O.	R.N.	
Entwistle, Robert	Atlantic Avenue	Private	Y.C.V.	
Erskine, Alex.	Cavehill Road	Lance-Corporal	R.I.F.	Died of Wounds.
Ferguson, Wm.	Garden Street	Lieutenant	M. Gun Corps	
Freeman, Samuel	Mervue Street	Lance-Corporal	R.E.	Bravery Cert.
Fullerton, John	14 Rosemount Gardens	Corporal	R.D.F.	
Gillespie, J.	Duncairn Gardens	Private	York & Lanc. Regt.	
Gilliland, George	Kilronan Street	Private	R.I.R.	
Girvan, J. W.	Shore Road	Lieutenant		Wounded.
Girvan, S. K.	Shore Road	Sergeant	R.I.R.	Wounded.
Graham, George	Spamount Street	Engineer	R.N.	
Graham, Thomas	Orient Gardens	Private	R.F.C.	
Graham, Thomas	Spamount Street	Private	R.I.R.	Wounded.
Greenlees, Thomas	Duncairn Gardens	F. Mechanic	R.A.F.	
Greer Thos. J.	Gainsborough Drive	...	...	
Hamilton, W. J.	Up. Meadow Street	Private	R.I.R.	Wounded.
Hayes, John	Duncairn Gardens	Private	N.I.H.	
Heaney, Anthony	Mileriver Street	E.R.A.	R.N.	
Hosie, Jas. A.	Mountcollyer Street	Private	R.C.D.	Wounded.
Hosie, John	Mountcollyer Street	Private	I. Guards	Wounded.
Hosie, Joseph	Mountcollyer Street	Private	R.I.R.	
Hosie, Wm.	Mountcollyer Street	Private	Y.C.V.	
Jamison, Harry	Stratheden Street	Private	R.I.R.	
Jamison, Samuel	Stratheden Street	Private	R.I.R.	
Johnston, Joseph	Cosgrave Street	Private	A.S.C.	
Kane, Hugh	Cosgrave Street	Sergeant	A.S.C.	
Kane, Robert	Halliday's Road	Corporal	R.A.M.C.	Wounded.
Keith, Edward	Mountcollyer Street	Lance-Corporal	R.I.R.	Wounded.
Keith, George	Mountcollyer Street	Private	R.I.R.	
Keith, James	Mountcollyer Street	Private	R.I.R.	
Keith, Robert	Mountcollyer Street	Private	R.I.R.	Wounded.
Kelso, George G.	Duncairn Gardens	Sergeant	R.I.R.	
Kidd, Robert	Up. Meadow Street	Private	R.I.R.	Wounded.
Kyle, David	Up. Meadow Street	Private	R.M.L.I.	
Kyle, Robert	Up. Meadow Street	Corporal	R.I.R.	M.M., Wounded
Lamont, Thomas	Up. Meadow Street	Private	Labour Corps	
Lamont, Thomas	Upper Meadow Street	Private	Y.C.V.	
Larmour, Fred.	Stratheden Street	Private	R.I.R.	
Lenaghan, T.	Brookvale Street	Private	R.E.	Killed.
Lunn, James	Spamount Street	Sergeant	R.I.R.	
Lunn, William	Spamount Street	Private	R.I.R.	
McBride, James	Glenrosa Street	Private	A.S.C.	
McConkey, Fred. R.	Duncairn Gardens	Private	A.S.C.	
McConnell, J. K.	Rosemount Street	Lieutenant	74 Punjabs, I. Army	
McConnell, R. B.	Rosemount Street	Lieutenant	R.I.F.	M.C.
McConnell, S. B.	Rosemount Street	Lieutenant	R.I.F.	
McFall, George	Spamount Street	Private	R.I. Rifles	
McFall, John	Spamount Street	Private	R.I. Rifles	
McFall, Robert	Spamount Street	Private	R.I. Rifles	Killed.
McKay, Alex.	Spamount Street	Gunner	R.F.A.	Drowned.
McKeown, John	Cedar Avenue	Private	R.A.M.C.	Died.
Magill, A.	Fedora Terrace	Corporal	A.S.C.	Killed.
Magill, Hugh	Fedora Terrace	Private	Manchester Regt.	Killed.
Mitchell, Jim	Spamount Street	Private	Cam. Highldrs.	Wounded.
Moore, Hugh	Carlisle Street	Gunner	R.F.A.	Wounded.
Moore, Thos. H.	Brookhill Avenue	Lieutenant	Inn. Fus.	Wounded.
Moore, Wm.	Carlisle Street	1st C. P.O.	R.N.	
Morrison, Alex.	Spamount Street	Private	R.I.R.	Wounded.
Patterson, James	Brougham Street	Lance-Corporal	N.I.H.	
Rainey, Thomas	Shore Road	Sergeant	R.I.R.	Killed.
Reid, Edward	Stratheden Street	Sergeant	R.I.R.	
Reid, Gregory	Stratheden Street	Sergeant	R.E.	Killed, M.M.
Reid, William	Kilronan Street	Private	A.S.C.	
Rodgers, Alex.	Bentinck Street	A.B.	R.N.	Killed.
Ross, Adam T.	Clanchattan Street	A.B.	R.N.	
Ross, E. L.	Clanchattan Street	Private	R.E.	
Ross, G. V.	Clanchattan Street	Private	N.I.H.	Wounded.
Ross, T.	Clanchattan Street	Private	Y.C.V.	Wounded.
Rusk, John	Cavehill Road	Private	N.I.H	
Scott, A.	Henderson Avenue	Sergeant	R.I.R.	Wounded.
Scott, D.	Henderson Avenue	Lieut. Commander	R.N.	
Scott, John	Spamount Street	Private	R.I.R.	Wounded.
Smyth, H. P.	Limestone Road	Lieutenant	R.E.	
Stewart, James	Eia Street	Lieutenant	R.N.V.R.	
Stewart, J. C.	Eia Street	Private	A.S.C. M.T.	
Stewart, M. C.	Eia Street	O.S.	R.N.	
Stewart, Robert	Eia Street	Sergeant	R.E.	

BELFAST PRESBYTERY.   MACRORY MEMORIAL.

Name.	Home Address.	Rank.	Regiment, Battalion or Unit.	Remarks.
Stuart, Jack	Glantane Street	Private	R.F.A.	
Tate, Johnston	Cedar Avenue	Lieutenant	R. Irish Fus.	Killed.
Tate, Robert	Cedar Avenue	Lieutenant	K.S.L.I.	
Thompson, David	Fleet Street	Private	R.I.F.	Killed.
Turkington, Isaac	Alloa Street	Lieutenant	R.F.C.	
Walker, Edmund	Cliftonpark Avenue	Sergeant	A.S.C.	
Wallace, Wm.	Up. Canning Street	Private	R.G.A.	Killed.
Watt, James	Kilronan Street	Private	A.S.C.	Killed.
Yorke, Robert	Up. Meadow Street	Lance-Corporal	R.I.R.	Killed.
Young, Frank	Adam Street	Private	R.I.R.	
COLONIAL FORCES.				
Erskine, Thomas		Driver	Australn. Force	
Ferguson, D. B.		Sapper	R.E., N.Z.	
Ferguson, James		Private	N.Z. Inftry.	
Fullerton, William	Rosemount Gardens	Trooper	M.G. Squad, Can. Inftry.	Wounded.
Gemmell, Gordon		Private	N.Z. Rifles	Wounded.
Gemmell, Robert		Private	M.G. Corps, N.Z.	
Gemmell, Ronald		Private	Otago R. N.Z.	Wounded.
Hook, Henry J.		Private	52 B. Canadians	
McClements, Frank		Private	Can. R.A.M.C.	
McClements, Robert		Private	S. African Inftry.	
Mitchell, Jim		Private	Canadian Horse	
Moore David		Sergeant	Canadian Force	
Mullan, S.		Lieutenant	Australian Force	
Shannon, Herbert V.		Sergeant	Canadian Force	
Stewart James		Lieutenant	Can. Engineers	
Walker, Harry		Lieutenant	R.N.	
Yorke, Wm.		Sergeant	Canadian Force	Wounded.
MALONE.				
Allen, William McCreight	Ashbury, Balmoral Av.	Private	10th R.I. Fus.	
Armstrong George	51 Moonstone Street	A.B.	R.N.	
Armstrong, Joseph	51 Moonstone Street	Stoker	H.M.S. Dominion	
Barclay, Norman	83 Eglantine Avenue	Private	6th Batt. R. Highldrs. B. Wch.	
Beck, W. Edmund	Balmoral	Probation Surgeon	R.N.	
Bell, David H.	5 Charleville Avenue	Stoker	H.M.S. Vengeance	
Black, Samuel	Balmoral	Q.M. Sergt.	10th Batt. R.I.R.	Wounded.
Breadon, John	21 Maryville Avenue	Private	9th Batt. Inn. Fus.	
Burton, Jack	Tassagh, Cranmore Park	Sergeant	14th Batt. R.I.R.	Killed in Action.
Boyd, John	35 Maryville Avenue	Private	Arg. & Suth. Highldrs.	Killed in Action.
Condy, Edgar	29 College Gardens	Lieutenant	R.A.M.C.	
Condy, Robert	29 College Gardens	Captain	R.A.M.C.	
Coulter, J. W. G.	Balmoral	Sergeant	6th Batt. R. Highldrs.	
Cox, William	Balmoral	Lieut. Commander	H.M.S. Progress	Torpd. & Drown'd
Curry, Charles John	Malone Cottage	Chief Engineer	S.S. Bray Head	Torpd and Drown'd
Douglas, George	44 Windsor Road	Private	R.M.L.I.	
Douglas, Robert	44 Windsor Road	Rifleman	19th Batt. R.I. Rifles	
Downey, Andrew	1 Maryville Avenue	Rifleman	19th Batt. R.I. Rifles	Killed in Action.
Downey, John	1 Maryville Avenue	Private	9th Batt. Inn. Fus.	Killed in Action.
Elwood, Fred. B.	13 University Square	Lieutenant	R.A.M.C.	M.C.
Elwood, Herbert	13 University Square	Captain	Croix Rouge Francais	
Ferguson, William V.	1 Mowhan Street	Private	N.I.H.	Wounded.
Giles, H. C.	Beech Lodge, Malone Pk.	Petty Officer	R.N.A.S.	
Gilmore, Alfred	Cloverlea, Stockman's Le.	Trooper	South Irish Horse	
Gregg, James	11 Capstone Street	Private	9th Batt. Inn. Fus.	
Gregg, Samuel	11 Capstone Street	Sapper	R.E.	
Hamilton, William	Magdala Street	2nd Lieutenant	3rd Conn. Rangers	Killed in Action.
Heslip, Isaac	68 Wellington Park	Major	3rd Batt. R.I.R.	
Hilditch, William	22 Ferndale Place	Driver	A.S.C.	
Houston, Samuel	6 Capstone Street	Lance-Corporal	N.I.H.	Wounded.
Hunter, William	475 Lisburn Road	Corporal	Despatch Rider R.E.	
Henderson, J. O.	3 Cranmore Avenue	Lieutenant	King's African Rifles	
Henderson, Robert	3 Cranmore Avenue	Writer	R.N.	
Hall, William H.	3 Osborne Terrace	Private	R.E.	
Irwin, Robert	26 Rathcool Street	Private	9th Batt. Inn. Fus.	
Jelly, Herbert	Rubyville, Balmoral	Private	South Irish Horse	Died Pris. in Ger.
Jamison, James	29 Brookland Street	Lance-Corporal	10th Batt. R.I.R.	Wounded.
Jamison, John	29 Brookland Street	Private	2nd Batt. Inn. Fus.	Wounded.
Jamison, William	29 Brookland Street	A.B.	H.M.S. Pactolus	
Jamison, Henry	29 Brookland Street	Private	6th Batt. Black Watch	
Johnston, William	Malone Church	P.O.	R.N.A.S.	
Kirkwood, Alexander	9 Marlborough Place	Rifleman	10th Batt. R.I.R.	Wounded.
Leitch, Jas. Lyle Finlay	Finaghy	2nd Lieutenant	6th Batt. R.I.R.	
Leitch, Walter	116 Melrose Street		R.N.	
Mackenzie, Horace	Malone	Captain	A.S.C.	
Mackenzie, J. R. Morell	Malone	Lieutenant	R.A.M.C.	
Magee, Fredk. Herb.	Fruithill Park	Engineer	H.M.S. Emperor of India	
Martin, W. H.	2 Myrtlefield Park	Sergeant	N.I.H.	
Mahaffy, Thomas	29 Hugh Street	Private	12th Batt. R.I.R.	Killed in Action.
Mateer, Norman Cooper	Cranmore Crescent	Lieutenant	R.I. Fus.	
Martin, Joseph J.	15 Prospect Street	Private	14th Batt. R.I.R.	

BELFAST PRESBYTERY. **MALONE.**

NAME.	HOME ADDRESS.	RANK.	REGIMENT, BATTALION OR UNIT.	REMARKS.
MANDERSON, HAROLD	Malone	Lieutenant	Transport Section	Died in Service.
MATTHEWS, GEORGE	Ruskey, Cranmore Av.	Lance-Corporal	9th Batt. R.I. Fus.	Wounded.
MATTHEWS, THOMAS	Ruskey, Cranmore Av.	Corporal	Field Ambulance	
MAXWELL, ROBERT H.	671 Lisburn Road	Sergeant	R.E.	
MURDOCH, W. J. HUGHES	8 Adelaide Avenue	2nd Lieutenant	King Edward's Horse	
MILLAR, EDWARD	44 Lisburn Avenue	Private	Air Force	
McCOUBRIE, EDWARD H.	Balmoral Avenue	Private	19th Batt. R.I.R.	
McCURDY, JOHN	Charleville Avenue	A.B.	H.M.S. Severn	Wounded.
McCUTCHEON, GEORGE	40 Rathcool Street	Private	Middlesex Regt.	
McCUTCHEON, GEORGE	40 Rathcool Street	Private	A.S.C.	
McCUTCHEON, HUGH	40 Rathcool Street	Private	Air Service	
McCUTCHEON, JOSEPH	40 Rathcool Street	Private	Inn. Fus.	
McDOUGALL, ARTHUR	Rue Royale, Finaghy	Private	17th Batt. R.I.R.	
McDOUGALL, ROBERT	Rue Royale, Finaghy	Private	A.S.C.	
McDOWELL, ALFRED	West End Park	2nd Lieutenant	14th Batt. R.I. Rifles	
McKELVEY, ROBERT	Beersbridge Road	Private	6th Batt. R. Highldrs.	D.C.M.
McVEA, JAMES	Poplar Grove, Balmoral	Corporal	6th Batt. R. Highldrs.	
McWILLIAM, W. J.	Balmoral Nursery	Private	14th Batt. R.I.R.	
McWILLIAM, ALBERT	8 Hugh Street	Rifleman	19th Batt. R.I.R.	
McWILLIAM, ANDREW	8 Hugh Street	Sergeant	10th Batt. R.I.R.	
NEILLY, THOMAS	1 Mayfield Street	Trooper	4th Hussars	
NIXON, WILLIAM	Lisburn Road	Private	9th Batt. Inn. Fus.	Killed in Action.
PRIESTLY, GEORGE	61 Wellesley Avenue	2nd Lieutenant	R.F.C.	Wounded.
PRIESTLY, HERBERT S.	61 Wellesley Avenue	Lieutenant	15th Ser. Batt. Manch. Regt.	Wounded.
PRESS, FINLAY	Ivanhoe, M'borough Park	Sergeant	M.T. A.S.C.	
RANKIN, ROBERT H.	Meadowlands, Balmoral	2nd Lieutenant	14th Batt. R.I. Rifles	Killed in Action.
REA, R. L.	5 Myrtle Terrace	Captain	R.A.M.C.	
REID, JOHN	The Rowans, C'more Av.	Sergeant	Headquarters Staff	
RUSK, WILLIAM	Martinville, Malone Rd.	Driver	M.T. A.S.C.	
RANKIN, HAROLD	Meadowlands, Balmoral	Gunner	R.H. Artillery	
SHAW, ERNEST H.	Strathavon, Balmoral	2nd Lieutenant	5th R. Inn. Fus.	Wounded.
STEVENSON, JAMES	Lynwood, Malone Park	2nd Lieutenant	R.I.R.	
STEVENSON, STANLEY	Lynwood, Malone Park	2nd Lieutenant	10th R.I.R.	Wounded.
STEVENSON, THOMAS	Riversdale, A'town	Private	6th Inn. Fus.	
THOMPSON, HERBERT	Finaghy	Sergeant	R.I.R.	
WEIR, AUSTIN	Riverview, Shaw's Bge.	Private	14th R.I.R.	
WEIR, JOSEPH	Riverview, Shaw's Bge.	Private	2nd Borderers	Killed in Action.
WHITE, WM. J.	Blackstaff Road	Private	13th R.I.R.	
WHITESIDE, R. P.	Donore, Cranmore Av.	Driver	M.T.	
WILGAR, WM. J.	Fernleigh, Balmoral	2nd Lieutenant	R.N. Lancs.	
WILSON, CHARLES M.	The Manse, Malone	Captain	A.O. Dept.	
WILSON, JAMES	13 Ulsterville Gardens	Corporal	20th R.I.R.	
WILSON, WILLIAM	Rose Lodge, A'town	Private	I.G.	Killed in Action.

COLONIAL & U.S.A. FORCES.

NAME.	HOME ADDRESS.	RANK.	REGIMENT, BATTALION OR UNIT.	REMARKS.
AGNEW, JAMES	3 Osborne Terrace	Private	Can. Contingent	
ALDERDICE, WALTER	Malone Park	Private	1st N.Z. Contingent	
ALLEN, GEORGE	Balmoral Avenue	Private	Can. Contingent	Wounded,
ANDERSON, DAVID	Andersonstown	Private	Can. Contingent	
DORNAN, JOHN	29 Maryville Avenue	Farrier	Can. Contingent	
EDMUNDSON, F. M.	Balmoral	Sergeant	Can. Contingent	
MATEER, FRED. MILLS	Cranmore Crescent	Private	Aust. Contingent	
MATTHEWS, JAMES	Cranmore Avenue	Private	U.S. Army	
MATTHEWS, WM.	Cranmore Avenue	Private	Can. Contingent	
McALLEN, WM.	Balmoral		S.A. R.E.	
REILLY, J. B.	Reformatory Avenue		Can. Med. Corps	
WEIR, THOMAS	Riverview, Shaw's Bge.	Private	Can. Contingent	

MAY STREET

NAME.	HOME ADDRESS.	RANK.	REGIMENT, BATTALION OR UNIT.	REMARKS.
ACHESON, SAMUEL	207 Albertbridge Road	Surgeon Lieut.	R.N.	
ADAIR, JOHN	27 Eversleigh Street	Private	R.I.R.	
ADGEY, DAVID	50 Lagan Street	Lance-Corporal	R.I.R.	
ADGEY, THOMAS	50 Lagan Street	Private	R.I.R.	
ALLEN, FRED. M.	168 Newtownards Road	Surgeon Lieut.	R.N.	
ALLEN, SAMUEL	168 Newtownards Road	Cadet		
ALLEN, WM. K.	3 Townhall Street	Trooper	N.I.H.	
ANDERSON, SAMUEL	Ansley, Cregagh Road	Private	R.I.R.	Wounded.
ANDERSON, ERNEST	418 Woodstock Road	Cadet		
ANDREWS, DAVID	114 Grosvenor Road	Sergeant	R.I.R.	Killed in Action.
ANDREWS, HENRY	114 Grosvenor Road	Rifleman	R.I.R.	
AULD, ANDREW	7 Up. Newtownards Rd.	Rifleman	R.I.R.	
BAILEY, JOHN	25 Lindsay Street	Private	A.S.C.	
BALLENTINE, JAMES	21 Walnut Street	Rifleman	R.I.R.	
BALLENTINE, LOUIS	21 Walnut Street	Rifleman	R.I.R.	M.M.
BALLENTINE, ROBERT	21 Walnut Street	Rifleman	R.I.R.	
BEATTIE, WM.		Gunner	R.F.A.	
BELL, JOSEPH	32 Canterbury Street	Captain	Royal Scots	Wounded.
BENNETT, MALCOLM	10 Ormeau Road	Trooper	Rhodesian Regt.	
BERRINGTON, CHARLES	302 Cupar Street	Private	A.S.C.	
BERRINGTON, HENRY	302 Cupar Street	Rifleman	R.I.R.	
BLACK, ROBERT H.	30 Spruce Street	Rifleman	R.I.R.	Killed in Action.
BLAKELEY, HERBERT J.	Ardmore, Newtownbreda	Lance-Corporal	R.I.R.	Wounded.

BELFAST PRESBYTERY.   MAY STREET.

NAME.	HOME ADDRESS.	RANK.	REGIMENT, BATTALION OR UNIT.	REMARKS.
BRAMSTON, WM. J.	12 Rodner Street	Sergeant	R.I.R.	
BRYARS, DAVID L.	45 Cromwell Road	Petty Officer	Armoured T.S., Russia	
BURNS, GEORGE	17 Copeland Street	Private	R.I.R.	Killed in Action.
BURNS, JOHN	6 Burmah Street	Private	Canadians	
CAMPBELL, FRED.	Fitzwilliam Avenue	Lieutenant	C.L.I.	Killed in Action.
CARDWELL, THOMAS	12 Lt. Charlotte Street	Private	R.I.R.	
CASSON, JOHN	28 Kimberley Street	Corporal	R.I. Fus.	
CLARK, DONALD R.	Woodside, Ravenhill Rd.	2nd Lieutenant	R. Mun. Fus.	
CLARK, FRED. S.	Woodside, Ravenhill Rd.	Corporal	R.I.R.	
CLEMENTS, DAVID M.	2 North Parade	Captain	R.A.M.C.	
COBURN, FRED.	5 Hatfield Street	Sergeant	R.I.R.	
COOPER, WM.	25 Malcolm Street	Private	Canadians	
CORBETT, VICTOR	29 Riverview Street	Private	R.I.R.	
COWAN, MARSHALL	53 Lindsay Street	Private	R.I.R.	Killed in Action.
COWAN, JAMES	53 Lindsay Street	Private	R.I.R.	
COWDEN, ROBERT	29 Malcolm Street	Private	R.I.R.	
DODDS, WM.	15 Howard Street South	Lance-Corporal	R.I.R.	Wounded.
DUNCAN, JAMES	29 Tyrone Street	Rifleman	R.I.R.	Killed in Action.
DUNCAN, WILLIAM	29 Tyrone Street	Rifleman	R.I.R.	Killed in Action.
DUNN, JOSEPH S.		Gunner	R.F.A.	
DOWDS, JAMES	12 Lindsay Street	Private	Army Cyclist C.	
DOWNIE, ARCHIBALD		Lieutenant	Scottish Borderers	
DYER, WM. J.	80 Roden Street	Private	R.I.R.	Killed in Action.
ELLIOTT, RICHARD	97 Rugby Avenue	Trooper	N.I.H.	
FARLEY, WM.	21 Walnut Street	Driver	A.S.C.	
FLETCHER, ALFRED J.	54 South Parade	Paymaster	R.N.	
GALLAGHER, BARRY	3 Ravenscroft Avenue	Seaman	R.N.	
GAMBLE, SAMUEL M.	Glendun, Cregagh	Private	R.A.F.	
GEMMELL, ALEXANDER	8 Cromwell Road	Lance-Corporal	R.I.R.	
GIBSON, GEORGE		Sapper	R.E.	
GIBSON, WILLIAM		Quartermaster	R.A.M.C.	
GILLILAND, HARRY	8 Milner Street	Rifleman	R.I.R.	Killed in Action.
GILLILAND, JAMES G.	8 Milner Street	Gunner	R.F.A.	
GORDON, JOHN		Rifleman	R.I.R.	
GORMAN, ROBERT	93 Thorndyke Street	Rifleman	R.I.R.	
GOULDING, THOMAS	3 Princess Ter., Creg. Rd.		R.N.	
GOULDING, WM.	3 Princess Ter., Creg. Rd.		R.N.	
GRAHAM, JOSEPH	3 Lavinia Street	Driver	A.S.C.	
GREER, JAMES	10 Shaftesbury Avenue	Sapper	R.E.	Killed in Action.
GREER, WALLACE	10 Shaftesbury Avenue	Private	R.I.R.	Killed in Action.
GRIBBEN, GEORGE	32 Pine Street	Private	R.I.R.	
HALL, THOMAS		Private	R.I.R.	
HAMILTON, FRED. S.	37 Elgin Street	Private	R.I.R.	
HAMILTON, JOHN	14 Holmes Street	Stoker	R.N.	
HANNA, SAMUEL	244 Roden Street	Gunner	Tank Corps	
HANNA, WM. H.	244 Roden Street	Lance-Corporal	R.I.R.	Wounded.
HARPER, JAMES	95 Rugby Avenue	Private	R.I.R.	Killed in Action.
HARVEY, FORSYTHE	Inverary, Downshire Rd.	Private	R.I.R.	Killed in Action.
HASLETT, HORACE R.	Kintora, Donaghadee	Major	R.I.R.	Wounded, Croix-de-Chevalier.
HASLETT, JAMES	Kintora, Donaghadee	Captain	A.S.C.	
HIGGINS, HUGH	216 Ravenhill Avenue	Trooper	N.I.H.	
HIGGINS, JOHN	216 Ravenhill Avenue	Lieutenant	R.I.R.	
HILL, STANLEY	Stanleyville, Cregagh	Lieutenant	R.A.F.	
HILL, THOMAS E.	Stanleyville, Cregagh	Captain	R.A.M.C.	
HOBSON, ANDREW	2 Annette Street	Private	R.I.R.	Died.
HUNTER, JOSEPH	6 Stranmillis Road	Lieutenant	Leinster Regt.	Wounded.
JACKSON, JOHN	23 London Street	Seaman	R.N.	
JOHNSTON, JAMES	26 Charlotte Street	Rifleman	R.I.R.	Killed in Action.
JOHNSTON, JOSEPH	104 Rugby Avenue	Sapper	R.E.	
JOHNSTON, ROBERT	104 Rugby Avenue	Private	Cyclist Corps	
JOHNSTON, THOMAS	2 Annette Street	Rifleman	R.I.R.	
JOHNSTON, WILLIAM M.	183 Cupar Street	Private	Canadian Army	Died of Wounds.
KEITH, WM. H.	44 Shaftesbury Avenue	Sapper	R.E.	
KELMAN, JAMES	8 Glandore Avenue	Lance-Corporal	N.I.H.	
KENOLTY, DAVID	10 Hamilton Street	Private	R.I.R.	
KENOLTY, EDWARD C.	10 Hamilton Street	Lance-Corporal	R.I.R.	
KIRKLAND, JOHN	114 Ravenhill Road	Private	London Scottish	Killed in Action.
KNOX, SAMUEL	83 Bloomfield Avenue	Private	R.I.R.	Killed in Action.
LOVE, JOHN	48 Raby Street	Private	R.I.R.	
MAGEE, JOHN	Tacton, Newtownbreda	Sapper	Canadian Railway Troops	
MARTIN, WM. H.	Montana, Glandore Av.	Lieutenant	Yorkshire Regt.	
MILLAR, ARTHUR J.	89 Eglantine Avenue	Captain	R.I. Fus.	Killed in Action.
MOLES, EDWARD	64 Bendigo Street	Trooper	Irish Guards	
MOORE, DAVID S.	147 University Street	Lieutenant	Royal Scots	Killed in Action.
MOORE, ROBERT		Private	R.M.L.I.	
MORROW, ARTHUR G.	10 India Street	Private	R.I.R.	Killed in Action.
MORTON, SIDNEY	4 Atlantic Avenue	Corporal	A.S.C.	
MOTHERWELL, DAVID	133 University Street	Lieutenant	R.I.R.	
MOTHERWELL, JAMES	133 University Street	Sergeant	R.I.R.	
MOTHERWELL, J. ERNEST	133 University Street	Lieutenant	H.L.I.	Killed in Action.
MOYGANNON, DAVID	13 Lindsay Street	Private	R.I.R.	
MOYGANNON, DAVID, JUN.	13 Lindsay Street	Private	West Kent Yeomy.	
MOYGANNON, JAMES A.	13 Lindsay Street	Private	R.I. Fus.	Killed in Action.

BELFAST PRESBYTERY.   MAY STREET.

Name.	Home Address.	Rank.	Regiment, Battalion or Unit.	Remarks.
Murphy, James	99 Westmoreland Street	Rifleman	R.I.R.	
Murphy, Samuel	99 Westmoreland Street	Private	R.I.R.	
Murphy, Wm. John	99 Westmoreland Street	Private	R.I.R.	Killed in Action.
McAllister, Alexander	10 Sussex Place	Gunner	R.F.A.	
McAllister, Isaac	10 Sussex Place	Lance-Corporal	R.I. Fus.	
McAllister, John	10 Sussex Place	Driver	R.E.	
McAllister, Wm.	10 Sussex Place	Private	R.I. Fus.	
McBride, Bertie	65 Woodstock Road	Private	R.I.R.	Wounded.
McCance, George	Knockbreda Road	Cadet	R.N.	
McCartney, John		Signaller	R.I.R.	
McCartney, George				Inn. Fus.
McCaughan, David	29 Little May Street	Gunner	R.F.A.	
McCaw, James	52 Limestone Road	Corporal	R.I.R.	
McCloy, Harrison		Sergeant	Tank Corps	
McCloy, John		Captain	R.A.M.C.	
McConnell, Wm. J.	24 East Street	Driver	A.S.C.	
McConnell, Brian	Cranmore Park	Lieutenant	K.O.S.B.	Killed in Action.
McConnell, James	Cranmore Park	Lieutenant	Tank Corps	
McConnell, Thomas B.	Cranmore Park	Lieutenant	R.I.R.	
McConnell, Isaac	1 Roden Street	Corporal	R.E.	Killed in Action.
McConnell, Bertie	1 Roden Street	Sergeant	R.I.R.	
McCormack, Robert	37 Hartington Street		A.O.C.	
McCurdy, Alexander	144 University Street		Canadians	
McCarthy, Robert	8 Milner Street	Sergeant	R.I.R.	
McCue, Albert	33 Haywood Avenue	Private	Seaforth Highldrs.	
McCue, Ernest	33 Haywood Avenue	Private	R.I.R.	Killed in Action.
McCue, John	33 Haywood Avenue	Private	R.I.R.	
McCue, Robert	33 Haywood Avenue	Private	R.I.R.	
McCullough, James	19 Howard Street South	Private	R.I.R.	
McCullough, Wm.	19 Howard Street South	Private	R.I.R.	Killed in Action.
McDowell, John B.	22 Erin Street	Private	R.I.R.	Killed in Action.
McDowell, James	22 Erin Street	Private	R.I.R.	Killed in Action.
McGown, Jackson	6 Linenhall Street	Captain	A. Ord. Dep.	
McGown, Melville	Derryvolgie Avenue	Major	A. Ord. Dep.	M.C.
McKibbin, Fred.	3 Eglantine Avenue	Captain	R.A.M.C.	
McKinlay, George	43 Thorndale Avenue		Paymaster's Staff	
McNally, Wm. J.	15 Lindsay Street	Private	Canadians	
McNally, Samuel	11 Lt. Charlotte Street	Private	R.I.R.	
McNaught, Andrew	22 Fitzroy Avenue	Private	R.I.R.	
McNaught, James C.	22 Fitzroy Avenue	Lieutenant	H.L.I.	
McNeill, Fred.	103 Tate's Avenue	Trooper	N.I.H.	
McQuiston, Brice	106 North Parade	Trooper	N.I.H.	
McQuiston, Thos. E.	106 North Parade	Lieutenant	R.I.R.	
McWilliams, John	3 Maryville Street	Driver	R.F.A.	
McMullan, Wm.	27 Hopefield Avenue	Lieutenant	R.I.R.	
Norrie, Wm.	3 Vernon Street	Private	Canadians	
Norrie, James	3 Vernon Street	Private	Canadians	
Orr, Herbert J.	Orlock, Cregagh	Lance-Corporal	R.I.R.	
Patterson, Alexander		Lieutenant	M.G.C.	
Pollock, Hugho	11 College Gardens	Captain	W.A.F.F.	
Pollock, Norman	11 College Gardens	Lieutenant	R.I.R.	
Prichard, Walter	9 Malcolm Street	Private	R.I.R.	
Reid, John	57 Hatfield Street	Private	R.I.R.	
Ritchie, Arthur	60 Castlereagh Road	Lance-Corporal	Royal Scots	
Robinson, Thomas	10 Hamilton Street	Sergeant	R.I.R.	
Robinson, Wm.		Private	R.I.R.	
Rodgers, Wm.	21 Howard St. South	Private	R.I.R.	Killed in Action.
Ross, Wm.	22 Rainey Street	Private	R.I.R.	
Stewart, Thomas	12 Bankmore Street	Private	R.I.R.	
Stewart, Andrew	14 Rainey Street	Private	R.I.R.	
Stewart, David	22 Charlotte Street	Private	R.I.R.	
Stewart, Wm.	12 Bankmore Street	Seaman	R.N.	
Stewart-Carlile, Alfred	Duncairn Gardens	Lieutenant	R.E.	
Stewart-Carlile, Wm.	Duncairn Gardens	Corporal	R.E.	
Scott, Andrew	Musgrave St. Barracks	Private	Irish Guards	
Smith, James Tennent	22 Cyprus Avenue	Trooper	N.I.H.	
Smyth, Joseph	49 Gt. Patrick Street	Private	Black Watch	Killed in Action.
Smyth, Lewis	21 Walnut Street	Private	R.E.	
Stafford, David				
Stanfield, Thomas	29 Pine Street	Rifleman	R.I.R.	
Stone, Hugh	86 Holywood Road	Sergeant	R.I.R.	
Strain, Walter	10 Candahar Street	Pioneer	R.E.	
Straney, James	21 Lindsay Street	Private	R.I.R.	
Tate, James	24 Jerusalem Street	Lance-Corporal	N.I.H.	
Tumath, Edward S.	663 Lisburn Road	Corporal	R.E.	
Tumath, Wm.	12 Little May Street	Private	A.S.C.	
Woodside, Charles		Trooper	N.I.H.	Killed in Action.
Whyte, James G.	Central Fire Station	Sergeant	R.I.R.	
Williamson, Fred.	22 Stranmillis Road	Lieutenant	Gurkha Regt.	Killed in Action.
Wotherspoon, Norman F.	Brekka, Ardenlee Av.	Sergeant	Black Watch	
Wright, Thomas	47 Maryville Street	Private	R.A.F.	
Wylie, Julius H.	2 Lr. Mount Street	Lieutenant	R.I.R.	
Wylie, David	2 Lr. Mount Street	Rifleman	R.I.R.	
Young, James M.	8 Madrid Street	Rifleman	R.I.R.	Killed in Action.

BELFAST PRESBYTERY.   MEGAIN MEMORIAL.

Name.	Home Address.	Rank.	Regiment, Battalion or Unit.	Remarks.
	MEGAIN MEMORIAL.			
ADAMS, GEORGE	8 Witham Street	Private	8th R.I.R.	Killed.
ADAMS, HUGH JAMES	35 Severn Street	Private	10th R.I.R.	Wounded.
ADAMSON, JOHN B.	27 Hornby Street	Private	8th R.I.R.	Wounded.
AGNEW, EDWARD	32 Adam Street	Private	10th R.I.R.	
AGNEW, JAMES	147 Dee Street	Private	14th R.I.R.	Killed.
AGNEW, SAMUEL	147 Dee Street	Private	R.A.F.	
ALLEN, GEORGE	8 Carlton Street		R.M.L.I.	Died.
ALLEN, ROBERT JOHN	3 Parker Street	Private	4th R.I.R.	
ALLEN, SAMUEL	8 Carlton Street	Private	R.A.M.C. and R.F.A.	
ALLOLY, WILLIAM	38 Avoniel Road	Private	8th R.I.R.	Wounded.
ANDERSON, JAMES	56 Avoniel Road	Private	8th R.I.R. and N.F.	Wounded.
ANDERSON, WILLIAM	56 Avoniel Road	Private	R.F.A.	Wounded.
ANDERSON, WILLIAM	16 Kenbaan Street	Private	8th R.I.R. and R.A.F.	
ARMSTRONG, JOSEPH	88 Thistle Street	Driver	A.S.C.	
ARMSTRONG, WILLIAM	53 Ribble Street	Private	Black Watch	Killed.
BAINS, GEORGE	76 Bloomfield Avenue	Sapper	R.E.	Wounded 3 times.
BAINS, JAMES	76 Bloomfield Avenue	Sapper	R.E.	
BAINS, JOHN	76 Bloomfield Avenue	A.B. Seaman	R.N.	
BAKER, EDWARD	31 Carew Street	Private	R.I.R. and N.F.	Wounded.
BARR, WILLIAM	35 Hilltoot Street	Sergeant	12th R.I.R.	Wded., D.C.M.
BARRY, SAMUEL	226 Newtownards Road	Private	8th R.I.R.	Prisoner of War.
BAXTER, ALFRED	14 Cuba Street	Private	R.A.F.	
BAXTER, JOHN	14 Cuba Street	Private	17th R.I.R.	Wounded.
BAXTER, ROBERT	14 Cuba Street	Private	R.G.A.	Gassed twice.
BAXTER, SAMUEL J.	14 Cuba Street	Private	R.G.A.	
BAXTER, WILLIAM	14 Cuba Street	Private	14th R.I.R.	Killed.
BAXTER, SAMUEL	65 Bright Street	Private	R.A.F.	
BEATTIE, EDWARD	14 Laburnum Street	Private	17th R.I.R.	Wounded.
BEATTIE, MARTIN	14 Laburnum Street	Private	A.S.C.	
BELSHAW, JAMES	67 Bright Street	Leading Seaman	R.N.	
BENNETT, ALEXANDER	22 Frome Street	Driver	R.E.	Wounded.
BENNETT, FRANK	93 Mersey Street	Private	14th R.I.R.	
BENNETT, WILLIAM	93 Mersey Street	Private	R. Inn. Fus.	
BENNETT, JOSEPH	9 Carew Street	Private	8th R.I.R.	Prisoner of War.
BINGHAM, THOMAS	46 Medway Street	Private	10th R.I.R.	Killed.
BINGHAM, THOMAS	46 Medway Street	Lance-Corporal	6th R. Inn. F.	Killed.
BLACK, JOHN	160 Island Street	Private	4th R.I.R.	
BLACK, WILLIAM	160 Island Street	Private	A.S.C.	
BLACKSTOCK, JAMES	86 Island Street	Sapper	R.E.	
BLACKSTOCK, THOMAS	5 Mersey Street	Sapper	R.E.	
BOND, EDWARD	59 Severn Street	Private	North Staffordshire	
BOWMAN, JAMES	73 Woodstock Road	Private	9th R. Irish F.	Wounded 3 times.
BOWMAN, DAVID	73 Woodstock Road	Private	A.S.C.	
BOWMAN, SAMUEL	51 Witham Street	Private	2nd R.I. Fus.	Killed.
BOYD, ARTHUR	7 Carew Street	Private	R.A.M.C.	Killed.
BOYD, DAVID	57 Newcastle Street	Private	17th R.I.R.	
BOYD, WILLIAM	22 Mourne Street	Private	1st R.I.R.	Wounded.
BOYD, WILLIAM	28 Chadolly Street	Private	R.E.	
BRANLEY, JAMES	17 Westbourne Street	Private	R.I.R.	
BRENNAN, CECIL	21 Kensington Avenue	Telegraphist	R.E.	
BROWN, RICHARD W.	83 Hornby Street	Driver	A.S.C.	
BRYARS, G. P.	108 North Parade	Lieutenant	R. Irish F.	Wounded.
BRYARS, WILLIAM	108 North Parade	Captain	R.A.M.C.	
BUGLASS, DAVID J.	91 Cheviot Avenue	Engineer	R.N.	
BURNS, THOMAS	44 Medway Street	Private	R. Inn. F.	Wounded 4 times.
BURROWS, DAVID R.	101 Solway Street	Private	R.F.A.	
BURROWS, ROBERT J.		Sapper	R.E.	Killed.
BUSTARD, SAMUEL	17 Bloomfield Avenue	Stoker	R.N.	
CARLISLE, ROBERT	13 Westminster Avenue	Private	8th R.I.R.	
CARROLL, WILLIAM	42 Bloomfield Avenue	Private	R.A.F.	
CARSE, GEORGE	30 Chadolly Street	Chef in Officers' Mess	R. Highldrs.	
CHIVERS, JOHN	15 Tower Street	Private	R. Inn. F.	Prisoner of War.
CLARKE, JOHN	118 Dee Street	Sapper	R.E.	
CONNERY, CHARLES	16 Tamar Street	Private	R.A.M.C.	Wounded.
COPE, JAMES	13 Dundela Street	Private	1st R. Inn. F.	Prisoner of War.
CORBETT, JOHN E.	7 Roseberry Street	Private	R.I.R.	Wded., lost arm.
CORRY, JAMES	20 Cable Street	Private	S. Lancs.	Killed.
COULTER, CHARLES	33 Montrose Street		18th R.I.R.	
COWAN, ALBERT	Ashley Villa, B'field	Lieutenant	R.N.	
COWAN, JAMES	Ashley Villa, B'field	Captain	R.A.M.C.	
COWAN, WM. J.	Ashley Villa, B'field	Captain	R.A.M.C.	
CRAIG, THOMAS	24 Comber Street	Private	R.I.R.	Wounded.
CRAIG, WM. J.	24 Comber Street	Private	R.I.R.	Wounded.
CRAIG, WILLIAM	29 Roundhill Street	Private	A.S.C. and R.F.A.	
CROSSEN, JOHN	93 Derwent Street	Private	6th R.I.R.	Killed.
CROSSEN, JAMES	4 Westminster Avenue	Private	2nd R. Inn. F.	Wded., lost arm.
CROSSEN, WILLIAM	4 Westminster Avenue	Lance-Corporal	S.H. and R. Inn. F.	
DALES, HUGH	73 Tower Street	Private	1st Life Guards	
DARRAGH, SAMUEL	58 Chadolly Street	Private	10th R.I.R.	Wounded.
DAVIDSON, GEORGE	15 Lisavon Street	Private	A.S.C.	
DAVIDSON, WM.	15 Lisavon Street	Private	16th R.I.R.	
DAVIDSON, THOMAS	38 Avoniel Road	Sergeant	8th R.I.R.	Killed.

BELFAST PRESBYTERY. MEGAIN MEMORIAL.

Name.	Home Address.	Rank.	Regiment, Battalion or Unit.	Remarks.
Dempsey, Hugh	121 Dee Street	Corporal	2nd R. Inn. F.	Killed.
Donnan, Albert	78 Montrose Street	Private	N.I.H.	
Donnan, Charles	78 Montrose Street	Sergeant	8th R.I.R.	Croix-de-Guerre.
Donnan, David	78 Montrose Street	Private	8th R.I.R.	
Donnelly, Alfred	10 Avon Street	Private	8th R.I.R.	
Donnelly, Hugh	190 Templemore Street	Private	R.A.F.	
Donnelly, John	71 Chadolly Street	Private	8th R.I.R.	
Douglass, James	3 Carew Street	Private		
Douglass, John J.	34 Baskin Street	Private	Gordon Highldrs.	
Duncan, Edward	4 Ravenscroft Street	Private	8th R.I.R.	Wounded.
Ervine, John	14 Frome Street	Private	8th R.I.R.	
Ervine, Jun., John	14 Frome Street	Private	R. Horse Artillery	
Ervine, Thomas	14 Frome Street	Private	5th R. Inn. F.	
Ferguson, Samuel	Baskin Street	Private	A.S.C.	
Finlay, Samuel	8 Newcastle Street	Private	8th R.I.R.	M.M., Wounded, Prisoner of War.
Fisher, Hugh	6 Templemore Avenue	Private	8th R.I.R.	Wounded.
Fisher, Thomas	62 Templemore Street	Private	2nd R. Inn. F.	Killed.
Fitchie, Samuel	41 Kenbaan Street	Driver	R.F.A.	Wounded.
Fleming, John	28 Evelyn Avenue	Private	R.I.F.	
Fleming, John	25 Tower Street	Private	R.A.F.	
Fowler, Robert J.	160 Woodstock Road	Sergeant	5th R. Inn. F.	Wounded.
Fraser, Thomas	92 Montrose Street	Private	1st Scottish Rifles	Killed.
Fraser, William	92 Montrose Street	Private	10th Northumberland Fus.	Killed.
Fraser, Walter G.	92 Montrose Street	Sergeant	6th R.I.R.	
Galbraith, David	34 Altcar Street	Private	8th R.I.R.	Prisoner of War.
Gilliland, Wm.	35 Pomona Avenue	Private	8th R.I.R.	
Gordon, Alexander	36 Chadolly Street	Private	14th R.I.R.	
Gordon, Francis J.	35 Banbury Street	Private	5th R.I.R.	
Gordon, Robert	38 Belvoir Street	Private	8th Hussars	
Gourley, Samuel	25 Connswater Street	Private	8th R.I.R.	Wounded.
Gourley, Wm. H.	25 Connswater Street	Private	9th R.I.R.	
Graham, Alex. N.	73 Mersey Street	Lance-Corporal	Argyle & Sutherland	
Graham, David	4 Hunt Street	Private	R.A.F.	
Graham, James	4 Hunt Street	Private	R.A.M.C.	
Graham, John	11 Chadolly Street	Driver	A.S.C.	
Graham, Wm.	15 Ulsterdale Street	Private	A.S.C.	
Graham, Wm.	69 Bright Street	Private	8th R.I.R.	
Graham, —	71 Tower Street	Private		
Grant, Robert	15 Tower Street	Private	R.I.R.	Wounded, King's Parch Cert.
Greer, Thomas	33 Eversleigh Street	Private	6th Inn. Dragoons	Prisoner of War.
Haire, Joseph	29 Stonyford Street	Sapper	R.E.	Killed.
Hall, Herbert	Laurington, Up. N'ards R	Private	N.I.H.	Wounded.
Hamill, Robert	12 Shamrock Street	Driver	R.E.	
Hamilton, David S.	38 Mersey Street	Leading Stoker	R.N.	
Hamilton, Alan	38 Mersey Street	Private	1st R.I.R.	Killed.
Hamilton, Robert J.	38 Mersey Street	1st Cl. Stoker	R.N.	Killed.
Hand, Joseph	5 Temple Street	Private	R.I.R.	
Hanna, James	6 Medway Street	Sergeant	R.I.R.	Wounded 3 times.
Hanna, Thomas	6 Medway Street	Private	17th R.I.R.	Wded., lost eye.
Hanna, Joseph	10 Beechfield Street	Joiner	Mercantile Marine	
Harding, Alfred	6 Medway Street	Private	R.I.R.	Prisoner of War.
Harvey, Wm.	33 Nevis Avenue	Private	A.S.C.	
Harvey, Robert	18 Whitestar Street	Private		Killed.
Henderson, Robert	93 Mountpottinger Road	Private	King's Liverpool	Wounded.
Herron, James	28 Hornby Street	Mechl. Stoker	R.N.	
Hiles, Hector	93 Derwent Street	Stoker	R.N.	Killed.
Hillen, Ernest	99 Bridge End	Gunner	R.M.	
Hillen, George	99 Bridge End	Lance-Corporal	4th R.I.R.	
Hillis, Jas. Herbert	25 Newcastle Street	Leading Stoker	R.N.	Killed.
Hodgen, James	83 Mersey Street	Private	10th R.I.R.	
Hunter, George	58 Dee Street	Private	10th R.I.R.	
Irvine, Wm.	43 Bread Street East	Private	17th R.I.R.	
James, Thomas	21 Armitage Street	Sapper	R.E.	
Johnston, Robert	8 Chater Street	Private	8th R.I.R.	Killed.
Jones, David	22 Hind Street	Private	8th R.I.R.	Killed.
Kay, James	3 Carew Street	Private	8th R.I.R.	
Kelly, Thomas	12 Derwent Street	Private	8th R.I.R.	
Kennedy, James	29 Frome Street	Private	14th R.I.R.	Killed.
Kerr, Robert	5 Carlton Street	Seaman	R.N.	
Kerr, Robert C.	30 Hornby Street	Corpl. Mechanic	R.N.A.S. and R.A.F.	
Keilty, Robert	42 Hornby Street	Engineer	Mercantile Marine	
Keilty, Wm. J.	66 Avon Street	Private	8th R.I.R.	
Kitchen, Joseph	30 Mourne Street	Private	2nd R.I.R.	Killed.
Kynes, William	46 Medway Street	Private	9th R. Inn. F.	Wounded 3 times.
Laverty, James	41 Severn Street	Private	8th R.I.R.	Wounded twice.
Laverty, Robert	41 Severn Street	Private	9th R. Inn. F.	
Laverty, William	41 Severn Street	Private	8th R.I.R.	Wounded.
Lecky, Robert	78 Solway Street	Lance-Corporal	9th R. Inn. F.	Killed.
Lemon, John G.	2 Chobham Street	Driver—Motor	A.S.C.	
Lewis, James	88 Bright Street	Private	6th Black Watch	Wded., Disabled.
Lewis, John	88 Bright Street	Sapper	R.E.	
Lightbody, Robert	25 Constance Street	Private	R.A.F.	

BELFAST PRESBYTERY. MEGAIN MEMORIAL.

Name.	Home Address.	Rank.	Regiment, Battalion or Unit.	Remarks.
LINDSAY, WILLIAM	250 Newtownards Rd.	Captain	King's Liverpool	Wounded.
LINDSAY, WILLIAM	200 Newtownards Road	2nd Lieutenant	Worcester	
LOWRY, JAMES	43 Humber Street	Sergeant	8th R.I.R.	
LOWRY, THOMAS	43 Humber Street	Private	8th R.I.R.	Wounded.
MAGILL, THOMAS B.	25 Severn Street	Private	A.S.C.	
MAJURY, HUGH	54 Hornby Street	Sergeant	16th R.I.R.	
MARSHALL, JAMES	12 Bloomfield Street	Private	R.F.A.	Killed.
MARSHALL, JAMES	12 Bloomfield Street	Seaman	Mercantile Marine	Killed.
MARTIN, WM. J.	28 Hornby Street	Sapper	R.E.	
MAY, JAMES	29 Dagmar Street	Lance-Corporal	K.O.S.B.	Killed.
MILLER, THOMAS	17 Fraser Street	Private	16th R.I.R.	
MILLS, THOMAS	51 Constance Street	Private	R.F.A.	Wounded.
MILLS, JAMES	51 Constance Street	Private	2nd R.I.R.	Killed.
MILLS, WILLIAM	51 Constance Street	Private	R. Inn. F.	
MITCHELL, DAVID	75 Holywood Road	Lance-Corporal	8th R.I.R. and A.S.C.	Wounded.
MITCHELL, FREDK.	75 Holywood Road	Lance-Corporal	3rd R. Inn. F.	Wded., Pris. of War
MITCHELL, GEORGE	75 Holywood Road	Private	R.F.A.	
MONTGOMERY, JAMES	3 Hemp Street	Private	8th R.I.R.	Killed.
MOORE, SAMUEL	25 Montrose Street	Private	8th R.I.R.	
MOORHEAD, HENRY	Kenilworth Street	Private	16th R.I.R.	Killed.
MORGAN, GEORGE	13 Chamberlain Street	Private	2nd R.I.R.	Killed.
MORRISON, JAMES	74 Montrose Street	Private	8th R.I.R.	
MORROW, JAMES	20 Derwent Street	Sergeant	R. Inn. F.	
MORROW, RICHARD	30 Hornby Street	Private	8th R.I.R.	Wounded twice.
MORROW, WILLIAM	140 Bread Street	Driver	R.F.A.	
MORTON, WM. T.	101 Ardenlee Avenue	Chief Engineer	Mercantile Marine	
MURPHY, T. H.	90 Tamar Street	Private	16th R.I.R. and A.S.C.	
McCANN, ROBERT	15 Tower Street	Lance-Corporal	2nd R. Inn. F.	Wounded.
McCARTNEY, SAMUEL	22 Welland Street	Private	R.M.L.I.	
McCLEAN, D. J.	14 Athens Street	Private	8th R.I.R.	
McCLUNG, WILSON	85 Tamar Street	Private	R.A.F.	
McCLURE, SAMUEL	39 Kensington Avenue	Private	R.A.M.C.	
McCLURG, WM.	20 Dunraven Avenue	Private	R.A.F.	
McCLUSKEY, HENRY	2 Hunt Street	Private	8th R.I.R.	
McCLUSKEY, JOHN	2 Hunt Street	Private	R.A.F.	
McCONNELL, ROBERT WALLACE	Ulidia, Holywood Road	2nd Lieutenant	The King's Own R.L.	Killed.
McCOSKRIE, JOHN	49 Belvoir Street	Private	2nd R.I.R.	Killed.
McCOUBREY, THOMAS	78 Tamar Street	Co. Q.M. Sergeant	R.E.	
McFARLAND, GEORGE	7 Rosebery Street	Private	2nd R.I.R.	Killed.
McILROY, HENRY	19 Welland Street	Corporal	A.S.C.	
McILROY, WILLIAM	19 Welland Street	Corporal	R.I.R.	Died in Hospital.
McILVEEN, JAMES	41 Swift Street	Private	14th R.I.R.	Wounded.
McINTOSH, THOMAS	8 Stormount Street	Private	Seaforth Highldrs.	
McILWRATH, JAMES	8 Queen Victoria St.		R.M.L.I.	Killed.
McKEE, JOHN R.	40 Solway Street		R.I.R.	Killed.
McKENDRICK, WM.	34 Mourne Street	Lance-Corporal	Seaforth Highldrs.	Wounded.
McKERNAN, JAMES J.	15 Convention Street		7th R.I.R.	Killed.
McKERNAN, THOMAS	15 Convention Street		8th R.I.R.	Killed.
McKENZIE, JOHN	14 Armitage Street		R.N.	Killed.
McKIMM, JAMES	6 Methuen Street	Private	R.I.R.	Died in Camp.
McLEAN, WM.	Wye Street	Private	Inn. Dragoons	
McMILLAN, JAMES	14 Ina Street	Sergeant	8th R.I.R.	Men. in Despatches, D.C.M., & French M.M.
McMILLAN, ROBERT	14 Ina Street	Lance-Corporal	Irish Guards	Killed.
McMILLAN, WM.	14 Ina Street	Lance-Sergeant	8th R.I.R.	
McMILLAN, JOHN W.	13 Derwent Street	Private	A.S.C.	
McMILLAN, THOMAS	13 Derwent Street	Private	R.A.F.	
McROBERTS, ALEX.	22 Welland Street	Private	R.I.R.	Killed.
McWILLIAMS, ADAM	11 Montrose Street	Private	8th R.I.R.	Wounded.
NELSON, GEORGE	15 Hart Street	Private	R.A.F.	
NEVILLE, RICHARD	63 Beersbridge Road	Coy. Sergt.-Major	R.I.F.	Twice Mentioned in Des., D.C.M., and French M.M.
NEVILLE, ROBERT J.	63 Beersbridge Road	Private	R.A.M.C.	Died in Hospital.
NEVILLE, WM.	63 Beersbridge Road	Private	R.I.R.	
NORRIS, FRANCIS	107 Church Street E.	Private	1st R. Inn. F.	Killed.
NORRIS, WM. J.	107 Church Street E.	Private	1st R.I.R.	Killed.
O'NEILL, HUGH	90 Mount Street	Private	R.A.F.	
PATTERSON, JOHN	70 Avon Street	Private	A.S.C.	
PATTERSON, ROBERT	10 Chater Street	Private	R.A.M.C.	M.M.
PEARSON, PHILIP	100 Solway Street		R.N.	
POLLOCK, THOMAS W.	Clonallon Street	Private	R.I.R.	Drd. at Seaforth.
QUINN, JOSEPH	53 Methuen Street	Private	R.I.R.	
QUINN, THOMAS	53 Methuen Street	Stoker	R.N.	Killed.
QUINN, WM. G.	28 Hornby Street	Private	8th R.I.R.	Killed.
RENNIE, GEORGE	104 Newcastle Street	Seaman	R.N.	
RENNIE, JOHN	104 Newcastle Street	Seaman	R.N.	
REYNOLDS, WM.	135 Dee Street	Private	8th R.I.R.	
RINGLAND, JAMES	190 Templemore Street	Sergeant	9th R. Inn. F.	M.M., Wounded.
RODGERS, DAVID M.	129 Parkgate Avenue	Private	R.E. and Seaforth Highldrs.	Killed.
RODGERS, ROBERT	129 Parkgate Avenue	Corporal	R.E.	
ROGERS, SAMUEL	47a Hornby Street	Private	R.E.	
ROLSTON, JAMES	20 Downpatrick Street	Private	R.I.R.	Prisoner of War.

BELFAST PRESBYTERY. MEGAIN MEMORIAL.

Name.	Home Address.	Rank.	Regiment, Battalion or Unit.	Remarks.
Rolston, Robert	45 Glenallen Street	Sapper	R.E.	
Rolston, William	80 Bright Street	Private	R.F.A.	Wounded.
Savage, Robert	20 Glenallen Street	Private	R.A.M.C. and R.F.A.	
Saville, Sydney	5 Pomona Avenue	Private	2nd Suffolks	Wounded twice.
Scott, George	25 Frome Street	Seaman	R.N.	
Scott, James	25 Frome Street	Private	8th R.I.R.	
Scott, John	25 Frome Street	Sapper	R.E.	
Scott, Hugh	35 Severn Street	Private	8th R.I.R.	
Scott, Robert J.	71 Island Street	Private	2nd R.I.R.	Killed.
Scott, Thomas	25 Frome Street	Private	Irish Guards	
Shields, Wm.	12 Tern Street	Signaller	R.N.	
Sleator, Henry	76 Seaforde Street	Private	R.I.R.	
Sleator, James	76 Seaforde Street	Private	R.I.R.	Killed.
Sloan, Thomas	10 Chamberlain Street	Private	1st R. Inn. F.	
Smith, Thomas	75 Derwent Street	Driver	R.F.A.	
Smyth, Wm.	19 Well Street	Driver—Motor	A.S.C.	
Smyrl, Norman	240 Newtownards Road	Private	R.A.M.C.	
Spence, James	20 Mersey Street	Private	8th R.I.R.	Prisoner of War.
Spence, John	20 Mersey Street	Sapper	R.E.	
Spratt, David John	32 Mersey Street	Private	R.M.L.I.	Prisoner of War.
Spratt, Wm.	17 Avon Street	Private	8th R.I.R.	Prisoner of War.
Spratt, Robert	1 Ravenscroft Street	Sergeant	S. Wales Borderers	Killed.
Stannage, Fras. M.	58 Stonyford Street	Private	R.E.	
Stewart, Alex.	73 Bright Street	Private	2nd R.I.R.	
Stewart, Robert J.	73 Bright Street	Lance-Corporal	2nd R.I.R.	Wounded twice.
Stewart, Valentine	38 Witham Street	Stoker	Mercantile Marine.	
Stewart, Samuel	3 Woodstock Place	Private	R.M.L.I.	Killed.
Sturrock, Walter	12 Grampian Street	Private	Seaforth Highldrs.	
Tarbett, Robert	34 Roundhill Street	Sergeant	R.A.M.C.	M.M.
Tarbett, Wm.	34 Roundhill Street	Private	R.I.R.	
Tate, James	30 Solway Street	Sergeant	8th R.I.R.	Killed.
Thompson, John	89 Island Street	Private	10th R.I.R. and Seaforths	
Thompson, Frank		Mechanic	R.A.F.	
Treliving, Harold	21 Kingscourt Street	Petty Officer	R.N.	
Turner, Robert	40 Ardilaun Street	Sapper	R.E.	
Vincent, David	10 Armitage Street	Private	R.I.R. and A.S.C.	
Waddell, James	58 Bright Street	Corporal	R.E.	
Waddell, John	58 Bright Street	Private	R.A.F.	
Walker, Fredk.	33 Montrose Street	Private	8th R.I.R.	
Wallace, James	5 Hart Street	Private	R.A.F.	
Wallace, John	5 Hart Street	Private	A.S.C.	
Wallace, Robert	5 Hart Street	Private	R. Inn. F.	Wounded twice.
Watton, James	36 Bright Street	Private	R.A.F.	
Weir, Andrew	6 Hunt Street	Private	R.E.	
Weir, Hugh	6 Hunt Street	Private	6th R.I.R.	Wd., Pris. of War.
Weir, James	6 Hunt Street	Private	8th R.I.R.	
White, James	49 Severn Street	Private	8th R.I.R.	Wounded.
White, Hugh	49 Severn Street	Lance-Corporal	8th R.I.R.	Killed.
White, Thomas	49 Severn Street	Private	N.I.H.	
Wilson, James	20 Chater Street	Private	London Irish Rifles	
Wilson, Wm.	20 Chater Street	Private	R.I.R.	
Wilson, Robert	87 Hornby Street	Gunner	8th R.I.R.	Killed.
Wilson, Wm. J.	87 Hornby Street		10th R.I.R.	Wounded.
Wilson, Samuel	105 Dee Street	Armourers' Crew	R.N.	
Wilson, Thomas	105 Dee Street	Armourers' Crew	R.N.	
Wilton, Albert	4 Hind Street	Private	Horse Guards	
Woods, Smuel	46 Altcar Street	Private	8th R.I.R. and R.G.A.	
Young, George	77 St. Leonard's Street	Private	1st R. Munsters	Wded, Disabled.
Young, Herbert	77 St. Leonard's Street	Private	1st R. Inn. F.	Wounded 4 times, Killed.
Young, Thomas	77 St. Leonard's Street	Sapper	R.E.	
Young, Thomas	77 St. Leonard's Street	Private	1st R.I.R.	Died of Wounds.
COLONIAL FORCES.				
Beattie, James V.	39 Welland Street	Corporal	C.E.F.	
Campbell, Alex.	Cedar Grove, North Rd.		C.E.F.	
Campbell, John	26 Montrose Street		C.E.F.	Killed.
Campbell, John	59 Belvoir Street		4th Otago Regt., N.Z.	
Graham, John	4 Hunt Street		C.A.M.C.	
Rodgers, James	129 Parkgate Avenue	Lieutenant	Canadian Scottish	Rose from ranks, M.M., M.C., Wd.
Storey, John	26 Mayflower Street		Australian E.F.	
Wilde, Thomas		Sergeant	C.E.F.	M.M.
Hillen, Samuel	99 Bridge-End	Private	C.A.M.C.	Wded., lost eye.
Hillen, Wm. J.	99 Bridge-End	Private	C.F.A.	
MOUNTPOTTINGER.				
Alley, Wm.	38 Avoniel Road	Private	8th Batt. R.I.R.	
Barr, A.	29 Cluan Place	Private	R.I.R.	
Baxter, Nathaniel	60 Epworth Street		R.E.	
Beattie, James	121 Roseberry Road			
Bell, J. M.	24 Crystal Street	Private	8th Batt. R.I.R.	

BELFAST PRESBYTERY.   MOUNTPOTTINGER.

NAME.	HOME ADDRESS.	RANK.	REGIMENT, BATTALION OR UNIT.	REMARKS.
BELL, ROBERT	63 Bloomfield Avenue	Private	Black Watch	Killed.
BELL, WILLIAM	63 Bloomfield Avenue	Private	18th Batt. R.I.R.	
BELL, WILLIAM	38 Rosslyn Street			
BELL, WILLIAM	4 Stranmillis Gardens	Private	N.I.H.	
BLACK, CHAS.	Templemore Street	Private	14th Batt. R.I.R.	
BLACK, CHARLES	Templemore Avenue	Private	18th Batt. R.I.R.	
BLACK, ROBERT	2 Moorgate Street	Private	8th Batt. R.I.R.	
BLACK, THOMAS	2 Moorgate Street	Private	8th Batt. R.I.R.	
BLACK, THOMAS	Templemore Avenue	Private	16th Batt. R.I.R.	
BLAIR, JAMES	42 Christopher Street		A.S.C.	
BOLTON, ALEXANDER	15 Glentoran Street			
BOLTON, THOMAS	39 Eversleigh Street	Corporal	10th R.I.R.	
BRERETON, THOS. C.		A.B.	R.N.	
BROWN, JOHN	Bangor			
BROWN, JOSEPH	Euston Street	Driver	A.S.C.	
BUICK, WM.	21 Channing Street			
CAMPBELL, JOSEPH	Woodstock Road	Private	14th R.I.R.	
CAMPBELL, ROBERT	8 Dunvegan Street	Private	8th R.I.R.	
CARRUTHERS, JOSIAH	4 Glenbrook Avenue	Private	1st Inn. Fus.	Killed.
CARRUTHERS, MAT.	4 Glenbrook Avenue	Private	8th R.I.R.	
CHRISTIE, ROBT. Y.	148 Woodstock Road	Sergeant	12th Inn. Fus.	
CLARKE, J. HOWARD	Upper Frank Street	Corporal	A.S. Corps	
CLARKE, ROBT. D.	51 Magdala Street	Q.M. Sergt.	Edin. Fus.	
CLARKE, WM.	3 Grove Street E.		A.S.C.	
CLEMENTS, HENRY	Mount Street	Private	4th Seaforth Highldrs.	
CRAIG, ROBERT	32 Redcar Street	Sergeant	14th R.I.R.	
CUNNINGHAM, WM.	19 Ballarat Street			
CURRAGH, ROBERT	16 Swift Street	Private	R.A.M.C.	
DAVISON, THOMAS	38 Avoniel Street	Sergeant	8th R.I.R.	Killed.
DAWSON, SAMUEL	43 Woodcot Avenue	Sergeant	14th R.I.R.	
DEMPSEY, JOHN	154 Connsbrook Avenue	Private	14th R.I.R.	
DOHERTY, JOS.	28 Beechfield Street		A.S.C.	
DOUGLAS, DAVID	67 Dunvegan Street	Private	8th Inn. Fus.	Killed.
DOUGLAS, JAS.	67 Dunvegan Street	Private	14th R.I.R.	
DOUGLAS, ROBERT S.	119 Euston Street	Private	14th R.I.R.	
DOUGLAS, SAMUEL	67 Dunvegan Street	A.B.	H.M.S. Magic	Killed.
EDGAR, T. A.		Private	6th R.I.R.	
ERVINE, A. G.	Cregagh Road	Sergeant	14th R.I.R.	Killed.
ERVINE, CHAS. J.	Cregagh Road	Lieutenant	Northld. Fus.	Killed.
FIRTH, E.	Quinton Street	Private	A.S.C.	
FLEMING, WM.	3 Castlereagh Road	Corporal	8th R.I.R.	
FOSTER, N. R.	Cregagh Road	Stoker	H.M.S. Birkenhead	
FRACKLETON, SAMUEL S.	3 Endsleigh Gardens	Sergeant	14th R.I.R.	Wounded.
GEORGE, JAMES		Driver	Heavy Artillery	
GORDON, F.	16 Spring Street	Sapper	R.E.	
GORMAN, ALEX.	44 Cheviot Avenue	Bugler	8th R.I.R.	
GORMAN, THOMAS H.	44 Cheviot Avenue	Bugler	8th R.I.R.	
GRAHAM, EDWARD	198 My Lady's Road		N.I.H.	Killed.
GRAHAM, JOHN		Private	M.G.C.	
GRAY, JAMES				
HALLIDAY, JAMES	15 Frankfort Street	Private	4th Q's O. Hussars	
HAMILTON, J. T.	Shamrock Street		8th R.I.R.	
HAMILTON, WM. H.		Private	18th R.I.R.	
HANNA, SYDNEY	North Road	Cadet	R.A.F.	Prisoner of War.
HARDING, THOS. G.		Pioneer	Signalling Corps	
HARPER, JAMES	Orangefield	Private	10th R.I.R.	
HARVEY, JAMES		Petty Officer	Armoured Cars	
HAWTHORNE, DAVID	72 Mount Street		A.S.C.	
HOWARD A.	16 Evelyn Avenue	Private	14th R.I.R.	
HOWARD, WILLIAM	16 Evelyn Avenue		N.I.H.	
HUNTER, ALEX.		Gunner	R.G.A.	
HUNTER, SAMUEL		Private	R. Inn. Fus.	
HUTTON, JAMES	30 Euston Street	Private	8th R.I.R.	
IRWIN, ROBERT J.	Cregagh Road		R.A.F.	
IRWIN, WM. JAMES	Cregagh Road	2nd Lieutenant	3rd R.I.R.	Killed.
LOGAN, JAMES	Glenwherry Street	Private	2nd Inn. Fus.	Killed.
McCLEAN, WALLACE	Albertbridge Road	Driver	R.F.A.	
McCORMICK, WM.		A.B.	H.M.S. Fury	
McCULLOUGH, JAMES	52 Fitzwilliam Street	Private	N.I.H.	Killed.
McCULLOUGH, JOHN	Fern Street			
McGOWAN, ROBT. JAS.	17 Isoline Street			
McKERSIE, WM.	420 Woodstock Road		E.R.A. Home Defence	
MACKIE, JAMES	120 Beersbridge Road			
McWILLIAMS, JAMES		Private	Seaforth Highldrs.	
MAGOWAN, R. J.		Driver	A.S.C.	
MATHERS, JOHN	80 Rosslyn Street	Private		
MEARES, THOMAS	25 Halcombe Street	Private	8th R.I.R.	
MEARNS, S.	48 Euston Street	A.B.	R.N.R.	
MILLAR, THOMAS	Belmont Street	Sergeant	8th R.I.R.	Killed.
MILLER, JOHN	100 Lord Street	Private		
MILLER, THOMAS	47 Castlereagh Street	Private	14th R.I.R.	
MONAGHAN, A. A.	9 Roundhill Street		R.N.	
MONTGOMERY, STEPHEN	17 Lyons Street	Private		
MORROW, JOHN	38 Moorfield Street		R.F.A.	

BELFAST PRESBYTERY.   MOUNTPOTTINGER.

NAME.	HOME ADDRESS.	RANK.	REGIMENT, BATTALION OR UNIT.	REMARKS.
NEILLY, J. B.	Ogilvie Street	Private	R.A.M.C.	
PARKHILL, JAMES	7 Castlereagh Place	Sapper	R.E.	M.C.
PARKHILL, MOORE	7 Castlereagh Place	Private	14th R.I.R.	
PATTERSON, T.	...	Stretcher-bearer	R.I.R.	
REID, JAMES	8 Ravensdale Street	Lance-Corporal	2nd R.I.R.	Killed.
REID, S.	4 Bloomdale Street	Private	R.A.M.C.	
REID, WM.	8 Ravensdale Street	Private	R.I.R.	
ROBINSON, JOHN	...	...	...	
ROBINSON, W. R.	...	Private	8th R.I.R.	Killed.
RODGERS, ROBERT	18 Evelyn Avenue	Private	14th R.I.R.	
RODGERS, WM.	Evelyn Avenue	Private	A.S.C.	
ROY, WILLIAM	56 Mourne Street	Private	14th R.I.R.	
SAVAGE, ROBERT	20 Glenallen Street	Private	R.A.M.C.	
SAVAGE, WM.	20 Glenallen Street	A.B.	R.N.	
SCOTT, R.	...	Driver	A.S.C.	
STEWART, JOS. O.	126 My Lady's Road	Private	R.A.M.C.	
SIMMS, GEORGE	81 Grove Street East	Private		
TANNAHILL, ANDREW	26 Mount Street	Private	14th R.I.R.	
TATE, ALEX., M.D.	56 Mourne Street	Private		
TRASH, CONSTABLE	M'pottinger Rd. Bks.	Private	I.G.	
THOMPSON, ROBERT	93 Madrid Street	Private	N.I.H.	
TOTTON, DAVID	67 Dunvegan Street	Private	8th R.I.R.	
TODD, SAMUEL	...	Private	Seaforth Highldrs.	
TODD, WILLIAM	...	Private	9th R.I.R.	
WATSON, A. T.	25 Cluan Place	...	R.E.	
WATSON, HUGH	25 Cluan Place	Private	4th Inn. Fus.	
WATSON, J. W.	25 Cluan Place	Private	R.E.	
WHITE, HUGH	50 Lichfield Avenue	Private		
WILSON, JAMES	25 Grampian Avenue	Private	N.I.H.	
WILSON, THOMAS	25 Grampian Avenue	Writer	H.M.S. Russel	
WRIGHT, SAML. JAS.	129 Beersbridge Road	Private	A.S.C.	
	COLONIAL AND U.S.A. FORCES.			
DORNAN, GEO. IRVINE	Madrid Street	Private	Aust. Inft.	
DORNAN, JOHN	Madrid Street	...	Aust. Inft.	
DOUGLAS, JAS. M.	Eversleigh	Private	26th Aust. Inft.	
FALCONER, JOHN	Cregagh	Sergeant	Can. Ex. Force	
McBRIDE, FREDERICK	21 Calender Street	Private	39th Can. Ex. Force	
MELVILLE, NELSON	97 Bloomfield Avenue	Private	10th Winnipeg L.I.	
WATSON, CHARLES J.	Cyprus Avenue	Private	74th Can. Ex. Force	
WHITESIDE, WM.	My Lady's Road	Private	Can. A.M. Corps	
YOUNG, THOS.	My Lady's Road	Private	150th Can. Inft.	
	McQUISTON MEMORIAL.			
ATKINSON, R.	30 Bangor Street	Trooper	21st Lancers	
ALLEN, W.	92 Grove Street East	Private	2nd R.I.R.	
ANDERSON, D.	Earlswood Road	Sergeant	9th R.E.	
ARMOUR, W.	48 Beersbridge Road	Private	1st R.I.R.	
ARNOLD, A.	11 Ravenscroft Avenue	Sergeant	R.A.F.	
ALLEN, S. E.	1 Roden Terrace	Gunner	R.F.A.	
BEATTIE, WM.	66 My Lady's Road	A.M.	R.A.F.	
BARR, W. J.	Glyneath, Cregagh Rd.	2nd Lieutenant	15th Manchesters	
BALLANTINE, F.	1 Cregagh Road	2nd Lieutenant	10th R.I.F.	
BAILLIE, B.	15 Willowfield Street	Private	14th R.I.R.	
BAILLIE, S.	15 Willowfield Street	Private	14th R.I.R.	
BAILLIE, ROBERT	15 Castlereagh Place	Private	14th Leicesters	
BALLANCE, WM.	12 Chadolly Street	Private	R.I.R.	
BEGGS, W. J.	10 Swift Street	Private	R.E.	Killed in Action.
BELL, GEORGE	11 Chatsworth Street	Trooper	N.I.H.	
BENSON, JOSEPH	12 Bangor Street	Private	R.E.	Died.
BINGHAM, J. K.	9 Channing Street	Rifleman	16th R.I.R.	
BLACK, W. C.	14 Kenbaan Street	Private	R.E.	Killed in Action.
BIRCH, S.	1 Park Parade	Private	14th R.I.R.	
BOTHWELL, A.	10 Ashfield Street	Private	6th Inn. Fus.	Killed in Action.
BOYD, JAMES	Douglas Street	Rifleman	4th R.I.R.	Died.
BOYD, COURTLAND	21 Douglas Street	Rifleman	6th R.I.R.	
BOYD, DAVID	21 Douglas Street	Rifleman	4th R.I.R.	
BOYD, WM.	28 Foxglove Street	Lance-Corporal	15th R.I.R.	Prisoner of War.
BOYD, WM., M.B.	Ravenscroft Avenue	Captain	R.A.M.C.	
BRODY, D.	24 Ravensdale Street	Rifleman	10th Ord. Dept.	
BROWN, R.	5 Paxton Street	Rifleman	2nd R.I.R.	Prisoner of War.
BROWN, J.	5 Paxton Street	Rifleman	17th R.I.R.	
BROWN, H.	47 Castlereagh Place	Private	M.T., 17th	
BROWN, W. T.	47 Castlereagh Place	Sergeant	14th R.I.R.	Prisoner of War.
BROWN, J. D.	47 Castlereagh Place	R.N.	H.M.S. Highflyer	
BOWERS, T.	25 Canton Street	Private	R.E.	
BURTON, W.	138 Woodstock Road	Rifleman	R.I.R.	
BURTON, WM.	20 Chater Street	Private	Royal Warwick Regt.	
BELL, G. F.	11 Chatsworth Street	Trooper	6th Dragoon Guards	
BLACK, ALEXANDER	16 Euston Street	Rifleman	17th R.I.R.	
CAIRNS, J.	147 Euston Street	Gunner	R.F.A.	
CAIRNS, J.	103 Rathmore Street	Corporal	M.M.P.	

BELFAST PRESBYTERY.   McQUISTON MEMORIAL.

Name.	Home Address.	Rank.	Regiment, Battalion or Unit.	Remarks.
Carmichael, W.	30 Oakland Avenue	Private	14th R.I.R.	
Caughey, A. E.	230 Beersbridge Road	Driver	R.E.	
Cinnamond, J.	38 Isoline Street	Private	8th R.I.R.	
Caruth, J. H.	84 Euston Street	Sapper	R.E.	
Clarke, D.	98 Omeath Street	Bugler	14th R.I.R.	
Clarke, W.	7 Ribble Street	Private	R.A.M.C.	
Close, James	Canton Street	Private	8th R.I.R.	Killed in Action.
Cobbe, F. C.	113 Castlereagh Road	Lance-Corporal	14th R.I.R.	
Cochrane, F. B.	Ardenlee Street	Private	R. Inn. Fus.	
Coey, D.	67 Redcar Street	Private	H.M.S. Minotaur	
Coey, A.	67 Redcar Street	Private	2nd R. Inn. Fus.	Prisoner of War.
Cole, Gerald M.	80 Richardson Street	Private	R.A.M.C.	
Cole, David M.	80 Richardson Street	Midshipman	R.N. Transport Service	
Cole, Alex. E.	80 Richardson Street	Engineer	R.N. Transport Service	
Cole, Albert W.	80 Richardson Street	Chief Engineer	R.N. Transport Service	
Collins, S.	22 Bangor Street	Private	1st Irish Guards	
Collins, J.	64 Glenvarlock Street	Private	1st Irish Guards	
Coulter, C.	40 My Lady's Road	Lieutenant	13th Royal Welsh Fus.	M.C.
Courtney, S.	63 Canton Street	Private	R.A.M.C.	
Craig, J. T.	78 Portallo Street	Private	R.M.L.I.	
Cromie, Robert	77 Killowen Street	Sergeant	M.G. Section	
Cowdy, E.	25 Ravensdale Street	Private	R.A.F.	
Cromie, Richard	77 Killowen Street	Private	14th R.I.R.	
Cull, D. D.	158 Beersbridge Road	Lance-Corporal	M.G. Corps	
Cull, J.	158 Beersbridge Road	Private	14th R.I.R.	Missing.
Cull, S.	158 Beersbridge Road	Private	2nd Seaforth Highldrs.	Killed in Action.
Crothers, S.	32 Chamberlain Street	Private	6th Inn. Dragoons	
Currie, James	14 Canton Street	Private	8th R.I.R.	Killed in Action.
Clarke, —	8 Mashona Street	A.B.	R.N.	Drowned in attempting to save life.
Cairns, Alex.	103 Rathmore Street	Private	9th R.I.R.	
Cahill, James	81 Portallo Street	Private	Ayr Yeo. Barracks	
Davidson, James	38 Dunraven Avenue	Sergeant	R.F.A.	M.M.
Davidson, S.	92 Grove Street East	Private	A.S.C.	
Davis, J.	21 Madrid Street	A.M.	R.A.F.	
Dickson, W. J.	42 Douglas Street	Corporal	8th R.I.R.	
Dorman, James	17 Cregagh Road	Trooper	2nd K.E. Horse	
Dorman, T. B.	17 Cregagh Road	Corporal	10th R.I.R.	
Dunlop, E.	Earlswood Road	Private	M.T. A.S.C.	
Dyer, T.	157 Woodstock Road	Sergeant	R.A.F.	
Edgar, J. H.	2 Reid Street	Sergeant	Royal Marines	
Ervine, A. G.	Cregagh Road	Q.M. Sergt.	14th R.I.R.	M.M. and M.S.M.
Ervine, C. J.	Cregagh Road	2nd Lieutenant	27th Northumberland Fus.	Died of Wounds.
Ellison, W.	37 Douglas Street	Private	19th R.I.R.	
Flavelle, Albert E.	128 My Lady's Road	C. A/m	Cyclist Batt.	
Fulton, S.	48 Glentoran Street	Sergeant	75th Inft. Brigade	Missing.
Fleming, G.	213 Templemore Avenue	Private	R.A.F.	
Gabbey, Alex.	Ballynahinch	Private	17th R.I.R.	Prisoner of War.
Gabbey, A.	8 Wayland Street	2nd Lieutenant	116th M G	
Gault, Joseph	70 Mountpottinger Rd.	Asst. Adjutant	19th R.I.R.	
Gardner, Joseph	33 Glenallen Street	Private	2nd R.I.R.	Killed in Action.
Gardner, A. W.	39 Hatton Drive	Private	A.S.C.	Killed in Action.
Gardner, Wm.	39 Hatton Drive	Drummer	2nd R. Inn. Fus.	Missing.
Geary, John	147 Avoniel Road	Sergeant	2nd R. Inn. Fus.	
Gillespie, W.	38 Ogilvie Street	Shipwright	H.M.S. Campania	
Gilliland, E. S.	235 Cregagh Street	2nd Lieutenant	3rd R. Inn. Fus.	
Girvan, D.	18 Bangor Street	Private	8th R.I.R.	
Gowdy, John	47 Portallo Street	Sergeant	109th Inft. Brigade	M.M.
Gowdy, Joseph	47 Portallo Street	Q.M.S.	109th Inft. Brigade	M.M. and M.S.M.
Grachey, Alex.	13 Evelyn Avenue	Driver	R.F.A.	
Gray, R. J.	52 Canton Street	Lance-Corporal	10th R.I.R.	M.M.
Gray, R. J.	97 Killowen Street	Lance-Corporal	10th R.I.R.	
Grange, John	24 Hatton Drive	Private	14th R.I.R.	
Ground, John	50 Newry Street	Corporal	105th R.F.A.	Killed in Action.
Gamble, R.	Ogilvie Street	Private	Northumberland Fus.	
Hadden, James	40 Isoline Street	A /M.	R.A.F.	
Halliday, S.	39 Douglas Street	Private	5th R.I.R.	Died.
Hadden, John	40 Isoline Street	2nd A /m	R.A.F.	
Hamilton, J. T.	Cregagh Road	Lieutenant	9th R.I. Fus.	
Hamilton, Ed.	Cregagh Road	Lieutenant	9th R.I. Fus.	Killed in Action.
Hamilton, J. S.	15 Lr. Frank Street	Private	R.F.A.	
Hamilton, R.	157 Cregagh Road	1st A/m.	R.N.A.S.	
Hamilton, C.	33 Bangor Street	Private	2nd R.I. Fus.	Killed in Action.
Hamilton, R.	7 Bangor Street	Private	5th York & Lancs. Regt.	
Hanna, Francis	67 Church Street East	Private	R.I.F.	Killed in Action.
Herron, John	11 Bangor Street	Private	8th R.I.R.	
Herron, John	4 Canton Street	Private	2nd R.I.R.	
Harper, W.	92 My Lady's Road	Private	8th London Regt.	Killed in Action.
Higgins, Hugh	216 Ravenhill Avenue	Private	R.I.F.	Prisoner of War.
Hill, Gilbert	63 Omeath Street	Private	Seaforth Highldrs.	
Hodgen, James	118 Castlereagh Road	Private	7/8 R. Inn. Fus.	Killed in Action.
Hodgen, John	118 Castlereagh Road	Lance-Corporal	2nd R. Inn. Fus.	
Houston, T.	28 Canton Street	Sapper	R.E.	
Houston, W.	28 Canton Street	Stoker	H.M.S. Terror	

BELFAST PRESBYTERY.   McQUISTON MEMORIAL.

Name.	Home Address.	Rank.	Regiment, Battalion or Unit.	Remarks.
Houston, John	13 Moneyrea Street	Private	12th R.I.R.	Prisoner of War
Houston, Samuel	13 Moneyrea Street	Private	2nd R.I. Fus.	
Houston, S.	19 Douglas Street	Private	2nd R.I.R.	
Hoy, W.	23 Ashfield Street	Private	R.I. Regt.	
Hoy, John	23 Ashfield Street	Private	5th R.I.R.	
Hoy, John F.	9 Channing Street	Private	2nd R.M.L.I.	
Hogg, W. G.	London	Lieutenant	15th R.I.R.	Killed in Action.
Hughes, James	52 Douglas Street	Private	7th R.I.R.	Killed in Action.
Hughes, R.	52 Douglas Street	Private	1st R.I.R.	
Hutchinson, Wm.	6 Euston Street	Private	108th Field Ambulance	
Hanna, R.	9 Rokeby Street	Private	1st East Lancs. Regt.	
Houston, W.	Bangor Street	Rifleman	8th R.I.R.	
Ireland, S. J.	21 Madrid Street	2nd Lieutenant	17th King's L'pool Regt.	Killed in Action.
Irvine, R.		Gunner	R.G.A.	Prisoner of War.
Jackson, Jonathan	104 Castlereagh Road	Private	A.S.C.	
Jackson, Lister	104 Castlereagh Road	Private	2nd R.I.R.	Killed in Action.
Jamieson, Gordon	15 Willowholme Street	Gunner	R.F.A.	
Johnston, W.	Frankfort Street	Private	H.S.	
Johnston, James	24 Canton Street	Private	8th R.I.R.	Killed in Action.
Kelly, S.	16 Bangor Street	Sapper	R.E.	
Kelly, D.	16 Bangor Street	Sapper	R.E.	
Kelly, W. A.	97 Woodstock Road	Lance-Corporal	1st R.I. Regt.	
Keown, W. S.	Norwood, Cregagh Road	2nd Lieutenant	R.E.	
Keith, W. J.	1 Pottinger Street	Sergeant	14th R.I.R.	Died.
Keith, Thomas	1 Pottinger Street	Lance-Corporal	8th R.I.R.	
Kerr, A. C.	13 Toronto Street	Private	9th R. Inn. Fus.	
Kerr, J. F.	13 Toronto Street	Private	1st R. Inn. Fus.	
Kerr, Samuel	13 Toronto Street	Private	R.A.M.C.	Killed in Action.
Killop, W.	Cyprus Gardens	Sub-Lieutenant	I.W. Transport	
Killop, H.	Cyprus Gardens	Sub-Lieutenant	S.S. Orbita	
Kitchen, E.	42 Ravenhill Road	Private	A. & S. Highldrs.	
Law, Joseph	40 Canton Street	Private	3rd R.I.R.	
Lemon, W.	30 Bangor Street	Driver	R.F.A.	
Lemon, J.	30 Bangor Street	Seaman	H.M.S. Repulse	
Lemon, John	11 Willowfield Street	Private	R.A.M.C.	
Larmour, H.	36 Moorfield Street	Sapper	R.E.	
Laughlin, H.	141 Castlereagh Road	Stoker	H.M.S. Beagle	
Laverty, A.	11 Ravenscroft Street	L. Seaman	H.M.S. Thunderer	
Laverty, W.	11 Ravenscroft Street	L. Seaman	H.M.S. Pelrous	Killed in Action.
Laverty, D.	11 Ravenscroft Street	L. Seaman	H.M.S. Hawke	Killed in Action.
Lawther, J. A.	4 Dunluce Avenue	Wireless Operator	H.M.S. Cochrane	
Lilley, T.	38 Eversleigh Street	Private	1st Irish Guards	
Lemon, Alexander	11 Willowfield Street	3rd A/m.	R.A.F.	
Lagan, P.	10 Frankfort Street	Private	4th R.I.F.	
Magee, Hugh	47 Willowfield Street	Sergeant	3rd R.I.R.	
Magee, James	65 Ballarat Street	Lance-Corporal	2nd R.I.R.	
Martin, Robert	7 Rokeby Street	Private	6th R.I.R.	
Matier, W.	21 Bangor Street	Private	8th R.I.R.	Killed in Action.
Maxwell, S.	26 Bangor Street	Rifleman	2nd R.I. Fus.	
Maxwell, James	26 Bangor Street	Private	14th R.I.R.	
Maxwell, John	26 Bangor Street	Rifleman	8th R.I.R.	
Mercer, D.	246 Woodstock Road	Private	14th R.I.R.	
Miles, J.	11 Canton Street	Rifleman	3rd R.I.R.	
Milling, S.	Athens Street	Sapper	R.E.	
Millar, James	22 Glenvarlock Street	Private	R.A.M.C.	
Mills, John	91 Ardenvohr Street	Private	10th R.I.R.	Missing.
Mills, D.	37 Delaware Street	Private	A.S.C.	Died.
Miskelly, H.	7 Bangor Street	Driver	R.F.A.	
Miskelly, J.	7 Bangor Street	Gunner	R.F.A.	
Miskelly, John	40 Willowfield Street	Private	R. Inn. Fus.	
Miskelly, Jas.	40 Willowfield Street	Private	10th R.I.R.	
Miskelly, Alex.	40 Willowfield Street	Private	7th R.I.R.	
Mitchell, Gordon	153 Albertbridge Road	Sergeant	14th R.I.R.	M.M.
Mitchell, David	153 Albertbridge Road	A.M.	R.T.C.	
Mitchell, George	252 Castlereagh Road	Sapper	R.E.	
Moore, T. A.	214 Ravenhill Avenue	Private	M.T.	
Moore, James	214 Ravenhill Avenue	Corporal	11/13 R.I.R.	
Muir, A.	93 Killowen Street	Corporal	A.S.C.	
Murdoch, John	85 The Mount	Private	R.E.	
Murdoch, Wm.	85 The Mount	Private	R.E.	
Mills, John	91 Ardenvohr Street	Private	10th R.I.R.	
Muir, Wm.	18 Oberon Street	A.M.	R.A.F.	
Martin, W. J.	55 Willowfield Street	Private	R.A.F.	
McKinlay, Jim	13 Roseberry Road	L. Sergeant	R. N. Division	
McAvoy, W. J.	25 Bangor Street	Sergeant	2nd R.I.R.	
McAvoy, E.	25 Bangor Street	Private	15th R.I.R.	
McAvoy, Samuel	25 Bangor Street	Private	14th R.I.R.	Prisoner of War.
McAlpine, James	48 Canton Street	Rifleman	16th R.I.R.	
McAlpine, Wm.	48 Canton Street	Rifleman	16th R.I.R.	
McBride, J.	29 Bangor Street	Sapper	R.E.	
McBride, S.	29 Roseberry Road	Corporal	17th R.I.R.	Died.
McCarter, J.	11 Bangor Street	Rifleman	8th R.I.R.	
McCarter, W.	9 Bangor Street	Private	Lab. Batt.	
McComb, C.	1 Cliftonpark Avenue	2nd Lieutenant	14th R.I.R.	

BELFAST PRESBYTERY. McQUISTON MEMORIAL.

Name.	Home Address.	Rank.	Regiment, Battalion or Unit.	Remarks.
McConnell, W. R.	193 Templemore Avenue	2nd Lieutenant	N.I.H.	
McCready, S.	92 Thorndyke Street	Lance-Corporal	10th R.I.R.	
McDonald, W. B.	6 Isthmus Street	Private	2nd R. Inn. Fus.	Died.
McDowell, R.	17 Jocelyn Gardens	Captain	N. Staffords	M.C., K'd. in Act.
McDowell, T.	17 Jocelyn Gardens	Lance-Corporal	R.F.A.	
McBurney, Herbert	128 My Lady's Road	Private		
McPhail, G.	66 Redcar Street	Sergeant	R.E.	
McKay, W.	15 Moneyrea Street	2nd A/m.	R.A.F.	
McIlhenny, J.	Sunnyside, Ardenlee Av.	Corporal	8th Horse Trans.	
McKeen, W.	Cherryville Street	Sapper	R.E.	
McKeen, T.	44 Cherryville Street	Bugler	8th R.I.R.	
McKnight, J.	64 Richardson Street	Sergeant	R.F.A.	
McKnight, H.	11 Bangor Street	Rifleman	8th R.I.R.	Prisoner of War.
McKee, T.	146 Ravenhill Avenue	Private	14th R.I.R.	
McMonagle, J.	10 Bangor Street	Pioneer	R.E.	
McMillan, R.	8 Jocelyn Gardens	Private	A.S.C.	
McMillan, A.	8 Jocelyn Gardens	Sapper	R.E.	
McMullan, D.	13 Ardgowan Street	Lance-Corporal	8th R.I.R.	M.M.
McKnight, Wm.	64 Richardson Street	Gunner	R.G.A.	
McQuoid, Ben.	81 Willowfield Street	2nd Lieutenant	N.I.H.	
McConnell, S.	198 My Lady's Road	Lance-Corporal	R.I.F.	
McCormack, C. F.	90 Greenore Street	A.M.	R.A.F.	
McGuigan, James	North Road		Irish Guards	
McKenzie, Tom	31 Madrid Street		R.A.F.	
Nelson, D.	15 Isoline Street	Corporal	A.S.C.	
Noble, H.	98 Castlereagh Road	Lieutenant	King's Liverpool	
Noble, E.	98 Castlereagh Road	Private	1st Innis. Fus.	
Noble, A.	98 Castlereagh Road	Private	Irish Guards	
Nolan, E. J.	42 Ravenhill Road	Major	R.F.A.	
Orr, D. E.	98 Channing Street	Private	Royal Marines	Killed in Action.
Orr, John	1 Canton Street	Sergeant	Labour Batt.	
Orr, W. James	26 Roseberry Street	Private	19th R.I.R.	
Orr, Fred.	26 Roseberry Street	Driver	R.F.A.	
Pascoe, H.	53 Canton Street	Sapper	R.E.	Died.
Parsons, S.	10 Ravensdale Street	Gunner	R.F.A.	
Patterson, R.	1 Channing Street	Private	2nd R.I.R.	Killed in Action.
Parkes, Jos.	22 Isoline Street	Sergeant	R.F.C.	
Pauley, F.	17 Ashfield Street	Rifleman	R.I.R.	
Pauley, R.	17 Ashfield Street	Private	M.T.	
Pavis, C.	14 Woodlee Street	Bandsman	4th Div., H.Q. Staff, B.E.F.	
Pentland, W.	Athens Street	Private	R.I.R.	
Phillips, W. J.	2 Frankfort Street	Rifleman	12th R.I.R.	Prisoner of War.
Phillips, J.	2 Frankfort Street	Private	R.I.R.	Prisoner of War.
Pirret, J. L.	43 Ardenlee Avenue	Sergeant	A.S.C.	
Pirret, J. K.	43 Ardenlee Avenue	2nd Lieutenant	11th King's R. Rifles	Killed in Action.
Porter, F.	19 Jocelyn Gardens	Corporal	7th Cadet Batt.	
Porter, R.	19 Jocelyn Gardens	A/m	R.A.F.	
Pratt, T.	20 Bangor Street	Private	1st R.I. Fus.	
Pollen, Edward	90 Portallo Street	Private	Royal Marines	Died.
Pearse, Samuel	Canton Street	Private	A.S.C.	
Rankin, S.	Canton Street	Private	3rd R.I.R.	
Rankin, T.	Canton Street	Stoker	H.M.S. Osprey	
Reid, W.	58 Douglas Street	Private	199th Labour Coy.	
Reid, R.	58 Douglas Street	Private	241st S.B.A.C.	
Reid, H.	7 Canton Street	Private	9th R.I. Fus.	Prisoner of War.
Reynolds, D.	5 Douglas Street	Driver	R.F.A.	
Reynolds, Wm.	5 Douglas Street	Corporal	49th C.C.S.	
Richardson, E.	26 Bangor Street	Private	8th R.I.R.	
Richey, B.	Sunnymede, Ormiston C.	2nd Lieutenant	3rd R.I.F.	Prisoner of War.
Rice, F.	Hamburg Street	Private	R.I.R.	
Richmond, A. T.	31 Rochester Street	Captain	R.N.	D.S.O.
Ritchie, S. J.	144 Templemore Avenue	Private	Mechl. Trans.	
Ringland, W.	Canton Street	Seaman	H.M.S. Musketeer	
Ringland, M.	Canton Street	Private	G.G. Batt.	
Rolston, James	10 Athens Street	Private	11th R.I.R.	
Rowan, A.	28 Athens Street	Rifleman	19th R.I.R.	
Rodgers, T.	97 Chadolly Street	Gunner	R.G.A.	
Ritchie, Thomas	13 Moneyrea Street	Driver	A.S.C.	
Sandes, M.	173 Witham Street	Sapper	R.E.	
Scott, John	258 Woodstock Road	Private	2nd R.I.R.	Killed in Action.
Scott, James	42 Cheviot Avenue	Private	Royal Marines	Killed in Action.
Scott, J. A.	151 Albertbridge Road	Telegraphist	Indian Army	
Scott, J. J.	9 Isoline Street	Petty Officer	R.N.	
Scott, John	90 Killowen Street	Private	8th R.I.R.	Killed in Action.
Scott, George	90 Killowen Street	Stoker	R.N.	
Shields, S.	28 Canton Street	Driver	R.F.A.	
Smyth, Alex.	58 Jocelyn Street	Warrant Officer	R.N.	
Smyth, Robert	111 Euston Street	A.B.	R.N.	
Snowden, J.	14 Carlton Street	Corporal	17th R.I.R.	Killed in Action.
Snowden, M.	14 Carlton Street	Sergeant	2nd R.I.R.	
Somerville, A.	58 Jocelyn Street	Corporal	17th R.I.R.	
Smyth, Stanley	29 Ravenhill Avenue	2 A/m	R.A.F.	
Smyth, Thos. L.	29 Ravenhill Avenue	3 A/m	R.A.F.	
Spence, J.	21 Bangor Street	Lance-Corporal	8th R.I.R.	Prisoner.

BELFAST PRESBYTERY. McQUISTON MEMORIAL.

Name.	Home Address.	Rank.	Regiment, Battalion or Unit.	Remarks.
Spence, W.	4 Flora Street	Private	9th R.I.R.	
Spence, J.	4 Flora Street	Private	14th R.I.R.	
Steenson, T.	9 Bangor Street	Rifleman	12th R.I.R.	Prisoner of War.
Stewart, O. W.	92 Greenore Street	Sergeant	16th R.I.R.	
Stewart, W. J.	92 Greenore Street	Driver	R.F.A.	
Stewart, W.	99 Tildarg Street	A.B.	H.M.S. Hecla	
Steenson, Bertie	128 Ravenhill Road	A/m	R.A.F.	
Shepherd, D.	57 Omeath Street	A/m	R.A.F.	
Thompson, S.	47 Halcombe Street	Captain	8th Northamptons	
Trotter, F. C.	11 Hamburg Street	R.Q.M. Sergeant	5th Seaforth Highldrs.	
Truesdale,	19 Solway Street	Private	R.I.R.	
Wightman, W.	Newry Street	Sapper	R.E.	
Waddell, Dav.	352 Woodstock Road	Private	3rd Wilts	
Waddell, D.	84 Castlereagh Road	Signal.	14th R.I.R.	
Waid, H.	Cregagh Road	Private	A.S.C.	
Ward, W.	82 Jocelyn Avenue	Gunner	R.F.A.	
Wauchope, G. W.A.	3 Oakland Avenue	Sub-Lieutenant	R.N.V.R.	Killed in Action.
Whitley, R. J.	Flordia, Ardenlee Av.	Lieutenant	R.F.A.	
Whitley, George	Flordia, Ardenlee Av.	Lieutenant	King's Liverpool	Killed in Action.
Winnington, A.	98 Portallo Street	Corporal	R.E.	
Woods, R.	Hollyville, Ardenlee Av.	Lieutenant	R.E.	
Wilson, James	20 Chater Street	Rifleman	1/18 London Irish Fus.	
Wade, Richard	Canton Street	Private	5th R.I. Fus.	
Young, W. J.	134 Templemore Avenue	Private	1st Gloucester Regt.	Prisoner of War in Austria.
COLONIAL FORCES.				
Brown, G. A.	47 Castlereagh Place	Private	Canadians	
Barr, George	Cregagh Road	Private	Canadians	
Best, Tom	460 Oberon Street	Rifleman	N.Z.R.	
Caughey, F. W.	230 Beersbridge Road	Private	Canadians	
Cowdy, E.	25 Ravensdale Street	Private	Canadians	
Faulkner, G.	106 Templemore Avenue	Private	Canadians	
Ferguson, T.	109 Killowen Street	Gunner	S. Africans	Died.
Galbraith, S. T.	44 London Street	Sergeant	Canadians	
Galbraith, W.	44 London Street		Australians	
Gordon, S.	Templemore Avenue	Private	N. Zealanders	
Grant, F. C.	Ardenlee Parade	Private	Canadians	Killed in Action.
Hogg, R. G.	233 Mt.pottinger Rd.	Private	241st Canadians	
Larmour, Wm.	36 Moorfield Street	Q.M. Sergt.	Canadians	
Maybery, J. S.	184 Albertbridge Road	Private	Australians	Killed in Action.
McConnell, H.	227 Cregagh Street	Private	Canadians	Killed in Action.
Pirret, W. R.	43 Ardenlee Avenue	Sapper	6th Canadians	
Pentland, A.	Athens Street	Private	Canadians	
Ritchie, James	144 Templemore Avenue	Sergeant	N. Zealanders	
Shiels, R.	40 Lichfield Avenue	Private	Canadian Railway Troops	
Scott, Jas. N.	225 Holywood Road	Private	Canadians	
Smyth, John	111 Euston Street	Lance-Corporal	21st Canadians	
Taylor, W. H.	18 Newry Street	L. Stoker	H.M.A.S. Una	Died.
Thompson, J.	57 Willowfield Street	Private	78th Canadians	
Turnbull, James	Haddington Gardens	Gunner	Canadians	
Waid, R. R.	Cregagh Road	Private	Canadians	M.M. with Bar.
Waid, W.	Cregagh Road	Private	Canadians	
Welch, John	31 Park Parade	Private	Canadians	Killed in Action.
NELSON MEMORIAL.				
Agnew, James	63 Woodvale Road		R.E.	
Agnew, John	104 Clonard Gardens	Private		
Aiken, Victor	6 Emerson Street			
Allen, Jack	21 Lawnview Street	Private	A.S.C.	
Allen, Wm.	23 Emerson Street	Private		
Aiken, John	136 Agnes Street			
Andrews, Archie	17 Elswick Street	Driver	A.S.C.	
Andrews, John W.	17 Elswick Street			Killed in Action.
Andrews, Richard	17 Elswick Street	Rifleman		
Andrews, Thomas	17 Elswick Street	Sapper	R.A.	
Armstrong, Geo.				
Barr, Gordon	6 Esmond Street	Corporal		
Beattie, Albert	165 Canmore Street			
Beattie, Albert	60 Crosby Street			Killed in Action.
Beattie, David	60 Crosby Street		Dragoon Guards	
Beattie, Samuel	165 Canmore Street			
Beggs, Thomas	3 Tennyson Street	Private		
Bell, Henry	37 Lawnbrook Avenue	Rifleman	R.I.R.	Killed in Action.
Bennett, Wm.	2 Morris Street	Sapper	R.E.	
Bingham, Alfred	51 Sugarfield Street			Killed in Action.
Bingham, J.	51 Sugarfield Street	Private		
Blair, David	Fourth Street			Killed in Action.
Blair, Joseph	Fourth Street			Killed in Action.
Blair, Samuel	Fourth Street			Killed in Action.
Boston, James	22 Bromley Street			
Boston, Joseph	22 Bromley Street			Killed in Action.
Boston, Samuel	22 Bromley Street			Killed in Action.

BELFAST PRESBYTERY. NELSON MEMORIAL.

Name.	Home Address.	Rank.	Regiment, Battalion or Unit.	Remarks.
BOYD, ALEX.	189 Crimea Street	Rifleman	R.I.R.	
BOYD, W. R.	230 Leopold Street	Gunner	R.F.A.	
BOYLE, WM.	33 Dewey Street	Sapper	R.E.	
BRADFORD, JAMES	2 Acton Street	Private	Seaforth Highldrs.	
BREEN, W. H.	4 Annsboro Street			Killed in Action.
BROWN, JOHN	43 Bellevue Street			Killed in Action.
BROWN, JOSEPH	256 Cambrai Street	Private	R.I.R.	
BROWN, SAMUEL	8 Fourth River Gdns.			Killed in Action.
BROWN, S. G.	46 Spring Street	Sergeant	R.E.	M.M.
BROWN, W. R.	21 Moscow Street	Private	R.I.R.	
BROWNLEE, EDWARD	6 Bracken Street			
BROWNLEE, JAMES	142 Leopold Street	Sergeant	R.I.R.	
BYRON, ARCHIE	138 Glenwood Street	Private	R.I.R.	
BYRON, DAVID	138 Glenwood Street	Sergeant	R.E.	M.M.
BYRON, WM.	138 Glenwood Street	Rifleman	R.I.R.	
CAMPBELL, CHARLES	22 Snugville Street	Private	R.A.M.C.	
CAMPBELL, R.	31 Benwell Street			
CAMPBELL, SAM.	31 Benwell Street	Private	R.I.R.	
CAMPBELL, S. F.	33 Moscow Street	Rifleman	R.I.R.	
CARLISLE, FRED.	13 Lillie Street	Trooper	N.I.H.	
CHAMBERLAIN, ROBERT	41 Jersey Street	Sergeant	R.A.M.C.	
CHAPMAN, JOHN	90 Glenwood Street	Private		
CHAPMAN, R. J.	90 Glenwood Street	Private	R.I.F.	
CHRISTIE, JOHN	15 Emerson Street	Driver		
CHRISTIE, JOSEPH	77 Palmer Street			
CLARKE, DAVID	150 Disraeli Street	Private		
CLARKE, JOHN	97 Glenwood Street	Private		
CLARKE, THOMAS	150 Disraeli Street			
CLARKE, WM.	41 Eighth Street	Rifleman	R.I.R.	
COOK, R. W.	41 Lanark Street	Private		
COOPER, ROBERT	19 Legum Street	Lance-Corporal	R.I.F.	
CORBETT, W.	89 Emerson Street	Private		
COULTER, WM.	21 Esmond Street	Trooper	18th Hussars	
CRAIG, JOHN	90 Mountjoy Street	Private		
CRAIG, ROBERT	2 Dunmoyle Street	Lance-Corporal	R.A.M.C.	M.M.
CRAIG, W. E.	4 Esmond Street	Sergt.-Major	A.S.C.	M.C.
CRAIG, WM. R.	2 Dunmoyle Street	Airman	R.F.C.	
CRANGLE, SAMUEL	2 Glentilt Place	Sapper	R.E.	
CREIGHTON, WM.	64 Shankill Road	Private		Died.
CROWE, CHAS.	66 Orkney Street			Killed in Action.
CULLAN, ROBERT	2 Annsboro' Street			
CUNNINGHAM, WM.	16 Aberdeen Street	Rifleman	R.I.R.	
DONALDSON, THOMAS	Newtownards	Sergeant		
DONNAN, ROBERT	36 Lawnbrook Square	Private		
DOUGLAS, WM.	17 Collingview Street	Private	A.S.C.	
EAGLESON, W. JAS.	73 Northumberland St.	Private	R. Inn. Fus.	
EDGAR, ALEX.	3 Tennyson Street			M.M.
ESLER, JAMES	Canmore Street	Trooper		
FERGUSON, W. J.	1 Dunmoyle Street	Private	Northumberland Fus.	
FERRIS, E. D.	226 Cupar Street	Private		
FINLAY, DAVID	187 Cambrai Street		R.N.	
FINLAY, S. J.	288 Conway Street	Private		
FLECK, JAMES	2 Weallen Street	Private	A.S.C.	
FLEMING, JOSEPH	106 Sugarfield Street	Corporal	A.S.C.	
FOWLER, JOSEPH	18 Bracken Street	Private	R.A.M.C.	
FRASER, JAMES	220 Mayo Street	Private	R. Inn. Fus.	
FRASER, THOMAS	77 Palm Street			
FREEBURN, OSCAR	19 Silvio Street			
FRYAR, ROBERT	75 Old Lodge Road			
GALLAGHER, FRED.	264 Cambrai Street	Sapper	R.E.	
GALLAGHER, JAMES	264 Cambrai Street			Killed in Action.
GARDNER, SAM.	58 Cumberland Street	Private		Killed in Action.
GAULT, JAMES	1 Azenone Street	Lance-Corporal		
GIBSON, DAVID	149 Agnes Street	Private	R. Leinsters	
GIBSON, WM.	7 Seventh Street			
GILBERT, ROBERT	27 Sugarfield Street			
GILLESPIE, FRANK	19 Bromley Street	Gunner		
GILLESPIE, R. S.	24 Mayo Street	Sergeant	R.A.M.C.	M.M. and Bar.
GILLILAND, JOSHUA	5 Fifth Street	Private		
GLENCROSS, GEORGE	119 Brookmount Street	Rifleman	R.I.R.	
GLENCROSS, HUGH	119 Brookmount Street			
GLENCROSS, JAMES	119 Brookmount Street	Rifleman	R.I.R.	Killed in Action.
GLENCROSS, MALCOLM	36 Crimea Street	Stoker	R.N.	
GRAHAM, JOHN	47 Glenwood Street	Stoker	R.N.	
GRAHAM, W. JAMES	25 Matchett Street	Sergeant	R.I. Regt.	
GRAINGER, ALFRED	174 Cambrai Street	Rifleman		
GRAINGER, WM.	174 Cambrai Street	Private		
GRAY, ANDREW	222 Mayo Street	Private		
GRAY, JAMES	222 Mayo Street	Private		
GRAY, JOHN	222 Mayo Street	Corporal		
GRAY, JOHN	4 Caledon Street		R.N.	
GRIFFITHS, DAVID	60 Argyle Street	Rifleman		
GRIFFITHS, ROBERT	60 Argyle Street	Rifleman		
HAGAN, W. J.	1 Sugarfield Street	Sapper	R.E.	

BELFAST PRESBYTERY. NELSON MEMORIAL.

Name.	Home Address.	Rank.	Regiment, Battalion or Unit.	Remarks.
HARLAND, ALF.	Whiteabbey	Private	R.A.M.C.	
HARLAND, THOMAS	Whiteabbey	Sergt.-Major	R.A.M.C.	M.C.
HARLAND, WM.	Whiteabbey		R.A.F.	
HARRIS, GERALD	56 Oregon Street	Private	R.I.R.	
HARVEY, THOS.	266 Cambrai Street	Sergeant		M.S.M.
HIGGINSON, JAMES	1 Broom Street	Sapper	R.E.	
HODKINS, JAMES	26 Olive Street	Rifleman	R.I.R.	
HUSTON, SAM	1 Eastland Street	Rifleman	R.I.R.	
HUSTON, SAMUEL	106 Emerson Street	Sapper	R.E.	
HUTCHINSON, ALEX.	182 Sugarfield Street	Rifleman		
HUTCHINSON, JOHN	182 Sugarfield Street	Rifleman		
HYNDMAN, JOSEPH	197 Cupar Street			
HYNDMAN, PERCY	6 Springmount Street	Private	R.A.M.C.	
HYSLOP, DAN	Money Street	Rifleman		
INGRAM, ARTHUR	33 Keswick Street	Rifleman		
JACKSON, FRANK	208 Cupar Street	Rifleman	R.I.R.	
JACKSON, FRANK, JUN.	208 Cupar Street	Private		
JOHNSTON, ANDREW	40 Bellevue Street	Rifleman		
JOHNSTON, JOHN	173 Up. Meadow Street	Lance-Corporal	R.I.R.	
JOHNSTON, WM.	173 Up. Meadow Street	Lance-Corporal	R.I. Fus.	
JOHNSTON. WM.	309 Shankill Road	Rifleman	R.I.R.	
KENNEDY, SAMUEL	79 Bellevue Street	Sergeant		
KERNAGHAN, JOSEPH	32 Mountjoy Street	Private	Northumberland Fus.	
KILPATRICK, W. J.		Corporal		Killed in Action.
KING, T. E.	35 Dower Street	Rifleman		
KIRKLAND, ROBERT	38 Ninth Street	Gunner	R.G.A.	
KNOX, HERBERT	19 Ashmore Street	Private	King's O.L. Regt.	Killed in Action.
KYLE, JACK	19 Broadway	Sergeant		
LEANAY, JAMES	18 Courtree Street	Private	R. Inn. Fus.	
LEWIS, FRANK	243 Mayo Street	Rifleman	R.I.R.	
LEWIS, WM.	23 Ambleside Street	Lance-Corporal		
LITTLE, GEORGE	58 Glenfarne Street	A.C.	R.A.F.	
LOGAN, WM.	33 Macky Street	Sapper	R.E.	
LONG, JOHN	18 Emerson Street	Gunner	R.F.A.	
LOUGHLIN, WM.	329 Shankill Road	Private	I.G.	Killed in Action
MACAULEY, JAMES	65 Paris Street		R.I.R.	
McBRETTNAY, HERBERT	10 Mountcashel Street			Died.
McCLEAN, JACK	Springfield Parade	Sergeant		
McCLEAN, WM.	Springfield Parade	Corporal		
McCLEERY, JAMES	96 Oregon Street			
McCLEERY, SAM.	167 Cambrai Street	Driver	R.F.A.	
McCLEERY, W. J.	167 Cambrai Street	Rifleman	R.I.R.	
McCLELLAND, DAVID	45 Glenwood Street	Sergeant	R. Inn. Fus.	
McCLELLAND, GEORGE	45 Glenwood Street	Stoker	R.N.	
McCOMB, ARCHIE	156 Cupar Street			
McCORMICK, HENRY	30 Brookmount Street	Sergeant	R.I.R.	
McCORMICK, JACK			R. Inn. Fus.	Killed in Action.
McCORMICK, WM.	55 Beverly Street	Private	R.A.M.C.	K'd. in Act., M.M.
McCULLAGH, ROBERT	63 Lanark Street	Sergeant	R.I.R.	
McCULLAGH, THOMAS	56 Glenfarne Street		R.N.	
McFALL, ROBERT	Whitehouse			Killed in Action.
McGLADDERY, JACK	21 Madras Street	Lieutenant	Black Watch	
McGLADDERY, JOE	21 Madras Street	Sergt.-Major		
McGRATH, W. J.	47 Lanark Street	Sergeant	R.I.R.	
McILROY, WILLIAM	1 Yew Street	Private		
McINTYRE, DAVID	4 Bootle Street	Rifleman	R.I.R.	
McINTYRE, GILBERT	4 Bootle Street			Killed in Action.
McKEAN, JOHN	181 Cupar Street	Rifleman	R.I.R.	M.M.
McKENDRY, JOHN	182 Cupar Street			
McKEOWN, ROBERT C.	120 Bellevue Street	Rifleman	R.I.R.	
McKIBBEN, L.	15 Fairfax Street	Rifleman		
McLENAGHAN, SAM.	51 Lawnbrook Avenue			
McLENAGHAN, T.	51 Lawnbrook Avenue			
McMENEMY, S.	20 Woodvale Street	Sapper	R.E.	
McNEIL, JOHN	85 Old Lodge Road	Fitter	R.A.F.	
McVEIGH, DAVID	223 Mayo Street		M.T.	
MAGEE, WM.	Springfield Parade	Private		Killed in Action.
MARTIN, DAVID	64 Glenfarne Street	Driver	A.S.C.	
MARTIN, JAMES	Bangor	Sapper	R.E.	
MARTIN, JAMES	25 Bellevue Street	Private		
MARTIN, THOMAS	Whiterock Houses	Rifleman	R.G.A.	Killed in Action.
MEEK, JAMES	18 Courtree Street	Private	R.A.F.	
MERCER, SAMUEL	276 Shankill Road	Lieutenant		
MERCER, WALTER	276 Shankill Road	Private	R.A.M.C.	
MILLAR, J. T.	48 Cranmore Street	Sergeant	R.I.R.	
MILLAR, W. J.	48 Cranmore Street	Private	R.A.F.	
MILLIGAN, DAVID	16 Jersey Street			Killed in Action.
MILLIGAN, DAVID	28 Brookmount Street	Private		
MILLIGAN, ROBERT	134 Ainsworth Avenue			
MOLYNEUX, ARTHUR	1a Genoa Street	Private		
MOLYNEUX, T. J.	1a Genoa Street	Driver		
MONTGOMERY, WILLIAM	113 Westmoreland Street	Driver	A.S.C.	
MORRISON, ERNEST	61 Southport Street	Private	Sig. Co	
MORRISON, JAMES	61 Southport Street	Sapper	Sig. Co.	

BELFAST PRESBYTERY.   NELSON MEMORIAL.

Name.	Home Address.	Rank.	Regiment, Battalion or Unit.	Remarks.
Morrison, Samuel	61 Southport Street	Sapper	R.E.	
Morsden, Fred.	158 Ainsworth Avenue			
Murray, George	30 Springfield Village			
Neil, Samuel	5 Daisyfield Street		R.I.R.	
Nesbitt, W. E.	54 Ninth Street	Rifleman	R.I.R.	
Parkes, James	172 Cupar Street			
Parr, W. J.	30 Brookmount Street	Gunner	R.F.A.	
Penman, Charles	10 Lyle Street	Sergeant	R.I.R.	Killed in Action.
Pepper, W. J.	30 Glenwood Street	Rifleman		
Phillips, James	Mossvale Street			
Popham, Henry	126 Glenwood Street			
Popham, Hugh	126 Glenwood Street			
Porter, W. John	4 Bootle Street			
Pratt, Thomas	36 Benwell Street			Killed in Action.
Quail, John	44 Glenwood Street	Private		
Quigg, Tom	Cookstown			
Richardson, George	61 Springfield Road			
Ritchie, Tom	12 Glenwood Street		Seaforth Highldrs.	
Ritchie, Wm.	89 Glenwood Street			
Robinson, R.	34 Hillman Street		R.A.F.	
Roney, Hugh	38 Urney Street			
Ross, Fred.	Bangor			
Ross, Robert	318 Springfield Road	Trooper	N.I.H.	Killed in Action.
Ross, R.	20 Linview Street			Killed in Action.
Scott, Alex.	146 Argyle Street		R.N.	
Scott, Samuel L.	146 Argyle Street			
Shannon, Herbert	71 Bellevue Street	Private	R.I. Fus.	
Shannon, James	316 Shankill Road	Trooper	N.I.H.	
Shannon, Joseph	71 Bellevue Street			Killed in Action.
Shaw, Alex.	54 Groomsport Street			
Shaw, Thomas	325 Shankill Road			
Smith, Edward	118 Crimea Street	Driver	R.F.A.	
Smith, Sydney	61 Cambrai Street	Private	R.I.R.	
Smyrl, James	36 Esmond Street	Rifleman	R.I.R.	
Smyrl, Robert	36 Esmond Street	Stoker	R.N.	
Smyrl, Samuel	36 Esmond Street	Private	R. Inn. Fus.	
Smyth, Jas.	37 Jersey Street	Rifleman		
Smyth, Robert	166 Cupar Street			
Smyth, Samuel	12 Thomas Street	Lance-Corporal	R.I.R.	
Spence, Robt.	19 Legann Street	Lance-Corporal		
Steen, Sam.	82 Tennant Street			
Steer, Wm. H.	25 Orkney Street	Private		
Stephenson, James	4 Crimea Street	A.M.	R.A.F.	
Stephenson, Joseph	31 Tennant Street			Killed in Action.
Stephenson, Wm.	13 Yarrow Street	Gunner		
Stevenson, Wm.	69 Canmore Street		M.G. Corps	
Stewart, David	98 Sugarfield Street	Rifleman	R.I.R.	
Stewart, James	21 Columbia Street	Rifleman		
Stinson, Moses	47 James Street		R.I.F.	
Stinson, Samuel	47 James Street		R.I.F.	
Symmons, R. H.	50 Broadbent Street	Rifleman	R. Brigade	
Telford, John	59 Emerson Street	Driver	A.S.C.	
Telford, Robert	59 Emerson Street	Private	R.I.R.	
Telford, Samuel	59 Emerson Street	Lance-Corporal	R.I.R.	
Telford, Wm.	59 Emerson Street	Sergeant	R.G.A.	
Thompson, David	13 Whitworth Street		R.N.	
Thompson, Harry	13 Whitworth Street	Private		
Thompson, Hugh	57 Carnan Street			Killed in Action.
Thompson, John	57 Carnan Street			Killed in Action.
Thompson, Robert	59 Ashmore Street	Rifleman		
Thompson, Wm.	41 Lanark Street			
Tool, Joseph	214 Leopold Street	Private		
Topping, Allan	145 Mayo Street	Corporal	R.I.R.	Killed in Action.
Topping, Robert	145 Mayo Street	Private	R. Inn. Fus.	
Turner, Stewart	279 Springfield Road	Trooper	N.I.H.	Killed in Action.
Wallace, David	270 Springfield Road	Rifleman	R.I.R.	
Wallace, Robert	270 Springfield Road	Private	Seaforth Highldrs.	Killed in Action.
Wallace, Robert	28 Acton Street	Corporal	R.I.R.	
Walker, Thomas M.	11 Tennent Street		R.N.	
Warren, George	49 Glenwood Street			
Waugh, Alex.	29 Lanark Street	Rifleman		
Waugh, Alex., Jun.	29 Lanark Street			
West, John	70 Sugarfield Street		R.N.	
Wilson, Hugh	2 Seventh Street	Private	R.I.R.	
Wilson, James	235 Conway Street			
Wilson, Robert	40 Roden Street	Private		
Wilson, Robert, Jun.	40 Roden Street			Killed in Action.
Wilson, Wm.	40 Roden Street	Sapper		
Woodside, W.	Shankill Road	Lieutenant	Rf. Brigade	M.M.
Young, Albert	17 Lawnview Street	Private	R. Fus.	
Young, Charles	17 Lawnview Street	Sergeant		Killed in Action.

BELFAST PRESBYTERY.   NELSON MEMORIAL.

Name.	Home Address.	Rank.	Regiment, Battalion or Unit.	Remarks.
	COLONIAL FORCES.			
Foster, Leonard	21 Esmond Street	Private	Canadians	Killed.
Gray, Frank	222 Mayo Street		Canadians	Killed.
Hagan, Alf. J.	22 Bromley Street	Private	Australian Army	
Harland, Thos., Jun.	Whiteabbey	Sergt.-Major	Canadians	
Larmour, David	122 Brookmount Street	Sergeant	Canadians	D.C.M.
Young, J. W.	182 Cupar Street		Canadians	
	NEWINGTON.			
Adair, John	1 Clanmorris Street	Private	18th W D.	Prisoner of War.
Agnew, Andrew	12 North Derby Street	Private	15th R.I.R.	Pris. of War., Wounded.
Alexander, James	65 Bentinck Street	Seaman	Mercantile Marine	Boat torpedoed.
Allen, John	Glayndwr, Shore Road	E.R.A.	R.N.	
Allen, Robert	112 Duncairn Gardens	Private	M.T. R.A.S.C.	
Anderson, Ben.	42 Adam Street	Private	9th R.I.R.	Killed in Action.
Anderson, Geo. P.	42 Adam Street	Private	Black Watch	
Anderson, John	42 Adam Street	Private	4th Hussars	
Angus, James	50 Alexandra Park Av.	Corporal	A.S.C.	Gassed.
Angus, Norman	50 Alexandra Park Av.	Private	15th R.I.R.	
Armstrong, Charles	North Queen Street	Private	R.I.R.	
Atkinson, W. J.				
Auld, John	55 Cosgrave Street	Private	9th R.I.R.	Wounded.
Bailie, J. A.	62 Alexandra Park Av.	Lance-Corporal	Wireless Sig. Co., R.E.	
Barr, Robert	15 Seaview Street	Private	18th R.I.R.	Wounded.
Barron, R. J.	17 Limestone Road	Private	16th Pioneers	Killed in Action.
Beare, Harry C.	12 Atlantic Avenue	Lance-Corporal	14th R.I.R.	Wounded twice.
Beattie, Alexander	20 St. Aubyn Street	P.O.	R.N.	
Beattie, S. A.	96 Hillman Street	Seaman	R.N.	
Beggs, Hugh				
Bell, John	82 Cosgrave Street	Private	2nd R. Inn. Fus.	Died of Wounds.
Bell, Robert	3 Hogarth Street	Sapper	Signal Section R.E.	Wounded twice.
Bennet, Clarence	82 Lilliput Street	Rifleman	2nd R.B.	
Beresford, Wm.	15 Rowan Street			
Best, Andrew	21 Cosgrave Street	Private	R.A.F.	
Best, Francis	21 Cosgrave Street	Stoker	R.N.	
Best, George	198 North Queen Street	Sapper	R.E.	Wounded.
Best, John	198 North Queen Street	Private	9th R.I.R.	Killed in Action.
Best, Robert	21 Cosgrave Street	Stoker	R.N.	
Best, Samuel	21 Cosgrave Street	Private	R.A.F.	
Best, Wm. John	21 Cosgrave Street	Corporal	15th R.I.R.	Twice Wounded, Prisoner of War.
Blair, Ernest	65 Seaview Street	Private	3rd Yorks.	Prisoner of War, Wd. twice, D.C.M.
Blair, John	65 Seaview Street	Private	R.A.F.	
Blair, Samuel	109 Up. Canning St.	Private	1st R.I.R.	
Boal, Adam	18 Cosgrave Street	Private	12th Manchesters	Killed in Action.
Boal, Thomas	18 Cosgrave Street	Leading Stoker	R.N.	Wounded.
Boyd, Adam	18 York Road	Private	9th R.I.R.	Wounded.
Boyd, George	11 Cultra Street	Stoker	R.N.	Killed in Action.
Boyd, Thomas	18 York Road	Private	8th R.I.R.	Killed in Action.
Boyles, Hugh	25 Cosgrave Street	Private	15th R.I.R.	
Boyles, John	25 Cosgrave Street	Private	10th R.I.R.	Killed in Action.
Bready, Richard	32 Mervue Street	Private	2nd R.I.R.	Killed in Action.
Breckie, Edward	Mackey Street	Private	R.I.R.	
Bryars, John S.	18 Edlingham Street	Private	15th R.I.R.	Wounded.
Cain, William	55 Adam Street	P.O.	R.N.	
Cairns, Alexander	36 Cosgrave Street	Private	4th Hussars	Killed in Action.
Cairns, James	36 Cosgrave Street	Stoker	R.N.	
Cairns, Robert	36 Cosgrave Street	Gunner	R.G.A.	
Cairns, Samuel	36 Cosgrave Street	Private	1st I.G.	
Calderwood, W. L.	85 Parkmount Street	Gunner	R.N.	
Caldwell, John	61 Mackey Street	Private	R.A.M.C.	Died of Wounds.
Caldwell, Wm.	28 Baltic Avenue	Private	2nd R. Inn. Fus.	
Campbell, Archie	36 Lilliput Street	Rifleman	15th R.I.R.	Gassed.
Campbell, John	36 Lilliput Street	Rifleman	15th R.I.R.	Wounded.
Campbell, R. A.	18 Evolina Street	Private	R.E.	Wounded.
Campbell, W. H.	82 Cosgrave Street	Private	R.A.F.	
Campbell, Wm.	65 Seaview Street	Lance-Corporal	9th R.I.R.	Prisoner of War.
Campbell, Wm.	86 Upper Meadow Street	Private	Army Ordnance Corps	
Campbell, Wm.	44 Lilliput Street	Private	9th R.I.R.	Wounded.
Carrick, Wm.	2 Victoria Gardens	Driver	A.S.C.	
Carson, James	170 North Queen Street	Private	15th R.I.R.	Died.
Carson, John	170 North Queen Street	Private	15th R.I.R.	Missing.
Cathcart, James	84 Up. Canning Street	3rd Engineer	Mercantile Marine	
Caughey, Percy	51 Victoria Terrace	Sapper	R.E.	Killed in Action.
Charters, Thomas	95 Lilliput Street	Trooper	6th Ir. Dragoons	Wounded.
Clyde, T. H.				
Cooke, George	27 Upper Mervue Street	Private	R.A.S.C.	Killed in Action.
Coote, Tom	6 Lewis Street	Private	Cheshire Regt.	
Coulter, Alexander	8 Upper Canning St.	Private	R. Engineers	
Cowden, James	22 Bentinck Street	Corporal	15th R.I.R.	Wounded.

(136)

BELFAST PRESBYTERY. NEWINGTON.

Name.	Home Address.	Rank.	Regiment, Battalion or Unit.	Remarks.
Craig, John	99 Cosgrave Street	Private	12th U.V.F.	Wounded.
Craig, Thos. Thompson	99 Cosgrave Street	Boy Cook	R.N.	
Crook, Hamilton	51 Ivan Street	Private	Tank Corps	
Cunningham, Robert	61 Hanna Street	2nd A.C.	R.M.A.F.	
Curran, Robert	6 Carnalea Street	Private	10th R.I.R.	
Currell, John	31 Limestone Road	Chief Engineer	Mercantile Marine	
Dalgleish, Robert	20 Lewis Street	Gun Layer	R.N.	
Dalgleish, Wm.	259 North Queen Street	Private	16th R.I.R.	Gassed.
Darragh, Alex.	33 Henderson Avenue	Trooper	N.I.H.	
Darragh, Richard	Henderson Avenue	Private	9th R.I.R.	
Davidson, Wm.	183 Spamount Street	Private	Mechanical Transpts.	
Davis, James				
Dawson, Jas. E.	117 Duncairn Gardens	Co. Quartermaster	Irish Guards	Twice Wounded.
Dickey, John	53 Cosgrave Street	Private	2nd R. Inn. Fus.	Died of Wounds.
Dickson, Ross				
Doak, John J.	139 Cosgrave Street	Private	3rd R.I.R.	Wounded.
Dobbin, Samuel	22 Limestone Road	Private	Cyclist Corps	M.M.
Doey, J.				
Dorman, Richard Samuel	24 Trevelyan Terrace	Ship's Officer	Mercantile Marine	
Douglas, Charles	66 Gainsborough Drive	Officer	Mercantile Marine	
Douglas, Daniel	Norbrae, Linden Gdns.	Private	Mech. Transports	
Douglas, John	Norbrae, Linden Gdns.	Sergeant	R.E.	
Douglas, Wm.	Norbrae, Linden Gdns.	Private	R.I.R.	Wounded.
Duncan, Edward	7 Lewis Street	Lance-Corporal	15th R.I.R.	Prisoner of War.
Duncan, John	7 Lewis Street	Private	15th R.I.R.	Disabled.
Dyer, Joseph	20 Kilronan Street	A.B.	Submarine Service	Wounded.
Dykes, George	33 Up. Mervue Street	Private	15th R.I.R.	Wounded.
Dykes, John	114 Mountcollyer Av.	Gunner	R.N.	
Ekin, Fred.	Ashley Gardens	Private	20th R. Inn. Fus.	Killed in Action.
Ekin, Leslie	Ashley Gardens			
Elder, John	68 Lilliput Street	Sergeant	R. Inn. Fus.	Killed in Action.
Elliot, James	10 Alexandra Park Av.	Private	14th R.I.R. (Y.C.V.)	Killed.
English, Arthur	76 Lilliput Street	Private	Mech. Transports	
English, J. B.	31 Osborne Street	Private	R.A.S.C.	
English, Thomas	76 Lilliput Street	Private	Mech. Transports	
English, Wm.	79 Up. Mervue Street	Private	N.I.H.	
Erwin, Abe	11 Syringa Street	2nd Lieutenant	R. Flying Corps	
Fee, Samuel	83 Lilliput Street	Private	15th M.G.S.	Wounded.
Fee, William	83 Lilliput Street	Private	10th R.I.R.	Killed in Action.
Ferguson, Archie	5 Tramway Street	Sapper	R.E.	
Ferguson, Robert	107 Limestone Road	Private	3rd Dragoon Guards	Wounded.
Fleming, Donald	23 Ophir Gardens	Sergeant	9th R.E.	Wounded.
Fleming, Douglas	23 Ophir Gardens	Lance-Corporal		
Fleming, James	23 Ophir Gardens	Private	15th R.I.R.	
Fleming, John	23 Ophir Gardens	Sergeant	Can. Engineers	
Foster, John	117 Cosgrave Street			
Fullerton, R. H.	Lilliput Street	Private	R. Inn. Fus.	Killed in Action.
Gaston, Stafford	77a Up. Meadow Street	Private	15th R.I.R.	Wounded.
Getty, James	4 Cliftonville Avenue	Private	Duke of Wellington's Regt.	
Gibb, James	16 Mountcollyer Road	Private	15th R.I.R.	
Gibson, John	78 Lilliput Street	Private	15th R.I.R.	Killed in Action.
Gibson, L. A.	1 Bellevue Tce, F'william	Private	Mech. Transports	Gassed.
Gillespie, John	45 Up. Mervue Street	Fireman	R.N.	
Gilmour, Robert J.	100 Mountcollyer Road	Private	15th R.I.R.	Killed in Action.
Gilpin, Albert	100 Duncairn Gardens			
Gordon, James				
Graham, Skeffington	138 Up. Canning Street	P.O.	Armoured Car Section	Died.
Green, William	34 Hogarth Street	Private	9th R. Inn. Fus.	Wd. twice, Gassed
Greenwood, Albert	Newington Avenue		R.A.M.C.	
Greenwood, John	Newington Avenue		R.A.M.C.	Killed in Action.
Greer, Henry	9 Mackey Street	Private	15th R.I.R.	Killed in Action.
Guinea, William	51 Glenrosa Street	Private	R.F.A.	Twice wounded.
Hale, Joseph	Mountcollyer Road			
Hall, Samuel	34 Osborne Street	Private	Cameron Highldrs.	Twice wounded.
Hamilton, Hugh	Mervue Street			
Hamilton, James	2 Loughview Terrace	E. Officer	Mercantile Marine	
Hamilton, John	2 Loughview Terrace	Corporal	15th R.I.R.	Killed.
Hamilton, Robert	2 Loughview Terrace	Lance-Corporal	R.E.	
Hamilton, John	67 Adam Street	Private	R.A.F.	
Hamilton, John	12 Hillman Street	Private	R.A.S.C. M.T.	Died.
Hanna, J.				
Harkness, Robert	106 Mountcollyer Avenue	Sergeant	9th R. Inn. Fus.	M.M.
Harper, Jas. A.	103 Lilliput Street	Sapper	R.E.	
Harpur, Thomas	10 Glandore Street	C.Q.M.S.	10th R. Inn.	Twice Wounded.
Harpur, Thompson	10 Glandore Street	Trooper	N.I.H.	Killed in Action.
Harris, Arthur	9 Alexandra Avenue	Eng. Sub-Lieut.	R.N.R.	
Henry, W. J.	28 Lilliput Street	Temp. Lt.-Eng.	R. Naval Transport	Wounded.
Hillis, Joseph	Shore Road	Sergeant	R.I.R.	M.M.
Hoey, Wm. Jas.	41 Up. Canning Street	Private	R.A.S.C.	
Holmes Hugh	31 Glenrosa Street	2nd Corporal	R.E.	
Holmes, James J.	3 Glenrosa Street	Sergeant	R.E.	M.M. & Ulster Cert.
Houston, Robert	11 Mervue Street	Private	R.A.S.C.	
Houston, Thomas	11 Mervue Street	Lance-Corporal	12th R.I.R.	
Howard, Matthew	30 Edlingham Street	Private	3rd R.I.R.	

BELFAST PRESBYTERY. NEWINGTON.

Name.	Home Address.	Rank.	Regiment, Battalion or Unit.	Remarks.
Hume, W. J.	15 Up. Mervue Street	Private	Mech. Transports	
Hunter, Andrew	90 Lilliput Street	Private	15th R.I.R.	Wounded.
Hunter, Henry	70 Hogarth Street	Corporal	R.A.S.C.	
Hunter, James	19 Limestone Road	Corporal	R.F.A.	1914 Star, Croix-de-Guerre, M.M., Prisoner of War.
Irwin, James	52 Harrisburg Street	Private	R.A.S.C.	
Irwin, Stewart	52 Harrisburg Street	Private	6th R. Inn. Fus.	
Jackson, John	45 Limestone Road	Bandsman	15th R.I.R.	Missing.
Jackson, W. B.	54 Hogarth Street	Co. Sergt.-Major	Cyclist Corps	
Johnson, Wm.				
Kane, James	92 Mervue Street	Stoker	R.N.	
Kane, John	92 Mervue Street	Stoker	R.N.	
Kane, William	92 Mervue Street	Corporal	1st R. Inn. Fus.	Killed in Action.
Kells, William	Lilliput Street			
Kennedy, Peter				
Kernaghan, Alex.	15 Collyer Street	Private	2nd R.I.R.	Wounded 3 times.
Kernaghan, James	14 Limestone Road	Sergeant	15th R.I.R.	Killed in Action.
Kernaghan, Hugh	68 Mountcollyer Street	Driver	R.G.A.	
Kernaghan, John	68 Mountcollyer Street	Private	R.A.S.C.	
Kernaghan, William	4 Cliftonville Avenue	Captain	Mercantile Marine	
Kerr, R. J. Steele				
Kidd, Isaac	11 Mervue Street	Corporal	R.A.S.C.	
King, James	28 Limestone Road	E.R.A.	R.N.	
King, Joseph	28 Limestone Road	Private	Cyclist Corps	Wounded.
Kirkpatrick, David	72 Cosgrave Street	Lance-Corporal	1st R. Inn. Fus.	Killed in Action.
Kirkpatrick, Thomas	34 Mervue Street	Sapper	R.E.	
Knox, William	71 Lilliput Street	Lance-Corporal	2nd R.I.R.	Killed in Action.
Larmour, Alex.	1 Indiana Avenue	Private	N.I.H.	
Larmour, James	103 Lilliput Street	Stoker	R.N.	Killed in Action.
Lee, James	38 Lilliput Street	Gunner	R.G.A.	
Liddle, Archie	73 Glenrosa Street	Lance-Corporal	14th R.I.R.	Wounded.
Liggett, Frederick	50 Lewis Street	Gunner	5th R. Inn. Fus.	Killed in Action.
Liggett, John	50 Lewis Street	Stoker	R.N.	
Little, Henry	12 N. Derby Street	Stoker	R.N.	
Livingstone, George	48 Duncairn Gardens	Private	R.E.	Gassed.
Livingstone, John	48 Duncairn Gardens	Rifleman	15th R.I.R.	Missing.
Livingston, Wm.	9 Mervue Street	Private	3rd R.I.R.	
Logan, James	19 Ilchester Street	Private	R.E.	
Lorimer, Wm., Sen.	113 Cosgrave Street	Private	2nd R.I.R.	
Lorimer, Wm., Jun.	106 Mountcollyer Avenue	Private	14th R.I.R.	Died of Wounds.
Lowry, Joseph	27 Mackey Street	Private	16th R.I.R.	
Lowry, Samuel	39 Collyer Street	Private	1st R. Inn. Fus.	Wounded.
Luke, Alexander	46 Ivan Street	Carpenter	R.N.	
Luke, James	46 Ivan Street	Signaller	R.I.R.	
Luke, John	46 Ivan Street	Sapper	R.E.	
Luke, Robert	46 Ivan Street	Private	16th R.I.R.	Wounded.
Luke, William	46 Ivan Street	Private	Scotch Regt.	Twice Wounded.
Magee, Adam	59 Cavehill Road	Trooper	N.I.H.	
Magowan, James	86 Seaview Street	Private	5th R. Inn. Fus.	Wounded.
Magowan, John	86 Seaview Street	Private	5th R.E.	Killed in Action.
Magowan, W. J.	York Street	Captain	Tank Corps	
Malcolm, William	13 Mountcollyer Avenue	Sapper	R.E.	Wounded.
Marne, Robert				
Marshall, Joseph	61 Willowbank Street	Lance-Corporal	N.I.H.	
Mearns, Robert	13 Lilliput Street	Lance-Corporal	R.A.M.C.	
Mehaffy, Matthew	138 Mervue Street	Q.M. Sergt.	2nd Inniskillings	Wounded.
Mehaffy, Robert	31 Hillman Street	Corporal	R.A.S.C.	
Mellon, Henry	22 Steen Street	Lance-Corporal	R.E.	Cert. of Gallantry.
Millar, James	13 Lilliput Street	Gunner	R.N.	
Millar, Robert	76 Bentinck Street	Sergeant	15th R.I.R.	Prisoner of War.
Milligan, Fred. Robt.	62 Ruth Street	P.O.	R.N.	
Milligan, T. A.	62 Ruth Street	Co. Sergt.-Major	15th R.I.R.	Twice Wd., D.C.M.
Milligan, Wm.	62 Ruth Street	Private	2nd R.I.R.	Wounded.
Mitchell, Irvine	61 Up. Mervue Street	Private	15th R.I.R.	3 times Wounded.
Montgomery, Stephen	39 Up. Meadow Street	Private	R.I.R.	
Montgomery, Wm.	39 Up. Meadow Street	Private	N.I.H.	Gassed.
Montgomery, Robert	Fernbank Villas	Private	9th R.I.R.	Killed in Action.
Montgomery, Wm.	Fernbank Villas	Trooper	N.I.H.	Wounded.
Moon, John	44 Ruth Street	Leading Stoker	R.N.	Killed on bd. ship.
Moore, Robert	62 Fortwilliam Par.	Sergeant	R.E.	Belgian M.M., 1915 Star, Mentioned in Despatches.
Mullan, David	108 Mervue Street	Stoker	Mer. Mar. Reserves	
Murphy, John				
Murray, Alex. B.	33 Mervue Street	Private	R. Inn. Fus.	Prisoner of War.
Murray, James	33 Collyer Street	Rifleman	15th R.I.R.	Wounded.
McAdam, Samuel	Canning Street	Private	R.I.R.	
McAlister, John	14 Moyola Street	Private	R.A.F.	
McAlister, Wm.	14 Moyola Street	Sergeant	15th R.I.R.	
McBride, F. L.	24 Marsden Gardens	Private	13th R.I.R.	Wounded.
McBride, Robert	24 Marsden Gardens	Private	A.S.C. M.T.	
McBride, Thomas	36 Canning Street			
McBride, Victor Wm.	127 Alexandra Park Av.		R.N.	Killed in Action.

BELFAST PRESBYTERY.   NEWINGTON.

Name.	Home Address.	Rank.	Regiment, Battalion or Unit.	Remarks.
McBroom, Thomas	38 Mackey Street	Private	10th R.I.R.	Wounded.
McCartney, John				
McCartney, Robert				
McCaulay, Samuel	Mountcollyer Avenue	Private	R.I.R.	Killed in Action.
McCaw, E. J.	32 Limestone Road	Private	9th Inniskillings	Wounded.
McClean, John	55 Up. Mervue Street	Private	R.I.R.	Wounded.
McClure, H. A.	8 Evolina Street	Lance-Corporal	16th R.I.R.	Wounded.
McClure, James	40 Mackey Street	Private	R.A.S.C.	Missing.
McComiskey, James	52 Parkmount Street	Private	9th R.I.R.	Killed in Action.
McCullough, Robert	57 Collyer Street	Private	Tank Corps	
McCullough, T. A.	57 Collyer Street	Driver	15th R.I.R.	
McCullough, Thos.	57 Collyer Street	Rifleman	15th R.I.R.	
McCullough, W. J.	57 Collyer Street	Gunner	21st R.F.A.	
McDermott, Joseph	Cosgrave Street		R.N.R.	
McDevitt, W. J.	5 Craigavad Street	Sergeant	3rd R. Inn. Fus.	Wounded twice.
McFarland, R. F.	76 Gainsborough Drive	Trimmer	R.N.	
McFetridge, David	12 Mackey Street	Lance-Corporal	6th Inniskillings	
McFetridge, George	4 Collyer Street	Private	R.A.M.C.	
McFetridge, Richard	4 Collyer Street	Private	L.C.	
McGaffin, James	28 Baltic Avenue	Private	15th R. Inn. Fus.	Wounded twice.
McGarrell, James	50 Greenmount Street	Stoker	R.N.	
McGaughan, David	55 Harrisburg Street	Corporal	2nd Inniskillings	Wounded.
McGaughan J. C.	55 Harrisburg Street	Private	3rd Cheshires	
McGaughan, Wm. H.	55 Harrisburg Street	Sapper	R.E.	
McGee, Henry	10 N. N. Queen Street	Private	15th R.I.R.	Wounded.
McGee, James	10 N. N. Queen Street	Private	5th R.I.R.	Died.
McGookin, John	28 Lilliput Street	Private	2nd R. Inn. Fus.	Wd., Pris. of War.
McGrugan, Alex.	27 Mervue Street	Private	A.S.C. M.T.	
McKeown, John	39 Copperfield Street	Private	6th R.I.R.	
McKeown, R. G.	39 Copperfield Street	Private	London Irish	
McKillen, Samuel	40 Alexandra Park Av.	Lieutenant	R.A.F.	
McLean, James P.	87 Seaview Street	Private	15th R.I.R.	Wounded.
McMichael, Joseph	35 Up. Meadow Street	Private	2nd R. Inn. Fus.	
McMillan, James	116 Mervue Street	Private	15th R.I.R.	Gassed.
McMillan, Samuel	116 Mervue Street	Lance-Corporal	15th R.I.R.	Wounded.
McNeilly, John	134 Spamount Street	Private	R. Marines	Gassed twice.
McQuillan, Matthew	15 Limestone Road	Private	15th R.I.R.	Wounded.
McRobb, James	49 Ballycarry Street	Private	R.F.A.	
McVea, Jack	28 Cedar Avenue	Trooper	N.I.H.	Killed in Action.
McVea, Victor	28 Cedar Avenue	Lieutenant	R.I.R.	Wounded.
Neil, William	81 Cosgrave Street	Stoker	R.N.	
Neil, William	16 Collyer Street	Private	Young Citizens	Wounded twice.
Nicholson, Albert	74 Ruth Street	Sergeant	R. E.	Wd., M.M. & Bar.
Nicholson, James A.	74 Ruth Street	2nd Engineer	Mercantile Marine	
Nicholson, John	74 Ruth Street	Lance-Corporal	Cyclist Corps	Wounded.
Nicholson, John	35 New North Queen St.	Corporal	R.A.M.C.	
Nisbitt, S.				
OHara, Wm.	15 Jennymount Terrace	Lance-Corporal	15th R.I.R.	Prisoner of War.
Park, Frank	99 Mountcollyer Road	Private	R.E.	
Park, Thos. C. W.	99 Mountcollyer Road	Private	R.H.A.	Wounded.
Parker, Ed. Phillips	50 Gainsborough Drive	Officer	R.N.	
Parker, John	90 Up. Meadow Street	Seaman Gunner	R.N. Reserves	
Parker, Richard	90 Up. Meadow Street	Private	15th R.I.R.	Wounded twice.
Patterson, James	St. Aubyn Street	Private	R.I.R.	
Patterson, Joseph	St. Aubyn Street	Private	R.I.R.	
Pattison, James				
Patrick, James	80 Cosgrave Street	Private	16th R.I.R.	Wounded.
Patrick, John	80 Cosgrave Street	Sergeant	11th R. Inn. Fus.	Killed in Action.
Patrick, Johnston	80 Cosgrave Street	Private	R.A.F.	
Patrick, Wm., Sen.	90 Cosgrave Street	Private	11th R. Inn. Fus.	
Patrick, Wm., Jun.	80 Cosgrave Street	Stoker	R.N.	
Pelan, Wm. James	74 Up. Canning Street	Corporal	R.G.A.	K'd. in Act., D.C.M.
Phillips, John	40 Lewis Street	Lance-Corporal	R.E.	
Pollock, Edward	31 Collyer Street	Private	8th R. Inn. Fus.	
Pollock, Robert	31 Collyer Street	Driver	R.F.A.	
Pollock, George	114 Up. Canning Street	Corporal	R.E.	
Pyper, Robert	Gainsborough Drive			
Quate, Wm.	34 Mileriver Street	Sapper	R.E.	
Quirey, Frank	40 Mackey Street	Private	R. Inn. Fus.	Died.
Quirey, Robert	40 Mackey Street	Gunner	R.G.A.	Wounded.
Reid, Alfred				
Reid, George	61 Up. Mervue St.	Stoker	R.N.	Killed in Action.
Reid, Robert				
Reilly, John	68 Oldpark Road	Lieutenant	R.A.F.	
Rippard, Joseph	158 Hillman Street	Private	2/2 London Regt.	Wounded twice.
Rippard, Wm.	158 Hillman Street	Private	R. Flying Corps	
Robinson, John	36 Collyer Street	Corporal	R.A.M.C.	
Roddy, Edward	39 Mackey Street	Private	10th R.I.R.	
Rodgers, James				
Rodgers, James (Junr.)				
Ross, Samuel	36 Wensley Street	Private	R.I.R.	Killed in Action.
Ross, William	134 Mervue Street	Private	1st R. Inn. Fus.	Killed in Action.
Rowley, James	55 Ivan Street	Lance-Corporal	R.A.M.C.	Wounded.
Rush, Andrew	77 Fortwilliam Parade	Private	R.A.S.C.	

(139)

BELFAST PRESBYTERY. NEWINGTON.

Name.	Home Address.	Rank.	Regiment, Battalion or Unit.	Remarks.
SHARPE, WM.	343 N. Queen Street	Lance-Corporal	5th R.I. Lancers	Gassed.
SHAW, WM. JAMES	51 Mackey Street	Private	1st R. Inn. Fus.	
SHERRARD, SAMUEL	11 Craigavad Street	Private	R. Inn. Fus.	
SINCLAIR, NORMAN				
SKELLY, ROBERT	51 Glenrosa Street	Private	15th R.I.R.	Killed in Action.
SMITH, HARRY P.	117 Limestone Road	Lieutenant	Army Ordnance Corps	Wounded.
SMITH, JAMES	224 York Street	Private	R.G.A.	
SMITH, ROBERT	30 Hillman Street	Private	R. Inn. Fus.	
STARRETT, DAVID	29 Spamount Street	Private	9th R.I.R.	
STEAD, JAMES	32 Osborne Street	Private	R.A.F.	Wounded.
STEVENSON, STEVEN	91 Henderson Avenue	Bugler	1st R.I.R.	Wounded twice.
STEWART, ALEX.	47 Adam Street	Chief Officer	Mercantile Marine	
STEWART, FREDERICK	47 Adam Street	Private	1st R. Inn. Fus.	Wounded.
STEWART, JOSEPH	47 Adam Street	Private	R.E.	
STEWART, H. J.	Fernbank Villas			
STRAIN, CHARLES M.	46 Rowan Street	Gunner	6th R.I.R.	
STRAIN, W. H.	46 Rowan Street	Lance-Corporal	2nd Leinsters	
SWANN, T. G.	Hogarth Street	Lieutenant	R. Inn. Fus.	
THOMAS, R. W.	22 Queen Victoria Gdns.	Private	R.A.S.C.	
THOMPSON, JAMES	33 Limestone Road	Private	15th R.I.R.	Killed in Action.
THOMPSON, JOHN	33 Limestone Road	Private	15th R.I.R.	Wounded.
THOMPSON, SAMUEL	87 Cedar Avenue	Sergeant	6th Black Watch	Wounded.
THOMPSON, SAMUEL	20 Little Ship Street	Private	15th R.I.R.	
THOMPSON, THOMAS	16 Mountcollyer Road	Private	R.F.C.	
TOWNLEY, JAMES	13 Mackey Street	Private	18th R.I.R.	Killed in Action.
TOZER, WM. JAMES	Kincraig, Antrim Road	Sergeant	R.A.S.C. M.T.	M.M.
TURNER, ANDREW	9 Glandore Street	Driver	R.E.	
TURNER, WM.	9 Glandore Street	Sapper	R.E.	
TURNER, JAMES	109 Mervue Street	Sapper	Inland Water Transport	
WALKER, WM.	8 Collyer Street	Lance-Corporal	5th R.I.R.	Twice Wd., M.M.
WALKER, WM.	35 Glenrosa Street	2nd Cl. Air Mech.	R.A.F.	
WALLACE, DAVID	29 Weaver Street	Private	3rd C. R.	
WALLACE, GEORGE	29 Weaver Street	Stoker	R.N.	
WALLACE, SAMUEL	29 Weaver Street	Sergeant	Leinster Regt.	Wounded twice.
WALLACE, JOHN	28 Mountcollyer Road	Driller	R.E.	
WALLACE, JOSEPH	14 Limestone Road	Private	11th R.I.R.	Killed in Action.
WALLACE, ROBERT	6 Collyer Street	Private	2nd R.I.R.	Wounded.
WASSON, ROBERT	173 Crumlin Road	Sergeant	8th R.I. Regt.	Wounded.
WASSON, SAMUEL	22 Indiana Avenue	Private	4th Field Ambulance	Wounded.
WATSON, ARCHIBALD	36 Mervue Street	Private	R. Inniskillings	Wounded & Gassed.
WATSON, JOHN	84 Mountcollyer Road	Sapper	R.E.	
WATSON, JOHN	51 Mervue Street	Private	15th R.I.R.	Killed in Action.
WARING, SAMUEL	111 Mervue Street	Stoker	R.N.	
WHITE, JAMES	114 Up. Canning Street	P.O.	R.N.R.	
WHITE, JOSHUA	8 Sylvan Street	Private	R.A.M.C.	
WHITE, SAMUEL	52 Mackey Street	Private	R. Inn. Fus.	Wounded.
WILKINSON, ISAAC	126 Cosgrave Street	Sergeant	5th U.V.F.	
WILLIAMSON, JOSEPH	40 Mackey Street	Private	3rd R.I.R.	
WRIGHT, HERBERT G.	165 Duncairn Gdns.	Private	R.F.A.	Wounded.
WILKINSON, SAMUEL	15 Craigavad Street	Rifleman	2nd R.I.R.	
YOUNG, CHARLES				
YOUNG, THOS. F.	37 Newington Avenue	Major	R.E.	M.C. and D.S.O.
YOUNG, WM.				
COLONIAL AND U.S.A. FORCES.				
DOHERTY, ROBERT	40 Hillman Street	Private	Can. M.S.S.	
DOHERTY, W. J.	40 Hillman Street	Sergeant	Can. O. Corps	
FLACK, J. W.	4 Camberwell Terrace	Sergeant	76th Canadians	Wounded.
GILPIN, FREDK.	100 Duncairn Gardens	Private	Canadians	Killed in Action.
HARPER, MATTHEW	10 Glandore Street	Private	Aust. Engineers	Wounded.
LIVINGSTONE, T. M.	48 Duncairn Gardens	Private	U.S.A. 12th Cav.	
MILLAR, M. HARRY	Glandore Avenue	Private	Canadian Tanks	
MILLAR, SAMUEL	Glandore Avenue	Corporal	49th Canadians	Wounded.
MONTGOMERY, JAMES A.	39 Up. Meadow Street	Lance-Corporal	47th Canadians	Wounded.
ROSS, GEORGE RAPHAEL	27 Henderson Avenue	Private	9th Canadians	Killed in Action.
THOMPSON, HUGH	42 Fortwilliam Parade	Sergeant	13th Australians	Wounded.
WHITE, WM. THOS.	114 Up. Canning St.	Private	S.A. Inft.	
NEWTONBREDA.				
ALLAN, DUNCAN		Lance-Corporal	R.E.	
ARLOW, JACK	10 Rushfield Street	Trooper	M.G. Corps	
BLAIR, G.		Stoker	R.N.	
BLAIR, J. KIRKWOOD	57 Candahar Street	Cadet	No. 7 Cadet Batt.	Killed in Action.
BRITTAIN, ALBERT E.	327 Ormeau Road			
BROWN, FRED.	Ormeau Road	Private		
BRYARS, GUY	108 North Parade	Lieutenant	8th Ir. Fus.	
BRYARS, WM.	108 North Parade	Lieutenant	R.A.M.C.	
CARSER, WM.	Cherryvale Lodge	3rd Engineer	Transport S.	
CLARKE, IVAN	69 South Parade	Private	109 M.G. Corps	Wounded.
CLARKE, LINDSAY	69 South Parade	Lance-Corporal	K.O. Liverpool	
CORRY, R. ERIC	Redroofs, N'breda	2nd Lieutenant	R.G.A.	
CRYMBLE, JACK	College Green	Lieutenant	R.I. Fus.	Killed in Action.

BELFAST PRESBYTERY. NEWTONBREDA.

Name.	Home Address.	Rank.	Regiment, Battalion or Unit.	Remarks.
Dobbin, Jack	Annadale	Lieutenant	Indian Army	
Dobbin, Wm.	Annadale	Private	23rd Inn. Fus.	Killed in Action.
Drean, Fred.	Rosetta Avenue		Transport Ser.	
Drean, Stanley	Rosetta Avenue	Lieutenant	11th Inn. Fus.	M.C., Wounded.
Drean, Wm. C.	Rosetta Avenue	Lieutenant	8th R.I.R.	
Duff, Thomas	7 Parkmore Street	Signaller	3rd R. Inn. Fus.	
Gaston, Wm.	40 Jamison Street	Private	A.S.C.	
Graham, Robert			R.N.A.S.	
Graham, Wm.		Private	A.S.C.	
Graham, Wm.	Purdysburn	Colonel	R.A.M.C.	Died.
Hall, Thomas	Knockbreda Road	Rifleman	R. Ir. R.	Wounded.
Hayes, Wm.	31 Deramore Street	Sergeant	8th R.I.R.	
Henderson, Leslie	Knockbreda Road		R.N.	
Hill, Harry	36 University Avenue	Private		Wounded.
Hyndman, Norman		Private	14th R.I.R.	
Hyndman, Valentine	Antrim Road	Captain	Y.C.V., R.I.R.	Killed in Action.
Jackson, Balfan	South Parade	Private	24th Ir. Fus.	Killed in Action.
Jackson, Geo.	South Parade	Private	23rd Ir. Fus.	Killed in Action.
Jamison, Bertie	473 Ormeau Road	Private	14th R.I.R.	Killed in Action.
Jamison, James	473 Ormeau Road	Captain	10th R.I.R.	Killed in Action.
Jardin, Andrew	Newtonbreda	Corporal	Headquarters U. Division	Wounded.
Killen, Edward O.	Bedford	Lieutenant	R.E.	Killed in Action.
Kirk, Alister	The Pines, Newtonbreda	Lieutenant	R.F.C., Egypt	Wounded.
Kirk, Stanley	The Pines, Newtonbreda	Lance-Corporal	N.I.H.	
Leitch, Gordon	22 Burmah Street	Private	14th R.I.R.	Wounded.
Lindsay, Richard	Eglantine Avenue	Rifleman	7th R.I.R.	Wounded.
McAlery, John	Moyallon, Annadale	Captain	R.A.F.	Wd., Killed in Act., Italian Silver Med.
McAnoy, Geo.	Newtonbreda	Private	Indian Army	
McAnoy, John	Newtonbreda	Rifleman	16th R.I.R.	
McCartney, Harry	Rossmore Avenue	Lieutenant	Indian Army	
McCartney, James	17 Walmer Street	Corporal	8th R.I.R.	
McCausland, Jack	Cherryvale	Lieutenant	9th R. Ir. Fus.	
McCausland, Samuel	Cherryvale	Cadet	R.N.A.S. in Russia	Russian Medal
McCrea, Wm.	36 Sunnyside Street	Bombardier	R.H.A.	Wounded.
McCullagh, J. R.	95 South Parade	Major	85th Labour Coy.	
McDowell, John	Florenceville Avenue	Lieutenant	R. Innis. Fus.	
McDowell, Wm.	Florenceville Avenue	Private	R.A.M.C.	
McFadzean, Wm.	**Rubicon, Cregagh**	**Private**	**14th R.I.R.**	**V.C., Killed in Act.**
McKee, James	25 Deramore Street	Private	8th R.I.R.	Killed in Action.
McKee, Thomas		Stoker	R.N.	
McKee, Wm.				
McLardy, Angus	6 Monalto, S. Parade	Lieutenant	R.I.R.	
McMillan, Arnold	Rosetta Park	Surgeon	R.N.	
Majury, James	36 Raby Street	Trooper	N.I.H.	Wounded.
Majury, Samuel	36 Raby Street	Private	M.T. A.S.C.	
Malcolm, Harry	Knockbreda Road	Captain	R.A.M.C.	
Martin, Jack	Haslar, Galwally Park	Lieutenant	9th R.I.R.	Wounded.
Mather, Norman		Private	M.T. A.S.C.	
Maxwell, John	Ormeau Road	Trooper	N.I.H.	
Mercer, Harold	Haypark Avenue	Sergeant	Chinese Lab. Co.	
Milliken, Robert	Dunvegan Street	Private	R.M.L. Inf.	
Mitchell, James	388 Ravenhill Road	Sergeant	36th Div. Engineers	
Murray, James	120 University Avenue	Private	10th R.I.R.	Wounded.
Murray, William	120 University Avenue	Lieutenant	1st Middlesex	Killed in Action.
Nesbitt, Samuel	Inglemere, F'ville Av.	P.O.	R.N.A.S.	
Patterson, Alex.	Rosetta Avenue	Lieutenant	10th R.I.R.	
Patterson, Clawson	South Parade	Sergeant	14th R.I.R.	
Patterson, Harold	South Parade	Lance-Corporal	14th R.I.R.	Killed in Action.
Patterson, Jack	South Parade	Gunner	5th Machine Gun	Wounded.
Ramsey, Thos.		Private	2nd Cam. Highldrs	Killed in Action.
Rea, Herbert	Dalzieu	Lieutenant	14th R.I.R.	Wd., Kd. in Action.
Rea, Norman	Dalzieu	Lieutenant	10th R.I. Fus.	
Rea, Robert	Dalzieu	Lieutenant	R.I.R.	
Rea, Wm.	Ormeau Road	2nd Lieutenant	R.I.R.	Prisoner
Reid, Wm.	Rosetta Avenue	Corporal	10th Field Co. R.E.	
Riddell, Sam.		Sapper	R.E.	
Robb, Alfred	Lisnabreeny	Captain		
Robb, Frederick	Charlesville	Lieutenant	2nd Scots Fus.	Wounded.
Rutherford, W.		Lieutenant	Yorkshire Regt.	Killed in Action.
Stanley, Jack	Knockbreda Road	Corporal	8th R.I.R.	
Stanley, R. O.	Knockbreda Road	Lieutenant	10th R.W. Fus.	Killed in Action.
Stevenson, Jack	Glencregagh	Lieutenant	9th R.I.R.	M.C., Prisoner.
Tate, James	Rosetta Villas	Captain	R.A.M.C.	Prisoner
Tate, Wm.	Knockbreda Park		Transport S.	
Thompson, David	33 Jamison Street	Private	Labour Corps	
Thompson, Ernest	Knock	Private	14th R.I.R.	
Thompson, Joseph	Knock	Captain	12th Manchesters	
Tougher, R. A.	Annadale Avenue	Captain	A.S.C., Egypt	Ment. in Des.
Williamson, John	Cregagh	Lance-Corporal	R.A.M.C.	
Workman, Franz	Newtonbreda Manse	Captain	R.A.F.	M.C.
Workman, Jas. H.	Newtownbreda Manse	Private	A.S.C.	M.M., Wounded.

BELFAST PRESBYTERY. NEWTONBREDA.

Name.	Home Address.	Rank.	Regiment, Battalion or Unit.	Remarks.
COLONIAL AND U.S.A. FORCES.				
Anderson, Alex.	2 Fitzwilliam Avenue	Private	N.Z. Field Amb.	
Bennett, John	...	Major	Canadian Contgt.	
Courtney, Samuel	Rosetta Park	Private	N.Z. Territorials	
Curlis, Rollo	1 Belvoir Place	Trooper	Aus. L. Horse	Killed in Action.
Deans, Thos.	Knockbreda Park	Private	Canadian Contgt.	
Hall, Wm.	Knockbreda Road	Private	Canadian Contgt.	
Harvey, George	Islet Hill, Groomsport	Sergeant	American Army	
Harvey, Maxwell	Islet Hill, Groomsport	Private	Canadian A.M. Corps	
Mateer, Fred.	...	Sapper	Australian Force	
Workman, E. G.	The Manse, N'breda	Private	1st Batt. Can. Engineers	
OLDPARK.				
Archer, Joseph	249 Oldpark Road	Private	14th R.I.R.	Wounded.
Beattie, Wm.	45 Ballymoney Street	Private	R.A.M.C.	
Bennett, Frederick	23 Rosevale Street	Sergeant	14th R.I.R.	Killed in Action.
Blair, Wm.	188 Oldpark Road	Private	R.A.M.C.	
Blair, Wm. Joseph	8 Barrow Street	Private	9th R.I.R.	
Bradford, Robert	186 Oldpark Road	Private	9th R.I.R.	Wounded.
Brown, James	14 Hillview Street	Private	R.A.M.C.	Killed in Action.
Brown, Samuel	14 Hillview Street	Private	14th R.I.R.	
Cameron, Samuel	392 Oldpark Road	Private	R.A.M.C.	Prisoner.
Cargill, Jack	3 The Gables, C'ville	Sergeant	14th R.I.R.	Prisoner.
Comer, Edward	62 Charleville Street	Private	6th R.I.R.	Wounded.
Comer, Walter	62 Charleville Street	Private	6th R.I.R.	
Dempster, Wm.	25 Louisa Street	Gunner	Machine Gun Corps	
Dogherty, Frank	388 Oldpark Road	Private	Royal Air Craft	
Ellison, James	39 Keswick Street	Private	1st R.I.R.	Prisoner.
Ellison, Shaw	39 Keswick Street	Private	R.E.	
Esler, Maybin	Westland Gardens	Private	2nd Leinster Regt.	
Esler, Wm. John	Westland Gardens	Private	B Division, V. Stores	
Falls, Robert	208 Oldpark Road	Driver	R.E.	
Falls, Thomas	208 Oldpark Road	Private	A.S.C.	
Fletcher, Robert	3 Waterproof Street	Private	R. Inn. Fus.	Wounded.
Forbes, Alexander	Kingsmere Avenue	Private	14th R.I.R.	
Forbes, John R.	Kingsmere Avenue	Cadet	South Camp, Newtownards	
Forbes, Wm.	Kingsmere Avenue	Private	14th R.I.R.	Killed in Action.
Fraser, John Holden	14 Alliance Avenue	Private	R.E., Rail. Con. Corps.	
Gault, James	8 Oldpark Avenue	Private	R.E. (Sapper)	
Gilmore, Alexander	28 Oldpark Avenue	Saddler	R.A.M.C.	
Graham, Robert	210 Cliftonville Road	Air Mechanic	Seaplane Squadron	
Graham, William	210 Cliftonville Road	Gunner	112th Siege Battery	
Gowdy, Wm.	Raleigh Street	Sapper	R.E.	
Gormall, Robert	15 Benwell Street	Private	R.A.F.	
Gormall, Thomas	15 Benwell Street	Seaman	H.M.S. Dominion	
Hanley, Robert	30 Southport Street	Private	14th R.I.R.	Wounded.
Harris, Hugh	40 Linwood Street	Sergeant	14th R.I.R.	Wounded.
Hawthorne, Joseph	45 Westland Road	Corporal	14th R.I.R.	Wounded.
Houston, John S.	60 Southport Street	Corporal	2nd R.I.R.	
Hunter, H. G. R.	Oldpark Road	2nd Lieutenant	5th R.I. Regt.	
Kyle, Alfred	52 Danube Street	Private	17th R.I.R.	
Larmour, Alfred	172 Cliftonville Road	Corporal	14th R.I.R.	
Lawther, Ernest	29 Hillview Street	Private	8th R.I.R.	
Love, Arthur	Cavehill Road	Corporal	8th R.I.R.	
McCairley, Andrew	133 Manor Street	Private	9th R.I.R.	Died.
McCairley, George	133 Manor Street	Seaman	R.N.	
McCalmont, Hugh G.	21 Bandon Street	Private	R.A.M.C.	
McCalmont, John	21 Bandon Street	Corporal	15th R.I.R.	Wounded.
McClatchey, James	41 Battenberg Street	Private	9th R.I.R.	
McCullough, Andrew	39 Keswick Street	Private	15th R.I.R.	
McIvor, Lawrence	8 Walton Street	Private	4th R.I.R.	
McKee, Herbert	176 Oldpark Road	Private	R.E.	
McLean, John	51 Manor Street	Engineer	R.N.	Drowned.
McLean, Robert	51 Manor Street	Sergeant	N.I.H.	
McMaster, Samuel	88 Oldpark Avenue	Private	R.A.S.C.	
McMichael, Alfred	40 Louisa Street	Stoker	R.N.	
McMordie, Alfred	201 Oldpark Road	Gunner	R.F.A.	
Mahood, Thos. J.	16 Linden Gardens	Sergeant	14th R.I.R.	
Mark, Thomas	17 Ballycarry Street	Sergeant	15th R.I.R.	
Minnis, Robert	267 Oldpark Road	Private	A.S.C.	Prisoner.
Mooney, Daniel	40 Ballyclare Street	Private	R.A.M.C.	
Murdock, Wm.	12 Oldpark Village	Private	15th R.I.R.	
Murdock, Wm., Junr.	12 Oldpark Village	Private	3rd R.I.R.	
Neill, Robert	9 Ballymoney Street	Private	15th R.I.R.	Killed in Action.
Patton, Wm.	4 Ballycastle Street	Private	R.I. Fus.	Wounded.
Ramsey, James	405 Oldpark Road	Private	N.I.H.	
Ramsey, Thomas	405 Oldpark Road	Seaman	R.N.	
Reid, Samuel	68 Roseleigh Street	Corporal	17th R.I.R.	Wounded.
Risk, Harold	24 Clifton Drive	Corporal	14th R.I.R.	
Robertson, Robert	6 Cliftonville Street	Private	14th R.I.R.	Wounded.
Russell, William	176 Oldpark Road	Bombardier	R.G.A.	
Sloane, A. C.	21 Manor Street	Private	R.A.M.C.	

(142)

BELFAST PRESBYTERY. OLDPARK.

Name.	Home Address.	Rank.	Regiment, Battalion or Unit.	Remarks.
Smith, James	14 Oldpark Village	Seaman	R.N.R.	
Smyth, Thomas	Kingsmere Avenue	Private	R.A.F.	
Sterling, Robert H.	10 Avonbeg Street	Trooper	N.I.H.	
Streight, Robert	40 Hillview Street	Private	Royal Air Craft	
Streight, Thomas	40 Hillview Street	Private	R.A.M.C.	
Stuart, John H.	50 Newington Street	Private	R.F.A.	Wounded.
Sullivan, Thos. H.	Knutsford Drive	2nd Lieutenant	13th R.I.R.	Wounded.
Thompson, Jas. H.	8 Westland Gardens	Engineer	H.M.S. Hunsbrook	
Thompson, Thos. J.	40 Linwood Street	Gunner	R.F.A.	Wounded.
Weir, Hugh	37 Linwood Street	Private	Royal South Downs	Killed in Action.
Weir, Wm.	37 Linwood Street	Private	15th R.I.R.	
Wilkinson, David	427 Oldpark Road	Private	7th R.I.R.	Wounded.
Wilson, David	29 Vistula Street	Private	R.A.M.C.	Wounded.
Wilson, Isaac	29 Vistula Street	Private	R.A.M.C.	
Wilson, John	9 Linwood Street	Private	15th R.I.R.	Killed in Action.
Wilson, Joseph	29 Vistula Street	Private	15th R.I.R.	
Wilson, Wm.	9 Linwood Street	Private	15th R.I.R.	M.M.
COLONIAL FORCES.				
Carothers, Alen	120 Oldpark Avenue		Can. E.F.	
Comer, Herbert	62 Charleville Street		Can. E.F.	
Falls, Joseph	208 Oldpark Road		Aust. E.F.	
McNabb, John	Stratheden Street		Can. E.F.	Killed in Action.
ORMISTON.				
Bell, Alex.	Ballyhackamore	Private	N.I.H.	Wounded.
Bell, Thomas	Ballyhackamore	Private	14th R.I.R.	
Bell, William	Ballyhackamore		R.A.F.	
Bottcher, Henry	29 Kerrsland Crescent	Private	18th R.I.R.	Wounded.
Boyd, Robert	10 Sandown Road	Private	R.F.A.	
Browne, Fred.	Kensington Road	Private	R.M.L.I.	
Carlisle, Wm.	Ormiston Park	Corporal	18th R.I.R.	Killed in Action.
Coates, Samuel	21 Sinclair Street	Private	8th R.I.R.	
Corry, Robert	4 Bethany Street		R.N.	
Corry, Robert, Jun.	4 Bethany Street	Private	A.S.C.	
Corry, William	4 Bethany Street	Corporal	4th R.I.F.	Killed in Action.
Crilly, Robert	15 Irvine Street	Corporal	16th R.I.R.	Twice Wounded.
Davis, Robert	Sydenham	Private	N.I.H.	
Dickey, John	Ormiston Gardens	Private	8th R.I.R.	Wounded.
Donaldson, Robert	5 Irvine Street	Private	8th R.I.R.	Wounded.
Duffield, Harry	Knock	Private	A.S.C.	
Duffield, Hugh	Knock	Private	A.S.C.	
Fisher, John	Ballyhackamore	Private	8th R.I.R.	
Fisher, Samuel	Ballyhackamore	Private	8th R.I.R.	Wounded.
Fraser, Henry	Ballyhackamore	Private	17th R.I.R.	
Garnett, John	19 Wilcar Street	Private	16th R.I.R.	Wounded.
Garnett, Thomas	19 Wilcar Street	Private	6th Innis. Dragoons	
Garnett, Wm.	19 Wilcar Street	Private	R.E.	
Gourly, Samuel	9 Hillview Avenue	Private	8th R.I.R.	
Hamilton, H. B.	5 Houston Street	Private	6th R.I.R.	Twice Wounded.
Hamilton, R.	5 Houston Street	Private	4th R.I.F.	Killed in Action.
Hamilton, W. J.	5 Houston Street	Private	6th R.I.F.	Wounded.
Hanna, Samuel	2 Castleview Terrace	Private	14th R.I.R.	Wounded.
Hanna, Wm.	2 Castleview Terrace	Private	10th Canadian Force	
Herron, Samuel	24 Sandown Road	Private	R.E.	
Hewitt, Joseph	16 Sandown Road	Private	4th R.I.R.	
Hewitt, Robert John	16 Sandown Road	Private	8th R.I.R.	
Hudson, Wm.	69 Sandown Road	Private	8th R.I.R.	Killed in Action.
Hynes, George	36 Houston Street	Private	25th Seaforth Highldrs.	
Hynes, Robert	36 Houston Street	Private	9th R.I.R.	Wounded.
Hynes, Samuel	36 Houston Street	Private	8th R.I.R.	Killed in Action.
Jackson, Wm.	10 Castlereagh Street	Private	14th R.I.R.	Killed in Action.
Johnston, E. S.	Charlotte Villas	Private	14th R.I.R.	Wounded.
Jones, Thos. Wally	108 Montrose Street	Sergeant	R.I.F.	
Kennedy, R.	141 Parkgate Avenue	Private	M.T.	
Kerr, G. P.	Ormiston Gardens		R.N.	
Little, Harry	7 Houston Street	Private	R.F.A.	Wounded.
McDougall, F.	Sandown Road	Private	M.T.	
McIlvenny, David	17 Houston Street	Private	17th R.I.R.	
McKee, James	1 Irvine Street	Private	16th R.I.R.	Wounded.
McKee, John	1 Irvine Street	Private	16th R.I.R.	Wounded.
McKee, Richard	1 Irvine Street	Private	R.E.	Wounded.
McKee, Wm.	1 Irvine Street		R.N.	
Montgomery, Robert	15 Sinclair Street	Private	9th R.I.R.	Killed in Action.
Montgomery, Wm.	15 Sinclair Street		N.I.H.	
Percy, Ernest	14 Ebrington Gardens	2nd Lieutenant	Inn. Dragoons	Wounded.
Percy, T. R.	14 Ebrington Gardens		R.N.	
Proctor, H.	Southview	Private	8th R.I.R.	
Reid, Charles	13 Irvine Street	Lance-Corporal	20th R.I.R.	Wounded.
Reid, Samuel	13 Irvine Street	Private	20th R.I.R.	
Richie, Samuel	44 Hillview Avenue	Private	M.T.	
Robson, David	41 Dundela Street		6th R.I.R.	Wounded.

BELFAST PRESBYTERY.   ORMISTON.

Name.	Home Address.	Rank.	Regiment, Battalion or Unit.	Remarks.
ROBSON, JOHN	11 Dundela Street	...	16th R.I.R.	
RODGERS, JAMES	20 Houston Street	...	2nd L.F	Wounded.
RODGERS, SAMUEL	20 Houston Street	...	R.I.F.	Killed in Action.
SCULES, JOHN	16 Sandown Road	...	Cycling Corps	
SLOANE, DAVID	42 Oakland Avenue	2nd Lieutenant	16th R.I.R.	M. Cross.
SLOANE, WM. R.	42 Oakland Avenue	2nd Lieutenant	3rd London Rifles	
SMITH, R.	Anchorage, Cregagh	...	R.A.F.	
SMYTH, HUGH	42 Sandown Road	Private	20th R.I.R.	
STEWART, W. J.	10 Houston Street	...	1st Garr. Batt. R.I.R.	
TEMPLETON, J. C.	71 Belmont Ch. Road	Corporal	14th R.I.R.	Wounded.
TEMPLETON, R.	71 Belmont Ch. Road	Corporal	Seaforth Highldrs.	
THOMPSON, DAVID	16 Sinclair Street	Private	2nd R.I.F.	
TORRENS, J. C.	Knock	Lieutenant	14th R.I.R.	Killed in Action.
VANCE, CHARLES	9 Irvine Street	Corporal	8th R.I.R.	Twice Wounded.
VANCE, FRED.	1 Irvine Street	Private	6th R.I.R.	Wounded.
VANCE, JAMES	8 Sandown Road	Private	8th R.I.R.	
VANCE, JOSEPH	1 Irvine Street	Private	6th R.I.R.	Killed in Action.
VANCE, ROBERT	9 Irvine Street	Lance-Corporal	10th R.I.R.	Wounded.
VANCE, ROBERT	265 Up. N'ards Road	Private	R.A.F.	
VANCE, SAMUEL	44 Sandown Road	Private	14th R.I.R.	Wounded.
WALKER, HENRY	...	...	R.N.	
WARD, FRANCIS	18 Sandown Road	Private	8th R.I.R.	
WARD, HAMILTON	18 Sandown Road	...	3rd Batt. S.H.	
WARD, SAMUEL	18 Sandown Road	Private	R.F.A.	
WARD, W. J.	18 Sandown Road	Private	5th Seaforth Highldrs.	Wounded.
WATSON, ROBERT	13 Houston Street	Private	R.A.S.C.	
WATSON, THOMAS	13 Houston Street	...	10th R.I.R.	Killed in Action.
WHITESIDE, WM.	5 Irvine Street	Private	8th R.I.R.	
YOUNG, JOHN	9 Houston Street	Private	M.T.	
RAVENHILL ROAD.				
AGNEW, RICHARD	Sunwich Street	Private		
AGNEW, SAMUEL	Sunwich Street	Private		
BAGLEY, JAMES	Park Parade	Private		
BINGHAM, DAVID	Coburg Street	Private		
BLACK, ROBERT J.	Woodstock Road	Private		
BOYD, GILBERT	My Lady's Road	Private		
BUICK, JAMES	Rosslyn Street			
CHAMBERS, THOMAS	...			
COATES, HAMILTON	India			
COCHRANE, ERNEST	Cregagh Road	2nd Lieutenant		
COCHRANE, HUGH	Cregagh Road	Lance-Corporal		
CRAIG, FRED	Ravenhill Street	Private		
CRAIG, ROBERT W.	Redcar Street	2nd Lieutenant		
CUNNINGHAM, ALFRED	Ravenhill Road	Private		
DAVISON, E.	Ardenlee Parade			
DOUGLAS, BERTIE	Ravenhill Avenue	Private		
ESDALE, JOHN C.	Delhi Street	Sergeant		
ESDALE, SAMUEL	Delhi Street	Sergeant		
FRAZER, ROBERT	Ardenlee Avenue			
FRAZER, THOMAS	Ardenlee Avenue	Private		
GALBRAITH, JAMES	...			
GIFFIN, ROBERT	Rosslyn Street			
GILCHRIST, JOHN	Sherwood Street	Private		
GILL, JOHN	Ravenhill Avenue			
GILL, WILLIAM	Ravenhill Avenue	Private		
GILLESPIE, WM. J.	My Lady's Road			
GORDON, JOHN	...	Private		
HALL, THOMAS	Rosetta Park			
HILLIS, SAMUEL	Richardson Street			
HILLIS, THOMAS	Richardson Street			
IRWIN, WILLIAM	...			Killed in Action.
JOHNSTON, JOHN	Shamrock Street			
JOHNSTON, STEWART	Ravenhill Terrace	2nd Lieutenant		
JOHNSTON, WM.	Shamrock Street			
KELLY, JAMES	Mount Street			
KELLY, WILLIAM	Mount Street			
KERNOHAN, HUGH	Killowen Street			
LARMOUR, GEORGE	Fitzroy Avenue	Private		Killed in Action.
LARMOUR, JAMES	Roseberry Road			
LARMOUR, JAMES	Roseberry Road	Petty Officer		
LARMOUR, JOHN	Fitzroy Avenue			
LARMOUR, JOSEPH	Roseberry Road			
LARMOUR, WM.	Fitzroy Avenue			
LENNON, JAMES	Donard Street			Killed in Action.
LENNON, THOMAS	Donard Street			Killed in Action.
LYTTLE, JAMES	Willowholme			
McCHESNEY, DOUGLAS	Omeath Street		R.N.	
McCONNELL, ALEX.	My Lady's Road	Lance-Corporal	R.N.	
McCONNELL, SAMUEL	My Lady's Road	Lance-Corporal		
McCOUBREY, SAMUEL J.	Rochester Street			
McCRACKEN, JAMES	Albertbridge Road			
McGEOWN, JACK	University Avenue	2nd Lieutenant		Killed in Action.

BELFAST PRESBYTERY.   RAVENHILL ROAD

Name.	Home Address.	Rank.	Regiment, Battalion or Unit.	Remarks.
McGeown, Thomas	University Avenue	...	...	
McKee, William	Balfour Avenue	...	...	
McKeown, Thomas	Ranleigh Street	...	...	
Martin, Harold	Ravenhill Avenue	Sergeant	...	
Millar, Albert	Glendower Street	...	...	
Millar, John	Glendower Street	Sergeant	...	
Morrow, Herbert	Ardenlee Avenue	Sergeant	...	
Morrow, Stanley	Ardenlee Avenue	...	...	
Murphy, W. J.	Roslyn Street	Sergeant	...	
Orr, David	Channing Street	...	...	Killed in Action.
Orr, Samuel	Albertbridge Road	...	...	
Patton, Arthur	Reid Street	...	...	Killed in Action.
Ritchie, James	Donard Street	...	...	Killed in Action.
Robertson, Malcolm	...	...	...	
Robinson, Harry	London Street	...	...	
Robinson, James	London Street	...	...	
Robinson, Wm.	Donard Street	...	...	Killed in Action.
Rooney, John	Delaware Street	...	...	
Ross, Herbert	Park Parade	Lance-Corporal	...	
Seaton, Donald	Delaware Street	Corporal	...	
Shields, James	...	...	...	
Stevenson, Thomas	...	...	...	
Vance, Harry	Donard Street	...	...	
Watson, Jas. Ross	Fitzroy Avenue	...	...	
Wasson, George	Park Parade	...	...	
Wasson, Wm.	Park Parade	...	...	
Weir, John	...	...	...	
COLONIAL FORCE.				
Finlay, George	...	...	Canadians	
Finlay, Robert	...	...	Canadians	
Hall, William	...	...	Canadians	
Heron, Jack	...	Sergeant	Canadians	
Honar, George	...	...	Canadians	
Orr, Arthur	...	...	Canadians	
Weir, Norman	...	...	Canadians	
ROSEMARY STREET.				
Anderson, William	236 York Street	Corporal	A.S.C.	
Atkinson, Harry	77 Glasgow Street	Private	14th R.I.R.	
Aspell, Robert C.	238 Leopold Street	A.B.	H.M.S.	
Aspell, Joseph	238 Leopold Street	Lieutenant	A.S.C.	
Adair, Samuel	2 Sackville Street	Private	A.S.C.	
Archer, Joseph	249 Oldpark Road	Lance-Corporal	8th R.I.R.	Wounded.
Alexander, William	166 Roden Street	Private	14th R.I.R.	Military Medal.
Austin, John	7 Clifton Street	Lieutenant	Mac. G. Corps	
Archer, Richard	131 York Road	Sergeant	U.S.A. Army	
Allen, John	4 Conlon Street	Private	R.M.L.C.	
Bailey, William	...	Private	R.A.M.C.	
Ballard, William	84 Glenwood Street	Private	R.A.M.C.	
Bellis, George R.	15 Memel Street	A.B.	Naval Reserve	Died.
Buick, John	44 Mount Street	Private	C.R.C.	
Best, A. J.	18 Ormeau Road	Captain	R.A.M.C.	
Brown, Wm.	11 Lt. George's Street	Private	R.E.	Killed in Action.
Bryce, George	24 Mountcharles	Lieutenant	R.N.V.R.	
Bill, John	61 University Street	Lieutenant	R.A.M.C.	Killed in Action.
Boyles, Robert	77 Wall Street	Lance-Corporal	17th R.I.R.	
Boyles, John	77 Wall Street	Private	16th R.I.R.	
Boyd, Alex.	79 Howard Street South	Private	10th R.I.R.	
Bond, Harry	33 Jennymount Street	Private	A.S.C.	
Bothwell, Thomas	7 Hatfield Street	Private	5th Can. In. Brig.	
Boyd, Samuel	79 Howard Street South	Private	10th R.I.R.	
Burgess, Samuel	131 Tennent Street	Private	109th F.A.	Prisoner of War.
Bell, John	5 Clanmorris Street	Private	R.E.	
Bond, Thomas	33 Jennymount Street	Private	R.A.M.C.	
Brown, David	29 Bute Street	Private	9th R.I. Fus.	
Boyd, Wm.	Sancroft Street	Private	15th R.I.R.	Killed in Action.
Bingham, Henry	54 Westland Street	Private	9th R.I.R.	Missing.
Bond, Robert	Donegall Road	...	H.M.S.	
Bell, Samuel	5 Claremorris Street	Private	6th R.I.R.	
Baxter, Richard	25 Hillman Street	Private	R.I.R.	Killed in Action.
Barrett, David	22 Shannon Street	Private	A.S.C.	
Bell, Joseph	2 Shaftesbury Street	Private	R.I.R.	Lost at sea.
Brown, John	2 Thomas Street	Private	R.A.M.C.	
Bryson, Thomas	136 Nelson Street	Private	15th R.I.R.	Prisoner of War.
Bryson, Robert	136 Nelson Street	Private	20th R.I.R.	
Bell, Ernest	43 Third Street	Private	R.A.M.C.	Prisoner of War.
Barr, James	21 Ivan Street	Private	R.A.M.C.	M.M., Pris. of War.
Bennett, Harry	28 Q. Victoria Gdns.	Private	14th R.I.R.	
Boyles, W. J.	22 Orkney Street	Private	R.I. Fus.	Killed in Action.
Blackwood, George	43 Beechpark Street	Private	R.I.R.	Killed in Action.
Barrett, Samuel	22 Shannon Street	Corporal	S. Lancs.	Died of Wounds.

BELFAST PRESBYTERY. ROSEMARY STREET.

Name.	Home Address.	Rank.	Regiment, Battalion or Unit.	Remarks.
Brooks, Wm.	Tramway Street	Private	R. Inn. Fus.	Killed in Action.
Brown, Hugh	Corporation Street	A.B.	H.M.S.	
Bristow, John	48 Canmore Street	Private	R.I.R.	
Branagh, John	3 Abbey Street W.	Stoker	H.M.S.	
Brooks, Henry	Tramway Street	Private	R.E., E. Ex. F.	
Bristow, Wm.	7 Bisley Street	Lance-Corporal	R.I.R.	
Burns, George	23 Nile Street	Private	9th R.I.R.	Killed in Action.
Burgess, Ernest	131 Tennent Street	Lance-Corporal	R.I.R.	
Bell, Geo. S.	6 Earl Street	A.B.	H.M.S.	Lost at sea.
Boyd, Harry	78 Hillman Street	Sergeant	R.I.R.	Lost at sea.
Barnes, Wm.	60 Sixth Street	Private	A.S.C.	
Bleakley, Robert	Craig's Cot., Whitehouse	Private	R.I.R.	Killed in Action.
Barkley, James	165 Earl Street	Private	R.I.R.	Killed in Action.
Birney, S. A.	28 Earl Street	A.B.	H.M.S.	
Birney, James	28 Earl Street	A.B.	H.M.S.	
Brooks, Hamilton	6 Tramway Street	Private	3rd Dorsets	
Bowes, William	56 Clanmorris Street	Stoker	H.M.S.	
Bowes, William	9 Cambridge Street	Private	9th R.I.R.	Wounded.
Bristow, Thomas	49 Canmore Street	Private	R.I.R.	Killed.
Brown, Alfred	Depot Terrace	Private	Winnipeg Rifles	
Boyd, Thomas	Duncairn Gardens	Private	14th R.I.R.	
Burke, James	Garmoyle Terrace	Private	15th R.I.R.	
Bowman, John	9 Crossby Street	Private	H.L.I.	Prisoner of War.
Carmichael, Janie	Lismore, Windsor Avenue		Soldiers' Club, Rouen	
Carmichael, Charles	Lismore, Windsor Av.	Private	" Reserve "	
Carmichael, Robert	Lismore, Windsor Av.	Private	Can. Contg.	
Campbell, Ernest	Q. Victoria Gardens	Private	R.I.R.	
Campbell, C. S.	37 Hillview Street	Lance-Corporal	17th R.I.R.	Wounded 5 times.
Campbell, James	31 Up. Townsend Street	Private	R.E.	
Campbell, William	131 York Road	Private	R.I.R.	Prisoner of War.
Callendar, Jack	10 Earl Street	Private	15th R.I.R.	
Currie, Wm.	41 Royal Avenue	Private	R.I.R.	Killed in Action.
Cairns, James	40 Jamison Street	Sergeant	10th R.I.R.	M. Medal.
Cunningham, Hugh	22 Steen Street	Air Mechanic	R.A.F.	
Currie, John	15 Nile Street	Private	110th F.A.	
Creighton, James	Various lodgings	Private	19th R.I.R.	
Crawford, David	Craigavad Street	Private	2nd R.I.R.	
Connolly, Wm. J.	26 Sixth Street	A.B.	H.M.S.	
Charters, Brice	8 Marine Street	Corporal	Tank Corps	
Cousins, Isaac	52 Sixth Street	Private	R. Irish Fus.	Killed in Action.
Cunningham, George	8 Earl Street	Private	R.I.R.	
Courtney, George	249 Oldpark Road	Private	9th R.I.R.	
Close, Samuel	50 Dundee Street	Private	R. Inn. Fus.	
Caughey, Wm.	28 Newport Street	Private	R.I.R.	
Cooper, Joseph	21 Delaware Street	Private	R.A.M.C.	Prisoner of War.
Colville, Samuel	73 Alexandra Park Av.	Sergeant	20th Hussars	
Clyde, Thomas	Earl Place	Sergeant	R.F.A.	Wounded.
Cardwell, Samuel	104 Snugville Street		H.M.S.	
Carson, Robert	41 Carnalea Street	Private	19th R.I.R.	
Campbell, Archie		A.B.	H.M.S.	
Cinnamond, Geo.	Marine Street	Private	2nd R.I.R.	Prisoner of War.
Craig, David	4 Earl Street	Private	R.E.	
Craig, Robert	4 Earl Street	Private	17th R.I.R.	Wounded.
Craig, Samuel	4 Earl Street	Private	2nd R.I.R.	Killed.
Craig, John	4 Earl Street	A.B.	H.M.S.	
Campbell, Frank	38 Hillview Street	Private	R.I.R.	Wounded.
Connor, Byron		Private	Canadians	
Carrick, John		Private	A. & S. Highldrs.	
Cook, George	17 Ayr Street	Private	R.I.R.	
Cooper, Albert	Dunmurry	Private	R.I.R.	Prisoner of War.
Crowe, Edward	99 Mayo Street	A.B.	H.M.S.	
Crawford, R.	9 Up. Townsend Street	Private	R.I.R.	
Craig, John	7 Springmount Street	A.B.	H.M.S.	
Cunningham, Josias	Fernhill	Sub-Lieutenant	R.N.V.R.	
Crawford, James	Craigavad Street	O.S.	H.M.S.	
Dalgleish, R. W.	152 Mountcollyer St.	Sergeant	14th R.I.R.	
Dunwoody, John	7 Sheridan Street	Corporal	1st R.I.R.	Wounded.
Diamond, James	81 Ravenhill Road	Private	14th R.I.R.	
Dennison, Samuel	16 Jennymount Street	Private	18th Manchester Regt.	Missing, Killed.
Dickson, Edward	18 Lilliput Street	Private	R.E., M.E.F.	Killed.
Dunn, Tom	4 Earl Street	Private	15th R.I.R.	
Daly, Wm.	5 Mountcollyer Road	Private	15th R.I.R.	
Dougan, Fred.	134 Roden Street	Sergeant	R.E.	
Dixon, Ross	6 Carnalea Street	Private	17th R.I.R.	
Dickson, R.	Hanna Street	Lance-Corporal	R. Inn. Fus.	Wounded.
Duggan, Humphrey	41 Seventh Street	Private	R.I.R.	Died of Wounds.
Doran, J.	Greencastle	Private	57th Bat. R.F.A.	
Duggan, Matt.	41 Seventh Street	Private	R.I.R.	
Dickson, Thomas	18 Lilliput Street	Private	R.A.M.C.	
Dykes, George	114 Mountcollyer Av.	Private	15th R.I.R.	Prisoner of War
Drummond, Wm.	6 Sixth Street	Private	R. Irish Regt.	
Davidson, Wm.	94 N. Howard Street	Private	R.I.R.	
Dougan, T. J.	167 Canmore Street	Private	R.I.R.	
Dinsmore, Samuel	Mountcollyer Road	Private	3rd R.I.R.	

(146)

BELFAST PRESBYTERY. ROSEMARY STREET.

Name.	Home Address.	Rank.	Regiment, Battalion or Unit.	Remarks.
Duff, James	122 Ormeau Road	Lieutenant	R.E.	Wounded.
Davidson, Thomas	120 Nelson Street	Private	R.I.R.	
English, Joseph	Hopeton Street	Private	19th R.I.R.	
Ellis, Wm.	22 Fleet Street	Private	14th R.I.R.	
Evans, Wm.		Private	S. Staffs.	Prisoner of War.
Elliott, Samuel	29 Matlock Street	Private	R.E., Mesopotamia	
Elliott, Cecil	4 Windsor Gardens	Private	R.A.F.	
Ferris, George	20 Vernon Street	Sergeant	9th R.I.R.	Wounded.
Fowler, Johnson	42 Weaver Street	Private	15th R.I.R.	Wounded.
Freeman, John	27 Trafalgar Street	Private	R.I.R.	Killed in Action.
Fullerton, John	North Ann Street	Private	15th R.I.R.	
Foster, Wm.	Lodgings	Private	5th R.I.R	
Ferris, Wesley	84 North Howard St.	A.B.	H.M.S. Racoon	Lost at sea.
Flanagan, James	29 North Ann St.	Private	R.M. Fus.	Wounded.
Flanagan, John	29 North Ann St.	Private	R.M. Fus.	Pris. War. B'garia.
Finnegan, Dr. John	23 Botanic Avenue	Captain	R.A.M.C.	Military Cross.
Finnegan, Robert	23 Botanic Avenue	Private	M.T. A.S.C.	Died of Wounds.
Foley, Ernest	7 Dundela Gardens	Private	5th Can. Reserves	
Fleming, Joseph	48 Broadbent Street	Private	14th R.I.R.	Died of Wounds.
Grant, James	15 Mountcollyer Road	Private	A.S.C.	
Gordon, Alex.	20 Balfour Avenue	Corporal	M.T. A.S.C.	
Graham, J.	N. Queen Street	Private	A.S.C.	
Gray, Hugh	4 Sackville Street	Private	R.E.	
Gray, Alex.	4 Sackville Street	Private	9th R.I.R.	Killed in Action.
Graham, George	25 Paris Street	Private	R.I.R.	
Gilmore, Harry	2 Sixth Street	Private	R.I.R.	
Graham, R.	22 Rathlin Street	Private	A.S.C.	
Gilmore, David	2 Sixth Street	Private	R.I.R.	
Graham, Gerald	North Queen Street	A.B.	H.M.S.	
Graham, Ernest	N. Queen Street	Lance-Corporal	R.I.R.	
Gilliland, Edward	9 North Thomas Street	Private	15th R.I.R.	Wounded.
Gilmore, Samuel	2 Sixth Street	Private	R.A.M.C.	
Gilmore, Matt.	Shankill Road	Private	R.F.A.	
George, John	Nelson Street	Private	C.R's.	Killed in Action.
Gilmore, James	17 Seventh Street	Private	Aust. L.I.	
Glasgow, Thomas	34 Fourth Street	Private	R.F.A.	
Glasgow, Robert	34 Fourth Street	Private	R.F.A.	Killed in Action.
Gamble, Robert	Earl Place	Private	15th R.I.R.	
Gamble, Henry	Earl Place	Private	M.E.F.	
Grey, Robert	74 South Parade	Private	9th R.I.R.	
Gamble, Wm.	Earl Place	Private	15th R.I.R.	
Gibson, John	12 Trafalgar Street	Private	9th R.I.R.	
Grant, E.	Thomas Street	Private	1st R.I.R.	
Grant, George	Thomas Street	Private	A. & S. H.	
George, Wm.	67 Crosby Street	Private	R.A.M.C.	M.M., Pris. of War.
Graham, George		Private	R.I.R.	
Graham, W. J.	97 Whitla Street	Private	R. Marines Batt.	
Grant, Abr.	Thomas Street	Private	R.I.R.	
Graham, William	22 Rathlin Street	Private	R.I.R.	
Green, Alfred	46 Mountcollyer Street	Private	A.S.C.	
Gordon, J.	20 Balfour Avenue	Private	M.T. A.S.C.	
Hamilton, James	20 Fitzwilliam Street	Lieutenant	R.I.R., Eg. Ex. Force	
Hamilton, J. G.	10 Fairview Street	M. at Arms	"Olympic"	
Harrison, Albert	43 Waring Street	Corporal	R.I.R.	Died of Wounds.
Humphries, T. L.	72 North Parade	Corporal	R.I.R.	Prisoner of War.
Hume, Wm.	27 Tudor Place	A.B.	H.M.S.	
Heenan, David	62 Oberon Street	A.B.	H.M.S.	
Hull, John	6 Earl Street	Driver	R.I. Fus.	
Hull, Wm.	6 Earl Street	Private	R.I.R.	
Haslett, John	43 Seventh Street	Private	R.I.R.	
Hanna, John	12 Hanna Street	Private	17th R.I.R.	
Hughes, Wm.	86 Henry Street	A.B.	H.M.S.	
Hogg, F.	6 Sussex Street	Private	R.I.R.	Killed in Action.
Harper, Martin	18 Earl Street	Private	R.E.	
Hermon, Wm.	32 Lime Street	Private	14th R.I.R.	Wounded.
Hazley, F.	20 Jamison Street	Private	R.I.R.	
Harrison, J.	Sussex Street	Private	R.E.	
Hill, David	30 Wilton Street	Lance-Corporal	R.I.R.	
Horner, F.	Seaview Street	Private	18th R.I.R.	
Hanna, Henry	12 Hanna Street	Private	15th R.I.R.	
Harkness, Hugh	Argyle Street	Private	3rd R.I.R.	Died of Wounds.
Harris, Hugh	32 Linwood Street	Sergt.-Major	109th L.T.M.B.	M.M., Wounded.
Heenan, Harry	62 Oberon Street	A.B.	H.M.S.	
Henderson, Robert	Hanna Street	Private	15th R.I.R.	Killed in Action.
Hagan, Joe	25 York Road	Private	R.E.	
Hoey, F.	102 Nelson Street	Private	A.S.C.	
Harper, Charles	18 Earl Street	Private	19th R.I.R.	
Howes, W.	48 Earl Street	Private	4th R.I.R.	
Hart, Wm.	71 Hopeton Street	Private	R. Warw. Regt.	
Hayden, D.	1 Coolderry Street	Private	R.I.R.	
Hobbs, James	Hanna Street	Private	R.I.R.	
Hughes, Isaac	71 Tennent Street	Private	U.S.A. Army	
Hughes, Shep.	71 Tennent Street	Private	U.S.A. Army	
Humphries, Jack	92 North Parade	Private	A.S.C.	

BELFAST PRESBYTERY. **ROSEMARY STREET.**

Name.	Home Address.	Rank.	Regiment, Battalion or Unit.	Remarks.
HILL, JACK	18 Nore Street	Private	London Irish Rifles	Prisoner of War.
HILL, HARRY	18 Nore Street	Private	N. Lanc. Regt.	
HENDERSON, WM.	Hanna Street	Private	15th R.I.R.	Killed in Action.
HAYES, ALLAN	Leadbetter Street	Private	R.I.R.	
HEENAN, JOHN	62 Oberon Street	Private	R.I.R.	
HOEY, CHARLES	84 Wilson Street	Private	M.T. A.S.C.	
HAIRE, JAMES	...	Private	U.S.A. Army	
HALLEY, JAMES	...	Private	A.S.C.	
IRWIN, ROBERT	Isabella Street	Private	15th R.I.R.	
IRVINE, ARTHUR	8 Denmark Street	Private	14th R.I.R.	
JENKINS, EDWARD	5 Sixth Street	Private	R.I.R.	Killed in Action.
JOHNSTON, EDWARD	3 Seventh Street	Corporal	R.I.R.	
JOHNSON, SAMUEL	9 Glenwood Street	Corporal	A.S.C.	
JOHNSTON, WM.	29 Mervue Street	Private	R.I.R.	
JOHNSTON, ALEX.	27 N. Boundary Street	Private	R.I.R.	Died of Wounds.
JOHNSTON, JAMES	14 St. Vincent Street	Corporal	R.E.	Wounded.
JOHNSTON, WM.	46 Fourth Street	Private	R.I.R.	
JOHNSTONE, JOSIAS	14 St. Vincent Street	Staff Sergt.	A.O.C., E.E.F.	
JAMIESON, D.	65 Hopeton Street	Private	M.T.A.S.C.	
JOHNSTONE, HARRY	14 St. Vincent Street	Private	T.W.T. R.E.	
JOHNSTONE, ANDREW	...	Sergeant	75th Batt. Can.	Killed in Action.
JACKSON, JOHN	Lewis Street	Private	15th R.I.R.	Killed in Action.
KERR, ROBERT	10 Barrow Street	Private	R.A.M.C.	
KNOX, DAVID	10 Rowan Street	Private	R.I.R.	Prisoner of War.
KIRK, JOHN	243 Oldpark Road	Corporal	R.I.R.	
KNOX, JOHN	40 Lower York Street	A.B.S.	R.N.R.	
KIRK, EDWARD	8 Craig's Terrace	Lance-Corporal	R.I.R.	
KENNEDY, D.	64 Northumberland St.	Sergeant	R.I.R.	
KENNEDY, DAVID	16 Clanmorris Street	Private	15th R.I.R.	Wd., Pris. of War.
KEITH, JAMES	33 Gainsboro' Drive	Private	15th R.I.R.	
KERR, JAMES	10 Barrow Street	A.B.	H.M.S.	
KERR, SAMUEL	10 Barrow Street	Private	R.F.A.	
KERR, JOHN	7 Rutherford Street	Private	A.S.C.	
KENNEDY, F. J.	Nelson Street	Private	A.S.C.	
KELLY, JOHN	5 Rotterdam Street	Private	1 R. Irish Fus.	
KELLS, JOS.	15 Lindsay Street	Lance-Corporal	L. N. Lancs.	Prisoner of War.
LOWRY, HARRY	8 Candahar Street	Captain	A.V.C.	Died of Cholera.
LEITH, SAMUEL	154 Mountcollyer Street	Lieutenant	1/5 York & Lanc. Regt.	
LARMOR, WM.	252 Conway Street	Private	R.I.R.	
LORIMER, ANDREW	7 Donnybrook Street	R.Q.M.	9th R.I.R.	
LOCKHART, J.	155 Silvio Street	Private	R.I.F.	
LYNAS, JOHN	4 St. Mary's Street	Sergeant	R.I.R.	
LEE, SAMUEL	Townsend Street	Lieutenant	4th R. Irish Fus.	
LEWIS, ANDREW	88 N. Howard Street	Private	N.I.H.	Prisoner of War.
LARKHAM, HENRY	14 Earl Street	Private	5th R.I.R.	Killed in Action.
LILBURN, HENRY K.	Dunedin, Belfast	Private	Can. Contg.	Wounded.
LIVINGSTONE, RICH.	14 James Street	Private	Can. Contg.	
LEDLIE, R. J.	6 Strangemore Terrace	Captain	R.A.M.C.	
LEDLIE, E. R.	6 Strangemore Terrace	Lieutenant	6th R.I.R., E.E.F.	Wounded, M.C.
LAVERY, JOHN	8 North Thomas Street	Private	R.I.R.	Died of Wounds.
LILLICRAP, J. H.	...	P.O.1	H.M.S. Glorious	
LYSKE, H.	30 Devonshire Street	Private	R.I.R.	
MYERS, ROBERT	48 Fife Street	A.B.	Trawlers, R.N.	
MURRAY, JOHN	Mountcollyer Road	Private	A.S.C.	
MAGILL, JOHN	76 Cambrai Street	Corporal	C. Corps	
MEHAFFY, WM.	14 Portallo Street	Private	R.I.R.	
MERCER, T. W.	31 Berlin Street	A.B.	H.M.S. "Electra"	
MALCOLM, HENRY	4 Fourth Street	Private	R.I.R.	
McCLATCHIE, W. A.	14 Donegall Sq. W.	Corporal	R.F.C.	M.C.
McCLURKIN, THOMAS	Ashley Gardens	Captain	R.A.M.C.	
McCLEERY, JOHN	Bank Buildings	Private	L.E.R.	
MORROW, SAMUEL	122 Ormeau Road	Lieutenant	19th R.I.R.	
MILLIKEN, JOHN	76 Old Lodge Road	Private	15th R.I.R.	
McBRIDE, HENRY	11 University Street	Lieutenant	A.S.C.	
MATTHEWS, SAMUEL	Central Fire Station	Sergeant	Cheshires	
MARSHALL, W. H.	Bank Buildings	Private	Can. Contg.	Prisoner of War.
MAGILL, ROBERT	2 Thorndale Avenue	Private	N.I.H.	Prisoner of War.
MOORHEAD, J.	13 St. Paul's Street	Private	R.A.M.C.	
MOORE, SAMUEL	33 Gainsboro' Drive	Private	15th R.I.R.	
MURRAY, W.	27 Mountcollyer Road	Private	6th R. Inn. Fus.	
MURPHY, JAMES	96 Henry Street	Sergeant	R. Inn. Fus.	Died of Wounds.
MURPHY, HENRY	18 Parker Street	Corporal	8th R.I.R.	Died of Wounds.
MOORHEAD, MATT.	13 St. Paul's Street	Private	R.A.M.C., E.E.F.	
MARSDEN, JAMES	3 Eighth Street	Private	9th R.I.R.	Killed in Action.
MITCHELL, JOSEPH	112 Earl Street	Private	15th R.I.R.	
MOORE, ROBERT	33 Gainsboro' Drive	Private	14th R.I.R.	
MARTIN, DAVID	19 Earl Street	Sergeant	A.O.C.	
MILLS, DAVID	Central Fire Station	Corporal	R.A.M.C.	
MEARNS, ROBERT	13 Lilliput Street	Private	R.A.M.C.	
MITCHELL, IRWIN	20 Clanmorris Street	Lance-Corporal	14th R.I.R.	Wounded.
MARTIN, ALBERT	31 Unity Street	V.A.	H.M.S.	
MARTIN, FRED.	19 Earl Street	Private	C. Corps	Wounded.
MONTGOMERY, GEORGE	...	Private	5th R.I.R.	
MILLIKEN, ANDREW	11 Oranmore Street	Lance-Corporal	R.I.R.	

BELFAST PRESBYTERY. ROSEMARY STREET.

NAME.	HOME ADDRESS.	RANK.	REGIMENT, BATTALION OR UNIT.	REMARKS.
MILLIGAN, JOHN	50 Lower York Street	Private	R.I.R.	
MILLAR, ROBERT	12 Nile Street	Private	15th R.I.R.	Killed.
McMULLAN, ROBERT	6 Geoffrey Street	Private	19th R.I.R.	Wounded.
McNAB, HUGH	3 Keadyville Avenue	Private	R.I.R.	Wounded.
McDONALD, JOHN	Central Fire Station	Stoker	Submarine	Lost at Sea.
McLELLAN, ALEX.	Old Cavehill Road	Private	N.I.H.	Pris. of War. M.M.
McCULLOUGH, J. S.	58 South Parade	Private	Can. Contg.	
McCONNELL, ISAAC	1 Roden Street	Sergeant	R.E.	Killed in Action.
MEWHA, JAMES	20 Sixth Street	Private	R.A.M.C.	
McGOOKIN, DANIEL	51 Meadow Street	Private	R.A.M.C.	
McILVEEN, JOHN	32 Gt. George's Street	Sergeant	12th R.I.R.	
McCONNELL, WM.	20 Fourth Street	Private	R.A.M.C.	
McKEAN, GEORGE	18 Canning Street	Private	15th R.I.R.	
McLEAN, JOHN	89 Lilliput Street	Private	Labour Corps	
McCULLOUGH, THOS.	54 Geoffrey Street	Private	R.F.A.	
McNIECE, JOHN	4 Hudson Street	Private	M.T. A.S.C.	
McCULLOUGH, H.	51 Townsend Street	Private	R.I.R.	
McKERGAN, JAMES	64 Agnes Street	Private	R.I.R.	
McILROY, JAMES	25 Rowan Street	Private	R.I.R.	Killed.
McCARROLL, JAMES	12 Lime Street	Private	14th R.I.R.	Missing.
McADOREY, JOSEPH	10 Clanmorris Street	Private	15th R.I.R.	Killed.
McDOWELL, THOMAS	40 Israel Street	A.B.	H.M.S.	
McDOWELL, THOMAS	26 Up. Charleville St.	Private	A.S.C.	
McMEEKIN, ALFRED	30 Linwood Street	Private	R.E.	
McCREA, WM.	14 Ship Street	Private	R.I.R.	
McCLURE, JOHN	15 Seventh Street	Sergeant	R.I.R.	
McLEAN, JOHN	32 Collyer Street	Private	R.I.R.	
McMINN, JAMES	15 Trafalgar Street	Private	1st R.I.R.	
McMINN, THOMAS	15 Trafalgar Street	Private	4th R.I.R.	
McCAW, JAMES	32 Limestone Road	Private	R.I.R.	
McCREADY, R.	43 Oldpark Road		H.M.S.	Lost at Sea.
McCRACKEN, WM.	63 Matchett Street	Private	R.I.R.	Killed in Action.
McCRACKEN, A.	8 Back Ship Street	Private	Hussars	Killed.
McCOMISH, WM.	5 Weir Street	Private	15th R.I.R.	
MACFARLANE, DAVID	24 Fifth Street	Private	R.A.M.C.	
MACFARLANE, JAMES	20 Harrisburg Street	Private	16th R.I.R.	
McCULLY, EDWARD	M'Tier Street	Corporal	1st R.I.R.	
McKERGAN, JOHN	60 Agnes Street	Private	N.I.H.	
McDOWELL, WILLIAM	107 Mountcollyer Av.	Sergeant	4th Hussars	
McILHAGGER, W. B.	42 Gainsboro Drive	Private	R.E.	
MACDONALD, HARRY	40 Little York Street	Private	S. Lancs.	
McALEES, THOMAS	20 Roxburgh Street	Private	8th R.I.R.	
McCLUNE, WILLIAM	17 Woodford Street	Private	6th Worcs.	
McCLURE, HUGH	9 Evolina Street	Private	R.I.R.	
McALLISTER, ROBERT	27 Clanmorris Street	Corporal	15th R.I.R.	
McCORMICK, WM.	31 Jennymount Street	Private	15th R.I.R.	Prisoner of War.
McCLUNE, JOHN	17 Woodford Street	A.B.	H.M.S.	
MACMILLAN, WM.	8 Grove Street	Private	M.G.C.	
McCAUGHRAN, WILSON	Albany Street	Private	R.I.R.	
McCLURE, JAMES	55 Glenwood Street	Private	R.I.R.	
McALPINE, W.	131 Little York Street	Sergeant	R.I.R.	
McCRUM, ALBERT	17 Ritchie Street	Private	R.A.M.C.	
McCARROLL, GEO.	14 Lime Street	Private	R.I.R	
MACDONALD, H.	36 Up. Townsend Street	Private	Seaforth Highldrs.	
McROBERTS, JOS.	Clanmorris Street	Private	R.I.R.	
McCAW, JOHN	32 N. Howard Street	Private	R. Inn. Fus.	
McCORMICK, ROBERT	31 Jennymount Street	Private	15th R.I.R.	Killed in Action.
McCAW, SAMUEL	Ambleside Street	Private	R.E.	
McCAW, STANLEY	North Parade	Private	M.T. A.S.C.	
McBRIDE, THOS. H.	York Street	Private	R.I.R.	
McKINNEY, WILLIAM	11 Berlin Street	Private	R.A.F.	
McCLURE, THOS.	55 Glenwood Street	Private	R.I.R.	
McMURRAY, W. J.	62 Earl Street	Private	16th R.I.R.	
McKAY, WM.	60 Hillview Street	Private	R.I.R.	
McKEOWN, HUGH	135 Lower York Street	Private	Liverpool Rifles	Wounded.
McCORMICK, ROBERT	31 Jennymount Street	Private	R.T.F., Salonika	Wounded.
McKEOWN, MARTIN	135 Little York Street	Private	9th R.I.R.	
McKINNIE, WM.	78 Hopeton Street	Private	R.E.	
McCOY, A.	Harrisburg Street	Private	R.I.R.	Wounded.
McALLISTER, ALEX.	Nile Street	Private	2nd R.I.R.	Killed.
McMINN, JACK	Cross Street	Private	R.E.	Killed.
McCORMICK, JOHN	31 Jennymount Street	Private	R.I.R.	
McCRACKEN, WM.	8 Back Ship Street	Private	4th Hussars	Wounded.
McCRACKEN, JAMES	8 Back Ship Street	Private	6th Inn. Dragoons	
McLAUGHLIN, CHARLES	11 Bentinck Street	Private	15th R.I.R.	Killed in Action.
McILWAINE, A.	32 Paris Street	Private	Labour Corps	
McWILLIAMS, WM.	102 Clementine Street	Private	R.I. Fus.	Wounded.
McCARROLL, ALEX.	12 Lime Street	Private	16th R.I.R.	Killed in Action.
McLEAN, DANIEL	89 Lilliput Street	Private	Labour Corps	
McCARTER, R.	2 Fife Street	Corporal	Infant. B. Train	
McCLATCHIE, DERM.	14 Donegall Sq. W.	Lieutenant	R.I.R.	
McDONALD, WM.	Central Fire Station	Private	Can. Pioneers	Wounded.
MACFARLAND, GEORGE	Late Belfast	Captain	R.A.M.C.	Died of Wounds.
McCONNELL, JAMES W.	1 Roden Street	Private	A.S.C.	Youngest M.M. in British Army (16).

BELFAST PRESBYTERY. ROSEMARY STREET.

Name.	Home Address.	Rank.	Regiment, Battalion or Unit.	Remarks.
Millar, Alex.	66 Little York Street	Private	R.I.R.	
Millar, Francis	66 Little York Street	Private	R.E.	
Millar, Thomas	66 Little York Street	Private	R.I.R.	
Mullan, Joseph	56 Ottawa Street	Private	M.T., Egypt	
Martin, Robert	72 Little York Street	Private	R.E.	
Mills, James A.	Malvern Street	Private	R.M.L.C.	
Moore, Hugh	14 Weaver Street	Private	19th R.I.R.	Prisoner of War.
Murdough, Richard	44 Fife Street	Private	B.H., Italy	
Millar, John	66 Little York Street	Private	R.I.R.	
Millar, Frank	66 Little York Street	Private	15th R.I.R.	
Moody, Matthew	3 St. James Street	Private	C.F.A.	Wounded.
Magill, W. J.	16 Bute Street	Private	R.E.	
Moorhead, W. J.	13 St. Paul's Street	Private	R.I.R.	Wd., Pris. of War.
Morton, James	10 Molyneaux Street	Private	14th R.I.R.	
McAleese, Joseph	20 Roxburgh Street	Private	R.I.R.	
McKibbin, Isaac	4 Lr. George's Street	Private	R.I.R.	
Martin, James	19 Earl Street	Private	R.E.	
McCarroll, George	12 Lime Street	Private	R.I.R.	
McClements, John	23 Craigavad Street	Private	A.S.C.	
Morton, George	Nelson Street	Private	R.I. Dragoons	Killed.
Millar, W	66 Little York Street	Private	4th R. Inn. Fus.	Killed.
Milligan, James	Wall Street	Private	A.S.C.	
Morton, James	4 Beechpark Street	Private	8th Hussars	...
Malcolm, James	49 Sixth Street	Private	R.I.R.	
McFadden, James	...	Lance-Corporal	R. Inn. Fus.	Wounded.
Mulligan, William	12 Moscow Street	Private	R.A.F.	
Nelson, Samuel	Nelson Court	Private	R.E., 121 Coy.	Died of Wounds.
Neill, Samuel	17 Haldane Street	Private	R.I.R.	
Netting, W. H.	...	S.B.A.	H.M.S. Monitor	
Nesbitt, John	40 Parkmount Street	Private	14th R.I.R.	Wounded.
Nelson, Thomas	Robb & Co.	Private	N.I.H.	Wounded.
Newell, Robert	1 Comber Street	Corporal	10th R.I.R.	
Neill, Wm.	101 Sugarfield Street	Private	R.I.R.	Missing.
Nelson, Samuel	7 Trafalgar Street	Private	R.A.	
O'Neill, John S.	9 Wellington Park	Captain	F.A., Ind. Ex. F.	
Omerod, A.	74 Argyle Street	Private	R.I.R.	
Orr James	5 Dagmar Street	Stoker	H.M.S.	
Osborne, Arthur	...	P.O.1	H.M.S. Glorious	
Officer, Henry	104 Cosgrave Street	Private	R.I.R.	
Park, William	Garthowen	Major	R.A.F.	
Proctor, Thomas	33 Jennymount Street	Stoker	H.M.S. Mandate	
Patterson, Thomas	14 Glasgow Street	Private	R.A.M.C.	Killed.
Peden, James	23 Tyne Street	Private	R. Mun. Fus.	
Pepper, John	110 York Road	E.R.A.	H.M.S. Talbot	
Phillips, S.	55 Cultra Street	Private	3rd R.I.R.	
Patterson, Samuel	14 Glasgow Street	Private	R.A.M.C.	Wounded.
Parker, George	96 Dover Street	Private	9th R.I.R.	Wounded.
Patterson, James	54b York Street	Private	5th R.I.R.	
Palmer, John	73 Glasgow Street	Sergeant	R.I.R.	Killed.
Porter, Samuel	60 Brown Street	Private	R.I.R.	
Purse, C.	Nelson Street	Private	15th R.I.R.	
Pollock, Herbert	Messrs. Robb & Co.	Private	R.A.F.	
Purse, James	175 Nelson Street	Private	R.I.F.	
Quin, John	51 Fifth Street	Private	R.A.M.C.	
Quinn, John	45 Glenwherry Street	Private	8th R.I.R.	
Quaite, George	5 Trafalgar Street	Private	L.C.	
Rentoul, Rev. J. L.	Late Asst. Rosemary St. Church	Private	R.A.M.C.	
Rentoul, W.	Lodgings	Lieutenant	E. Lancs.	Killed in Action.
Rowley, James	55 Ivan Street	Lance-Corporal	R.A.M.C.	
Ross, Herbert	Church Lane	Private	R.I.R.	
Richards, W.	...	A.B.	H.M.S. Monitor	
Rogerson, Wm.	188 Ormeau Road	Private	R.E.	Wounded.
Rogers, James	...	Private	R.I.R.	
Robinson, John	North Thomas Street	Private	R. Inn. Fus.	
Robb, William	Earl Street	Private	R.I.R.	
Robb, S. A.	Earl Lane	Private	R.I.R.	Prisoner of War.
Rea, Isaac	...	Private	A.S.C.	
Robinson, William	98 Wilton Street	Private	R.A.M.C.	
Rea, James	38 Dagmar Street	Private	2nd R. Ir. Fus.	
Rice, James	14 College Street W.	A.B.	H.M.S.	
Riley, William	55 Glenrosa Street	Private	R.M.L.C.	
Richmond, Harry	43 Lanark Street	Private	3rd Shipyard Co.	
Rowan, Samuel	5 Melrose Street	Private	R.I.R.	
Sinclair, Thomas	22 University Square	Colonel	A.M.S.	C.B.
Sinclair, J. M.	38 Windsor Park	Captain	R.I.R.	Wounded.
Sinclair, Sam	32 Seventh Street	Private	A.S.C.	
Seawright, James	Manor Street	Private	R.I.R.	Killed in Action.
Sheeran, Braiden	35 Earl Street	Private	R.I.R.	
Sinclair, John	32 Seventh Street	Private	R.I.R.	
Stewart, James A.	3 Virginia Street	Private	14th R.I.R.	Killed in Action.
Shaw, James	Penrose Street	Private	R.F.A., E.E.F.	
Sydney, Geo.	...	Private	R.A.M.C.	
Strain, Wm. H.	46 Rowan Street	Private	6th R.I.R.	

BELFAST PRESBYTERY.   ROSEMARY STREET.

Name.	Home Address.	Rank.	Regiment, Battalion or Unit.	Remarks.
Spiers, Vincent	44 Collyer Street	Private	R.I.R.	
Swan, Richard		Private	R.A.M.C.	
Sloan, Robert	69 Townsend Street	Private	R.E.	
Sweeney, David	Earl Street	Private	R.I.R.	
Stitt, John	20 Sixth Street	Bombardier	R.F.A.	Killed in Action.
Sloan, Alec	50 Sixth Street	Private	R.A.M.C.	
Stitt, Thomas	20 Sixth Street	Private	R.A.M.C.	Prisoner of War.
Smith, Wm.	42 Aberdeen Street	Private	R.I.R.	
Stronge, Joseph	50 Canmore Street	Private	R.I.R.	
Shanks, Wm.		Private	R. Mun. Fus.	M. Medal.
Stockman, Wm.	Ritchie Street	Private	6th Inn. Dragoons	
Sempey, Mat.	41 Meadow Street	Private	20th R.I.R.	
Sloan, Alec. C.	168 Manor Street	Private	9th R.I.R.	
Strange, W. J.	Lodgings	Private	19th R.I.R.	
Seawright, M.	27 Virginia Street	Private	N.I.H.	
Seawright, Alf.	27 Virginia Street	Private	K's. R.R.	
Smith, John		A.B.	H.M.S.	
Stitt, Nath.	20 Sixth Street	Private	R.H.A.	
Starrit, Thos.	71 Fortingale Street	Private	R. Inn. Fus.	
Smith, Samuel		Private	R.I.R.	
Starrit, James	23 Carnalea Street	Private	13th R.I.R.	Missing.
Stewart, S. K., Miss	R.V. Hospital	Sister	Lord Derby Hosp.	
Scott, L. G., Miss	Lr. Windsor Avenue	Sister	3rd Gen. Hosp.	
Scott, James	Gardiner Street	Private	R.E.	
Spratt, Alex.	11 North Derby Street	A.B.	H.M.S.	
Shaw, John	Messrs. Robb & Co.	Private	R.A.F.	
Stewart, James	4 Southland Street	Private	R.A.F.	
Tate, Robert M.	444 Oldpark Road	Lieutenant	R.E.	
Thomas, John	48 Dagmar Street	Private	N.I.H.	
Thompson, John	Nelson Street	Corporal	R. Inn. Fus.	
Thompson, T.	152 Conway Street	Drummer	R. Inn. Fus.	
Turtle, John	27 Mountcollyer Road	Private	15th R.I.R.	
Thompson, James	13 Aberdeen Street	Private	R.I.R.	
Thompson, D.	Deacon Street	A.B.S.	H.M.S.	
Tanner, Robert	31 Seventh Street	Sergeant	R. Inn. Fus.	
Taylor, William	Turin Street	Private	9th R.I.R.	Killed.
Tanner, Hugh	51 Third Street	Private	A.S.C.	
Templeton, S.	43 New Dock Street	Private	C. Corps	
Templeton, Geo.	8 Moscow Street	Private	R.E., Salonika	
Thompson, Percy	5 Beverley Street	A.B.	H.M.S.	
Telford, Robert	24 Trafalgar Street	Private	1st R.I.R.	Killed.
Taylor, Greaves			H.M.S. Glorious	
Upton, Wm.		Private	1st Wilts.	
Vance, M.	50 Lindsay Street	Stoker	H.M.S.	
Wales, Samuel	136 Nelson Street	Private	R. Mun. Fus.	Killed.
Warnock, Thomas	North Ann Street	A.B.S.	H.M.S. Goliath	Lost at Sea.
Welch, James	48 Eia Street	Private	M.T. A.S.C.	
Walker, Wm. Jas.	37 Dundee Street	Private	R.I.R.	
Walker, William	37 Dundee Street	Private	R. Irish Regt.	
Woodside, Wm.	43 Waring Street	Sergeant	R.I.R.	
Woodside, Isaac	43 Waring Street	Private	R.I.R.	
Welsh, Robert	48 Eia Street	Private	R.I.R.	Killed in Action.
Wilson, Matt.	81 Hopeton Street	Private	R.I.R.	Killed in Action.
Weir, Wm.	37 Linwood Street	Private	R.I.R.	
West, Robert	Fortingale Street	Private	R.A.M.C.	
Weir, E. J.	31 Seventh Street	Private	R.I.R.	
Wright, James	Ulverston Street	Private	Irish Guards	Wounded and Discharged.
Wilson, Alex.	140 Earl Street	Private	R. Inn. Fus.	Killed.
Wales, John	Malvern Street	Private	A.S.C.	
Wright, Samuel	Mountcollyer Street	Private	R.F.A.	Killed.
Wylie, James	5 M'Candless Street	Corporal	8th Hussars	Prisoner of War.
Woods, Thomas	113 Durham Street	Private	14th R.I.R.	
Wylie, Robert	12 Westland Street	Private	N.I.H.	
Wright, Wm.	Glenrosa Street	A.B.	H.M.S. Cressy	Lost at Sea.
Wilson, J. S.	36 Lincoln Avenue	Private	L.L. Corps	
Weatherup, Wm.	Church Lane	Lance-Corporal	R.I.R.	M.M., Pris. of War.
Whitters, Thos.	30 Eglinton Street	Q.M.S.	R.W. Fus.	
White, James	28 Mountcollyer Road	Private	107th M.G. Corps	
Woods, Joseph	20 St. Kilda Street	A.B.	H.M.S. Good Hope	Lost at Sea.
Weaver, Robert	122 Ormeau Road	Lieutenant	H.M.S. Avoca	
Wales, W. J.	Malvern Street	Private	4th R. Inn. Fus.	Prisoner of War.
Wheeler, Albert	50 Carlow Street	Private	R.I.R.	
Weir, Richard	38 Christopher Street	Private	R.I.R.	
Wilson, Wm.	140 Earl Street	Private	R.E.	
Wilkinson, S.	83 Glenmathan Street	Private	2nd R.I.R.	Prisoner of War.
Wright, Adam	Rowan Street	Private	9th R.I.R.	Wounded.
Watson, Samuel	150 Up. Earl Street	Private	9th Fus.	Died of Wounds.
Walker, John	North Ann Street	Private	15th R.I.R.	Killed in Action.
Walker, Leonard	58 Tennent Street	Private	C. Corps	Wounded.
Wales, Wm.	Malvern Street	Private	R.I. Fus.	
White, Thomas	Nelson Street	Private	R. Inn. Fus.	
Wallace, Wm.	140 Up. Canning Street	Private	T.M. Battery	Wounded.
Welch, Kathleen	48 Eia Street	Sapper	W.A.A. Corps	

BELFAST PRESBYTERY. ROSEMARY STREET.

Name.	Home Address.	Rank.	Regiment, Battalion or Unit.	Remarks.
Wales, Robert	Nelson Street	Private	5th R.I.R.	
Warren, Samuel	170 Cupar Street	Private	R.I.R.	Prisoner of War.
Watson, Tom	14 Ravenhill Park	Private	R.G.A.	
Watson, Alex.	35 Limestone Road	Private	R.F.A.	
Waring, Alfred	Central Fire Brigade	Bandsboy	R.I.R.	
Young, James R.	Rathvarna	Captain	A.S.C.	
Young, John	1 Valentine Street	Private	15th R.I.R.	Killed.
Yates Thomas	25 Springmount Street	Private	R.I.R.	
Yates, John	Springmount Street	Stoker	H.M.S. Hawk	Lost at Sea.
Young, Wm.	64 Snugville Street	Private	R.E.	
Young, James	54 Boyd Street	Private	9th R.I.R.	
ST. ENOCH'S.				
Adair, James	87 Cavehill Road	2nd Lieutenant	11th R. Inn. Fus.	Invalided.
Adair, George	87 Cavehill Road	3rd A/m.	R.A.F.	
Adair, Robert	87 Cavehill Road	Sergeant	R.A.F.	Wounded.
Adams, Alexander	119 Riga Street		8th R.I. Rifles	Wounded.
Adams, Andrew	119 Riga Street	Sergeant	King's Liverpools	Mons Star, Wded.
Adams, Hugh	119 Riga Street		Lancashire Fus.	Gassed.
Adams, Robert	119 Riga Street		R. Irish Fus.	
Adjey, Alfred	44 Twickenham Street		5th A.S.C.	
Agnew, Hugh J.	114 Up. Meadow Street		9th R.I. Rifles	Wounded.
Agnew, Samuel	114 Up. Meadow Street		R.A.M.C.	
Agnew, Thomas R.	138 Spamount Street		H.M.S. Vanguard	Killed in Action.
Allen, James A.	59 Rosemount Gardens	Lieutenant	R.N.R.	
Allen, Robert J.	72 Duncairn Gardens	Sergt.-Major	G.H.Q.	Ment., Invalided.
Allister, Robert	38 Townsend Street	Corporal	A.S.C.	
Baillie, George	66 Christopher Street		A.S.C.	
Baillie, William	66 Christopher Street	Sergeant	15th R.I. Rifles	M.M. Wded., Pris.
Barkley, James	122 Earl Street		15th R.I. Rifles	Killed in Action.
Biggar, John	14 Greenmount Street		9th R.I. Rifles	
Biggar, John, Jun.	1 Carnalea Street		2nd R.I. Rifles	
Boyd, Hugh	68 Townsend Street		9th R.I. Rifles	Prisoner.
Boyd, James	Lyndhurst, Knock	Lieutenant	18th Canadians	Wounded, Gassed, Twice mentioned.
Boyd, Robert	17 India Street		10th R.I. Rifles	Killed in Action.
Boyd, William H.				Killed in Action.
Boylan, John	23 Annadale Street		15th R.I. Rifles	Killed in Action.
Boyle, James	Charnwood Avenue	Sergeant	9th Black Watch	
Brennan, James	123 Brookmount Street		A.S.C.	Wounded.
Brooks, William	4 Burlington Street	Corporal	R.E.	
Brooks, John	4 Burlington Street		4th R.I. Rifles	
Brown, Alexander C.	74 Bristol Street	Sergeant	17th R.I. Rifles	Wounded.
Brown, Henry	14 Earl Lane		15th R.I. Rifles	
Brown, Henry	18 Burke Street		H.M.S. Vindictive	
Brown, James	18 Burke Street		R.F.A.	Gassed.
Brown, John	18 Burke Street		R.E.	
Brown, William R.	18 Burke Street		H.M.S. Miranda	
Brown, John	Southampton	Commander	H.M.S. City of Oxford	
Brown, John, Jun.	Southampton		R.I. Rifles	Killed in Action.
Brown, Hugh	Southampton	2nd Lieutenant	2nd R.I. Rifles	Killed in Action.
Brown, Robert	Southampton	2nd Lieutenant		
Brown, John L.	8 North Thomas Street		A.S.C.	
Brown, John McM.	9 Ponsonby Avenue		1st R.I. Rifles	Wounded.
Brown, Robert	81 Agnes Street	Lance-Corporal	15th R.I. Rifles	Wounded.
Brownlee, John	12 Up. Charleville Street		122nd R.E.	Wounded.
Brownlee, William	12 Up. Charleville Street		2nd R. Inn. Fus.	M.M., Prisoner.
Butler, James	63 Kashmir Road		15th R. Irish Rifles	Wounded.
Cameron, James	52 Brookhill Avenue	Sergeant	50th Canadians	M.M., Killed in Act
Cameron, David K.	52 Brookhill Avenue		N.I.H.	
Campbell, Charles	22 Snugville Street		R.A.M.C.	Wounded.
Campbell, Frank	7 Gardner Street	Corporal	R.E.	
Campbell, Fred.	107 Up. Meadow Street		107th T.M.B.	Wounded.
Campbell, James E.	107 Up. Meadow Street		9th R.I. Rifles	Wounded.
Campbell, Henry	22 Victoria Gardens		R. Inn. Fus.	Gassed.
Campbell, William	22 Victoria Gardens	Sergeant	Canadian A.S.C.	
Campbell, Joseph	22 Victoria Gardens		Strathcona's Horse	
Campbell, William K. (MB., Ch.B.)	47 Glandore Avenue	Major	R A.M.C.	D.S.O., M.C., Bar, 4 times ment.
Carlisle, Hugh M.	170 Duncairn Gardens	Chief Engineer	Transport	Thrice torpedoed
Carlisle, William				Killed in Action.
Carson, John	Trades Hotel		2nd N.Z. Rifles	Killed in Action.
Carson, Samuel D.	Trades Hotel	Lieutenant	3rd Machine Gun Corps	
Caughey, Edward	83 Richardson Street		Durham Lt. Inft.	
Caulfield, John C.	18 Greenmount Street	Corporal	N.I.H.	
Charlton, George A.	8 Antrim Road	2nd Lieutenant	5th S. Staffords	
Charlton, Ernest H.	8 Antrim Road	Lieutenant	S. African Forces	
Christie, David	46 Royal Avenue		9th R.I. Rifles	Wounded.
Clark, William	40 Christopher Street		2nd R. Inn. Fus.	
Clow, Henry C.	9 Newington Avenue		3rd Canadian Art.	
Clow, William M.	9 Newington Avenue		9th R. Irish Fus.	
Coburn, John	16 Beechpark Street	Major	R.G.A.	M.C., Belg. Cross.
Copeland, Fred. J.	Alliance Avenue	2nd Lieutenant	3rd R. Irish Fus.	Mentioned.

BELFAST PRESBYTERY. ST. ENOCH'S.

Name.	Home Address.	Rank.	Regiment, Battalion or Unit.	Remarks.
Copeland, Joseph H.	Alliance Avenue	2nd Lieutenant	12th R. Irish Rifles	
Copeland, Samuel C.	Alliance Avenue	Corporal	U.S.A. Field Art.	Gassed.
Cordner, James	The Manse, Drumbo	Lieutenant	2nd R.I. Rifles	M.C., Kd. in Act.
Crawford, Ed. L.	3 Trinity Street	Corporal	20th R.I. Rifles	
Crawford, Hampton	14 Fortingale Street		12th Inn. Fus.	Killed in Action.
Crichton, Jack	Downview Avenue	Lance-Corporal	Canadians	Died of Wounds.
Crozier, Albert	42 Dock Street		H.M.S. Sobo	
Cuddy, George C.	150 Agnes Street		A.S.C.	
Cullen, James	42 Harcourt Street		Canadian Field Art.	
Curry, William S.	9 Keswick Street	Sergeant	9th R.I. Rifles	Wounded.
Devine, John	123 Cosgrove Street		R.A.M.C.	
Dickson, Joseph	39 Alloa Street		R.E.	
Dickson, Joseph A. V.	28 Up. Townsend St.		5th R. Inn. Fus.	Prisoner.
Donald, Robert J.	38 Mountcollyer Street		Irish Guards	Wounded.
Dunn, James	93 Bristol Street		12th R.I. Rifles	Prisoner.
Finlay, Robert	29 Christopher Street		R.G.A.	
Finn, James	Shipbuoy Street		17th R.I. Rifles	
Finn, Thomas	Shipbuoy Street		18th R.I. Rifles	
Foster, Harry	6 Kells Street		R.A.M.C.	Gassed.
French, Fred. G.	26 Cumberland Street		27th Canadians	Killed in Action.
French, John A.	26 Cumberland Street	2nd Lieutenant	3rd R.I. Rifles	
Fulton, Stewart	11 Rosewood Street		U.S. National Guards	Killed.
Fulton, Thomas	8 Yarrow Street	E.R.A.	H.M.D. Nymptic	Wounded.
Garvey, David S.	197 Agnes Street		14th R.I.R. (Y.C.V.)	Wounded.
Garvey, Henry S.	197 Agnes Street	Corporal	14th R.I.R. (Y.C.V.)	Wounded.
Garvie, Charles	74 Denmark Street	Corporal	R.E.	
Gaston, James G.	151 Oldpark Road		15th R. Irish Fus.	
Gault, Ernest	120 Oldpark Avenue	Sergeant	R.A.M.C.	
Gault, Samuel H.	120 Oldpark Avenue	2nd Lieutenant	E. African Forces	
Girvan, Frederick	24 Easton Gardens	Captain	Devonshires	Killed in Action.
Girvan, Walter	24 Easton Gardens	2nd Lieutenant	3rd R.I. Rifles	M.M.
Girvan, John			R.A.M.C.	
Gordon, John	14 Carlisle Street		15th R.I. Rifles	Wounded.
Graham, Albert	303 Crumlin Road		15th R.I. Rifles	Wounded.
Graham, Joseph A.	303 Crumlin Road	2nd Lieutenant	15th R.I. Rifles	Wounded.
Graham, Robert	303 Crumlin Road	Sergeant	15th R. Irish Fus.	D.C.M., Wounded.
Graham, Evan McJ.	Dungannon R.I.C.	Lieutenant	4th R. Irish Fus.	
Gray, Thomas	1 Twickenham Street	Corporal	R.E.	Wounded.
Greene, Joseph			H.M.S. Agamemnon	
Greer, Alexander	14 Dagmar Street		R. Marine Art.	
Greer, Archibald	14 Dagmar Street		H.M.S. Gurkha	Invalided.
Greer, Henry	14 Dagmar Street		1st Inn. Fus.	Killed in Action.
Greer, William	14 Dagmar Street		Seaforths	Killed in Action.
Hackney, George	Lansdowne Road	Lance-Corporal	14th R.I.R. (Y.C.V.)	Wounded.
Hanna, Archibald M.	27 Court Street		15th R.I. Rifles	Killed in Action.
Hanna, Harry R.	27 Court Street		R.E.	
Hanna, Charles H.	Canada		Canadians	Killed in Action.
Hanna, Frederick	Canada		Canadians	Wounded.
Hanson, J. Henry	29 Up. Townsend St.	Corporal	14th R.I.R. (Y.C.V.)	M.M.
Hart, William M.	29 Brookhill Avenue	Electrician	H.M.S. Orontes	
Hazel, James	60 Langford Street		H.M.S. Duke of Albany	Torpedoed.
Hazel, Samuel	66 Belgrave Street		8th Inn. Fus.	Wounded, Gassed.
Hazel, Thomas	38 Hanna Street	King's Corporal	2nd Dragoon Guards	
Heenan, Arthur	8 Suir Street		1st R.I. Rifles	Killed in Action.
Henry, Robert				
Henry, Thomas				
Hogg, Robert J.	5 Trinity Street		Army Cycle Corps	
Hull, Charles E.	6 Knutsford Drive		R.G.A.	
Hunter, David H.	71 Glenrosa Street	Corporal	14th R.I.R. (Y.C.V.)	
Hunter, Robert	71 Glenrosa Street		R.M.E.	
Hutchison, Arch.	Old Lodge, Cliftonville	Sergt.-Major	Canadian R.E.	Wounded.
Jackson, George G.	29 Cliftonpark Avenue		1st Canadians	Wounded.
Jackson, William	11 Manor Drive		Australians	Wounded.
Johnson, Geo. R.	36 Penrith Street	Corporal	R. Inn. Fus.	
Johnston, John	40a Ravenhill Road		R.E.	
Jones, Hugh	211 York Street		9th R.I. Rifles	Wounded.
Kelly, John	278 Crumlin Road	Lance-Corporal	6th R.I. Rifles	Killed in Action.
Kennedy, Thomas	21 Lawrence Street	Corporal	R.E.	Wounded.
Keys, Samuel	155 Roden Street		15th R.I. Rifles	
Kirkwood, George	"Afton," Ashgrove Pk.	Sergeant	Canadians	
Kirkwood, Walter	38 Wyndham Street	Telegraphist	H.M.S. Erin	
Knox, David H.	10 Rowan Street		15th R.I. Rifles	Prisoner.
Laverty, William J.	36 Willowbank Street		1st R.I. Rifles	Died in India.
Larkin, Henry	13 Ambrose Street		9th R.I. Rifles	Killed in Action.
Lee, Thomas	23 N. Thomas Street		9th R.I. Rifles	Killed in Action.
Leitch, Norman	106 Limestone Road		14th R.I.R. (Y.C.V.)	Prisoner.
Leitch, Walter	106 Limestone Road	2nd Lieutenant	London Irish	
Leitch, Harold V.	106 Limestone Road		108th F.A.C.	
Livingstone, Andrew	53 Carnalea Street		2nd Inn. Fus.	Wded, Mons Star.
Lowry, William J.	212 Grosvenor Road		H.M.S. Canada	
Lowry, Robert E.	212 Grosvenor Road		14th R.I.R. (Y.C.V.)	Killed in Action.
Lowry, Thomas E.	33 Matlock Street	Lance-Corporal	9th R.I. Rifles	Died.
Lynn, Hugh Alex.	100 Dover Street	Sergeant	Canadian A.S.C.	
Lynn, James E.	100 Dover Street		9th R.I. Rifles	Prisoner.

(153)

BELFAST PRESBYTERY.   ST. ENOCH'S.

Name.	Home Address.	Rank.	Regiment, Battalion or Unit.	Remarks.
Lyons, Hugh	Montreal, Canada		Canadians	Wounded.
Magill, Albert	75 Duncairn Gardens	Qr. Mr. Sgt.	2nd R.I. Rifles	Wounded.
Manning, —	Canada		Canadians	
Mateer, John	44 Riga Street		18th A.S.C.	
Megaw, James	31 Vernon Street	Corporal	14th R.I.R. (Y.C.V.)	
Mercer, David C.	34 N. Boundary Street	Corporal	N.I.H.	Wounded.
Mercer, William J.	161 Agnes Street		15th R.I. Rifles	
Millar, Alexander	206 York Street		R.F.A.	
Millar, William				Killed in Action.
Milligan, Charles S.	Ligoniel Dispensary		2nd R.I. Rifles	Wounded.
Milligan, John	Ligoniel Dispensary		1st N.I.H.	
Mitchell, Albert	234 Spamount Street		Canadians	Prisoner.
Mitchell, David H.	16 Regent Street	Lance-Corporal	14th R.I.R. (Y.C.V.)	Wounded.
Moore, William M.	115 Cosgrove Street	Lance-Corporal	R. Irish Fus.	
Morrison, John	36 Heather Street		15th R.I. Rifles	Wounded.
Morrow, Andrew K.	62 Hopewell Street		H.M.S. Egmont	
Morrow, Hugh	62 Hopewell Street		R.E.	Mons Star, Wded.
Murphy, James	96 Henry Street	Sergeant	5th R. Irish Fus.	Killed in Action.
Macauley, Fred. C.	17 Cardigan Drive		7th Canadians	
McAteer, Hugh	4 Blenheim Street		14th R.I.R. (Y.C.V.)	Wounded, Blind.
McAteer, John	4 Blenheim Street		14th R.I.R. (Y.C.V.)	Killed in Action.
McCandless, John	13 Roe Street		6th Dragoon Guards	
McCartney, Wm.	6 St. Albans Gardens		R.A.F.	
McClatchey, Robert	234 Spamount Street	Sergeant	1st R. Irish Fus.	
McClelland, Arthur	96 Henry Street		A.S.C.	Died of Wounds.
McClure, Alfred E.	46 Jaffa Street		15th R.I. Rifles	Wounded.
McClure, Hugh	197 Crumlin Road		R.E.	Killed in Action.
McClure, George	17 Percy Street		11th Northumberland Fus.	Mons Star, M.M.
McClure, Robert	17 Percy Street	Petty Officer	H.M.S. Queen	Wounded.
McClure, James	1 Tyne Street	Sergeant	K.O. Yorkshire Lt. Inft.	
McComb, Ch. Henry	Dunedin, Antrim Road	Lieutenant	9th Inn. Fus.	Wounded.
McComb, M.B., CH.B., Samuel	Ben Vista, Antrim Road	Captain	R.A.M.C.	
McConkey, Fred. W.	129 Snugville Street		H.M.S. City of Oxford	
McCullough, Thomas	256 Cupar Street	Sergeant	Signalling School	
MacDowell, Jas. E.	11 Eglantine Gardens	Captain	Machine Gun Corps	St. George's Cross, Russian Order of St. Anne, Russian Order of St. Stanislaus.
McElrath, R. Harper	Marlborough Park		10th R. Dublin Fus.	Killed in Action.
McGookin, James	7 Foreman Street		R.A.M.C.	
McGookin, Wm.	7 Foreman Street		1st R. Irish Fus.	Killed in Action.
McGookin, Robert	12 Foreman Street	Corporal	R.E.	Wounded.
Macivor, Wm. A.	57 Ponsonby Avenue	Corporal	King's Liverpools ("Pals")	Wounded.
McKee, Robert	66 Alexandra Park Av.		Royal Marines	
McKnight, Wm.	Greenmount Street		9th R.I. Rifles	
McMullan, Hugh W.	29 Jersey Street	Captain	R. Horse Artillery	
McMullan, John	146 Cliftonpark Avenue		14th R.I.R. (Y.C.V.)	Wounded.
McMullan, Martin S.	146 Cliftonpark Avenue		N.I.H.	Wounded.
McMurtry, James Alex.	11 Crumlin Road		Irish Guards	Wounded.
McMurtry, W. Killen	9 Thorndale Avenue	Sergeant	14th R.I.R. (Y.C.V.)	Wounded.
McNair Robert	32 Ilchester Street	Corporal	3rd R.I. Rifles	Wounded.
McNamara, Wm. B.	Peter's Hill Baths	Lance-Corporal	15th R.I. Rifles	Wounded.
McQuillan, Henry	120 Up. Meadow Street		R.A.M.C.	
McQuoid, Jas. B.	94 Chief Street	Corporal	1st Inn. Fus.	Killed in Action.
McQuoid, Wm. C., Jun.	94 Chief Street	Lance-Corporal	15th R.I. Rifles	Wded, Prisoner.
McWhirter, Joseph	Glencot, Glenburn Park		H.M.T. Aragon	Twice torpedoed.
McWhirter, Robt. J.	Glencot, Glenburn Park	Lieutenant	9th R. Inn. Fus.	Wounded.
McWhirter, Samuel	Glencot, Glenburn Park	Sergeant	R.A.F.	
Neill, William	17 Mayo Street		14th R.I.R. (Y.C.V.)	Wounded, Gassed.
Nelson, David	32 Marsden Gardens		Canadians	Killed in Action.
Nicholson, Albert	74 Ruth Street	Sergeant	R.E.	M.M. and Bar.
Nimick, William	27 Landscape Terrace		R.F.C.	
Nutt, Frederick	14 Vistula Street	Lance-Corporal	15th R.I. Rifles	Wounded.
Orr, Edmund	130 Mountcollyer Street		H.M.T. Hunsdon.	
Parker, George G.	96 Dover Street		Army Ordnance Corps	Wounded.
Patton, Henry	31 Beechpark Street		2nd Warwickshires	
Patton, John	59 Foyle Street		R.A.M.C.	Wounded.
Patton, Matthew	3 Baskin Street		A.S.C.	
Patton, Samuel	53 Cambrai Street		H.M.S. Vanquisher	
Patton, Thomas	53 Cambrai Street		H.M.S. Queen	
Patton, William	53 Cambrai Street		D.L.I.	Killed in Action.
Patton, Thomas	23 Conlon Street		H.M.S. Monarch	
Peden, Robert G.	102 Antrim Road		A.S.C.	Wounded.
Pelling, Ernest C.	88 Bristol Street		H.M.S. Garry	
Pollock, M.B., CH.B. (Edin.) A. Norman,	7 Glandore Park	Surgeon Lt.	H.M.S. Hibernia	
Pollock, Paul G.	7 Glandore Park	Lance-Corp. (Scout)	14th R.I.R. (Y.C.V.)	Killed in Action.
Percy, Edward G. M.	15 Daisyfield Street		R.F.C.	
Purse, Robert	169 Nelson Street		15th R.I. Rifles	
Purse, William	175 Nelson Street		R.N.	
Reavey, Daniel	14 Dagmar Street		R.I. Regiment	
Reid, Herbert F. McC.	St. Enoch's N.S.	Captain	12th Northumberland Fus.	Wounded.
Reid, Samuel	104 Bristol Street		R. Irish Fus.	Wounded.

BELFAST PRESBYTERY.   ST. ENOCH'S.

Name.	Home Address.	Rank.	Regiment, Battalion or Unit.	Remarks.
Ritchie, John	24 Carnalea Street	...	36th R.E. Signallers	...
Robinson, John S. H.	St. Enoch's N.S.	Captain	The Welsh	Killed in Action.
Robinson, John	61 N. Thomas Street	Lance-Corporal	R.I. Rifles	...
Roy, Joseph	32 Ballycastle Street	...	15th R.I. Rifles	Killed in Action.
Roy, Robert	32 Ballycastle Street	...	15th R.I. Rifles	...
Service, Caulfield	144 Antrim Road	...	R.G.A.	Wounded.
Shanks, Jerry	201 York Street	...	1st London Irish Rifles	...
Shaw, Thomas	20 Harcourt Street	...	7th R.I. Rifles	Wded, Prisoner, Escaped.
Shilliday, John	9 Madrid Street	...	R.A.F.	...
Sillars, Thomas	60 Dover Street	Lance-Corporal	8th R.I. Rifles	Killed in Action.
Smith, B.D., C.F., Rev. Fred	7 Glandore Park	Captain	48th Gen. Hospital, Salonica	...
Smith, Henry	16 Regent Street	Corporal	1st W. Yorks	Wounded.
Smyth, Louis	12 Ewart's Row	...	R.E.	...
Smyth, R. Reuben	7 Thorndale Avenue	Corporal	Canadian Rifles	M.M.
Skelly, Frank	36 Woodvale Road	...	Canadians	...
Spence, Thomas	36 Landscape Terrace	Sergt.-Major	R.F.A.	...
Stead, Thomas A.	3 Craigavad Street	Sergeant	15th R.I. Rifles	Killed in Action.
Stewart, Robert	65 Dover Street	...	Army Ordnance Corps	...
Stewart, Samuel	5 Ivan Street	Lance-Corporal	1st R. Irish Fus.	...
Strong, Joseph	50 Canmore Street	...	15th R.I. Rifles	Gassed.
Sturgeon, Samuel	236 Duncairn Gardens	Reg. Q.M.S.	10th R.I. Fus.	...
Sullivan, John	21 Up. Meadow Street	Corporal	15th R.I. Rifles	Gassed.
Taggart, Joseph C.	41 Court Street	Lance-Corporal	11th R. Inn. Fus.	Wounded.
Taylor, William McD.	10 Orkney Street	Qr. Mr. Sgt.	9th R.I. Rifles	M.S.M.
Taylor, Wm. Thos.	42 Cliftonpark Avenue	Captain	R.A.F.	...
Templeton, Wm. H.	8 Baltic Avenue	...	Irish Canadians (208th)	Gassed.
Templeton, George	Ponsonby Avenue	Major	3rd R.I. Rifles	...
Thompson, John, Jun.	22 Lime Street	...	A.S.C.	...
Thompson, Robert J.	35 Hanover Street	...	15th R.I. Rifles	Killed in Action.
Thompson, Thomas	35 Hanover Street	...	15th R.I. Rifles	Wounded.
Townsley, David	147a Antrim Road	Sergeant	122nd R.E.	M.M.
Townsley, Samuel	147a Antrim Road	...	122nd R.E.	...
Trew, Albert D.	36 Willowbank Street	...	2nd Rifle Brigade	Wounded.
Trew, James A.	36 Willowbank Street	...	12th R.I. Rifles	Prisoner.
Walker, Frederick R.	107 Donegall Street	Captain	Argyle & Sutherlands	Died.
Walker, Wm. John	94 Henry Street	...	Submarine, R.N.	...
Waring, John K.	27 Regent Street	Sergeant	14th R.I.R. (Y.C.V.)	Gassed.
Watson, Charles	121 Manor Street	...	9th R. Irish Fus.	Wounded.
Watson, Daniel	88 Bristol Street	...	6th R.I. Rifles	Wounded.
Watson, Wm. D.	14 Raleigh Street	...	8th R.I. Regiment	Wounded.
Willis, Eric M.	17 Cavehill Road	Cadet	" Huntress " (Head Line)	...
Willis, J. Henry M.	17 Cavehill Road	Cadet	R.A.F.	...
Wilson, Thomas A.	33 Landscape Terrace	Lance-Corporal	A.S.C.	...
Wilson, Frank	24 Thorndale Avenue	...	2nd R. Munster Fus.	...
Wilson, Thomas G.	48 Carlisle Street	...	1st N.I.H.	Wounded.
Wright, James	...	...	...	...
Wright, Robert S.	263 N. Queen Street	...	Canadian Machine Corps	Wounded, Died.
Wright, Thos. H.	263 N. Queen Street	...	15th R.I. Rifles	Gassed.
SHANKILL ROAD MISSION.				
Adams, Andrew	95 Bellevue Street	...	...	Wounded.
Alister, Wm.	30 Matchett Street	Private	...	Killed in Action.
Alister, David	30 Matchett Street	Private	Res. Army Signal Coy.	...
Allen, Wm.	27 Northumberland St.	Rifleman	R.I. Rifles	...
Allen, James	50 Paris Street	Private	A.S.C.	...
Alexander, T. J.	14 Woodvale Street	Bombardier	R.F.A.	...
Anderson, James	38 Flax Street	Private	R.I.R.	...
Anderson, Louis	38 Flax Street	Private	M.T. A.S.C.	...
Anderson, Edward	24 Crosby Street	Private	R.I.R.	Wounded.
Anderson, Wm.	24 Crosby Street	Corporal	R.I.R.	Wounded.
Anderson, Francis	1b Malvern Street	...	...	...
Arnold, Thos.	24 Glenwood Street	Corporal	R.I.R.	...
Armstrong, Samuel	23 Acton Street	Lance-Corporal	16th Cheshires	Wounded.
Armstrong, David	74 Hopeton Street	...	...	...
Bell, Samuel	28 Glentilt Street	Private	R.I. Fus.	Wounded.
Bell, James	28 Glentilt Street	Private	M.T.	...
Bell, Wm.	2 Paris Street	Driver	A.S.C.	Prisoner of War.
Belshaw, Hugh	34 Derry Street	Private	Innis. Dragoons	...
Blakely, Herbert	22 Ninth Street	Rifleman	R.I.R.	Wounded.
Black, George	76 N. Howard Street	Stoker	Navy	...
Boyd, Frank	29 Up. Charleville St.	Stoker	Navy	...
Boyd, J. A.	9 Dunn Street	Private	R.I.R.	...
Boyd, R. B.	9 Dunn Street	Staff-Sergt.	Transport Supply Corps	...
Boyd, William	41 James Street	...	...	Killed in Action.
Boyd, Edwin	53 Hopeton Street	...	...	...
Boyd, Wm.	Craven St. R.I.C. Barracks	Sergeant	Irish Guards	Killed in Action.
Boyd, Alexander	63 Lawnbrook Avenue	...	R.I.R.	Killed in Action.
Boyd, Wm.	67 Downing Street	...	...	...
Bell, J. K.	25 Carlow Street	Sergeant	...	Killed in Action.
Beattie, R. J.	20 Aberdeen Street	...	...	Killed in Action.
Bell, R. J.	51 Langford Street	...	...	Died of Wounds.
Bowden, James	69 Sugarfield Street	Private	R.A.M.C.	...

BELFAST PRESBYTERY. SHANKILL ROAD MISSION.

Name.	Home Address.	Rank.	Regiment, Battalion or Unit.	Remarks.
BOYCE, THOMAS	96 Agnes Street	Rifleman	R.I.R.	
BRIGGS, R. J.	44 Beresford Street	Driver	R.E.	
BRIGGS, RALPH	44 Beresford Street	Sapper	R.E.	
BROWN, DAVID	28 Westmoreland St.	Cyclist	Cyclist Corps	
BROWNE, T.	41 James Street		50th Batty., 34th Brig.	
BURCH, THOMAS	Raleigh Street	Lance-Corporal	R.I.R.	Wounded.
CALDERWOOD, BILL	32 Beverley Street		Navy	Killed in Action.
CALDERWOOD, THOMAS	32 Beverley Street	Trooper	6th I. Dragoons	
CALDERWOOD, SAMUEL	32 Beverley Street	Private	R.I.R.	
CALLEN, DAVID	24 Ardmoulin Avenue	Sapper	R.E.	
CAMPBELL, WILLIAM	Killarney Street	Sergeant	R.I.R.	Wounded.
CAMPBELL, JOHN	7 Tenth Street	Private	R.I.R.	Wounded.
CAMPBELL, WM.	Glenwood Street	Private	R.I.R.	
CAMPBELL, T. J.	3 Kitchener Street	Private	Salvage Corps, Canadians	
CAMPBELL, CHARLES	18 Haddow Street			
CAMPBELL, CHAS., JUN.	18 Haddow Street		Navy	
CAMPBELL, JOHN M.	18 Haddow Street			
CATHCART, WILLIAM	51 Israel Street	Gunner	R.F.A.	
CHAMBERS, J. A.	27 Hopewell Street	Lance-Corporal	R.I. Fus.	
CHAMBERS, JOHN	Riversdale Street	Sapper	R.E.	
CHESTNUTT, A.	68 Silvio Street	Private	R. Dublin Fus.	Prisoner of War.
CLARE, JAMES	27 Coniston Street	Rifleman	R.I.R.	Killed in Action.
CONNOLLY, ALEX.	170 Agnes Street		Irish Guards	Died of Wounds.
CONNOLLY, WM. J.	26 Sixth Street	Stoker	Navy	
CONNOLLY, THOMAS	Sugarfield Street			
COCHRANE, —	2 Chichester Avenue	Private	M.T.	
CRAIG, JOHN	7 Springmount Street	Stoker	Navy	
CROTHERS, JOHN			Navy	Killed in Action.
CROZIER, J. J. A.	90 Chief Street	Sergeant	A.V.C.	
CRYMBLE, CHARLES	Mountjoy Street		R.I.R.	Killed in Action.
CUNNINGHAM, JAMES	92 N. Howard Street	Rifleman	R.I.R.	Wounded.
CUSH, JAMES	10 Ceylon Street	Rifleman	R.I.R.	
CUMMINS, JOHN	175 Canmore Street	Private	Inn. Fus.	
DALZELL, BERTIE	32 Universty Avenue	Private	Canadian F.A.	
DEMPSTER, BOYD	82 Sugarfield Street	Private	Irish Guards	
DICKSON, WM.	Shore Road	Driver	R.E.	
DOUGLAS, GEORGE	43 Lawnbrook Avenue	Staff Sergeant	R.G.A.	
DRENNAN, WM.	40 Carnan Street	Corporal	Overseas Batt., Canada	
DALTON, T. J.	Hopeton Street	Private	R.I.R.	Killed in Action.
ESLER, DAVID	193 Crimea Street	Rifleman	R.I. Rifles	Wounded.
FORDE, SAMUEL L.	Rutherglen Street	Sergeant	R. I. Fus.	
FERGUSON, WM.	37 Lorton Street	Petty Officer	Navy	
FINLAY, JAMES	56 Dundee Street			
FLEMING, JOHN	63 Lawnbrook Avenue	Lance-Corporal	R.I.R.	
FOSTER, WM.	Cambrai Street	Corporal	R.I.R.	
FOSTER, ANDREW	Westmoreland Street	Private	N.Z.R.B.	
FLETCHER, ROBERT			Navy	Killed in Action.
FRENCH, DAVID	25 Foreman Street	Private	R.I.R.	
GAULT, SAMUEL H.	120 Oldpark Avenue	Lieut.	King's African Rifles	
GAULT, ERNEST	120 Oldpark Avenue	Sergeant	R.I.R.	
GALBRAITH, —	Hopewell Street	Sergt.-Major	R.E.	
GIBSON, ALEXANDER	42 Tennent Street	Private	R.H., Canada	
GIBSON, JOHN	60 Wilton Street			
GILMOUR, R. J.	30 Oldpark Avenue	Private	R.A.M.C.	
GILMOUR, SCOTT	30 Oldpark Avenue	Lance-Corporal	27th Training Reserve Batt.	
GOWAN, SAMUEL	28 Harrybrook Street	Private	R. Innis. Fus.	Killed in Action.
GOULD, GEORGE	Dover Street	Driver	R.G.A.	
GOULD, RICHARD	Conway Street		R.M.L.I.	
GOULD, SAMUEL	Conway Street		Navy	
GRAHAM, THOMAS	Beverley Street		A.S.C.	
GRAHAM, WM.	66 Tennent Street	Rifleman	R.I.R.	
GRAHAM, R.	66 Tennent Street	Sapper	R.E	
HAMILTON, W. T.	90 Old Lodge Road	Warrant Telegraphist	Navy	
HAMILTON, JOSEPH	44 Raleigh Street	Stoker	Navy	
HALL, WM.	48 Wilton Street	Rifleman	R.I.R.	Wounded.
HANNA, DANIEL	Disraeli Street	Sergeant	R.I.R.	
HARKNESS, JAMES	Beresford Street	Private (Drums)	Duke of Wellington Regt.	
HAIRE, J. MARTIN	Sixth Street	Private	R.I. Fus.	
HARRIS, ALBERT	9 Brennan Street			
HASTINGS, JAMES	25 Sixth Street	Rifleman	R.I.R.	Prisoner of War.
HENDERSON, WM.				Killed in Action.
HENRY, ALEXANDER	Snugville Street	Private	R.I.R.	
HENRY, SAMUEL	Seventh Street	Private	R.I.R.	
HENRY, JOHN	Byron Street	Private	R.I.R.	Prisoner of War.
HISLOP, T. W.	18 Landscape Terrace	Private	R.I.R.	
HILL, JOHN	Byron Street	Rifleman	R.I.R.	Prisoner of War.
HILL, SAMUEL	Byron Street	Private	R.I.R.	
HOOKS, JOSHUA	4 Elswick Street	Sergeant	Headquarters	
HOOKS, JAMES	4 Elswick Street	Rifleman	R.I.R.	
HOOKS, JOHN				Killed in Action.
HOSICK, ALFRED	66 Aberdeen Street	Private	R.I.R.	
HOSICK, ALFRED, SEN.	66 Aberdeen Street	Private	R. Irish Regt.	
HOLYWOOD, WM.	166 Silvio Street			
HUGHES, JAMES			R.E.	Killed in Action.

(156)

BELFAST PRESBYTERY.   SHANKILL ROAD MISSION.

Name.	Home Address.	Rank.	Regiment, Battalion or Unit.	Remarks.
Hunter, T. J.	1 Kinnaird Terrace	Sergt.-Major	A.S.C.	
Hunter, David	39 Moscow Street	Private	Ulster Field Bakery	
Hunter, John	Agnes Street	Private	R.I.R.	
Hutchinson, D.	3 Lawnbrook Avenue	Rifleman	King's Royal Rifles	
Harper, Robert	31 Ghent Street		R.I. Rifles	Prisoner of War.
Irwin, Charles	Sixth Street	Rifleman	R.I.R.	
Jardine, David	10 Alloa Street	Rifleman	R.I.R.	
Johnston, W. J.	9 Up. Charleville St.			Killed in Action.
Johnston, Thomas	Huss Street	Private	I. Fusiliers	Died of Wounds.
Johnston, W. J.	104 Ainsworth Avenue	Sergeant	R.I.R.	Wounded.
Johnston, Wm.	Glentilt Street	Rifleman	R.I.R.	
Johnston, Thomas	Glentilt Street	Private	R. Inn. Fus.	
Johnston, R. G.	38 Wigton Street	Sapper	R.E.	
Johnston, R. J.				
Johnston, Wm. James				
Johnston, Wm.	35 Cumberland Street		Canadians	Killed in Action.
Johnston, John	35 Cumberland Street		Inn. Fus.	Missing.
Kane, Archibald	84 Bray Street	Rifleman	R.I.R.	
Kane, David	Crosby Street	Driver	Transport	
Kernaghan, Robert	158 Agnes Street	Sergeant	R.I.R.	
Kernaghan, Wm.	158 Agnes Street	Private	R.I.R.	Wounded
Kernaghan, David	159 Agnes Street	Sapper	127 Batt. (O.S.) Rail. Con.	
Keenan, Hugh	Lorton Street	Rifleman	R.I.R.	Prisoner of War.
Keenan, Frank	Lorton Street	Rifleman	R.I.R.	
Keenan, George	Lorton Street		Navy	
Kidd, John H.	Daisyfield Street	Gunner	R.F.A.	
Kinkaid, Robert	Sugarfield Street			
Kinkaid, James	Sugarfield Street			
Kinkaid, Andrew	Sugarfield Street			
Kinkaid, John	Sugarfield Street			
Kirkwood, George	Sixth Street	Saddler	A.S.C., Canadians	
Kirkpatrick, Thomas	41 Enfield Street	Private	1st Cheshire Regt.	
Kitson, David	Crosby Street	Driver	R.E.	
Lewis, Wm.	N. Howard Street	P.O.	Navy	
Lewis, Andrew	N. Howard Street	Private	R.I. Fus.	Prisoner of War.
Lyons, John	27 Morpeth Street	Private	R.I.R.	
McBride, Kirker	41 Up. Charleville St.	Sergeant	R.I.R.	Killed in Action.
McBride, T. J.	41 Up. Charleville St.	Lance-Corporal	R.I.R.	
McBride, John	41 Up. Charleville St.	Corporal	Navy	
McCauley, James	Weir Street	Driver	A.S.C.	
McCallen, Wm.	58 Fifth Street		Inn. Fus.	Killed in Action.
McCleery, Austin	44 Arkwright Street	Private	R.I.R.	Killed in Action.
McClean, J. A.	44 Arkwright Street	Rifleman	R.I.R.	
McClung, Wm.	31 Cumberland Street	Rifleman	R.I.R.	
McClung, James	31 Cumberland Street	Private	R.I.R.	Wded, Pris of War.
McClure, H.	227 Mayo Street	Private	B.M.L.C.	
McClung, James	107 Canmore Street	Private	H.L.I.	Died of Wounds.
McCleave, Edward	51 Langford Street			Killed in Action.
McConaghy, John		Private	Inn. Fus.	Killed in Action.
McComich, Chas.			Navy	
McCoubrey, Jack	81 Springfield Village	Private	R.I.R.	Killed in Action.
McCluney, John	34 Mountjoy Street	Private	Training Res. Batt.	Wounded.
McCluney, W. J.	34 Mountjoy Street		Navy	
McCreary, James	7 Dunmoyle Street	Private	R.A.F.	
McCreary, John	7 Dunmoyle Street		Navy	
McCreedy, Albert	32 University Avenue	Sapper	A.S.C. C.E.	Died.
McCreedy, Robert	Mayo Street	Gunner	M.G.C.	Prisoner of War.
McCreedy, Joseph	20 Caledon Street	Sergeant	R.I.F.	
McCullough, Wm.	27 Springmount Street	Private	R. Inn. Fus.	
McCullough, Wm., Jun.	27 Springmount Street	Private	R.I.R.	
McCurdy, R.	107 Palmer Street	Sergeant	R.A.M.C.	
McCurry, Thos.	67 Wall Street	Private	R.I.F.	Prisoner of War.
McDonald, George	45 Emerson Street	Private	Canadians	
McDonald, S. G.	45 Emerson Street		Navy	
McDowell, Wm.	26 Matlock Street	Rifleman	R.I.R.	
McEvoy, W. J.	14 Sydney Street W.	Private	R.I.R.	Killed in Action.
McEvoy, Thomas	14 Sydney Street W.	Sapper	R.E.	
McGready, John	Glencairn Street	Private	R.I.R	
McFarlane, Wm.	Beresford Street	Rifleman	R.I.R.	
McKee, Joseph	Westmoreland Street	Q.M. Sergeant	Inf. Detail, Base Depot	
McKeown, Robert	87 Glenwood Street	Lance-Corporal	R.I.R.	
McKibbin, Edward	24 Dewey Street		Navy	
McKibbin, James	24 Dewey Street	Private	Australians	
McKinley, Joseph	19 Downing Street	Private	R.A.M.C.	
McMullan, D.			R.A.F.	
McIlroy, Wm.	31 Aberdeen Street		R.I.R.	Killed in Action.
McKnight, James	236 Cupar Street	Private	R.I.R.	Killed in Action.
McAnally, John	1 Linen Street		Navy	Killed in Action.
McAnally, W.	13 Tennent Street	Sergeant	R.I.R.	
McNabney, George	21 Klondyke Street	Gunner	R.F.A.	
McTear, James	Sixth Street	Rifleman	R.I.R.	
McQuillan, Wm.	39 Tenth Street		Navy	Killed in Action.
Mailey, John H.	Cupar Street	Private	R.I.R.	Killed in Action.
Martin, Wm.				Killed in Action.

BELFAST PRESBYTERY.   SHANKILL ROAD MISSION.

Name.	Home Address.	Rank.	Regiment, Battalion or Unit.	Remarks.
MATIER, SAMUEL	171 Ainsworth Avenue	Rifleman	R.I.R.	Killed in Action.
MATTHEWS, JAMES	6 Wimbledon Street			
MATTHEWS, W. J.	42 Lorton Street	Rifleman	R.I.R.	Wounded.
MAJURY, JOHN	82 N. Howard Street	Sergeant	R. Inn. Fus.	
MILLS, SAM.	21 Arkwright Street	Sapper	Canadian Div. Engineers	
MILLAR, W.			Navy	
MILES, ALEXANDER	44 Mountjoy Street	Private	R.A.M.C.	
MONTGOMERY, NOEL	5 Lower Crescent	Captain	R.A.M.C.	
MONTGOMERY, F. P.	5 Lower Crescent	Captain	R.A.M.C.	M.C.
MONTGOMERY, W. E.	5 Lower Crescent	Lieutenant	Chinese Labour Corps	
MONTGOMERY, WM.	98 Boundary Street	Private	R.E.	
MONTGOMERY, RICHARD	98 Boundary Street	Corporal	Irish Guards	
MONTGOMERY, STEPHEN	98 Boundary Street	Rifleman	R.I.R.	
MONTGOMERY, ALEX.	Mayfair Street	Private	Seaforth Highldrs.	Killed in Action.
MONTGOMERY, DAVID	Conway Street	Private	Seaforth Highldrs.	Wd., Pris. of War.
MORELAND, JAMES	34 Daisyfield Street	Private	R.I. Fus.	
MORELAND, H.	34 Daisyfield Street	Sergeant	R.I.R.	
MORRISON, W. J.	55 M'Tier Street	Lieutenant	16th Officers' Cadet Batt.	
MORRISON, R.	55 M'Tier Street	Driver	R.G.A.	
MORRISON, IRVINE	55 M'Tier Street	Driver	A.S.C.	
MORROW, JOHN	Carlow Street			
MURPHY, THOMAS	Bellevue	Private	Field Amb.	
NEILLY, WM.	123 Agnes Street	Lance-Corporal	R.E.	D.C.M.
NEILLY, WM.	18 Warkworth Street	Sapper	R.E.	
NEILLY, ROBERT	21 Morpeth Street	Driver	A.S.C.	Wounded.
NEILLY, D. C.	21 Morpeth Street	Private	R. Inn. Fus.	
NEILL, JOHN	Westmoreland Street	Sapper	R.E.	
NELSON, ROBERT	13 Canmore Street	Private	A.S.C.	
NESBITT, HENRY	25 Ballycarry Street	Private	R.I.R.	
NEVILLE, ROBERT	46 Snugville Street		A.S.C.	
NIMICK, JOHN	8 Bromley Street	Private	R.I. Fus.	
NUGENT, ARTHUR	57 Beverley Street	Sapper	R.E.	
ORR, JOSEPH	30 Tyne Street			
PLAYFAIR, WM.	Percy Street	Sergeant	R.I. Fus.	
PORTER, THOMAS			Inn. Fus.	Killed in Action.
PORTER, WM.			R.I. Rifles	Killed in Action.
PENMAN, CARL	3 Craig's Terrace	Sergeant	R.I.R.	Killed in Action.
PATTENDEN, WM.				Killed in Action.
PURDY, RICHARD	4 Ottawa Street		Navy	Killed in Action.
QUIGG, SAMUEL J.	23 Northumberland St.		Navy	
REID, JAMES	51 Bellevue Street	Private	R.I.R.	
REID, THOMAS	51 Bellevue Street	Private	R.I.R.	Killed in Action.
REID, SAMUEL	44 Raleigh Street	Rifleman	R.I.R.	Killed in Action.
REILLY, JAMES	41 Sugarfield Street	Private	Inn. Fus.	Killed in Action.
RICHMOND, WM.	159 Canmore Street	Private	Inn. Fus.	
RICE, JAMES	53 Fairview Street	Private	R.E.	
RICE, WM.	53 Fairview Street	Private	R.I.R.	
RIDDELL, F. W.	44 Beresford Street	Gunner	Navy	
ROBINSON, R. J.	63 Crosby Street	Private	Scottish Rifles	Killed in Action.
ROBINSON, THOMAS	63 Crosby Street	Private	Inn. Fus.	Prisoner of War.
ROBINSON, WM.	32 Roe Street		South Lancashire	Killed in Action.
ROBINSON, ALBERT	32 Roe Street		King's Own Liverpool Regt.	Killed in Action.
ROBINSON, HERBERT	32 Roe Street		Navy	
RUSSELL, W. L.	30 Westland Street	Sergeant	R.I.R.	
RUSSELL, FRED.	159 Agnes Street	Sapper	General Base Depot	
SANDERS, THOMAS	26 Bristol Street	P.O.	Navy	Died.
SANDS, EDWARD	63 Aberdeen Street	Private	R.I.R.	Wounded.
SCOTT, STEWART	65 Aberdeen Street	Rifleman	R.I.R.	Died of Wounds.
SCOTT, ROBERT	180 Sugarfield Street			
SEEDS, THOMAS	13 Crosby Street	Private	Innis Fus.	Killed in Action.
SHIELDS, T. J.	62 Lonsdale Street	Private	Seaforth Highldrs.	
SHORTT, ROBERT	54 Dundee Street	Private	R.I.R.	Killed in Action.
SILVEY, ROBERT	224 Cupar Street	Sergt.-Major	R.I.R.	
SMITH, ARTHUR	2b Aberdeen Street	Rifleman	R.I.R.	
SMITH, ARTHUR, JUN.	2b Aberdeen Street	Gunner	R.F.A.	
SMITH, J. C.	2b Aberdeen Street	Rifleman	R.I.R.	Killed in Action.
SMITH, WM.	2b Aberdeen Street	Rifleman	R.I.R.	
SMITH, JOSEPH	58 Aberdeen Street	Sergeant	M.G.C.	
SMITH, ISAAC	54 Beverley Street	Private	R.I.R.	
SMITH, ROBERT	20 Elswick Street			
STEVENSON, J.	18 Warkworth Street	Private	Canadians	
STEVENSON, W. H.	18 Warkworth Street	Corporal	Canadian Forestry Corps	
STEVENSON, THOMAS	19 Ballycastle Street	Sergeant	C.E. Canadians	Wounded.
STEPHENS, HENRY	18 Eccles Street	Sergeant	A.S.C.	
STEWART, JOHN	44 Hopeton Street	Lance-Corporal	R.I.R.	
THOMAS, GEORGE	97 Broom Street	Gunner	M.G.C.	Wounded.
THOMPSON, SAMUEL	68 Percy Street	Private	R.I.R.	
THOMPSON, WM.	43 Percy Street	Sapper	R.E.	
THOMPSON, W.	15 Huss Street	Rifleman	R.I.R.	
THORNTON, R.	14 Sydney Street W.	Private	Inn. Fus.	
TOPPING, W.	125 Agnes Street	Driver	A.S.C.	
TORRENS, J. B.	2 Collingwood Avenue	Private	Life Guards	
WARNOCK, ROBERT	7 Diamond Street	Sergeant	North Irish Horse	
WATSON, WM.	38 Seventh Street	Private	A.S.C.	

BELFAST PRESBYTERY.   SHANKILL ROAD MISSION.

Name.	Home Address.	Rank.	Regiment, Battalion or Unit.	Remarks.
WEST, JOHN	70 Sugarfield Street	...	Navy	
WHITESIDE, MELVIN	103 Conlig Street	Rifleman	R.I.R.	Wd., Pris. of War.
WHITESIDE, THOMAS	103 Conlig Street	Private	A.S.C.	
WILSON, R. J.	221 Mayo Street	Lance-Corporal	C.C.S.	
WILSON, HUGH	16 Springmount Street	Pioneer	R E.	
WILSON, FRANK	16 Springmount Street	Rifleman	R.I.R.	
WILSON, J. E.	16 Springmount Street	...	R.I. Fus.	Prisoner of War.
WILSON, HUGH, JUN.	16 Springmount Street	...	...	
WILSON, JOHN	16 Springmount Street	Private	R.G.A.	
WILKINSON, R. J.	51 Bray Street	Sergeant	R.I. Fus.	
WOOD, HENRY	13 Riga Street	...	...	
WRIGHT, J.	89 Snugville Street	Sergeant	R.I.R.	
WRIGHT, ROBERT	7 Herron's Row	Lance-Corporal	R.I.R.	
	SINCLAIR SEAMEN'S.			
ANDERSON, DAVID	Brougham Street	...	R.A.F.	
ANDERSER, F. W.	Earl Street	Lieutenant	L.M. Lancs.	
ANDERSER, EDWARD	Earl Street	Corporal	R.I.R.	
ALEXANDER, WILLIAM	Cambridge	Private	R.F.A.	
ACHESON, WM. J.	Gt· George's Street	Sergeant	15th Hussars	
ANDERSON, HARRY	Brougham Street	Sergeant	R.A.M.C.	
ANDERSON, FRED.	Brougham Street	Sergeant	Devonshires	
AULD, ARCHIBALD	Ambrose Street	Private	R.I.R.	
BAIRD, JOHN D.	Spencer Street	Private	R.I.R.	Killed.
BAIRD, SAMUEL B.	Spencer Street	Sergeant	R.I.R.	Killed.
BAIRD, WM. JOHN	Spencer Street	Corporal	R.I.R.	
BARBOUR, T. W.	Kilronan Street	Private	R.I.R.	
BARKLIE, JOHN	Clanmorris Street	Sapper	R.E.	
BELL, ROBERT	Michael Street	Sapper	R.E.	
BENNETT, HAROLD C.	St. Aubyn Street	Private	R.I.R.	
BENNETT, HARRY S.	Queen Victoria Gardens	Private	R.I.R.	
BENNETT, JAMES	Orlington	Private	A.S.C.	
BERKELEY, LOWRY EDMONDS	Bangor	Lieutenant	20th R. Inn. Fus.	Wounded.
BERKELEY, W. L.	South Africa	Private	S.A. Inft.	Killed in Action.
BIGGAR, JOHN	Greenmount Street	Private	R.I.R.	
BODEL, WM. D.	Earl Lane	Private	R.A.F.	
BOYD, SAMUEL	Meadow Street	Private	R.I.R.	
BROWN, JOHN	North Thomas Street	Private	A.S.C.	
BROWN, HARRY	Earl Lane	Private	R.I.R.	
BROWN, WM.	North Thomas Street	Private	R.I.F.	
BROWN, ANDREW	Dock Street	Private	C.D.S.C.	
BROWN, JAMES	Dock Street	Private	Anzacs	
BURCH, ALEX	Caroline Street	Private	R.I.R.	
BRIERS, WILLIAM	Earl Lane	Sergeant	R.F.A.	
BURCOMBE, CHAS. W.	Meadow Street	Private	A.S.C.	
CARSON, ROBERT	Hogarth Street	Corporal	R.I.F.	
CHARTERS, BRYCE	Marine Street	Private	C.C.	
CHARTERS, JAMES	Marine Street	Private	R.I.R.	Killed.
CALDER, LEONARD	Ambrose Street	Private	R.I.R.	
COWAN, ROBERT	N. Thomas Street	Private	R.I.F.	
COCHRANE, ROBERT	Gt. George's Street	Private	R.I.F.	
CALDER, JOHN	Ivan Street	Private	R.I.R.	
CLARKE, THOMAS	Limestone Road	Private	R.I.R.	
CLARKE, ISAAC	Limestone Road	Private	Anzacs	
CLARKE, JAMES	Lt. Ship Street	Corporal	R.I.R.	
CHALMERS, G. S.	Lincoln Avenue	Private	U.S.A.	
CHALMERS, GEORGE	Clifton Crescent	Private	A. & S. Highldrs.	
CLELAND, ROBERT	Tomb Street	Private	R.I.R.	
CLELAND, E.	Tomb Street	Private	A.S.C.	
CLELAND, A.	Tomb Street	Private	R.I.R.	
CARGILL, H. G.	Osborne Street	Sergeant	R.I.F.	
CAMPBELL, ALBERT	Ambrose Street	Private	R.A.F.	Killed.
CAMPBELL, JAMES	Michael Street	Private	R.I.R.	
CAMPBELL, JOHN	Ambrose Street	Private	R.I.R.	
CHRISTIE, SAMUEL	Nile Street	Private	Cam. Highldrs.	
CRAWFORD, C. W.	Cliftonville	Private	C.F.A.	
CRAIG, ROBERT	Nile Street	Private	R.I.R.	
CRAIG, THOMAS	Lt. Ship Street	Private	R.I.F.	Killed.
CRAIG, SAMUEL	Trafalgar Street	Private	R.I.R.	Killed.
COOKE, E.	Shipbuoy Street	Private	R.I.R.	Killed.
CREIGHTON, HARRY	Spencer Street	Private	A.S.C.	Killed.
CROZIER, JOHN	Castleton Avenue	Private	R.I.F.	
COLHOUN, ANDREW	Greenisland	Sergeant	N.I.H.	
CLYDE, T. H.	Earl Place	Corporal	R.F.A.	
COLLINS, WM. JAMES	Nelson Street	Private	A.S.C.	
DAVISON, JOHN	Spamount Street	Private	R.I.R.	
DAVISON, HUGH	Spamount Street	Private	Canadians	Killed.
DAVISON, THOMAS	Spamount Street	Private	Canadians	Killed.
DAVEY, JAMES	Ruth Street	Sergeant	Canadians	
DICK, JOHN M.	Newington Avenue	Sergeant	A.S.C.	
DICKSON, ROBERT R.	Nelson Street	Private	R. Inn. Fus.	
DIXON, THOMAS	Nelson Street	Sapper	R.E.	
DODD, THOMAS	N. Thomas Street	Private	A.S.C·	

BELFAST PRESBYTERY. — SINCLAIR SEAMEN'S.

Name.	Home Address.	Rank.	Regiment, Battalion or Unit.	Remarks.
DORNAN, THOMAS	Kensington Street	Private	R.I.F.	Killed.
DUNWOODY, JAMES	Corporation Street	Private	R.I.R.	
EARLEY, HU.	Alexandra Park Av.	Sergeant	Canadians	
EARLEY, JOHN	Alexandra Park Av.	Private	R.A.F.	
EASDALE, H.	Pilot Street	Private	R.I.R.	
ELLIOTT, BERTIE	Mountcollyer Street	Sapper	R.E.	
ELLIOTT, JAMES	Spamount Street	Private	R.A.F.	
FREEMAN, JOHN	Trafalgar Street	Private	R.I.R.	Killed.
FLACK, WM.	Greenmount Street	Sergeant	R.I.R.	
FLACK, GEORGE M'C.	Holywood Road	Private	A.S.C.	
FLACK, DAVID W. B.	Holywood Road	Sergeant	R.I.R.	Killed.
FLACK, JOHN P.	Greenmount Street	Private	R.I.R.	
GAW, JAMES	Osborne Street	Private	R.I.R.	Killed.
GAGEBY, WILLIAM	Earl Place	Corporal	R.E.	
GEORGE JAMES	Earl Place	Sergeant	Conn. Rangers	Killed.
GILCHRIST GEORGE	Crosscollyer Street	Sergt.-Major	R.I.R.	
GILCHRIST WM.	Crosscollyer Street	Private	Canadians	Killed.
GILCHRIST JAMES	Crosscollyer Street	Private	R.F.A.	
GIBSON, JAMES	Little York Street	Private	R.I.R.	
GRAHAM WM.	Alexandra Park Avenue	Sapper	R.E.	
GORDON ALEX.	Balfour Avenue	Private	R.A.F.	
GORDON JOHN	Nelson Street	Private	R.I.R.	
GORDON JOSEPH	Balfour Avenue	Private	A.S.C. M.T.	
GRAY GEO.	Snugville Street	Private	R.F.A.	
HARPER JOHN L.	Beverley Street	Sergeant	R.I.R.	
HARPER JOHN	Beverley Street	Private	N.I.H.	
HARPER PAUL	Beverley Street	Private	R.I.R.	Killed.
HARRISON ELIAS JOHN	Seaview Street	Lance-Corporal	R.I.R.	Killed.
HEGGAN JAMES	Spamount Street	Private	R.I.R.	
HAMILTON JAMES L.	Carnalea Street	Corporal	R.I.F.	Killed.
HENDRY DAVID	Cultra Street	Private	R.I.R.	
HENDERSON JAMES	Alexandra Park Av.	Sapper	R.E.	
HESLIP HARRY	Fleet Street	Private	R.I.R.	Killed.
HOBBES, JAMES	Nile Street	Private	R.I.R.	
HOPPER, J. D.	Chichester Park	Lieutenant	Bedfords	
HUTCHINSON, ALEX.	Spamount Street	Private	R.I.R.	Killed.
HUTCHINSON, ISAAC	Spamount Street	Private	A.S.C.	
HUTCHINSON, WM. J.	Queen's Road	Private	R.I.R.	
HUTCHINSON, ROBERT R.	Spamount Street	Private	R.I.F.	
HARVEY, WM. R.	Michael Street	Private	R.A.M.C.	
HEARST, W.	Grove Street	Private	R.I.R.	
HOUSTON, WM.	Cambridge Street	Sapper	R.E.	
HOLLAND, JAMES	Lt. Corporation St.	Private	R. Inn. Fus.	
HUNTER, ALEX.	Upper Meadow Street	Private	R.I.R.	
HOLMES, ALEX.	Canterbury Street	Lieutenant	U.S.A.	
IRVINE, CLEMENTS	Valentine Street	Private	R.I.R.	
IRVINE, JOHN	Valentine Street	Private	Seaforth Higldrs.	Killed.
IRVINE, T. H	Valentine Street	Private	R.F.A.	Killed.
JAMISON, DAVID	Whitla Street	Private	R.I.R.	
JACKSON, JOHN C.	Glenburn Park	Private	R.I.R.	
JAMISON, JOHN	Whitla Street	Private	R.F.A.	
JERWOOD, HARRY	Mervue Street	Private	K.R.R.C.	
JONES, WM.	Stratheden Street	Private	R.I.R.	
KELSO, THOMAS	Nelson Street	Private	R.I.R.	
KENNEDY, WM.	Canning Street	Private	R.I.R.	
KENNEDY, JOHN	Hillman Street	Sergeant	R.I.R.	
KERR, ERNEST R.	Stratheden Street	Private	R.I.R.	
KING, HARRY S.	Brookvale Avenue	Private	A.S.C.	
KNOCKER, DAVID	Lt. York Street	Private	Canadians	
KILLOW, HUGH A.	Meadow Street	Private	R.I.R.	
LEWIS, ROBERT	Valentine Street	Corporal	R.F.A.	
LEE, ROBERT M.	Meadow Street	Corporal	Irish Guards	Killed.
LYNAS, RICHARD	Milewater Road	Private	R.A.F.	
LYNAS, WM. J.	Up. Meadow Street	Private	R.I.R.	
LYTTLE, THOMAS	Up. Meadow Street	Private	R.I.R.	
LIVINGSTONE, COLIN	Garden Street	Private	H.L.I.	
LEE, JAMES	Meadow Street	Private	R.I.F.	
LEE, JOSEPH	Gamble Street	Private	R.I.R.	
LEATHEM, CRANSTON	Fleet Street	Private	I.W.T.	
MAGILL, WM.	N. Thomas Street	Sapper	R.E.	
MAGUIRE, WM.	Gt. George's Street	Corporal	R.I.R.	
MARTIN, GEORGE	Townsend Street	Private	R.A.F.	
MARTIN, ROBERT	Back Ship Street	Private	R.I.R.	
MORROW, WM. JAMES	Earl Lane	Private	R.G.A.	
MOORE, WM. S.	Ship Street	Private	A.S.C. M.T.	
MILLAR, ROBERT	Bentinck Street	Sergeant	R.I.R.	
MORRISON, WM. ROSS	Nelson Street	Private	2nd Hants.	Killed.
MORRISON, JOHN Q.		Sapper	R.E.	
MORELAND, HARRY	Tasmania Street	Private	R.I.R.	
MORELAND, FRED.	Tasmania Street	Private	R.I.R.	
MORELAND, WM.	Nelson Street	Private	R.I.R.	
MORLEY, THOMAS	Sussex Street	Sergeant	R.I.R.	
MURPHY, HUGH	Michael Street	Private	R.I.R.	
MULHOLLAND, MORTIMER	Michael Street	Private	Anzacs	

BELFAST PRESBYTERY. — SINCLAIR SEAMEN'S.

NAME.	HOME ADDRESS.	RANK.	REGIMENT, BATTALION OR UNIT.	REMARKS.
MONTGOMERY, A.	Lincoln Avenue	Private	R.I.R.	
McADAM, THOMAS	Lt. Ship Street	Private	R.I.R.	
McALISTER, EDWARD S.	Ruth Street	Private	R.A.F.	
McALISTER, JAMES	Gt. George's Street	Private	R.I.R.	
McALISTER, ISAAC	Gt. George's Street	Lance-Corporal	R.I.R.	Killed.
McCLEMENTS, JOHN	Fortwilliam Parade	Private	A.S.C.	
McCLEMENTS, SAMUEL	Fortwilliam Parade	Private	A.S.C.	
McCALLUM, JOSEPH	Queen Victoria Gdns.	Private	R.I.R.	
McALPIN, WM. J.	Lt. York Street	Private	R.I.R.	
McBRIDE, SAMUEL	Mountcollyer Road	Private	R.I.R.	
McBRIDE, DAVID	Oldpark Place	Corporal	R.A.M.C.	
McATAMNEY, WM.	Adam Street	Corporal	R.G.A.	
McCARTNEY, ROBERT	Ship Street	Sapper	R.E.	Killed.
McFALL, GEORGE	New Lodge Road	Private	Canadians	
McCLURG, JAMES	Old Lodge Road	Private	N.I.H.	
McCOMB, BERTIE	Edenderry Gardens	Corporal	R.I.R.	
McCORMICK, DAVID	Greenmount Street		R.A.F.	
McCREA, WM.	Ship Street	Lance-Corporal	R.I.R.	
McFARLAND, JAMES	St. Vincent Street	Private	R.I.R.	
McILROY, JAMES	Rowan Street	Private	R.I.R.	Killed.
McILROY, ROBERT J.	Rowan Street	Private	17th Royal Scots	
McILROY, ROBERT D.	Hanna Street	Private	R.I.R.	
McKEOWN, ROBERT	Spamount Street	Sergeant	M.M.P.	
McKEOWN, ROBERT	Brougham Street	Private	Canadians	
McKINLY, SAMUEL	Corporation Street		R.A.F.	
McKNIGHT, WM.	Ship Street	Private	R.I.R.	
McLAUGHLIN, HARRY	Whitehouse	Private	R.I.R.	
McMILLAN, ALEX.	Shipbuoy Street	Private	R.I.R.	
McMILLAN, RICHARD	Shipbuoy Street	Sergeant	R.I.R.	Killed.
McVICKER, JOSEPH	Hillman Street	Private	R.I.R.	
McVICKER, ARCHIE	Michael Street	Private	R.I.R.	
McKISSOR, GEORGE	Lt. Ship Street	Private	R.I.R.	
McQUOID, BEN.	Willowfield Street	Lieutenant	Lond. Nth. Lancs.	
McCORMICK, SAMUEL	Greenmount Street	Private	A.S.C.	
McNEILL, JAMES O.	Fleet Street	Private	5th Cheshire	
McCORMICK, WM.	Greenmount Street	Private	I.W.T.	
NORRIS, JOHN	Copperfield Street	Private	Seaforth Highldrs.	
McMURTRY, JOHN	Fleet Street	Private	R.F.A.	
McMURTRY, M.	Fleet Street	Private	Irish Guards	Killed.
NELSON, SAMUEL	Trafalgar Street		R.A.F.	
OSBORNE, H. C.	Hopefield Terrace	2nd Lieutenant	Lond. Nth. Lancs.	Killed.
OSBORNE, E. G.	Duncairn Gardens	Private	Canadians	
PAISLEY, NORMAN	Oldpark Avenue	Private	R.I.R.	
PALMER, JOHN	Ivan Street	Sergeant	R.I.R.	Killed.
PATTERSON, WILLIAM	Earl Street		R.A.F.	
PATTISON, JAMES	Hanna Street	Private	R.I.R.	
PERRY, WILLIAM	Earl Street	Private	R.I.R.	Killed.
PERRY, JAMES	Earl Street	Private	R.I.F.	Killed.
PURSE, CHARLES	Nelson Street	Private	R.I.R.	
PURSE, JAMES	Nelson Street	Private	R.I.F.	
PURSE, WILLIAM	Nelson Street		R.A.F.	
POLLOCK, WILLIAM	South Parade	Private	R.I.R.	
POLLOCK, ALEX.	Shipbuoy Street	Private	R.I.R.	
PROCTOR, JAMES	Hanna Street	Corporal	R.I.R.	
PROCTOR, WM.	Hanna Street	Sapper	R.E.	
PURDY, WM.	Corporation Square	Lance-Corporal	R.I.R.	
QUAITE, WM.	Trafalgar Street	Private	R.I.R.	Killed.
QUAITE, GEORGE	Earl Lane	Private	R.I.R.	
REA, JOHN	Earl Street	Private	A.S.C.	
RIGBY, WM. J.	Lt. George's Street	Private	R.I.R.	Killed.
ROBINSON, JOHN	Shore View	Private	R.I.R.	
ROBINSON, JOHN T.	Shore Terrace	Private	R.I.F.	Killed.
ROBINSON, THOMAS	Lt. York Street	Private	Canadians	Killed.
RIDDELL, HUGH	Nile Street	Private	R.A.M.C.	
ROBINSON, JAMES	Shore View	Private	R.I.R.	
ROSS, WM. S.	Gainsboro' Drive	2nd Lieutenant	R.I.R.	Killed.
RUSSELL, JOHN	Oldpark Place		R.A.F.	
SMITH, THOMAS	Meadow Street	Private	R.I.R.	
SMYTH, FIELDING	Bedeque Street		R.A.F.	
SPENCE, JOSEPH	Spamount Street	Private	R.A.M.C.	
STEPHENSON, W. J.	Derwent Street	Private	R.I.F.	
STEPHENSON, J. T.	Up. Meadow Street	Private	R.I.R.	
STEWART, JAMES	Nelson Street	Private	R.I.R.	
SEMPEY, HUGH	Meadow Street	Private	A.S.C.	
SEMPEY, MATTHEW	Meadow Street	Private	R.I.R.	
SINCLAIR, NORMAN	Fleet Street	Sapper	R.E.	M.M.
TAYLOR, THOMAS	Mervue Street	Private	A.S.C.	
TAYLOR, GEORGE	Kansas Avenue	2nd Lieutenant	R.E.	Killed.
TEMPLETON, ANDREW	Up. Meadow Street	Private	R.I.R.	Killed.
TODD, JOHN	Ambrose Street	Private	R.I.R.	
TODD, THOMAS	Ambrose Street	Private	A.S.C.	
TORRENS, JOHN	Gresham Buildings	Corporal	R.I.R.	
TURNBULL, JOHN	Gt. George's Street	Private	R.I.R.	
TURTLE, JOHN	Mountcollyer Road	Private	R.I.R.	Killed.

BELFAST PRESBYTERY. SINCLAIR SEAMEN'S.

Name.	Home Address.	Rank.	Regiment, Battalion or Unit.	Remarks.
Turtle, Alex.	Mountcollyer Road	Private	I.W.T.	
Thompson, Wm.	Rowan Street	Private	A.S.C.	
Thompson, George	Rowan Street	Private	R.I.R.	Killed.
Turner, Wm.	Spamount Street	Sapper	R.E.	
Walker, Robert	Ruth Street	Private	R.G.A.	
Walker, Wm.	Corporation Street	Private	R.I.F.	
Wilson, James	Nelson Street	Private	R.I.R.	
Wilson, Robert	Nelson Street	Private	Cam. Highldrs.	
Wallace, Wm.	Bentinck Street	Private	R.G.H.	
Wilson, David	Cavour Street	Corporal	R.I.R.	
Young, James	Corporation Street	Sapper	R.E.	
Young, William	Mountcollyer Street		R.A.F.	
ROYAL NAVY.				
Alexander, J.	6 Cambridge Street	Seaman	H.M.S. Gibraltar	
Bennett, H. McG.	9 St. Aubyn Street		R.M.L.I.	
Boyd, John	39 Meadow Street	Seaman	H.M.S. Charon	
Boyd, Wm.	68 Templemore Avenue	E.R.A.		
Bowes, Francis	56 Clanmorris Street	Seaman	H.M.S. Egremont	
Bowes, Wm.	56 Clanmorris Street	Seaman	H.M.S. Panther	
Beggs, Joseph	39 Ship Street	Seaman	R.N.V.R.	
Brien, Joseph	38 Marine Street	Stoker	R.N.R.	
Birney, Samuel	28 Earl Street	Seaman	H.M.S. Centurion	
Cleland, James	43 Tomb Street		R.M.L.I.	
Craig, John	20 Nile Street	Stoker	H.M.S. Drake	
Craig, Robert	167 Alexandra Pk. Av.	Skipper	R.N.V.R.	
Craig, Robert	20 Nile Street	Stoker	H.M.S. Victory	
Chambers, James	11 Nile Street	Stoker	H.M.S. Devonshire	
Costello, Thomas	23 Trafalgar Street	Stoker	R.N.R.	
Connor, Harry	20 City Street	Signaller	H.M.S. Blanche	
Duff, Aaron	26 Earl Street	Seaman	H.M.S. Bellerophon	
Elliott, Samuel	90 Cosgrove Street	Eng. Sub. Lieut.	R.N.R.	
Edmondson, Wm.	Probate Office	Steward	R.N.V.R.	
Erskine, Hamilton	6 Lt. Corporation Street	Seaman	H.M.S. Indomitable	
Gardner, George	16 Spencer Street	Seaman	R.N.R.	
Gray, Wm.	Grove Street	Stoker	H.M.S. Bulwark	Died.
Gordon, Alex.	20 Balfour Avenue	Aux. Eng. Lieut.	R.N.V.R.	
Harpur, David	65 Beverley Street	Seaman	H.M.S. Brilliant	
Herron, David	143 Rugby Avenue	Aux. Eng. Lieut.	R.N.V.R.	
Houston, Samuel	15 Boyne Street	Seaman	R.N.V.R.	
Houston, James	11 Cambridge Street	Stoker	R.N.V.R.	
Hunter, James	83 Up. Meadow Street	Stoker	R.N.R.	
Hume, James	18 Ambrose Street	Seaman	H.M.S. Circe	
Heggen, Daniel	123 Spamount Street	Seaman	H.M.S. Sunshine	
Ingram, Samuel	7 Hanna Street	Stoker	R.N.	
Gillis, George	28 New Andrew Street	Seaman	R.N.R.	
Jelly, Henry	162 New Lodge Road	Stoker	H.M.S. Indefatigable	Died.
Jamison, John	122 Up. Meadow Street	Seaman	R.N.V.R.	
Knox, John	40 Lt. York Street	Stoker	H.M.S. Springhall	
Lee, Joseph	35 Meadow Street	R.M.L.I.	H.M.S. Neptune	
Lee, Joseph	30 Gamble Street	Stoker	H.M.S. Vengeance	
Lyttle, John	Trafalgar Street	Seaman	A.S.R.N.	
Leslie, Wm. J.	20 Earl Lane	Stoker	R.N.R.	Died.
Lyttle, James	29 Trafalgar Street	Stoker	H.M.S. Africa	
Leathem, Wm.	Ormiston Park	Stoker	R.N.R.	
Marshall, Wm. E.	Nelson Street	Stoker	H.M.S. Gibraltar	
Mulholland, Bryce	12 Sylvan Street	Stoker	R.N.R.	
Montgomery, Alex.	2 Carnalea Street	Seaman	R.N.V.R.	
Moore, Wm.	112 Nelson Street	Stoker	R.N.R.	
McCullough, Thomas	27 Adam Street	Stoker	H.M.S. Drake	
McNeill, William	20 Fleet Street	Seaman	H.M.S. Sydney	
McMillen, Samuel	2 Shipbuoy Street	Stoker	H.M.S. Agincourt	
McWilliams, H.	Fleet Street	Stoker	H.M.S. Revenge	
McIlwrath, James	5 Grove Street	Stoker	H.M.S. Illustrious	Died.
McVicker, Archie	Hillman Street	Seaman	A.S.R.N.	
McIlwrath, Samuel	7 Cambridge Street	Stoker	H.M.S. Invincible	
McKeown, Thos. D.	69 Collyer Street	E.R.A.	H.M.S. Aquarius	
McKirdy, Alex.	63 Gainsborough Drive	Eng. Lieut.	R.N.R.	Died.
McMullan, Wm. James	20 Marine Street	Seaman	H.M.S. Poppy	
Neill, Robert	2 Nile Street	Stoker	R.N.R.	
Patterson, Arthur	9 Singleton Street	Signaller	H.M.S. Suffolk	
Patterson, James	9 Singleton Street	Seaman	H.M.S. Bonetta	
Proctor, John	31 Hanna Street	Seaman	H.M.S. Lowestoft	
Sloane, Douglas	22 Nile Street	Stoker	H.M.S. Indefatigable	Died.
Smyth, David	Whitehead	Sub-Lieutenant	R.N.V.R.	Died.
Smyth, David	Whitehead	Seaman	R.N.V.R.	
Todd, John	22 Earl Lane	Stoker	H.M.S. Bayard	Died.
Steele, Archie	Carnalea Street	Stoker	R.N.V.R.	
Todd, Hugh	Brougham Street	Eng. Lieutenant	R.N.V.R.	Died.
Rodgers, Fred.	Nelson Street	Seaman	A.S.R.N.	Killed.
Robinson, Francis	Cosgrove Street	Stoker	R.N.	
Thompson, James	Up. Mervue Street	Seaman	H.M.S. Ellerslie	
Thompson, George	Rowan Street	Seaman	R.N.R.	

BELFAST PRESBYTERY. SINCLAIR SEAMEN'S.

Name.	Home Address.	Rank.	Regiment, Battalion or Unit.	Remarks.
Whitford, Alex.	Shipbuoy Street	Stoker	H.M.S. Margarita	
Wilson, Hugh	Up. Meadow Street	Seaman	A.S.R.N.	
Wright, Edward	Tennent Street	Stoker	P.O., R.N.	
Youell, James	Dock Street	Stoker	P.O., R.N.	
Wheatley, G. A.	13 Castlereagh Place	Eng. Lieutenant	R.N.V.R.	
STRAND, SYDENHAM.				
Adams, H.	43 Park Avenue	Private	R.I.R.	Wounded.
Anderson, J.	22 Kimona Street	Private	N.I.H.	
Ballentine, T.	158 Connsbrook Avenue	Private	R.E.	
Barron, J.	64 Lisavon Street	Private	R.I.R.	
Black, A. J.	192 Connsbrook Avenue	Corporal	R.F.A.	
Black, J.	31 Fernvale Street	Private	R.F.A.	Gassed.
Blanchflower, J.	21 Third Avenue	Private	R.I.R.	
Brown, A.	15 Connsbrook Street	Private	R. Inn. Dragoons	Wounded.
Camlin, E.	59 Victoria Road	Sergeant	R.I.R.	Wounded.
Clugston, W. B.	93 Connsbrook Avenue	Sergeant	R.I.R.	Wounded.
Cobain, E.	43 Park Avenue	Corporal	R.I.R.	
Cobain, R.	43 Park Avenue	Private	Seaforth Highldrs.	
Connery, D. P.	35 Ravenscroft Avenue	Private	R.E.	
Crothers, J.	258 Newtownards Rd.	Private	R.E.	
Culbert, J.	67 Kyle Street	Corporal	R.I.R.	Wounded.
Dempsey, J.	158 Connsbrook Avenue	Private	R.I.R.	Gassed.
Dempsey, S.	158 Connsbrook Avenue	Private	R.E.	
Dobbin, J. G.	Sandringham, Sydenham	Sergeant	R.A.M.C.	Wounded.
Dunbar, R.	28 Fernvale Street	Sergeant	R.I. Regt.	
Finlay, J.	14 Grampian Avenue	Corporal	Life Guards	Wounded.
Finnieson, B.	81 Park Avenue	Sergt.-Major	R.E.	
Finnieson, F.	81 Park Avenue	Private	Can. Seaforth Highldrs.	
Gilbert, T.	30 Fernvale Street	Private	R.I.R.	Killed in Action.
Gilbert, J.	30 Fernvale Street	A.B.	"The Cadmus"	
Gray, W.	64 Pim's Avenue	Private	Seaforth Highldrs.	Killed in Action.
Gray, T.	64 Pim's Avenue	Private	Seaforth Highldrs.	Wounded.
Gregg, A.	3 Laburnum Street	Trooper	N.I.H.	
Gunning, E.	Newtownards Road	Sergeant	A.O.C.	Thrice ment. Des.
Gunning, W.	Newtownards Road	Private	R.E.	
Halleron, T.	1 Westcott Street	Engineer	R.N.R.	
Halleron, Mrs. M.	1 Westcott Street	V.A.D.	V.A.D.	
Hamilton, N.	17 Lisavon Street	Corporal	R.I.R.	M.M.
Hamilton, W.	5 Third Avenue	Private	R.I.R.	M.M.
Harding, H.	7 Fernvale Street	Sergeant	R.I.R.	
Harte, J.	17 Kyle Street	Private	R.I.R.	Killed in Action.
Harvey, I. F.	Downshire Road	Captain	Inn. Fus.	Killed in Action.
Hewitt, J.	Margaret Villa L'field Rd.	Private	A.I.F.	Killed in Action.
Houston, R. F.	15 Methuen Street	Sergeant	R.I.R.	Killed in Action.
Hunt, D.	16 Dundela View	1st Mate	R.N. Res.	
Hunt, J.	16 Dundela View	3rd Mate	R.N. Res.	
Hunt, W.	16 Dundela View	3rd Mate	R.N. Res.	
Hunter, J.	89 Nevis Avenue	Private	R.I.R.	
Hunter, C.	3 Oakdene Ter., Park Av.	Stoker	R.N.	Wounded.
Ireland, S.	47 Victoria Road	Lieutenant	Liverpool Regt.	Killed in Action.
Knowles, G.	28 Lisavon Street	Private	Seaforth Highldrs.	
Knowles, J.	28 Lisavon Street	A.B.	R.N.	
Langridge, J.	16 Westcott Street	Corporal	Pioneers	
Langridge, J.	16 Westcott Street	Corporal	R.A.S.C.	
Larkin, J.	11 Kimona Street	Stoker	R.N.	
Larkin, J.	11 Kimona Street	Sergeant	R.I.R.	
Lewis, J.	27 Kyle Street	Sergeant	R. Inn. Fus.	
Lewis, I.	56 Tamar Street	Stoker	"Hawke"	Killed.
Magee, A.	72 Cheviot Avenue	Sergeant	R. Inn. Fus.	Killed in Action.
Magee, D.	72 Cheviot Avenue	Private	R. Inn. Fus.	Killed in Action.
Magee, W. J.	72 Cheviot Avenue	Private	R.I.R.	Died of Wounds.
Maxwell, J.	15 Kimona Street	Sergeant	R.I.R.	
Milford, J.	28 Kimona Street	Stoker	R.N.	
McCormick, W.	8 Westminster Avenue	Private	R.I.R.	
McCormick, F.	25 Nevis Avenue	Trooper	N.I.H.	
McClurg, W.	286 Connsbrook Avenue	Private	R.I.R.	Wounded.
McClean, S.	5 Fernvale Street	Private	R.A.M.C.	
McClean, W.	20 Shaw Street	Private	R.I.R.	
McDowell, W.	25 Nevis Avenue	Sergeant	R. Inn. Fus.	Killed in Action.
McCoubrey, T.	81 Park Avenue	Sergt.-Major	R.E.	
McFerran, T.	284 Connsbrook Avenue	Trooper	N.I.H.	Killed in Action.
McIlveen, T.	13 Fernvale Street	Private	R.A.M.C.	
McIntosh, J.	293 Connsbrook Avenue	Private	R.I.R.	
McKinstry, J.	18 Lisavon Street	Sergeant	R.I.R.	Killed in Action.
Murphy, J.	24 Lisavon Street	Private	Cam. Highldrs.	Killed in Action.
Orr, T.	6 Church Street E.	Private	R.E.	Wounded.
Orr, S.	1 Welland Street	Sergeant	N.I.H.	
Pepper, A.	21 Greenville Terrace	Private	N.I.H.	Killed in Action.
Reynolds, D.	28 Welland Street	Private	R.F.A.	
Riddick, H.	5 Third Avenue	Private	Seaforth Highlanders	Killed in Action.
Ross, J.	22 Lisavon Street	Private	R.I.R.	Wounded.
Russell, R.	61 Connsbrook Avenue	Corporal	R.I.R.	

BELFAST PRESBYTERY.   STRAND, SYDENHAM.

Name.	Home Address.	Rank.	Regiment, Battalion or Unit.	Remarks
Shaw, W. J.	61 Pim's Avenue	Corporal	R.I.R.	
Shaw, M.	61 Pim's Avenue	Private	R.I.R.	
Sheriff, J.	14 Victoria Avenue	Corporal	R.I.R.	Wounded.
Simms, J. M.	69 Victoria Road	Private	R. Inn. Fus.	Killed in Action.
Simms, R. J.	69 Victoria Road	Shipwright	R.N.	
Simms, T.	69 Victoria Road	Sergeant	R. Inn. Fus.	
Skimin, H.	24 Shaw Street	Stoker	"The Lion"	Wounded.
Skimin, S.	24 Shaw Street	Private	R.I.R.	Wounded.
Somerville, T. H.	39 Cheviot Avenue	Lieutenant	R.A.F.	Wounded.
Silvey, W. J.	Inverary Avenue	Lance-Corporal	R.I.R.	Killed in Action.
Thompson, C.	3 Kimona Street	Private	R.I.R.	
Thompson, E. E.	11 Connsbrook Street	Wireless Operator	R. Navy	
Thompson, G.	3 Kimona Street	Corporal	H.L. Inft.	Killed in Action.
Truesdale, W.	127 Parkgate Avenue	Private	Seaforth Hghldrs.	M.M.
Tully, J.	41 Ravenscroft Avenue	Corporal	M.M.P.	
Wright, T.	14 Kimona Street	Driver	R.N.A.S	

TOWNSEND STREET.

Name.	Home Address.	Rank.	Regiment, Battalion or Unit.	Remarks
Adair, Samuel	2 Sackville Street	Rifleman		
Agnew, Samuel	34 Westmoreland Street	Sergeant		
Alexander, W. H.	10 Berry Street	Private		
Allison, C. F.	8 Easton Crescent	Colonel		M.C., Mons Medal.
Aicken, George	5 Malvern Place	Sergeant		M.M., bar, Mons M.
Aicken, Henry	5 Malvern Place	Private		Wded and Pris.
Armstrong, John	Cliftonpark Avenue	Sergt.-Major		Missing.
Armstrong, Wm. John	54 Westland Street	Rifleman		
Ash, Joseph	68 Northumberland St.	Private		
Babington, Samuel	11 Annesley Street	Private		Killed in Action.
Bingham, Harry	54 Westland Street	Rifleman		Killed in Action.
Bingham, Thos. J.	11 Castleton Gardens	Rifleman		Prisoner.
Bowden, Herbert	Ballygomartin Road	Rifleman		
Boyd, John	15 Hampden Street	Rifleman		
Bradley, George	85 Westmoreland St.	Engineer		
Bradley, Thomas	85 Westmoreland St.	Bandsman		
Bradley, Wm. J.	85 Westmoreland St.	Corporal		Wounded twice.
Bradshaw, Scott	3 Bradford Street	Corporal		Wounded.
Brown, David	28 Westmoreland Street	Private		Wounded.
Brown, Henry Edward	48 Edinburgh Street	Private		
Buchanan, J. C.	7 Albany Street	Rifleman		
Burgess, James	29 Eccles Street	Rifleman		
Burke, Wm.	59 Hopeton Street			
Cairns, James A.	3 Matlock Street	Lance-Corporal		Prisoner.
Campbell, James	9 Howe Street			
Campbell, Henry	47 Peter's Hill	Sergeant		
Campbell, John	9 Howe Street	Trooper		
Carson, John	32 Howe Street	Rifleman		
Campbell, Samuel	14 Queensland Street	Rifleman		Prisoner.
Carson, John	32 Howe Street	Rifleman		
Cathcart, Hugh	14 Lime Street	Private		Wounded.
Christie, Jack	23 Shankill Road	Sergeant		
Clements, John H.	59 Downing Street			
Clements, John McR.	69 Hooker Street			
Connery, Robert	14 Courtrai Street	Rifleman		
Cooper, Hugh	36 Rosewood Street	Sapper		
Corry, James	2 Somerville Gardens	Rifleman	14th R.I.R.	Killed in Action.
Coulter, Joseph	18 Penrith Street	Rifleman		
Coulter, Wm.	18 Penrith Street			
Coulter, Wm.	368 Shankill Road	Trooper		
Craig, James	103 Up. Canning Street	Rifleman	4th R. Inniskillings	Killed in Action.
Craig, Wm. James	103 Up. Canning Street	Private		
Crawford, J.	7 Up. Townsend Street	Sergeant		
Crawford, Robert	2 Shankill Road	Rifleman	14th R.I.R.	Killed in Action.
Crawford, Robt. B.	7 Up. Townsend St.	Bandsman		Wounded.
Crawford, Wm.	7 Up. Townsend St.	Rifleman		
Crothers, Wm.	30 Sackville Street			
Crymble, John	79 Palmer Street	Lance-Corporal		
Dalgleish, Thomas	22 Clifton Drive	Sergeant		
Darragh, James	26 Sylvan Street	Trooper		
Dickey, —	86 Antrim Road	Captain		
Dickey, Herbert Thomas	86 Antrim Road			Wounded.
Dickey, Stanley	86 Antrim Road			
Dickson, Reuben	Bangor	Trooper		
Duncan, James	60 Orkney Street			
Duncan, Thomas	60 Orkney Street	Lance-Corporal		
Duncan, Wm.	60 Orkney Street	Sergeant		
Duncan, Wm.	102 Peter's Hill	Private		
Edmondson, Samuel	18 Tyne Street	Private		W'ded and Missing.
Ellis, Wm.	36 Mountcashel Street	Rifleman		Wounded.
Fee, Wm. Jordan	3 Trevelyan Terrace			Wounded.
Fenton, J. A.	27 Thorndale Avenue	Flight Lieutenant		Killed in Action.
Finlay, Thomas	16 Castleton Gardens	Private		Killed in Action.
Finlay, William	18 Snugville Street	Sergeant	16th R.I.R.	Killed in Action.

BELFAST PRESBYTERY.   TOWNSEND STREET.

Name.	Home Address.	Rank.	Regiment, Battalion or Unit.	Remarks.
GIBSON, MAT. H.	62 Antrim Road			
GIBSON, SAMUEL MOORE	62 Antrim Road			
GILLESPIE, JAMES H.	9 London Street	Private		
GILLIES, JOHN	16 Hopeton Street			
GIRVAN, J. W.	4 Glenarm Terrace	Lieutenant		
GIRVAN, S. K.	1 Earl Street	Sergeant		
GORDON, R. J.		Private	11th R.I.F.	Killed in Action.
GOUDY, HARRY	100 Tennent Street	Rifleman		
GOUDY, ROBERT	100 Tennent Street	Rifleman	18th R.I.R.	Killed in Action.
GRACEY, GEORGE	148 Mountcollyer St.	Captain		Prisoner of War.
GRAY, DAVID	55 Shankill Road			
GREER, ALEX.	29 Cromwell Road	Lieutenant		
GREER, WM.	43 Bristol Street	Corporal		
HARBINSON, ROBERT	39 Brookmount Street	Rifleman		
HARPER, ROBERT	91 Dundee Street	Private		
HART, W. J.	49 McCandless Street	Private		
HASTINGS, J. A.	59 Hopeton Street	Corporal		
HENDERSON, J. C.	10 Perth Street	Rifleman		Wounded twice.
HENRY, JOHN	110 Tennent Street			
HENRY, RICHARD	31 Cranmore Street			
HIGGINSON, R. ERNEST	1 Mt. Royal, Antrim Rd.	Lieutenant	R.A.F.	
HUGHES, ARTHUR	25 Geoffrey Street	Sergeant		
HUTTON, GEORGE	13 Danube Street	Private		Wounded.
IRWIN, ALEX.		Private	A.S.C.	Missing.
JACKSON, S. J.		Private		
JACKSON, W. A.	24 Arkwright Street	Private		
JOHNSTON, ANDREW	48 Hudson Street	Trooper		Wounded.
JOHNSTON, FREDERICK	9 Cranburn Street	Rifleman		
JOHNSTON, GEO.	23 Lonsdale Street	Private		
JOHNSTON, HUGH	77 Beverley Street	Rifleman		Wounded.
JOHNSTON, WM.	36 Kensington Street		Northumberland Fus.	
JORDON, WM.	88 Stanhope Street		R.N.	
KERNS, ROBERT	23 Lonsdale Street	Lance-Corporal		
KINNAIRD, JOHN	54 Ambleside Street	Sergeant		D.C.M.
KNOX, ROBERT G.	13 Ilchester Street	Commander		
LEATHEM, JAMES	34 Windsor Road	Sapper		
LEEBURN, WM. JAS.	25 Cargill Street	Sergeant		Mons. M., M.M. Wd
LEEMAN, JAS. ALEX.	68 Dover Street	Private		
LONG, JAMES	25 Virginia Street	Rifleman		
LORIMER, ANDREW	268 Leopold Street	Rifleman		
LORIMER, JOHN D.	28 Evolina Street	Sergeant		
LYNN, ROBERT	16 River Terrace	Rifleman		
LYNN, SAMUEL	16 River Terrace	Rifleman		
McATEER, JAMES	33 Lorton Street	Lieutenant		Wounded.
McATEER, WM.	33 Lorton Street	Private		Wounded.
MACAULEY, W. J.		Major	A.D., V.S.	Killed in Action.
McBURNEY, RICHARD	37 Berlin Street			
McBURNEY, WM.	28 Lorton Street	Private		
McCLEAN, WALLACE	Springfield Road			
McCLINTOCK, JOHN	33 Erin Street	Private	U.S. Army	
McCLURG, ALBERT E.	29 Esmond Street	Trooper		
McCLURG, WM.	248 Leopold Street	Lance-Corporal		
McCOMB, SAMUEL	102 Percy Street	Sapper		Croix-de-Guerre.
McGOWAN, W. J.	34 Antrim Road	Private	N. Zealanders	Killed in Action.
McILHAGGA, SAMUEL	12 Castleton Gardens			Wounded.
McLAY, WM.	79 Palmer Street	Rifleman		
McMAHON, F. J.	26 Wyndham Street	Rifleman		
McMEEKIN, WM.	33 Kendal Street			
MAGILL, ROBERT	56 Rugby Avenue	Sapper		Wounded.
MARTIN, HARVEY	31 Dublin Road	Private		
MARTIN, J. S.		Lieutenant	2nd R.I.R.	Killed in Action.
MARSHALL, R.	25 Bedeque Street			
MELLON, JAMES	23 Bristol Street			
MILLAR, DAVID		Lance-Corporal	1st R.I.R.	Killed in Action.
MILLAR, JOHN	60 Orkney Street	C.S.M.		
MILLS, A. M.	50 Woodvale Road	Lieutenant		
MILLS, JOSEPH	50 Woodvale Road	Rifleman		Wounded.
MILLS, THOMAS	50 Woodvale Road			
MOLLOY, WM.	20 Christopher Street	Sapper		Killed in Action.
MORRISON, WM.	15 Westmoreland St.	Rifleman		
MORRISON, WM.	85 Peter's Hill	Private		
MOORE, GEORGE	11 Shaftesbury Square	Rifleman		
MOORE, JOHN	123 Northumberland St.			
MOORE, WM. S.	137 Up. Meadow St.	Trooper		
MORROW, H.M.	59 Downing Street			Wounded.
MORROW, JOSEPH	55 Downing Street	Rifleman		
MURRAY, ALBERT	60 Devonshire Street	Rifleman	14th R.I.R.	Gassed.
MURRAY, WM.	60 Devonshire Street		14th R.I.R.	Wounded.
NEILL, ROBERT		2nd Lieutenant	R.G.A.	
NEILL, WM.	52 Kendal Street	Sergeant		
NESBITT, ROBERT	Jaffa Street	Trooper		
NESBITT, WM. A.	Old Lodge Road	Rifleman		Prisoner.
NEWELL, THOS. B.		Rifleman	4th R.I.F.	Killed in Action
NIXON, JOHN		Rifleman	15th R.I.R.	Died of Wounds.

BELFAST PRESBYTERY.   TOWNSEND STREET.

Name.	Home Address.	Rank.	Regiment, Battalion or Unit.	Remarks.
Nixon, John	50 Israel Street	...	...	
Oliver, Wm.	4 Dover Street	Private	...	
Parker, Joseph	38 Alloa Street	Lieutenant	...	
Parker, Robert	54 Lawnbrook Avenue	Rifleman	...	
Parker, Wm.	54 Lawnbrook Avenue	...	...	
Rea, John	12 Century Street	Trooper	...	
Reid, J. C.	188 Agnes Street	...	...	
Reid, John	179 Dunluce Avenue	...	...	
Rice, George	5 Cumberland Street	...	...	
Rice, George	21 Cumberland Street	...	...	
Rice, Samuel	5 Cumberland Street	Private	...	
Risk, Harold	20 Wyndham Street	...	...	
Roddy, Wm.	...	Rifleman	14th R.I.R.	Wded and Missing.
Saunderson, Jas. A. M.	...	Lance-Corporal	15th R.I.R.	Killed in Action.
Scott, Alex. P.	91 Lawnbrook Avenue	...	...	Killed in Action.
Scott, John C.	37 Bedeque Street	Corporal	R.E.	D.C.M., Killed.
Shearer, Wm.	...	Sergeant	R.I.R.	
Simpson, S.	41 Westmoreland St.	...	...	
Sloan, Alex.	69 Townsend Street	...	...	
Sloan, Robert	69 Townsend Street	...	...	
Smith, Thomas	2 Mount Easton	Captain	...	
Smith, Wm.	2 Mount Easton	Q.M.	...	
Smyth, Alfred J.	...	Private	Durham Light Inft.	Killed in Action.
Stewart, Alex.	68 Perth Street	...	...	
Stewart, Tom	Irene, Oldpark Road	...	...	
Storey, John	37 Woodvale Road	...	...	
Storey, J. T.	37 Woodvale Road	...	...	
Teacey, Marshall	56 Agincourt Avenue	Rifleman	...	
Thompson, Geo.	Ollarba Terrace	Major	...	Croix-de-Guerre.
Thompson, Samuel H.	69 Percy Street	Rifleman	...	
Torrance, James	223 Cambrai Street	...	...	
Tougher, R. A. H.	Danesfort, Annadale Av.	Captain	...	
Walker, George	16 Cedar Avenue	Private	...	Wounded.
Ward, Stephen H.	...	Petty Officer	...	Died.
Watson, Chas. P.	The Myrtles, C'ville Rd.	Captain	...	Wded, M.C. & Bar.
Watson, James	66 Downing Street	...	...	
Williamson, Robert	5 Hopeton Street	...	...	
Wilson, David	30 Paris Street	...	...	
Wilson, James Harold	...	Private	2nd Black Watch	Killed in Action.
Wilson, John	30 Paris Street	...	...	
Wilson, John	65 Shankill Road	...	...	
Wright, Archie	Brown Street	Rifleman	...	
Wright, Robert	10 Campbell Street	Rifleman	...	
Young, Wm.	44 Up. Townsend St.	...	...	
Zebedee, Fred. W.	10 Newington Street	Lieutenant	...	
ULSTERVILLE.				
Alexander, Robert	44 Edinburgh Street	Private	R.F.A.	
Armstrong, John	23 Windsor Road	Private	R.F.A.	Wounded.
Arnold, Robert	Surrey Street	Private	R.A.F.	
Beggs, Wm.	368 Donegall Road	Wireless Operator	R.N.	
Bell, Harry	Donnybrook Street	Private	R.I.R.	Killed in Action.
Black, Alfred	Northbrook Street	Private	Black Watch	Wounded.
Black, Charles	Tate's Avenue	Private	R.I.R.	Wounded.
Carson, Samuel	213 Dunluce Avenue	Sergeant	R.S.	
Cartlidge, Wm. Percy	115 Edinburgh Street	Private	R.A.M.C.	
Connolly, Charles	Edinburgh Street	Sergeant	A.S.C.	
Craig, Edward	Cussick Street	Private	R.I.R.	
Craig, Wm.	Cussick Street	Private	R.I.R.	Killed in Action.
Dorrity, Edward	Edinburgh Street	Private	R.I.R.	Wounded.
Fairley, Wm.	7 Northbrook Street	Private	R.I.R.	Wounded.
Fitzsimons, S. E. S.	Roden Street	Lieutenant	R.I.R.	
Gibson, Wm.	Lisburn Avenue	Private	R.I.R.	
Graham, Archibald	1 Stranmillis Street	Private	S.H.	Wounded.
Grattan, Wm.	Cussick Street	Private	R.I.R.	Wounded.
Haslett, Frank W.	1 Ulster Terrace	Cadet	R.I.R.	
Hendry, James	Dunluce Avenue	Sergeant	R.E.	
Hopkins, John	Northbrook Street	Private	R.I.R.	
Hopkins, John, Jun.	Northbrook Street	Private	R.I.R.	
Hopkins, Robert	Northbrook Street	Private	R.I.R.	
Houston, Fred.	Gt. Northern Street	Private	R.I.R.	Died.
Jackson, John	83 Edinburgh Street	Private	A.S.C.	
Jamison, Samuel	Ferndale Street	Private	R.I.R.	Wounded.
Johnston, Charles	57 Edinburgh Street	Sergeant	R.I.R.	
Lee, Wm.	Lisburn Avenue	Private	R.A.F.	
Lynn, Alex.	Ferndale Street	Private	R.I.R.	
McBurney, Wm.	3 Edinburgh Street	Private	R.I.R.	Wounded.
McCartney, John	52 Melrose Street	Private	R.E.	Wounded.
McCashin, Harry	Dunluce Avenue	Private	R.I.R.	Killed in Action.
McCullough, Robert	Meadowbank Place	Sergeant	R.F.A.	Wounded.
McFarland, Geo.	16 Tate's Avenue	Lieutenant	R.I.R.	Wounded.
McIlreavey, Alex.	Ethel Street	Private	C.C.	
McIlreavey, Hugh	Ethel Street	P. Officer	R.N.	

BELFAST PRESBYTERY.   ULSTERVILLE.

Name.	Home Address.	Rank.	Regiment, Battalion or Unit.	Remarks.
McKee, Alan	115 Tate's Avenue	Private	R.I.R.	Wounded.
McKittrick, Wm.	Lr. Windsor Avenue	Private	R.S.	
McLoughlin, John	Meadowbank Place	Private	R.I.R.	Killed in Action.
McLoughlin, Walter	Meadowbank Place	Private	M.T.	Wounded.
McMaster, Robert	Gt. Northern Street	Private	R.I.R.	
McNeill, Fred.	Northbrook Street	Private	N.I.H.	
McWhirter, Robert	135 Tate's Avenue	Private	R.E.	
Mason, Richard	Rathcool Cottage	Sergeant	R.A.F.	
Mason, Wm.	Rathcool Cottage	Private	S.H.	
Neill, George	5 Windsor Terrace	Private	Black Watch	
Nicholson, Hugh	Ferndale Place	Private	R.I.R.	Killed in Action.
Patterson, James	38 Edinburgh Street	Private	R.I.R.	
Patterson, Samuel	38 Edinburgh Street	Private	R.I.R.	Wounded.
Patton, Joseph	78 Edinburgh Street	Private	A.S.C.	
Patton, Wm.	78 Edinburgh Street	Private	R.I. Fus.	Wounded.
Rodgers, Robert	Marlborough Avenue	Private	R.I.R.	Died.
Rossborough, Alex.	Dumbarton, Scotland	Private	R.I.R.	Wounded.
Sloan, Joseph	10 Donnybrook Street	Private	R.I.R.	Killed in Action.
Smith, John	Clough, Co. Antrim	Lieutenant	R.I.R.	Killed in Action.
Sterne, Robert	Edinburgh Street	Private	R.M.	Wounded.
Stevenson, Samuel	16 Edinburgh Street	Stoker	R.N.	
Walker, William	Adelaide Avenue	Private	A.S.C.	
Wigson, J.	Napier Street	Private	R.E.	Killed in Action.
Wilson, D.	Melrose Street	Private	R.I.R.	
Wilson, J.	Melrose Street	Private	R.I.R.	Wounded.
COLONIAL FORCES.				
Glover, Geoff.	Lisburn Road	Sergeant	Can. University Unit	
McAree, Thomas	Donegall Road	Private	Can. F.A.	
McBurney, James	3 Edinburgh Street	Private	Can. E.F.	
McFarland, J. H.	16 Tate's Avenue	Sergeant	Can. E.F.	
WESTBOURNE.				
Adams, S.	50 Clandeboye Street	Eng. W.O.	R.F.A.	
Adair, F.	10 Templemore Avenue	Corporal	R.I.R.	
Addison, R.	87 Grove Street East	Private	R.A.M.C.	Killed in Action.
Addison, W.	87 Grove Street East	A.B.	R.N.	
Agnew, J.	19 Ravenscroft Avenue	Private	R.I.R.	Killed in Action.
Agnew, W.	19 Ravenscroft Avenue	Private	Seaforth Highldrs.	Killed in Action.
Allister, R. H.	93 Up. Newtownards Rd.	Lieutenant	S.A.E.F.	
Allen, A.	...	Driver	R.A.S.C.	
Allen, T.	...	Sergeant	R.I.R.	
Anderson, J.	...	Private	R.I.R.	
Anderson, J.	...	Private	R.E.	
Anderson, R.	15 Chatsworth Street	Private	R. Inn. Fus.	Killed in Action.
Andrews, W.	...	Sergt.-Major	R.A.M.C.	
Atkinson, J.	45 Paxton Street	Corporal	R.I.R.	
Atkinson, J.	...	Lance-Corporal	R.I.R.	Killed in Action.
Bailie, A. F.	33 Wolff Street	A.B.	R.N.	
Baillie, H.	10 Montrose Street	Private	South Lancs.	Killed in Action.
Bailie, T.	83 Tower Street	Private	R.I.R.	
Bailie, R. A.	83 Tower Street	Private	N.Z. E.F.	
Bailie, W.	32 Roundhill Street	Private	R.A.O.C.	
Barnes, H.	...	Engineer	Mer. Ser.	
Bell, A.	...	Lance-Corporal	R.I.R.	
Bell, T.	...	Private	R.I.R.	
Bingham, T. H.	105 Solway Street	Private	Seaforth Highldrs.	Killed in Action.
Birch, H.	...	Stoker	R.N.	Killed in Action.
Black, W.	100 Tower Street	C.E.R.A.	R.N.	
Blair, T.	...	Private	S. Lancs.	Killed in Action.
Bothwell, T. H.	...	Private	R.I.R.	
Bowers, A.	54 Hornby Street	Private	R.I.R.	D.C.M.
Boyd, W.	Tower Street	Gunner	R.G.A.	Killed in Action.
Brackenridge, W. H.	6 Clara Street	Sapper	R.E.	
Brown, R.	24 Fox Street	Private	R.I.R.	
Campbell, J.	73 Bloomfield Avenue	Stoker	R.N.	
Childs, E.	11 Brandon Terrace	Private	R.I.F.	
Collier, D.	19 Belvoir Street	Co. Sergt.-Major	R.I.R.	Killed in Action.
Connolly, J.	52 Thistle Street	Bos'n's Mate	R.N.R.	
Connolly, J., Jun.	57 Thistle Street	Sapper	R.E.	
Coulter, J.	75 Cheviot Avenue	Private	M.G.C.	
Conway, M.	...	Lance-Corporal	R.I.R.	
Craig, A.	47 Lendrick Street	Sergeant	R.M.F.	
Craig, S. A.	47 Lendrick Street	Q.M.S.	R.I.R.	
Creighton, J.	...	Sergeant	R.A.F.	Killed in Action.
Cranston, S.	4 Gawn Street	...	R.I.R.	
Creelman, A.	12 Lendrick Street	Private	R.I.R.	
Cull, J. H.	3 Colville Street	Lance-Corporal	R.I.R.	Killed in Action.
Cull, S.	3 Colville Street	...	Seaforth Highldrs.	Killed in Action.
Cully, W.	7 Thistle Street	A.B.	R.N.R.	
Dales, J.	...	Private	R.A.F.	

BELFAST PRESBYTERY. WESTBOURNE.

Name.	Home Address.	Rank.	Regiment, Battalion or Unit.	Remarks.
Dale, J. H.	13 Belvoir Street	Reg. Sergt.-Major	R.I.R.	M.M., Kd. in Act.
Davidson, R.	89 Tower Street	Ft· Sergeant	R.F.A.	
Deans, J.	27 Tower Street	Corporal	R.W.R.	
Dickson, J.	...	A.B.	R.N.	
Dickson, W.	...	Private	R.I.R.	
Dobson, F. J.	...	Private	R.A.F.	
Doloughan, A.	1 Finmore Street	Lance-Corporal	I.D.	
Doloughan, J.	1 Finmore Street	Corporal	R. Inn. Fus.	Killed in Action.
Donnan, J.	28 Medway Street	Sapper	R.E.	
Donnan, S.	28 Medway Street	Private	R.A.S.C.	
Donnan, T.	28 Medway Street	Private	London Fus.	
Donnan, W.	28 Medway Street	...	R. Inn. Fus.	
Douglas, J.	...	Driver	R.A.S.C.	
Dunwoody, W. J.	7 Thistle Street	Corporal	R.F.	
Elliott, T.	...	Private	R.I.R.	Killed in Action.
Emerson, J.	45 Paxton Street	Private	R.I.R.	Killed in Action.
Esler, J.	...	Sergeant	R.A.S.C.	M.M.
Fisher, D.	35 Solway Street	Private	R.I.R.	Killed in Action.
Flannigan, J. A.	...	Private	R.I.R.	
Forsythe, A.	3 Bryson Street	Sapper	R.E.	
Forsythe, F.	3 Bryson Street	Gunner	R.N.	
Forsythe, G·	...	Private	R.I.R.	Killed in Action.
Forsythe, H.	...	Lance-Corporal	M.G.C.	Killed in Action.
Forsythe, R.	3 Bryson Street	Private	R.I.R.	
Forsythe, W.	72 Bryson Street	Private	R.G.A.	
Foster, J.	11 St. Leonard's Street	Private	R.E.	
Foster, R. M.	11 St. Leonard's Street	Private	R.I.R.	Killed in Action.
Gardner, W. A.	55 Westbourne Street	Private	Seaforth Highldrs.	
Gatenby, E.	12 Tower Street	Sergeant	R.I.R.	
Gibson, J·	...	Private	R.I.R.	
Gilliland, J.	56 Bryson Street	Private	I. Guards	Killed in Action.
Gilliland, W.	56 Bryson Street	Private	R.I.R.	
Gilmore, E.	13 Baskin Street	Private	R.E.	
Girvan, A·	...	Sapper	R.E.	
Gordon, R.	...	Private	R.I.R.	
Goudy, T.	28 Tower Street	Sapper	R.E.	
Grant, W. J.	34 Saunders Street	Private	R. Inn. Fus.	Killed in Action.
Gray, W.	52 Canton Street	Lance-Corporal	R.A.M.C.	
Gray, R. J.	52 Canton Street	Lance-Corporal	R.I.R.	M.M.
Hall, A.	57 Mourne Street	Co. Sergt.-Major	R.I.R.	Killed in Action.
Hanna, W.	40 Montrose Street	Lance-Corporal	R.E.	
Henry, S.	15 Thistle Street	Corporal	R.I.R.	
Hewitt, W.	41 Bryson Street	Sapper	R.E.	Killed in Action.
Hill, R.	...	Private	R.A.F.	
Hives, S.	118 Mountpottinger Rd.	Corporal	N.I.H.	
Hook, H.	6 Templemore Avenue	P.O.	R.N.	
Hoy, S.	83 Newcastle Street	Private	R.I.R.	Killed in Action.
Hume, G.	...	Private	Scot. R.	
Hurst, W.	28 Ribble Street	Sto. P.O.	R.N.	
Irvine, J.	...	Private	R.A.S.C.	
Irvine, G.	...	Corporal	R. Inn. Fus.	
Jackson, A.	9 Paxton Street	Corporal	R.I.R.	
Jamison, R.	12 Beechfield Street	Private	R.I.R.	
Johnston, J.	...	A.B.	R.N.	
Johnston, R.	...	Private	R.I.R.	Killed in Action.
Johnston, W.	...	Signaller	R.W.R.	Killed in Action.
Johnston, W. J.	...	Private	R.I.R.	
Jones, T.	...	Private	N.I.H.	
Kennedy, D.	...	Private	R.I.R.	Killed in Action.
Kennedy, J.	...	Gunner	M.G.C.	Killed in Action.
Kerr, A.	23 Sintonville Avenue	Engineer W.O.	R.N.	Killed in Action.
Kerr, N.	23 Sintonville Avenue	Sapper	R.E.	
Kerr, W.	23 Sintonville Avenue	Jun. E.O.	R.N.R.	
Kernaghan, J.	...	Private	R.A.F.	
Kirk, W.	3 Dee Street	Sapper	R.E.	
Kirk, D.	3 Dee Street	Driver	R.E.	
Law, D.	...	Private	N.I.H.	
Lee, G.	...	Gunner	R.G.A.	
Lee, W.	...	Private	R. Inn. Fus.	
Leebody, J.	27 Bright Street	Corporal	R.I.R.	
Leebody, R.	27 Bright Street	Private	R.I.R.	Killed in Action.
Lewis, J.	...	Lance-Corporal	R.E.	
Liggett, E.	109 The Mount	Bombardier	R.F.A.	
Liggett, G.	109 The Mount	Gunner	R.F.A.	Killed in Action.
Little, J.	...	Sergeant	R.E.	
Long, J.	90 Tower Street	Private	R.I.R.	Killed in Action.
Long, R.	...	Driver	R.A.S.C.	
Long, S.	90 Tower Street	Private	R.I.R.	Killed in Action.
Long, S.	...	Private	H.L.I.	
Long, W.	...	Private	R. Inn. Fus.	Killed in Action.
Lowry, A.	...	Private	R.I.F.	Killed in Action.
Lyons, W. G.	79 Fraser Street	Private	R.A.M.C.	
Magee, J.	79 Fraser Street	C.P.O.	R.N.R.	
Mallard, J.	52 Woodcot Avenue	Sec. A.M.	R.A.F.	

BELFAST PRESBYTERY. WESTBOURNE.

Name.	Home Address.	Rank.	Regiment, Battalion or Unit.	Remarks.
Marshall, D.	22 Crystal Street	Private	R.I.R.	
Martin, W. C.		Private	R.I.R.	
Martin, G.		Private	R.I.R.	
Matthews, H.	91 Solway Street	Private	R.I.R.	
Matthews, J.	3 Susan Street	Private	R.I.R.	
Matthews, W. J.	34 Hornby Street	Private	R.I.R.	
Millar, J.		Sergeant	R.I.R.	
Milligan, S. J.		Sergeant	R.I.F.	
Milligan, T.		Private	I.G.	
Mills, A.	174 Connsbrook Avenue	Private	R.I.R.	
Milne, J.	28 Crystal Street	A.B.	R.N.V.R.	
Moffatt, H. S.	17 Gawn Street	Lance-Corporal	R. Inn. Fus.	Killed in Action.
Moffatt, E.	Larkfield Villa	Private	R.I.R.	
Munro, G.	8 Oakland Avenue	Captain	M.G.C.	M.M. and Bar.
Moore, T.	3 M'Master Street	Sergeant	R.I.R.	
Morrow, J.		Lance-Corporal	R.I.R.	Killed in Action.
Morrow, T.		Private	R. Inn. Fus.	Killed in Action.
Murphy, F.		Private	R.I.R.	
McBratney, J. H.		Private	R.I.R.	Killed in Action.
McBride, J.		Major	R.F.A.	Killed in Action.
McCann, J. E.		Private	R.I.R.	Killed in Action.
McCarroll, W.	15 Chadolly Street	Private	Seaforth Highldrs.	M.M.
McConnell, A.	198 My Lady's Road	Lance-Corporal	R.I.R.	
McConnell, S. M.	198 My Lady's Road	Lance-Corporal	R.I.R.	M.M., Kd. in Act.
McCoubrey, P.	4 Roxburgh Street	Private	R.E.	
McCrudden, C.		Stoker	R.N.	
McCulloch, A.		Private	R. Inn. F.	
McCullough, E.		Sapper	R.E.	
McDowell, J. E.	4 Derwent Street	Sapper	R.E.	
McElroy, W.		Corporal	R.I.R.	Killed in Action.
McGiffen, T.	58 Templemore Avenue	P.O.	R.N.A.S.	
McGuffin, S.	50 Belmont Road	A.B.	H.M.A.N.	
McIlroy, A.	313 Albertbridge Road	Lance-Corporal	R.I.R.	
McIlroy, R.	313 Albertbridge Road	Lance-Corporal	R.I.R.	
McLean, D. W.	36 Mersey Street	Ld. Stoker	R.N.	
McLean, J. J.	36 Mersey Street	Lance-Corporal	R.A.S.C.	
McLean, J. W.	36 Mersey Street	Lance-Corporal	R.I.R.	Killed in Action.
McMaster, D.	94 Castlereagh Road	Private	R.A.S.C.	Killed in Action.
McMaster, J.	3 Susan Street	Qr. M.S.	R.G.A.	
McMillan, H.		Lance-Corporal	R.I.F.	
McNally, R.	24 Baskin Street	A.B.	R.N.	
McNeice, D.	17 Convention Street	Private	R.I.R.	
McVeigh, T. S.	132 Dee Street	Driver	R.A.S.C.	
McVeigh, W. T.	132 Dee Street	Sapper	R.E.	Killed in Action.
Napier, J.	132 Beersbridge Road	Lance-Corporal	R.I.R.	Killed in Action.
Napier, R.	132 Beersbridge Road	Private	R.I.R.	
Nicholl, D.		Private	R.I.R.	
Nickle, A.	17 Hillview Avenue	P.O.	R.N.	
Orr, H. G.		Private	A.C.I.	
Orr, S.		Private	R.A.S.C.	
Parker, A. E.	82 Tower Street	Reg. S.M.	Cheshire Regt.	
Patience, W. H.	5 Up. Frank Street	Steward	Mer. Ser.	
Patterson, J.		Driver	R.F.A.	
Patterson, R.		Driver	R.F.A.	
Pearson, G. H.	44 Dee Street	P.O.	R.N.	
Poag, J. S.	35 Austin Street	Lance-Corporal	R.I.R.	Killed in Action.
Pollock, T.	45 Lecumpher Street	Sergeant	R.A.S.C.	Killed in Action.
Poots, W. J.	20 Derwent Street	Sergeant	R. Inn. F.	
Price, T.	271 Newtownards Road	Private	R.A.S.C.	
Quinn, J.	40 Frank Street	Corporal	S.S.R.	
Ritchie, J.		Private	R.I.R.	Killed in Action.
Rodgers, J.	30 Grampian Avenue	Private	R.I.R.	
Rodgers, H. F.	30 Grampian Avenue	Sergeant	R.I.F.	
Russell, A.	76 Beechfield Street	Private	Cameron Highldrs.	Killed in Action.
Savage, R.	1 Clonallen Street	Sapper	R.E.	
Scilly, J. F.	344 Newtownards Road	2nd Lieutenant	R.I.R.	Killed in Action.
Scott, A.	37 Comber Street	Private	R.E.	
Scott, J.	26 Sherwood Street	Lance-Corporal	R.I.R.	
Scott, S.	8 Duke Street	Private	R.I.R.	
Semple, R. J.	83 Portallo Street	Private	R.I.R.	
Shaw, S. J.	7 Ina Street	E.R.A.	R.N.	
Shaw, T. H.	7 Ina Street	Private	R.I.R.	
Sloan, J.	218 Ravenhill Avenue	Eng. Lieutenant	R.N.R.	
Smith, J.		Private	R.I.R.	
Smyly, J. L.	20 Templemore Avenue	Corporal	R.F.C.	
Smyly, C. S.	20 Templemore Avenue	Private	R.A.S.C.	
Smyth, S.	85 Woodstock Road	Ft. Sergt.	R.A.F.	
Somerset, J.	32 Kenilworth Street	Private	R.I.R.	Killed in Action.
Somerset, T.	32 Kenilworth Street	Private	R.I.R.	
Somerset, W.	32 Kenilworth Street	Private	R.I.R.	
Stewart, W.		Private	R.I.F.	
Sturgeon, J.		Sergeant	R.E.	Croix-de-Guerre
Templeton, N.	19 Church Street East	Private	R.I.R.	
Thompson, D.	86 Bryson Street	P.O.	R.N.	

BELFAST PRESBYTERY. WESTBOURNE.

Name.	Home Address.	Rank.	Regiment, Battalion or Unit.	Remarks.
Thompson, J.		A.B.	R.N.	
Thompson, R. J.		Private	R.I.R.	
Vincent, D.	14 Humber Street	Private	I.D.	
Wallace, H.		Private	R.I.F.	
Watson, W. J.		Private	M.G.C.	Killed in Action.
Williams, F. A.	60 Montrose Street	Private	R.A.M.C.	
Williams, W. J.	60 Montrose Street	Driver	R.A.S.C.	
Wilkinson, R. J.	Up. Newtownards Road	Co. Q.M.S.	B.W.	
Winters, J.	7 Baskin Street	Private	R.E.	
Wilson, J.		Private	R.A.M.C.	
Wilson, W., Sen.		Private	R.I.F.	Killed in Action.
Wilson, W. Jun.		Private	R. Inn. Fus.	Killed in Action.
Wilson, T.		Gunner	R.F.A.	
Witherow, T. H.	8 Kirkliston Drive	Lieutenant	R.I.R.	
Wright, C.		Sapper	R.E.	
Wright, J.	11 Glenmore Street	Private	R.I.R.	
Wright, S.		Sec. A.M.	R.A.F.	
Wylie, D.	2 Lower Mount Street	Private	Seaforth Highldrs.	
Wylie, J. K.	2 Lower Mount Street	Lieutenant	R.I.R.	
COLONIAL FORCES.				
Douglas, R.		Private	Aust. E.F.	Killed in Action.
Ferguson, D.	33 The Mount	Private	Can. E.F.	Killed in Action.
Jamison, F.	128 Templemore Avenue	Private	Can. E.F.	Killed in Action.
Leebody, S.	27 Bright Street	Sergeant	Can. E.F.	M.M., D.C.M.
Kirkland, G.	248 Newtownards Road	Lieutenant	Aust. E.F.	Killed in Action.
McGimpsey, S.	Vancouver	Sergeant	Can. E.F.	Killed in Action.
McGimpsey, T.	Vancouver	Driver	Can. E.F.	Killed in Action.
Morrison, J. G.	1 Lombard Avenue	Private	Can. E.F.	Killed in Action.
Rosemond, D.	181 Madrid Street	Private	N.Z.E.F.	
Scilley, R. A.	344 Newtownards Road	Private	Can. E.F.	Killed in Action.
Smith, E.	85 Woodstock Road	Private	Can. E.F.	
WHITEABBEY.				
Baxter, John	Monkstown	Corporal	12th R.I. Rifles	Prisoner.
Beattie, Thomas	Whiteabbey	Private	N.I.H.	
Bell, Samuel	Whiteabbey	Private	Royal Irish Rifles	
Bell, William	Whiteabbey	Private	Marine	
Blair, James	Bleach Green	Corporal	12th R.I. Rifles	Wounded.
Blair, Samuel	The Corners, Whiteabbey	Corporal	12th R.I. Rifles	Military Medal.
Brennan, Thomas	Whiteabbey	Corporal	12th R.I. Rifles	
Brown, George		Lieutenant	Durham Regt.	
Caithness, Will	Whiteabbey	Surg. Prob.	Torpedo Boat Destroyer	
Cameron, John	Whiteabbey	Gunner	Field Artillery	
Connery, John	Whiteabbey	Sergt.-Major	Veterinary Corps	
Coulter, Samuel	Whiteabbey	Private	12th R.I. Rifles	Killed in Action.
Crawford, David	Whiteabbey	Private	12th R.I. Rifles	
Cunning, James	Whiteabbey	Corporal	12th R.I. Rifles	
Dubois, Joseph	Monkstown	Private	12th R.I. Rifles	
Erskine, Pakenham	Whiteabbey	Lieutenant	East Africa	
Erskine, William R.	Whiteabbey	Private	1st Royal Fusiliers	Killed in Action.
Farquhar, Douglas	Monkstown	Sergeant	12th R.I. Rifles	
Gourley, James	Bleach Green, W'abbey	Private	12th R.I. Rifles	
Gray, Robert		Private	12th R.I. Rifles	
Greer, James	Greenisland	Private	12th R.I. Rifles	Wounded.
Haffern, Robert	Monkstown	Private	12th R.I. Rifles	
Harkin, Andrew	Bleach Green	Private	11th R.I. Rifles	Killed in Action.
Harkin, Wm.	Bleach Green	Private	11th R.I. Rifles	Killed in Action.
Harland, Thomas	Monkstown	Sergt.-Major	R.A.M.C.	Military Medal.
Henderson, Stanley	Whiteabbey	Captain	Garrison Artillery	Wounded.
Houston, John	The Corners, Whiteabbey	Private	12th R.I.R.	
Houston, Wm.	The Corners, Whiteabbey	Private	12th R.I.R.	
Jackson, David	Whiteabbey	Corporal	Garrison Artillery	
Lee, William	Whiteabbey	Private	12th R.I. Rifles	
Logan, James	Whiteabbey	Private	12th R.I.R.	
Logan, Robert	Whiteabbey	Private	R.A.S.C.	
Lough, Joseph	Monkstown	Private	R.A.F.	
Loughlin, John	Greenisland	Private	R.I. Rifles	
Loughran, Wm.	Whitehouse	Private	R.I. Rifles	
McCracken, James	Greenisland	Lieutenant	N.I.H.	
McCready, Andrew	Whiteabbey	Private	R. Engineers	
McCready, Henry	Whiteabbey	Sergeant	R.I. Rifles	
McCready, James	Whiteabbey	Sergeant	R.I. Rifles	
McCready, William		Sergeant	Canadians	
McDowell, John	Whiteabbey	Sergeant	R.N.	
McFetridge, Alex.	Whiteabbey	Sergeant	Mesopotamia Force	
McKeeman, John	Bleach Green	Private	12th R.I. Rifles	Killed in Action.
Mackie, Frazer	Hazelbank, Whitehouse	Lieutenant	R.E.	
Mackie, John	Monkstown	Private	R.A.F.	
McKinney, Wm.	Whiteabbey	Private	12th R.I. Rifles	
McLoughlin, Wm	Whiteabbey	Private	12th R.I. Rifles	
McMurray, Gawn	Whiteabbey	Private	12th R.I. Rifles	

BELFAST PRESBYTERY.   WHITEABBEY.

Name.	Home Address.	Rank.	Regiment, Battalion or Unit.	Remarks.
McMurray, Wm.	Whiteabbey	Private		
McShane, John	Whiteabbey	Private	12th R.I.R.	
McShane, Thomas	Whiteabbey	Private	12th R.I.R.	
Magill, Wm.	Jordanstown	Private	Public Schoolboys' Batt.	Wounded.
Magilton, Valentine	Whitehouse	Seaman	R.N.	
Mahaffy, Robert	Whiteabbey	Private	R.A.F.	
Major, Samuel	Cloughfern	Private	12th R.I.R.	Killed in Action.
Martin, Joseph	Monkstown	Sergeant	Egyptian Army	
Mawhinney, Thomas	Bleach Green	Private	12th R.I. Rifles	Wounded.
Miller, Andrew	Whiteabbey	Private	12th R.I. Rifles	
Mitchell, Joseph	Whiteabbey	Private	R.A.F.	
Mulholland, Samuel	Cloughfern, Whiteabbey	Corporal	A.S.C.	
Peake, Hugh	Monkstown	Private	12th R.I. Rifles	
Robinson, George	Monkstown	Private	12th R.I. Rifles	Gassed.
Saunderson, Thomas	Jordanstown		R.N.	
Saunderson, Wm.	Monkstown	Private	12th R.I.R.	
Shaw, Geoffrey	Greenisland	Lieutenant	N.I.H.	
Shaw, Harold	Greenisland	Lieutenant	Artillery	
Sloan, Charles	Whiteabbey	Private	12th R.I. Rifles	Prisoner.
Sloan, Robert	Whiteabbey	Private	12th R.I.R.	Killed in Action.
Sloan, Samuel	Whiteabbey	Private	12th R.I.R.	
Smyth, Thos. Hugh	Whiteabbey	Corporal	12th R.I.R.	
Smyth, Thomas Jackson	Cloughfern	Private	12th R.I. Rifles	
Smyth, Wm. John	The Bleach Green	Private	12th R.I. Rifles	Killed in Action.
Stevenson, J. H.	Jordanstown	Sub-Lieutenant	R.N.V.R.	
Stevenson, Wm.	Jordanstown	Lieutenant	12th R.I. Rifles	
Stewart, Jackson	Whiteabbey	Private	12th R.I.R.	
Stewart, Samuel	Whiteabbey	Private	12th R.I.R.	Killed in Action.
Stewart, William	Whiteabbey	Corporal	12th R.I.R.	
Stewart, Wm.		Seaman	R.N.	
Thomas, Phillip	Greenisland	Private	18th R.I. Rifles	Killed in Action.
Trimble, Adam	Greenisland	Private	R.A.S.C.	
Wright, John	Whiteabbey	Private	R.A.F.	
Wright, Robert		Private	R.A.F.	
Wright, Thomas	Whiteabbey	Private	R.I. Rifles	
COLONIAL FORCE.				
Farquhar, Wm.	Monkstown	Corporal	Canadian Army	
Greer, Andrew	Greenisland	Corporal	Canadian Army	
WHITEHOUSE.				
Agnew, William	10 Barbour Street	Sapper	R.E.	D.C.M., M.M., Twice Wounded.
Andrews, James	9 Front Row, Whitewell	Private	2nd R.I. Fus.	Invalided.
Anderson, James	Longwood Crescent	Rifleman	15th R.I. Rifles	
Anderson, James	7 Harrisburg St., Belfast	Corporal	9th Inn. Fus.	Wounded.
Anderson, Robert	7 Harrisburg St., Belfast	Private	9th Inn. Fus.	Killed in Action.
Anderson, William	7 Harrisburg St., Belfast	Private	9th Inn. Fus.	Prisoner of War.
Armer, William J.	Carlton Villas	Sergeant	15th R.I. Rifles	
Beck, William H.	Brick Row	Private	R.A.M.C.	
Beggs, William	Lower Whitehouse	Rifleman	15th R.I. Rifles	Invalided.
Blair, W. J.	Cavehill View	Rifleman	15th R.I. Rifles	
Black, Francis	Barbour Street	Rifleman	9th R.I. Rifles	Wounded.
Black, John	Parkmore Terrace	Rifleman	2nd R.I. Rifles	Invalided.
Bradley, Robert	Henderson Avenue	Private	2nd Inn .Fus.	Wounded.
Bradley, George	Henderson Avenue	Sergeant	M.G.C.	M.M., K'd in Act.
Bruce, James	Whitewell Road	Sergeant	15th R.I. Rifles	
Brennan, James	Erskine's Terrace	Rifleman	15th R.I. Rifles	Wounded.
Coey, Edward	Merville	Captain	107th M.G. Co.	
Coey, Arthur	Merville	Lieutenant	107th B.H.Q.	Ment. in Des.
Coey, George	Merville	Lieutenant	1st R.I. Rifles	Wounded.
Chambers, Henry	Lowwood Terrace	R.S.M.	Inn. Fus.	
Campbell, W. E.	Granville Terrace	1st Cl. Air Mech.	R.A.F.	
Cowan, Joseph	Lower Whitehouse	Rifleman	12th R.I. Rifles	Wounded.
Capper, Joseph	Skegoniel	Staff Sergt.	A.S.C.	
Clark, Jack	Parkmount Cottages	Rifleman	8th R.I. Rifles	Wounded.
Dack, James	Lilac Cottage	Rifleman	9th R.I. Rifles	Wounded.
Davison, James	Racart House	Private	N.Z. Infantry	
Diamond, Owen	Tate's Row	Rifleman	16th R.I. Rifles	
Dunwoody, Eric	Ballygolan Villa	Rifleman	15th R.I. Rifles	Wounded.
Dickson, H. L.	Bawnmore	Captain	R.I. Rifles	W'd, Ment. in Des.
Dickson, C.	Bawnmore	Lieutenant	Cheshires	
Dickson, W. W.	Bawnmore	Captain	R.A.M.C.	
Dickson, J. H.	Bawnmore	Private	364th Inf., Am. Army	American M.M.
Elliott, Louis R.	Ashley, Greencastle	Private	107th M.G.C.	
Elliott, J. Patton	Ashley, Greencastle	Private	2nd R. I. Fus.	Torpedoed.
Eliott, Clark	11 Bell's Row	Rifleman	15th R.I. Rifles	Prisoner of War.
Elliott, Samuel	15 Cultra St., Belfast	Private	Northumberland Fus.	Wounded.
Erskine, Jack	Longwood	Lieutenant		D.C.M., Ment. in Despatches.
Finlay, William	Dandy St., Whitehouse	Sergeant	15th R.I. Rifles	M.M., Wounded, Ment. in Des. Prisoner of War.

BELFAST PRESBYTERY. — WHITEHOUSE.

Name.	Home Address.	Rank.	Regiment, Battalion or Unit.	Remarks.
Ferguson, William	48 Canning St., Belfast	Private	9th R. Inn. Fus.	Killed in Action.
Forrester, George	Dandy St., Whitehouse	Rifleman	15th R.I. Rifles	Killed in Action.
Fittis, Samuel	Concrete Row, W'abbey	Lance-Corporal	15th R.I. Rifles	
Graham, Edward	Whitehouse	Gunner	R.F.A.	Killed in Action.
Graham, David	Ritchie's Row	Private	1st R. I. Fus.	Killed in Action.
Graham, Joseph	Ritchie's Row	Private	107th M.G.C.	
Gilmore, Joseph	Whitewell	Rifleman	15th R.I. Rifles	
Gracey, Samuel	Carntall	Rifleman	9th R.I. Rifles	
Holding, Stanley	Sycamore House	Lieutenant	14th R.I. Rifles	Invalided.
Humphrey, Robert	Lower Whitehouse	Rifleman	15th R.I. Rifles	Killed in Action.
Humphrey, W. J.	Lower Whitehouse	Lance-Corporal	12th R.I. Rifles	Wd., Pris. of War.
Humphrey, Robert	Bessbrook	Lieutenant	2nd R. Dub. Fus.	Wounded, M.M.
Hull, Richard	Lower Whitehouse	Rifleman	15th R.I. Rifles	Wounded.
Heslip, Thomas	Ivy Cottage, Whitehouse	Rifleman	12th R.I. Rifles	Wounded.
Heslip, George	Ivy Cottage, Whitehouse	Sergeant	A.S.C.	
Hull, James	Barbour Street	Sapper	R.E.	Wounded.
Houston, Thomas	Doagh Rd., Whitehouse	Private	Aust. L. Horse	Wounded.
Houston, Charles	Doagh Rd., Whitehouse	Corporal	1st R. Inn. Fus.	Killed in Action.
Hilditch, Robert	Bell's Square	Rifleman	18th R.I. Rifles	
Hamilton, Reginald Lamont	Sunnyside	Lieutenant	8th R.I. Rifles	
Jenkins, S. J.	Cavehill View	Captain	5th Inn. Fus.	D.C.M., Wounded.
Kerr, John	Longwood Terrace	Sergeant	11th R.I. Rifles	Invalided.
Killen, William	Lower Whitehouse	Rifleman	15th R.I. Rifles	Wounded.
Lynn, Hugh	Ritchie's Row	Private	2nd Inn. Fus.	Wounded.
Lynn, Samuel	Erskine's Terrace	Rifleman	15th R.I. Rifles	
Lynn, Samuel	Ritchie's Row	Private	R.A.F.	
Larmour, Fred.	Avondale Terrace	Sergeant	R.E.	
Millar, William	11 Raleigh St., Belfast	Corporal	2nd R.I. Rifles	Wounded.
Marquis, W. J.	Lower Whitehouse	Rifleman	15th R.I. Rifles	Killed in Action.
Moore, Thomas A.	Erskine's Row	Sergeant-Major	15th R.I. Rifles	Wd., Pris. of War.
Marks, William	2 Maple Terrace	Private	2nd R.I. Rifles	Prisoner of War.
Maxwell, Joseph	Barbour St., Greencastle	Private	R.A.F.	
Moore, Thomas H.	Lower Whitehouse	Private	9th R.I. Fus.	Wounded.
Molloy, Alfred	4 Seaview Street	Private	Mech. Transport	Died in Hospital.
Morrison, John	Seaview Terrace	Private	9th R.I. Fus.	M.M., Pris. of War.
McWatters, John	Barbour Street	Rifleman	9th R.I. Rifles	
McMaster, John	Seaview Ter., Grencastle	Corporal	15th R.I. Rifles	Wounded.
McCallum, Gilbert	Greencastle	Private	1st R.I. Fus.	Prisoner of War.
McTernaghan, Wm.	Dandy Street	Rifleman	15th R.I. Rifles	
McWilliams, David	Ritchie's Row	Sergeant	15th R.I. Rifles	M.S.M.
McCartney, Matthew	Whitewell Road	Corporal	15th R.I. Rifles	Prisoner of War.
McAllister, W. J.	Erskine's Terrace	Corporal	15th R.I. Rifles	
McRoberts, Robert	Whitewell	Rifleman	15th R.I. Rifles	
McRoberts, David	Dunaney, Carnmoney	Rifleman	16th R.I.R.	Killed in Action.
McFall, Robert	Craig's Cottages	Lance-Corporal	9th R.I. Rifles	Killed in Action.
McConnell, Robert	High Street, Greencastle	Private	6th R.I. Fus.	Killed in Action.
McConnell, Thomas	High Street, Greencastle	Private	R.F.A.	
McConnell, Alex.	10 Barbour Street	Rifleman	9th R.I. Rifles	
McConnell, Alex., Jun.	10 Barbour Street	Rifleman	9th R.I. Rifles	Killed in Action.
McWilliams, Andrew	Ritchie's Row	Gunner	R.F.A.	
McCartney, Thomas	Granville Terrace	Air Mechanic	R.A.F.	Invalided.
McCartney, John	Lower Whitehouse	Private	9th R. Inn. Fus.	Killed in Action.
Pherson, James	Carrowdore, W'house	Rifleman	15th R.I. Rifles	
Peden, Richard	Bell's Square	Private	R.E.	Wounded.
Porter, H. C.	11 Shamrock Terrace	Private	R.A.M.C.	Invalided.
Patton, Joseph	Whitewell	Rifleman	8th R.I. Rifles	Killed in Action.
Patton, Robert	Whitewell	Sergeant	15th R.I. Rifles	Wounded.
Payne, James	Skegoniel Road, Belfast	Rifleman	15th R.I. Rifles	Prisoner of War.
Robinson, Harold	Bawnmore	Major	A.S.C.	
Reid, John	Laburnum Cottage	Sergeant	15th R.I. Rifles	Killed in Action.
Shaw, Samuel	M'Cormick's Row	Corporal	2nd R.I. Rifles	
Simms, Thomas	Whitewell	Private	Aust. Inf. F.	
Stewart, Andrew	Boyd's Bridge	Rifleman	15th R.I. Rifles	Invalided.
Stewart, William	Boyd's Bridge	Rifleman	15th R.I. Rifles	Wounded.
Shaw, Alex.	Dandy St., Whitehouse	Lance-Corporal	6th Inn. Fus.	M.M.
Sinclair, William	Rose Cottage, W'house	Sergeant	12th R.I. Rifles	Prisoner of War.
Sinclair, Andrew	Rose Cottage, W'house	Sergeant	15th R.I. Rifles	Killed in Action.
Sinclair, George	Rose Cottage, W'house	Sapper	R.E.	
Snoddy, Thomas	5 Dandy Street	Driver	A.S.C.	Died of Wounds.
Smythe, Bryce	Edgewood		Anglo-Fr. Red Cross	
Smythe, Allan	Edgewood	Lieutenant	A.S.C. M.T.	
Sutherland, Allen	Throne Ter., Whitehouse	Sergeant	Armoured Car, M.G. Co.	
Thompson, James	Mt· Pleasant, W'house	Private	R.A.F.	
Taylor, William	Thompson Sq., W'house	Private	9th R.I. Fus.	
Vint, Jonathan	Mount Maon, G'castle	Captain	4/5 Black Watch	Wounded.
Wilson, W. H.	Longlands	Rifleman	15th R.I. Rifles	Prisoner of War.
Wilson, James	Rose Cottage, W'house	Rifleman	15th R.I. Rifles	Twice wounded.
ROYAL NAVY AND MERCANTILE MARINE.				
Anderson, W. H.	Cranmore Terrace	Stoker	H.M.S. Serbol	
Boyd, Samuel	Barbour Street	Stoker	H.M.S. Ophir	
Boyd, James	Whitehouse	Petty Officer	H.M.S. Rugby	Wounded.
Bruce, Samuel	Whitehouse	A.B. Seaman	H.M.S. Cordova	1914 Med. O'seas, L.S.R.N. Medal.

BELFAST PRESBYTERY.   WHITEHOUSE.

NAME.	HOME ADDRESS.	RANK.	REGIMENT, BATTALION OR UNIT.	REMARKS.
BRYSON, SAMUEL	Whitehouse	Gunner Electrician	Canadian Navy	
BURNIE, SAMUEL	Greencastle	Gunner	Centurion	
CRAWFORD, JAMES	Ivy Row, Whitehouse	Stoker	Duchess of Devonshire	
CHARLTON, JOHN	Erskine's Terrace	Fireman	H.M.T. St. Aubyn	
COEY, JOHN SMILEY	Merville, Whitehouse	Midshipman	H.M.S. Formidable	Lost at Sea.
DACE, HERBERT	Erskine Terrace	Stoker	H.M.S. Mantua	
ELLIOTT, W. NORMAN	Ashley, Greencastle	Chief Engineer	S.S. Ganges	
ELLIOTT, HOWARD A.	Ashley, Greencastle	Engineer	S.S. Lord Downshire	Twice torpedoed.
FEE, SAMUEL	Barbour Street	Stoker	H.M.S. Hawke	Lost at Sea.
FERGUSON, WM.	Rockview, Whitehouse	Trimmer	H.M.S. London Bell	Died in Hospital.
GALLAGHER, EZEKIEL	Concrete Row, W'well	Stoker	H.M.S. Marmora	Lost at Sea.
MAXWELL, JAMES	Barbour St., Greencastle	Stoker	Princess Irene	Lost at Sea.
McCARTNEY, WILLIAM	High St., Greencastle	Stoker	Slieve Bearnagh	
McCARTNEY, SAMUEL	High St., Greencastle	Stoker	H.M.S. Mantua	
McDONALD, WILLIAM	Seaview Terrace	Steward	Garron Head	Lost at Sea.
SIMMS, JOHN	Whitewell	Stoker	H.M.S. Africa	Twice torpedoed.
WILLIAMSON, W. A.	Ballycraigy House	Lieut.-Commander	H.M.S. Canopus	Invalided.
WINDSOR.				
ADAMS, THOMAS	Kilrea, Co. Derry	Captain	R. Inn. Fus.	M. Cross.
ANDERSON, HARRY	18 Meadowbank Street	Corporal	10th R.I.R.	
AYER, GEORGE	Ballyclare	Private	Army Reserve	Killed in Action.
BAILIE, JOHN	Windsor Avenue	Captain	R.A.S.C.	
BEATTIE, NORMAN	Bangor	Sergeant	R.I.R.	Died of Wounds.
BEATTY, ROBERT L.	Eglantine Avenue	Cadet	R.I.R.	
BEATTIE, WM. H.	Bangor	Lieutenant	R.I.R.	
BEVERIDGE, JOHN R.	Balmoral Avenue	Lieutenant	R.N.T.S.	
BLAIR, ALEX.	Stranmillis Road	Private	N.I.H.	Died of Wounds.
BLAIR, W. W.	Strabane	Captain	R.A.M.C.	
COCKS, ROBERT	Lisburn Road	Lieutenant	R.I.R.	Wounded.
CONNOR, BERTIE	Lisburn Road	Lieutenant	R.I.R.	Prisoner.
CURLEY, FRANK	Lisburn Road	Lieutenant	R.E.	Killed in Action.
CURLEY, JAMES	Lisburn Road	Lieutenant	R. Inn. Fus.	M. Cross.
ERVINE, GEORGE	Derryvolgie Avenue	Corporal	R.F.A.	
FERRIS, WILLIE	Knock	2nd Lieutenant	R.I.R.	Killed in Action.
GILLESPIE, H. A.	Newry	Captain	R.A.M.C.	
HANNA, HENRY	Adelaide Avenue	Sergeant	R.I.R.	
HENDERSON, JAMES	Windsor Park	Lieutenant	R.A.S.C.	
HENDERSON, LILBURN	Windsor Park	Captain	R.I.R.	Wounded.
HENDERSON, OSCAR	Windsor Park	Lieutenant	R.N.	Croix-de-Guerre, D.S.O.
HENDERSON, YORKE	Windsor Park	Lieutenant	R.I.R.	M.C., Kd. in Action
IRWIN, FRED.	Castleblayney	Corporal	R.I.R.	Killed in Action.
LATHAM, EDWARD	Bawnmore Road	Captain	E. Yorkshire Regt.	
LYTTLE, GEORGE	Lisburn Road	Captain	R.A.M.C.	
MacARTHUR, W. P.	Arnside, Windsor Park	Lieut.-Colonel	R.A.M.C.	Wd., D.S.O., O.B.E
McCAUGHEY, DON	Derryvolgie Avenue	Lieutenant	M.G. Corps	Wounded.
McCAUGHEY, JACK	Derryvolgie Avenue	Sub-Lieutenant	R.N.	
McCAUGHEY, WM.	Bawnmore Road	Lieutenant	R.G.A.	
McCAUL, CHARLES	Lisburn Road	Captain	R.I.R.	
McCONKEY, ERNEST	Ethel Street	Private	R.I. Fus.	Died.
McCONNELL, JOHN D.	College Green House	Lieutenant	M.G. Corps	
McILDOWIE, JIM	Deramore Drive	2nd Lieutenant	3rd R.I. Fus.	
McKANE, ROBERT	Osborne Park	Lieutenant	R.A.	
McKINNEY, J. COLVILLE	Wellington Park	Lieutenant	R.I.R.	Wounded.
McKINNEY, THOMAS	Wellington Park	Captain	17th Batt. Tank Corps	
McNEILL, ARTHUR	37 Ashley Avenue	Lieutenant	R.I. Fus.	
MacNEILL, NORMAN	37 Ashley Avenue	Lieutenant	K.O.S.B.	Wounded.
MARTIN, JOHN	Derryvolgie Avenue	Lieutenant	R.A.F.	Wounded.
MONTGOMERY, EDWARD	Eglantine Avenue	Lieutenant	Manchester Regt.	
NEVIN, WM.	14 Chadwick Street	Co. Sergt.-Major	14th R.I.R.	Killed in Action.
NICHOLSON, HOWARD	Myrtlefield Park	Lieutenant	R.I.R.	Wounded.
PATTERSON, D. KNOX	Lisburn Road	Captain	A.S.C.	
PHILLIPS, THOMAS	Mount Charles	Captain	R.I.R.	Killed in Action.
PRING, ESAU	Rathdrum Street	Petty Officer	R.N.	
PRING, JOSEPH	Rathdrum Street	Sergeant	R.I.R.	
PRING, WALTER	Rathdrum Street	Seaman	R.N.	
PROCTOR, DAVID	Thalia Street		Mine-sweepers	
PROCTOR, JOHN	Thalia Street		Mine-sweepers	
ROBERTSON, ERNEST	Dunluce Avenue	2nd Lieutenant	R.I.R.	Wounded.
ROGERS, ROBERT	Marlborough Avenue	Corporal	R.E. Signals, R.F.A.	Died.
SHAW, MARTIN	Chlorine Gardens	Lieutenant	R.I.R.	
SHAW, WILLIAM	Chlorine Gardens	Major	R.E.	M.C., Kd. in Action
STEWART, LEWIS	Wellesley Avenue	Major	R.I.R.	D.S.O., Kd. in Act.
STRAIN, ALBERT	Windsor Park	Lieutenant	R.I.R.	
STRAIN, ERIC	Windsor Park	2nd Lieutenant	R.I. Fus.	
STRAIN, ERNEST	Windsor Park	Lieutenant	M.G.C.	Wounded.
THOMSON, BERTIE	Eglantine Avenue	Lieutenant	Welsh Fus.	
THOMSON, HUGH	Ashley Avenue	Private	R.A.F.	
THOMPSON, WILLIAM	Ashley Avenue	Private	R.I.R.	
WHYTE, STANLEY	Gortin, Strabane	Lieutenant	R.E.	
WRIGHT, SAMUEL	Derryvolgie Avenue	Captain	R.A.M.C.	

BELFAST PRESBYTERY.   WINDSOR.

Name.	Home Address.	Rank.	Regiment, Battalion or Unit.	Remarks.
COLONIAL FORCES.				
Blair, Arthur	Stranmillis	Staff Sergeant	N.Z. Force	Wounded.
Dalzell, Bertie	Wellington Park Avenue	Private	Canadians	
Doran, Harry	Dunluce Avenue	Driver	Can. A.S.C.	
Doran, Joe	Dunluce Avenue	Private	Canadians	Wounded.
Glover, Geoffrey	Lisburn Road	Private	196 Batt. Canadians	
McConnell, John D.	College Green House	Private	Canadians	
McNeill, Howard	37 Ashley Avenue	Major	Canadian For. Corps	
Nelson, John	1 Surrey Street	Corporal	Canadian Dragoons	
Shannon, John	Chichester Terrace		Canadians	Killed in Action.
WOODVALE PARK.				
Abernethy, Herbert	16 Woodvale Avenue			
Arthur, George	71 Cambrai Street	A.C.	R.A.F.	
Aspell, Robert C.	238 Leopold Street	Seaman	R.N.	
Aspell, Joseph	238 Leopold Street	2nd Lieutenant	1st Batt. R.I.R.	
Bennett, James	35 Springfield Village	Private	9th Batt. R.I. Rifles	Killed.
Bennett, Hugh	35 Springfield Village	Private	1st Batt. R. Inns.	Killed.
Beattie, Robert	51 Bracken Street	Lance-Corporal	R.E.	
Black, Robert	237 Cambrai Street			
Black, James	237 Cambrai Street	Private	15th Batt. R.I.R.	Killed.
Blair, Thomas	137 Lawnbrook Avenue	Private	1st Batt. R.I.R.	
Birnie, Robert	3 Broom Street	Private	12th Batt. R.I.R.	Killed.
Boyd, James	27 Heather Street	Private	13th Batt. R.I.R.	
Boyd, Samuel	27 Heather Street	Private	15th Batt. R.I.R.	
Boyd, James	34 Bootle Street	Lance-Corporal	N.I.H.	
Brown, Edmund	158 Canmore Street	Private	2nd Batt. R.I.R.	
Brown, Robert	33 Silvio Street	Gunner	Royal Marines	
Caldwell, Alexander	91 Enfield Street	Torpedo Gunner	R.N.	
Caldwell, George	91 Enfield Street	Marine	R.N.	Wounded.
Campbell, John	30 Heather Street	Lance-Corporal	15th Batt. R.I.R.	Wounded.
Crawford, Matthew	24 Mossvale Street	Trooper	N.I.H.	
Cochrane, Joseph	102 Palmer Street	Private	15th Batt. R.I.R.	Killed.
Coleman, Robert	233 Springfield Road		24th London R.F.	
Collins, Samuel				
Collins, Frederick E. C.	41 Disraeli Street	Sapper	12th Pioneer Batt. R.E.	Wounded.
Collins, Wm. Thos.	41 Disraeli Street	Private	12th Batt. R.I.R.	Died of Wounds.
Connolly, Henry	67 Cambrai Street	Private	15th Batt. R.I.R.	Wounded, M.M.
Cooper, David	105 Disraeli Street	Private	2nd Batt. R.I.R.	
Copeland, Charles	71 Woodvale Road	Gunner	Tank Corps	
Crothers, Thomas	136 Disraeli Street	Private	11th Batt. R. Inn. Fus.	Wounded.
Crothers, Alexander	136 Disraeli Street	Private	8th Batt. R.I.R.	
Crothers, David	136 Disraeli Street	Private	2nd Batt. R.I.R.	Killed.
Crothers, Samuel	136 Disraeli Street	Private	R.F.A.	
Crowe, Edward	Mayo Street	Stoker	R.N.	
Crowe, John	7 Clovelly Street	Private	9th Batt. R.I.R.	
Crowe, James	51 Clovelly Street	Private	9th Batt. R.I.R.	
Cumings, Thomas	32 Ottawa Street	Private	15th Batt. R.I R.	Wounded.
Crowe, Thomas	Bray Street	Private	15th Batt. R.I.R.	
Dempster, Samuel				
Dodds, John	45 Disraeli Street	Private	2nd Batt. Inn. Fus.	Died of Wounds.
Donnelly, William	222 Leopold Street	Lance-Corporal	1st Batt. Inn. Fus.	Killed.
Donnelly, Alexander	21 Broom Street	Private	2nd Batt. Irish Fus.	Wounded.
Donnelly, Samuel	Ballygomartin Road	Private	104th Batt. R.I.R.	
Donnelly, Joseph	Ballygomartin Road	Private	103rd Batt. R.I.R.	
Dougherty, James	106 Disraeli Street	Private	14th Batt. R.I.R.	Wounded.
Dougherty, Thomas	106 Disraeli Street	Private	14th Batt. R.I.R.	Wounded.
Dunwoody, George	27 Fingal Street	Private	9th Batt. R.I.R.	Killed.
Eakin, David	64 Carnan Street	Corporal	4th Batt. Inn. Fus.	
Ellison, Samuel	5 Glenvale Street	Lance-Corporal	9th Batt. R.I.R.	
Frazer, John	12 Rutherglen Street	Chief Writer	R.N.	
Fleming, Thomas	15 Mountcashel Street	Private	14th Batt. R.I.R.	Killed.
Ferguson, W. G.	22 Esmond Street			
Fletcher, James	62 Heather Street	Trooper	N.I.H.	
Fulton, James Norman	41 Woodvale Road	Lieutenant	Inn. Fus.	
Galway, Frederick	298 Springfield Road	Chief E.R.A.	R.N.	
Grainger, David	266 Leopold Street	Private	15th Batt. R.I.R.	Wounded.
Halley, James, Sen.	3 Enfield Street	Staff Sergeant	M.G.C.	
Halley, James, Jun.	3 Enfield Street	Private	R.I. Fus.	
Hamilton, James H.	121 Mayo Street	Able Seaman	R.N.	Drowned.
Harbinson, Robert	39 Brookmount Street	Private	R.A.M.C.	
Harbison, Robert J.	Ballygomartin Road	Corporal	R.G.A.	
Harkley, Robert	Ballymurphy	Private	R.E.	
Harrison, Thomas	8 Rathlin Street	Private	A.S.C.	
Harvey, W. J.				
Hastings, Robert J.	174 Cupar Street		Mechanical Transport	
Henderson, Frederick	126 Leopold Street	Driver	A.S.C.	
Henderson, William				
Herron, Albert	Crumlin Road		Mechanical Transport	
Hill, Arthur	89 Enfield Street	Sergt.-Major	9th Batt. R.I.R.	Wounded.

(174)

BELFAST PRESBYTERY.   WOODVALE PARK.

Name.	Home Address.	Rank.	Regiment, Battalion or Unit.	Remarks.
Hyndman, James	65 Mossvale Street	Private	9th Batt. R.I.R.	
Ingham, Graham	360 Springfield Road	Private	Mechanical Transport	
Ingham, James	360 Springfield Road	Private	17th Batt. R.I.R.	
Irvine, Richard	13 March Street	Private	2nd Batt. R.I.R.	Wounded.
Jamison, Robert	25 Heather Street	Corporal	2nd Batt. R.I.R.	Killed.
Johnston, Thomas				
Jones, Thomas	24 Oregon Street	Private	15th Batt. R.I.R.	Wounded.
Kinkaid, James	80 Oregon Street	Private	2nd Batt. R.I.R.	
Kinkaid, John	80 Oregon Street	Private	4th Batt. R.I.R.	Killed.
Lawson, Walter	17 Enfield Street	Private	16th Pioneer Batt.	
Lindsay, John	22 Mossvale Street	Private	9th Batt. R.I.R.	
Lindsay, Samuel	Ballygomartin Road	Lance-Corporal	9th Batt. R.I. Fus.	Gassed.
Logan, Robert	222 Leopold Street	Private	2nd Batt. Irish Guards	Killed.
Loughins, Samuel	24 Esmond Street	Leading Seaman	R.N.	
Lyle, James	1 Bracken Street	Private		
Lyle, William	1 Bracken Street	Private	2nd Batt. R.I. Fus.	
Lyttle, Charles	32 Heather Street	Private	9th Batt. R.I.R.	
Mackey, Robert J.	5 Bracken Street	Sapper	R.E.	
Magee, William	22 Heather Street	Sergeant	15th Batt. R.I.R.	Gassed.
Majury, Andrew	4 Pollard Street	Gunner	R.G.A.	
Mann, John	58 Esmond Street	Private	15th Batt. R.I.R.	Wounded.
Mann, Robert	58 Esmond Street	Private	11th Batt. Inn. Fus.	Killed.
Martin, James	240 Leopold Street	Stoker	R.N.	
Mawhinney, William	61 Mayo Street	Private	1st Inn. Fus.	
Melville, Samuel	Ballygomartin Road	Corporal	N.I.H.	Gassed.
Milliken, Joseph	60 Heather Street	Private	A.S.C.	
Moore, Matthew	211 Cambrai Street	Lance-Corporal	Seaforth Highldrs.	M.M.
Moreland, Joseph	Oldpark	Private	Cycling Corps	
Morrison, John	36 Heather Street	Private	15th Batt. R.I.R.	Wounded.
Morrison, John	24 Ottawa Street	Private	15th Batt. R.I.R	Lost Limb.
Morrison, William	24 Ottawa Street	Private	R.I.R.	
Mulholland, Samuel	30 Rosebank Street		R.N.	
Murdock, Alexander	222 Leopold Street	Corporal	A.S.C.	
McCallion, Robert	24 Heather Street	Lance-Corporal	15th Batt. R.I.R.	Wounded.
McCann, James	18 Rathlin Street	Gunner	R.N.	
McCleery, Alexander	114 Woodvale Avenue	Private	9th Batt. R.I.R.	
McCleery, William J.	114 Woodvale Avenue	Sergeant	A.S.C.	
McClinton, John	8 Fingal Street	Private	15th Batt. R.I.R.	Wounded.
McClurg, Albert	248 Leopold Street	Lance-Corporal	1st N.I.H.	
McConnell, Samuel	231 Cambrai Street	Private	14th Batt. R.I.R.	
McCoy, James	124 Disraeli Street	Private	10th Batt. R.I.R.	
McCrea, Samuel	40 Ottawa Street	1st Lieutenant	2nd Batt. R.I.R.	Gassed.
McCrossan, James	Crumlin Road	Private	Mechanical Transport	
McDonald, William	28 Rutherglen Street		A.S.C.	
McDowell, William				
McFall, Thomas	122 Disraeli Street	Stoker	R.N.	
McFarland, William				
McGladery, Samuel	Ballygomartin Road			
McGready, John	23 Glencairn Street	Private	16th Batt. R.I.R.	
McKibbin, Robert	Chief Street			
McLean, Ramsay	5 Ohio Street	Private	16th Batt. R.I.R.	Killed.
McMeekin, Charles	74 Chief Street		R.A.F.	
McMeekin, James	74 Chief Street	Private	Y.C.V., M.G.C.	
Nugent, Thomas	10 Ohio Street	Trooper	8th Hussars	
Patterson, Joseph				
Playfair, Robert	33 Silvio Street	Gunner	Royal Marines	
Prenter, W. J.	51 Hooker Street	Private	6th Batt. Inn. Fus.	Wounded.
Pullens, John	144 Disraeli Street	Private	6th Batt. Inn. Fus.	Wounded.
Strahan, John	43 Leopold Street	Private	10th Batt. Hampshires	Wounded.
Shanks, John	11 Cambrai Street	Trooper	N.I.H.	
Shaw, Charles	106 Cambrai Street	Corporal	15th Batt. R.I.R.	M.M.
Shaw, Charles	8 Rathlin Street	Private	R.I.R.	
Shaw, George	4 Rathlin Street	Private	8th Batt. R.I.R.	
Sterling, William	Ballygomartin Road	Captain	King's Liverpools	
Sterling, Robert	Ballygomartin Road	Lieutenant	Royal Air Service	
Stewart, William	155 Mayo Street	Private	9th Batt. R.I.R.	Killed.
Stewart, John	155 Mayo Street	Private	9th Batt. R.I.R.	
Stewart, Thomas	155 Mayo Street	Corporal	2nd Batt. R.I.R.	
Shields, Samuel	11 Broom Street	Private	15th Batt. R.I.R.	
Stitt, Thomas	29 Mayo Street	Private	9th Batt. R.I.R.	
Scott, Robert	15 Oregon Street	Private	2nd Batt. R.I.R.	Killed.
Taylor, William, Sen.	15 Woodvale Street	Drum-Major	12th Batt. R. Inn. Fus.	
Taylor, Wm., Jun.	15 Woodvale Street	Mechanic	R.A.F.	
Tweed, John	194 Leopold Street	Private	15th Batt. R.I.R.	
Todd, Frank				
Thompson, Robert H.	7 Dewey Street			
Thompson, Alexander	110 Woodvale Avenue	Private	9th Batt. R.I.R.	Killed.
Watson, John	Ohio Street	Corporal	6th Batt. R. Inn. Fus.	
Weir, Wm. J.	88 Mayo Street	Sapper	R.E.	
Weir, Joseph	88 Mayo Street	Private	1st Batt. R. Inn. Fus.	
Weir, W. H.	88 Mayo Street	Private	8th Batt. R.I.R.	
Wilson, Hugh	237 Cambrai Street	Sergeant	A.S.C.	
Wilson, Robert	Ballygomartin Road			
Woods, James	Glencairn Road	Private	A.S.C.	

BELFAST PRESBYTERY. WOODVALE PARK.

Name.	Home Address.	Rank.	Regiment, Battalion or Unit.	Remarks.
COLONIAL FORCES.				
Callan, James	286 Cambrai Street	Corporal	1st Aust. L.H. Brigade	
Crothers, William	136 Disraeli Street	Private	5th Can. Engineers	
Dougan, John W.	B. Columbia	Sergeant	54th Bn. Kootney	
YORK STREET.				
Beattie, R. J.	7 Alexandra Park Av.	Corporal	12th R.I.R.	
Boyd, Samuel	52 Duncairn Gardens	Private	14th R.I.R.	Killed in Action.
Boyd, Thomas	52 Duncairn Gardens	Driver	Y.C.V., A.S.C.	Wounded.
Brown, Francis	5 Ambrose Street	Lance-Corporal	R.E.	
Browne, Robert	St. Jude's Avenue	Private	Lewis G.S., 4th Seaforth H.	
Campbell, Samuel	73 Lt. York Street	Lance-Corporal	16th R.I. Fus.	
Carse, John	104 Mountcollyer Road	Driver	121st R.E.	
Cathcart, Matthew	6 Deacon Street	Private	N.I.H.	Killed in Action.
Christy, Samuel	29 Meadow Street	Sapper	R.E.	
Colville, Alexander	73 Alexandra Park Av.	Sergeant	15th R.I.R.	
Colville, Samuel	73 Alexandra Park Av.	Sergeant	3rd Troop M.G. Sq.	Wounded.
Colville, Thomas	73 Alexandra Park Av.	Private	N.I.H.	
Colville, James	16 Rowan Street	Private	R.F.A.	
Cooper, John	Lansdowne Road	Lieutenant	9th Inn. Fus.	Wounded.
Cunningham, F. J.	63 Agincourt Avenue	Sapper	352nd R.E.	
Dawson, William	24 Adam Street	Shipwright	R.N. Barracks, P'mouth	
Dunn, Thomas	16 Ship Street	Private	15th R.I.R.	
Ellis, William	22 Fleet Street	Corporal	14th M.G.C., R.I.R.	...
Ferguson, Thomas	98 Mervue Street	Stoker	R.N.	
Ferguson, William	48 Canning Street	Private	9th R. Inn. Fus.	Killed in Action.
Gilchrist, John	46 Sherwood Street	...	...	
Gorman, Alexander	Fire Station, Whitla St.	Band Boy	3rd R.I.R.	
Gray, William	57 Hogarth Street	Stoker	H.M.S. Bulwark	Killed in Explosion
Grogan, Alfred	34 Dock Street	Bombardier	R.F.A.	Gassed.
Grogan, Charles	34 Dock Street	Staff-Sergeant	17th Essex Regt.	
Haddock, William	50 Brookhill Avenue	Midshipman	Rathlin Head	
Hearst, M.	7 Spamount Street	Driver	107th M.G. Corps	
Hearst, William	3 Grove Street	Private	15th R.I.R.	
Hedley, David	61 Bentinck Street	Lieut. Engineer	R.N.	
Hogg, Dr. W. J.	120 Cliftonpark Avenue	Captain	R.A.M.C.	
Hunter, Wm. A. T.	Fortwilliam	Lieutenant	9th R.I.R.	
Hylands, Samuel	26 Vere Street	Cook	R.N.	
King, William	4 Bentinck Street	Private	Y.C.V.	Killed in Action.
Knox, John	11 Grove Street	Private	9th R.I.R.	
Lemon, Moses	33 Hillman Street	Sergt.-Major	4th R.I. Fus.	
McAdam, Thomas	Cosgrave Street	Private	12th R.I.R.	
McClelland, Arthur	92 Henry Street	Driver	A.S.C.	Died of Wounds.
McClelland, Alexander	24 Rowan Street	O. Seaman	R.N.	
McConkey, Thomas	30 Gamble Street	Private	M.T. A.S.C.	
McCullough, James	62 Bentinck Street	Sapper	R.E.	
McCullough, Walter	62 Bentinck Street	Private	9th R.I.R.	
McCullough, Walter	7 Fleet Street	Lance-Corporal	15th R.I.R.	Killed.
McCullough, Thomas	35 Dock Street	Private	15th R.I.R.	Killed in Action.
McCleery, Albert	43 Adam Street	Q.M. Sergeant	A.S.C.	
McCleery, Samuel A.	43 Adam Street	Private	26th L. of Sup., A.S.C.	
McCleery, Wm. J.	43 Adam Street	Chief Engineer	R.N. Res.	
McGowan, Thomas	39 New N. Queen Street	Private	Seaforth Highldrs.	Killed in Action.
McIlroy, James	Glenburn Park	Private	92nd F. Amb., R.A.M.C.	
McIlwrath, James	57 Hogarth Street	1st Cl. P. Officer	H.M.S. Vengeance	
McIlwrath, Samuel	57 Hogarth Street	Stoker	H.M.S. Invincible	Killed in Action.
McKean, George	24 Canning Street	Private	15th R.I.R.	1914-15 Star.
McKean, James	24 Canning Street	Leading Seaman	R.N.	Drowned.
McKean, William	24 Canning Street	Sapper	R.E.	
McMaster, William	Grove Ter., Shore Rd.	Junior Engineer	M.F. Aux.	
McMillan, Samuel	55 Southport Street	Sergeant	1st R.I. Fus.	
McMinn, Robert	11 Cross Street	Lance-Corporal	4th R.I. Fus.	
McMurtry, James	12 Moyola Street	Private	8th R.I.R.	
McMurtry, William	12 Moyola Street	Private	8th R.I.R.	
McVicker, Joseph	76 Hillman Street	Private	14th R.I.R.	Prisoner of War.
McVicker, William	76 Hillman Street	Private	9th R.I. Fus.	
Meeke, Wm. S.	253 York Street	Private	S.I. Horse	Cert. for Gallantry, Wd., twice gassed.
Middleton, Luke	30 Hogarth Street	Private	14th R.I.R.	
Millar, James	5 Mountcollyer Road	Private	15th R.I.R.	
Nelson, Samuel	7 Trafalgar Street	Air Mechanic	R.A.F.	
Paton, Wm. S.	Henderson Avenue	Engineer	H.M.S. Jackal	
Porter, William	34 Bute Street	Private	1st R.I. Fus.	Wounded.
Prentiss, Dr. H. H.	Kettering	Captain	R.A.M.C.	Twice Wounded.
Rea, Wm. S.	42 Canning Street	Private	1st Irish Guards	
Reilly, Kennedy	1 Grove Street	Private	15th R.I.R.	
Seymour, T. H.	13 Ship Street	Gunner	13th R.G.A.	
Taylor, J. A.	63 Agincourt Avenue	Sapper	121st R.E.	
Taylor, Samuel	63 Agincourt Avenue	...	...	
Thomson, Andrew	Fire Station, Whitla St.	Driver	A.S.C.	
Wade, Alfred	29 Spencer Street	Private	5th Cameron Highldrs.	Twice Wounded.
Walls, James	69 Gainsboro' Drive	Private	1st R.I.R.	Wounded.

BELFAST PRESBYTERY.   YORK STREET.

Name.	Home Address.	Rank.	Regiment, Battalion or Unit.	Remarks.
Wilson, James	17 Gt. George's Street	Private	19th R.I.R.	Wounded.
Wilson, Robert	39 Bentinck Street	Sapper	R.E.	
Woodside, Charles	29 Lawther Street	Corporal	R.E.	1914 Star.
COLONIAL FORCES.				
Dixon, Robert	10 St. Paul's Street	Private	47th Canadians	Killed in Action.
McCleery, Henry	43 Adam Street	Co. Sergt.-Major	Canadians	
McCullough, Matthew	63 Bentinck Street	Sergeant	24th Canadians	Wounded and Died
McIlroy, John	42 Eia Street	Sapper	1st Field Co. Canadians	
Scott, Hugh G.	2 Gainsboro' Drive	Private	90th Winnipeg Rifles	Gassed twice, Wounded, Killed.

CARRICKFERGUS PRESBYTERY.

Name.	Home Address.	Rank.	Regiment, Battalion or Unit.	Remarks.
BALLYCARRY.				
Baird, Wm.	Islandmagee	Officer	Mercantile Marine	
Brennan, Wm. A.	Ballycarry	Captain	Mercantile Marine	
Cameron, James	Ballycarry	Private	R.E.	
Cameron, John	Ballycarry	Private	R.I.R.	Wounded.
Cameron, Robert	Ballycarry	A.B.	Mercantile Marine	
Cameron, Samuel	Ballycarry	Private	R.I.R.	Wounded.
Cameron, Wm.	Ballycarry	A.B.	Mercantile Marine	Prisoner of War.
Creighton, Wm. D.	Whitehead	P.O.	Armoured Cars	St. George and St. Stanislaus Medals.
Doherty, Patrick	Ballycarry	Private	R.D. Fusiliers	Prisoner of War.
Dundee, Charles	Ballycarry	Captain	R.A.M.C.	Wounded. Awarded M.C.
Dundee, Wm. B. H.	Ballycarry	Captain	R.A.M.C.	
Erskine, Pardoe	Ballycarry	Sailor	Mercantile Marine	
Haveron, James	Ballycarry	Sailor	Mercantile Marine	
Hay, Robert	Ballycarry	Ldg. Signaller	R.N.	Torpedoed.
Hawkins, Boyd	Ballycarry	Sailor	Mercantile Marine	Torpedoed.
Irvine, John	Ballycarry	Officer	Mercantile Marine	Torpedoed.
Johnston, George	Whitehead	Captain	Mercantile Marine	
Macauley, W. J.	Islandmagee	Seaman	R.N.	
Magill, Charles	Ballycarry	Private	R.I.R.	
Martin, Wm. J.	Ballycarry	Stoker	R.N.	
Milliken, R. J.	Ballycarry	Sailor	Mercantile Marine	
McAllister, John	Ballycarry	A.M.	R.A.F.	
McConnell, John	Ballycarry	Captain	Mercantile Marine	
McCready, John	Ballycarry	Sailor	Mercantile Marine	Torpedoed.
McGarry, Wm.	Ballycarry	Sailor	Mercantile Marine	Torpedoed.
McKee, John	Ballycarry	Officer	Mercantile Marine	
McKinty, Patrick	Magheramorne	Private	R.A.S.C.	Wounded.
McMurran, Henry	Ballycarry	Private	R.I.R.	
Noble, Randal	Ballycarry	Sailor	Mercantile Marine	
Niblock, John	Ballycarry	Sailor	Mercantile Marine	
Orr, Samuel C.	Ballycarry	Captain	Mercantile Marine	
Peoples, Thomas	Ballycarry	Private	R.I.R.	
Steele, James S.	Ballycarry	Lieutenant	R.I.R.	Awarded M.C.
Stevenson, Nathaniel	Ballycarry	Captain	Mercantile Marine	Torpedoed (2).
Wilson, John	Ballycarry	Private	R.I.R.	
Wilson, John	Ballycarry	Sailor	Mercantile Marine	
Wilson, Robert	Ballycarry	Sailor	Mercantile Marine	
COLONIAL FORCES.				
Barry, David	Ballycarry		Canadians	Died of Wounds.
Hume, Hugh	Ballycarry		Canadians	Wounded.
McKee, James	Ballycarry		Canadians	Died.
McKinty, Wm.	Magheramorne		Canadians	
Penny, Robert	Whitehead		Canadians	Wounded.
Stevenson, James	Ballycarry		Canadians	
Wilson, Wm.	Ballycarry		Americans	
BALLYCLARE.				
Adrain, Alfred	North End	Private	N.I.H.	
Adrain, Hugh	Le-Ballyclare	C.Q.M.S.	R.I.R.	
Beggs, Andrew	Market Square	Private	R. In. Fus.	Wounded.
Brown, Alex.	Ballyclare	Private	R.I.R.	

CARRICKFERGUS PRESBYTERY.   BALLYCLARE.

Name.	Home Address.	Rank.	Regiment, Battalion or Unit.	Remarks.
Brown, Samuel J.	Ballyclare	Private	R.I.R.	
Creeth, David	Ballyclare	Private	R.I.R.	
Graham, William	Moss Road	Private	R.I.R.	
Grange, Robert	Mill Lane	Corporal	R.E.	M.M.
Grant, John	The Cottage	Corporal	R.I.R.	
Grant, Robert	The Cottage	Lieutenant	R. In. Fus.	Wounded.
Greer, Edward	Moss Road		R.N.	
Hayes, William	Moss Road	Private	R.E.	
Kirk, William	Ballyclare	Private	R.I.R.	
Kirk, Wm. John	Green Road	Private	R. In. Fus.	Wounded.
Logan, Wm. A.	Craig Hill	Private	Labour Batt.	Wounded.
Lorimer, Andrew	North End	Private	R.E.	
Lorimer, James	Main Street	Private	R.I.R.	Wounded.
Lorimer, John	Market Square	Private		
McAulay, Henry	Mill Lane	Private	R.N.	
McAulay, Robert	Mill Lane	Private	R.I.R.	
McAulay, William	Mill Lane	Private		
McCalmont, James	Green Road	Private	R.I.R.	Wounded 4 times.
McClean, James	Green Road	Private	R.I.R.	
McCrea, Bertie	Le-Ballyclare	Private	R.I.R.	Killed in Action.
McCreary, Francis	Green Road	Private	R.I.R.	Wounded.
McGaw, Robert	Park Place	Private	Labour Batt.	
McGladdery, James	Green Road	Private	M.T. A.S.C.	
McGuigan, Arthur	Green Road	Private	R.I.R.	Wounded.
McGuigan, Wm.	Green Road	Private	R.I.R.	Wounded.
McKeown, John	Melvale	Private	R.I.R.	Wounded twice
McKeown, Robert	Melvale	Private	R.I.R.	Wounded.
McMeekin, Robert	Main Street	2nd Lieutenant	Seaforth Highlanders	Wounded twice.
McMillan, Wm.	Cogry	Private	R.I.R.	
Mewhirter, James	Ashlea Villas	Sergt.-Major	A.S.C.	
Morrison, Wm. Jas.	Caldhame	Private	R.I.R.	Wounded.
Montgomery, Nathaniel	Cogry	Private	R.I.R.	
Patton, Robert	Green Road	Private	R.I.R.	Wounded twice.
Patton, Thomas	Ashlea Gardens	Sergt.-Major	A.S.C.	
Reid, Wm. John	Ballycor Road	Private	R.I.R.	Killed in Action.
Ross, Dixon	Fairview	Private	Armoured Motor	
Ross, John	Fairview	Captain	A.S.C.	
Smyth, Robert	Green Road	Private	R.I.R.	
Smyth, Wm.	Green Road	Private	R.I.R.	Died.
Spence, Wm.	Le-Ballyclare	Sergt.-Major	A.S.C.	
Walker, Thos. M.	Moss Road	Private	R.I.R.	
Warnick, John	Market Square	Captain	R.A.M.C.	Wounded.
Williams, Benjamin	Main Street	Private	R.E.	
Williams, Fred	Main Street	Private	K.O. Yorkshire	
Williams, John	Main Street	Private	R.G.A.	
Wilson, Thos. Hugh	Green Road	Private	R.I.R.	
Wilson, William	Le-Ballyclare	Private	R.I.R.	Wounded twice.
Workman, Robert	Green Road		R.N.	
Workman, Wm. J.	Green Road	Private	R.I.R.	
Young, Jas. Johnston	Doagh Road	Cadet	O.T.C.	
COLONIAL FORCES.				
Beattie, John	Ballyclare	Corporal	Canadians	Wounded.
Hunter, Robt. Thos.	Little Ballymena	Private	Can. F.A.	
Kerr, James	Main Street	Private	Can. Infт.	Wounded.
FIRST BALLYEASTON.				
Adair, J.	Ballyeaston	Sapper	R.E.	Wounded.
Beggs, Robert				
Buchannan, F.	Ballyclare	Private	M.T. A.S.C.	
Caruth, John	Rashee	Private	18th R.I.R.	
Clugston, W. H.	Dunamoy	Corporal	Cyclist Corps	Wounded twice.
Davidson, H. Stewart	Cogry	Private	1st Dorsets	Wounded thrice. Twice Gassed.
Marshall, T. J.	Ballyalbanagh	Private	6th R.I.R.	Wounded twice.
Moore, E.		Private	27th R.F.A.	
Moore, —				
McCauley, C.	Ballyalbanagh	Sapper	R.E.	Killed in Action.
McCauley, D.	Ballyalbanagh	Lance-Corporal	12th R.I.R.	
McConnell, R.	Rashee	Private	12th R.I.R.	
McConnell, S.	Rashee	Private	A.S.C.	
McConnell, S.	Rashee	Sergeant		
McConnell, W. J.	Rashee	Private	M.T. A.S.C.	
McKenzie, D.	Ballyclare	Private	11th R.I.R.	Killed in Action.
Reid, R.	Gateside	Private	12th R.I.R.	Prisoner of War.
Stevenson, S.	Ballyclare	2nd Lieutenant	Not Posted	
Taylor, Joseph	Springvale	Sergeant	12th R.I.R.	Killed in Action.
Todd, S.	Drumadarragh	Private	12th R.I.R.	Killed in Action.
White, J.		Private	M.T. A.S.C.	
Wilson, F. C.	Ballyalbanagh	Private	6th R.D.F.	Wounded.
Wilson, Wm.	Upper Ballyalbanagh	Private	R.I.R.	

CARRICKFERGUS PRESBYTERY.   FIRST BALLYEASTON.

Name.	Home Address.	Rank.	Regiment, Battalion or Unit.	Remarks.
COLONIAL FORCES.				
ADAIR, T.	Ballyeaston	Sapper	75th Can. Batt.	
ADAIR, J.	Ballyeaston	Private	75th Can. Batt.	
AGNEW, S.	Ballyclare	Corporal	1st W.I.B.	
CRAIG, B. W.	Ballyboley	Private	9th Field Amb. A.I.F.	
SEMPLE, A.	Ballynashee	Private	Can. Forestry Corps	
SECOND BALLYEASTON.				
BEGGS, SAMUEL	Ballyeaston	Private	12th R.I.R.	Wounded.
DAVIDSON, SAMUEL	Ballyeaston	Private	12th R.I.R.	Wounded.
HAYES, ROBERT	Ballyclare	Private	12th R.I.R.	Killed in Action.
JENKINS, ANDREW	Castletown	Private	14th R.I.R.	
LAIRD, ROBERT JOHN	Ballyclare	Lance-Corporal	12th R.I.R.	Wounded.
LEITH, WM. JAMES	Dunamoy	Private	63rd Brigade R.F.A.	Wounded.
LOUGHRAN, WM. H.	Ballyclare	Corporal	M.T. R.A.M.C.	
LYNN, SAMUEL	Ballycorr	Private	9th R.I. Fus.	
McALISTER, ROBERT	Tildarg	Private	18th R.I.R.	
McCLEAN, ROBERT	Cogry	Lance-Corporal	12th R.I.R.	Wounded.
McCLEAN, WM.		Private	12th R.I.R.	Wounded.
McGOOKIN, ARTHUR	Rashee	Private	Farrier, A.S.C.	
McGOOKIN, ARTHUR, JUN.	Rashee	Trooper	N.I.H.	Gassed.
McGOOKIN, THOMAS	Rashee	Private	I. Guards	Killed in Action.
McILWAINE, JAMES	Ballyalbana	Private	12th R.I.R.	Wounded.
McNALLY, FRED.	Brookfield	2nd Lieutenant	5th R.I. Regt.	
MANSON, ROBERT	Ballyclare	Private	12th R.I.R.	Killed in Action.
MAYNE, WILLIAM	Dunamoy		R.N.	
MOORE, ANDREW	Ballyeaston	Corporal	12th R.I.R.	Wounded, M.M.
ROBINSON, SAMUEL	Cogry	Private	12th R.I.R.	Killed in Action.
SMITH, HUGH F.	Kilbride		R.N.	
STEWART, HUGH	Cogry	Private	Labour Corps	Wounded.
SURGEONER, JAMES	Ballyclare	Private	3rd K.O.R.L.	
TODD, BRYSON	Ballyeaston	Private	R.E.	
TODD, JAMES	Ballyclare	Lance-Corporal	12th R.I.R.	
WADDELL, GEORGE	Cogry	Private	12th R.I.R.	Killed Accidentally
WHITE, JOHN	Rashee	Lance-Corporal	12th R.I.R.	Gassed.
WILSON, ALEX.	Cogry	Private	12th R.I.R.	
COLONIAL FORCES.				
BLAIR, JOHN	Cogry	Private	1st Can. Div.	Wounded.
GILMOUR, WM. ANDREW	Ballyeaston	Private	Can. Div.	
McCLELLAND, WM.	Ballynashee	Private	N.Z.	Killed in Action.
McCREARY, SAMUEL	Ballyclare	Private	Can. Div.	
SEMPLE, ALAN	Kilbride	Private	1st Aust. Div	Wounded.
WHITE, JAMES	Rashee	Drummer	78th Canadians	
BALLYLINNEY.				
ADAMS, THOMAS	Ballyclare	Stoker	R.N.	
ADAMS, WM.	Ballyclare	Private	M.T.	
ALEXANDER, JOHN	Bruslee	Trooper	N.I.H.	Wounded.
ALEXANDER, SAMUEL T.	Bruslee	Captain	R.A.M.C.	
BEGGS, JOSEPH	Ballyclare	Private	R.I.R.	Wounded.
BEGGS, WM.	Ballyclare	Sergeant	R.I.R.	Prisoner of War.
BELL, SAMUEL	Ballylinney	Private	R.D. Fus.	Wounded.
BLAIR, JOSEPH	Le-Ballymena	Private	R.I.R.	Killed in Action.
BLAIR, SAMUEL	Le-Ballymena	Stoker	R.N.	
BOYD, JOHN	Ballycraigy	Driver	A.S.C.	Wounded.
CALWELL, SAMUEL	Ballyclare	Sergeant	R.I.R.	Killed in Action.
CAMPBELL, S. W.	Lisnalinchy	2nd Lieutenant	R.D. Fus.	Wounded.
COWAN, WM.	Ballyclare	Private	R.I.R.	
CRYMBLE, FRANCIS	Ballyclare	Private	R.A.F.	
DOOLE, JOSEPH	Ballylinney	Private	R.E.	
DUNDEE, ALBERT	Straidnahanna	Lieutenant	N.I.H.	Wounded.
DUNDEE, ALEX.	Straidnahanna	Lieutenant	R.I.R.	M.C., Wounded.
DUNDEE, CHAS.	Straidnahanna	Lance-Corporal	Y.C.V.	Wounded.
DUNDEE, ROBERT	Straidnahanna	Lance-Corporal	N.I.H.	
DUNDEE, WM. J.	Straidnahanna	Sergeant	S.A. Rifles	
FERRIS, GEORGE	Bruslee	Signaller	N.I.H.	
GAULT, JOSEPH	Carntall	Private	R.I.R.	
GAULT, ROBERT	Carntall	Lance-Corporal	R.I.R.	Killed in Action.
HAMILL, J. J.	Ballylinney	Private	R.I.R.	
HAMILL, SAMUEL	Ballyclare	Seaman	R.N.	
HARVEY, JOSEPH	Ballyclare	Sergeant	R.I.R.	M.M. Killed.
HETHERINGTON, R.	Le-Ballymena	Private	R.M.	
HUNTER, JOHN	Lisnalinchy	Private	R.I.R.	Wounded.
McKINTY, HUGH	Lisnalinchy	Lance-Corporal	R.E.	
MILLIKEN, ROBERT	Bruslee	Private	M.T.	
MOORE, HUGH	Ballyclare	Private	10th Hussars	
MOORE, JOHN	Ballyclare	Corporal	R. Inn. Fus.	
MOORE, ROBERT	Ballylinney	Sergeant	R.E.	
MOORE, WILLIAM	Ballylinney	Private	R.I.R.	

CARRICKFERGUS PRESBYTERY.

BALLYLINNEY.

Name.	Home Address.	Rank.	Regiment, Battalion or Unit.	Remarks.
Nimmons, Joseph	King's Moss	Private	R. Inn. Fus.	Wounded & Pris.
Nimmons, Sidney	King's Moss	Signaller	Marine Artillery	
Nimmons, Wm. R.	King's Moss	Driver	M.T.	
Owens, H. H.	Lisnalinchy	Private	R.I.R.	Wounded.
Patterson, Thomas	Ballylinney	Corporal	R. Inn. Fus.	
Patterson, Wm.	Ballylinney	Trooper	N.I.H.	Wounded.
Reid, Thomas	Ballylinney	Private	L.C.	
Reid, William	Ballylinney	Private	A.S.C.	
Rowney, John	Carntall	Sergeant	R.E.	
Smyth, Wm. P.	Le-Ballymena	Signaller	R.M.	Wounded.
Smyth, Wm. R.	Le-Ballymena	Gunner	T.C.	Wounded.
Strange, Wm. J.	Ballyclare	Lance-Corporal	R.I.R.	Wounded.
Templeton, Ab.	Ballyclare	Private	R.I.R.	Prisoner.
Templeton, Alex.	Ballyclare	Private	R.E.	
Sempy, Joseph	Ballyclare	Corporal	R.I.R.	Killed in Action.
Wilson, Robert H.	Ballylaggan	Captain	R.A.M.C.	Killed in Action.
COLONIAL FORCES.				
Coleman, John R.	Lisnalinchy	Private	Can. E.F.	Killed in Action.
Dundee, S. Blair	Bruslee	Lieutenant	Can. E.F.	M.C., Wounded.
Milliken, Samuel	Bruslee	Private	Aust. I.F.	Killed in Action.
Wilson, Wm. J.	Le-Ballymena	Bombardier	Aust. Art.	
BALLYNURE.				
Adair, John Scott	Headwood	Rifleman	Scottish Rifles	
Adrain, Andrew	Ballynure	Rifleman	R.I.R.	Killed in Action.
Auld, John	Ballyrickard	Gunner	R.F.A.	
Burnim, William	Ballyboley	Rifleman	R.I.R.	
Cameron, Robert	Straid	Private	Labour Corps	
Cameron, Samuel	Straid	Rifleman	R.I.R.	Wounded & Pris.
Davidson, James	Headwood	Rifleman	R.I.R	Killed in Action.
Dundee, Wm. B. Hill	Ballynure		R.A.M.C.	
Gamble, Thos. Henderson	Straid	Artificer	R.E.	
Geary, Wm.	Ballyboley	Lance-Corporal	R.I.R.	
Gettingby, Thos. John	Lismenary	Rifleman	R.I.R.	Prisoner.
Gyle, Thomas	Ballynure	Rifleman	R.I.R.	
Hawthorn, Wm.	Ballycorr	Rifleman	R.I.R.	
Henderson, James	Little Ballymena	Driver	R.E.	
Hetherington, Robert	Dunturkey	Stoker	R.N.	
Hill, John	Skilganaban	Rifleman	R.I.R.	Killed in Action.
Hutchinson, Alex.	Dairyland	Rifleman	R.I.R.	
Hutchinson, John	Dairyland	Rifleman	R.I.R.	Wounded.
Jenkins, John	Dunturkey	Engineer	H.M. Transports	
Laird, Robert John	Ballyboley	Rifleman	R.I.R.	Killed in Action.
McClellan, Allen John	Ballyboley	Lieutenant	R.I.R.	Killed in Action.
McClellan, Peter	Ballyboley	Lieutenant	R.N.	
McConkey, Matt. Geo.	Ballygowan	Lance-Corporal	R.I.R.	Twice Gassed.
McConkey, Samuel	Ballygowan	Sergeant	R.I.R.	Prisoner of War.
McCreary, Robert	Straidlands	Major	R.E.	M.C.
McCreary, Samuel Fulton	Straidlands	2nd Lieutenant	Cavalry Reserve	
McFerran, James	Dunturkey	Sergeant	R.I.R.	M.M., M.S.M.
McWilliam, David	Ballynure	Private	Gordon Highlanders	
Millar, Andrew	Ballyboley	Trooper	N.I.H.	
Montgomery, Eldred M.	Ballyboley	Lieutenant	Indian Army Guides	
Montgomery, Hector	Scotch Hill	Seaman	R.N.	
Montgomery, Verus C.	Ballyboley	Captain	R.A.M.C.	
Moore, Robert	Ballygowan	Private	Highland Light Infantry	Killed in Action.
Park, Richard	Ballynure	Private	M.T. A.S.C.	
Patton, Wm. Andrew	Haystown	Lance-Corporal	R.I. Fus.	Wounded & Pris.
Robinson, Robt. John	Lismenary	Rifleman	R.I.R.	
Shannon, Robt. John	Haystown	Rifleman	R.I.R.	Thrice Wounded.
Shannon, Thomas	Haystown	Rifleman	R.I.R.	Twice Wounded.
Sherrard, John	Headwood	Rifleman	R.I.R.	5 times Wounded.
Stewart, Joseph H.	Dunturkey	Rifleman	R.I.R.	
Stewart, Thos. John	Dunturkey	Rifleman	R.I.R.	
Turner, James	Ballycorr	Rifleman	R.I.R.	
Woodside, Robert	Lismenary	Captain	R.A.M.C.	
COLONIAL FORCES.				
Adrain, Wm.	Ballynure	Private	Canadians	
Crooks, Samuel	Ballygowan	Trooper	N.Z. Forces	
Elliott, Wm.	Headwood	Private	Canadians	Killed in Action.
Hill, Matthew Geo.	Castletown	Private	Australian Forces	
Jackson, Thomas	Skilganaban	Gunner	U.S. Army	
Jenkins, Wm.	Ardboley	Private	Canadians	
McClellan, Watson	Ballyboley	Lieutenant	Canadians	
McClintock, Jas. Thompson	Ballyboley	Private	Canadians	Killed in Action.
McConkey, Alex.	Ballygowan	Sergeant	Canadians	
McIlroy, James	Ballygallough	Rifleman	N.Z. Forces	
Park, James Shaw	Clements Hill	Trooper	Australian Forces	
Robinson, Thos. Alex.	Irish Hill	Sergeant-Major	Canadians	

CARRICKFERGUS PRESBYTERY. CAIRNCASTLE.

Name.	Home Address.	Rank.	Regiment, Battalion or Unit.	Remarks.
CAIRNCASTLE.				
Clarke, Robert	Brookfield	Private	9th R.D. Fus.	Died.
Crawford, James	Lisnahay	Private	4th King's Liverpool	Killed in Action.
Crawford, Samuel H.	Lisnahay	C.Q.M.S.	1st King's Liverpool	Wounded.
Crawford, W. Stewart	Corkermain	Corporal	R.E.	Wounded.
Graham, James	Clough	Private	9th R.I. Fus.	
Hunter, Robert	Ballygailey	Private	1st R.I.R.	Wounded.
Sittlington, Robert	Droagh	Private	1st R.I.R.	Wounded.
Sittlington, Thomas	Droagh	Private	9th R.I. Fus.	Killed in Action.
Steele, Andrew	Sallagh	Private	12th R.I.R.	Wounded.
Steele, Arch.	Sallagh	Private	20th R.I.R.	
Steele, Hugh	Sallagh	Private	8th R.I.R.	Killed in Action.
Steele, James	Sallagh	Lance-Corporal	11th R.I.R.	Wounded.
Steele, Samuel	Sallagh	Private	12th R.I.R.	
Todd, Montgomery	Ballywillan	Private	2nd R.I.R.	
Todd, Robert	Ballygally	Private	12th R.I.R.	
COLONIAL FORCES.				
Brown, James	Corkermain	Private	N.Z. Ex. F.	Killed in Action.
Brown, John C.	Corkermain	Private	N.Z. Ex. F.	
Brown, Thomas M	Corkermain	Private	N.Z. Ex. F.	Wounded.
McMullan, Joseph A.	Lisnahay	Private	Aust. Ex. F.	Died of Wounds.
McMullan, Wm. James	Lisnahay	Private	Aust. Ex. F.	Wounded.
Steele, Joseph	Sallagh	Private	Aust. Ex. F.	Wounded.
Stewart, Robt. James	Ballyhacket	Private	N.Z.	Killed in Action.
FIRST CARRICKFERGUS.				
Barkley, Thomas M.	Greenisland	Lieutenant	H.M. Patrol Service.	
Baird, James				
Bodels, Samuel	Prospect Street	Gunner	H.M.S. "Westmoreland"	
Cameron, Robt. Edmond	Rhanbuoy Park	Private	M.S. A.S.C.	
Campbell, Bruce	Upper Woodburn	Private	9th R.I.R.	
Carrey, John	Meadowbank	Lieutenant	1/9 Manchesters	
Carrey, Thomas	High Street	Officer	S.S. Transport	
Close, Joseph	Green Street		H.M.S. "Impereuse"	
Craig, George	Irish Quarter South	Private	12th R.I.R.	
Crymble, James	Greenisland	Driver	22nd Brigade F.A.	
Dalton, Robert	Lower Woodburn	Sergeant	12th R.I.R.	Killed in Action.
Davey, Allan	Lancasterian Street		9th R.I. Fus.	
Davey, Wm. H.		Major	27th Northumberland Fus.	
Forsyth, Alex.	Violet Cottage	Lieutenant	16th R.I.R.	
Forsyth, Alex., Jun.	Violet Cottage	Cadet	16th R.I.R.	
Gilmour, Albert	Irish Quarter South		Army Ordnance	
Haggan, Alex.	Knockagh	Private	12th Batt. R.I.R.	
Haggan, John	Knockagh	Private	12th Batt. R.I.R.	
Haggan, Thomas	West Street	2nd Lieutenant	Gar. Batt. Fusiliers	
Hamilton, Henry	Joymount Bank		Special Service Squadron	
Hamilton, Henry	Albert Road	Sergeant	12th Batt. R.I.R.	Killed in Action.
Hamilton, John	West Street	Chief Writer	H.M.S. "Zetland"	
Hamilton, John	Nelson Street	Baker	H.M.S. "Macedonia"	
Hamilton, Richard	West Street	2nd Lieutenant	19th R.I.R.	
Harper, John	Victoria Street		36th Div. Train A.S.C.	
Hilditch, John	North Street	Private	10th R. Inn. Fus.	
Hilditch, Wm.	North Street	Private	M.T. A.S.C.	
Houston, James	Unity Street	Gunner	Garrison Artillery	
Kellet, Hugh	Irish Quarter South	Private	12th R.I.R.	
Kerr, David	West Street	Private	R. Dub. Fus.	
Kerr, Jack	West Street	Engineer	Ship "Matawa"	
Law, William	North Street	Seaman	S.S. "Oceano"	
Legg, Charles	Bayview	2nd Lieutenant	R.E.	
Legg, Hugh G.	Bayview	2nd Lieutenant	11th R. Inn. Fus.	
Logan, Wm.	Knockagh	Trooper	N.I.H.	
Lusk, James	Davys Street			
McAtamney, Samuel	Albert Road	Private	R.I. Fus.	
McBride, Alex.	Lower Woodburn	2nd Lieutenant	12th R.I.R.	
McBride, John	Lower Woodburn	Private	20th Batt. R.I.R.	
McKendry, George	Lancasterian Street		H.M.S. "Buester"	
McKendry, John	Lancasterian Street	Stoker	H.M.S. "Tenacious"	
McKeown, Harold		2nd Lieutenant	Connaught Rangers	Killed in Action.
McKeown, Hugh	Prospect Street	Sapper	R.E.	
McMinn, John	Albert Road	Carpenter	S.S. "Britannic"	
McMurtry, John	Scotch Quarter	Officer	Trans. "Cambrian Range"	Prisoner of War.
Middleton, Wm.	Nelson Street	Private	12th Batt. R.I.R.	
Millar, Wm.	Fairymount	Lieutenant	R.N. Reserve	
Mills, Charles	Joymount Parade	Private	Co. London Regiment	
Miscampbell, Alex.	Governor's Place	Captain	A.S.C.	
Miskimmon, Cecil	Woodlawn	Private	9th Batt. R.I. Fus.	
Miscampbell, T. P.	Governor's Place	2nd Lieutenant	R.E.	
Morrison, Wm.	Irish Quarter	Private	R.I.R.	Killed in Action.
Porter, Harold	Silverdale	Captain	R.E.	
Porter, Robert	Silverdale	Lieutenant	4th R.I.R.	

(181)

CARRICKFERGUS PRESBYTERY.
FIRST CARRICKFERGUS.

Name.	Home Address.	Rank.	Regiment, Battalion or Unit.	Remarks.
Porter, Stanley	Silverdale	2nd Lieutenant	R. Garrison Artillery	
Ross, Ekin	Nelson Street	Seaman	Transport "Clandeboye"	
Stewart, Edmond	Green Street	Private	12th Batt. R.I.R.	
Taylor, Wm.	Hopefield	Private	G.B. R.I. Fus.	
Watson, Charles	Green Street	Seaman	H.M.S. "Imperieuse"	
White, Edward	M'Keen's Row	Private	12th Batt. R.I.R.	
White, John	M'Keen's Row	Private	12th Batt. R.I.R.	
Young, John	Agnes Street	Sergeant	R.G.A.	
Young, Robert	Agnes Street	Private	Royal Welsh Fus.	
Young, Paul	Agnes Street	Stoker	H.M.S. "Buttercup"	
Young, Joseph	Agnes Street	Corporal	Loyal North Lancashires	
Young, Thomas			RN.. Air Service	
COLONIAL FORCES.				
Brett, Wm.	North Street	2nd Lieutenant	Canadians	
Cambridge, Thomas	High Street	Lieutenant	King's African Rifles	
Haggan, Paul	Knockagh	Sapper	Can. Engineers	
Moore, Alex.		Private	72nd Batt. Can.	
Morris, David	Ellis Street	Cadet	Aust. Engineers	
McVea, M. E.	High Street	2nd Lieutenant	5th Batt. Aust.	
Porter, William	Hawthorn Cottage	Sergeant	Can. Force	
Reilly, James B.	Thornfield Cottage	Private	Can. F.A.	
Robinson, Arthur	Marine Terrace	Captain	49th Can.	
Smyth, Henry	Governor's Place	Sergeant	Canadians	
CARRICKFERGUS, JOYMOUNT.				
Adamson, James	Carrickfergus	Private	R.F.A.	
Adamson, John	Carrickfergus	Seaman	R.N.	
Anderson, John	Carrickfergus	Private	R.A.F.	
Atkins, Harry	Carrickfergus	Seaman	R.N.	
Bamford, Wm.	Woodburn	Private	N.I.H.	
Barr, Bruce	Carrickfergus	Private	R.A.F.	
Barry, John	Carrickfergus	Seaman	R.N	
Beattie, Thomas	Carrickfergus	Private	R.E.	
Beattie, Thomas	Carrickfergus	Private	12th R.I.R.	
Birney, Wm.	Eden	Seaman	M.M.	
Boyd, James	Carrickfergus	Private	18th R.I.R.	
Boyd, Robert H.	Carrickfergus	Sergeant	C.C.	
Boyd, Thos. W.	Carrickfergus	Lieutenant	10th R.I. Fus.	
Boyd, Wm. G.	Carrickfergus	Lieutenant	10th R.I.R.	Killed in Action.
Brennan, Robert	Woodburn	Private	12th R.I.R.	Died.
Brennan, Wm.	Carrickfergus	Private	R.G.A.	
Burgess, Sidney	Carrickfergus	Private	R.A.M.C.	
Cameron, James	Carrickfergus	Seaman	M.M.	
Campbell, Alex.	Carrickfergus	Private	78th R.I.R.	
Campbell, James	Greenisland	Private	R.E.	
Carlisle, David	Carrickfergus	Private	12th R.I.R.	M.M.
Carlisle, Edward	Carrickfergus	Private	12th R.I.R.	Killed in Action.
Carson, Robert	Woodburn	Private	8th E.F.	
Caruth, David	Carrickfergus	Private	M. Transport	
Clarke, Wm. J.	Carrickfergus	Seaman	R.N.	
Close, Alex.	Carrickfergus	Private	12th R.I.R.	Wounded.
Coulter, Samuel	Carrickfergus	Seaman	R.N.	
Craig, Robert	Carrickfergus	Seaman	R.N.	
Craig, Wm.	Carrickfergus	Private	R.M.L.C.	
Crawford, Angus	Carrickfergus	Private	12th R.I.R.	
Crawford, Robert	Carrickfergus	Sergeant	R. Office	
Crawford, Thomas	Carrickfergus	Private	N.I.H.	
Curran, Samuel	Carrickfergus	Private	R.E.	
Davey, James	Carrickfergus	Private	12th R.I.R.	Wounded.
Davidson, Charles	Eden	Seaman	M. Marine	
Elliott, Wm. James	Carrickfergus	Private	R.F.A.	
Endis, Wm.	Carrickfergus	Private	12th R.I.R.	
Ferguson, John	Carrickfergus	Private	12th R.I.R.	Wounded.
Finlay, Thomas	Carrickfergus	Private	78th R.I.R.	
Forsythe, Alex.	Carrickfergus	Lieutenant	16th R.I.R.	
Forsythe, Alex.	Carrickfergus	2nd Lieutenant	16th R.I.R.	
Gardiner, Alex.	Carrickfergus	Private	R.A.F.	
Gardiner, Andrew	Carrickfergus	Seaman	R.N.	Drowned.
Giffen, Samuel	Carrickfergus	Lieutenant	19th R.I.R.	
Haggan, Ezekiel	Carrickfergus	Private	A.S.C.	
Haggan, E. S. J.	Carrickfergus	Private	12th R.I.R.	Killed in Action.
Hamilton, Robert	Carrickfergus	Private	12th R.I.R.	
Hamilton, Thomas John	Greenisland	Private	A.S.C.	Wounded.
Hay, David	Carrickfergus	Seaman	R.N.	
Highlynds, George	Carrickfergus	Seaman	M.M.	
Hill, Alex.	Carrickfergus	Seaman	R.N.	Drowned.
Hill, Samuel	Carrickfergus	Private	12th R.I.R.	Killed in Action.
Hunter, John	Carrickfergus	Seaman	R.N.	
Hunter, Robert	Carrickfergus	Seaman	R.N.	
Hunter, Wm.	Carrickfergus	Private	78th R.I.R.	
Kelly, Joseph	Carrickfergus	Private	A.V. Corps	

CARRICKFERGUS PRESBYTERY. CARRICKFERGUS (Joymount).

Name.	Home Address.	Rank.	Regiment, Battalion or Unit.	Remarks.
Lewis, Wm.	Carrickfergus	Private	R.E.	
Lisk, Wm.	Carrickfergus	Seaman	R.N.	
Logan, Harry	Castleton, Belfast	Lieutenant	London Irish	
Logan, James F.	Castleton, Belfast	Sergeant	14th R.I.R.	
Logan, John W.	Castleton, Belfast	Private	9th R.I. Fus.	
Lyle, Samuel	Carrickfergus	Private	12th R.I.R.	
Lyle, Thomas	Carrickfergus	Private	M.T. A.S.C.	
McAllister, Alex.	Carrickfergus	Sergeant	...	Wounded.
McAllister, Andrew	Carrickfergus	Seaman	R.N.	Drowned.
McAllister, Arthur	Carrickfergus	Private	12th R.I.R.	
McAllister, Felix	Carrickfergus	Private	12th R.I.R.	
McAllister, Henry	Carrickfergus	Private	12th R.I.R.	Died.
McAllister, Matthew	Carrickfergus	Private	12th R.I.R.	
McAllister, Samuel	Carrickfergus	Private	R.B.R.	Wounded.
McAlpine, William	Carrickfergus	Private	12th R.I.R.	Wounded.
McAtamney, John	Carrickfergus	Private	Middlesex Regt.	
McAuley, David	Carrickfergus	Sergeant	R.I.R.	Wounded.
McCabe, John	Carrickfergus	Private	12th R.I.R.	Wounded.
McConkey, John	Carrickfergus	Lieutenant	R.N.	
McDermott, Thomas	Carrickfergus	Private	12th R.I.R.	Wounded.
McDermott, Wm. J.	Carrickfergus	Private	12th R.I.R.	M. Medal.
McDonald, Wm. R.	Carrickfergus	Private	12th R.I.R.	Killed in Action.
McDowell, Wm.	Carrickfergus	Private	12th R.I.R.	
McIlwaine, Gilbert	North Street	C.M. Sergeant	A.S.C.	
McIlwaine, James C.	North Street	C.M. Sergeant	12th R.I.R.	
McIlwaine, John	North Street	Sergeant	12th R.I.R.	Killed in Action.
McKee, Robert	Carrickfergus	Private	R.B.R.	
McKeown, Wm.	Carrickfergus	Private	18th R.I.R.	
McKibbin, Walter	Woodburn	Private	N.I.H.	Wounded.
McKinney, Edward	Carrickfergus	Seaman	R.N.	
McKinney, George	Carrickfergus	2nd Lieutenant	17th R.I.R.	Killed in Action.
McMurran, George	Carrickfergus	Private	12th R.I.R.	
McMurran, Joseph	Carrickfergus	Seaman	R.N.	
McNeill, Hugh	Carrickfergus	Private	12th R.I.R.	Wounded.
McNeilly, John	Carrickfergus	Private	12th R.I.R.	Wounded.
McNeilly, Wm.	Carrickfergus	Private	12th R.I.R.	
McQuitty, Wm.	Carrickfergus	Seaman	R.N.	
Malcolm, Isaac	Greenisland	Private	R.E.	
Millar, George	Carrickfergus	Private	12th R.I.R.	
Millar, James	Carrickfergus	Private	12th R.I.R.	
Millar, Robert	Carrickfergus	Seaman	R.N.	
Millar, Wm.	Carrickfergus	Sergeant	12th R.I.R.	Wounded.
Milliken, James	Scoutbush	2nd Lieutenant	Cadet Corps	Killed in Action.
Milliken, Robert	Carrickfergus	Private	18th R.I.R.	
Milliken, Wm.	Carrickfergus	Private	R.E.	
Milliken, Wm.	Carrickfergus	Private	R.I.R.	
Montgomery, Andrew	Carrickfergus	Private	78th R.I.R.	
Montgomery, James	Carrickfergus	Private	12th R.I.R.	
Ogilvie, David	Carrickfergus	Seaman	R.N.	
Owens, George	Carrickfergus	Private	12th R.I.R.	Killed in Action.
Owens, Matthew	Woodburn	Private	R.A.M.C.	
Perry, Henry	Carrickfergus	Private	12th R.I.R.	Wounded.
Reid, Thomas	Carrickfergus	Seaman	R.N.	
Robinson, David	Greenisland	Private	4th R.I.R.	
Robinson, George	Carrickfergus	Seaman	R.N.	
Robinson, John	Carrickfergus	Seaman	R.N.	
Robinson, Robert	Carrickfergus	Private	15th C.R.	Wounded.
Robinson, Samuel	Woodburn	Private	12th R.I.R.	Wounded.
Robinson, Thomas	Greenisland	Private	12th R.I.R.	
Robinson, Thomas	Carrickfergus	Private	...	
Robinson, Wm. John	Greenisland	Private	R.G.A.	
Sempie, James	Carrickfergus	Private	12th R.I.R.	Killed in Action.
Shearer, James	Bonybefore	Private	3rd R.I.R.	Wounded.
Simms, Thomas	Bonybefore	Private	12th R.I.R.	
Sloan, Kyle	Carrickfergus	Seaman	R.N.	
Sloan, Samuel	Carrickfergus	Private	3rd R.I.R.	Died.
Smyth, John	Carrickfergus	Private	12th R.I.R.	Killed in Action.
Smyth, Robert	Carrickfergus	Private	12th R.I.R.	Killed in Action.
Smyth, Robert	Carrickfergus	Private	12th R.I.R.	
Smyth, Samuel	Carrickfergus	Private	12th R.I.R.	
Sterling, David	Carrickfergus	Seaman	R.N.	
Stewart, Edward	...	Seaman	R.N.	
Stewart, Thomas	Carrickfergus	Private	R.I.R.	
Stewart, William	Carrickfergus	Seaman	R.N.	Died.
Wallace, John	Carrickfergus	Private	12th R.I.R.	
Wallace, Robert	Church Lane, Belfast	Corporal	17th R.I.R.	M.M.
Weatherup, Wm.	Woodburn	Private	12th R.I.R.	
Weir, Wm.				

COLONIAL FORCES.

Name.	Home Address.	Rank.	Regiment, Battalion or Unit.	Remarks.
Barr, James	Carrickfergus	Sergeant	Canadian M.R.	Wounded.
Birney, James	Eden	Seaman	Canadian Navy	
Millar, George	Carrickfergus	Private	Can. E.F.	
Minnis, James	Woodburn	Private	Canadian R.	Killed in Action.

CARRICKFERGUS PRESBYTERY. — FIRST ISLANDMAGEE.

Name.	Home Address.	Rank.	Regiment, Battalion or Unit.	Remarks.
FIRST ISLANDMAGEE.				
Dick, William	Islandmagee	Seaman	Mercantile Marine	
Donald, Edward	Islandmagee	Seaman	Transport Service	
Duff, James	Islandmagee	Seaman	Mercantile Marine	
Harvey, John	Islandmagee	Lance-Corporal	2nd Batt. R.I.R.	Killed in Action.
Hawthorne, James	Islandmagee	Seaman	Mercantile Marine	
Jackson, John McC.	Islandmagee		Aust. Imp. Force	
Johnston, Alex.	Islandmagee	Seaman	Mercantile Marine	
Kane, Jas. Macaulay	Islandmagee	Seaman	Mercantile Marine	
Macaulay, Robert	Islandmagee		Transport Service	
McKay, Hugh	Islandmagee		Transport Service	
McKay, Wm.	Islandmagee	Chief Engineer	Mercantile Marine	
McLernon, Patrick	Islandmagee	Seaman	Mercantile Marine	
McMaster, John	Islandmagee	Seaman	Mercantile Marine	
Mawhinney, Andrew	Islandmagee	Lance-Corporal	Irish Guards	Killed in Action.
Nicol, Thos. Falconer	Islandmagee		5th High. Light In.	Killed in Action.
Ross, Wm. Samuel Baird	Islandmagee	Lieutenant	15th Batt. R.I.R.	Killed in Action.
Stewart, Albert	Islandmagee	Seaman	Mercantile Marine	
Wilson, Wm. Johnston	Islandmagee	Seaman	Mercantile Marine	
Woodside, David	Islandmagee	Seaman	R.N.	Killed in Action.
Woodside, Thomas	Islandmagee	Seaman	R.N.	Killed in Action.
Wright, James	Islandmagee	Lance-Corporal	Irish Guards	Killed in Action.
SECOND ISLANDMAGEE.				
Boyd, Robert	Islandmagee		R.N.R.	
Dick, Charles	Islandmagee	Trooper	N.I.H.	
Ford, James	Islandmagee	Private	Garrison Batt.	Wounded.
Ford, Stewart	Islandmagee	Private	18th R.I.R.	
Hill, Allan	Islandmagee	Private	32nd Aust. Inft.	
Hill, Hugh	Islandmagee		R.N.R.	
Holmes, Jas. McA., M.B.	Belfast	Fleet Surgeon	R.N.	D.S.O.
Holmes, John V., M.B.	Belfast	Major	R.A.M.C.	
Holmes, Thos. S. S., M.B.	Belfast	Captain	R.A.M.C.	
Hunter, John	Islandmagee		R.N.R.	
Jackson, John	Islandmagee	Private	14th R.I.R.	
Jones, Andrew	Islandmagee	Private	19th R.I.R.	
Jones, John A.	Islandmagee	Lieut. in Command	R.N.R.	
Jones, Robert	Islandmagee	Lieut. in Command	R.N.R.	
Jones, Wm.	Islandmagee	Gunner	R.G.A.	
Kerr, David	Islandmagee	Private	18th R.I.R.	Died.
Kerr, Davis	Islandmagee	Lieut. in Command	R.N.R.	
Kerr, Hugh	Islandmagee	Lieut. in Command	R.N.R.	
Kerr, James	Islandmagee	Private	10th R.I.R.	
Kerr, Wm. A.	Islandmagee	Private	17th R.I.R.	
Laird, David	Islandmagee	Sapper	R.E., Naval Div.	
McCalmont, George	Islandmagee	Trooper	N.I.H.	
Macready, Oscar H.	Islandmagee	Captain	16th R.I.R.	Men. Despatches twice. Died of Wounds.
Mann, James	Islandmagee	Sub-Lieutenant	R.N.R.	
Martin, Wm. H.	Islandmagee	Trooper	N.I.H.	
Montgomery, Edward	Islandmagee	Private	18th R.I.R.	
Ross, John	Islandmagee	Lance-Corporal	1st London Regt.	Killed in Action.
Ross, Thomas	Islandmagee	Trooper	N.I.H.	
Tearl, James		Private	U.S. Inft.	
Templeton, Thomas		Trooper	N.I.H.	Wounded.
KILBRIDE.				
Allison, Wm. Walker, M.B.	Kilbride Manse	Captain	E.E.F.	
Bell, James	Ballybracken	Private	12th R.I.R.	Killed in Action.
Christie, John	Doagh	Private	12th R.I.R.	
Craig, James	Muckamore	Corporal	2nd Dragoon Guards	
Crawford, James	Ballyclare	Private	12th R.I.R.	Prisoner.
Coulter, Chas. Wm.	My Lady's Road, Belfast	Lieutenant	R.W. Fus.	M.C.
Gardiner, Samuel	Belfast	Private	R.M.L.I.	
Harper, Samuel John	Ballyhamage	Stoker	R.N.	
Higginson, John	Ballyhamage	Private	R.I.R.	
Hill, Alex.	Kilbride	Gunner	R.F.A.	Killed in Action.
Hunter, Chas. Edward	Ballyclare	Private	R.M.L.I.	
Kelly, Charles	Ballyhamage	Sergeant	12th R.I.R.	
Logan, Wm. James	Doagh	Private	11th R.I.R.	Wounded
Lorimer, Wm. Hugh	Whiteabbey	Private	12th R.I.R.	
McCrory, Samuel	Kilbride	Private	18th R.I.R.	
McNally, Fred. J.	Brookfield	Lieutenant	R.A.M.C.	
Mayne, Samuel	Cogry	Private	12th R.I.R.	
Montgomery, Henry	Kilbride	Private	R.A.S.C.	
Nevin, Alex.	Brookfield	Private	5th R.I.R.	
Nevin, John	Holestone	Private	12th R.I.R.	Killed in Action.
Nevin, Matthew	Holestone	Private	5th R.I.F.	Wounded.
Nevin, Wm. Hugh	Holestone	Private	18th R.I.R.	Wounded.
Orr, John	Church Lane	Private	Indian Army.	

CARRICKFERGUS PRESBYTERY.

KILBRIDE.

Name.	Home Address.	Rank.	Regiment, Battalion or Unit.	Remarks.
Orr, William	Brookfield	Private	R.I.R.	
Robinson, Andrew	Kilbride	Lance-Corporal	R.E.	
Robinson, Wm.	Kilbride	Sapper	R.E.	Wounded
Robson, James A.	Doagh	Private	R.A.M.C.	
Robson, Robert B.	Doagh	Trooper	6th Inn Dragoons	
Robson, Wm.	Doagh	Lieutenant	Black Watch	Wounded, Prisoner of War
Semple, James	Kilbride	Private	12th R I R	Wounded, Prisoner of War
Steele, Joseph	96 Ravenhill Rd., Belfast	Private	3rd K O R Lanc	
Smyth, Thos. John	Springvale	Q. Master	12th R I R	Prisoner of War
Taylor, Thomas	Doagh	Private	16th R.I.R.	
Whiteside, Jas. Bryson	Ballybracken	Private	9th R.I.F.	
Wicklow, Edward	Springvale	Private	12th R.I.R.	Wounded.
Wicklow, Wm.	Springvale	Private	R.I. Fus.	Wounded.
Wilson, John	Doagh	Stoker	R.N.	
COLONIAL FORCES.				
Allison, Robert Arthur	Kilbride Manse	Lieutenant	Canadian	Wounded.
Beggs, Thomas	Cogry	Private	Canadian	
Cameron, Wm.	Doagh	Gunner	Canadian F.A.	
Harper, Wm. Jas.	Ballyhamage	Private	13th Australian	
Kirk, Wm.	Doagh	Private	27th Canadian	Killed in Action.
Lorrimer, John	Ballyhamage	Lieutenant	Canadian R.A.F.	
Mahood, David	Ballynure	Corporal	Canadian	Killed in Action.
Milford, John	Doagh	Private	43rd Canadian	
Milford, Wm.	Doagh	Gunner	Canadian	
Wilson, James	Doagh	Driver	Canadian	
Wilson, Samuel Milliken	Doagh	Gunner	Canadian F.A.	
FIRST LARNE.				
Adams, Robert	Castle Terrace	Rifleman	12th R.I.R.	
Adams, R. McFerran	Castle Terrace		12th R.I.R.	Killed in Action.
Adams, William James	Newington	Pioneer	R.E.	
Agnew, Robert	Waterloo Road	Corporal	12th R.I.R.	Wounded.
Agnew, Wm. Henry	Inver	Rifleman	12th R.I.R.	
Andrews, James	Meetinghouse Street	Lance-Corporal	R.I. Fus.	
Armstrong, Wm.	Coronation Terrace	Lieutenant	R.I.R.	
Bailie, James	Meetinghouse Street	Corporal	12th R.I.R.	Wounded.
Bailie, James	Circular Road	Rifleman	12th R.I.R.	Killed in Action.
Baine, John E.			Canadians	Killed in Action.
Baxter, Samuel	Circular Road	Rifleman	12th R.I.R.	Wounded.
Beggs, James	Dunluce House		R.N.R.	
Beggs, Wm.	Dunluce House		R.A.M.C.	
Bell, Alex.	Carson Street			Killed in Action.
Bell, James	Newington Avenue	Corporal	R.I.R.	
Brennan, Bryce	Hope Street	Rifleman	12th R.I.R.	Killed in Action.
Brennan, Robert	Carson Street	Rifleman	4th R.I.R.	
Brownlees, John	Newington Avenue	Private	Irish Guards	
Bryson, Samuel	Drummond Street	Rifleman	12th R.I.R.	
Bryson, William	Fleet Street		R.N.R.	
Burns, Wm. A. L.				
Caldwell, James				Killed in Action.
Campbell, Wm.	Waterloo Road	Lance-Corporal	12th R.I.R.	Killed in Action.
Carmichael, James				Killed in Action.
Carmichael, John				
Carmichael, Wm.				Killed in Action.
Carson, Fred.	The Knowe	Captain	R.A.M.C.	Military Cross.
Carson, Herbert W.	The Knowe	Lieut.-Colonel	R.A.M.C.	D.S.O., Killed in Action.
Carson, Holden	The Knowe	Captain	R.A.M.C.	
Carson, Jas. A. B.	The Knowe	Captain	R.A.M.C.	Killed in Action.
Carson, Hugh	Ballymena Road		12th R.I.R.	
Carson, James	Ballymena Road	Rifleman		
Carson, Samuel	Ballymena Road	Rifleman	12th R.I.R.	Wounded.
Carson, Wm.				
Clarke, Christopher	Mill Brae	Private	R.I.F.	
Clarke, Edmund	Mill Brae	Lance-Corporal	R.I.F.	Killed in Action.
Clarke, John M.	Mill Brae	Private	R.I.F.	Wounded.
Clements' John	St. John's Place	C.P.O.	R.N.	
Close, Andrew	Hope Street	Stoker	R.N.R.	
Connor, Joseph	Bank Road	Private	R.I.R.	
Craig, Robert				
Crawford, Joseph	Mill Street	Lance-Corporal	12th R.I.R.	
Davidson, James	Hightown			
Davis, John				
Davis, Robert	Erection Villas	C.P.O.	R.N.	
Dooris, John	Inver Cottage	Rifleman	12th R.I.R.	
Erskine, Robert			R.G.A.	Killed in Action.
Erskine, Thomas	The Cliff	Private	R.G.A.	
Fergie, Archie	Bay Road	Stoker	R.N.R.	...
Fergie, Chas.	Bay Road	Private	R.A.F.	

CARRICKFERGUS PRESBYTERY. FIRST LARNE.

Name.	Home Address.	Rank.	Regiment, Battalion or Unit.	Remarks.
Fergie, James	Bay Road	Rifleman	12th R.I.R.	Killed in Action.
Ferguson, Albert	Newington Avenue	Sergeant	R. Defence Corps	
Ferris, Alec	Rathmore	Captain	4th R.I.R.	
Ferris, James	Rathmore	Lieutenant	R.A.F.	
Fleming, John	Mill Brae	Private	A. Vet. Corps	
Gettingby, Thomas	Meetinghouse Street	Sergeant	12th R.I.R.	Killed in Action.
Gilliland, John	Pound Street	Private	12th R.I.R.	
Gordon, R. Graham				
Greenlees, James	Kilwaughter	Private	R.A.M.C.	
Greer, Arthur	Greenland Terrace	Rifleman	6th R.I.R.	Wounded.
Hanna, James	Glynn Road	Rifleman	8th S. Rifles	Killed in Action.
Havelin, Saunderson	Ballymena Road	Rifleman	12th R.I.R.	Wounded.
Hayes, Joseph	Inver	Coy. Sergt.-Major	12th R.I.R.	
Henderson, P.				
Hill, John				
Hoey, Thomas				
Hood, Wm.	Olderfleet Road		R.N.R.	
Houston, John	Portland Street	Private	12th R.I.R.	
Houston, Robert	Portland Street	Private	12th R.I.R.	
Huey, W. Wallace	Chelmsford Place			Killed in Action.
Hylands, Frank	Waterloo Road	Private	In. Fus.	Killed in Action.
Hylands, John	Quay Lane	Stoker	R.N.R.	Killed in Action.
Hyslop, James	Meetinghouse Street	Private	R.I.R.	
Hyslop, Robert	Old Glenarm Road	Private	R.I.R.	
Hyslop, Thomas	Meetinghouse Street	Private	12th R.I.R.	
Jackson, George	Main Street	Captain	R.A.S.C.	
Jenkins, Wm.	Dunluce Street	Sergeant	12th R.I.R.	
Johnston, Arch. M.	34 Carson Street	Lance-Corporal	12th R.I.R.	Died of Wounds.
Johnston, Frank	Kilwaughter	Trooper	N.I.H.	
Johnston, Robert	Meetinghouse Street	Private	M.T. R.A.S.C.	
Johnston, Thomas	Kensington Terrace	Sergeant	12th R.I.R.	Wounded.
Kilpatrick, Thomas	Millbrook			Killed in Action.
Kilpatrick, Wm.	Millbrook			Killed in Action.
Kilpatrick, Wm. Jas.				Killed in Action.
King, James	St. John's Place			
King, John	Ballysnod	Private	12th R.I.R.	
Kirkwood, Nathaniel	Mill Street	Sergeant	12th R.I.R.	D.C.M.
Lilley, Andrew	Meetinghouse Street	Sergeant	R.G.A.	
Lilley, Wm.	Meetinghouse Street	Private	R.E.	
Lynas, Robert	Meetinghouse Street	Rifleman	12th R.I.R.	Wounded.
Lyttle, Samuel	Browndodd	Rifleman	12th R.I.R.	
McClelland, Earnfaunce	Curran Street	Captain	Leinster Regt.	Men. Des.
McCluggage, Andrew	Station Road			
McCluggage, William	Ballyboley	Lieutenant	12th R.I.R.	Killed in Action.
McClure, Hugh	Newington Avenue	Sapper	R.E.	Killed in Action.
McClure, James	Newington Avenue	Sapper	R.E.	
McClure, Robert	Newington Avenue	Rifleman	12th R.I.R.	
McConnell, John				
McDowell, Robert	Mission Lane	Rifleman	12th R.I.R.	Killed in Action.
McDowell, Wm. H.	Drumalis	Sergeant	12th R.I.R.	Killed in Action.
McFall, James	Millbrook	Rifleman	12th R.I.R.	
McFall, Samuel John	Glynn			Killed in Action.
McFerran, David				
McGarel, Archibald	Glynn Road	Rifleman	12th R.I.R.	Wounded
McGarel, William	Glynn Road	Rifleman	12th R.I.R.	
McIlwaine, Thomas	Ballysnod			
McIlwaine, William	Ballysnod			
McKay, James	Millbrook			
McKay, Samuel	Millbrook	Private	12th R.I.R.	Killed in Action.
McKeen, William				
McKenzie, D.				
MacKey, Robert John	Circular Road	Sapper	R.E.	
MacKey, Samuel Ross	Circular Road	Stoker	R.N.R.	Killed in Action.
MacKey, Wm. Leslie	Circular Road	Stoker	R.N.R.	
McManus, James	Mountpleasant	Sergeant	12th R.I.R.	Killed in Action.
McMorran, James	Coronation Terrace	Private	12th R.I.R.	Wounded.
McMurtry, Andrew	Bay Road	Rifleman	12th R.I.R.	
McNally, Thomas	Millbrook			Killed in Action.
McNeill, Andrew	Pound Street	Rifleman	12th R.I.R.	
McNeill, John				
McNeill, Wm.	Pound Street		R.N.	
Magee, Harry	Main Street			
Magill, John	Main Street			Killed in Action.
Magill, Spencer	Main Street			Killed in Action.
Manson, Hugh	Carson Street	Corporal	1st R.I.R.	Wounded.
Manson, Thomas	Carson Street	Rifleman	12th R.I.R.	
Melville, Wm.	Clonlee	Sergeant	12th R.I.R.	
Meneilly, John	Circular Road	Rifleman	12th R.I.R.	Wounded.
Mills, Wm. John	Carson Street	Rifleman	12th R.I.R.	Wounded.
Mitchell, James	Glynn Road	Corporal	N.I.H.	
Murray, Wm.	Point Street			Killed in Action.
Orr, Arthur	Ballysnod		R.N.	
Orr, James	Ballysnod	Lieutenant	R.N.	
Orr, Matthew	Circular Road	Sergeant	12th R.I.R.	

CARRICKFERGUS PRESBYTERY.

FIRST LARNE.

Name.	Home Address.	Rank.	Regiment, Battalion or Unit.	Remarks.
Owens, Alex.	Point Street	Private	12th R.I.R.	
Owens, Alex. E.	Clonlee	Sergeant	12th R.I.R.	
Owens, Jack	Clonlee	Private	12th R.I.R.	
Owens, Thomas	Point Street	Private	12th R.I.R.	
Patterson, John	Park Street	Sapper	R.E.	
Pierce, George F.	Meadow Street	Gunner	R.N.R.	
Porter, Wm.	Agnew Street		R.N.R.	
Ramsey, Robert John		Corporal	12th R.I.R.	
Reid, James	Waterloo Road	Rifleman	12th R.I.R.	Killed in Action.
Reid, Wm.	25 Glynn Road	Private	12th R.I.R.	
Richmond, Robert	Drummond Street	Stoker	R.N.	
Richmond, Samuel	Drummond Street		R.N.	
Robinson, Archibald	Fleet Street	Rifleman	12th R.I.R.	
Robinson, Daniel	Bay Road		R.N.R.	
Robinson, John				
Robinson, Samuel				
Robinson, Thomas	29 St. John's Place	Sergeant	1st R.I.R.	Killed in Action.
Robinson, Thomas	Meetinghouse Street	Rifleman	12th R.I.R.	Died of Wounds.
Robinson, Wm.	Meetinghouse Street	Private	Worcester Regt.	
Robinson, Wm. James				
Ross, James	Rossville	Trooper	N.I.H.	
Ross, John	Rossville	Private	R.A.S.C.	M.M.
Savage, Thomas	Victoria Street	Lieutenant	3rd Rifle Brigade	Killed in Action.
Semple, Adam	Invergordon Terrace	Stoker	R.N.R.	
Shannon, Thomas	Castle Terrace		R.N.R.	
Shannon, Wm.	Portland Street		R.N.R.	
Shain, David	Newington Avenue	Private	12th R.I.R.	
Shain, John	Newington Avenue	Corporal	12th R.I.R.	
Shain, Samuel	Newington Avenue	Private	12th R.I.R.	
Simms, David S.	Carson Street	Private	Lancaster Regt.	Killed in Action.
Simms, Ernest	Main Street			
Simms, Robert	Main Street	Rifleman	12th R.I.R.	
Sloan, John				
Smiley, Hubert	Drumalis			
Smiley, Sir John R.	Drumalis			
Smiley, Peter Kerr	Drumalis			
Smith, Albert	Old Glenarm Road	Sergeant	R.G.A.	
Smythe, Charles	Fleet Street	Private	12th R.I.R.	
Snoddy, George	Ballysnod	Rifleman	12th R.I.R.	
Snoddy, Samuel	Ballysnod	Sergeant	12th R.I.R.	
Snoddy, Wm.	Ballysnod	Rifleman	12th R.I.R.	
Steele, Robert				
Stewart, Barkley	Bay Road	Stoker	R.N.R.	
Thompson, George	Ollarba, Larne Hbr.	Major	12th R.I.R.	D.S.O.
Walker, John	Park Street	Rifleman	12th R.I.R.	Wounded.
Workman, Wm.	Bridge Street	Private	12th R.I.R.	
Wright, Archie	Old Glenarm Road	Rifleman	12th R.I.R.	
Yeates, Samuel	Dalaraida, Magheramorne		R.A.M.C.	
COLONIAL FORCES.				
Fergie, Robert	Bay Road	Private	Canadians	
Greenlees, Andrew	Main Street	Private	Can. R.A.M.C.	
Greenlees, James F.	Main Street	Trooper	S.A. Mt. Rifles	
Greenlees, Thomas	Main Street	Trooper	S.A. Mt. Rifles	
McNeill, James	Mount Pleasant	Private	Aust. I.F.	
Melville, Alex.	Clonlee	Private	Aust. I.F.	Killed in Action.
Mitchell, Alex. Scott	Glynn Road	Trooper	Strath. Horse	Killed in Action.
Moore, Archibald	Ballymena Road	Private	Canadians	M.M. and Bar.
Orr, James	Meetinghouse Street	Lieutenant	Canadians	
LARNE, (GARDENMORE.)				
Agnew, Andrew	81 Mill Street	Private	12th Batt. R.I.R.	Killed in Action.
Allison, F.	"Mervue"	Captain	R.A.M.C.	
Armstrong, James	Adelaide Terrace		H.M. Trawler "Rose"	
Armstrong, John	Adelaide Terrace	Private	12th Batt. R.I.R.	
Barklie, John	2 Clonlee		H.M.S. "Acquarious"	
Birch, Gerald A.		2nd Lieutenant	2nd Batt. Man. Regt.	
Brown, W. N.	"Lisnamoyle"	Private	Croix Rouge Française	
Buchanan, Hugh	12 Meadow Street	Private	12th Batt. R.I.R.	
Campbell, Wm. J.	38 Waterloo Road	Private	12th Batt. R.I.R.	Killed in Action.
Carmichael, W. J.	112 Main Street		R.N.R.	
Clarke, John	Kilwaughter	Private	12th Batt. R.I.R.	
Clarke, Samuel James	90 Old Glenarm Road	Private	R.E.	
Clarke, Stewart	Kilwaughter	Private	G. Highlanders	
Clarke, Wm.	43 Mill Street	Private	6th Batt. R.I. Fus.	
Clements, Alexander	Meetinghouse Street	Private	Labour Batt. R.E.	
Clements, Houston	20 Glynn View Avenue	Private	12th Batt. R.I.R.	Killed in Action.
Clements, Jackson	Carson Street	Private	Worcester Regt.	
Clements, James	15 Queen Street	Private	18th Batt. R.I.R.	
Clements, Wm.	15 Queen Street		R.N.	
Coey, John Smiley	Merville, Belfast	Midshipman	R.N.	Killed in Action.
Craig, David	13 Newington Avenue	Private	2nd R. Inn. Fus.	

CARRICKFERGUS PRESBYTERY. **LARNE (Gardenmore).**

Name.	Home Address.	Rank.	Regiment, Battalion or Unit.	Remarks.
Craig, Joseph	Mill Street	Private	12th Batt. R.I.R.	
Crawford, James	38 Old Glenarm Road	Private	Irish Guards	
Crawford, James	38 Old Glenarm Road	Private	R.A.M.C.	
Crooks, James	40 Newington Avenue	Sergeant	12th Batt. R.I.R.	
Crooks, James	2 Balneum Terrace	Private	17th Batt. R. Welsh Fus.	
Crooks, James	Balneum Terrace	Private	4th Batt. R. Inn. Fus.	
Davison, Charles	Station Road	Captain	R.I. Fus.	
Davison, Wm. H.		Captain	R.A.M.C.	
Doole, James	89 Old Glenarm Road	Private	R.E.	
Erwin, Hugh	Invergordon Terrace	Private	Shipyard Co. R.E.	
Ferguson, Albert	6 Newington Avenue	Private	6th Batt. R.I.R.	
Finlay, Samuel	26 Waterloo Road	Private	12th Batt. R.I.R.	
Forbes, James	30 Glynn Road	Private	Inns of Court O.T.C.	
Fraser, William	Old Glenarm Road	Private	Fife and Forfarshire Yeo.	
Gardiner, Allan	21 Circular Road	Private	12th Batt. R.I.R.	
Gardiner, George		Private	12th Batt. R.I.R.	Killed in Action.
Gilchrist, Richard	32 Fleet Street	Private	12th Batt. R.I.R.	
Girvan, James	20 Herbert Avenue	Private	12th Batt. R.I.R.	
Goudy, Robert	4 Curran Street	Private	12th Batt. R.I.R.	
Gourley, Hugh	24 Carson Street	Private	12th Batt. R.I.R.	
Gourley, Thomas	3 Waterloo Road	Private	12th Batt. R.I.R.	Killed in Action.
Greenwood, Adam	16 Gardenmore Place	Private	12th Batt. R.I.R.	
Hamilton, Alexander	33 Circular Road	Private	3rd Batt. R.I.R.	
Hanson, Rev. D. H., B.A.	Gardenmore Manse	Lieut-Colonel	Chaplain Dep.	C.B.E.
Hanson, R. S.	Gardenmore Manse	Captain	12th Batt. R.I.R.	M.C.
Hart, W. T. G.	Olderfleet Road	Sergeant	12th Batt. R.I.R.	
Henderson, John O.	Victoria Street	2nd Lieutenant	10th Batt. R.I.F.	
Hill, John	99 Circular Road	Private	12th Batt. R.I.R.	
Hoy, Robert	4 Fleet Street	Lance-Corporal	12th Batt. R.I.R.	
Hoy, Thomas	8 Fleet Street		H.M.S. "Mercury"	
Jamison, Samuel	56 Bank Road	Private	3rd Batt. R.I.R.	Killed in Action.
Kerr, William	51 Waterloo Road		R.N.R.	
Kerr, Wm., Jun.			R.N.R.	
Lennon, Norman	12 Main Street	Corporal	Motor Despatch Rider	
Logan, John	3 Curran Street	Private	12th Batt. R.I.R.	
Logan, Joseph	29 Thorndale Avenue	Private	12th Batt. R.I.R.	Killed in Action.
Mackell, Robert	11 Clonlee	Private	R.F.A. Motor Gun Section	
Magee, Samuel	Back Road	Sergeant	12th R.I.R.	
Mellin, Samuel	The Open	Private	12th Batt. R.I.R.	Killed in Action.
Millar, Thomas	10 Newington Avenue	Private	12th R.I.R.	
Mooney, Joseph	Glynn	Private	12th R.I.R.	
Mooney, Robert J.	Glynn Road		Royal Navy	
Moore, Robert	14 Newington Avenue		R.N.R. Trans. Service	
Moore, William	Mill Lane		H.M.S. "Queen Mary"	Killed in Action.
McAteer, James	26 Fleet Street		H.M.S. Trawler "Rose"	Drowned.
McBroom, John H.	Glynn		H.M.S. "Canopus"	
McBroom, Samuel	Glynn		H.M.S. Trans. "Slemish"	
McBroom, Thomas S.	Glynn	Private	12th Batt. R.I.R.	
McCord, William	17 Newington Avenue	Private	Arg. and Suth. High.	Killed in Action.
McCrea, Wm.		Private	18th R.I.R.	
McCullough, Joseph	35 Waterloo Road	Private	6th Batt. R.I.R.	
McIlhenny, Thomas	4 St. John's Place E.		R.N.R.	
McIlhenny, Wm.	4 St. John's Place E.		H.M.S. "Mantuce"	
McIntyre, Robert S.	11 Mill Lane	Private	12th Batt. R.I.R.	
McIvor, W. J.		Private	Lab. Batt. R.E.	
McKernon, Edward	Back Road	Private	3rd Batt. R. Inn. Fus.	
McKernon, Robert	Back Road	Private	R.F.A.	
McMullan, Robert	Shamrock Lodge	Private	Inns of Court O.T.C.	
McNeill, Alexander	Greenland Terrace	Private	11th Batt. R. Inn. Fus.	Killed in Action.
McNeill, David	Roddens Road	Private	R.E.	
McVeigh, James Murphy	Droagh		H.M.S. "Benbow"	Killed in Action.
McVeigh, Wm. Alfred	Droagh		R.N.R.	Drowned
McVeigh, John		Private	R.E.	
Peoples, Thomas	Waterloo	Private	18th Batt. R.I.R.	
Poag, William	Droagh	Private	N.I.H.	
Reid, Jack	22 Circular Road		R.N.R. Trans. Service	
Reid, Joseph, Jun.	16 Adelaide Terrace	Private	12th Batt. R.I.R.	Killed in Action.
Reid, W. B.		Private	Sig. Co. R.E.	
Ritchie, David		Private	9th Batt. R.I.R.	Killed in Action.
Robinson, Daniel	23 Bay Road	Engineer	R.N.R.	
Robinson, Samuel, Jun.	Barnhill	Private	12th Batt. R.I.R.	Killed in Action.
Scullion, Robert	87 Circular Road	Private	12th Batt. R.I.R.	
Simpson, Archie	103 Old Glenarm Road	Private	Z Batt. R.H.A.	
Simpson, William	Point Street	Corporal	12th Batt. R.I.R.	
Steele, James	Mill Street	Private	12th Batt. R.I.R.	Killed in Action.
Sutherland, George	Uril Lodge	2nd Lieutenant	3rd Batt. R.I. Fus.	Died of Wounds.
Taggart, Alfred C.	Larne Harbour	Captain	7th Batt. R.I. Fus.	
Taggart, Robert S.		2nd Lieutenant	R.A.M.C.	
Todd, Andrew	20 Old Glenarm Road	Private	18th Batt. R.I.R.	
Todd, John	Glynn	2nd Officer	H.M. Trans. Coll. "Divis"	
Todd, John	20 Old Glenarm Road	Private	R.A.M.C.	
Torbit, Robert	153 Old Glenarm Road	Private	12th Batt. R.I.R.	
Torbit, Thomas	153 Old Glenarm Road	Private	12th Batt. R.I.R.	
Torbit, Wm.	153 Old Glenarm Road	Private	12th Batt. R.I.R.	Killed in Action.

CARRICKFERGUS PRESBYTERY.

LARNE (Gardenmore).

Name.	Home Address.	Rank.	Regiment, Battalion or Unit.	Remarks.
WALKER, JAMES, JUN.	The Laurels	Private	12th Batt. R.I.R.	Killed in Action.
WILLIAMS, W. W.	Barnhill	Asst. Paymaster	R.N.R.	
WILSON, H. G.	Ard Lodge	Lieutenant	R.A.M.C.	
WILSON, J. A. LAWTHER	Chaine Villa	Major	R.A.M.C.	
WILSON, W. A.	Ard Lodge	Sergt.-Major	12th Batt. R.I.R.	
COLONIAL FORCES.				
BARKLIE, WHITEFORD	2 Clonlee	Private	U.S. E.F.	
CLARKE, HENRY	Kilwaughter	Private	Aust. Med. Corps	
CROOKS, MARCUS	Model Farm	Private	Can. R.A.M.C.	
DAVIS, ROBERT	Glynn View Avenue	Private	U.S. E.F.	
DOOLE, JOSEPH	...	Private	Can. E.F.	
GIFFIN, HUGH	...	Private	Can. E.F.	
GILLILAND, JACK	Victoria Street	Private	2nd Rhodesian Regt.	
HOLDEN, THOMAS	Killyglen	Private	Can. E.F.	
SIMPSON, JAMES	163 Old Glenarm Road	Private	Aust. E.F.	Killed in Action.
STREIGHT, SAMUEL	Cairnduff	Private	Can. Horse Art.	
LOUGHMORNE.				
BOYD, JAMES	Loughmorne	Private	12th R.I.R.	Wounded and Pris. of War.
POAG, ROBERT	Bellahill	Corporal	46th Can.	
STEWART, JAMES A.	Commons, Carrickfergus	Private	2nd R.I.R.	Killed in Action.
WELSH, ROBERT G.	Commons, Carrickfergus	Private	8th Argyle and Suth. High.	
WELSH, WM.	Commons, Carrickfergus	Private	R.E. Labour Corps	
MAGHERAMORNE.				
AGNEW, WM. J.	Magheramorne	Officer	Mercantile Marine	
BLAIR, JOHN	Magheramorne	Corporal	12th R.I.R.	Wounded.
BODLES, ROBERT	Magheramorne	Seaman	M. Marine	Drowned.
BROWN, JAMES	Magheramorne	Stoker	R.N.	
BROWN, JOHN	Magheramorne	Private	I.G.	
BROWN, SAMUEL	Magheramorne	Private	2nd R. Scots Fus.	Prisoner.
BROWN, WILLIAM	Magheramorne	Seaman	M.M.	Drowned.
BURNS, JOHN	Magheramorne	Seaman	M.M.	
BURNS, WM. ORR	Magheramorne	Officer	M.M.	
CLOSE, JAMES	Magheramorne	Officer	M.M.	Torpedoed thrice.
CLOSE, ROBERT	Magheramorne	Engineer	M.M.	
CLOSE, WM. J.	Magheramorne	Lieut. Commander	M.M.	
COBURN, ALBERT	Magheramorne	Private	R.A.M.C.	
CORBETT, WM.	Magheramorne	Private	R.E.	Wounded.
CRAIG, WM.	Magheramorne	Seaman	M.M.	
GEORGE, JAMES	Magheramorne	Seaman	M.M.	
GEORGE, JOHN	Magheramorne	Seaman	M.M.	
GIBBONS, WM.	Magheramorne	Private	R.A.M.C.	
HOUSTON, JOSEPH	Magheramorne	Seaman	M.M.	
HOUSTON, ROBERT J.	Magheramorne	Private		
HUME, JOHN	Magheramorne	Seaman	M.M.	
HUME, ROBERT	Magheramorne	Seaman	M.M.	
HUNTER, DAVID	Magheramorne	Seaman	M.M.	Torpedoed.
HUNTER, HUGH	Magheramorne	Captain	M.M.	
HUNTER, JOHN	Magheramorne	Private	12th R.I.R.	Killed in Action.
HUNTER, MATTHEW	Magheramorne	Seaman	M.M.	
HUNTER, WM. J.	Magheramorne	Seaman	M.M.	Torpedoed.
KIRKALDY, WM. J.	Magheramorne	Private	R.A.M.C.	Killed in Action.
LIDDLE, ALEX.	Magheramorne	Seaman	M.M.	
LOUGH, SAMUEL	Magheramorne	Seaman	M.M.	
LOUGH, WM.	Magheramorne	Seaman	M.M.	
McCALLION, HENRY	Magheramorne	Seaman	M.M.	
McCALLION, JOHN	Magheramorne	Seaman	M.M.	
McCALLION, WM.	Magheramorne	Lance-Corporal	12th Batt. R.I.R.	Wounded.
McCLURE, JAMES	Magheramorne	Seaman	M.M.	
McCLURE, JOHN	Magheramorne	Captain	M.M.	
McCONNELL, JAMES	Magheramorne	Seaman	M.M.	Drowned.
McCONNELL, WM.	Magheramorne	Seaman	M.M.	
McCONNELL, WM.	Magheramorne	Private	12th R.I.R.	Wounded.
McILWAINE, WM.	Magheramorne	Seaman	M.M.	
McKINTY, HUGH	Magheramorne	Seaman	M.M.	
MAGILL, CHARLES	Magheramorne	Private	12th R.I.R.	
MILLIKEN, J. J.	Magheramorne	Seaman	M.M.	
MORROW, ALEX.	Magheramorne	Seaman	M.M.	
MULHOLLAND, HENRY	Magheramorne	Seaman	M.M.	
NICKLE, THOMAS	Magheramorne	Seaman	M.M.	
O'NEILL, JOHN	Magheramorne	Private	12th R.I.R.	Pris. and Died.
O'NEILL, JOSEPH	Magheramorne	Engineer	M.M.	Twice Torpedoed.
O'NEILL, JOSEPH	Magheramorne	Seaman	M.M.	
ORR, MATTHEW	Magheramorne	Sergeant	12th R.I.R.	Wounded.
RICE, BRICE R.	Magheramorne	Seaman	M.M.	
SEMPLE, ROBERT	Magheramorne	Seaman	M.M.	
SEMPLE, THOMAS C.	Magheramorne	Seaman	M.M.	

CARRICKFERGUS PRESBYTERY. **MAGHERAMORNE.**

Name.	Home Address.	Rank.	Regiment, Battalion or Unit.	Remarks.
Stuart, John	Magheramorne	Seaman	M.M.	
Wilson, W. J.	Magheramorne	Seaman	M.M.	Killed in Action.
Wright, James	Magheramorne	Private	2nd I.G.	
Young, James	Magheramorne	Seaman	M.M.	
Young, Samuel	Magheramorne	Seaman	M.M.	
Young, Wm. J.	Magheramorne		R.N.	
COLONIAL FORCES.				
Caldwell, Thomas	Magheramorne	Private	Can. A.S.C.	
Gibb, A. B.	Magheramorne	Sergeant	Lord Strath. Horse	
Gibb, John	Magheramorne	Private	Canadian	Killed in Action.
Houston, Thomas	Magheramorne	Private	U.S.A. Force	
Hume, Robert	Magheramorne	Private	Cameron High.	
McDowell, J. B.		Lance-Corporal	Can. Ry. Con. Corps.	
RALOO.				
Agnew, Alfred	Ballynerry	Private	R.E.	
Burns, Hugh	Gleno	Private	R.I.R.	Gassed.
Burns, John	Gleno	Private	R.I.R.	Killed in Action.
Carleton, Hugh	Ballygowan	Private	R.I.R.	
Carson, Hugh	Ballymena Road	Private	R.I.R.	
Carson, Samuel	Ballymena Road	Private	R.I.R.	Wounded.
Dawson, Wm. Jas.	Ballyvallough	Private	R.I.R.	
Dobbin, James	Kilwaughter	Private	R.I.R.	Killed in Action.
Donald, S. J. W.	Ballyrickard	Captain	R.A.M.C.	
Ferguson, James	Carnduff		Merchant Service	Drowned.
Graham, Andrew	Ballyboley		R.I.R.	
Graham, John	Altalevelly	Sergeant	R.I.R.	
Graham, Martin	Altalevelly		R.I.R.	Killed in Action.
Graham, Wm. James	Altalevelly		N.I.H.	Wounded.
Hamilton, James	Altalevelly		R.N.	
Laverty, Samuel	Ballyfore	Private	Devonshires	
Lyttle, Samuel	Browndodd		Devonshires	
McAllister, Wm. John	Ardboley	Sergeant	Army Cycle Corps	
McBride, Wm.	Ballynerry	Private	R.I.R.	Wounded.
McCluggage, Wm. Hugh	Ballyvernstown	Private	R.I.R.	Killed in Action.
McIntyre, John Lyle	Toomebridge	Lieutenant	R.E.	
McKee, David C.	Kilwaughter	Sergeant	R.I.R.	Killed in Action.
McKee, James	Toreagh	Private	R.I.R.	Killed in Action.
Moore, Archibald	Browndodd		R.N.	
Moore, Hugh	Browndodd		R.N.	
Moore, Robert	Ballygowan	Private	Highland Light Inft.	Killed in Action.
Murry, Wm.	Larne	Private	Gordon Highlanders	
Orr, Alex.	Toreagh		Black Watch	
Semple, Adam	Commons, Carrickfergus	Captain	Merchant Service	
Semple, Adam, Jun.	Commons, Carrickfergus		R.N.	
Semple, John	Commons, Carrickfergus		Merchant Service	
Snoddy, George	Ballysnodd	Private	R.I.R.	
Snoddy, Samuel	Ballysnodd	Sergeant	R.I.R.	
Weatherup, Thomas	Ardboley		R.E.	
Weir, Joseph	Kilwaughter		R.I.R.	
Wharry, Robert	Kilwaughter		R.I.R.	Wounded.
Woods, John	Gleno		R.I.R.	
COLONIAL FORCES.				
Baxter, Matt.	Ballygowan		Canadians	
Crawford, James	Toreagh		Australians	Died of Wounds.
Hamilton, Will	Altalevelly		Australians	
Johnston, Matt.	Belfast		Australians	
McClean, James	Toreagh		Canadians	
McWilliam, Andrew	Ballyrickard		Canadians	
McWilliam, James	Ballyrickard		Canadians	
McWilliam, Nathaniel	Browndodd		Australians	
Moore, Samuel	Browndodd		Canadians	Killed in Action.
Shaw, John H.	Ballyrickard	Q.M. Sergt.	Canadians	Killed in Action.
Streight, Samuel	Carnduff		Canadians	
WHITEHEAD.				
Auld, Donald	Blackhead		Australian E.F.	
Barbour, Thomas W.	Ford Cottages	Signaller	12th R.I.R.	Twice Wounded.
Bonugli, Pietro	Whitehead	Private	Army of Italy	Wounded.
Boyd, Henry	Ebenezer Villa	Lance-Corporal	H.M.S. "Lady Corywright"	Torpedoed, lost.
Brown, Fredk.	Ebenezer Villa	Private	226th Batt. C.E.F.	Twice Wounded.
Carroll, George	Whitehead	Lieutenant	H.M.S. "Alecto"	Sub. Service
Carroll, John	Whitehead	Engineer	Can. Eng. 5th Div. Sig. C.	
Cathcart, James	Whitehead	Telegraphist	B.E.F., France	
Connell, Samuel	Whitehead	Officer	H.M.S. "Vendetta," R.N.	
Creighton, G. Herbert	Whitehead	Captain	R.F.C.	
Creighton, W. D.	Rosemount		Armoured Cars	
Graham, Vaughan	Beach House	Lance-Corporal	18th Batt. R.I.R.	

CARRICKFERGUS PRESBYTERY.   WHITEHEAD.

Name.	Home Address.	Rank.	Regiment, Battalion or Unit.	Remarks.
Greer, John	Whitehead	Stoker	H.M.S. "Calais," R.N.	
Greer, Thomas	Whitehead	Private	British Army in Italy	
Haddick, R. J.	India	Captain	12th Inn. Fus.	
Haddick, Victor	India	Captain	Regular Army	Twice Wounded.
Haddick, Thomas E.	Palestine	Lieutenant	1st Leinster	
Heddles, F. E.	Eastbourne	Commander	H.M.S. "Chalkis"	Torpedoed, Res.
Henderson, Thomas	Whitehead	Cook	14th Batt. R.I.R.	
Hunter, Jos. M.	6 Stranmillis Rd., Belfast	Lieutenant	Leinster Regt.	Wounded.
Johnston, Robert	Whitehead		H.M.S. "Sandhurst"	
Knox, Fergus Y.	Whitehead	Acting Captain	2nd Batt. R.I.R.	Twice Wounded.
Kyle, David J.	Whitehead		South African Scottish	Wounded.
Kyle, George	Whitehead	Gunner	23rd Div. R.F.A.	Gassed.
Larmour, Wm.	Whitehead	Lieutenant	Transport "Royal George"	
Lilley, Wm.	Whitehead	Cadet	Royal Arsenal, Woolwich	
Magill, Harry	Whitehead	Private	Canadian Army	
McCoull, Walter Hanley	Whitehead	2nd Lieutenant	U.S. Field Artillery	
McElroy, Alfred	Whitehead	Private	12th Batt. R.I.R.	Pris. of War.
Mitchell, W.	Whitehead	Ship's Writer	H.M.S. "Dreadnought," R.N.	
Morton, W. E.	Craig Ailsa	M.T. & Signaller	R.E. 36th Div. B.E.F.	
Niblock, James	Wellhead	2nd Lieutenant	12th Batt. R.I.R.	
Reid, Leonard	Whitehead	Private	9th Batt. R.I.R.	Gassed.
MERCANTILE MARINE.				
Bury, Percy	Whitehead			Torpedoed.
Bury, Robert	Whitehead			
Creighton, Harry	Whitehead	Engineer		Lost with Ship.
Duff, Stanley	Whitehead			
Duff, Jack	Whitehead			
Gray, Captain	Whitehead			
Hagan, Samuel	Blackhead			
Hay, John, Jun.	Whitehead			
Hay, William	Whitehead			Lost with ship.
Magill, Ernest E.	Whitehead			
Smyth, David	Whitehead			
Smyth, Wm.	Whitehead			
WOODBURN.				
Hetherington, Robert	Ballynure		R.N.	
Hilditch, Wm.	Woodburn	Stoker	R.N.	
Horner, Henry	Hamilton's Row	Private	12th R.I.R.	
Lough, Thomas	Monkstown	Private	Can. Ex. Force	Wounded.
McAlister, Wm. K.	Commons	Private	R. Marines	Killed in Action.
McAuley, Wm. J.	Knockagh	Private	Can. Ex. Force	Died.
Shaw, Edward	Unity Street	Private	12th R.I.R.	Wounded.
Wilson, Thomas	Woodburn	Sergt.-Major	R.A.M.C.	M. Medal.

CAVAN PRESBYTERY.

Name.	Home Address.	Rank.	Regiment, Battalion or Unit.	Remarks.
BALLYHOBRIDGE.				
Thompson, Jas. Wm.	Legmacaffrey		4th Canadian M.G.C.	
BELTURBET.				
Berry, Rowan J.		Lieutenant	5th Lancers	
Maxwell, W. E.		Captain	Indian Army	
Warner, J. W.		Driver	R.A.S.C.	
CARRIGALLEN.				
Boyd, Harris	Mohill	Private	N.I.H.	
Gray, John	Moy	Private	Irish Guards	Killed in Action.
Irwin, Samuel H.	Derren, Mohill	Lieutenant	R.E.	
Laing, Herbert	Ballyconnell	Private	18th R.I.R.	Wounded.
McAdoo, Samuel	Monaghan	Private	Irish Guards	Died of Wounds.
McElroy, Alfred	Ballyconnell	Private	12th R.I.R.	Prisoner. Died in Germany.
McElroy, Fred	Ballyconnell	Captain	H.B. M.G.C.	Died. Men. in Des., D.S.O.
Rogers, Richard	Anghavore	Private	12th R. In. Fus.	
Stratton, B. R.	Mohill	Private	M.T. A.S.C.	
Tease, John	Kells	Sergeant	Irish Guards	Wounded.

CAVAN PRESBYTERY.   CARRIGALLEN.

Name.	Home Address.	Rank.	Regiment, Battalion or Unit.	Remarks.
COLONIAL FORCES.				
Arnold, Richard J.	Cullies	Private	Canadian Ex. Force	Died of Wounds.
Faris, Henry	Sonagh	Private	Canadian Ex. Force	Wounded.
Flood, Robert	Oakhill	Private	Canadian Ex. Force	
CAVAN.				
Agnew, David	Farnham	Farrier	A.S.C.	
Armstrong, Samuel	Drumkeeran	Private	108th M.G. Coy.	Wounded.
Callan, J.	Cavan	Sergeant	2nd R.I.F.	Home Service.
Crosbie, John			R.N.A.S.	
Fluke, —	Aughnacloy	Sergeant	2nd R.I.F.	Killed in Action.
Lindsay, Arch.	Berwick-on-Tweed		2nd R.I.F.	Wounded.
Parke, James	Castlederg	Private	London I.R.	Wounded, Killed.
Pollock, John J. McE.	Cavan	Lieutenant	108th T.M.B.	Prisoner of War.
Pollock, S. Norman F.	Cavan	Cadet	O.T.C.	
CLONES.				
Armstrong, Bertie	Woodbine Cottage	Private	Lancashire Fus.	Killed in Action.
Brown, William	Clara Street	Private	R.I.F.	Killed in Action.
Currie, Samuel Hans	Manse, Clones	Cadet	R.A.F.	
Davidson, J. H.	Clones	Private	R.I.F.	Killed in Action.
Dunn, David J.	Clones	Private	R.E	
Fairburn, Albert	Clones	Petty Officer	R.N.	
Francey, S. J.	Clones	Trooper	N.I.H.	
Grimson, Jack, M.B.	Clones	Lieutenant	R.A.M.C.	
Grimson, Thomas, M.B.	Clones	Surgeon	R.N.	
Henry, Thomas	Clones	Captain	R.I.F.	
M'Ilrath, R.	Clones	Private	R.I.F.	Killed in Action.
Malone, J. J.	Clones	Private	R.I.F.	Died of Wounds.
Moorhead, John	Clones	Petty Officer	R.N.	
Parke, J. C.	Clones	Major	Essex Regt.	Wounded.
Pringle, Harold, M.B.	Clones	Captain	R.A.M.C.	
Pringle, James A.	Clones	Driver	British Red Cross	
Pringle, J. C.	Clones	Captain	R.E.	
Potts, William	Clones	Private	R.E.	
Reid, James A.	Newtownbutler	Private	K.O.S.B.	Wounded.
Russell, Alexander	Newtownbutler	Private	R.I.F.	
Shields, Robert	Clones	Private	R.I.F.	Killed in Action.
Watt, Robert	Clones	Private	R.I.R.	
COLONIAL FORCES.				
Fyffe, Alfred	Clones	Private	Canadian Force	
Greer, James A.	Clones	Private	Canadian Force	Wounded.
McHardy, John	Clones	Lieutenant	Canadian Force	Killed in Action.
Thompson, James W.	Clones	Private	Canadian Force	
COOTEHILL.				
Brown, Andrew	Cootehill	Sergeant	R.E. Postal Service	
Brown, William	Cootehill	2nd Lieutenant	R. In. Fus.	Killed in Action.
Doherty, Joseph	Cootehill	Sergeant	R.E.	M.M.
Fairburn, George J.	Anahard	Private	A.S.C.	
Flood, Robert S.	Millvale	Captain	9th R.I.F.	K'd in Action, M.C.
Flood, Samuel B.	Millvale	Private	5th K.R.R.	
Flood, W. J. Lowe	Millvale	Lieutenant	108th T.M.B.	
Hall, Thomas	Cootehill	Lance-Corporal	1st R.I.R.	Killed in Action.
Moffatt, David	Latsey	Regt. Sgt.-Major	R.A.M.C.	M.M.
Ronaldson, J. Victor	Cabra	Lance-Corporal	N.I.H.	
Stephenson, Robert W. W.	Ashfield	Captain	1st R. Inn. Fus.	Wounded, M.C.
Stephenson, William J.	Lattyloo	Co. Sgt.-Major	9th R. Irish Fus.	Wounded, M.M.
White, Edwin	Cootehill	Signalman	R.N.	
White, Thomas	Cootehill	Corporal	9th R.I.F.	
COLONIAL FORCES.				
Brown, Alexander	Corglass	Private	1st Otago inf., N.Z.	
Brown, James D.	Drumherriff	Private	N.Z. A.S.C.	
Brown, Robert H.	Corglass	Private	14th Otago Reg., N.Z.	Killed in Action.
Fairburn, J. Angus	Cootehill	Private	45th Can. Highlanders	Killed in Action.
Fairburn, Thomas	Cootehill	Sergeant	5th Cav. Corps, U.S.A.	
Flood, John A.	Millvale	Lance-Corporal	7th Canadian Infantry	Wounded.
Stoddart, Henry	Dartrey	Private	1st Canadian M.G.C.	
Stoddart, William	Dartrey		1st Canadian M.G.C.	

CAVAN PRESBYTERY.   FIRST AND SECOND DRUM.

Name.	Home Address.	Rank.	Regiment, Battalion or Unit.	Remarks.
FIRST AND SECOND DRUM.				
Crawford, John	Drum	Private	...	Wounded.
Hull, George	Drum	Private	N.I.H.	
McCrackin, Joseph	Drum	Sergeant	...	Wounded.
Stewart, John James	Drum	Sergeant	...	Wounded.
Potts, John	Drum	...	American Army	
DRUMKEERAN.				
Armstrong, Charles	...	2nd Lieutenant	3rd R.I. Reg.	
Armstrong, Samuel	...	Corporal	M.G.C.	
Rogers, Jack	...	Corporal	M.G.C.	
Rogers, Richard	...	Private	10th R. Inn. Fus.	
Rogers, J. Trevor	...	Private	Canadians	
KILLESHANDRA.				
Carson, Oliver	Main Street	Private	R.N.A.S.	
Clarke, Douglas H.	Church Street	Private	R.E.	
Clarke, William	Church Street	Private	R.E.	
Henderson, William	Aughavadrin	Private	N.I.H.	
Paton, Henry	Killeshandra	Private	Irish Guards	Killed in Action.
KILMOUNT.				
Lindsay, James	Canningstown	Private	4th R.I.F.	Gassed.
McFadden, Thomas	Drumartin	Private	R. Inn. Fus.	Wounded.
Pogue, Abraham	Tonnymaclduff	Sgt.-Major	Irish Guards	Wounded, M.M.
Thompson, Joseph	Ardmore	Private	R.G.A.	Wounded.
Watson, David	...	...	...	Wounded.
COLONIAL FORCES.				
Anderson, Joseph	Leighan	Sergeant	U.S. Army	
Barnett, Edward	Drumoyn	Corporal	Canadians	Killed in Action.
Gibson, Isaiah	Ratrussan	Private	U.S. Army	
Wade, James	Ardmore	Private	U.S. Army	

CLOGHER PRESBYTERY.

Name.	Home Address.	Rank.	Regiment, Battalion or Unit.	Remarks.
AUGHNACLOY.				
Boyle, J.	Aughnacloy	Private	R.I.R.	
Burton, John	Aughnacloy	Private	R.I. Reg.	
Corbitt, R. J.	Aughnacloy	Private	S.G	
Fluke, S.	Aughnacloy	Captain	R.I.F.	Killed in Action
Galbraith, W.	...	Sergeant	R.I.F.	
Hall, John	Aughnacloy	Private	R. In. Fus.	Killed in Action.
Leaney, W.	Glencull	Private	R.I. Reg.	
McCleery, R.	Aughnacloy	Private	R.M.F.	
McDonald, James R.	Doolargy	Private	R.A.M.C.	Killed in Action.
McDonald, Wm. T.	Doolargy	Signaller	R.G.A.	
Moore, A.	Aughnacloy	Sergeant	R.I.F.	
Pringle, Geo., M.D.	Aughnacloy	Captain	R.A.M.C.	
Robinson, A.	Aughnacloy	Private	R.I.F.	
Smith, Wm. Thos.	Aughnacloy	Private	R. In. Fus.	Killed in Action.
White, Alexander	Aughnacloy	Private	R. In. Fus.	Killed in Action.
White, S.	Aughnacloy	Private	R.I.F.	
COLONIAL FORCES.				
Boyd, John	Aughnacloy	Private	N.Z.R.B.	Twice Wounded.
Wilson, B.	Aughnacloy	Private	Canadians	
Wilson, C.	Aughnacloy	Private	Canadians	
BALLYGAWLEY.				
Coote, W. J.	Lisdourl	Captain	9th R. In. Fus.	
Henderson, William	Ballygawley	Corporal	9th R. In. Fus.	Killed in Action.
Hopper, Joseph	Lisbeg	Private	9th R. In. Fus.	Twice Wounded.
McCollum, Robert J.	Findrum	Private	R.A.M.C.	
Martin, William	Ballygawley	Private	R.A.M.C.	
Patterson, William	Knockonney	Private	9th R In. Fus.	
Sloan, Anthony	Martray	Private	9th R. In. Fus.	

CLOGHER PRESBYTERY. BALLYGAWLEY.

NAME.	HOME ADDRESS.	RANK.	REGIMENT, BATTALION OR UNIT.	REMARKS.
COLONIAL FORCES.				
Boyd, Samuel	Armaloughy	Private	208th Irish Canadians	
Macartney, David	Knockonney	Private	86th Canadian M.G.	
Oliver, Samuel	Cavankilgreen	2nd Lieutenant	1st Wellington Batt., N.Z.E.F.	Wounded.
CAVANALECK.				
Fenton, J.	Fivemiletown	Sergeant	R. In. Fus.	
Fails, George	Bigh	Private	R. In. Fus.	
Jordon, Andrew	Creagh	Private	R. In. Fus.	Wounded.
Menaul, Samuel	Stachan	Corporal	R. In. Fus.	Wded. and Pris.
Mulligan, James	Fivemiletown	Private	R. In. Fus.	
CLOGHER.				
Bailey, Robert N. H.	The Manse, Clogher	Major	O.C., 42 P.O.W. Co., France	Wounded.
Cooke, James	Mallybeney	Private	9th R. In. Fus.	
Cuthbertson, H. S.	Townagh	Sergeant	R.A.S.C.	
Donaldson, Robert	Dromore	Private	9th R. In. Fus.	Died.
Donaldson, William	Dromore	Private	G.A. Suffolk Regt.	
Hacket, J.		Corporal	6th R. In. Fus.	Wounded, G.M.
Kirkpatrick, John	Ferrew	Private	9th R. In. Fus.	
Monaghan, Robert J.	Ratory	Private	10th R. Grenadiers	
Ramsay, William J.	Carntall	A.B.	R.N.	
Rennick, Samuel J.	Carryclogher	Private	15th R.I.R.	
Rennick, William John	Carryclogher	Private	12th M.G. Corps	
Rooney, Clarence	Eskernabrogue	Corporal	9th R. Inn. Fus.	Wounded.
COLONIAL FORCES.				
Adams, Charles	Aghendromen	Sapper	1st Anzac	Wounded.
Adams, Edward	Aghendromen	Sapper	1st Anzac	Wounded.
Cuthbertson, William	Townagh	Sergeant	N.Z.	Wounded, M.M.
Fleming, Alexander	Fogart	Private	Can. A.S.C.	
Johnston, Jas. Hogarth	Broomhill	Private	Can. Highlanders	Killed in Action.
Ramsay, John	Carntall	Private	29th Canadians	Missing.
Ramsay, Thomas	Carntall	Private	29th Canadians	Wounded.
ENNISKILLEN.				
Caldwell, Andrew Victor	Henry Street	Private	16th R.I.R.	Gassed.
Caldwell, Edwin H.	Henry Street	Private	R.I.G.	
Caldwell, Herbert	Henry Street	Private	R.I.R.	Wded., Pris., Died.
Caldwell, Hugh C.	Henry Street	Sergeant	11th R. In. Fus.	
Caldwell, William	Henry Street	Private	11th R. In. Fus.	
Carson, Ralph	Enniskillen	Lieutenant	R.I.F.	
Caughey, Samuel	Castle Place	Private	11th R. In. Fus.	Wounded.
Crothers, W.	Henry Street	Col.-Sergt.	4th R. In. Fus.	
Darling, John	Erne View	Lieutenant	Munster Fus.	Wded., M.C. & Bar. Killed in Action.
Erwin, George	Wellington Place	Private	R.A.F.	
Erwin, John	Wellington Place	Lieutenant	11th Inn. Dragoons	
Erwin, Joe	Wellington Place	Private	R.E.	Gassed.
Garret, George	Alma Terrace	Captain	4th R. In. Fus.	
Griffiths, George	Darling Street	Private	11th R. In. Fus.	Wounded.
Hanna, Henry Lyle	Silver Hill	Captain	A.S.C.	
Harvey, Hamilton M.	Belmore Street	Lieutenant	11th R. In. Fus.	
Harvey, Thomas J.	Belmore Street		R.A.F.	
Inglis, R. H.	Belmore Street	Private	18th H.L.I.	Wounded.
Inglis, William	Belmore Street	Flight-Lieutenant	R.A.F.	
Lynn, David	Paget Square	Private	11th R. In. Fus.	
Lynn, J. H.	Paget Square	Private	R.A.F.	
Lynn, Robert	Paget Square	Private	11th R. In. Fus.	Wounded.
McCorkell, George	Ulster Hotel	Private	R.G.A.	Wounded.
McCorkell, Robert	Ulster Hotel	Private	28th R.I.R.	
McGowan, J.	Castle Barracks	Col.-Sergt.	4th R. In. Fus.	
McKean, Harry	Sedan Terrace	Private	28th R.I.R.	
McKean, Jack	Sedan Terrace	Lieutenant	12th R. In. Fus.	M.C. and Bar.
Marcus, Leo M.	Fair View	Private	R.A.M.C.	
Mitchell, Fred.	The Manse	Lieutenant	10th R.I.F.	Killed in Action.
Mitchell, Victor	The Manse		10th R.I.F.	
Morrison, William	Forthill	Private	16th R.I.R.	Killed in Action.
Myles, T.	Orchard Terrace	Q.M.S.	4th R. In. Fus.	
Porter, R. J.	The Brook	Lieutenant	4th R. In. Fus.	
Rankin, James	Darling Street	Private	R.E.	
Shaw, Mercer	Belmore Street	Private	14th R.I.R.	Wounded.
Shaw, Samuel	Belmore Street	Private	R.E.	Wounded.
Shaw, Thomas	Belmore Street	Private	R.E.	Thrice Wounded.
Shaw, William	Belmore Street	A.B.	R.N.	
Steenson, John	Castle Street	Private	11th R. In. Fus.	

CLOGHER PRESBYTERY. ENNISKILLEN.

Name.	Home Address.	Rank.	Regiment, Battalion or Unit.	Remarks.
Stewart, Chas. M.	Dublin	Lieutenant	Vet. Surgeon	
Stewart, Jack	Dublin	Lieutenant	A.S.C.	
Stewart, James Brian	Henry Street	Lieutenant	11th R. In. Fus.	
Stuart, J. M. B.	Alexandria Terrace	Lieutenant	12th Sappers and Miners	
Trimble, Aylwin	E. Bridge Street	Captain	7th R. In. Fus.	Men. in Des., Wded
Trimble, Noel D.	E. Bridge Street	Lieutenant	12th R. Inn. Fus.	Killed in Action.
Trimble, Rex	E. Bridge Street	Lieutenant	6th R.I.F.	
Whaley, Cecil D.	High Street	Lieutenant	12th Welsh Regt.	Wounded.
Whaley, George B.	High Street	Private	50th Gordon Highlanders	
Wilson, W.	Henry Street	Sgt.-Major	4th R. In. Fus.	Died of Wounds.
COLONIAL FORCES.				
Briscoe, Harry		Lieutenant	Canadian Army	Killed in Action.
Caldwell, John C.	Henry Street		Can. Sig. Corps	Decorated by the King. Killed in Action.
Erwin, James	Enniskillen	Private	R.F.A., U.S.A. Army	
Erwin, Samuel	Enniskillen	Sergeant	R.A.M.C., U.S. Army	
Erwin, William	Enniskillen		U.S. Army	
Mitchell, G. C.	The Manse	Private	Can. Home Defence	
Wylie, —	Willoughby Place	Private	Australian Force	
GLENHOY.				
Comac, William J.	Garvaghey	Private	9th R. In. Fus.	
Hardy, Samuel	Kilgaun	Private	R.F.A.	
Howard, Gilbert A.	Eskemore	Drummer	2nd R. In. Fus.	Killed in Action.
McMullin, William J.	Claremore	Private	9th R. In. Fus.	
Mulligan, George	Glenhoy	Corporal	King's L.R.	
Mulligan, James	Glenhoy	Private	King's L.R.	
COLONIAL FORCES.				
Glassey, James	Claremore	Private	N.Z. Army	Wounded
Glassey, Joseph	Claremore	Private	N.Z. Army	
Glassey, Robert	Claremore	Private	N.Z. Army	Killed in Action.
Glassey, Thomas	Claremore	Private	N.Z. Army	Wounded.
Howard, William	Eskemore	Private	U.S. Army	
Irwin, Carson	Eskemore	Sergeant	Canadian Force	
McMullin, Alexander	Claremore	Private	Canadian Force	
Mulligan, Joseph	Tyehany	Private	U.S. Army	
Welsh, James	Annagarvey	Sergeant	5th Canadians	Killed in Action.
LISBELLAW.				
Boyle, J. C. C.	Manse	2nd Lieutenant	3rd R. In. Fus.	Wounded.
Carrothers, J. S.	Farnaght	2nd Lieutenant	R. In. Fus.	Killed in Action.
Eadie, E.	Lisbellaw	Lieutenant	R. In. Fus.	M.C., Wounded.
Eadie, J. T.	Lisbellaw	2nd Lieutenant	R. In. Fus. M·G.C.	Wounded.
Eadie, W.	Lisbellaw	Driver	R.A.S.C.	
Faussett, J. R.	Montreal	Private	Canadian Horse	Wounded.
McAuley, J. J.	Lisbellaw	Private	R. In. Fus.	Wounded.
MAGUIRESBRIDGE.				
Bates, John	Lisnaskea	Sergeant	R. In. Fus.	D.C.M.
Dick, Robert C.	Lisnaskea	Lieutenant	R.E.	M.C.
Fairburn, Albert	Lisnagole	P.O.	H.M.S. "Prince Eugene"	
Graham, William J.	Maguiresbridge	2nd Lieutenant	R. In. Fus.	
Lawe, Hiram	Lisnaskea	Private	R. In. Fus.	
Lawe, James	Lisnaskea	Private	R. In. Fus.	
Lawe, William	Lisnaskea	Private	R. In. Fus.	
Lough, Robert	Maguiresbridge	Sergeant	Canadian Inf.	Wounded.
Lough, S. P.	Maguiresbridge	Captain	Canadian Inf.	M.C.
McCalden, Joseph	Lisnaskea	Captain	R.A.M.C.	
McKeaney, William	Lisnaskea	Private	R. In. Fus.	Killed in Action.
Wilson, D. L.	Maguiresbridge	Lance-Corporal	R. In. Fus.	Wounded.
TEMPO.				
Johnston, Jas. E.	Emaroo	Surgeon Lt.-Com.	R.N.	
Johnston, R. A.	Emaroo	Captain	R.A.M.C.	
McIntyre, Robert J.	Tempo	Private	M·G.C.	
Nelson, W. V.	Emaroo	Private	R. In. Fus.	Wounded.
Wallace, David	Grathgower	Private	R. In. Fus.	Wounded.
Wallace, Hugh	Grathgower	Private	R.I.F.	Wounded.
Wylie, James	Killee	Private	N.I.H.	

COLERAINE PRESBYTERY.

Name.	Home Address.	Rank.	Regiment, Battalion or Unit.	Remarks.
AGHADOWEY.				
Archibald, George	Aghadowey	Trooper	Egypt. Ex. F.	
Archibald, Samuel		Private	Coldstream Guards	
Barr, William		Private	R. Inn. F.	
Bolton, Sloan M.		2nd Lieutenant	R.I.R.	Wounded.
Boyd, John M'A.			R.N.	
Devenney, James		Private	R. Inn. F.	
Devenney, James		Lance-Corporal	Royal Scots	Died of Wounds.
Dinnen, Robert		Private	R.F.A.	Killed in Action.
Dinnen, William		Private	R. In. Fus.	Died of Disease.
Donaghy, William		Private	R. In. Fus.	Wounded.
Downs, John			R.N.	
Ferris, William W.		Private	R. In. Fus.	
Forgrave, James		Private	R. In. Fus.	
Grissam, James		Private	R. In. Fus.	
Harkin, Andrew		Private	R.I.R.	Killed in Action.
Harkin, W. J.		Private	R.I.R.	Killed in Action.
Hunter, Joseph		Private	N.I.H.	
Kennedy, Gilbert M.		Lieutenant	Scotch Rifles	Killed.
Kennedy, Norman R.		Lieutenant	Royal Scots	M.C.
Knox, Robert		Private	R. In. Fus.	Killed in Action.
Livingston, Albert H.		Sergeant	1st Inft. Brigade	Killed in Action.
Livingston, J. Ernest		Private	London Rifles	Wounded.
Macauley, Matthew		Private	Black Watch	
Macauley, Samuel		Private	R. In. Fus.	Killed in Action.
Macauley, William John		Private	R.I.R.	
McIlroy, J. Clarke		Lieutenant	R.F.A.	M.C.
McIlroy, R. Ernest		Private	K.O.R.	
McIlroy, William		Sergeant	R. In. Fus.	
McMurtry, Samuel		Private	R.E.	
McQuigg, James T.		Private	R.W.F.	
Millar, Edward		Private	R. In. Fus.	
Millar, Henry		Private	N.I.H.	
Millican, Frank		Private	R. In. Fus.	
Millican, George		Private	R.I. Fus.	
Millican, Samuel		Sergeant	R. In. Fus.	
Moon, W. J. K.	Ballydevitt House	Captain	R. In. Fus.	M.C.
Moore, James		Lance-Corporal	R. In. Fus.	Wounded.
Morrison, A. J. McC.		Captain	R.A.M.C.	Thrice Wounded.
Morrison, H. Rankin	Meath Park	Lieutenant	M. Transport	Serb. Decoration.
Moffatt, David		Corporal	R.G.A.	
Moffatt, W. J.		Private	R.E.	
Neill, James		Private	Scottish Horse	Killed in Action.
Neill, Richard		Private	R. Inn. Fus.	M.M. Wounded.
Neill, Robert		Lance-Corporal	R. In. Fus.	Wounded.
Patterson, Alexander		Sergeant	R.F.E.	
Patterson, Andrew		Lieutenant	R. In. Fus.	M.C.
Perry, William J.		Corporal	N. Somerset Yeo.	
Stuart, James		Private	M. Police	
Stuart, Robert		Private	R.I.R.	Killed in Action.
Stuart, Thomas		Private	R. In. Fus.	Killed in Action.
Stuart, Wilson		Private	R.I.R.	
Taylor, Hugh		Private	R. In. Fus.	Killed in Action.
Wallace, James		Private	R.I.R.	
Wilson, G. W.		Private	R.G.A.	
Wilson, Robert		Lance-Corporal	R. In. Fus.	
Woodend, David		Private	R. In. Fus.	
Woodend, John		Private	R. In. Fus.	Killed in Action.
Workman, William		Private	R. In. Fus.	Killed in Action.
COLONIAL FORCES.				
Archibald, Alexander		Captain	Can. A.M.C.	
Duff, Thompson		Private	Can. M.G.C.	
Faith, Matthew P.		Private	Aust. Imp. Force	
Kane, William J.		Private	Aust. Imp. Force	Killed in Action.
Lynn, Thomas L.		Private	Aust. Imp. Force	Killed in Action.
Macauley, Jamison		Private	Canadians	
Wallace, Stephen		Private	N.Z. Force	
BALLYRASHANE.				
Acheson, Robert T.	Islandeffrick	Trooper	N.I.H.	Wounded.
Boyd, W. Frank	Benvarden	Lance-Corporal	Machine Gun Squadron	
Cox, Samuel	Islandheaghy	Private	R. In. Fus.	Killed in Action.
Dunlop, John	Blaugh	Private	Labour Batt.	
Getty, John S.	Railway Road	Corporal	Marine Transport	
Getty, Robert J.	Articrunnagh	Gunner	R.G.A.	
Irwin, William	Newmills	Private	R. In. Fus.	Killed in Action.
Logue, Samuel	Ballyrashane	Sapper	R.E.	
Lyons, James	Carnglass	Sergeant	R. Dublin Fusiliers	
Macauley, Hugh	Ballyrashane	Corporal	N.I.H.	
McDowell, James T.	Ballyrashane	Writer	R.N.	

COLERAINE PRESBYTERY.   BALLYRASHANE.

Name.	Home Address.	Rank.	Regiment, Battalion or Unit.	Remarks.
M'Dowell, Samuel	Ballyrashane	Private	M.T. R.A.S.C.	
McIntyre, William J.	Articrunnagh	Private	R. In. Fus.	Killed in Action.
McMullen, George	Ballylaggan	Private	R.I.R.	
McNab, Wilson	Loughan Reagh	Gunner	R.G.A.	Gassed.
McNaughten, James	Ballyversal	Private	R. In. Fus.	Wounded.
Martin, Charles W.	Liswatty	Sapper	R.E.	Killed in Action.
Martin, David	Liswatty	Lance-Corporal	R. In. Fus.	Wounded, Pris. of War.
Meehan, William	Ballyversal	Sapper	R.E.	
Morrow, William	Boghill	Corporal	R. In. Fus.	Wounded.
Patton, Joseph	Liswatty	Private	R. In. Fus.	Wded and Gassed.
Quinn, Edward	Ballyrashane	Sergeant	R.F. Artillery	Awarded D.C.M. & M.M. Gassed.
Quinn, Joshua	Ballyrashane	Private	M.T. R.A.S.C.	Wounded.
Ramsey, Wilson	Ballyboggy	Rifleman	R.I.R.	
Ross, John	Tullans	Private	R. In. Fus.	Wounded.
Stirling, Thomas	Liswatty	Lieutenant	R.I.R.	Gassed.
Watton, Harry	Damhead	Lance-Corporal	N.I.H.	
Wright, John	Damhead	Sergeant	R. In. Fus.	Killed in Action.
Wright, Thomas	Damhead	Trooper	N.I.H.	Killed in Action.
COLONIAL FORCES.				
Dalzell, Robert	Loughan Reagh	Corporal	N.Z. Inft.	
Lyons, John S.	Carnglass	Private	Can. Inft.	Killed in Action.
McBride, Andrew	N. Buildings, B'money	Corporal	N.Z. E.F.	Killed in Action.
BALLYWATT.				
Andrews, Robert	Ballyrock	Private	R.I.R.	Died.
Blair, J.	Carnglass	Gunner	Exp. School of Gunnery	
Chestnut, H.	Lisnisk	Lance-Corporal	M.G.C.	Wounded.
Currie, William	Cloyfin	Private	R.I.R.	
Dorrans, W. J.	Ballyohme	Rifleman	R.I.R.	
Downs, Alexander	Ballyrock	Private	R.I.R.	Wounded.
Downs, F.	Ballyrock	Private	R.I.R.	
Downs, Joseph	Ballyrock	Private	R.I.R.	Wounded.
Erewin, William	Ballymagarry	Private	R. In. Fus.	Wounded.
Knox, W. R.	Ballyhome	Sergeant	Arm. Car. Brigade	Received M.M. and Cross of St.George (Rus.)
Lynn, W. J.	Ballyhome	Private	R.I.R.	Wounded.
Miller, R.	Tullycapple	Private	H.L.I.	Wounded.
Miller, W. J.	Tullycapple	Gunner	R.G.A.	Wounded.
Murdock, A.	Revallagh	Gunner	R.G.A.	
McCurdy, W. J.	Kilmoyle	Sergeant	R. Air F.	
McGonigal, William	Ballyhome	Corporal	R.I.R.	Wounded and Pris.
McLaughlin, Alexander	Priestland	Private	R.I.R.	
McNabb, John	Islandcarragh	Private	R. In. Fus.	Killed in Action.
McNabb, Robert	Islandcarragh	Corporal	R.I.R.	Died of Wounds in Germany.
Rankin, J. W.	Ballyhome	Cadet	R. Air F.	
Rankin, J.	Ballyhome	Mechanic	R. Air F.	Wounded.
Stewart, J.	Cloughan	Private	R. Inn. Fus.	
Stinson, S.	Ballyhome	Lance-Corporal	R.I.R.	Prisoner
Stirling, William	Cloughan	Private	R. In. Fus.	Prisoner.
Thompson, William T.	Ballylough	Private	R. Air F.	
Walker, F. W.	Ballyrock	Captain	R.F.A.	Received M.C.
Walker, S. E.	Ballyrock	Lieutenant	R.I.R.	Wounded.
Walker, John	Kilmoyle	Gunner	R.G.A.	
Wallace, Daniel	Ballybogey	Private	R.I.R.	
Watton, Alexander	Carnglass	Gunner	R.G.A.	
Watton, R. J.	Carnglass	Sapper	R.E.	
Watton, Samuel	Carnglass	Gunner	R.G.A.	
COLONIAL FORCES.				
Murdock, D. J.		Private	U.S.A.	
Nevin, T.		Private	N.Z.	Wounded.
Nevin, William		Private	N.Z.	
Patterson, R. J.		Bombardier	Canadian	
Thompson, James		R.A.M.C.	N.Z.	
Thompson, Joseph		R.A.M.C.	N.Z.	Killed in Action.
BALLYWILLAN.				
Brownlow, Robert	Islandmore	Private	10th R.I.R.	
Campbell, Fred W.	Crossreagh	Captain	R.A.M.C.	
Clarke, James	Knockertoiton	Driver	R.F.A.	
Clarke, Joseph	Knockertoiton	Private	A.S.C. M.T.	
Dixon, Henry R.	Eglinton Place	Private	A.S.C.	
Glenn, James	Maddybenny	Private	15th R.I.R.	
McCaughan, Andrew	Islandmore	Private	10th R.I.R.	Wounded.
McLaughlin, John	Portstewart	Colonel	R.A.M.C. and R.F.A.	

COLERAINE PRESBYTERY.   BALLYWILLAN.

NAME.	HOME ADDRESS.	RANK.	REGIMENT, BATTALION OR UNIT.	REMARKS.
McMullen, James	Bellemont	Private	1st R.I.R.	Killed in Action.
McNeill, Andrew	Islandflackey	Private	15th R.I.R.	Killed in Action.
McNeill, Samuel	Macilvennon	E.R.A.	R.N.	
Purdy, William J.	Maddybenny	Private		
Rankin, Alfred	Glenmanus	Private		
Rankin, John	Glenmanus	Private	12th R.I.R.	Wounded.
Rankin, Matthew	Glenmanus	Corporal	12th R.I.R.	M.M. Wounded.
Richardson, William	Islandmore	Private		
Sloan, Robert	Corvally	S.M.	N.I.H.	
Stewart, William J.	Loguestown	Driver	12th R.I.R.	Wounded.
Taggart, H. Lyle	Glenmanus	Gunner	R.G.A.	Wounded.
Taggart, Percy	Glenmanus	Trooper	N.I.H.	
Taggart, Robert J.	Glenmanus	Sergeant	12th R.I.R.	Wounded.
Taggart, William	Glenmanus	Sergeant	R.E.	D.C.M.
COLONIAL FORCES.				
Cairns, Robert	Glenmanus	Private	Can. E.F.	Wounded.
Campbell, Edward	Crossreagh	S.M.	Can. E.F.	Killed in Action.
Edgar, Jesse	Islandmore	Corporal	Canterbury Reg., N.Z.	Killed in Action.
Rankin, James George	Glenmanus	Corporal	U.S. Army	Killed in Action.
BOVEEDY.				
Henry, Hugh	Boveedy	Stoker	R.N.	
Henry, Robert	Boveedy	Private	G. Highlanders	Killed in Action.
Hill, Fred. R.	Boveedy	Sergeant	M.G.C.	
McCracken, Robert	Boveedy	Private	R. In. Fus.	Killed in Action.
McCracken, Samuel	Boveedy	Private	R. Irish Fus.	
McIlwrath, Robert	Boveedy	Corporal	R. In. Fus.	Men. Desp. Killed in Action.
McLaughlin, William	Boveedy	Private	R. In. Fus.	
May, Samuel	Boveedy	Private	Can. I.F.	
Moore, Samuel	Boveedy	Gunner	R.G.A.	Twice Wounded.
Moore, Thomas	Boveedy	Signaller	R.G.A.	
Moore, William	Boveedy	Corporal	R.F.A.	
Stewart, David	Boveedy	Driver	R.F.A.	
Thompson, William J.	Boveedy	Corporal		Killed in Action.
Wilson, James W.	Boveedy	Sergeant	A.I.F.	M.M. Twice Wd.
Witherow, —	Boveedy	Corporal	Lanc. Fus.	Wounded.
CASTLEROCK.				
Blair, R. J.	Carnowry	Private	In. Fus.	
Clarke, Jack	Castlerock	Private	In. Fus.	Killed in Action.
Elliott, Robert	Castlerock	Private	In. Fus.	
Glenn, Thomas	Castlerock	Private	In. Fus.	M.M. & Mons Star. Wounded.
Glenn, William	Castlerock	Private	In. Fus.	Wounded.
McCarter, Fredk., M.B.	Castlerock	Captain	R.A.M.C.	M.C. and Bar.
McCarter, William, M.B.	Castlerock	Captain	R.A.M.C.	Men. in Desp. Pris. of War.
McCullough, Ross	Castlerock	Sergeant	R.F.A.	Wounded.
Maguire, John	Downhill	Private		
Orr, Samuel	Articlave	Private	In. Fus.	Killed in Action.
Scott, William	Downhill		R.E.	
Swann, Hugh	Castlerock	Private	R.A.F.	
Swann, S. T.	Castlerock	Private	R.E.	
Swann, W. J.	Castlerock	Private	In. Fus.	Killed in Action.
FIRST COLERAINE.				
Allen, John	Coleraine	Private	R.A.M.C.	
Arthur, Samuel	Glasgow	Driver	M.T. A.S.C.	
Armstrong, George	Coleraine	Corporal	R.I.R.	Killed.
Barr, William	England	Sergeant	Army Pay Office	
Barrie, Frank	Coleraine	Lieutenant	R.A.F.	Pris. of War.
Bell, Ernest	Argentine	Cadet	O.T.C.	
Bell, Martin	Coleraine	Private	R. In. Fus.	
Black, Charles	Portrush	Private	M.T. A.S.C.	
Black, William	Portrush	Private	London Irish Rifles	
Boone, John	Coleraine	Corporal	R. In. Fus.	Killed.
Boyd, George	Coleraine	Private	R. In. Fus.	Wounded. Pris. of War.
Cameron, A. H.	Portrush	Private		
Cameron, William	Portrush	Private		Killed.
Carson, John	Liverpool	R.S.M.		Wounded.
Carson, William	Coleraine	Trooper	N.I.H.	
Caskey, Henry	Coleraine	Corporal	Black Watch	
Caskey, James	Coleraine	Lieutenant	R. In. Fus.	M.C.
Crawford, Percy	Coleraine	Lieutenant	I.R.	
Dunlop, William	Coleraine	Sergeant	R.A.M.C.	Wounded.
Finlay, Malcolm	England	Private		
Gardiner, William	Coleraine	Private	R. Irish Fus.	Wounded.

COLERAINE PRESBYTERY.

FIRST COLERAINE.

Name.	Home Address.	Rank.	Regiment, Battalion or Unit.	Remarks.
Grundle, James	Coleraine	Sergeant	R. In. Fus.	Killed.
Grundle, John	Coleraine	Private	R.I.R.	Wounded.
Grundle, Richard	Coleraine	Corporal	R. In. Fus.	
Grundle, Samuel	Coleraine	Private	R. In. Fus.	
Grundle, William	Coleraine	Corporal	R. In. Fus.	Wounded.
Harte, Hugh	Coleraine	Private	R.A.M.C.	
Henderson, J. A.	Coleraine	Private		
Hunter, Benjamin	Coleraine	Private	A.S.C.	
Hunter, John	Coleraine	Private	R. In. Fus.	
Hunter, William	Coleraine	Gunner	R.G.A.	
Hunter, Robert	Coleraine	Gunner	R.G.A.	
Hutchinson, Ernest	Coleraine	Lieutenant	R. In. Fus.	
Hutton, Henry	Coleraine	Private	K.O.S.B.	
Hutton, Miller	Coleraine	Private	R. In. Fus.	Killed.
McAfee, Jacob	Coleraine	Private	R. In. Fus.	Wounded.
McElwee, John	Coleraine	Corporal	Machine Gun Section	
McKenzie, John	Coleraine	Trooper	N.I.H.	Injured on Duty.
McLarnon, J. Starritt	Coleraine	Lieutenant	R. In. Fus.	Wounded.
McNeill, Robert	Coleraine	Private	A.S.C.	Died.
McNeill, James	Coleraine	Gunner	R.G.A.	
Macaulay, Jack	Coleraine	Signaller	R.G.A.	
Martin, Thomas	Coleraine	Seaman	Navy	Lost at Sea.
Martin, Robert	Coleraine	Sergeant	R. Marine Artillery	
Miller, Knox	Coleraine	Private	R. In. Fus.	Wounded.
Moody, Thomas	Coleraine	Gunner	R.G.A.	Died in Service.
Moore, Wilson	Coleraine	Private	R. In. Fus.	
Mullan, Hugh	Coleraine	Sergeant		Killed.
Paul, William	Coleraine	Sergeant	Black Watch	Prisoner of War.
Simpson, James	Coleraine	Private	Despatch Rider	
Sweeny, James	Coleraine	Sergeant	Field Amb. Corps	
Telfer, Alec	Scotland	Corporal	K.O.S.B.	Wounded.
Todd, Arnold	Coleraine	Private	Black Watch	Killed.
Todd, Walter	Coleraine	Private	M.T. A.S.C.	
Tosh, William	Coleraine	Sergeant	R.A.F.	
Troy, James	Coleraine	Gunner	R.G.A.	
Troy, John	Coleraine	Private	R. In. Fus.	
Walker, John	Coleraine	Private	R. In. Fus.	Wounded.
COLONIAL FORCES.				
Barr, James		Sergeant	Canadians	
Bell, Alfred		Private	Aust. I. Force	Killed in Action.
Carson, Graham		Private	Canadians	
Crawford, Alexander		Private	Canadians	
Crawford, Henry		Private	Canadians	
Crawford, William		Lieutenant	Canadians	Croix de Guerre & Rus. Cross.
Glassey, Samuel		Trooper	Canadians	Wounded.
Hunter, James		Private	U.S. Army	Wounded.
Macaulay, James		Sapper	Canadians	
McCandlis, John		Private	Canadians	
McCandlis, John, Jun.		Private	Canadians	
McKenzie, Hugh		Private	U.S. Army	
McKenzie, James		Private	U.S. Army	
McKenzie, Robert		Private	U.S. Home Service	
Mackey, Thompson		Private	N.Z. Force	
Martin, William		Private	Canadians	Killed in Action.
Moody, Alan		Signaller	Canadians	Wounded.
Mulholland, Daniel		Private	Canadians	
Mulholland, Thomas		Private	Canadians	
Mulholland, William		Private	Canadians	Killed in Action.
Pollock, Joseph				
COLERAINE, NEW ROW.				
Adams, John Wilson	Spital Hill	Seaman	Royal Navy	Killed.
Allen, David	Strand Road	Private	R. In. Fus.	Killed in Action.
Allen, Joseph	Strand Road	Private	R. In. Fus.	Died of Wounds.
Anderson, Robert	Terrace Row	Private	R. In. Fus.	Wounded.
Anderson, Samuel	Spoutfields	Gunner	R.G.A.	
Anderson, Wilfred	Spring Gardens	Cadet	R.G.A.	
Bacon, Samuel	Victoria Terrace	Sergeant	R.E. (Railway Ord. Dep.)	
Barr, Alexander	Mount Street	Bombardier	R.F.A.	
Barr, Joseph	Mount Street	Gunner	R. Marine Art.	
Barr, Leslie	Mount Street	Private	R.I.R.	
Barr, Richard	Mount Street	Private	R.I.R.	
Barr, Robert	Mount Street	Private	R. In. Fus.	
Barr, William	Mount Street	Private	R. In. Fus.	Prisoner.
Blair, Charles S.	Union Street	Private	Lancashire Fus.	Killed in Action.
Boyce, Nathaniel	Desert	Seaman	R.N.	
Burnett, Henry	Reid's Terrace	Gunner	R.G.A.	
Cameron, Hector	Upper New Row	Private	R. In. Fus.	
Campbell, Thomas	Brook Street	Sergeant	R.G.A.	Killed in Action.
Clements, James	Park View	Private	R. In. Fus.	

COLERAINE PRESBYTERY. NEW ROW, COLERAINE.

Name.	Home Address.	Rank.	Regiment, Battalion or Unit.	Remarks.
CONNELL, THOMAS G.	Boghill	A.B.	R.N.	
CONOLLY, ALFRED	Cairnview Cottages	Private	R. In. Fus.	Wounded & Pris.
CONOLLY, JAMES	Cairnview Cottages	Private	Argyle & Suth. Highlanders	Wounded.
DALLAS, EDWARD REID	Church Street	Private	Royal Dub. Fus.	Killed in Action.
DALZELL, JAMES MORRISON	Waterford Terrace	Driver	R.G.A.	
DUFFIN, DOUGLAS	Formerly Gateside	Private	Black Watch	
DUNLOP, WILLIAM J.	Formerly Eastbourne	Lieutenant	R.A.	Killed in Action.
DUNNE, DAVID	Nursery Avenue	Sergeant	R.A.M.C.	
DUNNE, JOHN M.	Nursery Avenue	Lance Corporal	R. In. Fus.	Wounded.
DUNNE, SAMUEL	Nursery Avenue	Private	R. In. Fus.	
FORSYTHE, HUGH	Union Street	Signaller	R.G.A.	
FULTON, JOHN A.	Mount Street	Lieutenant	Royal Irish Regt.	
GILLESPIE, DONALD	Formerly Captain St.	Lieutenant	Dorsets	
GILMOUR, ROBERT WALLACE	Diamond	Lieutenant	R. In. Fus.	Killed in Action.
GILMOUR, WILLIAM ECCLES	Diamond	Private	Royal Dub. Fus.	
GRAHAM, WILLIAM	Shell Hill	Lance Corporal	Royal Scots	Prisoner.
GRAHAM, JACK	Shell Hill	Private	Royal Scots	
GRAHAM, SAMUEL	James Street	Private	R. In. Fus.	
HENRY, JAMES ALFRED	Nursery Avenue	Private	Black Watch	Killed in Action.
HENRY, ROBERT NOEL	Nursery Avenue	Lieutenant	R.I.R.	
HENRY, THOMAS	Rathanna	2nd Lieutenant	R. In. Fus.	
HENRY, WALKER	Taylor's Row	Private	R. In. Fus.	Killed in Action.
HENRY, JOHN	Taylor's Row	Private	R. In. Fus.	
HILL, J. ROLAND, M.D.	Formerly New Row	Captain	R.A.M.C.	
HILL, ROBERT	Bellhouse Lane	Private	R. In. Fus.	Wounded.
INNES, JAMES	Formerly Diamond	Lieutenant	Gordon Highlanders	Killed in Action.
JAMISON, JAMES	Brook Street	Sergeant	R. In. Fus.	Certificate.
KANE, WILLIAM	Strand Road	Private	R. In. Fus.	
KELLY, WILLIAM R.	Formerly Railway Road	Private	R.I.R.	
KENNEDY, HENRY	Formerly Ratheane	Cyclist	Motor Despatch Corps	
KILGORE, JOSEPH	Millburn Terrace	Private	R. In. Fus.	
KNOX, ROBERT S.	Formerly Adelaide Av.	Lieut.-Colonel	R. In. Fus.	D.S.O. & 3 Bars.
LAW, CAMPBELL	Commons	Private	R. In. Fus.	
LIKEN, FREDERICK	Dunedin Terrace	Lieutenant	R. In. Fus.	
LIKEN, THOMAS A.	Formerly Dunedin Ter.	Gunner	R.G.A.	
LOGUE, SAMUEL	Mount Street	Sapper	R.E.	
MACAULAY, DAVID	Bar View	Private	R. In. Fus.	
MILLAR, WILLIAM	The Lodge	Corporal	R.G.A.	
MILLIKEN, JOHN A. W.	Ballysally	Seaman	R.N.	
MULLAN, WILLIAM	New Row	Private	R. In. Fus.	Wounded, Leg off.
MULLAN, WILLIAM	The Lodge	Private	R.G.A.	Killed in Action.
MURPHY, JAMES	Brook Street	Private	R. In. Fus.	Prisoner.
MURPHY, THOMAS	Brook Street	Private	R. In. Fus.	Prisoner.
MACONACHIE, WILLIAM	Nursery Avenue	Major	Machine Gun Corps	Men. in Desp.
McAFEE, GEORGE H.	Abbey Street	Q.M. Sergt.	R. In. Fus.	
McAFEE, JOHN	Strand Road	Private	A.S.C.	
McAFEE, ROBERT	Strand Road	Cyclist	Army Cyclist Corps	
McAFEE, ALBERT	Strand Road	Private	R.A.F.	
McAULAY, WILLIAM	Stable Lane	Private	R. In. Fus.	Prisoner.
McCLELLAND, DAVID	Dunlop Street	Private	R. In. Fus.	Killed in Action.
McCLELLAND, JAMES	Baptist Lane	Private	R. In. Fus.	
McCLELLAND, JOSEPH	James Street	Private	R. In. Fus.	
McCLELLAND, JOHN	James Street	Private	R. In. Fus.	
McALEESE, WILLIAM	Abbey Street	Lance-Corporal	Leinsters	
McELWAINE, J. C.	Northern Bank		R.I.R.	
McGREGOR, JOHN	New Row	Private	Gordon Highlanders	Killed in Action.
McKINNEY, WILLIAM J.	Eastbourne	Lieutenant	Highland L. Inf.	Killed.
McKINNEY, EDWARD R.	Eastbourne	2nd Lieutenant	R. In. Fus.	Killed in Action.
McKEOWN, ROBERT	Brook Street	Lance-Corporal	R. In. Fus.	Wounded.
McKEOWN, THOMAS	Brook Street	Lance-Corporal	R.I.R.	Wounded.
McLAUGHLIN, ROBERT	James Street	Private	R. In. Fus.	
McLAUGHLIN, JAMES S.	Railway Road	Private	R.I.R.	
McQUILKEN, JOHN	Upper New Row	Private	R. In. Fus.	Pris. Wounded.
McQUILKEN, WILLIAM	Upper New Row	Private	R. In. Fus.	Prisoner.
McSEVENEY, ROBERT	Westbrook Terrace	Private	R. In. Fus.	
McWILLIAMS, JOHN	Margretta Terrace	Private	K.O.S.B.	
McWILLIAMS, JAMES	Margretta Terrace	Private	R.A.F.	
NEILL, JOHN	Taylor's Row	Private	R.I. Fus.	
PATTERSON, ALEXANDER	Nursery Avenue	Private	R. In. Fus.	
PATTERSON, DAVID	Nursery Avenue	Private	R. In. Fus.	
PATTERSON, ROBERT	Nursery Avenue	Trooper	N.I.H.	Killed in Action.
RANKIN, HENRY, SEN.	Park Street	Private	R. In. Fus.	Wounded.
RANKIN, HENRY, JUN.	Park Street	Private	R. In. Fus.	
RANKIN, GEORGE	Park Street	Stoker	R.N.	
RODMONT, JOHN	Killowen	Private	R. In. Fus.	Killed in Action.
SINCLAIR, SAMUEL	Railway Place	Lieutenant	H.L.I.	Wounded.
SMYTH, JAMES	Cross Lane	Private	R. In. Fus.	Killed in Action.
SMYTH, JOHN	Burnside	Lance-Corporal	R. In. Fus.	
STEEN, HUGH B., M.D.	Formerly Balleney	Major	R.A.M.C.	
STEEN, ROBERT, M.D.	Formerly Balleney	Major	R.A.M.C.	
STEWART, HUGH B.	Eastbourne	Major	D.A., A.V.S.	
STIRLING, JAMES	Circular Road	Artificer	R.N.	
STIRLING, JAMES	Tullans	Sapper	R.E.	
STIRLING, JOHN	Tullans	Private	Motor Transport	

COLERAINE PRESBYTERY.   NEW ROW, COLERAINE.

Name.	Home Address.	Rank.	Regiment, Battalion or Unit.	Remarks.
Watt, Samuel B.	Westbrook Terrace	Sergeant	R. In. Fus.	Prisoner.
Wilkie, James	Railway Terrace	Private	R. In. Fus.	
Wilkie, Samuel	Railway Terrace	Corporal	Royal Scots Fus.	
Wilmott, George	Cairnview Cottages	Private	A.S.C.	
Wilmott, John	Cairnview Cottages	Private	R. I. F.	
Wilson, Joseph	Diamond	Private	Black Watch	
Wilson, Joseph	Church's Walls	Sapper	R.E. (Ry. Lab. Co.)	
Wilson, Robert N. D.	Ashbrook	Cadet	R.G.A.	
Wilson, Robert	Formerly Bridge Street	Lance-Corporal	R. In. Fus.	
Wright, Matthew	Cross Lane	Private	R. In. Fus.	Wounded.
Wright, Thomas	Cross Lane	Lance-Corporal	R. In. Fus.	Killed in Action.
Young, William	Stone Row	Private	R. In. Fus.	
COLONIAL FORCES.				
Blair, Jesse	Union Street	Private	Canadians	
Boyce, William	Desert	Private	Americans	Killed in Action.
Craig, S.	Killowen	Sergt.-Major	S. African Inft.	
Currie, John	New Row	Private	Americans	
Duffin, Edward	Gateside	Private	N.Z. Contingent	
Duffin, Malcolm G.	Gateside	Private	N.Z. Contingent	
Edmiston, David	Commons	Sergeant	Canadians	Wounded.
Gibson, Samuel	Park Street	Sergeant	Canadians	
Henry, Richard T.	Rathanna	Private	Can. Mt. Rifles	
Keenan, William	Ballindreen	Private	Canadians	Killed in Action.
Logue, Thomas	Mount Street	Gunner	American Army	Killed in Action.
Moffatt, Robert	Abbey Street	Sergeant	Canadians	
Patterson, James	Nursery Avenue	Private	Canadians	Killed in Action.
Pollock, Stormonth	Half Mile	Private	Americans	Killed in Action.
Shannon, A. Gilbert	Coleraine	Corporal	Canadians	
Wilson, James	Diamond	Private	Canadians	Killed in Action.
TERRACE ROW.				
Abraham, J. J.	Lodge Road	Lt.-Col. (A.D.M.S.)	R.A.M.C.	D.S.O. and White Eagle of Servia.
Acheson, Robert	Coleraine	Private	Durham Lt. Inft.	Killed in Action.
Anderson, Alec	New Row	Lance-Corporal	R.I.R.	
Anderson, John	New Row	Private	Canadians	
Anderson, Samuel	New Row		Liverpool Scottish	
Anderson, Thomas	New Row		M.T. R.A.S.C.	
Anderson, William	New Row	Private	R. In. Fus.	Killed in Action.
Anderson, William	New Row	Private	R. In. Fus.	Killed in Action.
Bellas, James	Cronbanagh			
Barbour, John	Brook Street	Lance-Corporal	K.O.R.L.	
Black, Harry	Dundoran	Corporal	A.N.Z.A.C.	Killed in Action.
Black, Joseph	Dundoran	Corporal	R. Irish Fus.	
Boyd, S. R.	Adelaide Avenue	Private	R. In. Fus.	Prisoner.
Boyd, Thomas	Adelaide Avenue	Sergeant	C.A.M.C.	
Baird, John H.	Castletoothery	Gunner	R.G.A. (Canada)	
Clarke, William	Nursery Avenue	Corporal	R. Irish Fus.	
Cochrane, Harry	Loughan	Rifleman	R.I.R.	
Cochrane, John	Loughan	Private	R.A.F.	
Cochrane, Thomas	Loughan	Rifleman	R. In. Fus.	
Cox, Joseph	New Market Street	Rifleman	R.I.R.	
Cox, Samuel	New Market Street	Private	R. In. Fus.	
Cox, William	New Market Street	Sergeant	R. In. Fus.	
Creelman, James	Brook Street	Rifleman	R.I.R.	
Creelman, Joseph	Brook Street	Private	R. In. Fus.	Killed in Action.
Creelman, Robert	Taylor's Row	Private	R. In. Fus.	Prisoner.
Creelman, Samuel	Brook Street	Corporal	R. In. Fus.	
Davis, W. J.	Coleraine			
Doherty, James	Carthall	Private	I Guards	Wounded.
Dymond, James	Terrace Row	Private	Scottish Rifles	Killed in Action.
Dymond, John	Terrace Row	Private	R.M.L.I.	Rus. Decoration.
Dymond, Robert	Terrace Row	Private	R. In. Fus.	Pris. Escaped.
Dymond, Samuel	Terrace Row	Private	R. In. Fus.	Mons Star.
Eakin, Harry		Private	R. Can. Vol. Reserves	
Eaton, James	Ballysally	Corporal	Gordon Highlanders	
Eaton, Samuel	Ballysally	Private	Black Watch	
Eyre, Charles	Railway Road	Lance-Corporal	R. In. Fus.	Killed in Action.
Eyre, T. A.	Railway Road	Rifleman	R.I.R.	
Finlay, James	Society Street	Private	R. In. Fus.	Wounded twice.
Given, Harry	Captain Street	Sapper	R.E.	
Givins, John	Castleroe	Sapper	R.E.	
Glen, Knox	Coleraine	Private	R. In. Fus.	
Hamill, J.	Ballinteer	Private	R.A.F.	
Henry, James W.	Railway Road	Private	Civil Service Rifles	Killed in Action.
Henry, John A.	Railway Road	Private	Civil Service Rifles	
Henry, Roy	Railway Road	Corporal	R.G.A.	D.C.M.
Hutchinson, A.	Bellhouse Lane	Sergeant	R. In. Fus.	M.M.
Hutchinson, Charles	Bellhouse Lane	Private	R. In. Fus.	Mons Star.
Hutchinson, John	Bellhouse Lane	Private	R. In. Fus.	Killed in Action.
Hutchinson, William	Bellhouse Lane	Private	R. In. Fus.	

COLERAINE PRESBYTERY.   TERRACE ROW.

Name.	Home Address.	Rank.	Regiment, Battalion or Unit.	Remarks.
IRWIN, R. B. W.	Union Street	Lieutenant	R. In. Fus.	M.C. Men. Desp. Prisoner.
IRWIN, W. W.	Union Street	Trooper	N.I.H.	
KELLY, ALFRED	James Street	Private	A.S.C.	
KELLY, ARCHIE	James Street	Private	R. In. Fus.	Killed in Action.
KELLY, ALFRED	James Street	Private	A.S.C.	
KELLY, JAMES	James Street	Private	Seaforth High.	
KELLY, JOSEPH	James Street	Private	A.S.C.	
KENNEDY, HUGH	Captain Street	A/Staff Sergt.	R.A.S.C.	
KEYS, W. G.	New Row	Captain	Army Dental Service	
LECKY, JOHN	Adelaide Avenue	Lance-Corporal	Black Watch	
LEEBURN, S. G.	Beresford House	Sergeant	R.A.F.	
LEES, JOSEPH	Castletoothery	Private		
LEES, ROBERT	Castletoothery	2nd Lieutenant	R.N.R.	Killed in Action.
LEONARD, ISAAC	Abbey Street	Private	R. West Surrey	Killed in Action.
LEONARD, JOHN	Abbey Street	Sergeant	R. In. Fus.	
LOVE, GEORGE	Lismurphy	Private	R.N.A.S.	
LOVE, R. S.	Lismurphy	Lance-Corporal	Munster Fus.	
LYND, E. C.	Rathanna	Engineer Officer	Transport Service	
LYND, W. L.	Rathanna	Navig. Officer	Transport Service	
McAFEE, G. G.	Abbey Street	C.Q.M.S.	R. In. Fus.	
McFARLANE, T.	Church Street	2nd A/M	R.A.F.	Thrice Wounded.
McINTOSH, A.	Lodge Road	Corporal	I. Guards	Wounded.
McINTYRE, JAS.	Coleraine	Sapper	R.E.	M.M.
McLAUGHLIN, R.	New Row	Private	R.M.L.I	
McMULLAN, T.	Blindgate Street	Private	R.G.A.	
MARSHALL, J. J.	Captain Street	Staff-Sergt.	R.A.S.C.	
MAXWELL, W.	Brook Street	Sergeant	R. Dub. Fus.	Wounded.
MITCHELL, JOSEPH	Killowen Street	Private	R. In. Fus.	
MOORE, J. A.	Duneden Terrace	2nd Lieutenant	R.N.A.S.	
MOORE, S. J.	Duneden Terrace	Sergeant	R.A.M.C.	
MORROW, E. A.	Island Leaghy	Sergeant	R.G.A.	Wounded.
MURPHY, A.	Stone Row	Lance Corporal	R. In. Fus.	Killed in Action.
MURPHY, JAMES	Stone Row	Private	Argyle & Suth. High.	
MURPHY, JOHN	Stone Row	Private	R. Hants Regt.	
MURPHY, H.	Stone Row	Private	R. In. Fus.	Killed in Action.
NEELY, JAMES	New Row	Lance-Corporal	R. In. Fus.	
PATON, REV. J. G., M.A.	Edenmore	Captain	Chaplain	Men. Desp. M.C. 2 Bars.
PEACOCK, T.	Spittalhill	Sergeant	Canadians	
PORTER, J.	Stone Row	Lance-Corporal	R.A.M.C.	
RICHARDSON, WILLIAM	Castletoothery			
RODGERS, R.	Coleraine	Private	R.O.D.	
SCOTT, A.	Station House	Cadet Sergt.	O.T.C.	
SCOTT, W.	Station House	Major	Indian Army	
SHANNON, JOSEPH	Adelaide Avenue	Lieutenant	R. In. Fus.	Wounded & Pris.
SHIRLEY, GEORGE	James Street	Private	R. Scots. Fus.	Killed in Action.
SHIRLEY, R. J.	James Street	Private	R. In. Fus.	Killed in Action.
SLOAN, ROBERT	Killowen Street	Gunner	R.F.A.	
SLOAN, THOMAS	Killowen Street	Gunner	R.F.A.	
SLOAN, W. J.	Killowen Street	Sergeant	R. In. Fus.	Wounded.
SMALL, DANIEL	Ballywilliam	Private	A.N.Z.A.C.	
SOMMERVILLE, R.		Private	R. In. Fus.	
STEWART, JOSEPH	Boghill	Cadet	R.A.F.	
STUART, E. M. W.	Bridge Street	Private	M.T. A.S.C.	
STUART, J. H. J.	Bridge Street	Lieutenant	Dental Surg., R.N.	
TODD, W.	Nursery House	Lance-Corporal	M.T. R.A.S.C.	
WATT, F.	Longcommons	Private	R. In. Fus.	Killed in Action.
WILMOT, G. A.	Brook Street	C.S.M.	R. In. Fus.	M.M. & Certificate.
WILMOT, JAMES	Longcommons	Sergeant	R. In. Fus.	M.M. Wounded.
WILSON, D.	Woodbine Terrace	A.B.	R.N.	
WILSON, G.	Woodbine Terrace	Private	Naval Brigade	Died in Hospital.
WORKMAN, A. H.	Abbey Street	Com. Armourer	R.N.	
CROSSGAR.				
ANDERSON, ALEXANDER	Castleroe	Private	R. In. Fus.	Killed in Action.
BLAIR, DAVID M.	Crossgar	Airman	R.A.F.	
CALVIN, J. OLIVER	Kiltinney		R.A.F.	
CARRICK, ROBERT JOHN	Ballyclough	Fireman	Transport Ship	
McCLEMENTS, WILLIAM	Ballylintagh	Private	3rd R. In. Fus.	
McKEEMAR, ISAAC	Drumcroon	Private	10th R. In. Fus.	Wounded.
SIMON, THOMAS JAMES	Ballynacannon	Private	A.S.C.	
COLONIAL FORCES.				
KENNEDY, EDWARD S.	Ballyclough	Private	Can. Force	Wounded.
MacLAUGHLIN, JOHN	Moneybrannon	Sergeant	Can. Force	
MAYRS, DAVID K.	Crosscandley	Sergeant	Can. Force	Killed in Action.
MAYRS, JOSEPH C.	Crosscandley	Private	Can. Force	
MAYRS, WILLIAM B.	Crosscandley	Private	Can. Force	

COLERAINE PRESBYTERY. **FIRST DUNBOE.**

Name.	Home Address.	Rank.	Regiment, Battalion or Unit.	Remarks.
FIRST DUNBOE.				
Aiken, Alexander	Articlave	Sergeant	I.G.	
Bell, Thomas	Articlave	Private	10th R. In. Fus.	Missing.
Callaghan, James	Castlerock	Private	R.G.A.	
Callaghan, William	Castlerock	Private	...	Killed in Action.
Cameron, Donald	Bellaney	Private	A.O.C.	
Crawford, Joseph	Castlerock	Lieutenant	R.I.R.	
Cummins, John	Milltown	Private	R. Ir. Fus.	Prisoner.
Johnston, David	Pottagh	Private	...	
Johnston, James	Pottagh	Private	...	Killed in Action.
Johnston, John	Pottagh	Private	...	Killed in Action.
Johnston, Robert	Pottagh	Private	...	Pris. in Germany.
Keers, Joseph	Blakes	Private	R.I.R.	
McCarron, Thomas	Milltown	Sergeant	R. In. Fus.	Killed in Action.
McCarron, William	Milltown	Private	R. In. Fus.	Killed in Action.
McConaghie, Samuel	Bratwell	Trooper	N.I.H.	
McFarland, George	Milltown	Private	R. In. Fus.	
McFarland, John	Milltown	Private	R. In. Fus.	
McKay, James	Castlerock	Signaller	10th R. In. Fus.	Prisoner.
McNab, William	Altibrian	Private	8th B.W.	
Macready, Austin	Articlave	Corporal	...	Prisoner.
Macready, H. John	Articlave	Lieutenant	R.A.F.	
Pollock, James	Ballyhacket	Corporal	R. In. Fus.	
Pollock, John	Quilly Head	...	...	
Savage, Robert	Altibrian	Private	R. In. Fus.	
Thorpe, John	Sconce	Lance-Corporal	...	Wounded.
COLONIAL FORCES.				
Dugan, Joseph	Castlerock	Lieutenant	Canadians	
King, James	Gorticavin	Private	Australians	Killed in Action.
Lynch, John	Altidillan	Private	Canadians	
McNab, Robert	Altibrian	Sapper	Australians	
SECOND DUNBOE.				
Acheson, James	Ringrash	Corporal	3rd R.I.R.	
Cameron, James Steel	Ballinrees	Cadet	R.A.F.	
Cameron, Thomas J.	Ballinrees	Captain	R.A.F.	
Cameron, William C.	Ballinrees	Private	N.I.H.	
Campbell, James A.	Balteagh	Private	R.A.F.	
McKee, John	Balteagh	Private	R.F.A.	
McKee, Joseph	Balteagh	Private	R.G.A.	
McKee, Matthew	Balteagh	Private	R. Irish Fus.	
Purcell, Archibald	Fermoyle	Private	12th R.I.R.	Killed in Action.
Smyth, James W.	Ballyvennox	Private	10th Canadian Batt.	
Smyth, Martin	Ballyvennox	Private	Dub. Fus.	Killed in Action.
Vincent, James	Gorticowan	Private	American Forces	
DUNLUCE.				
Brown, Gordon	Portballintrae	Private	12th R.I.R.	Killed in Action.
Burns, Henry	Urblereagh	Private	N.I.H.	
Carson, Robert	Bushfoot	Private	12th R.I.R.	Killed in Action.
Carson, Robert John	Ballyrock	Private	12th R.I.R.	Wounded & Pris.
Carson, Samuel	Ballyrock	Private	12th R.I.R.	Killed in Action.
Hammill, William	Ballymagarry	Private	12th R.I.R.	
Liken, John	Bushmills	Private	Lancashire Fus.	Killed in Action.
Liken, Richard	Bushmills	Private	R.E.	
Liken, William	Bushmills	Private	1st Batt. R.I.R.	
McAlister, David	Bushmills	...	R.N.	
McAlister, Isaac B.	Bushmills	Private	12th R.I.R.	Died of Wounds.
McAlister, James	Bushmills	Private	12th R.I.R.	Wounded.
McClements, Robert W.	Ballymagarry	Private	...	Killed in Action.
McKay, David	Ballyclough	Private	Scots Guards	
McKay, Matthew	Ballyclough	Private	12th R.I.R.	Killed in Action.
McLean, James S.	Priestland, Belfast	2nd Lieutenant	R.F.A.	Killed in Action.
Mitchell, Samuel	Craigaboney	Private	12th R.I.R.	Wounded and Died.
Moorehead, James	Portballintrae	Private	12th R.I.R.	
Moorehead, Joseph	Portballintrae	Private	12th R.I.R.	Wounded.
Stewart, William	Ballynaris	Private	N.I.H.	
White, James	Main St., Bushmills	Private	R.A.F.	
Wilmont, Robert	Ballylough	Private	...	
COLONIAL FORCES.				
Fullerton, John	Ballyness East	Private	Canadian Force	
Fullerton, Wilson	Ballyness East	Private	N.Z. Force	Died of Wounds.
McNabb, David	...	Private	Canadian Force	Died of Wounds.

COLERAINE PRESBYTERY. FIRST GARVAGH.

Name.	Home Address.	Rank.	Regiment, Battalion or Unit.	Remarks.
FIRST GARVAGH.				
Cathcart, William	Garvagh	Private	9th Batt. R.I.F.	Mons Star.
Curry, John			R.N.	
Faith, James	Caw	Private	10th Batt. R.I.F.	Killed in Action.
Ferguson, William	Garvagh	Lance-Corporal	12th Batt. R.I.F.	Wounded.
Gibson, Joseph	Metican	Private	R.I.F.	
Gibson, Robert		Gunner	R.G.A.	
Gould, Robert Allen	Crockindolg	Trooper	5th Light Horse Reg.	
Graham, John A.		Corporal	R.I.F.	
Gray, William		Sapper	R.E.	
Linton, William John	Carhill	2nd Lieutenant	10th Batt. R.I.R.	
McCaughey, Alexander		Lance-Corporal	R.I.F.	
McIntyre, David J.	Drumacrow	Sergeant	10th Batt. R.I.F.	M.M., Men. in Des
McMichael, William		Corporal	2nd Dragoons	
Madill, Jos. Herbert		Captain	R.A.M.C.	
Madill, Thomas		Surgeon	R.N.	
Mullan, Hugh	Garvagh	Private	9th Batt. R.I.F.	Pris. in Germany.
Mullan, James	Garvagh	Lance-Corporal	2nd Border Regt.	
Smyth, William Johnston	Gortnamoyagh		A.S.C.	
Thompson, Alfred	Kewrin	Private	N.I.H.	
Wilson, James	Movenis	Trooper	N.I.H.	Mons Star.
COLONIAL FORCES.				
Black, Hugh Clarke			N.Z. Forces	
Linton, Robert		Lance-Corporal	N.Z. Forces	
Moody, William			N.Z. Forces	
Moore, John			S. A. Infantry	
McCooke, John			Australian Forces	
Torrens, Thomas		Private	Australian Forces	Killed in Action.
SECOND GARVAGH.				
Adams, T. A.	Garvagh	Captain	R.A.M.C.	
Blake, Robert	Garvagh	Private	R.I.R.	Prisoner.
Burnside, Samuel	Eden Bann	Trooper	N.I.H.	Prisoner.
Davidson, Thomas	Garvagh	Private	R.I.R.	Wounded.
Fleming, Samuel	Garvagh	Gunner	R.G.A.	
Gibson, Thomas	Metican	Private	R.I.R.	Wounded.
Graham, John	Garvagh	Corporal	R.I.F.	
Kelly, Robert John	Cah	Sergt.-Major	Middlesex Regt.	Wounded.
McMaster, James T.	Inchaleen	Private	R.I.F.	
Robertson, Ralph	Ardavon	Corporal	R.E.	Awarded M.M.
Wilson, Alexander	Ballyagan	Gunner	R.G.A.	
Wilson, Thomas	Ballyagan	Gunner	R.G.A.	
COLONIAL FORCES.				
Dallis, George	Garvagh	Private	N.Z. Rifles	Wounded.
Lamont, William	Garvagh	Private	Can. Rifles	Wounded.
Linton, Samuel Scott	Carhill	Sergeant	N.Z. Rifles	Wounded.
Moore, David	Bellury	Private	Aust. I.F.	
Scott, Alexander	Moyletra	Sergeant	Aust. I.F.	
MACOSQUIN.				
Allen, James	Coole	Private	R. In. Fus.	
Allen, Joseph	Coole	Private	R. In. Fus.	Killed in Action.
Allen, William		Private		
Dickson, David	Society Street	Private	R. In. Fus.	
Downs, J.	Keely	Private	R. In. Fus.	Killed in Action.
Downs, Thomas	Keely		R. In. Fus.	Killed in Action.
Gault, David	Castlerow	Private	R. In. Fus.	Killed in Action.
Gault, Henry	Castlerow	Private	R. In. Fus.	
Gault, J.	Castlerow	Private	R. In. Fus.	
Gault, Kennedy	Castlerow	Private	R. In. Fus.	Killed in Action.
Gault, Robert	Castlerow	Private	R. In. Fus.	
Gray, James	Killure	Private	R. In. Fus.	M.M.
Gray, Samuel	Cullyveny	Private	R. In. Fus.	Prisoner at Kut.
Gray, W. J.	Garvagh	Private		
Harbinson, Robert	Cullyveny	Private	R. In. Fus.	M.M.
Kane, John	Ballylaggan	Private	R. In. Fus.	Killed in Action.
Lawrence, David	Ballylaggan	Private	R. In. Fus.	Wounded.
Lawrence, William	Ballylaggan	Private	R. In. Fus.	Wounded.
Loughrey, William	Macleary	Private	R. In. Fus.	
McQuilkan, Alexander	Camus	Private	R. In. Fus.	
McQuilkan, J.	Coleraine	Private	R. In. Fus.	
McQuilkan, William	Coleraine	Private	R. In. Fus.	
Morrison, A. J. McC., M.B.	Blackhill	Captain	R.A.M.C.	Wounded.
Morrison, H. R.	Meath Park	Lieutenant	A.S.C.	Serb Decoration.
Moore, D.	Macosquin	Sergeant		Killed in Action.
Tracey, Robert J.	Dromore	Private	R. In. Fus.	Wounded.
Wallace, Joseph	Coole	Private	R. In. Fus.	Killed in Action.
Wallace, Robert	Coole	Private	R. In. Fus.	Killed in Action.

COLERAINE PRESBYTERY.　　　　　　　　　　　　　　　　　　　　　　　　　　　　　　　　　　　　MACOSQUIN.

Name.	Home Address.	Rank.	Regiment, Battalion or Unit.	Remarks.
COLONIAL FORCES.				
Allen, J.	...	Private	Canadian Force	
Allen, R.	...	Private	Canadian Force	
Cunningham, C.	...	Private	U.S. Army	
McQuilkan, A.	...	Private	N.Z. Force	
McQuilkan, John	...	Private	N.Z. Force	Killed in Action.
McQuilkan, J.	...	...	N.Z. Force	
Marshall, James	...	...	Canadian Force	Wounded.
Moore, W. H.	...	...	Australian Force	Killed in Action.
Peden, S. J.	...	...	Canadian Force	Killed in Action.
MONEYDIG.				
Adams, Thomas	Carnroe	Captain	9th R.I. Fus.	M.C.
Archibald, William A.	Caheney	Private	9th Batt. R.I.F.	Wounded.
Calderwood, Hugh	Claggan	Driver	Transport A.S.C.	
Gilmore, Alexander	Drumeene	Private	174 Labour Corps	
Gilmore, William	Drumeene	Private	R.I. Fus.	Died.
Gilmore, William	Killyvalley	Private	R.F.A.	
Hogg, James	Carnroe	Private	10th R.I. Fus.	Died.
Kennedy, William	Caheney	Private	8th R.I.R.	
Lyttle, William McCay	Moyletra	Able Seaman	S.S. "Australia"	
McIlfatrick, Samuel	Cooleyrammer	Private	36th R.I. Fus.	Killed in Action.
McIlroy, Robert	Moneydig	Private	1/6 A.C.S.H.	
Morrison, H. Rankin	Moneydig	Private	36th Div. A.S.C.	
Morrison, Jos. Dickey	Moneydig	Lance-Corporal	9th R.I. Fus.	Killed in Action.
Orr, Adam	Ballyagan	...	No. 1 Tech. Advisor	
Stewart, Rev. Wm. H.	Moneydig	Captain	C.F.	
Stewart, David	Moneydig	Private	R.I. Fus.	
Stewart, James	Gorton	Private	R.I. Fus.	Killed in Action.
Stewart, John	Moneydig	Private	10th R.I. Fus.	
Stewart, Thomas	Moneydig	Sergeant	27th Black Watch	Thrice Wounded.
Stewart, William	Moneydig	Private	10th R.I. Fus.	Wounded.
Torrens, David	Carnroe	Lance Corporal	M.T. R.A.S.C.	
Torrens, James	Tamlaght	Private	9th R.I. Fus.	Twice Wounded.
Toye, Robert Ernest	Cooleyrammer	Co. Q.M. Sergt.	15th R.I.R.	Killed in Action.
Toye, William	Cooleyrammer	Chief P. Officer	R.N.	
Warwick, J. Alexander	Drogheda	Private	13th Batt. Tank Corps	
COLONIAL FORCES.				
Archibald, Matthew	Caheney	Private	A.I.F.	Killed in Action.
Archibald, William H.	Caheney	...	A.A.	
Hazlett, Jos. Bamford	Moneydig	Private	2nd Otago Batt., N.Z.	Killed in Action.
Hogg, Archibald	Carnroe	Private	Col. Force	Killed in Action.
Hogg, Sandy	Tamlaght	Private	A.I.F.	
McAtamney, James	Moneydig	Private	S.S.U. 506	
McLaughlin, John	Mayoughill	Sergeant	27th Batt. 2nd Can.	
Peden, James	Mayoughill	Sergeant	American A.C.	
Peden, Robert William	Mayoughill	...	Canadian Engineers	
Stewart, John	Culnaman	Private	N.Z.F.	
Toye, David A. Wilson	Cooleyrammer	Co. Sergt.-Major	N.Z.F.	Twice Wounded. Gassed.
Toye, Samuel Perry	Cooleyrammer	Private	N.Z.F.	Severely Wounded.
PORTRUSH.				
Adams, Thomas	Causeway Street	Private		
Allison, Robert M.	Causeway Street	Sergeant		M. Medal.
Black, Charles E.	Coleraine Road	Private		
Black, William	Coleraine Road	Corporal		
Cameron, Alexander H.	Causeway Street	Private		
Cameron, William	Causeway Street	Private		Killed in Action.
Elkin, Robert	Bazaar Street	...		
Elkin, William	Bazaar Street	...		Died.
Esdale, W. J.	Causeway Street	Sergeant		
Foreman, John	Causeway Street	Lance-Corporal		Killed in Action.
Frazer, Edmund	Portrush	Corporal		Killed in Action.
Frazer, William	Portrush	Private		Died. Prisoner.
Gilfillan, David	Mark Street	Private		Wounded.
Gilfillan, James	Mark Street	Private		
Graham, Daniel	Causeway Street	Private		
Graham, John	Landsdown Crescent	Private		
Hamill, John	...	Private		
Hemphill, John	Main Street	Lance-Corporal		
Hunter, James	Eglinton Terrace	Private		Died. Prisoner.
Hunter, James D.	Eglinton Terrace	Private		
Hunter, William	Croc, na-mac	Private		
Lamont, Samuel	Ballyreagh	Private		
Lyons, Stewart	Mark Street	...		
MacCaw, Daniel	Causeway Road	Sergeant		
McCulloch, Jim	Main Street	Private		
McCulloch, William	Main Street	Lieutenant		

COLERAINE PRESBYTERY. PORTRUSH.

Name.	Home Address.	Rank.	Regiment, Battalion or Unit.	Remarks.
McCulloch, William	Bazaar Street	Private		Killed in Action.
McFarlane, Samuel	Landsdown Crescent	Private		Died in France.
McMillan, Andrew	Causeway Street	Private		
McMullen, George	Causeway Street	Sergeant		
McNabb, James	Ballymagarry	Lance-Corporal		
McNabb, Samuel	Ballymagarry	Sapper		
Matthews, James	Manse Avenue	Corporal		
Matthews, Robert	Manse Avenue	Private		
Matthews, Thomas	Manse Avenue	Private		
Miller, John	Craig Vara	Petty Officer		Died.
Miller, William	Craig Vara	Sapper		
Moffett, James	Dunluce Street	Private		
Moffett, John	Dunluce Street	Private		
Moffett, John	Main Street	Private		
Moorhead, Samuel	Kerr Street	Private		
Morrow, Edmund	Dhu Varren	Lieutenant		
Mullan, Waldo	Dhu Varren	Private		Killed in Action.
Murray, Matthew	Princess Street	Private		Killed in Action.
Murray, Samuel	Princess Street	Private		Wounded.
Peden, Alec	Main Street	Sergeant		
Peden, Bertie	Main Street	Lance-Corporal		
Pepper, Bertie	Main Street	Lieutenant		Killed in Action.
Porter, Bertie	Mir-a-mer	Doctor	R.A.M.C.	M.C. Men. Desp.
Ramage, Alec	Princess Street	Private		
Riddell, Eddie	Main Street	Corporal		Killed in Action.
Shaw, Arthur	Manse Avenue	Private		
Shaw, David	Manse Avenue	Private		
Smith, Thomas	Bath Street	Private		Killed in Action.
Stewart, Andrew	Main Street	Sergeant		
Strathdee, Charles	Princess Street	Seaman	R.N.	
Strathdee, Ernest	Princess Street	Sergeant		
Strathdee, George	Princess Street	Sergeant		Wounded.
Strathdee, William	Princess Street	Paymaster	R.N.	
Todd, Andrew	Causeway Street	Sapper		
PORTSTEWART.				
Boggs, William	Portstewart	Cadet	R.A.F.	
Boyd, William	Portstewart	Private	10th In. Fus.	
Brown, William	Mullaghacall	Private	R. In. Fus.	
Brown, William	Portstewart	A.B.S.	R.N.	
Burke, Robert	Portstewart	Private	R.A.F.	Died in Hospital.
Burke, William	Portstewart	Private	Tank Corps	
Campbell, Edward	Portstewart	A.B.S.	R.N.	
Crawford, Theodore A.	Portstewart	Lieutenant	R.F.A.	
Davidson, George	Portstewart	Private	London Regiment	
Davidson, James	Doey	Private	9th In. Fus.	
Douglas, Daniel	Roseleeth	Private	10th In. Fus.	
Ferguson, Alexander	Portstewart	Major	1st R. In. Fus.	M. Cross
Gray, John	Burnside	Private	6th R. In. Fus.	Killed in Action.
Hamilton, Henry	Portstewart	Private	10th R. In. Fus.	
Hamilton, Joseph	Portstewart	Private	10th R. In. Fus.	
Hayes, James	Burnside	Private	10th R. In. Fus.	Killed in Action.
Hayes, Thomas	Burnside	Private	1st R. In. Fus.	Killed in Action.
Henry, S. Stuart	Portstewart	Lieutenant	R.A.F.	Pris. in Germany.
Kilpatrick, William	Burnside	Private	R. In. Fus.	Killed in Action.
Logan, Andrew	Portstewart	Lance-Corporal	10th R. In. Fus.	
Logan, William	Portstewart		R.N.	
Lyons, James	Portstewart	Private	10th R. In. Fus.	
McCurdy, James	Mullaghacall	Private	10th R. In. Fus.	Killed in Action.
McCurdy, James, Jun.	Portstewart	Private	N.I.H.	
McIlreavy, Alexander	46 Ethel Street, Belfast	Private	Cycling Corps	
McIlreavy, Hugh	46 Ethel Street, Belfast		R.N.	
McMichael, William	Cromore	Private	1st I.G.	Died in Hospital.
Martin, Alan	Portstewart	Private	10th R. In. Fus.	
Moreland, George	Cromore	Private	1st N.I.H.	
Reid, Daniel, Jun.	Portstewart	Private	R.A.F.	
Reid, William James	Portstewart	Corporal	N.I.H.	Killed in Action.
Sinclair, John	Cappagh	Private	10th R. In. Fus.	
Sinclair, Samuel	Cappagh	Private	10th R. In. Fus.	Killed in Action.
Sinclair, William J.	Cappagh	Private	10th R. In. Fus.	
COLONIAL FORCES.				
Campbell, Daniel		Private	Canadians	
Hunter, Hugh		Private	Canadians	
Linton, James		Private	S. African Reg·	
Lynch, Robert		Private	N Z·	
McCandless, David		Sergeant	Australians	Killed in Action.
McCready, James		Sergeant	Canadians	
McCready, William		Sergeant	Can. Inft.	

COLERAINE PRESBYTERY.

RINGSEND.

Name.	Home Address.	Rank.	Regiment, Battalion or Unit.	Remarks.
RINGSEND.				
Carson, Andrew	Macosquin	Sapper	R.E.	Twice Wounded.
Cochrane, James	Camm	Sapper	R.E.	Killed in Action.
Crowe, Charles	Letterloan	Private	Royal Army Vet. Corps	Wounded.
Leese, John	Ringsend	Signaller	R.G.A.	
McCloskey, Alfred	Macosquin	Private	R. In. Fus.	
Millen, Robert	Ringsend	Private	R. In. Fus.	Killed in Action.
Moffat, Robert	Ringsend	Gunner	R.G.A.	
Morrison, George	Camm	Trooper	N.I.H.	Wounded and Died. P.O.W.
Morrow, James	Craigmore	Trooper	R.I. Hussars	
Patterson, Hugh	Crossmakever	Private	R.E.	
Ross, James	Leck	Private	R. In. Fus.	
Thompson, John	Belraugh	Private	R. In. Fus.	
COLONIAL FORCES.				
Boyd, John Brown	Ringsend	Corporal	American E.F.	
Cochrane, John	Camm	Private	Mounted Engineers, U.S.A.	
Crowe, Robert A.	Letterloan	Private	58th Can. Res.	
Gibson, Albert	Ringsend	Private	20th Reinforcements, N.Z.	
Gibson, Ernest	Ringsend	Batt. Grenadier	E.L.Q., N.Z.	
McCloskey, Robert	Letterloan	Trooper	Can. Light Horse	Wounded.
Maxwell, David	Ballynacally	Rifleman	R.B., N.Z.	
Morrison, David	Belraugh	Lance-Corporal	Otago Regt., N.Z.	
Ritchie, Thomas	Cashel	Private	Can. Inft.	Killed in Action.
Steen, Robert John	Blackhill	Private	2nd Rhodesian Regt.	

COMBER PRESBYTERY.

Name.	Home Address.	Rank.	Regiment, Battalion or Unit.	Remarks.
BALLYGOWAN.				
Boyce, James	Magherascouse	Private	14th R.I.R.	Twice Wounded.
Brown, William	Ballygowan	Private	Sutherland Highlanders	W'ded 5 times.
Burrows, Robert	Ballygowan	Private	R.I.R.	Killed in Action.
Burrows, Robert J.	Ballygowan	Private	R.E.	
Clarke, James	Ballygowan	Private	19th R.I.R.	Killed in Action.
Clarke, Samuel	Ballygowan	Private	R.E.	
Connolly, Samuel	Ballygowan		R.N.	
Craigan, Robert	Magherascouse	Private	N.I.H.	Wounded.
Davidson, John	Ballycloughan	Private		Wounded.
Dickson, A. McC.	Ardmore	Lieutenant	18th R.I.R.	Wounded, M.C.
Dickson, J. E.	Ardmore	Lieutenant	13th R.I.R.	
Dumican, Samuel	Ardmore	Lieutenant	R.I.R.	
Gabby, William	Magherascouse	Private	17th R.I.R.	
Galbraith, David	Ballygowan		M.T. A.S.C.	Prisoner of War.
Garrett, Hugh	Ballygowan	Sapper	R.E.	
Gibson, Joseph	Ballygowan	Private	R.A.M.C.	
Gibson, Joseph	Ballygowan	Private	19th R.I.R.	
Gibson, Robert	Ballygowan	Private	19th R.I.R.	Prisoner of War.
Gibson, Robert	Ballygowan	Private	Irish Guards	
Gibson, Samuel	Ballygowan	Private	16th R.I.R.	Killed in Action.
Grant, John	Ballyknockan	Private	Dublin Fus.	Wounded.
Hanna, David	Ballykeigle	Private	13th R.I.R.	Wounded and Pris.
Hill, Charles	Ravara	Private	13th R.I.R.	Killed in Action.
Jordan, Alexander	Ballygowan	Private	A.S.C.	Twice Wounded.
Jordan, Lowry	Ballygowan	Lance-Corporal	2nd Rf. Brigade	M.M. and Bar.
Jordan, Wallace	Ballygowan	Private	13th R.I.R.	Killed.
McDowell, Samuel	Ballygowan	Private	13th R.I.R.	Prisoner of War.
McIlwaine, James	Ballygowan	Corporal	14th Y.C.V.	
McMurray, Robert	Ballygowan		High. Lt. Inf.	
McNally, James	Ballygowan	Private	14th Y.C.V.	
Mannis, Daniel	Ballygowan	Private	12th R.I.R.	
Mannis, George	Ballygowan	Sergeant	13th R.I.R.	M.M.
Mannis, Robert	Ballygowan	Sapper	R.E.	
Massey, Robert	Ballygowan	Private	16th Cyclists' Co.	Prisoner of War.
Maxwell, John	Carnesure, Comber	Private	10th R.I.R.	
Meharry, John	Ballygowan	Private	R.I.R.	Wounded.
Mills, John	Ardenvohr St., Belfast		17th R.I.R.	Killed.
Mills, William	Ballygowan	Private	A.S.C.	
Murray, David	Magherascouse	Corporal	8th Lancers	
Murray, John	Magherascouse		R.N.	
Nixon, Alexander	Ballygowan	Private	13th R.I.R.	

COMBER PRESBYTERY. BALLYGOWAN.

Name.	Home Address.	Rank.	Regiment, Battalion or Unit.	Remarks.
Nixon, John	Ballygowan	Private	R. Marines	
Pyper, Thomas	Moneyrea, Ballygowan	Private	N.I.H.	
Pyper, William	Moneyrea, Ballygowan		19th R.I.R.	
Rea, John	Ballygowan	Private	13th R.I.R.	Wounded.
Reid, William	Ballygowan	Private	13th R.I.R.	
Stevenson, William	Ballygowan	Private	R.A.M.C.	
Young, George	Ballygowan	Private	A.S.C.	Killed.
Young, Harry		Private	R.M.	Killed in Action.
COLONIAL FORCES.				
Gibson, Robert	Ballygowan	Private	N.Z.L.I.	
Grant, Samuel	Ballyknockan	Private	Can. Inf.	Killed in Action.
McDowell, Harry	Ballygowan	Private	Can. Inf.	
McDowell, R. J.	Ballygowan	Lance-Corporal	Can. Inf.	Killed in Action.
Millar, Wm. Barry	Ballygowan	Corporal	13th Australian Inf.	Killed in Action.
Shiels, Robert	Magherascouse	Private	Can. Inf.	Wounded.
Stevenson, Samuel	Ballygowan	Private	A.S.C., Aust. L.H.	
THIRD BALLYNAHINCH.				
Bain, James	Ballymacarn	Farrier	Ind. E.F.	
Ellis, Henry	Ballynahinch	Corporal	R.B., C.T.D.	Wounded.
English, James	Ballynahinch	Lieutenant	15th R.I.R.	Men. in Des.
Hill, Charles	Creevytenant	Corporal	R.E.	
Hill, James	Creevytenant	Major	R.A.M.C.	Wounded, M.C.
Johnston, Thomas	Ballymacarn	A.C.I.	R.A.F.	
Lawther, James	Newcastle	Captain	R.F.A.	Wounded.
McMaster, William J.	Glassdrummond	Wheeler	C.F.A.	Wounded.
Martin, William	Ballynahinch	Captain	R.A.M.C.	
Moore, James	Ballynahinch	Corporal	13th R.I.R.	Killed in Action.
Moore, Thomas	Ballynahinch	Private	A.S.C.	
Morrow, Robert	Ballynahinch	Private	Can. E.F.	Wounded.
Newell, William	Cumber Bridge	Rifleman	19th R.I.R.	
FIRST COMBER.				
Beers, Robert	Comber	Rifleman	13th R.I.R.	
Beers, William	Comber	Rifleman	13th R.I.R.	Killed in Action.
Boyd, George	Comber	Sergeant	13th R.I.R.	Killed in Action.
Boyd, James	Comber	Corporal	3rd R.I.R.	
Burgess, Samuel R.	Comber	Corporal	13th R.I.R.	Wounded.
Caldwell, Victor	Comber	Private	Royal Irish Reg.	
Campbell, William	Comber	Rifleman	13th R.I.R.	
Cassey, George	Comber	Rifleman	13th R.I.R.	Killed in Action.
Cassey, James	Comber	Rifleman	13th R.I.R.	Killed in Action.
Cassey, Thomas	Comber	Driver	A.S.C.	
Cassey, William	Comber	Private	Worcester Regt.	
Cooke, William	Comber	Private	R.D.C.	
Dickson, John	Comber	Stoker	H.M.S. Urchin	
Dickson, William	Comber	Rifleman	13th R.I.R.	
Donnan, William	Comber	Private	R. In. Fus.	Wounded.
Finlay, James	Comber	Sergeant	13th R.I.R.	Died.
Fisher, George	Comber	Corporal	Trench Mortar Battery	
Fisher, Thomas J.	Comber	Private	13th R.I.R.	Killed in Action.
Galway, James	Comber	Gunner	R.F.A.	Wounded.
Galway, Samuel	Comber	Private	13th R.I.R.	Wounded.
Gamble, David J.	Comber	Private	13th R.I.R.	Died in Germany.
Gamble, John	Comber	Private	4th Seaforth High.	
Gibson, George	Comber	Private	A.S.C.	Wounded.
Glover, Alex.	Comber	Private	16th R.I.R.	Died.
Glover, John	Comber	Private	13th R.I.R.	Prisoner of War.
Graham, Donald	Comber	Captain	R.A.M.C.	
Graham, Louis	Comber	Captain	R.A.M.C.	
Graham, Norman	Comber	Captain	R.A.M.C.	M.C.
Graham, William	Comber	Captain	R.A.M.C.	
Grainger, Thomas	Comber	Surgeon-General		C.B.
Gunning, James	Comber	Sergeant	13th R.I.R.	Wounded.
Headley, James	Comber	Corporal	R.E.	
Headley, Mathew	Comber	Corporal	R.E.	
Hood, J.	Comber	Sapper	R.E.	
Hood, W. J.	Comber	Stoker	R.N.	
Horner, Jacob	Comber	Trooper	N.I.H.	Wounded.
Johnstone, James	Comber	Rifleman	13th R.I.R.	
Kennedy, Robert	Comber	Private	Labour Corps	
Kirk, James	Comber	Rifleman	13th R.I.R.	
Lieberman, Charles	Comber	Corporal	Labour Corps	
Loughran, James	Comber	Sergeant	R.F.A.	
Megraw, Ainsley	Comber	Sergeant	13th R.I.R.	
Minnis, George	Comber	Private	13th R.I.R.	Prisoner of War.
Mitchell, David	Comber	Captain	R.A.M.C.	Wounded.
Moore, Thomas	Comber	Private	R.E.	
McBurney, Edward	Comber	Engineer-Lieut.	R.N.R.	
McBurney, James	Comber	Lieutenant	20th R.I.R.	Killed in Action.

(208)

COMBER PRESBYTERY. FIRST COMBER.

Name.	Home Address.	Rank.	Regiment, Battalion or Unit.	Remarks.
McCann, Albert	Comber	Engineer-Lieut.	R.N.R.	
McCann, Robert	Comber	Lieutenant	R.N.V.R.	
McCulloch, John	Comber	Private	13th R.I.R.	Killed in Action.
McMillan, William	Comber	Private	Labour Corps	
McQuoid, W. J.	Comber	Corporal	A.S.C.	
Oliver, Ellis	Comber	Private	13th R.I.R.	Killed in Action.
Oliver, John	Comber	Ass. Mech.	R.A.F.	
Oliver, John	Comber	Corporal	19th R.I.R.	
Oliver, Thomas	Comber	Private	20th R.I.R.	
Patton, David	Comber	Stoker	R.N.	
Patton, James	Comber	Private	13th R.I.R.	Killed in Action.
Patton, Joseph	Comber	Private	13th R.I.R.	
Price, John	Comber	Sergeant	13th R.I.R.	Killed in Action.
Proctor, Hugh	Comber	Lieutenant	R.F.C.	Wounded.
Proctor, James	Comber	Sergeant	13th R.I.R.	Killed.
Proctor, John	Comber	Bombardier	R.F.A.	
Quinn, John	Comber	Sergeant	R.N.M.	Killed.
Quinn, William	Comber	Sergeant	R.E.	
Ritchie, J. A.	Comber	2nd Lieutenant	A.S.C.	
Scott, Albert	Comber	2nd A.M.	R.F.C.	
Scott, William	Comber	Private	18th R.I.R.	
Shannon, William	Comber	Sergeant	2nd R.I.R.	
Shaw, Alexander	Comber	Corporal	A.V.C.	
Skillen, John	Comber	Private	13th R.I.R.	
Skillen, Matthew	Comber	Rifleman	Labour Corps	
Speers, James	Comber	Sergeant	13th R.I.R.	Wounded.
Speers, William	Comber	Private	13th R.I.R.	Wounded.
Stevenson, Alexander	Comber	Private	13th R.I.R.	Prisoner of War.
Strange, George	Comber	Lieutenant	2nd R.G.A.	
Strange, Girvan	Comber	Private	12th R.I.R.	
Smythe, Bertie	Comber	Engineer-Lieut.	R.N.R.	
Swindle, John	Comber	Private	18th R.I.R.	Killed.
Thompson, Alexander	Comber	Sapper	R.E.	
Thompson, George	Comber	Sapper	R.E.	
Thompson, Hans	Comber	Rifleman	13th R.I.R.	
Thompson, James	Comber	Private	1st King's Liverpool	
Thompson, Robert	Comber	Rifleman	12th R.I.R.	
Thompson, Wm. J.	Comber	Rifleman	13th R.I.R.	Killed.
Todd, Hugh	Comber	Private	13th R.I.R.	Prisoner of War.
Todd, John	Comber	Private	13th R.I.R.	Wounded.
Todd, Joseph	Comber	Lance-Corporal	12th R.I.R.	
Vogan, Samuel	Comber	Rifleman	2nd R.I.R.	Wounded.
Watt, W. H.	Comber	Corporal	26th R.F.A.	Wounded.
Wherry, Alexander	Comber	Private	R.E.	
Wherry, David	Comber	Private	13th R.I.R.	

SECOND COMBER.

Alexander, James	Comber	Trooper	N.I.H.	
Allen, John	Comber	Rifleman	13th R.I.R.	Killed,
Allen, John	Comber	Private	3rd Border Regt.	
Allen, Thomas	Comber	Rifleman	13th R.I.R.	
Anderson, John	Comber	Stoker	R.N.	
Barry, Alexander	Comber	Bandsman	13th R.I.R.	Wounded.
Basset, James	Comber	Rifleman	18th R.I.R.	Wounded.
Bennet, Andrew	Comber	1st Class Stoker	Naval Brigade	Wounded.
Bennet, John	Comber	Sergeant	R.F.A.	
Bennet, William	Comber	Sergeant	13th R.I.R.	Wounded.
Blackstock, James	Comber	Lance-Corporal	A.S.C.	Wounded.
Bowman, Harry	Comber	Rifleman	13th R.I.R.	
Boyd, James	Comber	Private	19th R.I.R.	
Brown, David	Comber	Private	13th R.I.R.	Wounded.
Brown, William J.	Comber	Sergeant	13th R.I.R.	Killed.
Brown, Joseph	Comber	Sergeant	13th R.I.R.	Wounded.
Campbell, George	Comber	Private	18th R.I.R.	
Cannavan, William	Comber	Private	R.E.	
Clarke, John	Comber	Rifleman	18th R.I.R.	
Coey, Thomas	Comber	Rifleman	13th R.I.R.	Killed.
Coleman, William	Comber	Rifleman	13th R.I.R.	Wounded.
Crawford, Robert	Comber	Bandsman	13th R.I.R.	Wounded.
Donaldson, —	Comber	Private	R.M.L.I., "Collingwood," Home Fleet.	
Donaldson, James	Comber	Rifleman	13th R.I.R.	Killed.
Donaldson, John	Comber	Rifleman	13th R.I.R.	Killed.
Donaldson, Samuel	Comber	Rifleman	13th R.I.R.	Killed.
Drain, Harry	Comber	Corporal	18th R.I.R.	
Dunseith, Hugh	Comber	Rifleman	19th R.I.R.	Wounded.
Gabbey, Hugh	Comber	Private	18th R.I.R.	
Gabbey, James	Comber	Private	12th R.I. Fus.	Wounded.
Gabbey, W.	Comber	Private	3rd Irish Guards	
Geddis, S. M.	Comber	2nd Lieutenant	Army Cyclists Corps	Wounded.
Glover, Joseph	Comber	Private	18th R.I.R.	
Glover, William	Comber	Private	13th R.I.R.	Wounded.
Graham, John	Comber	Rifleman	13th R.I.R.	

COMBER PRESBYTERY. SECOND COMBER.

Name.	Home Address.	Rank.	Regiment, Battalion or Unit.	Remarks.
Hare, James	Comber	Rifleman	13th R.I.R.	Killed.
Hedley, Matthew	Comber	Private	R.E.	
Herron, Albert	Comber	Sergeant	A.S.C.	
Herron, Samuel	Comber	Rifleman	13th R.I.R.	
Herron, William	Comber	Trooper	N.I.H.	
Ireland, William	Comber	Bandsman	13th R.I.R.	
Keilty, John	Comber	Private	R.A.M.C.	
Kelly, Hugh	Comber	Private	18th R.I.R.	Killed.
Kelly, James	Comber	Rifleman	17th R.I.R.	Wounded.
Lowry, Samuel	Comber	Sergeant	3rd H.L.I.	Wounded.
Lowry, William	Comber	Corporal	R.E.	D.C.M.
Lundy, Samuel	Comber	Rifleman	18th R.I.R.	
Maguire, James	Comber	Private	18th R.I.R.	Wounded.
Maitland, Samuel	Comber	Rifleman	13th R.I.R.	Wounded.
Marshall, Robert	Comber	Rifleman	13th R.I.R.	
Mawhinney, Robert	Comber	Rifleman	13th R.I.R.	
Maxwell, Thomas	Comber	Driver	14th R.I.R.	Wounded.
Moham, James	Comber	4th Engineer	Hospital Ship	
Morgan, Robert	Comber	Rifleman	18th R.I.R.	
Murray, D. J.	Comber	2nd Lieutenant	16th Liverpool Regt.	
Murray, George	Comber	Rifleman	13th R.I.R.	Wounded.
McAllister, John	Comber	Rifleman	13th R.I.R.	Wounded.
McAllister, Samuel	Comber	Private	1st R. In. Fus.	Wounded.
McBratney, J. H.	Comber	Rifleman	14th R.I.R.	Killed.
McBratney, Samuel	Comber	Sapper	R.E.	
McClurg, Robert	Comber	Seaman	H.M.S. General Crawford	
McConnell, Rev. Thos., B.A.	Comber	Captain	C.F.	
McCutcheon, James	Comber	Rifleman	13th R.I.R.	
McCutcheon, John	Comber	Rifleman	13th R.I.R.	Killed.
McIlveen, Alexander	Comber	Rifleman	13th R.I.R.	Wounded.
McIlveen, John	Comber	Rifleman	13th R.I.R.	Killed.
McIlveen, William	Comber	Rifleman	13th R.I.R.	
McMorran, James	Comber	Saddler	No. 7 Depot Coy.	
Orr, Robert	Comber	Rifleman	13th R.I.R.	Killed.
O'Prey, William	Comber	Trooper	N.I.H.	
Patterson, James	Comber	Lance-Corporal	13th R.I.R.	Killed.
Purdy, William	Comber	Driver	A.S.C.	
Quinn, John	Comber	Private	A.S.C.	
Rodney, Robert	Comber	Private	A.S.C.	
Savage, James	Comber	Private	Royal Marines	
Seales, Hugh	Comber	Driver	A.S.C.	
Seales, William J.	Comber	Petty Officer	H.M. Torpedo Boat 29	
Semple, William	Comber	Plumber	H.M.S. Transport	
Smyth, David	Comber	Rifleman	13th R.I.R.	Killed.
Smyth, Hugh	Comber	Rifleman	13th R.I.R.	
Smyth, Thomas	Comber	Driver	A.S.C.	
Smyth, Samuel	Comber	Trooper	N.I.H.	
Wallace, James	Comber	Rifleman	13th R.I.R.	
Wallace, John	Comber	Private	R.A.M.C.	
Watt, R.	Comber	Private	18th R.I.R.	
Wilson, Harry	Comber	Sergeant	R.I.F.	Gassed.
Withers, S. H.	Comber	Lt.-Colonel	O.C. 29th General Hospital	
Withers, William	Comber	Trooper	N.I.H.	
Wright, John	Comber	Private	R.I.R.	
COLONIAL FORCES.				
Drake, J. Edgar	Comber	Private	Can. E.F.	
Kelly, Hugh	Comber	Lance-Corporal	Can. F.A.	
Montgomery, J. H.	Comber	Sergeant	Can. F.A.	
DUNDONALD.				
Auld, James				
Bell, Archie				Killed in Action.
Bell, Thomas				
Cairns, Hugh				
Carruthers, Wm.				
Conkey, Robert				Killed in Action.
Courtney, William				
Dempster, Samuel				Killed in Action.
Donaldson, Robert				
Donaldson, William H.				
Fisher, Hugh				
Ferguson, David				
Ferguson, James				Killed in Action.
Ferguson, Samuel J.				
Frew, Philip W.				
Galway, James L.				
Galway, Robert McB.				Killed in Action.
Galway, William G.				
Gibson, Hugh				
Glenn, Alexander				
Glenn, James				

COMBER PRESBYTERY. DUNDONALD.

Name.	Home Address.	Rank.	Regiment, Battalion or Unit.	Remarks.
Gourley, Hugh	...	...	...	
Gourley, Henry	...	...	...	
Gourley, Robert	...	...	...	
Gourley, Samuel	...	...	...	
Gray, J. Logan	...	...	...	Killed in Action.
Gray, Edward	...	...	...	
Hare, John	...	...	...	
Harris, James	...	...	...	
Henry, Arthur H.	...	...	...	
Herriott, James	...	...	...	
Holmes, Thomas	...	...	...	
Hunter, John	...	...	...	
Irvine, Alexander	...	...	...	
Kennedy, Edwin R.	...	...	...	
Kenny, Robert	...	...	...	
Lindsay, James	...	...	...	Killed in Action.
Majury, James	...	...	...	
Majury, Hans	...	...	...	
Majury, Wm. J.	...	...	...	Killed in Action.
McClean, Donald	...	...	...	
McClean, Cornelius G.	...	...	...	
McClenaghan, George	...	...	...	
McClenaghan, Henry	...	...	...	
McConnell, James	...	...	...	
McCullough, David	...	...	...	Killed in Action.
McIlvenny, Hugh	...	...	...	
McKittrick, David	...	...	...	Killed in Action.
Mawhinney, Thomas A. M.	...	...	...	
Montgomery, William K.	...	...	...	
Montgomery, David K.	...	...	...	
Moore, James	...	...	...	
Morrow, Thomas H.	...	...	...	
Reid, James H.	...	...	...	
Reynolds, Henry H.	...	...	...	
Robb, A. Bryson	...	...	...	
Robb, John C.	...	...	...	
Stevenson, Hamilton	...	...	...	
Thompson, Arthur	...	...	...	
Thompson, William	...	...	...	
Walker, John	...	...	...	Killed in Action.
Wallace, John	...	...	...	
Wallace, George	...	...	...	
Ward, William J.	...	...	...	
Ward, Francis	...	...	...	
Ward, Hamilton	...	...	...	
Ward, Samuel	...	...	...	
Woods, Richard W.	...	...	...	
Wylie, George	...	...	...	
	GILNAHIRK.			
Boyd, Joseph	Gilnahirk	Private	2nd R.I. Regt.	
Boyd, R. C. H.	Gilnahirk	Gunner	R.F.A.	
Boyd, William	Gilnahirk	Private	13th R.I.R.	
Brand, Andrew	Gilnahirk	1st Lieutenant	R. Berkshire Regt.	
Coulter, J. W. C.	Gilnahirk	Captain	A.P.D.	
Dugan, James M.	Gilnahirk	Lance-Corporal	10th R.I.R.	Died of Wounds.
Harper, John W.	Gilnahirk	Major	14th R.I.R.	
McCaw, William G.	Gilnahirk	Sergeant	8th R.I.R.	Killed in Action.
McConnel, Harold	Gilnahirk	1st Lieutenant	R.A.F.	Killed in Action.
McCune, D. S. K. C.	Gilnahirk	Private	R.A.F.	
McDowell, Samuel L.	Gilnahirk	Private	R.A.M.C.	
McDowell, William J.	Gilnahirk	Sapper	R.E.	
Miller, James	Gilnahirk		R.A.F.	
Mills, William J.	Gilnahirk	Private	14th R.I.R.	
Moorhead, Roy	Gilnahirk	1st Lieutenant	4th R.I.R.	
Morrow, James	Gilnahirk	Private	London Irish Rif.	Wounded.
Niblock, Alexander	Gilnahirk	Driver	M.G.C.	
Niblock, Frank	Gilnahirk	Rifleman	14th R.I.R.	
Perry, Harry	Gilnahirk	Sergeant	R.G.A.	
Skates, William	Gilnahirk	Rifleman	8th R.I.R.	
Stewart, Thomas	Gilnahirk	Sergeant	R.N.A.S.	
Wilson, Wyndham S.	Gilnahirk		R.H.A.	
	COLONIAL FORCES.			
Harper, Robert	Gilnahirk		1st Depot Batt. B.C.	
Magill, Harry	Gilnahirk	Private	1st Canadian Div.	
McCune, William H.	Gilnahirk	Corporal	1st Canadian Div.	Killed in Action.
Morrow, Hugh H.	Gilnahirk	Private	31st Can. Div.	Wounded.
Watson, John F.	Gilnahirk	Sergeant	1st Can. Div.	
Watson, Robert	Gilnahirk	Gunner	5th Canadian Div.	

COMBER PRESBYTERY. GRANSHAW.

Name.	Home Address.	Rank.	Regiment, Battalion or Unit.	Remarks.
GRANSHAW.				
Black, James	43 Oldpark Av., Belfast	Private	Canadians	Wounded.
Dempster, Andrew J.	Moneyrea	Private	R.I.R.	Killed in Action.
Dempster, Hugh	Moneyrea	Private	R.I.R.	Wounded.
Dempster, William	Moneyrea	Private	Canadians	
McKee, Samuel	Granshaw	Private	Australians	Killed in Action.
Millar, John	55 Lord Street, Belfast	Private	R.I.R.	Wounded.
Wilson, Frank	Ballyrussell	Private	R.I.F.	
KILLINCHY.				
Adams, William	Lisbane	Corporal	M.G.C.	Gassed.
Calvert, James	Ballygigan	Private	R.I.R.	Killed in Action.
Calvert, William	Ballygigan	Private	R.I.R.	Twice Wounded.
Cromie, David	Ballyministra	Private	R.I.R.	Killed in Action.
Haslett, John	Drumreagh	Lieutenant	R.I.R.	M.C.
Hay, Thomas	Ballyministra	Gunner	R.I.R.	Wounded.
Heaney, James	Lisbane	Private	H.L.I.	Wounded.
Heaney, Samuel	Lisbane	Lance-Corporal	R.I.R.	Twice Wounded.
Jamison, John	Lisbane	Private	A.S.C.	Prisoner.
Keenan, William	Ballymacreely	Sergeant	A.S.C.	
Lawther, David	Carragullen		M.T., Russia	
Lowry, Andrew	Lisbane	Private	R.S.F.	Killed in Action.
McMaster, Andrew	Killinchy	Private		Prisoner.
McMaster, William	Killinchy	Private	R.D.F.	Prisoner.
Marshall, Andrew	Ballymorran	Stoker	R.N.	
Marshall, Hugh	Ballymorran	Sergeant	Vic. R.C.	
Marshall, John	Ballymorran	Stoker	R.N.	
Marshall, Morrow	Derryboye	Sergeant	E.A.E.F.	
Marshall, Robert	Ballymorran	Private	Seaforth Highlanders	Wounded.
Minnis, Thomas	Tullymagee	Private	N.I.H.	
Morrison, James	Lisbane	Private	Y.C.V.	Killed in Action.
Morrison, James	Ballyministra	Q.S.	R.A.	M.M.
Montgomery, Hans	Ringhaddy	Private	Labour Batt.	
Parker, William J.	Ballydrain	Driver	Horse Transport	
Robinson, Robert	Balloo		Motor Transport	
Snodden, William J.	Killinchy	Private	R.I.R.	Killed in Action.
Tate, James	Ballyministra	Sergeant	R.I.R.	Killed in Action.
Wallace, J.	Ballyleghorn	Private	Cycle Batt.	
COLONIAL FORCES.				
Cooper, William J.		Sergeant	S.A. Force	
Hewitt, Robert		Private	Canadian Force	Killed.
Hewitt, Wellington		Private	American Force	
Jamison, William		Private	N.Z. Force	
Jelly, David		Private	Australian E. Force	Wounded.
Johnston, Thomas		Observer	Canadian R.A.F.	
Keenan, James		Private	Canadian Force	Wounded.
Lyttle, Andrew		Private	Canadian Force	Killed in Action.
Lyttle, Hamilton		Private	Canadian Force	
Lyttle, Robert		Private	Canadian Force	
Lyttle, William		Private	Canadian Force	
McMullen, John		Private	American Force	
Montgomery, William		Private	Canadian Force	Killed in Action.
Moore, David		Private	American Force	
Russel, Samuel		Private	Canadian Force	
FIRST KILLYLEAGH.				
Andrews, Samuel	Killyleagh	Private	R.I.R.	
Calvert, Robert	Killyleagh	Private	R.I.R.	
Calvert, Samuel	Killyleagh	Private	R.I.R.	
Calvert, William James	Killyleagh	Private	R.I.R.	Killed in Action.
Campbell, Robert	Killyleagh	Corporal	R.I.R.	Killed in Action.
Casement, James	Killyleagh	Private	R. In. Fus.	
Coffey, Samuel	Killyleagh	Corporal	R.I.R.	Killed in Action.
Dornan, John	Killyleagh	Private	R.I.R.	Wounded.
Dornan, James	Killyleagh	Corporal	R.I.R.	Wounded.
Duff, James	Crossgar	Lieutenant	Yorkshire Regt.	
Fee, Robert	Killyleagh	Corporal	R.I.R.	Wounded.
Geddis, John	Killyleagh	Private	R.I.R.	
Heron, Charles	Killyleagh	Captain	R.I.R.	
Houston, James	Killyleagh	Corporal	R.I.R.	Wounded.
Hunsdale, Arthur	Killyleagh	Private	R.I.R.	
Kennedy, Edward	Killyleagh	Private	R.I.R.	Wounded.
Kennedy, John	Killyleagh	Private	R.I.R.	
Kennedy, Joseph	Killyleagh	Private	R.I.R.	Killed in Action.
Kilpatrick, James	Killyleagh	Sergeant	R.I.R.	Wounded.
Kilpatrick, Thomas	Killyleagh	Sergeant	R.I.R.	Wounded.
Lawther, Henry	Killyleagh	Engine-Lieut.	R.N.	
Magill, Robert	Killyleagh	Stoker	R.N.	Killed.
Magill, James	Killyleagh	Corporal	Canadian Force	

(212)

COMBER PRESBYTERY. FIRST KILLYLEAGH.

Name.	Home Address.	Rank.	Regiment, Battalion or Unit.	Remarks.
Martin, James	Killyleagh	Private	R.I.R.	Wounded.
Martin, Samuel	Killyleagh	Corporal	R.I.R.	Killed in Action.
Mathews, Edward	Killyleagh	Private	R.I.R.	
Mawhinney, R. J.	Killyleagh	Private	R.I.R.	
Moore, William	Killyleagh	Corporal	R.I.R.	Killed in Action.
Morrow, James	Killyleagh	A.B.	R.N.	Killed in Action.
McBride, Charles	Druse Street, Belfast	Private	R.I.R.	Wounded.
McBride, James	Druse Street, Belfast		R.I.R.	
McBride, John	Druse Street, Belfast		R.I.R.	Wounded.
McBride, Robert	Druse Street, Belfast		R. In. Fus.	Wounded.
McCleery, James Moore	Killyleagh	Sergeant	R.I.R.	Killed in Action.
McCleery, Robert	Killyleagh	Private	R.I.F.	Pris. in Germany.
McKelvey, William	Killyleagh	Private	R.I.R.	
Patterson, Thomas	Killyleagh	Sergeant	Irish Guards	Wounded.
Quinn, Joseph	Killyleagh	Private	R.I.F.	Wounded.
Quinn, Joseph, Jun.	Killyleagh	Private	R.I.R.	Wounded.
Rea, John	Ballygowan	Private	R.I.R.	
Ringland, Hans	Killyleagh	Sergeant	R.I.R.	
Ringland, James	Killyleagh	A.B.	R.N.	
Ringland, Thomas B.	Killyleagh	Engineer-Lieut.	R.N.	
Roye, David	Ballygalley	Private	R.I.R.	Pris. in Germany.
Roye, Edward	Ballygalley	Private	R.I.R.	
Sheppard, Thomas	Killyleagh	Mechanic	R.N.	
Stott, John	Killyleagh	Private	R.I.R.	Pris. in Germany.
Stott, Robert	Killyleagh	Private	R.I.R.	
Sullivan, Matthew	Killyleagh	Private	R.I.R.	
Sullivan, Samuel	Killyleagh	Private	R.I.R.	Died a Prisoner in Germany.
Thompson, Hugh	Crossgar	Private	R.I.R.	Wounded.
Watson, Robert	Killyleagh	Private	R.I.R.	Wounded.
Weaver, Robert	Ballytrim	Surgeon-Lieut.	R.N.	
Young, Thomas	Killyleagh	Private	R.I.R.	
COLONIAL FORCES.				
McBride, James	Toye	Corporal	N.Z. Force	Wounded.
McCleery, John R.	Killyleagh	Private	Canadian Force	
Magill, Hubert	Killyleagh	Sapper	Canadian Force	
Patterson, Robert	Killyleagh	Corporal	Canadian Force	
SECOND KILLYLEAGH.				
Beers, John	Killyleagh	Private	R.I.R.	
Calvert, Robert	Killyleagh	Private	R.I.R.	
Clarke, John	Comber	Private	R.I.R.	
Clarke, Robert	Comber	Private	R.I.R.	Killed in Action.
Connolly, Robert	Killyleagh	Private	R.I.R.	
Dynes, Alexander	Comber	Private	R.I.R.	Killed in Action.
Dynes, George	Comber	Private	R.I.R.	
Dynes, Thomas	Comber	Private	R.I.R.	Killed in Action.
Ferguson, William J.		Private	R. Scots	
Geddis, Hans		Private	R. In. Fus.	
Gracey, David	Killyleagh	Private	R.I.R.	
Jennings, Francis	Killyleagh	Private	R.I.R.	Killed in Action.
Jennings, Robert	Killyleagh	Private	R.I.R.	
McClurg, Charles	Killyleagh	Private	R.I.F.	
McClurg, James	Killyleagh	Private	A.S.C.	
McClurg, Robert	Killyleagh	Private	R.N.	
McClurg, Thomas	Killyleagh	Private	M.T.	
McKnight, Henry K.	Shrigley	Sergeant	R. In. Fus.	Croix de Guerre.
Matthews, Thomas	Killyleagh	Private	R.I.R.	M.M.
Morrison, James		Sergt.-Major	R.F.A.	D.C.M.
Morrison, Samuel		Private	R.I.R.	
Morrow, David	Shrigley	Private	R.I.R.	
Neill, James		Private	R.I.R.	
Sproule, Charles L.	Killyleagh	Captain	R.A.M.C.	
Sproule, Wallace	Killyleagh	Captain	M.G.C.	Wounded. Twice Men. in Des.
Stevenson, Hamilton	Killyleagh	Private	R.I.R.	
Walkingshaw, Francis	Killyleagh	Private	R.I.F.	
Walkingshaw, Francis, Jun.	Killyleagh	Private	R.I.R.	
Walkingshaw, John	Killyleagh	Private	R.I.R.	
Watson, Hugh	Killyleagh	Private	R.I.R.	
Wilson, Joseph	Shrigley	Private	R. In. Fus.	
Withers, Alexander	Killyleagh	Private	South Lancashires	
Woodside, William J.	Killyleagh			
COLONIAL FORCES.				
Beers, Thomas			Canadians	
Lang, Leonard			Canadians	
McCord, William			Canadians	
McVeigh, William			Canadians	
Robinson, James			Canadians	

COMBER PRESBYTERY. NEWTONARDS (Strean).

Name.	Home Address.	Rank.	Regiment, Battalion or Unit.	Remarks.
NEWTOWNARDS, STREAN.				
Simms, Rev. J., D.D., K.H.C., C.M.G.	Newtownards	Major-General	Principal Chaplain	Men. in Des.
Allen, Charles	Ulsterville, Newtownards	2nd Lieutenant	6th Black Watch	D.C.M., Promoted on Field.
Amberson, William	Regent Street	Corporal	13th R.I.R.	Wounded.
Armstrong, William W.	Clandeboye	2nd Lieutenant	Black Watch	Killed in Action.
Armstrong, John	Clandeboye	Petty Officer	R.N.A.S.	Medal of St. Geroge Russia.
Bailie, J.	Church Street	Private	R. In. Fus.	
Bennett, J. Gordon	...	...	R.F.C.	
Brown, James	Court Street	Rifleman	R.I.R.	Prisoner.
Crowe, Hugh	Frances Street	Sergeant	R. In. Fus.	
DeVoy, Samuel	South Street	Sergeant	R.I.R.	Killed in Action.
DeVoy, John Forbes	South Street	2nd Lieutenant	N.I.H.	Promoted on Field.
Doggart, William	Frances Street	Private	M.T. A.S.C.	
Dooley, T. J.	Frances Street	Private	M.T. A.S.C.	
Gordon, J. D.	Regent Street	Signaller	10th R.E.	
Gordon, Claude R.	Regent Street	Corporal	13th R.I.R.	
Heron, James	North Street	Sergt.-Major	R.I.R.	
McClements, Robert	Forde Street	Corporal	R.I.R.	
McKee, William	Forde Street	Private	M.T. A.S.C.	
McLean, Charles	Mark Street	Private	A. & S. Highlanders	Killed.
McLean, Duncan	Balfour Street	Private	R.I.R.	Killed.
McLean, Norman	Mark Street	Private	R.E.	Wounded.
McLean, Peter	Mark Street	Private	C.C. Highlanders.	
Meikle, George	Dunalton	2nd Lieutenant	King Edward's Horse	Promoted on Field.
Muir, Andrew	Church Street	Corporal	M.M. G.S.	
Muir, James	Church Street	Private	Glasgow R.E.	
Murray, Thomas	Wallace Street	Private	R. In. Fus.	Wounded.
Orr, Hamilton	James Street	Private	R.I.R.	Killed in Action.
Patterson, James	Killarn	Private	Canadian Exp. Force	
Patterson, Joseph	Killarn	Private	M.T. A.S.C.	
Simms, John S.	Woodgarth, N'ards	Captain	2/12 London Rifles	Killed in Action.
Stevenson, John	James Street	Private	Seaforth Highlanders	
Stevenson, Samuel	James Street	Private	R.G.A.	
Stevens, George	Kiltonga	Private	A & S. Highlanders	
Stevens, John	Kiltonga	Sapper	R.E., Ulster Division	
Stevens, W. M.	Kiltonga	Driver	R.G.A.	
Stouppe, Norman	Frances Street	Private	R.I.R.	Wounded.
Torry, Alexander	Greenwell Street	Private	R. In. Fus.	
SPA.				
Bailie, John	Drumaness	Private	13th R.I.R.	M.M., Wounded.
Bailie, Samuel	Drumaness	Private	13th R.I.R.	
Cleland, Thomas P.	Spa	Lance-Corporal	10th R.I.R.	
Lowry, John	Drumaness	Private	18th R.I.R.	
Moss, Andrew	Drumaness	Private	1st N.I.H.	
McCoubrey, Harry	Spa	Gunner	6th F.A., B.A.C.	
McCoubrey, Robert J.	Spa	Private	12th R.I.R.	Wounded.
McCoubrey, John A.	Spa	Corporal	38th Ottawa Batt.	Wounded.
Scandrett, Robert	Dunmore	Private	13th Batt. A.I.F.	Killed in Action.

CONNAUGHT PRESBYTERY.

Name.	Home Address.	Rank.	Regiment, Battalion or Unit.	Remarks.
BALLINA.				
Hamilton, Cecil C.	Ballina	2nd Lieutenant	3rd Con. Rangers	Killed in Action.
Hamilton, Hector M.	Ballina	2nd Lieutenant	1st Inniskillings	Killed in Action.
Hamilton, William	Ballina	2nd Lieutenant	3rd Connaughts	Killed in Action.
Laing, St. Clair, K.N.	Ballina	2nd Lieutenant	Royal Munsters	Died of Disease.
Petrie, Norman	Rosserk	Cadet	O.T.C.	
Reid, William	Ballina	Private	3rd Lancashire Fus.	Prisoner of War.
Shannon, John J.	Cloona	Captain, R.A.M.C.	Lincoln Yeomanry	Killed in Action.
Stevenson, Thomas	Coolcronan	Private	12th Inniskillings	
COLONIAL FORCES.				
Irwin, Bertie	...	...	Canadian Army	
Irwin, David	...	...	Canadian Army	
Laing, Cecil	Ballina	Private	Canadian A.S.C.	
Petrie, Frederick	Ballina	Private	Canadian Artillery	

CONNAUGHT PRESBYTERY.

BALLYMOTE.

Name.	Home Address.	Rank.	Regiment, Battalion or Unit.	Remarks.
BALLYMOTE.				
Ashmore, Richard	Manse, Creevelea	Lieutenant	Can. E.F.	Killed in Action
Boreland, H.	Bricklieve	Private	I.G.	Killed in Action.
Gamble, David	Ballymore	2nd Lieutenant	R.I.R.	Wounded.
Gamble, George	Ballymore	...	R.N.	
Gamble, John	Ballymore	...	R.N.	Torpedoed.
Gamble, Thomas	Ballymore	...	R.N.	Torpedoed.
Gass, ——	Gurteen	A.B.	R.N.	
Gorman, Richard	Ballymore	Captain	R. Vet. Corps	
Hunter, James	Riverstown	2nd Lieutenant	H.L. Inft.	Wounded.
Hunter, John A.	Riverstown	Lieutenant	R. Inn. Fus.	Wounded.
Kerr-Taylor, John M.	Castlebaldwin	Corporal	I.G.	Wounded.
Knox, Thos. Witherow	The Manse	Lieutenant	R.I.R.	Wounded.
Knox, W. H.	The Manse	Captain	R. Inn. Fus.	M.C., Men. Des.
Knox, H. Watt	The Manse	Cadet	R.A.F.	Torpedoed.
McComb, H.	Ballymore	Lieutenant, A.B.	R.N.	Killed in Action
Morrison, H. N.	Ballymore	Instructor	R.N.	
Orr, James F.	Greyfield	Bombardier	R.F.A.	
Smith, E. Wm.	Ballymore	Bombardier	R.F.A.	
Stuart, James	Temple House, B'more	...	...	
Stuart, John	Temple House, B'more	...	...	Killed in Action
Stuart, Wm.	Temple House, B'more	...	...	
Smith, John Robt.	Ballymore	Lieutenant	U.S. E.F.	
Wilson, Robert	Bricklieve	Private	Can. Force	Died.
BOYLE AND CLOGHER.				
Connolly, Jack		Private	R.I.R.	
Garland, Willie		Private	S.I.H.	
McDonald, Henry		Private	Con. Rangers	
Poynton, Basil		Lieutenant	Dub. Fusiliers	
Smith, F. F. S. Smith		Captain	I.M.S.	
Smith, Henry		Lieutenant		
Smith Melville J.		Lieutenant	R.A.	
Smith, W. A.		Captain	A.V.C.	
Stewart, Herbert		Sergeant	Canadians	
Watson, John H.		Sergeant	Royal Scots	
Watson, Wm. T.		Private	S.A. Rifles	
CASTLEBAR.				
Andrews, Robert	Banbridge	2nd Lieutenant	N.I. Horse	Killed in Action.
McHolmes, James	Ellison St., Castlebar	Sergeant	6th Conn. Rangers	Killed in Action.
Morrison, John Alex.	Castlebar	2nd Lieutenant	Dub. Fus.	4 Years' Service.
HOLLYMOUNT.				
Coupar, A. B.	Ashford	Private	Army Service Corps	
Coupar, R.	Scotland	Private	16th H.L. Inft.	
McIntosh, Alex.	Ashford	Private	I.G.	Wounded.
McIntosh, John	Ashford	Private	I.G.	Killed in Action.
Ireland, Thomas	Creagh	Private	Can. H.L. Inft.	Wounded.
KILLALA.				
Boyle, Robert M.	The Manse, Killala	Captain	2nd Royal Inn. Fus.	M.C. Twice W'ded.
Carson, Robert John	Killala	Private	I.G.	Killed in Action.
Carson, John	Newtonwhite, Killala	Private	R. Inn. Fus.	Twice Wounded.
Carson, Thomas E.	Ballintean, Killala	Private	I.G.	Twice Wounded.
Carson, Charles W.	Ballintean, Killala	Private	R. Inn. Fus.	
Leitch, Charles A.	Ballysakeery, Killala	Pilot	Royal Flying Corps	Killed in Action.
Leitch, Henry B. J.	Ballysakeery, Killala	Sergt.-Major	R. Irish Regt.	
Leitch, Oswald J.	Ballysakeery, Killala	Corporal	8th Royal Hussars	
Leitch, Wm. L.	Ballysakeery, Killala	Corporal	I.G.	Killed in Action.
Massey, T. H.	Court Hill, Killala	Capt. Surgeon	King's African Rifles	M.C.
Robertson, F. W.	Killala	Surg. Probationer	R.N.V.R.	
COLONIAL FORCES.				
Alexander, Wm.	Lisglennon, Killala	Corporal	3rd Aust. Light Horse	Wounded, Died.
Carson, S. G.	Newtonwhite, Killala	Captain	C.E.F	M.C.
Sharpe, R. Paton	Mullafarry, Killala	Corporal	C.E.F.	Killed in Action.
Sharpe, Thomas	Mullafarry, Killala	Sergeant	C.E.F.	Wounded.
SLIGO.				
Acheson, John	Keady, Armagh	Lieutenant	R.A.F.	
Blackwood, Arthur	Stephen St., Sligo	Private	36th (Ulster) Div. R.I.R.	Wounded and Pris.
Bryce, Wm.	753 Pollockshaws, G'gow	2nd Lieutenant	Machine Gun Corps	
Clarke, Alex.	Bridge St., Sligo	Corporal	R.S.F.	4 times Wounded.
Clarke, John	Bridge St., Sligo	Lance-Corporal	2nd Batt. S.R.	M.M. and Bar.
Clarke, Richard	Bridge St., Sligo	Gunner	R.F.A.	Wounded.
Crozier, Samuel	7 Ratcliffe St., Sligo	Private	R.I.F.	

CONNAUGHT PRESBYTERY.

SLIGO.

Name.	Home Address.	Rank.	Regiment, Battalion or Unit.	Remarks.
Cruickshank, Wm.	Gray's Inn. Sligo	Sergeant	R.A.V.C. 26th A.F.A.	M.S.
Cunningham, Robert	Fermoyle, Sligo	Co. Sergt.-Major	1/8th London Regt.	Killed in Action.
Kerr, Harold	Thornhill, Sligo	2nd Lieutenant	36th (Ulster) R.I.R.	
Lougheed, Alfred	Albert St., Sligo	Captain	Wiltshire Regt.	
MacArthur, James	Knox St., Sligo	Lieut.-Colonel	Essex Yeomanry	
McLean, James	Priestland, Co. Antrim	Lieutenant	R.F.A.	M.C. Killed.
McMeekin, Robert	Finnisklin, Sligo	Sub.-Lieutenant	R.N.R.	Twice Torpedoed.
McMeekin, Wm. J.	Finnisklin, Sligo	Lance-Corporal	R.I.F.	Prisoner of War.
Meldrum, Cosmo	John Street, Sligo	Private	Army O. Corps	1914 Star.
Meldrum, Gordon	John Street, Sligo	Driver	R.F.A.	
Meldrum, James	John Street, Sligo	Sergeant	A.O.C.	
Meldrum, John	John Street, Sligo	Private	A.O.C.	
Meldrum, Thomas	John Street, Sligo	Rifleman	6th Batt. R.I.R.	
Morrison, Fredk.	Cyprus Park Belfast	2nd Lieutenant	North Staff. Regt.	Wounded.
Murrow, Stuart	Albert Street, Sligo	Trooper	N.I.H.	
Perry, Wm.	1 William Street, Sligo	Driver	5th Aux. Bus. Co.	
Quin, James	Ulster Bank House, Sligo	Captain	R.A.M.C.	
Quin, Joseph	Ulster Bank House, Sligo	Surg. Prob.	R.N.	
Rankin, W. J.	Coleraine, Co. Derry	Private	R.A.F.	
Robertson, A. Linton	Kiltycooley, Sligo	M.R.C.V.S.	Royal Army Vet. Corps	Wounded.
Robertson, J. Gilfillen	Kiltycooley, Sligo	2nd Lieutenant	R.I.F.	Killed in Action.
Robertson, N. Alistair	Kiltycooley, Sligo	Private	2nd Royal Scots	Killed in Action.
Robertson, Walter O. D.	Kiltycooley, Sligo	Private	R.G.A.	
Reid, Robert	William Street, Sligo	Private	N.I.H.	
Reid, William	William Street, Sligo	Private	R.I.R.	Killed in Action.
Sinclair, Cadzow	The Mall, Sligo	Surgeon	R.N.	
Sinclair, James	The Mall, Sligo	2nd Lieutenant	R.G.A.	
Sinclair, Roy	The Mall, Sligo	Lieutenant	R.A.F.	Wounded.
Sinclair, Hugh Reid	The Mall, Sligo	Private	R.A.F.	
COLONIAL FORCES.				
Blackwood, John	Stephen Street, Sligo	Private	3rd B. Australians	Wounded.
Blackwood, Wm.	Stephen St., Sligo	Sergeant	Australian E.F.	
Paul, John McNeill	Wine Street, Sligo	Private	R.F.A., Canada	Died.
Robertson, James	Lynn's Place, Sligo	Private	Nairobi D.C., Brit. E. Africa	
Watters, James	The Manse, Sligo	Private	S.A. Heavy Artillery	Killed.
Thompson, David R.	6 Union Place, Sligo	Trooper	4th Garry Horse, Canada	
WESTPORT AND NEWPORT.				
Aitken, W. J. L.	Newport	Sub.-Lt. R.N.V.R.		Died.
Davidson, John	Westport	1st Engineer	R.N. Transport	
Girvin, James	Westport	Private	S. Lancashire	Pris. in Germany.
Newell, John	Rossmoney, Westport	Coastguard	Stoker, R.N.	
Simpson, James	Skene House, Ballyglass	Corporal	H.L.I.	
Simpson, William	Royculla, Westport	Lieutenant	H.L.I.	

CORK PRESBYTERY.

Name.	Home Address.	Rank.	Regiment, Battalion or Unit.	Remarks.
BANDON.				
Armstrong, William	95 Edinburgh St., Belfast	Sergeant	R.A.M.C.	
Bishop, Cecil	Castle Bernard	Gunner	R.F.A.	
Bishop, J. Harold	Castle Bernard	Driver	R.F.A.	
Boyle, Thomas	Kilbeg	Trooper	S.I.H.	
Boyle, William	Kilbeg	Private	A.S.C.	
Grieg, J.	Shannon Street	Sergeant	R. Marine Art.	
Harman, Robert	Myrtle Grove	A.B.	R.N.	
Johnston, Fred	Bandon	Gunner	R.F.A.	
McLean, George	Laragh	Gunner	R.F.A.	Died of Wounds.
McLean, John	Laragh	Rifleman	R.I.R.	Killed in Action.
McLean, Robert	Laragh	Private	Cheshire Regt.	Killed in Action.
Thomson, George	Kilbrogan	Private	R.A.F.	
Wilson, William	Bray	Sergeant	R.E.	
COLONIAL FORCES.				
Bishop, William	Castle Bernard	Private	Canadian Force	
Bunker, William E.	Castle Road	Trooper	U.S. Army	
Dixon, James	Bandon	Private	Australian Force	Died in Hospital.
Dixon, William	Bandon	Sergeant	Canadian Force	Died of Wounds.
Dow, William	Bandon	Private	Canadian Force	
Wyllie, Jack	Hill Ho., Dunmanway	Sergeant	King's African Rifles	

CORK PRESBYTERY. QUEEN STREET, CORK.

Name.	Home Address.	Rank.	Regiment, Battalion or Unit.	Remarks.
CORK (QUEEN STREET).				
Adam, Andrew				M.M.
Adam, James				
Adam, Robert				
Boyd, James			R.N.	
Boyd, Samuel			Canadian Rifle Brigade	Killed in Action.
Baker, Eddie			Canadian Ex. Force	
Baker, Jack			New Zealand Rif. Brig.	Killed in Action.
Birrell, Robert			M.G.C.	Wounded.
Burbridge, Henry			Middlesex	Wounded.
Cummins, Andrew			M.T. A.S.C.	
Cooper, George			Munster Fusiliers	Wounded.
Cooper, Louis			Connaught Rangers	Wounded.
Dalton, Richard			Canadian Pioneers	
Dalton, William			A.S.C.	
Greig, George			R.N. Transport	
Goodall, Archibald			R.N. Transport	
Gray, William				
Harper, Prof.		Lieutenant		Killed in Action.
Houston, Edmund			Connaught Rangers	Wounded.
Houston, Richard			Canadian Ex. Force	Prisoner of War.
Houston, Thomas			M.T. A.S.C.	
Hogg, Albert			R.M.F.	Wounded.
Hatton, Gerald			R.E.	
Hill, Isaac			R.D.F.	
Munro, John			R.S.R.	
Munro, Herbert			R.A.F.	
McCallum, Campbell			R.A.F.	
McNaughton, Hector			R.I.	
McArthur, Lindley			S.I.H.	
MacIlwraith, William			Mine Sweepers	
Mahony, George		Captain	I.M.S.	
Miller, J.			R.M.F.	Killed in Action.
Minto, Thomas			London Scottish	Died.
Paterson, John			H.L.I.	
Paterson, David			Cameron Highlanders	
Paterson, Alexander			Scots Guards	Killed in Action.
Rollo, John			R.A.	Prisoner of War.
Ross, John Popham				Wounded.
Redmond, Thomas			R.M.F.	Prisoner of War.
Souter, Peter		Lieutenant	Royal Scots	Wounded.
Welch, Thomas			M.T. A.S.C.	
Wyllie, John				Wounded.
Warriner, James			R.N.	
CORK (TRINITY CHURCH).				
Barrie, Alex. B.	10 Patrick Street	Chief Engineer	Transport Service	Killed in Action.
Beatson, James	11 Myrtle Hill Terrace	Engineer	R.N. Transport	
Beatson, Robert	11 Myrtle Hill Terrace	Engineer	R.N. Transport	
Bennie, Harold E.	Blackrock Road	Lieutenant	R. Marines	Died of Wounds.
Berry, Rowan J.	Frankfield Terrace	Lieutenant	S.I.H.	
Buchan, Walter J.	Alexandria Terrace	Corporal	O.T.C., Dublin Univ.	
Cairnduff, Andrew	Fernhurst Avenue	Lieutenant	R.A.F.	Prisoner of War.
Cairnduff, John	Fernhurst Avenue	Captain	Indian Army	Wounded.
Cairnduff, Norman	Fernhurst Avenue	Lieutenant	R.G.A.	Killed in Action.
Dale, John Francis	16 Morrison's Island	Lieutenant	R. Welsh Fus.	Wounded.
Flood, Wm. J. Lowe	Summerhill South	Lieutenant	Leinster Regt.	
Greadon, Arthur	5 Little William St.		R.N.	Drowned.
Hall, Norman	4 Sunmount	Lieutenant	R.I. Reg.	Wounded.
Hatton, Fred.	Douglas Road		Railway Brigade	
Henderson, George Logan	Ardrum	Private	R. In. Fus.	Wounded, M.C.
Henderson, Thomas	Ardrum	Private	R. Tank Corps	W'ded & Missing.
Highet, Dr. Hugh	Strawan Villas	Captain	R.A.M.C.	
Leavis, Henry	Ellerslie	Major	R.A.S.C.	
Lunham, Dr. John L.	Lotamore	Major	Indian Medical Service	
McCluskey, Alan Jas.	3 Ossery Place	Private	R.E.	
McCluskey, John Grieve	3 Ossery Place	Corporal	R.A.S.C.	
McElnay, George H.	1 Victoria Terrace	Lieutenant	R.D.F.	Wounded.
McKechnie, John W.	Buxton House	Driver	Mech. T. Corps	
McKenzie, Alastair	15 Myrtle Hill Terrace		R.N.R.	
McKenzie, James M.	15 Myrtle Hill Terrace	Captain	Indian Cavalry	M.C.
McMillan, Jas. Patterson	48 L. Glanmire Road	Private	Irish Guards	Wounded.
Mark, Ernest Campbell	4 Park Villas	Captain	R.G.A.	Gassed.
Mark, John M.	4 Park Villas	Surgeon-Dentist	R.N.V.R.	
Munro, Robert	Summerhill South	Lieutenant	R.I.F.	Wounded.
Murphy, John Howard B.	The Manse	Lieutenant	Egyptian Labour Corps	
Murray, Alexander	13 Telephone Terrace, Blarney	Private	Cameron Highlanders	
Patterson, William	29 Alexandria Villas	Private	R.M.F.	Wounded.
Ridge, Arthur	6 Sidneyville	Lieutenant	R.E.	
Ridge, Dr. Percy B.	6 Sidneyville	Captain	R.A.M.C.	Died.
Robinson, James	18 Crown Park	Captain	R.M.F.	

CORK PRESBYTERY. **TRINITY CHURCH, CORK.**

Name.	Home Address.	Rank.	Regiment, Battalion or Unit.	Remarks.
Robinson, Maurice	18 Crown Park	Lieutenant	Leinster Regt.	
Ross, Dr. George	Fernhurst Avenue	Major	R.A.M.C.	
Ross, Dr. Henry	Fernhurst Avenue	Colonel	Indian Medical Service	
Ross, Percy C.	Sunday's Well	Corporal	A.S.C.	
Smith, Dr. John B.	2 Verdon Place	Colonel	Indian Medical Service	
Sutton, Richard T.	Ellesmere	Lieutenant	R.I.F.	Killed in Action.
Thomson, Benjamin	Blarney	Private	W. Yorks	
Thomson, David M.	3 St. Helen's Terrace	Lieutenant	R. Berkshires	Wounded.
Thomson, Dr. John	3 St. Helen's Terrace	Captain	R.A.M.C.	
Thomson, Norman	3 St. Helen's Terrace	Private	A.S.C.	
Thompson, Dr. Logan	2 Strowan Villas	Captain	R.A.M.C.	M.C.
Tyrie, Donald Grant	6 Ferncliffe Villas	Lieutenant	R.N.V.R.	
Wallace, Alexander	Old Blackrock Road	Trooper	Queen's Light Hussars	Wounded.
Whitaker, Samuel	York House	Lieutenant	Connaught Rangers	
Wilson, James V.	1 Lansdown	Captain	R. Fus.	Wounded.
COLONIAL FORCES.				
Highet, Campbell McGregor	2 Strowan Villas	Lieutenant	Canadian Engineers	
Langlands, John G.	Richmond Hill	Corporal	S.A. Ex. Force	Wounded.
McKenzie, John K.	15 Myrtle Hill Terrace		N.Z. Engineers	
Mark, Arthur Russell	4 Park Villas	Lieutenant	Canadian R.A.F.	
Milligan, Jos. Edmund	70 Gardiner's Hill	Private	1st Canadians	Died of Wounds.
Murray, Thomas	Blarney	Lance-Corporal	Canadian Transport	
Smith, Louis G.	Egerton Villas	Private	Can. Vict. Rifles	Wounded.
FERMOY.				
Dixon, Charles George	Bawnaglough	2nd Lieutenant	R.I.	Killed in Action.
Flack, Rev. W. T., M.A.	Curragh Camp	C.F.	C.F.	
Heathcote, Stanley	Buxton	Sergt.-Major	A.S.C.	Men. in Des.
Kyle, David L., B.A., B.E.	RatheaIy Road	2nd Lieutenant	R.E.	Killed in Action.
McBride, William	Barrack Hill	Ass.-Paymaster	R.N.	
McBride, James Tait	Barrack Hill	Ass.-Paymaster	R.N.	
McCausland, Jas. Ed., M.D.	Coole Abbey	Surgeon	R.N.	
Tyers, Arthur	Newark	Sergeant	Leicester	Missing.
LISMORE.				
Glynn, Arthur	...	Private	R.I.F.	Killed in Action.
Glynn, Jack	...	Private	R.I.F.	
Grant, William	...	Private	English Regt.	
Young, John	...	Private	R.E.	
MALLOW.				
Robinson, Victor	R.I.C. Barracks, Castletownroche	Private	Irish Guards	
QUEENSTOWN.				
Elliott, James	Castlemary	Private	M.T.C.	
Humphreys, Carl	Rostellan	Private	K.R.R.	
Humphreys, Jim	...	Corporal	Irish Guards	Wounded.
McFie, Robert	Plunket Terrace	Mate	R.N.R., H.M. Tug "America"	Died.
McQueen, Campbell	Rushbrooks	Major	R.A.M.C.	M.C.
Ryan, Fred. C. P.	Plunket Terrace	Q.-M.-Sgt.	2nd Wiltshire Regt.	W'ded & Gassed.
Wilson, William	Ballincarrig	Private	Black Watch	Killed in Action.

DERRY PRESBYTERY.

Name.	Home Address.	Rank.	Regiment, Battalion or Unit.	Remarks.
BALLYARNETT.				
Bell, John	Brookhall	Corporal	R. In. Fus.	
Bell, R. J.	Silverdale	Corporal	R. In. Fus.	Wounded.
Bell, Samuel	Brookhall	Private	R. In. Fus.	
Burns, Andrew	Steelstown	Private	R. In. Fus.	Wounded.
Burns, David	Steelstown	Q.M. Sergt.	R.E.	Wounded.
Burns, Dysart	Steelstown	Gunner	Royal Marine	
Burns, James	Steelstown	Rifleman	R. In. Fus.	
Burns, John	Steelstown	Private	R. In. Fus.	Wounded.
Burns, Joseph	Steelstown	Lance-Corporal	R. In. Fus.	Wounded.
Burnside, Walter	Steelstown	Sergeant	R.G.A.	W'ded and Pris.
Byres, James	The Collon	Private	R. In. Fus.	Killed in Action.

DERRY PRESBYTERY.

BALLYARNETT.

Name.	Home Address.	Rank.	Regiment, Battalion or Unit.	Remarks.
Carruthers, David	The Collon	Gunner	R.G.A.	Wounded.
Christie, Daniel	Ballyarnett	Private	R. In. Fus.	Wounded.
Colhoun, I.	Phillip Street, Derry	Private	R. In. Fus.	Killed in Action.
Crockett, John	Dundrain	Private	R. In. Fus.	Wounded.
Crockett, Joseph A.	Dundrain	Gunner	Machine Gun Section	Killed in Action.
Dinsmore, John	Shantallow	Sergeant	R. In. Fus.	Killed in Action.
Doak, John	Shantallow	Private	Black Watch (R.H.)	Killed in Action.
Donnell, Thomas	Boomhall	Private	R. In. Fus.	Wounded.
Falconer, Samuel	Shantallow	Private	A. and S. Highlanders	
Gamble, Robert	Myrtle Cottage, Collon	Corporal	R. In. Fus.	Wounded.
Gray, John	The Glen, Derry	Private	R. In. Fus.	Died of Wounds.
Henry, Robert	Collon Terrace, Derry	Private	R.I.R.	
King, Robert	Lenamore, Muff	Private	1st R.I.R.	
Laird, J.	Lenamore, Muff	Gunner	R.G.A.	
Long, Harry	Ardmore, Muff	Cadet	Cadet Corps	
Lyttle, Jack	Ballyarnett	A.B.	Royal Naval Division	Wounded.
MacBride, Thomas	Shantallow	Private	Transport, Manchester Regt.	
MacCarter, R. A.	Ture	Gunner	R.H.A.	
MacClintock, William	Gallagh	Private	R. In. Fus.	Killed in Action.
MacFeely, Robert	Ballynagard	Lance-Corporal	R.I.F.	Wounded.
McKimm, John	Ballynagard	Private	1st Royal Marines	W'ded and Pris.
Mitchell, John	Michellstown, Ture	Private	R. In. Fus.	Killed in Action.
Montgomery, Robert	Boomhall	A.B.	R.N.	
Neely, William	Shantallow	Private	R. In. Fus.	Wounded.
Ramsey, Jack	Shantallow	Private	R. In. Fus.	
Smyth, James	Boomhall	Private	R. In. Fus.	Wounded.
Starritt, Samuel	Troy	Sergeant	R. In. Fus.	Gassed.
Stewart, Andrew	Springtown	Gunner	R.F.A.	
Struthers, Alexander	Belmont	Private	R. In. Fus.	Wounded.
Struthers, James	Belmont	Gunner	E.R.G.A.	Wounded.
Struthers, Robert	Belmont	Sapper	R.E.	Wounded.
Struthers, Allan	Belmont	Mine Sweepers	R.N.V.R.	Lost an eye.
Thompson, James	Shantallow	Private	R. In. Fus.	Wounded.
Wilson, Hugh	Ballyarnett	Private	R. In. Fus.	Wounded.
Wylie, Thomas	The Misk, Derryvane	Private	R. In. Fus.	Wounded.
Wylie, William	The Misk, Derryvane	A.B.	Royal Naval Division	Wounded.
COLONIAL FORCES.				
Cunningham, John	Gt. James' St., Derry	Private	Can. Inf.	Died.
Cunningham, R. A.	Gt. James' St., Derry	Private	Can. M. Amb. Corps	
Gallagher, Thomas	Springfield	Corporal	Can. Force	
Kenna, Robert	Nicholson Square	Private	Can. Highlanders	Killed in Action.
Vine, James A.	Ballynagard	Private	Australian Inf.	Wounded.
BUNCRANA.				
Cole, Albert W.	Buncrana	Driver	8th Army Brigade, Can.	
Crawford, Ernest	Victoria Park		M.T A.S.C.	
Johnston, H. W.	Buncrana	Lieutenant	5th R. In. Fus.	
Johnston, J. A. L.	Buncrana	Captain	9th R.I.F.	Wounded.
Mee, Ernest Campbell	Buncrana	Lieutenant	Duke of Wellington's W.R.	Killed in Action.
Mee, J. Norman	Buncrana	Lieutenant	31st Batt. Can.	
Wright, David	Lisfannan	Lieutenant	9th R.I.F.	Prisoner.
BURT.				
Buchanan, M. S.	Inchlevel	Lieutenant	9th R.I.F.	Wounded.
Buchanan, Stewart		Private	11th R. In. Fus.	Killed in Action.
Buchanan, Thomas		Lieutenant	R.A.F.	
Buchanan, William	Inchlevel	1st Lieutenant	3rd Leinsters	
Downey, Joseph	Derry	Private	10th R. In. Fus.	Killed in Action.
Holden, Joseph	Skeog	Private	11th R. In. Fus.	
Lynch, Samuel	Speenogue	Lance-Corporal	N.I.H.	
McDowell, Robert J.	Inchlevel	Private	11th R. In. Fus.	Pris. in Germany.
McNutt, John	Burnfoot, Derry	Private	N.I.H.	
McNutt, William, B.A.	Hillhall, Lisburn	Captain	Army Chaplains' Depart.	
Robinson, Andrew	Toolette	Corporal	R.E.	Wounded.
Robinson, Calvin	Toolette	Private	11th R. In. Fus.	Wounded.
Robinson, Percy	Toolette	Private	10th R. In. Fus.	
Ross, Leslie N.	Burt Manse, Derry	Lieutenant	16th R.I.R.	Wounded.
Walker, William	Coshquin	Private	11th R. In. Fus.	Wounded.
Wallace, Joseph	Derry	Private	11th R. In. Fus.	
COLONIAL FORCES.				
Buchanan, John	Inchlevel	Private	49th Canadians	Died.
Robinson, Ernest	Toolette	Trooper	New Zealand Conting.	Wounded.
Ross, George H.	Burt Manse, Derry	Lieutenant	10th Canadians	Wounded.

DERRY PRESBYTERY.   **CROSSROADS.**

Name.	Home Address.	Rank.	Regiment, Battalion or Unit.	Remarks.
CROSSROADS.				
Campbell, Thomas J.	Castruse, Bogay	Private	R. In. Fus.	Wounded.
Creswell, Thomas	Castruse, Bogay	Private	R. In. Fus.	
McGowan, Joseph	Monglass, Bogay	Private	R. In. Fus.	Killed.
McGowan, Samuel	Bohillion, Burt	Private	R. In. Fus.	
McGowan, Samuel	Brayhead, Derry	Private	R. In. Fus.	
Porter, Robert	Castruse, Bogay	Sergeant	R. In. Fus.	
Robb, William	Gortlush, Bogay	Private	R. In. Fus.	
Rutherford, James	Garshuey, Bogay	Private	R. In. Fus.	Killed.
COLONIAL FORCES.				
Black, Andrew	Ballyhaskey	Sergt.-Major	2nd Co. Canadians	
Dougherty, James	Creevagh, Derry	Private	4th Co. Canadians	W'ded & Missing.
McGowan, William	Braehead, Derry	Private	1st Co. Canadians	
FIRST DERRY.				
Anderson, James	12 Barrack Street		R.N.	
Anderson, John	20 Dark Lane	Gunner	R.F.A.	
Anderson, Robert	20 Dark Lane	Driver	R.F.A.	
Anderson, Robert	31 Windmill Terrace	Private	R. In. Fus·	Wounded.
Anderson, Robert	12 Barrack Street	Private	R. Irish Regt.	
Anderson, Samuel	12 Barrack Street	Sergeant	R.F.A	Wounded.
Anderson, William	12 Barrack Street	Private	R In Fus	Killed in Action
Anderson, William John	Fountain Street	Private	R. Irish Regt.	
Andrews, Herbert	1 Abercorn Place	Lance-Corporal	R. In. Fus.	
Andrews, Matthew	1 Abercorn Place	Private	R. In. Fus.	
Andrews, Samuel	5 Charlotte Street	Corporal	Northumberland Fus.	
Ballantine, J. Douglas	Marlboro' Street	Sub.-Lieut.	R.N.R.	
Ballantine, William	Fountain Street	Private	R. In. Fus.	Killed in Action.
Bell, Robert		Private	R. In. Fus.	
Bovaird, John R.	Marlboro' Terrace	Private	R.A.F.	
Braid, William		Private	R. In. Fus.	Killed in Action.
Brown, A. A.	39 Barry Street	Lance-Corporal	Seaforth Highlanders	
Brown, James	67 Fountain Street	Private	R. In. Fus.	
Brown, James	46 Fountain Street	Private	R. In. Fus.	Wounded.
Brown, R. E.	Fairman Place	Lance-Corporal	R. Ir. Fus.	
Brown, William John	Rosemount Avenue	Sub.-Lieut.	R.N.	
Browne, L.D.S.I., David John	28 Pump Street	Captain	R. In. Fus.	
Buchanan, David	Alt-an-aros	Lieutenant	Seaforth Highlanders	Killed in Action.
Burns, William		Private	R. In. Fus	
Burnside, John	31 Lewis Street	Private	R. In. Fus.	
Burnside, Joseph	High Street	Sergeant	R. In. Fus.	
Byers, Robert		Private	R. In. Fus.	
Caldwell, John F.	May Street	Lieutenant	R. Irish Fus.	
Caldwell, John V.	Victoria Road	Private	Lothian and Border Horse	
Caldwell, S. J.	Alexandria Terrace	Lieutenant	E. African Forces	
Campbell, James	28 Phillip Street	Sub.-Lieut.	R.N.	
Campbell, John	2 Glasgow Street	Private	R. In. Fus.	
Campbell, Samuel	28 Phillip Street	Private	R. In. Fus.	Gassed.
Carson, Robert	Nicholson Square	R.Q.M.S.	5th Lancers	
Carruth, Matthew	Model School	Lieutenant	R. Ir. Fus.	Killed in Action.
Colhoun, James	Alt-an-righ	Major	R. In. Fus.	M.C.
Colhoun, John H.	Alt-an-righ	Major	R.F.A.	
Colhoun, William A.	Alt-an-righ	Captain	29th Punjab	M.C. and Bar.
Colhoun, James	21 Fountain Street	Private	R. In. Fus.	
Crawford, Charles O.	Northland Road	Lieutenant	R.I.R.	W'ded., M.C. & Bar
Crawford, George		Private	R. In. Fus.	
Creswell, Andrew	1 Gordon Terrace	Sergeant	R. In. Fus.	
Creswell, Henry		Private	R. In. Fus.	
Creswell, Henry C. P.	45 Marlboro' Street	Lieutenant	Canadian Rifles	
Creswell, John	Hogg's Folly	Private	R. In. Fus.	Killed in Action.
Creswell, Samuel	1 Gordon Terrace	Private	R. In. Fus.	Wounded.
Creswell, William James	4 Hogg's Folly	Lance-Corporal	R. In. Fus.	Killed in Action.
Crockett, William	28 Elmwood Terrace	Sapper	R.E.	
Currie, David	14 Stewart's Terrace	Coy. Sgt.-Major	R. In. Fus.	
Currie, George	14 Stewart's Terrace	Private	I. Guards	
Currie, John	14 Stewart's Terrace	Rifleman	N.Z. Rifles	
Dinsmore, Edmund	London Street	Lieutenant	R.A.M.C.	Died in Camp.
Diver, George	5 North Street	Private	R. In. Fus.	
Diver, Thos. Wilson	24 Creggan Road	Lance-Corporal	R. In. Fus.	Killed in Action. M.M. and Cert. for Gallantry.
Dougherty, Joseph	Foyle Road	Private	R. In. Fus.	
Dougherty, Robert	Foyle Road	Private	R. In. Fus.	
Douglas, George		Private	R. In. Fus.	Killed in Action.
Downs, John	15 Stewart's Terrace	Drummer	R. In. Fus.	Killed in Action.
Downs, Wm. Maurice	15 Stewart's Terrace	Sapper	R.E.	
Duffin, Douglas	Belfast Bank	Q.-M. Sergeant	Black Watch	
Duncan, R. G.	Marlboro' Street	Flight-Cadet	R.A.F.	
Dunseath, James	Albert Place	Private	R. In. Fus.	
Edgar, John	16 Windmill Terrace	Private	R. In. Fus.	Wounded.

DERRY PRESBYTERY. FIRST DERRY.

Name.	Home Address.	Rank.	Regiment, Battalion or Unit.	Remarks.
Edmiston, R. Max.	Maybrook	Lieutenant	Canadians	Wounded.
Elliott, Thomas	8 Lewis Street	Sapper	R.E.	
English, Maurice G.	5 Marlboro' Street	Lieutenant	R.N.A.S.	Killed in Action.
Fulton, Ernest	34 Edenmore Street	Lance-Corporal	H.L.I.	
Fulton, Thomas A.	34 Edenmore Street	Sergeant	R.A.M.C.	
Gillies, David	10 Crawford Square	Captain	R.A.M.C.	
Gillies, John B., D.S.	10 Crawford Square	Captain	R.A.M.C.	
Glenn, James	Albert Place	Private	R. In. Fus.	Killed in Action.
Glenn, Richard	Albert Place	Private	R. In. Fus.	
Grant, Douglas J.	5 Clarence Avenue	Private	King's Shropshire L. Horse	
Greer, D. Niven	1 Woodleigh Terrace	E.R.A.	R.N.	
Greer, Fred. J.	1 Woodleigh Terrace	Cadet	Inns of Court O.T.C.	
Greer, Stewart P.	1 Woodleigh Terrace	Lieutenant	M.G.C.	Wounded.
Greer, Wm. Nevin	1 Woodleigh Terrace	Captain	R.A.M.C.	O.B.E.
Grisold, Edward	Victoria Road	Private	Can. Survey Section	
Hamilton, John P.	...	A/Corporal	R.A.F.	
Hamilton, Robert	19 Ebrington Street	Sergeant	R. In. Fus.	
Hamilton, William	26 Belview Avenue	Gunner	R.G.A	
Hassan, David	11 Carrigan's Lane	Private	H.L.I.	
Hassan, James	11 Carrigan's Lane	Lance-Corporal	R.I.R.	Wounded.
Hassan, William	11 Carrigan's Lane	Corporal	R.Dub. Fus.	
Hastings, Albert V.	Templemore Park	Lieutenant	1st R. Dub. Fus.	
Hastings, Thomas E.	Templemore Park	Captain	R. In. Fus.	M.C.
Henderson, Arthur A.	Bayview Terrace	Private	R.A.S.C.	
Hogg, G. C.	Lisowen	Private	Canadians	
Howieson, Thomas	1 Cedar Street	Private	R. In. Fus.	
Huffington, Albert	7 Millar Street	Private	R.A.F.	
Huffington, William J.	7 Millar Street	Lance-Corporal	Black Watch	
Hunter, John A.	29 Lewis Street	Private	R. In. Fus.	Gassed.
Hunter, Thomas	29 Lewis Street	Private	R. In. Fus.	
Hunter, William W.	29 Lewis Street	Driver	R.F.A.	
Hunter, D. N.	37 Edenmore Street	Sapper	R.E.	
Johnston, H. Wallace	Buncrana	Lieutenant	R. In. Fus.	Wounded.
Johnston, J. A. L.	Buncrana	Captain	R. In. Fus.	Wounded.
Johnston, J. A. Weir	Crawford's Square	Major	A.O.C.	
Jordan, William	Great James' Street	Sapper	R.E.	
Joyce, Thos. Victor	13 Fairman Place	Captain	H.L.I.	
Kelly, Robert	Mountjoy Street	Sergeant	R. Inn. Fus.	Killed in Action.
Kennedy, S. S.	9 Simpson's Brae	Lieut.-Colonel	R.A.F.	O.B.E.
Killen, Jas. M., F.R.C.S.	Northland Road	Captain	R.A.M.C.	
Kincaid, David	21 Fairman Place	Lieutenant	R.I.R.	
Kincade, George	72 Fountain Street	Lance-Corporal	R.E.	
Kincade, Robert	72 Fountain Street	Private	R.I.R.	
Kyle, David Logan	Woodleigh Terrace	Lieutenant	R.E.	Killed in Action.
Lang, Christopher D.	41 Clooney Terrace	Lieutenant	R.A.F.	
Lang, Leonard	41 Clooney Terrace	Private	Can. Garr. Art.	
Lang, Norman	41 Clooney Terrace	Private	R.A.S.C.	
Lang, Walter	41 Clooney Terrace	Sergeant	R.F.A.	
Lapsley, James H.	Henry Street	Private	R. In. Fus.	
Lapsley, Samuel E.	Henry Street	Sergeant	R. In. Fus.	M.S.M.
Lawrence, George	21 Orchard Row	Sergeant	R. In. Fus.	
Lindsay, George F.	Elagh House	Lance-Corporal	R.I.R.	
Lindsay, Robert A.	Elagh House	Corporal	17th Lancers	
Loughlin, J.	Ivy Terrace	Private	R.A.S.C.	
Lumsden, John	2 Orchard Row	Lance-Corporal	R. In. Fus.	
Lynch, Robert J.	19 Ebrington Street	Private	Labour Batt.	
Lyons, William C.	Lawrence Hill	Captain	R.A.M.C.	
MacAlister, Sidney C.	Fern Cottage, Creggan	Lieutenant	Mah. Light. Inf.	
McCaughey, James	34 Abercorn Road	Cadet	D. University O.T.C.	
McClintock, James	Harding Street	Private	R. In. Fus.	Killed in Action.
McClure, Ernest	Beechview Avenue	Lieutenant	R. In. Fus.	Killed in Action.
McClure, Norman	Beechview Avenue	Q.M. Sergeant	R.F.A.	
McDermott, Charles	Pitt Street	Private	R. In. Fus.	Wounded.
McDermott, William	Pitt Street	Private	R. In. Fus.	
McDermott, David	Pitt Street	Private	R. In. Fus.	
McDermott, Jacob	Pitt Street	Private	R. In. Fus.	
McGarrigle, George	96 Spencer Road	Lance-Corporal	R.A.M.C.	
McGarrigle, George, Jun.	96 Spencer Road	Gunner	R.F.A.	
McGarrigle, Matthew	96 Spencer Road	Private	R. In. Fus.	Wounded.
McGranahan, J. Benson	Crawford's Square	Captain	R.A.M.C.	
McGranaahan, James N.	Crawford's Square	Lieutenant	R.I.R.	M.C.
McGregor, Alex.	9 Kennedy Street	Corporal	R. In. Fus.	Wounded.
McGregor, John	5 Barrack Street	Private	R. In. Fus.	Killed in Action.
McGregor, Samuel	5 Barrack Street	Private	R. In. Fus.	Killed in Action.
McGregor, William R.	5 Barrack Street	Lance-Corporal	Canadians	
McHugh, James	Creggan Road	Private	R.A.M.C.	
Macintosh, Norman D.	Northland Road	Lieutenant	R.E.	
Mackey, Samuel	...	Lieutenant	R. In. Fus.	
McKinley, John	25 Moore Street	Sergeant	R. In. Fus.	
McKinley, Thomas A.	1 Moore Street	Corporal	Scottish Rifles	Wounded.
McLaughlin, W. J.	Foyle Road	Lieutenant	R.I.R	Wounded.
McLean, A. D.	5 Demesne Terrace	Lieutenant	Queen's R.W. Surreys	
McLean, Matthew	5 Demesne Terrace	Sergeant	Canadians	
MacMaster, John S.	3 College Avenue	Lieutenant	107th T. Mortar Batt.	

DERRY PRESBYTERY.   FIRST DERRY.

Name.	Home Address.	Rank.	Regiment, Battalion or Unit.	Remarks.
MADILL, JOSEPH	West End Park	Corporal	R.E.	
MATHERS, WILLOUGHBY	...	Corporal	Black Watch	Wounded.
MAXWELL, A. C.	Northland Road	Private	10th Can. Signal Sec.	
MAXWELL, A. F.	Northland Road	Lieutenant	R.I.F.	
MAXWELL, ERNEST V.	Northland Road	Private	R.A.M.C.	
MAXWELL, J. C.	Northland Road	Sergeant	N.Z. Med. Corps	
MAXWELL, C. A.	14 Bennett Street	E.R.A.	R.N.	
MILLAR, JAMES	Farm Hill, Groarty	Sergeant	Australian Light Horse	
MILLAR, WILLIAM	Farm Hill, Groarty	Lieutenant	R.I.F.	
NEELY, SAMUEL	Rosemount	Sapper	R.E.	
NEILL, JAMES	Fountain Street	Private	R. In. Fus.	Killed in Action.
NELSON, JOHN	Clarendon Street	Private	N.I.H.	
NEWELL, PETER BROWN	Aberfoyle Terrace	Private	Cameron Highlanders	
NORRIS, JOHN	34 Fountain Street	Private	R. In. Fus.	Killed in Action.
ORR, ALEX.	14 Mountjoy Street	Driver	R.F.A.	Wounded.
ORR, JAMES S.	Glasgow	Sergeant	R.F.A.	Wounded, M.M. & Cert.
ORR, ROBINSON	14 Mountjoy Street	Sapper	R.E.	Gassed.
OWENS, RICHARD	Fountain Street	Sergeant	R. In. Fus.	Killed in Action.
PILGRIM, JAMES	Cedar Street	Sergeant	R. Scots Fus.	
PORTER, GEORGE	32 Lower Bennett St.	Lieutenant	R. In. Fus.	
PORTER, JAMES	32 Lower Bennett St.	Sergeant	R. In. Fus.	Killed in Action, Cert. for Gall.
PORTER, SAMUEL	32 Lower Bennett St.	A.B.	R.N.	
PORTER, THOMAS A.	32 Lower Bennett St.	L.S.	R.N.	
REED, ROBERT E.	15 Princes Street	Private	P.O. Rifles	Died in Camp.
REID, FOREST	The Elms	Private	Canadians	
ROBERTS, CHARLES	Fort James	Private	R.A.F.	
ROBERTS, DAVID R.	Northland Road	Captain	R.A.M.C.	
RUTHERFORD, JACK R. S.	Barrack Street	Lance-Corporal	M.G.C.	Wounded.
SEMPLE, J. R.	Glenavon, Creggan	Lieutenant	Rifle Brigade	Gassed.
SEMPLE, WILLIAM J.	Glenavon, Creggan	Lance-Corporal	R.E.	
SHEATH, JOSEPH	Orchard Row	Private	Hants Regt.	
SHEPPARD, RALPH	Park Avenue	Lance-Corporal	R. In. Fus.	Killed in Action.
SHIELDS, FRANCIS	Wapping Lane	Sergeant	R. In. Fus.	
SHIELDS, ROBERT	Wapping Lane	Private	R.A.F.	
SHIELDS, WILLIAM	Moat Street	Private	R.A.F.	Killed in Action.
SIMMONS, F. S.	Rose Cottage, Waterside	Sub.-Lieutenant	R.N.	
SIMMONS, J. GLASSON	Rose Cottage, Waterside	E.R.A.	R.N.	
SMITH, JAMES	...	Private	R. In. Fus.	
SMITH, R. J.	Charlotte Street	Private	15th Worcesters	
SMYTH, JOHN B.	7 Rosemount Terrace	Private	R. Irish Regt.	
SMYTH, SAMUEL J.	7 Rosemount Terrace	Private	M.G.C.	
SMYTH, WILLIAM G.	7 Rosemount Terrace	Q.M. Sergeant	M.T. R.A.S.C.	
SPROTT, THOMAS	Portadown	Sergeant	R.A.M.C.	Killed in Action.
STARRETT, DAVID	5 Barrack Street	Private	R. In. Fus.	
STARRETT, JAMES	27 Princes Street	Private	R. Scots	
STEVENSON, ARCHD. McC.	2 Sydney Terrace	Lieutenant	M.T. A.S.C.	
STEVENSON, DAVID	The Collon	Gunner	R.F.A.	
STEVENSON, HUGH	The Collon	Lieutenant	Lancashire Fus.	Killed in Action.
STEVENSON, LEONARD W. H.	Hampstead Hall	Lieutenant	R. In. Fus.	Killed in Action, M.C.
STEVENSON, MAURICE	Hampstead Hall	Captain	Bengal Lancers	
STEWART, J. C.	Clarendon Street	Lieutenant	N.I.H.	
STEWART, WILLIAM	Bennett Street	Drummer	R. In. Fus.	
SWEENY, JAMES Y.	Clarendon Street	Lieutenant	78th Canadians	Wounded.
SWEENY, T. CAMPBELL	Clarendon Street	Lieutenant	R. In. Fus.	Wounded, M.C.
TAYLOR, JOHN	High Street	Lieutenant	R. In. Fus.	Wounded, M.C.
THOMPSON, JAMES	Shantallow	Private	R. In. Fus.	
TILLIE, ARNOLD REED	Elstow	Flight-Com.	R.A.F.	Killed in Action.
TILLIE, JOHN ARCHD.	Elstow	Lieutenant	Black Watch	Killed in Action.
TILLIE, TALBOT LEE	Elstow	Captain	Cameronians	
TILLIE, WM. KINGSLEY	Elstow	Lieut.-Colonel	M.G.C.	M.C., D.S.O.
TILLIE, CHAS. GORDON	Duncreggan	Captain	R. In. Fus.	Killed in Action.
TORRENS, ALEX.	28 Elmwood Terrace	Sapper	R.E.	
TORRENS, JOSEPH	Omagh	Corporal	R. In. Fus.	
WALKER, SAMUEL	Belfast Bank	Lieutenant	Black Watch	
WALLACE, ALEX.	46 Creggan Road	Private	R.A.F.	
WALLACE, JOSEPH	46 Creggan Road	Private	R. In. Fus.	
WALLACE, ROBERT	11 Albert Street	Sergeant	R.E.	
WALLACE, WILLIAM	46 Creggan Road	Private	R. In. Fus.	
WILLIAMSON, LAWRENCE	Clarence Avenue	Lieutenant	H.L.I.	
WILSON, R. H.	7 North Street	Bombardier	R.G.A.	Wounded, Gassed.
WILSON, THOMAS	22 Lewis Street	Drummer	R. In. Fus.	
WILSON, W. J.	Abercorn Road	Lieutenant	R. In. Fus.	
WILSON, W.	Fountain Street	Private	2nd Cheshires	
WYLIE, BERTIE	8 Albert Place	Sergeant	R. In. Fus.	Wounded.
WYLIE, JOHN	8 Albert Place	Gunner	R.G.A.	Wounded.
SECOND DERRY.				
ALEXANDER, SAMUEL	14 Princes Street	2nd Lieutenant	N.I.H.	
ALLEN, JOHN	23 Glasgow Terrace	Private	R.E.	
ALLEN, ROBERT R.	...	...	...	Killed in Action.

DERRY PRESBYTERY.

SECOND DERRY.

Name.	Home Address.	Rank.	Regiment, Battalion or Unit.	Remarks.
Barker, William Alex.	Lawrence Hill	Cadet	D.U.O.T.C.	
Barnett, Edward	43 Lower Bennett Street	Private	R.E. Signal Corps	
Barnett, William	43 Lower Bennett Street	Private	10th R. In. Fus.	Wounded.
Beatty, Richard	7 De Burgh Terrace	Private	Canadian Dragoons	
Beatty, Thomas	7 De Burgh Terrace	Private	Canadian Dragoons	Killed in Action.
Best, Walter George Kelly	Sackville Street	2nd Lieutenant	1/2 R. In. Fus.	
Bingham, Andrew	7 College Terrace	Private	N.I.H.	
Boggs, James	5 Asylum Road	Private	Black Watch	Wounded.
Boyd, James	8 Mary Street	Private	10th R. In. Fus.	Killed in Action.
Boyd, John	8 Mary Street	2nd Lieutenant	9th R.I.F.	Wounded.
Burnside, Alex.	53 Argyle Street	Private	A.S.C.	
Burnside, Charles	Sheriff's Mtn.	Private	Motor Transport	
Burnside, Harry				Killed in Action.
Burnside, Walter	20 Edenmore Street	Private	10th R. In. Fus.	
Calderwood, William C.	12 Laburnum Terrace	Corporal	12th R. In. Fus.	
Chambers, Fredk. William	Clarence Avenue	Lieutenant	R.F.C.	Wounded.
Chambers, James	4 Carrigan's Lane	Corporal	2nd R. In. Fus.	
Chambers, Joseph	65 Abercorn Road	Sergeant	N.I.H.	
Conn, Thomas	Aberfoyle Terrace	Boy Artificer	R.N.	
Connor, William C.	4 Albert Place	Ordinary Seaman	H.M.S. "Royal Oak"	
Connor, William J.				
Cooke, Andrew	37 Clarendon Street	Sergeant	R.A.F.	
Cordner, George	6 Abercorn Road	Private	R.F.A.	
Cottrell, Benjamin	8 Northland Terrace	Private	Middlesex	Killed in Action.
Crockett, Charles Love	Templemore Park	2nd Lieutenant	12th R. In. Fus.	Killed in Dublin.
Crockett, John A.	Templemore Park	Lieutenant	9th R. In. Fus.	
Cully, Andrew	13 Westland Avenue	Corporal	10th R. In. Fus	Prisoner of War.
Dickey, Eric	58 Burton Hill, Melton Mowbray, Leicester	Flight Sub.-Lieut.	R.N.A.S,	Wounded.
Douglas, Robert Martin	131 Creggan Road	Private	3rd R. In. Fus.	Gassed.
Dunlop, Edgar	c/o J. Dunlop, Buncrana	Private	Motor Transport	Wounded.
Frankland, Arthur	33 Marlboro' Street	Lance-Corporal	Signal Coy., R.E.	
Galbraith, Joseph	20 Creggan Road	Private	Auxiliary Horse Transport	
Gamble, John	34 Chamberlain Street	Private	R.G.A.	Wounded.
Gardiner, James	Richmond Villas, Meadowbank Avenue	Private	R.A.F.	
Gentle, Andrew	117 Foyle Road	Private	K.O.S.B.	Killed in Action.
Gentle, Neil	117 Foyle Road	Private	Black Watch	Killed in Action.
Hall, James Henry	7 Asylum Road	A.B. Seaman	H.M.S. "Paladin"	
Hall, Lindsay	7 Asylum Road	Lance-Corporal	10th R. In. Fus.	Wounded.
Henderson, Samuel	c/o James Rankin, 82 Michelbairne Ter.	A. B. Seaman	H.M.S. "Albemarle"	
Kennedy, James	24 Governor Road	Private	Rifle Brigade	
Kilgore, James	35 Governor Road	Sergeant	10th R. In. Fus.	
Kilgore, Robert	18 Mary Street	Private	2nd H.L.I.	Wounded.
Laird, James	Sheriff's Mtn.	Corporal	10th R. In. Fus.	Wounded.
Lee, Robert	Sackville Street	Private	Auxiliary Horse Transport	
McAlonen, John E.				
McCarter, John	6 Demesne Terrace	2nd Lieutenant	9th R. In. Fus.	Killed in Action.
McComb, William	10 Upper George Street	Sergeant	A.S.C.	Wounded.
McCullagh, Wm. Lennox	Demesne Terrace	Private	R.F.A.	
McCurdy, William	Springtown	Private	R.F.A.	Wounded twice.
Martin, John L.	G.P.O.	Private	R.E.	
Miller, Alex.	73 Fountain Street	Lance-Corporal	10th R. In. Fus.	Killed in Action.
Mitchell, Jack	26 Governor Road	Private	17th R.I.R.	
Mitchell, Robert A.	77 Long Tower Street	Corporal	8th R.I.R.	Prisoner of War.
Montgomery, Alec R.	De Burgh Terrace	Corporal	R.F.A.	
Montgomery, Jack M.	De Burgh Terrace	2nd Lieutenant	10th R. In. Fus.	Died.
Neely, Adam	213 Bishop's Street	Corporal	11th R. In. Fus.	Wounded.
Neely, William J.				
Nicholl, Matthew	10 Queen Street	2nd Lieutenant	R.A.F.	Wounded.
Nicholl, William	10 Queen Street	Flight-Cadet	R.A.F.	Wounded.
Orr, Harry	6 Charlotte Street	Sergeant	10th R. In. Fus.	Prisoner of War.
Paris, Henry	M'Crea-Magee College	Sgt. & Drill Instr.		
Porter, Robert	The Farm	Corporal	3rd R.I.F.	
Rankin, John A.	39 Francis Street	Sergeant	10th R. In. Fus.	Wounded.
Reilly, Edward	12 Mary Street	Private	R.I.R.	
Reilly, William				
Robb, David	Springtown	Private	R.A.F.	
Robb, John	Springtown	Private	R.F.A.	
Robb, William	Springtown	Lance-Corporal	Canadians	Killed in Action.
Roulston, Andrew	Park Avenue	Gunner	R.G.A.	
Roulston, Robert	Park Avenue	Private	26th Royal Fusiliers	Killed in Action.
Speer, George	Ballymaconragh	Private	A.S.C.	
Speers, George	21 Lewis Street	Private	R.A.F.	
Speers, Thomas	21 Lewis Street	Private	R.N.A.S.	
Steele, Andrew	Academy Terrace	Sergeant	10th R. In. Fus.	
Thompson, David	4 Marlboro' Street	Sergeant	A.S.C.	
Thompson, John	5 Upper Nassau Street	Private	1st R. In. Fus.	Wounded.
Thompson, Robert	5 Upper Nassau Street	Private	10th R. In. Fus.	Wounded & Gassed
Walker, Adam	Coshquin	Private	A.S.C.	
Walker, David John	Coshquin	Private	Cameron Highlanders	Died.
White, D. Gordon	Clarence Avenue	2nd Lieutenant	R. In. Fus.	Killed in Action.
White, Wilfred	Clarence Avenue	2nd Lieutenant	R.I.F.	

DERRY PRESBYTERY. SECOND DERRY.

Name.	Home Address.	Rank.	Regiment, Battalion or Unit.	Remarks.
WILEY, ALEX.	Aberfoyle Terrace	A.B. Seaman	R.N.	Wounded.
WILEY, FRED.	Aberfoyle Terrace	Lance-Corporal	3rd R. In. Fus.	
WILEY, WILLIAM	Aberfoyle Terrace	Purser	Canadian Transport Service	
WILSON, JAMES	3 Cranagh Terrace	Private	A.S.C.	
WRAY, D. H.	Carrick, Limavady	Captain	1st R. Irish Regt.	Killed in Action.
WRAY, E. J.	Carrick, Limavady	Private	1st Canadian Mounted Rifles	Prisoner of War.
WRAY, HERBERT H.	Carrick, Limavady	2nd Lieutenant	East Lancs.	
WRAY, W. L.	Carrick, Limavady	Lieutenant	72nd Seaforth Highlanders	Wounded.
DERRY, GREAT JAMES' STREET.				
ANDERSON, W. R.	Londonderry	Lieutenant	King's Liverpools	Wounded.
BARBOUR, DAVID	Londonderry	Artificer	H.M.S. "Indus V"	
BARBOUR, FRED.	Londonderry	Artificer	R.N.	
BIGGER, EDGAR G.	Londonderry	Cadet	Inns of Court	
BIGGER, W. FINLAY	Londonderry	2nd Lieutenant	Gloucester Regt.	Wounded.
BLACKLAY, OLIVER H.	Londonderry	Captain	R.A.M.C.	Wounded, M.C. and Bar.
BOYD, ALBERT	Londonderry	Lance-Corporal	R. In. Fus.	Prisoner of War.
BOYD, ALEXANDER	Londonderry	Sergeant	R. In. Fus.	
BOYD, GEORGE	Londonderry	Private	R.I.F.	Wounded.
BOYD, PATRICK G.	Londonderry	Gunner	R.F.A.	
BOYLE, ROBERT E. A.	Londonderry	Private	R. Welsh Fus.	
BOYLE, W. P. O.	Londonderry	Private	142nd Squad R.A.F.	
CAMERON, JAMES	Londonderry	Cadet	R.A.F.	
CAMPBELL, JAMES E.	Moville	Private	R. In. Fus.	Killed in Action.
CAMPBELL, JOHN	Londonderry	Private	R. Munster Fus.	
CAMPBELL, JOHN	Londonderry	Private	R. In. Fus.	
CAMPBELL, SAMUEL	Londonderry	Private	K.O.Y.L.I.	
CARSON, SOLOMON	Londonderry	Private	R. In. Fus.	Wounded.
CLAYTON, ERNEST	Londonderry	2nd Lieutenant	R.I.R.	
COCHRANE, I. S.	Londonderry	2nd Lieutenant	R.I.R.	
CRAIG, GEORGE D. M·A.	Londonderry	Captain	R.I.F.	Staff.
CUNNINGHAM, JOHN	Londonderry	Private	R. In. Fus.	Died.
CUNNINGHAM, W. J. B.	Londonderry	Private	109th Light T.M.B.	
CURRY, ROBERT	Londonderry	Private	R. In. Fus.	Prisoner of War.
CURRY, THOMAS	Londonderry	Lance-Corporal	R. In. Fus.	Killed in Action.
DAVISON, W. A.	Dungiven	Sergeant	R. In. Fus.	Wounded.
DONALDSON, JOHN	Londonderry	Lance-Corporal	R. In. Fus.	
DONALDSON, R. J·	Londonderry	Engineer	Naval Transport	
DONALDSON, W.	Londonderry	Sapper	R.E.	
DONALDSON, W. G.	Londonderry	Lance-Corporal	R. In. Fus.	Wounded.
DONNELL, JOHN C.	Londonderry	Private	R.A.S.C.	
DONNELL, REGD. A.	Londonderry	Signaller	Scottish Rifles	Wounded.
DONNELL, ROBERT M.	Londonderry	Private	R. In. Fus.	
DOUGAN, ROLAND H.	Londonderry	Cadet	R.A.F.	
DOUGHERTY, EDWARD	Londonderry	Private	R.I.F.	
DOUGHERTY, ROBERT	Londonderry	Corporal	R. In. Fus.	Prisoner of War.
FERGUSON, HERBERT	Londonderry	Private	10th R. In. Fus.	Prisoner of War.
FERGUSON, WILLIAM	Londonderry	Private	M.T. A.S.C.	
FLETCHER, ALBERT	Londonderry	2nd Lieutenant	Leinster Regt.	
FOSTER, SAMUEL R.	Londonderry	Major	R.A.M.C.	M.C. & Bar, Croix de Guerre.
GAILEY, N. W.	Londonderry	Lieutenant	R.E.	
GALBRAITH, HUGH	Londonderry	Private	R. In. Fus.	Killed in Action.
GALBRAITH, FRANK	Londonderry	Marine	H.M.S. "Viknor"	Drowned in Viknor.
GARDINER, GILBERT	Londonderry	Private	Worcester Regt.	Wounded.
GARDINER, THOMAS	Londonderry	Private	Irish Com. Labour Corps	
GARDINER, WILLIAM	Londonderry	Lance-Corporal	M.G.C.	Wounded.
GILLILAND, DAVID	Londonderry	Sapper	R.E. Signals	
GILLILAND, JAMES	Londonderry	Private	R. In. Fus.	Killed in Action.
GLENDINNING, WILLIAM	Londonderry	2nd Lieutenant	R. In. Fus.	
GRIEVE, ALEXANDER	Londonderry	A.N.S.	H.M.S. "Ramillies"	
GRIEVE, JOHN	Londonderry	Sapper	R.E.	
GRIEVE, THOMAS	Londonderry	Private	R.I.F.	
HADDEN, JOHN	Londonderry	2nd Lieutenant	R.I.R.	Killed in Action.
HARTE, JOHN	Londonderry	Private	R. In. Fus.	
HARTE, THOMAS	Londonderry	Private	Mec. Transport	
HARPUR, THOMAS	Londonderry	Sergeant	R. In. Fus.	
HARPUR, THOMSON	Londonderry	Lance-Corporal	N.I.H.	Wounded.
HEANEY, GEORGE	Londonderry	2nd Lieutenant	R.G.A.	Died. Pris. of War
HEGAN, WILLIAM	Londonderry	Corporal	Transport Service	
HENRY, JOHN	Londonderry	Private	R. In. Fus.	Killed in Action.
HENRY, MARCUS	Londonderry	Private	8th Hussars	
HENRY, THOMAS	Londonderry	Private	R.A.F.	
HEPBURN, WILLIAM	Londonderry	2nd Lieutenant	R.I.F.	
HOLMES, R. G.	Londonderry	Private	14th Black Watch	
HUTCHISON, ROBERT	Londonderry	A.N.S.	H.M.S. "Goliath"	Drowned.
IRONS, S. DOUGLAS	Londonderry	2nd Lieutenant	19th R.I.R.	Gassed.
IRWIN, FREDERICK	Limavady	2nd Lieutenant	R. In. Fus.	M.C. Killed in Action.
IRVINE, GERARD	Londonderry	Captain	Warwickshire Regt.	Died of Wounds.
IRWIN, I. BOYD	Donegal	Captain	K.O.R.L.R.	M.C. Wounded.
JACK, ALBERT	Londonderry	Private	R. In. Fus.	Killed in Action.

DERRY PRESBYTERY.   **GREAT JAMES' STREET, DERRY.**

Name.	Home Address.	Rank.	Regiment, Battalion or Unit.	Remarks.
Jack, W. H.	Londonderry	Captain	R. Irish Regt.	
Jarmeny, Robert	Londonderry	A.N.S.	H.M.S. "Grenville"	
Kellock, Edward	Londonderry	2nd Lieutenant	R. In. Fus.	
Kelly, William R.	Londonderry	Rifleman	R.I.R.	Wounded.
Keys, Thomas	Londonderry	Sergeant	R. In. Fus.	Prisoner of War
Keys, Walter	Londonderry	Captain	R.A.M.C.	
Kilpatrick, David	Londonderry	Private	44th Ordnance	
Kilpatrick, Joseph	Londonderry	Private	M.G.C.	Killed in Action.
Laird, James	Londonderry	Lance-Corporal	R. In. Fus.	Wounded.
Leebody, H. A.	Edinburgh	Major	R.A.M.C., D.A.D.M.S. Scottish Command	
Lemon, A. M.M.	Londonderry	Corporal	143rd Co. A.S.C.	
Lemon, Herbert	Londonderry	C.Q.M.S.	879th Co. A.S.C.	M.M.
Logan, James	Londonderry	Private	R. In. Fus.	Prisoner of War
Logue, John	Londonderry	Private	R. In. Fus.	Killed in Action.
Logue, Joseph	Londonderry	Sergeant	R. In. Fus.	Wounded.
Lynn, Albert	Londonderry	Rifleman	R.I.R.	
Lynn, Rev. Jos., B.A., B.D.	Londonderry	Major	S. Chaplain 34th Div.	Men. in Des.
McAdoo, Robert	Londonderry	Captain	R.A.M.C.	
McCauley, William	Londonderry	Private	R. In. Fus.	
McClelland, R. G.	Londonderry	Private	5th Scottish Rifles	
McClure, Edward	Ballymena	Private	R.I.F.	
McDermott, William	Londonderry	Gunner	90th Siege Batt.	
MacDonald, W. H. R.	Londonderry	Cadet	R.M.C., Camberley	
McElhinney, Charles		Trooper	12th Lancers	
McMichael, John	Londonderry	Private	R. In. Fus.	
McMichael, William	Londonderry	Private	M.G.C	
McMonagle, David	Londonderry	2nd Lieutenant	R.A.F.	
McMonagle, Hugh	Londonderry	Private	R.A.M.C.	
McMonagle, Hugh Reynolds	Londonderry	2nd Lieutenant	2nd Durham L.I.	
Menmuir, Glennie	Londonderry	Wireless Op.	R.F.A.	
Mitchell, Alex.	Londonderry	Private	R. In. Fus.	Wounded.
Mitchell, James	Londonderry	Private	R. In. Fus.	Killed in Action, 3 times W'ded.
Mitchell, Joseph	Londonderry	Sergeant	R. In. Fus.	
Mitchell, Robert	Londonderry	Lance-Corporal	R. In. Fus.	M.M., D.C.
Mitchell, Robt. J.	Londonderry	Private	R. In. Fus.	Prisoner of War.
Mitchell, William	Londonderry	Private	R. In. Fus.	Killed in Action.
Moncrieff, Robert J.	Londonderry	Rifleman	R.I.R.	
Moon, John	Londonderry	Private	R. In. Fus.	Killed in Action.
Morrison, Alfred H.	Londonderry	Lieutenant	50th Batt. M.G.C.	Wounded
Morrison, Haslett	Londonderry	Major	M.G.C.	Killed in Action.
Morrison, Leonard	Londonderry	Surg. Prob.	H.M.S. "Lapwing"	
Morrison, Robert V.	Londonderry	Captain	I.M.S.	
Morrison, Samuel	Londonderry	Private	R. In. Fus.	
Morrison, William	Londonderry	Private	R. In. Fus.	Killed in Action.
Neill, Robert G.	Londonderry	Lieutenant	Staff 2nd Class	
Orr, David	Londonderry	Private	R. In. Fus.	
Orr, John James	Londonderry	Private	Supply Depot	
Orr, Robert	Londonderry	Private	R. In. Fus.	
Orr, Samuel	Londonderry	Private	R. In. Fus.	Died of Wounds.
Orr, William	Londonderry	Driver	R.G.A.	
Robertson, Alexander	Londonderry	Sergeant	R. Munster Fus.	M.M. P. of War.
Robertson, James	Londonderry	Engineer	M. Marine	
Robinson, James	Londonderry	Private	R. In. Fus.	
Robinson, William	Londonderry	Seaman	M. Marine	P for duration of War.
Rock, Robert	Londonderry	Cadet	R.A.F.	
Smith, Robert	Londonderry	Private	R. In. Fus.	
Smyth, D. W.	Londonderry	Private	R. Irish Regt.	
Smyth, R. I.	Londonderry	Private	R.I.F.	Died.
Spence, Harry	Londonderry	Lieutenant	Leinster Regt.	Wounded.
Stevenson, Joseph	Londonderry	Sapper	R.E.	
Stewart, Robert J.	Londonderry	Bombardier	R.G.A.	Wounded.
Thompson, James A. F.	Londonderry	Cadet	R.M.C., Camberley	
Thompson, Robert G. F.	Londonderry	2nd Lieutenant	Yorks and Lancaster Regt.	
Thompson, S. Scott	Londonderry	2nd Lieutenant	Tank Corps	
Tosh, William	Londonderry	Private	R. In. Fus.	Killed in Action.
Wallace, Thomas G.	Londonderry	Sapper	R.E.	
Wightman, Alex.	Londonderry	2nd Lieutenant	R.I.F.	Wounded.
Wightman, William	Londonderry	Mechanic	R.A.F.	
Wilton, James M.	Londonderry	Captain	R. In. Fus.	M.C., Wounded.
Whyte, Scott	Londonderry	Private	R. In. Fus.	
Woodburn, D. B.	Londonderry	Captain	R.G.A.	Wounded.
Wylie, Albert	Londonderry	Private	R. In. Fus.	
COLONIAL AND U.S.A. FORCES.				
Blacklay, Francis P.	Londonderry	Private	Can. Cameron Highlanders	Killed in Action.
Browne, Harry	Londonderry	Private	6th Reserve Batt. Canadians	Wounded.
Craig, Robert J.	Londonderry	Captain	B.N. Indian Regt.	M.C., M. in Des.
Forrester, Charles	Australia	Private	A.E. Force	Wounded.
Forsythe, James	Canada	Sergeant	78th C.E. Force	
Forsythe, Samuel	Canada	Sergeant	78th C.E. Force	M.M.

DERRY PRESBYTERY. **GREAT JAMES' STREET DERRY.**

Name.	Home Address.	Rank.	Regiment, Battalion or Unit.	Remarks.
Forsythe, William J.	Canada	Private	78th C.E. Force	Killed in Action.
Glendinning, Henry	New Zealand	Private	Wellington Infantry	
Harper, Matthew	Australia	Lance-Corporal	A.I. Force	Wounded.
Irvine, Herbert	Victoria B.C.	Private	C.E.F.	
McGregor, Samuel	Sydney	Private	8th Australian Field Amb.	
Maclean, J.	S. Africa	Private	S. African Force	
Maclean, D.	S. Africa	Private	S. African Force	
Platt, R. M.	Canada	Trooper	C. Light Horse	
Smyth, William Scott	Canada	Private	C.E. Force	Killed in Action.
Wray, Harry	U.S.A.	Sergeant	60th U.S. Infantry	
DERRY, CARLISLE ROAD.				
Andrews, J. H.	Templemore Park	2nd Lieutenant	R.I.R.	Killed in Action.
Arbuckle, David	Abercorn Road	Driver	R.G.A.	
Arbuckle, R.	Abercorn Road	Bombardier	R.G.A.	
Arbuckle, Ernest			Ammunition Department	
Barbour, James	Dublin	Lieutenant	R. Dublin Fus.	
Barbour, John	Portadown	Q.M. Sergeant	R.I.F.	
Barr, J. H.	Aubrey Street	2nd Lieutenant	18th Royal Rifles	
Bell, Victor	Westland Avenue	Trooper	N.I.H.	Killed in Action.
Beattie, George	Beechwood Avenue	Private	5th R. In. Fus.	
Boyd, Ernest	George Street	Lance-Corporal	Service Batt. M.G.C.	
Boyd, Thomas	George Street	Sapper	R.E.	
Boyd, John	Spencer Road	Private		Prisoner of War.
Browne, James	Derry View	Driver	17th Field Co., Salonica	
Browne, Andrew	Moore Street		Military Police	
Campbell, E.	Grafton Terrace	Sergeant	12th R. In. Fus.	
Caldwell, John	Carlisle Road	Gunner	R.G.A.	Wounded.
Colhoun, Robert	Park Avenue	Private	M.G.C.	Wounded.
Colhoun, Thomas	Park Avenue	Private	10th R. In. Fus.	Wounded.
Colhoun, T. J.	Charlotte Street	Private	R. In. Fus.	
Colhoun, James	Charlotte Street	Private	R. In. Fus.	Killed in Action.
Craig, A. N.	Carlisle Terrace	Doctor	R.A.M.C.	
Craig, M. N.	Carlisle Terrace		Mercantile Marine	
Craig, Fred. W.	Carlisle Terrace	Doctor	R.A.M.C.	
Craig, Eric E.	Carlisle Terrace	2nd Lieutenant	R.I.R.	Killed in Action.
Currie, Andrew	Melrose Terrace	Corporal	10th R. In. Fus.	
Currie, R. J.	Melrose Terrace	Lance-Corporal	2nd R. In. Fus.	
Donnelly, Ernest	Clarence Avenue	Lance-Corporal	R. In. Fus.	Killed in Action.
Fulton, John	Kennedy Street	Private	10th R. In. Fus.	
Given, Bertie	Hawkins Street	2nd Lieutenant	R.I.R.	
Given, Tom	Hawkins Street	Private	R.A.M.C.	
Glass, John A.	Foyle Road	Lance-Corporal	10th R. In. Fus.	
Glass, William	Foyle Road	Private	M.T. A.S.C.	Wounded.
Graham, Frank A.	Philips Street	A.B.	R.N.	
Greer, A. D.		Sergeant	R. In. Fus.	
Greer, William L.	Henry Street	Private	R. In. Fus.	Killed in Action.
Guthrie, W. J.	Foyle Road	Private	R.A.M.C.	M.M.
Holmes, David	Fountain Street	Private	R. In. Fus.	
Holmes, Samuel	Fountain Street	Private	R. In. Fus.	Wounded.
Houston, John	Windmill Terrace	Sapper	R.E.	
Hunter, John T.	Moat Street	Sapper	R.E.	
Hyndman, John	Carrickmore House	Sergeant	A.S.C.	
Johnston, William	Harding Street	Private	M.T. A.S.C.	
Jordan, Samuel	Henry Street	Private	R. In. Fus.	
Jordan, Thomas	Society Street	Private	R. In. Fus.	Wounded.
Laird, William H.	Princes Street		R.A.M.C.	
Lapsley, Alexander	Aubrey Street	Driver	M.T. A.S.C.	
Little, William T.	Abercorn Place			
Logue, John	Fountain Street	Private	R. In. Fus.	
Lyttle, George	Charlotte Street	Driver	R.G.A.	
Lyttle, John	Charlotte Street	Sapper	R.E.	
McConnell, David	Fountain Street	Private	R. In. Fus.	Died of Wounds.
McConnell, Thomas	Bennett Street	Private	R. In. Fus.	
McGowan, D.	Fountain Street	Lance-Corporal	R. In. Fus.	Killed in Action.
McGowan, George	Fountain Street	Private	R.I.F.	Wounded.
Mackey, Samuel	Up. Bennett Street	Lieutenant		
MacLaughlin, J. L.	Victoria Park	2nd Lieutenant	R.I.R.	Wounded.
McNeill, Charles	Wesley Street	Bombardier	R.G.A.	Wounded.
McNeill, J. E.	Wesley Street	Sergeant	R.A.M.C.	Wounded, M.M.
McNutt, Henry	Aubrey Street	Private	R. In. Fus.	D.C.M.
McNutt, John	Aubrey Street	Lance-Corporal	R. In. Fus.	
McNutt, R. A.	Aubrey Street	Signaller	R. In. Fus.	
Mitchell, J.	Major Row	Gunner	R.G.A.	
Mitchell, R. S.	Major Row	Private	R. In. Fus.	
Mitchell, Robert	Major Row	Private	R. In. Fus.	
Mitchell, William	Major Row	Private	R. In. Fus.	
Mooney, W. H. S.	Dacre Terrace	Private	A.S.C.	
Morrow, Stanley	Abercorn Road	Lieutenant	R. In. Fus.	Wounded.
Murray, Robert				
Patterson, J. K.	Dacre Terrace	2nd Lieutenant	Royal Fus.	
Patterson, J. R.	Dacre Terrace	Lance-Corporal	Grenadiers	Wounded.
Patterson, Robert	Fountain Street	Gunner	R.G.A.	

DERRY PRESBYTERY.   CARLISLE ROAD, DERRY.

Name.	Home Address.	Rank.	Regiment, Battalion or Unit.	Remarks.
Russell, John	Miller Street	Trooper	N.I.H.	
Russell, Robert	Miller Street	Private	A.S.C.	
Russell, William	Miller Street	A.B.	R.N.	
Shannon, H. S.	Pump Street	Sergeant	Army Ord. Corps	
Shannon, L. C.	Pump Street	2nd Lieutenant	West Kent Y.	Wounded.
Shannon, R. W.	Pump Street	Sergeant	M.T. A.S.C.	Wounded.
Stevenson, Joseph	Abercorn Road	Private	10th R. In. Fus.	
Stevenson, William	Abercorn Road	Private	A.S.C.	
Stewart, Adam	Albert Street	Private	R In. Fus.	Killed in Action.
Wallace, R. J.	Henry Street	Lance-Corporal	R. In. Fus.	
Williams, Robert	Charlotte Street	Private	R. In. Fus.	Killed in Action.
Wray, James	Mountjoy Street	Private	R. In. Fus.	Wounded.
COLONIAL FORCES.				
Anderson, James	Carlisle Road	Sergeant	Canadians	Wounded.
Anderson, Norman	Carlisle Road	Co. Sgt.-Major	Australians	Killed in Action.
Andrews, S. H.	Templemore Park	Bombardier	Can. F.A.	
Boyd, Hugh	Spencer Road	Driver	Can. F.A.	
Chambers, W. K.	Bishop Street	Sergeant	Can. Mounted Rifles	Wounded.
Kelly, Samuel	Moat Street	Corporal	Can. Scottish	
McNeill, H. G.	Wesley Street	Trooper	Australian Light Horse	Killed in Action.
Patterson, W. L.	Dacre Terrace	Driver	Canadians	Wounded.
DERRY, CLAREMONT.				
Chambers, Fred.	Grafton Street	Private	R.A.F.	
Colhoun, Thomas	Fairman Place	Carpenter	R.N.	
Craig, Harward	Northland Avenue	Captain	King's Liverpool Regt.	
Finlay, James	Argyle Street	Sapper	R.E.	
McBride, Herbert	Creggan Road	Private	R.A.F.	
McClean, David	Barry Street	Sergeant	R.I.F.	
McCleery, William	Templemore Terrace	Corporal	4th Hussars	
McNee, George	Barry Street	Private	Seaforth Highlanders	
McNee, Thomas	Barry Street	Seaman	R.N.	Drowned.
Millar, Samuel	Asylum Road	Signaller	R.G.A.	
Neely, Robert	Stewart's Terrace	Rifleman	Worcester Regt.	
Parkinson, John	Barry Street	Private	R.I.F.	
Robinson, J. M.	Clarence Avenue	Lieutenant	R.E.	
Rodden, Robert	Wesley Street	Private	R.I.F.	
Roulstone, Samuel	The Collon	Lance-Corporal	R.I.F.	
Rutherford, Fred.	Groarty	Corporal	R.I.F.	
Rutherford, Henry	Groarty	Corporal	R.I.F.	
Sinclair, Andrew	Hawthorne Terrace	Corporal	R.I.F.	Died of Wounds.
Sinclair, Hugh	Hawthorne Terrace	Private	Canadian Highlanders	Died from gas.
Sinclair, John	Hawthorne Terrace	Sergeant	R.I.F.	Killed in Action.
Smith, Arthur	Claremont Street	Captain	M. Marine	
Stewart, Samuel	Fairman Place	Private	N.I.H.	
Walker, James	Fairman Place	Corporal	N.I.H.	
Woods, Fred.	Governor Road	Signaller	R.I.R.	
DERRY, EBRINGTON.				
Adair, John	Ebrington Terrace	Private	R. Inn. Fus.	Killed in Action.
Adair, William	Ebrington Terrace	Bombardier	R.F.A.	
Alford, Matthew	Ashcroft Place		R.F.A.	
Alford, Thomas	Ashcroft Place		R.F.A.	
Allen, Henry S.	Dungiven Road	Coy. S.M.	R. Inn. Fus.	Killed in Action.
Allen, W. J.	Dungiven Road	Gunner	R.G.A.	
Anderson, Robert	Fountain Street	Private	R. Inn. Fus.	
Anderson, Samuel	Fountain Street	Sapper	R.E.	
Anderson, Wm.	Bennet Street	Lieutenant	R. Inn. Fus.	
Arbuckle, Robert	Ivy Terrace	Sergeant	R. Inn. Fus.	Killed in Action.
Arbuckle, William	Ivy Terrace	Rifleman	R.I.R.	
Barr, Hamilton	King Street	Private	R. Inn. Fus.	Twice Wounded.
Barr, Robert	King Street	Corporal	M.G.C.	
Bell, William	Abercorn Place	Drum-Sergt.	R. Inn. Fus.	Thrice Wounded.
Black, David J.	Strabane Old Road	Private	R. Inn. Fus.	Killed in Action.
Black, Henry	Meekin's Row	Private	R. Inn. Fus.	
Black, Robert	Clooney	Private	R. Inn. Fus.	
Black, Robert J.	Strabane Old Road	Sergeant	Canadians	
Black, Samuel	Meekin's Row	Private	R. Inn. Fus.	
Boyd, Alexander	Fountain Hill	Sergeant	R. Inn. Fus.	
Boyd, Henry	Chapel Road	Gunner	R. Marines	
Boyd, John	Fountain Street	Private	R.I.R.	Killed in Action.
Boyd, Joseph	Alfred Street		R.A.M.C.	
Bratton, David	Bonds Street	Private	R. Scotch Rifles	
Bruce, John	Cuthbert Street	1st Class Stoker	R.N.	
Caldwell, Herbert	King Street	Private	R. Inn. Fus.	
Caldwell, Joseph	King Street	Private	R. Inn. Fus.	
Caldwell, Robert	King Street	Gunner	R.F.A.	
Caldwell, Samuel	Belfast		A.O. Corps	
Caldwell, Stephen	King Street	Sergt.-Major	Irish Guards	Killed in Action.
Caldwell, Stewart	King Street	Private	R. Inn. Fus.	

DERRY PRESBYTERY. EBRINGTON, DERRY.

Name.	Home Address.	Rank.	Regiment, Battalion or Unit.	Remarks.
Caldwell, Thomas	King Street	Corporal	R. Inn. Fus.	
Cambridge, Neill	Glendermott Road	Gunner	R.G.A.	
Campbell, Alex.	Fountain Hill	C.Q.M.S.	R. Inn. Fus.	M.M.
Campbell, John	Fountain Hill	Private	Irish Guards	
Campbell, Robert	Fountain Hill	Sergeant	R. Inn. Fus.	
Campbell, Thomas	Fountain Hill	Private	R. Inn. Fus.	
Carruthers, John A.	George Street	Private	R.I.R.	
Carruthers, Wm.	George Street		R.N.	
Cavanagh, James	Pine Street	Corporal	R. Inn. Fus.	
Clark, David	Violet Street	Private	R. Inn. Fus.	
Clark, Fred.	America		R.A.M.C.	
Clark, Wm. J.	Primrose Street	Signaller	R.G.A.	Wounded.
Colhoun, Hugh	Derry	Gunner	R.G.A.	
Colhoun, James	Alfred Street	Private	R. Inn. Fus.	Died.
Colhoun, John	Alfred Street	Private	R. Inn. Fus.	Killed in Action.
Colhoun, John	Tamneymore	Sergeant	R. Inn. Fus.	
Cowan, Robert	Abercorn Place	Private	R. Inn. Fus.	
Crawford, Albert	Strabane Old Road	Private	R. Inn. Fus.	
Crawford, James	Strabane Old Road	Private	Canadian F.A.	
Curry, John J.	Lower Road	Gunner	R.G.A.	
Curry, Joseph	Lower Road	Private	R. Inn. Fus.	
Davidson, George	Ivy Terrace	Private	A.S.C.	
Davidson, Robert H.	Bond's Hill	Private	A.S.C.	
Denning, Robert S.	Bond's Street	Corporal	R. Inn. Fus.	Wounded.
Diamond, John	Bond's Street	Private	R. Inn. Fus.	
Dockett, Henry W.	Derwent Place	Corporal	A.S.C.	
Donaghy, John	Ferguson Street	Private	R. Inn. Fus.	Wounded.
Donaghy, Samuel	Kilfennan	Private	R. Inn. Fus.	Thrice Wounded.
Donaghy, Thomas J.	Dunfield Terrace		A.O. Corps	
Donnell, John	Glendermott Road	Private	R. Inn. Fus.	
Donnell, Robert	Emerson Street	Private	R. Inn. Fus.	Died.
Donnell, Wm. J.	Glendermott Road	Corporal	R. Inn Fus.	
Doris, Christopher	Clooney Terrace	Rifleman	R.I.R.	
Dornan, Samuel	Emerson Street	Private	R.E.	
Duddy, Alex.	Pine Street	Private	R. Inn. Fus.	
Duddy, William	Pine Street	Private	R. Inn. Fus.	
Ferguson, Alex.	Ebrington Terrace	Major	R.I Fus.	M.C., D.C.M.
Gibson, D.	Emerson Street	Private	R. Inn. Fus.	
Gibson, William	Emerson Street	Private	R. Inn. Fus.	
Gibson, William	Bond's Street	Corporal	R. Scotch Fus.	Lost Leg.
Godfrey, William	Emerson Street	Corporal	R.A.F.	
Graham, Alex.	Spencer Road	Private	R. Inn Fus.	
Graham, John	Spencer Road	Private	R. Inn. Fus.	Wounded.
Gray, James N.	Benvarden Avenue	Private	R. Inn. Fus.	Lost Arm.
Hamilton, Wm. J.	Fount Hill	Private	R. Inn. Fus.	Wounded.
Handcock, David	Benvarden Avenue		R.A.M.C.	Killed.
Harvey, John	Ivy Terrace	Private	R. Inn. Fus.	
Haslett, J. Holmes	Australia		R.A.M.C.	Killed.
Haslett, John S.	Clooney Terrace	Private	R. Inn. Fus.	Killed in Action.
Heaney, Thomas	Prehen	Private	R. Inn. Fus.	
Henderson, Andrew	Spencer Road	Private	R. Inn. Fus.	
Henderson, Matthew	Spencer Road	Private	R. Inn. Fus.	
Hines, Joseph W.	Princes Street	Corporal	R. Marines	
Houston, James A.	Clooney	Sergeant	R.I.R.	
Houston, John	Clooney	Private	R. Inn. Fus.	Twice Wounded.
Hughes, Robert	Olive Terrace	Private	R. Inn. Fus.	
Hutcheson, Daniel	Wapping Lane	Sergeant	R. Inn. Fus.	
Irwin, Edward	Cross Street	Lance-Corporal	R. Inn. Fus.	Wounded.
Irwin, Leonard	Olive Terrace	Sergeant	M.G.C.	Killed in Action.
Jack, Albert W.	Melrose Terrace	Private	R. Inn. Fus.	
Jack, James S.	Melrose Terrace	Driver	A.S.C.	
Jamieson, Herbert W.	Duke Street	Lieutenant	R. Inn. Fus.	
Jamieson, James A.	Duke Street	Lieutenant	R. Inn. Fus.	
Kelly, Robert	Mountjoy Street	Sergeant	R. Inn. Fus.	
Kennedy, John W.	Kennedy Place	Reg. Sergt.-Major	R. Inn. Fus.	Killed in Action.
Kerr, Thomas R. S.	Ebrington Barracks	Sergeant	R. Inn. Fus.	M.C.
Keys, Alex.	Spencer Road	Private	R. Inn. Fus.	Killed in Action.
Kyle, William	Lower Road	Private	R. Inn. Fus.	
Kilgore, John	Bentley Street	Corporal	R. Inn. Fus.	Lost hand.
Lang, Walter	Alfred Street	Sergeant	R.F.A.	
Le Sal, Frank	Cuthbert Street	Private	1st Dorsets	
Lowthers, James	Drumahoe	Saddler	R.A.S.C.	
Lowthers, Marcus	Carlisle Road	2nd Lieutenant	R Inn. Fus.	
Lowthers, Thomas D.	Lismacarrol		R.N.	
Love, John	Kennedy Street	Private	R. Inn Fus.	
Lynch, David J.	Bond's Street	Private	R. Inn. Fus.	Killed in Action.
Lynch, David	Bond's Street	Private	R. Inn. Fus.	
Lyttle, Robert	Spencer Road	Private	R.A.F.	
McBain, James	Cuthbert Street	C.Q.M.S.	R. Scots Fus.	Killed in Action. D.C.M.
McCarter, Andrew	Alexander Place	Private	R. Inn. Fus.	
McCarter, William	Alexander Place	Private	R. Inn. Fus.	
McCarter, Wm.	Alexander Place	Lance-Corporal	A.S.C.	
McClay, William	Fountain Hill	Corporal	R. Inn. Fus.	M.M., Kd. in Act.
McClean, Thomas	Ballyowen	Lance-Corporal	R. Inn. Fus.	Wounded.

DERRY PRESBYTERY.   EBRINGTON, DERRY.

Name.	Home Address.	Rank.	Regiment, Battalion or Unit.	Remarks.
McClean, William	Ballyowen	Corporal	R. Inn. Fus.	Wounded.
McConnell, Wm. C.	Clooney Terrace	Sapper	R.E.	Killed in Action.
McDermott, John A.	Spencer Road	Lance-Corporal	R. Inn. Fus.	
McDermott, Robert	Spencer Road	Gunner	R.G.A.	
McDermott, Samuel	Spencer Road	Private	Irish Guards	
McDermott, William	Spencer Road	Gunner	R.N.	
McDonnell, George	Emerson Street	Corporal	1st Dorsets	
McFadden, James A.	Maydown	Private	R. Inn. Fus.	Killed in Action.
McFadden, Robert J.	Maydown	Private	R. Inn. Fus.	Killed in Action.
McFaul, Andrew	Cuthbert Street	Lance-Corporal	M.G.C.	
McFaul, David J.	Dunfield Terrace	Gunner	R.F.A.	
McFaul, William	Dunfield Terrace	Private	R. Inn. Fus.	Lost leg.
McFeeters, James	Alexander Place	Private	R. Inn. Fus.	
McGowan, David	Bond's Place	Private	R. Inn. Fus.	Killed in Action.
McGowan, Joseph	Bond's Place	Private	R. Inn. Fus.	
McGowan, Thomas	Bond's Place	Lance-Corporal	R. Inn. Fus.	Killed in Action.
McIlroy, Andrew	Albert Street	Private	R.I.R.	
McIlroy, Robert J.	Albert Street	Corporal	R. Inn. Fus.	Killed in Action.
McKaig, Joseph	Carlisle Road	Coy. Sergt.-Major	R.E.	
McKane, Robert	Glendermott Road	Private	R. Inn. Fus.	Lost leg.
McKane, Wm. J.	Pine Street	Private	R. Inn. Fus.	
McKay, Peter	King Street	Driver	R. Scots Fus.	
McLaughlin, Patrick	Dark Lane	Private	R.A.S.C.	
McLucas, Archibald	Wessley Street	Driver	R.F.A.	
McMichael, Samuel	Glendermott Road	Gunner	R.F.A.	
McMenemin, John	Bond Street	Sergeant	R. Inn. Fus.	Wounded, Pris.
McMonagle, Alex.	Dungiven Road	Private	R. Inn. Fus.	Killed in Action.
McMonagle, Arch.	Dungiven Road	Private	R. Inn. Fus.	
McMonagle, David	Dungiven Road	Private	R. Inn. Fus.	
McMonagle, Joseph	Dungiven Road	Stoker	R.N.	
McNulty, John	Spencer Road	Private	R. Inn. Fus.	
Magee, Robert	Glendermott Road	Sapper	R.E.	
Malseed, Henry	Edendale	Lieutenant	R. Inn. Fus.	Wounded.
Matson, William	Maydown	Private	R. Irish Fus.	
Mellick, John J.	Bond's Street	Mechanic	Aust. Air Force	
Mernor, Edward	Pine Street	Sergt.-Major	R. Inn. Fus.	
Mills, Alex.	Orchard Row	Lance-Corporal	R. Inn. Fus.	
Mills, Robert	Orchard Row	Private	R. Inn. Fus.	
Mills, Thomas A.	Orchard Street		R.N.	Killed in Action.
Mitchell, George S.	Bentley Street	Corporal	R.I.R.	
Mitchell, Wm. J.	Bentley Street	Private	R. Inn. Fus.	
Mooney, Patrick	King Street	Private	R. Irish Fus.	
Moorehead, Samuel	Clooney	Private	R. Inn. Fus.	
Mowbray, Joseph	Orchard Row	Rifleman	R. Scotch Rifles	
Mowbray, Thomas	Orchard Row	Sergeant	R. Inn. Fus.	Killed in Action.
Munn, John	Alma Place	Private	R. Inn. Fus.	
Murtland, James	Bond's Street	Private	R. Inn. Fus.	Killed in Action.
Myers, William	Ebrington Terrace	Sergeant	R. Scotch Fus.	
Orr, John	Fountain Hill	Private	R. Inn. Fus.	
Orr, Joseph	Fountain Hill	Lance-Corporal	R. Inn. Fus.	
Orr, Joseph	Bond's Street	Private	R. Inn. Fus.	
Orr, Ruben	Bond's Street	Private	R. Inn. Fus.	Killed in Action.
Orr, William	Bond's Street	Private	R. Inn. Fus.	
Owan, Richard	Ebrington Barracks	Sergeant	R. Inn. Fus.	Killed in Action.
Pickens, James	Violet Street	Driver	R.A.S.C.	
Pickens, Robert	Violet Street	Private	M.G.C.	
Pickens, Matthew	Violet Street	Gunner	R.G.A.	
Pilgrim, James	Ebrington Barracks	Sergeant	R. Scotch Fus.	
Platt, Alex.	Lower Road		R.A.F.	Lost arm.
Quinlin, Hugh	Ebrington Street	Sergeant	R. Inn. Fus.	Killed in Action.
Radcliff, Fred. J.	Fountain Hill	Private	R. Inn. Fus.	
Razn, Arthur	York Street	Private	R Scotch Fus.	
Reid, Alexander	Bornwell Place	Sergeant	R. Inn. Fus.	Killed in Action.
Reilly, John	Bond's Street	Private	R. Inn. Fus.	Wounded.
Richardson, Allen	Olive Terrace	Private	R. Scotch Fus.	Killed in Action.
Rodgers, John	Simpson's Brae	Private	R. Irish Fus.	
Sherrard, Matthew	Clooney Terrace	Private	R. Inn. Fus.	
Simpson, Robert	5 King Street	Corporal	R. Inn. Fus.	
Simpson, Robert	4 King Street	Private	R. Inn. Fus.	
Simpson, Samuel	King Street	Private	R. Inn. Fus.	Killed in Action.
Simpson, Samuel	5 King Street	Driver	R.F.A.	
Slater, Frederick C.	Foyle View	Private	R. Inn. Fus.	Killed in Action.
Smallwoods, James	Florence Street	Sergeant	R. Inn. Fus.	Wounded.
Smallwoods, John	Clooney	Private	R.I.R.	
Smallwoods, Joseph	Clooney	Private	R. Inn. Fus.	
Smallwoods, William	Clooney		R.N.	
Smallwoods, Wm.	St. Columb's	Sergeant	R. Inn. Fus.	
Smyth, James	Cuthbert Street	Private	R. Inn. Fus.	
Smyth, John	Cuthbert Street	Private	Can. F.A.	
Smyth, William	Cuthbert Street	Sergeant	R. Inn. Fus.	M.S.M.
Smyth, William	Cuthbert Street	Sapper	R.E.	
Smyth, Samuel	York Street	Private	R. Inn. Fus.	
Smyth, William	York Street	Private	R. Scotch Rifles	
Spence, Alex.	Ebrington Terrace	Sergeant	R. Inn. Fus.	

DERRY PRESBYTERY. EBRINGTON, DERRY.

Name.	Home Address.	Rank.	Regiment, Battalion or Unit.	Remarks.
Stevenson, Joseph	St. Columb's	Sergeant	R. Inn. Fus.	Wounded.
Strawbridge, David	Herbert Street	Private	R.F.A.	Wounded.
Strawbridge, James	Herbert Street	Private	R. Inn. Fus.	
Strawbridge, William	Herbert Street	Driver	R.F.A.	
Stuart, Stephen H.	Prehen	Private	R.I.R.	
Taggart, Albert	Spencer Road	Air Mechanic	R.A.F.	
Taggart, John	Spencer Road	Private	A.S.C.	
Taggart, Samuel	Spencer Road	Private	R.I.R.	
Tait, William J.	Fountain Place	Private	R. Inn. Fus.	
Thompson, H. Norman	Melrose Terrace	2nd Lieutenant	R. Inn. Fus.	Killed in Action.
Thompson, Thomas B.	Melrose Terrace	Private	Black Watch	Killed in Action.
Thompson, Victor L.	Melrose Terrace	Sergeant	Black Watch	Killed in Action.
Torrens, David	Violet Street	Private	R. Inn. Fus.	Killed in Action.
Urquehert, James	Bentley Street	Private	R. Scotch Rifles	
Ussher, David	King Street	Private	R. Inn. Fus.	
Ussher, John	King Street	Sergeant	M.G.C.	D.C.M.
Venables, Charles	Bond's Place	Private	R. Scotch Fus.	
Verschuur, William	Spencer Road		R. Marines	
Walker, Andrew	Florence Street		R.A.M.C.	
Walker, Albert	Alfred Street	Private	R. Inn. Fus.	
Walker, David	Alfred Street	Private	R. Inn. Fus.	Wounded.
Walker, Fred.	Alfred Street	Private	R. Inn. Fus.	Wounded.
Walker, Robert	Alfred Street	Private	R. Inn. Fus.	
Walker, Wm.	Alfred Street	Private	R.E.	
Wallace, Andrew	Irish Street	Private	R. Inn. Fus.	Killed in Action.
Wallace, George	Irish Street	Private	Dragoon Guards	
Westfrowd, Leonard	Ebrington Terrace	Private	R. Scotch Fus.	
Wilmont, George	Dunfield Terrace	Q.M.S.	R. Inn. Fus.	M.M.
Wray, William	Bond's Street	Gunner	R.F.A.	
Young, Robert	Primrose Street	Q.M.S.	R. Inn. Fus.	M.M.
DERRY, WATERSIDE.				
Anderson, Howard	Arnside	Cadet	R.E.	
Bailey, William	Emerson Street	Private	R.I.F.	
Ballard, Ernest	Alexandra Terrace	Private	1st Hampshires	W'ded & Pris. of War.
Begley, James	Distillery Brae	Private	R.I.F.	
Black, Joseph	Fountain Street	Lance-Corporal	R.I.F.	
Black, William Alfred	Chapel Road	2nd Air Craftsman	R.A.F.	Wounded.
Blair, Robert	Glendermott Road	Private	R.A.M.C.	
Blair, William	Glendermott Road	Private	R.A.M.C.	
Brown, Alexander	Duke Street	Lance-Corporal	R.I.F.	Wounded.
Brown, William J.	Ferguson Street	Lance-Corporal	R.I. Regt.	
Bryars, Samuel	Henry Street	Private	R.I.F.	Killed in Action.
Bryars, William	Henry Street	Private	R.I.F.	Gassed.
Burke, James	Aubrey Street	Corporal	R.I.F.	Wounded 3 times D.C.M.
Campbell, Samuel	Dungiven Road	Private	R.I.F.	Wounded.
Campbell, William	King's Street	Private	R.I.F.	W'ded and Killed in action.
Carnwath, Andrew	Caw	Lance-Corporal	R.I.F.	Wounded.
Carnwath, David	Caw	Mechanic	R.A.F.	
Carton, William Phillips	Ebrington Terrace	Lance-Corporal	R.I.F.	Killed in Action
Chambers, Alexander	Bentley Street	Private	R.I.R.	
Crockett, Joseph	Duke Street	Private	R.I.F.	Killed in Action
Crockett, W. J.	Spencer Road	Sapper	R.E.	
Crooks, Thomas L.	Spencer Road	Dispenser	R.A.M.C.	
Curry, James	Emerson Street	Co. Sergt.-Major	R.I.F.	Wounded twice.
Curry, John	Emerson Street	Private	R.I.F.	
Curry, Thomas	Emerson Street	Private	R.I.F.	
Curry, William	Emerson Street	Private	R.F.A.	
Darragh, David	Florence Street	Private	R.I.F.	Wounded.
Davidson, James	Riverview Terrace	Seaman	Mercantile Navy	
Deans, Donald	Cuthbert Street	Private	R.A.F.	
Deans, Hamilton	Cuthbert Street	Private	R.I.F.	Died.
Dickson, John P.	Glendermott Road	Sergeant	R.I.R.	
Dinsmore, James	Kennedy Street	Driver	R.E.	Wounded.
Dixon, R. J.	Mary Street	Private	R.I.F.	W'ded & Killed in Action.
Downie, Joseph	Spencer Road	Lance-Corporal	R.S.F.	Killed in Action.
Duff, J.	Ebrington Terrace	Pipe-Major	R.S.F.	
Dunlop, William	Violet Street	Private	R.I.F.	Killed in Action.
Eaton, Arthur H. M.	Altnagalvin	Sub.-Lieut.	R.N.V.R.	
Eaton, Charles	Altnagalvin	Lieutenant	R.I.R.	Wounded.
Eaton, Richard O.	Altnagalvin	Lieutenant	R.I.F.	Wounded 4 times. M.C.
Edgar, H. Alexander	Maple Street	Corporal	R.I.F.	Wounded thrice.
Edgar, John	Maple Street	Private	R.I.F.	
Edgar, John, Jun.	Maple Street	Private	R.I.F.	
Fairweather, Ernest	Cuthbert Street	Private	The King's Liverpools	Wounded.
Ferguson, James	Baronet Street	Seaman	R.N.C.	Died of Wounds.
Finlay, John	Moore Street	Sergeant	R.I.F.R.	Drowned.
Gillan, George	York Street	Private	R.I.F.	Killed in Action.

DERRY PRESBYTERY.   WATERSIDE, DERRY.

Name.	Home Address.	Rank.	Regiment, Battalion or Unit.	Remarks.
Gillan, Robert	York Street	Private	R.I.F.	
Gillan, William	York Street	Private	R.A.S.C.	Wounded 3 times.
Godfrey, Willie	Emerson Street	Private	R.A.F.	
Gordon, Joseph	Alexandra Place	Private	R.I.F.	
Gourley, Alexander	Dungiven Road	Private	R.I.F.	Wounded twice.
Gourley, Samuel	Dungiven Road	Private	R.I.F.	Killed in Action.
Griffs, H. E.	Clooney Terrace	Sergeant	R.I.F.	Wounded twice, M.S.M.
Haire, Samuel	King Street	Sapper	R.E.	
Hamilton, Hugh	Violet Street	Private	R.I.F.	
Hamilton, Willie	Violet Street	Private	R.I.F.	Died.
Haslett, George	Maple Street	Sapper	R.E.	Gassed.
Haslett, Ralph	Maple Street	Private	R.I.F.	
Hatrick, Alexander	Bond Street	Private	R.I.F.	
Heaney, James	Benvarden Avenue	Leading Stoker	R.N.D.	Killed in Action.
Heaney, Fred. G.	Benvarden Avenue	Co. Sergt.-Major	R.I.F.	Wounded twice.
Heaney, Archie	Benvarden Avenue	Stoker	R.N.	
Heaney, Joseph	Benvarden Avenue	Private	R.I.F.	Gassed and Pris. of War.
Jeffrey, Archie	Violet Street	Private	R.I.F.	
Jeffrey, Robert	Violet Street	Lance-Corporal	M.G.C.	Wounded, Prisoner, M.M. & Parchment Cert.
Jeffrey, William	Violet Street	Private	M.G.C.	
Jervis, Thomas	Robert Street	Sergeant	R.I.F.	Killed in Action.
Jordan, F.	Society Street	Sergeant	R.I.F.	Wounded.
Kilgour, Robert	King Street	Private	R.E.	
Kincaid, James	Alfred Street	Lieutenant	R.I. Lancers	
Kincaid, William	Alfred Street	Drummer	R.I.F.	
Leitch, William	Pine Street	Lance-Corporal	R.I.F.	Killed in Action.
Love, James	Prehen	Private	R.I.F.	Killed in Action.
Lyttle, John	Cuthbert Street	Private	R.I.F.	Killed in Action.
Lyttle, Robert	Cuthbert Street	Driver	R.F.A.	
Lyttle, William	Cuthbert Street	Private	R.I.F.	Wounded.
Lyttle, William James	Cuthbert Street	Private	R.A.S.C.	
Magee, James	Barnwell Place	Private	A.M.C.	Gassed.
Malseed, Alfred, M.B.	Bond's Hill	Captain	R.A.M.C.	W'ded and Gassed M.C.
Milloy, John	Strabane Road	Private	O.S.B.	W'ded & Men. in Despatches.
Mitchell, William H.	Benvarden Avenue	Private	R.I.F.	
Mitchell, Joseph	Benvarden Avenue	Private	R.I.F.	
Mitchell, Hugh	Benvarden Avenue	Private	R.I.R.	
Moore, Thomas	Irish Street	Private	R.I.F.	
Morrison, Edward	Fountain Hill	Private	R.I.F.	
Morrison, T. A.	Chapel Road	Signaller	R.E.	
McCarter, Alexander	Glendermott Road	Private	R.I.F.	
McCarter, Andrew	Glendermott Road	Private	R.I.F.	Killed in Action.
McClay, S. A.	Irish Street	Leading Stoker	R.N.	
McClay, Thomas	Irish Street	Private	R.I.F.	W'ded and Gassed.
McClelland, James	Robert Street	Stoker	R.N.	
McCrea, Joseph	Mount View	Private	R.I.F.	Killed in Action.
McCrea, William	Mount View	Corporal	R.I.F.	Died of Wounds.
McCready, John	Pine Street	Lance-Corporal	R.I.F.	Wounded twice.
McDermott, James	Bellevue	Lieutenant	R.W.F.	Torpedoed.
McFarland, Andrew	Lower Bennett Street	Private	R.I.F.	Killed in Action.
McFarland, John	Lower Bennett Street	Lance-Corporal	R.I.F.	Wounded twice.
McGinley, William	Emerson Street	Private	R.I.F.	Wounded.
McKay, John	Bishop Street	Private	R.I.F.	Wounded.
McKeegan, David	Orchard Row	Corporal	M.G.C., R.I.F.	Wounded thrice.
McKeegan, Robert	Orchard Row	Private	R.I.R.	Prisoner of War.
McMillan, William	Violet Street	Corporal	R.I.F.	Wounded twice, Pris. of War.
Orr, Joseph	Fountain Street	Private	R.I.F.	W'ded 3 times.
Parker, Arthur	Wapping	Private	R.A.F.	Wounded twice.
Patterson, James	Florence Street	Private	R.I.F.	
Patterson, Joseph	Dungiven Road	Private	R.I.F.	Wounded twice & Pris. of War.
Quigley, Robert	Fountain Hill	Private	R.I.F.	Wounded 3 times.
Rankin, William	Fountain Hill	Private	R.I.F.	Wounded 3 times.
Rankin, William John	Pine Street	Lance-Corporal	R.I.F.	W'ded and Killed in Action.
Reid, John	Bond's Hill	Corporal	R.I.F.	Wounded.
Roulstone, Charles	Bond's Hill	Gunner	R.F.A.	
Roulstone, John	Bond's Hill	Trumpeter	F.A.	
Roulstone, Robert	Bond's Hill	Boy	F.A.	
Roulstone, Tom	Bond's Hill	Boy	F.A.	
Roulstone, William	Bond's Hill	Signaller	R.A.	
Rutherford, Robert	Alexandra Place	Lance-Corporal	R.I.F.	Wounded.
Rutherford, Samuel	Alexandra Place	Private	R.I.F.	
Rutherford, Samuel, Jun.	Alexandra Place	Lance-Corporal	R.I.F.	Wounded.
Sherrard, Edward	Glendermott Road	Private	R.I.F.	Gassed.
Sherrard, William	Glendermott Road	Private	R.I.F.	Wounded 3 times.
Simpson, Joseph	Irish Street	Act. Sergeant	R.A.S.C.	

DERRY PRESBYTERY. WATERSIDE, DERRY.

Name.	Home Address.	Rank.	Regiment, Battalion or Unit.	Remarks.
Simpson, William S.	Dunfield Terrace	Hospital Orderly	R.A.M.C.	
Smith, Hubert	Dunfield Terrace	Dentist	R.A.F.	
Smith, John	Dunfield Terrace	Private	R.I.F.	Killed in Action.
Smith, Joseph	Bond's Hill	Private	A. and S. Highlanders	Wounded.
Smith, Robert M.	Bond's Hill	Cadet	R.A.F.	
Smyth, John	Glendermott Road	Lieutenant	R.I.F.	Wounded.
Smyth, Joseph Lindsay	Chapel Road	Private	R.S.F.	Wounded.
Smyth, Samuel	Glendermott Road	Sergeant	R.I.F.	Killed in Action.
Smyth, William M.	Glendermott Road	Lance-Corporal	Royal Marines	Wounded.
Speers, William James	Dunfield Terrace	Private	R.I.F.	Killed in Action.
Stewart, John	Duke Street	Sapper	R.E.	Wounded twice.
Stirling, George	George's Street	Private	R.I.F.	Wounded & Killed in Action.
Swan, Robert James	Glendermott Road	Corporal	R.F.C.	
Swan, Samuel Hunter	Glendermott Road	Private	R.I.F.	Killed in Action.
Taylor, John	Moore Street	Private	R.I.F.	
Warke, Joseph	Emerson Street	Corporal	R.I.F.	Wounded.
Watson, James	The Cottage	Major	R.A.S.C.	M.C., M. in Des.
Watson, James	Bond's Hill	Lieutenant	The Manchester Regt.	Killed in Action.
Watson, John	The Cottage	Captain	R.A.M.C.	Wounded.
Watson, Andrew	The Cottage	Lieutenant	M.O. R.A.F.	
Watson, Thomas	Bond's Hill	Sapper	R.E.	
Whiteside, Joseph	Henrietta Street	Private	R.I.F.	Wounded.
Whiteside, Robert	Henrietta Street	Private	R.I.F.	Wounded.
Williamson, Joseph	Pine Street	Lance-Corporal	R.I.F.	Wounded 3 times.
Williamson, John	Pine Street	Private	R.I.F.	Killed in Action.
Williamson, Robert	Pine Street	Private	R.A.F.	
Williamson, Charles	Pine Street	Private	R.I.R.	
Williamson, Chas. Hugh	Bond Street	Private	R.I.R.	
Williamson, William James	Bond Street	Private	R.I.F.	
Wilson, William J.	Wapping	Sergeant	R.I.F.	Wounded & Killed in Action.
Wilson, Henry	Wapping	Corporal	R.I.F.	Wounded 3 times.
Wilson, Robert	Moore Street	Driver	M.G.C.	Wounded.
Young, Robert W.	King Street	Private	M.T. A.S.C.	Wounded.
COLONIAL FORCES.				
Leitch, Robert	Pine Street	Private	Canadian Force	Killed in Action.
Love, John	Prehen	Private	Canadian M.G.C.	Killed in Action.
Reid, J. Smith	Spencer Road	Trooper	Canadian Cavalry	Wounded 4 times.
FAHAN AND INCH.				
Adams, J. A.	Fahan	Corporal	5th R.E.	
Adams, W. M.	Fahan	2nd Lieutenant	Reserve Brigade	
Brewster, H.	Fahan	Captain	R.G.A.	
Creswell, D. A.	Inch	Lieutenant	2nd R.I.R.	Wounded.
Creswell, T.	Inch	Captain	2nd R.I.R.	Wounded.
Hamilton, A. S.	Fahan	Driver	A.S.C.	Wounded.
Hamilton, J.	Fahan	Surgeon	R.N.	
McClean, G. S.	Fahan	2nd Lieutenant	R.E.	
Mitchel, A.	Fahan	2nd Lieutenant	R.I.F.	Killed in Action.
Pinkerton, R.	Burnfoot	Private	R.I.F.	Wounded.
Tomb, J. S.	Fahan	Captain	Welsh Fus.	
Tomb, J. W.	Fahan	Gunner	R.G.A.	
Tomb, T. H.	Fahan	Private		
COLONIAL FORCES.				
Adams, R. F.	Fahan	Assist. Chaplain	75th Canadian Regt.	
McClean, W. S.	Fahan	Corporal	Calcutta Scot. Vol.	
Porter, J. R.	Inch	Private	79th Canadians	Killed in Action.
GREENBANK.				
Ayton, John	Quigley's Point			
Ewing, Robert	Greenbank Cottage	Driver	Gordon Highlanders	
Simpson, Samuel	Quigley's Point			
Stewart, Moses	The Collin	Private	Ulster Division	Wounded.
Taylor, Henry			American Army	
KNOWHEAD.				
Bell, Robert	Drumacross	Private	2nd Life Guards	Died.
Burns, John	Muff	Private	R.E.	Wounded.
Dinsmore, Henry	Muff	Lieutenant	K.R.R.	M.C.
Hadden, John	Muff	2nd Lieutenant	R.I.R.	Killed in Action.
Keys, John	Birdstown	Private	10th R. In. Fus.	Killed in Action.
Keys, Thomas	Muff	Private	9th R. In. Fus.	Wounded.
Long, Samuel	Muff	Private	9th R. In. Fus.	Wounded.
Moorehead, Andrew	Muff	Private	Canadians	Wounded.
Thompson, James	Muff	Private	2nd Gar. Batt. R. Inn. Fus.	Wounded.
Thompson, John	Culmore	Corporal	Canadian Police	

DERRY PRESBYTERY. KNOWHEAD.

Name.	Home Address.	Rank.	Regiment, Battalion or Unit.	Remarks.
WYLIE, ALBERT	Ardmore	Private	R.F.A.	
WYLIE, ARTHUR	Muff	Private	9th R. In. Fus.	
WYLIE, JOSEPH	Muff	2nd Lieutenant	9th R. In. Fus.	Wounded.
WYLIE, SAMUEL	Muff	Mechanic	R.N.R.	
MAGHERAMASON.				
BROWN, JOHN	Desertone	Private	15th Cheshire Regt.	
CAMPBELL, ANDREW	Rossnagalliagh	Private	12th R. In. Fus.	
CAMPBELL, JOHN	Rossnagalliagh	Private	12th R. In. Fus.	
COLHOUN, HUGH	Gortavea	Private	12th R. In. Fus.	
FALCONER, JOHN JAMES	Gortavea	Private	9th R In. Fus.	Wounded.
HUNTER, JOHN	Cloughogle	Private	12th R. In. Fus.	
HUTCHINSON, ALEX. B.	Bready	Private	9th R. In. Fus.	Wounded.
HUTCHINSON, JAMES	Bready	Private	9th R. In. Fus.	Wounded.
McKINLAY, ROBERT	Ardmore	Private	12th R. In. Fus.	Killed.
McKINLAY, SAMUEL	Ardmore	Private	12th R. In. Fus.	
McKINLAY, THOMAS	Ardmore	Private	12th R. In. Fus.	
MONTGOMERY, JOSEPH	Gortavea	Private	9th R. In. Fus.	Killed in Action.
MILLAR, THOMAS	Gortavea	Private	3rd R. In. Fus.	
MITCHELL, SAMUEL	Craigtown	Private	3rd R. In. Fus.	Killed in Action.
RODEN, DAVID	Cloughogle	Private	9th A. and S. Highlanders	Wounded.
RODEN, JOHN	Cloughogle	Private	12th R. In. Fus.	
RODEN, THOMAS	Cloughogle		10th R.G.A.	
ROULSTON, EDWARD	Drumagor		65th Coy. R.G.A.	
WALKER, THOMAS	Desertone	Private	12th R. In. Fus.	
COLONIAL FORCES.				
BROWNE, GEORGE	Vancouver	Private	7th Can. Inf.	
DOHERTY, JOSEPH	Cloughogle	Private	Canadian Rly.	Killed.
HAMILTON, ROBERT	Cloughogle	Private	49th Can. Inf.	Killed.
HUTCHINSON, DAVID		Sergeant	4th Can. Inf.	M.M.
JEFFREY, ALEX.	Waikato, N.Z.	Private	N.Z. Force	Wounded.
LYNCH, ALEX.	Fetersburg, Va. U.S.A.	Private	5th Batt. Rifle Brigade	
LYNCH, WILLIAM JOHN		Private	208th Can. Inf.	
McIVOR, SAMUEL G.	Toronto	Private	38th Can. Inf.	Wounded.
MITCHELL, DAVID ALEX.	Malvern, Australia	Driver	Australian Artillery	Wounded.
MALIN.				
BAIRD, R. J.	Ballycrampsie	Sergeant	Canadian Div.	
BOGGS, JAMES	Malin	Private	Black Watch	Wounded.
COLHOUN, GEORGE	U.S.A.	Private	9th Rec. Co., Q.M.C.	
DYKES, GEORGE	Malin	Private	R.E.	
DYKES, JERRY	Malin	Sergeant	R.I.R.	
HENDERSON, A.	Dunargis, B'gorman	Sergeant	Australian Force	
HENDERSON, ARCHIE	Dunargis, B'gorman	Corporal	Canadian Force	
HENDERSON, SAMUEL	Dunargis, B'gorman	Private	Irish Guards	
NELSON, THOMAS M.	Malin	Private	R. In. Fus.	
MONREAGH.				
BEATTY, THOMAS	St. Johnston	Private	11th R. In. Fus.	Wounded.
BOYD, ALEXANDER	Cross, Churchtown	Private	11th R. In. Fus.	Killed in Action.
BOYD, WILLIAM	Cross, Churchtown	Private	5th R.I.F.	
BROWN, JAMES, M.D.	St. Johnston	Captain	R.A.M.C.	
BURKE, GEORGE	Dooish	Gunner	R.G.A.	
BURKE, JAMES	Dooish	Gunner	P. Batt. R.H.A.	
BURKE, JOHN	Dooish	Gunner	H. Batt. R.H.A.	Killed in Action.
COLE, SAMUEL	Legnaduff	Lieutenant	N.I.H.	
DONAGHY, JAMES	Leitrim, Bogay	Private	10th R.I.F.	
DONAGHY, JOHN	Leitrim, Bogay	Private	11th R.I.F.	Killed in Action.
DONAGHY, WILLIAM	Leitrim, Bogay	Private	11th R.I.F.	Killed in Action.
HUNTER, JAMES	Monreagh	Lance-Corporal	9th R.I.F.	
HUNTER, JOHN	Legnaduff	Private	11th R.I.F.	Killed in Action.
McCLELLAND, WILLIAM	Carrigans	Private	9th R.I.F.	Wounded.
MASON, JAMES	Killea	Private	11th R.I.F.	Killed in Action.
OSBORNE, JOSEPH	Bready	Private	Australian Imp. Forces	Killed in Action.
PARK, JOSEPH	St. Johnston	Private	11th R.I.F.	
PAYNE, JAMES	Monglass	Private	11th R.I.F.	Wounded.
ROULSTON, JOHN	Monreagh	Private	11th R.I.F.	Killed in Action.
RUTHERFORD, ANDREW	Imlick	Private	11th R.I.F.	Wounded.
RUTHERFORD, FRED.	Molenan	Private	11th R.I.F.	
RUTHERFORD, HARRY	Molenan	Private	11th R.I.F.	
WALKER, SAMUEL	Ruskey	Private	10th R.I.F.	Wounded.
WILKIN, JOHN	Carrigans	Private	Aircraft	
MOVILLE.				
AYTON, DAVID	Balleghan	Private	R.E.	
CAMPBELL, JAMES E.	Ballyrattan	Private	10th R. In. Fus.	Wounded twice.
McCORKELL, WILLIAM	Greencastle	Private	R.F.A.	
McCREA, JAMES	Greencastle	Sergeant	11th R. In. Fus.	
MORGAN, JAMES H.	Riverview	Private	A.S.C.	
PARKE, JAMES	Rosebank	Sergeant	11th R. In. Fus.	Killed in Action. Wounded, M.M.

DERRY PRESBYTERY. SECOND RAPHOE,

Name.	Home Address.	Rank.	Regiment, Battalion or Unit.	Remarks.
SECOND RAPHOE.				
Craig, Robert	Drumcrow	Private	Innis. Dragoons	
Gibson, Alex.	Raphoe	Private	11th R. In. Fus.	
Gilfillan, Albert	Momeen, Raphoe	Private	11th R. In. Fus.	Killed in Action.
Gilfillan, Andrew	Momeen, Raphoe	...	11th R. In. Fus.	Killed in Action.
Hamilton, Thomas	Raphoe	2nd Lieutenant	11th R. In. Fus.	
Kelly, John	Momeen, Raphoe	Private	R.A.M.C.	
Lapsley, James	Raphoe	Private	12th R. In. Fus.	
Lapsley, Samuel	Raphoe	...	11th R. In. Fus.	
Lindsay, Andrew	Argery	...	12th R. In. Fus.	Killed in Action.
Rogers, Thomas	Raphoe	...	11th R. In. Fus.	
Wallace, J. Waldo	Raphoe	Lieutenant	10th R.I.R.	Men. in Des.
COLONIAL FORCES.				
Craig, John	Drumcrow	Private	Canadian Force	
Hamilton, Richard	Raphoe	Lieutenant	Canadian Force	...
McFeeters, R. E.	Raphoe	Private	Canadian Mounted Rifles	
McGregor, Samuel	Raphoe	Private	8th Australian Field Amb.	Wounded.
Moore, Thomas	Raphoe	Private	47th Canadians	

DONEGAL PRESBYTERY.

Name.	Home Address.	Rank.	Regiment, Battalion or Unit.	Remarks.
BALLYSHANNON.				
Berry, W. E.	Bundoran	Captain	R.A.M.C.	
Caldwell, Hugh	Ballyshannon	Sergeant	11th Batt. R. In. Fus.	
Gilmour, Bryce	Ballyshannon	Private	I.G.	Killed in Action.
Hamilton, John	Ballyshannon	Lieutenant	11th Batt. R. In. Fus.	Killed in Action.
Hunter, W. M.	Barnhill, Letterkenny	Lieutenant	R. Irish Fus.	Killed in Action.
Myles, J. Sproule	Ballyshannon	Major	11th Batt. R. In. Fus.	M.C. Wounded.
Potter, Scott	Bundoran	Captain	R.A.M.C.	
Potter, Ross	Bundoran	Lieutenant	R.N.	
Rodgers, Marshall	Bundoran	...	...	
Thompson, Jack	Ballyshannon	Private	R. In. Fus.	
Vaughan, Fred	Ballyshannon	Private	R. In. Fus.	
Wright, Rev. J. Jackson	Ballyshannon	3rd Class	R.A.C.D.	M.C.
COLONIAL FORCES.				
Caldwell, John	Ballyshannon	Private	Canadian Force	Killed in Action.
Gilmour, Cecil	Ballyshannon	Private	Canadian Force	Wounded.
Kyle, Oliver	Ballyshannon	Private	Canadian Force	Died of Wounds.
Wray, Frank	Ballyshannon	Private	Canadian Force	
FIRST CASTLEDERG.				
Bogle, R.	Drumclamph	Private	9th Batt. R. In. Fus.	
Bogle, William	Ballylennon	Sergeant	9th Batt. R. In. Fus.	
Burke, David	Crawfordstown	Private	Black Watch	
Burke, J.	Crawfordstown	Private	2nd Batt. R. In. Fus.	
Burke, James	Crawfordstown	Lance-Corporal	9th Batt. R. In. Fus.	Wounded.
Burke, Robert	Crawfordstown	Private	9th Batt. R. In. Fus.	Wounded.
Caldwell, James	Carrick	Private	2nd Batt. Royal Scots	
Crawford, Bradley	Clare	Private	R.G.A.	
Derry, George	Goland	Captain	R.A.M.C.	
Derry, Joseph	Goland	Private	N.I.H.	Killed in Action.
Glenn, David	Castlegore	Private	9th R. In. Fus.	Wounded.
McCay, Andrew William	The Manse	Captain	15th R.I.R.	Wounded.
McCay, C. A. R.	The Manse	Major	R.A.M.C.	Wounded.
McCay, J. F. D.	The Manse	Act.-Captain	15th Batt. R.I.R.	Killed in Action.
McErvel, W. A.	Spamount	Captain	M.G.C.	Men. Des.
Porter, George	Garvetagh	Private	9th R. In. Fus.	Wounded.
Porter, Robert	Ballylennon	Sergeant	C.A.V.C.	
Robinson, A.	Adenagee	Sergeant	I.G.	
Robinson, A.	Garvetagh	Corporal	R.A.M.C.	
Robinson, Bertie	Ardbarren	Private	R.F.A.	Wounded.
Robinson, John	Garvetagh	Private	2nd Batt. R. In. Fus.	Wounded.
Rutledge, Robert	Garvetagh	Corporal	9th Batt. N. Staffs.	
Young, J. J.	Carncorn	Private	9th R. In. Fus.	Wounded.

DONEGAL PRESBYTERY. SECOND CASTLEDERG.

Name.	Home Address.	Rank.	Regiment, Battalion or Unit.	Remarks.
SECOND CASTLEDERG.				
Beattie, George	Cavan, Castlederg	Trooper	N.I.H.	
Elliott, Thomas	Castlederg	Private	9th R. In. Fus.	
Henderson, James	Fyfin	Private	9th R. In. Fus.	
Huey, Fred.	Erganagh	Private	R.A.F.	
Katterson, Robert	Pullyarnon	Trooper	N.I.H.	
Kerrigan, William	Kilewagh	Private	9th R. In. Fus.	Died pris. in Germany.
Leary, G. F. N.	Castlederg	Major	R.A.M.C.	
McCormick, Andrew H.	Kilclean	Trooper	N.I.H.	
McCutcheon, Matthew	Castlederg	Private	9th R. In. Fus.	
Millar, David	Crew	Private	R.I.R.	
Mitchell, William	Pullyarnon	Trooper	N.I.H.	
Patrick, James	Castlederg	Private	9th R. In. Fus.	
Roulston, William	Castlederg	Private	R.H.A.	
Watt, Thomas	Castlederg	Private	9th R. In. Fus.	Wounded.
Young, Hugh	Castlederg	S.Q.M.S.	A. Ord. Corps	
COLONIAL FORCES.				
Condy, James	Luremore	Private	Canadians	
Gourley, Robert	Castlederg	Private	Australians	
Henderson, Andrew	Scansherin	Private	Canadians	
Katterson, J.	Pullyarnon	Private	N.Z.	
Leary, S. W. S.	Castlederg	Captain	S.A. A.M.C.	
Leary, T. G. S.	Castlederg	Captain	Aust. A.M.C.	
Millar, Thomas	Crew	Private	Canadians	
DONEGAL.				
Crawford, David	Tullycullion	Private	R.F.C.	
Harron, William	Drumgowan	2nd Lieutenant	Border Regt.	
Irwin, Joseph Boyd	Diamond	Captain	King's Own Lan. Regt.	M.C., D.S.O.
Irwin, James Ross		2nd Lieutenant	Irish Regt.	Killed in Action.
Kee, Robert	Quay Street	Private	I.G.	
Lyons, Robert	Drumcoe, Inver	Private	27th Canadians	
Neilson, Daniel B.	The Manse	1st Officer	S.S. "Eurybeates"	
Neilson, Edwin F.	The Manse	Sergt.-Major	27th City of Winnipeg Regt.	Wounded.
Neilson, Matthew Hale	The Manse	Private	25th R. Fus.	
Smith, Albert	Bayview	Sergt.-Instructor	R. In. Fus.	
Smith, George	Bayview	Seaman	R.N.	
Stewart, David	Ulster Bank	Private	A.S.C.	
Stewart, Samuel P.	Ulster Bank	2nd Lieutenant	S. Irish Horse	
Wray, John	Townlough	Private	R. In. Fus.	
KILLETER.				
Blackburn, Thomas	Lislaird	Private	R. In. Fus	Wounded.
Cather, Robert G.	Creeduff	Private	N.I.H.	Pris. of War.
Duncan, James	Killeter Manse	1st A.M.	R. Air Force	
Monteith, Henry	Lisnacloon	Sergeant	R. In. Fus,	Twice Wounded.
McCormick Thomas J.	Woodside	Corporal	N.I.H.	Killed in Action.
Robb, William G.	Lislaird	Sergeant	R.G.A.	
Sproule, Graham	Drumahon	Gunner	R.F.A.	
COLONIAL FORCES.				
Hamilton, William H.	Carricoghan	Private	Canadian L.I.	Wounded.
Monteith, William J.	Lisnacloon	Private	Canadian Engineers	
Sproule, Richard	Clegernagh	Private	Australians	Wounded.
Young, Gilbert	Lislaird	Private	Canadian L.I.	Killed in Action.
Young, Stewart	Altamullan	Private	Australians	Wounded.
Young, William A.	Altamullan	Private	Australians	
STRANORLAR.				
Bennett, Richard	Ballybofey	Private	R.E.	
Brookes, John	Edenmore	Private	10th R. In. Fus.	
Ewing, William	Stranorlar	Private	10th R. In. Fus.	
Fleming, Thomas	Stranorlar	Private	10th R. In. Fus.	Killed in Action.
Gregory, George	Ballybofey	Private	10th R. In. Fus.	Killed in Action.
Gregory, Thomas	Ballybofey	Private	10th R. In. Fus.	
Hutchinson, Matthew	Stranorlar	Private	10th R. In. Fus.	
Lucas, Adam	Cavan	Seaman	R.N.	
Lucas, Frederick	Cavan	Private	Scotch Regt.	Died in Action.
Lucas, John	Cavan	Private	10th R. In. Fus.	Wounded.
Pollock, James	Meenavoy	Private	Scotch Regt.	
Russell, Joseph	Cavan	Private	10th In. Fus.	Wounded.
Taylor, Peter	Stranorlar	2nd Lieutenant	Scotch Regt.	Wounded.
Whyte, Horace	Castlebane	Private	R. In. Fus.	
Whyte, Howard	Castlebane	2nd Lieutenant	R. In. Fus.	
Wilson, John	Stranorlar	Private	10th R. In. Fus.	

DONEGAL PRESBYTERY. STRANORLAR.

Name.	Home Address.	Rank.	Regiment, Battalion or Unit.	Remarks.
COLONIAL FORCES.				
Caldwell, Robert	Ballybofey	Private	Can. Force	Prisoner.
Harper, James	Liskerran	Private	Can. Force	
Lucas, Edward	Cavan	Private	Aust. Force	
Tynan, Samuel	Carricknamane	Private	Can. Force	Prisoner.
Wauchope, Charles	Trusk	Private	Aust. Force	
Wauchope, James	Trusk	Private	Aust. Force	
Wauchope, Robert	Trusk	Private	Can. Force	
Wauchope, William	Trusk	Private	Can.	Died in Action.

DOWN PRESBYTERY.

Name.	Home Address.	Rank.	Regiment, Battalion or Unit.	Remarks.
ARDGLASS.				
Ball, John C. G.	The Manse	Captain	R.A. Ch. D.	Men. in. Desp.
Dougherty, James	Burnside	Corporal	14th R.I.R.	Wounded.
Gillett, Edward John	Killough	Chief Officer	R.N.	
Gillett, Ed. John, Jun.	Killough	Signalman	R.N.	
Gillett, Thomas L.	Killough	Midshipman	R.N.R.	
Herron, Thomas	Tullycarnon	A.B.	R.N.	
Mackenzie, Donald	Killough	L.B.	R.N.	Wounded.
Mawhinney, Samuel	Ardglass	Sergeant	5th R.I.R.	Wounded.
Williams, David	Burnside	Lance-Corporal	Ox. and Bucks. L.I.	
Williams, Walter	Burnside	2nd Lieutenant	R. In. Fus.	
FIRST BALLYNAHINCH.				
Adams, Samuel	Raleagh	Private	Old Contemptibles	Wounded.
Cochrane, William	Oughill, Ballykelly	Trooper	N.I.H.	
Dunlop, John	Ballymacarn	Private	3rd I.G.	
Farr, John	Ballynahinch	Private	M.T. A.S.C.	
Gourley, James	Ballynahinch	Private	420th Battery R.F.A.	
Gourley, Robert	Ballynahinch	Private	4th R.I.R.	
Hamilton, Andrew Rowan	Ballynahinch	Lieutenant	R.A.M.C.	
Hamilton, Thomas Witherow	Ballynahinch	Lance-Corporal	12th R.I.R.	Wounded.
Hill, Samuel F.	Ballynahinch	Corporal	36th M.G.C.	Prisoner. Twice Wounded.
Hunter, Robert John	Magheraknock	Corporal	20th London Regt.	3 Medals. Killed.
Johnston, Frank	Ballynahinch	Rifleman	6th R.I.R.; R.A.S.C.	Gassed and Twice Wounded.
Johnston, Wm. John	Ballynahinch	Lance-Corporal	13th R.I.R.	
Jordan, Wm.	Tonaghmore	A.B.	R.N.	
McAuley, John	Ballynahinch	Rifleman	12th R.I.R.	Twice Wounded.
McIlwaine, James	Mourne View	Lance-Corporal	17th R.I.R.	
Patterson, George	Mourne View	Driver	M.T. A.S.C.	Wounded.
Patterson, Jas. Alex.	Mourne View	Private	11th R.I.R.	Wounded.
Patterson, Martin	Bann Hill	Private	6th Royal Scots	M.M. Wounded.
Scott, David Harden	Station Hill	Lieutenant	R.A.F.	M.C. Killed in Action.
Simpson, David H.	Creevytennant	Private	Motor Section, D.H.Q.	Twice Wounded.
Simpson, Johnston H.	Creevytennant	Rifleman	14th R.I.R.	Killed in Action.
Simpson, Wm. A.	Creevytennant	Private	M.T. A.S.C.	
Thompson, Frank	Ballynahinch	Private	M.T. A.S.C.	
Thompson, Hugh	Ballynahinch	Private	M.T. A.S.C.	
Watson, John	Ballynahinch	Private	13th R.I.R.	Killed in Action.
COLONIAL FORCES.				
Bothwell, Robt. McC.	Magheraknock	Private	3rd Can. Div.	
Bothwell, Thos. H.	Magheraknock	Private	9th Can. Batt.	
Clokey, James	Ballykine		4th Can. M.G.C.	Killed in Action.
Hill, Wm. George	Ballykine	Private	50th Can. L. Inft.	Wounded. Killed in Action.
Lemon, Carl	Ballynahinch	Private	194th Can. Highlanders	
Lemon, Samuel	Ballynahinch	Corporal	3rd Can. Div.	Wounded.
Lemon, Wm.	Ballynahinch	Private	50th Can. Div.	
McLean, David	Dunmore	Private	Aust. A.M.C.	
Martin, James	Drumaness	Private	2nd Div. Winnipeg Rifles	Killed in Action.
Martin, Robert	Drumaness	Trooper	Auckland Mt. Rifles	
Purdy, Hugh	Drumaness	Private	S.A. Police	
Reid, James	Magheralone	Private	1st Batt. Can. High.	Wounded.

Name.	Home Address.	Rank.	Regiment, Battalion or Unit.	Remarks.
SECOND BALLYNAHINCH.				
Carlisle, John	Ballynahinch	Private	R.I.R.	Twice Wounded.
Cooper, H. B. S.	Spa	Cadet	O.T.C.	
Earls, Wm.	Ballykine	Lance-Corporal	13th R.I.R.	
Harper, M. T.	Clintnagooland	Lance-Sergeant	13th R.I.R.	M.M. K'd. in Act.
Heron, W. S.	Ballynahinch	Lieutenant	R.A.M.C.	
Kingan, Joseph	Ballynahinch	Private	Mechanical Transport	
McConnell, Hamilton	Ballynahinch	Cadet	O.T.C.	
McConnell, W. F.	Ballynahinch	Major	C.F. France	
McGinnis, John	Ballynahinch	Lance-Corporal	13th R.I.R.	Killed in Action.
McKibbin, Wm.	Cahard	Private	R.A.M.C.	
Mathers, W. C.	Ballynahinch	Cadet	O.T.C.	Wounded.
Milling, Thomas	Ballynahinch	Captain	R.A.M.C.	
Patterson, Thomas	Ballynahinch	Private	11/13 R.I.R.	Wounded.
Russell, Wm.	Ballynahinch	Major	R.A.M.C.	M.C.
Weir, Wm.	Ballynahinch	S. Lieutenant	2nd King's Own R.L. Regt.	Wounded. Comm'ded for Bravery
COLONIAL FORCES.				
Hunter, S. M.	Ballynahinch	Private	Australian Force	Killed in Action.
Kingan, Alex.	Ballynahinch	Private	3rd Can. Div. Cyc. Corps	Killed in Action.
McCalla, James	Cargygray	Sergeant	S. African Rifles	Wounded. Died.
BOARDMILLS.				
Brown, Samuel	Bresagh House	Captain	R.A.M.C.	Wounded. M.C.
Caughey, Robert	Bresagh	Private	M.T. A.S.C.	
Caughey, Samuel D.	Bresagh	Private	R.I.R	Wounded.
Davis, Robert	Killaney Lodge	1st Officer	R. Fleet Aux.	
Gibson, Thomas J.	Creevytenant	Lieutenant	A.S.C., Forage Dept.	
Gurnell, Robert M.	Boardmills	2nd Lieutenant	R.I.R.	Killed in Action.
Hilland, William	Cargycroy	Private	M.T. A.S.C.	
Jackson, Wm. J.	Drumra	Private	R.I.R	Prisoner of War.
Kirkpatrick, John A.	Mossgrove	Private	R.I.R.	Cert. for devotion to duty.
Kirkpatrick, John B.	Lakeview	Private	M.T. A.S.C.	
Moreland, Martin	Mealough	Private	R.I.R.	Gassed.
McCandless, John B.	Boardmills	Private	M.T. A.S.C.	
McCandless, Leslie I.	Boardmills	Lieutenant	Sherwood Foresters	Wounded.
McCarroll, David	Kilmarnock	Private	A.S.C.	
McCarroll, Lindsay McC.	Kilmarnock	Private	Tank Corps	Wounded.
McCarroll, Martin	Lisban	Private	Royal Field Artillery	
McCarroll, Robert H.	Kilmarnock	Private	Argyll & Suth. High.	Wounded. M.M.
McCarroll, Wm. J.	Kilmarnock	Private	R.F.A.	
Patterson, David	Lisban	Sergeant	R.I.R.	Wounded.
Scott, David L.	Carricknaveagh	Private	R.I.R.	
Scott, Norman A.	Carricknaveagh	Private	R.I.R.	Wounded.
Smylie, Wm. J.	Carricknaveagh	Private	R. In. Fus.	Killed in Action.
Stewart, Alex.	Carricknaveagh	Private	R.I.R.	
Stewart, Hugh H.	Carricknaveagh	Private	R.I.R.	Killed in Action.
Stewart, John	Carricknaveagh	Private	R.I.R.	
COLONIAL FORCES.				
Ferguson, John B.	3 Canadahar St., Belfast	Private	Canadians	Killed in Action.
Gibson, George A.	Ballynahinch	Private	Australian A.S.C.	
CLOUGH, CO. DOWN.				
Bell, Andrew	Clough	Private	13th R.I.R.	Wounded.
Burtney, John	Upper Clara	Private		Prisoner of War.
Campbell, Wm. John	Magherasaul	Private	N.I.H.	
Connor, Eddie	Clough	Private	13th R.I.R.	Wounded.
Connor, Harold W.	Clough	Private	13th R.I.R.	Wounded.
Connor, John A. C.	Clough	Private	13th R.I.R.	
Cromie, James	Clough	Private	13th R.I.R.	
Fitz, John	Knocksticken	Private	13th R.I.R	Wounded.
Heenan, Alfred Thomas	Drummanaghan	Private	10th R. In. Fus.	
Heenan, John	Drummanaghan		N.I.H	
Irwin, Hugh		Private	2nd I.G.	
Kidd, T. H.	Dundrum	Private	20th A.I.F.	Wounded.
Lewis, Hugh D.	Knocksticken	Private	8th R.I.R.	Wounded.
Lewis, Samuel	Knocksticken	Private	4th R.I.R.	
McBride, Samuel	Ballywillwill	Private	Pioneers, 5th Can. Battery	
McCammon, Hugh	Moneycarra	Private		
McMechan, James	Annsboro'	Private	13th R.I.R.	Wounded.
McMechan, John	Annsboro'	Private		
Maitland, Robert	Dundrum	2nd Lieutenant	19th R.I.R.	
Maitland, William S.	Dundrum	2nd Lieutenant	1st R.I.R.	M.C.
Megaw, Robert	Clara	Gunner	5th Can. F.A.	Wounded.
Potter, Wm. John	Dundrum	Private	9th R.I.R.	Killed in Action.
Robinson, Richard	Waterask	Private	13th R.I.R.	
Shaw, Herbert	Magherasaul	Private	13th R.I.R.	
Summers, J. Andrew	Seaforde	Private		Killed in Action.

DOWN PRESBYTERY. DOWNPATRICK.

Name.	Home Address.	Rank.	Regiment, Battalion or Unit.	Remarks.
DOWNPATRICK.				
Banford, J.	Saul Street	...	...	...
Banford, N. J.	Saul Street	...	...	...
Banford, W.	Saul Street	...	...	...
Brown, Craig J.	Saul Street	...	...	...
Brown, Ernest	Saul Street	...	R.I. Fus.	Wounded. M.M.
Cargo, John	Magheracranmoney	Sergeant	...	...
Cargo, Wm. Henry	Magheracranmoney	...	...	...
Cleland, Wm. T.	Raholp	Sergeant	...	...
Clydesdale, John Wilson	New Bridge Street	Private	...	Killed in Action.
Clydesdale, Joseph	New Bridge Street	Private	...	Killed in Action.
Crichton, Malcolm Nichol	Dun-beth-glas	Private	R.F.A.	...
Emerson, Guy	Bawnmore Av., Belfast	Gunner	R.I. Regt.	Wounded.
Ferguson, Robert	Irish Street	Lieutenant	16th R.I.R.	Killed in Action.
Gaddis, John	Bridge Street	Private	16th R.I.R.	...
Green, James, Jun	Bridge Street	Private	A.S.C.	...
Green, Hugh	Bridge Street	Private	A.S.C.	...
Hamilton, Wm.	Scotch Street	Private	A.S.C.	...
Henry, James	Belfast	Sergeant	R.I.R.	Killed in Action.
Henry, Samuel	Belfast	Sergeant	...	...
Heron, James	Ardragale	Private	R.I.R.	Wounded.
Kennedy, John	Irish Street	Sergeant	R.I.R.	Prisoner of War.
Lascelles, John	Killavees	...	R.A.M.C.	...
Lascelles, Walter	Killavees	Lieutenant	...	...
Lascelles, Wm. James	Killavees	Fleet Surgeon Prob.	R.A.M.C.	...
Law, David	Church Street	Captain	...	...
Law, J.	Church Street	Sergeant	...	Wounded.
Law, William	Church Street	Private	...	...
Leathem, John	Scotch Street	Private	...	Wounded.
Leathem, Richard	Scotch Street	Sergeant	...	Wounded.
Leathem, William	Scotch Street	Private	...	...
McBride, Frank J.	New Bridge Street	Private	R.I.R.	Wounded.
McBride, James	New Bridge Street	Private	R.I.R.	Wounded.
McBride, Joseph	New Bridge Street	Sergeant	R.F.A.	Killed in Action.
McBride, Joseph	Laurel Lodge	Major	Navy	...
McCormick, William	Fountain Street	Gunner	R.I.R.	...
McCracken, Samuel	New Bridge	Sergeant	R.I.R.	...
McDonald, Edward	Asylum Road	Corporal	American Army	...
McElney, Robert Gerald	The Manse	Private	R.A.M.C.	Killed in Action. M.C.
McElney, Wm. H. Campbell	The Manse	Captain	R. Air Force	
MacLeod, John	Stream Street	2nd Lieutenant	R.I.R.	...
Martin, James	Northern Banking Co.	Sergeant	R.I.R.	Wounded.
Maxwell, James	Church Street	Lieutenant	R.I.R.	Wounded. M.C.
Maxwell, Thomas B.	Church Street	Captain	R.E.	...
Moody, Thomas J.	Irish Street	Private	9th R.I.R.	Died.
Moore, William	Irish Street	Private	A.S.C.	...
Morrow, Samuel C.	Downpatrick	Lieutenant	R.I.R.	...
Nixon, Hugh Copeland	Bridge Street	2nd Lieutenant	R.I.R.	...
Patterson, David	The Quoyle Bridge	Sergeant	R.I.R.	...
Patterson, Robert	The Quoyle Bridge	Private	R.I.R.	Wounded.
Patterson, William	The Quoyle Bridge	Private	R.I.R.	...
Stopford, James	Bridge Street	Sergeant	R. Air Force	...
Whiteside, Alex. Forester	Belfast	2nd Lieutenant	Canadian Inft.	Killed in Action.
Young, George	Bridge Street	Captain	R.A.M.C.	...
		Sergeant		
SECOND DROMARA.				
Beck, William	Ballykeel	Private	...	Wounded.
Bell, Henry	Crossgar	Private	R.A.M.C.	...
Cardwell, Wm.	Derry	Private	R.F.A.	...
Corbett, Joseph	Derry	Private	9th Batt. R.I.R.	...
Ervine, Brownlow	Levalleyreagh	Sergeant	1st R.H.G.	W'ded and Missing.
Heron, A. G.	Crossgar	Captain	R.A.M.C.	...
Holmes, J. Logan	Leapox	Private	16th Batt. R.I.R.	...
Johnston, George	Derry	Lance-Corporal	10th Batt. R.I.R.	Wounded.
Lager, Albert	Dromara	Private	Belgian Army	...
McClurg, Samuel	Crossgar	Private	16th Batt. R.I.R.	...
McDowell, Samuel	Dromara	Private	13th Batt. R.I.R.	...
McMurray, Fred.	Crossgar	Private	4th King's Own R.L.R.	Wounded.
Nelson, Thomas	Crossgar	Trooper	N.I.H.	...
Welsh, Norman	Leapox	Private	M.T. A.S.C.	...
COLONIAL FORCES				
Barr, Dick	Dromara	Private	U.S. Army	...
Beck, Henry	Ballykeel	Private	46th C.M.R.	Wounded.
Beck, James	Ballykeel	Private	46th C.M.R.	...
Bothwell, Hamilton	Dromara	Private	Australians	...
Ervine, Stanley	Levalleyreagh	Private	U.S. Army	...
Jess, John Andrew	Dromara	Sergeant	5th C.M.R.	Twice Wounded.

DOWN PRESBYTERY. KILMORE.

Name.	Home Address.	Rank.	Regiment, Battalion or Unit.	Remarks.
KILMORE.				
Alexander, J. H.	Kilmore Manse	Lance-Corporal	N.I.H., Trans. Tank Corps	
Bailie, James	Listooder	Private	R.I.R.	Killed in Action.
Bailie, John	Drumaness	Private	R.I.R.	
Bailie, Samuel	Drumaness	Private	R.I.R.	
Cleland, James	Ballydian	Cadet		
Galloway, Harry	Drumaghlis	Private	R.I.R.	Wounded.
Graham, James	Drummatticonnar	Private	R.I.R.	
Graham, William	Drummatticonnar	Private	R.I.R.	
Hall, David	Ballynahinch	Private	R.I.R.	
Lightbody, John	Crossgar	Private	R.I.R.	
Lightbody, Roden	Crossgar	Private	R.I.R.	
McClements, Hugh	Clontmaglare	Private	R.I.R.	
McClurg, Andrew	Crossgar	Private	R.I.R.	
McClurg, Hugh	Crossgar	Private	R.I.R.	
McClurg, Robert	Crossgar	Sergeant	R.I.R.	Wounded.
McComb, Thomas	Listooder	Corporal	C.M.P.	Wounded.
McCoubrie, Harry	Creevy	Private	Can. Gun Corps	
McCoubrie, Percy	Listooder	Private	R.E.	
McCoubrie, Thomas	Listooder	Sergeant	R.I.R.	Killed in Action.
McVeigh, Samuel	Listooder	Lance-Corporal	R.I.R.	
Martin, Nathaniel	Drumaghlis	Private	R.I.R.	
Newell, Joseph	Creevyargon	Private	Can. L. Batt.	
Newell, Thomas	Drumaghlis			Killed in Action.
Nixon, Hugh C.	Drumaghlis	S.M. Far.	N.I.H.	
Patterson, Thomas C.	Listooder	Sergeant	I.G.	
Patterson, Samuel	Ballydian	Lieutenant	In. Fus.	Wounded.
Patterson, William	Ballydian	Lieutenant	In. Fus.	M.C.
Ralph, Dan	Rademon	Corporal	Machine Gun Corps	M.M.
Smith, William	Crossgar	Lance-Corporal	C.A.P.C.	Wounded.
Watson, David	Drumaghlis	Private	R.I.R.	
Wilson, William	Crossgar	Private	R.I.R.	
LISSARA.				
Adams, Hugh James	Crossgar	Sergeant	16th R.I.R.	
Adams, Wm. John	Crossgar	Private	16th R.I.R.	
Beatty, George	Crossgar			
Bingham, John	Crossgar	Private		Killed in Action.
Bingham, Robert	Crossgar	Private	12th R.I.R.	Wounded.
Campbell, Thomas				
Dickson, James	Crossgar	Lance-Corporal	16th R.I.R.	
Dickson, Robert	Crossgar	Private	16th R.I.R.	
Duff, James	Cluntagh	Lieutenant	R.E.	
Edgar, George	Crossgar	Lieutenant	Cadet Corps	
Frazer, Thomas	Crossgar	Private		
Kelly, John	Crossgar	Private	12th R.I.R.	
Kelso, Wm.				
Kerr, Samuel	Lissara	Private		Killed in Action.
Lightbody, John	Crossgar	Private	16th R.I.R.	
McCorriston, John				
McKnight, John				
McMordie, Francis	30 S. Parade, Belfast		R.E.P.S.	Killed in Action.
McMordie, Jas. W.	30 S. Parade, Belfast	Lieutenant		Killed in Action.
McMullan, Robert	Crossgar		8th R.I.R.	Killed in Action.
McMullan, Thomas	Crossgar	Private	8th R.I.R.	Killed in Action.
Martin, John	Crossgar	Corporal	16th R.I.R.	
Moffat, Samuel	Glasswater	Private		
Neill, James	Crossgar	Private	20th R.I.R.	
Patterson, Robert	Shrigley, Killyleagh	Private	16th R.I.R.	
Ringland, Hugh	Crossgar	Private	16th R.I.R.	
Ringland, Joseph	Crossgar	Private	M.T. A.S.C.	
Robertson, Edward W.	Crossgar		20th R.I.R.	Killed in Action.
Scott, Joseph	Crossgar	Private	20th R.I.R.	
Scott, Wm. J.	Crossgar	Private	1st R.I.R. Regt.	
Shaw, Hans	Annacloy	Sergt.-Major	A.S.C.	
Silcock, Fred. A.	Crossgar	Corporal	A.S.C.	
Silcock, Jas. H.				
Smyth, Wm.	Crossgar			Wounded.
Tate, Henry				
Thompson, Hugh	Crossgar	Private		Wounded.
Watson, Wm.				Killed in Action.
Woods, Robert	Crossgar		A.S.C.	
COLONIAL FORCES.				
Gordon, W. Ernest	Crossgar	Private	8th Canadians	
McMullan, David	Crossgar	Private	8th Canadians	Prisoner.
Patton, James A.	Crossgar	Private	40th Aust. Force	
Wilson, Samuel W.		Sergeant	Canadians	Wounded.

DOWN PRESBYTERY. MAGHERAHAMLET.

Name.	Home Address.	Rank.	Regiment, Battalion or Unit.	Remarks.
MAGHERAHAMLET.				
Clarke, Thomas S.	Deneight, Lisburn	2nd Lieutenant	R. Dub. Fus.	
Reid, Charles	Ballymaglane	Private	15th Div. R.I.R.	
RAFFREY.				
Bailie, Andrew	Derryboy	Driver	108th Machine Gun Corps	
Bailie, John	Derryboy	Private	12th R.I.R.	Wounded.
Calvert, James	Derryboy	Private	16th R.I.R.	
Calvert, Thos. G.	Derryboy	Private	88th Lab. Corps	
Coates, John	Raffrey	Signaller	13th R.I.R.	
Corbett, Hugh	Ballyalgin	Private	13th R.I.R.	Prisoner of War.
Corbett, Robert	Ballyalgin	Private	13th R.I.R.	Killed in Action.
Coulter, Wm. Robert	Barnamaghery	Private	2nd Rifle Brigade	Wounded.
Crockard, James	Carsonstown	Private	M.T. A.S.C.	
Elliott, David	Cluntagh	Corporal	4th R.I.R.	
Elliott, James	Cluntagh	Private	7th R. Scots Fus.	Killed in Action.
Elliott, Robert	Cluntagh	Private	110th Field Amb. R.A.M.C.	
Friars, Thomas	Killinchy Woods	Private	102nd Lab. Co.	
Geddes, Hans	Ballygoskin	Private	9th In. Fus.	
Hay, John	Derryboy	Farrier	A.S.C.	
Jackson, John	Derryboy	Private	A.S.C.	Died.
Johnston, Richard	Raffrey	Driver	251st Co. A.S.C.	
Johnston, Samuel	Raffrey	Driver	A. Batt. R.F.A.	
Matthews, Edward	Killyleagh	Driver	M.T. A.S.C.	
Marshall, Morrow Frew	Derryboy	Corporal	M.T. A.S.C.	
Minnis, David	Lisbane	Sergeant	14th R.I.R.	Twice Wounded. M.M.
Miskimmin, Samuel	Ballybunden	Sergeant	Machine Gun Corps	Killed in Action.
Moffett, Andrew	Derryboy	Private	18th R.I.R.	
Murray, Andrew	Ballymacashin	Private	2nd R.I.F.	
Murray, David	Ballymacreely	Gunner	196th Heavy Batt. R.G.A.	
Murray, Robert	Ballyminstra	Sergt.-Major	147th Heavy Batt. R.G.A.	Wounded.
Murray, Thos. J.	Ballyminstra	Lance-Corporal	5th R.I.R.	
McBride, Robert	Raffrey	Private	14th R.I.R.	
McIlveen, Robert	Derryboy	Private	M.T. A.S.C.	
McWhirter, Thomas	Ballyalgin	Lance-Corporal	16th R.I.R.	
Quinn, Alex.	Clea	Rifleman	13th R.I.R.	Killed in Action.
Quinn, Robert	Clea	Rifleman	9th R.I.R.	Prisoner.
Quinn, Thomas	Clea	Rifleman	182nd Lab. Co.	
Quinn, Thomas	Raffrey	Corporal	12th R.I.R.	Wounded.
Riley, Wm.	Derryboy	Private	2nd In. Fus.	Killed in Action.
Shaw, Hans	Derryboy	Far. Staff Sergt.	110th Div. Train	
Shaw, Robert	Derryboy	Private	13th R.I.R.	
Smyth, Andrew	Derryboy	Private	13th R.I.R.	
Smyth, Wellington	Derryboy	Private	13th R.I.R.	
Thompson, John	Barnamaghery	Private	12th R.I.R.	Prisoner.
Woods, Robert	Ballyalgin	Private		
COLONIAL FORCES.				
Calvert, Hugh	Derryboy	Private	2nd Can. L.B.	
Cunningham, Thomas A.	Ballywoolen	Private	Australians	Killed in Action.
Dickson, Wm.	Ballyalgin	Corporal	Toronto Regt.	Wounded.
Edmons, Robert	Ballygigan	Private	4th Can. Batt.	
Hanna, Robert	Carrickmannon	Private	N.Z.	
Kirk, Albert	Raffrey	Private	1st Can.	Killed in Action.
McCloy, J. L.	Ballyalgin	Private	4th Can. Div.	
McWhirter, Wm.	Ballyalgin	Private	Aust. Batt.	Wounded.
Miskimmin, Robert	Ballybronden	Trooper	N.Z. Cont.	Wounded.
FIRST SAINTFIELD.				
Bailie, Samuel	Carsonstown	Private		
Clarke, Samuel	Saintfield	Private		
Connolly, Albert	Ravarra	Private		
Connolly, Hugh Henry	Ravarra	Private		
Craig, Henry	Ravarra			
Davidson, David Alex., B.Sc.	Jennyvale	Lieutenant		
Davidson, Samuel	Aughnadarragh	Private		
Donnan, Robert	Cahard	Private		
Gibson, John	Tonaghmore	Private		
Graham, David		Private		
Hayes, Hugh Scott	Creevyloughare	Private		
Hewitt, William	Creevyloughare	Private		
Jackson, John	Carsonstown	Private		
Johnston, James	Saintfield	Private		
Jordon, Thomas	Lisdalgin			
Jordon, Thomas	Saintfield	Private		Wounded.
Leckey, Alex.	Saintfield	Private		Died of Wounds.
Leckey, Wm.	Saintfield	Private		
Magowan, Thomas	Saintfield			
Mannus, George	Ravarra	Private		

DOWN PRESBYTERY.   FIRST SAINTFIELD.

Name.	Home Address.	Rank.	Regiment, Battalion or Unit.	Remarks.
Mannus, Robert	Ravarra	...	...	
Moreland, Wm.	Saintfield	Private	...	
Morrison, John H.	Tonaghnieve	Sergt.-Major	...	
Morrison, Wm.	...	Private	...	
Morrow, Samuel John	Lisbane	Private	...	
Mundell, James	Creevylonghare	Private	...	
Neill, Andrew	...	Private	...	
Neill, Thomas	Saintfield	Private	...	Killed in Action.
Neill, William	...	Private	...	
Roy, Robert	Saintfield	Private	...	Killed in Action.
Russell, David	...	Private	...	
Shaw, William	...	Private	...	
Simpson, Robert E.	Saintfield	...	R.A.F.	
Skelly, Hugh Victor	Saintfield	Private	...	
Smiley, Robert	...	Private	...	
Wade, John	Carricknacessna	Private	...	
Walkinshaw, Robert	Saintfield	Private	...	
SECOND SAINTFIELD.				
Gillespie, Joseph	Saintfield	Private	R.I.R.	
Gregg, David	Saintfield	Private	R.I.R.	
Kennedy, John	Saintfield	Private	R.I.R.	Wounded.
Kinghan, James	Saintfield	Private	R. In. Fus.	Wounded.
McClenaghan, John	...	Lance-Corporal	R. In. Fus.	
Martin, James	...	Private	R.I.R.	Wounded.
Speedy, M.B., William	Saintfield	Captain	R.A.M.C., R.I.R.	
Withers, George	Saintfield	Bombardier	R.G.A.	
SEAFORDE.				
Cherrie, William	Clara	Private	N.I.H.	
McNerlin, James	Seaforde	Private	English Regiment	
McNerlin, Daniel	Seaforde	Private	English Regiment	
Nixon, Sandy	Drumgooland	Private	R.I.R.	
Stewart, H. J. L.	Seaforde Manse	Lieutenant	3rd R.I.R.	
Stewart, J. C. P.	Seaforde Manse	Sergeant	N.I.H.	
Stewart, R. C.	Seaforde Manse	Lance-Corporal	N.I.H.	
STRANGFORD.				
Cooper, Adam Porter	...	Corporal	2nd Can. B.E.F.	Wounded.
Cooper, Samuel Seed	...	Private	2nd Can. B.E.F.	Killed in Action.
McIlheron, John	Toberdoney	Private	R.F.A.	Wounded.
Monan, James	Green Row	Lance-Corporal	13th R.W.F.	Twice Wounded.

DROMORE PRESBYTERY.

Name.	Home Address.	Rank.	Regiment, Battalion or Unit.	Remarks.
ANAHILT.				
Christie, William	Hillsborough	Private	R.I.F.	
Coburn, Beattie	Ballyworphy	Staff Sergeant	Forage Dept.	
McCloughan, R. J.	Drumlough	Private	R.I.R.	
Marks, Alexander	Ballykeel	Private	R.I.R.	Wounded.
Marks, George	Ballykeel	Private	R.I.R.	Wounded.
Martin, Samuel	Cabra	Staff-Sergeant	Forage Dept.	
Patterson, David	Ballylintagh	Private	R.I.R.	Wounded.
COLONIAL FORCES.				
Marks, Robert	Ballykeel	Private	Canadian Force	Wounded.
Marks, Thomas	Ballykeel	Private	Canadian Force	
Patterson, Robert	Ballylintagh	Private	Australian Force	Wounded Twice
Patterson, William	Ballylintagh	...	Canadian Force	Wounded.
Philpott, Thomas Henry	...	Private	Canadian Force	Killed in Action.
BALLINDERRY.				
McConnell, J. F.	Ballinderry	Private	R.A.M.C., F.A.	
McMurtry, W.	Magheragall	Lance-Corporal	R.I.R.	
Spence, T.	Magheragall	Private	49th Can. Batt.	
Todd, F. E.	Ballinderry	Private	London I.R.	Wounded.
Todd, H. G.	Ballinderry	...	N.I.H.	Wounded.
Todd, S. H.	Ballinderry	Corporal	R.D. Fus.	

DROMORE PRESBYTERY.   BALLYCAIRN.

Name.	Home Address.	Rank.	Regiment, Battalion or Unit.	Remarks.
BALLYCAIRN.				
Atcheson, Thomas	Drumalig	Corporal	10th Batt. R.I.R.	
Burton, William James	Milltown	Private	Northumberland Fus.	Killed in Action.
Cochrane, George	Ballyaughlis	Private	11th Batt. R.I.R.	
Copeland, Samuel	56 Edenderry	Private	108th Field Amb. R.A.M.C.	
Crossley, Robert	Purdysburn	Private	R.A.F.	
Dornan, William	Milltown	Private	Northants Regt.	
Gibson, Thomas	Ballylesson	Private	2nd Batt. R.I. Fus.	Killed in Action.
McBride, James	Ballylesson	Private	19th Brigade R.F.A.	Salonica.
McClure, James Alen	Ballylesson	Private	A. Co. 54th Batt. M.G.C., Egyptian E.F.	
McClure, Melville	Ballylesson	Private	95th Brigade R.F.A.	
McIlwaine, Herbert	Drumbo	Private	20th French M.B., R.F.A.	
Nelson, William	Milltown	Private	R.A.F.	
Rutherford, John	Ballylesson	Private	R.F.A.	
Smyth, James	Upper Malone	Private	10th Batt. R.I.R.	
Smyth, John	Upper Malone	Private	1st Batt. R.I.R.	
Smyth, Joseph	Upper Malone	Sergeant	2nd Batt. R.I.R.	M.M.
Weir, Austen Chamberlain	Shaw's Bridge	Private	14th Batt. R.I.R.	
Weir, Joseph	Shaw's Bridge	Private	11th Border Regt.	Killed in Action.
COLONIAL FORCES.				
Marshall, Thomas George	Ballylesson	Private	1st Can. Corps R.F.A.	
Milligan, John	Monlough	Corporal	6th N.Z. Div.	
Weir, Thomas Victor	Shaw's Bridge	Private	90th Winnipeg Rifles	
BELVILLE.				
Cassells, Edward	Derrymacash	Private	R.A.F.	
Monaghan, William	Derryadd	Private	R.I. Fus.	
Stevenson, Lewis Lett	Derryinver	Private	N.I.H.	
COLONIAL AND U.S.A. FORCES.				
Adamson, William John	Bannfoot	Private	U.S.A. Army	
Castles, Edward	Derrytagh North	Drummer	Canadian Contingent	
Hamill, Joshua	Ardmore	Private	Canadian Contingent	
Hamill, Samuel Gordon	Ardmore	Private	Canadian Contingent	
Monaghan, Edward	Derryadd	Private	U.S.A. Army	Killed in Action.
Monaghan, David	Derryadd	Private	U.S.A. Army	
SECOND BOARDMILLS.				
Gill, Dr. Fred.	Rockvale	Lieutenant	R.A.F.	
Graham, James L.	Boardmills	Lieutenant	R. In. Fus.	Wounded.
Graham, Joseph	Boardmills	Driver	A.S.C.	
Hanna, William S.	Boardmills	Private	I.G.	
Jackson, William J.	Boardmills	Rifleman	R.I.R.	Prisoner of War.
Kelso, Rev. Robert	Boardmills Manse	Captain	Chaplain	
Lecky, Joseph	The Temple	Rifleman	R.I.R.	
Lecky, Samuel	The Temple	Driver	R.O.D.	
Shaw, Martin	Creevy	Private	R.I.R.	
COLONIAL FORCES.				
Dunwoody, James	Cargycroy	Private	Can. Force	
Dunwoody, Stewart	Cargycroy	Private	Can. Force	
Dunwoody, W. D.	Cargycroy	Private	Can. Force	
Lecky, Edward	The Temple	Private	Can. Force	
Walker, Hugh	Creevy	Private	Can. Force	
CARGYCREEVY.				
Davis, Charles	Magheraknock	Private	Machine Gun Corps H.L.I.	Killed in Action.
Davis, James	Magheraknock	Lance-Corporal	11th Batt. H.L.I.	Killed in Action.
Wilson, James	Stubby Hill	Private	31st Batt. Can.	Killed in Action.
Wilson, John	Stubby Hill	Private	8th Batt. Can.	Wounded.
FIRST DROMARA.				
Doake, S. Henry	Glenlagan	Major	R.F.A.	Killed in Action.
Gorman, Gilbert	Moybrick	Lance-Corporal	R.I.R.	Killed in Action.
Kane, John	Kinallen	Private	R.I.R.	
Kerr, Alexander	Skeogh	Private	R.I.R.	Killed in Action.
Lowry, Robert	Finis	Private	R.C.S.A.	
McIlveen, William James	Kinallen	Private	R.I.R.	
Murphy, John	Tullindoney	Private	R.A.M.C.	
Murray, Samuel	Leapoughs	Corporal	R.I.R.	
Steele, Alexander	Artana	Lance-Corporal	R.F.A.	
Steele, William John	Artana	Lance-Corporal	R.I.R.	

DROMORE PRESBYTERY. **FIRST DROMARA.**

Name.	Home Address.	Rank.	Regiment, Battalion or Unit.	Remarks.
Steenson, Samuel J.	Kinallen	Private	A.E.F.	
Tallerton, Alexander	Aughnaskeogh	Private	R.I.R.	
Truesdale, Fred.	Gransha	Private	R.I.R.	Died in Hospital.
Truesdale, George	Gransha	Private	R.I.R.	Wounded.
FIRST DROMORE.				
Agnew, W. J.	Greenan	Private	Scottish Lanc. Regt.	Wounded.
Arbuthnot, William	Meeting Street	Private	11th R.I.R.	Killed in Action.
Barr, Augustus	Ballysallagh	Trooper	S. Irish Horse	
Baxter, James	Gallows Street	Private	R.I.R.	Prisoner of War.
Beggs, John	Quilly	Private	R.I.R.	Killed in Action.
Bell, James	Market Square	Private	13th Batt. R.I.R.	Wounded.
Coburn, Robert	Gallows Street	Private	R.I.R.	
Cochrane, Albert	Gallows Street	Private	M.G.C.	Wounded.
Cochrane, Thomas, Sen.	Gallows Street	Sergeant	R.I.R.	
Cochrane, Thomas, Jun.	Gallows Street	Private	R.I.R.	Killed in Action.
Dobbin, Samuel J.	Weir's Row	Private	R. Irish Fus.	
Edgar, Hamilton	Lower Mount Street	Lance-Sergeant	R. Marines	
Edgar, Thomas	Lower Mount Street	Private	I.G.	Killed in Action.
Ellison, David	Lisnaward	Corporal	I.G.	
English, Douglas	Ballaney	Captain	R.I.R.	
English, Samuel	Ballaney	Captain	R.A.M.C.	
Gordon, William	Meeting Street	Private	13th R.I.R.	Killed in Action.
Graham, Noah	Bann Road	Private	R.I.R.	
Hunter, Kirker	Bann Road	Lieutenant	R.F.A.	Killed in Action.
Jamison, William	Drumbroneth	Private	12th R.I.R.	Wounded.
Kelly, John	Quilly	Lance-Corporal	R.I.R.	
Kernaghan, Victor	Skeogh	Private	R.I.R.	Wounded.
Kerr, Eric	Lower Mount Street	Private	R.A.F.	
Kerr, Leslie	Lower Mount Street	Private	16th R.I.R.	Wounded.
Kerr, Thomas R. S.	Lower Mount Street	Lance-Sergeant	1st R.I.F.	Killed in Action.
McCandless, James	Drumoghadore	Private	R. Marines	Wounded.
McCandless, Robert	Kilsallough	Private	R.I.R.	Killed in Action.
McDonald, Albert	Ballaney	Private	2nd R. In. Fus.	Killed in Action.
McDonald, David	Ballaney	Private	16th R.I.R.	
Martin, Shaw	Drumbroneth	Private	R.I.R.	Killed in Action.
Martin, William J.	Rampart Street	Corporal	R.I.R.	Wounded.
Mercer, Maurice	Bridge Street	Private	Royal Fus.	Prisoner of War.
Mulligan, David	Quilly	Private	2nd R.I.R.	
Nicholson, Hugh	Lurganbane	Private	R.I.R.	Died.
Nutt, Alexander	Meeting Street	Private	R. In. Fus.	
Nutt, Mark	Meeting Street	Private	2nd R.I.R.	Killed in Action.
Nutt, Robert	Meeting Street	Private	R.F.A.	Wounded.
Patterson, William	Gallows Street	Sapper	R.E.	
Poots, W. J.	Weir's Row	Private	R.I.R.	
Scott, Fred.	Meeting Street	Trooper	N.I.H.	Wounded.
Scott, Thomas	Lurganbane	Q.-M.S.	M.G.C.	Wounded.
Shields, John	Holm Terrace	Corporal	13th R.I.R.	Prisoner of War.
Smyth, Dobbin	Tullyglush	Private	R.I.R.	Wounded.
Smyth, Robert	Tullyglush	Private	R.I.R.	Killed in Action.
Wallace, Herbert	Regentville	Captain	R.G.A.	Wounded, M.C.
Watson, Harry	Meeting Street	Trooper	S. Irish Horse	
Young, John	Rampart Street	Private	R.I.R.	Died of Fever.
COLONIAL FORCES.				
Archer, Arthur	Coolsalla	Private	Canadian Army	
Hunter, Campbell	Bann Road	Lieutenant	Indian Army	
Poots, Thomas S.	Magherabeg	Private	Canadian Regt.	
Prenter, William	Ballaney	Private	Canadian Army	Killed in Action.
Reid, Stanley	Skeogh	Private	Canadian Army	
Todd, George F.	Lurganbane	Private	Aust. Ex. Force	Prisoner.
DROMORE, BANBRIDGE ROAD.				
Boyd, Robert	Holm Terrace	Private	R. In. Fus.	
Bryson, Samuel	Meeting Street	Lance-Corporal	R.I.R.	Killed in Action.
Campbell, R. K.	Quilly		R.A.M.C.	
Carson, David	Drumskeagh	Private	R.I.R.	Wounded.
Chambers, Edmund	Church Street	2nd Lieutenant	R. Irish Fus.	Wounded.
Chambers, James	Holm Terrace	2nd Lieutenant	R. Irish Fus.	
Cowden, C. H. C. A.	Church Street	Sergeant	R.A.F.	
Cunningham, J. H.	Mount Street	Private	R.I.R.	Killed in Action.
Dykes, Jeremiah	Police Office	Sergeant	R.I.R.	
Edgar, John H., M.A., B.L.	Dromore	Lieutenant	Durham Light Inft.	Killed in Action.
Ferguson, George	Holm Terrace	Private	R.I.R.	
Gibson, James	Quillyburn	Private	R.I.R.	
Gouley, Ernest	Skeogh	Private	R.I.R.	Killed in Action.
Gourley, John	Skeogh	Private	R.I.R.	Killed in Action.
Hunter, H. C.	Bann Road	Lieutenant	Indian Army	
Hunter, J. S. K.	Bann Road	2nd Lieutenant	R.F.A.	Killed in Action.
Hutchinson, George	Meeting Street	Mechanic	R.A.F.	
Hutchinson, Samuel	Gallows Street	Private	Northumberland Fus.	

DROMORE PRESBYTERY. BANBRIDGE ROAD, DROMORE.

Name.	Home Address.	Rank.	Regiment, Battalion or Unit.	Remarks.
Hutchinson, W. J.	Meeting Street	Lieutenant	R.F.C.	Killed in Action.
Jess, Isaac	Greenogue	Corporal	R.I.R.	Wounded.
Kerr, William J.	Ballymacormick	Sergeant	R.I.R.	
Lilley, Alexander	Cross Lane		Gordon High.	Killed in Action.
Lilley, Anthony	Cross Lane		S. Africans	
Lilley, James	Cross Lane	Stoker	R.N.	
McCandless, James	Drumaghadone	Gunner	R.N.	
McClatchey, John	Bellaney	Private	R.I.R.	
McCormick, W. J.	Mossvale	Lance-Corporal	R.I.R.	Died.
McCracken, Robert	Lagan View Terrace	Sergeant	R.F.A.	
McDonald, Albert	Gallows Street	Private	R.I.R.	
McDonald, George	Gallows Street	Private	R.I.R.	
McDonald, Henry	Gallows Street	Sergeant	R.I.R.	Wounded.
McDonald, Hugh	Gallows Street	Private	R.I.R.	Killed in Action.
McDonald, Joseph	Ballaney	Private	R.I.R.	
McDonald, Robert	Ballaney	Private	R.I.R.	
McDonald, R. J.	Gallows Street	Sergeant	R.I.R.	
McKean, J.	Police Office	Lieutenant	R. Irish Fus.	
McKee, Francis, F.R.C.S.	Prince's Street	Captain	R.A.M.C.	Died.
McMullan, Rev. W. J., B.A.	The Manse	Captain	Chaplain to Forces	
Magowan, S. W.	Bann Road		R.E.	
Mercer, J. W.	Listullycurran		R.A.M.C.	
Mitchell, George, M.D.	Drumenocken	Lieutenant	R.A.M.C.	
Rentoul, J. L., M.D.	Lisburn	Captain	R.A.M.C.	
Smith, Cecil	Church Street	Lieutenant		
Smyth, Aubrey, M.D.	Bedeque House	Staff-Surgeon	R.N.	
Thompson, Samuel J.	Church Street	Private	R. In. Fus.	
Towell, J. H.	Lagan View Terrace	2nd Lieutenant	R. Irish Fus.	Wounded.
Towell, William	Lagan View Terrace		R.A.M.C.	
Turner, Samuel	Holm Terrace	Private	R.I.R.	Prisoner of War.
Wallace, T. H., B.A., LL.B.	Regentville	Captain	R.G.A.	Wounded.
Walsh, Oliver L.	Railway Hotel	Sergt.-Major	R. In. Fus.	Wounded.
Ward, James	Ballymacormick	Corporal	Life Guards	
COLONIAL FORCES.				
Crane, David	Gallows Street		Canadians	
McCracken, John	Holm Terrace		1st Aust. Div.	Killed in Action.
McCracken, Samuel	Holm Terrace		1st Aust. Div.	
McDowell, William	Ballymacormick		M.G. Canadians	
DRUMBO.				
Allen, Robert	Edenderry	Private	R.I.R.	Killed in Action.
Brown, Robert	Edenderry	Private	R.S.F.	
Campbell, David		Private	A.E.F.	
Campbell, John		Private	A.E.F.	
Carmichael, Samuel	Leverogue House	Private	R.I.R.	
Cordner, James	Drumbo Manse	Lieutenant	R.I.R.	Killed in Action. M.C.
Cowan, Andrew	Drumbeg	Private	C.E.F.	Killed in Action.
Cowan, Robert	Drumbeg	Private	R.I.R.	
Crossley, Robert	Purdysburn	Private	R.A.F.	
Deans, Samuel, M.B., B.Sc.	Ballymacbrennan	Lieutenant	R.A.M.C.	
Dick, Samuel	Drumbeg	Lance-Corporal	R.I.R.	Killed in Action.
Dodds, Carlisle	Edenderry	Private	M.G.C.	
Gamble, John M.	Ballylesson	Private	R.I.R.	M.M.
Gill, William	Ballyskeagh	Private	R.I.R.	Killed in Action.
Gray, Alexander	Ballycoan, Purdysburn	Private	R.I.R.	
Gray, Thomas	Ballycoan, Purdysburn	Private	R.I.R.	Killed in Action.
Gray, William	Ballycoan, Purdysburn	Private	R.I.R.	
Hanna, Daniel	Drumbeg	Sergeant	R.I.R.	
Jackson, James	Ballylesson	Private	R.I.R.	
Jamison, Thomas	Ballycarngannon	Private	R.I.R.	
Kane, William J.	Edenderry	Private	R.I.R.	
Logan, Samuel	Ballymagarrick	Private	R.S.F.	
Logan, Thomas	Ballyskeagh, Lambeg	Private	R.I.R.	
McAvoy, James	Edenderry	Private	C.E.F.	
McCormack, Campbell McNeill, M.B.	Drumbo	Major	R.A.M.C.	Killed in Action. M.C., 2 Bars.
McCracken, William	Ballymullen	Private	R.I.R.	
McGowan, James B.	Clogher	Private	R.A.F.	
McKeown, William John	Edenderry	Lance-Corporal	R.I.R.	
McMaster, Samuel	Tullyard House		Canadian Navy	
McMaster, Philip George	Tullyard House	Lieutenant	M.G.C., R.I.R.	Killed in Action.
McWilliam, James	Edenderry	Sapper	R.I.R.	
McWilliam, John	Edenderry	Rifleman	R.I.R.	
McWilliam, William	Edenderry	Private	R.I.R.	
Maxwell, John	Ballycoan	Private		M.M.
Maxwell, William	Ballycoan	Private	R.A.F.	
Morrow, Hans Lowry, M.B.	Ballylesson	Captain	R.A.M.C.	
Murphy, Robert	Ballymacbrennan	Driver	R.E.	
Patterson, William Samuel	Ballymacbrennan	Sergeant	R.I.R.	

DROMORE PRESBYTERY. DRUMBO.

Name.	Home Address.	Rank.	Regiment, Battalion or Unit.	Remarks.
Reid, James	Edenderry	Rifleman	R.I.R.	
Reid, Samuel John	Edenderry	Rifleman	R.I.R.	
Tiffin, William	Drumbo	Private	R.T.S.	
Thompson, John	Ballylesson	Captain	R.I.R.	
Thompson, S. H. Hall	28 Col. Green, Belfast	Major	R.I.R.	
Waterworth, Herbert	Edenderry	Sergeant	R.I.R.	
Wilgar, William John	Farnlea, Balmoral	2nd Lieutenant	M.G.C.	
DRUMLOUGH.				
Andrews, George Camlin	Edentullick	Private	R.I.R.	Wounded.
Cains, James	Edentullick	Private	2nd I.G.	Wounded 4 times.
Chambers, William	Dromore	Private	R.I.R.	Killed in Action.
Crothers, William	Hillsborough	Private	R.G.A.	
Hamilton, Edward	Leappoges	Private	R.I.R.	Killed in Action.
Hamilton, James Alex.	Leappoges	Corporal	R. In. Fus.	
Jess, Joseph	Ballykeel	Private	R.I.R.	
Jess, Robert	Ballykeel	Private	R.I.R.	
McCone, Thomas	Drumlough	Private	R.I.R.	
Murdock, Alexander	Drumough	Private	R.G.A.	
Nicholson, S. John	Drumlough	Private	5th R.I.R.	
Presha, John	Drumlough	Private	11th R.I.R.	
Spence, William	Drumlough	Private	R.I.R.	
Strong, James	Drumlough	Private	R.G.A.	
COLONIAL FORCES.				
Jess, Howard	Hillsborough	Private	124th Can. Pioneers	
Mulholland, John	Drumlough	Trooper	5th Can. M. Rifles	
Thompson, Robert S.	Drumlough	Private	124th Can. Pioneers	Gassed.
Wilson, David	Ballykeel	Trooper	42nd Can. M. Rifles	Killed in Action.
HILLHALL.				
Armour, Thomas	Hillhall	Private	A.S.C.	
Black, William	Ballyskeagh	Private	R.I.R.	
Blakley, Samuel	Hilden View	Rifleman	R.I.R.	
Blakley, Samuel, Jun.	Hilden View	Rifleman	R.I.R.	Killed in Action.
Blakley, Thomas	Hilden View	Rifleman	R.I.R.	
Boyd, Harry	Lisnatrunk	Rifleman	R.I.R.	
Browne, James	Connolly Row	Rifleman	R.I.R.	Killed in Action.
Browne, James	55 Mercer Street	Rifleman	R.I.R.	
Browne, Robert	55 Mercer Street	Rifleman	1st Inn. Fus.	
Browne, Samuel	Late Connolly Row	Rifleman	R.I.R.	
Cairns, Robert	125 Gregg Street	Rifleman	R.I.R.	
Cairns, William	125 Gregg Street	Rifleman	R.I.R.	
Colvin, Samuel	Drumbeg	Private	11th R.I.R.	
Crookshank, William	Hillhall	L.-Corporal	16th R.I.R.	
Downing, James	Late Hillhall	2nd Lieutenant		Killed in Action.
Ferris, Alfred	Hillhall	Private	12th Manchester Regt.	
Ferris, Fred.	Hillhall			
Frazer, Robert	Tannabrick	Corporal	R.I.R.	
Fulton, John	Hillhall Road	Lance-Corporal	11th and 18th R.I.R.	Wounded.
Fulton, Stephen	East Down View	Private	A.S.C. and R.F.A.	
Gallagher, William	Bridge Street	Private	R.I.R. and Lab. Corps	Wounded.
Harrison, Albert	Hillhall	Private	R. In. Fus.	Died of Wounds.
Hunter, Robert	Hillhall Road	Rifleman	R.I.R.	Wounded.
Hunter, William	Hillhall Road	Rifleman	R.I.R.	Died.
Irvine, David	4 Low Road		11th R.I.R.	Killed in Action.
Irvine, Robert	Low Road	Private	Lincoln Regt.	
Irvine, Samuel	Low Road	Rifleman	11th R.I.R.	Killed in Action.
Irvine, William	Carman's Row	Rifleman	11th R.I.R.	Missing.
Kennedy, Campbell	Lambeg	Corporal	6th R.I.R.	Killed in Action.
Killips, John	Lower Plantation	Private	11th R.I.R.	
Leinster, James	44 Grand Street	Private	R.M.L.I.	
Lewis, Edward	Tullynacross	Private	R.I.R.	Killed in Action.
Lockhart, Robert	Tullyard	Rifleman	11th R.I.R.	Wounded.
Lockhart, Samuel	Mercer Street	A.B.	R.N.	Torpedoed.
Logue, John	Lower Plantation	Private	R.I.R.	
McCaugherty, John	Lisnatrunk	Private	Tank Corps	
McCaugherty, Archie	Lisnatrunk	Private	13th R.I.R.	Killed in Action.
McCullough, Andrew	Lower Plantation	Rifleman	R.I.R. and K.R.R.C.	Wounded. Killed in Action.
McKeown, Francis K.	Ballynahinch Road	Private	R.I.R.	Wounded.
McKeown, William	Hillhall	Private	11/13th R.I.R.	Missing.
McMillan, John	Late Masonic Hall	Corporal	14th R.I.R. (Y.C.V.)	Killed in Action.
McNair, John	Lower Plantation	Rifleman	11th R.I.R.	Killed in Action.
McNair, William	Lower Plantation	Rifleman	11th R.I.R.	
McNeill, Robert	Mercer Street	Private	11th R.I.R.	Wounded and Disabled.
McNeill, Victor	Mercer Street	Lance-Corporal	18th R.I.R.	
McNutt, Rev. William	Hillhall Manse	Captain	R.A. Chaplain Dept.	
Morrow, Robert	Hillhall Road	Rifleman	11th R.I.R.	Killed in Action.
Murdock, Thomas	Tullynacross	Corporal	N.I.H.	Wounded.

DROMORE PRESBYTERY. HILLHALL.

Name.	Home Address.	Rank.	Regiment, Battalion or Unit.	Remarks.
Porter, Richard	Hillhall	Rifleman	13th R.I.R.	Wounded and Pris.
Rainey, Henry	Gregg Street	Rifleman	11th R.I.R.	Wounded & Missing
Rainey, Samuel	Woodview Cottage	Sergeant	N.I.H.	M.M.
Rainey, Samuel	Hillhall Road	Rifleman	11th R.I.R.	Wounded.
Rainey, William	Woodview Cottage	Corporal	11th R.I.R.	Wounded.
Ringland, George	Tullynacross	Private	R.I.R. and 15th Worc. Regt.	Wounded.
Rush, Joshua	Ballymullen	Rifleman	2nd R.I.R.	Missing.
Scott, Thomas	Hilden View	Rifleman	13th R.I.R.	Wounded.
Smith, William	Ellenville	Rifleman	11th R.I.R.	Wounded.
Stewart, James	Ballymullen			Killed in Action.
Stewart, John	98 Gregg Street		6th R.I.R.	
Stewart, Thomas	Ballymullen			Killed in Action.
Taylor, James	Lockview	Gunner	R.G.A.	Gassed.
Turner, Edward	Mossview	A.B.	R.N.	
Turner, George	Mossview	Rifleman	10th R.I.R.	Killed in Action.
Turner, Lorenzo	Mossview	Rifleman	11/13th R.I.R.	
Turner, Robert	Hillhall	Rifleman	11/13th R.I.R.	Wounded thrice.
Turner, Samuel	Mossview	Rifleman	11/13th R.I.R.	Wounded.
Webb, Ernest	Bridge Street	Private	R.A.M.C.	Wounded.
Webb, Herbert	Bridge Street	Rifleman	11th R.I.R.	Wounded.
Whitley, Albert	36 Wesley Street	Corporal	R.E.	
Wilson, Fred.	Grand Street	Rifleman	11/13th R.I.R.	
Wilson, John	Grand Street	Rifleman	R.I.R., A.S.C.	
COLONIAL FORCES.				
Carson, James	Hillhall Farm	Private	Canadians	
Downing, Alexander	Late Hillhall	Sergeant	Canadians	
Frazer, William	Tannabrick		19th Can. Batt.	
Fulton, David	East Down View		Aust. Imp. Forces	Wounded.
McNair, John	Late Millbrook		11th R.I.R.	Killed in Action.
Magowan, Charles	Clogher		N.Z. Forces	Killed in Action.
Morrow, Robert	63 Bachelors' Walk			
HILLSBOROUGH.				
Baxter, W. E.	Hillsborough	Private	13th R.I.R.	Wounded.
Beattie, Robert	Becknamullagh	Private	R.A.M.C.	
Boyd, David	Aughindunvarren	Sergeant	R.E.	
Chalmers, Robert	Culcavey	Corporal	M.M.P.	
Coburn, Thomas	Culcavey	Private	13th R.I.R.	
Crothers, William	Aughindunvarren	Private	13th R.I.R.	
Dorman, William J.	Carnbane	Private	13th R.I.R.	Died on Service.
Freeland, Samuel	Aughindunvarren	Corporal	11th R.I.R.	Wounded.
Hamilton, Samuel	Park Street	Private	13th R.I.R.	Killed in Action.
Lillie, Edwin	Ballykeelartifinny	Private	1st R.I.R.	
McAdam, James	Culcavey	Private	13th R.I.R.	
McKee, John	Culcavey	Corporal	11th R.I.R.	Wounded.
McKenzie, Duncan	The Gardens	Private	R.A.M.C.	
Mahood, David	Aughindunvarren	Private	13th R.I.R.	Wounded.
Martin, Robert				
Martin, Samuel	Cabra	2nd Lieutenant	R.F.C.	
Milligen, Samuel	Carnreagh	Air-Mechanic	R.F.C.	
Orr, Rev. J. Herbert	The Manse	Captain	Chaplain	
Orr, Stanley H.	Belfast	Lieutenant	11th Loyal N. Lanc.	Wounded.
Robinson, William	Lisadian	Corporal	A.S.C.	
Smyth, William J.	Toughblane	Private	1st I.G.	
Spratt, Richard	Newport	Corporal	1st R.I.R.	
Toman, Henry	Ravarnette	Private	11th R.I.R.	Killed in Action.
Woods, Richard	Carnreagh	Lieutenant	R.E.	Wounded.
LEGACURRY.				
Bowers, James	Ravarnette	Sergeant	16th R.I.R.	W'ded. Lost leg.
Boyd, Alexander	Ravarnette	Private	1st R.I.R.	Killed in Action.
Boyd, Robert	Ravarnette	Private	R.E.	
Boyd, William	Ravarnette	Sergeant	2nd R.I.R.	Twice Wounded.
Heathwood, R.	Ravarnette	Corporal	R.F.A.	
McCloy, James	Cabra	Private	11th R.I.R.	
Presha, John	Ravarnette	Lance-Corporal	3rd R.I.R.	Wounded.
FIRST LISBURN.				
Adams, Edward	Hill Street	Private	Scottish Rifles	
Adams, Ralph	Hill Street	Private	R.I.R.	
Adams, Samuel	Hill Street	Private	53rd N. Fus.	Killed in Action.
Beck, Hugh H.	Longstone Street	Private	R.I.R.	
Beck, James	Longstone Street	Private	R.I.R.	
Beck, Robert	Longstone Street	Private	2nd In. Fus.	Killed in Action.
Black, David	Lambeg	Stoker	R.N.	
Blakely, Alexander F.	Lambeg	Private	R.I.R.	
Blakely, Edward C.	Hill Street	Private	R.I.R.	
Blakely, Thomas	Lambeg	Private	R.I.R.	
Campbell, David		Private		

DROMORE PRESBYTERY. FIRST LISBURN.

Name.	Home Address.	Rank.	Regiment, Battalion or Unit.	Remarks.
Campbell, Hubert	Castle Street	Cadet	R.I.R.	
Campbell, Wilfred S. H.	Chelsea, London	Captain	R.A.M.C.	
Carlisle, William	Gregg Street	Captain	R.E.	
Caughey, Joseph	Hillhall Road	Sergeant	R.I.R.	
Chambers, James	Lisburn	Private	R.I.R.	Killed in Action.
Clarke, William		2nd Lieutenant	R.I.R.	
Clay, John	Lambeg	Private	R.I.R.	Died of Wounds.
Clay, Thomas	Lambeg	Q.-M. Sergt.	109th Mortar Battery	Killed in Action.
Cooke, Fredk. G.	Walk	Private	N.I.H.	Killed in Action.
Coulter, James	Bow Street	Private	R.I.R.	Prisoner
Coulter, P. B.	Bow Street	Private	R.I. Fus.	
Coulter, Theodore	Bow Street	Sergeant	R.I.R.	
Coulter, Victor	Railway Street	Lieutenant	R.I.R.	
Coulter, W. Ernest	Railway Street	Captain	Leinster Regt.	
Cree, George	Low Road	Private	R.I.R.	
Cree, William	Low Road	Private	R.I.R.	Prisoner.
Crothers, Jack	Llewellyn Avenue	Private	R.I.R.	
Deane, Laurence	Mercer Street	Sapper	R.E.	
Dickson, Robert	Gregg Street	Private	R.I.R.	
Dickson, Samuel	Gregg Street	Private	R.I.R.	Killed in Action.
Douglas, Samuel	Ravarnette	Private	R.I.R.	Killed in Action.
Duff, Ernest	Old Hillsborough Road	Lieutenant	King's Rifles	
Fisher, David J.	Lambeg	Sergeant	R.I.R.	
Fisher, Joseph	Lambeg	Private	M.G.C., R.I.R.	
Fisher, William J.	Lambeg	Stoker	R.N.	
Gill, David	Balliskeagh	Lance-Corporal	R.I.R.	
Gill, James	Balliskeagh	Private	R.I.R.	Prisoner.
Gill, Robert	Balliskeagh	Private	R.I.R.	
Gill, William	Balliskeagh		R.I.R.	Killed in Action.
Gillespie, J. E. Stanley	Seymour Street	Q.-M. Sergt.	R.I.R.	
Gillespie, R. C. V.	Seymour Street	Corporal	E. Yorkshires	Killed in Action.
Gillespie, W. C. D.	Seymour Street		H.M.S. "Duke of Edinburgh"	
Greenfield, Richard B.	Walk		H.M.S. Duke of Edinburgh	
Greenfield, Robert S.	Walk	Private	108th Field Amb.	
Hull, Frederick G.	Castle Street	Captain	R.I.R.	
Johnston, Joseph G., M.D.	Railway Street	Lieut.-Colonel	R.A.M.C.	M.C.
Kinkead, Henry	Ardmore	2nd Lieutenant	R.A.	
Kirkwood, T. J.	Lisburn	Private	R.I.R.	Died.
Knox, Charles	Lambeg	Sergeant	R.A.	Died of Wounds.
Ledlie, James	Lambeg	Private	R.I.R.	
Ledlie, Samuel	Lambeg	Private	R.I.R.	
Ledlie, Thomas	Lambeg	Private	R.I.R.	
Lindsay, Robert	Low Road	Private	R.I.R.	Killed in Action.
Logan, Charles				
Logan, Jack				
Logan, Simon	Lisburn	Cadet	N.I.H.	
McClenaghan, John	Low Road	Lance-Corporal	R.I.R.	
McClenaghan, Richard	Low Road	Private	Trench M. Batt.	
McClenaghan, W. J.	Hilden	Sergeant	Northumberland Fus.	
McCloy, Matthew	Lisburn	Private	Labour Batt.	
McCumiskey, Harold	Bridge Street	Private	R. In. Fus.	Wounded.
McCumiskey, Herbert	Bridge Street	Private	R.I.R.	Wounded.
McCumiskey, James	Bridge Street	Gunner	R.F.A.	
McCumiskey, William	Bridge Street	Private	R.I.R.	
McKibbin, Joseph				
McLean, James P.	Lisburn	Private	R.I.R.	
McNeill, John		Private	R.I.R.	
Magee, James	Low Road		Worcester Regt.	
Magee, William		Private	Labour Batt.	
Malcomson, Norman D.	Ulster Bank	Lieutenant	Manchester Regt.	
Malcomson, Thomas	Ulster Bank	Captain	Manchester Regt.	Wounded.
Malcomson, Rodney				
Maze, Andrew	Antrim Street	Sergeant	S. African Corps	
Mines, Charles	Mercer Street	Private	R.I.R.	
Mines, John				
Mines, Thomas	Mercer Street	Private	R.I.R.	Died of Wounds.
Mitchell, Anthony	Low Road	Sergeant	R.I.R.	Wounded.
Moore, Joseph	Hillhall Road	Private	R.I.R.	
Murphy, Robert	Eia Street	Sapper	R.E.	Wounded.
Newell, James	Low Road	Sapper	R.E.	Killed in Action.
Patterson, Phares	Smithfield	Private	R.I.R.	
Patterson, W. J.	Hill Street		R.I.R.	
Pearson, David	Longstone Road	Private	R.I.R.	
Pearson, William				
Pelan, Thomas	N.C.R.	Private	S. African Force	
Perry, Robert	Low Road		R.N.	
Reid, John	Lambeg	Private	R.I.R.	Prisoner.
Rodgers, Marshall	Church Street	Private	R.I.R.	
Rush, Edward	Lambeg	Private	R.I.R.	
Shaw, John	O. H. Road	Sergeant	R.I.R.	Wounded.
Simpson, Herbert	Cremorne	Captain	R.I.R.	
Simpson, John	Low Road	Private	R.I.R.	
Simpson, Joseph	Low Road	Private	R.I.R.	Killed in Action.
Simpson, William	Wilson Street	Private	R.I.R.	

DROMORE PRESBYTERY.   FIRST LISBURN.

Name.	Home Address.	Rank.	Regiment, Battalion or Unit.	Remarks.
Skillen, Fred A.	Railway Street	Captain	King's Liverpool	
Skillen, William	...	...	...	
Smyth, W. James	Walk	Private	R.I.R.	Wounded.
Stewart, Robert	Lambeg	Private	R.I.R.	
Thompson, James	Market Square	Private	R.I.R.	Wounded.
Thompson, John	Market Square	Private	R.I.R.	Wounded.
Todd, Francis	Low Road	Private	R.I.R.	Killed in Action.
Walker, Joseph	Church Street	Sergeant	N.I.H.	Killed in Action.
Walker, Robert	Church Street	Lance-Corporal	R.I.R.	
Waring, Alfred	Linenhall Street	Private	R.I.R.	Killed in Action.
Waring, John	Linenhall Street	Private	R.I.R.	Killed in Action.
Watson, William	Millbrook	Private	R.M.L. Inft.	
Watton, Thomas	Antrim Street	Sergeant	R.I.R.	
Wilson, Joseph	44 Castle Street	Sergeant	R.A.F.	
Wilson, Thomas H.	Brooklyn	Captain	R.I.R.	Wounded and Pris.
Wilson, W. A.	Fintern	Captain	R.I.R.	Died in Hosp., S.A.
Wilson, W. J. B.	Brooklyn	Captain	R.I.R.	Wounded
COLONIAL FORCES.				
McCumskey, Albert	...	...	Can. Dragoons	Wounded.
Maze, William	...	...	Can. E.F.	
Moore, Albert	...	...	Can. F.A.	
Morrow, Robert	...	Corporal	2nd Canadians	
Smyth, Andrew	...	Private	Can. Cavalry	
RAILWAY STREET.				
Alexander, J. B., M.B.	Lisburn	Lieutenant		
Archer, William	Lisburn	Gunner		
Beattie, Ernest	Lisburn	Private		
Beattie, Robert	Lisburn	Private		
Beattie, Victor	Lisburn	Sergeant		M.M.
Bell, Andrew	Lisburn	Private		
Bell, Harry	Lisburn	Private		
Bell, John	Lisburn	Private		
Bell, John, Jun.	Lisburn	Private		Killed in Action.
Blakely, Samuel	Tullynacross	Private		
Blakely, William J.	Tullynacross	Private		
Boyd, Ernest A.	Lisburn	Lieutenant		
Boyd, H. S.	Lisburn	Cadet		
Boyd, James R.	Lisburn	Sergt.-Major		
Boyd, John, M.B.	Lisburn	Lieutenant		
Bowman, Robert	Lisburn	2nd Lieutenant		
Braithwaite, James	Lisburn	Sergeant		Killed in Action.
Braithwaite, Rene	Lisburn	Sergeant		D.C.M.
Braithwaite, Samuel	Lisburn	Sergt.-Major		
Braithwaite, William	Lisburn	Signalman, R.N.		
Carson, J. C., M.B.	Lisburn	Lieutenant		M.C.
Carson, T. J.	Lisburn	Private		
Cathcart, Robert	Lisburn	Private		Killed in Action.
Cathcart, Thomas	Lisburn	Private		
Cathcart, Thomas, Jun.	Lisburn	Lance-Corporal		Killed in Action.
Chambers, J. O.	Lisburn	Sergeant		
Connolly, Henry	Lisburn	Sergeant		M.M.
Connolly, Jack	Lisburn	Private		
Coulter, Andrew	Lisburn	Private		
Cousins, Robert	Lisburn	Corporal		
Cree, John	Lambeg	Sergeant		
Cunningham, William	Lisburn	Guardsman		Killed.
Curran, David	Lambeg	Corporal		
Dunlop, Daniel	Lisburn	Private		
Dunlop, Quinton	Lisburn	Corporal		Killed in Action.
Dunlop, William	Lisburn	Sergeant		
Dowds, John	Lisburn	Private		
Egerton, Harry	Lisburn	Lance-Corporal		
Fraser, J. H., B.Sc.	Lisburn	Sapper		
Freeman, James	Lisburn	Private		
Freeman, W. J	Lisburn	Private		
Fullerton, David	Lisburn	2nd Lieutenant		
Gillian, R. J.	Lisburn	Private		
Graham, James	Lisburn	Private		
Griffin, George	Lisburn	R.N.		
Griffin, Martin	Lisburn	Lance-Corporal		
Guinn, Robert	Lisburn	Private		
Hamilton, Robert	Lisburn	Private		
Hamilton, E. S. B., M.B.	Manchester	Captain	R.A.M.C.	M.C.
Hanna, David	Lambeg	Private		
Harvey, Gordon	Lisburn	2nd Lieutenant		
Henry, James	Hilden	Private		
Hillis, John	Lisburn	Private		
Hopkins, John	Lisburn	Private		Killed in Action.
Hunter, H. G. R.	Lisburn	2nd Lieutenant		
Innes, Samuel	Lisburn	2nd Lieutenant		

DROMORE PRESBYTERY.   RAILWAY STREET.

Name.	Home Address.	Rank.	Regiment, Battalion or Unit.	Remarks.
Irvine, James A.	Lisburn	Corporal		
Johnston, John	Lisburn	Lance-Corporal		
Keery, Henry	Hilden	Private		
Keightly, M. F.	Lisburn	Lieutenant		
Keightly, P. C. R.	Lisburn	Captain		Killed in Action.
Killips, John	Lisburn	Private		
King, George	Lisburn	Private		Killed in Action.
King, James	Lisburn	Private		
Kissack, James	Lisburn	Private		
Lennox, Francis	Lisburn	Private		Killed in Action.
Lewis, George	Lisburn	Private		
Lewis, James	Lisburn	Private		
Lewis, William	Lisburn	Private		Killed in Action.
Lutton, John	Lisburn	Sergeant		
Lutton, John, Jun.	Lisburn	Corporal		
Lyness, Albert	Lisburn	Private		
Lyness, David	Lisburn	Private		
Lyness, Matthew	Lisburn	Sergeant		Killed in Action.
McCarthy, Joseph	Lisburn	Private		
McCaw, James	Lisburn	Private		
McConnell, Edward	Lisburn	Private		
McConnell, Samuel	Lisburn	Lance-Corporal		
McCormick, Thomas	Lisburn	Private		
McDowell, J. H.	Ballymacash	Private		
McDowell, James	Ballymacash	Private		
MacGregor, G. G.	Lisburn	Cadet		
MacGregor, R. P.	Lisburn	Lieutenant		M.C.
McMordie, Joseph	Lisburn	Private		
McNair, Isaac	Lisburn	Private		Killed in Action.
McNair, John	Lisburn	Private		
McNeice, Alex.	Lisburn	Private		
McNeice, J.	Lisburn	Private		
McNeill, Robert	Lisburn	Sergeant		M.M.
McNeill, William	Lisburn	Corporal		
Magill, William	Lisburn	2nd Lieutenant		
Maginnis, Alex.	Lisburn	Private		Killed in Action.
Martin, Samuel	Lisburn	Private		
Moore, Fred.	Lisburn	Sergeant		
Moore, James	Lisburn	Sergeant		
Moore, John	Lisburn	Sergeant		
Moore, William	Lisburn	Private		
Morrison, D. St.G., B.A.	Lisburn	Lieutenant		Killed in Action.
Murdoch, Alex.	Lisburn	Sergeant		
Neagle, Francis	Lisburn	Private		
Neagle, William James	Lisburn	Sergeant		Killed in Action.
Neill, Thomas	Lisburn	Private		
Philpott, G. H.	Lisburn	Private		Killed in Action.
Ramsey, James	Lisburn	Private		
Ramsey, John	Lisburn	Private		Killed in Action.
Rentoul, J. L., M.B.	Lisburn	Captain	R.A.M.C.	
Ritchie, William	Lisburn	Lance-Corporal		Killed in Action.
Rogan, Arthur	Lisburn	Private		
Rogan, Robert	Lisburn	Private		
Rose, Albert	Lisburn	Corporal		
Rose, George	Lisburn	Corporal		
Scott, David	Lisburn	Private		
Shirlow, William	Lisburn	Private		
Spence, D. A.	Lisburn	Private		
Skelly, George	Belsize	Private		
Skelly, James	Belsize	Private		Killed in Action.
Skelly, John	Belsize	Corporal		
Skelly, James	Lisburn	Private		
Skelly, J. R.	Lisburn	Private		
Skelly, Walter	Lisburn	Private		
Skelly, William	Lisburn	Private		Killed in Action.
Stewart, Jos.	Lambeg	Private		
Stewart, William	Lambeg	Private		
Stranwick, William	Lisburn	Private		
Stuart, William, Constable	Lisburn	Corporal		
Taylor, D. R., B.A., M.B.	Lisburn	Lieutenant		
Thompson, John	Lisburn	Private		
Thompson, J. H.	Lisburn	Sergt.-Major		
Wallace, S. B.	Lisburn	Lieutenant		
Weir, William	Lisburn	Lieutenant		
Whitfield, William, M.B.	Lambeg	Lieutenant, R.N.		
Whitfield, Charles A., M.B.	Lambeg	Lieutenant		
Wilson, R. H.	Lisburn	Sergt.-Major		
LISBURN, SLOAN STREET.				
Baxter, Isaac	Low Road	Rifleman	R.I.R.	
Campbell, John		Lance-Corporal	Royal Berks.	Missing, believed dead.
Campbell, Thomas	The Cottage, Low Road	Q.M. Sergeant	Middlesex	

DROMORE PRESBYTERY.   SLOAN STREET, LISBURN.

Name.	Home Address.	Rank.	Regiment, Battalion or Unit.	Remarks.
CARLISLE, JAMES	71 Mercer Street	Stoker 1st Class	R.N.	
CARLISLE, WILLIAM	62 Hillhall Road	Pioneer	R.E.	
CARUTH, HUGH	1 Colin View	Seaman	R.N.	
CARUTH, SAMUEL	1 Colin View		R.A.F.	
CATHCART, DAVID	87 Ballynahinch Road	Sergeant	11th R.I.R.	Killed in Action.
CORBETT, HENRY	Lambeg		R.A.F.	
CREIGHTON, ROBERT	Plantation	Rifleman	11th R.I.R.	W'ded and Gassed.
CROTHERS, JOHN	Westbourne Crescent	Signaller	R.F.A.	M.M.
CROTHERS, VICTOR	Westbourne Crescent	Private	R.A.S.C., M.D.	
FOYE, SILAS	Gregg Street	Rifleman	R.I.R.	Wounded.
FOYE, THOMAS	15 Sloan Street	Lance-Corporal	R.I.R.	Wounded.
GIBSON, JOHN	49 Sloan Street	Private	18th R.I.R.	Killed in Action.
GIBSON, JAMES	49 Sloan Street	Signaller	R.E.	
HAYES, WILLIAM	Saintfield Road	Staff-Sergeant	R.G.A.	
HOLMES, THOMAS	Low Road	Corporal	I.G.	
HOLMES, WILLIAM	Low Road	Sergt.-Major	I.G.	D.C.M., W'ded.
HOLMES, JAMES	Low Road	Seaman	R. Marines	Killed in Action.
LYNESS, JAMES	32 Hillhall Road	Seaman	R.N.	
McKINSTRY, CHALMERS	The Manse, R'stown			
MAXWELL, CHARLES	Mercer Street	Private	R.I.R.	
MILLIGEN, WILLIAM	Deneight	Corporal	A.E.T.	
MILLIGEN, SAMUEL	Deneight	Sergeant	R.A.F.	
MILLIGEN, JOHN P.	Deneight	Corporal	A.E.T.	
MILLIGEN, LEWIS A.	Deneight	Corporal	A.E.T.	
NEWELL, JAMES	129 Gregg Street	Lance-Corporal	R.E.	Killed in Action.
RICHARDSON, GORDON	7 Laganvale Terrace	Trooper	N.I.H.	
ROBERTS, SAMUEL	10 Canal Street	Lance-Corporal	R.I.R.	M.M. and Bar.
SPENCE, ALEXANDER	Low Road	Private	R.I.R.	
STEWART, HUGH	40 Old Hillsborough Rd.	Rifleman	11th R.I.R.	
STOREY, JOHN	Belsize Road	Rifleman	R.I.R.	
TEENEY, WILLIAM H.	Bachelors' Walk	Sapper	R.E.	
TORANCE, RICHARD	Laurel Vale	Trooper	N.I.H.	
VOGAN, WILLIAM	5 Mercer Street	Signaller	Machine Gun Corps	
WHAN, DAVID S.	Smithfield	Lance-Corporal	15th R.I.R.	Prisoner of War.
WRIGHT, WILLIAM	34 Seymour Street	Private	11th R.I.R.	Wounded twice.
WRIGHT, WILLIAM J.	Old Hillsborough Road	Lance-Corporal	R.E.	
LOUGHAGHERY.				
MARTIN, WILLIAM	Legacurry	Corporal	B.E.F., E. Africa	
RUTHERFORD, JOSEPH B.	Carricknadarriff	Driver	R.F.A.	
SCOTT, JAMES HERBERT	Ballymurphy	Rifleman	14th R.I.R.	Killed in Action.
SCOTT, THOMAS	Ballymurphy	Driver		
FIRST LURGAN.				
BAXTER, CHARLIE	Robert Street	Private	H.L.I.	Killed in Action.
BELL, HARRY	Queen Street	Private	M.A.C.	
BELL, R. J.	Queen Street	Lance-Corporal	16th A. & S.H.	
BLACK, W. S.	Church Place	Sergeant	R.A.M.C.	
BULLICK, JOSEPH	Prince's Street	Lance-Corporal	R.N. Lancs.	Prisoner of War.
CALLAGHAN, R.	Church Place	Sergeant	20th R.I.R.	Wounded.
CAMPBELL, JOHN	Market Street	S.M.	A.S.C.	M.S.M.
CARSON, SAM	Toberhuiney	Private	R.I.R.	
CONNOLLY, BOB	Queen Street	Private	9th R.I.F.	
CONNOLLY, JOHN	Queen Street	Private	IC. War Hospital	Wounded.
CRAWFORD, W. B. S.	The Manse	Gunner	R.G.A.	
CROZIER, GEORGE	Wellington Street	Corporal	N.I.H.	
CROZIER, HARRY	Cornrainey	Private	R.A.F.	
CROZIER, JAMES	Hamilton Street	Private	Labour Corps	Wounded.
CROZIER, WILLIE	Hamilton Street	Private	R.A.F.	
CULLY, JAMES	Bowen's Lane	Corporal	1st R.I.F.	Prisoner of War.
CUNNINGHAM, JOHN	Albert Street	C.S.M.	10th R.I.F.	
CUNNINGHAM, TOM	Ram Park	Private	16th R.I.F.	
DOWDS, GEORGE	Factory Lane	Private	R.A.M.C.	
DUFFY, WILLIAM	Union Street	Lance-Corporal	10th R.I.F.	Wounded.
DUKE, W. THOMAS	Union Street	Lieutenant	16th R.I.R.	
ENGLISH, W. L., M.B.	Oakley	Lieutenant	R.A.M.C.	
FERGUSON, R.	Dollingstown	Sergeant	21st Batt. O.C.	
FERGUSON, SAM	Factory Lane	Sergeant	6th R.I.R.	Died.
FITZIMONS, BOB	Robert Street	Private	9th R.I.F.	Died.
FITZIMONS, JIM	Robert Street	Corporal	M.G.C.	Wounded.
FOSTER, FRED.	Market Street	Sergeant	9th R.I.F.	Killed in Action.
FOYE, WILLIAM	Robert Street	Private	R.A.M.C.	
FOYE, ALEX.	Robert Street	Private	5th R.I.R.	
GIBSON, HARRY	Union Street	Private	9th R.I.F.	Killed in Action.
GIBSON, JAMES	Brown's Yard	Private	R.E.	
GIBSON, ROBERT	Union Street	Driver	R.I.F.	
GIBSON, THOMAS	Queen Street	Private	1st E. Lancs.	Killed in Action.
GIBSON, WILLIAM	Brown's Yard	Lance-Corporal	9th R.I.F.	Killed in Action.
GIBSON, W. J.	Union Street	Sergeant	N.I.H.	Wounded.
GLENN, JAMES	Church Place	Private	R.A.F.	
GLENN, WILLIAM	Church Place	Private	9th R.I.F.	Killed in Action.

DROMORE PRESBYTERY. FIRST LURGAN.

Name.	Home Address.	Rank.	Regiment, Battalion or Unit.	Remarks.
Gordon, Samuel	Barris's Yard	Private	R.A.M.C.	
Gordon, William	Turmoyra	Lance-Corporal	R.F.A.	
Graham, Albert	Queen Street	Private	9th R.I.F.	Wounded.
Graham, Albert	Factory Lane	Private	9th R.I.F.	Killed in Action.
Graham, John	Factory Lane	Private	3rd N. Fus.	
Hadden, Ralph	Avenue Road	Sergeant	N. Fus.	
Hall, James	Ram Park	Private	9th R.I.F.	
Hall, William	Rooney's Yard	Private	5th R.I.R.	Wounded.
Hall, W. J.	Ram Park	Private	I.G.	Wounded.
Hamilton, Alex.	Avenue Road	Private	9th R.I.F.	Killed in Action.
Hanna, Alex.	North Street	Private	M. Marine	
Hanna, Robert	Watson's Lane	Private		
Hanna, William	Watson's Lane	Private	1st A. & S.H.	
Hanna, William	North Street	Private	A.S.C.	Wounded.
Haskis, George	Avenue Road	Private	R.A.M.C.	
Hayes, Charles, B.A.	Moorefield	Gunner	R.G.A.	
Henry, James	Barris's Yard	Private	R.A.F.	
Henry, John	Barris's Yard	Private	9th R.I.F.	Killed in Action.
Hill, Thomas	Hill Street	Lance-Corporal	Labour Corps	Wounded.
Houston, Thomas	Northern Bank	Lieutenant	10th R.I.R.	
Johnston, Arch.	Cornrainey	Private	R.A.F.	
Johnston, Ernest	Grace Hall	Lieutenant	8th S. Staffs.	Killed in Action.
Johnston, Herbert	Grace Hall	Sergeant	21st O.C.B.	Killed in Action.
Johnston, Percy	Grace Hall	Lieutenant	R.G.A.	
Lyttle, Isaac	Edward Street	Private	10th R.I.F.	Wounded.
McCaw, G. T, M.A.	Tegnavin	Lieutenant	R.E.	
McCleery, G. A.	Corcreeny	Private	R.I.R.	
McCleery, James	John Street	Private	R.I.R.	
McKinstry, John	Belfast	Lieutenant	R.I.R.	
McMurray, A.	Flush Place	Private	R.A.F.	
Magee, Edward	Victoria Street	Private	Garr. Guard Co.	
Maguire, William	Hill Street	Lance-Corporal	5th R.I.R.	
Malcomson, David	Church Place	Lieutenant	R.G.A.	
Malone, Thomas	George Street	Private	9th R.I.F.	Killed in Action.
Matthews, Robert	Gilford Road	Private	Trench Mortar Batt.	
Mitchell, F. D.	Ulster Bank	Captain	10th R.I.F.	Died of Wounds.
Montgomery, E. M.	Ulster Bank	Lieutenant	Indian Army	
Patterson, Samuel	Ronney's Yard	Corporal	R.I.R.	
Patrick, R. J.	William Street	Private	R.E.	
Pedlow, Robert	Market Street	Surgeon Prob.	R.N.	
Plenderleith, George	Beech Hill	Paymaster	R.N.	
Reid, Norman	Corcreeny	Corporal	9th R.I.F.	Died of Wounds.
Seawright, Ritchie	Gilford Road	Private	3rd H.L.I.	Wounded.
Smyth, Richard	Union Street	Driver	R.F.A.	
Smyth, Robert	Union Street	Private	9th R.I.F.	Killed in Action.
Sparkes, Richard	Avenue Road	Private	16th R.I.R.	Wounded.
Sproule, A. B.	The Manse	Private	R.A.F.	
Stewart, Thomas	Victoria Street	Private	Garr. Batt. R.I.F.	
Thompson, Charles, V.S.	Church Place	Captain	1st Batt. Buffs	Wounded.
Thompson, John M.B.	Church Place	Captain	R.N.	
Walls, Fred.	Queen Street	Cadet	Inns of Court	
COLONIAL AND U.S.A. FORCES.				
Aiken, Hanna	Watson's Lane	Private	U.S. Army	
Clarke, Jim	High Street	Corporal	Can. L.I.	
Clarke, Mac.	High Street	Lieutenant	19th R.I.R.	
Clarke, Thomas	High Street	Lieutenant	Can. Grenadiers	
Clarke, William	High Street	Lieutenant	R.I.R.	
Donaldson, David	William Street	Lance-Corporal	Can. F.A.	
Foster, Archie	Victoria Street	Sergeant	75th Can.	
Geddis, James	High Street	Gunner	R.F.A.	
Hunter, Thomas	Legacorry	Private	Canadians	
McIlwaine, James	Dollingstown	Q.-M.S.	Canadians	
Ruddy, Alfred	Victoria Street	Seaman	R.N.	
LURGAN, HILL STREET.				
Alexander, Samuel	27 George Street	Private	1st E. Lancs.	Killed in Action. Mons Star.
Boyce, Norman	182 Union Street	Captain	R.A.M.C.	Men. in Des.
Brown, David J.	40 George Street	Corporal	9th R.I. Fus.	1915 Ribbon.
Brown, John	High Street	Corporal	R.E.	1914 Ribbon.
Calvert, Albert	Victoria Street	Private	2nd R.I.R.	Killed in Action.
Campbell, John	4 Victoria Place	Corporal	R.M. Fus.	
Carson, John	Hill Street P.O.	Sergeant	2nd Leinster Regt.	Prisoner.
Carson, Robert	Hill Street P.O.	Private	R.E.	
Carson, Thomas	Hill Street P.O.	Lieutenant	2nd Leinster Regt.	
Cassells, Bertie	6 Woodville Street	Private	R.I. Fus.	
Chambers, Samuel	39 Princes Street	Private	R.A.F.	
Clarke, Frank	20 Albert Street	Corporal	2nd R.I.R.	Killed in Action.
Clarke, John	20 Albert Street	Private	15th R.I.R.	W'ded. 1915 Rib.
Clarke, Thomas	20 Albert Street	Private	9th R.I. Fus.	1915 Ribbon.
Clarke, William	20 Albert Street	Sapper	122nd R.E.	1915 Ribbon.

DROMORE PRESBYTERY. HILL STREET, LURGAN.

Name.	Home Address.	Rank.	Regiment, Battalion or Unit.	Remarks.
COLVILLE, JOHN	Victoria Street	Private	9th R.I. Fus.	
COOPER, ALBERT E.	64 John Street	Private	R.A.F.	
COOPER, WILLIAM	64 John Street	Private	12th R.I.R.	
CORKIN, ROBERT	46 Avenue Road	Private	9th R.I. Fus.	
CRABBE, W. J.	Hill Street	Private	1st I.G.	W'ded. 1914 Star.
CRANEY, HUGH	Wellington Place	Corporal	12th R.I.R.	1915 Ribbon.
CUMMINS, JOSEPH	13 Victoria Street	Bombardier	R.G.A.	M.M.
CURRAN, W. J.	140 Hill Street	Private	2nd R.I.R.	Wounded.
DILLON, JOSEPH	5 Prince's Street	Sergeant	9th R.I. Fus.	W'ded. 1915 Rib.
DILLON, VICTOR	5 Prince's Street	Private	9th R.I. Fus.	Killed in Action.
DOAK, FRED.	Ann Street	Private	Connaught Rangers	Killed in Action.
FRIAR, WILLIAM	18 Hill Street	Private	16th R.I.R.	
FULTON, HUGH	George Street	Private	9th R.I. Fus.	Killed in Action.
GIBSON, REV. ANDREW, B.D.	The Manse	Captain	Chaplain	M.C.
GILKINSON, JAMES	14 Hill Street	Private	9th R.I. Fus.	Killed in Action.
GILKINSON, JOHN	14 Hill Street	Private	3rd R.I.R.	
GILKINSON, WILLIAM	14 Hill Street	Private	9th R.I. Fus.	
GILKINSON, WILLIAM	14 Hill Street	Private	M.G.C.	
GRACEY, DAVID	Drumgor	Private	11th H.L.I.	Killed in Action.
GRAHAM, GEORGE	14 Brownlow Terrace	Sapper	R.E.	
HARLAND, W. J.				
HOBBS, ANDREW	Bridge Street	Private	9th R.I. Fus.	Killed in Action.
HOBBS, DAVID	143 Union Street	Private	9th R.I. Fus.	Killed in Action.
HOBBS, HERBERT	143 Union Street	Private	9th R.I. Fus.	Wounded.
HOBBS, ROBERT	143 Union Street	Sergeant	9th R.I. Fus.	Killed in Action.
HOUSTON, SAMUEL	94 John Street	Private	9th R.I. Fus.	Killed in Action.
HUTCHESON, JOHN	42 John Street	Private	R.A.F.	
HUTCHESON, R. W.	42 John Street	Private	R.I. Fus.	Wounded.
HUTCHESON, S. J.	42 John Street	Private	R.E.	
HUTCHINSON, ALFRED	Drumgor	Private	R. In. Fus.	Wounded.
HUTCHINSON, JOSEPH	Drumgor	Private	1st Seaforths	Wounded. M.S.
HUTCHINSON, RICHARD	Drumgor	Corporal	20th R.I.R.	
JONES, RUPERT C.	William Street	Sergeant	16th R.I.R.	
KELLY, WILLIAM	Victoria Street	Private	9th R.I. Fus.	Killed in Action.
KINKEAD, WILLIAM	11 Hamilton Street	Drummer	R.I. Regt.	
LONG, GEORGE	William Street	Corporal	9th R.I. Fus.	
LONG, JAMES	William Street	Private	9th R.I. Fus.	Killed in Action.
LYNN, SAMUEL	High Street	Private	9th R.I. Fus.	
LYTTLE, ABRAM	Ballnamoney	Private	R.M.L.I.	Killed in Action.
LYTTLE, SAMUEL	Ballnamoney	Corporal	2nd R.I. Fus.	Wounded.
McCARROLL, C. A.	48 Prince's Street	Private	2nd R.I. Fus.	
McCARROLL, GEORGE	Victoria Street	Private	9th R.I. Fus.	
McCARROLL, ROBERT	48 Prince's Street	Private	6th R.I.R.	
McCARROLL, W. J.	Charles Street	Private	19th Hussars	
McCLATCHEY, GEORGE	2 Albert Street	Private	9th R.I. Fus.	Wounded.
McCLATCHEY, SAMUEL	2 Albert Street	Bombardier	R.F.A.	Killed in Action.
McCONNELL, JAMES	100 Victoria Street	Private	R.I.R.	Wounded.
McCONVILLE, JAMES	120 Victoria Street	Private	R.I. Regt.	
McCONVILLE, THOMAS	120 Victoria Street	R.Q.M.S.	9th R.I.F.	M.S.M.
McCORMICK, SAMUEL	Lough Road	Private	R.G.A.	Wounded.
McDOWELL, C.	Ann Street	Private	R. In. Fus.	Wounded.
McDOWELL, JOHN	Queen Street	Private	M.G.C.	
McDOWELL, SAMUEL	John Street	Sergeant	R.I.R.	
McDOWELL, S. J.	32 George Street	Sergeant	9th R.I. Fus.	Wounded.
McDOWELL, SOLOMON	134 Union Street	Sergeant	9th R.I. Fus.	
McDOWELL, W. JAMES	134 Union Street	Private	9th R.I. Fus.	Killed in Action.
McGEOWN, JACKSON	William Street	Private	9th R.I. Fus.	W'ded & P.O.W.
McGEOWN, J. S.	William Street	Lieutenant	R.A.F.	Wounded.
McILROY, ALFRED	45 Avenue Road	Private	9th R.I. Fus.	Killed in Action.
McILROY, JAMES	45 Avenue Road	Private	9th R.I. Fus.	
McILWAINE, DAVID	Dukestown	Private	12th R.I.R.	Wounded.
McILWAINE, JAMES	Prince's Street	Private	R. Warwicks	
McILWAINE, JAMES	110 Hill Street	Private	5th R.I.R.	
McILWAINE, JOSEPH	110 Hill Street	Private	16th R.I.R.	
McILWAINE, RICHARD	Queen Street	Private	N.I.H.	Men. in Des.
McILWAINE, SAMUEL	Moyraverty	Sapper	R.E.	
McILWAINE, SAMUEL	Dukestown	Private	14th R.I.R.	Wounded. M.M.
McILWAINE, WILLIAM	Dukestown	Private	5th R.I.R.	
McILWAINE, WILLIAM	33 Hill Street	Private	M.G.C.	M.M.
MAGEE, H. J.	Charles Street	C.S.M.	R. Dub. Fus.	
MAGILL, JOHN	Mark Street	Private	R.I.R.	
MAGUIRE, H. H.	High Street	Private	R.A.M.C.	
MALCOMSON, JOHN	High Street	Sergeant	A.S.C. M.T.	
MARTIN, THOMAS	Drumgash	Private	2nd R. In. Fus.	Killed in Action.
MAXWELL, WILLIAM	Drumgor	Sergeant	R.I. Fus.	W'ded and P.O.W.
MAWHIRT, GEORGE	6 James Street	Private	R.I. Fus.	
MENABENY, JAMES	56 Hill Street	Private	16th R.I.R.	Killed in Action.
NEILL, ROSS C.	Brownlow Terrace	Sergeant	R.I.R.	Killed in Action.
ORR, CHARLES	Flush Place	Private	R.I.R.	
PHILLIPS, H. J.	14 Albert Street	Private	R.A.M.C.	
PRESTON, R.	Lough Road	Private	3rd Scottish Rifles	
ROBINSON, HARRY	William Street	Private	R. In. Fus.	
ROBINSON, THOMAS	William Street	Private	R.I. Fus.	
SMITH, THOMAS	Dollingstown	Private	11th R.I.R.	Died of Wounds.

DROMORE PRESBYTERY.   HILL STREET. LURGAN,

Name.	Home Address.	Rank.	Regiment, Battalion or Unit.	Remarks.
Sparks, John	Hill Street	Private	R.I.R.	
Taylor, Alex.	19 George Street	Private	9th R.I. Fus.	Wounded.
Tedford, H.	18 Hill Street	Private	R.I. Fus.	
Thompson, John	Avenue Road	Sergeant	16th R.I.R.	
Thompson, William	Avenue Road	Wireless Operator	Merchant Service	
Twinan, Richard	Moyraverty	Sergeant	General Service	
Watson, Alex.	Victoria Street	Private		
Watson, W. J.	Victoria Street	Lance-Corporal	9th R.I. Fus.	Killed in Action.
Watson, Samuel	Avenue Road	Lieutenant	Leinster Regt.	Wounded.
Watson, Victor	Avenue Road	Private	9th R.I. Fus.	Killed in Action.
Wright, Alex.	42 Ann Street	Private	R.I. Fus.	
Wright, Harry	42 Ann Street	Private	R.A.F.	
Wright, James	19 Bridge Street	Private	9th R.I. Fus.	Killed in Action.
Wright, John	19 Bridge Street	Private	2nd R.I. Fus.	W'ded and P.O.W.
	COLONIAL FORCES.			
Crabbe, James	George Street	Private	32nd Canadian E.F.	Wounded.
Crozier, Joseph	Queen Street	Sergeant	Canadian E.F.	Wounded.
Gilmore, William R.	Church Place	Lance-Corporal	87th Canadian E.F.	Killed in Action.
Gracey, H.	Drumgor	Sergeant	Canadian E.F.	Wounded.
Hutchinson, S.	Drumgor	Private	Canadian E.F.	Wounded.
Hutchinson, J. A.	Drumgor	Private	Canadian E.F.	
Kane, Matthew	George Street	Private	Canadian R.A.M.C.	
McIlwaine, Isaac	Moyraverty	Private	Canadian E.F.	
Sturgeon, Joseph	George Street	Private	24th Canadian E.F.	Killed in Action.
	MAGHERAGALL.			
Belshaw, Joseph	Aughnabough	Private	11th R.I.R.	Wounded.
Fleming, James	Aughnabough	Private	11th R.I.R.	Killed in Action.
Fleming, Richard	Aughnabough	Corporal	Can. Gren. Guards	Killed in Action.
Green, Richard	Magheralisk	Sergeant	11th R.I.R.	
Lattimore, John	Stoneyford	Corporal	R.G.A.	
Lattimore, William	Stoneyford	Private	R.G.A.	
Scott, Henry	Ballycarrickmaddy	Private	11th R.I.R.	Killed in Action.
Thompson, Joseph	Killultagh	Private	R.F.A.	
Withers, Thomas	Ballypitmane	Private	S.A. Inft.	
	MAZE.			
Adams, Harry	Culcavey	Corporal	R.A.M.C.	
Adams, Oliver	Culcavey	Sergeant	1st R. Irish Fus.	Prisoner of War.
Blain, Edward	Lake View	Private	1st Wellington Batt. E.F., N.Z.	Died of Wounds.
Chapman, Jonathan	Culcavey	Private	Egypt. Ex. Force	
Emerson, Thomas H.	Culcavey	Rifleman	14th Batt. R.I.R.	Killed in Action.
Faulkner, John	Aughnatrisk	Rifleman	13th Batt. R.I.R.	Killed in Action.
Jamieson, Robert F.	Maze	Rifleman	13th Batt. R.I.R.	Wounded.
Kane, Samuel	Culcavey	Rifleman	13th Batt. R.I.R.	Killed in Action.
Kane, Thomas	Culcavey	Sergeant	13th Batt. R.I.R.	
Montgomery, James	Culcavey	Private	6th Batt. R. In. Fus.	Wounded.
Neill, Albert E.	Maze	Rifleman	20th Batt. R.I.R.	Died.
Nelson, William	Culcavey	Rifleman	13th Batt. R.I.R.	Missing.
O'Hara, James	Maze	Lieutenant	Can. 2nd Contingent	Wounded.
O'Hara, Thomas Kennedy	Maze	C.P.O.	H.M.S. "Manxman"	
Smith, Robert Hugh	Aughnatrisk	Rifleman	14th Batt. R.I.R.	Wounded.
Smith, James	Aughnatrisk	Private	R.A.M.C.	
Wright, Thomas	Maze	Private	R.A.M.C.	
	MOIRA.			
Baxter, George	Ballymagin	Lance-Corporal	13th R.I.R.	M.M.
Beattie, William	Grove Hill			
Crookshanks, William	Toughlomny	Private	16th R.I.R.	
Davison, Hall	Yew Tree, Megabery	Rifleman	11th Batt. R.I.R.	Killed in Action.
Duff, Samuel, M.D.			R.A.F.	
Hanna, James	The Acres, Maralin	Staff Sergeant	R.F.A.	
Lamie, S.	Edenmore	Rifleman	14th Batt. R. In. Fus.	
Lowry, Henry	Railway Tavern	Rifleman	15th R.I.R.	Killed in Action.
McCracken, James	Maralin		15th R.I.R.	Killed in Action.
Magill, Samuel J.	Kircassock	Private	R.I. Fus.	
Swain, John	Moira		R.A.	
	WARINGSTOWN.			
Allen, Robert	Waringstown	Private	R.E.	Died.
Baxter, Ernest	Donacloney	Rifleman	1st Batt. R.I.R.	
Baxter, John	Donacloney	Rifleman	1st Batt. R.I.R.	Killed in Action.
Campbell, James	Milltown	Bombardier	R.F.A.	Killed in Action.
Ferris, James	Ballymacateer	Rifleman	16th Batt. R.I.R.	Wounded.
Foye, Robert	Annaghanoon	Q.-M. Sergeant	I.G.	Wounded.
Gregson, Thomas James	Edenballycoghill	Rifleman	13th Batt. R.I.R.	Killed in Action.
Kennedy, William	Tullyheron	Rifleman	9th Batt. R. Irish Fus.	
Kernaghan, William	Waringstown Road	Rifleman	16th Batt. R.I.R.	

DROMORE PRESBYTERY.   WARINGSTOWN.

Name.	Home Address.	Rank.	Regiment, Battalion or Unit.	Remarks.
McCollum, Archie	Tullyheron	Lance-Corporal	16th Batt. R.I.R.	
McCollum, John	Waringstown	Sergeant	16th Batt. R.I.R.	
McConnell, Harry	The Valley	Private	Labour Batt.	
McCormick, Henry	Tullynacross	Private	9th Batt. R. Irish Fus.	Killed in Action.
McCormick, James	Tullynacross	Rifleman	16th Batt. R.I.R.	
McMurray, Samuel	Knocknashane	Rifleman	13th Batt. R.I.R.	
Maguire, John	Lurgan	Private	R.A.M.C.	
Maguire, Robert	Lurgan	Private	R.A.M.C.	
Middleton, John	Banoge	Captain	Canadian R.A.M.C.	
Moore, Alexander	Belfast	Seaman	H.M.S. "Havelock"	
Moore, Henry	Belfast	Q.-M. Sergeant	16th Batt. R.I.R.	Gassed.
Moore, Robert	Corcreaney	Private	Royal Irish Fus.	Killed in Action.
Moore, Samuel George	Gilford Road	Rifleman	4th R.I.R.	
Perry, Robert	Lurgan	Rifleman	16th Batt. R.I.R.	
Turtle, James	Tullyheron	Private	Despatch Rider	
Turtle, John	Tullyheron	Private	16th Batt. R.I.R.	Wounded.
Whaley, William	Knockboy House	Corporal	7th Batt. R.I. Fus.	Killed in Action.

DUBLIN PRESBYTERY.

Name.	Home Address.	Rank.	Regiment, Battalion or Unit.	Remarks.
DUBLIN, ADELAIDE ROAD.				
Anderson, Alfred	Dublin		R.E.	
Anderson, F. A.	Dublin	Captain	R.A.	M.C.
Anderson, Henry	Dublin		Artists' Rifles	Killed in Action.
Bamford, John Raymond	Dublin		1st Guards	
Bennie, Harold	Dublin	Lieutenant	Royal Marines	Killed in Action.
Blackadder, Fred.	Dublin		R.A.	
Blackadder, Charles	Dublin	Sergeant	City of London	Killed in Action.
Bolton, Reginald R.	Dublin	Lieutenant	R.F.A.	
Bourke, Edmund Cecil	Dublin	Lieutenant	Dublin Fus.	
Bourke, Henry	Dublin	Sergeant	Canadian E.F.	
Bourke, Robert	Dublin	Lieutenant	R.D. Fus.	
Bourke, Thomas Leslie	Dublin	Lieutenant	R.A.F.	Killed in Action.
Boyd, Robert	Dublin	Captain	R.D.F.	
Boyd, Patrick	Dublin		R.A.F.	
Brown, Thomas	Dublin		Essex Regt.	
Buchanan, George	Dublin	Major	R.A.M.C.	
Carruthers, J. S.	Dublin	2nd Lieutenant	R. Inn. Fus.	Killed in Action.
Chambers, A. Ferguson	Dublin	2nd Lieutenant	Warwicks	Killed in Action.
Charlton, S. A.	Dublin		South Irish Horse	
Chrisrian, Henry	Dublin		Australian Light Infantry	Killed in Action.
Christian, Robert	Dublin		R.D.F.	Killed in Action.
Clarke, Norman	Dublin	Sub-Lieutenant	R.N.V.R.	
Clarke, Norman	Dublin		R.I. Rifles	
Clarke, Thomas	Dublin		Black Watch	
Corbett, Stanley G.	Dublin		South Irish Horse	
Cowan, A. E.	Dublin	Lieutenant	R.E.	Killed in Action.
Craig, James Ferguson	Dublin	Lieutenant	R. Army Vet. Corps	
Crawford, Alfred	Dublin	Petty Officer	H.M.S. Centurion	
Crawford, Fred.	Dublin		R.G.A.	
Cunningham, W. E.	Dublin	Lieutenant	52nd Sikhs	
Davies, R. L.	Dublin	Sergeant	R.A.M.C.	
Deery, Joseph	Dublin		North Irish Horse	Killed in Action.
Denham, C. Holmes	Dublin	Captain	R.A.M.C.	
Dickson, W. Arthur	Dublin	Lieutenant	Royal Irish Regt.	
Dickson, John	Dublin	Lieutenant	Roya Irish Rifles	
Dickson, James A.	Dublin	Lieutenant	M.G.C.	
Dixon, Gilbert	Dublin		Can. E.F.	
Donaldson, John C.	Dublin	Lieutenant	M.G.C.	
Dougherty, J. Gerald	Dublin	2nd Lieutenant	R.D. Fus.	
Dunlop, J. P.	Dublin	2nd Lieutenant	R.A.M.C.	
Dunlop, Cyril	Dublin		N.Z. Mtd. Rifles	
Eadie, William	Dublin		M.T., A.S.C.	
Eaglesham, J. S. J.	Dublin		A. & S. Highldrs.	Killed in Action.
Edgar, Robert	Dublin	Sergeant	R.A.M.C.	
Edgar, John	Dublin	Captain	Lincolnshire Regt.	
Ellerker, William	Dublin	Captain	R.F.A.	
Elliot, William	Dublin	Captain	R.A.M.C.	M.B.E., Died.
Fraser, Alex. Victor	Dublin		South Irish Horse	
Fraser, James A.	Dublin	2nd Lieutenant	R.A.F.	
Fraser, Jack H.	Dublin	Sergeant	Irish Guards	
Fraser, Robert P.	Dublin		R.A.M.C.	
Gillies, Forbes	Dublin	2nd Lieutenant	Lincolnshire Regt.	Killed in Action.

DUBLIN PRESBYTERY.   ADELAIDE ROAD.

Name.	Home Address.	Rank.	Regiment, Battalion or Unit.	Remarks.
Guilgault, D.	Dublin	Cadet	Can. Light Infantry	Died.
Grene, George	Dublin	Private	R.E.	
Harper, Frank	Dublin	Sergeant	R. Dub. Fus.	Killed in Action.
Henderson, G. York	Dublin	Lieutenant	R. Irish Rifles	M.C., Kd. in Action
Henry, John Alex.	Dublin		R.I. Fus.	
Hewat, Cecil	Dublin	Captain	Sherwood Foresters	
Hewat, William	Dublin	Captain	East York Regt.	
Hogg, William F.	Dublin	Captain	R. Irish Rifles	M.C.
Hope, Archie	Dublin	Lieutenant	R. Dublin Fus.	
Houston, Wylie	Dublin	Lieutenant	R. Engineers	Killed in Action.
Hume, John	Dublin	Captain	R.I. Fus.	
Hume, John	Dublin	Captain	R.I. Fus.	
Hume, Norman	Dublin	2nd Lieutenant	R.A.F.	
Hutchinson, A. D.	Dublin	2nd Lieutenant	Black Watch	
Irwin, S. W.	Dublin	Captain	R.E.	
Johnson, F. W.	Dublin	2nd Lieutenant	Connaught Rangers	M.C.
Johnson, Reginald	Dublin	Captain	R.A.M.C.	
Kelly, Gavin	Dublin	Cadet	Inns of Court O.T.C.	
Kyle, David	Dublin	2nd Lieutenant	R.E.	Killed in Action.
Leask, J. Cunliffe	Dublin	Captain	Northumberland Fus.	Killed in Action.
Lindsay, Wilson	Dublin	Corporal	Mech. Trans.	
McClelland, John	Dublin	Lieutenant	R.I. Fus.	
McClelland, Wm. E.	Dublin	Captain	R. Munster Fus.	
McClintock, Wm.	Dublin	Surgeon Lieutenant	R.N.	
McConnell, Reginald	Dublin	Cadet	Inns of Court O.T.C.	
McElwaine, Eric	Dublin	Captain	16th Punjabs	O.B.E.
McElwaine, Percy	Dublin	Lieutenant	R. Irish Rifles	
McKeeman, Frank	Dublin	2nd Lieutenant	R.I. Rifles	
McKeeman, Robert	Dublin	Private	R.F.A.	
MacKeowen,	Dublin	Private	South Irish Horse	
MacMaster, P. L. G.	Dublin	Lieutenant	M.G.C.	Killed in Action.
McNicol, Robert	Dublin	Major	R.A.M.C.	
MacNie, George	Dublin	2nd Lieutenant	R.D. Fus.	Killed in Action.
MacNie, William	Dublin	Surgeon		
Martin, Andrew	Dublin	Private	R.A.S.C., M.T.	
Mathews, S. W.	Dublin	Captain	R.A.M.C.	Died.
Mathews, James	Dublin	Lieutenant	Irish Guards	Killed in Action.
Mein, Cranston	Dublin	Lieutenant	Royal Scots	
Middleton, John Alan	Dublin	Lieutenant	R.A.S.C.	
Mooney, C. Douglas	Dublin	Lieutenant	R.A.S.C.	M.C.
Nevin, W. Kerr	Dublin	Captain	Loyal North Lancs.	
Nevin, W. Milllar	Dublin	2nd Lieutenant	Lanc. Fus.	
Paisley, J.	Dublin		North Irish Horse	
Patton, Thomas	Dublin		R.A.S.C.	
Percy, David B.	Dublin		R. Lincoln Regt.	Killed in Action.
Percy, James C.	Dublin		R.N.V.R.	
Plant, J. B. L.	Dublin	2nd Lieutenant	R.D.F.	Died.
Pringle, Harold	Dublin	Major	R.A.M.C.	
Pringle, Seton	Dublin	Lieut-Colonel	R.A.M.C.	
Reid, Robert McMinn	Dublin	Lieutenant	Highland L.I.	
Robertson, Alex.	Dublin		R.D.F.	
Robson, James	Dublin		R.A.M.C.	
Robson, William	Dublin	Lieutenant	Black Watch	
Ronald, Ross	Dublin	Major	N. Irish Horse	M.C.
Scott, R. T. Millie	Dublin	Captain	M.G.C.	
Small, Robt. A.	Dublin		R.A.S.C. M.T.	
Sinclair, S.	Dublin	Lieutenant	R.A.F.	
Smith, A. E.	Dublin		R.A.S.C. M.T.	
Smith, Duncan McCallum	Dublin	Lieutenant	R.A.M.C.	
Stephen, J. Griffin	Dublin		Army Cyclist Corps	
Stephen, William	Dublin		R. Dub. Fus.	
Stewart, Charles	Dublin	Captain	R.A. Vet. Corps	
Stewart, John F.	Dublin	Lieutenant	R.I. Fus.	
Stodart, Holden	Dublin	Superintendent	St. John's Am. Brigade	Killed in Dublin.
Taylor, William	Dublin	Colonel	R.A.M.C.	C.B.
Taylor, W. H. H.	Dublin		R.F.A.	
Todd, Drew P.	Dublin	Captain	R.A.M.C.	
Todd, Hugh	Dublin		North Irish Horse	
Wade, William	Dublin	Captain	R.A.M.C. (African Rifles)	
Wilson, Daniel	Dublin	Captain	R Inn. Fus.	
Wilson, James	Dublin		Irish Guards	
Wylie, W. E.	Dublin	Lieutenant	Dublin University O.T.C.	
LOWER ABBEY STREET.				
Armstrong, Reginald	Beechfield Ho., Clontarf	Trooper	N.I.H.	Killed in Action.
Blyth, Robert	26 Wigan Road	Corporal	4th R.D. Fus.	
Burns, Hamilton	35 Smithville	2nd Lieutenant	1st R.D. Fus.	
Campbell, William	31 Finglas Road	Lieutenant	R.F. Corps	Killed in Action.
Campbell, Andrew W.	31 Finglas Road	Lieutenant	12th A. & S. Highldrs.	Wounded.
Carson, Robert	33 Bachelors' Walk	Gunner	S.S. Ansonia	
Cook, John J.	Scotland	Corporal	10th R.D. Fus.	
Downing, John	Belfast	Lieutenant	10th R.D. Fus.	Killed in Action.
Eakin, Norman	75 Blessington Street	Signaller	Sig. Corps, 36th Div.	

DUBLIN PRESBYTERY. LOWER ABBEY STREET.

Name.	Home Address.	Rank.	Regiment, Battalion or Unit.	Remarks.
EAKIN, ROBERT A.	75 Blessington Street	Sergeant	2nd Vic. T.B.	
EARNSHAW, FREDERICK	5 Hollybank, Drumcondra	2nd Lieutenant	R.I. Fus.	
EARNSHAW, W. V.	5 Hollybank, Drumcondra	Private	7th Hussars	
FOGGO, ROBERT	North Strand	Private	6th Dragoon Guards	...
FOGGO, JAMES	North Strand	C.C.	H.M.S. London	
FOGGO, WILLIAM	North Strand	L. Corporal	2nd Batt. Irish Guards	
GILMORE, ROSS GEORGE	Kenilworth Square	2nd Lieutenant	6th R.D. Fus.	Wounded.
GREY, R. G.	102 Cabra Park	Trooper	21st Army Corps	
HENDERSON, A. VICTOR	86 Botanic Road	Private	A. & S. Highldrs.	
ISAAC, DAVID	Leinster House	Private	7th R.D. Fus.	Died.
JONSTON, D. PERCY	Gracehall, Lurgan	2nd Lieutenant	R.G.A.	
JOHNSTON, ERNEST	Gracehall, Lurgan	2nd Lieutenant	South Staffords	Killed in Action.
JOHNSTON, SAMUEL	Cookstown	Sergeant	A/102 Brigade R.F.A.	M.M.
KERR, THOMAS J.	Dublin	Private	6th Dragoon Guards	Wounded.
KINNEAR, C. ANNESLEY	Albany Ho., Ranelagh	Lieutenant	R.F.A.	Killed in Action.
LAIRD, ALEX.	39 St. Lawrence Road	Rifleman	15th R.I. Rifles	
LYONS, J. V. B.	Clontarf	Corporal	A.P.O.	
MANLY, JOHN	Trinity College	Sergeant	R.A.M.C.	
MARSHALL, ALEX.	Dublin	Lieutenant	15th M.G. Co.	
MERHETTE, FRANK	82 Hollybank Road	Sergeant	5th R.I. Fus.	
MILLER, JACK	97 Phibsborough Road	2nd Lieutenant	11th R.D. Fus.	Wounded.
MILLER, W. ROBERT	Lr. Gardiner Street	Private	10th Essex Reg.	
NEILL, R. G.	Londonderry	2nd Lieutenant	63rd I.B.D.	
POLLOCK, SAMUEL A.	42 Mt. Pleasant Square	Private	A.S.C.	
POLLOCK, ROBERT	42 Mt. Pleasant Square	Driver	R.F.A.	
SHEPHERD, ALFRED	Daisyhill, Co. Armagh	2nd Lieutenant	8th R.I. Fus.	Wounded.
SHEPHERD, J. MACKAY	Daisyhill, Co. Armagh	Lieutenant	173rd M.G. Co.	
SCOTT, LEONARD	Lr. Sackville Street	2nd Lieutenant	R.D. Fus.	Killed in Action.
STEWART, H. R.	Banbridge, Co. Down	2nd Lieutenant	6th O. & B.L. Inft.	
SMITH, JAMES	Elm Park, Drumcondra	2nd Lieutenant	9th Gurkhas, I.A.	
SINCLAIR, SAMUEL	9 Dolphin Avenue	2nd Lieutenant	R.F.C.	
THOMPSON, R. M.	Delamere, Ballsbridge	Lieutenant	9th Delhi Inft., I.A.	Wounded.
TAYLOR, ROBERT	36 Claude Rd., D'condra	Private	H.A.C.	
TODD, W. P.	Cowper Gdns., Ranelagh	Private	5th Manchester Regt.	
WARNER, ALBERT	Molind Place, Dublin	Private	2nd R.D. Fusiliers	Wounded.
WILSON, A. S.	Frankfort Av., Rathgar	2nd Lieutenant	7th R.D. Fus.	Killed in Action.
COLONIAL FORCES.				
CAMPBELL, DUNCAN D.	Glasnevin	Private	S. African Regt.	
HOWE, EDWARD	Sandymount	Bugler	3rd Canadians	Wounded.
PORTER, HUBERT D.	26 Rathdrum Road	Sergeant	31st Canadians	Wounded.
PORTER, JOHN E.	26 Rathdrum Road	Private	10th Canadians	Wounded.
YOUNG, WILLIAM	Fairview	Private	Can. Highldrs.	Killed in Action.
BLACKROCK.				
McCLEAN, GEORGE	Blackrock	Private	R.I.R.	Killed in Action.
McCLEAN, JAMES	Blackrock	Private	R.F.A.	Killed in Action.
McCLEAN, ROBERT	Blackrock	Private	R.W.F.	Killed in Action.
SLOAN, HAROLD	Blackrock	2nd Lieutenant	R.G.A.	Killed in Action.
STODART, HODDER	Blackrock		St. John's Amb.	Killed in Dub., '16.
WYLIE, WILLIAM	Blackrock	Lieutenant	Lincoln Regt.	Killed in Action.
CLONTARF.				
ALEXANDER, WM.	11 Addison Road	Trooper	N.I.H.	
ALLEN, NORMAN	4 Charlemont Terrace	Cadet	R.A.F.	
ARMSTRONG, REGINALD	Beechfield	2nd Lieutenant	N.I.H.	Killed in Action.
BAILEY, ALBERT		Private	A.I.F.	Killed in Action.
BAILEY, CHARLES	Kelburne, Howth Rd.	Captain	R.D.F.	M.C.
BENTLEY, F.	92 Amiens Street	Private	R. Inn. Fus.	
BROWN, A.	80 Leinster Avenue		R.E.	
CORRY, ALEXANDER	Victoria Rd., Howth Rd.	Engineer	R.M.M.	Torpd. & Drowned.
CROZIER, ALAN	62 St. Lawrence Road	Cadet	R.M.C.	
CROZIER, WM.	62 St. Lawrence Road	Private	G.H.	Wounded.
DALLAS, ALFRED	81 St. Lawrence Road	Lieutenant	R.A.	Wounded.
DALLAS, ERNEST	81 St. Lawrence Road	Lieutenant	N.I.H.	
DALLAS, WILLIAM R.	81 St. Lawrence Road	2nd Lieutenant	R.A.F.	Killed.
GALT, NOEL	Woodfield, Howth Road	Corporal	C. of London R.F.	Killed in Action.
GILBERT, GEORGE	St. John's, Donnycarney	Lieutenant	R.A.	
GIBSON, JOHN	40 Clonliffe Road	Private	R.E.	
GREER, T.	26 Waverley Avenue	Private	R.A.M.C.	
HOLMES, JOHN	Mt. Dillon	Private	R.A.F.	
KERR, JOHN	49 Hollybrook Road	A.P.	R.N.V.R.	
LAWRIE, ERNEST	Willowbrook	Private	R.A.F.	
LAWRIE, JOHN	Willowbrook	Private	R.I.F	
LAWSON, DAVID	15 Fairview Avenue	Trooper	N.I.H.	
LAWSON, STIRLING	15 Fairview Avenue	Private	R.A.F.	
LEWIS, STANLEY	52 Hollybrook Road	Trooper	N.I.H.	
LEWIS, THOMAS	52 Hollybrook Road	Private	R.A.S.C.	
LYLE, ARTHUR	Dalriada, Howth Road	Lieut.-Colonel	R.E.	
MACMI, FRANK	Warrenpoint	Captain	C.R.	Killed in Action.
McBRATNEY, JAMES	Royal Terr., Fairview	Private	R.A.F.	

DUBLIN PRESBYTERY. CLONTARF.

Name.	Home Address.	Rank.	Regiment, Battalion or Unit.	Remarks.
McClure, George	5 St. Lawrence Road	Trooper	N.I.H.	Wounded.
McDaniel, James	Warrenpoint, Clontarf	Lieutenant	R.A.F.	Killed in Action.
Munro, John L.	110 Clapham Rd., London	Private	110th T.R.B.	
Paul, Alex.	Glenvale, Howth Road	2nd Lieutenant	R.I.R.	Killed in Action.
Paul, Walter	Glenvale, Howth Road	Private	R.I.F.	Killed in Action.
Pope, R. A. D.	Palmyra, Vernon Avenue	Private	R.A.	
Porter, Cyril	Vernon Parade, Clontarf	Private	R.D.F.	Killed in Action.
Porter, G. R.	Vernon Parade, Clontarf	Captain	K.O.Y.L.I.	Killed in Action.
Poynton, B.	26 St. Lawrence Road			
Russell, James	Tullyherron, Clontarf	Private	R.I.R.	Wounded.
Scott, Geo. W.	Bellevue, Clontarf	Lieutenant	R.A.	
Shott, Eustace	Auburn, Clontarf	Captain	R.A.	
Stafford, A. J.	Rushfield House	Private	R.A.S.C. M.T.	
Taylor, Arthur	Graham Villas	2nd Lieutenant	R.M.F.	Killed in Action.
Telford, W. T.		Captain	C. of London R.F.	M.C.
Tennant, Alex.	24 Hollybrook Road	Sergeant	A.I.F.	Killed in Action.
White, Bertie	Hughenden, Clontarf	2nd Lieutenant	2nd K.E.H.	
White, Horace	101 St. Lawrence Road	Private	R.D.F.	Wounded.
Williams, Charles	Janeville, Donnycarney	Lieutenant	R.I.F.	Wounded.
Williams, Edward	Janeville, Donnycarney	2nd Lieutenant	K.O.R.L.R.	
Wilson, James	83 Philipsburg Avenue	Sergeant	R.A.M.C.	
DONORE.				
Barkley, Frederick	8 St. Anthony's Road	2nd Lieutenant	Indian Army	
Calwell, Arthur James	12 Grove Park, R'mines	Co. Sergt.-Major	R. Irish Fus.	Killed in Action.
Calwell, Harold	12 Grove Park, R'mines	Leading Seaman	H.M.S. Donegal	
Calwell, William M.	12 Grove Park, R'mines	Captain	R. Dub. Fus.	M.C., Wounded.
Cunningham, Thomas	37 Reuben Avenue	Army Scrip. Reader	A.S.R. Society	Served in France.
Fairlie, Edward	South Circular Road	Private	R.A.M.C.	
Gilmore, William	South Circular Road	Sergeant	New Zealand Rifles	
Gowdy, Andrew	Royal H., Kilmainham	Sergeant	R.A.S.C.	
Gramshaw, Harold	Hamilton Street	Private	S.I.H., Leinster Regt.	
Hamilton, James Brown	7 Eaton Sq., Terenure	Private	R.A.M.C.	
Lamont, William	Spencer Avenue	Private	Irish Guards	Killed in Action.
Lauder, Alf. Norman	26 Parnell Place	Seaman	R.N.	
Laurie, William	Roy. Hos., Kilmainham	Captain	R.A.S.C.	
Law, Harold	28 Hamilton Street	Private	R.A.M.C.	
Law, Stanley	28 Hamilton Street	Private	Connaught Rangers	Killed in Action.
Matthews, George	St. Catherine's Terrace	Conductor	Army Ord. Corps	M.C.
McCullagh, Thompson	Thorn Villa, Dublin	Private	R.A.F.	
McNeill, Neil	St. Kilda, Grove Park	Private	Officers' Training Corps	
Russell, Wallace	Olney, Terenure	Lieutenant	R Dub. Fus.	Killed in Action.
Sands, James L.	116 Leinster Road	Engineer-Commander	R.N., H.M.S. Southampton	Ment. in Dis.
Sands, John Drummond	116 Leinster Road	Captain	Indian Med. Ser.	
Sands, Thomas	116 Leinster Road	Major	South African Med. Corps	
Sargeant, Benjamin	St. Catherine's Terrace	Lance-Corporal	R.A.S.C.	
Sargeant, Henry	St. Catherine's Terrace		R.E.	
Spratt, Robert	Dublin	Private	Irish Guards	
Thompson, George	Ontario Terrace	Private	Royal Marines	
Watson, Alexander	Grove Park, Rathmines	Private	Machine Gun Corps	
Watson, David	Grove Park, Rathmines	Private	R.A.M.C.	
Watson, George	Grove Park, Rathmines	Private	R. West Kent Regt.	
ORMOND QUAY.				
Anderson, H. McD.	32 Dargle Road	Lieutenant	Machine Gun Corps	Killed in Action.
Anderson, W.	32 Dargle Road	Lieutenant	Northumberland Fus.	
Anderson, G.	32 Dargle Road	Engineer Officer	R.N.R.	
Beattie, S. H.	46 Fitzwilliam Square	Lieut.-Colonel	R. West Kents	Mons M., M.C.
Beattie, A. E.	46 Fitzwilliam Square	Major	R.A.S.C.	Mons Medal.
Beattie, J. O.	46 Fitzwilliam Square	Captain	16th Rajputans	
Beggs, Samuel	107 Botanic Road	Trooper	21st Lancers	
Binnie, Norman	110 Drumcondra Road	Lieutenant	R.I. Fus.	
Bowler, H.		Private	21st Northumberland Fus.	
Bowler, Edward		Private	R.I. Rifles	Killed in Action.
Browne, A. J.	52 Lr. Leeson Street	Corporal	R.M. Police	
Campbell, Wm.	31 Finglas Road	Lieutenant	R.F.C.	Killed in Action.
Colter, George	18 Carlisle Avenue	Q.M.S.	R. N. Lancs.	
Cooper, Thomas	Harding Home	Private	H.L. Infantry	
Coupar, Allan	Harding Home	Private	Royal Scots	Killed in Action.
Coupar, Henry	Harding Home	Private	R.D. Fus.	
Dunckley, Samuel	1 Vernon Grove, Rathgar	Captain	R.F.C.	
Fortune, Jack	Glenone, D'condra Park	Private	A.S.C.	
Fyffe, Robert	Bellacolla, Queen's Co.	Private	R.D. Fus.	
Gunning, Edward		Private	A.O.C.	
Heggie, Thomas	Home Farm Road	Trooper	S.I.H.	
Horne, Alexander		Private	Irish Guards	
Jamieson, William	7 Anglesea Street	Private	R.D. Fus.	
Keilty, John	Andrew's Hall, Comber	Private	R.A.M.C.	
Lambert, M.		Q.M.S.	Army Pay Corps	
Little, Sidney	91 Botanic Road	Private	R.E.	
Low, Gavin	Sabblestown	Captain	R.E.	
Lowe, Bertie	58 Grove Park	Captain	R.V.C.	

DUBLIN PRESBYTERY.   ORMOND QUAY.

Name.	Home Address.	Rank.	Regiment, Battalion or Unit.	Remarks.
LUCAS, HENRY	3 Up. Ormond Quay	Lance-Corporal	R.D. Fus.	
LUCAS, T. G.	3 Up. Ormond Quay	Private	M.G.C.	
MACKIE, ALEXANDER	3 Up. Ormond Quay	Cadet	H.L.I.	
MAGEE, H. G.	3 Up. Ormond Quay	Sergeant	R.I. Fus.	
McCLEAN, J. N.	3 Up. Ormond Quay	Private	A. & S. Highldrs.	Killed in Action.
McCONNELL, HEDLEY	203 N. Circular Road	Lieutenant	R.F.A.	
McCONNELL, NORMAN	203 N. Circular Road	Private	6th Black Watch	Wounded.
McCONNELL, ROBERT	3 Little Strand Street	Private	R.G.A.	
McCLELLAND, WILLIAM	Up. Leeson Street	Lieutenant	R.I.Fus.	
McCLELLAND, JACK	Up. Leeson Street	Lieutenant	R.I. Fus.	
McDONALD, WM.	Up. Leeson Street	Private	Cameron Highldrs.	
McENTIRE, JAMES	23 Pembroke Park	Major	R.A.M.C.	Legion of Honour.
McENTIRE, GORDON	23 Pembroke Park	Captain	R.A.M.C.	
McENTIRE, HENRY	23 Pembroke Park	Captain	125th Rajputans	
McENTIRE, DRUMMOND	23 Pembroke Park	Captain	R.A.M.C.	
McFARLANE, WM.	23 Pembroke Park	Sapper	R.E.	Prisoner of War.
McMASTER, DAVID	23 Pembroke Park	Private	A.S.C.	
McNEIGHT, HERBERT	Lorne Ter., N.C.R.	Cadet	O.T.C., Dublin	
METHVEN, COLIN	Harding Home	Private	R.F.C.	
MORRIS, W. O.		Lieutenant	King's Liverpool Regt.	Killed in Action.
MORRIS, WILLIAM	63 Cadogan Road	Telegraphist Officer	R.N.R.	
MYLES, FINLAY	7 Adelaide Terrace	Q.M.S.	R.D. Fus.	
MYLES, DAVID	7 Adelaide Terrace	Sergeant	R.D. Fus.	
MYLES, JOHN	7 Adelaide Terrace	Private	R.D. Fus.	
NELSON, WILLIAM	74 Seaview St., Belfast	Sapper	R.E.	Killed in Action.
NIMMO, THOMAS	44 Cadogan Road	Sergeant	Connaught Rangers	
NIMMO, JAMES	44 Cadogan Road	Private	Connaught Rangers	Killed in Action.
PETTERS, CONSTANCE	11 Suffolk Street	Private	R.A.M.C.	
PINKERTON, DAVID	Edinburgh	Sapper	R.E.	
SLOAN, NORMAN ED.	Dunsinear, Dublin	Lieutenant	R.I. Fus.	
SLOAN, HAROLD	Dunsinear, Dublin	Lieutenant	R.G.A.	Killed in Action.
SEYMOUR, R.	Dunsinea, Dublin	Corporal	R.F.A.	
SEYMOUR, EDWARD	Dunsinea, Dublin	Private	5th R.D. Fus.	
SMYTH, ALBERT	14 Cabra Park	Lieutenant	Machine Gun Corps	Wounded.
SMYTH, JAMES	14 Cabra Park	Gunner	Motor M.G. Section	Killed in Action.
SMYTH, SAMUEL	14 Cabra Park	Cadet	Sandhurst M.T.C.	
TAYLOR, R. G.		Corporal	S.I.H.	
TUCKER, A. W.	Four Courts, Dublin	Lance-Corporal	R.D. Fus.	
TUCKER, RICHARD	Four Courts, Dublin	Trooper	S.I.H.	
WATTERS, ALEXANDER	17 Harold's Road	Sapper	R.E.	
WATSON, HARVEY		Lieutenant	2nd R.I. Regt.	
WHYTE, T. J.		Army Scrip. Reader	Scripture Reader	
ROBINSON, WILLIAM	51 Capel Street	Private	Motor Transport	
COLONIAL AND U.S.A. FORCES.				
BATTISON, PETER	7 Citric Road	Sergeant	Can. E.F.	
BEATTIE, VERNON	46 Fitzwilliam Square	Private	R.M. American E.F.	
CAMPBELL, E.		Private	Can. E.F.	Killed in Action.
STUART, W. S.	Kimage Road	Sergeant	Can. E.F.	Wounded.
RATHGAR.				
ADAM, ALFRED C.	Holywood House	Captain	R.G.A.	
ADAM, WILLIAM B.	Holywood House	Midshipman	R.N.V.R.	
ANDERSON, ALFRED W.	Brentford, Orwell Park	Captain	1st Batt. R.I. Regt.	
ANDERSON, LIONEL J.	Brentford, Orwell Park	Private	London R.A.M.C.	
ANDERSON, M. KEBBLE	Brentford, Orwell Park	Lieutenant	R.I. Regt.	Died of Wounds.
ANDERSON, ROBERT W. G.	Brentford, Orwell Park	Corporal	Sussex Yeomanry	
BARLAS, A. R., M.B.	Palmerston Gardens	Captain	R.A.M.C.	
BARLAS, THOS. W. C.	Palmerston Gardens	Lieutenant	Gordon Highldrs.	
BLUE, ARCHIBALD J.	London	Captain	R.A. Ord. C.	
BLUE, DUGALD		Private	A.S.C.	
BROWNE, WM. H.	41 Ashdale Road	Private	R. Dub. Fus.	
BUCKHAM, BERT. T.	14 Airfield Road	Private	2nd R.I. Regt.	
BURROWS, OSWALD, M.B.	30 Kenilworth Square	Captain	R.A.M.C.	M.C.
CARSON, GEO. W.	51 Palmerston Road	Lieutenant	King's Liverpool Regt.	M.C.
CARTER, ROBERT W.	17 Ashdale Road	Lieutenant	R. Dub. Fus.	
CHERRY, JAMES F.	Clonallen, Kimmage Rd.	Private	A.S.C.	
CHERRY, ROBIN	Orchardtown House	Boy, 1st Class	R.N.	
CLELAND, T. W.	32 Berea Terrace	2nd Lieutenant	A.S.C.	
CLOUSTON, NOEL S.	Ashmere, Orwell Road	Lieutenant	R.E.	
COLLIE, ALEXANDER	9 York Avenue	Private	Gordon Highlandrs	
CRAIG, SAMUEL M.	6 Kenilworth Road	2nd Lieutenant	123rd Outram Rifles	
CUNNINGHAM, JAMES P.	37 Grosvenor Square	S. Sergt.-Major	S.I.H.	
DALGETTY, ALEXANDER	1 Ashfield Villas	Sergeant	R.E	
DRAFFIN, JAMES A. L.	41 St. Kevin's Park	Captain	Welsh Regt.	
DRURY, G. MAURICE	22 Victoria Road	Captain	A.S.C.	
DRURY, NOEL E.	Swiftbrook, Saggart	Lieutenant	6th R. Dub. Fus.	
DUNCKLEY, SAMUEL W.	1 Vernon Grove	Captain	R.F.C.	
DUNLOP, R. GORDON	10 Ashfield Terrace	Gunner	Hon. Artillery Co.	
DUNLOP, THOMAS QUINTON	38 Moyne Road	Private	R. Dub. Fus.	
EATON, OSCAR A. M.	3 Belgrave Terrace	2nd Lieutenant	1st Queen's Westminster R.	M.C.
FALLON, ROBERT	Terenure Road S.	Private	R.I. Regt.	

DUBLIN PRESBYTERY. RATHGAR.

Name.	Home Address.	Rank.	Regiment, Battalion or Unit.	Remarks.
Fallon, Thomas H.	Falburg, Terenure	Private	10th R. Dub. Fus.	
Fawcett, Robert	Kincora, Zion Road	Private	A.S.C.	
Ferguson, Augustus K.	49 Brighton Road	2nd Lieutenant	R.I. Regt.	
Ferguson, Karl E. A.	49 Brighton Road	Lieutenant	R.I. Regt.	
Harris, Alfred	14 Highfield Road	2nd Lieutenant	12th R. Inn. Fus.	M.C.
Harris, Basil M.	14 Highfield Road	Cadet	R.A.F.	
Harris, David W.	14 Highfield Road	2nd Lieutenant	1st R. Dub. Fus.	
Henchie, Wm. H.	7 Ashfield Terrace	Private	A.S.C.	
Hughes, Lancelot E.	2 Winton Avenue	Sergeant	London Irish Rifles	
Hunter, Herbert	Elsinore, St. Kevin's Pk.	Captain	A.S.C.	
Inglis, C. H.	Leinster Road	2nd Lieutenant	A.S.C.	
Inglis, H. F.	Leinster Road	2nd Lieutenant	Leinster Regt.	
Jones, Walter V.	67 Grosvenor Square	Sergeant	R.A.M.C.	
Kirker, James A.	28 Grosvenor Square	Lieutenant	R.A.F.	
Larmour, Arthur	1 Vesey Tce., Garville A.	Lance-Corporal	R.E.	
Leask, J. Cunliffe	Newcastle-on-Tyne	Captain	Northumberland Fus.	Died, M.C.
Lees, David W.	1 Victoria Road	2nd Lieutenant	R.A.F.	
Lees, G. Martin	1 Victoria Road	Lieutenant	R.A.F.	M.C.
Lemon, David W.	2 Winton Avenue	Lieutenant	7th Leinster Regiment	Killed, M.C.
Lemon, Gilbert M.	2 Winton Avenue	Lance-Corporal	10th R. Dub. Fus.	Killed in Action.
Martin, R. S.	16 Edenvale Road	Signaller	R.N.V.R.	
Mitchell, Donald O.	Edenvale Road	Lance-Corporal	6th Black Watch	Killed in Action.
Moore, Oldham S.	18 Belgrave Road	Private	Black Watch	
Moore, Robert, M.D.	Grosvenor Road	Captain	R.A.M.C.	
Munro, J. Bayne	25 Charlesville Road	2nd Lieutenant	R. Inn. Fus.	
McAlister, Wm. C.	38 Hannahville Park	2nd A.M.	R.A.F.	
Macaulay, Rev. Jas J., B.A.	6 Palmerston Villas	Captain	Chaplain	
McElnay, G. Herbert	16 Grosvenor Place	Lieutenant	R. Dub. Fus.	M.C.
McGugan, James N.	36 St. Kevin's Park	Private	R.I. Regt.	
MacHutchinson, Wm. F.	6 Mount Temple Terrace	2nd Lieutenant	7th R. Dub. Fus.	Died of Wounds.
McKean, Lionel	4 Rostrevor Terrace	Flight Lieutenant	R.N.A.S.	
McKnight, Matthew, M.D.	Nevara, Temple Gardens	Captain	R.A.M.C.	
McMurtry, Alex. D.	43 Ashdale Road	2nd Lieutenant	R.I. Fus.	
Nisbet, Robert H.	Rosenau, Zion Road	Lieutenant	R.F.A.	
Nixon, Arthur Cecil	Ardmore, Highfield Road	Lieutenant	R.F.A.	
Preston, George D.	Bardowie, Orwell Park	Lieutenant	Yorkshire Regt.	
Quirk, Phinlo St. John	31 Garville Avenue	Private	R.A.M.C.	Died.
Robertson, Ian W.	Dunbrody, Orwell Park	Cadet	R.A.F.	
Robertson, John B.	11 Whitton Road	Private	M. Transport	
Robinson, D. P.	19 Terenure Park	2nd Lieutenant	A.S.C.	
Robson, Ernest	North Shields	Lieutenant	5th Durham L.I.	
Robson, Jack C.	North Shields	Driver	Heavy Artillery	
Rodgers, David H. C.	Acrebrook, Rathfarnham	Gunner	R.G.A.	
Rodgers, George	Acrebrook, Rathfarnham	Private	7th Leinster Regt.	Died of Wounds.
Rodgers, Richard	Acrebrook, Rathfarnham	Private	M.G. Corps	Killed in Action.
Scott, Robert T. M.	33 Garville Avenue	Lieutenant	Yorkshire Regt·	
Semple, J. Mervyn	Frankfort Avenue	2nd Lieutenant	R.I.R.	
Seyers, William G.	6 Moyne Road	Private	R. Warwickshire Regt.	Killed in Action.
Smyth, Nelson	Kincora, Zion Road	Private	A.S.C.	
Taylor, W. J.	18 Mountainview Road	Private	R.F.A.	
Thomson, R. Peel, M.B.	39 Harcourt Street	Lieutenant	R.A.M.C.	
Trotter, James A.	30 Kenilworth Park	Private	R. Dub. Fus.	
Woods, John McB.	Terenure Road	Captain	1st Batt. R. Marines	
Woods, Wm. W.	Terenure Road	Private	R. Dub. Fus.	
COLONIAL FORCES.				
Buckham, Andrew G.	14 Airfield Road	Trooper	Can. Cavalry	
Eaton, John Wallace	3 Belgrave Terrace	Lieutenant	Intel. Corps 2nd Can. Div.	
McGregor, Wm. J.	61 Frankfort Avenue	Corporal	66th Can. E.F.	
RUTLAND SQUARE.				
Bell, Jack	Gencairn, N.C. Road	2nd Lieutenant	R. Dub. Fus.	
Bell, Joseph	Gencairn, N.C. Road	Captain	Army Vet. Corps	Ment. in Dis.
Bell, Randal	Gencairn, N.C. Road	Private	R.I. Fus.	Wounded.
Burns, Digby	6 Charleville Road	Captain	R.A.M.C.	
Burns, John Wm.	6 Charleville Road	Captain	R.A.M.C.	
Cree, R. Ewart	27 Mespil Road	Captain	R.A.M.C.	M.C.
Crowe, George D.	46 Kildare Street	Sergeant	R.A.M.C.	Wounded.
Crowe, John Colvin	46 Kildare Street	Colour-Sergeant	R.I. Regt.	Wounded, M.M.
Cumming, Joseph C.	Lindsay Rd., Glasnevin	Private	R. Dub. Fus.	Wounded.
Cunningham, J. R.	Hillcrest, Drumcondra	Trooper	S.I.H.	Wounded.
Duncan, Alex.	64 Connaught Street	Major	Army Vet. Corps	
Dunwoody, Wm.	Shamrock Vs., D'condra	Private	S.I.H.	
Eustace, Wm. N., M.D.	Lisronagh, Glasnevin	Lieutenant	R.A.M.C.	
Fannin, E. M.	3 Rutland Square	Captain	R.A.M.C.	
Gordon, Alan S.		2nd Lieutenant	A.S.C.	
Harper, —		Qr.-Master Sergeant	R. Dub. Fus.	Killed in Action.
Linden, Samuel M.	31 Adelaide Road	2nd Lieutenant	R.G.A.	Killed in Action.
Lyon, John Alex.	111 Botanic Road	Corporal	R.I.R.	
McAdam, T. A.	85 Lindsay Road	Private	R.E.	
Macalister, J. Denham	7 Albany Terrace	Sergeant	R.A.M.C.	
McCleery, Henry	80 Botanic Road	2nd Lieutenant	Indian Army	

DUBLIN PRESBYTERY. RUTLAND SQUARE.

Name.	Home Address.	Rank.	Regiment, Battalion or Unit.	Remarks.
McCleery, R. J.	80 Botanic Road	Lieutenant	Indian Army	
McNair, Charles J.	Tower House, Launtry	Private	M.G.C.	
Moore, Francis M.	11 Ailesbury Road	Lieutenant	52nd Sikhs F.F.	Wounded.
Meikle, A.	Wharf Road	Pipe-Major	R. Scots Fus.	Prisoner of War.
Morrison, John	Riverview, Botanic Av.		194th Brigade H.Q.	
Osborne, W. H.	4 Mountjoy Square	Lieutenant	Leinster Regt.	M.C., Wounded.
Roberts, E. G.	1a Wharf Road	Sergeant	R.A.	Wounded.
Russell, Norman	Rathmines Road	Captain	A.S.C.	Wounded.
Russell, James Joseph	173 Botanic Road	Private	R.A.M.C.	
Russell, Samuel D.	173 Botanic Road	Cyclist	Army Cyclist Corps	
Shanks, E.	7 Claude Road	Lance-Corporal	R. Dub. Fus.	Wounded.
Shott, Eustace J.	50 Iona Road	Captain	R.F.A.	
Shott, Richard H.	50 Iona Road	2nd Lieutenant	R.E.	
Squires, Peter	11 Annesley Bridge Av.	Gunner	H.M.S. Red Gauntlet	
Squires, James	11 Annesley Bridge Av.	Private	R. Dub. Fus.	
Strachan, Andrew	6 Iona Crescent	2nd Lieutenant	R. Dub. Fus.	Wounded.
Thompson, George	27 Ellesmere Avenue	E.R.A.	H.M.S. Viking	
COLONIAL FORCES.				
Gourlie, George	4 St. Albans Terrace	Private	Can. E.F.	Wounded.
McCleery, Wm.	80 Botanic Road	Private	N.Z. Mtd. Rifles	
McMurtry, John H.	20 Auburn Street	Sergeant	E. African Regt.	
McNair, Andrew T.	Tower House	Private	Can. Highldrs.	
McNair, Robert H.	Tower House	Private	Can. Highldrs.	
Sutherland, Wm.	Lindsay Road	Sergeant	Can. Inft.	M.M.
SANDYMOUNT.				
Aitken, George T.	32 Gilford Road	Sergeant	Alberta Dragoons	Killed, M.M.
Aitken, John James	32 Gilford Road	Lt.-Colonel	Army Vet. Corps	D.S.O.
Aue, Ronald P. F.	4 Gilford Road	Private	R.D.F.	Wounded.
Campbell, Cecil G.	2 Gilford Road	Private	75th Canadians	Killed in Action.
Campbell, Charles J.	24 York Terrace	2nd Lieutenant	R.A.F.	
Campbell, Douglas, N.	1 Herbert Road	Sergeant	H.A.C.	
Colvin, Walter C.	23 Cambridge Avenue	Private	A.S.C.	
Cooper, Herbert W.	17 Newbridge Avenue	Private	R.A.F.	
Cumming, Andrew M.	Ballsbridge Grounds	Sergeant	A.S.C.	
Cumming, John F.	Ballsbridge Grounds	Sergeant	A.S.C.	
Grant, Stanley C.	1 Molesworth Street	Lieutenant	1st R.I. Regt.	Killed in Action.
Greer, James C.		Q.M. Sergeant	R.E.	
Hawthorne, Wm.	Ringsend	Private	Lancashire Regt.	
Johnstone, Robert S.	52 Tritonville Road	Sergeant	S.I.H.	
Kerr, David		Private	R.D.F.	
Lamond, William	Thorncastle Street	Private	R.I.R.	Killed in Action.
McConnell, James W.		Capt. and Adjutant	R.G.A.	
McNair, Andrew	Gilford Road	Private	17th Canadians	
McNair, Robert	Gilford Road	Private	17th Canadians	Killed in Action.
McNair, Charles	Gilford Road	Private	75th Canadians	
McWilliam, Thomas A.	83 Strand Road	Captain	Indian Army	
McWilliam, Wm. N.	83 Strand Road	Capt. and Adjutant	Black Watch	
Masson, Wm. J.	3 Newgrove Avenue	Gunner	R.M. Artillery	
Murphy, Alex.	3 Bath Street	Private	R.D.F.	Killed in Action.
Murray, Wm.		Lieutenant	Middlesex Regt.	Killed in Action.
Rawson, Charles S.	68 Tritonville Road	Corporal	Mechanical Transport	
Rawson, Richard E.	68 Tritonville Road	Lance-Corporal	R.D.F.	
Reid, John	116 Stephen's Green	Sergeant	7t. A. & S. Highldrs.	M.M.
Smith, Alban G.	74 Serpentine Avenue	Lieutenant	R.I.R.	M.C., Wounded.
Simms, J. H. A.	Oakland Park	Private	S.I.H.	
Thompson, Henry J.	78 South Lotts Road	Sapper	R.E.	
Walker, David	23 Newbridge Avenue	Private	R.A.F.	
Walker, John	23 Newbridge Avenue	Private	R.A.F.	
Walker, William	23 Newbridge Avenue	Private	R.E.	
ATHY.				
Coupar, Allan	Kildougan	Private	H.L. Inft.	Killed in Action.
Coupar, Henry	Kildougan	Private	R. Dub. Fus.	
Hosie, Henry	Coursetown	Captain	A.S.C.	
Melrose, George		Captain	R.G.A.	
Mullins, David			17th K's O. Rifles	Wounded.
Murray, John	Ardreigh	Cadet		
Neill, Wm.	Foxhill	Lieutenant	S.I. Horse	
Pinkerton, E. S.	Athy	Private	R. Dub. Fus.	
Sutherland, David	Monasterevan		Wood-cutting, U.S.A.	
Sutherland, Walter	Monasterevan	Private	Scottish Rifles	
Telford, D. A.	Athy	Lieutenant	1st Life Guards	
Telford, R. A.		Captain	Yorkshire Dragoons	
Wilkie, John	Mageney	Private	Leinster Regt.	
Wilkie, William	Mageney	2nd Lieutenant	Leinster Regt.	

DUBLIN PRESBYTERY.   BALLACOLLA.

Name.	Home Address.	Rank.	Regiment, Battalion or Unit.	Remarks.
	BALLACOLLA.			
Clarke, George H.	Ballacolla	2nd Lieutenant	3rd R. Inn. Fus.	
Fyffe, Hugh B.	Abbeyleix	Private	R.D.F.	
Fyffe, Robert M.	Abbeyleix	Private	R.D.F.	Wounded.
Mitchell, Thomas	Abbeyleix	2nd Lieutenant	R. Ir. Dragoon Guards	Ment. in Dis.
Mitchell, Wm.	Abbeyleix	Lieutenant	R.I.R.	Wounded.
Smeaton, Wm.	Rathdowney	Corporal	Scottish Horse	
	BIRR.			
Brown, D.	Gardens, Birr Castle	Private	Black Watch	Wounded.
Hunter, W.	Gardens, Birr Castle	Private	Scotch Guards	
O'Hara, Wm.	Green Street, Birr	2nd Lieutenant	3rd Leinsters	Wounded.
Roe, George	Cumberland Street	Sergt.-Major	R.A.M.C.	Wounded.
Thompson, Thomas	Boulanarig, Birr	Private	S.I.H.	
Young, D. R.	Gashouse, Birr	Driver	R.F.A.	
Young, George H.	Gashouse, Birr	Private	51st Royal Warwicks	
Young, James	Gashouse, Birr	Sergt.-Major	A. Ord. Corps	M.M.
Young, John	Gashouse, Birr	Corporal	R.A.F.	
	COLONIAL FORCES.			
McDowell, Frazer	Frankfort, King's Co.	Rifleman	Australian E.F.	Wounded.
McDowell, James	Frankfort, King's Co.	Rifleman	N.Z. E.F.	Died of Wounds.
McDowell, Joseph	Frankfort, King's Co.	Driver	Transport Service	
	BRAY.			
Austin, Alfred C.		Reg. Sergt.-Major	R.A.M.C.	
Austin, Arden		Major	R.A.M.C.	M C.
Boyd, Thomas		Private	R.D.F.	Died, Pris. of War.
Clarke, T. C.		Sapper	R.E.	
Fleming, Thomas		Private	Inn. Fus.	
Gilmour, Wm.		Private	R.D.F.	
Graydon, Fredk.		Private	R.D.F.	
Harris, Wm.		Sapper	R.E.	
Henry, Arnold		Captain	R.A.M.C.	
John, Herbert		2nd Lieutenant	York and Lanc.	
John, Percy		Lieutenant	Welsh Fus.	
Killick, Bruce		Petty Officer	Coastguard, R.N.	
Luggar, Richard		Private	S.I.H.	
McFarland, Vivian		Private	Inn. Fus.	Killed in Action.
McFarland, William		Sergeant	Inn. Fus.	
Rogers, Eldon		Petty Officer	Coastguard R.N.	
Sherran, James			Gordon Highldrs.	
Thomas, Ernest			R.N.R.	
Wilson, William		Sergeant	R.E.	
	COLONIAL FORCES.			
Buckham, Andrew		Private	Canadian Force	
Buckham, Robert		Private	Canadian Force	
Gibson, David		Private	Canadian Force	
Hilton, William		Private	Canadian Force	
Luggar, Alec		Lance-Corporal	Canadian Force	
McFarland, Cecil		Private	Canadian Force	
	CARLOW.			
Bailey, Alex.	Pembroke	Lance-Corporal	Can. L. Inft.	Killed in Action.
Belshaw, Gilbert	Dublin Street	Private	R.A.M.C.	
Belshaw, John	Dublin Street	Private	Motor Transport	
Belshaw, Robert	Dublin Street	Private	Motor Transport	
Belshaw, Thomas	Dublin Street	Private	Cyclist Corps	
Brough, John	Coollattin	Lieutenant	R.A.S.C.	
Field, J. W.	Brown's Hill	Captain	R.I.R.	Killed in Action.
Gray, David	Montgomery Street	Private	Engineers	
Henry, Jack	Athy Road	Trooper	N.I.H.	Wounded.
Johnstone, Robert	Ballintemple	Cadet		
Mullins, David	Tullow Street	Private	A.S.C.	Wounded.
Murray, W. E.	Dunleckny	Trooper	N.I.H.	Wounded.
Purves, Mercer	Boherduff	Private	S. African Regt.	
Stevenson, William	Bagnalstown	Trooper	S.I.H.	Wounded.
Wright, James	Strawhall, Carlow	Lieutenant	R.I.R.	Wounded.
Wright, William	Strawhall, Carlow	Private	R.I.R.	Wounded.
	DROGHEDA.			
Barrett, Percival R.	Glasnevin		O.T.C.	
Brown, John	Drogheda	Lance-Corporal	R.E.	
Cahoun, Hugh	Omagh	2nd Lieutenant	Gordon Highldrs.	
Campbell, Hugh	Beauparc	Private	Seaforth Highldrs.	Killed in Action.
Connolly, Charles	Drogheda	Private	R.I.R.	

DUBLIN PRESBYTERY. DROGHEDA.

Name.	Home Address.	Rank.	Regiment, Battalion or Unit.	Remarks.
Connolly, Robert	Drogheda	Private	R.I.R.	
Inglis, Charles A.	Drogheda	2nd Lieutenant	R. Dub. Fus.	
Inglis, Ian Douglas	Drogheda	2nd Lieutenant	R. Dub. Fus.	Killed in Action.
Jordan, James E.	Drogheda	2nd Lieutenant	R. Dub. Fus.	
Jordan, Victor Ernest	Drogheda	Midshipman	R.N.	
Lawson, Alex.	Drogheda	Sergeant	R.I.R.	
Smartt, Arthur	Sevenoaks	Private	R.A.F.	
Smartt, David	Drogheda	Private	Australians	
Telfer, William	Drogheda	Private	Middlesex Regt.	
Walker, Eric	Newcastle-on-Tyne	Captain	Northumberland Fus.	
Watt, Hugh J.	Drogheda	Warrant Officer	Australians	

ENNISCORTHY.

Arnold, Ernest	24 Brighton Av., Rathgar	Lieutenant	52nd Brigade R.F.A.	Wded and Gassed.
Arnold, M.B., John Irwin	24 Brighton Av., Rathgar	Captain	R.A.M.C.	
Johnston, George	Templeshambo	Private	West Kents	Wd. and Disabled.
Kirkpatrick, Rev. W. S., B.A.	The Manse, Enniscorthy	Captain	Chaplain	
Williamson, Andrew	The Quay, Enniscorthy	2nd A.M.	R.A.F.	
McCartney, John	Late The Manse	Private	Can. A.S.C.	

GREYSTONES AND KILPEDDER.

Beatty, Charles	Greystones		R.A.M.C.	
Beatty, Thomas	Greystones	Signaller		
Evans, Robert James	Kilpeddar	Private	R.I. Regt.	
Evans, Samuel Henry	Kilpeddar	Private	R.I. Regt.	Wounded.
Farrell, John George	Eden Cottage, G'stones	Sergeant	1st R.I. Guards	Wounded.
Kerr, James	Kilpeddar	Private	R.I.S.	
King, Alfred	Canada	Private	5th Canadians	
King, Frank Irwin	Newtown, Mt. Kennedy	Private	Northumberland Fus.	Killed in Action.
Thornton, Fredk.	Greystones	Cadet	R.A.F.	
Wilson, Geo. Heatley	Greystones	Sergeant	R.A.M.C.	

HOWTH AND MALAHIDE.

Bannerman, John	St. Fintan's	Stretcher Bearer	R.A.M.C.	
Dickie, R. Kelso	Seatown House	2nd Lieutenant	R.A.F.	
Hunter, J. Kenneth	Baymount	Cadet	R.A.F.	
Hunter, R. Gordon	Baymount	2nd Lieutenant	1st R.D.F.	Wounded & Pris., Died in Germany.
Kirker, James	Casino	Captain Surgeon	R.A.M.C., R.N.	
Moore, Thomas W.	Sunnymead	Lieutenant	R.A.F.	
Porter, Geo. F. L.	5 Corbridge Terrace	Captain	W. Yorkshire Regt.	Killed in Action.
Towell, Robert N. C.	Banbridge	Lieutenant	R.G.A.	
Wilkes, John F.	25 Cherryfield Avenue	Lieutenant	1st R.M.F.	
Wilkinson, Wm. G.	Wymberg	Captain	A.S.C.	

KILKENNY.

Borthwick, Cecil	Jerpoint Hill	Private	R.F.A.	
Brennan, H. W.	The Manse	Sub.-Lieutenant	R.N.R.	
Hanna, Acheson K.	John St., Kilkenny	Private	A.S.C.	
Hogg, William	Flood Hall	Private	A.S.C.	
Hunter, —	Talbot's Inch	Private	G. Highldrs.	
McDonald, Charles	Glendine Cottage	Surgeon	R.N.	
McDonald, Kenneth	Glendine Cottage	Lieutenant	R.A.F.	Killed in Action.
McPetrie, James	Dunmore Park	Private	G. Highldrs.	
Murison, Robert	Farmley	Captain	V. Corps	
Murray, William	Bagnalstown	Private	S.I.H.	
Stevenson, William	Bagnalstown	Private	S.I.H.	
Woods, Christie	Kilkenny	Lieutenant		

COLONIAL FORCES.

Bothwick, Dick	Jerpoint Hill		Can. Inft.	
Cantley, Alex.	Blancheville	Private	Can. B.W.	Killed in Action.
Walsh, Frank	Grange House	Private	N.Z. Inft.	Lost leg and eye.

KILLUCAN.

Bailey, Thos. Robert	Rose Lodge	Lance-Corporal	R.M. Fus.	
Bailey, Wm. John	Rose Lodge	Private	R.M. Fus.	Wounded.
Duncan, Lowry Sinclair	The Manse	Capt. and Adjut.	14th R.I.R.	M.C. and Bar.

KINGSTOWN.

Anderson, Ernest	Monkstown	Signaller	B.W.	
Bailey, Samuel	Glenageary	Corporal	R. Inn. Fus.	
Barret, Charles	Kingstown	Sergeant	4th Bedfordshire Regt.	Wounded.
Brabazon, Alan	6 Clarinda Park E.	Captain	6th Leinster Regt.	Wounded.
Dickinson, Francis	Pilot View, Dalkey	Corporal	R.A.M.C.	
Douglas, Archibald	Derrynane Terrace	Captain	R. Inn. Fus.	Wounded.
Douglas, Robert	Derrynane Terrace	Captain	R. Dub. Fus.	

DUBLIN PRESBYTERY.   KINGSTOWN.

Name.	Home Address.	Rank.	Regiment, Battalion or Unit.	Remarks.
Eason, E. Keith	Harvieston, Dalkey	Lieutenant	R. Dub. Fus.	
Kelly, E. Gordon	Rosebank, Kingstown	2nd Lieutenant	Civil Service Rifles	
McClintock, Hugh	Dreghorn, Dalkey	Surgeon	R.N.	
McFarlane, John W.	Kingstown	Private		Killed in Action.
McFerran, Robert	Pier View House	Lieutenant	R. Dub. Fus.	Wounded.
McFerran, Thomas	Pier View House	2nd Lieutenant	R.A.F.	
Murdock, Percy	Glenageary	2nd Lieutenant	R.N.A.S.	
Patrick, James	25 Adelaide Street	Lieutenant	B.W.	
Sutton, Richard	Blenheim	Captain	Leinster Regt.	Wounded.
Walker, William	Kingstown	Private	R.E.	
Wallace, Milo	Dalkey	2nd Lieutenant	R.E.	M.C.
Weatherill, Edward	6 Ailesbury Rd., Dublin	2nd Lieutenant	Dublin Fus.	Killed in Action.

LUCAN.

Name.	Home Address.	Rank.	Regiment, Battalion or Unit.	Remarks.
Abel, George	Celbridge	Private	10th R. Dub. Fus.	Missing.
Abel, John	Celbridge	Private	20th Northumberland Fus.	Wounded.
Abel, William	Celbridge	Gunner	R.G.A.	Wounded.
Gailey, Samuel A.	Lucan	Surgeon Prob.	H.M.S. Obedient	
Gailey, James L.	Lucan	Sergeant	110th Field Amb. R.A.M.C.	Killed in Action.
Laidlaw, Robert	Somerton, Castleknock	Lieutenant	Scots Greys	Wounded.
McFadyen, T.	Chapelizod	Private	R.E.	
Ronaldson, W. P.	Leixlip	Lieutenant	King's African Rifles	Wounded.
Ronaldson, G. E.	Leixlip	Private	R. Dub. Fus.	Missing.
Younger, Alex.	Chapelizod	Corporal	R. Irish Fus.	W'd., M.M. & Bar.
Younger, James	Chapelizod	Private	S.I.H.	Wounded.
Younger, Roderick	Chapelizod	Private		Killed in Action.

MOUNTMELLICK.

Name.	Home Address.	Rank.	Regiment, Battalion or Unit.	Remarks.
Brown, Thomas A.	Portarlington	Private	Inniskillings	Wounded.
Burns, Wm. H.	Mountmellick	Private	London Territorials	Killed in Action.
Chambers, Wm.	Mountmellick	Sergeant	Canadian Contgt.	Wounded.
Crowe, George	Maryborough	Sergeant	R.A.M.C.	
Lemon, John	Maryborough	Sergeant	Grenadier Guards	Wounded.
McComas, George A.	Mountmellick	Private	Inniskillings	Killed in Action.
Moyles, David A.	Mountmellick	2nd Lieutenant	R.I.R.	Wd., M.C., & M..M
Moyles, John	Mountmellick	Cadet	Flying Corps	
Moyles, Samuel	Mountmellick	2nd Lieutenant	Gurkhas, India	
Wilkie, Wm.	Mountmellick	2nd Lieutenant	Leinster Regt.	Wounded.

NAAS.

Name.	Home Address.	Rank.	Regiment, Battalion or Unit.	Remarks.
Clements, W. H.	Belfast	2nd Lieutenant	7th R. Dub. Fus.	Killed, M.M.
Cockburn, Malcolm	Newbridge	Private	R.E.	Killed in Action.
Cockburn, Stuart	Newbridge	Private	R.E.	
Gray, D.	Naas	Qr. M. Sergt.	R. Dub. Fus.	
Knox, W. H.	The Manse, Sligo	Acting Captain	Connaught Rangers	M.C.
Longmuir, James	Curragh Grange	Sergeant	R.G.A.	
McLeish, Peter	Irishtown, Straffan	Corporal	I.G.	Killed in Action.
Morrison, Matthew	Naas	Sergeant	Leinster Regt.	
Morrison, Samuel	Naas	Sergeant	R. Dub. Fus.	
Ramsay, Clement	Dunlavin	Captain	R.A.M.C.	

NENAGH.

Name.	Home Address.	Rank.	Regiment, Battalion or Unit.	Remarks.
Clarke, S. G.	Crowl, Cloughjordan	Private	2nd Home Ser. Gar. Batt.	
Gray, William	Drummond, Borrisokane	Private	A.S.C.	
Smith, John	Traverstown, Nenagh	Private	Gordon Highldrs.	

TULLAMORE.

Name.	Home Address.	Rank.	Regiment, Battalion or Unit.	Remarks.
Allen, Milby	Clara	Private	A.S.C.	
Bennett, Archie	Tullamore	Sergeant	B. Watch	Wounded.
Black, Norman	Clara	Private	R.A.F.	
Conolly, Robert	Tullamore	Sergeant	R.A.M.C.	Prisoner of War.
Henderson, Allan	Tullamore	Private	Motor Eng. Corps	
McFarlane, Malcolm	Clara	Private		
McNeill, George	Tullamore	2nd Lieutenant	R.I. Regt.	Wounded.
McNeill, John C.	Tullamore	2nd Lieutenant	2nd Essex Regt.	Killed in Action.
Young, H.	Tullamore	Sergt.-Major	A.S.C.	

WEXFORD.

Name.	Home Address.	Rank.	Regiment, Battalion or Unit.	Remarks.
Brown, William W.	64 Main Street	Private	R.A.M.C.	
Curry, Daniel		Q.M.S.	A.S.C.	
Fortune, Frank	Richmond Terrace	Lieutenant	A. & S. Highldrs.	Wounded.
Reid, Edgar	Abbey Street	Private	I. Guards	Killed in Action.
Rennie, William	Talbot Street	Private	R.F.A.	Wounded.
Rettie, Frank	Emmett Place	Private	A.S.C.	Drowned.
Scott, John	Emmett Place	Private	R. Leinster Regt.	Wounded.

DUNGANNON PRESBYTERY.

Name.	Home Address.	Rank.	Regiment, Battalion or Unit.	Remarks.
BALLYMAGRANE.				
Morrow, Frederick	Curlough	Private	Australians	
Morrow, Thomas	Curlough	Lance-Corporal	R.I.R.	Wounded.
McCullagh, Wilson	Crilly	Private	R.I. Fus.	
Smith, Thomas	Mulnahorn	Private	R.I. Fus.	
Williamson, Robert	Curlough	Private	Lancashire Regt.	Wounded.
Wilson, George	Glenkeen	Lance-Corporal	Liverpool Scottish	
Wilson, Robert	Glenkeen	Private	R.A.M.C.	
BALLYREAGH.				
Clarke, Andrew	Bockets	Private	3rd R.I. Fus.	
Dunbar, John	Legaroe	Lance-Corporal	R.I. Fus.	Wounded.
Houston, David	Millix	Private	9th R.I. Fus.	
Houston, Robert A.	Millix	Private	N.Z. E.F.	Wounded.
McDaniel, David	Tullyvannon	Sergeant	R.I. Fus.	Wounded.
McDaniel, Edward	Tullyvannon	Sergeant	4th Can. E.F.	
McDaniel, Richard T.	Tullyvannon	Sergt.-Major	Can. O Corps	Wounded.
McDaniel, William James	Tullyvannon	Bombardier	R.F.A.	
CARLAND.				
Cross, William	Carland	Private	R.I. Fus.	
Howard, Jackson	Carland	Private	R.I. Fus.	
Moore, Ernest	Carland	Private	R.I. Fus.	
Morrow, Robert	Carland	Private	1st R.I. Fus.	Killed in Action. V. Cross, Mons Star, Russian Medal, and 3 other Medals.
COLONIAL FORCES.				
McIvor, John	Tullyarran	Corporal	N.Z. Regt.	
McIvor, William	Tullyarran	Sergeant	N.Z. Regt.	Wounded.
McMinn, Hugh	Crondermott	Private	N.Z. Regt.	
McMinn, Jeremiah	Crondermott	Sergeant	N.Z. Regt.	
CASTLECAULFIELD.				
Acheson, Malcolm K., M.D.	Castlecaulfield	Captain	R.A.M.C.	
Acheson, Vincent A.	Castlecaulfield	Captain	6th R. In. Fus.	Killed in Action.
Brown, Lawrence	Donaghmore	2nd Lieutenant	8th R. In. Fus.	Killed in Action.
Brown, Oliver N.	Donaghmore	Private	R.A.M.C.	
Kelly, William	Drumnafern	Private	R.E.	
Loughran, Alexander	Killyharra	Corporal	oth Durham Light Infy.	Killed in Action.
McAteer, Charles	Cormullagh	Sapper	R.E.	
McAteer, David	Cormullagh	Sergeant	Gordon Highlanders	Prisoner.
McAteer, Hugh	Glasgow	Regt. Sergt.-Major	H.L.I.	
McIvor, James	Derryalskea	Lance-Corporal	5th R.I.R.	
Sothers, Nathaniel	Glassmullagh	Corporal	9th R. In. Fus.	Wounded.
Waddell, Nicholson	Castlecaulfield	Private	R.A.F.	
Watt, Joseph	Aughnaskea	Lance-Corporal	9th R. In. Fus.	Wounded.
COLONIAL FORCES.				
Ferry, Rev. D.	Castlecaulfield	Chaplain	U.S. Army	
Kelly, Frederick	Dresderna	Private	S.A. Fus.	
Kelly, Hanson	Dresderna	Private	S.A. Fus.	
Loughran, Joseph	Killyharra	Private	Australian Force	
Loughran, Samuel	Castlecaulfield	Private	N.Z. Force	
Wilson, Robert	Castlecaulfield	Corporal	Canadian M.G.	
CLENANEES, UPPER AND LOWER.				
Alexander, James	Mullycar	Private	R.I.F.	Killed in Action.
Dickson, William	Carricklongfield	Private	R.I.F.	
Ewing, Craig	Edentilone	Gunner	R.G.A.	
Fair, William	Coolhill	Driver	R.F.A.	
Kelly, H. Mitchell	Moghan	Sergeant	Black Watch	Killed in Action.
McAteer, Joseph	Mulnahunch	Sapper	R.E.	
McAteer, William Robert	Mulnahunch	Private	A.S.C.	
McKee, Albert	Cranslough	Gunner	R.F.A.	
McMillen, John	Kiltyclaven	Private	R.I.F.	Wounded.
Reid, Joseph	Ennish	Private	R.I.F.	Wounded.
Sloane, William	Dergina	Private	R.G.A.	
Stinson, John	Clintyfallow	Sergeant	R.I.F.	Died in France.
Williamson, Joseph	Lisferty	Gunner	R.F.A.	
Williamson, Thomas	Lisferty	Lance-Corporal	R.I.F.	M.C. Killed in Action.
Williamson, William James	Dernaborey	Gunner	R.F.A.	

DUNGANNON PRESBYTERY. CLENANEES, UPPER AND LOWER.

Name.	Home Address.	Rank.	Regiment, Battalion or Unit.	Remarks.
COLONIAL FORCES.				
Alexander, James	Mullycar	Private	Canadians	
Alexander, William	Mullycar	Private	Canadians	
Condy, Archy	Lisferty	Private	U.S.A.	
Conlon, Ben	Ennish	Private	Canadians	Killed in Action.
Cuddy, Hugh C.	Aughintober	Private	U.S. Air Squad.	
Cuddy, Robert	Aughintober	Private	U.S Air Squad	
Cuddy, Samuel	Aughintober	Corporal	Canadian Inft.	M.M.
Curry, Walter	Carricklongfield	Private	19th Can. Inft.	Killed in Action.
Goodwin, David	Knocknarney	Sergeant	Can. Inft.	Wounded.
Hadden, George	Farrater	Lance-Corporal	Q O. Regt., Canada	Killed in Action.
Jamieson, John	Mullyrodden	Private	Q.O. Regt., Canada	
McMillan, Angus	Clintyclaven	Private	Can. Inft.	
McMillan, Dugald	Clintyclaven	S. Sergeant	Princess Pat's	Wounded.
Millar, James	Mullyrodden	Private	Q.O. Regt., Canada	Killed in Action.
Simpson, Andrew	Greenmount	Gunner	N.Z. Field Art.	
Simpson, T. M.	Greenmount	Lance-Corporal	N.Z. Field Art.	
FIRST DUNGANNON.				
Anderson, James	Dungannon	Private	9th R. In. Fus.	Wounded.
Anderson, Robert	Dungannon	Private	9th R. In. Fus.	Killed in Action.
Anderson, William	Dungannon	Private	9th R. In. Fus.	Prisoner of War.
Averill, Robert	Dungannon	Private	3rd R. In. Fus.	Killed in Action.
Bell, Alexander	Dungannon	Private	R.N.V.R.	
Bell, Robert	Dungannon	Sergeant	1st R. In. Fus.	Wounded.
Bell, Ross	Dungannon	Sergeant	12th R. In. Fus.	Wounded.
Best, William	Dungannon	Lieutenant	R. Irish Fus.	Wounded.
Blair, Thomas	Dungannon	Drummer	12th R. In. Fus.	
Coleman, James	Dungannon	Private	R.E.	
Dickson, T. C. Harold	Dungannon	Captain	4th R. Dub. Fus.	Wounded.
Dickson, William T.	Dungannon	Captain	6th R. In. Fus·	Died of Wounds.
Henry, John	Dungannon	Private	9th R. In. Fus.	
Henry, Robert	Dungannon	Private	9th R. In. Fus.	
Henry, Thomas	Dungannon	Private	9th R. In. Fus.	
McClean, Robert	Dungannon	Corporal	Irish Guards	
M·Ferran, David	Dungannon		R.N.	
McGrath, John	Dungannon	Private	9th R. In. Fus.	Wounded & Pris.
McMenemy, William	Dungannon	Private	9th R. In. Fus.	Killed in Action.
Reid, H. F. M.	Dungannon	Lieutenant	Northumberland Fus.	Wounded.
Reid, Samuel E.	Dungannon	Private	Irish Guards	
Sloan, James Z.	Dungannon	Lieutenant	R.E.	
Somerville, Robert	Dungannon	Private	R. In. Fus.	Killed in Action.
Sugars, Harold	Dungannon	Captain	R.A.M.C.	M.C. and D.S.O. Wounded.
Sugars, John C.	Dungannon	Lieutenant	R.F.A.	
Todd, George	Dungannon	Private	R.A.M.C.	
Todd, Henry	Dungannon	Private	A.S.C.	
Williamson, Isaac	Dungannon		R.N.	
Wilson, Thomas A.	Dungannon	Lieutenant	7th E. Lancs. R·	Wounded.
Young, Joseph	Dungannon	Private	12th R. In· Fus.	Wounded.
COLONIAL FORCES.				
Burrows, Hamilton	Dungannon	Private	S.A.M. Rifles	Accid. Killed.
Burrows, John	Dungannon	Private	S.A. Imp. L.H.	Died on Service.
Ferguson, Joseph	Dungannon	Private	Canadians	
Johnston, Ernest	Dungannon	Private	S. Africans	
Johnston, Harold	Dungannon	Private	Canadians	
McMenemy, James	Dungannon	Private	Canadians	Wounded.
SECOND DUNGANNON.				
Bell, John	Market Square	Sergeant	Irish Guards	Wounded.
Belshaw, George Cook	Coolhill	Sergt.-Major	R. In. Fus.	W'ded & D.C.M.
Carter, Isaac	Drumkee	Trooper	N.I.H.	
Finney, Henry	The Park	Private	M.T. A.S.C.	
Gedge, Hamilton	Miltown	Private	R.I.R.	
Gray, James	Coolhill	Lance-Corporal	R. In. Fus.	Wounded.
Harper, Edgar H.	College View	Lieutenant	South Staffs. Regt.	Killed in Action.
Harper, Ernest M.	College View	Lieutenant	R. Munster Fus.	Killed in Action.
Kelly, William J.	Henry Street	Private	R.G.A.	
Lambe, David	Lisnahull	Lance-Corporal	R. In. Fus.	
Lambe, Edwin T.	Lisnahull	Corporal	Irish Guards	
Lambe, Samuel Victor	Lisnahull	Private	R. In. Fus.	Killed in Action.
Lawson, Albert	Miltown	Private	M.T. A.S.C.	
Lawson, Joseph	Miltown	Sapper	R.E.	
Lawson, Samuel J.	Miltown	Sapper	R.E.	Wounded.
Lawson, Thomas	Miltown	Corporal	R. In. Fus.	Twice Wounded.

DUNGANNON PRESBYTERY. SECOND DUNGANNON.

Name.	Home Address.	Rank.	Regiment, Battalion or Unit.	Remarks.
Lawson, William	Miltown	Corporal	R.I.R.	Wounded.
Lemon, Samuel G.	Miltown	Private	R. In. Fus.	
Lemon, William James	Miltown	Sergt.-Major	Grenadier Guards	Wounded.
Mackie, John	Killyquinn	Sergeant	R.I.R.	
McAlister, James	Scotch Street	Private	R.A.M.C.	Wounded.
McConaghy, William	Union Place	Private	R. In. Fus.	Wounded.
McCrea, Alexander	Miltown	2nd Lieutenant	R.G.A.	Killed in Action.
McCrea, James	Miltown	Trooper	Queen's R. Lancers	
McCrea, John	Miltown	Trooper	Queen's R. Lancers	
McCrea, Robert	Miltown	Private	R.G.A.	
McCrea, Thomas	Miltown	Trooper	Queen's R. Lancers	
McDonald, John	Granville	Sergeant	Cycling Corps	Died of Wounds.
O'Hara, David	Killyquinn	Private	R.I.R.	Killed in Action.
Orr, Alexander	Moygashel	Private	R. In. Fus.	
Orr, Robert	Moygashel	Private	R. In. Fus.	Killed in Action.
Orr, Thomas	Moygashe.	Private	R. In. Fus.	
Price, Vincent C.	Beech Valley	Private	Anti-Aircraft Co.	
Rainey, Joseph	Rossmore	Private	R. In. Fus.	
Ringland, James	Perry Street	Sergeant	R. In. Fus.	
Shannon, Robert	Moygashel	Private	R.G.A.	
Simpson, William A.	The Manse	Captain	R. Air Force	
Smith, Alexander	Royal School	Private	R. In. Fus.	
Steenson, William C.	Beech Valley	Private	R. In. Fus.	
Taylor, Robert	Moygashel	Private	R. In. Fus.	Killed in Action.
Watson, Joseph Henry	Dromore	Private	R. Irish Regt.	Prisoner of War.
Wray, William James	Miltown	Lance-Corporal	R. In. Fus.	
Young, Joseph	Miltown	Private	R. In. Fus.	
COLONIAL FORCES.				
Lawson, George Robert	Miltown	Private	3rd Batt. Can. Pioneers	Died of Wounds.
Scott, Robert	M'Kee's Terrace	Private	28th Batt. of Canada	Killed in Action.
Watson, Robert James	Dromore	Gunner	Canadian Artillery	
EGLISH.				
Anderson, Robert	Coolhill	Gunner	R.F.A.	Gassed Twice.
Cumberland, James	Kilnacart	Private	9th R. In. Fus.	Killed in Action.
Cumberland, John	Kilnacart	Private	9th R. In. Fus.	Killed in Action.
Cumberland, Wm. George	Kilnacart	Private	9th R. In. Fus.	
Reid, John	Crosteely	Sergeant	9th R. Irish Fus.	Wounded.
Reid, W. E.	Shanmoy	Lieutenant	11th R.I.R.	Gassed Twice.
MINTERBURN.				
Allen, David	Ballagh	Private	R. Irish Fus.	Killed in Action.
Busby, Isaac	Dyan	Lance-Corporal	R. Irish Fus.	Killed in Action.
Clarke, Thomas	Ballagh	Private	R. In. Fus.	Killed in Action.
Galway, Andrew	Tannaghlane	Private	R. Irish Fus.	Killed in Action.
Irvine, William	Larrykean	Private	A.S.C.	
Rutherford, Thomas	Dyan	Private	R. Reg. Artillery	Killed in Action.
Trotter, Hugh	Minterburn	Private	S. Lancers	
Woods, Thomas	Carrycastle	Private	I G.	
Wright, Bennie	Ballyboy	Private	S. Lancers	
Wright, George Henry	Ballyboy	Gunner	26th Battery	Killed in Action.
COLONIAL FORCES.				
Campbell, Robert L.	Legain	Private	Can. F. Amb.	Died of Wounds.
Edwards, John	Crievelough	Private	16th Canadians	
Fleming, Willie	Minterburn	Private	Auckland Inft.	
Gray, Frank	Kilinaul	Private	Australians	
Jenkinson, William J.	Tannagh	Driver	Canadians	
McKeown, H. R.	Ballyvady	Corporal	B.S.A.P.	Wounded.
Robinson, Andrew	Caledon	Private	39th Batt. A.D., B.D.	
POMEROY.				
Adams, Ralph	Limehill	Private	R. In. Fus.	
Boyd, John	Turnabarson	Private	R.H. Art.	
Boyd, William	Mabuoy	Private	I. Guards	Killed in Action.
Forde, Andrew	Bardahessiagh	Private	Can. L. Inft.	
Forde, Robert	Bardahessiagh	Private	R. In. Fus.	Died.
Gilkinson, Edward	Gortavoy	Private	M.G.C.	
Irwin, James	Altmore	Private	U.S. Army	Wounded 9 times.
Irwin, Robert	Altmore	Private	R. In. Fus.	D.C.M.
Irwin, Thomas	Altmore	Private	N.I. Horse	
Kerr, Robert John	Sessiaghscott	Private	R. In. Fus.	Wounded.
McIvor, Samuel	Gortavoy	Private	R. In. Fus.	Wounded.

GLENDERMOTT PRESBYTERY.

Name.	Home Address.	Rank.	Regiment, Battalion or Unit.	Remarks.
BANAGHER.				
Brown, Samuel	Mulderg	Corporal	1st Canterbury Inft. Batt.	Died of Wounds.
Connell, Robert McAlister	Loughtilube	Sergeant	9th Batt. R. Inn. Fus.	Twice Wounded.
Eakin, Isaac	Tirglasson	Private	R.E.	
Eakin, James Leslie	Terrydreen	Private	55th Batt. A.I.F.	Wounded.
Eakin, Joseph Reid	Terrydreen	Private	R.I. Regt.	
Miller, Matthew James	Cleggan	Private	9th Batt. R. Inn. Fus.	
McArthur, Henry	Killycor	Private	9th Batt. R. Inn. Fus.	Wounded.
McArthur, Wm. John	Killycor	Private	9th Batt. R. Inn. Fus.	
Quigley, Jack	Park	2nd Lieutenant	9th Batt. R·I. Rifles	
Rosborough, Archibald	Letterlougher	Private	A.I.F.	
Rosborough, Henry	Letterlougher	Private	9th Batt. R. Inn. Fus.	Killed.
Warnock, Robert	Straidarran	2nd Lieutenant	6th Batt. R.I. Rifles	Wounded.
Withrow, Alex. Hunter	Kincull House	2nd Lieutenant	8th Batt. R.I. Rifles	Died of Wounds.
Withrow, John Thos., B.A.	Kincull House	2nd Lieutenant	9th Batt. R.I. Rifles	Died of Wounds.
CUMBER.				
Cairns, Thomas	Mallabuoy	...	...	
Campbell, Alex.	Fawney	...	...	
Campbell, Marcus	Fawney	Lance-Corporal	9th R.I.F.	
Chambers, T. C.	Ardground	Private	9th R.I.F.	M.C.
Christie, Andrew	Gortnaraw	Private	9th R.I.F.	Killed in Action.
Christie, Samuel	Gortnaraw	Private	A.S.C.	
Cochrane, Jack	Fawney Fort	...	10th R. Inn. Fus.	Killed in Action.
Craig, Geo. Lyle	The Oaks	Lieutenant	4th Dragoon Guards	
Dickson, David	Killaloo	Private	10th R. Inn. Fus.	Killed in Action.
Gourley, Alex.	Ballyarton	Private	10th R. Inn· Fus.	Killed in Action.
Gourley, Samuel	Ballyarton	Private	...	Wounded.
Gilfillan, Wm. G.	Ballinamoor	Lieutenant	R.E.	
Hamilton, Wm.	Tonduff	Private	10th R. Inn. Fus.	Prisoner.
Henderson, David	Tamneymore	Private	10th R. Inn. Fus.	Wounded.
Henderson, James H.	Tamneymore	Sergeant	19th Camp Base Depot	
Henderson, Samuel	Tamneymore	Corporal	A.I.F.	
Irwin, R. T.	Goshaden	Private	9th R.I.F·	Killed in Action.
Kelly, Thomas	Goshaden	Private	10th R. Inn. Fus.	Killed in Action.
Lowry, John S.	Gortnasky	Private	10th R. Inn. Fus.	
Mackenzie, Kenneth	Ballyarton	Lieutenant	12th R. Inn. Fus.	Wounded.
Millar, Joseph	Tamneymore	Private	10th R. Inn. Fus.	Killed in Action.
Mitchell, James	Killaloo	Sergeant	10th R. Inn. Fus.	Killed in Action.
Moore, James	Tamneymore	Private	10th R. Inn. Fus.	Killed in Action.
Moore, Joseph	Tamneymore	Private	R. Scots	
Pinkerton, Samuel A.	Cross	Private	9th R.I.F.	Killed in Action.
Quigley, Jack	Killaloo	Private	10th R. Inn. Fus.	Killed in Action.
Quigley, Samuel	Killaloo	Private	10th R. Inn. Fus.	Killed in Action.
Thom, James	Tamneymore	Private	10th R. Inn. Fus.	Wounded.
Thompson, J. D.	Breakfield	Private	9th R.I.F.	
COLONIAL FORCES.				
Colhoun, T. S.	Ballyarton	Rifleman	N.Z.R.B.	
Irwin, Thomas W.	Goshaden	Lance-Corporal	Can. For. Corps	Wounded.
Kennedy, Albert J.	Glenlough	Sergeant	Canadians	
McCorkell, Joseph	Glenlough	Private	1st Can. A.S.P.	
McCorkell, Henry	Glenlough	Private	Canadians	
Marshall, Harry	Breakfield	Corporal	Aust. Regt.	Died at Cairo.
Nutt, John	Gortnaskea	Private	Canadians	
UPPER CUMBER.				
Craig, David	Claudy	Private	12th R. Inn. Fus.	
Deehan, Edward	Lyng, Claudy	Private	2nd Inn. Fus.	
Dixon, Robert J.	Claudy	Private	10th R. Inn. Fus.	Military Cert.
Laird, Archibald	Claudy	Private	N.I.H.	
Lamrock, Charles	Lettermuck	Private	10th R. Inn. Fus.	Wounded.
McDermott, W. D.	Sallowilly	Private	R. Inn. Fus.	Wounded.
Milliken, John	Kincull	Private	3rd R. Inn. Fus.	
Montgomery, John	Tullentrain	Private	Motor Transport	
Montgomery, Sam.	Tullentrain	Private	Machine Gun	
Reilly, James	Sallowilly	Private	10th R.I. Fus.	Wounded.
Reilly, John	Sallowilly	Private	12th R. Inn. Fus.	Wounded.
Reilly, William	Sallowilly	Private	King's O. Scott. Borderers	Killed in Action.
Robinson, David	Claudy	Driver	M.G., Salonica Force	
Rosborough, Thomas	Bond's Glen	Trooper	Can. Mtd. Rifles	
FIRST DONAGHEADY.				
Colhoun, Francis	Cloughoor	Seaman	R.N.	
Cooke, Thomas	Gortin	Private	R. Inn. Fus.	Twice Wounded.
Currie, John	Peter's Hill	Private	R. Inn. Fus.	Twice Wounded.
Doherty, George	Altreste	Private	R. Inn. Fus.	Killed in Action.
Doherty, Stephen	Altreste	Private	R. Inn. Fus.	Killed in Action.
Logue, Benjamin	Ballinabuoy	Private	R. Inn. Fus.	

GLENDERMOTT PRESBYTERY.   FIRST DONAGHEADY.

Name.	Home Address.	Rank.	Regiment, Battalion or Unit.	Remarks.
Lowry, David	Glencush	Private	R. Inn. Fus.	Twice Wounded.
Lynch, John	Killyclooney	Private	R. Inn. Fus.	Wounded 4 times.
McCrea, Robert	Fairview	Lieutenant	R.E.	
McMorris, J. N.	Altreste	Captain	R.A.M.C.	
Whiteside, Robert	Collermoney	Private	R. Inn. Fus.	Killed in Action.
COLONIAL FORCES.				
Colhoun, John	Cloughcor	Corporal	Canadian Force	Killed in Action.
Colhoun, Robert	Cloughcor	Private	Canadian Force	
Colhoun, William	Cloughcor	Seaman	Canadian Navy	
Cooke, John	Gortin	Sergeant	Canadian Force	Killed in Action.
Cooke, William	Gortin	Private	Canadian Force	
Falconer Alexr.	Castlemellon	Private	Canadian Force	
Lowry, Harry	Cloughcor	Private	New Zealand Force	Killed in Action.
Lowry, Samuel	Cloughcor	Private	New Zealand Force	Wounded.
Lowry, William	Glencush	Private	Canadian Force	Killed in Action.
McCloy, William	Gortmonley	Private	Canadian Force	
McCrea, Joseph	Fairview	Private	Australian Force	
Mitchell, John P.	Castlemellon	Private	Canadian Force	Wounded.
Neely, James	Killyclooney	Private	Canadian Force	Wounded.
Neely, Robert	Killyclooney	Private	Canadian Force	
Thompson, Harry	Cullion	Private	Canadian Force	
Thompson, Samuel	Cullion	Sergeant	Canadian Force	
SECOND DONAGHEADY.				
Adair, Robert	Cullion		R.A.F.	
Barr, David	Bogagh	Private	11th R. Inn. Fus.	
Boak, William	Killyclooney	Gunner	R.F.A.	
Fulton, David	Maghereagh	Private	R.I.R.	Wounded.
Lowry, Stephen	Cullion	Corporal	R.E.	M.M., Bar, D.C.M.
McGowan, John	Ballylaw	Private	5th R. Inn. Fus.	
McGowan, Thomas	Ballylaw	Private		Wounded, Ypres.
Porter, Robert	Thornhill	1st Air Mechanic	R.A.F.	
Woods, James	Drumgauty	Private	R.I.R.	
Woods, Wm.	Drumgauty	Private	R.I.R.	Twice wounded.
COLONIAL AND U.S.A. FORCES.				
Brown, John	Killymallagh	Private	Canadian Force	
Carnwath, Thomas	Collermoney	Captain	R.A.M.C.	D.S.O.
Currie, George H.	Gloudstown	Private	Canadian Force	
Currie, Ralph	Sandville	Private	Canadian Force	Wounded.
Daly, John James	Toronto	Private	Canadian Force	Wounded.
Love, Albert	Toronto	Private	Canadian Force	
Love, James	Toronto	Sergeant	Canadian Force	Wounded.
Love, Walker	Toronto	Private	Canadian Force	
McCay, William	Killycurry	Corporal	Canadian Force	
McCourt, Samuel	Mountcastle	Private	Canadian Force	Killed in Action.
Mitchell, David	Tarnatrine	Lance-Corporal	Cameron Highldrs.	Killed in Action.
Mitchell, James B.	Tarnatrine	Corporal	Canadian Force	Wounded.
Mitchell, John	Tarnatrine	Sergeant	Canadian Force	Wounded.
Mitchell, Thomas M.		Gunner	Canadian Force	Wounded.
Stevenson, Thomas	Killyclooney	Trooper	Australian Force	Died.
Woods, Robert	Drumgauty	Private	U.S. Engineers	
Wray, Samuel J.	Mountcastle	Sergeant	Can. M. Rifles	
DONEMANA.				
Arbuckle, Fred.	Donemana	Private	R. Inn. Fus.	
Brown, William	Tyboe	Private	R. Inn. Fus.	
Chambers, Thomas	Liscleen	Sergeant	R.A.S.C.	
Cummings, Robert	Benowen	Private	R. Inn. Fus.	
Dunlop, W. J.	Donemana	Private	R. Inn. Fus.	Died.
Forbes, John	Donemana	Private	Seaforth Highldrs.	
Forbes, Robert	Donemana	Private	R. Inn. Fus.	
Holmes, James	Tryconnolly	Private	R. Inn. Fus.	
Holmes, Wm. S.	Tryconnolly	Private	R. Inn. Fus.	Killed in Action.
Jeffrey, Archie	Aughtermoy	Private	Royal Air Service	
Jeffrey, Thomas	Cregan	Private	R. Inn. Fus.	
Key, Samuel	Tyboe	Private	R. Inn. Fus.	
Keys, Thomas	Tyrkernaghan	Private	R. Inn. Fus.	
Killen, Joseph	Ballynenor	Private	R. Inn. Fus.	
Laughlin, David	Donemana	Private	R. Inn. Fus.	Killed in Action.
Laughlin, Jacob	Donemana	Private	R. Inn. Fus.	Killed in Action.
Laughlin, Wm. E.	Donemana	Private	R. Inn. Fus.	
McKinley, James	Donemana	Sergeant	R. Inn. Fus.	
McKinley, John	Donemana	Private		
McKinley, William	Donemana	Private	R. Inn. Fus.	Killed in Action.
Neely, George	Castlemelon	Private	R.G.A.	
Sayers, Samuel	Drummond	Private	R. Inn. Fus.	Died of Wounds.
Shaw, Samuel	Fawney	Private	R. Inn. Fus.	
Taylor, Alexr. M.	Tyboe	Private	R. Inn. Fus.	Killed in Action.

GLENDERMOTT PRESBYTERY. DONEMANA.

Name.	Home Address.	Rank.	Regiment, Battalion or Unit.	Remarks.
Taylor, Wm. J.	Tyboe	Private	R. Inn. Fus.	
Thompson, Joseph	Drean	Private	R. Inn. Fus.	
COLONIAL FORCE.				
Allen, John	Donemana	Private	Canadians	
Allen, Robert	Donemana	Private	Canadians	
Callaghan, R. H.	Donemana	Private	Canadians	
Cochrane, James	Benone	Private	Canadians	
FAUGHANVALE.				
Archibald, James B.	Orchardstown	Sergeant	3rd R. Inn. Fus.	
Archibald, Robert R.	Orchardstown	Private	R.N.A.S.	
Barr, James	Glebe	Private	14th Batt. Highland L.I.	
Barr, Samuel	Glebe	Private	14th Batt. Highland L.I.	
Colhoun, Joseph	Maydown	Private	M.G.C.	
Donald, William	Campsie	Private	10th Batt. R.I.F.	Wounded.
McLeod, John	Willsboro'	Private	M.T. A.S.C.	
McCarron, David	Eglinton	Private	R.I.F.	Wounded.
McConnell, Alfred B.	Derryarkin	Private	3rd Batt. R.I.R.	
McConnell, Vincent	Derryarkin	Private	Army Cyclist Corps	
McConnell, William	Derryarkin	Private	R.E.	
McElroy, John	Derryarkin	Private	9th Batt. R.I.F.	
Richmond, Robert James	Campsie	Private	12th Batt. R.I.F.	Wounded.
Ross, William	Tullanee	Private	12th Batt. R.I.F.	Wd. by accident.
Smyth, Samuel	Eglinton	Private	10th Batt. R.I.F.	Wounded.
Smyth, William	Eglinton	Private	A.S.C.	
COLONIAL AND U.S.A. FORCES.				
Colhoun, John	Maydown	Private	207th Australian I. Force	
Colhoun, Robert	Maydown	Private	75th Canadians	
Colhoun, Samuel	Maydown	Private	Canadian Force	
Colhoun, William	Maydown	Private	Australian Force	
Semple, John	Eglinton	Private	American Force	
Smyth, James Edward	Killylane	Private	1st Can. Mounted Rifles	Wounded.
Smyth, Thomas	Longfield	Private	Australian Force	
Wray, Albert	Tully	Private	U.S. Army	
Wray, Alex.	Tully	Private	Canadian Force	
FIRST AND SECOND GLENDERMOTT.				
Anderson, Adam, B.A., B.E.	Curryfree	Lieutenant	S.W.B.	Wounded.
Austin, John	Londonderry	Private	S.B.	Killed.
Austin, William	Londonderry	Private	R. Inn. Fus.	Wounded.
Bredin, Ezekiel	Drumcoran	Private	R.F.C.	
Brolly, John	Drumahoe	Private	R.F.C.	Wounded.
Cresswell, John	Ardlough	Private	R. Inn. Fus.	Killed.
Curry, John	Londonderry	Private	R. Inn. Fus.	Killed.
Curry, Joseph	Londonderry	Private	R. Inn. Fus.	Wounded.
Doak, Robert	Carrody	Private	R. Inn. Fus.	Wounded.
Donaghy, David	Ardmore	Private	R. Inn. Fus.	
Donaghy, William	Ardmore	Sergeant	R. Inn. Fus.	Wounded.
Gillen, Thomas	Drumahoe	Private		Wounded.
Goligher, Thomas	Cross	Private	R. Inn. Fus.	
Hamilton, Hugh	Londonderry	Private	R. Inn. Fus.	Wounded.
Hamilton, Robert	Monaghmore		R.N.	
Hatrick, John	Carnafern	Engineer	R.N.	
Henderson, George	Londonderry	Private	R. Inn. Fus.	Invalided.
Jamison, James	Londonderry	Private	R. Inn. Fus.	Prisoner.
Jenkins, Samuel	Londonderry	Private	R.I.R.	Invalided.
Hunter, James	Ardmore	Private	R. Inn. Fus.	
Hillier, Herbert	Londonderry	Private	R. Inn. Fus.	
Hillier, John James	Londonderry	Private	R. Inn. Fus.	Wounded.
Kelly, James	Drumahoe	Private	R. Inn. Fus.	Wounded.
King, William	Londonderry	Private	R. Inn. Fus.	Wounded.
Laird, William	Londonderry	Private	R.A.M.C.	
Lynch, Robert	Tirbracken	Private	R. Inn. Fus.	Wounded.
McBrien, Robert	Lisdillon	Private	R. Inn. Fus.	Killed.
McClay, Allen	Londonderry	Private	R. Inn. Fus.	Wounded.
McClay, John James	Londonderry	Private	R. Inn. Fus.	Wounded.
McClay, Robert	Londonderry	Private	R. Inn. Fus.	Killed.
McNerlen, John	Londonderry	Private	R. Inn. Fus.	Wounded.
Norris, David	Londonderry	Private		Killed.
Norris, William	Drumahoe	Corporal	Scottish Borderers	Killed.
Orr, James	Lisdillon	Private	R. Inn. Fus.	Wounded.
Rosborough, James	Lisdillon	Private		
Rosborough, J. F.	Lisdillon	Private	R. Inn. Fus.	Wounded.
Shields, William	Ardmore	Private	R. Inn. Fus.	Wounded.
Simpson, William	Altnagelvin	Private	R. Inn. Fus.	
Stevenson, George	Tultyalley	Private	R. Inn. Fus.	Missing.
Strawbridge, Robert, B.A.	Gortgranagh	Cadet	Artists' Rifles	
Smyth, Alexander	Londonderry	Private	N.I.H.	Wounded.

GLENDERMOTT PRESBYTERY.

FIRST AND SECOND GLENDERMOTT.

Name.	Home Address.	Rank.	Regiment, Battalion or Unit.	Remarks.
Taylor, Hamilton	Altnagelvin	Private	R. Inn. Fus.	Wounded.
Taylor, Robert	Altnagelvin	Private	R. Inn. Fus.	Pris. & Wounded.
Thompson, Thomas	Londonderry	Surgeon		
Thompson, John	Londonderry	Engineer		
Thompson, Alfred	Brookmount	Private		
Thompson, T. R.	Gobnascale	Quartermaster		
Thompson, Richard G.	Gobnascale	Private	R. Inn. Fus.	Wounded.
Thompson, Mat.	Gobnascale	Private	R. Inn. Fus.	
Thompson, Lance	Gobnascale	Private	R. Inn. Fus.	Wounded & Pris.
Thompson, Robert	Gobnascale	Sergeant	R. Inn. Fus.	Missing.
Thompson, J. W.	Gobnascale	Lieutenant	R. Inn. Fus.	Killed.
Thompson, W. (Fred.)	Gobnascale	Private	R. Inn. Fus.	Killed.
Wade, Albert	Altnagelvin	Engineer		
Wade, Fred.	Altnagelvin	Private	R. Inn. Fus.	
COLONIAL FORCES.				
Campbell, David	Drumahoe	Private	N.Z. Force	Invalided.
Campbell, Thomas	Drumahoe	Private	N.Z. Force	Invalided.
Campbell, Thomas	Drumahoe	Private	N.Z. Force	
Campbell, Wm. John	Drumahoe	Private	N.Z. Force	
Leslie, William	Londonderry	Sergeant	Australian Force	
McCrea, Henry	Gorticross	Private	N. Z. Force	
McCrea, James	Gorticross	Private	Canadian Force	Wounded.
McCrea, Robert	Gorticross	Corporal	N.Z. Force	Killed in Action.
Norris, Joseph	Londonderry	Corporal	Australian Force	
Smyth, John C.	Tanneymore	Private	Canadian Force	
Snodgrass, Wm.	Carnafern	Corporal	Canadian Force	Wounded.
Thompson, S. J.	Gobnascale	Private	Canadian Force	Wounded.
GORTNESSY.				
Baird, J. E A.	Eglinton	2nd Lieutenant	R. Inn. Fus.	
Hall, Rev. W. P., M.A.	The Manse	Captain	C.F.	
Lamberton, Wallace	Aughill	Private	Australian Force	
Matson, William	Ardnajuniog	Private	R. Inn. Fus.	
Perry, Joseph	Falloward	Private	Canadian Force	
Quigley, Robert	Gortnessy	Private	R. Inn. Fus.	

LETTERKENNY PRESBYTERY.

Name.	Home Address.	Rank.	Regiment, Battalion or Unit.	Remarks.
CARRIGART.				
Fisher, James	Umlagh	Sergeant	M.G. Corps	D.C.M. Killed in Action.
Munro, Charles	Carrigart	C.Q.M.S.	A. and S. High.	Killed in Action.
Munro, George	Carrigart	Sergeant	R. In. Fus.	
Speers, William	Glenree	Lance-Corporal	H.L.I.	Killed in Action
Sweeney, T. C.	10 Clarendon St., Derry	Captain	R. In. Fus.	M.M. Wounded
DUNFANAGHY.				
Jacob, Samuel	Dunfanaghy	Private	11th Batt. R. In. Fus.	
Montgomery, John	Fougher	Private	Motor Transport	
Wilson, Harry	Horn Head	Private	Machine Gun Corps	Wounded.
FANNET.				
Clarke, George	Edmonton	Private	R.E. Can. Force	
Elliot, James	Kerrykeel	Lance-Corporal	R. In. Fus.	Drowned.
Inkster, Andrew	Kerrykeel	Lance-Corporal	R. Highlanders	Killed in Action.
McIlwain, James	Drumfad	Lance-Corporal	R. In. Fus.	M.C.
McConnell, Dr. George	Kerrykeel	Captain	R.A.M.C.	
KILMACRENAN.				
Burns, Charles H.	Kilmacrenan	Trooper	N.I.H.	Wounded.
Burns, Robert A.	Kilmacrenan	Corporal	U.S. Army	
Patterson, Moses	Portlean	Sergeant	Can. Army	Killed in Action.
Stewart, R. E.	Gortnaskeagh	Private	Canadians	
Stewart, S. B.	Gortnaskeagh	Corporal	R.A.M.C., Egypt Ex. F.	
Stewart, W. J.	Gortnaskeagh	Driver	Canadian Force	W'ded and Gassed.

LETTERKENNY PRESBYTERY.   FIRST LETTERKENNY.

Name.	Home Address.	Rank.	Regiment, Battalion or Unit.	Remarks.
FIRST LETTERKENNY.				
Ashe, George	Corravaddy	Private	R A F	
Birnie, Robert	Dromore	Lieutenant	Munster Fus	
Black, William	Glencar	Sergeant	R A M C	
Campbell, John	Letterkenny	Wireless Op.	R A F	
Galbraith, Joseph	Letterkenny	Private	A S C	
Gregg, Richard	Killydesert	Private	R In Fus	Died
Gregg, Robert	Killydesert	Private	Labour Corps	
MacLennan, Allen	Letterkenny	Wireless Op.	R A F	Killed in Action
MacLennan, Bruce	Letterkenny	Corporal	11th R. In. Fus.	
MacLennon, Donald	Letterkenny	Sapper	R.E.	
MacLennon, Hector	Letterkenny	Corporal	R. In. Fus.	Wounded.
Porter, Robert	Letterkenny	Private	11th R. In. Fus.	
Scott, James	Killylasten	Private	11th R. In. Fus.	
Speer, Albert	Letterkenny	Sergeant	11th R. In. Fus.	Killed in Action
Stoops, Samuel	Letterkenny	Driver	A.S.C.	
LETTERKENNY, TRINITY CHURCH.				
Boal, John	Letterkenny	Private	R.I.F.	
Corry, M.	...	Lieut.-Colonel	I.M.S.	
Corry, S. B.	Letterkenny		R.I.F.	Wounded.
Cowen, Jacob	Letterkenny	Private	R.I.F.	Wounded.
Duffy, J S.	Letterkenny	Sergeant	R.E.	
Elliott, Joseph	Letterkenny	Private	N.I.H.	Wounded.
Henderson, J.	Letterkenny			
Hunter, W. M.	Letterkenny	Lieutenant	R.I.F.	Killed.
Kerr, Arthur	Letterkenny	Private	R.I.R.	
Kerr, R. J.	Letterkenny	Private	R.I.F.	
Knipe, W. H.	Letterkenny	Private	R.E.	
Knipe, E.	Letterkenny	Private	R.I.F.	Wounded.
Knipe, A. M.	Letterkenny	Private	R.I.R.	Killed.
Leitch, A. G.	Letterkenny	Captain	R.A.M.C.	
McCoy, H.	Letterkenny	Private	A.S.C.	
McClure, C. J.	Letterkenny	Corporal	R.I.F.	Wounded.
McClure, John	Letterkenny	Lieutenant	R.I.F.	Killed.
McElhinney, C.	Letterkenny	Sergeant	N.I.H.	
Millar, J. L.	Letterkenny	Lieutenant	R.I.R.	Killed.
Robinson, Joseph	Letterkenny	Private	R.I.F.	Killed.
Sterritt, Joseph	Letterkenny	Private	R.I.F.	Killed.
Power, Alexander	Letterkenny	Sergeant	R.I.F.	
Rankin, William	Letterkenny	Private	A.S.C.	
Scott, William	Letterkenny	Private	Air Force	
White, Joseph	...	Private	R.I.F.	Wounded.
COLONIAL AND U.S.A. FORCES.				
Boal, Tom			Canada	
Cassidy, S. R.			N.Z.	Killed.
Cowen, William			Canada	
Healey, Samuel			N.Z.	
Hunter, Joseph			U.S.A.	
Hunter, R.			Canada	Wounded.
Hunter, J. H.			Canada	Wounded.
McCoy, D.			U.S.A.	
McNutt, D.			U.S.A.	
Peoples, F.			Canada	
Ramsay, Joseph			Canada	Killed.
MILFORD, CO. DONEGAL.				
Best, William	Tirhomin	Private	R. In. Fus.	
Burns, Alexander	Milford	2nd Lieutenant	Royal Air Service	
Burns, Joseph	Milford	Private	A.S.C.	
Burns, J. A. O.	Milford	Private	Queen's Hussars	
Hay, Frederick	Gortmecall	Private	R.I.R.	
Hunter, James	Cranford	Private	R.G.A.	
Hunter, William	Cranford	Private	Seaforth High.	
Johnston, Samuel	Tirhomin	Sergeant	R. In. Fus.	Pris. in Germany.
Moore, H.	Cranford	Private	A.S.C.	
Morrow, William	Milford	Private	R. In. Fus.	
Stevenson, David	Gortmecall	Private	A.S.C.	
Wilson, William	Magheradrummond	Private	N.I.H.	
Young, Hugh	Milford	Captain	R. In. Fus.	M.C.
COLONIAL FORCES.				
Allen, Hugh	Alberta	Sergeant	Canadian Inft.	
Gamble, Charles		Private	Canadian Inft.	
Hunter, John	...	Private	Australian Inft.	
Hunter, Joseph	Philadelphia	Private	U.S.A. Inft.	
Young, Cyril	Philadelphia	Private	U.S.A. Inft.	

LETTERKENNY PRESBYTERY.
FIRST RAMELTON.

Name.	Home Address.	Rank.	Regiment, Battalion or Unit.	Remarks.
FIRST RAMELTON.				
Black, William C.	Bogwell	Bombardier	R.F.A.	M.M. Wounded.
Buchanan, Joseph	High Cairn	Private	R. In. Fus.	Prisoner.
Campbell, John	Church Street	Lance-Corporal	R.A.F.	Wounded.
Colhoun, William	Glentidaly	Private	N.I.H.	
Elliott, Richard	Bank	Private	Scottish Fus.	
Fullerton, John C.	Shellfield	Lieut.-Colonel	R.F.A.	
Fullerton, S. C.	Shellfield	Lieutenant	S. Lanc. Fus.	Wounded.
Kennedy, James W.	Church Street	Private	R. In. Fus.	
Lockhart, Moses	Back Lane	Officer	R.N.	
Lockhart, Oliver	Back Lane	Stoker	R.N.	
Lockhart, Robert	Back Lane	A.B.	R.N.	
McAdams, James	Back Lane	Private	R. In. Fus.	Wounded.
McNevisin, Edward	Bridge End	Sergeant	R. In. Fus.	Wounded.
McNutt, John	Long Hill	Private	N.I.H.	
Malseed, Andrew	Church Street	Private	N.I.H.	
Malseed, Harry	Church Street	Private	N.I.H.	...
Malseed, John	Church Street	Private	R. In. Fus.	
Peoples, Charles	Bank Terrace	Private	A. and S. High.	Wounded.
Peoples, George	Bank Terrace	Private	R.I.F.	Killed in Action.
Peoples, John	Bank Terrace	Private	A. and S. High.	Killed in Action.
Peoples, William	Bank Terrace	Private	R. In. Fus.	
Porter, Alexander	Castle Street	Private	A.S.C.	
Porter, Nelson	Castle Street	Private	A.S.C.	
Stewart, Samuel	High Glen	Private	R.A.F.	
Thompson, Thomas	Aughnish	Lance-Corporal	N.I.H.	Wounded.
Wilson, D. W. J.	Cairn	Private	R. In. Fus.	
COLONIAL FORCES.				
Cheatley, Joseph D.	Ballyhenny	Lance-Corporal	Canadians	Wounded.
Cheatley, Patterson	Ballyhenny	Private	Canadians	Wounded.
Callan, John	Back Lane	Private	Can. High.	
Davidson, Hugh	The Mall	Corporal	Canadians	
Mackey, James D.	Dublin	Private	Canadians	Wounded.
SECOND RAMELTON.				
Aiken, Andrew	Drumherive	Private	R. In. Fus.	
Baird, David	Race End	Private	N.I.H.	Wounded.
Bates, Alexander	Glenleary	Private	N.I.H.	
Birney, George	Ramelton	Lance-Corporal	11th In. Fus.	Thrice Wounded.
Birney, James	Ramelton	Private	R.A. Force	
Birney, Robert	Ramelton	Private	12th R. In. Fus.	Wounded.
Corry, Fred.	Ramelton	Sergeant	Can. R.A.M.C.	
Duncan, James	Aughnagaddy	Lance-Corporal	R. Irish Fus.	
Galbraith, Joseph	Drummond	Driver	A.S.C.	
Galbraith, Joseph	Ardrummon	Lance-Corporal	R.E.	
Gallagher, George	Ballyconnolly	Private	R. In. Fus.	
Hamilton, Robert	Aughnagaddy	Private	11th R. In. Fus.	Killed in Action.
Hatrick, Andrew E.	Castleshanaghan	Sergeant	N.I.H.	Wounded.
Hunter, Thomas	Ramelton	Private	R. In. Fus.	Killed in Action.
Kennedy, David	Aughnish	Corporal	N.I.H.	
Kilpatrick, John	Tully	Private	A.S.C.	
Kilpatrick, William	Tully	Private	N.I.H.	
Loughhead, John	Ramelton	Private	R.F.A.	
Love, Matthew	Ramelton	Private	King's Liverpool Regt.	
Love, Thompson	Ramelton	Private	R. In. Fus.	Gassed.
McClure, Francis	Drumacloghan	Private	N.I.H.	
McClure, James	Drumacloghan	Sapper	Telegraph Dep., R.N.	
McDonald, William	Ramelton	Private	3rd In. Fus.	Gassed.
Montgomery, James	Ramelton	Private	A.S.C.	
Moore, Thomas	Aughnish	Private	11th In. Fus.	
O'Brien, James	Aughnish	Private	12th In. Fus.	Wounded.
O'Brien, Robert	Aughnish	Private	11th In. Fus.	
Osborne, Robert	Ramelton	Private	N.I.H.	
Osborne, William	Ramelton	Corporal	R.A. Force	
Reagh, James	Magheradrummond	Private	N.I.H.	
Reagh, Samuel	Magheradrummond	Corporal	N.I.H.	
Speer, George	Ballybocurragh	Driver	A.S.C.	
Taylor, George	Ramelton	Private	12th R. In. Fus.	Thrice Wounded.
Watson, Robert	Race End	Private	N.I.H.	Wounded & Gassed
Wilson, James	Magheradrummond	Private	N.I.H.	
Wilson, William	Magheradrummond	Private	N.I.H.	
RATHMULLEN.				
Mayrick, George	Rathmullen	Signaller	R.E.	
FIRST RAY.				
Colquhoun, A. L.	Rossbracken	Sergeant	N.I.H.	
Colquhoun, F. J.	Rossbracken	Private	N.I.H.	French M.M.

LETTERKENNY PRESBYTERY.

FIRST RAY.

Name.	Home Address.	Rank.	Regiment, Battalion or Unit.	Remarks.
Gallagher, Samuel	Corkey	Sapper	R.E.	
Gallaugher, H.	Balleighan	Captain	11th R. In. Fus.	D.S.O. Killed in Action.
Hutchinson, Alexander	Ballyholey	Private	9th R. In. Fus.	Died.
Hutchinson, John	Ballyholey	Private	9th R. In. Fus.	
Leckey, William	Manorcunningham	Private	9th R. In. Fus.	M.M.
McConnell, D.	Ballylevin	Private	11th R. In. Fus.	
McKee, Rev. E. J., LL.D.	Manorcunningham	Captain	Chaplain	Wounded.
Patterson, Samuel	Ardagh	Private	11th R. In. Fus.	Wounded.
Roulstone, Alexander	Castleblaugh	Private	11th R. In. Fus.	Wounded & Died in Germany.
COLONIAL AND U.S.A. FORCES.				
Gallaugher, David	Balleighan	Private	Canadians	
Gallaugher, David	Balleighan	Cadet	54th Brigade Can. F.	M.M.
Leckey, J. C.	Train	Private	2nd Otago Regt., N.Z.	Wounded.
Leckey, R. C.	Castlefoley	Private	32nd Air Sq. A.E.F.	
Leckey, Thomas	Castlefoley	Private	78th Can. Div.	Wounded.
McClintock, John	Galdonagh Point	Private	1st Can. Div.	
McConnell, James	Ballylevin	Private	N.Z.	Killed in Action.
Patterson, Archibald	Ardagh	Private	Canadian Div.	
SECOND RAY.				
Barnhill, David	Ballylawn	Sergeant	11th In. Fus.	M.M. Killed.
Chambers, William	Moneyhaughley	Sapper	108th Div. R.E.	
Clarke, John A. W.	Coalfield	Private	N.I.H.	Wounded.
Hay, William A.	Trimragh	Signaller	27th R.F.A.	
Hughes, Robert	Finvoy, Co. Antrim	Private	N.I.H.	
Hutchinson, John	Manorcunningham	Corporal	R.F.A.	Killed in Action.
Irwin, George L.	Errity House	Captain	R.A.M.C.	
Kilgore, Robert J.	Magherabeg	Private	N.I.H.	Wounded.
McClean, Francis G.	Rossbrakin	Sergeant	N.I.H.	
McConnell, Alexander	Errity	Sergeant	N.I.H.	Invalided.
McConnell, Frederick	Errity	Private	N.I.H.	Died.
McConnell, James A.	Manorcunningham	Private	N.I.H.	
McElhinney, Charles	Ray	Private	N.I.H.	
McElhinney, William	Manorcunningham	Private	N.I.H.	
McKinley, Robert	Moneyhaughley	Private	6th In. Dragoons	
McKinley, Robert W.	Woodside	Captain	11th & 9th In. Fus.	M.C. Wounded.
McLaughlin, Samuel	Dromore, Letterkenny	Private	3rd In. Fus.	Killed in Action.
Moore, John	Labadish	Private	11th In. Fus.	Wounded.
Phillips, Robert J.	Pluck	Corporal	10th In. Fus.	Prisoner of War in Germany.
Phillips, Samuel	Pluck	Private	N.I.H.	
Phillips, William J.	Pluck	Private	R.M. Artillery	
Rainey, William J.	Beragh	Corporal	I.G.	Killed in Action.
Ramsey, Archibald	Manorcunningham	Staff-Sergeant	A.S.C.	
Ramsey, James A.	Corkey	Private	N.I.H.	Wounded.
Rodgers, James	Mondooey	Private	N.I.H.	Prisoner of War in Germany.
Russell, Samuel N.	Ballylawn	Private	Home Defence, London	
Stevenson, Henry	Aughliard	Sergeant	9th R. In. Fus.	Killed in Action.
Wallace, George	Galdonagh	Private	11th R. In. Fus.	Invalided.
COLONIAL AND U.S.A. FORCES.				
Arthur, Samuel	Pluck	Private	14th Can. Batt.	Wounded.
Barnhill, James	Ballylawn	Private	27th Can. Batt.	Died.
Barnhill, John	Ballylawn	Corporal	2nd Batt. N.Z. E.F.	Wounded.
Stevenson, David	Aughliard	Private	Aviation, U.S.A.	
TRENTA.				
Buchanan, Edmund	Rathdonnell	Corporal	N.I.H.	1914 Star. Died.
Dunlop, D.	Dromore, Trenta	Private	N.I.H.	Wounded.
Ferguson, T.	Gartan	Private	R.I.R.	
Michael, James P.	The Manse	Cadet	R.A.F.	
Michael, William, M.B.	The Manse	Surgeon-Lieut.	R.N.	
Sproule, William	Trenta	Private	R. In. Fus.	Wounded.
Tease, John L.	Trenta	Corporal	N.I.H.	1914 Star. W'ded.
Tease, Samuel	Trenta	Private	R. In. Fus.	Wounded.
COLONIAL AND U.S.A. FORCES.				
Neely, D.	Cloncarney	Private	N.Z. Force	Wounded.
Nelson, T.	Cloncarney	Private	N.Z. Force	Wounded.
Rankin, John	Lisdonnelly	Staff-Sergeant	S.A. Force	
Tease, F. G.	Trenta	2nd Lieutenant	Canadians	M.M. Wounded.
Tease, James R.	Trenta	Private	Canadians	

LIMAVADY PRESBYTERY.

Name.	Home Address.	Rank.	Regiment, Battalion or Unit.	Remarks.
BALLYKELLY.				
Allen, John	Dromore	Private	10th R. In. Fus.	
Blair, James	Ballykelly	Lance-Corporal	T.M.B., 10th R.I.R.	Wounded.
Blair, Robert	Ballykelly	Private	10th R. In. Fus.	
Campbell, Tom	Ballykelly	Private	11th R.I.F.	Thrice Wounded.
Cochrane, William	Ballykelly	Trooper	N.I.H.	
Douglas, John	Tamlaght	Private	M.T. A.S.C.	
Douglas, Wilson	Ballykelly	Private	3rd R.I.F.	
Forsythe, George	Carnamuff	Private	12th R.I.F.	Killed in Action.
Gilloway, James	Bessbrook	Private	H.S. Garrison	Wounded.
Gilloway, Joseph	Bessbrook	Private	11th R.I.F.	
Hamilton, Samuel	Ballykelly	Private	Scot. Rifles	
Harper, Sam	Ballykelly	Private	Scots Guards	
Irwin, Joseph	Carrichue	Private	9th R. In. Fus.	
Marshall, Robert	Ballykelly	Private	11th R. Dub. Fus.	
McFaul, Robert	Ballykelly	Lance-Corporal	10th R. In. Fus.	Killed in Action.
McFaul, William	Ballykelly	Private	10th R. In. Fus.	Twice Wounded.
Rodden, Charles	Ballykelly	Private	R.G.A.	
Rodden, James	Ballykelly	Corporal	10th R. In. Fus.	Wounded.
Wark, James	Culmore	Private	10th R. In. Fus.	
Wark, Joseph	Ballykelly	Private	10th R. In. Fus.	Killed in Action.
Whyte, Robert	Ballykelly	Private	10th R. In. Fus.	Wounded.
COLONIAL FORCES.				
Cochrane, Robert		Private	78th Canadians	Wounded.
Guthrie, Robert			N.Z. Mounted	
Marshall, Thomas		Driver	A.S.C. Australians	
BALTEAGH.				
Irwin, Thomas	Ballyness	Lance-Corporal	R. In. Fus.	
Irwin, William	Ballyness	Lance-Corporal	R. In. Fus.	Killed in Action.
McGinnis, John	Maine, Drumsurn	Lance-Corporal	R.I.R.	Killed in Action.
McIntyre, William C.	Lislane	Private	R. In. Fus.	Wounded.
Mullan, John	Little Derry	Corporal	Post Office Rifles	Wounded.
Rentoul, William John	Maine, Drumsurn		R.N.	
Scott, John	Ardmore	Private	R. In. Fus.	Wounded.
Young, John A.	Ballymully	Private	R. In. Fus.	Killed in Action.
Young, William	Cloghan	Private	R.G.A.	
COLONIAL AND U.S.A. FORCES.				
Adams, William	Ballyquin	Corporal	American Force	
Craig, Alex. Lyle	Gortnarney	Private	Canadians	Wounded.
Ross, James	Aughansillagh	Private	Canadians	Died of Wounds.
Ross, Robert	Ballyleighery	Private	Canadians	
BOVEVA.				
Falls, Joseph	Bovevagh	Private	3rd R. In. Fus.	Wounded.
Ferguson, John	Drumneechy	Rifleman	2nd King's R. Rifles	Good Con. Medal.
Jackson, Joseph	Ardinariff	Gunner	110th Battery R.F.A.	
McConachy, Chas. Geo.	Strath	Seaman	R.N.	Lost in N. Sea.
Sinclair, James	Bovevagh	Private	Wireless Squad.	
Smyth, David H.	Mulkeeragh	Guardsman	5th Platoon I.G.	
COLONIALS AND U.S. ARMY.				
Ferguson, Robert	Drumneechy	Bomb.	Aust. L. Horse	
Hull, Robert	Ballymaceever	Private	Aust. Imp. Horse	Killed in Action.
Stewart, James	Derryork	Private	U.S. Inft.	Killed in Action.
Stewart, Robert	Derryork	Private	U.S. F. Artillery	
Wray, James Ernest	Gortgarn	Private	Can. Air Force	
Wray, John Nutt	Gortgarn	Private	Can. Air Force	
DERRAMORE.				
Dickson, Henry	Killybready	Private	R.A.F.	
Dickson, John	Killybready	Private	R. In. Fus.	Died from Gas.
Dickson, William	Limavady	Private	R.E.	
Hamilton, James	Drumalief	Private	R. In. Fus.	
Lynch, David	Mullane	Private	R.G.A.	
Madden, Robert	Artikelly	Sergeant	R.F.A.	D.C.M.
Madden, Thomas	Scotland	Private	Scottish Rifles	Killed in Action.
Sherrard, Robert		Private	U.S. Army	
Taylor, James	Kiltinney	Private	King's R. Rifles	
Taylor, John		Private	Aust. Force	
DRUMACHOSE.				
Anderson, Samuel	Limavady	Private	M.T. A.S.C.	
Carson, Andrew	Carrick	Sapper	R.E	
Connell, Charles J.	Limavady	Rifleman	11th R.I.R.	Gassed.

LIMAVADY PRESBYTERY.   DRUMACHOSE.

Name.	Home Address.	Rank.	Regiment, Battalion or Unit.	Remarks.
Connell, John H.	Limavady	Corporal	7th R.I.R.	
Douglas, James	Limavady	Lieutenant	10th R. In. Fus.	Wounded.
Douglas, John A.	Limavady	Corporal	11th R. In. Fus.	
Dunn, John	Keady	Private	12th R. In. Fus.	
Elder, William	Limavady	Lance-Corporal	10th R. In. Fus.	
Kennedy, David	Enagh	Private	R.A.F.	Died.
Kennedy, William	Enagh	Private	R.A.F.	
Lawson, George Fowler	Limavady	Private	Hussars	Died.
Lyndsay, Fred.	Derramore	S.S.	S.A.A.B.	
McIntosh, Albert	Ballymoney	Corporal	N.I.H.	
McLeod, John F.	Drummond	Gunner	R.F.A.	Wounded.
Marshall, James	Limavady	Lance-Corporal	H.L.I.	Wounded.
Neely, Alfred	Limavady	Corporal	N.I.H.	
Oliver, James	Derrybeg	Cadet	R.A.F.	
Oliver, Thomas	Dungiven Road	Private	R. In. Fus.	
Sherrard, John	Drumalief	Private	12th R. In. Fus.	Died.
Tait, John	Killane	Private	6th R. In. Fus.	Died of Wounds.
Tait, Robert	Killane	Private	1st I.G.	Wounded.
Tait, William	Limavady	Private	R. In. Fus.	Died.
COLONIAL AND AMERICAN ARMY.				
Barbour, William	Drummond	Private	Canadian	Killed in Action.
Loughrey, James	Carrick	Private	Canadian	Croix de Guerre.
Love, William	Drumbane	Mechanic	U.S. Ambulance	
McCormick, Robert S.	Limavady	Private	Canadian M.G. Co.	
McKittrick, William	Limavady	Private	Canadian Signal S.	
DUNGIVEN.				
Armstrong, Hamilton	Dungiven	Lance-Corporal	Post Office Rifles	Wounded.
Davison, William A.	Dungiven	Sergeant	10th R. In. Fus.	Wounded.
Deane, Samuel	Dungiven	Private	Scottish Rifles	Wounded.
Deane, William	Dungiven	Private		Killed in Action.
Flemining, William A.	Dungiven	Corporal	10th R. In. Fus.	Wounded.
Gibson, William	Dungiven	Private	A.S.C.	
Macartney, Samuel	Dungiven	2nd Lieutenant	R.E.	
McCay, Thomas F.	Dungiven	2nd Lieutenant	19th R.I.R.	Killed in Action.
McSparron, Archibald	Dungiven	2nd Lieutenant	N.I.H.	
Moorhead, Joseph	Dungiven	Corporal	Royal Scots	Wound. and Pris.
Parke, John	Dungiven	Private	9th R. In. Fus.	Wounded.
Scott, Andrew	Dungiven	2nd Lieutenant	R.I.R.	Prisoner.
Stewart, Isaac I.	Dungiven	Private	14th R.I.R.	Wounded.
COLONIAL AND U.S.A. FORCES.				
Douglas, Robert	Dungiven	Private	110th Canadians	
Haslett, John	Dungiven	Private	36th Canadians	Wounded.
Hutton, Alexander	Dungiven	Private	American Amb. Co.	
Hutton, James	Dungiven	Private	Canadian Engineers	
Hutton, William	Dungiven	Private	Canadian Railway Troops	
Irwin, Henry	Dungiven	Private	43rd Canadians	Killed in Action.
Irwin, Robert J. S.	Dungiven	Private	N.Z. Mounted Rifles	
Moorehead, William	Dungiven	Corporal	18th Canadians	
Rosborough, John	Dungiven	Private	N.Z. Rifles	Wounded.
Stewart, George A.	Dungiven	Private	1st Montreal Regt.	Killed in Action.
Stewart, Hugh F.	Dungiven	Staff-Sergeant	56th Canadians	Wounded.
Stewart, William M.	Dungiven	2nd Lieutenant	5th Brigade A.I. Force	Killed in Action.
LARGY.				
Baird, Thomas	Roe Park	Private	12th R.I. Fus.	Killed in Action.
Campbell, J. E.	Largy	Corporal	C.A.S.C.	
Campbell, John McC.	Largy	Signaller	36th Div. R.I. Fus.	
Forrest, James	Largy	Private	R.I. Fus.	Died of Wounds.
Forrest, John	Glasgow	Private	A.S.C.	
Forrest, William	Largy	Lance-Corporal	H.L.I.	Twice Wounded.
Hazlett, John	Tillydrum	Private	7th H.L.I.	Died of Wounds.
Lyons, Joseph	Moyse	Private	R. Air Force	
Moore, Hugh	Moyse	Fireman	H.M.S. "Hildebrand"	
Moore, James	Slate Row	Private	37th Batt. H.L.I.	
Moore, William	Slate Row	Private	Lothian and Border Horse	Died.
Moorehead, Robert	Limavady	Private	10th R.I. Fus.	Killed in Action.
Neely, William J.	Largy	Trooper	N.I. Horse	
Orr, William	Largy	Private	R.A. Force	
Spinks, Edmund	Largy	Private	R.A.M.C.	
Spinks, William	Largy	Private Signaller	9th Batt. R.I. Fus.	
COLONIAL AND U.S.A. FORCES.				
Campbell, William	Largy	Private	72nd Can. Inft.	Killed in Action.
Dunseith, Thomas	Carrick	Private	20th Can. Batt.	
Hynds, Samuel	Moyse	Private	Can. R.F. Troops	
Morrison, John	Terrydremond	Private	311th Inf. Am. Ex. Force	

LIMAVADY PRESBYTERY.   FIRST LIMAVADY.

Name.	Home Address.	Rank.	Regiment, Battalion or Unit.	Remarks.
FIRST LIMAVADY.				
Brown, John	Drumgesh	Private	R.A.F.	
Crumley, John	Keady	Private	R. In. Fus.	Wounded.
Gault, William	Ballyclose Street	C.Q.M.S.	Labour Corps	
Lyndsay, H.	Deramore	Private	R.F.A.	
McAllister, Joseph	Streeve	Private	R.I.R.	Wounded.
Morrison, George	Connell Street	Private	R. In. Fus.	Killed in Action.
Morrison, James	Connell Street	Private	R. In. Fus.	Killed in Action.
Oliver, Thomas	Catherine Street	Sergeant	R.A.M.S.	
Rankin, John	Kennaught Street	Private	R. In. Fus.	Wounded.
Thompson, Benj.	Main Street	Private	R.I.R.	Invalided.
COLONIAL FORCES.				
McCullough, E. C.	Main Street	Sergeant	Can. F.A.	
Rankin, James	Roe Green	Private	C.C.S., Can.	
Rankin, John	Roe Green	Private	Can. F.A.	M.M.
Thompson, Hugh	Main Street	Private	Australian Force	
Thorpe, Jack	Catherine Street	Private	Can. F.C.	
SECOND LIMAVADY.				
Alcorn Henry	William Street	Sergeant	10th Inniskillings	
Baird, William	Roemill Road	Sergeant	10th Inniskillings	Wounded.
Blackburn, James	Irishgreen Street	Sergeant	10th Inniskillings	Wounded.
Bond, Alexander	Kennaught Street	Private	10th Inniskillings	Killed in Action.
Boyd, Harris	Barley Park	Signaller	N.I.H.	
Boyd, Robert J.	Roemill Road	Sergeant	5th Can. Siege Battery	
Campbell, Daniel H.	Main Street	Lance-Corporal	Dub. Fus.	Wounded.
Drennan, James W.	Carse Hall	2nd Lieutenant	10th Inniskillings	Killed in Action.
Gault, William	Main Street	Q.M. Sergeant	Labour Corps	
Hunter, Benn M.	Market Street	Sergeant	10th Inniskillings	Wounded. Military Medal.
Irwin, Fred.	Roemill Cottage	2nd Lieutenant	10th Inniskillings	Killed in Action. M.M.
Irwin, Harry	Main Street	Signaller	10th R.I.R.	Wounded.
Kyle, James B.	Main Street	Gunner	R.M.A.	Wounded.
Livingstone, Samuel	Protestant Street	Private	10th Inniskillings	
Lowry, Henry	White Hill	Corporal	2nd Anzac Corps	
Marshall, Robert	Bovally	Sapper	121st Co. R.E.	M.M.
Martin, James	Carbullion	2nd Lieutenant	R.I.R.	Wounded.
Montgomery, Thomas V.	Catherine Street	Sergeant	Irish Guards	
Moody, David	Main Street	Private	Australian Field Force	Wounded.
Morrison, Thomas A.	Terrydremond	Corporal	Signals R.E.	
McCay, Alexander	Isle of Man Street	Corporal	10th Inniskillings	
McLaughlin, John	Irishgreen Street	Corporal	10th Inniskillings	Wounded.
Purcell, Charles	Railway Place	Signaller	10th Inniskillings	
Purcell, W. P.	Railway Place	2nd Officer	H.M.T. " Vancura "	
Purdy, John	Terrydremond	Private	10th Inniskillings	
Simpson, James	Deerpark	Private	10th Inniskillings	Wounded.
Smyth, James	Linenhall Street	Private	10th Inniskillings	Missing.
Smyth, John	William Street	Private	10th Inniskillings	Wounded.
Warke, Henry	Ballymullen	Private	10th Inniskillings	Wounded.
White, Gerald	Albert Terrace	Private	Tank Corps	
White, John	Albert Terrace	Captain	1/8 Lancashire Fus.	
White, Wallace	Albert Terrace	Rifleman	10th R.I.R.	
MAGILLIGAN.				
Glenn, Thomas	Bellarena	Corporal	Scotch Guards	Wounded.
Kelly, Samuel	Tircrevin	Private	R. In. Fus.	Wounded.
Lawson, John	Tircrevin	Bombardier	R.F.A.	
Martin, Samuel John	Tircrevin	P.O. 1st Class	R.N.	Three Medals.
McLaughlin, Alexander	Bellarena	Corporal	R. In. Fus.	Killed in Action.
Sherrard, James Lucas	Drummonds	Private	Royal Highlanders	
Sherrard, Joseph Connell	Drummonds	Corporal	I.G.	Twice Wounded.
MYROE.				
Brewster, Robert H.	Carrowmudle	Co. Sergt.-Major	5th R. In. Fus.	
Cromie, Joseph	Carrowmena	Driver	R.G.A.	
Devine, John	Ballymecran	Private	10th R. In. Fus.	Killed in Action.
Gardiner, John	Ballymecran	Private	Am. Army	
Kealey, Samuel	Culmore	Lance-Corporal	Am. Army	M.M. Wounded.
McCullagh, Ben.	Carryclare	Private	N.I.H.	Wounded.
McCurry, Daniel	Carrowreagh	Private	10th R. In. Fus.	Wounded.
McCurry, John	Carryclare	Private	12th R.I.R.	W'ded. Lost Eye.
McCurry Robert	Carryclare	Private	10th R. In. Fus.	
McLaughlin, Joseph	Carrowmena	Private	10th R. In. Fus.	Killed in Action.
Mark, Samuel M. H.	Carrowmena	Captain	12th R. In. Fus.	Men. Despatches. Wounded.
Martin, Israel	Carse Hall	Private	10th R. In. Fus.	
Moore, Mark	Back, Myroe	Sergeant	10th R. In. Fus.	Wounded.

MAGHERAFELT PRESBYTERY.

Name.	Home Address.	Rank.	Regiment, Battalion or Unit.	Remarks.
BELLAGHY.				
Bruce, Hugh	Mullaghboy	...	R.A.F.	
Burnside, James	Ballymacombs	2nd Lieutenant	R. Inn. Fus.	
Chesney, James	Church Cottage	Lance-Corporal	8th Scottish Rifles	Wounded.
Dawson, Samuel	Bellaghy	Private	R. Inn. Fus.	Killed in Action.
Ewing, Matthew	Killyberry	Stoker	R.N.	Wounded.
Ewing, William	Killyberry	Private	R. Inn. Fus.	
Gray, Samuel	Bellaghy	Private	R. Inn. Fus.	
Hunter, Joseph	Killyberry	Private	R.F.A.	Killed in Action.
McCarroll, John	Glenvale	Private	...	
McClelland, Robert	Edenreagh	...	R. Inn. Fus.	Killed in Action.
McCrea, Thomas	The Manse	Lieutenant	11th R. Inn. Fus.	M.C., Wounded.
McIlroy, William	Glenvale	Lance-Corporal	R.E.	Killed in Action.
McKelney, Adam	Ballyscullion	Private	R.I.R.	Killed in Action.
Martin, Leslie	Glenvale	Private	R. Inn. Fus.	
Moore, Henderson	Tamladuff	Private	R. Inn. Fus.	Killed in Action.
Pollock, John	Oldtown	Private	N.I.H.	
Russell, Alex.	Tamladuff	Private	R. Inn. Fus.	Killed in Action.
Sloss, Andrew	Tamladuff	Private	R. Irish Fus.	
Stewart, John	Oldtown	Private	R.I. Rifles	
Thompson, Arthur	The Castle	Lance-Corporal	R.I. Rifles	
Thompson, George	The Castle	Surgeon Prob.	R.N.	
Wylie, William	Bellaghy	Private	R.I. Rifles	Wounded.
COLONIAL AND U.S.A. FORCES.				
Campbell, Wilson	Ballyscullion	...	Aust. Imp. Force	
Clarke, James	Tamladuff	...	N.Z. Inft.	
Dawson, Samuel	Bellaghy	...	American Army	Killed in Action.
Ewing, Fred.	Killyberry	...	Aust. Impl Force	Killed in Action.
Ewing, Thomas	Killyberry	...	Aust. Light Horse	
Hutchinson, Fred.	Glenvale	...	Canadian Force	
Kennedy, Thomas	Oldtown	...	Canadian Force	
McCrea, Harold A.	The Manse	...	Aust. Imp. Force	Wounded.
McCullough, Herbert	Ballyneare	...	N.Z. Force	
McIlroy, James	Glenvale	...	N.Z. Force	
McKee, Thomas	Drumlamph	...	N.Z. Force	Killed in Action.
Norwell, James	Bellaghy	...	African Military Post	
Wilson, George	Bellaghy	...	N.Z. Force	
Wilson, Hugh	Ballymacombs	...	N.Z. Force	
Wilson, Robert	Ballymacombs	...	N.Z. Force	Killed in Action.
Wilson, Robert	Bellaghy	...	N.Z. Force	Killed in Action.
CASTLEDAWSON AND CURRAN.				
Anderson, Matthew	Castledawson	Lieutenant	R.N. Reserve	
Browne, Robert	Castledawson	Corporal	R. Inn. Fus.	
Brown, Henry	Toberhead	Corporal	R. Inn. Fus.	
Brown, Wm. F.	Curran	Private	R. Inn. Fus.	
Campbell, Samuel	Toberhead	Private	R. Inn. Fus.	Killed in Action.
Ellis, Samuel	Toomebridge	Private	R. Inn. Fus.	Killed in Action.
Evans, John	Castledawson	Private	R. Inn. Fus.	
Fulton, David	Aughrim	Private	R. Inn. Fus.	Wounded.
Hammond, Wm. J.	Castlesawson	Private	R. Inn. Fus.	Died of Wounds.
Hawe, John	Castledawson	Private	R. Inn. Fus.	Wounded.
Houston, Francis	Toberhead	Private	R. Inn. Fus.	
Johnstone, John	Castledawson	Private	R. Inn. Fus.	Killed in Action.
Johnstone, William	Castledawson	Stoker	R.N.	
Kane, Thomas	Grange	Private	R. Inn. Fus.	
Kerr, Hiram	Lemnaroy	Lance-Corporal	R. Inn. Fus.	Wounded.
Kirkwood, Fred.	Curran	Private	R. Inn. Fus.	
Lennox, Tom	Toomebridge	Corporal	R.A.	
Leslie, Alex.	Castledawson	Private	R. Inn. Fus.	
Leslie, Hugh	Castledawson	Private	R. Inn. Fus.	
Leslie, James	Castledawson	Private	R. Inn. Fus.	
Leslie, John	Castledawson	Private	Seaforth Highldrs.	Killed in Action.
Leslie, Robert	Castledawson	Private	R. Inn. Fus.	
Leslie, Wm.	Castledawson	Private	R. Irish Fus.	Killed in Action.
McCool, William	Castledawson	Private	Highland Light Inft.	Killed in Action.
McFadden, James	Broagh	Private	R. Inn. Fus.	
McKelvey, Adam	Belfast	Private	R.I.R.	Killed in Action.
McKendry, James	Toberhead	Private	R. Inn. Fus.	Killed in Action.
Mawhinney, Edward	Castledawson	Private	R. Inn. Fus.	
Mawhinney, Henry	Castledawson	Private	R.E.	
Mawhinney, James	Castledawson	Private	1st Scots Guards	Wounded.
Mawhinney, Samuel	Castledawson	Private	R. Inn. Fus.	Wounded.
Milligan, James	Castledawson	Private	R. Inn. Fus.	Wounded.
Morton, Samuel	Toberhead	Gunner	R.G.A.	
Pickering, Tom	Tamnadace	Lance-Corporal	R. Inn. Fus.	
Robinson, Alex.	Tamnadace	Private	...	Wounded.
Sampson, George	Leitrim	Corporal	R. Inn. Fus.	Twice Wounded.
Speers, Robert	Drumlamph	Private	R. Inn. Fus.	
Stewart, John	Curran	Private	R. Inn. Fus.	

MAGHERAFELT PRESBYTERY.   CASTLEDAWSON AND CURRAN.

Name.	Home Address.	Rank.	Regiment, Battalion or Unit.	Remarks.
Weir, George	Toberhead	Sergt.-Major	R. Inn. Fus.	Wounded.
Woodend, Arthur	Castledawson	Private	R. Inn. Fus.	Wounded.
Woodend, Thomas	Castledawson	Private	R. Inn. Fus.	Killed in Action.
Woods, Robert	Castledawson	Lance-Corporal	R. Inn. Fus.	Twice Wounded.
Woods, Samuel	Castledawson	Private	R. Inn. Fus.	
COLONIAL & U.S.A. FORCES.				
Anderson, John	Toberhead	Private	Australian Force	
Davison, Andrew	Castledawson	Private	N.Z. Force	
Davison, Joseph	Castledawson	Private	N.Z. Force	
Evans, Thomas	Castledawson	Private	Canadians	
Hueston, Tom	Castledawson	Private	U.S. Army	
Leslie, Henry	Derrygarve	Private	Canadians	
Leslie, Robert J.	Derrygarve	Private	Canadians	Killed in Action.
McCarrol, Alec	Toberhead	Private	Canadians	
McCleery, Jack	Aughrim	Private	Australians	
McKendry, Stewart	Toberhead	Private	U.S. Army	
Mawhinney, John	Leitrim	Private	Australians	
Sampson, John	Leitrim	Private	Australians	
Speers, John	Drumlamph	Private	Australians	
Wright, Robert	Edenreagh	Private	Canadians	
CULNADY.				
Anderson, J. A.	Culnady	Private		
Armstrong, Wm.	Dungleady	Private	N.I.H.	
Brady, Spencer	Tirgarvil	Private	R.G.A.	
Ferguson, James	Upperlands	Private	10th R. Inn. Fus.	
Hill, J.	Upperlands	Private	3rd R. Inn. Fus.	
Johnston, G.	Upperlands	Private	10th R. Inn. Fus.	
Johnston, J.	Upperlands	Private	10th R. Inn. Fus.	
McFadden, Charles	Upperlands	Private	10th R. Inn. Fus.	
McGuinness, D.	Culnady	Private	10th R. Inn. Fus.	
McGuinness, Tom	Culnady	Private	9th R. Inn. Fus.	
Montgomery, John	Upperlands	Private	R.E.	
Montgomery, Wm. L.	Upperlands	Private	3rd R. Inn. Fus.	Died of Wounds.
Pink, James	Upperlands	Private	Black Watch	
COLONIAL FORCES.				
Bruce, H. S.	Dungledy	Private	Australian Force	
Clarke, M. A.	Dungledy	Private	N.Z. Force	
Dripps, A. B.	Dungledy	Private	Australian Force	
Dripps, A. W.	Dungledy	Private	Australian Force	
Fleming, John	Tiernageragh	Private	Canadian Force	
Kyle, William	Culnady	Private	Canadian Force	Missing.
Paul, S.	Culnady	Lieutenant	Canadian Force	
Paul, W. G.	Culnady	Lieutenant		
Riddell, Harry	Drumuck	Private	Australian Force	
Riddell, J.	Drumuck	Private	Australian Force	
Riddell, J. A.	Drumuck	Private	Australian Force	
SWATERAGH.				
Bolton, J.	Lismoyle	Private		Died a Prisoner.
Caskey, Marshall	Culnagrew	Private		Killed in Action.
McIlfatrick, S.	Ballynian	Private		
Witherow, W.	Laragh	Private		
DRAPERSTOWN.				
Barclay, William	Draperstown	Private	R.E.	
Barnett, Robert	Sixtowns	Lance-Corporal	King's Own Scot. Borderers	
Bodkin, Alexander	Draperstown	Corporal	4th R. Irish Fus.	
Diamond, James McN.	Draperstown	2nd Lieutenant	18th London Irish Rifles	Wounded.
Dickey, Alfred C., M.B.	Draperstown	Captain	R.A.M.C.	
Kenning, David J.	Coolsara	Lance-Sergeant	13th Batt. Rifle Brigade	
McLean, Wallace	Draperstown	Private	R.A.M.C.	
Mundell, James	Draperstown	Private	9th Batt. R. Inn. Fus.	
Taylor, Samuel	Draperstown	Private	10th Batt. R. Inn. Fus.	
COLONIAL FORCE.				
Brooke, Wm. J.	Draperstown	Private	15th Canadians	
Diamond, Gerald G.	Draperstown	Corporal	2nd Canadians	Wounded.
Henderson, George	Draperstown	Private	Can. Entrenching Batt.	
McLean, Robert T.	Draperstown	Captain	199th Ir. Can. Rifles	
Patterson, Alex.	Draperstown	Private	Can. Rifles	Killed in Action.

MAGHERAFELT PRESBYTERY.   FIRST KILREA.

Name.	Home Address.	Rank.	Regiment, Battalion or Unit.	Remarks.
FIRST KILREA.				
ADAMS, THOMAS	Claragh, Kilrea	Private	Gordon Highldrs.	Killed in Action.
BAMFORD, JOSEPH L.	Kilrea	Lieutenant	R.A.F.	Killed in Action.
DEMPSEY, EPHRAIM	Mullan, Kilrea	Private	R. Inn. Fus.	
DINSMORE, SAMUEL	Lower Tamlaght	Private		
DOOLE, WM.	Lislea	Private	Australian Force	
GILMORE, WM.	Kilrea	Private	R. Inn. Fus.	
GRAHAM, DAVID	Kilrea	Private	Seaforth Highldrs.	Killed in Action.
GREEN, HUGH	Tivaconway	Private	R. Inn. Fus.	
HAMILTON, JOSEPH	Kilrea	Private	Cameron Highldrs.	
HOLMES, ROBERT	Lislea	Private	R. Inn. Fus.	Wounded.
JOHNSTON, JAMES T.	Drumsara, Kilrea	Surgeon	Naval Prob.	
JOHNSTON, JOHN D.	Drumsara, Kilrea	Private	Army Service Corps	
KNOX, JAMES H.	Kilrea	Private	R. Inn. Fus.	Killed in Action.
KNOX, JOHN	Kilrea	Lieutenant	London Rough Riders	
LOUGHLIN, ARCHIE	Lislea	Private	R. Inn. Fus.	Killed in Action.
McCAHON, ROBERT	Kilrea,	Lieutenant	R.E.	Died of Wounds.
McCLEERY, JAMES W.	Kilrea	Private	A.S.C.	
McMATH, ANDREW	Kilrea	Private	R. Inn. Fus.	
McMATH, THOMAS	Kilrea	Private	R. Inn. Fus.	Killed in Action.
McMULLAN, JOHN	Reastown	Private	Royal Artillery	
MICHAEL, ALEXANDER	Gortmacrane	Private	R. Inn. Fus.	Killed in Action.
MICHAEL, WILLIAM	Gortmacrane	Private	R. Inn. Fus.	
NELSON, JAMES	Lislea	Private	R. Inn. Fus.	Wounded.
RITCHIE, WILLIAM	Kilrea		N.I.H.	Died in France.
TAYLOR, JOHN	Reastown		A.S.C.	
TAYLOR, ROBERT G.	Reastown		South Irish Horse	
TURNER, ROBERT			Army Pay Departmt.	
WILKINSON, HUGH			N.I.H.	
COLONIAL FORCES.				
DOOLE, JOHN	Lislea	Private	Australian Force	
GORDON, ROBERT JAMES	Lislea	Private	Australian Force	Killed in Action.
GRAHAM, GEORGE	Kilrea	Private	S.A. Force	
GRAHAM, JAMES	Kilrea	Private	S.A. Force	
GRAHAM, JOHN	Kilrea	Private	Australian Force	
GRAHAM, ROBERT		Private	Australian Force	Killed in Action.
SMYRELL, ARTHUR G.	Ballymaconly	Private	Australian Force	
TORRENS, ROBERT			Australian Force	Wounded.
TURNER, JOHN			S. African Cav.	
WILSON, JAMES WALLACE			Australian E. Force	Wounded.
SECOND KILREA.				
ADAMS, DAVID C.	Kilrea	Sergeant	R.I. Fus.	Wounded.
BOLTON, SLOAN	Agivey House	Lieutenant	R.I.R.	Wounded.
GAMBLE, JOHN	Kilrea	Private	Scots Guards	Killed in Action.
GAMBLE, THOMAS	Kilrea	Sergeant	R.H.A.	
GILMORE, ROBERT	Drumane	Private	R.I. Fus.	Killed in Action.
GILMORE, WM. JAMES	Kilrea	Private	R. Inn. Fus.	Wounded.
McMASTER, JAMES	Drumane	Private	R.I.R.	
MICHAEL, SAMUEL	Drumagarner	Private	A.S.C.	
MOON, JAMES	Kilrea	Private	R.I. Fus.	Wounded.
PAUL, EDWARD	Trinaltinagh	Private	R.I. Fus.	
PEDEN, HUGH	Drumane	Private	R.A.F.	
REA, JOSEPH	Kilrea	Sergeant	1st R. Highldrs.	
WATSON, JOSEPH	Ballymaconnolly	N.C.O.	H.L. Inft.	Killed in Action.
WOODEND, EDWARD	Kilrea	Private	A.S.C.	
COLONIAL FORCES.				
McCAHON, ROBERT GEORGE	Kilrea	Lieutenant	Aus. Imp. Force	
PAUL, ROBERT J.	Trinaltinagh	Rifleman	N.Z. Rifle Brigade	
RICHMOND, ALEX.	Kilrea	Private	Aus. Imp. Force	
RICHMOND, WM.	Kilrea	N.C.O.	Aus. Imp. Force	Killed in Action.
MAGHERA.				
ANDERSON, S. C.	Fallagloon	Private	M.T. A.S.C.	
BOLTON, S. E.	Maghera	Trooper	N.I.H.	
BOYD, CHRISTIE	Carrickakielt	Private	10th R. Inn. Fus.	M.M., Died of Wds.
BRADY, T. G.	Knocknakielt	Private	9th R. Inn. Fus.	
BROWNLOW, GEORGE	Maghera	Private	9th R. Inn. Fus.	
BROWNLOW, HUGH	Maghera	Private	6th R. Inn. Fus.	
BROWNLOW, JOHN	Maghera	Gunner	R.F.A.	
DUNLOP, THOMAS	Tullyheron	Rifleman	20th R.I.R.	
FLEMING, JOHN	Carrickakielt	Sergeant	10th A. & S.H.	
GROGAN, WM.	Maghera	Sergeant	13th R.I.R.	Wounded.
HOUSTON, ARTHUR	Maghera	2nd Lieutenant		Killed in Action.
HOUSTON, GERALD	Maghera	2nd Lieutenant		
HOUSTON, T. H.	Maghera	Private	8th R.I. Fus.	
KELLY, JOHN	Slatiebogie	Driver	14th Bgde A.F.A.	

MAGHERAFELT PRESBYTERY.   MAGHERA.

Name.	Home Address.	Rank.	Regiment, Battalion or Unit.	Remarks.
Kelly, William	Slatiebogie	Private	C.A.S.C.	
Kissick, James L.	Craigmore	Private	106th Canadians	
McCracken, Thomas	Knocknakielt	Gunner	265th S. Battery	Wounded.
McCracken, W. J., M.B.	Knocknakielt	Lieut. Commander	R.N.	M.C., 2 bars, D.S.O.
McCracken, Wm.	Tamneymullen	Private	10th R.I. Fus.	
McGowan, Cecil	Maghera	Captain	Hon. Artillery Co.	Twice Wounded.
McIlroy, T. G.	Upperlands	Lance-Corporal	10th R.I. Fus.	M.M., Killed.
McKeown, A.	Maghera	Private	6th Leinster Regt.	
McKinney, Joseph	Maghera	2nd Lieutenant	R.I.R.	Killed in Action.
Mason, James	Maghera	Gunner	283rd S. Battery	
Moore, W. J.	Maghera	Signaller	6th R. Inn. Fus.	
Nelson, R. J.	Maghera	Private	A.O. Corps	
Nelson, Samuel	Maghera	Private	11th R.I. Fus.	
Paul, David	Creive	2nd Lieutenant	A.S.C.	Killed in Action.
Paul, Joshua	Creive	Trooper	N.I.H.	Wounded.
Paul, Robert	Mullagh	Private	R.A.M.C.	
Paul, Wm. G.	Creive			
Porter, Henry J.	Knocknakielt	Private	3rd R.E.	
Porter, Smyth	Knocknakielt	Private	6th N.F. Brigade	
Porter, W. J.	Knocknakielt	Lance-Corporal	11th R.I. Fus.	
Porter, Thomas	Beagh	Private	2nd Garrison Fus.	
Shiels, John	Mullagh	Lance-Corporal	11th R.I. Fus.	Died of Wounds.
Sloss, Joseph	Creive	Private	10th R.I. Fus.	
Stockman, R. J.	Maghera	Private	10th R.I. Fus.	Wounded.
Young, Samuel	Maghera	Private	R.I. Regt.	
FIRST MAGHERAFELT.				
Brown, Robert	Magherafelt	Sergeant	A.S.C.	
Clarke, James	Tillinkesy	Private		Wounded.
Corbett, Thomas	Motalee	Private		
Campbell, James	Magherafelt	Private	10th Batt. Inn. Fus.	Died, Pris. of War.
Evans, Jack	Magherafelt	Private	Air Service	
Foster, Thomas	Ballymulderg	Private	Irish Guards	
Finn, Wm.	Motalee	Private	10th Batt. R.I.F.	Killed at Somme.
Hammond, John	Grange	Private	9th Batt. R.I.F.	Killed in Action.
Hammond, Joseph	Grange	Private	10th Batt. R.I.F.	
Hawe, Samuel Mc.	Drumrainey	2nd Lieutenant		
Hure, Alfred	Magherafelt	Private	R.A.F.	
Hure, Robert J.	Magherafelt	L. Seaman	R.N.	
Kennedy, James	Motalee	Lance-Corporal	10th Batt. R. Inn. Fus.	
Love, Angus	Dunamoney	Private	A.S.C.	
Love, Daniel	Dunamoney	Lance-Corporal	10th Batt. R. Inn. Fus.	Killed at Somme.
McCleery, John	Magherafelt	Lance-Corporal	Mesopotamia Ex. F.	
McIvor, Thomas	Magherafelt	Private	61st Div. Sup. Column	
Magill, John	Magherafelt	Private	5th Batt. R. Inn. Fus.	
Montgomery, E. A. V.	Magherafelt	2nd Lieutenant	3rd Manchesters	
Parke, Robert	Grange	Private	R. Irish Fus.	Killed in Action.
Palmer, William	Roshure	Private	10th Batt. R. Inn. Fus.	
Semple, James	Dunarnon	Private	10th Batt. R. Inn. Fus.	
Semple, William	Dunarnon		R.N.	Died in Hospital.
Staunton, S. G.	Drumrainey	Private	R.N.A.S.	
Stewart, Robert A.	Dunamoney	Private	R.G.A.	
Stewart, Thomas	Magherafelt	Private	10th Batt. R. Inn. Fus.	
Tucker, Peter	Magherafelt	Lance-Corporal	Res. Emp. Co.	
COLONIAL AND U.S.A. FORCES.				
Atkinson, Matt. James	Magherafelt	Private	American Ex. Force	
Boden, Chesney	Magherafelt	Private	Australian Ex. Force	Wounded.
Duncan, George	Magherafelt	Private	S. African Ex. Force	
Duncan, James	Magherafelt	Private	Canadian Ex. Force	Wounded.
Eakin, Hugh	Magherafelt	Private	Canadian Ex. Force	
Given, Wm.	Magherafelt	Private	N.Z. Ex. Force	Killed in Action.
Hure, Andrew	Magherafelt	Private	Canadian Ex. Force	
Hure, George	Magherafelt	2nd Lieutenant	Australian Ex. Force	M.M.
Hure, Hugh	Magherafelt	Sergeant	Canadian Ex. Force	
Hure, Thomas	Magherafelt	Private	Canadian Ex. Force	
Love, Thomas	Magherafelt	Private	Canadian Ex. Force	
McLernon, Bruce	Magherafelt	Private	N.Z. Ex. Force	
Montgomery, Alex.	Magherafelt	Private	Canadian Ex. Force	
Montgomery, H.	Magherafelt	Private	S. African Ex. Force	
Munro, Wm. H.	Magherafelt	Sergeant	Australian Ex. Force	Killed at Gallipoli.
Nevin, Thomas	Magherafelt	Private	Canadian Ex. Force	
Parke, Wm.	Magherafelt	Private	Canadian Ex. Force	Killed in Action.
Ritchie, Henry Hanna	Magherafelt	Private	American Ex. Force	Died in training.
Ritchie, Samuel J. Evans	Magherafelt	Private	American Ex. Force	
Ritchie, Wm. John	Magherafelt	1st Lieutenant	American Ex. Force	
Scott, Robert	Magherafelt	Private	N.Z. Ex. Force	
Stewart, James	Magherafelt	Private	American Ex. Force	

MAGHERAFELT PRESBYTERY.
FIRST MAGHERAFELT.

Name.	Home Address.	Rank.	Regiment, Battalion or Unit.	Remarks.
Stitt, Hugh	Magherafelt	Private	Canadian Ex. Force	
Stitt, James	Magherafelt	Private	Canadian Ex. Force	
Wright, Andrew	Magherafelt	Private	Canadian Ex. Force	
Wright, George	Magherafelt	Private	Canadian Ex. Force	
SALTERSLAND.				
Carnaghan, Wm. E.	Druminard, Coagh	Lieutenant	Connaught Rangers	Wounded.
Ferguson, James	Ballyronan	Private	R.I. Fus.	
Kerrigan, H. W.	Ballynenagh	Capt.	R.A.M.C., Sherwood Foresters	
Lammey, Wm. J.	Ballynenagh	Sergeant	R.I.R.	Wounded.
McKinney, Alex.	Ballyriff	Private	R.I. Fus.	Killed in Action.
Milliken, Charles	Ballymulderg	Private	R.I. Fus.	
TOBERMORE.				
Bradley, Robert	Tobermore	Private	10th R. Inn. Fus.	
Clarke, Henry	Tobermore	Private	R.A.S.C.	
Clarke, John	Tobermore	Private	M.T. A.S.C.	
Devlin, William	Tobermore	Driver	R.A.S.C.	
Donnelly, Daniel	Tobermore	Private	R. Inn. Fus.	Wounded.
Hassin, Robert	Tobermore	Driver	R.A.S.C.	
Henderson, Samuel	Tobermore	Driver	5th R.H.A.	
Henderson, Thomas	Tobermore	Trooper	N.I.H., attd. R.I.R.	Killed in Action.
Henry, Robert	Tobermore	Private	9th R. Inn. Fus.	Killed in Action.
Johnston, Andrew	Tobermore	Sergeant	12th C.E.F.	Killed in Action.
Johnston, Andrew	Tobermore	Private	R.A.M.C.	
Johnston, J. W.	Tobermore	Corporal	1st Gordon Highldrs.	
Redfern, Thomas	Tobermore	Private	H.L.I.	Wounded.
Stone, S.	Tobermore	Private	11th R. Inn. Fus.	
Todd, Wm.	Tobermore	Private	2nd R. I. Fus.	
Winton, Edward	Tobermore	Private	3rd R. Inn. Fus.	
Winton, Matthew	Tobermore	Private	10th R. Inn. Fus.	Wounded.
Winton, Thomas	Tobermore	Private	10th R. Inn. Fus.	Cert., Kd. in Action
Wisoner, Daniel	Tobermore	Private	10th R. Inn. Fus.	
Wisoner, James Semple	Tobermore	Private	10th R. Inn. Fus.	
Wisoner, John	Tobermore	Private	6th R. Inn. Fus.	Wounded.
Wisoner, Joseph	Tobermore	Signaller	2nd R. Inn. Fus.	Mil. Cert., W'ded.
Wisoner, William	Tobermore	Private	10th R. Inn. Fus.	
Yearl, James	Tobermore	Private	7/8 R. Inn. Fus.	Wounded.
Young, Samuel	Tobermore	Private	9th R. Inn. Fus.	
Young, Thomas		Private	9th Royal Inn. Fus.	
COLONIAL AND U.S.A. FORCES.				
Anderson, David		Private	Canadians	Killed in Action.
Anderson, Samuel	Tobermore	Lieutenant	Canadians	
Esler, Henry	Tobermore	Sergeant	20th Canadians	Wounded.
Johnston, Samuel	Tobermore		20th Canadians	Killed in Action.
McKee, Gerald	Tobermore	Private	U.S.A. Army	Wounded.
McLaughlin, Wm.	Tobermore	Private	Australians	
Martin, David	Tobermore	Private	4th Canadians	
Martin, William	Tobermore		4th Canadians	
Stewart, David	Tobermore	Private	19th Canadians	Wounded.
Wallace, John	Tobermore		15th Canadian Highldrs.	
Wallace, Samuel	Tobermore		135th Co. C.F. Canadians	
Winton, David	Tobermore	Private	14th Batt. Canadians	Killed in Action.
Wisoner, Alex.	Tobermore	Private	2nd M. Gun Canadians	Wounded.
Wisoner, William	Tobermore	Private	15th Canadians	Wounded.
KNOCKLOUGHRIM.				
Boyd, Christie	Knocknakielt	Private	3rd Batt. Inn. Fus.	Died of Wounds.
Ewing, George	Ballynahone	2nd Lieutenant	R.A.F.	
Ewing, John	Ballynahone	Private	A.S.C. M.T.	
Fullerton, F. John	Slatabogie	Lance-Corporal	3rd R. Inn. Fus.	
Lennox, Wm. James	Ballinacross	Private	3rd R. Inn. Fus.	
Martin, F. John	Ballinacross	Private	12th Batt. R. Inn. Fus.	Died in Hospital.
Young, Thomas	Dergnagh	Private	Attd. 25th Batt. M.G.C.	Twice Wounded.
COLONIAL FORCES.				
Anderson, George	Ballinacross	Private	Can. Machine Gun	
Elliott, Andrew	Ballinacross	Private	N.Z. Ex. Force	Seriously wounded.
Lennox, Robert	Ballinacross	Sergeant	18th Batt. Can. Ex. Force	
McCaughey, Wm. James	Ballinacross	Private	15th Batt. Can. Ex. Force	

MONAGHAN PRESBYTERY.

Name.	Home Address.	Rank.	Regiment, Battalion or Unit.	Remarks.
BALLYALBANY.				
Bryans, Robert G.	Feduff	Corporal	I.G.	
Crawford, Robert	Monaghan	Lance-Corporal	R.I. Fus.	Wounded.
Gibson, Dick	Monaghan	Q.-Sergt.	R.A.M.C.	
Gibson, William	Monaghan	Sea Officer	R.N.	Wounded.
Gillanders, Edward	Aughnaseda	Corporal	9th R.I. Fus.	Wounded.
Gordon, James	Tamlet	Private	9th R.I. Fus.	
Gordon, William	Tamlet	Private	9th R.I. Fus.	
Greacen, Robert	Monaghan	Lieutenant	6th R.I.R.	Wounded.
Harveson, Wm.	Corragh	Private	10th R.I. Fus.	Wounded.
Houston, Wm.	Monaghan	Private	R.I.R.	Wounded.
Jackson, Ed.	Rackeragh	Lance-Corporal	9th R.I. Fus.	M.M., Wounded.
Jenkins, R.	Monaghan	Air Mechanic	R.A.F.	
Kennedy, T. J.	Monaghan	Lieutenant	R. Inn. Fus.	Killed in Action.
McKee, Harry	Newgrove	2nd Lieutenant	12th R.I.R.	Wounded.
Mitchell, Stewart	Latlurcan	Corporal	9th R.I. Fus.	Twice Wounded.
Stuart, John	Sheetrim	Private	I.G.	Killed in Action.
Swan, George	Monaghan	2nd Lieutenant	R.G.A.	
Swan, Walter	Monaghan	Lieutenant	16th R.I.R.	
Vance, William	Tullyvogie	Private	R.I. Fus.	
Walker, Samuel		Private	R.I.R.	
Walker, Thomas		Private	R. Inn. Fus.	
Walker, Wm. J.		Private	R. Inn. Fus.	
Wright, John	Sheetrim	Wheeler	Artillery	
COLONIAL FORCES.				
Gibson, Jack	Monaghan	Private	Canadians	Died.
Graham, William	Billis	Private	Can. Art.	
Greacen, Thos. E.	Monaghan	Captain	4th Canadians	Twice Wounded.
Holdcroft, William	Billis	Private	Canadians	
Pollock, W. H.	Cormeen	Corporal	Australians	
Shannon, Gilbert	Monaghan	Corporal	Canadians	
CAHANS.				
Bell, Thomas	Radrum	W. Operator	R.E.	
Black, David	Banaghroe	Private	9th R.I. Fus.	Killed in Action.
Black, John	Banaghroe	Private	9th R.I. Fus.	Wounded.
Black, Samuel	Banaghroe	Private	9th R.I. Fus.	W'ded & Prisoner.
Fleming, Wm. James	Slieveroe	Private	9th R.I. Fus.	Killed in Action.
McClelland, Benjamin	Drumlinney	Gunner	R.G.A.	
McClelland, Hugh Geo.	Drumlinney	Sergeant	R.F.A.	Wounded.
McClelland, John	Drumlinney	Gunner	R.G.A.	
McCullagh, Geo. David	Slieveroe	Corporal	10th R. Dub. Fus.	Wounded, M.M., Killed in Action.
McCullagh, John A.	Slieveroe	Private	W. Yorkshire Regt.	Twice Wounded.
McCullagh, John B.	Stranoodin	Private	A. & S. Highldrs.	Wounded.
Middleby, Robert	Lossett	Trooper	N.I.H.	
Nelson, David	**Derraghland**	**Major**	**L Battery R.H.A.**	**V.C. Died of Wounds**
Turbitt, David	Urcher	Private	R. Inn. Fus.	Killed in Action.
Turbitt, Gordon	Urcher	Private	N. Lanc. Regt.	
Turbitt, James	Urcher	Trooper	N.I.H.	
Waddell, Samuel	Lisnavane	Corporal	R.F.A.	Wounded.
COLONIAL FORCE.				
McClelland, Fred	Banaghbane	Private	Canadian Contgt.	Wounded.
McClelland, Robert	Banaghbane	Private	20th Can. E.F.	Wounded.
Turbitt, Thomas	Urcher	Private	Can. Cyclist Corps	Wounded.
CLONTIBRET.				
Allen, James Carson	Letterban	Private	R.I.F.	
Crawford, Sydney	Castleshane	Cadet	Indian Army	
Duffy, Samuel	Sallagh	Driver	R.F.A.	
Gilanders, Robert Hugh	Castleshane	Private	R.I.F.	Twice Wounded.
Gray, William	Bradox	Lance Corporal	R.A.M.C.	
Groves, Thomas	Clontibret	Gunner	Anti-Aircraft	W'ded and Gassed.
Houston, John	Bradox	Private	R.I.F.	Killed in Action.
Houston, Robert	Bradox	Private	R.I.R.	
Huggard, William	Bradox	Trooper	N.I. Horse	
Irvine, Joseph Knox	Clontibret	Lieutenat	R.A. Vet. Corps	
Irvine, Robert C.	Clontibret	Major	R.A.M.C.	Died in France.
Jebb, Thomas	Clontibret	Private	Sherwood Foresters	
McClelland, John	Clontibret	Private	Dub. Fus.	
M'Comb, John	Clontibret	Gunner	R. Marines	
Pattison, Samuel	Castleshane	Sergeant	Civil Service Rifles	M.M.
Thompson, John Knox S.	The Manse, Clontibret	Cadet	R.I.R.	
Wallace, William	Bradox	Trooper	N.I.H.	Wounded
Wilson, Isaac Howard	Clontibret	Corporal	S.I. Horse	Prisoner of War.

MONAGHAN PRESBYTERY. CLONTIBRET.

Name.	Home Address.	Rank.	Regiment, Battalion or Unit.	Remarks.
COLONIAL AND U.S.A. FORCES.				
Kinnear, James	Derrynoose	Trooper	3rd Auckland M. Rifles	
Knox, Robert	Bradox	Private	U.S.A. Army	
McBride, Thomas	Clontibret	Lance-Corporal	Canadian Army	
DRUMHILLERY AND MIDDLETOWN.				
Campbell, Leonard	Tirnacree	Sergeant	R. Irish Fus.	Wounded.
Dixon, Thomas	Drumhillery	Corporal	R. Irish Fus.	Killed in Action.
Flannigan, Joseph	Drumhillery	Private	R. Irish Fus.	
Irons, Joseph	Cavanagarvin	Private	R. Irish Fus.	
Leyburn, James	Raws, Keady	Sergeant	R.I.R.	Wounded.
Leyburn, John	Raws, Keady	Sergeant	N.I.H.	Wounded.
McCrea, John	Madden, Keady	Private	R. Irish Fus.	Killed at Mons.
Mitchell, Thomas	Keady	Private	R. Irish Fus.	Wounded.
Tecey, Marshall	Drumgrenagh	Private	R.I.R.	
Walker, William	Curryhughes	Driver	A.S.C.	
COLONIAL FORCES.				
Anderson, Edward	Drumneil	Private	Canadians	
Cargill, John	Glenickney	Q.M.S.	Canadians	
Gordon, Robert	Crossdall	Sergeant	Australians	
Graham, Samuel	Crann	Private	Australians	
Kerr, Robert	Cargybolie	Private	Canadians	
Kinnear, Cosbie	Drummond	Private	Australians	
Stewart, James	Feyduff	Private	Canadians	
GLENNAN.				
Anderson, W. J.	Emyvale	Private	9th R.I.R.	
Boyd, Allan	Emyvale	Private	9th R.I.R.	Killed in Action.
Cargill, Jack	Glasslough	Sergeant	12th R.I.R.	Prisoner of War.
Dunn, Thomas	Tydavnet	Lieutenant	Canadians	
Foster, Kelvey	Glasslough	Sergeant	9th Batt. R.I.R.	Prisoner of War.
Gillanders, Joseph	Glasslough	Lance-Corporal	12th Batt. R.I.R.	
Gillanders, Robert	Glasslough	Sergeant	12th Batt. R.I.R.	
Gillanders, Samuel	Glasslough	Private	9th Batt. R.I.R.	
Gillanders, William	Glasslough	Private	A.S.C.	
Gilroy, William	Glasslough	Sergeant	Gordon Highldrs.	
Mitchell, Wm.	Glasslough	Sergeant	152nd Coy. R.E.	
Nixon, James	Glasslough	Private	R.A.M.C.	Died.
Nixon, Thomas	Glasslough	Private	12th R.I.R.	Wounded.
Steenson, Samuel	Tynan	Private	12th R.I.R.	Killed in Action.
Steenson, Wm.	Mullapike	Lieutenant	Canadians	
Stewart, Robert	Glasslough	Private	9th R.I.R.	
Sturgeon, Daniel	Glasslough	Private	12th R.I.R.	Killed in Action.
Sturgeon, Samuel	Glasslough	Sergeant	12th R.I.R.	Killed in Action.
Vance, Samuel	Glasslough	Private	9th R.I.R.	Killed in Action.
Vance, William	Glasslough	Private	R.I.R.	
Wilson, Alec	Glasslough	Private	9th R.I.R.	Killed in Action.
Wilson, John	Glasslough	Private	9th R.I.R.	Wounded.
Woods, Wm.	Glasslough	Q.-Master Sergt.	2nd I. Guards	
LISLOONEY.				
Currie, Robert	Tynan	Private	8th R.I.F.	
Ewart, John	Killylea	Private	R.I.F.	
Garmony, Hugh	Killylea	Private	Australian Force	
Garmony, Robert	Killylea	Private	9th R.I.F.	Wounded.
Greenaway, Wm.	Tynan	2nd Lieutenant	R.I.F.	
McKee, Edward	Tynan	Sergeant	9th R.I.F.	Killed in Action.
Mills, Joseph J.	Killylea	Captain	10th Vet. Hospital	
Mills, R. J.	Killylea	Private	Australian Force	
Mills, Thomas	Killylea	Private	Australian Force	Wounded.
Scott, Thomas	Tynan	Sergeant	8th R.I.F.	
FIRST MONAGHAN.				
Barnes, Thomas	Hill Street	Sergt-Major	3rd Batt. R.I. Fus.	Wounded.
Barnes, William	Hill Street	Private		
Black, John Traver Cecil	Ballyleck	Lieutenant	R.M.L.I.	Killed in Action.
Black, Thos. Saml. Culbert	Ballyleck	Sergeant	7th R. Dublin Fus.	Died of Wounds.
Bothwell, John	Beaghbarton	Corporal	3rd Batt. Cheshires	
Boyd, James	Ballinagall	Corporal	N.I.H.	
Clarke, David Joseph	Tamlet	Corporal	9th Batt. R. Irish Fus.	
Clarke, Geo. Henry	Tamlet	Private	Motor Transport	
Clarke, Geo. Herbert	Aughnaseda	Private	9th Batt. R. Irish Fus.	Wounded.
Dunne, Joseph D.	Drumcoo Jackson	Private	R.E.	
Ferris, Edward	Tanderageebrack	Corporal	N.I.H.	Wounded.
Flack, Wm. Henry	Dublin Street	Private	8th Hussars	
Johnston, Hugh	Crosses	Sergeant	1st Bedfordshire Regt.	
Jackson, Alexander	Tanderageebann	Sergeant	R.E. (U.D.)	

MONAGHAN PRESBYTERY.

FIRST MONAGHAN.

Name.	Home Address.	Rank.	Regiment, Battalion or Unit.	Remarks.
Jackson, Edward	Rakeeragh	Lance-Corporal	9th Batt. R. Irish Fus.	Wounded, M.M.
Jackson, Moore	Tanderageebann	Lance-Corporal	9th Batt. R. Irish Fus.	Wounded.
Jackson, Noble	Tanderageebann	Private	9th Batt. R. Irish Fus.	Wounded.
Jackson, Thomas	Tanderageebann	Private	9th Batt. R. Irish Fus.	Killed in Action.
Johnston, Walter	Monaghan	2nd Lieutenant	3rd Batt. R. Dub. Fus.	
Kennedy, Walter	Feragh	Private	9th Batt. R. Irish Fus.	Killed in Action.
Keown, Robert	Dublin Street	Lieutenant	R.A.M.C.	
Latimer, Samuel Hugh	Kilnadrain	Sergt.-Major	5th Batt. R. Irish Fus.	Killed in Action.
McAllan, Edwin	Monaghan	Sergt.-Major	9th Batt. R. Irish Fus.	
McAuley, Wm. Ingham	Cliftonville, Belfast	Major	A.V.C.	Killed in Action.
McWilliam, Rev. J.	Corlatt House	Captain	Chaplain to Forces	
McWilliam, Wm.	Corlatt House	Lieutenant	4th Connaught Rangers	
Methvin, Colin	Rossmore Park	Private	Flying Corps	Wounded.
Montgomery, John	Dancenaire	Private	N.I.H.	Wounded.
Mullan, Wm.	Leagh	Sergeant	9th Batt. R. Irish Rifles	Killed in Action.
Somerville, Johnston	Crumlin	Private	M.T. R.A.S.C.	
Taylor, William	Dublin Street	Captain	R.A.M.C.	
Wallace, John	Killygoan	Sapper	R. Engineers	
Wallace, Mark	Killygoan	Corporal	9th Batt. R. Irish Fus.	Killed in Action.
Wright, James M. W.	Aghaboy	Private	R.A.M.C.	
COLONIALS AND U.S.A. FORCES.				
Allister, James	Feragh	Sergt.-Major	U.S. Engineers	
Breakey, Leo	Hill Street	First Lieutenant	R.A.F., Can.	Killed by accident.
Caldwell, Robert	Hill Street	Sergeant	S.A. Inft.	Wounded.
Dunn, James	Drumcoo (Jackson)	Private	Canadian Force	Killed in Action.
Dunwoody, Will	Blackwatervale	Sergeant	Australian F. Corps	
Erskine, Alfred	Crosses	Private	Australian Force	Wounded.
Erskine, Henry	Crosses	Private	Australian Force	Killed in Action.
Hastings, Robert	Tullycruman	Private	Transport U.S.A.	
Jackson, Alfred	Tanderageebann	Private	Canadian Inft.	
Jackson, Fred	Mullyknock	Corporal	S.A. Motor Cycle Corps	
Jackson, Harry	Tanderageebann	Sergeant	Can. Inft.	Killed in Action.
Jackson, Samuel	Tanderageebann	Private	Can. Field Art.	
Johnston, Thomas	Ballyleck	Corporal	1st Can. Regt.	
McAllan, Geo.	Monaghan	Private	E.A.F Corps	
NEWBLISS.				
Carson, Hugh	Rawdery	Private	R.I.F.	Killed in Action.
Carson, Wm.	Rawdery	Corporal	Cameron Highldrs.	Wounded.
Clarke, Joseph	Newbliss	Corporal	R.I.F.	Wounded.
Clarke, Wm.	Newbliss	Private	R.I.F.	Killed in Action.
Dale, Albert	Edengoash	Sergt-Major	Northumberland Fus.	Kd. in Action, M.M.
Dale, John	Edengoash	Sergt.-Major	R.I.R.	Kd. in Action, M.M.
Dixon, Thomas	Mullagreenan	Private	R.F.A.	
Johnston, Matthew	Cottage, Smithboro'	Captain	R.A.M.C.	
Keers, William (Rev.)	Newbliss	Private	R.A.M.C.	
Moore, James	Drumgarley	Private	R.I.F.	Killed in Action.
Nesbit, James	Cashland	Private	Labour Corps	Died.
Pollock, Geo. Foster	Killykeeragh	Private	R.A.M.C.	Died.
Scott, George	Boghill	Private	R.A.F.	
Scott, John Wm.	Boghill	Private	Tanks	
Williamson, John Jos.	Carn	Private	Northumberland Fus.	Wounded.
COLONIAL AND U.S.A. FORCES.				
Agnew, Andrew		Private	Canadians	
Whiteman, Samuel		Private	U.S.A.	
Wilson, —		Corporal	U.S.A.	
STONEBRIDGE.				
Andrews, Robert	The Island, Roslea	Private	Irish Guards	Wounded.
Black, George	Drumcaw	Private	Canadians	Killed in Action.
Black, Hugh	Drumcaw	Private	R.I. Fus.	
Black, William	Drumcaw	S.Major	Canadians	
Coulson, Wm.	Tyranny, Stonebridge	Sergeant	R.I. Fus.	Wounded.
Francey, Samuel	Lisoarty, Stonebridge	Trooper	N.I.H.	
Haslett, Lewis	Roslea	Corporal	R. Inn. Fus.	M.M., Wounded.
Moore, Richard	Lisroom	Private	R.E.	
Norris, Wm.	Gransha, Clones		R.I. Fus.	Wounded.
White, Charles W.	The Manse	Lieutenant	R.I.R.	Killed in Action.
White, Wm. C.	The Manse	Captain	R.A.M.C.	
SCOTSTOWN.				
Armstrong, David	Killalion	Sergeant	N.I.H.	Wounded.
Heastie, Joseph	Iterea	Private	Canadian Army	Twice Wounded.

MONAGHAN PRESBYTERY.

SMITHBOROUGH.

Name.	Home Address.	Rank.	Regiment, Battalion or Unit.	Remarks.
Bryans, T. E.	Lissinan	Lieutenant	17th Batt. R.I.R.	Wounded.
Gibson, Wm. C.	Smithboro'	Private	R.A.M.C.	Wounded.
Gibson, Walter D.	Smithboro'	Private	14th Batt. R.I.F.	Killed in Action.
McMahon, David	Smithboro'	Corporal	M.M. Police	
McMahon, Samuel	Smithboro'	Private	A.S.C.	
Martin, John L.	Killacoghill	Private	R.E. Signal	
Martin, Thos. D.	Killacoghill	Private	U.S. Army	
Moorhead, Andrew	Keenogue	Lance-Corporal	9th Batt. R.I.F.	Killed in Action.
Welsh, Fred. J.	Carnowen	Private	9th Batt. R.I.F.	Killed in Action.

MUNSTER PRESBYTERY.

Name.	Home Address.	Rank.	Regiment, Battalion or Unit.	Remarks.
CLONMEL.				
Anderson, Wm.	Cahir	Private	R. Irish	Killed in Action.
Copestake, —	Mill House	Lieutenant	R.I.R.	
Forbes, John	Clonmel	Private	Secretary's Office	Kd. b'ring Message.
Forbes, Donald	Clonmel	Sergeant	R. Irish Regt.	
Gordon, Hay	Cahir	Private	Col. Charteris' Corps	
Graham, James	Cahir	Private	A. Field Force	
Hendry, Wm.	Clonmel	Sergeant	I. Guards	Wounded.
Massie, Douglas	Cahir	Private	A. Field Force	
Massie, Henry	Cahir	Private	Indian Army	
McCullagh, John	Cahir	Private	R.I.R.	Wounded.
Rankin, Hugh	Clonmel	Private	R. Irish Regt.	
Rankin, John	Clonmel	Private	R. Irish Regt.	
Rentoul, W. W.	The Manse	Captain	7th E. Lancs.	Wounded.
Whisker, Thomas	Clonmel	Sergeant	Amb. Corps	
LIMERICK.				
Agar, Wm. J.	Limerick	Corporal	6th R.I.R.	
Austin, Harold	Limerick	Cadet	7th Leinster Regt.	Killed in Action.
Barnett, J. Bolton	Limerick	Lieutenant	12th R. Inn. Fus.	
Barnett, John H. N.	Limerick	Lieutenant	18th King's Liverpool Regt.	Wounded.
Beckett, James	Limerick	Captain	India Recruiting Staff	
Bell, —	Limerick		R.G.A.	
Bruce, George B.	Limerick	Private	10th R.D. Fus.	Wounded.
Buchanan, Francis J.	Limerick	Pioneer	R.E.	
Cooper, Jas. Corbett	Limerick	Sergeant	M.G.C., Notts	Prisoner.
Donald, John	Limerick	Coy. Sgt.-Major	42nd R. Highldrs.	
Dunn, James S.	Limerick	2nd Lieutenant	2nd K's.O.S.B.	Killed.
Dunn, John D.	Limerick	2nd Lieutenant	1st Leinster Regt.	
Ferguson, Geo. J.	Limerick	Private	M.T. R.A.S.C.	
Ferguson, Thomas W.	Limerick	Sapper	R.E.	
Goodwin, Alfred E.	Limerick	Lieutenant	R.A.S.C.	
Holliday, Julis O.	Limerick	Flight Lieutenant	R.A.F.	
Hutchinson, Wm. G.	Limerick	3rd Air Mechanic	R.A.F.	
Hutchinson, Anthony A.	Limerick	3rd Air Mechanic	R.A.F.	
Hutchinson, Adam N. C.	Limerick	Sapper	R.E.	
Hutchinson, David S.	Limerick	Sergeant	R.E.	
Jennings, Richard B.	Limerick	Private	M.T. R.A.S.C.	
Kirkpatrick, Daniel	Limerick	Lieutenant	A.P. Dept.	
Lee, Arthur S.	Limerick	Captain	R.A.S.C.	
McLeod, George	Limerick	Sergeant	2nd R.I. Regt.	D.C.M., Twice Wd.
McLeod, Hector	Limerick	Private	7th R.I. Regt.	
McLeod, Kenneth	Limerick	Private	4th Leinster Regt.	
McLeod, Norman	Limerick	Private	5th R.I. Regt.	
Morrison, Wm.	Limerick	Private	7th R.I.R.	Killed in Action.
Murray, Alfred S.	Limerick	Captain	3rd Lincoln Regt.	
Oliver, John	Limerick	1st Air Mechanic	R.A.F.	
Owens, C. Arnold	Limerick	Lieutenant	13th W. Yorks Regt.	Killed in Action.
Owens, Wm. B.	Limerick	2nd Lieutenant	R.E.	Wounded, Died.
Paul, Hugh	Limerick	Surgeon Prob.	R.N.	Jutland Battle.
Paul, Robert J.	Limerick	Captain	W. India Force	
Rennie, James	Limerick	Private	42nd R. Highldrs.	
Snell, P. Sidney	Limerick	2nd Lieutenant	6th R.I. Fus.	Killed Sulva Bay.
Stewart, Alex.	Limerick	Private	R. Scots	Wounded.
Sutherland, Donald	Limerick	Private	M.T. R.A.S.C.	
Waters, Geo. A.	Limerick	Gunner	R.F.A.	
Whisker, Thos. G.	Limerick	Sergeant	R.A.M.C.	
Wickham, Wm. A.	Limerick	2nd Lieutenant	1st City of London Regt.	

MUNSTER PRESBYTERY.

LIMERICK,

Name.	Home Address.	Rank.	Regiment, Battalion or Unit.	Remarks.
	COLONIAL FORCES.			
Cleland, John		Trooper	4th N.Z.M.R.	
Goodwin, James		Sergeant	Can. Force	
Holliday, Eldrid I.		Private	Can. Force	
McLeod, John		Private	2nd Aust. Inft.	Twice wounded.
	TIPPERARY.			
Harris, Geo. Arthur	Ballykisteen	Lieutenant	S.I.H.	Wounded.
Harris, J. C. B.	Ballykisteen	Captain	9th Lancashire Fus.	Wounded twice.
Lamie, A. R	Tipperary	Assist. Paymaster	R.N.	
	WATERFORD.			
Athol, G. G.	18 Bean Street	Private	Royal Fus.	Wounded.
Brown, Alan	20 Morley Terrace		R.F.A.	
Brown, J. M. D.	20 Morley Terrace	Sergeant	R.A.M.C.	
Fernie, J.	Rosemount, Tramore	Mate	R.N. Transport	
Fernie, R. N.		Corporal	R.I.R.	D.C.M., Killed.
Patterson, John	Gas Works	Cadet	Artists' Rifles O.T.C.	
Torrie, W. J.	Rosemount	Lieutenant	R.N.V.R.	
Walker, A. E.		Lieutenant	Dublin Fus.	
	DUNCANNON.			
Auld, Thomas		Private	R.F.A.	
Fenton, Alfred	Fort Augusta	Lance-Corporal		Prisoner of War.
Fenton, A. Percy	Fort Augusta	Private	R.A.M.C.	Wounded.
Fenton, E.	Fort Augusta	Trooper	R. Irish Lancers	
	PORTLAW.			
Ferguson, Thomas		Rifleman	16th R.I.R.	
McGregor, James		Sergeant	8th Seaforth Highldrs.	Killed, Loos.
McLeod, Norman		Pioneer	R.I. Regt.	
McWhan, John	Curraghmore	Sergeant	R.F.A.	
Thompson, Wm.		Gunner	R.F.A.	
Wallace, Hugh		Driver	R.F.A.	
	COLONIAL FORCE.			
Brown, W. T.	20 Morley Terrace	Driver	Canadian F.A.	Wounded.
Fenton, James W.		Private	9th Can. Mounted Rifles	
Fernie, James	Rosemount, Tramore	Sergeant	1st Can. M.G. Corps	M.M. and Bar.

NEWRY PRESBYTERY.

Name.	Home Address.	Rank.	Regiment, Battalion or Unit.	Remarks.
	ANNALONG.			
Burden, Thomas	Ballyvea	1st Cl. P.O.	R.N.	
Campbell, Hugh	Mullertown	Private	Victoria Rifles	
Croskerry, Francis	Moneydara	Sergeant	R.I.R.	Killed in Action.
Eakins, Charles S.	Ballyvea	O.S.	R.N.	
Gordon, Alexander	Annalong	Driver	R.E.	
Gordon, James	Annalong	Corporal	A.O.C.	
Gordon, Leonard A.R.	Moneydara	Major	10th Cameronians	
Gordon, Wesley	Annalong	Corporal	Lancs. Hussars	Died on Service.
Haugh, James	Annalong	Private	R.I. Fus.	Wounded.
Hill, Harry	Mullertown	1st Cl. P.O.	R.N.	D.S.M.
Irvine, Robert	Ballyvea	Private		
Moore, James	Moneydarabeg	Gunner	S.A.H.A.	Wounded.
McBurney, George	Moneydarabeg	Gunner	R.G. Artillery	
McCullough, Samuel	Moneydara	Private		
McDowell, James	Moneydara	Private	R.I.R.	
Newell, John	Moneydara	A.B.	R.N.	
Parkinson, Robert	Moneydara	Private		
Pue, Robert	Ballyvea	Sergeant	R.M.L.I.	Persian Gulf Medal and Bar.
Pue, Thomas	Moneydara	Gunner	S.A.H.A.	
Robinson, Robert	Mullertown	Private	R.I.R.	
Russell, John	Annalong	Private	R.I.R.	
Scott, John	Annalong	Sergeant	R.I.R.	
Trimble, William	Annalong	Private	R.I.R.	Wounded.

NEWRY PRESBYTERY. ANNALONG.

Name.	Home Address.	Rank.	Regiment, Battalion, or Unit.	Remarks.
	COLONIAL FORCES.			
Chambers, John	Moneydara	Private	Can. M.G. Corps	
Donnan, Charles	Annalong	Private	Can. E.F.	
Gordon, John	Annalong	Private	Aus. Inft.	
Gordon, W. H.	Annalong	Private	Can. Pioneers	Wounded.
Haugh, Samuel	Annalong	Private	Can. E.F.	
Kernaghan, Samuel	Moneydarabeg	Sapper	Can. Eng.	
McBurney, James	Moneydarabeg	Sergeant	Aust. E.F.	
McCullough, James	Moneydara	Private	Can.	
Marks, Thomas	Annalong	Private	Can. Reserve	
Newell, Samuel	Annalong	Private	U.S. Inft.	
Newell, William	Moneydara	Private	Can. Rifles	Killed in Action.
Pue, Thomas	Ballyvea	Sapper	Can. Eng.	
Robinson, Samuel	Moneydarabeg	C.P.O.	Aust. Navy	
Skillen, Arthur	Ballyvea	Private	Otago Regt., N.Z.	
	BESSBROOK.			
Alderdice, Archibald	Maytown		Australians	
Alderdice, Thomas	Maytown	Private	R. Irish Fus.	
Baird, Joseph				Died.
Beattie, Alexander	College Square	Private	R. Irish Fus.	Killed in Action.
Beattie, James	College Square	Rifleman	R.I.R.	Killed in Action.
Beattie, John	College Square	Private	R. Irish Fus.	
Black, James	Fountain Street	Corporal	R.I.F. and M.G.C.	
Black, Samuel	Grosvenor House	Lance-Corporal	A.S.C. M.T.	
Black, William	Fountain Street	Sergeant	R.I.R.	Killed in Action.
Blakely, James	Charlemont Square	Private	R. Irish Fus.	Killed in Action.
Blakely, R. J.	Charlemont Square	Private	R. Irish Fus.	
Bradley, George	James Street	Private	R. Irish Fus.	
Bradley, James	College Square	Private	R. Irish Fus.	
Bradley, Joshua	College Square	Private	R. Irish Fus.	
Bradley, Samuel	James Street	Private	R. Irish Fus.	
Brady, Andrew	College Square	Private	R. Irish Fus.	Killed in Action.
Brady, Andrew	College Square	Rifleman	R.I.R.	
Brady, James, Jun.	Fountain Street	Private	R. Irish Fus.	
Brady, James	Fountain Street	Private	Labour Corps	
Brady, William John				
Brown, James	College Square	Lance-Corporal	R. Irish Fus.	Killed in Action.
Brown, Thomas	College Square		R. Air Force	
Burke, William	Diveinagh	Private	R. Irish Fus.	
Clarke, David	Maytown Terrace	Corporal	R. Irish Fus.	
Clarke, George	Maytown Terrace	Private	R. Irish Fus.	
Cromwell, William	College Square	Private	R.I.F. and M.G.C.	
Cunningham, J.	College Square	Private	R. In. Fus.	
Cunningham, W. J.				
Cully, George				
Davidson, James	James Street	Private	R. Irish Fus.	
Davidson, Robert	James Street	Private	R. Dub. Fus.	
Dunwoody, J.	The Hotel	Lieutenant	R. Dub. Fus.	Drowned.
Faulkner, George	The Cottage	Air Mechanic	R. Air Force	
Flood, R. S.	The Hotel	Captain	R. Irish Fus.	M.C. Killed in Action.
Graham, Thomas		Sergeant	R. Irish Fus.	
Gray, Edward	Orange Hall	Private	R. Irish Fus.	Killed in Action.
Gray, Rennie	Grosvenor House	Sergeant	R. Irish Fus.	
Gray, Thomas	Grosvenor House	C.Q.M.S.	R. Irish Fus.	
Gray, William	Grosvenor House	R.Q.M.S.	R. Irish Fus.	
Halliday, Thomas	Frederick Street	Lance-Corporal	N.I.H.	
Halliday, William	Fountain Street	Sapper	R.E.	
Hamilton, Alexander	Mountcallfield	Sergeant	R. Inn. Fus.	
Hamilton, Thomas	Fountain Place	Private	R. In. Fus.	Killed in Action.
Hanna, Edmond	Fountain Place	A.B.	R.N.	
Hanna, Samuel	Fountain Place	Rifleman	R.I.R.	
Hare, Thomas	Charlemont Square	Sergeant	R. Irish Fus.	
Hare, W. J. W.	Charlemont Square	Rifleman	R.I.R.	
Humphreys, James	College Square	Private	R. Irish Fus.	
Humphreys, Robert	College Square	Lieutenant	R. Dub. Fus.	M.M.
Johnston, Thomas	College Square	A.M.	R. Air Force	
Livingstone, Samuel	Maytown	Lieutenant	R. Air Force	
Logan, William	Crow's Walk	A.M.	R. Air Force	
McCullough, J.	Charlemont Square	Corporal	R. Irish Fus.	Killed in Action.
McCullough, William	High Street	Private	A.S.C.	
McCune, William	Fountain Street	Private	R. Irish Fus.	
McGaffin, Joseph	Fountain Street	Private	Canadians	
McKee, David	Mount Charles	C.Q.M. Sergeant	R.I.R.	
Maginnis, Henry				
Magowan, Thomas	College Square	Corporal	R. Irish Fus.	
Mitchell, John				
Moffitt, William	Diveinagh	Driver	R.G.A.	
Morrow, George	College Square	Private	R. Irish Fus.	
Morrow, James	Charlemont Square	Private	R. Irish Fus.	
Morrow, John	College Square	Sapper	R.E.	

NEWRY PRESBYTERY.   BESSBROOK.

Name.	Home Address.	Rank.	Regiment, Battalion or Unit.	Remarks.
Moses, Abraham	Deramore Terrace	Private	R. Irish Fus.	
Nelson, David	Craigmore	Private	R. Irish Fus.	
Nelson, William J.	Maytown Terrace	Private	R. In. Fus.	
Pike, John H.	Craigmore	Private	R. Irish Fus.	
Priestly, Andrew	M'Keain's Close	Sergeant	R. In. Fus.	
Priestly, John	M'Keain's Close		R. In. Fus.	
Roy, Samuel	Maytown Terrace		R.I.R.	Killed in Action.
Roy, William J.	Maytown Terrace		R.I.R.	Killed in Action.
Simpson, James H. H.	The School	Private	R. Irish Fus.	
Sterritt, Hugh	College Square	Private	R. Irish Fus.	Killed in Action.
Stevenson, James	Fountain Street	Corporal	R. Irish Fus.	
Stewart, W.	Thomas Street	Guardsman	I.G.	
Stuart, Rev. Alexander	The Manse	Captain	Chaplain	Killed in Action.
Taylor, William J.		Corporal	Canadians	
White, John				
White, Robert				
White, R. G.				
Williamson, T.				
Wilson, James	Rosemount	Private	R. Irish Fus.	

CARLINGFORD.

Forsythe, George		Lance-Corporal	R.F.A.	Died.

CASTLEBELLINGHAM.

Name.	Home Address.	Rank.	Regiment, Battalion or Unit.	Remarks.
Arthur, W. Primrose	Drumleck	Private	Aust. E.F.	Killed in Action.
Cleland, John	Ardee	Private	R. Irish Fus.	
Cleland, Thomas	Ardee	Signaller	R. Irish Fus.	
Donnan, Howard H.	Castlebellingham	Lance-Corporal	S. Irish Horse	1914 Star.
Donnan, Robert W.	Castlebellingham	Bombardier	R.F.A.	D.C.M. and M.M.
Forbes, John C.	Lurgangreen	Lance-Corporal	I. Guards	Wounded.
Hosie, James A.	Castlebellingham	Cadet	R.A.F.	
Hosie, W. Victor	Castlebellingham	Air Mechanic	R.A.F.	
McAllister, Alexander	Castlebellingham	Gunner	R.F.A.	
McAllister, Isaac	Castlebellingham	Corporal	R.I.F.	Wounded.
McAllister, John	Castlebellingham	Sergeant	R.E.	
McAllister, Thomas	Castlebellingham	Corporal	R.A.F.	
McAllister, William	Castlebellingham	Corporal	R.I.F.	W'ded 1914 Star.
McDowell, Ernest	Mullaharlin	Trooper	S. Ir. Horse	Killed in Action.
McKenna, John	Castlebellingham	Private	R.I.R.	
Nixon, Harold	Milestown	Engineer	R.N.	Drowned.
Stirling, Alexander	Castlebellingham	Lieutenant	R.A.F.	Wounded.

CLARKESBRIDGE.

Name.	Home Address.	Rank.	Regiment, Battalion or Unit.	Remarks.
Bell, James	Tullyvallen	Gunner	R.G.A.	
Blackwood, James	Cortamlet	Clerk	R.N.	
Blackwood, Joe	Ballinarae	Corporal	2nd I.G.	
Blackwood, W. J.	Ballinarae		R.N.	
Irwin, Fred. J.	Skerrymore	Corporal	10th R.I.R.	Killed in Action.
Irwin, Henry E.	Skerrymore	Sergeant	R.F.A.	
McClean, John	Altnamackin	Gunner	R.G.A.	
McConnell, William	Tullyvallen	Bombardier	R.G.A.	
Meeke, A.	Tullyvallen	Corporal	A.T. Corps	
Megaw, Tom	Skerriff	Private	R.F.A.	
Stoops, Samuel A.	Skerriff	Private	A.S.C.	
Thompson, John	Cortamlet	Gunner	25th R.F.A.	

COLONIAL AND U.S.A. FORCES.

Name.	Home Address.	Rank.	Regiment, Battalion or Unit.	Remarks.
Bell, William	Tullyvallen		American Army	
Blackwood, James A.	Altnamackin		5th Can. F.A.	Died of Wounds.
Carswell, John	Altnamackin	Sergeant	American E.F.	
McBride, Samuel	Armaghbrague	Private	U.S. Inft.	
Stoops, Herbert	Skerriff	Private	9th Aust. Inft.	

CREMORE.

Name.	Home Address.	Rank.	Regiment, Battalion or Unit.	Remarks.
Alderdice, John	Ballyreagh	Private	R.E.	Wounded.
Andrews, Joseph	Rathconvil	Private	A.S.C.	
Andrews, William A.	Rathconvil	Private	A.S.C.	
Brown, Robert	Ballygorman	Private	R.I.F.	
Clegg, James	Federnagh	Sergeant	N. Staffords	Killed in Action.
Hanna, Abraham	Liseraw		R.A.F.	
Hanna, William	Ballydogherty	Sergeant	R. Dub. Fus.	
Milne, Alexander	Tullylin	Private	A.S.C.	
Porter, John	Ballyreagh	Private	R.I. Fus.	
Porter, William James	Ballyreagh	Private	R.I. Fus.	Killed in Action.
Stewart, Adam K.	Crieve	Lieutenant	R.E.	
Turner, William	Crewbeg	Private	A.S.C.	

NEWRY PRESBYTERY. DONOUGHMORE, Co. Down.

Name.	Home Address.	Rank.	Regiment, Battalion or Unit.	Remarks.
DONOUGHMORE, CO. DOWN.				
Burnett, Henry W.	The Manse	Sergeant	5th Seaforth High.	Killed in Action.
Cummins, Wm. Robert	Ringclare	Private	25th Can. C.	
Donaldson, Andrew	Lisnarea	Sergeant	Can. M.G.	Twice Wounded.
Harshaw, Robert	Ringclare	Private	N.I.H.	
Harshaw, William James	Ringclare	Sergeant	12th R.I.R.	Wounded.
McCready, David	Ballymacratty	Private	R.I. Fus.	Twice Wounded.
McGaffin, William	Church View	Private	12th R.I. Fus.	Prisoner.
Marshall, Harry	Tulymurry	Sapper	R.F.A.	
Marshall, James F.	Tullymurry	Sergeant	R.E., C.C.	M.M.
FIRST DRUMBANAGHER AND JERRETTSPASS.				
Barton, Harold	Goraghwood	Sergeant	R.I. Fus.	D.C.M., Pris. of War
Bittles, William	Cullentraugh	Corporal	R.M., H.M.S. "Donegal"	
Clarke, Allen	Greenfield	Trooper	N.I.H.	
Henry, Thomas M.	Lisummon	Private	4th R.I.R.	
Henry, Trevor	Lisummon	Trooper	N.I.H.	
Lockhart, Maxwell	Kilmonaghan House	Lance-Corporal	N.I.H.	Mons Medal
Lockhart, William	Knockduff House	Sergeant	R. Irish Fus.	Mons Med. Pris.
Moody, Andrew	Lett	Private	4th R.I.R.	
Moody, William T.	Lett	Private	I.G.	Killed in Action.
Murray, Richard	Craigmore	Private	R.I.R.	Twice Wounded. Lost limb.
Porter, David Henry	Kilrea	Cadet	17th R.I.R.	
COLONIAL FORCES.				
Bittles, Isaac	Cullentraugh	Private	U.S.A. Navy	
Gordon, Thomas R.	Searce	R.A.M.C.	Aust. I.F.	Died of Wounds.
Irwin, Thomas	Ballylough	Private	Can. Contingent	Twice Wounded.
DUNDALK.				
Beamish, O. K.	19 Castle Road		R.E.	
Craig, F. W.	The Towers	Lieutenant	S. Lancashires	
Creighton, J. L.	Hemingway House	2nd Lieutenant	R.I. Hussars	
Cunningham, A. G.	49 Broughton Street	Sapper	R.E.	
Hardy, Ronald	48 Dublin Street	Private	R.E.	
Harkness, J. M.	Stapleton Place		R.N.R.	
Harvey, J. B.	Belfast	Sergeant	R.I.R.	
Harvey, Leslie	Belfast	Sergeant	R.I.F.	
Irwin, Henry	Clarkesbridge	Sergeant	R.F.A.	
Jennings, John	17 Dublin Street	Private	R.F.A.	
Jennings, Robert	17 Dublin Street	Private	N.I.H.	
Jennings, William	17 Dublin Street	A.B.	R.N.	
Lyons, Robert	Chapel Lane	Sapper	R.E.	
McAlister, Ben	Brunswick Row	Private	R.A.M.C.	
McConnell, J. F.	Lisburn	Lance-Corporal	R.A.M.C.	
McConnell, Samuel	Market Street	2nd Lieutenant	R. In. Fus.	
McCrum, Herbert	5 Mountain View	A.B.	R.N.	
McDonald, James	Castle Road	Private	A. Imperial Forces	
McDowell, E. V.	Mullaharlin	Private	S. Irish Horse	
McDowell, H. E.	Faughart	Private	R.F.A.	
McDowell, John	Faughart	Staff-Sergeant	A.S.C.	
McKenna, S. W.	Castle Road	R.Q.M.S.	Tyneside Irish	
Matho, Charles	Clermont Park	Private	8th Hussars	
Melville, James	Clanbrassil Street	Lance-Corporal	R.G.A.	
Melville, John R.	Clanbrassil Street	Private	R.A.M.C.	
Morrison, Ernest	30 Vincent Avenue	Private	M.T. A.S.C.	
Ramsey, Hugh	Proleek	Corporal	R.E.	
Ramsey, Robert	Proleek	Private	R.E.	
Stewart, John	47 Castle Road	Private	R.F.A.	
Stewart, William	47 Castle Road	Corporal	R.E.	
Thompson, John G.	Earl Street	Private	8th Hussars	
JONESBOROUGH.				
Barclay, G.	Adavoyle	Private	A.I. Force	
Barclay, N.	Adavoyle	Sergeant	London Regt.	D.C.M.
Barclay, R. W.	Adavoyle	Private	A.I. Force	
Paul, Robert W.	Adavoyle	Driver	N.Z. F.A.	
Paul, T. Fred.	Adavoyle	Gunner	N.Z. F.A.	
Walker, Robert	Jonesboro'	Private	N.I.H.	
FOURTOWNS.				
Close, Robert	Fourtowns	Signaller	13th Batt. R.I.R.	
Cunningham, Fred. James	Killysavan	Trooper	N.I.H.	
Kirkland, William	Ballymacrallymore	Private	3rd Batt. R. Scots	
Lyster, William	Killysavan	Private	A.S.C.	
McCready, Alexander	Drumantine	Rifleman	20th Batt. R.I.R.	
McCready, William	Drumantine	Private	10th Batt. R.I. Fus.	Died in France.

NEWRY PRESBYTERY. — FOURTOWNS

Name.	Home Address.	Rank.	Regiment, Battalion or Unit.	Remarks.
McKee, William	Ballymacrallymore	Rifleman	11th Batt. R.I.R.	
Miscimmins, Ringham J.	Killysavan	Private	16th R.I.R.	
Miscimmins, William	Legananney	Sapper	R.E.	
Purdy, James Allen	Poyntzpass	Private	2nd Batt. R.I. Fus.	Wounded.
Purdy, McDermott	Killysavan	Corporal	4th Brigade I.G.	
Taylor, Samuel Priestly	Killysavan	Sergeant	1st Batt. I.G.	Wounded.

KINGSMILLS.

Name.	Home Address.	Rank.	Regiment, Battalion or Unit.	Remarks.
Adams, John	Lisadian	Sergeant	9th R.I.F.	M.M. and Bar.
Andrews, Martin	Belleeks	Private	N.I.H.	
Crozier, David	Lisadian	Private	18th Batt. R.I. Fus.	
Crozier, Robert Thomas	Lisadian	Private	R.I.R.	
Crozier, W. J.	Lisadian	Sergeant	9th R.I. Fus.	
Edgar, Thomas H.	Drumhoney	Sergeant	N.I.H. and King's L.	
King, John	Lurganah House	Private	N.I.H.	Killed in Action.
King, William	Lurganah House	Private	5th Black Watch	Killed in Action.
McKnight, William	Drumhoney	Private	1st Batt. I. Fus.	Killed in Action.
Meeke, Rev. Hugh, M.A.	Warrenpoint	Lieut.-Colonel	Chaplain	D.S.O.
Meeke, William, L.D.S.	Warrenpoint	Lieutenant	R.A.M.C.	
Moffett, Samuel	Lisnalea	Corporal	R.I.R.	Wounded.
Moffett, Thomas	Lisnalea	Private	R.I.R.	
Patterson, Robert	Lurganah	Private	N.I.H.	
Torrie, Rev. E. G.	Kingsmills	Private	R.A.M.C.	
Watson, William	Belleeks	Private	R.I.R.	
Williamson, Robert	Rathcarbry	Private	4th Batt. R.I.R.	

COLONIAL AND U.S.A. FORCES.

Name.	Home Address.	Rank.	Regiment, Battalion or Unit.	Remarks.
Andrews, Moses	Belleeks	Private	Canadians	
Andrews, William John	Belleeks	Sergeant	Canadian Army	Died.
Harrison, Herbert J.	Tullywiney	Sergeant	Canadian Army	
King, Joseph	The Moor	Private	U.S. Army	
McMullan, Robert	Knockavannon	Corporal	Toronto Regt.	
Rankin, William	Tullyhappy	Private	Canadians	Wounded. Died.

SECOND MARKETHILL.

Name.	Home Address.	Rank.	Regiment, Battalion or Unit.	Remarks.
Conley, James	Ballindarragh	Private	9th R.I.F.	
Dougan, Arthur	Markethill	Private	16th R.I.R.	
Dougan, James	Markethill	Private	16th R.I.R.	
Ewart, Joseph	Ballindarragh	Seaman	H.M.S. "Assistance"	
Ewart, James	Ballindarragh	Private	A. and S. High.	
Marshall, Gilbert	Markethill	Captain	R.A.M.C.	
McConnell, W. J.	Fort Manse	Captain	Chaplain	Twice Men. in Des.
McCready, David	Markethill	Private	9th R.I.F.	Wounded.
Moore, Samuel	Markethill	Private	9th R.I.F.	
Muldrew, J.	Markethill	Driver	A.S.C.	
Rainey, James	Markethill	Private	1st R.I.F.	
Shepherd, Alfred	Daisy Hill	2nd Lieutenant	7/8 R.I.F.	Wounded.
Shepherd, J. N.	Daisy Hill	Lieutenant	15th K.R.	
Shepherd, George	Markethill	Captain	R.A.M.C.	
Stewart, W. J.	Markethill	Private	110th F.A., R.A.M.C.	
Stockdale, James	Markethill	Sapper	R.E.	
Thompson, Jack	Lattery	Private	2nd R.I.F.	Died.

COLONIAL FORCES.

Name.	Home Address.	Rank.	Regiment, Battalion or Unit.	Remarks.
Coburn, John	Drumahee	Private	7th Winnipeg Rifles	
Lyons, Frank	Rose Cottage	Sergeant	4th Canadian M.R.	D.C.M.
Lyons, Samuel D.	Rose Cottage	Private	4th Canadian M.R.	Killed.
Wilson, H. McF.	Markethill	Lance-Corporal	Canadian F.A.	

MOUNTNORRIS.

Name.	Home Address.	Rank.	Regiment, Battalion or Unit.	Remarks.
Culley, William S.	Tullyallen	Private	9th R.I. Fus.	Killed in Action.
Dale, Rev. J. M. R.	Seaview	Chaplain	10th Division	Twice Men. in Des.
Hadden, Harry	Tullyherron	Private	9th R.I. Fus.	Wounded Twice.
Hadden, James M.	Ballintate	Private	10th R.I. Fus.	Wounded.
Hadden, John	Lurgaross	Sapper	R.E.	
Halliday, George	Crankey	Corporal	11th R.I.R.	Killed in Action.
Halliday, John	Crankey	Private	Transport Corps	
Irwin, Archie	Keadymore	Private	N.I.H.	
McGaughey, William	Glenanne	Corporal	10th R.I. Fus.	Wounded.
McWhirter, James	Glenanne	Private	9th R.I. Fus.	Wounded. Pris.
McWhirter, Joseph	Glenanne	Private	9th R.I. Fus.	Wounded.
McWhirter, Samuel	Glenanne	Private	9th R.I. Fus.	Killed in Action.
Magowan, John Hall	Tullyherron	Lieutenant	R.A. and Intellig. Dept.	Wounded.
Magowan, William	Tullyherron	Private	R.A.F.	
Martin, Joseph James	Ballygorman	Private	14th R.I.R.	
Stewart, James	Glenanne	Sergeant	6th R.I.R.	
Whiteside, Thomas	Glenanne	Private	9th R.I.F.	
Whiteside, William	Glenanne	Private	R.E.	

NEWRY PRESBYTERY.   MOUNTNORRIS.

Name.	Home Address.	Rank.	Regiment, Battalion or Unit.	Remarks.
COLONIAL FORCES.				
Hadden, M. Albert	Tullyherron	Private	Canadians	Wounded.
Hadden, John Girvin	Tullyherron	Corporal	Canadians	
Halliday, David	Crankey	Private	Canadians	Wounded.
Henry, Thomas George	Crieve	Sergeant	Can. M.G.C.	Killed in Action.
McCullough, Thomas	Tullyallen	Lance-Corporal	Canadians	Died.
McElroy, William J.	Tullyherron	Private	Canadians	
Scott, Stewart B.	Cregans	Private	Can. M.G.C.	
MOURNE.				
Annett, Charles	Glenloughan	Private	16th R.I.R.	Wounded.
Annett, James	Ballyvea	Private		
Annett, Washington	Kilkeel	Gunner	R.N.	
Baird, James	Cargenagh	Private	Manchester Regt.	
Ballance, Thomas	Harbour Road	Private	13th R.I.R.	Killed in Action.
Beck, David	Aughnaloopy	Private	12th R.F.A.	
Beck, Gilbert	Maghery	Corporal	98th Brigade H.G.	
Bingham, William	Aghnahoory	Private	8th R.I.R.	Wounded.
Boyd, John	Benagh	Private	14th R.I.R.	Wounded.
Campbell, William	The Moor	Private	36th Div. R.E.	
Cousins, Albert	Harbour Road	Private	8th R.I.R.	Died.
Cousins, John	Harbour Road	A.B.	R.N.	Died.
Cousins, Robert	Maghery	Private	A.S.C. M.T.	
Cowser, Harry	Bayview Park	Cadet	R.A.F.	
Davidson, Thomas	Kilkeel	Private		
Ferguson, James H.	Harbour Road	Private	8th R.I. Fus.	Killed in Action.
Ferguson, Robert	Ballymartin	Corporal	23rd Ammunition Sub. Park	
Ferguson, Willie	Ballyinahatten	Stoker	R.N.	
Fisher, Rev. James	Ballymartin	Captain	Intelligence Office	
Galbraith, William	Harbour Road	Sergeant	13th R.I.R.	Croix de Guerre.
Girvin, Hugh	Maghery	Private	3rd R.I.R.	
Gordon, Samuel Laird	Beulah	Private		
Graham, Willie	Greencastle Street	Private	2nd In. Fus.	Prisoner of War.
Hanna, Harry	The Anchorage	Sergeant	8th R.I.R.	Wounded.
Hanna, James	Ballinran	A.B.	R.N.	
Hanna, William James	The Anchorage	Lieutenant	10th R.I.R.	Wounded.
Hanna, William James	Ballinran	Drill Instructor	R.N.	
Harper, George	Cranfield	Private	8th R.I. Fus.	Wounded.
Haugh, George	Dunavil	Sergeant	19th R.I.R.	Wounded.
Heron, Sydney	Greencastle Street	Private	8th R.I.R.	Prisoner of War.
Hunter, Willie	Ballinran	Private	13th R.I.R.	Killed in Action.
McAver, Robert J.	Harbour Road	Sergeant	49th M.G.C.	
McBride, Harry	Magheramurphy	Private	R.E.	Wounded.
McBride, Willie	Magheramurphy	Private	13th R.I.R.	
McKee, James	Harbour Road		N.I.H.	Wounded.
McKnight, James	Kilkeel		R.N.	
McKnight, John	Derryogue	Lance-Corporal	13th R.I.R.	
McKnight, Robert	Derryogue	Private	11th R.I.R.	Killed in Action.
McKnight, William T.	Newry Street	Sergeant	18th R.I.R.	Killed in Action.
Newell, Charlie	Harbour Road	Private	12th R.I.R.	Wounded.
Nicholson, Richard	Milboy	Private	Sig. Corps	
Perry, Samuel	Aghnahoory		R.N.	
Quinn, Willie	Mill Road	Private	11th R.I.R.	Wounded.
Rooney, John	Kilkeel	Private		
Scott, Samuel	Ballinran	Despatch Rider		Killed in Action.
Scott, Thomas	Ballinran	Cadet	R.A.F.	
Shannon, William John	Fintnamara	Lieut.-Colonel	16th Lancers	D.S.O. with Bar.
Skillen, James	Ballyvea	Lieut.-Colonel		
Sloan, George	Maghery	Private		
Sloan, Gerald	Greencastle Street	Private	N.I.H.	Wounded.
Spiers, Thomas	Aghnaloopy	Private	R.E.	
Stevenson, George	Milboy	Private	6th Leinst. Regt.	
Stevenson, Ira	Maghereagh	Private		
Stevenson, Tom	Maghereagh	Private		
Wilson, S. England	Ballymageough	Private		
Wilson, W. Henry	Ballymageough	Private		
COLONIAL AND U.S.A. FORCES.				
Annett, John	Brachney	Private	N.Z. Force	Killed in Action.
Annett, John	Ballyrea	Despatch Rider	S. African Force	
Annett, John	Glenloughan	A.B.	Canadian Navy	
Ballance, George	Harbour Road	Sergeant	Canadians	Wounded.
Chestnut, Robert J.	Cranfield	Private	American Army	
Cousins, Robert	Brackney	Private	American Army	
Crutchley, Leonard	Ballinahatten	Private	N.Z. E.F.	
Crutchley, Robert	Ballinahatten	Private	N.Z. E.F.	
Crutchley, Thomas H.	Ballinahatten	Private	N.Z. E.F.	
Ferguson, Willie	Ballinahatten	Private	American Army	
Galbraith, John	Harbour Road	Private	American Army	
Galbraith, Robert	Harbour Road	Private	American Army	
Gordon, Richard	Beulah	Major	S. African Force	

NEWRY PRESBYTERY.   MOURNE.

NAME.	HOME ADDRESS.	RANK.	REGIMENT, BATTALION OR UNIT.	REMARKS.
HANNA, JOHN	Bridge Street	Corporal	Can. F.A.	
HANNA, MAX	Bridge Street	Private	Can. E.T.D.	
HANNA, ROBERT	Cranfield	Private	N.Z.R.B.	Invalided.
KEYES, SAMUEL	Newcastle Street		Can. Contingent	Killed in Action.
LINTON, JOHN	Ballinran	Lieutenant	Indian Army	Wounded.
McBRIDE, JOHN	Magheramurphy	Private	Can. R. Troops	
McCUTCHEON, W. J.	Ballykeel	Corporal	Can. E.F.	
McKEE, WILLIE	Ballymageough	Private	Can. E.F.	
McMULLEN, ROBERT	Kilkeel	Private	N.Z.	
MATIER, HUGH	St. Ruans	Sergt.-Major	Can. Fus.	
MATIER, ROBERT	St. Ruans	Lieutenant	Canadians	
NEWELL, ROBERT	Ballykeel	Private	American Army	
NEWELL, SANDY	Harbour Road	Sergeant	American Army	D.C.M. Killed in Action.
NICHOLSON, ROBERT	Derryogue	Captain	U.S. Ex. Force	
PATTERSON, ARTHUR	Cranfield	Private	N.Z. Force	
QUINN, BOB	Newcastle Street	Private	U.S.A.	
QUINN, EDWARD	Maghereagh	Private	Can. H.A.	Killed in Action.
QUINN, SAMUEL	Newcastle Street	Private	U.S.A.	
QUINN, THOMAS	Maghereagh	Private	Australian E.F.	
FIRST NEWRY.				
ALDERDICE, L. G.	Newry	2nd Lieutenant	H.B., R.G.A.	Wounded.
ANDREWS, WILLIAM	Cowan Street	Sapper	R.E.	
BALLENTINE, W.	Damolly	Rifleman	19th R.I.R.	
CAIRNS, W.	Cloughenramer	Gunner	R.G.A.	
CLARKE, HENRY	Caulfield Place	Lance-Corporal	13th R.I.R.	Killed in Action.
COPELAND, WILLIAM	Arthur Street	Trooper	N.I.H.	
COWAN, A.	Cowan Street	Private	5th Reserve Training Batt.	
COWAN, G.	Cowan Street	Signaller	6th R.I.R.	
COWAN, R.	Cowan Street	Corporal	8th R.I.R.	Killed in Action.
COWAN, W.	Stream Street	Lance-Corporal	R.A.M.C.	Killed in Action.
DAVIS, JAMES				
DONALDSON, J. K.	Basin Walk	Sergeant	R.E.	Wounded.
DONALDSON, W. K.	Basin Walk	Private	E. Kent Regt.	
ENGLISH, J.	Windsor Hill	C.Q.M.S.	R.I.R.	Wounded.
FERRIS, JOSEPH	Talbot Street	Private	3rd R.I.R.	
FERRIS, JOHN	Cloughenramer	Rifleman	13th R.I.R.	Wounded.
FERRIS, R. EDWARD	Dublin Road	Cadet	R.A.F.	
FERRIS, SAMUEL	Damolly	Rifleman	13th R.I.R.	W'ded and Pris.
FERRIS, SAMUEL	Strain Street	Private	R.I.R.	
FISHER, F. C.	Bridge Street	Eng.-Comdr.	R.N.	
FISHER, J. ANNETT	Rockville	Captain	King's Liverpool	M.C. Wounded.
FISHER, REV. J. A., M.A.	Crossmichael	Lieutenant	K.O.S.B.	Wounded.
FISHER, J. S.	Rockville	Lance-Corporal	8th Scott. M. Amb.	
FISHER, T. A.	Bridge Street	Captain	4th Devons	
GILLESPIE, H. A., M.B., B.Ch.	Trevor Hill	Captain	R.A.M.C.	Wounded.
GRAY, ROBERT	Canal Street	Gunner	R.F.A.	
GRAY, S.	Canal Street	Rifleman	R.I.R.	Died.
GRAY, WILLIAM	Canal Street	Gunner	R.G.A.	
HADDEN, GEORGE	Canal Street	Drummer	R.I.F.	Wounded.
HUNTER, WILLIAM	Talbot Street	Corporal	I.G.	
KERR, W. P.	Sugar Island	Private	R.A.M.C.	
KINCADE, ROBERT	Canal Street	Private	18th R.I.R.	Died.
McBRIDE, WILLIAM	Drumcashlone	Gunner	R.F.A.	Killed in Action.
McGAFFIN, GEORGE B.	Crobane	Sergeant	6th In. Dragoons	
McGAFFIN, W. H.	Crobane	Private	8th E. Yorks	Killed in Action.
McKEE, JOHN	Kiln Street	Private	R. Dub. Fus.	Died of Wounds.
McKEE, W.	Arthur Street	Private	R.E.	
McKENZIE, A.	Helen's Terrace			
McKENZIE, J.	Helen's Terrace			
McKENZIE, W.	Helen's Terrace			
McWILLIAMS, J.	Derryboy	Private	9th R.I.F.	
MAGOWAN, S. E.	Windsor Villas	2nd Lieutenant	19th R.I.R.	
MARTIN, D. S., M.B., B.Ch.,	Sandy's Place	Captain	R.A.M.C.	
MARTIN, H. B.	Sandy's Place	Corporal	R.A.M.C.	Gassed.
MARTIN, J. N., T.C.D.	Sandy's Place	Lieutenant	K.R.R.	Wounded.
MARTIN, S. N.	Littleton	Sergeant	R.E.	
MAXWELL, G. S.	Imperial Hotel	2nd Lieutenant	R.F.A.	
MOFFIT, S.		Corporal	13th R.I.R.	Wounded.
MOORE, HERBERT E.	Beragh	Private	2nd Hants Regt.	Died of Wounds.
MORROW, HAROLD	Buttercrane Quay Ho.	Rifleman	6th R.I.R.	Wounded.
MORROW, W. S.	Buttercrane Quay Ho.	Corporal	R.F.A.	
NEILL, G.	Damolly	Drummer	13th R.I.R.	Wounded.
NESBITT, R.	Mountain View Ter.	R.Q.M.S.	18th R.I.R.	
O'DONAGHUE, W. B.	Bellevue	Lance-Corporal	1st N.I.H.	Wounded.
PATTERSON, J.	James' Street	Corporal	20th R.I.R.	
REID, JOHN	Loanda	Sergeant	9th R.I.F.	Wounded.
REID, S. E.	Ballyroney	Captain	Lancashire Fus.	Wounded.
RIDGES, J. S.	Dromalane	Corporal	R.E.	
SCOTT, H. T.	Caulfield Terrace	2nd Lieutenant	5th S. Lancashire	
SCOTT, J. K.	Caulfield Terrace	Sergeant	13th R.I.R.	
SCOTT, SAMUEL	Bridge Street	Corporal	R.E.	Died of Wounds.

NEWRY PRESBYTERY. FIRST NEWRY.

Name.	Home Address.	Rank.	Regiment, Battalion or Unit.	Remarks.
Spence, H. A.	Provincial Bank	Lieutenant	Leinster Regt.	Wounded.
Steele, J.	Barrack Street	Sergeant	57th R.G.A.	
Strahan, Thomas S.	The Manse	2nd Lieutenant	7th Gloucesters	
Tankard, B. J.	Ashgrove	Driver	A.S.C.	
Wauchope, G. A.	Daisy Hill	Sub-Lieutenant	R.N.V.R.	Killed in Action.
Wilson, A.	Erskine Place	Private	R.I.R.	
Wilson, S.	Erskine Place	Trooper	1st N.I.H.	
COLONIAL FORCES.				
Alderdice, A. E.	Newry	Private	Can. Trench Mortar	Wounded.
Alderdice, G. F.	Newry	Private	Can. Contingent	Wounded.
Andrews, A.	Commons	Private	S.A. Scottish	Killed in Action.
Bond, Thomas	Canal Street	Sergeant	N.Z. Dragoons	Wounded.
Crozier, H. C.	The Mart	Corporal	15th S.A. Signal Corps	
Donaldson, J. H.	Basin Walk	Sergeant	Canadian P.O.	
Morrow, S. E.	Quay House	Private	1st S.A. Inft.	Wounded.
O'Donoghue, J. J.	Bellevue	Lance-Corporal	18th Aust. I.F.	M.M. Wounded.
Wilson, J.	The Mart	Private	S.A. Inft.	
NEWRY, DOWNSHIRE ROAD.				
Barnes, John	Altnaveigh	Stoker	R.N.	Torpedoed 3 times.
Beatty, John	Carnegat	Private	5th R.I.F.	Died of Wounds.
Bothwell, William	Commons	Sergeant	6th R.B.	Wounded.
Boyd, Harry	Damolly	Private	R.G.A.	
Brown, D. Alexander	Canal Street	Private	1st Manchesters	
Campbell, Jack	Canal Street	Private	19th R.I.R.	
Carter, James	Sandy's Street	Private	5th R.I.R.	
Carter, Joseph	Sandy's Street	Corporal	A.O.C.	
Cartmill, Robert W.	Corrinshego	Private	18th R.I.R.	
Chambers, Jack	Penguin Place	Private	13th R.I.R.	Wounded.
Chambers, Robert	Penguin Place	Cook's Boy	R.N.	
Chambers, Thomas	Commons	Private	R.E.	
Chapman, James	Erskine Street	Private	A.S.C.	
Chapman, William	Damolly	Private	13th R.I.R.	
Clydesdale, Hugh	Cowan Street	Private	R.I.R.	Wounded.
Copeland, Alfred	Sheeptown	Sergeant	R.I.R.	Killed. D.C.M.
Copeland, Harrold	Sheeptown	Private	R.I.R.	
Copeland, James	Erskine Street	Sergeant	3rd R.I.R.	Wounded.
Copeland, Thomas	Sheeptown	Private	9th R.I.R.	
Copeland, William J.	Sheeptown	Private	10th R.I.R.	
Crozier, John	Sugar Island	Private	13th R.I.R.	
Crozier, Robert	Sugar Island	Lance-Corporal	13th R.I.R.	
Davenport, David	Penguin Place	Private		
Davenport, Emmet	Penguin Place	Private	2nd R.I.R.	Killed in Action.
Davenport, Joseph	Penguin Place	Private		
Davenport, Robert	Penguin Place	Private	1st R.I.R.	Killed in Action.
Davenport, Samuel	Penguin Place		157th Brigade 52nd Div.	
Dodds, George				
Dodds, James	Mullaglass	Corporal	R.I.R.	Prisoner & Wded.
Dodds, James	Stream Street	Lance-Corporal	2nd R.I.F.	
Dodds, Joseph	Stream Street	Private	R.A.M.C.	
Dodds, William	Pound Street	Private	13th R.I.R.	
Fegan, William	Cowan Street	Private	5th R.I.R.	
Ferris, D. Harry	Windsor Hill	Surgeon Prob.	R.N.	Killed.
Ferris, Joe	Talbot Street	Private	N.I.H.	Wounded.
Fleming, Ben	Corneyhaugh	Private	I.G.	
Gamble, James	Talbot Street	Private		
Gamble, Robert	Talbot Street	Private		
Gamble, William John	Talbot Street	Private	5th R.I.R.	
Grant, Harry	Crobane	Private	13th R.I.R.	Wounded.
Grant, John H.	Talbot Street	Private	10th RI·R.	Gassed.
Gray, Thomas	Cowan Street	Private	13th R.I.R.	
Hanna, Bob	Creive	Private	N.I.H.	
Hanna, Boyd	Creive	Private	13th R.I.R.	Wounded.
Hanna, Herbert	Aileen Terrace	Captain	14th R.I.R.	
Hanna, Joe	Creive	Private	13th R.I.R.	Wounded.
Hanna, Willie	Creive	Private	R.I.R.	
Hegan, Herbert	Damolly Park	Private	1st R.I.R.	Killed in Action.
Hegan, John	Talbot Street	Sergeant	N.I.H.	
Hendren, James	The Mall	Sergeant	15th R.I.R.	Wounded.
Hendren, William John	The Mall	Corporal	16th R.I.R.	
Johnston, Jack	Cowan Street	Private	I.G.	Wounded.
Jones, James	Stream Street	Private	13th R.I.R.	Killed in Action.
Kennedy, George	Barrack Street	Sergeant	R.H.A.	
Kerr, Charles E.	Badentoy	Lance-Corporal	6th Black Watch	Killed in Action.
Kerr, John N.	Altnaveigh	Private	N.I.H.	
Kerr, R. D.	Badentoy	Private	A.S.C.	
Kinlay, Joseph	Canal Street	Private	A.S.C.	
Lambe, John	Canal Street	Private	A.S.C.	
Livingston, William	Sugar Island	E.R.A	H.M.S. "Barham"	
McAnuff, Bertie	Canal Street	Sergeant	2nd R.I.R.	Wounded.
McConnell, Dr. George	Trevor Hill	Captain	R.A.M.C.	

NEWRY PRESBYTERY   DOWNSHIRE ROAD, NEWRY.

Name.	Home Address.	Rank.	Regiment, Battalion or Unit.	Remarks.
McCracken, Samuel	Sheeptown	Private	8th R.I.R.	Killed in Action.
McCrum, G. Albert	Chequer Hill	Private	2nd R.I.R.	Wounded.
McCrum, Joe	Chequer Hill	Private	R.G.A.	
McCutcheon, Robert	Edward Street	Private	13th R.I.R.	
McGladdery, Thomas	Crobane	Private	I.G.	Killed in Action.
McGladdery, William	Crobane	Private	R.I.R.	
McKinley, John R.	Damolly	Private	R.F.	
McMullan, Daniel	Canal Street	Private	A.S.C.	
McNeill, Bob	Hill Street	Private	A.S.C.	
McNeill, Joseph S.	Needham Street	E.R.A.	H.M.S. "Titania"	
Magowan, Thomas	Canal Street	Private	I.F.	Wounded.
Maitland, William	Turmore	Private	17th R.I.R.	
Martin, Joseph	Corrinshego	Private		
Masson, Harry	Kiln Street	Private	A.O.C.	Wounded.
Masson, William	Kiln Street		A.O.C.	
Mitchell, Albert	Commons	Private	Scotch Rifles	
Morrow, James	James Street	Private	2nd I.F.	
Morrow, John	James Street	Private	A.G.C.	
Morrow, Thomas	James Street	Private	2nd I.F.	
Morrow, William	James Street	Private	4th R.I.F.	Killed in Action.
Murphy, Isaac	Sandys Street	Private	10th R.I.F.	
Murphy, John	Sandys Street	Private	N.I.H.	
Murphy, John	Cowan Street	Private	13th R.I.R.	Wounded.
Murray, Richard	Edward Street	Private	2nd R.I.R.	Wounded.
O'Neill, Joseph	Downshire Road	Sergeant	I.D.G.	
Preston, David	Talbot Street	Private	R.A.M.C.	
Preston, W. J.	Sinclair Street	Sergeant	R.F.A.	
Scott, James	New Street	A.B.	H.M.S. "Rifleman"	
Scott, R. J. H.	New Street	2nd Lieutenant	17th R.I.R.	Wounded.
Scott, William H.	New Street	Private	17th R.I.R.	Prisoner.
Sheppardson, Samuel	Millvale	Sergeant		Died on Service.
Smith, William T.	Sugar Island	2nd Lieutenant	Con. Rangers	Wounded.
Sterritt, William	Canal Street	Corporal	A.S.C.	
Sturgeon, Samuel	Millvale	Lieutenant	H.A.C.	Wounded.
Todd, Fred.	Sugar Island	Private		
Truesdale, Albert	Downshire Road	Private	13th R.I.R.	Wounded.
Truesdale, Andrew	New Street	Private	3rd Cam. High.	
Truesdale, William	Corneyhaugh	Private	R.I.R.	Wounded.
Tweedie, Samuel	Damolly	Private	2nd R.I.R.	
Wheelan, Alec	Commons	Private	R.G.A.	Killed in Action.
Wylie, William J.	Canal Street	Private	A.S.C.	Gassed.
COLONIAL FORCES.				
Aiken, Matthew	Damolly	Private	Canadians	
Beggs, George	Lisdrumiska	Private	Canadians	
Beggs, Thomas	Lisdrumiska	Private	Canadians	
Brown, George	Canal Street	Private	Canadians	Killed in Action.
Copeland, John	Erskine Street	Private	Canadians	
Hamilton, Robert E.			Australians	Wounded.
Hegan, Walter	Damolly Park	Private	Canadians	Killed in Action.
Kerr, Alec	Badentoy	Private	Canadians	
Mathers, Henry	Canal Street	Private		
Masson, James	Kiln Street	Private	Canadians	
Mehaffy, Hugh	Edward Street	Private	Canadians	
SECOND NEWTOWNHAMILTON.				
Campbell, David	Newtownhamilton	Sergeant	I.G.	Wounded.
Campbell, William John	Newtownhamilton	Private	Scots Guards	
Cassels, George	Newtownhamilton	Private	H.L.I.	Wounded.
Cassels, Samuel	Newtownhamilton	Corporal	Lancers	Killed in Action.
Conn, John	Newtownhamilton	Private	R.I.F.	Wounded.
Copeland, Samuel	Newtownhamilton	Private	R.I.F.	Wounded.
Dixon, David	Newtownhamilton	Private	R.I.F.	Killed in Action.
Greer, William	Newtownhamilton	Private	R. In. Fus.	Killed in Action.
Hill, Jonathan	Newtownhamilton	Private		Killed in Action.
Johnston, Isaac	Newtownhamilton	Private		
McCulla, Walter	Newtownhamilton	Private	R. Air Force	
Patton, Robert	Newtownhamilton	Clerk	R.N.	
Robb, Isaac	Newtownhamilton	Private	N.I.H.	
Watson, John	Newtownhamilton	Private	H.L.I.	Wounded.
Watson, Thomas	Newtownhamilton	Private	N.I.H.	
COLONIAL FORCES.				
Andrews, Robert	Newtownhamilton	Private	Aust. Force	Killed in Action.
Campbell, Robert	Newtownhamilton	Private	Canadians	
Kinnear, John	Newtownhamilton	Private	Canadians	Wounded.
ROSTREVOR.				
Beck, George	Rostrevor	Sergeant	R.G.A.	Wounded. M.M.
Beck, Hugh	Rostrevor	Private	R.I.R.	

NEWRY PRESBYTERY.   ROSTREVOR.

Name.	Home Address.	Rank.	Regiment, Battalion or Unit.	Remarks.
Bell, J.	Rostrevor	Corporal	I. Guards	Wounded.
Donnan, E.	Rostrevor	Private	R.I.R.	
Feely, J.	...	Private	R.A.M.C.	M.M.
Hunter, C.	...	Sergeant	Can. Transport	
McKimm, G.	...	Sergeant	Territorials	
McKimm, S.	Rostrevor	Captain	Shropshires	Wounded. D.S.O.
Martin, R.	Rostrevor	2nd Lieutenant	A.S.C.	
Rentoul, Rev. J. L. B.A.	The Manse	Private	R.A.M.C.	Killed in Action.
Sinton, S.	...	Private	Canadians	
Sinton, W.	Rostrevor	Lieutenant	A.V.C.	
Sloan, George	Rostrevor	Private	Tank Corps	

RYANS.

Name.	Home Address.	Rank.	Regiment, Battalion or Unit.	Remarks.
Agnew, Rev. Robert	Finnards	Chaplain	R. Marines	
Cromie, Samuel	Ballykeel	Corporal	R.E.	
Ferguson, John	Finnards	Private	Labour Corps	
Hamilton, James	Crowreagh	Private	11/13th R.I.R.	Twice Wounded.
McCormick, Thomas	Shinn	Private	16th R.I.R.	Twice Wounded. Prisoner.
McKeown, Samuel	Sheeptown	Private	M.T. A.S.C.	Wounded.
McKeown, William	Sheeptown	Private	M.T. A.S.C.	
Murdock, Archibald	Savilbeg	Private	9th R.I.F.	Killed in Action.
Murphy, Isaac	Dysert	Private	9th R.I.F.	Wounded & Pris.
Murphy, John	Dysert	Private	R.I.F.	
Scot, Benjamin	Finnards	Bombardier	R.G.A.	Wounded and Torpedoed.
Trimble, R. John	Crowreagh	Private	3rd R. In. Fus.	Twice Wounded.

COLONIAL FORCES.

Name.	Home Address.	Rank.	Regiment, Battalion or Unit.	Remarks.
Copeland, Robert	Finnards	Mechanic	U.S.A Force	
McMinn, Gilbert	Dysert	Private	11th Canadians	
Sloan, James	Finnards	Private	Canadians	
Sloan, Robert	Ardaragh	Trooper	African Force	
Sloan, Thomas J.	Ardaragh	Private	Canadians	Wounded.

TULLYALLEN.

Name.	Home Address.	Rank.	Regiment, Battalion or Unit.	Remarks.
Baird, Hugh	Ballylane	Private	9th R.I.F.	
Byers, Mandale	Mawhan	Captain	R.A.M.C.	
Caldwell, Stephen	...	Sergeant	4th I. Guards	Died of Wounds.
Cully, Fred.	Crunagh	Private	9th R.I.F.	
Cully, Thomas	Crunagh	Private	3rd Canadian Troop	Wounded.
Kilpatrick, Thomas	Gass, Ballylane	Sergeant	13th R.I.R.	Wounded.
McCaldin, Robert	...	Private	4th R.I.F.	Killed in Action.
McCreary, Thomas	Glenanne	Private	9th R.I.F.	
Martin, John Sinclair	Belfast	Lieutenant	5th R.I.R.	Killed in Action.
Patterson, Dunwoody	Glenanne	Private	6th H.L.I.	
Patterson, John Andrew	Glenanne	Private	R.F.C.	
Patterson, William	Glenanne	Private	9th R.I.F.	
Somerville, Rich. Newman	72 Osborne Pk., Belfast	Lieutenant	R.E.	Killed in Action.
Somerville, Wm. Johnston	72 Osborne Pk., Belfast	Major	R.E.	D.S.O.
Vance, Thomas	...	Private	9th R.I.F.	Killed in Action.
Walker, David	Ballylane	Private	9th R.I.F.	
Whiteside, Samuel	Glenanne	Lance-Corporal	9th R.I.F.	M.M.
Whiteside, Wm. George	Killycarron	Corporal	Innis Dragoons	

WARRENPOINT.

Name.	Home Address.	Rank.	Regiment, Battalion or Unit.	Remarks.
Bourhill, E. R.	Post Office Street	...	R.N.	
Boyd, Harold	Golf House	Private	R.A.F.	
Boyd, J. B.	Golf House	Lieutenant	R.I.R.	
Boyd, R. A. E.	Golf House	Private	King's Liv. Regt.	
Campbell, J.	Hayes's Row	Private	R. In. Fus.	
Campbell, M.	Hayes's Row	Private	R.I.R.	Killed in Action.
Campbell, T.	Hayes's Row	Lance-Corporal	R.I.R.	
Erwine, James	Summer Hill	Sergt.-Major	Cornwalls	Killed in Action.
Johnson, E.	Duke Street	Captain	M. Marine	Prisoner of War.
Johnson, R. S.	Duke Street	Naval Engineer	R.N.	
Kerr, J.	Town Hall	Private	R.N.A.F.	
Lindsay, J.	Narrow Water	Private	R. In. Fus.	
McMurray, T.	Ballyrussell	Trooper	N.I.H.	
Marshall, H.	Warrenpoint	Private	R.E.	Died.
Megarry, R.	Hayes's Row	Private	R. In. Fus.	
Morrison, A.	Dundalk	Corporal	...	
Phoenix, William	Post Office Street	Corporal	R.N.A.F.	
Reid, John	Warrenpoint	Private	R. In. Fus.	
Reid, Joseph	Warrenpoint	Private	R.I.R.	
Rutherford, Rev. J. S., M.A.	The Manse	Private	R.A.M.C.	
Sheills, A.	Newry Road	Cadet	R.I.R.	
Steenson, H. A.	Church Street	Sergeant	C.A.M.C.	
Steenson, J.	Church Street	Private	R. In. Fus.	Killed in Action.
Steenson, J.	Church Street	Private	R.I.R.	

NEWRY PRESBYTERY.

WARRENPOINT.

Name.	Home Address.	Rank.	Regiment, Battalion or Unit.	Remarks.
Steenson, M.	Church Street	Corporal	R.E.	
Toombs, J.	Thomas Street	Private	R. In. Fus.	Killed in Action.
Toombs, R.	Thomas Street	Private	King's Own Liv.	Killed in Action.
Wilson, A.	Post Office Street	Private	S.A. Expd. Force	Died.
Wilson, R.	Newry Street	Trooper	N.I.H.	
COLONIAL FORCES.				
Donnan, J.			Australian Imp. Force	
McMurray, R. O.		Private	Canadian Exped. Force	
Marshall, J. F.		Lance-Corporal	Canadian Engineers	
Thompson, J.		Private	Canadian Exped. Force	
Wilson, H.		Gunner	R. Can. G.A.	

OMAGH PRESBYTERY.

Name.	Home Address.	Rank.	Regiment, Battalion or Unit.	Remarks.
BADONEY AND CORRICK.				
Alexander, William F.	Ballykeel	Private	9th R. In. Fus.	Wounded.
Hamilton, William S.	Droit	Private	N.I.H.	
Hamilton, Charles	Droit	Private	N.I.H.	
Hamilton, William C.	Woodbrook	Private	9th R.I.F.	
Lyons, Thomas McF.	Riversdale	Private	9th R.I.F.	Wounded.
McFadden, John, M.B.	Badoney Manse	Captain	R.A.M.C.	
McFadden, G. D. F.	Badoney Manse	Surgeon-Prob.	R.N.	
McNickle, Robert	Letterbratt	Private	9th R. In. Fus.	Wounded.
McNickle, John	Letterbratt	Private	9th R. In. Fus.	
Stark, James	Derbrough	Private	9th R. In. Fus.	Wounded.
Walker, James H.	Droit	Private	9th R. In. Fus.	Killed in Action.
Warnock, Thomas	Dunbunrawer	Private	9th R. In. Fus.	Killed in Action.
Wasson, George	Carrigans, Omagh	Private	9th R. In. Fus.	Killed in Action.
BALLYNAHATTY.				
Derry, Thomas	Relaghdooey	Private	Canadians	Wounded.
Fyffe, W. H.	Kiltamnagh	Lieutenant	31st M.G. Coy.	Wounded.
Young, Hugh	Loughmuck	Sergt.-Major	A.O.C.	
Young, R. O.	Blacksessiagh	Lieutenant	R. In. Fus.	
CLOGHERNEY.				
Ayre, Thomas	Gortaclare	Private	9th R. In. Fus.	
Chambers, Andrew	Dervaghroy	Private	Labour Corps	
Chambers, James	Dervaghroy	Private	9th R. In. Fus.	
Clarke, David	Redargan	Private	9th R. In. Fus.	
Clarke, Frederick O.	Beragh	Captain	R.A.M.C.	M.C.
Clarke, George	Redargan	Private	9th R.. In. Fus.	
Clarke, Thomas W.	Beragh	Major	R.A.M.C.	Wounded. M.C.
Corbett, George	Gortaclare	Private	9th R. In. Fus.	Wounded Twice.
Corbett, Robert	Gortaclare	Private	9th R. In. Fus.	Wounded.
Coulter, Robert	Gortaclare	Private	R. In. Fus.	Wounded.
Fenton, Robert	Beragh	Sergeant	9th R. In. Fus.	Wounded.
Hunter, John	Moylagh	Private	9th R. In. Fus.	
Kirkpatrick, Thomas H.	Dervaghroy	Co. Sergt.-Major	9th R. In. Fus.	Killed in Action.
McCausland, Joseph	Legacurry	Private	9th R. In. Fus.	
McCausland, Thomas	Legacurry	Private	Labour Corps	Wounded.
McDowell, James	Curr	Private	9th R. In. Fus.	Wounded.
McFarland, Joseph	Raw	Private	R.G.A.	
McKitterick, John, Sen.	Legacurry	Private	Labour Corps	
McKitterick, John, Jun.	Legacurry	Private	9th R. In. Fus.	
McKitterick, Thomas	Legacurry	Private	1st R. In. Fus.	Wounded.
McNaul, William J.	Beragh	Lance-Corporal	9th R. In. Fus.	Died.
Rainey, John	Garvaghy	Sergeant	Irish Guards	Killed in Action.
Rainey, Robert	Garvaghy	Private	9th R. In. Fus.	Died.
Steen, William	Osnagh	Private	9th R. In. Fus.	Wounded.
Watson, James	Donaghanie	Private	9th R. In. Fus.	
Watson, William	Ranelly	Private	9th R. In. Fus.	Killed in Action.
COLONIAL FORCES.				
Cunningham, John	Beragh	Private	Canadians	
Fenton, John	Beragh	Private	Canadians	
Rainey, James	Garvaghy	Private	Australians	Wounded.

OMAGH PRESBYTERY. DROMORE, CO. TYRONE.

Name.	Home Address.	Rank.	Regiment, Battalion or Unit.	Remarks.
DROMORE, CO. TYRONE.				
McFarland, Alexander	Gardrum	Private	9th R. In. Fus.	M.M.
McFarland, David	Gardrum	Sapper	R.E.	
Patterson, William J.	Aughnamo	Private	9th R. In. Fus.	Wounded.
COLONIAL FORCES.				
Blakely, John	Dromore	Private	P. Pat. Can. Imp. F.	Killed in Action.
Kirkpatrick, Hugh B.	Oldcastle	Driver	Australian Artillery	
Kirkpatrick, John F.	Old Castle	Driver	Am. Col., Aust. Are.	
Lynn, William John	Drumlish	Driver	Australian Artillery	
Lynn, Robert J.	Drumlish	Private	Australian Infantry	Wounded.
Moore, Robert		Private	Canadian Infantry	
Neelands, Robert	Drumardnagross	Private	15th Australian Inf.	Killed in Action.
Neelands, Samuel	Drumardnagross	Private	Australian Imp. F.	
DRUMQUIN.				
Duncan, Andrew	Drumquin	Bombardier	R.G.A.	Killed in Action.
Moody, Thomas	Drumquin	Private	M.G.C. 1st Canadian Div.	Killed in Action.
EDENDERRY.				
Chambers, Thomas	Arvalee			Killed in Action.
Johnston, Andrew	Racarson		Canadian Inf.	Killed in Action.
Lewis, Jack	Garvaghey			Killed in Action.
Watson, James	Camowen		R. Inn. Fus.	
FINTONA.				
Carson, Robert A.	Fintona	Private	8th R. In. Fus.	
Carson, William	Fintona	Private	A.S.C.	
Chambers, James	Fintona	Lieutenant	A.S.C.	
Chambers, John L.	Fintona	2nd Lieutenant	5th R. In. Fus.	
Chambers, Robert A.	Fintona	Captain	9th R. In. Fus.	M.C.
Crawford, Alexander	Fintona	M.T. Driver	A.S.C.	
Crawford, John	Fintona	Private	9th R. In. Fus.	Wounded.
Duncan, A. H. R.	Omagh	Captain	R.A.M.C.	Wounded.
Duncan, A. H. R.	Liverpool	Captain	R.A.M.C.	Wounded. M.C.
Irvine, George		Private	9th R. In. Fus.	Died.
Irvine, Robert	Fintona	Private	12th R. In. Fus.	Wounded 3 times.
Johnstone, Samuel	Fintona	Private	9th R. In. Fus.	
Kyle, Haslett	Fintona	Private	U.S. Army	
Kyle, Johnston	Fintona	Trooper	N.I.H.	
Martin, John	Fintona	Gunner	Garrison Art.	
McCoy, Thomas J.	Fintona	Private	9th R. In. Fus.	
Neely, Edwin E.	Scotland	M.T. Driver	A.S.C.	
Neely, Harold	Fintona	Bugler	12th R. In. Fus.	
Neely, Hubert	Fintona	Drummer	12th R. In. Fus.	
Neely, Samuel J. D.	Belfast	Sergeant	16th Lancers	Wounded. M.M.
Sproule, A. H. R.	South Africa	Captain	A.S.C.	
Sproule, G. J.	Fintona	Lieutenant	A.S.C.	
Sproule, J. C.	Aldershot	Captain	R.A.M.C.	
GILLYGOOLEY.				
Alexander John Joseph	Tarlum	Private	A.S.C.	Wounded.
Fyffe, Thos. Alex.	Tully Mills	Sergeant	37th Battery B.E.F.	
Graham, John	Kilmore	Private	9th R. In. Fus.	Wounded.
Graham, William Alex.	Dunewish	Private	R.I.F.	Wounded.
King, William	Tamlaght	Driver	189th Siege B.A.	
O'Donnell, William	Gillygolley	Private	9th R.I.F.	Killed in Action.
COLONIAL FORCES.				
Alexander, Thomas Henry	Tarlum	Trooper	Strathcona Horse	
Graham, David	Kilmore	Private	Canadian Pioneers	Wounded.
Watson, Robert	Botera	Private	15th Canadians	Wounded.
GORTIN.				
Forsythe, Cunningham	Lislap	Private	R. In. Fus.	
Forsythe, William J.	Lislap	Private	R. In. Fus.	
Hamilton, R. E.	Gortin	Corporal	N.I.H.	Gassed.
Knox, Armar	Lenamore	Private	N.I.H./R.I.R.	Killed in Action.
Knox, John	Lenamore	Private	R. In. Fus.	Wounded.
McFarland, Thomas				
Mathewson, Hamilton, M.B.	Dunbunrawer	Lieutenant	R.A.M.C.	Killed in Action.
Whyte, Fred. H., M.B.	Gortin	Captain	R.A.M.C.	
Whyte, J. Stanley, B.Sc.	Gortin	Lieutenant	R.E.	Wounded.

OMAGH PRESBYTERY.   IRVINESTOWN AND PETTIGO.

Name.	Home Address.	Rank.	Regiment, Battalion or Unit.	Remarks.
IRVINGSTOWN AND PETTIGO.				
Cuthbertson, Thomas	Pettigo	Corporal	H. Artillery	Wounded.
Cuthbertson, William	Pettigo	...	S.A. Army	
Dickson, Arthur	Pettigo	Lieutenant	R.I. Regt.	Wounded.
Dickson, Jack	Pettigo	Lieutenant	R.I.R.	
Dickson, James	Pettigo	Lieutenant	M.G.C.	Wounded.
Hilliard, George	Pettigo	Q.M.S.	R.I.R.	Wounded.
Johnston, Joseph	Crevinish	...	Am. Army	
McBride, William	...	Private	R. In. Fus.	Killed in Action.
McCubbin, Robert	Irvinestown	Lance-Corporal	Scottish Rifles	Killed in Action.
Nichol, James	Tievemore	Corporal	I. Guards	Wounded.
MOUNTJOY.				
Cooke, William	Dunbreen	Corporal	9th R. In. Fus.	
Cummins, Samuel	Lisnacreight	Wheeler	A.S.C.	
Donald, David	Mountjoy	Private	9th R. In. Fus.	
Donald, Samuel	Mountjoy	Private	9th R. In. Fus.	
Donald, Thomas	Mountjoy	Private	6th R. In. Fus.	
Fullerton, Archibald, M.B.	Mountjoy	Captain	R.A.M.C.	M.C., D.S.O.
Greer, John	Mountjoy	Corporal	9th R. In. Fus.	Killed in Action.
Lewis, William	Reylagh	Private	11th Scottish Rifles	
Lyons, Beattie, M.B.	Carnoney	Captain	R.A.M.C.	
Lyons, James, M.B.	Carnoney	Captain	R.A.M.C.	
Reddock, Samuel	Knockmoyle	Private	1st A. and S. Highlanders	
Wilkinson, Thomas	Castletown	Sergeant	2nd R. In. Fus.	Killed in Action.
COLONIAL FORCES.				
Cummins, James	Lisnacreight	Gunner	Aust. Inf. Brigade	Wounded.
Cummins, Oliver	Calkill	Private	35th Canadian Inf.	Wounded.
Henderson, James	Lislimnaghan	Trooper	11th Canadian Rifles	Killed in Action.
Jack, Andrew	Mountjoy	Private	Can. Oversea Batt.	
FIRST OMAGH.				
Adams, Alfred	High Street	Captain	R.A.M.C.	
Adams, R. H., F.R.C.S.I.	Tullyharm	Lieutenant	R.A.M.C.	
Adams, Albert P.	Tullyharm	Captain	R.A.M.C.	
Adams, W. I., F.R.C.S.I.	Tullyharm	Captain	R.A.M.C.	
Alexander, Benjamin	High Street	Private	R.A.M.C.	Killed in Action.
Armstrong, Hamilton	Asylum Cottages	Private	R.A.M.C.	
Campbell, Hugh	Lisnamallard	Sapper	R.E.	Killed in Action.
Campbell, John	Lisnamallard	Private	2nd R. In. Fus.	Wounded.
Campbell, William	Lisnamallard	Sapper	R.E.	
Carson, Robert	Dougery	Private	9th R. In. Fus.	
Carson, William John	Dougery	Lance-Corporal	9th R. In. Fus., M.Q.S.	Wounded.
Carson, Samuel	Dougery	Private	9th R. In. Fus.	Killed in Action.
Carson, Tom	Dougery	Private	9th R. In. Fus.	Wounded.
Chapman, W. O.	Edenderry House	Private	R.A.M.C.	
Clements, Charles	Dublin Road	E.R.A.	Submarine G7	Drowned.
Clements, Olley	Dublin Road	E.R.A.	H.M.S. " Ceres "	
Clements, Tom	Dublin Road	Lieutenant	9th R. In. Fus.	Killed in Action.
Clements, John	Dublin Road	Lieutenant	101st Field Art., U.S.A.	
Colquhoun, Hugh	Mullaghmena	Lieutenant	12th Royal Scots	W'ded and P O.W.
Colquhoun, Samuel	Mullaghmena	Lieutenant	10th R.I.F.	Wounded.
Coulter, Henderson	Drumragh	Private	9th R. In. Fus.	
Cruickshank, Philip	Campsie	Captain	9th R. In. Fus.	Killed in Action.
Duncan, A. H. R.	James Street	Captain	108th F.A., R.A.M.C.	Wounded.
Finney, John	Gt. Northern Rly.	Lieutenant	9th R. In. Fus.	Killed in Action.
Flood, Robt. Reginald	James Street	Lieutenant	M.G.C.	Wounded.
Fyffe, William	Wallbrook	Lieutenant	10th South Staffords	Wounded.
Hunter, Alfred	Drumragh	Sergeant	3rd King's R.R.	Killed in Action.
Logan, Simon	Campsie	Lieutenant	R.I.R.	M.C. and Bar.
Lynn, William Thomas	Dublin Road	Private	N.I.H.	Wounded.
Lynn, Samuel	Dublin Road	Driver	9th R. In. Fus.	
Lynn, John	Mullaghmore	Gunner	R.F.A.	
Lynn, James	Mullaghmore	Private	R.E.	Wounded.
McConnell, Samuel	Market Street	Lieutenant	5th R. In. Fus.	Wounded and Pris.
McConnell, John James	Kavlin Road	Private	1st R. Scots Fus.	
McConnell, Joseph	Kavlin Road	Private	6th Munster Fus., M.G.S.	
McConnell, Samuel	Kavlin Road	Private	E.E.F.	
McCormack, R. J.	Coneywarren	Major	R.A.M.C.	
McFarland, William	Killyclogher Road	Private	1st R. In. Fus.	
McFarland, William	Back Market	Private	A.S.C., Egypt	
McFarland, Robert	Lisnamallard	Private	R.I.R.	Wounded.
McKibben, Hamilton	Railway Terrace	Corporal	4th R. In. Fus.	
Magennis, Natheniel	Woodside Terrace	Sergeant	12th R. In. Fus.	
Montgomery, Samuel A.	Dergmoney	Captain	R.A.M.C.	Wounded.
Mullan, W. T.	Market Street	Sergeant	R.E., Egypt	
Neely, Jack	Camowen	Corporal	N.I.H.	
Patrick, William	Bridge Street	Private	3rd R. In. Fus.	Wounded.
Pollock, James	High Street	Private	R.A.M.C.	

OMAGH PRESBYTERY.   FIRST OMAGH.

Name.	Home Address.	Rank.	Regiment, Battalion or Unit.	Remarks.
Scott, W. Madden	Lisnamallard	Captain	London R.I.F.	Wounded.
Stevenson, Henry	Market Street	Private	9th R. In. Fus.	Killed in Action.
Tadley, John	Campsie Crescent	Lance-Corporal	12th R. In. Fus.	
Thompson, Ernest	Glenview Terrace	B. Telegraphist	R.N.	
Wilson, Robert	High Street	Lance-Corporal	9th R. In. Fus.	
Shields, James	Killabrack	Private	12th R. In. Fus.	
COLONIAL FORCES.				
Bassett, Edward		Lieutenant	Canadian Inf.	
Bassett, John		Major	Aide, Sir S. Hughes	
Campbell, Robert	Lisnamallard	Sergeant	38th Canadian Inf.	Killed in Action.
Cockburn, James	Lisnamallard	Sapper	Canadian Engineers	
Cockburn, Samuel	Lisnamallard	Private	8th Canadians	
Flood, Basil	James Street	Private	Canadian Inf.	Killed in Action.
Lynn, Robert	Dublin Road	Private	N.Z. Ex. F.	
McConnell, Joseph	Mullaghmore	Private	Canadians	
McCrindle, Andrew	Omagh	Captain	Canadians	
Miles, William	Drumragh	Sergeant	S.A. Horse	
Quigley, Andrew	Dergmoney	Sergeant	S.A. Contg.	
Quigley, Arthur	Dergmoney	Private	Canadian Inf.	
Watson, Robert	Mullaghmena	Private	9th Missisangra Horse	Killed in Action.
Watson, Robert E.	Mullaghmena	Sergeant	Canadian Highlanders	Wounded.
White, Joseph	Crevenagh	Private	2nd Canadian Pioneers	Died of Wounds.
OMAGH, TRINITY CHURCH.				
Allen, Thomas	Omagh	Sergeant	R. In. Fus.	
Anderson, J. B.	Omagh	Captain	R. In. Fus.	
Chisim, Maxwell	Omagh	Private	N.I.H.	
Christie, R. A.	Belfast	Private	R. In. Fus.	Wounded.
Clay, Thomas B. V.			R. In. Fus.	Wounded.
Dickie, J. McN.	Clonavon, Omagh		R.D. Fus.	Wounded. M.C.
Dickie, T. C.	Clonavon, Omagh		R.D. Fus.	Wounded.
Dickie, Wallace	Clonavon, Omagh	Major	R.D. Fus.	
Hall Frank	Omagh	Private	R. In. Fus.	Killed in Action.
Kyle, William	Omagh	Private	N.I.H.	
Lyons, R. H., M.B.	Omagh	Captain	R.A.M.C.	
McAdam, Jack	Omagh	Private	15th Coy. London Regt.	Died in training.
McAdam, Thomas A.	Omagh	Private	R.E.	
McNickle, George	Omagh		R.N.	
Montgomery, George	Omagh	Private	R.A.F.	
Mullan, William	Omagh		R. In. Fus.	
Nixon, William	Omagh	Private	R. In. Fus.	Killed in Action.
Parke, James	Inniscleen, Castlederg	Private	London Irish Rifles	Killed in Action.
Porter, R. J.	Omagh	Lieutenant	R. In. Fus.	
Torrens, Joseph	Omagh	Corporal	R. In. Fus.	
Wilson, E. F, M.B.	Omagh	Lieutenant	R.A.F.	
Wilson, V. J. F.	Omagh	Cadet	7th R. In. Fus.	Killed in Action.
Wray, John	Omagh	Private	R. In. Fus.	
COLONIAL FORCES.				
Colhoun, James	Mullaghmena	Private	7th C.R.F.	P.O.W.
Colhoun, John L.	Mullaghmena	Private	15th B. Can. Highlanders	
McAdam, W. J.	Omagh	Private	Canadian R.N. (Wireless)	
CREEVAN.				
Campbell, J. L.	Denamona	Private	R. In. Fus.	Killed in Action.
Kidd, Francis	Edenfogary	Corporal	R.I.F.	Wounded.
Shannon, Charles	Blacksessiagh	Private	R. In. Fus.	Wounded.
SESKINORE.				
Barr, Joseph	Eskra	Sergeant	R.F.A.	
Barr, Samuel	Eskra	Private	83 Infantry Brigade	Wounded.
Baxter, Edward	Legacurry	Private	9th R. In. Fus.	Killed in Action.
Bratton, William	Raveagh	Private	12th R. In. Fus.	Died.
Carter, William	Cuttor	Sergeant	C.F. Art.	Prisoner of War.
Christy, Hubert	Mullaghmore	Private	King's Liverpool Regt.;	
Cooke, Robert	Seskinore	Private	Warwick Regt.	
Cuthbertson, Joseph	Garvallagh	Private	9th R. In. Fus.	Killed in Action.
Hartley, William	Raveagh	Corporal	M.G.C.	Wounded.
McCausland, Thomas	Mullaghmore	Corporal	9th R. In. Fus.	Killed in Action.
McMeans, William	Kilfort	Private	Middlesex Regt.	
Maxwell, Thomas	Legacurry	Private	Canadian Regt.	Prisoner of War.
Mitchell, Fred.	Eskra	Private	U.S. Engineers	
Mitchell, John	Eskra	Corporal	9th R. In. Fus.	Wounded.
Morris, J. H.	Tullyrush	Private	1st R. In. Fus.	Killed in Action.
Noble, Alfred	Seskinore	Private	12th R. In. Fus.	Killed in Action.
Perry, William	Tullyrush	Sergeant	Canadian Regt.	
Riddell, James	Letfern	Corporal	12th R. In. Fus.	M.M. Wounded 3 times.

OMAGH PRESBYTERY.   SESKINORE.

Name.	Home Address.	Rank.	Regiment, Battalion or Unit.	Remarks.
Waddell, Andrew	Tullyrush	Warrant Officer	R.E.	
Waddell, George	Tullyrush	Private	2nd C. Regiment	Killed in Action.
Waddell, Samuel	Tullyrush	Private	1st R. In. Fus.	Killed in Action.
Young, Andrew	Tallyreagh	Private	Tank Corps	
Young, Jack	Tallyreagh	Private	38th Engineers	
SIXMILECROSS.				
Ashfield, George	Sixmilecross	Private	9th R. In. Fus.	Died of Wounds.
Ashfield, John	Sixmilecross	Private	R. In. Fus.	Pris. in Germany.
Ashfield, Joseph	Sixmilecross	Private	R. In. Fus.	Killed in Action.
Ashfield, Theophilus	Sixmilecross	Trooper	N.I.H.	Wounded.
Ashfield, Thomas	Cloghfin	Co. Sergt.-Major	9th R. In. Fus.	Wounded 3 times.
Ashfield, William James	Sixmilecross	Private	R. In. Fus.	Twice Wounded. Prisoner.
Chambers, Alexander	Sixmilecross	Private	9th R. In. Fus.	
Clements, John	Sixmilecross	Captain	R.A.M.C.	
Clements, Max	Beragh	Captain	R.A.M.C.	
Crawford, R. J.	Usnagh, Beragh	Private	9th R. In. Fus.	Killed in Action.
Crawford, Samuel	Sixmilecross	Sergeant	9th R. In. Fus.	M.M.
Ewings, John	Sixmilecross	Private	9th R. In. Fus.	Wounded.
Ewings, Joseph	Sixmilecross	Private	R. In. Fus.	Killed in Action.
Gibson, James	Redergan, Beragh	Private	9th R. In. Fus.	
Hilliare, Herbert	Remackin	Private	R. In. Fus.	Wounded.
Hilliare, Joseph	Ballintrain	Private	R. In. Fus.	
Junk, William	Sixmilecross	Private	R.A.F.	
Kyle, Thomas	Tanderagee	Private	R.A.F.	Died at Malta.
MacLaughlin, W. J.	Sixmilecross	Lieutenant	R.I.R.	Wounded.
Marshall, Fred.	Sixmilecross	Private	R.M. Fus.	Killed in Action.
Pauley, Thomas	Sixmilecross	Private	R. In. Fus.	
COLONIAL AND U.S.A. FORCES.				
Anderson, Henry	Cloghfin	Private	U.S.A.	
Anderson, George	Tyrooney	Lance-Corporal	Australians	Pris. in Germany.
Gillespie, James	Ballintrain	Private	N.Z. Contingent	Twice Wounded.
Robinson, Rankin	Cavanreagh	Sapper	N.Z. Contingent	
Forbes, James	Cooley	Private	U.S.A.	
Managh, Robert	Ballintrain	Private	N.Z. Contingent	

RAPHOE PRESBYTERY.

Name.	Home Address.	Rank.	Regiment, Battalion or Unit.	Remarks.
ALT.				
Barr, Tom	Alt	Private	A.S.C.	
Bogle, Joseph	Mullanbuoy	Private	Coldstream Guards	
Bogle, Robert	Mullanbuoy	Private	Coldstream Guards	Killed.
Donnell, Albert E.	Gortkelly	Gunner	S.A. Heavy Artillery	
Gilchrist, Saml.	Alt	Private	R. Inn. Fus.	Killed.
Harpur, John J. T.	Drumdoit	Sergeant	South Irish Horse	
Kerrigan, John	Mullanbuoy	Private	R. Inn. Fus.	Killed.
Wilson, John	Gortnamuck	Private	Canadian Queen's Rifles	Killed.
BALLINDRAIT.				
Blair, Alex. H.	Keelogs	Lieutenant	R.E.	
Blair, Andrew	Ardnaglass	Private	N.I.H.	
Buchanan, Robert	Argery	Private	R. Inn. Fus.	
Divin, Andrew	Ballindrait	Private	R. Inn. Fus.	
Gourley, David	Shannon	Private	R. Inn. Fus.	Wounded.
Gourley, John	Shannon	Private	R. Inn. Fus.	Killed in Action.
Gourley, Robert	Tober	Private	R. Inn. Fus.	
Guy, J. McF.	The Manse	Engineer	R.N.	
Guy, W. G. S.	The Manse	Lance-Corporal	Canadians	Wounded.
Guy, S. Thomas	The Manse	Lance-Corporal	M.T. Service	
Holmes, Alex.	Ballindrait	Private	R. Inn. Fus.	
Macbeth, Wm.	Monien	Sergeant	R. Inn. Fus.	Killed in Action.
McFarland, Andrew	Clonleigh	Private	R. Inn. Fus.	Wounded.
McGonigal, J.	Ballindrait		Mine-sweeper	
Quinton, Henry	Ballindrait	Private	Transport Service	Killed.
Roulston, Thomas	Cavan, Ballindrait	Private	R. Inn. Fus.	Killed in Action.
Smith, Matthew	Clonleigh	Private	Labour Batt.	
Snodgrass, Quinton	Murlog	Cadet		

RAPHOE PRESBYTERY. BALLINDRAIT.

Name.	Home Address.	Rank.	Regiment, Battalion or Unit.	Remarks.
Snodgrass, Rae	Murlog	Captain	R.A.M.C.	M.C.
Weir, Chas. D.	Park	Captain	Royal Lancers	M.C.
Weir, John	Drumbuoy	Captain	R. Inn. Fus.	Killed in Action.
Wray, William	Porthall	Private	R. Inn. Fus.	Wounded 3 times.
BALLYLENNON.				
Cooke, David	Craigadoish	Private	R.A.S.C.	
Cooke, Robert	Craigadoish	Lance-Corporal	Cameron Highldrs.	
Crawford, Andrew	Craigadoish	Private	Seaforth Highldrs.	Wounded.
Dunn, Andrew	Castletown	Private	11th R. Inn. Fus.	Killed in Action.
Dunn, William	Craigadoish	Private	11th R. Inn. Fus.	
Galbraith, Hugh	Carrickadawson	Private	11th R. Inn. Fus.	Prisoner.
Galbraith, John	Carrickadawson	Private	11th R. Inn. Fus.	Killed in Action.
Galbraith, Thomas	Ballylennon	Private	11th R. Inn. Fus.	Wounded.
Gourley, James	Carnshanagh	Lance-Corporal	11th R. Inn. Fus.	Killed in Action.
Gourley, Joseph	Carnshanagh	2nd Lieutenant	R. Inn. Dragoons	Wounded.
Kinkaid, Joseph	Ballylennon	Private	R.F.A.	
Lecky, John	Feddyglass	2nd Lieutenant	R.I.R.	Killed in Action.
McCausland, Joseph	Lettergall	Captain	R.A.M.C.	
McCausland, Samuel	Lettergall	Major	R.A.M.C.	M.C.
Porterfield, Alex.	Ballylennon	Sergeant	11th R. Inn. Fus.	Croix-de-Guerre, Died of Wounds.
Robinson, Ernest	Drumenon	Eng. Artificer	R.N.	Killed in Action.
Robinson, Joseph	Drumenon	2nd Lieutenant	11th R. Inn. Fus.	
Wilkie, Wm. A.	Ballyboe	Private	11th R. Inn. Fus.	
COLONIAL FORCES.				
Cooke, Samuel	Craigadoish	Sergeant	Can. L. Horse	
Cooke, Wm.	Craigadoish	Private	Can. M.G.C.	
McCobb, George	Woodland	Private	Australian Force	
CARNONE.				
Bates, David R.	Carnowen	Lieutenant	R.I.R.	
Bates, William	Carnowen	Private	Can. F.A.	
Harper, Robert T.	Carnowen	Private	R.I. Fus.	Wounded.
Harper, Wm. J.	Greenhill, Convoy	Private	116th Canadians	
Wallace, Thomas	Carnowen	Private		
Woods, John A.	Carnowen	Private	11th R.I.F.	
CONVOY.				
Allison, Archibald			R.N.	
Allison, David	Convoy		R.N.	Died.
Barrowman, John		Gunner	R.G.A.	
Barrowman, R. S.		Lieutenant	R. Inn. Fus.	M.C., Wounded.
Boal, John	Trentabuoy	Private	R. Inn. Fus.	
Burke, James H.	Calhame	Private	R. Inn. Fus.	
Caldwell, David	Convoy	A.M.	R.A.F.	
Cooke, Jas. Alex.	Convoy	Private	R. Inn. Fus.	Wounded.
Cowan, Alexander		Private	H.L.I.	Killed in Action.
Daisley, Thomas J.	Callin, Drumkeen	Private	R. Inn. Fus.	Wounded.
Daisley, Wm. J.	Callin, Drumkeen	Private	R. Inn. Fus.	Killed in Action.
Ewing, Wm.	Knockagarron	Private	M.T.S.	
Gallagher, James L.		Gunner	R.G.A.	
Gallagher, Thomas		Private	North Lancs.	Wounded.
Holmes, John	Convoy	Lieutenant	Yorkshire Regt.	
Holmes, R. J.	Convoy	Corporal	Black Watch	Wounded.
Hunter, William	Convoy	Corporal	Irish Guards	Wounded.
Malcolm, David	Agheygalt	Private	R. Inn. Fus.	Wounded.
McBride, Matthew	Kiltoal	Private	R. Inn. Fus.	Wounded.
McBride, Thomas	Kiltoal	Corporal	R. Inn. Fus.	Killed in Action.
McClure, David		Private	H.L.I.	
McClure, John		Private	R. Inn. Fus.	Wounded.
McClure, Robert		Private	R.G.A.	
McClure, Thos. J.		Sergeant	R.G.A.	D.C.M., M.M.
McConaghey, T. R.	Ruskey	Private	R.A.F.	
McConnell, James	Kiltoal	Private	R. Inn. Fus.	Wounded.
McKnight, James	Milltown	Private	R. Inn. Fus.	
McKnight, John	Milltown	Gunner	R.G.A.	
Roy, Joseph I.	Convoy	Lance-Corporal	R. Inn. Fus.	Wounded.
Shanklin, G. J.	Finnydurk	Captain	R.A.M.C.	
Wilson, James	Milltown	Private	R.E.	
COLONIAL AND U.S.A. FORCES.				
Gilchrist, John	Priestown	Private	S. African Inft.	
McBride, David	Kiltoal	Private	U.S. Army	
McBride, Robert	Kiltoal	Private	U.S. Army	Wounded.
Wilson, John G.		Private	Canadian Inft.	Wounded.

RAPHOE PRESBYTERY.   DONOUGHMORE.

Name.	Home Address.	Rank.	Regiment, Battalion or Unit.	Remarks.
DONOUGHMORE.				
Alexander, James	Castlefinn	Private	R.A.S.C.	
Baird, Galbraith	...	Private	11th R. Inn. Fus.	Killed in Action.
Black, Archibald	Adelaide, W. Australia	Private	11th R. Inn. Fus.	
Calderwood, Hugh	Castlefin	Sergeant	15th R.I.R.	Wounded.
Carson, Solomon	...	Private	11th R. Inn. Fus.	Wounded.
Carson, William	...	Private	11th R. Inn. Fus.	Killed in Action.
Coventry, Jack	Castlefinn	Private	11th R. Inn. Fus.	Killed in Action.
Coventry, Robert	Castlefinn	Private	3rd R. Inn. Fus.	Killed in Action.
Crawford, Thomas	...	Private	11th R. Inn. Fus.	
Elliott, Charles R.	Portrush	Colonel	R.A.M.C.	
Elliott, John	Drummurphy	Private	...	
Hamilton, James	Donoughmore House	Major	R.A.M.C.	
Holmes, James	Ballinacor	Private	11th R. Inn. Fus.	Killed in Action.
Kee, James	Ballinacor	Private	11th R. Inn. Fus.	
Long, Matthew	Killygordon	Private	...	
Lyttle, John	Killygordon	Private	...	
Lyttle, Matthew	Killygordon	Private	...	
McCullagh, Sandy	Ballinacor	Private	11th R. Inn. Fus.	Killed in Action.
McDermott, Samuel	Castlefinn	Captain	R.G.A.	
McKinlay, Alex.	Sessaghmore	Sergeant	N.I.H.	Wounded.
McKinlay, Archie	Sessaghmore	Cadet	R.N.	
McKinlay, Robert	Sessaghmore	Captain	R.A.M.C.	
Mortland, Joseph R.	Castlefinn	Private	3rd R. Inn. Fus.	Died of Wounds.
Mortland, Samuel	Castlefinn	Private	N.I.H.	
Patterson, Samuel J.	Killygordon	Private	R.A.F.	
Rodgers, Edmund	Killygordon	Private	...	
Roulston, Robert G.	Killygordon	Sergt.-Major	I.G.	
Rule, George	Gleneely	Private	R.A.F.	
Rule, Samuel	Gleneely	Private	R.A.F.	
Taylor, Andrew	Castlefinn	Sergeant	11th R. Inn. Fus.	
Taylor, Samuel	Castlefinn	Lieutenant	N.I.H.	
Wray, Hugh	Killygordon	Private	I. Guards	
COLONIAL FORCES.				
Baird, Alex.	...	Private	Australian Ex. Force	Wounded.
Black, James	Castlefinn	Private	Can. Ex. Force	
Crawford, James	Castlefinn	Private	Australian Imp. Force	Killed in Action.
Guthrie, Robert	Adelaide, W. Australia	Private	Australian Ex. Force	
Kincaid, William	...	Private	Canadian Ex. Force	
McCreary, Robert S.	Adelaide, W.A.	Private	Australian Imp. Force	
McCreary, Samuel	The Cross, Killygordon	Private	Canadian Ex. Force	Killed in training.
McCurdy, George	Meenahoney	Private	Australian Imperial Force	Killed in Action.
Moore, Samuel	Castlefinn	Private	Canadian Ex. Force	
Nelson, Jack	Castlefinn	...	Canadian Ex. Force	Wounded.
Wisely, John	Killygordon	Sergeant	Canadian Ex. Force	
Woods, Bertie	Killygordon	Private	Canadian Ex. Force	Killed in Action.
NEWTOWNCUNNINGHAM.				
Boal, Archibald	Moneymore	Trooper	Inn Dragoons	
Gardiner, Charles	Carrigans	Private	44th Battery R.F.A.	
Gardiner, Robert	Carrigans	Private	9th R. Inn. Fus.	
Gibson, John	Dooish	Private	11th R. Inn. Fus.	
Glenn, David	Moyle	Corporal	11th R. Inn. Fus.	Croix-de-Guerre.
Glen, James A.	Moyle Hill	Captain	R.G.A.	
Glenn, John J.	Moneymore	Captain	A.S.C.	Wounded.
Hunter, Matthew	Toulette	Trooper	Inn Dragoons	
Knowles, John	Newtowncunningham	C.F., 4th Class	...	
Law, Joseph	Drumbarnett	Private	R. Inn. Fus.	Wounded.
McKeever, William	Dooish	Sergeant	R.A.F.	
Roulstone, Robert	Gortree	Sergeant	11th R. Inn. Fus.	M.M.
Taylor, William	Ballyhaskey	Private	R. Inn. Fus.	
Walker, Samuel	Newtowncunningham	Corporal	11th R. Inn. Fus.	Wounded.
Watson, William	Moneygreggan	Private	11th R. Inn. Fus.	Discharged Sick.
Wilson, Thomas	Crieve	Gunner	154th Battery R.G.A.	
COLONIAL FORCES.				
Dunlop, John James	Lusticle	Driver	M.T. 2nd Aust. Div.	
Hunter, James	Dooish	Corporal	107th Batt. Can. Pioneers	
FIRST RAPHOE.				
Allen, Joseph	Craigs	Corporal	11th R.I. Fus.	Died of Wounds.
Baxter, William	Meeting-house Street	Staff Sergeant	Field Am., Egypt	
Doherty, Thomas	Glenmaquin	Corporal	Black Watch	
Hall, John	Drumucklagh	Sergeant	10th R.I. Fus.	
King, Basil	William Street	Private	R.A.F.	
King, William	William Street	Private	R.A.S.C.	
Laird, William	Cloughfin	2nd Lieutenant	9th R.I. Fus.	M.C. and bar.
McClay, James	Magheraboy	Private	11th R.I. Fus.	Wounded.

RAPHOE PRESBYTERY.

FIRST RAPHOE.

Name.	Home Address.	Rank.	Regiment, Battalion or Unit.	Remarks.
McClay, Samuel	Sheeplane	Lance-Corporal	M. Police	
McClay, Thomas	McBride Street	Private	9th R.I. Fus.	
McKnight, David	Glenmaquin	Private	7th R.I. Fus.	
McKnight, George	Meeting-house Street	Corporal	R.E.	Wounded.
McKnight, James	Ruskey	Lance-Corporal	11th R.I. Fus.	Killed in Action.
McKnight, John	Oakfield	Private	2nd Scots Guards	Wounded.
McKnight, Robert	Ruskey	Private	9th R.I. Fus.	Killed in Action.
Moody, Robert	Drumatoland	Lance-Corporal	N.I.H.	Wounded.
Parker, Jack	Irish Street	Private	2nd R.I. Fus.	
Porter, Joseph	Ardvarnock	Private	11th R.I. Fus.	
Smith, Andrew	Convoy	Corporal	9th R.I. Fus.	Killed in Action.
Smith, Ezekiel	Convoy	Corporal	9th R.I. Fus.	Killed in Action.
Welsh, James	Lismontigley	Lance-Corporal	9th R.I. Fus.	Wounded.
Wilkie, Wm.	Ballyholey	Private	3rd R.I. Fus.	Wounded.
Woods, John	Meeting-house Street	Private	9th R.I. Fus.	Wounded.
COLONIAL AND U.S.A. FORCES.				
Baxter, Harry	Meeting-house Street	Corporal	Can. Field Artillery	
Baxter, James	Meeting-house Street	Private	16th Australians	
Hyndman, Thomas	Oakfield	Private	American Army	
King, Jack	William Street	Corporal	Can. Inft.	
McLean, Thomas J.	Creggan	Private	9th Can. F.A.	
Parker, Joseph	Irish Street	Private	4th N.Z.	
ST. JOHNSTON.				
Allen, James	St. Johnston	Captain		
Callan, William	St. Johnston	Private	11th Batt. Inn. Fus.	
Galbraith, John	St. Johnston	Private	11th Batt. Inn. Fus.	Killed in Action.
Hamilton, Thomas	St. Johnston	Corporal	Machine Gun Corps	Wounded.
Jackson, John	St. Johnston	Private		
Jackson, William	St. Johnston			
Jackson, Robert	St. Johnston			
Laird, William	St. Johnston			
Logan, William	St. Johnston	Private	Labour Comp.	
Magee, William	St. Johnston	Private	11th Inn. Fus.	Wounded.
Magee, Thomas	St. Johnston	Private	11th Inn. Fus.	Wounded.
Millar, William	Carrigans			
McClellan, Thomas	Carrigans			Killed in Action.
McKeever, William		Sergeant	12th Inn. Fus.	
McLaughlin, Alexander	St. Johnston	Sergeant		Killed in Action.
McLaughlin, James	St. Johnston			
McLaughlin, John	St. Johnston	Corporal	Royal Irish Rifles	
McLaughlin, Joseph	St. Johnston	Q.M.S.	R.G.A.	M.M.
McLaughlin, William	St. Johnston	Corporal	R.E.	Ment. in D'patches, Died of Wounds.
Parke, Matthew	St. Johnston			
Porter, William	St. Johnston			
Quigley, James	St. Johnston			Killed in Action.
Radcliffe, John	St. Johnston	Private	2nd Inn. Fus.	Wounded.
Radcliffe, Joseph	St. Johnston	Private	9th Inn. Fus.	M.M.
Radcliffe, Thomas R.	St. Johnston	Private	11th Inn. Fus.	
Radcliffe, William	St. Johnston	Corporal	R. Inn. Fus.	Wounded.
Roulston, David	St. Johnston			
Roulston, John	St. Johnston			
Roulston, John	Carrigans			
Roulston, William G.	St. Johnston			
Rutherford, John	St. Johnston	Corporal	11th Inn. Fus.	
Rutherford, Samuel	St. Johnston	Private	11th Inn. Fus.	
Stephenson, John	St. Johnston	Private	11th Inn. Fus	
White, Robert	St. Johnston	Private	R.A.M.C.	
Wilson, Alan	St. Johnston	Corporal	11th Inn. Fus.	Wounded.

RATHFRILAND PRESBYTERY.

Name.	Home Address.	Rank.	Regiment, Battalion or Unit.	Remarks.
BALLYRONEY.				
Clydesdale, David	Seafin	Private	R.F.A.	Died.
Copes, Thos. James	Ballyroney	Lance-Corporal	R.I.R.	Killed in Action.
Cromie, Harry	Church Hill	Private	4th Hussars	Wounded thrice.
Cromie, James	Magheral			
Crorie, William	Drumadonald		Red Cross Amb. Corps	

RATHFRILAND PRESBYTERY. BALLYRONEY.

Name.	Home Address.	Rank.	Regiment, Battalion or Unit.	Remarks.
Davis, Wm. J.	Lakeview House	Corporal	M.M. Gun Corps	
Green, M.	Katesbridge	Private	Irish Guards	
Ingram, Arthur F.	Rathfriland	Lieutenant	R.A.F.	Wounded.
Kerr, Joseph Alex.				
Knox, John	Tierkelly	2nd Lieutenant	14th R.I.R.	M.C., Kd. in Act.
Ledlie, Robert	Airdrie, Scotland	Sergeant	Kilties	Gassed.
Ledlie, Wm. Hugh	Ballyroney		R.A.M.C.	
Mark, Fred. David	Ballybrick		R.E.	
Mawhinney, John	Lacken	Gunner	R.F.A.	Wounded.
Mawhinney, Wm.	Lacken	Private	R.I.R.	Wounded 3 times.
Moffatt, Archibald	Ballyroney	Private	R.I.R.	Wounded, Died.
Moffatt, Hugh John	Ballyroney	Private		Wounded.
Montgomery, Andrew	Ballyroney	Private		
Murphy, J. H.	Ballymacaraney		R.N.A.S.	
Park, Robert	Aughnavallog	Rifleman	R.I.R.	
Priestly, George	Drumadonald	Private	4th R. Inn. Fus.	Wounded, Ypres.
Reid, Edgar	Ballyroney	Captain	Shrop. L. Inft.	Prisoner.
Reid, Mayne	Ballyroney	Corporal Mechanic	R.N.A.S.	D.F.M.
Roy, Matthew	Lacken	Private	R.I.R.	
Russell, Wm.	Ballyward	Private	I. Guards	
Scott, David	Ballyward	Lance-Corporal	E. Lanc. Regt.	Wounded, lung taken out.
Scott, George	Ballyward	Rifleman	R.I.R.	Wounded.
Scott, John A.	Ballyward	Lance-Corporal	R.I.R.	Died U.V.F. Hosp.
Small, Wm. C.	Seafin	Lance-Corporal	9th R.I.R.	Killed, Messines.
Stewart, Herbert R.	Gargary	2nd Lieutenant	Oxford & Bucks. L.I.	
Strain, John	Lacken	Gunner	A. Battery, C.R.A.	
Strain, Robert James	Drumadonald	Private	R.A.S.C.	
Watt, Herbert Boyd	Magheral		N.I. Horse	
Watt, Wm.	Ballyroney	Rifleman	36th Ulster Div.	
Watt, Willie	Ballyroney	Private	11th R.I.R.	
Wilson, John	Lacken	Private	H.L. Inft.	Killed in Action.
Young, James	Seafin	Cadet		
Young, Robt. Alex., B.A.	Seafin	2nd Lieutenant	I. Guards	Wounded. Somme.
Young, Wm. John	Ballyroney	Rifleman	R.I.R.	Killed, Messines.
COLONIAL AND U.S.A. FORCES.				
Bell, Charles D.	Seafin	Gunner	Can. Res. Art.	
Cupples, Archie	Ballyroney	Sergeant	Can. Army	
Ledlie, Geo. Charles	Ballyroney	Private	Can. Army	
Martin, Albert D.	Annahinchago	Private	Field Sig., U.S.A.	
Martin, S. J.	Tierkelly	Private	S. African Force	Wounded.
Spiers, Thomas	Annahinchago	Private	U.S. Inft.	
Wilson, Robert	Toronto		Can. B.E.F.	Wounded.
BROOKVALE.				
Cromie, Thos.	Lisnacreevy	Private	R.I.R.	Escaped Prisoner
Cromie, William	Millvale	Lieutenant	R.A.S.C.	
Edgar, John, M.A.	Emdale	Private	Can. Amb. Corps	
Ervine, John	Ednagarry	Private	R.I.R.	
Gilmore, Samuel	Ballinamagna	Sergeant	R.I.R.	
McKnight, Frank	Rathfriland	Lance-Corporal	Aust. Inft.	Wounded.
Scott, William	Aughnavallog	Private	R.I.R.	Killed in Action.
Watt, James	Grallagh	Driver	Motor Transport	Killed.
Watt, John	Grallagh	Private	R.I.R.	
Watt, Wm.	Grallagh	Trooper	N.I.H.	M.M.
Wilson, John	Lissize	Gunner	H.M. Destroyer	
Wilson, Samuel	Lissize	Private	R.I.R.	Gassed.
CASTLEWELLAN.				
Bell, Richard	Castlewellan	Rifleman	13th R.I.R.	Wounded.
Blackwood, George	Castlewellan	Lance-Corporal	13th R.I.R.	
Cinnimond, Wm.	Kilmegan	Rifleman	9th R.I.R.	Wounded.
Donnan, Wm.	Annsboro'	Sergeant	13th R.I.R.	Prisoner.
Hamilton, Robert	Annsboro'	Rifleman	13th R.I.R.	Prisoner.
Jeffrey, Thos.	Annsboro'	Rifleman	17th R.I.R.	Wounded.
Johnston, John	Clonduff	Trooper	N.I.H.	
Jones, James	Ballymagreehan	Corporal	R.E.	
Jones, Samuel	Ballymagreehan	Stoker	R.N.	Died at Sea.
Lewis, John	Castlewellan	Rifleman	4th R.I.R.	
Lutton, Joseph	Castlewellan	Rifleman	13th R.I.R.	
Lyttle, Samuel	Castlewellan	Rifleman	19th R.I.R.	Prisoner.
McCracken, Samuel	Annsboro'	Rifleman	13th R.I.R.	
McNeilly, Wm. A.	Tullymore	Trooper	N.I.H.	Wounded.
Martin, David	Annsboro'	Rifleman	13th R.I.R.	
Nelson, Stephen	Castlewellan	Sergeant	13th R.I.R.	M.S. Medal.
Parker, Robert	Annsboro'	Rifleman	13th R.I.R.	
Parker, Walter	Annsboro,	Rifleman	13th R.I.R.	
Peters, Robert	Castlewellan	Rifleman	3rd Black Watch	Wounded.
Peters, Samuel	Castlewellan	Rifleman	2nd R.S.F.	Wounded.
Priestly, Wm.	Ballylough	Corporal	13th R.I.R.	Wounded.

RATHFRILAND PRESBYTERY. — CASTLEWELLAN.

Name.	Home Address.	Rank.	Regiment, Battalion or Unit.	Remarks.
Quinn, Alex.	Ballybannon	Rifleman	13th R.I.R.	Killed in Action.
Quinn, Thomas	Ballybannon	Rifleman	13th R.I.R.	Died of Wounds.
Richmond, Wm.	Annsboro'	Trooper	N.I.H.	
Thompson, Geo.	Castlewellan	Lance-Corporal	13th R.I.R.	Killed in Action.
Thompson, Ross	Castlewellan	Lance-Corporal	13th R.I.R.	Wounded.
Walsh, John	Annsboro'	Sergeant	1st K.O.Y.L.I.	Wounded, D.C.M.
Wright, Edward	Annsboro'	Q.M. Sergeant	13th R.I.R.	Wounded.
Wright, Herbert	Annsboro'	2nd Lieutenant	16th R.I.R.	
COLONIAL FORCE.				
Campbell, Samuel	Ballylough	Rifleman	11th Reserve Can.	
Hull, Harry	Annsboro'	Sergeant	5th P.P. Can. L. Inft.	Wounded.
Priestly, James	Ballylough	Sergeant	Win. Grenadiers	Wounded.
Shaw, Wm.	Clarkhill	Sergeant	1st Can. Pioneers	Wounded.
CLONDUFF.				
Adams, Charles	Ballynagappoge	Private	236th C.E.F.	
Henning, Matthew	Cabra	Private	S.I.H.	
Johnston, John	Moneygore	Private	N.I.H.	
McNeilly, Wm.	Lisnisk	Private	2nd K's. L. Regt.	
Newell, Joseph	Drumdrinagh	Private	4th Can. L. Batt.	
DRUMGOOLAND.				
Dickson, John	Drumadonald	Private	Irish Rifles	Wounded.
Malcomson, Richard	Drumadonald	Private	N.I.H.	Wounded twice.
Megaffin, James	Closkelt	Private	N.I.H.	Pris. in Germany.
McKee, Thomas	Drumadonald	Private	Irish Rifles	
Porter, Joseph, M.B.	Moneyslane	Captain	R.A.M.C.	
COLONIAL AND U.S.A. FORCES.				
Boyd, Paxton	Ballymacarainey	Private	American Force	
Cochrane, Alex.	Dechomet	Private	Canadian Force	Killed in Action.
Dickson, John	Drumadonald	Private	New Zealand Force	
Dickson, William	Drumadonald	Private	New Zealand Force	
Loughlin, Edwin	Dechomet	Private	Canadian Force	
Malcomson, Samuel	Closkelt	Private	Canadian Pioneers	
Megaffin, Hugh	Closkelt	Private	Canadian Force	Twice Wounded.
Morrison, Robert	Moneyslane	Private	American Force	
McBurney, Sandy		Private	Canadian Force	
McNeilly, Robert	Moneyslane	Private	American Force	
McNeilly, Samuel	Derryneil	Private	American Force	
Nicholl, Arthur			Canadian Force	
Redmond, John	Gransha, Dromara	Private	American Force	
DRUMLEE.				
Beattie, Robert	Annahinchago	Private	U.S. Army	
Beer, Henry Wm.	Ardaghy	Private	London Regt.	Wounded.
Buchanan, James Herbert	Ballyward	Lieutenant	R.I.R.	Killed in Action.
Dalzell, Alex.	Drumlee	Private	R.I.R.	
Dalzell, George	Drumlee	Private	R.I.R.	Wounded.
Dalzell, Joseph	Drumlee	Private	R.I.R.	Wounded.
Dalzell, Rowan	Drumlee	Private	R.I.F.	Killed in Action.
Dalzell, Wm.	Drumlee	Sergeant	R.I.F.	Killed in Action.
Gibson, Robert	Bryansford	Private	R.I.R.	Killed in Action.
Moffatt, Hugh John	Ballyward	Private	R. Inn. Fus.	Wounded.
Rowan, John	Gargory	Private	Australian Forces	Killed in Action.
Scott, George	Ballyward	Private	R.I.R.	Wounded.
Skelly, John	Gargory	Private	U.S. Army	Killed in Action.
Skillen, William	Clanawhillan	Private	N.I.H.	Wounded.
Small, James	Gargory	Private	R.I.R.	Wounded.
Small, John	Gargory	Private	R.I.R	
Spiers, James	Clenmaghery	Sergeant	Canadian Forces	Wounded.
Weir, James	Gargory	Lance-Corporal	R.I.R.	Killed in Action.
Weir, William	Gargory	Private	R.I.R.	
HILLTOWN.				
Brown, Geoffrey	Lisnamulligan	Private	R.I.R.	
Campbell, Samuel	Lisnamulligan	Private	R.I.R.	
Hall, William	Ballyaughian	Private	R.I.R.	
Woods, Walter	Ballygorrian	Private	Ulster Division	Killed in Action.
KILKINAMURRY.				
Johnston, William	Shanaghan	Lance-Corporal	17th R.I. Rifles	Wounded.
McMurray, Joseph	Enoch, Banbridge	Private	M.T. A.S.C.	M.M.
Malcomson, John	Gransha, Dromara	Gunner	R.G.A.	Wounded.

RATHFRILAND PRESBYTERY.   LEITRIM.

Name.	Home Address.	Rank.	Regiment, Battalion or Unit.	Remarks.
LEITRIM.				
McCoubrie, Francis	Derryneil	Lance-Corporal	5th R.I.R.	Killed in Action.
McCracken, Thomas	Slievenaboley	Lance-Corporal	5th R.I.R.	
McGregor, John A.	Derryneil	Private	17th R.I.R.	
COLONIAL AND U.S.A. FORCES.				
Campbell, Robert John	...	Lance-Corporal	319th A.F.A. Ex. F.	
Campbell, Samuel	...	Private	14th Battery Canadians	
Campbell, William	...	Private	5th Batt. Canadians	
Lowry, Charles Loftus	...	Private	U.S. Army	
Lowry, Thomas	...	...	Can. Light Inft.	Twice Wounded.
Lowry, William	...	...	F.A., U.S.A. Ex. Force	
NEWCASTLE.				
Bradford, Robert	Newcastle	Petty Officer	R.N.	
Bradford, Thomas	Newcastle	Private	R.A.F.	
Dodds, Thomas	Newcastle	Private	S. African Army	Died of Wounds.
Drennen, Robert	Newcastle	Private	R.A.M.C.	
Geddis, James	Newcastle	Private	R.I.R.	
Geddis, Joseph	Newcastle	Sergeant	R.I.R.	Died.
Heron, Robert	Newcastle	Private	N.I.H.	
McCaughey, Robert	Newcastle	Private	R.I.R.	Wounded.
McCullough, George	Newcastle	Private	R.I.R.	Wounded.
McSpadden, Wm.	Newcastle	Private	R.I.R.	Wounded.
Magill, Joseph	Newcastle	Captain	R.A.V.C.	
Magill, Robert	Newcastle	Colonel	R.A.M.C.	
Skillen, Nevin	Newcastle	Private	R.I.R.	Wounded.
Smyth, David	Newcastle	Private	R.I.R.	Wounded.
Smyth, Donard	Newcastle	Lieutenant	R.I.R.	Killed in Action.
Woods, Robert	Newcastle	Private	R.I.R.	
FIRST RATHFRILAND.				
Adams, James Beattie	Moneygore	Sergeant	R.A.S.C.	
Foster, Hugh John	Lurgancahone	Private	13th R.I.R.	Wounded and Pris.
Hart, Thos. Carlyle	Tierfergus	Private	19th R.I.R.	Drowned at Sea.
Lyttle, Joseph	Drumlough	Private	11/13th R.I.R.	Wounded.
McKnight, Joseph	Aughnavallog	Private	7th Reserve Artillery	
McKnight, Wm. John	Aughnavallog	Lance-Corporal	R.I.R.	Wounded, M.M.
Ross, Robert S.	Aughnavallog	Captain	R.A.M.C., R.F.A.	Wounded, M.C., Ment. in Desp.
COLONIAL AND U.S.A. FORCES.				
Foster, John	Rathfriland	Private	4th S. Africans	Wounded and Pris.
Foster, Samuel Annett	Rathfriland	Private	4th S. Africans	Killed in Action.
Foster, Matthew Small	Rathfriland	Private	4th S. Africans	Wounded.
McKnight, George	Aughnavallog	Private	American E.F.	
Smyth, Wm. G.	Dundrinagh	Sergeant	5th Canadians	
Weir, George	Lurgancahone	Private	R.C. Engineers	
SECOND RATHFRILAND.				
Graham, James	Aughnavallog	Corporal	M.T. A.S.C.	
Hall, J. J.	Downpatrick Street	Sergeant	20th R.I.R.	
Stranahan, Robert	Drumdrinagh	Corporal	R. Inn. Fus.	Died of Wounds.
Thompson, Andrew	Downpatrick Street	Sergeant	13th R.I.R.	
THIRD RATHFRILAND.				
Annett, Alex.	Rathfriland	Lance-Corporal	R.I. Rifles	
Annett, John	Rathfriland	Sergt.-Major	R.I. Fus.	
Cowper, W. H.	Rathfriland	2nd Lieutenant	R.I. Regt.	Wounded.
Elliott, J. H.	Rathfriland	Captain	R.A.M.C.	M.C.
Elliott, J. M.	Rathfriland	Captain	R.A.M.C.	
Elliott, W. H.	Rathfriland	Captain	R.A.M.C.	
Fryar, Hugh	Rathfriland	Private	R.I. Rifles	
Fryar, James	Rathfriland	Private	R.E.	
Geddis, Robert	Rathfriland	Private	R.I.F.	Killed in Action.
Graham, Samuel	Kiltariff	Private	Motor Transport	
Henning, Herbert	Rathfriland	Private	Yorkshire Regt.	Wounded.
Hudson, J. E.	Rathfriland	Sergeant	R.E	
Hudson, John C.	Rathfriland	Lieutenant	A.S.C.	
Hudson, H. Q.	Rathfriland	Sergeant	Tank Corps	
Hudson, R. K.	Rathfriland	Lance-Corporal	Training Reserve	
Hudson, R. J.	Rathfriland	Driver	Red Cross Service	
McAnuff, R.	Rathfriland	Lance-Corporal	R.I. Rifles	
McComb, John	Rathfriland	Private	Labour Company	
McKnight, T.	Rathfriland	Private	R.I. Rifles	
McNeilley, Alexander	Rathfriland	Private	R.I. Rifles	
Rowney, Alfred	Rathfriland	Private	R.I. Fus.	

RATHFRILAND PRESBYTERY.   THIRD RATHFRILAND.

Name.	Home Address.	Rank.	Regiment, Battalion or Unit.	Remarks.
	COLONIAL FORCES.			
Campbell, John	Rathfriland	Private	Can. R.A.M.C.	
Herron, W. W. M.	Rathfriland	Private	1st Canadians	
Kirk, Frank	Rathfriland	Private	S.A. Field Force	

Route Presbytery.

Name.	Home Address.	Rank.	Regiment, Battalion or Unit.	Remarks.
	ARMOY.			
Boyle, James	Ballybregagh	Private	H.L.I.	
Campbell, Samuel	Mullaghduff	Private	R.G.A.	
Connolly, George	Armoy	Carpenters' Crew	R.N.	
Connolly, John H.	Armoy	Private	R.F.A.	
Connolly, Robert J.	Drumdollagh	Private	Scottish Rifles	Wounded.
Ferguson, Samuel	Balleney	Private	N.I.H.	
Gibson, Alexander	Mullaghduff	Private	R.I.R.	Killed in Action.
Gibson, Robert	Park	Private	R.I.R.	Pris. in Germany.
Hamill, Alexander	Park	Private	Motor Transport	
Hartin, Robinson	Knocknahinch	Lance-Corporal	R.I.R.	Pris. in Germany.
Higgarty, Frank	Park	Private	R.I.R.	Killed in Action.
McCloy, Alexander	Ballybregagh	Staff-Surgeon	R.N.	
McGarry, Samuel	Park	Private	R.I.R.	
McKay, George	Moyaver	Private	R.I.R.	Pris. in Germany.
McLean, George	Clintyfinnin	Private	R.I.R.	Killed in Action.
McMillan, Joseph	Ballybregagh	Private	R.I.R.	
Neill, George	Armoy	Private	R.I.R.	Wounded.
Neill, Hugh	Armoy	Private	R.I.R.	
Neill, Robert	Armoy	Private	R.I.R.	
Smiley, William	Moyaver	Private	R.I.R.	Pris. in Germany
	COLONIAL AND U.S.A. FORCES.			
Carson, Robert	Ballybregagh	Private	American Force	
Connolly, Hugh W.	Drumdollagh	Private	Australian Imp. Force	Wounded.
Craig, John	Cromachs	Private	Australian Imp. Force	Killed in Action.
Gault, William	Summerhill	Private	N.Z. Ex. Force	
McBride, James	Turnarobert	Private	Can. Force	
McCloy, Henry	Ballybregagh	Private	S.A. Force	
McCormick, George	Mornaclough	Private	Can. Force	Killed in Action.
McMillan, Randal	Knocknahinch	Private	Can. Force	Wounded.
McMillan, Samuel	Knocknahinch	Private	N.Z. Force	
Kyle, James	Carrowcashel	Private	American Force	Died.
	BALLYCASTLE.			
Baillie, James	Ballycastle	Private	Motor Transport	
Douglas, Archer P.	Ballycastle		M. Marine	
Douglas, Keevers J.	Ballycastle		M. Marine	
Dunlop, Alexander	Ballycastle	Sergeant	R.I.R.	Wounded.
Dunlop, David	Ballycastle	Private	M.G.C.	Wounded.
Dunlop, William J.	Ballycastle	Private	R.F.A.	Killed in Action.
Farris, Robert	Broughinlea	Private	R.A.M.C.	
Galloway, Robert J.	Camsampson	Private	R.I.R.	
Greer, J. Kenneth M.	Ballycastle	Lieutenant	I.G.	M.C. Died of Wounds.
Hamill, Harry	Ballycastle	Private	R.I.R.	
Hamill, John	Ballycastle	Sergeant	R.I.R.	Prisoner of War.
Harper, R. W.	Ballycastle	Captain	R.A.M.C.	
Haughey, George F.	Ballycastle	2nd Officer	M. Marine	
Haughey, John A.	Ballycastle	Apprentice	M. Marine	Lost at sea.
Haughey, Thomas A.	Ballycastle	Engineer	M. Marine	
Henry, John	Ballycastle		R.N.	
Jackson, Frank	The Manse	Captain	6th R.I.F.	Wounded.
Jackson, H. M., M.B.	The Manse	Captain	R.A.M.C.	
Jackson, J. L., M.B.	The Manse	Major	R.A.M.C.	Croix de Guerre, Prisoner of War, Men. in Des.
Kennedy, James A.	Ballycastle	Apprentice	M. Marine	
Kerr, Richard	Ballycastle	Private	R.I.R.	
Kirkpatrick, Robert	Ballycastle	Private	Connaught Rangers	Killed in Action.
McDowell, Hugh	Garteoney	Private	R.I.R.	Wounded.
McGreggor, Randal	Ballycastle	Private	R.I.R.	
McIntyre, Joseph	Garteoney		R.N.	

ROUTE PRESBYTERY. BALLYCASTLE.

Name.	Home Address.	Rank.	Regiment, Battalion or Unit.	Remarks.
McLean, James	Ballycastle	Private	R.I.R.	Killed in Action.
McMullan, William	Ballycastle	...	...	
Robinson, James W.	Carneymoore	Captain	C.F.	
Spruce, Hugh	Moyarget	Corporal	R.I.R.	Killed in Action.
Spruce, Robert	Ballycastle	Private	R.I.R.	
Stars, Joseph	Ballycastle	Private	Motor Transport	
Steele, Alexandra	Ballycastle	Private	A.S.C.	
Stewart, S. O.	Ballycastle	Captain	C.F.	
Woodside, Alfred McB.	Ballycastle	Lieut.-Colonel	R.F.A.	Wounded.
Woodside, William A.	Ballycastle	Lieut.-Colonel	R.A.M.C.	D.S.O. Men. in Despatches.
COLONIAL AND U.S.A. FORCES.				
Henry, George	Ballycastle	Private	U.S. Army	
Kirkpatrick, Daniel	Ballycastle	Captain	U.S. Army	
McConachie, William	Ballycastle	Private	R.A.M.C., Australians	
McCormick, George	Ballycastle	Corporal	Canadians	Killed in Action.
McGuigan, Jack	Ballycastle	Private	Canadians	
McMullan, Hugh	Ballycastle	Private	M.G.C., U.S.A.	
Mitchell, Robert	Ballycastle	Private	U.S. Army	Killed in Action.
Smyth, Samuel C.	Ballycastle	Private	U.S. Army	
White, Hugh	Ballycastle	Private	Canadians	
White, William B.	Ballycastle	Private	Australians	Wounded.
Woodside, J. H.	Ballycastle	Private	U.S. Army	
Woodside, Robert	Ballycastle	Private	U.S. Army	
Woodside, William	Ballycastle	Private	U.S. Army	
FIRST BALLYMONEY.				
Archibald, Robert	Newhill	Seaman	R.N.	
Archibald, William	Linenhall Street	Trooper	N.I.H.	
Barklie, Joseph C.	Castle Street	Sergeant	R.F.A.	
Campbell, John	Balnamore	Private	10th R. In. Fus.	Wounded.
Campbell, Thomas C.	Ballymoney	...	R.E.	Killed in Action.
Chambers, Karl D.	Ballymoney	Leading Seaman	R.N.	
Chambers, Thomas	Ballymoney	Private	5th R.I.F.	Wounded.
Chambers, William	Ballymoney	Leading Seaman	R.N.	
Crawford, Alexander	Leck	Private	2/7th Black Watch	
Crawford, Harry	Leck	Private	3rd Seaforth Highlanders	Wounded.
Currie, James B.	Kilmoyle	C.Q.M.S.	7th R.I.R.	
Dooey, John	Miltown	Private	A.S.C.	
Elder, Alexander	Seacon	Private	12th R.I.R.	Wounded.
Elliot, J. R.	Ballymoney	Private	12th R. In. Fus.	
Getty, David	Balnamoney	Private	R.A.F.	Died.
Greer, James K. MacG.	Weston Crofts	Lieutenant	Irish Guards	M.C. Killed in Action.
Hamilton, William	Ballymoney	Captain	R.A.M.C.	
Henry, Daniel	Castle Street	Private	1st R.I.R.	Wounded.
Herd, Albert	Leaney	Private	5th R.I.F.	
Kane, David	Townhead Street	Private	R.A.F.	
Kane, William T.	Townhead Street	Leading Seaman	R.N.D.	Wounded.
Kinnaird, Andrew	Forttown	Private	12th R.I.R.	Killed in Action.
Knox, James B.	Charlotte Street	Lieutenant	12th R.I.R.	
Knox, Robert S.	Knowhead	Lieut.-Colonel	R. In. Fus.	D.S.O. & 3 Bars.
Leitch, Arthur	Ballymoney	Captain	R.A.M.C.	
Leyburn, George	Ballymoney	Private	12th R.I.R.	
Lusk, Andrew	Henry Street	Private	Royal Scots	
Lusk, Hugh	Henry Street	Trooper	N.I.H.	
Lusk, Samuel F.	Ballymoney	Captain	R.A.M.C.	
Lusk, William	Henry Street	Private	10th R.I.R.	
Macafee, William	Currysiskan	Lieutenant	A.S.C.	
McCloy, John	Ballymoney	Captain	R.A.M.C.	
McGugan, James	Ballymoney	Private	Irish Guards	
McKay, John	Brevallen	Gunner	R.F.A.	Killed in Action.
Murray, William James	Union Street	Sergeant	A.S.C.	
Neil, Thomas	Druckendult	Trooper	3rd Dragoon Guards	
Patterson, Gilmour	Ballymoney	Private	K.O. Scottish Borderers	Died.
Pollock, James H. H.	Ishlan	Captain	R.I.R.	Wounded.
Ross, Harry S.	Castle Street	Driver	A.S.C.	Wounded.
Semple, H.	Ballymoney	Gunner	Heavy Battery R.G.A.	
Stevens, John A.	Ballymoney	Private	9th H. L. I.	Wounded.
Stuart, James N.	John Street	Private	R.A.F.	
Stuart, John	John Street	Private	12th R.I.R.	
Taylor, David J.	Castle Street	Private	12th R.I.R.	Killed in Action.
Taylor, Samuel	Castle Street	Private	12th R.I.R.	Killed in Action.
Wilson, James	Townhead Street	Private	12th R.I.R.	Wounded.
Wilson, Robert	Townhead Street	Private	M.G.C.	Wounded.
Young, Redmond R.	Balnamore House	Lieutenant	R.E.	
Young, William	Balnamore House	Lieutenant	R. In. Fus.	Wounded.
COLONIAL AND U.S.A. FORCES.				
Baird, James	Ballymoney	Private	12th Reserve U.S.A.	
Biggart, Alexander	Ballymoney	Private	Canadians	

ROUTE PRESBYTERY.   FIRST BALLYMONEY.

Name.	Home Address.	Rank.	Regiment, Battalion or Unit.	Remarks.
Campbell, Edward	Ballymoney	Private	Canadians	Killed in Action.
Crawford, Charles	Portstewart	Gunner	Canadian Field Art.	
Crawford, Robert	Newhill	Corporal	319th Infantry, U.S.A.	
Darragh, Alexander	Ballymoney	Gunner	N.Z. Artillery	
Knox, William McA.	Main Street	Private	4th N.Z. Rifle Brigade	
Lilley, Daniel	Enagh	Private	Canadian Inf.	Gassed.
Perry, Samuel	Ballymoney	Private	Canadian Inf.	Wounded.
Pollock, Frederick	Ballymoney	Private	4th Australian Inf.	
BALLYMONEY, TRINITY CHURCH.				
Armour, W. S.	The Manse	Sup. of War Prop.	Indian Army	M.B.E.
Armour, J. B. M.	The Manse	Captain C.F.	14th Tank Corps	Men. in Des.
Armour, J. K. C.	The Manse	Lieutenant	R.G.A.	
Armour, R. L.	The Topp	Captain	A·V.C.	
Blair, S.	Roseyards	Sergeant	3rd Irish Guards	
Blair, W.	Roseyards	Sergeant	2nd Irish Guards	Wounded.
Chestnut, Joe	Meetinghouse Street	Private	19th R.I.R.	
Clements, W.	Ballymoney	Driver	48th Div. Signals, S.M.R.E.	Killed in Action.
Crawford, John	Ballymoney	Private	9th Scottish Rifles	
Culbertson, John	Ballymoney	Private	6th R.I.R.	Died in Hospital.
Getty, Andrew	Rodenfoot	Corporal	9th R. In. Fus.	Prisoner of War.
Hargy, Frank	Union Street	Guardsman	2nd Irish Guards	
Hargy, Tom	Union Street	Rifleman	11th R.I.R.	Wounded.
Henry, Thomas	Church Street	Trooper	1st N.I.H.	
Hogg, Gilmore	Balnamore	Private	12th R.I.R.	
Hogg, James	Balnamore	Corporal	18th R.I.R.	Wounded.
Hogg, John	Balnamore	Private	12th R.I.R.	Wounded.
Kirkpatrick, Andrew	Polantamny	Corporal	11th R. In. Fus.	
Kirkpatrick, John	Polantamny	Corporal	11th R. In. Fus.	
Lanigan, Robert	Ballyboyland	Private	12th R.I.R.	Prisoner of War.
Logan, S. J.	Castle Street	Private	9th Gordon Highlanders	Killed in Action.
Logan, W.	Castle Street	Private	10th Scottish Rifles	Killed in Action.
Logan, Matthew	Castle Street	Private	M.G.C.	
Logan, T.	Pleasure Step	Private	9th R.I.R.	Killed in Action.
Logan, T., Jun.	Pleasure Step	Private		
Loudan, Hugh	Townparks	Corporal	1st Irish Guards	
McAuley, Donald	Church Street	Corporal	Signal Section R.E.	D.C.M.
McClure, John	Rodenfoot		R.N.D.	
McConachie, Joe	Y.M.C.A.	Private	H.L.I.	
McConaghie, W. J.	Y.M.C.A.	Lance-Corporal	M.E.F., R.A.M.C.	
McComb, James	Market Street	Guardsman	3rd Irish Guards	
McComb, W.	Market Street	Private		
McCotter, Gordan	Rodenfoot	Trooper	N.I.H.	
McDowell, Andrew	Castle Street	Private	5th R. In. Fus.	
McElderry, S. B. B.	Charles Street	Cadet	211th Battery R.F.A.	
McGarry, Robert G.	Balnamore	Q.M. Sergeant	R.G.A.	
McLaughlin, James	Balliamonèy	Piper	7th R.I.R.	
McMaster, J. T.	Charlotte Street	Signaller	N.I.H.	Prisoner of War.
McMaster, David	Queen Street	Rifleman	4th R.I.R.	Prisoner of War.
Pattison, James	Union Street	Rifleman	6th R.I.R.	
Purce, George R. B.	Seymour Street	Major	R.A.M.C.	M.C.
Ramsey, James	Main Street	Private	R.I.R.	
Ramsey, James	Main Street	Lance-Corporal	327th Quarry Co., R.E.	
Robinson, Thomas	Roddenfoot	Private	9th R. In. Fus.	Killed in Action.
Scott, Robert W.	Meetinghouse Street	Trooper	Royal Horse Guards	Killed in Action.
Stuart, J. K.	Eastbourne	Trooper	N.I.H.	
Stuart, Samuel J.	Eastbourne	Lieutenant	R.A.F.	
Thomson, William	Conagher	Lance-Corporal	N.I.H.	Killed in Action.
Tweed, D.	Roddenfoot	Private	12th R.I.R.	
Wales, George	Market Street	Private	18th R.I.R.	Killed in Action.
Wales, James	Market Street	3rd Air Mechanic	R.A.F, R.F.C.	
Wales, Samuel	Market Street	Rifleman	6th R.I.R.	
Young, Robert	Market Street	Captain	R.I.R.	M.C.
Young, R. S.	Market Street	Captain	R.A.M.C.	
COLONIAL AND U.S.A. FORCES.				
Armour, S. B. B.	The Topp	Cadet	U.S.A.	
Atkinson, A.		Sergeant	27th Can. E.F.	
Beare, W.	Church Street	Sergeant	1st Can. E.F.	
Crawford, R.	Ballymoney	Private	62nd Can. E.F.	
Falconer, J. R.	Church Street	Sergeant	42nd Can. E.F.	
Halliday, Robert	Ballinamoney	Cadet	U.S. Army	
Halliday, Samuel	Ballinamoney	Private	122nd F.A., U.S. Army	
Hamilton, A. M. S.	The Manse	S.M.	R.A.M.C., B. East Africa	
Hamilton, F. W.	The Manse		R.A.M.C., U.S.E.F.	
Henry, James	Church Street	Rifleman	1st N.Z.E.F.	
Loudan, James	Ballymoney	Private	36th Can. Highlanders	
Young, W.	Market Street	Captain	1st Aust. F.A.	

ROUTE PRESBYTERY.   ST. JAMES' CHURCH, BALLYMONEY.

Name.	Home Address.	Rank.	Regiment, Battalion or Unit.	Remarks.
BALLYMONEY, ST. JAMES' CHURCH.				
Adams, Henry	Newbuildings	Rifleman		Killed in Action.
Bellingham, J.	Ballymoney	Private	A.S.C.	
Boyd, Thomas	Ballymoney	Private	R.I.R.	
Brown, Samuel	Ballymoney	Gunner	R.G.A.	
Campbell, James	Ballymoney	Private	Dublin Fusiliers	
Connell, Thomas	Ballymoney	Private	Motor Transport	
Crawford, J.	Ballymoney	2nd Lieutenant	R.I.R.	
Dickey, James	Culbrim	Rifleman	R.I.R.	Prisoner of War.
Dobbin, Robert	Ballymoney	Rifleman	R.I.R.	
Dobbin, Samuel	Ballymoney	Rifleman	R.I.R.	Prisoner of War.
Dunlop, William	Ballybrakes	Rifleman	R.I.R.	Prisoner of War.
Esler, Alexander	Calhame	Corporal	R.I.F.	
Fulton, Samuel	Seacon	Private	R.I.R.	Died.
Gray, Samuel	Dunaghy	Private	R.I.R.	Killed in Action.
Greene, Jackson	Ballymoney	Sergeant	R.I.R.	Wounded.
Hanna, John	Drumaheggles	Private	R.I.R.	Killed in Action.
Hogg, Gilmour	Balnamore	Private	R.I.R.	
Hunter, James	Ballymoney	Private	Irish Guards	W'ded and Gassed.
Kinnaird, James	New Buildings	Private	R.I.R.	
Kinnaird, Matthew	New Buildings	Private	R. In. Fus.	
Kirgan, John	Ballymoney	Private	R.I.R.	Killed in Action
Kirgan, Robert	Ballymoney	Private	R.I.R.	
Kirgan, Samuel	Ballymoney	Bombardier	Heavy Artillery	
Lamont, William	Ballymoney	Sapper	R.E.	
Lamont, William	Ballymoney	Rifleman	R.I.R.	
McArthur, Daniel	Ballymoney	Private	R.I.R.	Died.
McArthur, James	Ballymoney	Private	Norfolk Regt.	Wounded.
McAteer, William	Ballymoney	Trooper	N.I.H.	
McCabe, R. B.	Balnamore	Sapper	R.E.	
McCaw, James	Ballymoney	Gunner	R.G.A.	
McKinlay, J.	Balnamore	Private	M.G.C.	
McNaul, Robert	Ballygan	Rifleman	R.I.R.	Gassed. Died.
Moody, Andrew	Balnamore	Rifleman	R.I.R.	
Mooney, Henry	Ballymoney	Rifleman	R.I.R.	Wounded.
Mooney, Thomas	Coldagh	Rifleman	R.I.R.	
Mooney, William	Tullaghgore	Rifleman	R.I.R.	Wounded.
Murphy, Archie	Ballymoney	Private	R.I.R.	
Murphy, George	Ballywattick	Rifleman	R.I.R.	
Murphy, James	Ballywattick	Rifleman	R.I.R.	Wounded.
Murphy, Thomas	Ballywattick	Trooper	N.I.H.	Wounded.
Murphy, William	Ballywattick	Rifleman	R.I.R.	Died.
Murphy, James	Greenville	Rifleman	R.I.R.	Wounded & Pris.
Murphy, John	Greenville	Rifleman	R.I.R.	Killed in Action.
Murphy, Johnston	Ballymoney	Lieutenant	R.I.R.	Killed in Action.
Murphy, Robert	Ballymoney	2nd Lieutenant	R.I.R.	Killed in Action.
Neill, Richard	Ballymoney	Private	R. In. Fus.	
Nevin, Daniel	Coldagh	Rifleman	R.I.R.	Killed in Action.
Nevin, James	Coldagh	Rifleman	R.I.R.	
Reid, Hugh	Taughey	Rifleman	R.I.R.	Killed in Action.
Richard, Hugh	Ballymoney	Saddler	N.I.H.	
Richard, William	Ballymoney	2nd Lieutenant	R.G.A.	
Ross, John	Coldagh	Private	K's Liverpool Regt.	
Speers, William	Ballymoney	Rifleman	R.I.R.	Died a P.O.W.
Stewart, Robert	Ballywattick	Rifleman	R.I.R.	Killed in Action.
Stewart, Wilson	Ballywattick	Rifleman	R.I.R.	Prisoner.
Stroyan, John	Ballymoney	Private	R.I.F.	Wounded.
Stinson, Robert	Ballymoney	Rifleman	21st Lancers	
Taggart, Samuel	Ballymoney	Sergeant	A.S.C.	
BALLYWEANEY.				
Baird, John	Carnagall	Private	11th R.I.R.	Thrice Wounded.
Christie, Joseph	Ballyportery	Private	Australians	
Finlay, John	Mounthamilton	Private	12th R.I.R.	
Givin, Benjamin	Mounthamilton	Private	9th R.I.R.	Wounded.
Johnston, David	Mounthamilton	Private	R.I.R.	Killed in Action.
Johnston, John	Mounthamilton	Private	11th R.I.R.	
Kennedy, Thomas	Corkey	Private		
McAneaney, Thomas	Cloughmills	Private		
McCullough, Alexander	Ballyportery	Private	R.I.R.	
McIlhagga, Robert	Knockahollet	Private	R.I.R.	Killed in Action.
McLeod, Roderick	Carnbuck	Private	Seaforth Highlanders	Wounded.
Rock, Hugh	Carabeg	Private	11th R.I.R.	Killed in Action.
Thompson, James	Corkey	Corporal	N.I.H.	Wounded.
Turner, Robert	Cloughmills	Sergeant	Australians	Killed in Action.
Turner, Thomas	Cloughmills	Private	8th R.I.R.	Killed in Action.
BUSHMILLS.				
Alexander, Robert	Feigh	Private	N.I.H.	
Beverland, William	Ballyness	Rifleman	2nd R.I.R.	
Dunlop, David	Ballyness	Captain	R.A.M.C.	

ROUTE PRESBYTERY. BUSHMILLS.

Name.	Home Address.	Rank.	Regiment, Battalion or Unit.	Remarks.
Dunlop, Joseph	Ballyness	Captain	R.A.M.C.	
Dunlop, William	Ballyness	Major	R.A.M.C.	
Elliott, Andrew	Main Street	Private	12th R.I.R.	
Elliott, James	Main Street	Private	11th Royal Scots	Wounded.
Haughey, William	Bushmills	Rifleman	12th R.I.R.	Prisoner of War.
Kennedy, Thomas	Bushmills	Rifleman	12th R.I.R.	Killed in Action.
McAfee, John	Kilcubbin	Rifleman	12th R.I.R.	
McAllister, Eligha	Bushmills	Sergt.-Major	R.G.A.	
McAllister, John	Bushmills	Private	R. In. Fus.	
McAllister, William	Bushmills	Gunner	R.G.A.	
McAuley, Edward	Klondyke	Private	7th R. Scottish Fus.	Wounded.
McAuley, Robert	Klondyke	Private	2nd R. Scots	
McBride, William	Church Street	A.B.	R.N.	
McCallum, Charles	Bushmills	Private	12th R.I.R.	Prisoner of War.
McCallum, Hugh	Bushmills	Lance-Corporal	12th R.I.R.	Killed in Action.
McCallum, Joseph	Bushmills	Private	12th R.I.R.	
McCallum, Robert	Bushmills	Private	12th R.I.R.	Prisoner of War.
McEacheron, Robert	Bushmills	Gunner	R.G.A.	Wounded.
McKenzie, Matthew	Ballylough	Gunner	R.G.A.	Wounded.
McNeill, George	Bushmills	Captain	R.A.M.C.	
Martin, Daniel	Aird	Sergeant	12th R.I.R.	Twice Wounded.
Morrow, William	Church Street	Private	12th R.I.R.	Killed in Action.
Pursel, Hugh	Ballylaught	Private	12th R.I.R.	Died in Service.
Sharp, Archie	Bushmills		R.N.	
Sharp, Robert	Bushmills	Private	12th R.I.R.	Wounded.
Sinclair, Herbert	Bushmills	Lieutenant	R.A.M.C.	
Steel, John	Eagry	Private	7/8 R. In. Fus.	Wounded.
Steel, Samuel	Eagry	Private	1st R.I.R.	Wounded.
Stewart, Robert	Eagry	Private	Scotch Guards	
Taggart, John	Kilcubbin	Private	12th R.I.R.	
Taggart, Thomas	Bushmills	Captain	7th R.I.R.	
Tweed, William	Bushmills	Stoker	R.N.V.R.	
Watters, James	Bushmills	Sapper	R.E.	
COLONIAL AND U.S.A. FORCES.				
Alexander, Joseph	Feigh	Private	2nd Anzac	
Bain, G. C.	Bushmills	Lieutenant	Can. Ex. F.	
Cooke, Daniel	Bushmills	Private	Can. Ex. F.	Wounded.
Elliott, Alexander	Bushmills	Private	Can. Ex. F.	Killed in Action.
Galbraith, Alexander	Bushmills	Private	78th Winnipeg Gren.	Wounded.
Galbraith, Daniel	Bushmills	Corporal	78th Winnipeg Gren.	Wounded.
Galbraith, David	Bushmills	Lance-Corporal	78th Winnipeg Gren.	Wounded.
Galbraith, Robert	Bushmills	Private	16th Can. Scottish	Killed in Action.
Given, Arthur	Bushmills	Private	American Ex. F.	
Given, James Sharp	Bushmills	Private	American Ex. F.	Wounded.
McEacheron, Robert	Bushmills	Private	43rd Canadians	Died in Service
McNeill, Andrew	Bushmills	Private	78th Winnipeg Gren.	Wounded.
BUSHVALE.				
Biggart, Bertie	Gladhill	Private	N.I.H.	
Biggart, Samuel	Gladhill	Private	N.I.H.	Wounded.
Campbell, Robert	Islandmore	Private	19th Scots Guards	Killed in Action.
Chestnut, William	Clintyfinnan	Private	Irish Guards	
Gamble, David	Stranocum	Lieutenant		Wounded.
Gamble, George White	Stranocum		R.N.	
Gamble, John	Stranocum		R.N.	
Gamble, Thomas	Stranocum		R.N.	
Hegarty, Alexander	Knockanavery	Private	R.I.R.	
Henry, James L.	Stranocum	Private	R.A.M.C.	Wounded.
Holmes, Daniel	Stranocum	Private	R.I.R.	
Holmes, Robert	Dungorberry	Private		
Huey, Alexander	Ballycraigagh	Private	12th R.I.R.	Killed in Action.
Huey, James	Ballycraigagh	Private	12th R.I.R.	Killed in Action.
Lawson, James	Ballynafeigh		R.N.	
Lyle, Samuel	Topp		R.A.M.C.	
McAlea, Henry	Knockanavery	Private	A.S.C.	
McAleese, David	Knockanavery	Private	12th R.I.R.	Wounded.
McClure, John	Stranocum	Private		
McIlhatton, Robert	Kingarve	Private	R.I.R.	Killed in Action.
McIlhatton, W. J.	Clintyfinnan	Private	2nd Irish Guards	Wounded.
McMullan, Charles	Drumcrottagh	Private	M.T. A.S.C.	
McMullan, James	Drumcrottagh	Private	H.L.I.	
Patton, Joseph	Kingarve	Corporal	A.S.C.	
Patton, Robert	Kingarve	Private	2nd Irish Guards	Wounded.
Patton, William	Stranocum	Lance-Corporal	R.I.R.	Wounded.
COLONIAL AND U.S.A. FORCES.				
Blair, Hugh	Ballycraigagh		American Army	
Blair, W. J.	Ballycraigagh		American Army	
Cairns, Robert	Drumafivey		Canadian	
Holmes, Robert	Stranocum		Australian	Killed in Action.

ROUTE PRESBYTERY. BUSHVALE.

NAME.	HOME ADDRESS.	RANK.	REGIMENT, BATTALION OR UNIT.	REMARKS.
KNOX, GEORGE	Riverview		American	Wounded.
LAWSON, GEORGE	Ballynafeigh		American A.C.	
LAWSON, JOHN	Ballynafeigh		Canadian	Wounded.
LYLE, ROBERT	Topp		Canadian	
McCAW, ROBERT	Ballycraigagh		Canadian	
McCAW, SAMUEL	Ballycraigagh		Canadian	
McILHATTON, ANDREW	Kingarve		Australian	
PATTON, ARMOUR	Drumafivey		Australian	
WALKER, ALEXANDER	Stranocum		Australian	Killed in Action.
WALKER, DAVID	Stranocum		Australian	Wounded.
WALLACE, JOHN	Leitrim		Australian	Killed in Action.
CROAGHMORE.				
GAULT, JAMES	Islandranny	Private	R.I.R.	M.M.
GAULT, JOHN	Islandranny	Private	R.I.R.	
KANE, ARCHIE	Toberkeigh	Private	R.E.	
KERR, DANIEL, B.A.	Craignamaddy	Lieutenant	R. Cheshires	Killed in Action.
McCANN, JOHN	Ballinastraid	Stoker	R.N.	
McGEE, HUGH	Lisnagunagh	Private	R.I.R.	
McGEE, ROBERT	Lisnagunagh	Private	R.I.R.	M.M.
McKILLOP, PATRICK	Drumnagessin	Private	R.E.	
McPHERSON, DAVID	Clegnagh	Private	Black Watch	M.M.
DERVOCK.				
ADAMS, JAMES	Carncullagh	Private		Killed in Action.
CARTON, HUGH	Kirkhills	Q.M.S.	1st Irish Guards	Killed in Action.
CARTON, ROSS	Kirkhills	Sergeant	R.F.A.	
CONNELL, JAMES A.	Carnbore	Major	A.V.C.	Men. In Des.
ENGLISH, W. J.	Dervock	Private	12th R.I.R.	
GARDNER, GAMBLE	Dervock	Private	6th R.I.F.	
GAULT, JOSEPH	Drumcrotagh	Lieutenant	R.I.R.	
GRAHAM, GEORGE	Ballymacfin	Lieutenant	R. Dub. Fus.	Killed in Action.
HAMILTON, JOHN	Ballyrobin	Lieutenant	R. In. Fus.	Killed in Action.
HAMILTON, WILLIAM	Ballyrobin	Lieutenant	R.E.	
HUEY, WALLACE W.	Carncullagh	Private	1/7th Warwick Regt.	Killed in Action.
JAMESON, S.	Carncullagh	Private	12th R.I.R.	Killed in Action.
JOHNSTON, DANIEL	Derrykerghan	Lieutenant	R.G.A.	
LAVERTY, JOHN	Clunties	Private	R.I.R.	
LAVERTY, ROBERT	Clunties	Private	R.I.R.	
LIGGETT, ROBERT	Aughnacrosey	Q.M.S.	15th R.I.R.	
McCAW, DANIEL	Drumcrotagh	Corporal	12th R.I.R.	
McCAW, DAVID	Dervock		10th C.P.L.	
McCAW, ROBERT J.	Dervock		10th C.P.L.	
McCAUGHAN, WILLIAM	Dervock		R.E.	
McCOLLUM, R. J.	Dervock	Private	R.A.M.C.	
McMULLAN, ALEXANDER	Dervock	Sergeant	12th R.I.R	
McMULLAN, JOHN	Dervock	Private	12th R.I.R.	
McMULLAN, R. J.	Ballymacfin	Private	12th R.I.R.	Died in Hospital.
McMULLAN, WILLIAM	Dervock	Private	R.E.	
MAXWELL, W. N.	Dervock Manse	Captain	R.A.C.D.	
MENEELY, ADAM	Toberdoney	Private	R.A.F.	
MISKELLY, ROBERT J.	Carnfrogue	Private	R.I.F.	
MONTGOMERY, JOHN	Stranocum	Private	Irish Guards	Wounded.
SHIELDS, JOHN	Lisnabragh	Private		
SMYTHE, NEVIN	Stroan	Trooper	N.I.H.	
WRIGHT, W. J.	Ballymoney Road	Corporal	2nd Irish Guards	Killed in Action.
COLONIAL AND U.S.A. FORCES.				
BOYLAND, WILLIAM	Ballynafeigh	Private	U.S. Army	
McCAUGHAN GEORGE	Stroan	Private	Canadians	
McFAUL, MALCOLM	Ballyhunsley	Sergeant	U.S. Army	
McKENDRY, ANDREW	Stranocum	Private	A.N.Z.A.C.	
POLLOCK, TOM	Ballymacfin	Private	S.A. Force	
POLLOCK, WILLIAM	Ballymacfin	Private	U.S. Army	
DRUMREAGH.				
ADAMS, GEORGE	Charlotte Street	Private	Trench Mortar Battery	Wounded twice.
BLAIR, ALEXANDER	Drumskea	Lance-Corporal	20th R.I.R.	Wounded.
BLAIR, SAMUEL	Ballaghbeddy	Private	R.G.A.	Wounded.
BOYD, HUGH	Drumreagh	Private	2nd R.I.F.	
BOYD, JAMES	Drumreagh	Private	12th R.I.F.	Wounded & Pris.
BOYD, ROBERT	Drumreagh	Private	20th R.I.R.	
BOYD, WILLIAM	Drumreagh	Private	2nd Irish Guards	Wounded twice.
BROLLY, CLARKE	Balnamore	Private	12th R.I.R.	Wounded 4 times.
BROLLY, JAMES	Balnamore	Private	R.A.M.C.	
BROLLY, SAMUEL	Balnamore	Corporal	2nd R.I.R.	Wounded & Killed in Action.
BROLLY, THOMAS	Balnamore	Private	12th R.I.R.	Wounded twice.
BURNS, JOHN	Balnamore	Private	12th R.I.R.	Killed in Action.
BURNS, JOSEPH	Balnamore	Private	12th R.I.R.	Wounded twice.

ROUTE PRESBYTERY.   DRUMREAGH.

Name.	Home Address.	Rank.	Regiment, Battalion or Unit.	Remarks.
Burns, Robert	Balnamore	...	R.N.R.	Wounded.
Burns, Thomas Moody	Balnamore	Private	12th R.I.R.	Wounded 3 times.
Cairns, Alexander	Balnamore	L/Corporal	12th R.I.R.	Wounded & Killed in Action.
Campbell, Robert	Bendoorgah	Private	19th Scots Guards	Killed in Action.
Campbell, Bryce	Taitsfort	Private	8th R.I.R.	Killed in Action.
Campbell, William James	Killymaddy	Private	8th R.I.R.	Wounded.
Calvin, Robert	Ballymoney	Private	18th R.I.R.	Killed in Action.
Cooper, Dan S., M.B.	Bendoorgah	Captain	R.A.M.C.	
Cooper, John M., M.C.V.S.	Bendoorgah	Captain	A.V.C.	
Currie, Henry	Enagh	Private	12th R.I.R.	Wounded.
Currie, Samuel	Enagh	Private	Cameron Highlanders	Wounded 5 times.
Dickie, Robert	Moneycannon	Private	10th R.I.F.	Wounded 3 times.
Finlay, Samuel	Landaginey	Sergeant	3rd King's R. Rifles	
Forsythe, David J.	Balnamore	Corporal	12th R.I.R.	M.M. Prisoner.
Gillan, Felix	Balnamore	Private	12th R.I.R.	Wounded twice and Gassed.
Graham, Evan McI.	Enagh	2nd Lieutenant	10th R.I.F.	
Hendry, Thomas L.	Ballynagarvey	Lance-Corporal	Gordon Highlanders	Wounded. D.C.M. and Star.
Henry, Archie	Cobra	Private	King's West Surrey Regt.	Prisoner.
Hunter, Joseph	Drumnahaylis	Private	R.A.F.	
Maybin, Henry	Ballaghheddy	Private	12th R.I.R.	Wounded.
Mulholland, George	Balnamore	Sergeant	12th R.I.R.	M.M.
Mulholland, Hugh	Balnamore	Q.-M. Sergeant	36th M.G.C.	
Mulholland, Wm. James	Drumnahaglis	Private	N.I.H.	
McAuley, Joseph	Cobra	Private	Irish Guards	Wounded.
McClelland, Edward	Balnamore	Private	6th R. In. Fus.	Wounded.
McClelland, Samuel	Balnamore	Private	11th R. In. Fus.	Killed in Action.
McDowell, James	Clarehill	Private	10th R. In. Fus.	Wounded twice and Gassed.
McMaster, William James	Ballymoney	Private	12th R.I.R.	
McMillan, Samuel	Currysisken	Private	9th R. In. Fus.	Killed in Action.
McNabb, Samuel	Balnamore	Private	M.T. A.S.C.	
McNabb, William James	Balnamore	Private	M.G.C.	
McShane, John	Bendoorgah	L/Corporal	6th R.I.R.	
Park, James	Balnamore	Private	18th R.I.R.	
Smyth, John	Drumreagh	Private	Cameron Highlanders	Prisoner.
Smyth, Samuel	Drumreagh	Private	M.T. A.S.C.	
Steele, Hugh C.	Balnamore	Private	3rd R.I.F.	Wounded twice.
Taggart, Robert	Balnamore	Private	8th R.I.R.	
Taggart, William	Balnamore	Private	2nd R.I.R.	Gassed.
COLONIAL AND U.S.A. FORCES.				
Beare, Thomas H.	Canada	Private	Canadian Inf.	M.M. Wounded twice.
Campbell, Thomas	Canada	Lance-Corporal	Canadian M.G.C.	
Campbell, William	Canada	Private	27th Canadians	Wounded.
Campbell, William M.	Canada	Private	5th Canadian Inf.	Wounded twice.
Cooper, William M.	Canada	Private	Canadian Inf.	Wounded.
Dunn, Robert J.	Canada	Private	Canadian A.S.C.	
Hamill, Hugh	Canada	Private	4th Canadian Mounted Rifles	Gassed. Killed in Action.
Hamilton, Frank A.	Canada	Private	13th F.A., 4th Can. Div.	
Hamilton, Harry A.	Canada	Private	P.P.C.L.I.	
Hamilton, Samuel J.	America	Private	87th Engs., 1st Americans	
Hastings, William John	Canada	Private	M.G.C., Canadians	
Lusk, J. Sinclair	Australia	Private	Australian Inf.	Wounded.
Murphy, James	Canada	Private	13th R. Highlanders, Can.	Killed in Action.
Murphy, William J.	Canada	Private	13th R. Highlanders, Can.	Wounded.
McDowell, Samuel	Canada	Sergeant	7th Canadians	Killed in Action, Wounded. M.M.
McKinney, John	Canada	Private	Canadian Inf.	Killed in Action.
Purdan, John J. S.	Canada	Lance-Corporal	Canadian Inf.	Wounded.
Savage, Charles L.	Canada	Sergeant	42nd R. Highlanders, Can.	Wounded twice.
DUNLOY.				
Brownlow, Robert	Dunloy	Corporal	251st Coy. A.S.C.	
Elder, Samuel	Dunloy	Private	2nd R.I.F.	Wounded.
Fenton, James	Dunloy	Lance-Corporal	12th R.I.R.	Killed in Action.
Fenton, Thomas	Dunloy	Rifleman	12th R.I.R.	Wounded.
Given, Robert	Dunloy	Private	Scottish Regiment	Wounded.
Given, Samuel	Dunloy	Rifleman	6th R.I.R.	Wounded.
Heaney, William	Killagan	Captain	A.V.C.	
Lamont, James	Dunloy	Private	52nd Gordons	
McCracken, David	Dunloy	Private	H.L.I.	Missing.
McCracken, Robert	Dunloy	Corporal	M.G.C.	Wounded.
McDowell, Thomas J.	Dunloy	Lance-Corporal	11th R.I.R.	
McNeill, William	Dunloy	Corporal	20th R.I.R.	
Moore, Alexander	Dunloy	Private	H.L.I.	Prisoner.
Moore, Samuel	Dunloy	Rifleman	4th R.I.R.	
Surgenor, William	Dunloy	Drummer	5th Seaforth Highlanders	Wounded.

ROUTE PRESBYTERY. DUNLOY.

Name.	Home Address.	Rank.	Regiment, Battalion or Unit.	Remarks.
Templeton, David	Dunloy	Rifleman	12th R.I.R.	Wounded.
Wallace, John	Dunloy	Private	R.F.C.	
Young, John	Dunloy	Rifleman	12th R.I.R.	Prisoner.
Young, Robert	Dunloy	Gunner	286th Battery R.G.A.	
COLONIAL AND U.S.A. FORCES.				
Boyd, Wm. George	Dunloy	Lieutenant	R.F.C., Canadians	
Elder, James	Dunloy	Private	U.S.A. Troops	
Elder, William	Dunloy	Private	Canadian Troops	
Gault, William	Dunloy	Trooper	New Zealand Forces	Served in P'tine.
McMurray, William	Dunloy	Sergeant	Canadians	
McNeill, Herbert J.	Dunloy	Private	3rd Canadians	
Moore, Joseph	Dunloy	Sergeant	90th Canadians	
FINVOY.				
Boyd, William	Shanaghy	Private	N.I.H.	
Carson, James	Licheegan	Private	R.I.R.	
Coleman, R. J.	Ballymaconelly	Private	R.I.R.	Killed in Action.
Ferris, Hugh	Moneycammon	Private	Irish Guards	Wounded.
Graham, James	Carrowreagh	Private	H.L.I.	
Getty, David	Carrowreagh	Rifleman	R.I.R.	Wounded.
Henry, John	Upper Maddykeel	Private		Killed in Action.
Hanna, William	Knockan	Private		Killed in Action.
Hughes, Robert	Moneycannon	Private	N.I.H.	Wounded.
Lamont, Norman	Long Mountain	F-Corporal	R.E.	
Lamont, Archie	Long Mountain	Sapper	R.E.	
McCurdy, William	Artnagross	Rifleman	R.I.R.	Killed in Action.
McCurdy, John	Artnagross	Rifleman	R.I.R.	
McShane, Robert	Moneycannon	Private	Irish Guards	Wounded.
McShane, M. B.	Moneycannon	Rifleman	R.I.R.	Wounded.
McCurdy, G.	Artnagross	Gunner	R.F.A.	
McLean, Alexander	Knockan	Rifleman	R.I.R.	Wounded.
McMillan, Matthew	Mullan	Private	U. Division	
Madden, Andrew	Killymaddie	Private	Scotch Rifles	Killed in Action.
Madden, W. J.	Killymaddie	Private	Scotch Rifles	
Patton, James	Vow	Lance-Corporal	Cycling Corps	Killed in Action.
Sheals, Joseph	Carrowreagh	Rifleman	R.I.R.	
Steele, William	Drumlee	Private	Irish Guards	
Torrans, John	Balnagarry	Rifleman	Labour Corps	
Watson, James	Ballymaconelly	Private	R.I.R.	Killed in Action.
Wallace, Alexander	Craigs	Rifleman	R.I.R.	Prisoner of War.
Wallace, William	Craigs	Rifleman	R.I.R.	
Gray, James	Dirraw	Captain	R.A.M.C.	
Gray, John P.	Dirraw	Lieutenant	R. In. Fus.	Killed in Action.
Hart, James	Vow	Captain	Duke of Wellington's	M.C. Killed in Action.
Henderson, W. T.	Slavney	Captain	R.A.M.C.	
Hill, James	Dirraw	Captain	R.A.M.C.	M.C.
Hanna, A. M.	Artnagross	Lieutenant	N.T.E.F.	
Irvine, J. H.	Artnagross	Captain	N.T.R.B.	
McHenry, Joseph	Rasharkin	Lieutenant	Salonica Army	
COLONIAL AND U.S.A. FORCES.				
Blair, Alexander	Killans	Gunner	Canadian F.A.	
Blair, Hugh	Killans	Private	Canadians	
Boyd, David	Shanaghy	Waggoner	American E. Force	
Burns, T.	Slavney	Private	American E. Force	
Burns, John	Slavney	Private	American E. Force	
Campbell, Alfred	Craigs	Private	American E. Force	
Campbell, John James	Craigs	Sergeant	American E. Force	
Campbell, A.	Craigs	Gunner	Australian	
Ferris, William J.	Dirraw	Private	Canadians	
Ferris, David	Dirraw	Private	Canadians	Killed in Action.
Gault, John	Dirraw	Private	American E. Force	
Henry, John	Licheegan	Corporal	American E. Force	
Hunter, James	Slavney	Private	American E. Force	
Hill, D. C.	Killans	Private	Winnipeg Rifles	Killed in Action.
Hughes, John	Moneycannon	Private	American E. Force	
Mooney, Tom	Craigs	Sergeant	American E. Force	
Peacock, Alexander	Rasharkin	Pioneer	Aus. I. Force	
Savage, Matthew	Vow	Private	Canadians	
Savage, William	Vow	Private	Canadians	Wounded.
Shaw, C. F.	Tullaghan	Private	Canadians	Killed.
Scott, Tom	Lower Maddykeel	Rifleman	N.T.R.B.	
Torrans, David	Drumlee	Rifleman	American E. Force	
Falconer, James	Craigs	Sapper	Aus. I. Force	
Falconer, John	Craigs	Trooper	Aus. I. Force	
Falconer, Adam	Craigs	Driver	Aus. Mounted Division	

ROUTE PRESBYTERY. GARRYDUFF.

Name.	Home Address.	Rank.	Regiment, Battalion or Unit.	Remarks.
GARRYDUFF.				
Barkley, Joseph	Culduff	Sergeant	R.F.A.	
Boyd, George	Calhame	Private	R.I.R.	Wounded.
Carmichael, Andrew	Polintamney	Private	R.I.R.	
Carmichael, Robert	Polintamney	Private	N.I.H.	
Carmichael, Thomas	Polintamney	Private	R.I.F.	
Carmichael, William	Polintamney	Private	N.I.H.	
Carton, William James	Garryduff	Private	Military Transport	
Crawford, Alexander	Lecke	Private	Black Watch	
Crawford, Harry	Lecke	Private	Seaforth Highlanders	Wounded.
Dempsey, Isaac	Artiferral	Private	R.I.F.	Killed.
Hughes, Samuel	Garryduff	Private	R. In. Fus.	
Patton, James	Newbuildings	Private	R.I.R.	
Pollock, Thomas	Garryduff	Private	Northumberland Fus.	
Pollock, Robert	Garryduff	Private	A.S.C.	
Robinson, John C.	Garryduff	Private	N.I.H.	Wounded.
Robinson, James Ross	Newbuildings	Private	R.I.F.	
Semple, Hugh	Newbuildings	Private	R.G.A.	
Stirling, John	Galdonagh	Lance-Corporal	R.I.R.	M.M.
COLONIAL AND U.S.A. FORCES.				
Anderson, Thomas	Garryduff	Private	U.S. Army	
Brown, William	Burnquarter	Private	U.S.A. F. Sig.	
Cassidy, James	Unshinagh	Driver	Aust. I.F.	
McLaughlin, William	Garryduff	Private	Canadian Army	
Pollock, John	Eden	Private	Canadian Army	
Young, Thomas A.	Ballinamoney	Private	U.S. Army	
FIRST KILRAUGHTS.				
Alexander, Samuel	Kilraughts	Private	5th Transport, R. In. Fus.	
Anderson, Samuel Wallace	Drumdollagh	Private	R.I.R.	Died of Wounds.
Anderson, Robert Neill	Drumdollagh	Private	N.I.H.	
Bellingham, John	Kilraughts	Private	91st A. and S. Highlanders	Killed in Action.
Buick, Samuel Alexander	Culban	Private	10th Scottish Rifles	Killed in Action.
Doherty, William	Ballyboyland	Private	18th R.I.R.	Lost a leg.
Lanigan, Bob	Lisboy	Private	12th R.I.R.	
Moore, David	Blackhills	Private	12th R.I.R.	
Patton, Samuel	Ballyweaney	Lance-Corporal	1st R. In. Fus.	Killed in Action.
Patton, William	Ballyweaney	Private	2nd R. In. Fus.	
Taggart, Andrew F.	Friary, Armoy	Private	2nd R.I.R.	Killed in Action.
Taggart, Thomas	Friary, Armoy		H.M.S. "New Zealand"	
Taggart, John	Friary, Armoy	Gunner	R.G.A.	Died of Wounds.
Tweed, Hugh	Lisboy	Private	R.A.F.	
Wallace, Matthew	Turnagrove	Private	2nd R.I.R.	
Wallace, Robert William	Turnagrove	Corporal	3rd M.G.C.	M.M.
Workman, William	Kilraughts	Private	18th R.I.R.	Killed in Action.
Workman, Andrew	Kilraughts	Private	12th R.I.R.	
COLONIAL AND U.S.A. FORCES.				
Boyd, Samuel F.	Kilmoyangey	Private	A.E.F., M.T.	
Clyde, Robert	Ballyboyland	Private	Can. 18th Reserve	
Hanna, James	Culban	Private	158th U.S. Inf.	
Huey, John	Killagan	Private	Can. A.S.C.	
Kennedy, Archie	Ballyboyland	Private	Can. 1st Div. Supply Co.	Died of Wounds.
Kennedy, Robert	Ballyboyland	Private	Can. Inf.	
Kerr, James	Knockahollet	Private	A.E.F.	
Kerr, John	Knockahollet	Gunner	A.E.F., F.A.	
Lamont, William	Glennylough	Private	1st N.Z.R.B.	
Logan, Andrew B.	Knockahollet	Private	Can. Entrenching Batt.	
Moore, Alexander	Knockahollet	Corporal	A.E.F., M.T.	
Moore, Archie	Knockahollet	Electrician	Aust. Navy	
Moore, Jim	Knockahollet	Corporal	A.E.F. Engineers	
McMillan, David	Crosstagherty	Private	U.S.A. Mounted Guards	
Robinson, Samuel H.	Pharis	Private	Canadians	
Young, William James	Pharis	Private	13th Canadians	Died of Wounds.
MOSSIDE.				
Boyd, James	Mosside	Private	I.G.	Wounded.
Boyd, John	Mosside	Bombardier	R.F.A.	Killed in Action.
Boyd, Samuel	Mosside	Private	R.I.R.	
Chestnut, Alexander	Mosside	Trooper	N.I.H.	
Feeney, Daniel	Mosside	Trooper	N.I.H.	
Harte, Robert	Mosside	Private	R.I.R.	
Hodges, John	Carolelis	Trooper	N.I.H.	
Jamieson, Samuel	Whitehill	Private	R.I.R.	Killed in Action.
McAfee, William James	Carrowreagh	Corporal	Canadian Rifles	Wounded.
McFadden, Malcolm	Mosside	Private	R.I.R.	Killed in Action.
McLaughlin, Robert	Carolelis	Trooper	N.I.H.	
McLean, Samuel	Liscolman	Sapper	R.E.	

ROUTE PRESBYTERY. **MOSSIDE.**

Name.	Home Address.	Rank.	Regiment, Battalion or Unit.	Remarks.
McLeese, John	Gracehill	Private	R.I.R.	
McVicker, Albert	Lisnagab	Sergeant	R.I.R.	Wounded.
Mogey, Edward	Mosside	Private	R.I.R.	
Moore, William	Mosside	Private	R.I.R.	
Nichol, Archie	Liscolman	Private	Dublin Fusiliers	Killed in Action.
Simpson, Frank	Mosside	Private	R.I.F.	
Simpson, Samuel	Carnbore	Private	Canadians	
Taggart, James	Deffrick	Trooper	N.I.H.	
Taggart, Edward	Mosside	Private	R.I.R.	
Taggart, Daniel	Mosside	Private	R.I.R.	
Taggart, Robert	Mosside	Private	M.T. A.S.C.	
Wilkinson, Charles	Liscolman	Corporal	R.I.R.	Wounded.
RAMOAN.				
Campbell, Ross	Moyarget	Private	Scotch Regt.	
Campbell, William	Moyarget	Private	R.I.R.	
Colgan, James	Magheramore	Private	Seaforth Highlanders	
Colgan, Thomas	Capecastle	Private	R.A.M.C.	
Gatty, John B.	Carrycrowe	2nd Lieutenant	R.I.R.	Wounded.
Hartin, Joseph	Moyarget	Private	A.S.C.	
Hartin, Robert	Magheramore	Private	Canadians	Wounded.
McGowan, John	Moyarget	Private	R.I.R.	
McGregor, Randle	Ballycastle	Private	R.I.R.	
Matthews, Robert	Culkeany	Private	R.I.R.	Wounded.
Moore, William	Culkeany	Private	11th A. and S. Highlanders	
ROSEYARDS.				
Anderson, Stewart	Ballyrobin	Private	12th R.I.R.	
Barr, Samuel	Fernalizery	Private	7th R. Dublin Fus.	
Blair, William	Kirkhills	L.-Sergeant	2nd I. Guards	Prisoner of War.
Campbell, Alexander	Gladhill	Private	N.I.H.	Wounded.
Campbell, Hugh	Cuppidale	Sapper	R.E.	
Campbell, Robert	Cuppidale	Private	R.A.F.	
Campbell, Thomas C.	Cuppidale	Private	1st Munster Fus.	
Carton, Daniel	Fernalizery	Private	9th R. In. Fus.	
Crothers, C. A.	Manse, Stranocum	Cadet	R.A.F.	
Gordon, Samuel B.	Kirkhills	Lance-Corporal	12th R.I.R.	Wounded.
Hill, Alexander	Dunavarney	Private	8th R. In. Fus.	Killed in Action.
Holmes, Robert	Dromart	Private	9th R. In. Fus.	
McCaw, Daniel	Stroan	Private	19th R.I.R.	Prisoner of War.
McQuitty, Robert J.	Cuppidale	Private	11th R.I.R.	Wounded.
Munnis, John	Brackagh	Private	11th R.I.R.	
Reid, James	Ballyrobin	Private	11th R.I.R.	
Reid, Thomas	Dervock	Private	R.I.R., Home Defence	
Reid, William	Dervock	Private	8th Scottish Rifles	Wounded.
Shields, Robert	Kirkhills	Private	R.I.F.	
Wallace, Thomas	Kirkhills	Captain	8th R.I.F.	
White, David	Fernalizery	Private	11th R.I.R.	
White, John	Fernalizery	Private	11th R.I.R.	Wounded.
White, William	Fernalizery	Private	11th R.I.R.	Killed in Action.
COLONIAL FORCES.				
Campbell, Daniel	Cuppidale	Private	2nd Can. Reserve Batt.	Killed in Action.
Campbell, Robert	Cuppidale	Private	2nd Can. Reserve Batt.	Wounded.
Hill, Samuel	Dunaverney	Private	Can. Inf.	
Lilley, Archibald	Cuppidale	Private	28th Can. Highlanders	Wounded.
McQuitty, John	Cuppidale	Private	Australian I. Force	
TOBERKEIGH.				
Anderson, James	Prolusk	Private	R.I.R.	Wounded.
Bell, William	Toberkeigh	Private	R.I.R.	Killed in Action.
Brown, Samuel	Toberkeigh	Private	R.I.R.	Killed in Action.
Chestnut, Ezekiel	Carnan	Private	N.I.H.	
Currie, George	Magherintendry	Sergeant	R.I.R.	
Curry, Daniel	Toberkeigh	Sergeant	A.S.C.	Wounded.
Dunlop, Alfie	Straidkillen	Major	R.A.M.C.	M.C.
Dunlop W. J.	Straidkillen	2nd Lieutenant	R.F.A.	Killed in Action.
McAlister, Alexander	Arboy		S. African Regt.	
McAlister, Hugh	Cosy	Lieutenant	York and L. Regt.	Died in Hospital.
McAlister, John	Cosy	Private	S. African Regt.	
McCaughan, Daniel	Craignamaddy	Private	R.I.R.	
McCaughan, Samuel	Craignamaddy		R.N.	
McCaw, Daniel	Craignamaddy	Sergt.-Major	A.S.C.	
McCaw, Samuel R.	Ballyolgah	Sergeant	R.A.F.	
McFarland, Edward	Ballinlea	Private	R.I.R.	
McIntyre, John	Straid	Private		
McKay, James	Magherintendry	Private	I.G.	
McVicker, Daniel	Craignamaddy	Captain	R.A.M.C.	M.C.
McVicker, Joseph	Craignamaddy	Cadet	R.A.F.	
McVicker, J. W.	Craignamaddy	2nd Lieutenant	King's Liverpool	Killed in Action.

(316)

ROUTE PRESBYTERY. TOBERKEIGH.

Name.	Home Address.	Rank.	Regiment, Battalion or Unit.	Remarks.
McVicker, Samuel	Craignamaddy	Lieutenant	London Regt.	
Matthews, Robert	Ballinlea	Private	R.I.R.	Wounded.
Taggart, Samuel	Billy	Private	R.I.R.	
Taggart, W. J.	Mosside	Private	A.S.C.	
	COLONIAL AND U.S.A.	FORCES.		
Henderson, Daniel	Croagh		Canadians	
Henderson, James	Croagh		Canadians	
McCurdy, Daniel	Ballymoy	Private	Canadians	
McVicker, John	Islandrally		U.S.A.	
McVicker, Samuel	Islandrally	R.A.M.C.	U.S.A.	

STRABANE PRESBYTERY.

Name.	Home Address.	Rank.	Regiment, Battalion or Unit.	Remarks.
ARDSTRAW.				
Black, William	Ardstraw	Private	9th R. Inn. Fus.	Died of Wounds.
Brayden, Harry	Ardstraw	Private	9th R. Inn. Fus.	M.M., Died in Hosp.
Brayden, James	Ardstraw	Private	9th R. Inn. Fus.	
Bruce, Alex.	Ardstraw	Private	M.G.T.	
Burke, David	Ardstraw	Private	9th R Inn. Fus.	Killed in Action.
Cameron, William	Ardstraw	Trooper	N.I.H.	
Craig, Fredk.	Ardstraw	Lieutenant	16th Lancers.	
Devenny, James	Ardstraw	Private	9th R.I. Fus.	
De Zeeuw, Hugh	Ardstraw	Private	9th R.I. Fus.	
Forbes, Robert	Ardstraw	Private	A.I.F.	
Gallagher, James	Ardstraw	Private	9th R.I. Fus.	
Graham, John R.	Ardstraw	Sergeant	9th R.I. Fus.	M.M.
Gray, John J.	Ardstraw	Private	R.M.L.I.	
Hamilton, Charles	Ardstraw	Private	9th R.I. Fus.	
Hamilton, John J.	Ardstraw	Lance-Corporal	R.E.	M.M.
Johnston, George	Ardstraw	Sapper	R.E.	
Johnston, John	Ardstraw	Sapper	R.E.	
Knox, Alex.	Ardstraw	Private	9th R.I. Fus.	
Laird, John M.	Ardstraw	Sergeant	9th R. Inn. Fus.	Killed in Action.
McKnight, John	Ardstraw	Private	9th R.I. Fus.	
Magee, Robert	Ardstraw	Trooper	N.I.H.	
Maxwell, Charles	Ardstraw	Sapper	R.E.	Killed in Action.
Millar, Norman	Ardstraw	Trooper	N I. Horse	
Moore, Samuel	Ardstraw	Trooper	N.I. Horse	
Neilson, Matthew	Ardstraw	Surgeon	R.N.	
Noble, David	Ardstraw	Private	9th R. Inn. Fus.	Killed in Action.
Noble, Matthew	Ardstraw	Corporal	9th R. Inn. Fus.	Killed in Action.
Semple, Sir David, D.Sc., M.D.	Ardstraw	Colonel	R.A.M.S.	
Service, David	Ardstraw	Lieutenant	N. Lancs.	
Stewart, David	Ardstraw	Private	9th R.I. Fus.	
Todd, Robert H.	Ardstraw	Sergt.-Major	Scottish Horse	
Wilson, James	Ardstraw	Marconi Officer	Transport	
Young, John Fyfe	Ardstraw	Private	Motor Transport	
	COLONIAL FORCES.			
Aiken, David		Captain	Aust. A.M. Corps	
Aiken, James		Captain	Aust. A.M. Corps	
Kennedy, John F.		Bombardier	Can. E.F.	Died in Hospital.
Leitch, Samuel		Private	N.Z. E.F.	
McClurg, William		Lance-Corporal	Can. L.I.	Killed in Action.
DOUGLAS.				
Alexander, John	Douglas Bridge	Private	A. & S. Highldrs.	
Arthur, Wm. Fredk.	Douglas Bridge	Trooper	N.I.H.	Killed in Action.
Barbour, Edward	Douglas Bridge	Private	R. Inn. Fus.	
Dick, R. C., B.A.	Early Hill	Captain	R.E.	M.C.
Hamilton, Robert	Douglas Bridge	Private	Can. L.I.	
Hamilton, Robert	New Zealand	Private	N.Z. Rifles	
Hunter, John	Douglas Bridge	Sergeant	R.I.R.	M.M.
Hunter, Marshall	Douglas Bridge	Private	Scottish Rifles	Killed in Action.
McLoughlin, William	Douglas Bridge	Private	R.A.F.	
Reid, Andrew	Douglas Bridge	Trooper	N.I.H.	

STRABANE PRESBYTERY. DRUMLEGAGH.

Name.	Home Address.	Rank.	Regiment, Battalion or Unit.	Remarks.
DRUMLEGAGH.				
Fyffe, Alex.	Drumlegagh	Private	N.I.H.	Prisoner of War.
Heslipp, Robert	Baronscourt	Private	M.G. Corps	Wounded.
Hill, Robert	Aughacessey	Sergeant	9th R. Inn. Fus.	Wounded.
Hill, Sandy	Aughacessey	2nd Lieutenant	Leinster Regt.	
Kerr, Samuel	Meaghey	Bombardier	R.F.A.	
McBeth, Ross	Baronscourt	Lance-Corporal	N.I.H.	
Watson, Jack	Archill	Private	Can. Regt.	
Wasson, Thomas	Archill	Captain	A.S.C.	
Young, Joseph	Archill	Lance-Corporal	9th R. Inn. Fus.	Gassed.
GLENELLY.				
Glass, Robert	Aughalane	Private	Ulster Volunteers	Killed in Action.
Gordon, Charles	Eden	Private	Ulster Volunteers	Killed.
Lunney, Robert	Aughalane	Private	Ulster Volunteers	Killed.
Lunney, William	Aughalane	Private	Ulster Volunteers	Killed in Action.
LECKPATRICK.				
Allen, John	The Rock	Private	Canadians	Wounded.
Allen, Robert	The Rock	Private	Canadians	
Crawford, Robert	Ballee	Private	9th R. Inn. Fus.	
Darragh, Thomas	Ballymagorry	Private	9th R. Inn. Fus.	
Gourley, Fred.	Ballymagorry	Private	5th R. Inn. Fus.	
Hawthorne, Thomas	Ballymagorry	Private	9th R. Inn. Fus.	
Hawthorne, Wm.	Ballymagorry	Private	9th R. Inn. Fus.	Wounded.
Houston, Thomas	Woodend	Private	Canadians	
Huey, John James	Killynaught	Private	R.A.F.	
McCarter, William	Milltown	Private	9th R. Inn. Fus.	Wounded.
McCrea, Jack	Kennaghan	Private	Scotch Regt.	
McNeill, John	Milltown	Private	9th R. Inn. Fus.	
Nickle, Alex.	Ballymagorry	Private	9th R. Inn. Fus.	
Nickle, Robert	Ballymagorry	Private	9th R. Inn. Fus.	
Pollock, Jack	Artigarvan	Private	R.A.F.	
Pollock, John	Ballymagorry	Private	9th R. Inn. Fus.	Wounded.
Pollock, Robert	Artigarvan	Sergeant	9th R. Inn. Fus.	Died of Wounds.
Reid, Joseph	Ballee	Sergeant	9th R. Inn. Fus.	Wounded.
NEWTOWNSTEWART.				
Arthur, Alex.	Newtownstewart	Private		
Arthur, Fred.	Newtownstewart	Private	R. Inn. Fus.	Killed in Action.
Baird, Arthur G.	Newtownstewart	Sapper	Engineers	Wounded.
Bryden, Harry	Newtownstewart	Private	R. Inn. Fus.	M.C., Kd. in Act.
Dunbar, John	Newtownstewart	Lance-Corporal	R. Inn. Fus.	Killed in Action.
Dunbar, Samuel	Newtownstewart	Private	R. Inn. Fus.	
Dunbar, Wm.	Newtownstewart	Private	R. Inn. Fus.	Wounded.
Elkin, John	Newtownstewart	Private	R. Inn. Fus.	Wounded.
Elkin, Thomas	Newtownstewart	Private	R. Inn. Fus.	Wounded.
Ellis, Thomas	Newtownstewart	Private	Machine Gun Corps	Wounded.
Ellis, William	Newtownstewart	Private	R. Inn. Fus.	Prisoner.
Findlayson, John B.	Newtownstewart	Lance-Corporal	R. Inn. Fus.	
Gordon, R. McIlwaine	Newtownstewart	Private	R.A.F.	
Hall, John	Newtownstewart	Private	R. Inn. Fus.	Killed in Action.
Hall, Samuel	Newtownstewart		Pioneers	
Hall, William	Newtownstewart	Private	R. Inn. Fus.	
Hood, John H.	Newtownstewart	Captain	R.A.M.C.	
Jack, Robert	Newtownstewart	Lance-Corporal	R. Inn. Fus.	
Lyle, John S.	Newtownstewart	Surg. Prob.	R.N.	
McLaughlin, Andrew J.	Newtownstewart	Private	R. Inn. Fus.	
Morton, D. Hamill	Newtownstewart	Captain	R. Inn. Fus.	Wounded and Pris.
Murphy, Samuel	Newtownstewart	Lance-Corporal	R. Inn. Fus.	Wounded.
Murphy, Wm. J.	Newtownstewart	Private	R. Inn. Fus.	
Napier, James	Newtownstewart	Engineer Artificer		
Napier, John	Newtownstewart		M. Marine	
Patrick, Joseph	Newtownstewart	Captain	R.A.M.C.	
Robinson, Henry	Newtownstewart	Private	R. Inn. Fus.	Wounded.
Semple, Robert	Newtownstewart	Private	R. Inn. Fus.	Killed in Action.
Smyth, David P.	Newtownstewart	Corporal	R. Inn. Fus.	Killed in Action.
Walsh, Joseph G.	Newtownstewart	Lance-Corporal	R. Inn. Fus.	
Walsh, O. L.	Newtownstewart	Sergt.-Major	R. Inn. Fus.	
Wilson, Andrew	Newtownstewart	Lieutenant	R. Field Artillery	
COLONIAL AND U.S.A. FORCES.				
Arthur, Andrew	Canada	Sapper	Canadians	
Dunbar, Wm., Jun.	Canada	Corporal	8th Canadians	
Robinson, Stewart	Canada	Private	Canadian Forestry	
Robinson, William	Australia	Private	Australian Forces	Wounded.
Wauchob, David	S. Africa	Captain	S. African Force	
Wray, Alex.	America	Private	U.S. Army	

STRABANE PRESBYTERY. STRABANE.

Name.	Home Address.	Rank.	Regiment, Battalion or Unit.	Remarks.
STRABANE.				
Anderson, Robert	Strabane	Gunner	R.F.A.	
Anderson, Samuel	Strabane	P.S.M.	1/4 York and Lancaster	
Baird, James	Strabane	Private	11th R. Inn. Fus.	Killed in Action.
Barr, Samuel	Strabane	Private	12th R. Inn. Fus.	
Bates, William	Strabane	Private	R. Inn. Fus.	
Blair, Noel W.	Strabane	Private	R. Irish Fus.	
Blair, Wm. Wallace	Strabane	Captain	R.A.M.C.	
Britton, T. C.	Hazelwood	Captain	R.A.M.C.	
Britton, W. K. M.	Hazelwood	2nd Lieutenant	R.F.C.	Killed.
Burke, John	Drumboy	Private	R.I.R.	Died.
Clarke, John Kinghan	The Manse	Lieutenant	R.A.F.	Killed in Action.
Clarke, Thomas Veitch	The Manse	Lieutenant	Indian Army	
Craig, George	Strabane	Private	1st R. Inn. Fus.	Wounded 6 times.
Craig, John	Strabane	Gunner	R.F.A.	
Doherty, James	Strabane	Aircraftsman	R.A.F.	
Donnell, John	Strabane	Gunner	R.F.A.	
Elliott, Alfred	Strabane	Colonel	R.A.M.C.	
Elliott, Cecil Moore	Strabane	Private	7th R. Dub. Fus.	Killed, Sulva Bay.
Gordon, James	Strabane	Gunner	R.F.A.	Died of Wounds.
Gormley, W. J.	Flushtown	Private	R. Inn. Fus.	Died in Hospital.
Harpur, H. P.	Milltown	Captain	R.A.M.C.	
Hill, J. McAdam	Castle Street	Captain	R.A.M.C.	
Hill, J. Rowland	Castle Street	Lt.-Colonel	R.A.M.C.	
Hoy, Alfred	Ulster Bank House	Private	9th R. Irish Fus.	
Hunter, James	Lifford	Private	12th R. Inn. Fus.	
Ingram, Ernest	Strabane	2nd Lieutenant	R.E.	
Ingram, Wm. H.	Strabane	Corporal	9th R. Inn. Fus.	
Kinkaid, David	Strabane	2nd Lieutenant	R. Inn. Fus.	
McClements, George	Strabane	Private	13th A. & S. Highldrs.	
McCorkell, Robert	Lifford	Private	2nd R. Inn. Fus.	Killed in Action.
McGonigle, James	Ballindrait	Trooper	N.I.H.	
Nickle, Alex.	Strabane	Private	12th R. Inn. Fus.	
Orr, Charles	Strabane	Despatch Rider	R.A.F.	
Pollock, John	Strabane	Private	9th R. Inn. Fus.	
Porter, Robert	Strabane	Private	R. Inn. Fus.	
Porter, William	Strabane	Private	M.T. A.S.C.	
Porterfield, David A.	Lifford	Private	R. Inn. Fus.	Killed in Action.
Roulston, A. W.	Strabane	Air Mechanic	R.A.F.	
Roulston, James	Strabane	Private	9th R. Inn. Fus.	
Semple, Robert	Strabane	Private	N.I.H.	
Smith, David	Strabane	Private	1st R. Irish Fus.	
Smyth, W. B.	Strathfoyle	Lieutenant	N.I.H.	
Snodgrass, James	Strabane	Private	12th R. Inn. Fus.	
Stuart, John A. G.	Strabane	Lieutenant	R.G.A.	
Taylor, T.	Lifford	Captain	School of Musketry	
Taylor, W. John	Strabane	Gunner	R.F.A.	
Walls, Thomas A.	Strabane	Officer	R.N.	D.S.O., Killed Jutland Battle
Walls, Wm. D.	Strabane	Mechanic	Anti-Aircraft Ser.	
Weir, John	Drumbuoy	Captain	8th R. Inn. Fus.	Killed in Action.
White, George A.	Strabane	Trooper	SS. 6th Inn. Dragoons	
White, Samuel E.	Strabane	Trooper	SS. 6th Inn. Dragoons	
Young, James	Strabane	Private	R. Inn. Fus.	
COLONIAL FORCE.				
Blair, G. W.	Strabane	Sapper	20th Batt. Canadians	
Blair, Ross	Strabane	Driver	Can. H. Artillery	
Doherty, Harry	Strabane	Lance-Corporal	Can. Infantry	
Doherty, William	Strabane	Private	Can. Infantry	
Fyffe, J. J.	Strabane	Gunner	Can. Artillery	
McClements, R. J.	Bowling Green	Private	Canadians	
McCorkell, Joseph	Lifford	Sergeant	Canadians	
Porterfield, John	Lifford	Private	Canadians	Died of Wounds.
Porterfield, Sam. A.	Lifford	Private	Canadian Cameron Highldrs.	
Thompson, Stanley	Strabane	Driver	Con. A.S.C.	M.M.
URNEY AND SION.				
Adair, David	Church Square	Private	9th R. Inn. Fus.	
Adair, Francis	Church Square	Private	9th R. Inn. Fus.	
Adair, Wm.	Church Square	Corporal	R.F.A.	Wounded.
Adams, Day	Sion Mills	Private	R.A.F.	
Adams, Jack	Sion Mills	Sergeant	N.I.H.	
Cowan, Henry	Sion Mills	Lance-Corporal	9th R. Inn. Fus.	Killed in Action.
Crosbie, Jack	Sion Mills	Lieutenant	R.A.F.	
Dickson, Robert	Sion Mills	Sergeant	Cycling Corps	
Elliott, Herbert	Sion Mills	Private	R.E.	
Elliott, Samuel	Sion Mills	Private	14th R.I.R.	Wounded.
Elvin, George	31 Church Square	Private	9th R. Inn. Fus.	
Elvin, W. J.	31 Church Square	Sergeant	Cycling Corps	
Forrester, Charles	Sion Mills	Private	Can. Rifles	Wounded.

STRABANE PRESBYTERY.   URNEY AND SION.

Name.	Home Address.	Rank.	Regiment, Battalion, or Unit.	Remarks.
Haire, Alex.	Spamount	Private	9th R. Inn. Fus.	Killed in Action.
Haire, James	Albert Place	Private	9th R. Inn. Fus.	Prisoner of War.
Harper, John	Sion Mills	Sergeant	9th R. Inn. Fus.	
Holmes, Charles	Ballybogan	Lieutenant	12th R.I. Rifles	Wounded.
Holmes, William	Ballybogan	Trooper	N.I.H.	
Johnston, Thomas	Sion Mills	Lance-Corporal	9th R. Irish Fus.	Killed in Action.
Lindsay, Andrew	Sion Mills	Private	9th R. Inn. Fus.	Killed in Action.
Love, James	Glentown, Urney	Private	9th R. Inn. Fus.	Killed in Action.
McCallan, William	Tennent Street, Belfast	Private	9th R. Inn. Fus.	Killed in Action.
McConaghy, Fred.	Sion Mills	Driver	A.S.C.	
McConaghy, Harry	Sion Mills	Private	9th R. Inn. Fus.	Killed in Action.
McConaghy, John	Sion Mills	Sergt.-Major	9th R. Inn. Fus.	Wounded.
McConaghy, John	Sion Mills	Private	9th R. Inn. Fus.	Killed in Action
McConaghy, Robert	Sion Mills	Private	9th R. Inn. Fus.	Killed in Action.
McConaghy, Samuel	Sion Mills	Private	9th R. Inn. Fus.	Wounded.
McCrea, James	Sion Mills	Sergeant	2nd R. Inn. Fus.	Wounded and Pris.
McCrea, Joseph B.	Sion Mills	Corporal	1st R.I.R.	Wounded.
McCrea, W. J.	Sion Mills	Sergeant	Garrison Artillery	
McFarland, Andrew	Sion Mills	Corporal	11th R. Inn. Fus.	Killed in Action.
Maxwell, Charles	Castledale	Lieutenant	R. Inn. Fus.	
Maxwell, Charles	Sion Mills	Private	R. Inn. Fus.	Killed in Action.
Maxwell, Hamilton	Sion Mills		R.N.	
Maxwell, Jack	Sion Mills	Private	R. Inn. Fus.	Wounded.
Mills, Harry	Sion Mills	Private	9th R. Inn. Fus.	Killed in Action.
Mills, Joseph	Sion Mills	Private	9th R. Inn. Fus.	Wounded.
Neely, Andrew	Sion Mills	Private	M.G.C.	M.M., Ulster Certicate, Wounded.
Neely, Matthew	Sion Mills	Private	24th P.P. Canadians	Wounded.
Neill, Rev. Gilmour	The Manse, Sion Mills	Captain	Chaplain	
Neill, M. Craig	The Manse, Sion Mills	Sergeant	Can. R.A.M.C.	
Parke, James	Castlederg	Private	London Regt.	Killed in Action.
Parke, Thomas	Castlederg	2nd Lieutenant	Dublin Fus.	Wounded.
Stevenson, Charles	Sion Mills	Lieut-Colonel	Canadian Inft.	Wounded.
Thornton, Harry	Sion Mills	Corporal	R.E.	Wounded.
White, Edward	Sion Mills	Private	Canadian Inft.	Wounded.

TEMPLEPATRICK PRESBYTERY.

Name.	Home Address.	Rank.	Regiment, Battalion or Unit.	Remarks.
FIRST ANTRIM.				
Abernethy, William	Balloo	Private	11th and 12th R.I.R.	
Adair, James	Antrim	Trooper	N.I.H.	Died of Wounds.
Adams, Harry	Church Street	Private	11th R.I.R.	
Adams, James	Church Street	Rifleman	11th R.I.R.	Killed in Action.
Allen, Jack	Castle Street	Private	18th R.I.R.	
Allen, Johnnie	Church Street	Private	11th R.I.R.	
Allen, Thomas	Castle Street	Private	Labour Corps	
Allen, William	Creavery	Gunner	R.F.A.	
Allen, William	Castle Street	Private	11th R.I.R.	
Allen, Wm., Jun.	Castle Street	Private	18th R.I.R.	
Anderson, Harold	High Street	Lance-Corporal	R.G.A.	
Ashe, Samuel	Church Street	Private	Labour Corps	
Baird, Frank	Church Street	Trooper	N.I.H.	
Barbour, James	Boghead	Private	R.G.A.	
Barbour, Robert	Boghead	Private	12th R.I.R.	
Barkley, Arthur	Fountain Street	Private	11th R.I.R.	
Barnett, Robert G.	Canada	Private	R.A.F.	
Beresford, Edgar	The Steeple	Private	12th R.I.R.	
Beresford, Thomas	The Steeple	Private	12th R.I.R.	
Brown, John	Belmount	Private	11th R.I.R.	
Brown, Robert	Muckamore	Private	R.A.M.C.	
Buick, Jackson	Milltown	Sergeant	11th R.I.R.	Killed in Action.
Buick, James	Milltown	Lance-Corporal	11th R.I.R.	
Buick, Joseph	Milltown	Trooper	N.I.H.	
Cassidy, James	Balloo	Private	9th R.I. Rifles	
Christie, James	Riverside	Sergeant	R.A.F.	
Clarke, H.	Ballygrooby, Ran'town	Private	11th R.I.R.	
Clarke, Wm.	Islandreagh, Antrim	Corporal	4th R.I.R.	
Colgan, Thomas	Ballyclare	Private	R.A.M.C.	
Craig, James	Moylena, Muckamore	Private	M.G.C.	
Craig, William	Moylena, Muckamore	Trooper	N.I.H.	
Craig, Wm.	Church Street	Private	11th R.I.R.	
Donald, James	Canada	Private	7th Brigade C.F.A.	Prisoner of War.

TEMPLEPATRICK PRESBYTERY. — FIRST ANTRIM.

Name.	Home Address.	Rank.	Regiment, Battalion or Unit.	Remarks.
Donald, John W.	Templepatrick	Seaman	R.N. Depot	
Fleming, Harry	Kilbegs	Sergeant	12th R.I.R.	
Francey, John	Massereene	Private	R.A.M.C.	
Gleghorn, David	Crosshill, Crumlin	Corporal	12th R.I.R.	
Gleghorn, William	Potterswalls	Private	11th R.I.R.	Killed in Action.
Graham, Ezekiel	Massereene	Private	11th R.I.R.	
Gre n, David	Crosscannon	Private	11th R.I.R.	Prisoner of War.
Green, William	Crosscannon	Private	3rd R.I.R.	
Hall, Norman	High Street	Lieutenant	6th R. West Kent Regt.	
Jackson, Gordon	Muckamore	Cadet	O.C.B. Batt.	
Jackson, Samuel	Muckamore	Private	3rd R.I.R.	
Jackson, William	Castle Street	Lance-Corporal	10th R.I.R.	Prisoner of War.
Jamison, Thomas	Church Street	Sergeant	N.I.H.	M.M.
Kane, Joseph	Muckamore	Private	723rd Labour Corps	
Kirkpatrick, David	Burnside	Private	13th R.I.R.	
Kirkpatrick, Samuel	Burnside	Private	11th R.I.R.	Severely Wounded.
Kirkpatrick, Thomas	Burnside	Private	12th R.I.R.	Prisoner of War.
Kirkpatrick, Wm.	Bouverie St., Glasgow	Corporal	5th A. & S. Highldrs.	
Knox, William	Riverside	Private	3rd R.I.R.	
Lynn, Fred.	Creavery	Trooper	N.I.H.	
Lynn, James	Riverside			
McBurney, John	Massereene	Sergeant	18th R.I.R.	Wounded.
McCrory, Andrew	Riverside	Trooper	N.I.H.	
McCrubb, Daniel	Church Street	Private	11th R.I.R.	Wounded.
McCrubb, Thomas	Church Street	Lance-Corporal	1st R.I.R.	
McDonald, Edward	47 Harrisburg St., Belfast	Private	9th R.I.R.	
McDonald, James	47 Harrisburg St., Belfast	Private	9th R.I.R.	Prisoner of War.
McDonald, Thomas	47 Harrisburg St., Belfast	Lance-Corporal	9th R.I.R.	
McFadden, Wm.	Moylena	Private	11th R.I.R.	Killed in Action.
McFetridge, Thomas	Doncaster	Captain	R.A.M.C.	
McKillop, Andrew	High Street	Sapper	36th Sig. Corps R.E.	Severely Wounded.
McKittrick, Charles	Riverside	Private	1st R.I.R.	
McMurray, James	Randalstown	Corporal	11th R.I.R.	
Mawhinney, Samuel	Potterswalls	Sergeant	A.S.C.	
Millar, John	Fountain Street	Private	107th Labour Corps	
Millar, James	Fountain Street	Private	11th R.I.R.	Died of Wounds.
Millar, Samuel	Ballyno	Private	9th R.I. Fus.	
Millar, Wm. S.	Market Square	Private	A.S.C.	
Milliken, Wm.	47 Harrisburg St., Belfast	Private	R.A.F.	
Montgomery, Thomas	Parkhall	Lieutenant	R.A.M.C., R.A.F.	
Montgomery, Samuel	Parkhall	Lieutenant	Ministry of Food	
Moore, Frank W.	Railway Street	Private	R.A.M.C.	Died of Wounds.
Morton, William	Islandbawn	Trooper	N.I.H.	
Neilly, John	Massereene	Corporal	N.I.H.	
O'Neill, James	Riverside	Trooper	R.I.R.	
Pollock, James	Church Street	Co. Sergt. Major	7th R.I.R.	
Pollock, Thomas	Church Street	Private	R.A.M.C.	
Pollock, Victor	Church Street	Private	11th R.I.R.	Killed in Action.
Rainey, John	The Steeple	Private	11th R.I.R.	
Rainey, Robert	Church Street	Lance-Corporal	11th R.I.R.	
Reford, Allen	Cemetery Road	Private	5th R.I.R.	
Reford, Frank	Bouverie, Port-Glasgow	Private	11th R.I.R.	Gassed.
Reford, James	Cemetery Road	Lance-Corporal	W. Riding Regt.	
Scott, Jack	Ashville	Trooper	N.I.H.	
Steele, Harry	Castle Street	Lance-Corporal	12th R.I.R.	
Steele, Martin	Fountain Street	Sergeant	18th R.I.R.	Gassed and Wd.
Steele, Wm. H.	Church Street	Private	R.A.F.	
Swann, James	Fountain Street	Sergeant		Died of Wounds.
Thompson, Jonathan	Riverside	Private	18th R.I.R.	
Thompson, Thomas	Market Square	Sapper	Wireless, Mesop. Ex. Force	
Vance, Ezekiel	Riverside	Lieutenant	11th R.I.R.	Prisoner of War, Died of Wounds.
West, Bruce A.	Riverside	Captain	R.A.M.C., R.G.A.	Wounded.
West, John W.	Riverside	Lt.-Colonel	R.A.M.C.	French Legion of Honour, C.M.G.
Whiteside, Albert	High Street	2nd Lieutenant	14th R.I.R.	Killed in Action.
Wilkinson, William	Castle Street	Private	11th R.I.R.	Prisoner of War.
Wilson, Francis	Kilbegs	Lance-Corporal	13th R.I.R.	
Wilson, Geo. H.	Castle Street	Private	17th R.I.R.	Prisoner of War.
Wilson, Hugh G.	Ard Cottage, Larne	Captain	R.A.M.C., 12th R.I.R.	
Wilson, James	Potterswalls	Private	11th R.I.R.	
Wilson, T. A.	Kilbegs	Lance-Corporal	A.S.C.	
Wilson, Wm. A.	Ard Cottage, Larne	Q.M. Sergt.	12th R.I.R.	
Wright, John	Fountain Street	Lieutenant	C.P.O. Wireless	
Wright, Stanley	Fountain Street	Corporal	11th R.I.R.	Wounded.
Young, James	Church Street	Lieutenant	N.I.H.	Wounded, M.C.

COLONIAL AND U.S.A. FORCE.

Name.	Home Address.	Rank.	Regiment, Battalion or Unit.	Remarks.
Anderson, Norman	Canada	Private	4th Canadians	
Armstrong, James	America	Private	American Army	
Christie, Thomas	Canada	Sapper	23rd Canadians	
Christie, Walter	Antrim	Private	Canadians	
Donald, Wm.	Canada	Driver	Canadian F.A.	

TEMPLEPATRICK PRESBYTERY, FIRST ANTRIM.

Name.	Home Address.	Rank.	Regiment, Battalion or Unit.	Remarks.
Ellison, James	Canada	Private	Canadians	
Fletcher, Joseph S.	Canada	Corporal	2nd Canadians	
Heatly, Jack	Canada	Private	27th Canadians	
Henry, Robert	Canada	Private	1st N.Z. Force	
Hughes, James	Canada	Private	Canadians	
Lynn, Hugh	Antrim	Gunner	American M.G.	
McFerran, James H.	America	Lieutenant	U.S. Army	
Miller, James	New Zealand	Private	N.Z. Machine Brigade	
Moody, Matthew	Ballyharvey	Private	Can. R.A.	
Moore, Thomas	Canada	Driver	1st Can. Artillery	
Scott, James	Australia	Private	Australian Army	
West, Fred.	Antrim		S. African	

CRUMLIN.

Name.	Home Address.	Rank.	Regiment, Battalion or Unit.	Remarks.
Ayre, Samuel	Crumlin	Rifleman	11th R.I.R.	Killed in Action.
Campbell, J.	Crumlin	Rifleman	16th R.I.R.	Died in Hospital.
Campbell, J. H.	Cherryvalley	Rifleman	11th R.I.R.	Wounded.
Canning, C. C.	The Manse, Crumlin	Captain	11th R.I.R.	
Doyle, James Henry	Crumlin	Sergeant	11th R.I.R.	Wounded.
Fleming, J.	Crumlin	Rifleman	11th R.I.R.	Killed in Action.
Fleming, Robert	Crumlin	Rifleman	18th R.I.R.	
Fleming, S.	Crumlin	Rifleman	11th R.I.R.	Wounded.
Gillen, J.	Helen Street	Rifleman	18th R.I.R.	Wounded.
Gleghorn, David	Brysonstown	Corporal	11th R.I.R.	
Gray, S.	Milltown	Rifleman	11th R.I.R.	
Gray, W.	Milltown	Corporal	11th R.I.R.	
Harbinson, R.	Lough Neagh Terrace	Rifleman	11th R.I.R.	
Lindsay, H.	Crumlin	Rifleman	11th R.I.R.	
Lyle, J.	Crumlin	2nd Lieutenant	11th R.I.R.	
McConnell, A. E. P.	Cherryvalley	Captain	R.A.M.C.	M.C., Italian Medal.
McKee, R.	Crumlin	Private	Cam. Highldrs.	
McQuillan, W.	Crumlin	Sergeant	11th R.I.R.	Killed in Action.
Nicholl, S.	Crumlin	Rifleman	11th R.I.R.	
Nicholl, W.	Crumlin	Sergeant	11th R.I.R.	Wounded.
Park, Andrew	Ballydonaghy	Trooper	N.I.H.	
Rea, John	Crumlin	Trooper	N.I.H.	
Robinson, John	Crumlin	Private	A.S.C.	
Scott, Harry M.	Glen Oak	Lieutenant	R.N.V.R.	
Taggart, A.	Crumlin	Rifleman	11th R.I.R.	
Watterson, J. A.	Crumlin	Private	R.A.M.C.	
Williamson, Andrew	Crumlin	Rifleman	11th R.I.R.	Killed in Action.
Williamson, J.	Ballydonaghy	Rifleman	11th R.I.R.	
Williamson, Matt.	Ballydonaghy	Rifleman	3rd R.I.R.	
Williamson, W. J.	Crumlin	Corporal	11th R.I.R.	Killed in Action.

COLONIAL FORCES.

Name.	Home Address.	Rank.	Regiment, Battalion or Unit.	Remarks.
Campbell, A.	Cherryvalley	Private	3rd Canadian Force	
Hull, Robert	Dundesart	Sergeant	Australian Force	Killed in Action.
Johnston, Robert	Lough Neagh Terrace	Lance-Corporal	39th Canadian Force	

FIRST DONEGORE.

Name.	Home Address.	Rank.	Regiment, Battalion or Unit.	Remarks.
Agnew, Thomas	Parkgate	Private	R.I.R.	
Curry, Wm.	Parkgate	Sergeant	1st S.C.D.	Wounded.
Davison, Andrew	Dunadry	Private	12th R.I.R.	
Donald, Robert	Donegore	Private	12th R.I.R.	
Finlay, Thomas	Parkgate	Private	12th R.I.R.	Wounded.
Graham, C.	Dunadry	Private	R.F.A.	
Graham, N. C.	Dunadry	Captain	R.A.M.C.	M.C.
McCall, Thomas	Doagh	Private	R.I.R.	Wounded.
McClure, Frank	Parkgate	Private	12th R.I.R.	
McConnell, Thomas W.	Doagh	Major	G.P.O.	
McGrugan, Alex.	Parkgate	Private	B.T.S.	
McGrugan, George	Parkgate	Private	1st I.G.	Wounded.
McGrugan, Hugh	Parkgate	Private	12th and 13th R.I.R.	Wounded.
McKinney, George J.	Parkgate	Corporal	R.A.F.	
McQuade, Robert	Parkgate	Private	12th R.I.R.	
Minford, A. McK.	Parkgate	Lieutenant	R.A.M.C.	Died of Wounds.
Minford, J. B.	Parkgate	Lieutenant	R.A.M.C.	Wounded.
Nesbitt, Wm. John	Parkgate	Private	12th R.I.R.	Wd. and Pris.
Saunderson, Wm.	Doagh	Captain	R.A.M.C.	
Skelton, Dan	Templepatrick	Private	12th R.I.R.	Wounded.
Steele, David	Parkgate	Private	12th R.I.R.	
Steele, Frank	Parkgate	Private	12th R.I.R.	
Steele, James	Parkgate	Private	12th R.I.R.	
Steele, Samuel	Parkgate	Private	12th R.I.R.	
Stirling, George	Parkgate	Private	R.A.F.	

TEMPLEPATRICK PRESBYTERY.

FIRST DONEGORE.

Name.	Home Address.	Rank.	Regiment, Battalion or Unit.	Remarks.
COLONIAL FORCE.				
Jameson, John	Parkgate	Private	Can. M.R.	Killed in Action.
Lowry, Wm.	Donegore	Private	Can. Ex. F.	Wounded.
Saunderson, Henry	Doagh	Private	Winnipeg Rifles	Prisoner, escaped.
Todd, John	Doagh	Private	Winnipeg M.R.	Killed in Action.
Todd, William	Doagh	Private	Winnipeg M.R.	Wounded.
SECOND DONEGORE.				
Craig, Hugh	Manse, Templepatrick	2nd Lieutenant	R.I.R.	
Killen, David	Islandreagh	Private	Royal Marines	
Lyttle, Abram	Parkgate	Private	2nd King's Royal Rifles	
Ramsey, William	Newmill	Private	187th Coy. Royal Engineers	
COLONIAL FORCES.				
Adair, John	Ballywee	Private	78th Canadian M.G.C.	Killed.
Coulter, John	Browndod, Doagh	Corporal	2nd Batt. Can. Ex. F.	
Killen, James	Islandreagh	Private	26th N.Z. Rifles	
Moore, William	Ballyno	Sergeant	9th Can. M.G.	
Ramsey, W. J.	Ballycleverty	Sergeant	S. Africa R.A.M.C.	Wounded.
Stevenson, Alex.	Ballywoodock	Private	3rd Can. Labour Batt.	
Murdock, W. A.	Ballygowan	Private	No. 2. Regina Ex. Force	Died.
Warwick, Alex. C.	Browndod	Corporal	Can. R.E.	
DUNDROD.				
Brown, Adam	Torneroy	Driver	A.S.C.	Died in France.
Brown, George	Randox	Private	11th R.I.R.	Missing, Pres. Kd.
Brown, Hugh	Torneroy	Sergt.-Major	R.E.	
Carlisle, Samuel	Aughnamillan	Driver	15th R.I.R.	Wounded.
Clendinning, A.	Glenavy	Corporal	R.I.R.	
Corkey, Rev. D. S.	The Manse	Captain	Chaplain	Wounded, lost arm, Ment. in Des.
Henderson, William	Dundrod	Private	15th R.I.R.	Gassed.
Heaney, Thomas	Knockcairn	Private	11th R.I.R.	Killed in Action.
Henderson, F. G.	Dundrod	Private	R.A.S.C.	Wounded.
Irvine, Robert	Ballyhill	Private	10th Yorks. Regt.	
Johnston, Samuel	Hopevale	Trooper	N.I.H.	
Lowry, Robert	Ballydonaghy	Trooper	N.I.H.	Wounded.
McCartney, John	Glenavy	Driver	11th R.I.R.	Wounded.
McCartney, Samuel	Dundrod	Gunner	R.G.A.	
McCullough, Archibald	Knockcairn	2nd Lieutenant	2nd Inn. Fus.	
Mairs, John	Dundrod	Lance-Corporal	R. Marines	
COLONIAL FORCE.				
Armstrong, Wm. J.	Ballyhill	Private	Can. Forestry	
Calvert, David	Ballyhill	Private	Canadians	
Graham, Robert	Ballyhill	Private	Canadians	
McFarlane, Robert	Ballyhill	Sergeant	19th Can. E.F.	
McFarlane, W.	Ballyhill	Gunner	70th Battery Can. E.F.	
Milliken, Jos. T.	Ballyhill	Private	Canadians	
Spence, Sinclair A.	Ballykennedy	Corporal	Reserve Batt. Canadians	Gassed.
Upton, John	Budore	Driver	1st Can. M.G.	
DUNEANE.				
Andrews, R. J.	Duneane	Private	R.I.R.	
Canmer, J.	Duneane	Sergeant	R.I.R.	
Elliott, Rev. R. C., B.A.	The Manse	Captain	Chaplain	
King, Alfie	Toome	Private	R.A.F.	
McClure, Dr. S.	Artlone	Lieutenant	R.A.M.C.	
Macrory, James	Duneane	Private	R.I.R.	
Macrory, Robert	Duneane	Private	R.I.R.	
Russell, James	Duneane	Lieutenant	R.I.R.	
KILLEAD.				
Adair, George	Seacash	Private	R.I.R.	Killed in Action.
Adair, John	Seacash	Private	N.I.H.	
Adams, Robert	Tully	Private	R.I.R.	Wounded.
Ash, John	Rathmore	Private	R.M.L.I.	Wounded.
Boyd, Richard	Boghead	Private	R.I.R.	
Ceasar, Hugh	Ballyrobin	Private	R.I.R.	
Courtney, William	Killealy	Private	Scots Guards	Wounded.
Cummings, James	Tully	Private	Scots Guards	Killed in Action.
Cummings, Thomas	Tully	Private	Irish Guards	Wounded.
Erskine, Andrew	Seacash	Lieutenant	R.I.R.	
French, James	Ballyrobin	Private	R.I.R.	
Hunter, James	Killealy	Private	R.I.R.	Wounded.
McKelvey, Matthew	Boghead	Private	R.I.R.	Killed in Action.
McKibbin, Robert		Private	R.I.R.	

TEMPLEPATRICK PRESBYTERY. KILLEAD.

Name.	Home Address.	Rank.	Regiment, Battalion or Unit.	Remarks.
Megarry, James	Ballymacilhoyle	Corporal	R.I.R.	Killed in Action.
Molloy, Joseph	Lisnataylor	Private	R. Inn. Fus.	Wounded.
Moore, James	Aughnamillan	Private	R.I.R.	Prisoner.
Nicholl, James	Aughnamillan	Private	R.I.R.	
Officer, John	Aughnamillan	Lieutenant	R.A.F.	
Reid, Wm.	Killealy	Private	R.I.R.	Killed in Action.
Rodgers, Wm. James	Diamond	Private	A.S.C.	
Thursby, James	Ballyhill	Private	R.I.R.	
Wallace, Robert	Ballyrobin	Private	2nd Norfolk Regt.	Wounded.
White, Thomas	Lisnataylor	Private	N.I.H.	
Williamson, Samuel	Crumlin	Private	R.I.R.	Died of Wounds.
COLONIAL FORCES.				
Ansley, J. Taggart	Carnmany	Private	Canadians	
Fleming, George	Ballyhill	Private	Canadians	
Fleming, Robert	Ballyhill	Private	Canadians	
French, David	Ballyrobin	Private	Canadians	
Gault, William	Killealy	Private	Canadians	Wounded.
Gilmore, George	Ballyhill	Private	Canadians	
McComb, William	Cornhill	Private	Canadians	
Mackey, Blair	Killealy	Private		Twice wounded.
Mackey, Robert	Killealy	Private	S. African Regt.	
Mackey, W. Allen	Killealy	Private	S. African Regt.	
Molloy, Moody M.	Lisnataylor	Private	N.Z. Rifles	Wounded.
Molloy, Richard	Lisnataylor	Private	N.Z. Rifles	Wounded.
Morrison, Kennedy	Crookedstone	Private	Canadians	Wounded.
Morrison, Thomas	Crookedstone	Private	Canadians	
Robinson, Edmund	Aughnamillan	Private	N.Z. Rifles	
Williamson, Robert	Ardmore	Private	Canadians	
LYLEHILL.				
Barron, Humphrey	Umgall	Private	R.M.L.I.	
Barron, Samuel	Umgall	Lieutenant	R.A.M.C., Indian Army	
Blair, Samuel	Ballyutoag	Driver	159th Field Artillery	
Brown, John	Lylehill	Private	14th R.I.R.	
Hanna, Alexander	Ballymather	Flight Sub-Lieut.	R.N.A.S.	
Herdman, James	Ballyhill	Sergeant	Northumberland Fus.	Wounded.
Rea, David	Loanends	Lance-Corporal	11th R.I.R.	
Rea, James	Kilgreel	Driver	A.S.C., 7th Cav. Brigade	
Stewart, John	Lylehill	Private	M.G.C.	Killed in Action.
Woods, Thomas	Umgall	Lance-Corporal	A.S.C., A.P.O.	
COLONIAL FORCES.				
Alexander, Ezekiel Wylie	Ballyutoag	Private	124th P.N.R. Canadians	
Barron, Robert	Umgall	Private	New Zealand Forces	
Blain, Thomas	Ballyutoag	Sapper	1st Can. Railway Troops	
Carlisle, Samuel	Kilgreel	Private	21st Res. Canadians	Wounded.
George, David	Craigarogan	Private	5th Batt. 1st Can. Div.	Twice Wounded.
Mackey, David	Rickamore	Private	Canadian Highldrs.	Wounded.
Moore, James	Ballyutoag	Private	Can. Ex. Force	Killed in Action.
McMurray, George	Kilgreel	Private	15th Batt. Canadians	Killed in Action.
McMurray, Wm.	Kilgreel	Private	Canadian Highldrs.	Died.
MUCKAMORE.				
Alexander, James	Dunadry	Lieutenant	R.N.R.	
Allen, Robert	Dunadry	Private	R.E.	
Campbell, Samuel	Muckamore	Private	12th R.I.R.	Wounded.
Close, William	Muckamore	Private	R.E.	
Cowan, James	Clady Cottage	Lieut.-Colonel	R.A.M.C.	
Cowan, John	Clady Cottage	Private	A.S.C.	
Craig, James	Dunadry	Sergeant	2nd Dragoon Guards	
Craig, Thomas	Clady	Private	R.M.R.	
Cunningham, Joseph	Dunadry	Sergeant	12th R.I.R.	D.C.M.
Davidson, Hamilton	Dunadry	Private	R.N.R.	
Davidson, Walter	Dunadry	Private	R. Irish Fus.	
Davidson, W. C.	Dunadry	Private	Northumberland Fus.	Wounded.
Doole, Isaac	Muckamore	Private	12th R.I.R.	
Doole, William	Muckamore	Private	12th R.I.R.	
Eakin, Thomas	Clady	Sergeant	12th R.I.R.	
Elliott, Samuel	Clady	Private	11th R.I.R.	
Francey, Robert J.	Muckamore	Private	12th R.I.R.	
Goudy, Joseph	Muckamore	Private	12th R.I.R.	
Graham, William	Dunadry	Private	12th R.I.R.	
Harkin, Andrew	Dunadry	Private	12th R.I.R.	Killed in Action.
Harkin, William	Dunadry	Private	11th R.I.R.	Killed in Action.
Hunter, Edward	Dunadry	Private	12th R.I.R.	
Hunter, James	Dunadry	Lance-Corporal	12th R.I.R.	Wounded.
Jackson, Matthew	Clady	Private	N.I.H.	
Kerr, Hugh	Clady	Private	N.I.H.	
Lilley, Robert	Muckamore	Sergeant	A. & S. Highldrs.	M.M.

TEMPLEPATRICK PRESBYTERY. MUCKAMORE.

Name.	Home Address.	Rank.	Regiment, Battalion or Unit.	Remarks.
Lyle, S. F.	Ballyrobin	Private	12th R.I.R.	Wounded.
McAdam, John	Clady	2nd Lieutenant	Black Watch	M.C., Twice Wd.
McAulay, James	Dunadry	Private	12th R.I.R.	
McIvor, Samuel	Clady	Sergeant	12th R.I.R.	Killed in Action.
McQuillan, Wm.	Clady	Sergeant	R.I.R.	
Newton, John	Dunadry	Private	R.G.A.	
Rainey, John	Clady	Private	12th R.I.R.	
Reid, James	Muckamore	Private	12th R.I.R.	Twice Wounded.
Richardson, James	Muckamore	Private	Y.C.V.	Died.
Skelton, Arthur		Private	11th R.I.R.	
Smith, R. T.	Dunadry	Private	R.E.	
Smyth, W. J.	Muckamore	Private	12th R.I.R.	Killed in Action.
Stirling, David	Muckamore	Private	12th R.I.R.	Wounded.
Walker, James	Clady	Private	Y.C.V.	Killed in Action.
White, Joseph	Dunadry	Private	Y.C.V.	Wounded.
Wilson, James	Dunadry	Private	N.I.H.	
COLONIAL FORCES.				
Gray, Wilfrid	Dunadry	Private	Aust. L. Inft.	
Logan, A. P.	Kilmakee	Private	R.E., Canadians	
McGrath, David	Muckamore	Private	Canadians	Wd'd and Missing.
FIRST RANDALSTOWN.				
Clarke, Hugh	Randalstown	Private	11th R.I.R.	Twice Wounded.
Clarke, William	Randalstown	Corporal	11th R.I.R.	Wounded.
Craig, James	Randalstown	Captain	7th R.I.R.	Twice Wounded.
Ferguson, H. R. M., M.D.	The Manse, Randalstown	Captain	R.A.M.C., West Africa	Ment. in Des.
Ferguson, James M., M.B.	The Manse, Randalstown	Captain	R.A.M.C.	Ment. in Des. and Killed in Action.
Hughes, James	Randalstown	Private	11th R.I.R.	
Kernohan, D.	Mucklerammer	Lieutenant	N.I.H.	
McCaw, Alexander	Randalstown	Private	R.F.C.	
McFadden, George	Leitrim, Randalstown	Trooper	N.I.H.	
Millar, David	Magherabeg	Lance-Corporal	20th R.I.R.	Killed in Action.
Millar, William	Magherabeg	Sergeant	11th R.I.R.	Wounded and Pris.
Sloan, George	Randalstown	Sergeant	Egypt E.F., 54th E. An. Div.	
Speedie, T. J.	Clover Hill	Lance-Corporal	12th R.I.R.	Wounded.
Speedie, W.	Clover Hill	Captain	R.A.M.C.	
Wilson, Joseph	Randalstown	Corporal	11th R.I.R.	
COLONIAL AND U.S.A. FORCES.				
Duff, Thomas	Randalstown	Sapper	Can. Signal Corps	
Ferguson, C. G.	The Manse, Randalstown	Private	Can. M.G. Corps	
Ferguson, J. H. G.	The Manse, Randalstown	Sergeant	Can. A.S. Corps	
McFadden, William	Leitrim, Randalstown	Sergeant	R.A.F., U.S.A.	
Speedie, Henry	Clover Hill	Corporal	Can Cavl. Brigade	Killed in Action.
Swann, James	Randalstown	Corporal	Can. A.S.C.	
SECOND RANDALSTOWN.				
Agnew, W. L.	Randalstown	Captain	R.A.M.C.	
Agnew, W. R.	Ballymachroy	Sergt.-Major	Scots Greys	
Cameron, S.	Groggan	Private	R.A.F.	
Drennan, R.	Groggan	Private	11th R.I.R.	Missing.
Foster, A.	Cloughouge	Private	11th R.I.R.	Killed in Action.
Gordon, E.	Andraid	Corporal	N.I.H.	
Haire, J.	Ballytresna	Private	11th R.I.R.	
Haire, R.	Ballytresna	Private	11th R.I.R.	
Haire, Thomas	Ballytresna	Private	11th R.I.R.	
Houston, J.	Feehogue	Private	11th R.I.R.	
Jinkins, J.	Aghaboy	Private	11th R.I.R.	
Logan, R.	Groggan		R.N.	
Lynn, J.	Kilnock	Private	N.I.H.	
McAuley, W. J.	Tamlaght	Corporal	N.I.H.	Killed in Action.
McIlwaine, H.	Randalstown	Private	R.A.F.	
McKay, R.	Randalstown	Sergeant	R.A.M.C., 109th F.A.	M.M.
McLean, J.	Andraid	Private	11th R.I.R.	
McLean, J.	Andraid	Private	11th R.I.R.	Killed in Action.
Osborne, W.	Craigmore	Lance-Corporal	11th R.I.R.	Killed in Action.
Seymour, J.	Randalstown	Private	9th R. Inn. Fus.	
Smyth, A.	Caddy	Private	Gordon Highldrs.	
Smyth, T.	Caddy	Lance-Corporal	11th R.I.R.	Missing.
Young, J.	Caddy	Private	11th R.I.R.	
Young, W.	Caddy	Private	11th R.I.R.	
CANADIAN AND U.S.A. FORCES.				
Millar, H. H.	Magherabeg	Trooper	U.S.A.	
Nimmo, J.	Leitrim	Corporal	Canadian Force	
Nimmo, J.	Creggan	Private	Canadian Force	

TEMPLEPATRICK PRESBYTERY.   SECOND RANDALSTOWN.

Name.	Home Address.	Rank.	Regiment, Battalion or Unit.	Remarks.
Smyth, R. J.	Caddy	Private	U.S.A.	
Smyth, T.	Caddy	Private	U.S.A.	Killed in Action.
Smyth, W. J.	Caddy	Private	U.S.A.	
	TEMPLEPATRICK.			
Barnes, Charles	Carnanee	Private	A.S.C.	Wounded.
Bill, Hugh	Ballyrobert	Sergeant	R.E.	
Bill, John	Ballycushan	Rifleman	11th R.I.R.	
Davidson, J. L.	Ballypallady	Gunner	M.G.C.	Wounded.
Goudy, Wm.	Doagh	Private	R.I.R.	
Harper, David	Ballycraigy	Private	12th R.I.R.	
Hoy, Samuel	Ricamore	Private	R.I.R.	Killed in Action.
Hoy, Walter	Ricamore	Private	12th R.I.R.	
Ingram, Hugh		Private	R.I.R.	Wounded.
McBride, Arthur R.	Hydepark	Captain	12th R.I.R.	Twice Wd., Killed.
McCammond, Frank	Ballyrobert	Private	A.O.D.	
McCammond, James	Roughfort	Private	12th R.I.R.	
McCammond, Joseph	Ballyrobert	Private	18th R.I.R.	
McClay, Frank	Carnanee	Private	M.G.C.	
McClay, Robert	Carnanee	Private	18th R.I.R.	
McClay, Samuel	Roughfort	Private	12th R.I.R.	Killed in Action.
McCrum, Charles	Cloughinduff	Private	1st R. Dub. Fus.	Wounded.
McCrum, Robert	Cloughinduff			
McCrum, Robert C.	Kilgreel	Lieutenant	14th R.I.R.	Wounded.
McFarland, George	Ballyvesey	Private	8th R.I.R.	Wounded.
McFarland, John	Ballyvesey	Private	R.I.R.	Wounded.
McFarland, Robert	Ballyvesey	Lance-Corporal	5th R. Inn. Fus.	Killed in Action.
McIlwaine, Andrew	Templepatrick	Private	11th R.I.R.	
McIlwaine, John	Ballyvesey	Private	2nd I. Guards	Wounded.
McIlwrath, Rev. John	The Manse	Captain	Chaplain	
McNeilly, Robert	Ballypallady	Private	R.I.R.	Killed in Action.
McNeice, J.	Ballyvesey	Private	1st R.I. Fus.	Wounded.
McNeice, Tom	Ballyvesey	Corporal	R. Inn. Fus.	Twice Wounded.
Malcom, John	Roughfort	Private	R.I.R.	Wounded.
Mawhinney, John	Templepatrick	Private	11th R.I.R.	
Montgomery, Alex.	Ballycraigy	Private	12th R.I.R.	Wounded.
Montgomery, Andrew	Ballycraigy	Private	12th R.I.R.	
Moore, James		Private	11th R.I.R.	Prisoner.
Nawn, Charles	Cloughinduff	Private	3rd Northumberland Fus.	
Nesbitt, John	Roughfort	Private	B.W.	
Rea, David	Craigarogan	Corporal	11th R.I.R.	
Rea, John	Carnanee	Private	M.G. Corps	Twice Wounded.
Robinson, Joseph	Carnanee	Private	9th R. Inn. Fus.	Wounded.
Robinson, William	Templepatrick	Private	R.I.R.	
Spence, William	Roughfort	Private	12th R.I.R.	
Wilson, Francis	Kilgreel	Private	2nd R. Irish Fus.	
	COLONIAL FORCES.			
Davidson, Robert	Ballypallady	Corporal	Can. Ex. Force	Wounded.
Davidson, Thomas	Ballypallady	Corporal	2nd Aust. Ex. Force	Twice Wounded.
McClatchey, Wm. Bell	Ballymartin	Co. Sergt.-Major	S.A. Railway Section	
Taylor, David	Ballypallady	Private	Can. Ex. Force	

TYRONE PRESBYTERY.

Name.	Home Address.	Rank.	Regiment, Battalion or Unit.	Remarks.
	ALBANY.			
Martin, Alexander	Albany	Private	R. In. Fus.	Killed in Action.
Martin, James	Albany	Stoker	R.N.	
Martin, Robert	Albany	Private	14th R.I.R.	Wounded.
Watters, Hugh Henry	Albany	Corporal	H.L.I.	
	COAGH.			
Ashcroft, Albert	Coagh	Private	N.I.H.	
Ashcroft, Hugh	Coagh	Sergeant	N.I.H.	
Carson, Dr. Joseph T.	Coagh	Captain	R.A.M.C.	
Cowan, James	Annahavil	Cadet	R.N.R.	
Cowan, John H.	Annahavil	Lieutenant	R.N.V.R.	Prisoner.
Curry, Fred.	Coagh	Private	R. In. Fus.	Died of Wounds.
Curry, Joseph	Coagh	Private	R. In. Fus.	

TYRONE PRESBYTERY.   COAGH.

Name.	Home Address.	Rank.	Regiment, Battalion or Unit.	Remarks.
Greer, W. James	Mawillian	Rifleman	10th R.I.R.	Killed in Action.
Harkness, Thomas	Killygorland	Private	N.I.H.	
Jardine, George	Coagh	1st Class Stoker	R.N.	
MacKeown, Samuel	Coagh	Sergeant	14th Worcesters	
COLONIAL FORCES.				
Harkness, Alexander	Coagh	Private	N.Z. Force	
Harkness, Willie	Killygorland	Lieutenant	Canadian E.F.	
Sloan, Andrew	Coagh	Private	Australian I. Force	
Watters, Robert	Albany	Private	Canadian Force	
Watters, William James		Sergeant	Canadian Inf.	
BALLYGONEY.				
Burgess, Charles	Coagh	Captain	R.A.M.C.	
Gibson, Matthew	Ardtrea	Lieutenant	R.A.M.C.	
McKee, William	Ballygoney	Captain	R.A.M.C.	Croix de Guerre, Men. in Des.
MacKeown, George	Tamlaght	Sergeant	Leinster Regt.	
MacKeown, Robert W.	Tamlaght		R.N.A.S.	
Mullan, William	Annahavil	Private	R. In. Fus.	
Shaw, William		Drummer	3rd R. In. Fus.	
COLONIAL FORCES.				
Beattie, Edmond	Lurganbuoy	Driver	1st Canadian Div.	
Bell, Albert	Coagh	Lance-Corporal	N.Z. Force	Died of Wounds.
Burgess, Harold	Coagh	Sergeant	S.A. Rifles	
Burgess, Robert	Coagh	Sapper	E.A. Pioneers	Killed in Action.
Hogg, William	Knockinroe	Private	Devon Regt.	
Spritt, William James	Ringsend, Moneymore	Gunner	2nd Canadian Div.	
BRIGH.				
Donnelly, Samuel		Private	15th R. Scots	Killed in Action.
Farr, James		Private	R. In. Fus.	
Farr, Robert		Private	R. In. Fus.	Wounded.
Farr, Robert		Private	R. In. Fus.	
Smyth, William		Private	R. In. Fus.	
Whinnery, William		Private	R. In. Fus.	Wounded.
CLAGAN.				
Compton, Thomas J.	Dunmore	Farrier	A.S.C.	
Crooks, James	Ballybriest	Private		
Dale, Robert A.	Mobuy	Cadet	R.A.F.	
Donnelly, James	Ballynagilly	Private		
Johnston, Samuel	Knockadoo	Gunner	A 102nd Brigade, 23rd Div.	M.M. Wounded.
Lees, John	Ballybriest	Private		
Lyttle, Robert	Crievagh	Cadet	R.A.F.	
Maxwell, John	Ballynagilly	Private	5th N.I.H.	
Maxwell, Robert	Ballynagilly	Private	109th M.G.C.	
Maxwell, William	Ballynagilly	Corporal	R. In. Fus.	
Weir, John S. F., M.D.	Derrygennard	Lieutenant	R.A.M.C.	
COLONIAL FORCES.				
Bayne, Samuel	Letteran	Private	American E. Force	Killed in Action.
Crooks, William John	Ballybriest	Private	N.Z. Force	Died of Wounds.
Graham, Andrew McC.	Clagan	Private	Australian Force	Died of Wounds.
McClintock, Andrew	Clagan	Private	Australian Force	
McGarvey, James	Cairndaisy	Private	N.Z. Force	
Maxwell, James	Ballynagilly	Corporal	Canadian Force	
Mills, Thomas	Caneece	Private	American Ex. Force	
Mitchell, David C.	Dunmore	Private	N.Z. Force	Killed in Action.
FIRST COOKSTOWN.				
Bridgett, Andrew	Coagh Street	Corporal	24th M.G.C.	
Bridgett, Samuel James	Coagh Street	Corporal	M.T. A.S.C.	
Bridgett, William R.	Coagh Street	Sergeant-Major	6th Yorkshires	Killed Gallipoli.
Carnaghan, James	Cookstown	Private	Civil Service Rifles	Wounded.
Carson, Robert	Coagh Street	Private	R. In. Fus.	
Farr, Robert	Molesworth Road	Sergeant	6th R. In. Fus.	
Glasgow, Ernest	Cookstown	Private	R.E.	
Glasgow, Harry McDonald	Cookstown	Corporal	Special Brigade R.E.	Died.
Hopper, John	Cookstown	2nd Lieutenant	11th Bedfordshires	Lost right arm.
Hamilton, Herbert	Oldtown	Private	R.F.C.	
Lamont, William A.	Oldtown	Lieutenant	R.G.A.	
Lewis, James	Oldtown	Lieutenant	Anti-Aircraft Defence	
Lewis, Rev. Wilfrid	Oldtown	Captain	Chaplain	
Mayne, John	Union Street	Private	R.I.R.	Killed in Action.
Megarry, George Edward	Union Street	Sergeant	R. In. Fus.	Wounded.

TYRONE PRESBYTERY.   FIRST COOKSTOWN.

Name.	Home Address.	Rank.	Regiment, Battalion or Unit.	Remarks.
Miller, Samuel	Union Street	Private	R.I.R.	
McCord, William	Oldtown	Corporal	Royal Defence Corps	
McKeown, Frederick	Burn Road	Private	R.G.A.	Serving Gibraltar.
McKeown, Thomas	Burn Road		R.N.	Lost at sea.
McKinney, John	Glasgow	Private	R.G.A.	
McKinney, Robert	Glasgow	Private	R. In. Fus.	Severely Wounded
McClelland, Sidney	William Street	2nd Lieutenant	R.A.F.C.	
Murdock, George	Unagh	Private	Royal Scots	Wounded.
Murdock, William	Unagh	Sergeant-Major	Black Watch	Killed in Action.
Nelson, William	Oldtown	Private	M.T.C.	Wounded.
Penny, Norman	James Street	Private	R.A.F.	
Robinson, Robert	Union Street	Private	R.F.C.	
Scott, Samuel J. J.	James Street	Operator	Marconi Wireless R.N.	
Simpson, Robert	Coagh Street	Corporal	A.S.C.	
Spiers, James	Factory Square	Private	R. In. Fus.	Wounded.
Spiers, Samuel	Gortalowry	Private	R.I.R.	Killed in Action.
Thompson, William	Rock Cottage	Major	R.A.M.C.	
Whan, James	Cookstown	Private	Ulster Division	
Whan, William	Cookstown	Private	R.I.R.	Gassed.
Whan, William	Cookstown	Private	Ulster Division	Killed in Action.
COLONIAL FORCES.				
Best, William	Tulloch	Private	N.Z. Force	Wounded.
Bridgett, David	Coagh Street	Private	46th Canadians	
Fleming, Alexander	Cookstown	Private	10th Canadians	Killed in Action.
Gibson, Ivan	Cookstown	Private	Canadian Engineers	
Glasgow, Allan	Cookstown	2nd Lieutenant	10th Canadians	Twice Wounded.
Hogg, William	Tullyconnell	Private	8th Canadians	Killed in Action.
McCollum, Adam	James Street	Private	78th Winnipeg Gren.	Wounded.
SECOND COOKSTOWN.				
Brown, Samuel George	Cookstown	Sergeant	N.I.H.	
Cochrane, John H.	Cookstown	Private	R.I.R.	
Compton, Alexander	Loy Terrace	Sergeant-Major	R.G.A.	M.C.
Compton, George	Loy Terrace	Sergeant	2nd R.I.F.	Wounded.
Corbett, James	Killymoon Street	Private	9th R.I.F.	Killed in Action.
Corbett, Thomas A.	Killymoon Street	Private	R.A.F.	
Corbett, William J.	Killymoon Street	Private	R.A.F.	
Davis, William J.	Union Street	Private	A.S.C.	
Faris, William	Cookstown	3rd A.M.	R.A.F.	
Faulkner, John	Coolkeighan	Private	Y.C.V.	Killed in Action.
Fitzsimons, William E.	Cookstown	3rd A.M.	R.A.F.	
Fraser, William T.	Cookstown	Private	R.A.F.	
Freeburn, Alexander	Killymoon Street	Private	1st R.I.F.	Killed in Action.
Freeburn, Thomas	Killymoon Street	Gunner	R.G.A.	
Gilmour, Bryce	Ballymoney	Corporal	Irish Guards	Killed in Action.
Glasgow, B. G. L.	Cookstown	Cadet	Engineer Unit, D.U.O.T.C.	
Gourlay, W. Herbert	Cookstown	Private	R.A.F.	
Hamilton, Thomas	Cookstown	Sapper	Engineer Corps	
Hamilton, Wallace	Cookstown	Private	R.A.F.	
Henry, George A.	Cloghog	Sergeant	R.I.F.	M.M. Killed in Action.
Hill, Theodore P.	Canada	Private	31st Canadians	
Hughes, Alexander	Millburn Street	Private	R.A.F.	
Hughes, Thomas W.	Millburn Street	Private	Motor Transport	
Lavery, James S.	Oldtown Street	Private	2nd R.I.F.	Killed in Action.
Lavery, John P., B.A.	Oldtown Street	Private	R.G.A.	M.C. Wounded
Lavery, William D.	Oldtown Street	Cadet	R.A.F.	
McKenzie, Thomas J.	Tamnaskinney	Private	9th R.I.F.	
Nelson, Thomas	Union Street	Private	9th R.I.F.	Wounded 3 times.
Nobbs, Thomas W.	Oldtown Street	2nd A.M.	R.A.F.	
Warnock, James, M.D.	Tulloch	Captain	R.A.M.C.	
Warnock, William, M.B.	Tulloch	Captain	R.A.M.C.	
Williamson, Albert	Cookstown	Private	R.A.F.	
Williamson, Ernest	Cookstown	Private	R.A.F.	
THIRD COOKSTOWN.				
Allen, George H.	Derrycrummey	Air Craftsman	R.A.F. Wireless	
Anderson, Harry	Cookstown	Sergeant	M.G.C.	
Anderson, William	Duffless	Private	R. In. Fus.	
Artt, Andrew	Cookstown	Sergeant	R.E.	
Black, James	Drumnacross	Private	R. In. Fus.	
Blair, Robert	Toberlane	Private	R. In. Fus.	Died.
Bell, Robert James	Tamlaghtmore	Private	London Regt.	
Calders, Robert	Cookstown	Private	London Regt.	Wounded.
Crooks, Fred.	Dunman	Major	R.A.M.C.	
Crossan, Alfred	Unagh	Private	R. In. Fus.	
Devlin, Fred.	Cookstown	Private		
Doey, Fred.	Unagh		Motor Transport	Died of Wounds.
Doey, William	Unagh	Private		Wounded.
Espie, Samuel	Tullybuoy	Sergeant	R. In. Fus.	

TYRONE PRESBYTERY.   THIRD COOKSTOWN.

Name.	Home Address.	Rank.	Regiment, Battalion or Unit.	Remarks.
Ferguson, Harry	Cookstown	Private	R. In. Fus.	Wounded.
Ferguson, William	Cookstown	2nd Lieutenant	Gloucester Regt.	Wounded.
Harkness, Robert	Tyresson	Sergeant	M.G.C.	
Harris, Fred.	Ballyrea	Captain	H.L.I.	
Hogg, James	Cookstown	Private	R. In. Fus.	
Hogg, John	Cookstown	Private	R. In. Fus.	
Hogg, William	Cookstown	Private	R. In. Fus.	Wounded.
Kennedy, Thomas	Tyresson	2nd Lieutenant	I. Guards	Killed in Action.
MacKenzie, Joseph	Tullywiggan	Private	R. In. Fus.	
McKinney, James O.	Cookstown	Major	R.A.M.C.	
Mayne, Gerald	Cookstown	Major	R.A.M.C.	
Montgomery, Charles	Cookstown	Private	Scots Guards	Killed in Action.
Nelson, James	Lismoney	Private	R. In. Fus.	Died.
Porter, Hector McDonald	Cookstown	Private	R.A.S.C. M.T.	
Quigg, Thomas	Cookstown	2nd Aircraftsman	Wireless, Naval Wing	
Reid, James	Cookstown	Private	Dublin Fus.	
Reid, John	Cookstown	Private		
Reid, William	Cookstown	Private	R.A.M.C.	
Scott, William	Tullycall	Private	R. In. Fus.	
Seaton, William	Coolreaghs	Private	L.N. Lancashires	
Telford, Stanley	Cookstown	Private	R. In. Fus.	Wounded.
Thompson, Robert	Aughlish	Private		
Wilkinson, Jacob	Cookstown	Lance-Corporal	R. In. Fus.	Killed in Action.
Wilkinson, John	Cookstown	Private	R. In. Fus.	
Wilkinson, Thomas	Cookstown	Private	R. In. Fus.	
Woodburn, Thomas	Cookstown	Private	R. In. Fus.	Killed in Action.
Woodburn, William	Cookstown	Private	R. In. Fus.	Wounded.
COLONIAL AND U.S.A. FORCES.				
Crooks, John	Cookstown	Private	Canadian Regt.	Wounded.
Devlin, John	Cookstown	Private	S.A. Regt.	
Espie, Dick	Drumcraw	Private	Canadian Regt.	Wounded.
Espie, Robert	Drumcraw	Private	Canadian Regt.	
Knipe, John	Cookstown	Private	Canadian Regt.	
McKinney, Thomas	Toberlane	Private	U.S. Army	
Rankin, Thomas	Tullycall	Private	U.S. Army	
Rankin, —	Tullycall	Private	U.S. Army	
Shaw, William	Cookstown	Gunner	U.S. Army	Wounded.
Smyth, James	Cookstown	Private	Canadian Regt.	
Telford, Henry	Cookstown	Private	U.S. Army	
Telford, Robert	Cookstown	Sergeant	Australian Regt.	
Telford, Thomas	Cookstown	Private	Canadian Regt.	
LECUMPHER.				
Eakin, John	Larrycormick	Private	R. Highlanders	Wounded.
Finn, William	Megargy	Private	2nd R. In. Fus.	
Gibson, Andrew	Ballynagowan	Private	21st Div. Salvage Coy.	
Hanna, Robert Alex.	Ballynagowan	Lance-Corporal	1st N.I.H.	
Shannon, John Oliver	Carmean	Gunner	R.G.A.	
COLONIAL AND U.S.A. FORCES.				
Barefoot, George	Desertmartin	Private	Transport, U.S.A.	
Burns, Herbert	Cranny	Private	U.S. Army	
Fleming, Vesey	Roshure	Rifleman	N.Z.R.B.	Killed in Action.
Hanna, Thos. John Brown	Ballynagowan	Private	Can. Siege Battery	
Hanna, William Henry	Ballynagowan	Private	102nd Engineers, U.S.A.	
MAGHERAFELT, UNION ROAD.				
Brown, Isaac	Aughagaskin	Plate Layer	Irish Civilian B.E.F.	
Brown, John	Dunamoney	Private	10th R. In. Fus.	
Brown, John	Aughagaskin	Gunner	Siege Artillery	
Craig, John K.	Luney, Desertmartin	Private	11th Queen's Regt.	
Crossitt, J. Kennedy	Carmain	Corporal	9th R. In. Fus.	
Davison, Robert	Lisalbana	Private	10th R. In. Fus.	Died of Wounds.
Foster, Robert	Killyfaddy	Private	9th R. In. Fus.	
Houston, Thomas	Magherafelt	Lieutenant	10th R. In. Fus.	M.C.
Hunter, Joseph W.	Magherafelt	Private	9th R. In. Fus.	
Hunter, William M.	Magherafelt	Lieutenant	N.I.H.	
Magill, James	Rainey Street	Private	R.C.C., R.E.	
Magill, Malcolm	Rainey Street	Private	10th R. In. Fus.	M.M.
Magill, Thomas	Rainey Street	Corporal	Tank Corps	
FIRST MONEYMORE.				
Crawford, Frederick	Caneece	Private	R.A.F.	
Davison, Samuel	Drumrott	Lance-Corporal	R.I.R.	
Glover, Henry	Tamnadoey	Private	R.I.F.	
Junk, Robert	Drumrott	Private	R.A.F.	
Kissack, James	Quilly	Cadet	R.A.F.	
Kissack, William	Quilly	Gunner	R.A.F.	

TYRONE PRESBYTERY. FIRST MONEYMORE.

Name.	Home Address.	Rank.	Regiment, Battalion or Unit.	Remarks.
McIvor, Stewart L.	Moneymore	Captain	R.F.A.	M.C.
McIvor, William J.	Moneymore	Captain	R.A.M.C.	
McKee, Charles	Ballindrum	Private	R.G.A.	
Montgomery, John	Moneymore	Private	R. In. Fus.	
Montgomery, Robert	Coltrim	Private	R.I.F.	
Porter, Ernest	Moneyhaw	Rifleman	R.I.R.	
Rankin, Robert	Moneymore	Rifleman	R.I.R.	
Scilly, Thomas	Killybaskey	Private	R.I.F.	
Simpson, Allan	Magherascullion	Lieutenant	K.O.Y.L.I.	
Simpson, James	Ballymully	Private	R. In. Fus.	Killed in Action.
Simpson, Robert	Coltrim	Bombardier	R.G.A.	
Stewart, Oliver W.	Cairndaisy	Sergeant	R.I.R.	
Stewart, William J.	Cairndaisy	Gunner	R.F.A.	

COLONIAL FORCES.

Name.	Home Address.	Rank.	Regiment, Battalion or Unit.	Remarks.
Brown, Samuel J.	Moneyhaw	Private	Anzac	
Craig, Thomas G.	Tulnagee	Private	Anzac	
Davison, Andrew	Drumrott	Sergeant	C.E.F.	
Davison, James	Drumrott	Q.-M.S.	C.E.F.	Killed in Action.
Hunter, Thomas	Turnaface	Corporal	C.E.F.	
Johnson, Fred.	Coltrim	Private	C.E.F.	
McIvor, Albert E.	Moneymore	Captain	C.E.F.	
McIvor, David		Private	Anzac	
Montgomery, Thomas	Carradarragh	Private	C.E.F.	Killed in Action.
Reid, Carleton	Moneymore	Private	R.I.F.	
Scilly, William	Killybaskey	Sergeant	S.A.E.F.	Killed in Action.

SECOND MONEYMORE.

Name.	Home Address.	Rank.	Regiment, Battalion or Unit.	Remarks.
Duff, Thomas	Church Hill	Corporal	10th R. In. Fus.	Wounded.
Gilliland, Samuel	Moneymore	Private	Irish Guards	
Graham, Robert	Moneymore	Private	R.A.F.	
Harris, George A.	Moneymore	Private	4th R. In. Fus.	
Harris, Howard K.	Moneymore		R.A.F.	
Harris, Robert W.	Moneymore	Sergeant	M.T. A.S.C.	
Lowry, James V.	Moneymore	Chief Engineer	R.N.T.	
Murphy, Thomas	Cairndaisy	Private	10th R. In. Fus.	
Sandford, John H. E.	Moneymore	Captain	4th Bedfords	
Sharpe, Edward S., M.D.	Moneymore	Lieutenant	R.A.F.	
Sharpe, William McC.	Moneymore	Major	R.G.A.	Wounded, D.S.O., Twice M. in D.
Woods, John	Moneymore	Private	Irish Guards	Wounded.
Woods, Robert	Mowillion	Private	R.I.R.	

COLONIAL FORCES.

Name.	Home Address.	Rank.	Regiment, Battalion or Unit.	Remarks.
Boyce, Robert J.	Carradarragh	Private	A.E.F.	
Megaw, James	Moneymore	Private	S.A.E.F.	
Thompson, James		Private	M.G.C., Aus. E.F.	

NEWMILLS.

Name.	Home Address.	Rank.	Regiment, Battalion or Unit.	Remarks.
Carter, Isaac	Gortin	Sergeant	Dragoons	
Crossan, Robert	Gortnaglush	Private	Scottish Regt.	
Fulton, Robert	Roan Mills	Private	R. In. Fus.	Killed.
Hegarty, Hugh	Glencon	Private	R. In. Fus.	Wounded.
Hegarty, Samuel	Glencon	Private	R. In. Fus.	
Howard, Robert	Gortnaglush	Dispatch Rider	3/4th K.R.R.	
McDaniel, James	Coalisland	Private	R. In. Fus.	
McKeown, Robert	Drumreagh	Private	R. In. Fus.	Wounded.
Macky, Whiteside	Newmills	Lieutenant	2/3rd K.R.R.	Wounded.
MORROW, ROBERT	**Sessia**	**Private**	**R.I.F.**	**V.C. Died of Wounds.**
Wilkins, Bertie	Coalisland	Dispatch Rider	R. Artillery	

ORBITOR.

Name.	Home Address.	Rank.	Regiment, Battalion or Unit.	Remarks.
Davidson, H. C.	Montober	Private	M.T. A.S.C.	
Greer, George	Tamlaght	Private	Canadians	Gassed.
Henry, Robert	Drumearn	Lieutenant	Indian Army	
Kirkpatrick, Thomas	Killycurragh	Private	8th R.I.R.	Wounded.
Leeper, J. C.	Wellbrook	Lieutenant	1st R.I.R.	
Leeper, Nathaniel	Wellbrook	Midshipman	H.M.S. "Iron Duke"	
Loughlin, A. W.	Montober	Private	Canadians	
McKinney, Kenneth	Terrywinney	Private	9th R. In. Fus.	Wounded.
Mulholland, R.	Mackenny	Sapper	7th C.R.	Died on Service.
Parke, James	Drumearn	Private	1st Canadian Scottish	Killed in Action.
Parke, Thomas	Tattykeel	Gunner	R.G.A.	

TYRONE PRESBYTERY.   SANDHOLES.

Name.	Home Address.	Rank.	Regiment, Battalion or Unit.	Remarks.
SANDHOLES.				
Black, Isaac	Sandholes	Corporal	9th R. In. Fus.	Killed.
Eccles, Josiah	Gortavilly	2nd Lieutenant	R.G.A.	M.M.
Hegan, Jos. Alex.	Ballysudden	Sergeant	R.I.F.	
Hogshaw, Robert	Crossglebe	Private	9th R. In. Fus.	Killed.
Kerr, John	Sessiagh Scot	Corporal	9th R. In. Fus.	Wounded.
Little, Alexander	Killyneedan	Private	9th R. In. Fus.	Killed.
Little, Bruce	Killyneedan	A.B. Sailor	H.M.S. "Gloucestershire"	
Logan, Ernest Williamson	The Manse, Sandholes	Captain	I.A.R.O.	
McIvor, Andrew J.	Allen Cottage, Rock	Captain	R.A.M.C.	
Mason, Charles	Kiltyclay	Sapper		
Mayne, William	Anaghananam	Corporal	9th R. In. Fus.	Wounded. Killed in Action.
Mebin, Thomas	Kiltyclay	Private		
Munn, Andrew J.	Tolvin	Corporal	R.F.A.	
COLONIAL AND U.S.A. FORCES.				
Hamilton, Alfred	Finvey	Private	U.S. Transport	
Hegan, James	Ballysudden	Private	Canadians	Killed in Action.
Hegan, John	Ballysudden	Private	Canadians	
Leslie, Thomas	Donaghey	Private	N.Z. Rifle Brigade	Killed in Action.
Mayne, Jack	Kiltyclogher	Private	Canadians	
Parke, Alexander	Lisnanane	Private	Canadians	
Taylor, Samuel Albert E.	Tullyodonnell	Private	Canadians	
Trimble, Albert E.	Leggacurry House	Private	Canadians	
Trimble, Robert J.	Leggacurry House	Private	Canadians	
FIRST STEWARTSTOWN.				
Abernethy, Edwin	Aughnagrana	Lance-Corporal	12th R. In. Fus.	
Abernethy, John	Aughnagrana	Private	9th R. In. Fus.	Wounded.
Battersby, David	Dooragh	Sergeant	11th R. In. Fus.	
Battersby, John	Dooragh	Private	11th R. In. Fus.	
Hilliard, —		Sergeant		
Miller, Sinclair	Cloughfin	Lieut.-Colonel	R.A.M.C.	M.C., D.S.O. Twice Wounded.
Reid, Robert	Drumgornal	Private	R. Fus.	Killed in Action.
Shepherd, Robert	Aughlargue	Gunner	R.G.A.	
Stewart, Joseph	Gortin	2nd Lieutenant	R. Dublin Fus.	Killed in Action.
Stewart, Joseph	Templereagh	Private	A.S.C.	
Stewart, Samuel	Templereagh	Gunner	Can. F.A.	W'ded. Mons M.
Wallace, Thomas	Gortagammon	Private	R.A.F.	

UNITED FREE CHURCH.

Name.	Home Address.	Rank.	Regiment, Battalion or Unit.	Remarks.
BALLYFRENIS UNITED FREE CHURCH.				
Adams, William R.	Ballyhaskin	Private	R. Inn. Fus.	Twice Wounded.
Barkley, Hugh	Ballyfrenis	Private	N.I.H.	
Beck, James	Ballyblack	Private	Otago Division N.Z. E.F.	Killed in Action.
Bell, John	Ballyfrenis	Corporal	R.I.R.	
Burrows, James G.	Carrowdore	Corporal	R.I.R.	Died of Wounds.
Burrows, Robert, Sen.	Ballyfrenis	Private	R. Scots Fusiliers	
Burrows, Robert, Jun.	Ballyfrenis	Ord. Seaman	R.N.V.	
Forgie, John	Ballybuttle	Stoker	R.N.V.	
McIlwaine, Hugh	Ballyblack	Sergeant	A.S.C.	
McKibben, Thomas	Ballyrawer	Private	R.I.R.	
Reid, Hugh	Ballyfrenis	Stoker, 1st Class	R.N.V.	
Robinson, Thomas	Ballymacruise	Stoker, 1st Class	R.N.V.	
Robinson, Wm. James	Carrowdore	Private	Labour Corps	
BELFAST UNITED FREE CHURCH.				
Anderson, John	25 St. Kilda Street	Seaman	Minesweeper, R.N.	
Bain, John	67 Parkmount Street	Lance-Corporal	R.M.E.	
Bain, William	5 Skegoniel Avenue	Private	R.A.S.	
Baillie, Harry	Marino	Driver	Motor Transport	
Barr, Robert	77 Cheviot Avenue	Private	Motor Transport	
Barr, Thomas	77 Cheviot Avenue	Private	Royal Marines	
Barr, William	77 Cheviot Avenue	Private	R.I.R.	Prisoner
Berry, C. M.	14 Chambers Street	Private	R.I.R.	
Berry, Fred.	14 Chambers Street	Private	1st Batt. R.I.R.	Killed in Action.

UNITED FREE CHURCH. — BELFAST.

Name.	Home Address.	Rank.	Regiment, Battalion or Unit.	Remarks.
Berry, Harry	14 Chambers Street	Private	R.I.R.	
Blair, A. E.	30 Tate's Avenue	2nd Lieutenant	R. Leinsters	
Bray, John	61 Rosemount Gardens	Private	R.I.R.	Twice Wounded.
Brown, John	43 Avoca Street	Private	R.I.R.	D.C.M., Wounded
Brown, Thomas	43 Avoca Street	Private	Black Watch	
Brown, William	43 Avoca Street	Private	R.I.R.	
Boyd, Wm. Hugh	26 Gainsboro' Drive	Seaman	R.N.	Wounded.
Clark, David	30 Ulverston Street	Private	R.I.R.	
Clark, John	56 Paris Street	Private	R.I.R.	Died in Salonica.
Clark, Wm.	30 Ulverston Street	Private	R.I.R.	Killed in Action.
Coleman, James	14 Riga Street	Private	Cycle Corps	Wounded.
Cosgrave, James	18 Michael Street	Stoker	Mercantile Service	
Cosgrave, William	18 Michael Street	Private	R.I.R.	Killed in Action.
Coulter, William R.	24 Riga Street	Sapper	R.E.	M.M.
Craig, John	162 York Street	Sergeant	Seaforth Highldrs.	
Dougan, Matthew	58 Farnham Street	Private	R.I.R.	Wounded.
Davis, James	18 Jaffa Street	Chief Engineer	Mercantile Service	
Dunlop, William	5 Glenravel Street	Private	R.A.S.	
Dunn, Archibald	3 Gainsboro' Drive	Private	R.I.R.	
Dunn, David	3 Gainsboro' Drive	Private	R.I.R.	M.M., Wounded.
Dunn, George	3 Gainsboro' Drive	Sub-Lieutenant	T.S.	
Farrel, Jerry	19 Fairview Street	Private	R.I.R.	Wounded.
Fergus, George	83 Palmer Street	Private	R.A.M.C.	Wounded.
Fordyce, Alfred	17 Agra Street	Wireless Telegraphist	R.N.	
Fotheringham, William	13 Myrtle Ter., Balmoral	Sub-Lieutenant	T.S.	
Gillespie, Harry	14 Cosgrave Street	Stoker	R.N.	
Graham, Alexander	26 Gainsboro' Drive	Private	R.I.R.	Killed in Action.
Henderson, John	10 Perth Street	Private	R.I.R.	Twice Wounded.
Jackson, John	48 Dunvegan Street	P.O.	R.N.	
Johnston, Edward	49 Newport Street	Corporal	R.I.R.	
Knox, Francis	41 Kenilworth Street	Sergeant	R.I.R.	
Lowe, James	27 St. Kilda Street	Private	R.I.R.	Killed in Action.
Main, A.	21 Stranmillis Gardens	Lance-Corporal	P.P.C.L.I.	
Mathewson, Fred	7 Keswick Street	Sergeant	R.I.R	
Millar, Hugh	15 St. Vincent Street	Private	R.M.	
Millar, John	66 Mountcollyer Street	Private	R.I.R.	
Monro. Alex.	Alona, Knockdene Park	Captain	R. Vet. Corps	Wounded.
McArtney, S. W.	The Lodge, Campbell Col.	Private	P.P.C.L.I., Can. Army	
McDonald, S.	25 Fife Street	Private	R.I.R.	
McIntyre, Fred.	110 Ormeau Road	Private	R.I.R.	Killed in Action.
McKessor, A.	9 Little Ship Street	Private	R.I.R.	Wounded.
McLay, T. N.	30 Brookvale Avenue	Lieutenant	R.E.	Gassed.
McLean, Charles	34 Foreman Street	Private	Cycle Corps	Wounded.
McLean, Wm.	34 Foreman Street	Trooper	N.I.H.	
McLellan, S.	21 Farnham Street	Private	Cycle Corps	
Maneilly, Henry	174 N. Queen Street	Private	R.G.A.	Wounded.
Mitchell, Wm.	146 U. Meadow Street	Private	R.I.R.	
Nelson, Edward	15 Brougham Street	Private	R.A.S.	
Nelson, Fred.	31 N. Queen Street	Private	R.I.R.	Killed in Action.
Pollock, Lepper	Westwood, Salisbury Av.	Lieutenant	U.S. Navy	
Poore, John H.	Sabra House, Sydenham	C.W.C.	R.N.	
Poore, Harry	Sabra House, Sydenham	P.O.	R.N.	
Rennick, Robert	1 Becaville, Ormeau Rd.	Staff Captain	R.I.R.	M.C., Wounded.
Scott, Alexander	21 Stranmillis Gardens	Driver	Motor Service	Wounded.
Scott, John	21 Stranmillis Gardens	Corporal	Canadian Army	Killed in Action.
Scott, Walter	21 Stranmillis Gardens	Corporal	Canadian Army	Wounded.
Scott, William	21 Stranmillis Gardens	Private	Canadian Army	Wounded.
Sherman, George	123 Manor Street	Corporal	R.A.M.C.	Died.
Simpson, John, Sen.	197 Cliftonpark Avenue	Sub-Lieutenant	R.N.V.R.	
Simpson, John, Jun.	197 Cliftonpark Avenue	Clerk	T.S.	
Simpson, Victor	197 Cliftonpark Avenue	Private	R.A.M.C.	
Strong, A. E.	2 Abingdon Street	Private	Black Watch	
Swan, Duncan	33 Lewis Street	Seaman	Minesweeper, R.N.	
Taggart, George	Ballysillan	Lieutenant	R.N.	
Thom, William	5 Skegoniel Avenue	C.P.C.	R.N.	
Urquhart, John	113 My Lady's Road	Private	R.I.R.	
Wallace, James	66 New Lodge Road	Stoker	R.N.	
Watson, Archibald	18 Little York Street	Sailor	Mercantile Service	
Wilson, James	20 Deacon Street	Private	Black Watch	Killed in Action.
Wilson, William	20 Deacon Street	Private	R.I.R.	
Wiseman, Joseph	Edenbank, Cliftonville	Private	Black Watch	Killed in Action.
Wotherspoon, Walter	30 Tate's Avenue	Sub-Lieutenant	T.S.	Torpd. & Drowned.

DUBLIN—LOWER ABBEY STREET UNITED FREE CHURCH.

Name.	Home Address.	Rank.	Regiment, Battalion or Unit.	Remarks.
Anderson, James	16 Melrose Avenue	P.O.	Aust. Navy	
Armour, D. H.	Glasgow	Lance-Corporal	9th R. Inn. Fus.	M.M.
Armour, John	Glasgow	Private	9th R. Inn. Fus.	
Blackhall, David	Dublin	Signaller	174th Brigade R.F.A.	
Blyth, R.	Malahide Road	Private	7th R. Dub. Fus.	
Borland, James	5 Seaview Ter., Clontarf		H.M.T. Empress of Britain	
Borland, John	5 Seaview Ter., Clontarf	Sergeant	R.E.	
Bow, D. L.	9 Seaview Avenue	Private	Machine Gun Brigade	
Bowie, Neil	6 West Road	Stoker	R.N.	

UNITED FREE CHURCH. — DUBLIN.

Name.	Home Address.	Rank.	Regiment, Battalion or Unit.	Remarks.
Brown, J.	Clontarf	Lieutenant	10th R. Irish Fus.	
Brown, J. Harrison	Clontarf	Lance-Corporal	R. Fus.	Killed in Action.
Bryce, James	Hollybrook Road	2nd Lieutenant	17th R. Irish R.	Killed in Action.
Bryce, Ian Thomas	Hollybrook Road	Cadet	R.A.F.	
Christie, J. S.	Church Road		Black Watch	
Cossar, A. J.	59 Grove Park, R'mines	Lance-Corporal	Irish Guards	
Crossar, W. C.	59 Grove Park, R'mines	Sergeant	S. Irish Horse	
Dean, J. B.	...	...	R.N., S.B.R.	
Esselmont, J. S.	...	Trooper	Scottish Horse	
Ferguson, H.	112 St. Lawrence Road	Lieutenant	6th Inn. Fus.	
Fraser, A. A.	Ferguslie, Pembroke Park	Trooper	W. Kent Yeomanry	
Gallaher, John	39 Jones Road	Private	11th R. Dublin Fus.	
Henderson, Alex. M.	126 Up. Sheriff Street	Lance-Corporal	2nd R. Inn. Fus.	
Mackay, John	8 Cadogan Road	Cyclist	36th Army Cyclist Corps	
Mather, Robin	48 Rathdrum Road	Cadet	Indian Army	
Meiklejohn, John	56 Bella Street	Private	10th Batt. R. Inn. Fus.	
Mitchell, Alex.	40 Brighton Road	Staff Sergeant	S.A.M.C.	
Mitchell, Charles	40 Brighton Road	Sergeant	N. Zealand Forces	
Munro, John	Dublin	Sergeant	Army Vet. Corps	
Murray, A. G.	73 Dalymount Terrace	Sergeant	3rd Leinster Regt.	
Myers, G. A.	13 North Earl Street	Private	7th R. Inn. Fus.	Killed in Action.
McCrae, C.	14 Berkeley Road	2nd Air Mechanic	R.A.F.	
McCrea, Douglas	14 Berkeley Road	Private	Despatch Rider, M.G.C.	
McCrae, H.	14 Berkeley Road	Sergeant	R.E.	
McFarlane, G.	40 Bayview Avenue	Sergeant	11th Black Watch	
McMillan, J. K.	11 Leahy Ter., S'mount	2nd Lieutenant	5th A. & S. Highldrs.	
McRae, James	Iona Road, Glasnevin	2nd Lieutenant	R. Inn. Fus.	
McVey, R. B.	118 Brunswick Street	Drummer	London Scottish	
McVey, Wm.	118 Gt. Brunswick Street	Lance-Corporal	11th R. Dublin Fus.	
Nesbitt, James	54 North Strand	Private	6th R. Highlanders	Died of Wounds.
Nesbitt, R.	54 North Strand	Qr. Master Sergt.	13th R. Irish R.	
Palmer, David A.	Dublin	Captain	3rd R. Dublin Fus.	Kd. in Action., M.C.
Palmer, S. W.	Dublin	Lieutenant	11th R. Dublin Fus.	
Prentice, D. S.	Drumcondra	Surgeon	R.N.V.R.	
Robinson, George	28 Kenilworth Square	Captain	7th R. Irish Fus.	
Robinson, J. S., M.B., B.Ch.	Clontarf	Captain	R.A.M.C.	
Robinson, W. S.	Clontarf	Lieutenant	A.S.C., Transport Sect.	
Roddick, R.	185 Clonliffe Road	Sergeant	10th R. Dublin Fus.	Killed in Action.
Sanderson, C. H.	Effra Rd., Rathmines	Trooper	S. Irish Horse	Died of Wounds.
Sanderson, John	Effra Rd., Rathmines	Lance-Corporal	3/9th Highland L.I.	
Shaw, R.	Dublin	Private	R.A.M.C.	
Speedy, W. D.	6 Iona Rd., Glasnevin	2nd Lieutenant	R.F.A.	
Stephen, J. McBlain	St. David's Road	Private	2/6th Black Watch	
Urquhart, Kenneth	17 Windsor Avenue	E.R.A.	R.N.	
Watson, G.	3 Ulster St., Phibsboro'	Sergeant	10th Batt. R. Dublin Fus.	
Wilkin, J.	36 St. Mary's Terrace	Qr. Master Sergt.	Army Ord. Corp.	

CRAIGMORE UNITED FREE CHURCH.

Name.	Home Address.	Rank.	Regiment, Battalion or Unit.	Remarks.
George, James	...	Corporal	R.E.	
Haire, Thomas	...	...	1st Garr. Batt., R.I.R. Cawnpore	
Wilkinson, Rev. S. H.	...	Captain	Chaplain	

CULLYBACKEY UNITED FREE CHURCH.

Name.	Home Address.	Rank.	Regiment, Battalion or Unit.	Remarks.
Anderson, William	Harperstown	Private	18th R.I.R.	
Baird, Samuel	Craigs	Private	R.E.	
Craig, Adam	Galgorm	Private	12th R.I.R.	Killed in Action.
Craig, Archibald	Ballymena	Private	12th R.I.R.	
Craig, George	Galgorm	Private	12th R.I.R.	
Dunlop, Nathaniel	Loan	Signaller	4th R.I.R.	Killed in Action.
Gordon, James	Cullybackey	Private	8th R.I.R.	
Greenwood, Thomas	Harperstown	Private	12th R.I.R.	M.M.
Greenwood, William	Harperstown	Corporal	3rd H.L.I.	Killed in Action.
Harkness, Robert	Broughdone	Private	R.F.C.	
Harris, Hugh	Craigs	Private	18th R.I.R.	Killed in Action.
Hutchinson, Douglas	Hillmount	Private	R.E.	Wounded.
Hutchinson, James Wylie	Hillmount	Private	20th R.I.R.	
Johnston, John	Broughdone	Lance-Corporal	5th R.I.R.	Wounded.
Kennedy, Arthur	Craigs	Private	18th R.I.R.	Killed in Action.
Kennedy, George	Craigs	Private	18th R.I.R.	
Kennedy, Joseph	Craigs	Private	18th R.I.R.	
Kennedy, Robert	Craigs	Private	18th R.I.R.	Killed in Action.
Kilpatrick, Charles	Dreen	Private	8th Seaforths	Killed in Action.
Kilpatrick, David	Dreen	Private	16th R.I.R.	
Kilpatrick, Samuel	Dreen	Private	11th A. & S.H.	M.M.
McCrory, Matthew	Broughdone	Private	12th R.I.R.	Prisoner
McCrory, Samuel	Broughdone	Private	9th Irish Fus.	Wounded.
McCollum, Andrew	Cullybackey	Private	8th R.I.R.	Killed in Action.
McGowan, James	Broughdone	Seaforths	Seaforths	Killed in Action.
McMaster, James	Ballyconnolly	Private	16th R.I.R.	
McMaster, William	Ballyconnolly	Private	9th R.I.R.	Killed in Action.
McWhirter, William	Craigs	Private	2nd Scottish Rifles	Killed in Action.

UNITED FREE CHURCH. CULLYBACKEY.

Name.	Home Address.	Rank.	Regiment, Battalion or Unit.	Remarks.
Moore, James	Ahoghill	Private	R.E.	
Richmond, Henry F.	Craigs	Private	3rd R.I.R.	
Sands, Alexander	Ballyconnolly	Lance-Corporal	12th R.I.R.	Prisoner.
Sands, Thomas	Ballyconnolly	Private	11th R.I.R.	
Stewart, Samuel	Cullybackey	Private	8th R.E.F.	Prisoner.
Thompson, Cowan	Cullybackey	Lance-Corporal	R.A.M.C.	
Thompson, Robert K.	Cullybackey	Private	11th R.I.R.	
Wilkinson, Robert	Cullybackey	Private	19th R.I.R.	Prisoner.
Wilkinson, William	Cullybackey	Private	4th R.I.R.	Wounded.
Wylie, Archibald	Broughdone	Private	R.E.F.	Killed in Action.
Wylie, David	Broughdone	Private	India Reserves	Prisoner.
Wylie, James	Broughdone	Private	R.E.F.	Prisoner.
COLONIAL FORCE.				
Kernohan, John	Cullybackey	Driver	Can. F.A.	
McCloy, John	Craigs	Private	Canadian Contgt.	
McFadden, James	Broughdone	Private	180th Can. E.F.	
McFadden, Robert	Broughdone	Private	17th Can. E.F.	
Stewart, David	Craigs		Canadian Contgt.	
KILLAIG UNITED FREE CHURCH.				
Clarke, John W.	Killaig, Macosquin	Lieutenant	R.F.C.	
Clarke, Kennedy H.	Killaig, Macosquin	Lance-Corporal	Cyclist Corps	
Hamilton, John	Ballycann, Macosquin	Private	Rifle Brigade	Killed in Action.
Hamilton, Wm. James	Ballycann, Macosquin	Australians	Australians	Wounded.
Kennedy, Thomas	Ballycann, Macosquin	Lieutenant	R.A.M.C.	
Leighton, James	Camm, Macosquin	Trooper	R. Inn. Dragoons	
Peden, Robert A. G.	Clintagh, Macosquin	Gunner	R.G.A.	Wounded.
Rice, Robert	Ballywilliam, Macosquin	Lance-Corporal	Lab. Batt.	
Stewart, James	Ardverness, Macosquin	Trooper	R. Irish Horse	
Woods, John	Drumcroon, Macosquin	Private	R.I.F.	Wounded.
LISBURN UNITED FREE CHURCH.				
Bell, William	Lisnoe, Lisburn	Private	Labour Batt.	
Edgerton, Henry	Old Hillsboro' Road	Private	R.I. Rifles	Wounded.
Rowan, David	Ravarnette Road	Private	N.I.H.	
LOANENDS UNITED FREE CHURCH.				
Adams, Kenneth	Ballyhill	Private	11th R.I.R.	Wounded.
Bell, John Henry	Carnaghlis	Sergt.-Major	11th R.I.R.	D.C.M., Kd. in Act.
Bell, Robert	Carnaghlis	Private	R. Scots	Killed in Action.
Cunningham, Daniel	Muckamore	Lance-Corporal	11th R.I.R.	Wounded.
Goudy, James	Loanends	Private	11th R.I.R.	Killed in Action.
Goudy, Joseph H.	Loanends	Sergeant	11th R.I.R.	Wounded.
Green, George	Loanends	Lance-Corporal	19th R.I.R.	Prisoner.
Johnston, David	Wolfhill	Private	9th R.I.R.	
McBride, William	Ligoniel	Private	2nd R. Inn. Fus.	Wounded.
McClurg, Wm. J.	Loanends	Trooper	N.I.H.	
McIlree, Andrew	Loanends	Lance-Corporal	1st R. Inn. Fus.	
McIlwaine, Thomas	Templepatrick	Private	11th R.I.R.	Killed in Action.
COLONIAL FORCES.				
Annesley, Wm. John	Carmavey	Private	Canadians	
Bell, Alex.		Private	N.Z. Force	
Bell, Samuel	Carnaghlis	Private	N.Z. Force	
Brown, Hugh James	Ballyhill	P. Sergeant	Canadians	
Brown, James	Carnaghlis	Private	N.Z. Force	
Devlin, Robert	Ballysculty	Corporal	Canadians	Killed in Action.
McIlwaine, John	Templepatrick	Private	Canadians	Killed in Action.
Suffern, Harry	Lisnataylor	Surgeon	W. African Med. Service	Ment. in Dis.

THE PRESBYTERIAN CHURCH IN IRELAND.

Manse Roll of Honour.

1 Killed in Action. 2 Died of Wounds. 3 Died. 4 Wounded in Action. 5 Awarded Mons Star. 6 Awarded C.M.G. 7 Awarded D.S.O. 8 Awarded D.S.C. 9 Awarded M.C. 10 Mentioned in Despatches. 11 Awarded Prize for sinking German Submarine. 12 Awarded Italian Silver Medal for Valour. 13 Prisoners of War. 14 Awarded C.B. 15 Awarded K.C.M.G. 16 Missing. 17 Awarded O.B.E. 18 Awarded M.M. 19 Awarded Croix de Guerre. 20 Awarded K.B.E. 21 Promoted for Distinguished Service in the Field. 22 Awarded C.B.E. 23 Awarded Chevalier Legion of Honour. 24 Awarded Order Della Salute Publico.

NOTE.—The figures in brackets indicate number of times when it has happened more than once.

MINISTERS AND SONS OF MINISTERS.

NAME.	RANK.	BATTALION, REGIMENT, &c.	FATHER'S NAME.
ALEXANDER, JAMES HAROLD	Private	4th Sqn. N.I.H.	Rev. Thomas Alexander, Kilmore.
9 ALLISON, G. F.	Lieut.-Colonel	R.A.M.C.	Late Rev. J. A. Allison, Monaghan.
4 ALLISON, R. A.	Lieutenant	Canadian Engineers	Rev. R. Allison, Kilbride.
ALLISON, WM. WALTER, M.B.	Captain	R.A.M.C.	"
10 ARMOUR, REV. J. B. M., M.A.	Captain	Chaplain	Rev. J. B. Armour, Ballymoney.
ARMOUR, J. KENNETH C.	Lieutenant	R.G.A.	"
4 ARNOLD, JOHN CORRY, LL.B.	Captain	30th Batt. Northumberland Fus.	Late Rev. R. J. Arnold, Dunmurry.
ARNOLD, JOHN IRWIN	Captain	R.A.M.C.	Late Rev. Wm. Arnold, Enniscorthy
ARNOLD, RICHARD ERNEST	Lieutenant	R.F.A.	"
1 Ashmore Richard, M.A.	Lieutenant	Canadians	Late Rev. J. Ashmore, Creevelea.
1 Bailey, Alexander	Lance-Corporal	4th P.P. Canadian L.I.	Late Rev. R. T. Bailey, Carlow.
4 BAILEY, R. N. H.	Major	2nd Batt. H.L.I.	Rev. W. H. Bailey, Clogher.
BAIRD, WILLIAM	Engineer	H.M. Transport Service	Rev. W. J. Baird, Belfast.
BAIRD, WM. F.	Driver	R Battery, R.H.A.	Rev. David Baird, Garvaghy.
BALL, REV. J. C. G., B.A.	Captain	Chaplain	"
4 (3), 2 Bartley, William	Sergeant	52nd Batt. Canadian Cont.	Late Rev. J. R. Bartley, Tralee.
BEATTIE, H. H.	Captain	2nd Batt. Northamptons	Rev. Dr. H. H. Beattie, Belfast.
BEATTY, M. CECIL, M.B.	Lieut.-Colonel	R.A.M.C.	Late Rev. J. Beatty, Ballycopeland.
BELLIS, S. ARROTT	Lieutenant	R.N.V.R.	Late Rev. Dr. Bellis, Ramelton.
4 BERKELEY, LOWRY E.	Lieutenant	3rd Batt. Connaught Rangers	Late Rev. W. L. Berkeley, Belfast.
1 Berkeley, W L..	Private	3rd South African Infantry	"
1 Bodel, F. E.	Captain	King's Liverpool Regiment	Late Rev. J. Bodel, fy. of Ballyalbany
BOYD, JAMES ALEX.	Captain	The Essex Regt.	Late Rev. John Boyd, Ballynahinch.
4 BOYD, JOHN M.	Lieutenant	1st Canadian Res. Batt.	"
13 BOYD, ROBERT, B.A.	Captain	7th Batt. R. Dublin Fus.	Rev. Robert Boyd, Gujarat.
BOYD, PATRICK GARDNER	Cadet	R.A.F.	Rev. Robert Boyd, India.
BOYD, ROBERT HEANEY	Cadet	Royal Irish Fusiliers	Late Rev. R. H. Boyd, Ballyjamesduff
BOYD, THOMAS W.	Lieutenant	10th Batt. R.I.F.	Late Rev. R. H. Boyd, Ballyjamesduff
1 Boyd, W. Graham	Lieutenant	10th Batt. R.I.F.	"
BOYD, WM. RYDER	Lieutenant	R. Inniskilling Fus.	Late Rev. J. Boyd, Ballynahinch.
BOYLE, JAMES C. C.	2nd Lieutenant	R. Inniskilling Fus.	Late Rev. D. J. Boyle, Lisbellaw
4 (2), 9, 13 Boyle, Robert M.	Captain	2nd Batt. R. Inng. Fus.	Rev. Robert Boyle, Killala.
BRENNAN, HERBERT W.	Midshipman	H.M.S. "Caronia"	Rev. John Brennan, Kilkenny.
17 BURKITT, FRANK H.	Lieutenant	Guides of India	Rev. T. H. Burkitt, Athenry.
1 Burnett, Henry W.	Sergeant	5th Batt. Seaforth Highlanders	Rev. L. Burnett, Donoughmore.
BURNSIDE, FRANCIS M.	Captain	Royal Marine Artillery	Late Rev. S. D. Burnside, Carryduff.
10 BURNSIDE, GODFREY M.	Captain	Royal Marine Artillery	"
4 CALDWELL, S. A.	Bombardier	18th A.F.A. Brigade	Rev. S. E. Caldwell, Corboy.
CAMPBELL, J. J. B.	Lieutenant	R.A.F.	Late Rev. J. A. Campbell, formerly of Sandymount.
CAMPBELL, WM. W.	Trooper	S. A. Mounted Rifles	"
CANNING, CHARLES C.	Captain	11th Batt. R.I.R.	Rev. J. A. Canning, Crumlin.
4 CHAMBERS, FRED W.	Lieutenant	R.A.F.	Late Rev. F. Chambers, St. Johnston.
9 CHARLTON, DENHAM	Captain	South African Scottish	Rev. R. J. Charlton, formerly of Castledawson.
CHARLTON, R. J. WALLACE	Lieutenant	R.G.A., South Africa	"
10, 4, 1 Clarke, John K.	Lieutenant	R.A.F.	Rev. E. Clarke, Strabane.
CLARKE, THOMAS V.	Lieutenant	Indian Cavalry	"
1 Clarke, Robert	Private	9th Batt. R. Dub. Fus.	Late Rev. S. B. Clarke, Cairncastle.
7, 10 (4), 6 CLEMENTS, R. W., B.A., M.B.	Lieut.-Colonel	R.A.M.C., H.Q. Staff	Late Rev. W. Clements, Benburb.

(335)

MINISTERS AND SONS OF MINISTERS.

Name	Rank.	Battalion, Regiment, &c.	Father's Name.
4 Cochrane, John S.	Lieutenant	18th Batt. R.I.R.	Rev. John Cochrane, Gilford.
Cochrane, Wm. E.	Cadet	10th Batt. R.I.F.	,, ,, ,,
Colquhoun, J. W. C.	Lieutenant	3rd Batt. R.I.F.	Rev. Wm. Colquhoun, Belfast.
Colquhoun, W.	Midshipman	R.N.V.R.	,, ,, ,,
3 Cooke, Henry	Captain	10th Batt. 4th Div. Can. Con.	Late Rev. Wm. Cooke, Kilkenny.
4, 10 (2) Corkey, Rev. D. S., B.A.	Captain	Chaplain	Late Rev. Dr. Corkey, Glendermot.
Coulter, John W. C.	Captain	Army Pay Dept.	Rev. D. S. K. Coulter, Gilnahirk.
Cowper, Wm. Haslett	Lieutenant	The R.I. Regt.	Late Rev. G. T. Cowper, Rathfriland.
Craig, Hugh	2nd Lieutenant	R.I.R.	Rev. D. H. Craig, Donegore.
Crawford, Rev. R. G., B.A.	Captain	Chaplain	Late Rev. S. G. Crawford, formerly of Westport.
Currie, Samuel Hans	Cadet	R.A.F.	Rev. S. Currie, Clones.
10 (2), Dale, Rev. J. M. R., B.D.	Major	Chaplain	
Davey, Chas. Fredk., M.B.	Captain	R.A.M.C.	Late Rev. Dr. Davey, Belfast.
Davey, Thomas H.	Private	R.G.A.	,, ,, ,,
1 Davey, Wm. Edwin	Private	28th Batt. R.F.	,, ,, ,,
3 Davis, Rev. John, B.A.	Private	R.A.M.C.	Late Rev. John Davis, Ballynahinch.
Davison, Wm. A.	Sergeant	10th Batt. R. Inng. Fus.	Rev. Thomas Davison, Dungiven.
Deans, Theo. J.	2nd Lieutenant	Indian Army	Rev. John Deans, Richhill.
9 Dick, R. C., B.E.	Captain	R.E.	Rev. Robert Dick, Douglas.
Dickey, Alfred C., M.B.	Captain	R.A.M.C.	Rev. C. C. M. Dickey, Draperstown.
8 (3), 10, 4 Dickey, R. F. L.	Captain	R.A.F.	Late Rev. Dr. R. H. F. Dickey, Londonderry.
Dodds, Robert L.	Surgeon Probationer	R.N.V.R.	Rev. R. W. Dodds, Belfast.
Duncan, James	1st A.M.	R.A.F.	Rev. Wm. Duncan, Killeter.
9 (2), 4, 19 Duncan, Lowry S.	Captain	14th Batt. R.I.R.	Rev. S. Duncan, Killucan.
Edgar, Cyril	Private	N.Z. Mounted Rifles	Late Rev. Dr. R. M. Edgar Dublin.
Edgar, John W. W.	Lieutenant	9th Batt. Lincolns	,, ,, ,,
Edgar, R. McCheyne	Sergeant	R.A.M.C.	,, ,, ,,
Elliott, Brereton G.	Major	4th Batt. East Lancs.	Late Rev. John Elliott, Armagh.
Elliott, Charles J.	Captain	17th Australian A.S.C.	,, ,, ,,
Elliott, George M., M.B.	Captain	R.A.M.C., Hospl., Alexandria	Rev. Wm. Elliott, Ballinasloe.
Elliott, Oliver G.	Private	12th Batt. Royal Scots	,, ,, ,,
Elliott, Rev. R., M.A.	Lieutenant	8th Batt. Camerons	,, ,, ,,
Elliott, Robert B.	Private	R.A.M.C., 44th Fd. Amb.	Late Rev. John Elliott, Armagh.
Elliott, Rev. R. C., B.A.	Captain	Chaplain	,, ,, ,,
10 English, James	Lieutenant	20th Batt. R.I.R.	Late Rev. S. English, Ballynahinch.
Faris, Rev. George, B.A.	Captain	Chaplain	
Ferguson, H. R. M., M.D.	Captain	R.A.M.C., W. African Med. Stff	Rev. J. E. Ferguson, Randalstown.
10, 1 Ferguson, J. M., M.B.	Captain	R.A.M.C., 154th Brig. R.F.A.	,, ,, ,,
Ferris, Hugh	Private	S.A. Forces	Late Rev. J. C. Ferris, Belfast.
1 Ferris, Wm.	2nd Lieutenant	R.I.R.	,, ,, ,,
Flack, Rev. W. T., M.A., B.D.	Captain	Chaplain	
Fulton, Fleming, M.B.	Captain	R.A.M.C.	Rev. Dr. Fulton, Manchuria.
Gailey, Andrew J.	Private	R.G.A.	Rev. John Gailey, Ballysillan.
Gailey, John T.	Private	R.G.A.	,, ,, ,,
Gailey, S. A.	Surgeon Probationer	R.N. Vol. Reserve	Rev. A. Gailey, Lucan.
2 Gailey, J. L.	Sergeant	R.A.M.C., 36th Division	,, ,, ,,
9 Gibson, Rev. Andrew, B.A., B.D.	Captain	Chaplain	
Gibson, J. McIlrath, B.A., M.D.	Captain	R.A.M.C., St. Geo.'s Hosp., Malta	Late Rev. J. Gibson, Broughshane.
Gillespie, Donald S.	Lieutenant	7th Batt. Dorsets	Rev. S. Gillespie, Gujarat
Gilmore, John Jas. Alex.	Lieutenant	R.A.F.	Rev. W. J. Gilmore, N'crommelin.
Gilmore, William	Captain	R.A.M.C.	,, ,, ,,
Glass, James	Private	Australian Forces	Rev. T. Glass, fy. of Cookstown.
3 Gilmour, James M.	Private	N.Z. E.F.	Late Rev. James Gilmour, Boveedy.
Gilmour, Rev. R. H.	Private	Canadian Forces	Late Rev. John Gilmour, Mountjoy.
4 Gordon, Hugh N.	Captain	15th Batt. Northumberland Fus.	Rev. Dr. R. J. Gordon, Manchuria.
Gordon, R. D. L.	Cadet	Indian Army	,, ,, ,,
Graham, Donald S.	Private	N.I.H.	Late Rev. Dr. Graham, Comber.
Graham, L. J. D., M.B.	Captain	R.A.M.C.	,, ,, ,,
4, 9 (2) Graham, Norman B., B.A., M.B.	Captain	R.A.M.C., 86th Amb. C.	,, ,, ,,
Graham, Rev. Robert, B.A.	Captain	Chaplain	,, ,, ,,
Graham, W. S., M.B.	Captain	R.A.M.C.	
Greer, Alex.	Lieutenant	8th Batt. Hampshire Regt.	Late Rev. John Greer, Kilmount.
Guy, J. McFarland	Engineer	R.N.	Rev. J. M'F. Guy, Ballindrait.
4 Guy, W. G. S.	Lance-Corporal	Canadians	,, ,, ,, ,,
Hall, Rev. R., M.A., B.D.	Captain	Chaplain	
Hall, Rev. W. P., M.A.	Captain	Chaplain	
9, 13 Hamilton, E. S. B., M.B.	Captain	R.A.M.C.	Rev. R. W. Hamilton, Lisburn.
Hamilton, J. B.	Private	R.G.A.	Late Rev. Dr. J. M. Hamilton, Dublin.
9 Hamilton, Rev. John E., B.A.	Captain	Chaplain	Late Rev. J. S. Hamilton, Dublin.
22 Hanson, Rev. D. H., B.A., C.B.E.	Lieut.-Colonel	A.P. Chaplain	Late Rev. D. Hanson, Belfast.
4, 9 Hanson, Robert S.	Captain	12th Batt. R.I.R.	Rev. D. H. Hanson, Larne.
Harbinson, Charles H., M.B.	Captain	R.A.M.C., R.F.A.	Late Rev. W. Harbinson, Clarkesbridge.
9, 1 Haslett, T. Sinclair	Lieutenant	10th Batt. R.I.R.	Rev. Dr. Haslett, Ballymena.
6 Holmes, R. H., C.M.G.	Lieut.-Colonel	A.V.C.	Late Rev. John Holmes, Tipperary.
4 Hunter, J. F.	Lieutenant	6th Batt. R. Inng. Fus.	Rev. Wm. Hunter, Manchuria.
4 (2), 9 Hutchison, Rev. W. H.	Captain	Chaplain	
4, 18 Irwin, W. L.	2nd Lieutenant	2/7th Manchesters	Rev. Dr. C. H. Irwin, fy. of Bray.
9, 4 Jackson, C., B.Sc.	Lieutenant	11th Batt. R.I.R.	Late Rev. W. J. Jackson, Belfast.
4, 10 Jackson, Frank	Captain, G.S.O.	6th Batt. R.I.F.	Rev. Dr. Jackson, Ballycastle.
Jackson, H. M., B.A., M.B.	Captain	R.A.M.C.	,, ,, ,, ,,
9, 10, 13 Jackson, John L., M.B.	Major	R.A.M.C.	,, ,, ,, ,,

MINISTERS AND SONS OF MINISTERS.

Name.	Rank.	Battalion, Regiment, &c.	Father's Name.
4, 9, Jackson, J. S., B.A., B.Sc., A.M.I.C.E. ...	Lieutenant	70th Fd. Co. R.E.	Late Rev. W. J. Jackson, Belfast.
4 Jackson, Maurice	Captain	13th Batt. R. Inng. F.	" " " "
Keegan, James M., M.A., M.B.	Captain	R.A.M.C.	Late Rev. G. C. Keegan, Westport.
Keers, Rev. Wm., B.A.	Private	R.A.M.C.	
Kelso, Rev. Robert	Captain	Chaplain	
1 Kennedy, Gilbert M.	Lieutenant	6th Batt. The Cameronians	Late Rev. G. A. Kennedy, formerly of Aghadoey.
9, 10 Kennedy, Norman R.	Lieutenant	1st Batt. Royal Scots	" " " "
4, 13 Kennedy, John	Private	3rd Batt. R. Inng. F.	Late Rev. R. Kennedy, Myroe
17 Kimmitt, R. R.	Lieut.-Colonel	3rd London Irish Rifles	Late Rev. E. Kimmitt, Clonakilty.
Kirkpatrick, Rev. W. S., B.A.	Captain	Chaplain	
Knowles, Rev. John, B.A.	Captain	Chaplain	
4 (2) Knox, Fergus Y.	Captain	4th Batt. R.I.R.	Rev. D. B. Knox, Whitehead.
Knox, Hugh W.	Cadet	R.A.F.	Rev. H. M. Knox, Ballymote.
Knox, T. W.	Lieutenant	19th Batt. R.I.R.	" " " "
9, 10 Knox, W. H.	Captain	R. Inng. Fus.	" " " "
Latimer, Gordon D., M.D.	Captain	R.A.M.C.	Late Rev. J. Latimer, Groomsport.
1 Lecky, John	2nd Lieutenant	18th Batt. R.I.R.	Rev. A. G. Lecky, Ballylennon.
Legate, Rev. J. N. M., B.A.	Captain	Chaplain	Rev. E. M. Legate, Ballyclare
Legate, Rev. R. M.	Captain	Chaplain	
Logan, E. W.	Lieutenant	Indian Army	Rev. Dr. Logan, Sandholes.
Lowe, Alfred	Lieutenant	5th Batt. R.I. Regt.	Rev. Dr. Lowe, Belfast.
Lowe, John A.	Lieutenant	American Army	
17 Lyle, Arthur Nevin, B.A.	Lieutenant-Colonel	R.E.	Late Rev. T. Lyle, Dublin.
Lyle, T. M., B.E.	Captain	Indian Army	" " " "
Lynn, Frederick Charles	Private	R.A.F.	Rev. R. Lynn, Inch.
Lynn, John Brewster	Private	R.A.F.	" " " "
10 (2) Lynn, Rev. Joseph, B.A., B.D.	Major	Chaplain	" " " "
4 (2), 12 McAlery, John M.	Captain	R.A.F.	Late Rev. J. M'Alery, Ballycarry.
McCandless, John B.	Private	M.T. A.S.C.	Rev. J. L. M'Candless, Boardmills.
4 McCandless, Leslie I.	Lieutenant	10th Batt. Sherwood Foresters	" " " "
Macaulay, Rev. J. J., B.A.	Captain	Chaplain	Late Rev. M. Macauley, N'ards.
McCay, A. W.	Captain	15th Batt. R.I.R.	Rev. James M'Cay, Castlederg.
McCay, C. A. R.	Major	R.A.M.C.	" " " "
4, 1 McCay, J. F. D.	Lieutenant	15th Batt. R.I.R.	" " " "
14, 15, 20 McCay, The Hon. John W. T.	Major-General	Australian Imperial Forces	Late Rev. A. R. B. M'Cay, fy. of Ballynure.
1 McCleery, James Moore	Sergeant	13th Batt. R.I.R.	Rev. J. R. M'Cleery, Killyleagh.
McCleery, Robert	Private	North Irish Horse	" " " "
1 McClure, Hugh Cecil	Lieutenant	R.G.A.	Rev. Dr. M'Clure, fy. of Duneane.
4, 10, 3 McClure, J. R. S.	Captain	250th Ter. Co. R.E.	" " " "
McClure, Sam	Major	R.A.F.	" " " "
McClure, Rev. Wm., B.A.	Captain	Chaplain	
McComb, S., M.B.	Captain	R.A.M.C.	Late Rev. S. M'Comb, Belfast.
McComb, Thomas M.	Lieutenant	173rd Brig. R.F.A.	" " " "
1 McConnell, R. W.	2nd Lieutenant	10th K.O.R.L. Regt.	Rev. James M'Connell, Belfast.
10)2) McConnell, Rev. W. J., B.A.	Captain	Chaplain	
4 McCrea, Harold	Private	24th Batt. Australians	Rev. Thomas M'Crea, Bellaghy.
4, 9 McCrea, Thomas	Lieutenant	11th Batt. R. Inng. F.	" " " "
McCully, A. L., M.B.	Captain	R.A.M.C.	Late Rev. Jas. M'Cully, Broomfield.
McCully, W. C.	Private	2nd Batt. Kimberley, S.A.	" " " "
9 MacDermott, John Clarke	2nd Lieutenant	Machine Gun Corps	Rev. Dr. MacDermott, Belfast.
1 MacDermott, R. W., B.A., LL.B.	2nd Lieutenant	8th Batt. R.I.R.	" " " "
MacDermott, W., M.B.	Captain	R.A.M.C.	" " " "
McElfatrick, Rev. Thos. A., B.A.	Captain	Chaplain	
9, 1 McElney, R. G., M.B.	Captain	R.A.M.C., 77th Fd. Amb.	Rev. J. R. M'Elney, Downpatrick.
McElney, W. H. C.	2nd Lieutenant	R.A.F.	" " " "
McFadden, G. D. F.	Surgeon-Probationer	R.N.R., H.M.S. Victory	Rev. J. M'Fadden, Badoney.
McFadden, John B.	Captain	R.A.M.C., 12th Batt. R. In. F.	" " " "
1 MacFarland, George A., M.B.	Captain	R.A.M.C.	Late Rev. G. MacFarland, Belfast.
9 McGranahan, J. N.	Lieutenant	9th Batt. R.I.R.	Rev. Dr. M'Granahan, Londonderry
McGranahan, J. B., M.B.	Captain	R.A.M.C.	" " " "
MacLaughlin, Rev. David	Captain	Chaplain	
4 (5), 5, 16 MacLaughlin, A. W.	Lieutenant	R.A.F., No. 1 Squadron	Rev. D. Mac Laughlin, Drumminis.
McIlwrath, Rev. John, B.A.	Captain	Chaplain	
McKee, Alex. G.	Surgeon	R.N.	Late Rev. J. M'Kee, Drumkeen.
4 McKee, Rev. E. J., LL.D	Captain	Chaplain	
McKinney, George J.	Corporal	R.A.F.	Rev. A. M'Kinney, Parkgate.
McKinstry, E. Herbert	Lieutenant	17th Batt. R.I.R.	Rev. Jos. M:Kinstry, Randalstown.
McKinstry, Joseph	Lieutenant	3rd Batt. Wiltshire Regt.	" " " "
4 Macky, Whiteside	Lieutenant	17th Batt. R.I.R.	Rev. D. T. Macky, Newmills.
1 MacLurg, Wm.	Lance-Corporal	P.P. Can. L.I., Univ. Cont.	Rev. A. MacLurg, formerly of Ardstraw
McMullan, Rev. W. J., B.A.	Captain	Chaplain	
McNeill, Arthur V., B.A.	Lieutenant	5th Batt. R.I.F.	Late Rev. James M'Neill, Drumbo.
McNeill, James H.	Major	Can. For. Corps	" " " "
4 McNeill, Robt. N., B.A., LL.B.	Lieutenant	9th Batt. K.O.S.B.	" " " "
McNutt, Rev. Wm., B.A.	Captain	Chaplain	
10 (2), 2 Macready, Oscar H.	Captain	16th Batt. R.I.R.	Rev. H. H. Macready, Islandmagee.
Madill, J. T. Herbert, B.A., M.B.	Captain	R.A.M.C.	Late Rev. Dr. Madill, Garvagh.
Madill, Tom	Surgeon Probationer	R.N.V.R.	" " " "
4 Mark, Samuel M. H.	Captain	12th Batt. R. Inng. F.	Late Rev. John Mark, Dunboe.
9 Martin, Norman Todd	Lieutenant	R F.A.	Late Rev. Dr. W. Todd Martin, Belfast
1 Martin, Sidney Todd	Lieutenant	6th Batt. R. Inng. F.	" " " "

MINISTERS AND SONS OF MINISTERS.

NAME.	RANK.	BATTALION, REGIMENT, &c.	FATHER'S NAME.
MATTHEWS, C. C. D.	Private	S.A. Defence Force	Rev. S. Matthews, Wicklow
MATTHEWS, G. E.	Private	S.A. Defence Force	,, ,, ,,
2 Matthews, James Irwin	Private	Irish Guards	,, ,, ,,
MATTHEWS, J. S.	Private	S.A. Defence Force	,, ,, ,,
3 Matthews, S. W., M.B.	Captain	R.A.M.C.	,, ,, ,,
MAXWELL, REV. W. N., B.A.	Captain	Chaplain	
10 (4), 7, 21 MEEKE, REV. H. C., M.A.	Lieut.-Colonel	A.P. Chaplain	Rev. James Meeke, Kingsmills.
MEEKE, WM., L.D.S.	Captain	R.A.M.C.	,, ,, ,,
MEGAW, GEORGE L.	Private	Canad. A.S.C.	Rev. Dr. Megaw, Belfast.
MICHAEL, JAMES P.	Cadet	R.A.F.	Rev. Wm. Michael, Trenta.
MICHAEL, WM., M.B.	Surgeon	Royal Navy	,, ,, ,,
1 Millar, James L.	2nd Lieutenant	5th Batt. R.I.R.	Rev. Ross Millar, Letterkenny.
MILLING, THOMAS, M.B.	Captain	R.A.M.C., 169th R.F.A.	Late Rev. R. G. Milling, Ballynahinch
2 Mitchel, F. D.	Captain	10th Batt. R.I.F.	Late Rev. S. C. Mitchel, Enniskillen.
MITCHEL, G. C.	Private	Can. Home Def.	,, ,, ,, ,,
MITCHEL, V.	Lieutenant	1st Batt. R.I.F.	,, ,, ,, ,,
10 MITCHELL, REV. D. R.	Captain	Chaplain	Rev. D. K. Mitchell, Belfast.
MOFFETT, T. J. S., M.D.	Captain	R.A.M.C.	Late Rev. S. Moffett, Eskylane.
MONTGOMERY, ALEX., M.B.	Captain	R.A.M.C.	Late Rev. R. Montgomery, Belfast
MONTGOMERY, EDWIN	Captain	R.A.M.C., 77th Fd. Amb.	
9, 19 (2) MONTGOMERY, E. P., M.B.	Captain	R.A.M.C.	Rev. Dr. H. Montgomery, Belfast.
4 MONTGOMERY, H.	Major	Australian A.M.C.	Late Rev. R. Montgomery, Belfast.
MONTGOMERY, REV. W. E., B.D.	2nd Lieutenant	C.L.C.	Rev. Dr. Montgomery, Belfast.
10 (2) MONTGOMERY, W. N., M.B.	Captain	3rd Batt. R.I.F. & R.A.M.C.	,, ,, ,,
MOORE, C. C.	Lieutenant	1st Batt. Essex Regt.	Late Rev. J. C. Moore, Connor.
MOORE, D. B.	Captain	18th R.I.R.	
MOORE, HENRY R. D.	Lieutenant	Indian Army	Rev. H. H. Moore, Markethill.
MOORE, LOUIS L. P	Private	1st Batt. 18th London R. (L.I.R.)	Rev. J. C. Moore, formerly of Bellasi
MOORE, RUTHERFORD W.	Paymaster Lieutenant	R.N.	Rev. H. H. Moore, Markethill.
MORISON, EDGAR, M.B.	Captain	R.A.M.C.	Late Rev. J. Morison, Tullylish.
4 MORRISON, ALFRED E.	Staff Sergeant	10th Batt. Canadians	Rev. R. Morrison, Carndonagh.
4 (2), 13 MORTON, D. HAMILL, B.A., B.E.	Captain	7th R. Inng. F.	Rev. D. Morton, Newtownstewart.
4, 10 MULHOLLAND, H. C.	Captain	R.A.M.C., 38th Fd. Amb.	Rev. H. C. Mulholland, Churchtown.
MULLIGAN, JAMES A.	2nd Lieutenant	R.F.A.	Rev. J. A. W. Mulligan, fy. of G.port.
MURPHY, JOHN H. B.	Lieutenant	Egyptian Labour Corps	Rev. Dr. Murphy, Cork.
NEILL, REV. GILMOUR	Captain	Chaplain	Rev. M. Neill, Sion Mills.
NEILL, MATTHEW CRAIG	Sergeant	R.A.M.C., Canadian Cont.	,, ,, ,,
11 NEILSON, DANIEL B.	M. Mariner	Merchant Service	Rev. R. Neilson, Donegal.
4 NEILSON, EDWIN F.	Sergeant-Major	27th Batt. Winnipeg Regt.	,, ,, ,,
NEILSON, MATTHEW H.	Private	25th R.F. Legion of Frontiers-Men (E.A.)	,, ,, ,,
ORR, REV. J. H., B.A.	Captain	Chaplain	
4 (2), 9 OSBORNE, WM. H.	Lieutenant	4th Batt. Leinster Regt.	Rev. Dr. Osborne, Dublin.
PARK, REV. R. J. M, M.A.	Captain	Chaplain	
17 PARK, WILLIAM	Major	R.A.F.	Rev. Dr. Park, Belfast.
PARKE, JOSEPH B.	Lieutenant	18th Batt. R.I.R.	Late Rev. D. Parke, Donacloney.
PARR, J. F. F.	Major	R.A.M.C.	Late Rev. John Parr, Corlea.
9 (3), 10 PATON, REV. J. G., M.A., B.D.	Captain	Chaplain	
PATTON, GRAHAME	Captain	R.A.M.C.	Late Rev. Dr. Patton, Bangor.
PATTON, ERNEST	Lieutenant		Rev. Andrew Patton, Cloughwater.
PATTON, NOEL E.	Lieutenant	19th R.I.R.	,, ,, ,,
PATTON, T. W., B.A.	Lieutenant	5th Batt. R.I.F.	,, ,, ,,
PAUL, HAROLD S.	Private	Canad. Overseas Artillery	Late Rev. S. Paul, Gillygooley.
PERRY, R. J.	Corporal	19th Patt. R.I.R.	Rev. H. W. Perry, Portadown.
2 Phillips, T. McC., M.B.	Captain	R.A.M.C.	Late Rev. J. G. Phillips, Damascus.
POLLOCK, A. NORMAN, M.B.	Surgeon	R.N.	Rev. John Pollock, Belfast.
1 Pollock, Paul Gilchrist	Lance-Corporal	14th Batt. R.I.R.	,, ,, ,,
REA, JOHN T.	Major	Royal Engineers	Late Rev. G. T. Rea, Gujarat.
REID, REV. T. S., B.A.	Captain	Chaplain	
1 Rentoul, Rev. J. L., B.A.	Private	R.A.M.C.	Rev. R. W. R. Rentoul, Clonmel.
17 RENTOUL, REV. PROF. J. L., M.A., D.D.	Colonel	Chaplain-General	Late Rev. Dr. Rentoul, Garvagh.
RENTOUL, ALEX. C.	Private	Australian A.M.C.	Late Rev. A. Rentoul, Sandymount.
RENTOUL, A. H., M.B.	Major	R.A.M.C.	Rev. A. H. Rentoul, Longford.
RENTOUL, REV. J. B.	Captain	Chaplain	Late Rev. A. Rentoul, Sandymount.
10 RENTOUL, J. L., M.B.	Captain	R.A.M.C.	Late Rev. James Rentoul, Dromore.
4, 9, 10 RENTOUL, W. W.	Major	7th Batt. E. Lancs & 1st K.S.L.I.	Rev. R. W. R. Rentoul, Clonmel.
ROBINSON, ARCHIBALD	Private	19th Batt. 2nd Can. Cont.	Late Rev. W. C. Robinson, Ballykelly.
ROBINSON, J. M. C.	Lieutenant	R.E.	,, ,, ,,
ROBB, CAMPBELL, M.B.	Captain	R.A.M.C.	Late Rev. Dr. Robb, Galway.
ROBB, JAMES JACKSON, M.B.	Major	Ind. M.S.	,, ,, ,,
ROBSON, JOHN S. M.	Private	54th Batt. Can. Cont.	Late Rev. R. Robson, Hillhall.
4 ROSS, GEORGE H.	Lieutenant	10th Canadians	Rev. R. W. Ross, Burt.
4 ROSS, LESLIE N.	Lieutenant	16th Batt. R.I.R.	,, ,, ,,
4 SCOTT, HAROLD H.	Captain	R.A.M.C., 9th Lancs.	Late Rev. James Scott, Banbridge.
SCOTT, NORMAN	A.M.I.	R.A.F.	Rev. Richard Scott, Ennis.
17 SHANNON, REV. W. F., B.A.	Colonel	Chaplain	Late Rev. R. Shannon, Cladymore.
4, 10, 7 SHARPE, W. McC.	Major	16th Siege Battery R.G.A.	Rev. J. W. Sharpe, Moneymore.
SHARPE, EDWARD, M.B.	Lieutenant	R.A.M.C.	,, ,, ,,
6, 10 (7), 14 SIMMS, REV. J. M., C.B., C.M.G., D.D., LL.D., K.H.C.	Major-General	Principal Chaplain	
SIMPSON, HUGH	Captain	Labour Corps	Rev. E. F. Simpson, Ballymena.
SIMPSON, WM. A., M.B.	Captain	R.A.M.C.	Late Rev. R. T. Simpson, Dungannon.
3 Sinclair, R. L.	Driver	B Battery R.F.A.	Late Rev. R. W. Sinclair, Gujarat.

MINISTERS AND SONS OF MINISTERS.

NAME.	RANK.	BATTALION, REGIMENT, &C.	FATHER'S NAME.
SMITH, REV. FRED., B.D.	Captain	Chaplain	
SMITH, F. S. S., M.D.	Captain	Ind. M.S.	Late Rev. J. S. Smith, Clogher.
SMITH, JOHN B., B.A., M.B.	Lieut.-Colonel	Ind. M.S.	Late Rev. J. A. Smith, Cork.
SMITH, J. H., M.B.	Captain	Ind. M.S.	Late Rev. J. S. Smith, Clogher.
SMITH, J. M.	Lieutenant	R.F.A.	,, ,, ,,
SMITH, W. ALLEN	Lieutenant	A.V.C.	,, ,, ,,
1 Smyth, Gordon, D.L.	2nd Lieutenant	16th Batt. R.I.R.	Late Rev. J. Smyth, Crossgar.
SMYTH, JOHN A.	Corporal	187th Co. R.E.	,, ,, ,,
SMYTHE, R. HASTINGS	Captain	R.A.M.C.	Rev. R. H. Smythe, Castleblayney.
1 Steele, R. B., M.A.	Lieutenant	R.A.F.	Late Rev. Dr. Steele, India.
STEEN, JOHN	Gunner	61st Batt. Can. F.A.	Rev. John Steen, Glenelly.
STEVENSON ARCHIE M.	Private	1st Can. Mounted Rifles	Late Rev. M. Stevenson, formerly of Tobermore.
STEWART, A. K.	Lieutenant	R.E.	Late Rev. Hugh Stewart, Loughgilly.
STEWART, H. J. L.	Lieutenant	3rd Batt. R.I.R.	Rev. John Stewart, Seaforde.
STEWART, J. C. P.	Sergeant	N.I.H.	,, ,, ,,
18 STEWART, R. C.	Corporal	N.I.H.	,, ,, ,,
STEWART, REV. W. H., B.A.	Captain	Chaplain	
STRAHAN, THOMAS S.	Lieutenant	Gloucestershire Regt.	Rev. W. G. Strahan, Newry.
1 Stuart, Rev. A.	Captain	Chaplain	
1 Taylor, Alfred S., M.B.	Captain	R.A.M.C., 1st Batt. H.L.I.	Rev. Dr. D. A. Taylor, Belfast.
TAYLOR, D. R., M.B.	Lieutenant	R.A.M.C.	,, ,, ,,
THOMPSON, ARTHUR	2nd Lieutenant	2nd Batt. R. Innis. Fus.	Rev. Dr. Thompson, Londonderry.
THOMPSON, J. K. S.	2nd Lieutenant	19th Batt. R.I.R.	Rev. J. Thompson, Clontibret.
THOMPSON, ROBERT G. F.	2nd Lieutenant	1st Batt. York and Lancs.	Rev. Dr. Thompson, Londonderry.
TORRIE, REV. E. G., B.A.	Private	R.A.M.C.	
WADDELL, CHARLES	Lieutenant	3rd Batt. R.I.R.	Late Rev. Hugh Waddell, Manchuria
WADDELL, T. M. R.	Captain	R.A.M.C.	,, ,, ,,
WALKER, RALPH H.	2nd Lieutenant	R.A.F.	Rev. Professor Walker, Belfast.
8 WALKER, W. M., M.B.	Major	R.A.M.C.	Rev. S. Walker, Donaghadee.
10, 13 WALKER, S. H.	Lieutenant	5th Batt. R.I. Regt.	,, ,, ,,
4 (2), 10 WALLACE, JAMES W.	Lieutenant	19th Batt. R.I.R.	Rev. J. C. Wallace, Raphoe.
WALLACE, J. K. L.	Private	1st Can. Cont., Bomb-thrower	Late Rev. R. Wallace, Omagh.
1 Wallace, Robert C.	2nd Lieutenant	S. African Forces in E. Africa	,, ,, ,,
WATSON, REV. ANDREW	Captain	Chaplain	
1 Watson, John Hyndman	Sergeant	18th Batt. R. Scots	Late Rev. John Watson, Boyle.
WATSON, W. T.	Private	3rd Batt. S. African Infty.	,, ,, ,,
2 Watters, James C., B.A.	2nd Lieutenant	No. 1 Battery S.A. H.A.	Rev. F. O. M. Watters, formerly of Sligo.
WATTERS, THOMAS M.	Private	9th Batt. S. African Infantry	,, ,, ,,
9 (2), 19 WATTS, ROBERT	Captain	A.S.C., attd. 2nd Batt. R.I.R.	Late Rev. R. J. Watts, Kilmacrennan.
WEST, BRUCE A., M.D.	Captain	R.A.M.C.	Late Rev. Dr. West, Antrim.
10 (5), 6, 23, 24 WEST, JOHN WEIR, M.B.	Lieut.-Colonel	R.A.M.C.	,, ,, ,,
WHITE, P. W., M.B.	Captain	R.A.M.C., 108th Fd. Amb.	Rev. P. W. White, Stonebridge.
4, 9 WHITE, THOMAS J.	Lieutenant	16th Batt. R.I.R.	Late Rev. R. White, Kilkeel.
2, 10 White, Wm. C.	Engineer Lieutenant	R.N.R.	Rev. P. W. White, Stonebridge.
4, 9 WHITE, WM. R., B.A.	Captain	16th Batt. R.I.R.	Late Rev. R. White, Kilkeel.
WHYTE, FREDK. H., M.B.	Captain	R.A.M.C.	Rev. Adam Whyte, Gortin.
4 WHYTE, JOHN STANLEY, B.Sc.	Lieutenant	Royal Engineers	,, ,, ,,
4 WILKIN, CECIL	Lieutenant	5th Batt. R.I. Regt	Late Rev Jas. Wilkin, Ballinglen.
9, 10 WILSON, CHARLES MORELL	Captain	Army Ordnance Department	Late Rev. Dr. A. J. Wilson, Malone.
WILSON, CRAWFORD L.L.	Surgeon Probationer	R.N.V.R.	Late Rev. Dr. S. L. Wilson, Belfast.
WILSON, DAVID	Captain	107th Canadian Regt.	Late Rev. Dr. D. Wilson, Limerick.
WILSON, DANIEL M., K.C.	Captain	11th Batt. R. Inng. Fus.	,, ,, ,, ,,
1 Wilson, Edmund, E. F. B.	Major	South African R.A.M.C.	,, ,, ,, ,,
WILSON, HERBERT	Private	Australian Artillery	Late Rev. Dr. Wilson, Cookstown.
WILSON, ROBERT	2nd Lieutenant	R.F.A.	Late Rev. W. A. Wilson, Coleraine.
4 (3) WOODBURN, DAVID	Captain	R.G.A.	Rev. Prof. Woodburn, Londonderry.
WITHEROW, T. H., B.A.	Lieutenant	8th Batt. R.I.R.	Late Rev. Wm. Witherow, Belfast.
WORKMAN, E. G.	Private	1st Batt. Canadian Engineers	Late Rev. Dr. Workman, N'breda.
9, 10 WORKMAN, FRANZ	Flight Lieutenant	R.A.F.	,, ,, ,, ,,
18 WORKMAN, JAMES H.	Private	R.A.S.C. (M.T.)	,, ,, ,, ,,
9, 10 (3) WRIGHT, REV. J. JACKSON, B.A.	Major	Chaplain	Late Rev. Dr. Wright, Newtownards.
WRIGHT, ALFRED J.	Lieutenant	9th R. Inng. Fusiliers	,, ,, ,, ,,
4, 1 Wright, Matthew J.	2nd Lieutenant	14th Batt. R.I.R.	,, ,, ,, ,,
WRIGHT, RICHARD P. M.	Lieutenant	Inland Water Transport Ser.	,, ,, ,, ,,
17 WRIGHT, THOMAS	Engineer	Admiralty Work	,, ,, ,, ,,
4 WRIGHT, WM. M.	Captain	6th R. Dub. Fus.	,, ,, ,, ,,
4, 9, 10 YOUNG, HUGH	Captain	12th Batt. R. Inng. F.	Rev. W. J. Young, Milford.

DAUGHTERS OF MINISTERS.

NAME.	POSITION.	FATHER'S NAME.
*ALEXANDER, H. M.	Sister, St. Luke's Military Hospital, Halifax	Rev. Thomas Alexander, Kilmore.
BELLIS, CHARLOTTE H. S.	Nurse, French Red Cross	Late Rev. Dr. Bellis, Ramelton.
BLAIR, E. S.	V.A.D., H.M. Hospital, Gretna	Rev. J. C. Blair, Gujarat.
BOYD, NANCY	Nurse, Red Cross Hospital, Manchester	Rev. Robert Boyd, Gujarat.
BREAKEY, MAUD E.	Head Cook, W.A.A.C., Newmarket	Rev. J. J. C. Breakey, Lisburn.
BRENNAN, HELEN MAUD	Munitions Worker	Rev. John Brennan, Kilkenny.
BROWN, AELFREDA R.	War Office Worker	Rev. Thomas Brown, Bandon.
BROWN, PEARL RENTOUL	Intelligence Department, War Office	,, ,, ,,
BROWN, ZOE R.	,,	,, ,, ,,
CANNING, JANET B.	V.A.D., U.V.F. Hospital, Belfast	Rev. J. A. Canning, Crumlin.
*CLEMENTS, MAY	Matron, No. 8 General Hospital, B.E.F.	Late Rev. Wm. Clements, Benburb.
COWPER, A. H.	Cook, U.V.F. Hospital, Belfast	Late Rev. G. T. Cowper, Rathfriland.
COWPER, A. M.	Head Cook, Dumbarton House, Gilford	,, ,, ,,
**COWPER, MURIEL	Ministry of Food	,, ,, ,,
†EDGAR, AGNES McCHEYNE	Queen Alexandra N.N.S., H.S. "Asturias"	Late Dr. R. M. Edgar, Dublin.
HAMILTON, JANE BROWN	Nurse, Dublin Castle R.C. Hospital	Late Rev. Dr. Hamilton, Dublin.
HAMILTON, EILEEN NICHOLSON	Skilled Aeroplane Mechanic	Rev. J. G. Hamilton, Dromore.
‡HAMILTON, EMILY M.	Lieut.-Colonel, W.R.A.F.	Late Rev. John S. Hamilton, Dublin.
‡HAMILTON, J. ETHEL	Ministry of Munitions Office	,, ,, ,,
JACKSON, A. F.	V.A.D., U.V.F. Hospital, Belfast	Rev. Dr. Jackson, Ballycastle.
JACKSON, J. G.	V.A.D., U.V.F. Hospital, Belfast	,, ,, ,,
KENNEDY, MARGARET ADELAIDE	V.A.D., A.N., Stobhill, Glasgow, 24th General Hospital, B.E.F., and Royal Herbert Hospital, Woolwich	Late Rev. G. A. Kennedy, fy. of Aghadoey.
LEARMONTH, AGNES LIVINGSTONE, M.B.	Med. Officer, R.A.M.C., B.S.F.	Late Rev. John S. Hamilton, Dublin.
LYNN, HARRIET B.	Asst. Cook, Q.M.A.A.C., Dunstable	Rev. R. Lynn, Inch.
McELNEY, FLORENCE A.	V.A.D., U.V.F. Hospital, Belfast	Rev. R. M'Elney, Downpatrick.
McELNEY, MARY C.	Motor Driver, A.S.C.	,, ,, ,,
MacLAUGHLIN, NORAH T.	V.A.D., Secy. Aber Artro Military Hospital, N. Wales	Rev. D. MacLaughlin, Drumminis.
MEEKE, ISABEL	Nurse, 5th City of London Ter. Force	Rev. James Meeke, Kingsmills.
MEEKE, MRS. H. C.	Sister, St. Thomas Hospital, London	Rev. R. S. Coffey, fy. of Mullingar.
MILLAR, EDITH T. G.	Cook, Military Hospital, Londonderry	Rev. D. G. Millar, Londonderry.
MILLAR, ETHEL M. S.	Cook, Military Hospital, Londonderry	,, ,, ,,
†MISKELLY, NESSIE	Nurse, R.F. Hospital, Gray's Inn Rd., London	Late Rev. J. Miskelly, Armaghbrague.
MONTGOMERY, ELEANOR A. L.R.C.P. & S., Ed.	Med. Office i/c Q.M.A.A.C. Hospital, Isleworth	Rev. Dr. Montgomery, Belfast.
MONTGOMERY, MAUD J. E.	W.O. Officers' Casualty Dept.	Late Rev. R. Montgomery, Belfast.
MONTGOMERY, MARGERY	Nurse and Assistant Matron, Malta	Late Rev. A. Montgomery, Magherafelt.
NEILSON, HELEN	Nurse, R.F. Hospital, Gray's Inn Rd., London	Rev. R. Neilson, Donegal.
OSBORNE, KATHLEEN M.	W.R.A.F. (M.T.)	Rev. Dr. Osborne, Dublin.
OSBORNE, RUTH H.	W.R.A.F. (M.T.)	,, ,, ,,
POLLOCK, ELSIE ALEXANDER	Sister, U.V.F. Hospital, Belfast	Rev. John Pollock, Belfast
RENTOUL, ANNIE I. H.	Nurse, Australian Red Cross	Late Rev. Alex. Rentoul, Sandymount.
SHAW, INA	V.A.D., Bannvale Hospital, Gilford	Rev. G. B. Shaw, Clagan.
SIMPSON, EMILY C.	V.A.D., Military Hospital, Bath	Rev. E. F. Simpson, Ballymena.
SIMPSON, MAY O.	Sister, Q.A.I.M.N.S. (R.)	,, ,, ,,
SIMPSON, NORA J.	V.A.D., Waveney Hospital, Ballymena	,, ,, ,,
STEWART, ANNIE	Nurse, Q.A.I.M.N.S.B. St. Ignatius, Malta	Late Rev. Hugh Stewart, Loughgilly.
STUART, EILEEN	V.A.D., 24th General Hospital, B.E.F.	Rev. Dr. Stuart, Londonderry.
STUART, ETHEL	V.A.D., U.V.F. Hospital, Belfast	,, ,, ,,
THOMPSON, MAY	War Office Worker	Late Rev. Thos. Thompson, Glendermot.
WALKER, ELIZABETH S., M.B.	Military Hospital, Salonica	Rev. S. Walker, Donaghadee
WALKER, NORA McNEILL	X Ray Assistant, U.V.F. Hospital, Belfast	,, ,, ,,
WALKER, MAY	Asst. Horton War Hospital, Epsom	,, ,, ,,
WALLACE, ADA	Nurse, with S.A. Forces in E. Africa	Late Rev. R. Wallace, Omagh.
†WARNOCK M. E.	Nurse, Wandsworth Hospital, London	Late Rev. R. Warnock, Glenhoy.
WHITSITT, MAUD V.	V.A.D., 3rd London General Hospital	Rev. J. H. Whitsitt, Killeshandra.
WHYTE, HELEN E.	Women's Legion, Driver, A.S.C.	Rev. Adam Whyte, Gortin.
WHYTE, KATHLEEN W.	Sister, Q.A.I.M.N.S., Salonica and Bagdad	,, ,, ,,

* Mentioned in Despatches. † Awarded Royal Red Cross. ** Awarded O.B.E. ‡ Awarded M.B.E.